THE
UNIVERSAL
STORY

1. The main gate to the front lot, with the Alfred Hitchcock Theatre in the foreground and the famous Universal City sign on the hilltop behind.
3. A contemporary lobby card for *The Mummy* (1932)
4. On location in Paris during the filming of *The Concorde – Airport '79* (1980).
5. Dining with nostalgia – poster decor in the old commissary at the studios.
6. Carl Laemmle on 15th March 1915, the official opening day of Universal City.
7. The recreated office of the late Edith Head, Universal's famous costume designer, with her eight Oscars on the mantelshelf.
8. The vista which is Universal City nestling under the foothills of the Santa Monica mountains, photographed from the air in 1978.
10. The studio's main administration building and post office as they looked in 1953.

THE
UNIVERSAL
STORY
Clive Hirschhorn
OCTOPUS BOOKS

The publishers would like to thank John Douglas Eames for originating the concept for this series of studio histories.

WASHING
IRONING
The LAUGHS are MONSTERous!
Bud and Lou are in a stew when they tangle with the TITANS of TERROR!
BUD ABBOTT & LOU COSTELLO meet FRANKENSTEIN
The Wolfman
LON CHANEY
Dracula
When in Hollywood
Visit
Universal Studios

2. Elliott (Henry Thomas) and his famous friend in a scene from E.T. *The Extra-Terrestrial* (1982).
4. Every year nearly four million tourists enjoy the studio tour.
5. Filming a western on the back lot.
6. A contemporary lobby card for *Abbott And Costello Meet Frankenstein* (1948).
7. A portable electricity generating plant in the twenties.
8. A bird's-eye view of part of the studio's famous back lot, on which are built nearly 600 buildings and facades that can represent virtually any locale at almost any time in history.
10. Inside the Alfred Hitchcock Theatre – a 340-seat dubbing and screening room completed in 1980.

First published 1983 by
Octopus Books Limited
59 Grosvenor Street
London W1

Second Impression 1985

ISBN 0 7064 1873 5

Produced by Mandarin Publishers Limited
22a Westlands Road
Quarry Bay, Hong Kong

Printed in Hong Kong

Contents

Preface

Universal's total output of feature films to date, including those the studio released but did not make, is well over 2,600. Because of this it has been necessary to modify the approach used in previous titles of this series of studio histories, in order to include all the films in the available number of pages. By doing this I have managed to cover, in one form or another, every feature-length film (five reels or more, running 50 minutes or longer) released by Universal, or a subsidiary company, in the United States of America; the great majority of these have been produced by the studio, and released under its banner in Great Britain as well.

During the silent era alone (1912 to 1928), Universal made over 900 feature films. Space considerations apart, most of these silent films are, alas, lost forever and very little written material, let alone stills, is extant. What I have done therefore, is to single out what I consider to be the best and most representative of them for full treatment – that is, a critical and descriptive text, accompanied by a production still or portrait of a star from the film. The balance of the silent output, however, is not neglected altogether but appears in the form of contracted, unillustrated entries on the last page of the appropriate year. The entry for each of these films includes the director's name, the type of film it was (comedy, melodrama, western, etc.) and the leading players. I have also indicated the production imprimatur under which each film was originally released. The five principal ones – Super Jewel, Jewel, Bluebird, Butterfly and Red Feather – served, at least in part, as an indication of the prestige level of a film.

Up to and including 1929, the year to which a film is assigned here is the year it was copyrighted; the available records are more accurate in that respect than they are on release dates. In many, if not most, cases copyright year and release year would have been the same.

Also given abbreviated treatment are some of the studio's more routine productions, including the assembly-line westerns, between the arrival of sound and 1946. Unlike the silent listings, though, these entries also include the name of the producer (if known), a brief synopsis of the plot and the film's running time.

From 1930 onwards, the year under which a film appears is its year of theatrical release. A word of caution here, however: establishing the release year with certainty in a few cases, particularly some of the earlier films, can be difficult, as a comparative check on the same film in a number of reference works will often show. The first public showing may not be regarded as the release date, especially if the film was found wanting, withdrawn after a very short time to be revised, and then released again, but this time in the new year. Also, a film could have been given a limited release in the Los Angeles area, simply to enable it to qualify for an Academy nomination in that year, even though national release was not planned until early the following year, possibly even to coincide with the Awards presentation ceremony in April. For these reasons the reader may spot the occasional apparent discrepancy, but these are more likely to be uncertainties than errors.

In 1946 the studio experienced a major managerial upheaval, one result of which was that it embarked on a more ambitious production programme. From that year onwards, therefore, every film is presented with a full text and production still.

One of the biggest questions I was called upon to answer in collating the vast quantity of material relevant to the Universal story was what, exactly, constituted a Universal picture. In a number of cases this has proved to be a dauntingly difficult, and sometimes near impossible, task. So complex and variable are the possible connections and participation (both creative and financial) that a film studio can have with a product associated with its name, that it is simply not possible to draw a hard and fast line in every case. At the one extreme there is the picture that is conceived, administered and created on the studio's lot by staff on the studio payroll, fully financed by the studio and released world-wide by the studio or its distribution arm. At the other extreme we have the 'negative pick-up' – the film which is made and financed by an independent production company, who then negotiates over the distribution rights (probably in a restricted area) with a major studio, under whose banner the film is then released. Script approval, financial backing, making studio facilities available and many other opportunities for the studio to become involved with an independent's production, can so complicate any one case, that calling it a studio production, or not, becomes a very subjective decision indeed. There are several films in the book that could be argued either way, and in such cases I beg the reader's indulgence.

Giving due consideration to these problems, I have included in the main part of the book (pages 12 to 357) all Universal feature productions (except documentaries) that were released by the studio in the USA and by its distribution arm in the

United Kingdom. Films not yet released in the UK are also included if it is known that Universal holds the releasing rights there.

Before 1960, independent, 'non-studio' productions released by Universal (with or without restriction) do appear in the book, but they are in the appendix section (see page 368). From 1960 onwards, though, different criteria must be applied to reflect the changing policies that the major studios were forced to adopt when the Hollywood studio system started to break down, thanks chiefly to the advent of television and the huge decline in cinema audiences. From that time onwards the studios acted more and more as sole distributors for major productions made by independent bodies, while at the same time they concentrated their own efforts on producing fewer but more compelling films. Financial, and often creative, participation by the studio in independent productions became gradually more widespread, and the films came to be regarded as part of the output of the studio itself, even though it was clear that it did not actually make them. After 1960, therefore, I have relegated to the appendixes only those Universal releases that were made by foreign companies (that is, those based outside the USA) and also US-made independent productions if Universal's releasing rights included America but excluded the United Kingdom. Feature-length documentaries, too, are included in the appendixes, as are a handful of anomalous films that do not fit into any easily definable category.

The book does not deal with the many short subjects released by Universal throughout its long history, except to indicate which ones were nominated for, and/or won Academy Awards (see page 358). Nor are the serials made by the studio until 1946 included. Missing also are the films made specifically for television, even if they were subsequently released theatrically. Such films have figured with increasing prominence in the schedules of the major Hollywood studios since the early sixties. Indeed, when MCA took over Universal in 1959 its policy from the start was to develop, even concentrate on, television production. It was a policy that paid off, for it enabled the studio not only to survive but also to expand, at a time when other companies were being forced out of business. But that's a different story. This is a book about Universal's contribution to the world of cinema – I hope you enjoy it.

Clive Hirschhorn

Clive Hirschhorn
July 1983

Acknowledgements

Of the many people who so generously contributed their time to the book, I should first and foremost like to thank Robyn Karney who, in her capacity as general editor, devoted months of ceaseless work to the project. Similarly, my heartfelt thanks to Corin Moore, my diligent researcher, for the several hundred hours he spent at the British Film Institute searching for (and finding!) material that proved invaluable; without his painstaking involvement the book would have taken twice as long to write. I should also like to express my gratitude to David Burn of Octopus Books for so meticulously guiding each step of the work since it began.

George Baxt in New York brought his usual expertise and knowledge to bear on the finished manuscript, and for his many suggestions I am most grateful.

My particular thanks to Paul Lindenschmid of Universal City Studios, without whose help in gathering together the vast collection of stills the book would scarcely have been possible. My special thanks also to Louis Paul of the Library of the Performing Arts at New York's Lincoln Center for going way beyond the call of duty in helping to fill many of the inevitable gaps in the stills that were required. In this capacity, too, thanks are due to the staff of the National Film Archive of the British Film Institute, especially to Tise Vahimagi and Markku Salmi. Ian Cook, my photographer on the project, deserves my wholehearted appreciation as well.

For the various contributions of the people at Universal City, particularly those of Annette Welles, Nancy Cushing-Jones, Corinne de Luca and Sally Nichols, I am much indebted.

In their several capacities, my thanks to Peter Seward and the library staff of the British Film Institute, Dorothy Swerdlove and the staff of the Library of the Performing Arts, Lincoln Center, Mary Corliss of the stills archive at the Museum of Modern Art, Eric Spilker, Dion McGregor, Tony Slide, Critt Davis, Tony Sloman, Graham Bury, Tom Vallance, Anne Bennett of UIP, Sarah Harman and Charles Helliwell of UIP, Ray Block, David Bradley, William K. Everson, James Foscher and Eddie Brandt's Saturday Matinee.

Finally, I am also indebted to *The New York Times*, *Variety*, *Bioscope*, *Kine Weekly*, *The Monthly Film Bulletin* and *The Motion Picture Herald*.

For Pearl and Colin, my parents. With love.

Introduction

At 10 o'clock on Monday morning, 15th March 1915, ten thousand people cheered loudly as Carl Laemmle, the five-foot-two president of the Universal Film Manufacturing Company (known as 'The Universal') unlocked the gates to the main entrance of Universal City, five miles north of Hollywood on the 230-acre Taylor ranch across the Cahuenga Pass. He was presented with an outsized gold key (cost: $285) by actress Laura Oakley, 'chief of police' designate of the only city in the world built exclusively for the purpose of motion picture production. After announcing that there would be no long drawn-out speeches or 'meaningless ceremony', Laemmle turned the key and pronounced the studio, and its two days of inaugural festivities, open. As he did so, the thousands of onlookers who were standing in front of the gates behind the Universal band, marched into the impressive new premises, gaily singing 'The Star Spangled Banner' as they went.

In the front rank were the officers of Universal, exchange men, exhibitors and newspapermen who had journeyed from all parts of the country to be present on this historic occasion. They were followed by the tremendous crowds that had gathered from all over Los Angeles, many of whom had camped overnight outside the studio gates. The roads leading to Universal City were jammed with buses, street cars and automobiles as people continued to pour into the new studio complex. By the afternoon the crowd had swelled to twenty thousand, and still they flooded in.

As the first visitors – including Thomas Edison, who set the studio's electrical equipment in motion, as well as Buffalo Bill Cody – passed through the gates, they were met by Universal's roster of stars: Henry Rawlinson (Universal City's first mayor), Sydney Ayers, Pauline Bush, Grace Cunard, William Clifford, J. Warren Kerrigan, Francis Ford, Lon Chaney, Gertrude Selby, Jack Dillon and Vera Sissons; as well as by Carl Laemmle himself, his vice-president Robert H. Cochrane and treasurer Pat Powers.

In the afternoon, the actors returned to their respective sets on 'the greatest outdoor stage in the world', where their delighted fans were shown Francis Ford making the serial *Broken Coin*, as well as a spectacular flood which at one point went out of control.

During the course of the day (in which three minor accidents occurred and were promptly treated at Universal City Hospital), the thousands of visitors were shown, as part of their tour, the studio's barber shop and manicure parlour, its main restaurant, administration block, laboratory, theatre, ice plant, purchasing department, costume, make-up and dressing rooms, carpentry, paint and property shops, as well as the main stage which measured 300 feet by 65 feet. They were also shown a second, slightly smaller stage (measuring 200 feet by 50 feet) as well as the studio arsenal, the zoo, several horse corrals, blacksmith and harness shops, and a cavalry barracks providing quarters for 20 men. Finally, they saw the 150,000-gallon concrete reservoir at the back of the ranch, as well as the half million-gallon reservoir on the summit of Universal City's highest hill. The opening day's festivities closed with a rodeo show and, in the evening, a grand ball held in Universal's big 'electric studio'.

Carl Laemmle's dream had, at last, become a reality.

Yet just nine years earlier Laemmle, then a 39-year-old immigrant from Laupheim in Germany, had never even given motion pictures a thought. The tenth of estate agent Julius Baruch Laemmle's 13 children, Carl left school at the age of 13 and in 1884, after a short apprenticeship in a relative's store, purchased a one-way ticket from Bremerhaven to New York (cost: $22.50) to join his brother Joseph in Chicago. The next ten years of his life, in which he found employment in numerous badly paid jobs, could not have been less auspicious. But at least he learned to speak English during that period, and to assimilate himself into the American way of life. Then in 1894 he was offered his best job to date: book-keeper for the Continental Clothing Company in Oshkosh, Nebraska. Four years later he married Recha Stern, the niece of Sam Stern, the store's owner, and soon afterwards was appointed manager of the store. Nor did nepotism have anything to do with his new position. Over the years Laemmle had proved himself a most capable employee and full of initiative – especially in the areas of 'showmanship', such as the store's imaginative window displays and advertisements. This aspect of his work brought him into contact with Robert H. Cochrane, an employee in a Chicago advertising agency and a former journalist, whose pithy way with words and hard-hitting approach to advertising copy greatly impressed Laemmle. Though by now Carl could speak English fairly well he was no writer, and he came to an arrangement with Cochrane (who was twelve years his junior) whereby he would supply the general ideas for the advertisements, while the younger man would express those ideas in go-getting advertising jargon.

Five years later, in 1905, Laemmle journeyed from Oshkosh to Chicago (where Sam Stern, his uncle-in-law, was based) in order to persuade his employer to increase his salary. The meeting, however, did not go the way he had hoped and at the end of it Laemmle found himself out of a job. With the money he had managed to save in the eleven years he had been with the Continental Clothing Company, he decided to settle in Chicago and, on the advice of Robert Cochrane, to take advantage of his experience and open his own clothing store.

Then one day, while out looking for premises, Laemmle happened to notice that a moving picture show was being screened in a converted store or 'nickleodeon'. Though he had never set foot in such a place, nor had any interest in pictures that moved, his business sense was aroused when he noticed the large number of people standing in line, waiting for the next performance. After making some initial enquiries he learned how relatively inexpensive it was to project movies in a disused store or warehouse, and that for as little as $1,200 he could become the proprietor of such an establishment. As far as the actual movies themselves were concerned, he could, he learned, either purchase them outright from the

After just nine short years in the film business, Carl Laemmle is presented with the gold key to open Universal City on 15th March 1915.

above: Opening day at Universal City Studios. The teepee was set up as an attraction but Indians still lived in the hills around in 1914. *below left:* Special guest Buffalo Bill Cody (left) with Carl Laemmle on opening day at Universal City. *below right:* A still frame from the studio's newsreel *Universal Animated Weekly*, showing Thomas Edison laying the foundation tablet of the 'New Electric Studio' on 27th October 1915.

Biograph Company for 12 cents per foot, or rent programmes from the numerous film exchanges that were mushrooming all over the country.

Laemmle immediately decided to remodel a disused store at 909 Milwaukee Avenue, called it 'The White Front Theatre', and advertised it as 'The Coolest 5-cent Theatre in Chicago'. It's doors opened officially on 24th February 1906 and Carl Laemmle, former clothes salesman, found himself in the movie business. He recouped his initial investment (which turned out to be a little over $1,200) in the first month, his weekly take being $600 against expenses of $150. He engaged Robert Cochrane as his advertising manager and two months later opened a second theatre called 'The Family Theatre' at 1233 Halstead Street. In order to expand still further he borrowed $2,500 from Cochrane in return for 10 per cent of the profits. Thus began a business association that was to last for 30 years.

The Laemmle theatre chain was followed by the Laemmle Film Service, which became the largest picture exchange in the country, and by 1909 Laemmle and Cochrane were financially on top of the world, with weekly grosses of $10,000 in the Midwest and Canada.

But trouble was brewing. After spending years in the courts fighting for the ownership of certain motion picture patents, Thomas Edison (the very man who would help officiate at the opening of Universal City six years later) was given a court decision that supported his claims, resulting in the formation of the iniquitous Motion Picture Patents Company, or the 'Trust', as it came to be known – and feared. Basically, the Trust (comprising the Vitagraph, Essanay and Lubin film companies) was designed to eliminate not only independent film producers but also the country's 10,000 independent exchanges and exhibitors. Edison wanted absolute control of the burgeoning motion picture industry and insisted that all licenced producers pay him a fee for using his patents. Licence fees were also required from exchanges, and each exhibitor was expected to fork out two dollars each week for the use of Edison projectors. Furthermore, producers were forbidden to sell their product to any exchanges not fully paid up to the Trust. Those who violated these monopolistic strictures would be sued in court and would lose their licences to operate.

Laemmle, who was the Trust's biggest customer, was convinced that he would be excluded from these punishing rules. But the Trust's spokesman, one Jeremiah J. Kennedy, a powerful Wall Street banker, did not wish to make any exceptions and a state of war soon existed between them.

When Laemmle found that he no longer had any films to rent (being unable to purchase product from the Trust) there was only one honourable solution open to him – to make his own. On 12th April 1909 he officially severed all dealings with the Trust and publicly announced that it was his intention to move to New York and enter film production himself. To this end he rented a studio at 111 East 14th Street and, despite an injunction by Jeremiah Kennedy, he hired actor-director William Ranous. Together with a second-hand camera and the actress Gladys Hulette, he despatched Ranous to Coytesville, New Jersey, to film a one-reel version of *Hiawatha*. Laemmle's new film-making division was called IMP (Independent Motion Picture Company) and, though it took him four months to bring *Hiawatha* to the screen, the company's output soon averaged one film a week.

The following year IMP acquired the services of director Thomas H. Ince and, at a salary of $200 a week, lured Florence Lawrence (the Biograph Girl) away from Biograph, promising her the kind of publicity hitherto unknown in the industry (it wasn't until the 'teens that the 'star system' fully emerged).

Throughout this period of furious activity, Laemmle's battle with the Trust (who in 1910 formed the General Film Company to deal, often physically, with recalcitrant independents) continued. No fewer than 289 actions were brought against him, all of which he parried in an extraordinary show of determination. If it was a fight General Filmco (as Laemmle called it) wanted, a fight it would get, and after blasting Kennedy and his mob with vitriolic anti-Trust advertisements in the press (all of them written by Cochrane), his superhuman efforts to survive were finally vindicated. On 15th April 1912 the US Government filed a petition against the Motion Picture Patents Company and the General Film Company demanding their dissolution as 'corrupt and unlawful assocations'.

In the meantime IMP continued to flourish. King Baggott became the company's first big star, and Laemmle was also successful in luring another popular artist away from Biograph – little Mary Pickford. Pickford's first IMP production was *Their First Misunderstanding*, and Laemmle doubled her salary, as well as helping to create the star system by giving her star billing. Unfortunately they soon developed 'artistic and financial differences' which resulted in Pickford leaving the studio and Laemmle denouncing the very star system he had fostered.

Then, on 8th June 1912, just two months after his victory

above: A still frame from **Hiawatha**, a one-reel version of Longfellow's famous poem that marked Laemmle's film-making debut in 1909. *below:* The first anniversary of the Independent Motion Picture Company was celebrated in October 1910 with a banquet at New York's Hotel Imperial. Carl Laemmle (arrowed) may well have been the smallest man present but his professional stature was by that time very large indeed. *right:* As part of the build-up to the March 1915 opening day, special trains were chartered to bring guests from many parts of the nation to Universal City.

over the Trust, Laemmle amalgamated his IMP Company with Pat Powers's Picture Plays, Adam Kessel and Charles Baumann's Bison Life Motion Pictures (both founded three years earlier) as well as the Nestor Champion and William Swanson's Rex companies. Baumann was elected the company's first president, Pat Powers was vice-president, Carl Laemmle the treasurer and William Swanson the secretary. As a result of internal politicking however, this particular corporate structure was short-lived and, after a massive executive shake-up within weeks of the company's formation, Laemmle was appointed the new president with Robert H. Cochrane second in command and Pat Powers as treasurer.

Naturally, there was now the question of what to call the new company and it was Laemmle himself who came up with the answer – UNIVERSAL. The story has it that, while trying to find a suitable name, Laemmle happened to be looking out of the window of his New York office when he saw a wagon pass by in the street below; painted on its side were the words 'Universal Pipe Fittings'. The name 'Universal' appealed to Laemmle, on the grounds that the new company was the biggest film producing outfit in the world, and no one disagreed.

Universal's first picture was *The Dawn Of Netta*, a two-reeler directed by Tom Ricketts. Mary Miles Minter (then Juliet Shelby) appeared in a one-reeler called *The Nurse*, after which Laemmle moved his film-making outfit from New York to Los Angeles. Then, in 1912, the company had its first major success with a feature-length documentary called *Paul J. Rainey's African Hunt*. By the end of 1912 Universal operated two studios at the coast; the Nestor studio at Sunset and Gower in Hollywood, and one at Edendale. The stages were well and truly set for business.

1913-1926

When Silent Was Golden

In the early years, most of Universal's entertainment packages were made up of split-reel or one-, two- and three-reel shorts comprising a comedy, a melodrama and, from 1913, a newsreel called 'The Universal Animated Weekly'. For $105 a week, exhibitors received sufficient product to change their programmes daily, the full bill consisting of four reels of popular entertainment. Art for art's sake was rarely, if ever, a consideration.

Then, in 1913, came the first full-length feature in the form of the controversial and enormously successful drama dealing with white slavery called *Traffic In Souls*, which made half-a-million dollars. The year also brought to the screen featurette versions (shorter than five reels) of *Dr Jekyll And Mr Hyde*, *Ivanhoe*, *Robinson Crusoe* and *Uncle Tom's Cabin* and, in 1914, the company entered the weekly serial stakes with *Lucille Love, Girl Of Mystery* starring Grace Cunard and Francis Ford. The featurette *Jane Eyre* was filmed with Ethel Grandin and Irving Cummings; so was *The Merchant Of Venice* with Phillips Smalley as Shylock. Lon Chaney appeared in a two-reeler called *The Tragedy Of Whispering Creek*, but the big one was *Neptune's Daughter*, a seven-reeler starring swimming star Annette Kellerman as a mermaid who turns into a human. It was shot on location in Bermuda, took three months to complete, and cost $50,000. Despite the success of its lengthier film output, the studio continued to make literally thousands of one- and two-reel shorts, a practice that lasted well into the forties.

Early in 1914, 48-year-old Carl Laemmle, flushed with the success of his flourishing Universal Company, ordered his West Coast manager, Isidore Bernstein, to purchase the Taylor Ranch in Lankershim Township on the north side of the Hollywood Hills. The initial down-payment was $3,500 and the total cost of the property $165,000. Building began in June 1914, so did film production on the site, and the first completed picture to emerge from Universal City, late in 1914, was a costume epic feature called *Damon And Pythias*.

Laemmle intended the March 1915 opening of Universal City to be an historic occasion and, for several months prior to that date, he ran advertisements inviting exhibitors to attend the inauguration. In the trade paper *Universal Weekly* (a Laemmle subsidiary) he asked:

'Are you going to come out to Universal City on March 15th or not? Are you going to give your wife and kids a treat by bringing them to the wonder city of the world – or not? Just think of what it would mean to them and *YOURSELF* to see the inside workings of the biggest moving picture plant in the wide, wide world – a whole city where everybody is engaged in the making of motion pictures, a fairyland where the craziest things in the world happen – a place to think about and talk about all the rest of your days! See how we blow up bridges, burn

left: Universal's first full-length feature drama was **Traffic In Souls**, made in 1913. *right:* Carl Laemmle with Miss Universal, actress Lois Wilson, at Universal City's opening day celebrations.

down houses, wreck automobiles and smash up things in general in order to give the people of the world the kind of pictures they demand. See how buildings have to be erected just for a few scenes of one picture then have to be torn down to make room for something else. See how we have to use the brains God gave us in every conceivable way in order *TO MAKE THE PEOPLE LAUGH OR CRY OR SIT ON THE EDGE OF THEIR CHAIRS THE WORLD OVER.'*

It was an invitation exhibitors (and the general public) could not resist, and they turned up in their thousands. In fact, so successful was the launch, and so fascinated were the visitors by the techniques of film-making, that it occurred to Laemmle there was no reason why he shouldn't continue having organised tours of the studio – at a fee. The charge would be 25 cents a head – including a boxed lunch – and visitors would be permitted to watch, from specially erected bleachers, the filming of current productions. So popular were these Universal City tours, attracting some 500 people a day, that they continued until the advent of talkies, when the sensitive sound equipment in the enclosed stages made it impossible to have hundreds of visitors milling around on the set. The studio zoo – with its 30 lions, 10 leopards, several elephants, dozens of monkeys and scores of horses, dogs and cats – was also abandoned with the arrival of talkies, for animals couldn't be relied upon to keep quiet either!

In 1964 the studio resumed the tours, and today they contribute substantially to the company's profits; apparently the general public – and they flock from all corners of the globe – is still fascinated by the way movie-makers make 'people laugh or cry or sit on the edge of their chairs'.

Under Laemmle (or 'Uncle Carl' as he was known), Universal City grew and thrived. In 1915 alone it produced over 250 films, most of them two-reelers and serials, but also including several successful features such as *Mrs Plum's Pudding* starring British actress Marie Tempest, and *Garden Of Lies* with stage actress Jane Cowl.

There were, in all, three brands of features released by the studio at this time: the low-budget Red Feather programmers, the more ambitious Bluebird releases, and the occasional prestige or Jewel productions. Serials also continued to proliferate. The studio's roster of directors included George Marshall, Jack Conway, Rex Ingram, Robert Z. Leonard and Lois Weber – one of the few women directors working in Hollywood at this time; while the top stars were Harry Carey, Carmel Myers, Lon Chaney, Edith Roberts, Frank Mayo, Mae Murray and Priscilla Dean.

In 1917 Jack (John) Ford, who had started his career as an actor, made his directorial debut for Universal with a two-reeler called *The Tornado*; and in 1918 Rudolph Valentino made an appearance with Carmel Myers in *A Society Sensation*. The same year a 19-year-old youngster joined Universal's New York office at $35 a week and almost immediately became Uncle Carl's private secretary. His name was Irving Thalberg. The following year Thalberg was transferred to Universal City in Hollywood and made studio manager. Within months he became general manager in charge of production and, at the age of 21, the youngest studio head (answerable only to Laemmle) in Hollywood's history.

Making westerns, 1916-style. *above:* Visitors to the studio could watch from bleachers constructed beside the sets. *below:* Popular western star Harry Carey in a scene with Olive Golden.

above: After their success in **A Society Sensation** (1918), Rudolph Valentino and Carmel Myers were again paired in **All Night** (1918). *below:* Carl Laemmle (right) with his production protégé Irving Thalberg.

CARL LAEMMLE presents
MAY MURRAY
IN
"The Delicious Little Devil"
Supported by a big special cast including
RODOLPH VALENTINO WM.V. MONG AND BERTRAM GRASSBY
Directed by ROBERT Z. LEONARD
IT'S A UNIVERSAL

Carl Laemmle offers
Stroheim's
WONDER
PLAY
"BLIND
HUSBANDS"
Universal-Jewel
DE LUXE ATTRACTION
Produced by
Stroheim
himself
ERIC STROHEIM
FRANCELIA BILLINGTON

top: Mae (or May – she used both versions) Murray took top billing over Valentino in this 1919 success. *above:* Erich von Stroheim's debut picture for Universal was **Blind Husbands** (1919). *right:* Von Stroheim's extravagance is clearly evident in this picture of the huge set he built for **Foolish Wives** (1920). *below:* Publicity 1920-style; sandwich-board men set out to promote **The Virgin Of Stamboul**.

Erich von Stroheim – 'the man you love to hate' – joined the studio in 1919 and, with *Blind Husbands*, which he directed as well as starred in, gave Universal its most prestigious hit to date. John Ford also directed his most ambitious movie yet: Bret Harte's *The Outcasts Of Poker Flat* with Harry Carey and Cullen Landis.

The twenties began auspiciously with Von Stroheim's *The Devil's Passkey*, another hit; two year's later, however, this German genius's association with the studio soured after the completion of *Foolish Wives*, a million-dollar production which Thalberg reduced from 32 reels to a more manageable 14. Von Stroheim's extravagance resulted in his dismissal, the following year, from *The Merry-Go-Round* when, after five weeks of shooting, he was replaced by Rupert Julian. It was Thalberg who had him removed, and it was Thalberg who, the same year, initiated the triumphant, no-expense-spared production of *The Hunchback Of Notre Dame*, directed by Wallace Worsley and starring Lon Chaney in what many consider to be his greatest role.

Thalberg left Universal on 23rd February 1923 (one year before the formation of Metro-Goldwyn-Mayer) to join Louis B. Mayer as vice-president of Louis B. Mayer Productions; but he did make a point of attending the *Hunchback* premiere in New York on 16th September. The film was both a critical and financial smash and, in its initial release, was roadshown at admission prices well above the average. On the strength of this success Chaney became one of the studio's hottest stars, together with Herbert Rawlinson, Laura La Plante and Priscilla Dean.

The studio's next big hit, prestigiously as well as financially, was another Chaney vehicle, *The Phantom Of The Opera*, directed by Rupert Julian in 1925. Together with *Hunchback* it remains Universal's most celebrated silent production and nothing that the company released in the next five years came anywhere near it in terms of quality. After completing *Phantom* Chaney moved to MGM where his career failed to

top left: The enormous cathedral façade, specially built on the lot for **The Hunchback Of Notre Dame** (1923). *top right:* Hoot Gibson, popular western star of the twenties, in **The Bearcat** (1922). *above:* Lon Chaney played the title role in the 1925 classic, **The Phantom Of The Opera**.

equal the glorious heights it had reached at Universal, and in 1930, aged 47, he died of bronchial cancer.

The year of 1926 saw Laemmle's nephew William Wyler debuting as a director in several undistinguished two-reel westerns which gave no indication of his first-class gifts; while the irrepressible Cohens and Kellys made the first of several appearances in the comedy *The Cohens And The Kellys*.

Yet despite films such as *The Hunchback Of Notre Dame* and *The Phantom Of The Opera*, both released as Super-Jewel productions, the mid-twenties was not a particularly noteworthy period in the studio's history. Unlike MGM or Paramount, Universal had no affiliated theatre chain in which to exhibit its product and, with only limited access to first-run houses in the major cities, it was forced into independent theatres. As the majority of these theatres were rurally based, and catered to rural types, most of Universal's mid-twenties product was extremely unsophisticated. What Laemmle offered to his 'outback' exhibitors was, in the main, a formula programme consisting of a feature, a newsreel, a serial and a one- or two-reel short. These films, all part of a 'full service' contract, were produced efficiently, albeit economically. The most popular were stories with rural backgrounds and westerns starring the well liked Hoot Gibson. The studio's journeymen directors were in charge of these budget productions, while the more talented directors on the lot, such as Tod Browning, Rupert Julian and Clarence Brown were entrusted with the more ambitious projects.

With the cream of the first-run houses closed to him in America, Laemmle turned to Europe for the bulk of his profits, and found in the overseas market a large and willing audience for American westerns and action features. The studio became actively involved in European co-productions and by the end of the decade had on its books such 'foreigners' as Paul Kohner, whom Laemmle had promoted from the publicity department to head of European operations, Paul Leni, Paul Fejos, Karl Freund and Edgar Ulmer, all of whose work was distinctly more individual in flavour than most of what was being churned out at Universal City.

And then out of the blue, just as the silent film was reaching its maturity, the Warner brothers gambled everything they had on giving motion pictures a voice. The result was *The Jazz Singer*, premiered in New York on 6th October 1927 – and after that nothing was quite the same again.

1913-14

▽ One of the seminal works in the development of the feature film, **Traffic In Souls** (1913) launched the career of director George Loane Tucker, was one of the earliest 'sexploitation' films, and the first smash hit for the newly formed Universal Film Manufacturing Company. Allegedly based on the controversial Rockefeller White Slavery Report, though inspired by the White Slavery Report of New York district attorney Charles S. Whitman (as well as the success of the stage plays *The Flight* and *The Lure*), the film told the story of an innocent girl lured into a brothel by a procurer posing as the leader of a Purity Group, and rescued in the nick of time by a police officer. Ethel Grandin (2nd right) played the hapless victim, Matt Moore was her rescuer, and Howard Crampton (left) the heavy. The film also featured Jane Gail as Moore's fiancée who is also Miss Grandin's sister. Though producer-scenarist Walter McNamara relied far too much on coincidence for the resolution of his plot (Gail, after losing her job in a candy shop, just happens to be employed by vice-king Crampton as his secretary and, with the aid of a dictaphone machine, just happens to overhear a conversation with her sister's abductor), the film nevertheless skilfully managed to incorporate the story's 72-hour time span into six reels of screen time, and employed parallel editing (ie the cutting together of numerous plot lines to convey the impression that the events depicted were happening simultaneously), to excellent effect. **Traffic In Souls** took $5,000 in its first week, and within a month was playing in 28 theatres in New York alone. It made $450,000 on its initial $5,700 outlay.

▷ The first feature film to be made at Universal City in Hollywood, and completed before the studio's official opening in March 1915, **Damon And Pythias** (1914) was a six-reel epic that employed a cast of a thousand extras, as well as William Worthington (who dropped his director's mantle to appear as Damon) and Herbert Rawlinson (centre) as Pythias. Frank Lloyd (right), later a very successful film director, played the ambitious Dionysius, while the women in this familiar story of a self-sacrificing friendship between two men were Anna Little (left) and Cleo Madison (behind). All the performances were commensurate with the not-too-exacting demands of the scenario, and the direction, by Otis Turner, was at its best in the 'spectacle' sequences such as the battle outside the walls of Agrigentum – as well as an exciting chariot race in Syracuse, which city was impressively constructed on the large Universal City backlot. Particularly praised on its release was 'its fascinating and dramatic scenario, its splendid portraying company, its great scenes and perfection in photography'. At its glittering opening on November 30th, 1914, the public cheered its approval.

▷ Australian swimming star Annette Kellerman (illustrated) sent the critics into ecstasies of approval, not so much over her acting abilities but for the shapeliness of her body. Her superb physical frame was shown off to eye-catching advantage in **Neptune's Daughter** (1914), a fantasy, filmed on location in picturesque Bermuda with a cast that also included William Welsh (as Neptune, King of the Sea), William E. Shay, Edmund Mortimer, Lewis Hooper, Francis Smith, Leah Baird, Mrs Allen Walker, Millie Eisten, Katherine Lee and Herbert Brenon who also directed. The storyline had Miss Kellerman, as one of King Neptune's two daughters, setting out to avenge the death of her young sister (caught in a fishing net laid by a monarch of a nameless kingdom), in the course of which she loses her immortality, but falls in love with the monarch and becomes his queen. As the story unfurled, Miss Kellerman was called upon to exhibit her diving abilities and, like swimming star Esther Williams (who, in the fifties, appeared in an MGM biopic of Kellerman) revealed that there was a fortune to be made just by splashing about in the blue. Director Brenon successfully combined fantasy with reality and the public flocked to see it.

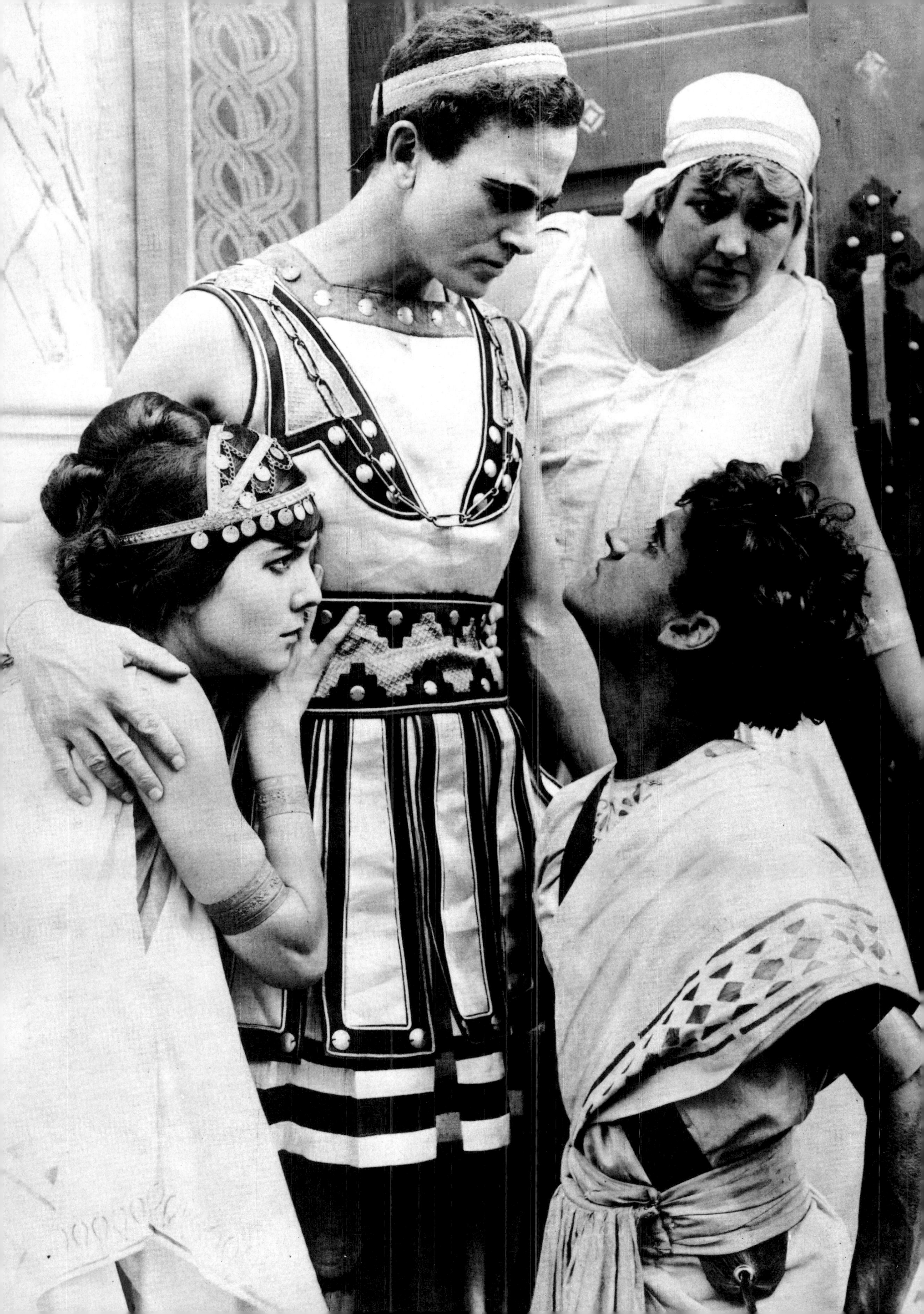

1915

▷ British star Marie Tempest (illustrated), in a rare American film performance, notched up a comedy success in the Broadway Universal release **Mrs Plum's Pudding**, playing a widow who, when oil is discovered on her ranch, becomes a millionairess overnight. In the big city, Miss Tempest is pursued by the opportunistic Lord Burlington but, when she pretends she has lost the deed to her farm and, consequently, is ruined, his love is found wanting. In the end, however, Burlington realises he loves the widow Plum not just for her 'pudding' but for herself and, at the fade, the couple are well on their way to living happily ever after. W. Grahame Brown played Burlington and Eddie Lyons was cast as Miss Tempest's son, with Violet MacMillan as the vivacious object of his affections. Lyons, together with James Dayton wrote it, and it was produced and directed by Al E. Christie.

▽ An unashamed tear-jerker, **My Old Dutch**, based on the celebrated Albert Chevalier song, was the homely tale of a happy-go-lucky young English couple who meet, fall in love, marry, have a son, then sit back and watch him grow until, after several set-backs, he finally achieves a position in the world they themselves were never able to attain. For a time, though, it looks as though the boy will be a huge disappointment but, in the end, he proves himself by rescuing his unhappy father and devoted mother from the poorhouse into which they have been driven by old age. Chevalier himself (right) played the father, and Florence Turner (centre left) was his wife. Between them, they made sure that after the film's five reels had unspooled, there wasn't a dry eye in the house. It was filmed on location in England, and directed by Larry Trimble. Henry Edwards (left) was also featured in support.

▽ A Universal Broadway release, **The Supreme Test** featured stage actress Henrietta Crosman (illustrated) as Violet Logan, a widow whose chief concern in life is to better conditions for the poor and needy. A somewhat complicated and melodramatic story (by L.V. Jefferson) found heroine Crosman reduced to poverty herself after her trustee misappropriates her money in a series of wild-cat speculations. But it all sorted itself out in the fifth reel with the *real* villain of the piece and a confirmed woman hater (Wyndham Standing) redeeming himself by proposing to Miss Crosman – who accepts. Completing the cast were Stella Razeto, Adele Farrington, Jack Wilson and Sylvia Ashton.

◁ In **Judge Not, Or The Woman Of Mona Diggings**, Julia Dean (illustrated) starred as the titular heroine of a quintessential melodrama which traced the fortunes of a destitute young woman (Dean) after her phoney marriage to Lee Kirk (Harry Carter), the no-good owner of a gambling joint. Harry Carey received top-billing as a dissolute young Easterner who becomes district attorney and, in reel six, successfully defends Miss Dean after she has been sent to prison for shooting Kirk in self-defence. A Universal Broadway feature, it also featured Marc Robbins as Judge Rand (Carey's father), was written by Peter B. Kyne, and directed by Robert Z. Leonard.

▷ **Garden Of Lies**, made by a company called Alco but distributed by Universal as a Broadway Universal Feature, starred New York stage actress Jane Cowl (illustrated) in a repeat performance of the role she created on Broadway. She played an American girl called Eleanor Mannering who, while living abroad, marries Prince Carl of Novodna. The couple are involved in a car accident on their wedding day, as a result of which Miss Cowl develops aphasia and cannot remember a thing. Her royal husband, meanwhile, has had to leave her bedside for that of his ailing father, the King. In her delirium, Cowl vaguely recollects that she has a husband, and so piteous are her pleas to see him, that her doctor persuades an adventurer called Mallory (William Russell) to pose as her absent Prince. Needless to say, she falls in love with the dashing Mr Russell, but on regaining her memory and being told of the deception, is furious at what has happened. It all ended happily, though, when, after the convenient death of the Prince, Cowl and her proxy lover wound up where you always knew they would – in each other's arms.

△ Comedienne Marie Cahill (illustrated), after delighting Broadway audiences with her performance in Avery Hopwood's **Judy Forgot**, gave cinema audiences a chance to chuckle over the misunderstandings caused by a girl who, everytime she smiles, cannot help winking. Mistaken identity also loomed large in Raymond L. Schrock's adaptation, with Miss Cahill, having lost her memory in a train wreck, being mistaken for a vaudeville star complete with husband and several children. Samuel B. Hardy co-starred as leading man Freddie, the bane of whose existence is Judy's infernal 'wink'. T. Hayes Hunter directed for maximum laughs, and seemed to get them.

OTHER PRODUCTIONS OF 1915

Business Is Business
Dir: Otis Turner. Comedy. Gretchen Lederer, Nat Goodwin, Maude George.

The College Orphan
Dir: William Dowlan. Comedy melodrama. Carter de Haven, Flora Parker de Haven.

Colorado
Dir: Norval MacGregor. Mining drama. Hobart Bosworth, Anna Lehr, Louise Baxter.

The Earl of Pawtucket
Dir: Harry C. Myers. Society comedy. Lawrence D'Orsay, Rosemary Theby.

Father And The Boys
Dir: Joseph de Grasse. Family comedy. Digby Bell, H. Ham, Bud Chase.

The Frame-up
Dir: Otis Turner. Political drama. George Fawcett, Maude George, Harry Carter.

Jewel
Dir: Phillips Smalley. Domestic drama. Ella Hall, Rupert Julian, Hilda Hollis.

Langdon's Legacy
Dir: Otis Turner. Comedy drama. J. Warren Kerrigan, Lois Wilson, Maude George.

A Little Brother Of The Rich
Dir: Otis Turner. Society Drama. Hobart Bosworth, Jane Novak, Hobart Henley.

The Long Chance
Dir: Edward le Saint. Western melodrama. Frank Keenan, Stella Razeto.

Love's Pilgrimage To America
Dir: Harry C. Myers. Immigrant comedy Lulu Glaser, Jack Richards, Adila Comer.

The Man Of Shame
Dir: Harry C. Myers. Drama. Wilton Lackaye, Rosemary Theby, Evelyn Dubois.

The Nature Man
Dir: none credited. Co-existence of Man and Nature. Knowles, the Nature Man.

The Primrose Path
Dir: Lawrence Martson. Romantic melodrama. Hal Forde, Gladys Hanson, William J. Walsh.

Scandal
Dir: Lois Weber and Phillips Smalley. Romantic drama. No cast credits.

Under Southern Skies
Dir: Lucius Henderson. Romantic melodrama. Mary Fuller, Paul Panzer, Milton Sills.

The White Scar
Dir: Hobart Bosworth. Northwest adventure. Jane Novak, Anna Lehr.

1916

▽ Based on Ludivoc Halevey's novel *L'Abbe Constantine*, **Bettina Loved A Soldier** was an effective piece of romantic flim-flam (in five reels), set in Longueval, France, and involving the purchase of Longueval Castle – on which the locals depend for their existence – by a wealthy American woman called Suzie Scott (Francelia Billington). Suzie has a pretty young sister of 17 called Bettina (Louise Lovely, centre), and the main business of E.J. Clawson's scenario, found Bettina being pursued by the gold-digging Paul de Lacardens, as well as by the more genuine Jean Reynaud, a cavalry lieutenant. She chooses Jean. Paul was played by Douglas Gerrard (right), Jean by Rupert Julian (left, who also directed), with George Berrill, Zoe DuRae and Elsie Jane Wilson completing the cast. (Bluebird).

▷ Based on Peter Bernard Kyne's much-filmed 1913 *Saturday Evening Post* story, **The Three Godfathers** was the perfect vehicle for Harry Carey (illustrated) who, in a screenplay by Harvey Gates, played one of a trio of outlaws fleeing from a sheriff's posse. After a particularly nasty desert sandstorm, the bandits encounter a dying woman in a wagon. She is about to become a mother and, just before she dies, implores the three outlaws to take care of her baby and to become its godfathers. At the risk of sacrificing their own lives, the three men agree to do as she asks, realising, as the narrative unfurls, that their chances of escaping the law are now impossible. Though several contemporary critics carped at the film's six-reel length, feeling that there was barely enough plot for five; as well as at some of the film's more gruesome moments (a vulture picking at the corpse of a dead outlaw came in for particular criticism), Edward J. Le Saint's gripping direction was generally praised; so was Harry Carey. Completing the cast were Stella Razeto, George Berrill, Frank Lanning, Joe Rickson and Hart Hoxie. It was remade in 1920 as *Marked Men*, in 1930 as *Hell's Heroes*, and in 1936 and 1948 by MGM as *Three Godfathers*. (Bluebird).

◁ Tyrone Power Sr starred in **Where Are My Children?**, a 'problem' drama dealing with birth control and its abuse which the National Board of Censors condemned. Basically the story of a District Attorney (Power, centre) who approves of contraception where misery might otherwise result, but who is all for having large families if the parents want and can afford them, it co-starred Helen Riaume (2nd right) as Power's wife – a woman who selfishly refuses to have children by pretending that she cannot. It was this deception that formed the basis of Lois Weber's scenario and provided it with its tension. More clarity of thought, however, was what was needed to define the issues at stake, and, in the absence of a definite point of view, the film lost much of its potential impact. Juan De La Cruz was cast as a physician whose abuse of birth control brings about his downfall, with other roles under the joint direction of Miss Weber and her husband Phillips Smalley going to Marie Walcamp, Cora Drew, Rene Rogers (2nd left), A.D. Blake (left), C. Norman Hammond and William J. Hope.

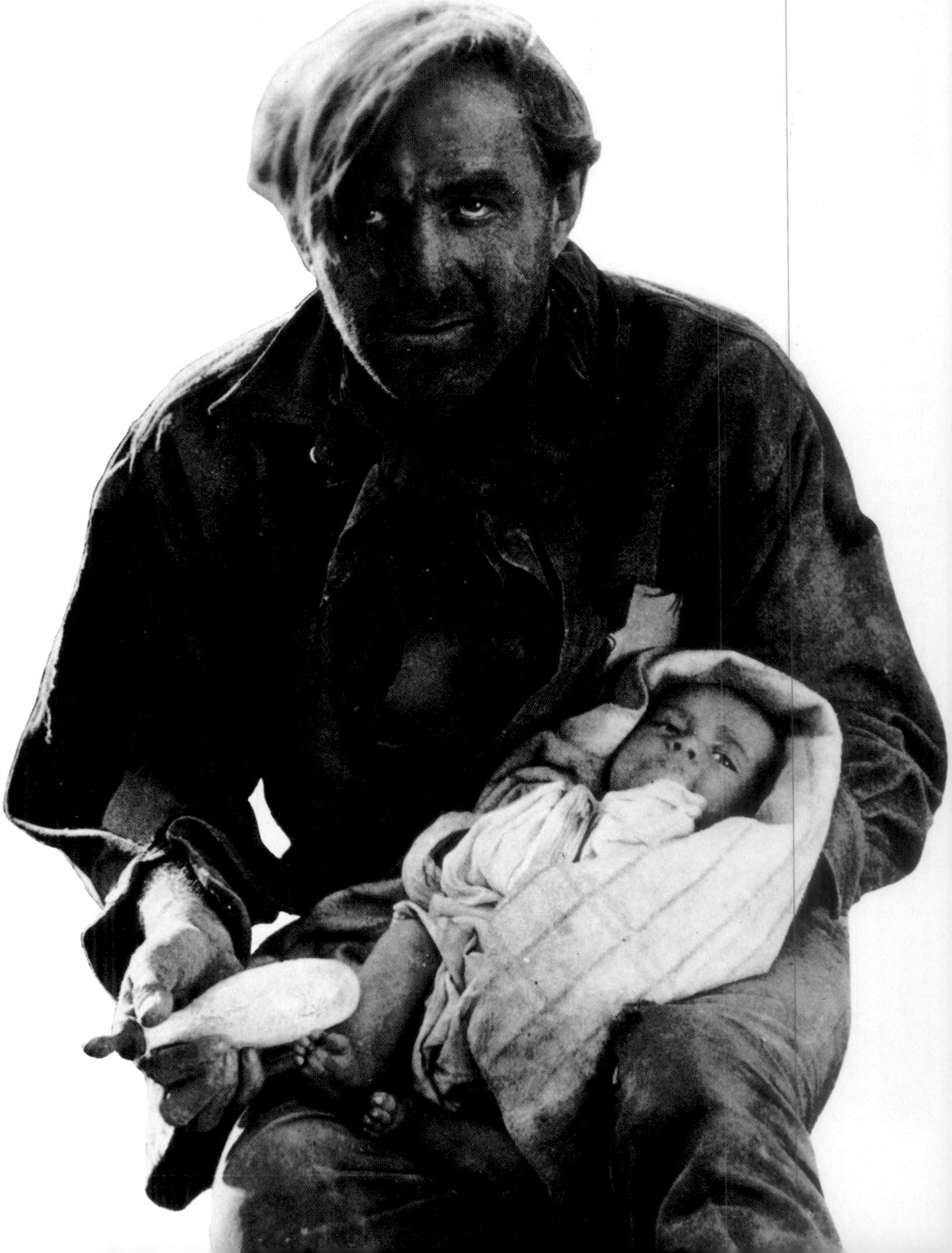

▽ One of the first attempts to expose the brutal treatment of the dispossessed Yaqui Indians, **The Yaqui**, a five-reeler Bluebird presentation, was based on Dane Coolidge's novel *The Land Of The Broken Promise*. It starred Hobart Bosworth (left) as Tambor, a stalwart Indian of the Broncho tribe who becomes the unfortunate butt of a conspiracy headed by an influential Mexican officer called Martinez, and is deprived of his wife and child through Martinez' cruelty. Jack Curtis played Martinez, with other roles under Lloyd B. Carleton's solid direction going to Golda Caldwell as Bosworth's wife and Dorothy Clark as his young daughter. Also cast: Charles Hickman, Gretchen Lederer, Alfred Allen (right), Yona Landowska (kneeling), and Emory Johnson. (Bluebird).

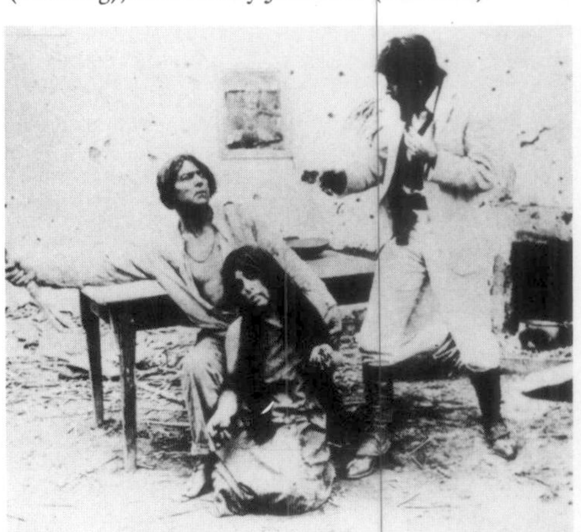

▽ The first of the studio's Red Feather features, **The Path Of Happiness** told the conventional story of a naive 'child of nature' who lives in the woods with her father, and a misshapen young man called Grekko. The birds and the squirrels are the girl's only friends and, until the death of her father and the arrival on the scene of a city gent (in search of some peace and quiet after an unhappy love affair), the harsh realities of life are unknown to her. How the visitor from the city teaches her, against the wishes of a jealous Grekko, the meaning of romantic love, formed the basis of Elaine Sterne's sentimental five-reel narrative which featured an ingenuous Violet Mersereau (illustrated) as the young woman of the woods, Harry Benham as the intruder from the city, Joseph Phillips as the father, and Sidney Bracey as Grekko. Also: Dorothy Benham, Florence Crawford and Leland Benham (as Little Grekko). It was directed by Elaine Sterne.

▽ Based on a story by Robert H. Davis that appeared in the *All Story Magazine*, **The Buglar Of Algiers** was one of the best films made by the studio in 1916. The story of two French soldiers, one of whom, Anatole (Kingsley Benedict, right), is the brother of Gabrielle (Ella Hall, centre), the other, Pierre (Rupert Julian, left) Gabrielle's sweetheart, it combined action with romance, though the film's underlying themes were friendship and patriotism. Separated by the vicissitudes of war, Gabrielle and her soldier are fated not to meet for many years. When, finally, they do, she is an old woman, unaware that her brother has recently died a hero in battle, and that Pierre, pretending to be Anatole, has been decorated in his friend's place. But Pierre has no intention of usurping the glory that rightfully belongs to Anatole, and the film ends with him decorating the dead body of his friend, which has been lying enshrouded in the flag of France in a small village. First-class performances from the three principals, and excellent direction by leading man Julian ensured the film both critical and public approval. (Bluebird).

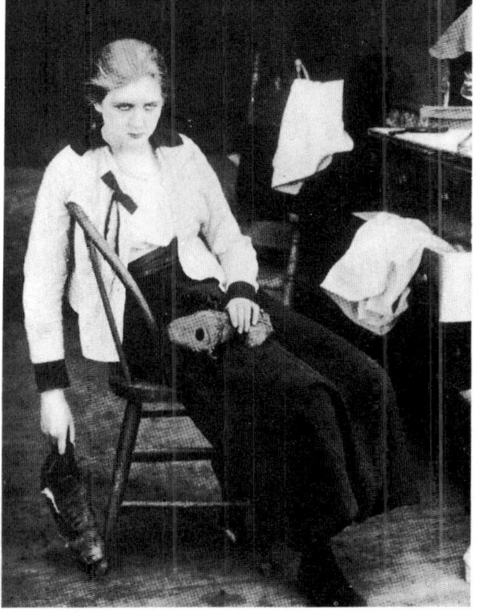

△ 'It reminds one of turning the pages of one of life's unhappiest chapters,' wrote a contemporary reviewer of **Shoes**, a heart-wrenching drama, directed by Lois Weber, about a working girl who, on only five dollars a week, has to keep her mother, her lazy father and three brothers and sisters from the breadline. The strain finally results in her selling her virtue for a pair of shoes. Based on a story by Stella Wayne Heron that appeared in *Collier's Magazine* (which in turn was inspired by a book by Jane Addams), the five-reel drama starred Mary MacLaren (illustrated) as the put-upon heroine, Harry Griffith as her father, Mrs Witting as her mother, Jessie Arnold as a chum, and William V. Mong as a hard-boiled cabaret singer. Director Weber also provided the scenario. (Bluebird)

△ Using Tennyson's poem 'Maud' as a guideline for **Naked Hearts**, scenarist Olga Printzlau fashioned a rather cloying narrative about the unfulfilled love of Maud and Cecil, two childhood sweethearts. On growing up, Maud finds herself betrothed to the foppish Lord Lovelace (Douglas Gerrard) against her will, while Cecil, after a duel with Maud's brother Howard (Jack Holt) leaves his childhood village for the Big City, where he becomes a celebrated musician and composes the song 'Come Into The Garden Maud'. War breaks out and, believing that Cecil has been killed in battle, Maud enters a convent. Unable to communicate with her, the hapless Cecil spends the rest of his life in sorrow, going to the convent walls every day, and playing his famous song in the fervent hope that Maud may hear it and know that, whatever may have happened, he has always remained faithful to her. Zoe Bech and Francelia Billington played Maud as a child and an adult respectively; while Gordon Griffith and Rupert Julian (who also directed, right) provided the two phases of Cecil. Completing the cast were George Hipp, Ben Horning, Paul Weigle and Nanine Wright (left). (Bluebird).

▽ Based on H. Rider Haggard's story *John Meeson's Will*, **The Grasp Of Greed** was the far-fetched yarn of a rising young authoress called Alice Gordon, who naively sells the rights of her future works to a miserly publisher called John Meeson. Appalled at the meanness of the contract, Meeson's nephew tears up the wretched agreement – a gesture which so embitters the curmudgeonly publisher that he draws up a will leaving his entire fortune to his business partners rather than to his nephew. Several plot complications, including a shipwreck, bring about a change of heart in Meeson, and the story's climax has him altering his will in his nephew's favour. As there's no paper on the desert island where Meeson lands up after the shipwreck, Alice (who was on the same ship and the same desert island), nobly agrees to have the new will tatooed on her back! The nephew shows his gratitude by marrying her. Louise Lovely (illustrated) played Alice, C.M. Hammond was Meeson and Jay Belasco the nephew. The scenario was by Ida May Park, and her husband, Joseph De Grasse, directed. Lon Chaney had a small part in it too. (Bluebird).

▽ The team of Ida May Park and Joseph De Grasse were also responsible for **The Grip Of Jealousy**, which again starred Louise Lovely (centre). She played the sister of a woman who dies in childbirth, and set in motion the convoluted plot about two feuding Southern families by leaving the new-born babe (which she mistakenly believes to be illegitimate) on the doorstep of an elderly slave (Walter Belasco). Lon Chaney played Silas Lacey, the villain of the piece, with other roles going to Jay Belasco as Miss Lovely's brother who Chaney murders and Harry Hamm (who is incorrectly blamed for the crime), as well as Marcia Morse and Grace Thompson. Though technically proficient – it was especially well photographed – the film's melodramatic plot failed to involve audiences and today its value to film historians lies solely in the malevolently effective performance by Chaney. (Bluebird).

▽ Ballet dancer Anna Pavlova, supported by members of the Ballet Russe, starred as Fenella, **The Dumb Girl Of Portici**, in Lois Weber's adaptation of Auber's opera *Masaniello*. The story of a poor Italian girl (Pavlova, foreground right) whose intemperate love for a Spanish Duke causes a revolution, it suffered from an excess of sub-titles, some confusing editing (which, at times, rendered the narrative almost incomprehensible), and from a central performance whose curiosity value far outstripped any actual dramatic achievement. After seven reels, audiences were finally given a glimpse of Pavlova the dancer in a brief aerial ballet (against moving clouds) depicting her flight to heaven after being stabbed. But it was scant compensation for much of the tedium, albeit beautifully photographed, that preceded it. Miss Weber co-directed with her husband Phillips Smalley, and the cast included Rupert Julian (as Masaniello), Douglas Gerrard, John Holt, Betty Schade, Edna Maison and Hart Hoxie. (Universal Special Feature).

▷ One of the studio's most prestigious films in 1916 was director Stuart Paton's visually breathtaking eight-reel version of Jules Verne's **20,000 Leagues Under The Sea.** Photographed not in a studio tank, but on location near the Bahamas, and utilising plot elements from Verne's *The Mysterious Island*, Paton surfaced with a splendid entertainment which, though popular with the public, did not make nearly as much money as Carl Laemmle had hoped. The reason for this was the film's escalating budget, much of which went on the development of Ernest and George Williamson's underwater camera, without which the film would have been far less visually striking. Jane Gail (right) provided the romantic interest (which, at best, was secondary to the action sequences, the most effective of these being a fight with an octopus), Allen Holubar (left) played Captain Nemo, the Indian Rajah who loses his wife and daughter prior to building the 'Nautilus', with other parts going to Dan Hanlon, Edna Pendleton and William Welsh. Remade by Disney in 1954.

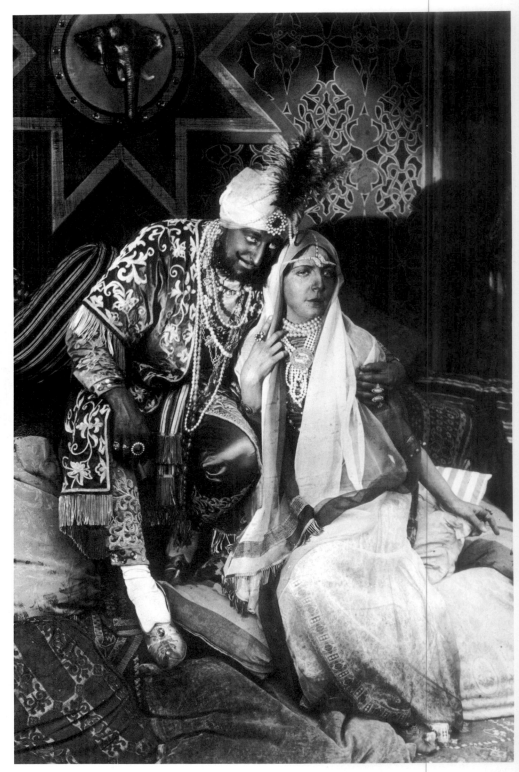

OTHER PRODUCTIONS OF 1916

Autumn (Red Feather)
Dir: O.A.C. Lund. Northwest saga. Violet Mersereau, Percy Richards.

Barriers Of Society (Red Feather)
Dir: Clark Irvine. Romantic drama. Dorothy Davenport, Emory Johnson.

The Beckoning Trail (Red Feather)
Dir: Jack Conway. Suspense melodrama. J. Warren Kerrigan, Maude George.

Behind The Lines (Bluebird)
Dir: Henry MacRae. Military drama. Harry Carey, Edith Johnson.

Black Friday (Red Feather)
Dir: Lloyd Carleton. Semi-historical drama. Dorothy Davenport, Richard Morris.

Black Orchids (Bluebird)
Dir: Rex Ingram. Romantic drama. Cleo Madison, Wedgewood Nowell, Howard Crampton.

The Black Sheep Of The Family (Red Feather)
Dir: Jay Hunt. Romantic melodrama. Francelia Billington, Jack Holt, Gilmore Hammond.

Bobbie Of The Ballet (Bluebird)
Dir: Joseph de Grasse. Domestic melodrama. Louise Lovely, Jay Belasco, Lon Chaney.

Brigadier Gerard (Red Feather)
Dir: Bert Haldane. Historical drama. Lewis Waller, A. E. George, Madge Titheridge, Fernand Mailly, Frank Cochrane.

Broken Fetters (Bluebird)
Dir: Rex Ingram. Oriental melodrama. Violet Mersereau, Frank Smith, William Garwood.

The Chalice Of Sorrow (Bluebird)
Dir: Rex Ingram. Heavy tragedy. Cleo Madison, Blanche White, Wedgewood Nowell.

The Child Of Mystery (Red Feather)
Dir: Hobart Henley. East Side suspense. Gertrude Selby, Thomas Jefferson, Paul Byron, Mark Fenton.

The Crippled Hand (Bluebird)
Dir: Robert Leonard and David Kirkland. 'Cinderella' tragedy. Ella Hall.

The Devil's Bondswoman (Red Feather)
Dir: Lloyd Carleton. Allegorical drama. Emory Johnson, Dorothy Davenport.

Doctor Neighbor (Red Feather)
Dir: Lloyd Carleton. Medical ethics drama. Gretchen Lederer, Hobart Bosworth, Dorothy Davenport, Emory Johnson.

Drugged Waters (Red Feather)
Dir: William Dowlan. Romantic comedy. Gloria Fonda, E.P. Evers.

The Eagle's Wings (Bluebird)
Dir: Rufus Steele. Patriotic drama. Rodney Ronous, Herbert Rawlinson.

Elusive Isabel (Bluebird)
Dir: Stuart Paton. Spy drama. Florence Lawrence, Sydney Bracey, Harry Millarde.

The End Of The Rainbow (Bluebird)
Dir: Lynn Reynolds. Redwoods melodrama. Myrtle Gonzales, Val Paul.

The Evil Women Do (Bluebird)
Dir: Rupert Julian. Morbid melodrama. Elsie Jane Wilson, Francelia Billington, Douglas Gerrard, Hobart Henley.

The Eye Of God (Bluebird)
Dir: Lois Weber and Phillips Smalley. Mystery melodrama. Lois Weber, Ethel Weber, Tyrone Power.

Fighting For Love (Red Feather)
Dir: Raymond Wells. Cowboy comedy. Ruth Stonehouse, Jack Mulhall, Noble Johnson.

The Flirt (Bluebird)
Dir: Lois Weber and Phillips Smalley. Small town drama. Marie Walcamp, Grace Benham, Antrim Short.

The Folly Of Desire (Red Feather)
Dir: George L. Tucker. Allegorical melodrama. Norman McKinnel.

From Broadway To A Throne (Red Feather)
Dir: William Bowman. Boxing drama. Carter de Haven, Yona Landowska, Malcolm Blevine, Duke Worne.

The Gay Lord Waring (Bluebird)
Dir: Otis Turner. Society suspense. J. Warren Kerrigan, Lois Wilson, Maude George.

The Gilded Spider (Bluebird)
Dir: Joseph de Grasse. Revenge melodrama. Louise Lovely, Lon Chaney.

The Girl Of Lost Lake (Bluebird)
Dir: Lynn Reynolds. Lumberjack romance. Myrtle Gonzales, Val Paul, Mary du Cello.

Gloriana (Bluebird)
Dir: E. Mason Hopper. Orphan drama. Zoe Rae, Virginia Foltz, William Canfield.

God's Crucible (Bluebird)
Dir: Lynn Reynolds. Western drama. George Hernandez, Val Paul, Myrtle Gonzales.

The Great Problem (Bluebird)
Dir: Rex Ingram. Prison reform drama. Violet Mersereau, Lionel Adams, Dan Hanlon.

Half A Rogue (Red Feather)
Dir: Henry Otto. Broadway romance. King Baggot, Clara Beyers, Joseph Castallaneous, Howard Crampton.

The Heart Of A Child (Red Feather)
Dir: Harold Shaw. Rags-to-riches drama. Edna Flugarth, Hayford Hobbs, Edward Sass.

Her Bitter Cup (Red Feather)
Dir: Cleo Madison. London slums drama. Edward Hearn, William V. Mong.

The Heritage Of Hate (Red Feather)
Dir: Burton George. Drama. William Quinn, Betty Schade, Roberta Wilson.

The Honor Of Mary Blake (Bluebird)
Dir: Edwin Stevens. Comedy. Violet Mersereau, Sidney Mason, Tina Marshall.

Hop, The Devil's Brew
Dir: Lois Weber and Phillips Smalley. Drugs drama. C. Norman Hammond, Marie Walcamp.

A Huntress Of Men (Red Feather)
Dir: Lucius Henderson. Society drama. Mary Fuller, Lon Chaney, Joseph Girard.

Idle Wives
Dir: Lois Weber and Phillips Smalley. Tragic drama. Lois Weber, Phillips Smalley, Neva Gerber, Mary MacLean.

If My Country Should Call (Red Feather)
Dir: Joseph de Grasse. Patriotic drama. Dorothy Phillips, Jack Nelson, Lon Chaney.

The Iron Hand (Red Feather)
Dir: Ulysses Davis. Political drama. Hobart Bosworth, Maude George, William V. Mong.

The Isle Of Life (Red Feather)
Dir: Burton George. Romantic adventure. Frank Whitson, Roberta Wilson, Hayward Mack.

It Happened In Honolulu (Red Feather)
Dir: Lynn Reynolds. Romantic comedy. Myrtle Gonzales, Val Paul, George Hernandez.

Jeanne Dore (Bluebird)
Dir: M. Mercanton. Mother-love drama. Sarah Bernhardt, Raymond Bernard.

John Needham's Double (Bluebird)
Dir: Lois Weber and Phillips Smalley. Tragic drama. Tyrone Power, Marie Walcamp.

Kinkaid, Gambler (Red Feather)
Dir: Raymond Wells. Crime puzzler. Ruth Stonehouse, R.A. Cavin, Raymond Whittaker.

A Knight Of The Range (Red Feather)
Dir: Jacques Jaccard. Western melodrama. Harry Carey, Olive Golden.

Little Eve Edgarton (Bluebird)
Dir: Robert Leonard. Comedy drama. Ella Hall, Thomas Jefferson, Dorris Pawn.

The Lords Of High Decision (Red Feather)
Dir: Jack Harvey. Suspense melodrama. Cyril Scott, Joseph Girard, Mildred Gregory.

The Love Girl (Bluebird)
Dir: Robert Leonard. Comedy drama. Ella Hall, Harry Depp, Adele Farrington.

Love Never Dies (Bluebird)
Dir: William Worthington. Sentimental romance. Ruth Stonehouse, Franklyn Farnum.

Love's Lariat (Bluebird)
Dir: George Marshall and Harry Carey. Western comedy. Olive Golden, Neal Hart.

The Madcap (Red Feather)
Dir: William Dowlan. Romantic comedy. Flora Parker de Haven, Richard Sterling.

The Main Spring (Red Feather)
Dir: Jack Conway. Social drama. Ben Wilson, Francelia Billington, Wilbur Higby.

The Man From Nowhere (Red Feather)
Dir: Henry Otto. Crime melodrama. King Baggot, Irene Hunt, Joseph Granby, Frank Smith.

The Man Inside
Dir: J.S. Schrock. Crime mystery. Edwin Stevens, Harry Benham, Tina Marshall.

The Mark Of Cain (Red Feather)
Dir: Joseph de Grasse. Ex-convict drama. Lon Chaney, Frank Whitson, Dorothy Phillips, Gilmore Hammond.

The Measure Of A Man (Bluebird)
Dir: Jack Conway. Religious drama. Louise Lovely, J. Warren Kerrigan, Harry Carter.

Mixed Blood (Red Feather)
Dir: Charles Swickard. Texan melodrama. Claire McDowell, George Beranger.

The Morals Of Hilda (Red Feather)
Dir: Lloyd Carleton. Romantic drama. Gretchen Lederer, Lois Wilson.

The Narrow Path (Red Feather)
Dir: Francis J. Grandon. Rags-to-riches drama. Violet Mersereau, Lenora Von Ottinger.

The People vs. John Doe
Dir: Lois Weber. Humanitarian drama. Harry de More, Evelyn Selby, Willis Marks.

The Piper's Price (Bluebird)
Dir: Joseph de Grasse. Marriage drama. Dorothy Phillips, William Stowell, Lon Chaney, Claire du Brey.

The Place Beyond The Winds (Red Feather)
Dir: Joseph de Grasse. Religious girl's exploits. Dorothy Phillips, Jack Mulhall.

Polly Put The Kettle On (Red Feather)
Dir: Douglas Gerrard. Family drama. Ruth Clifford, Zoe Rae, Thomas Jefferson.

The Pool Of Flame (Red Feather)
Dir: F. McGraw Willis. Adventure. Lois Wilson, Maude George, J. Warren Kerrigan.

The Price Of Silence (Bluebird)
Dir: Joseph de Grasse. Marriage drama. Dorothy Phillips, Vola Smith, Lon Chaney.

The Right To Be Happy (Bluebird)
Dir: Rupert Julian. 'A Christmas Carol'. John Cook, Claire McDowell, Emory Johnson.

A Romance Of Billy Goat Hill (Red Feather)
Dir: Lynn Reynolds. Deep South drama. Myrtle Gonzales, Val Paul, Joseph Jefferson.

Rupert Of Hentzau (Bluebird)
Dir: Geoffrey L. Tucker. Historical drama. Henry Ainley, Jane Gail, Charles Rock.

The Saintly Sinner (Bluebird)
Dir: Raymond Wells. Crime melodrama. Ruth Stonehouse, Jack Mulhall, Alida Hayman.

Saving The Family Name (Bluebird)
Dir: Lois Weber and Phillips Smalley. Family drama. Mary MacLaren, Gerrard Alexander, Phillips Smalley.

Secret Love (Bluebird)
Dir: Robert Leonard. Mining town melodrama. Helen Ware, Harry Carey, Jack Curtis.

Secret Of The Swamp (Bluebird)
Dir: Lynn Reynolds. Southern comedy drama. Myrtle Gonzales, George Hernandez.

The Seekers (Red Feather)
Dir: Otis Turner. Religious drama. Flora Parker de Haven, Edward Hearn, Paul Byron.

The Sign Of The Poppy (Bluebird)
Dir: Charles Swickard. Drugs melodrama. Hobart Henley, Mina Cunard, Gertrude Selby.

The Silent Battle (Bluebird)
Dir: Jack Conway. Alcoholic drama. J. Warren Kerrigan, Lois Wilson, Maude George.

The Social Buccaneer (Bluebird)
Dir: Jack Conway. Mystery. J. Warren Kerrigan, Louise Lovely, Maude George.

A Son Of The Immortals (Bluebird)
Dir: Otis Turner. European court drama. J. Warren Kerrigan, Lois Wilson.

The Sons Of Satan (Red Feather)
Dir: George L. Tucker. Crime melodrama. Gerald Ames, Lewis Gilbert, George Bellamy.

A Soul Enslaved
Dir: Cleo Madison. Sex melodrama. Irma Sorter, Thomas Chatterton.

The Sphinx (Red Feather)
Dir: Mr Adolphi. Comedy drama. Herbert Kelcey, Effie Shannon, Louise Luff.

A Stranger From Somewhere (Bluebird)
Dir: William Worthington. Comedy crime caper. Franklyn Farnum, Agnes Vernon.

The Strength Of The Weak (Bluebird)
Dir: Lucius Henderson. Romantic drama. Mary Fuller, Harry Hilliard, Edwards Davis.

Tangled Hearts (Bluebird)
Dir: Joseph de Grasse. Domestic drama. Louise Lovely, Agnes Vernon, Lon Chaney, Marjorie Ellisson.

The Target (Bluebird)
Dir: Norval MacGregor. Western melodrama. Hobart Bosworth, Anna Lehr, Maude George.

Temptation And The Man (Red Feather)
Dir: Robert F. Hill. Ex-convict drama. Hobart Henley, Sydell Dowling, Sidney Bracy.

Thrown To The Lions (Red Feather)
Dir: Lucius Henderson. Metropolitan drama. Mary Fuller, Clifford Gray, Joseph Girard.

Two Men Of Sandy Bar (Red Feather)
Dir: Lloyd Carleton. Western melodrama. Hobart Bosworth, Charles Hickman, Gretchen Lederer.

The Unattainable (Bluebird)
Dir: Lloyd Carleton. Domestic drama. Dorothy Davenport, Emory Johnson.

Under Suspicion
Dir: George Tucker. Crime comedy. Douglas Munro, Laura Cowie, Gerald Ames.

Undine (Bluebird)
Dir: Henry Otto. Aquatic fairy tale. Ida Schell, Douglas Gerrard, Edna Mason.

Wanted – A Home (Bluebird)
Dir: Lois Weber and Phillips Smalley. Social drama. Mary MacLaren, Nannie Wright, Grace Johnson.

The Way Of The World (Red Feather)
Dir: Lloyd Carleton. Domestic drama. Hobart Bosworth, Dorothy Davenport.

What Love Can Do (Red Feather)
Dir: Jay Hunt. Newspaper drama. Adele Farrington, C. Norman Hammond, O.C. Jackson.

The Whirlpool Of Destiny (Red Feather)
Dir: Otis Turner. City-girl saga. Flora Parker de Haven, Jack Mulhall, Charles H. Mailes, Edward Hearn.

The Wrong Door (Bluebird)
Dir: Carter de Haven. Farce melodrama. Carter and Flora Parker de Haven, Ernie Shields.

The Yoke Of Gold (Red Feather)
Dir: Lloyd Carleton. Pioneer drama. Dorothy Davenport, Alfred Allen, Emory Johnson.

The Youth Of Fortune (Red Feather)
Dir: Otis Turner. Domestic comedy. Carter and Flora Parker de Haven, Maude George.

△ Brand Whitlock, the US Minister to Belgium, furnished the story for a large-scale Civil War melodrama called **The Field Of Honor**. All about two men who love the same woman, it starred Louise Lovely as the sought-after heroine, M.K. Wilson as the man she eventually marries (only to discover that he is a coward in battle), and Allen Holubar (illustrated), who also directed, as the unsuccessful but worthier suitor. Elliott J. Clawson's scenario had the noble Holubar protecting Wilson's name after he believes he has fallen in battle; but Wilson, it turns out, isn't dead at all and his sudden reappearance causes all sorts of complications. A not especially distinguished effort – its main fault was Holubar's frenetic direction with its unvarying pace – the film also featured Sidney Dean, Helen Wright, Frank MacQuarrie and Frankie Lee. (Butterfly).

△ **Sirens Of The Sea**, loosely based on the legend of the Lorelei, was a self-consciously 'arty' attempt to justify the spectacle of star Louise Lovely and twenty of her chumbs cavorting along a rocky beach very scantily clad. In the sea, they wear even less. Co-star Jack Mulhall who, in the course of events, has a dream all about mermaids and sea sirens, pairs off with Miss Lovely (2nd left) shortly after arriving at this enchanted spot in his yacht; with co-star William Quinn (as a good-for-nothing playboy) finding solace in the arms of Carmel Myers (right). Allan Holubar wrote and directed it (story by Grace Helen Batley) and, in secondary roles, cast Sydney Dean, Evelyn Selbie and Helen Wright. (Jewel).

▷ Edward Everett Hale's patriotic story, **The Man Without A Country**, came to the screen in a scenario by Lloyd Lonergan, and with H.H. Herbert as the rather resistible hero who, after rejecting his country with the words, 'Damn the United States. I never want to hear her mentioned again', undergoes a dramatic change of heart when a friend gives him a copy of Hale's *The Man Without A Country* and implores him to read it. The book makes such an impression on Herbert that he wastes no time in rushing to the nearest recruiting office to enlist. Love interest was supplied by Florence LaBadie (illustrated), but the film's patriotic fervour was its *raison d'être*, and in the hands of director Ernest C. Warde, Hale's message was loud and clear. The cast was completed by J.H. Gilmour, Carey Hastings, Ernest Howard and Charles Dundan. (Jewel).

▷ The production team of Lois Weber and Phillips Smalley turned their attention to the problems of the indigent shopgirl in **The Price Of A Good Time.** Adapted by Miss Weber from Marion Orth's story *The Whim*, it told the cautionary tale of a girl (Mildred Harris, seated left) from a wretchedly unhappy background who, when offered a good time for a week by the son (Kenneth Harlan) of her employer, readily accepts. Her behaviour, however, is misunderstood by her brother who informs their parents of her relationship with Harlan, as a result of which the hapless shopgirl flings herself under the wheels of Harlan's car and is killed. There is a happy ending of sorts when Harlan's icy society girlfriend (Gertrude Astor) thaws and, as a result of what has happened, expresses a desire to do something useful in the world – such as becoming a shopgirl! A triumph of style over content and another hit for the Weber-Smalley combo, the film also featured Alfred Allen, Helene Rosson, Adele Farrington and Ann Schaeffer (right). (Jewel).

△ One of the studio's more successful 1917 releases, **Hell Morgan's Girl**, a five-reel Bluebird Production, was an ambitious drama set along California's rough-and-ready Barbary Coast, and climaxing in the San Francisco earthquake of 1906. The story concerned Roger Curwell, a young painter, who after being disowned by his wealthy father for refusing to give up his career as an artist, stumbles into Hell Morgan's disreputable saloon on the Barbary Coast and, in a state of inebriation, throws a glass of whiskey at a painting of a nude female which Morgan has recently purchased and hung over the bar. Morgan begins to thrash him, but his daughter Lola intervenes, persuades her father to give Roger a job as saloon pianist, and promptly falls in love with him, much to the chagrin of Sleter Noble, who is in love with her himself. The progress of Roger's romance with Lola, interrupted by a vamp called Olga, the San Francisco 'quake, and the deaths of both Sleter and Lola's father, formed the content of the film, many of whose violent 'underworld' scenes were labelled 'objectionable' in the press. Condemned by the police commissioner of New York City for its seaminess, the film had certain cuts made in the final print, but nothing that was removed damaged the realism that director Joseph De Grasse so successfully managed to bring to the subject. Dorothy Phillips (illustrated – wife of Allen Holubar) scored her biggest success as Lola, while William Stowell was equally successful as Roger Curwell. Hell Morgan was played by Alfred Allen, Sleter Noble by Lon Chaney and Olga by Lilyan Rosine. Joseph Gerard completed the cast.

▽ A lively and exciting western which, on its release, was favourably compared with *The Virginian* (Lasky, 1914), director Jack (later John) Ford's **Straight Shooting** was justifiably praised for realistically depicting a bitter clash between cattlemen and homesteaders. Harry Carey (illustrated) starred as Cheyenne Harry, a bad man with a good heart, with other roles in George Hiveley's stirring scenario going to George Berrill, Molly Malone, Duke Lee, Vester Pegg, Ted Brooks, Milt Brown and, in a small role, Hoot Gibson. (Butterfly).

▽ A story that 'brings both smiles and tears', as one wag wrote at the time, **Mother O' Mine** was a lump-in-the-throat weepie in which a son, through personal ambition, rejects his elderly mother when she comes to the city to visit him. By reel five, however, he has repented, and is even prepared to sacrifice his engagement to a society girl 'bred in the purple' in order to take care of the old woman who has returned to the country after overhearing a conversation in which she is described by her son as his erstwhile nurse. Written by Elliott J. Clawson from a story by Rupert Julian (right), who directed it and also appeared as the son, the film starred Ruby La Fayette (left) as the mother, as well as Elsie Jane Wilson, Ruth Clifford and W.E. Warner. (Bluebird).

◁ The effect that the hothouse atmosphere of Parisian society has on a basically charming young American girl was the subject of **Princess Virtue**, and it starred ex-Ziegfeld chorus girl Mae Murray (illustrated – making her Universal debut) as the titular heroine. Miss Murray's performance was on a par with the uninspired scenario Fred Myton cobbled out of Louise Winter's novel of the same name, the acting plaudits going to personable Wheeler Oakman who, despite hefty competition, managed to win MM for himself in reel five. Miss Murray's real-life husband, Robert Z. Leonard, directed it. Also cast were Jean Hersholt, Lule Warrenton, Clarissa Selwynne, Gretchen Lederer, Harry Van Meter and Paul Nicholson. (Bluebird).

△ Director Rupert Julian brought a certain charm to **A Kentucky Cinderella** whose plot, even in 1917, was distinctly old-fashioned. Its once-upon-a-time, happily-ever-after story traced the fortunes of a poor young girl who, after the death of her father, goes to her uncle in Kentucky where she is made distinctly unwelcome by his unpleasant second wife. But in the end it is she, rather than the wife's daughter, who nabs the handsome hero. Several black stereotypes – such as little Zoe Rae's pickaninny girl (foreground right) and Lucretia Harris' (centre right) coloured mammy (called Aunt Chlorinda) – infiltrated the scenario which Elliott J. Clawson fashioned from a story by F. Hopkinson Smith. The more serious acting chores went to Ruth Clifford (left) as the Cinderella of the title, to director Rupert Julian (as a character called Toulumne John) and to Harry Carter, Myrtle Reeves, Aurora Pratt, Eddie Polo, Emory Johnson and Frank Lanning. (Bluebird).

OTHER PRODUCTIONS OF 1917

The Almost Good Man
Dir: Fred A. Kelsey. Drama. Harry Carey, Clare du Brey, Vester Pegg, Frank MacQuarrie.

Anything Once (Bluebird)
Dir: Joseph de Grasse. Comedy drama. Franklyn Farnum, Lon Chaney, Claire du Brey.

Beloved Jim (Butterfly)
Dir: Stuart Paton. Sentimental drama. Harry Carter, Joseph Girard, Priscilla Dean.

The Birth Of Patriotism
Dir: E. Magnus Ingleton. War drama. Irene Hunt, Ann Kronan, Ernie Shields.

Bondage (Bluebird)
Dir: Ida May Park. Bohemian drama. Dorothy Phillips, William Stowell.

The Boy Girl (Bluebird)
Dir: Edwin Steven. Comedy. Violet Mersereau, Sidney Mason, Florida Kingsley.

Bringing Home Father (Bluebird)
Dir: William Worthington. Comedy drama. Franklyn Farnum, Brownie Vernon.

Broadway Love (Bluebird)
Dir: Ida May Park. Stage romance. William Stowell, Lon Chaney, Dorothy Phillips.

The Bronze Bride (Red Feather)
Dir: Henry MacRae. Squaw man romance. Claire McDowell, Frank Mayo, Frankie Lee.

Bucking Broadway (Butterfly)
Dir: Jack (John) Ford. Western comedy romance. Harry Carey, Molly Malone, Vester Pegg.

The Car Of Chance (Bluebird)
Dir: William Worthington. Family drama. Franklyn Farnum, Agnes Vernon, Molly Malone.

The Charmer (Bluebird)
Dir: Jack Conway. Juvenile comedy. Ella Hall, Martha Mattox, Belle Bennett.

The Circus Of Life (Butterfly)
Dir: Rupert Julian. Rooming-house saga. Pomeroy Cannon, Elsie Jane Wilson, Harry Carter.

The Clean-up (Bluebird)
Dir: William Worthington. Comedy drama. Franklyn Farnum, Brownie Vernon.

The Clock (Bluebird)
Dir: William Worthington. Romantic melodrama. Franklyn Farnum, Agnes Vernon, Frank Whitson, Mark Fenton.

Come Through
Dir: Jack Conway. Crime melodrama. Herbert Rawlinson, Alice Lake, George Webb.

The Co-respondent (Jewel)
Dir: Ralph W. Ince. Newspaper drama. Elaine Hammerstein, Wilfred Lucas.

The Cricket (Butterfly)
Dir: Elsie Jane Wilson. Sentimental drama. Zoe Rae, Harry Holden, Rena Rogers.

Desire Of The Moth (Bluebird)
Dir: Rupert Julian. Western melodrama. Ruth Clifford, Monroe Salisbury, W.H. Bainbridge.

The Devil's Pay Day (Bluebird)
Dir: William Worthington. Tragic drama. Franklyn Farnum, Gertrude Astor.

A Doll's House (Bluebird)
Dir: Joseph de Grasse. Ibsen drama. Dorothy Phillips, Lon Chaney, William Stowell.

The Door Between (Bluebird)
Dir: Rupert Julian. Drama. Monroe Salisbury, Ruth Clifford, George McDaniels.

The Double Room Mystery (Red Feather)
Dir: Hobart Henley. Suspense. Edwin H. Brady, Hayward Mack, Gertrude Selby.

The Double Standard (Butterfly)
Dir: Phillips Smalley. Crime drama. Roy Stewart, Hazel Page, Frank Brownlee.

The Edge Of The Law (Butterfly)
Dir: Louis Chaudet. Crime adventure. Ruth Stonehouse, Betty Schade, Lloyd Whitlock.

Eternal Love (Butterfly)
Dir: Douglas Gerrard. European romance. Ruth Clifford, Myrtle Reeves.

Even As You And I
Dir: Lois Weber. Allegoric drama. Maude George, Priscilla Dean, Ben Wilson.

Face Value (Bluebird)
Dir: Robert Leonard. Bad-girl-makes-good drama. Mae Murray, Wheeler Oakman, Clarissa Selwyn, Casson Ferguson.

Fear Not (Butterfly)
Dir: Allen Holubar. Crime drama. Myles McCarthy, Brownie Vernon.

The Fighting Gringo (Red Feather)
Dir: Fred A. Kelsey. Comedy western. Harry Carey, Claire du Bray, George Webb.

Fighting Mad (Butterfly)
Dir: Edward le Saint. Pioneer drama. William Stowell, Helen Wilson, Betty Schade.

Fires Of Rebellion (Bluebird)
Dir: Ida May Park. Young girl drama. Dorothy Phillips, Lon Chaney, William Stowell.

The Flame Of Youth (Butterfly)
Dir: Elmer Clifton. Adventure melodrama. Jack Mulhall, Donna Moon, Ann Kronan.

The Flashlight (Bluebird)
Dir: Ida May Park. Suspense melodrama. Dorothy Phillips, Lon Chaney, William Stowell.

Flirting With Death (Bluebird)
Dir: Elmer Clifton. Circus life comedy. Herbert Rawlinson, Brownie Vernon, Frank MacQuarrie, Marc Fenton.

The Flower Of Doom (Red Feather)
Dir: Rex Ingram. Chinatown melodrama. Yvette Mitchell, Gypsy Hart, Wedgewood Nowell.

Follow The Girl (Butterfly)
Dir: Louis Chaudet. Immigrant saga. Ruth Stonehouse, Jack Dill, Roy Stewart.

'49-'17 (Butterfly)
Dir: Ruth Ann Baldwin. Western melodrama. Joseph Girard, Jean Hersholt, Donna Drew.

The Gates Of Doom (Red Feather)
Dir: Charles Swickard. War romance. Claire McDowell, L.C. Shumway, Jack Connolly.

The Gift Girl (Bluebird)
Dir: Rupert Julian. Comedy. Louise Lovely, Emory Johnson, Wadsworth Harris.

The Girl And The Crisis (Red Feather)
Dir: William V. Mong. Capital punishment drama. Dorothy Davenport, Charles Perley.

The Girl By The Roadside (Bluebird)
Dir: Theodore Marston. Young girl mystery drama. Violet Mersereau, Allen Edwards.

The Girl In The Checkered Coat (Bluebird)
Dir: Joseph de Grasse. Criminal girls drama. Dorothy Phillips, Lon Chaney, William Stowell, Mrs A.E. Witting.

The Girl Who Won Out (Butterfly)
Dir: Eugene Moore. Orphan drama. Violet MacMillan, P.L. Pembroke, Barbara Conley.

The Greater Law (Bluebird)
Dir: Lynn Reynolds. Drama. Myrtle Gonzales, George Hernandez, Gretchen Lederer.

The Hand That Rocks The Cradle
Dir: Lois Weber and Phillips Smalley. Birth-control drama. Lois Weber, Phillips Smalley, Priscilla Dean, Evelyn Selbie.

Heartstrings (Red Feather)
Dir: Allen Holubar. Family saga. Maude George, Irene Hunt, Francelia Billington.

Hero Of The Hour (Red Feather)
Dir: Raymond Wells. Western melodrama. Jack Mulhall, Fritzi Ridgeway, Wadsworth Harris.

Her Soul's Inspiration (Bluebird)
Dir: Jack Conway. Drama. Ella Hall, Marc Robbins, Edward Hearn, Marcia Moore.

The High Sign (Butterfly)
Dir: Elmer Clifton. Romance. Herbert Rawlinson, Brownie Vernon, Nellie Allen.

High Speed (Butterfly)
Dir: George L. Sargent. Farce. Jack Mulhall, Fritzi Ridgeway, Harry Rattenbury.

A Jewel In Pawn (Bluebird)
Dir: Jack Conway. Sentimental saga. Ella Hall, Antrim Short, Walter Belasco.

John Ermine Of Yellowstone (Butterfly)
Dir: Francis Ford. Frontier epic. Mae Gaston, Burwell Hamrick, William Carroll.

The Lair Of The Wolf (Butterfly)
Dir: Charles Swickard. Murder melodrama. Gretchen Lederer, Donna Drew, Joseph Girard.

The Lash Of Power (Bluebird)
Dir: Harry Solter. Dream melodrama. Carmel Myers, Kenneth Harlan, Helen Wright.

Like Wildfire (Butterfly)
Dir: Stuart Paton. Romantic drama. Herbert Rawlinson, Neva Gerber, Johnnie Cook.

Little Miss Nobody (Bluebird)
Dir: Harry F. Millarde. Orphan drama. Violet Mersereau, Clara Beyers, Helen Lindroth.

The Little Orphan (Bluebird)
Dir: Jack Conway. War orphan drama. Ella Hall, Gretchen Lederer, Gertrude Astor.

The Little Pirate (Butterfly)
Dir: Elsie Jane Wilson. Juvenile adventure. Zoe Rae, Burwell Hemerick, Charley West.

The Little Terror (Bluebird)
Dir: Rex Ingram. Comedy romp. Violet Mersereau, Sydney Mason, Ed Porter, Ned Porter.

Love Aflame (Red Feather)
Dir: Raymond Wells. Comedy adventure Ruth Stonehouse, Jack Mulhall, Noble Johnson.

Man And Beast (Butterfly)
Dir: Henry MacRae. Wildlife adventure. Eileen Sedgewick, Park Jones, Harry Clifton.

The Man From Montana (Butterfly)
Dir: George Marshall. Mining crime drama. Neal Hart, Vivian Rich, George Berrill.

The Man Trap (Bluebird)
Dir: Elmer Clifton. Crook drama. Herbert Rawlinson, Sally Starr, Ruby La Fayette.

The Man Who Took A Chance (Bluebird)
Dir: William Worthington. Comedy. Franklyn Farnum, Agnes Vernon, Lloyd Whitlock.

A Marked Man (Butterfly)
Dir: Jack (John) Ford. Western melodrama. Harry Carey, Molly Malone, Harry Rattenbury.

Me An' Me Pal (Red Feather)
Dir: Harold Shaw. Cockney comedy. Hubert Willis, Gerald Ames, Edna Flugarth.

The Midnight Man (Butterfly)
Dir: Elmer Clifton. Crime melodrama. Jack Mulhall, Ann Kronan, Al McQuarrie.

Money Madness (Butterfly)
Dir: Henry MacRae. Detective drama. Don Bailey, Charles H. Mailes, Mary MacLaren.

Mr Dolan Of New York (Red Feather)
Dir: Raymond Wells. Boxing drama. Noble Johnson, Jack Mulhall, Julia Ray.

Mr Opp (Bluebird)
Dir: Lynn Reynolds. Small town saga Arthur Hoyt, George Cheesboro, Neva Gerber.

Mutiny (Bluebird)
Dir: Lynn Reynolds. Seafaring drama. Myrtle Gonzales, Val Paul, George Hernandez.

My Little Boy (Bluebird)
Dir: Elsie Jane Wilson. Christmas fable. Ella Hall, Zoe Rae.

My Unmarried Wife (Bluebird)
Dir: George Seigman. Comedy drama. Carmel Myers, Kenneth Harlan, Beatrice Van.

The Mysterious Mr. Tiller (Bluebird)
Dir: Rupert Julian. Drama. Ruth Clifford, Frank Brownie, Wedgewood Nowell.

The Mysterious Mrs. M (Bluebird)
Dir: Lois Weber. Occult mystery. Harrison Ford, Evelyn Selbie, Mary MacLaren.

Pay Me (Jewel)
Dir: Joseph de Grasse. Western melodrama. Dorothy Phillips, Lon Chaney, Evelyn Selbie.

The Phantom's Secret (Butterfly)
Dir: Charles Swickard. Mystery drama. Mignon Anderson, Hayward Mack, Marc Fenton.

The Plow Woman (Butterfly)
Dir: Charles Swickard. Pioneer saga. Mary MacLaren, H. C. de More, Andy McTavish.

Polly Redhead (Bluebird)
Dir: Jack Conway. Light comedy. Gertrude Astor, Charles H. Mailes, Gretchen Lederer.

The Pulse Of Life (Bluebird)
Dir: Rex Ingram. Suspense. Wedgewood Nowell, Gypsy Hart, William Dwyer.

The Raggedy Queen (Bluebird)
Dir: Theodore Marston. Light comedy. Violet Mersereau, Grace Barton, Frank Otto.

Red Saunders Plays Cupid
Dir: Jack (John) Ford. Adventure. Harry Carey, Claire du Brey, George Webb, Rex Rosselli.

The Reed Case (Butterfly)
Dir: Allen Holubar. Crime drama. Alfred Allen, Louise Lovely, Fred Montague.

The Rescue (Bluebird)
Dir: Ida May Park. Marriage drama. Dorothy Phillips, Lon Chaney, William Stowell.

The Reward Of The Faithless (Bluebird)
Dir: Rex Ingram. Tragic drama. Wedgewood Nowell, Betty Schade, Claire du Brey.

The Savage (Bluebird)
Dir: Rupert Julian. Northwest romance. Ruth Clifford, Colleen Moore, Monroe Salisbury.

The Scarlet Car
Dir: Joseph de Grasse. Melodrama. Franklyn Farnum, Lon Chaney, Edith Johnson.

The Scarlet Crystal (Red Feather)
Dir: Charles Swickard. New-girl-in-town drama. Herbert Rawlinson, Betty Schade, Dorothy Davenport.

The Secret Man (Butterfly)
Dir: Jack (John) Ford. Western melodrama. Harry Carey, Edith Sterling, Hoot Gibson.

The Show Down (Bluebird)
Dir: Lynn Reynolds. Desert island yarn. Myrtle Gonzales, George Hernandez.

The Silent Lady (Butterfly)
Dir: Elsie Jane Wilson. Romantic drama. Gretchen Lederer, Zoe Rae, Winter Hall.

Society's Driftwood (Butterfly)
Dir: Louis Chaudet. Revenge melodrama. Grace Cunard, Joseph Girard, Charles West.

Southern Justice (Bluebird)
Dir: Lynn Reynolds. Deep South drama. Myrtle Gonzales, George Hernandez.

The Spindle Of Life (Butterfly)
Dir: George Cochrane. Romantic comedy. Ben Wilson, Neva Gerber, Jessie Pratt.

The Spotted Lily (Bluebird)
Dir: Harry Solter. Romantic saga. Ella Hall, Gretchen Lederer, Victor Rottman.

A Stormy Knight (Bluebird)
Dir: Elmer Clifton. Mystery. Franklyn Farnum, Brownie Vernon, Jean Hersholt.

Susan's Gentleman (Bluebird)
Dir: Edwin Stevens. Romantic comedy. Violet Mersereau, Maud Cooling, Sidney Mason.

The Terror (Red Feather)
Dir: Raymond Wells and Frank Myton. Crime suspense. Jack Mulhall, Grace MacLaren.

Treason (Bluebird)
Dir: Allen Holubar. War drama. Lois Wilson, Dorothy Davenport.

Triumph (Bluebird)
Dir: Joseph de Grasse. Stage-struck girl drama. Dorothy Phillips, Lon Chaney.

Vengeance Of The West
Dir: Joseph de Grasse. No other information available.

The War Of The Tongs (Red Feather)
Dir: none credited. Oriental drama. Tom Hing, Lee Gow, Lin Neong, Hoo Ching.

Who Was The Other Man (Butterfly)
Dir: Francis Ford. Spy intrigue. Duke Worne, William T. Horne, Mae Gaston.

A Wife On Trial (Butterfly)
Dir: Ruth Ann Baldwin. Pollyanna romance. Mignon Anderson, Leo Pierson, L. Wells.

The Winged Mystery (Bluebird)
Dir: Joseph de Grasse. Mystery. Franklyn Farnum, Claire du Brey, Rosemary Theby.

The Wolf And His Mate (Butterfly)
Dir: Edward le Saint. Northwest adventure. Hart Hoxie, Louise Lovely, Betty Schade.

1918

▽ A handsome young actor called Rudolpho De Valentina (later Rudolph Valentino, centre right) received his first Universal credit in **A Society Sensation**, playing the son of a wealthy scion of society who falls in love with the daughter (Carmel Myers, centre left) of a Southern Californian fisherman (Alfred Allen). Perley Poore Sheehan's story, adapted by Hope Loring and Paul Powell, pivoted on the fisherman's belief, after discovering a steel engraving of an ancestor, that he should really be a member of the House of Lords. The movie also featured Lydia Yeamans Titus, Fred Kelsey, ZaSu Pitts and Harold Goodwin, and the appropriately lightweight direction was by Paul Powell. (Bluebird).

▷ 'A drama of intense emotions framed in commonplace surroundings' (as a promotional phrase insisted), **The City Of Tears** was the simple story of a chorus girl in an Italian opera company who, after the company has disbanded and the fifty dollars she has saved is stolen, finds solace with a kindly Italian delicatessen dealer called Tony. There wasn't much more to it than that, and it relied largely on the performances of Carmel Myers (illustrated) as the young singer and Edwin August as the man who befriends her, to keep Olga Printzlau's slender narrative on the boil. Very much a 'woman's picture', it was directed by Elsie Jane Wilson, and featured Earl Rodney, Leatrice Joy and Lettie Kruse. (Bluebird).

△ The pairing of M. De Valentina (right) and Miss Myers (centre) was successful enough to merit a repeat performance, and director Paul Powell brought them together for the second time in 1918 in **All Night**. The result was a really contrived farce from the pen of Edgar Franklin (with Edgar Myton scripting) which told the unlikely tale of a married couple (Charles Dorian and Mary Warren) who, after discharging their servants on the eve of an important dinner party they are giving for an eccentric millionaire (William Dyer, left), persuade two of their unmarried guests (De Valentina and Myers) to take their places while they, in turn, pretend to be the servants. The ensuing complications, as the unmarried couple pretend to be married for the sake of the millionaire, gave the film what little comic mileage it had, though none of the cast – including Wadsworth Harris and Jack Hull – was able to pummel much life into it. (Bluebird).

▷ Glossy production values from the Lois Weber-Phillips Smalley team kept the patrons amused at **For Husbands Only**, but underneath the surface sheen there wasn't much substance to G.B Stern's magazine story (adapted by Miss Weber) about a convent-bred girl who, on being introduced into society, immediately falls in love with a predatory bachelor. Discovering that the bachelor is merely toying with her affections, she marries a slow-witted man out of spite, then proceeds to make the flirtatious bachelor fall head over heels in love with her. Mildred Harris (illustrated) was the girl, Lewis J. (later Lew) Cody the object of her affections and Fred Goodwins the man she marries. (Jewel.)

OTHER PRODUCTIONS OF 1918

Beans (Bluebird)
Dir: Jack Dillon. Suspense comedy. Edith Roberts, William E. Lawrence.

Beauty In Chains
Dir: Elsie Jane Wilson. Spanish romance. Emory Johnson, Ruby La Fayette.

Borrowed Clothes
Dir: Lois Weber and Phillips Smalley. Drama. Mildred Harris, Edward J. Peel, Helen Rosson.

Brace Up (Bluebird)
Dir: Elmer Clifton. Secret Service drama. Herbert Rawlinson, Claire du Brey.

Brazen Beauty (Bluebird)
Dir: Tod Browning. Romance. Priscilla Dean, Thurston Hall, Gertrude Astor.

Bread
Dir: Ida May Park. Stage life drama. Mary MacLaren, Edward Cecil, Gladys Fox.

The Bride's Awakening (Bluebird)
Dir: Robert Leonard. Romantic drama. Mae Murray, Lewis Cody, Ashton Dearholt.

Broadway Scandal (Bluebird)
Dir: Joseph de Grasse. Comedy drama. Carmel Myers, Edwin August, Lon Chaney.

The Cabaret Girl (Bluebird)
Dir: Douglas Gerrard. Satire. Ruth Clifford, Ashton Dearholt, Carmel Phillips.

The Craving (Bluebird)
Dir: John Ford. Fantasy horror drama. Francis Ford, Mae Gaston, Peter Gerald.

Danger Go Slow
Dir: Robert Leonard. Comedy drama. Mae Murray, Jack Mulhall, Lon Chaney.

Danger Within (Bluebird)
Dir: Rae Berger. Child drama. Zoe Rae, Charles H. Mailes, William Carroll.

The Deciding Kiss (Bluebird)
Dir: Tod Browning. Satire. Edith Roberts, Hal Cooley.

Delirium
Dir: Francis Ford and Jack (John) Ford. Drama.

The Doctor And The Woman (Jewel)
Dir: Lois Weber and Phillips Smalley. Mystery drama. Mildred Harris, True Boardman, Albert Roscoe.

The Dream Lady (Bluebird)
Dir: Elsie Jane Wilson. Dream mystery. Carmel Myers, Thomas Holding.

The Eagle (Bluebird)
Dir: Elmer Clifton. Crime suspense. Monroe Salisbury, Edna Earle, Ward Wing.

The Empty Cab (Bluebird)
Dir: Douglas Gerrard. Mystery. Franklyn Farnum, Eileen Percy, Fred Kelsey.

Fast Company (Bluebird)
Dir: Lynn Reynolds. Light whimsy. Franklyn Farnum, Juanita Hanson, Lon Chaney.

The Fighting Grin (Bluebird)
Dir: Joseph de Grasse. Comedy. Franklyn Farnum, Edith Johnson, J. Morris Foster.

Fires Of Youth (Bluebird)
Dir: Rupert Julian. Marriage drama. Ralph Lewis, Ruth Clifford, George Fisher.

$5,000 Reward (Bluebird)
Dir: Douglas Gerrard. Detective yarn. Franklyn Farnum, Gloria Hope, William Lloyd.

The Flash Of Fate
Dir: Elmer Clifton. Financial crime-melodrama. Herbert Rawlinson, Mary MacGregor.

The Forbidden Box (Jewel)
Dir: Lois Weber and Phillips Smalley. Drama. Mildred Harris, Henry Woodward.

The Girl In The Dark (Bluebird)
Dir: Stuart Paton. Mystery adventure. Carmel Myers, Ashton Dearholt, Betty Schade.

The Girl Who Wouldn't Quit
Dir: Edgar Jones. Melodrama. Louise Lovely, Mark Fenton, Charles H. Mailes.

The Grand Passion (Jewel)
Dir: Ida May Park. Melodrama. Dorothy Phillips, William Stowell.

The Guilt Of Silence (Bluebird)
Dir: Elmer Clifton. Snow-country melodrama. Monroe Salisbury, Ruth Clifford.

Hands Down (Bluebird)
Dir: Rupert Julian. Western melodrama. Monroe Salisbury, Ruth Clifford.

Hell Bent
Dir: Jack (John) Ford. Western melodrama. Harry Carey, Neva Gerber, Duke Lee, Vester Pegg.

Hell's Crater
Dir: W.B. Pearson. Drama. Grace Cunard.

Her Body In Bond
Dir: Robert Leonard. Allegoric drama. Mae Murray, Kenneth Harlan, Al Roscoe.

Hugon, The Mighty (Bluebird)
Dir: Rollin Sturgeon. French-Canadian drama. Monroe Salisbury, Margery Bennett.

Hungry Eyes (Bluebird)
Dir: Rupert Julian. Western romance. Monroe Salisbury, Ruth Clifford.

The Kaiser, Beast Of Berlin
Dir: Rupert Julian. Semi-fiction drama. Ruth Clifford, Robert Gordon.

Kiss Or Kill
Dir: Elmer Clifton. Drama. Herbert Rawlinson, Priscilla Dean, Alfred Allen.

A Long Chance (Bluebird)
Dir: Jack Conway. Western adventure. Frank Keenan, Beryle Broughton.

The Love Swindle (Bluebird)
Dir: Jack Dillon. Romantic drama. Edith Roberts, Leo White, Clarissa Selwynne.

The Lure Of Luxury (Bluebird)
Dir: Elsie Jane Wilson. Sentimental romance. Ruth Clifford, Edward Hearn.

Madame Spy
Dir: Douglas Gerrard. Comedy drama. Jack Mulhall, Donna Drew, Wadsworth Harris.

The Magic Eye
Dir: Rae Berger. Juvenile drama. Zoe Rae, H.A. Burrows.

The Marriage Lie (Bluebird)
Dir: Harvey Gates. Comedy drama. Carmel Myers, Kenneth Harlan, Harry Carter.

Midnight Madness (Bluebird)
Dir: Rupert Julian. Mystery. Ruth Clifford, Kenneth Harlan, Harry M. Holden.

A Model's Confession
Dir: Ida May Park. Society drama. Mary MacLaren, Kenneth Harlan, Edna Earle.

Modern Love
Dir: Robert Leonard. Romance. Mae Murray, George Cheesboro, Philo McCullough.

Morgan's Raiders (Bluebird)
Dir: Bess Meredyth and Wilfred Lucas. Civil War drama. Violet Mersereau, Barbara Gilroy, Edward Burns.

The Mortgaged Wife
Dir: Allen Holubar. Drama. Dorothy Phillips, William Stowell, Albert Roscoe.

A Mother's Secret (Bluebird)
Dir: Douglas Gerrard. Romantic melodrama. Ella Hall, Mary Hirsch, Emory Johnson.

The Nature Girl (Bluebird)
Dir: O.A.C. Lund. Island drama. Violet Mersereau, Donald Stewart, Senorita de Cordoba.

New Love For Old
Dir: Elsie Jane Wilson. Romantic drama. Ella Hall, Emory Johnson, Gretchen Lederer.

Nobody's Wife
Dir: Edward le Saint. Northwest romance. Hart Hoxie, Louise Lovely, Betty Schade.

Painted Lips
Dir: Edward le Saint. Drama. Louise Lovely, Lewis Cody, Alfred Allen, Betty Schade.

The Phantom Riders
Dir: Jack (John) Ford. Western melodrama. Harry Carey, Buck Connor, Molly Malon, Vester Pegg.

Playthings (Bluebird)
Dir: Douglas Gerrard. Sentimental melodrama. Myrtle Reeves, Lewis Cody, Fritzi Brunette.

The Red, Red Heart (Bluebird)
Dir: Wilfred Lucas. Western romantic drama. Monroe Salisbury, Ruth Clifford, Val Paul.

A Rich Man's Darling (Bluebird)
Dir: Edgar Jones. Romantic comedy. Louise Lovely, Philo McCullough, Harry Holden.

The Risky Road
Dir: Ida May Park. Sex melodrama. Dorothy Phillips, William Stowell.

The Rough Lover (Bluebird)
Dir: Joseph de Grasse. Farce. Franklyn Farnum, Juanita Hansen, Catherine Henry.

Scandal Mongers (Bluebird)
Dir: Lois Weber and Phillips Smalley. Tragic drama. Rupert Julian, Adele Farrington, Lois Weber, Phillips Smalley.

The Scarlet Drop
Dir: Jack (John) Ford. Civil War drama. Harry Carey, Molly Malone, Vester Pegg.

The Sea Flower (Bluebird)
Dir: Colin Campbell. Secret Service adventure. Juanita Hansen, Al Whitman.

Set Free (Bluebird)
Dir: Tod Browning. Gypsy adventure. Edith Roberts, Harry Hilliard, Harold Goodwin.

She Hired A Husband (Bluebird)
Dir: Jack Dillon. Light romance. Priscilla Dean, Pat O'Malley, Marion Skinner.

Smashing Through
Dir: Elmer Clifton. Western melodrama. Herbert Rawlinson, Sally Starr, Neal Hart.

A Soul For Sale (Jewel)
Dir: Allen Holubar. Society drama. Dorothy Phillips, Albert Roscoe.

The Talk Of The Town
Dir: Allen Holubar. Society romance. Dorothy Phillips, William Stowell, Lon Chaney, George Fawcett.

That Devil, Bateese (Bluebird)
Dir: William Wolbert. Northwest action romance. Monroe Salisbury, Ada Gleason.

Thieves' Gold
Dir: Jack (John) Ford. Western melodrama. Harry Carey, Molly Malone, Vester Pegg, John Cook.

Three Mounted Men
Dir: Jack (John) Ford. Western melodrama. Harry Carey, Joe Harris, Harry Carter, Neva Gerber.

Together (Bluebird)
Dir: O.A.C. Lund. Family mystery. Violet Mersereau, Chester Barnett.

Tongues Of Flame (Bluebird)
Dir: Colin Campbell. Redwoods romance. Marie Walcamp, Al Whitman, Alfred Allen.

The Two-Soul Woman (Bluebird)
Dir: Elmer Clifton. Mystery drama. Priscilla Dean, Joseph Girard, Ashton Dearholt.

The Vanity Pool
Dir: Ida May Park. Political drama. Mary MacLaren, Thomas Holding, Franklyn Farnum.

The Velvet Hand (Bluebird)
Dir: Douglas Gerrard. Vendetta drama. Eugene Corey, Carmen Phillips, William Conklin.

When A Girl Loves (Jewel)
Dir: Lois Weber and Phillips Smalley. Psychological drama. Mildred Harris, William Stowell, Wharton Jones.

Which Woman? (Bluebird)
Dir: Harry Pollard. Mystery drama. Ella Hall, Eddie Sutherland, Edward Jobson.

The Wife He Bought (Bluebird)
Dir: Harry Solter. Romantic drama. Carmel Myers, Kenneth Harlan, Howard Crampton.

The Wild Cat Of Paris
Dir: Joseph de Grasse. Underworld drama. Priscilla Dean, Louis Barclay.

Wild Women
Dir: Jack (John) Ford. Cowboy comedy. Harry Carey, Vester Pegg, Ed Jones, Molly Malone.

The Wine Girl (Bluebird)
Dir: Harvey Gates and Stuart Paton. Romantic drama. Carmel Myers, Kenneth Harlan.

Winner Takes All (Bluebird)
Dir: Elmer Clifton. Western melodrama. Monroe Salisbury, Betty Schade.

A Woman's Fool
Dir: Jack (John) Ford. Comedy western. Harry Carey, Betty Schade, Vester Pegg, Ed Jones.

The Yellow Dog (Jewel)
Dir: Colin Campbell. Patriotic drama. Arthur Hoyt, Frank Clark, Clara Horton.

1919

▽ Olive Tell (left) starred in **The Trap**, an entertaining six-reel melodrama written by Eve Unsell from a story by Richard Harding Davis and Jules E. Goodman. She played a schoolteacher in the Yukon who promises to marry a successful prospector (Jere Austin), but marries his no-good brother (Earl Schenck) instead. After Schenck disappears and is reported to be dead, Miss Tell (left) travels to the States with her father (Joseph Burke), marries a good-looking broker from New York (Sidney Mason), bears him two children, then is threatened with blackmail by Rod La Rocque, the villain of the piece, whose intention it is to tell the unknowing Mr Mason all about his wife's previous marriage to Schenck. But it all ends happily with La Rocque meeting a dramatic end, and Austin marrying Miss Tell's sister (Tallulah Bankhead). The director was Frank Reicher.

◁ Dawson City during the gold-rush days in the Klondike was the spirited setting of **Paid In Advance**. Scripted by Allen Holubar (who also directed) from the story by James Oliver Curwood, it was the loosely constructed tale of Joan Gray, a lonely girl (Dorothy Phillips, centre) who, after being forced to leave home because of a fatal quarrel between two rival admirers, finds herself trapped by a lustful saloon-keeper known as Gold Dust Barker (Frank Brownlee). Rather than submit to Barker's advances, she offers herself as a wife to the highest bidder – and is purchased by prospector Jim Blood (William Stowell) who marries her, then disappears after killing Barker. Leaving the Lawless Klondike, Joan discovers she has inherited from the mysterious Jim Blood (also known as 'The Cur') a claim of great value and appoints a manager to look after it. Returning to Dawson City some time later, Joan discovers that the manager is none other than Jim Blood himself and the couple live happily ever after. Subtlety in plot and characterisation was rarely in evidence throughout Holubar's six-reel Jewel production, but life during the gold rush was realistically depicted and most of the exteriors beautifully photographed. Lon Chaney (left) appeared as one of Miss Phillips' rival suitors; Joseph Gerard was her father (killed en route to Dawson City), with other roles going to Priscilla Dean, Bill Buress and Harry De More.

▽ In **The Wicked Darling**, competently directed by Tod Browning, Priscilla Dean (illustrated) played a slum girl: a flower among weeds forced, as a consequence of her squalid environment, to steal for a living. After filching a necklace dropped by socialite Gertrude Astor, she finds refuge in the home of Wellington Playter, Miss Astor's one-time fiancé. Numerous plot complications in Waldemar Young's scenario (story by Evelyn Campbell) paved the way for a happy ending, and involved Miss Dean's attempts to go straight by becoming a waitress, as well as Playter's eventual bankruptcy after spending all his money on Miss Astor. Lon Chaney was third-billed as Stoop, a slum character in love with Miss Dean, and, together with Spottiswoode Aiken, another of the city's slum dwellers, received most of the critical acclaim in this fair-to-middling movie.

△ Director Robert Z. Leonard and his wife Mae Murray (left) joined forces for **The Delicious Little Devil**, (story by John Clymer and Harvey Thew, the latter also providing the scenario) which starred Mae as an Irish lass who helps eke out a meagre tenement existence for herself and her family by working as a hat-check girl in a restaurant. When she loses her job, she answers an ad for a dancer at a roadhouse, gets it, then falls in love with a 'gilded youth' whose father, believing the girl to be a notorious strumpet, sets out to disillusion his son at a supper party in which he attempts to make Mae drunk. But it doesn't quite work out that way and, in the end, the old boy, who's an Irishman himself, gives his son his unqualified approval. Audiences enjoyed seeing Miss Murray dancing – for it was as a dancer that she first came to prominence; and it was this aspect of her performance that attracted the most critical attention. Her leading man was Rudolpho De Valentina (right), with other roles going to Harry Rattenbury, Richard Cummings, Ivor McFadden, Bertram Grassby and Edward Jobson.

▽ Erich von Stroheim (right) made an auspicious directorial debut with **Blind Husbands**, a prestigious, eight-reel 'Jewel' release, which he also produced, and starred in as an Austrian army lieutenant who, while staying at a hotel in the Alps, turns his amorous attentions to the neglected wife (Francelia Billington, left) of an American surgeon (Sam de Grasse). Despite the surgeon's indifference, Miss Billington refuses to be unfaithful and informs Von Stroheim of this fact in a note which she slips underneath his door. Unaware of the attentions the lieutenant has been paying his wife, De Grasse agrees to join Von Stroheim on a perilous mountain-climbing expedition. When the pair finally reach the summit, De Grasse spots a letter which has dropped out of Von Stroheim's coat. He immediately recognises his wife's handwriting, but before he has a chance to read it, it is blown away. Thinking the worst, the surgeon picks a fight with the lieutenant and, after gaining the upper hand, promises to spare his life if he tells the truth about his relationship with his wife. Though, in reality, Von Stroheim is innocent of any real wrong-doing, he believes the truth will not be accepted and lies that he did, in fact, have an affair with the woman. Disgusted, De Grasse sets off, leaving the lieutenant alone on the mountain top. On his way down, however, De Grasse finds the letter proving both Von Stroheim's and his wife's innocence, but by then it is too late. Von Stroheim has thrown himself off the mountain, and is killed. Originally called *The Pinnacle*, but changed by Laemmle (against Von Stroheim's wishes) to the more commercial **Blind Husbands**, the film was an enormous critical success and it brought financial rewards as well as artistic respectability to the studio. Apart from drawing fine performances from his cast, Von Stroheim revealed a powerful ability to endow even the tritest story (which this one, written by himself, undoubtedly was) with a compelling cinematic quality – due, in the main, to his reliance on the camera rather than on subtitles – to advance the plot.

▽ **The Heart Of Humanity** was a nine-reel epic dealing, in general, with Canada's involvement in the Great War, and in particular with the agony suffered by a widow (Margaret Mann) who loses four of her sons on the battlefield. The fifth, a pilot (William Stowell, right), survives and, just in the nick of time, saves his young bride from the dastardly cluthes of the villainous Lieutenant von Eberhard. Dorothy Phillips (left) was top-billed as the bride, and Erich von Stroheim, who would soon become known as 'the man you love to hate' was cast as Eberhard. Both performances, under Allen Holubar's ambitious direction (it took a mammoth seven months to complete) received immense critical acclaim, especially von Stroheim's, whose brutality – seen at its worst in a sequence culminating in his throwing a baby out of a window – was truly shocking. Not unlike, in theme and construction, D.W. Griffith's *Hearts Of The World* (1918), it also contained some spectacular war scenes, but the film's major flaw was the prominence given to them in the scenario which Holubar and Olga Scholl devised from their own storyline. Hailed at the time as one of the best, most compassionate films to deal with the Great War, it was a Jewel Production and, in smaller roles, featured Robert Anderson, Frank Braidwood, George Hackathorne and, as Father Michael, in whose care Miss Phillips has been placed, Walt Whitman.

▷ Director Jack (John) Ford chose western star Harry Carey (illustrated) for his leading man in **The Outcasts Of Poker Flat**, an adaptation, by H. Tipton Steck, of Bret Harte's celebrated story. Utilising a plot-within-a-plot technique, the film featured Carey as the proprietor of a gambling hall in Arizona who cannot make up his mind whether to sacrifice the love he feels for his pretty ward (Gloria Hope) who he believes is in love with his buddy Tommy (Cullen Landis), or to try to win her for himself. Stumbling upon a copy of *The Outcasts Of Poker Flat*, he soon identifies with Harte's hero, John Oakhurst, whose predicament is similar to his own and, after reading all about Oakhurst (who befriends a girl on a steamboat, then magnanimously relinquishes her when a younger man claims her attention), Carey decides to fight for Miss Hope who, it turns out, has loved him all along. Ford was more successful with his re-creation of a California mining colony circa 1850 than in his handling of the film's big set-piece – a patently phoney studio-bound snow sequence; but on this occasion action took second place to the slow development of the plot, the principal interest being in the eventual outcome of the narrative, and in the dual roles played by the three principals. It was remade in 1937 (RKO) and in 1952 (20th Century-Fox).

OTHER PRODUCTIONS OF 1919

Ace Of The Saddle
Dir: Jack (John) Ford. Western melodrama. Harry Carey, Duke R. Lee, Vester Pegg.

After The War
Dir: Joseph de Grasse. Post-war melodrama. Grace Cunard, Herbert Prior.

The Amazing Wife
Dir: Ida May Park. Romantic drama. Mary MacLaren, Frank Mayo, Stanhope Wheatcroft.

Bare Fists (Powers)
Dir: Jack (John) Ford. Western melodrama. Harry Carey, Betty Schade, Joe Harris, Vester Pegg.

The Big Little Person
Dir: Robert Z. Leonard. Romantic drama. Mae Murray, Rudolph Valentino.

The Blinding Trail
Dir: Paul Powell. Romantic drama. Monroe Salisbury, Claire Anderson, Helen Eddy.

Bonnie Bonnie Lassie
Dir: Tod Browning. Young girl drama. Mary MacLaren.

The Brute Breaker
Dir: Lynn Reynolds. Action adventure. Frank Mayo, Kathryn Adams.

Common Property
Dir: Paul Powell. Drama. Robert Anderson, Nell Craig, Colleen Moore, Johnnie Cooke.

Creaking Stairs
Dir: Rupert Julian. Psychological drama. Mary MacLaren, Herbert Prior, Jack Mulhall.

The Day She Paid
Dir: Rex Ingram. Romance. Francelia Billington, Charles Clay, Harry Van Meter.

Destiny
Dir: Rollin Sturgeon. Family saga. Dorothy Phillips, William Stowell, Tom Ashton.

The Exquisite Thief
Dir: Tod Browning. Crime spoof. Priscilla Dean, Sam De Grasse, J. Milton Rose.

A Fight For Love
Dir: Jack (John) Ford. Western melodrama. Harry Carey, Neva Gerber, Joe Harris, Mark Fenton.

The Fire Flingers
Dir: Rupert Julian. Suspense drama. Clyde Fillmore, Fred Kelsey, Jane Novak.

Forbidden
Dir: Lois Weber and Phillips Smalley. Marital drama. Mildred Harris, Henry Woodward, Fred Goodwin.

The Game's Up (Bluebird)
Dir: Elsie Jane Wilson. Light comedy. Ruth Clifford, Al Ray, Harry Holden.

The Great Air Robbery
Dir: Jacques Jaccard. Air melodrama. Alan Forrest, Francelia Billington.

A Gun-fighting Gentleman
Dir: Jack (John) Ford. Comedy western. Harry Carey, Kathleen O'Connor, Barney Sherry.

Heads Win
Dir: Preston Kendall. No other information available.

His Divorced Wife
Dir: Douglas Gerrard. Mountain drama. Monroe Salisbury.

Home
Dir: Lois Weber. Country-girl drama. Frank Elliott, Mildred Harris, Clarissa Selwynne.

Lasca
Dir: Norman Dawn. Tragic drama. Edith Roberts, Frank Mayo, Veola Harty.

Light Of Victory (Bluebird)
Dir: William Wolbert. Patriotic drama. Monroe Salisbury, Betty Compson, Fred Kelsey.

A Little Brother Of The Rich
Dir: Lynn Reynolds. Social drama. Barney Sherry, Frank Mayo, Kathryn Adams.

The Little White Savage (Bluebird)
Dir: Paul Powell. Comedy adventure. Carmel Myers, Harry Hilliard, William Dyer.

Loot
Dir: William Dowlan. Crime adventure. Joseph Girard, Ora Carew, Frank Thompson.

The Man In The Moonlight
Dir: Paul Powell. Drama. Monroe Salisbury

The Millionaire Pirate (Bluebird)
Dir: Rupert Julian. Romantic fantasy. Monroe Salisbury, Ruth Clifford.

The Petal On The Current
Dir: Tod Browning. Courtroom drama. Mary MacLaren, Robert Anderson, Gertrude Claire.

The Pointing Finger
Dir: Edward Morrissey. Orphan drama. Mary MacLaren.

Pretty Smooth
Dir: Rollin Sturgeon. Underworld drama. Priscilla Dean, Francis McDonald.

The Rider Of The Law
Dir: Jack (John) Ford. Western melodrama. Harry Carey, Claire Anderson, Jennie Lee.

Riders of Vengeance
Dir: Jack (John) Ford. Western melodrama. Harry Carey, Seena Owen, Joseph Harris, Jennie Lee.

The Right To Happiness
Dir: Allen Holubar. Industrial unrest drama. Dorothy Phillips, William Stowell.

Roped
Dir: Jack (John) Ford. Western comedy drama. Harry Carey, Neva Gerber, Molly McConnell.

The Scarlet Shadow
Dir: Robert Leonard. Marital comedy. Mae Murray, Frank Elliot, Martha Mattox.

The Sealed Envelope (Bluebird)
Dir: Douglas Gerrard. Crime mystery. William A. Sheer, Fritzi Brunette.

The Silk Lined Burglar
Dir: Jack Dillon. Crime mystery. Priscilla Dean, Sam de Grasse, Ashton Dearholt.

The Sleeping Lion
Dir: Rupert Julian. Western melodrama. Monroe Salisbury, Alice Elliot, Sydney Franklyn.

The Spitfire Of Seville
Dir: George Seigman. Spanish adventure. Hedda Nova, Thurston Hall, Claire Anderson.

Sue Of The South (Bluebird)
Dir: Eugene Moore. Drama. Edith Roberts.

The Sundown Trail
Dir: Rollin Sturgeon. Pioneer comedy. Monroe Salisbury, A. Elliot, Clyde Fillmore.

The Taste Of Life
Dir: Jack Dillon. Drama. Edith Roberts.

The Trembling Hour
Dir: George Seigman. Crime suspense. Kenneth Harlan, Helen Jerome Eddy.

The Triflers
Dir: W. Christy Cabanne. Social comedy. Edith Roberts, David Butler, Forrest Stanley.

Under Suspicion
Dir: William Dowlan. Crook comedy. Forrest Stanley, Ora Carew.

The Unpainted Woman
Dir: Tod Browning. Rural melodrama. Mary MacLaren, David Butler, Thurston Hall.

The Weaker Vessel
Dir: Paul Powell. Comedy romance. Mary MacLaren, Anne Schaffer, Johnnie Cooke.

What Am I Bid?
Dir: Robert Z. Leonard. Mountain romance. Mae Murray, Ralph Graves, Willard Louis.

Who Will Marry Me? (Bluebird)
Dir: Paul Powell. Romantic drama. Carmel Myers, Thurston Hall, Betty Schade.

The Woman Under Cover
Dir: George Seigman. Murder melodrama. Fritzi Brunette, George McDaniels.

1920

▷ After his brilliant success with *Blind Husbands* (1919) Erich von Stroheim directed, but did not appear in the seven-reel Jewel presentation, **The Devil's Pass Key**, and again demonstrated that, when it came to telling a dramatic story solely in visual terms, there were few directors to equal him. Set in glittering Paris, it was the cautionary tale of an extravagant playwright's wife who runs up large clothes bills on the assumption that her husband's new play will be a resounding success. The play fails, and her modiste demands payment. The wife valiantly refuses to sacrifice herself for money, but is later (and innocently) lured into a blackmailing scheme involving the modiste, a dancer, and an American embassy attaché, and becomes the talk of Paris. Everyone has heard the gossip, except her husband who, after reading a newspaper report of the scandal in which the names have tactfully been omitted, writes a play about the situation. Ironically, the play is an enormous success, but the author is greeted with jeers. Tragedy threatens when he learns the truth but, in Von Stroheim's only miscalculation, a happy ending prevails. Sam De Grasse was top-billed as the unsuspecting author-husband, Una Trevelyan was his wife, Clyde Fillmore (centre) the American attaché, Maude George (right) the modiste who sets the plot in motion, and Mae Busch (left) the dancer involved in the blackmail. Von Stroheim scripted stylishly from a story (*Clothes and Treachery*) by Baroness De Meyer, and again emerged with one of the year's best films.

▽ A frenzied collection of movie clichés adroitly strung together against some decorative Oriental backgrounds by director Tod Browning, **The Virgin Of Stamboul** was also an action-packed romantic melodrama aptly described by one reviewer on its release as having 'all the thrills that may be derived from a race of wooden horses which go at high speed along fixed grooves to a predetermined result'. Priscilla Dean (right) starred as a beautiful beggar and the virgin of the title, Wallace Beery (left) was Achmet Bey, a wealthy sheik who covets Miss Dean for his thriving harem, and Wheeler Oakman (in real life he married Miss Dean) played the handsome hero who, in an exciting, no-holds-barred finale, rescues the heroine from the villain and claims her for his own. Eugene Forde, E.A. Warren, Edward Burns, Nigel de Brulier and Ethel Ritchie completed the cast. Tod Browning scripted, and the story was by H.H. Van Loan. (Jewel).

△ Mutiny at sea and a full-fledged revolution were two of the ingredients in **Under Crimson Skies**, a six-reel adventure whose love interest revolved around a romance between the captain of a sailing vessel and the wife of one of his passengers. Elmo Lincoln (left) starred as the Captain and Mabel Ballin (at piano) was the wife. Harry Van Meter was the jealous husband (who also happens to be shipping contraband munitions to Mexican rebels), with other roles under Rex Ingram's workaday direction going to Nancy Caswell, Frank Brownlee, Paul Weigel, Dick La Reno and Noble Johnson. It was written by J.C. Hawkes. (Jewel).

△ Though not unlike Goldwyn's 1917 release, *Polly Of The Circus*, director B. Reeves Eason's **Pink Tights**, a story with a circus background, was a crowd-pleaser in its own right – a heartwarming tale suitable for all the family. About a balloonist star of a one ring circus who, while dressed in pink tights, accidentally descends on the roof of a minister's home and, by so doing, finds she has compromised his stainless reputation, the film starred Gladys Walton (right) as Mazie, the girl in pink tights. Miss Walton's toughest competition wasn't leading man Jack Perrin (left) as the minister, but Reeves Eason Jr, the director's scene-stealing son who, in the course of J.U. Geisy's scenario, learns about Miss Walton's unorthodox descent on the minister, and precipitates a scandal. Dave Dyas, Stanton Hack, Rosa Gore, Dan Crimmins and Dorothea Wolbert completed the cast.

▽ A remake of the studio's 1916 release *The Three Godfathers*, directed by Edward J. Le Saint, **Marked Men**, this time directed by Jack (John) Ford, was another winner for Universal. Scripted by H. Tipton Steck from the *Saturday Evening Post* story by Peter Bernard Kyne, it was the moving tale of three bank robbers who, while escaping across the Mojave desert, discover a dying woman and her child in a covered wagon. Deciding that the child's life is more important than their own freedom, they become godfathers to the infant and attempt to return to civilisation with it. Harry Carey (top-billed, right), Joe Harris and Ted Brooks were the fugitives, and Winifred Westover (left) the dying mother. Also cast: J. Farrell MacDonald and Charles Lemoyne. It was remade in 1929 as *Hell's Heroes*, by MGM in 1936 and, again by John Ford (for Argosy and MGM) in 1948 with John Wayne.

OTHER PRODUCTIONS OF 1920

The Adorable Savage
Dir: Norman Dawn. Tropical island romance. Edith Roberts, Jack Perrin.

Alias Miss Dodd
Dir: Harry Franklin. Whimsical mystery. Edith Roberts, Johnnie Cook.

Beautifully Trimmed
Dir: Marcel de Sano. Crime suspense. Carmel Myers, Irving Cummings, Pell Trenton.

Blue Streak McCoy
Dir: Reaves Eason. Western romance. Harry Carey, Lila Leslie, Charles Arling.

The Breath Of The Gods (Jewel)
Dir: Rollin Sturgeon. Japanese tragic drama. Tsuri Aoki, Pat O'Malley.

Bullet Proof
Dir: Lynn Reynolds. Adventure romance. Harry Carey, Kathleen O'Connor, Fred Gamble.

Burnt Wings
Dir: W. Christy Cabanne. Infidelity drama. Josephine Hill, Frank Mayo, Rudolph Christians, Betty Blythe.

Everything But The Truth
Dir: Eddie Lyons and Lee Moran. Newly-weds comedy. Kathleen Lewis.

Fixed By George
Dir: Eddie Lyons and Lee Moran. Farce comedy. Lyons, Moran, Hazell Howell.

The Forged Bride
Dir: Douglas Gerrard. Crime drama. Mary MacLaren, Thomas Jefferson.

The Gilded Dream
Dir: Rollin Sturgeon. Society drama. Carmel Myers, Elsa Lorimer, Thomas Chatterton.

The Girl In Number 29
Dir: Jack (John) Ford. Comedy puzzler. Frank Mayo, Elinor Fair, Claire Anderson.

The Girl In The Rain
Dir: Rollin Sturgeon. Mystery. Lloyd Bacon, Anne Cornwall, Jessalyn Van Trump.

Hearts Up!
Dir: Val Paul. Western romance. Harry Carey, Arthur Millett, Charles LeMoyne.

Her Five-Foot Highness
Dir: Harry Franklin. Romantic saga. Edith Roberts, Ogden Crane, Stanhope Wheatcroft.

Hitchin' Posts
Dir: Jack (John) Ford. Pioneer drama. Frank Mayo, J. Farrell McDonald, Beatrice Burnham.

Honor Bound
Dir: Jacques Jaccard. Tropical island drama Frank Mayo, Edward Coxen, Helen Lynch.

Human Stuff
Dir: Reaves Eason. Western ranch romance. Harry Carey, Rudolph Christians.

In Folly's Trail
Dir: Rollin Sturgeon. Psychological drama. Carmel Myers, Thomas Holding.

La La Lucille
Dir: Eddie Lyons and Lee Moran. Farce comedy. Lyons, Moran, Gladys Walton, Ann Cornwall.

Locked Lips
Dir: William Dowlan. Japanese drama. Tsuru Aoki, Magda Lane, Stanhope Wheatcroft.

The Marriage Pit
Dir: Fred Thomson. Marriage drama. Frank Mayo. Lillian Tucker.

Once A Plumber
Dir: Eddie Lyons and Lee Moran. Comedy drama. Lyons, Moran, Sidney Deane, George B. Williams.

Once To Every Woman (Jewel)
Dir: Allen Holubar. Opera singer drama. Dorothy Phillips, William Ellingford.

Overland Red
Dir: Lynn Reynolds. Western melodrama. Harry Carey, Charles Lemoyne, Harold Goodwin.

The Path She Chose
Dir: Philip Rosen. Drama. Anne Cornwall, Claire Anderson, J. Farrell McDonald.

The Peddler Of Lies
Dir: William Dowlan. Mystery drama. Frank Mayo, Ora Carew, Ora Devereaux.

The Phantom Melody
Dir: Douglas Gerrard. Drama. Monroe Salisbury, Henry Barrows, Jean Calhorn.

The Prince Of Avenue A
Dir: Jack (John) Ford. Political comedy. James Corbett, Richard Cummings, Cora Drew.

The Red Lane
Dir: Lynn Reynolds. Borderland drama. Frank Mayo, Lillian Rich, James L. Mason.

Risky Business
Dir: Harry B. Harris. Social drama. Gladys Walton, Fred Malatesta.

The Road To Divorce
Dir: Philip Rosen. Married life drama. Mary MacLaren, Edward Pell, Bonnie Hill.

Rouge And Riches
Dir: Harry Franklin. Chorus girl romance. Mary MacLaren, Robert Walker.

The Secret Gift
Dir: Harry L. Franklyn. Immigrant drama. Lee Kohlmar.

Shipwrecked Among Cannibals (Jewel)
No information available.

Sundown Slim
Dir: Val Paul. Western romantic triangle. Harry Carey.

A Tokyo Siren
Dir: Norman Dawn. Japanese romance. Tsuri Aoki, Goro Kino, Jack Livingstone.

Two Kinds Of Love
Dir: Reaves Eason. No other information available.

Under Northern Lights
Dir: Jacques Jaccard. Northwest romance. William Buckley, Virginia Brown Faire.

Wanted At Headquarters
Dir: Stuart Paton. Crime melodrama. William Marlon, Eva Novak, Leonard C. Shumway.

West Is West
Dir: Val Paul. Western melodrama. Harry Carey.

White Youth
Dir: Norman Dawn. Drama. Edith Roberts, Thomas Jefferson, Alfred Hollingsworth.

1921

◁ Seventeen-year-old Gladys Walton (illustrated) was the chief (and only) attraction of **The Man Tamer**, a conventional romance with a circus background. She played a lion tamer who, in the course of A.P. Younger's scenario (story by John Barton Oxford), not only tames lions but also Roscoe Karns, the 'wild' son of millionaire C. Norman Hammond. William Welsh played a circus manager with unrequited designs on the heroine, and the rest of the cast included Rex De Rosselli as Miss Walton's father, C.B. Murphy and Parker J. McConnell. Cracking the whip – but not firmly enough – was director Harry B. Harris.

▷ 'They called her Flame Flower, and she was tabu to all men' was one of the catch-phrases advertising **The Shark Master**, an early forerunner of Universal's exotic series of Maria Montez-Jon Hall romances. Set on a Polynesian island called Amanu, it featured Frank Mayo who, despite being engaged to a girl back home, reluctantly falls in love with May Collins (Flame Flower, illustrated with Mayo) after his steamer is shipwrecked in the South Seas. It was 'Madame Butterfly' thinly disguised, except that when Mayo's fiancée finally arrives on the island to take him home, he refuses to leave Miss Collins, especially as she has since become the mother of his child. Dorris Deane played the hapless fiancée, with other roles under Fred LeRoy Granville's direction going to Herbert Fortier, Oliver A. Cross, 'Smoke' Turner and Nick De Ruiz. Granville also supplied the story and it was scripted by George C. Hull, whose captions were no match for the glorious scenery that provided the story's backdrop.

▷ 'Virtue is its own reward' was the uplifting message of **Outside The Law**, an eight-reel Jewel Production written, produced and directed by Tod Browning, and starring Priscilla Dean (left) as a society crook known as 'Silky Moll'. Miss Dean's co-star was Wheeler Oakman (centre) and, for much of Lucien Hubbard's scenario (story by Browning), the couple can't decide whether to continue their crooked life-styles or to go straight. In reel eight they opt for the latter. Plot took second place to Browning's vigorous depiction of his underworld milieu, with an all-out, no-expense-spared brawl in a Chinese restaurant being the film's big set-piece. Miss Dean received some of the best notices of her career for her work as 'Silky', but, thief though she was, couldn't quite match third-billed Lon Chaney (right) when it came to scene-stealing. In the dual role of arch-hood Black Mike Sylva, and Ah Wing, a Confucius disciple who teaches Dean and Oakman how to play it straight, Chaney notched up his greatest triumph to date, proving, at the same time, what a wizard he was with make-up (a climactic double exposure scene at the film's close has Black Mike stopping a bullet fired by Ah Wing). A child actor called Stanley Goethals, referred to as 'that kid' in the credits, also received critical attention, and the cast was completed by Ralph Lewis (as Miss Dean's father, a one-time crook), E.A. Warren, Melbourne McDowell and Wilton Taylor. It was remade in 1930.

▽ Hoot Gibson (right) received star billing in **Action**, a modestly budgeted but entertaining western from director Jack (John) Ford. All about a trio of trail rangers who buy a ranch owned by a pretty orphan girl, discover silver on it, and, despite the determined opposition of a gang of crooks, make a fortune, the film featured a somewhat over-coy Clara Horton as the orphan, as well as Francis Ford (left) and J. Farrell MacDonald as Hoot's travelling companions. Action and romance cohabited in the scenario fashioned by Harvey Gates from a story by J. Allen Dunn, the union being blessed with a healthy box-office bonanza. Also cast: Buck Connors, William Robert Daly, Dorothea Wolbert and Byron Munson.

◁ Priscilla Dean's range as a dramatic actress was stretched to the full in **Reputation**, an ambitious but ultimately unsatisfying drama, set in London and New York, against a theatrical background. Lucien Hubbard and Doris Schroeder's scenario (from a story by Edward Levin) told the story of an actress who abandons her daughter, becomes a drug addict, and hits rock bottom after her manager fires her from a production and replaces her with a young girl. Enraged, she shoots the manager, confessing to her crime only when the innocent young actress (who turns out to the older woman's daughter!) is blamed. Miss Dean (left) played both mother and daughter and did well enough in both roles, with other parts under Stuart Paton's disjointed and unconvincing direction going to Mae Giraci, Harry Van Meter, Harry Carter, Niles Welch, Spottiswoode Aitken and William Welsh. (Jewel).

△ Hoot Gibson (right) consolidated his reputation as Universal's leading western star in **Sure Fire,** a routine oater directed by Jack (John) Ford whose last western for the studio it turned out to be. Gibson starred as a vagabond cowpuncher who returns home to find his sweetheart (Molly Malone, centre) decidedly cool towards him. She disapproves of his lack of ambition – a state of affairs soon remedied in George C. Hull's scenario (story by Eugene Manlove Rhodes) after she is captured by outlaws and rescued by him. Fritzi Brunette (left) played Miss Malone's unfaithful married sister, and the cast was completed by B. Reeves Eason Jr, Murdock McQuarrie, George Fisher and Charles Newton.

OTHER PRODUCTIONS OF 1921

All Dolled Up
Dir: Rollin Sturgeon. Comedy. Gladys Walton, Edward Hearn, Richard Norton.

The Beautiful Gambler
Dir: William Worthington. Western melodrama. Grace Darmond, Jack Mower.

The Big Adventure
Dir: Reaves Eason. Rural drama. Breezy Eason Jr, Fred Herzog, Lee Shumway.

The Blazing Trail
Dir: Robert Thornby. Rural melodrama. Frank Mayo, Frank Holland, Mary Philbin.

Cheated Hearts
Dir: Hobart Henley. Desert adventure. Herbert Rawlinson, Warner Baxter, Marjorie Daw, Doris Pawn, Winter Hall.

Cheated Love
Dir: King Baggot. Romantic melodrama. Carmel Myers, Allen Forrest, John Davidson.

Colorado
Dir: Reaves Eason. Comedy romance. Alberta Vaughn, Donald Keith, John Steppling.

The Conflict (Jewel)
Dir: Stuart Paton. Society melodrama. Priscilla Dean, Herbert Rawlinson, Martha Mattox.

Danger Ahead
Dir: Rollin Sturgeon. Romantic melodrama. Mary Philbin, James Morrison, Jack Mower.

The Dangerous Moment
Dir: Marcel De Sano. Bohemian melodrama. Carmel Myers, George Rigas, Lule Warrenton.

A Daughter Of The Law
Dir: Jack Conway. Crook melodrama. Carmel Myers, Jack O'Brien, Fred Kohler.

Desperate Trails
Dir: Jack (John) Ford. Western melodrama. Harry Carey, Irene Rich, Georgie Stone.

Desperate Youth
Dir: Harry B. Harris. Orphan girl melodrama. Gladys Walton, J. Farrell MacDonald.

Dr Jim
Dir: William Worthington. Society melodrama. Frank Mayo, Claire Windsor, Oliver Cross, Stanhope Wheatcroft.

False Kisses
Dir: Paul Scardon. Melodrama. Miss Du Pont, Pat O'Malley, Lloyd Whitlock.

The Fighting Lover
Dir: Fred Leroy Granville. Comedy mystery. Frank Mayo, Elinor Hancock, Gertrude Olmstead, Jackson Read.

The Fire Cat
Dir: Norman Dawn. Melodrama. Edith Roberts, Walter Long, William Eagle Eye.

The Fire Eater
Dir: Reaves Eason. Western melodrama. Hoot Gibson, Louise Lorraine, Walter Perry.

The Fox (Jewel)
Dir: Robert Thornby. Western melodrama. Harry Carey, George Nichols.

The Freeze Out
Dir: Jack (John) Ford. Western melodrama. Harry Carey, Joe Harris, Helen Ferguson.

Go Straight
Dir: William Worthington. Melodrama. Frank Mayo, Cora Drew, Harry Carter, Lillian Rich.

High Heels
Dir: Lee Kohlmar. Society drama. Gladys Walton, William Worthington, Frederick Vogeding, Freeman Wood.

'If Only' Jim
Dir: Jacques Jaccard. Western melodrama. Harry Carey, Carol Holloway, Ruth Royce.

The Kiss
Dir: Jack Conway. Ranch melodrama. George Periolat, Carmel Myers, William E. Lawrence.

Luring Lips
Dir: King Baggot. Office melodrama. Darrel Foss, Ramsey Wallace, Edith Roberts.

The Mad Marriage
Dir: Rollin Sturgeon. Greenwich Village melodrama. Carmel Myers, Trueman Van Dyke.

The Magnificent Brute
Dir: Robert Thornby. Northwest melodrama. Frank Mayo, Dorothy Devore.

The Man Trackers
Dir: Edward Kull. Northwest melodrama. George Larkin, Barney Furey, Josephine Hill.

The Millionaire
Dir: Jack Conway. Melodrama. Herbert Rawlinson, Bert Roach, William Courtwright.

Moonlight Follies
Dir: King Baggot. Single-girl drama. Marie Prevost, Lionel Belmore, Marie Crisp.

No Woman Knows (Jewel)
Dir: Tod Browning. Businesswoman drama. Bernice Radom, Raymond Lee, Earl Schenck.

Nobody's Fool
Dir: King Baggot. Comedy romance. Marie Prevost, Helen Harris, R. Henry Guy.

Opened Shutters
Dir: William Worthington. Light drama. Joseph Swickard, Edith Roberts, Joe Singleton.

A Parisian Scandal
Dir: George L. Cox. Romantic drama. George Periolat, Marie Prevost, Lillian Lawrence.

Playing With Fire
Dir: Dallas M. Fitzgerald. Romantic comedy. Gladys Walton, Katherine McGuire, Hayward Mack, Hallam Cooley.

The Rage Of Paris
Dir: Jack Conway. Dance girl melodrama. Miss Du Pont, Elinor Hancock, Jack Perrin.

Red Courage
Dir: Reaves Eason. Western melodrama. Hoot Gibson, Joel Day, Molly Malone.

Rich Girl, Poor Girl
Dir: Harry B. Harris. Society melodrama. Gladys Walton, Gordon McGregor.

The Rowdy
Dir: David Kirkland. Sea drama. Rex De Rosseli, Anna Hernandez, Gladys Walton.

A Shocking Night
Dir: Eddie Lyons and Lee Moran. Bedroom farce. Lyons, Moran, Alta Allen.

Short Skirts
Dir: Harry B. Harris. Society melodrama. Gladys Walton, Ena Gregory, Jack Mower.

The Smart Sex
Dir: Fred Leroy Granville. Country comedy melodrama. Eva Novak, Frank Braidwood.

Society Secrets
Dir: Leo McCarey. Family satire. Eva Novak, Gertrude Claire, George Verrel.

Thunder Island
Dir: Norman Dawn. Seafaring drama. Edith Roberts, Fred De Silva, Fred Kohler.

Tiger True
Dir: J.P. McGowan. Mystery melodrama. Frank Mayo, Fritzi Brunette, Elinor Hancock.

The Torrent
Dir: Stuart Paton. South Seas adventure drama. Eva Novak, Jack Perrin, Oletta Ottis.

The Unknown Wife
Dir: William Worthington. Crime melodrama. Edith Roberts, Spottiswoode Aitken.

The Wallop
Dir: Jack (John) Ford. Western melodrama. Harry Carey, Mignonne Golden, William Gettinger.

Wolves Of The North
Dir: Norman Dawn. Snow-country drama. Herbert Heyes, Percy Challenger, Eva Novak.

1922

▷ Priscilla Dean (centre) gave a splendidly effective performance in **Under Two Flags**, the celebrated story by Ouida (Marie Louise de la Ramee), which first came to the screen via Fox in 1915, and again by Fox in 1917 with Theda Bara. She played Cigarette, the sweetheart of the French Foreign Legion, who falls hopelessly in love with Victor, an exiled Englishman, eventually sacrificing her life for him. James Kirkwood portrayed the object of her unrequited affections (he loves a titled Englishwoman), with Stuart Holmes (centre left) as the jealous villain who is also Victor's commanding officer and has Victor condemned to death on a false charge of treachery. John Davidson was prominently featured as Sheik Ben Ali Hammed, enemy of Algiers, with other roles in Edward T. Lowe Jr and Elliot J. Clawson's scenario (adapted by Lowe and Tod Browning) going to Ethel Grey Terry (centre, as the woman Victor loves), Robert Mack, Burton Law and Albert Pollet. Tod Browning also directed, his handling of the climactic battle scenes being especially skilful. He drew fine performances from all his leading players and, cinematically, made the most of Miss Dean's death scene when she courageously flings herself in front of a firing squad and stops a bullet intended for the man she loves. **Under Two Flags** was remade in 1936 with Ronald Colman and Claudette Colbert for 20th Century-Fox.

▽ Man-of-a-thousand-faces Lon Chaney wrestled bare-handed with a wolf in **The Trap**, a Jewel Production, in which he played a sympathetic trapper – a true child of nature whose innocence curdles after he is cheated out of his ranch and his girl by a total stranger (Alan Hale). Henceforth, he lives for just one thing – vengeance. His terrible plan? To trap a wolf and arrange things so that it will attack his enemy. However, the plan goes wrong, and it is his enemy's innocent young son (Stanley Goethals, left) who falls into the trap. Risking his life, Chaney (centre) kills the beast, and his bravery brings about a better understanding between the two men. Grippingly told by director Robert T. Thornby from a scenario by George C. Hull, and featuring Irene Rich (right) as the feminine interest, the film brought more plaudits for its star and was both a critical and financial success.

▷ Though the more perspicacious critics recognised that, embedded in the excesses of Erich von Stroheim's controversial **Foolish Wives** was a masterpiece on the subject of depravity, the majority of reviewers lambasted it as an ugly and degrading spectacle and an outrage to American womanhood. But the publicity it had garnered during the eleven months it took to complete paid off handsomely and, although after its initial release, the film underwent numerous censorship cuts and was truncated from fourteen reels (and 3½ hours running time) to ten reels, it was still a tremendous box-office success. The story of a bogus Russian count called Sergius Karamazin and his unscrupulous, indiscriminate use of women, it starred a compelling Von Stroheim (right) as Karamazin, with Maude George and Mae Busch as his accomplice cousins (bogus Princesses), and Miss Du Pont (left) as one of the 'foolish wives' of the title. Du Pont's husband, an American envoy, was played by Rudolph Christians, who died during production, and whose remaining scenes were completed by Robert Edeson (the film was so skilfully edited that it is difficult to tell the two actors apart). Most pathetic of all Karamazin's 'victims' is Malvine Polo, a half-wit whose vengeful counterfeiter father (Cesare Gravina) ultimately murders the count and symbolically throws his body in a sewer. Much of the film's astronomical cost (the final accounting was put at $1,103,736·38) was attributed to Von Stroheim's needlessly extravagant attention to detail, the lengthy shooting schedule, the massive construction of Monte Carlo on the backlot at Universal City, and the amount of footage actually shot (320 reels!). Though the film returned a handsome profit on its initial outlay, Von Stroheim's profligacy, and his autocratic manner, were fast rendering him unemployable. As well as starring in and directing **Foolish Wives**, Von Stroheim also wrote and produced it. The rest of his cast included Dale Fuller, Al Edmundsen, Louis K. Webb, C.J. Allen and Edward Reinach. (Super Jewel).

△ Dramatically, the high point of **The Storm** had nothing to do with rain or snow but was a massive, well-staged, colour-tinted forest fire. Audiences gasped and held their breaths wondering how the conflagration would affect the lives of three people who, for most of the winter, had been snowbound in a log cabin in the hills. The protagonists were a woodsman (House Peters, left), a city friend of his (Matt Moore), and a stranded French girl (Virginia Valli, right) whose father has been killed. A triangle situation soon develops, with Miss Valli eventually choosing top-billed Peters, the better man. It was written by J.C. Hawks from a play by Langdon McCormick and the director was Reginald Barker. It was remade by William Wyler in 1930.

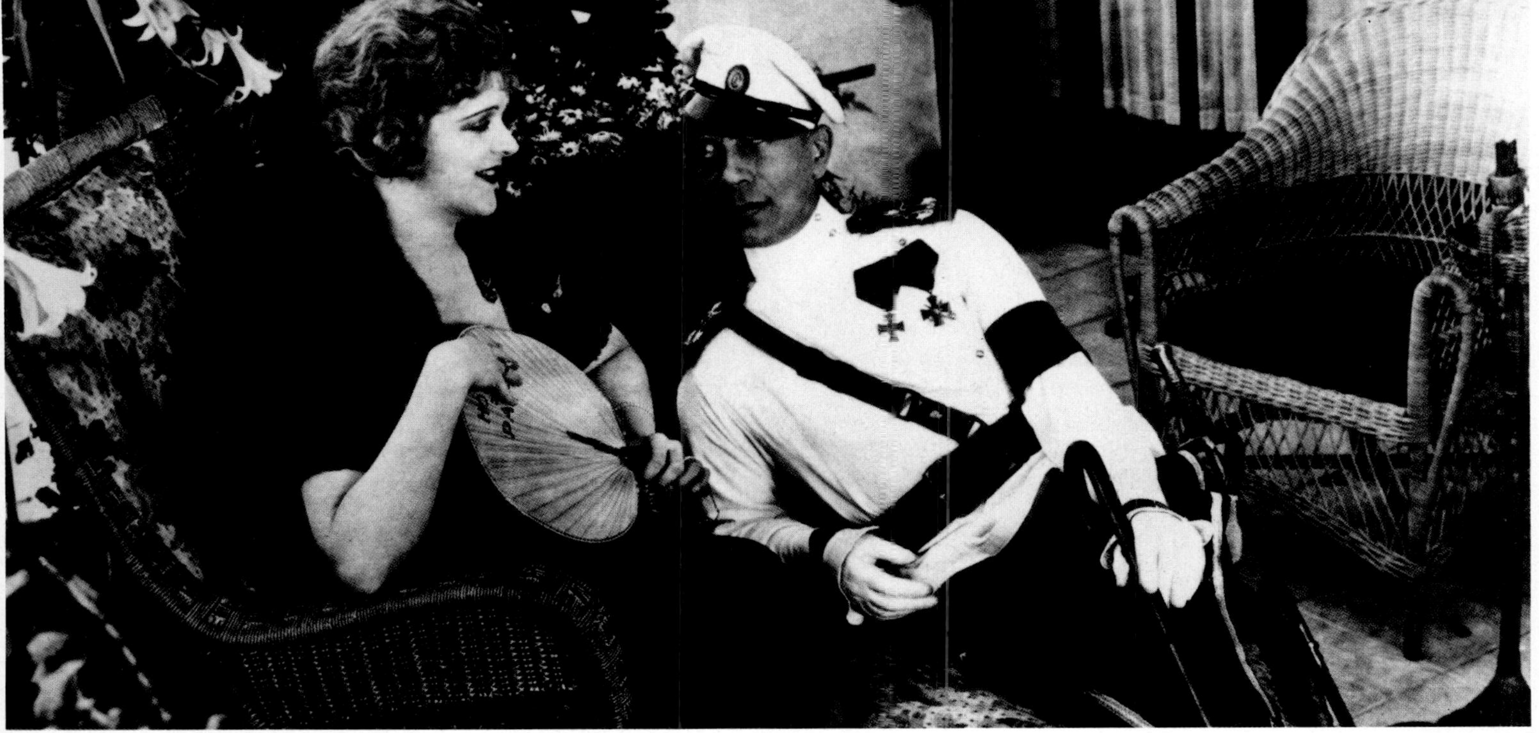

OTHER PRODUCTIONS OF 1922

Across The Dead-line
Dir: Jack Conway. Northwest drama. Frank Mayo, Russell Simpson, Molly Malone.

Afraid To Fight
Dir: William Worthington. Boxing melodrama. Frank Mayo, Lillian Rich, Lydia Knott.

The Altar Stairs
Dir: Lambert Hillyer. Crime melodrama. Frank Mayo, Louise Lorraine, Dagmar Godowsky.

Another Man's Shoes
Dir: Jack Conway. Comedy-melodrama. Herbert Rawlinson, Una Trevelyan, Barbara Bedford.

The Bearcat
Dir: Edward Sedgwick. Western romance. Hoot Gibson, Lillian Rich.

The Black Bag
Dir: Stuart Paton. Mystery drama. Herbert Rawlinson, Bert Roach, Virginia Valli.

Broad Daylight
Dir: Irving Cummings. Crime melodrama. Lois Wilson, Jack Mulhall, Ralph Lewis.

Caught Bluffing
Dir: Lambert Hillyer. Gambling melodrama. Frank Mayo, Wallace MacDonald, Edna Murphy.

Confidence
Dir: Harry Pollard. Rural comedy. Herbert Rawlinson, Harriet Hammond, Lincoln Plummer, William A. Carroll, Otto Hoffman.

A Dangerous Game
Dir: King Baggot. Drama. Gladys Walton, Otto Hoffman, Spottiswoode Aitken.

The Dangerous Little Demon
Dir: Clarence G. Badger. Comedy drama. Marie Prevost, Jack Perrin, Robert Ellis.

Don't Get Personal
Dir: Clarence G. Badger. Chorus-girl comedy. Marie Prevost, George Nichols.

Don't Shoot
Dir: Jack Conway. Crime drama. Herbert Rawlinson, Edna Murphy, William Dyer.

The Flaming Hour
Dir: Edward Sedgwick. Melodrama. Frank Mayo, Helen Ferguson, Melbourne MacDowell.

The Flirt (Jewel)
Dir: Hobart Henley. Small-town comedy drama. George Nichols, Lydia Knott.

Forsaking All Others
Dir: Emile Chautard. Vamp drama. Colleen Moore, Cullen Landis, Sam De Grasse.

The Galloping Kid
Dir: Nat Ross. Western comedy. Hoot Gibson, Edna Murphy, Lionel Belmore, Leon Barry.

The Girl Who Ran Wild
Dir: Rupert Julian. Western melodrama. Gladys Walton, Marc Robbins, Vernon Steele.

The Golden Gallows
Dir: Paul Scardon. Society melodrama. Miss Du Pont, Edwin Stevens, Eve Southern.

The Guttersnipe
Dir: Dallas M. Fitzgerald. Romantic satire. Gladys Walton, Walter Perry, Kate Price.

Headin' West
Dir: William J. Craft. Western melodrama. Hoot Gibson, Gertrude Short.

Her Night Of Nights
Dir: Hobart Henley. Romantic comedy. Marie Prevost, Edward Hearn, Hallam Cooley.

Human Hearts (Jewel)
Dir: King Baggot. Country drama. House Peters, Russell Simpson, Gertrude Claire.

The Jilt
Dir: Irving Cummings. Drama. Marguerite De La Motte, Ralph Graves, Matt Moore.

The Kentucky Derby (Jewel)
Dir: King Baggot. Horse-racing melodrama. Reginald Denny, Lillian Rich, Emmett King.

Kissed
Dir: King Baggot. Romantic comedy. Marie Prevost, Lillian Langdon, Lloyd Whitlock.

The Lavender Bath Lady
Dir: King Baggot. Domestic comedy. Gladys Walton, Edward Burns, Charlotte Pierce.

The Loaded Door
Dir: Harry A. Pollard. Western melodrama Hoot Gibson, Bill Ryno, Gertrude Olmstead.

The Lone Hand
Dir: Reaves Eason. Western comedy melodrama. Hoot Gibson, Marjorie Daw, Helen Holmes.

The Long Chance
Dir: Jack Conway. Western drama. Henry B. Walthall, Marjorie Daw.

Man To Man (Jewel)
Dir: Stuart Paton. Western melodrama. Harry Carey, Lillian Rich, Charles Le Moyne.

The Man Under Cover
Dir: Tod Browning. Crook melodrama. Herbert Rawlinson, George Hernandez, William Courtwright, George Webb.

The Man Who Married His Own Wife
Dir: Stuart Paton. Seafaring melodrama Frank Mayo, Sylvia Breamer, Marie Crisp.

The Married Flapper
Dir: Stuart Paton. Romantic comedy. Marie Prevost, Kenneth Harlan, Philo McCullough.

One Wonderful Night
Dir: Stuart Paton Mystery drama. Herbert Rawlinson, Lillian Rich, Sidney Bracey.

Out Of The Silent North
Dir: William Worthington. Northwest melodrama. Frank Mayo, Barbara Bedford.

Paid Back
Dir: Irving Cummings Melodrama. Gladys Brockwell, Mahlon Hamilton, Stuart Holmes.

The Power Of A Lie
Dir: George Archainbaud. Brother-sister drama. Mabel Julienne Scott, David Torrence, Maude George, Phillips Smalley.

Ridin' Wild
Dir: Nat Ross. Western melodrama. Hoot Gibson, Edna Murphy, Wade Boteler.

The Scrapper
Dir: Hobart Henley. Romantic drama. Herbert Rawlinson, Gertrude Olmstead, William Welsh, Franki Lee, Fred Kohler.

Second Hand Rose
Dir: Lloyd Ingraham. East Side romantic comedy. Gladys Walton, Wade Boteler, George B. Williams, Eddie Sutherland.

Shattered Dreams
Dir: Paul Scardon. Society melodrama. Miss Du Pont, Bertram Grassby, Herbert Heyes.

Step On It!
Dir: Jack Conway. Western melodrama. Hoot Gibson, Edith Yorke, Frank Lanning.

The Top O' The Morning
Dir: Edward Laemmle. Romantic drama. Gladys Walton, Harry Myers, Doreen Turner.

Tracked To Earth
Dir: William Worthington. Western melodrama. Frank Mayo, Virginia Valli.

Trimmed
Dir: Harry Pollard. Western melodrama. Hoot Gibson, Patsy Ruth Miller.

The Trouper
Dir: Harry B. Harris. Comedy drama. Gladys Walton, Jack Perrin, Thomas Holding.

Wild Honey (Jewel)
Dir: Wesley Ruggles. S. African melodrama. Priscilla Dean, Noah Beery, Lloyd Whitlock.

The Wise Kid
Dir: Tod Browning. Romantic comedy. Gladys Walton, David Butler, Hallam Cooley.

Wolf Law
Dir: Stuart Paton. Crook melodrama. Frank Mayo, Sylvia Breamer, Tom Guise.

A Wonderful Wife
Dir: Paul Scardon. Domestic melodrama. Miss Du Pont, Vernon Steele, Landers Stevens.

1923

▽ Herbert Rawlinson starred as an English aristocrat, the Hon Cecil Fitzhugh Waring, in **The Victor**, a pleasant romantic comedy which found Rawlinson (left) arriving in America to marry the daughter (Esther Ralston) of a wealthy chewing-gum baron (Otis Harlan) in order to save the family fortune, but his pride renders him unable to go through with it. Virtually on the breadline, he meets an impoverished actress called 'Teddy' Walters (Dorothy Manners), who kindly shares her meal of doughnuts with him. Touched by her generosity, he determines to look after her, and takes a job as a waiter. In an argument, he knocks out a well-known prizefighter, is immediately seized on by a fight promoter, and becomes so successful in the ring that he soon wins the British middleweight crown for himself. With his earnings he manages to save his father (Frank Currier) from financial ruin and, in return, is given his old man's blessing to marry Miss Manners. Based on Gerald Beaumont's story *Two Bells For Pegasus*, and scripted by E. Richard Schayer, it also featured Eddie Gribbon (right) and Tom McGuire, and was neatly directed by Edward Laemmle, who made a meal of most of the sequences in the ring – especially the climactic finale.

▷ Based on Frances Hodgson Burnett's 1877 novel *The Lass O'Lowrie's*, **The Flame Of Life**, set in a small mining town in Northern England, starred Priscilla Dean (right) as the daughter of brutal coal-miner Wallace Beery. Robert Ellis co-starred as the mine's new over-man who, despite his attempts to improve working conditions, incurs the hatred of Beery whom he fires for smoking in the mine. Deliberately ignoring Ellis' no-smoking-on-the-job rule, Beery defiantly returns to the tunnel and lights up inside it, causing an almighty explosion and, very nearly, Ellis' death. But the latter is rescued by Miss Dean who, despite such considerations as class barriers, loves him, and vice versa. The melodrama inherent in Burnett's story (screenplay by Elliott J. Clawson) was grippingly handled by director Hobart Henley who, throughout the film's seven reels, maintained the subject's northern England atmosphere, and kept the plot constantly moving. Fred Kohler, Beatrice Burnham, Emmett King, Kathryn McGuire (left) and Frankie Lee rounded out the cast. (Jewel).

△ Reginald Denny, who had made quite a reputation for himself in Universal's two-reeler series *The Leather Pushers* playing a refined boxer called Kid Robertson, returned to the ring in and as **The Abysmal Brute**. Suggested by a Jack London novel, the hold the scenario by A.P. Younger had on the original was, to put it mildly, tenuous, and after paring the complexities of the novel to a minimum, all that audiences were left with was a simple tale of a backwoods prizefighter whose romance with a society girl undergoes a hiccup when she learns of his true vocation. But love conquers all, and after winning the biggest fight of his life the champ retires to the backwoods with his new bride for a honeymoon. Denny's (left) leading lady was Mabel Julienne Scott (right), with other roles going to Charles French, Hayden Stevenson, David Torrence, George Stewart, Buddy Messinger, Crauford Kent and Dorothea Wolbert. Hobart Henley directed, his whirlwind boxing bouts in the ring, and an early sequence in which the hero rescues a man from drowning, offering patrons the best value for their money. (Jewel).

▽ A melodrama with a circus backdrop, **Sawdust** was the story of Nita Moore, a 'big-top' star who, after constant maltreatment by the circus' sadistic ringmaster, runs away to an elderly wealthy couple and convinces them that she is their long-lost daughter. The deception succeeds admirably, until Nita's lawyer, who is in love with her, reveals the truth to the girl's 'parents' after a quarrel. Nita attempts suicide by drowning, but is saved by the lawyer who forgives her, and they face a happy future together. Though Courtney Ryley Cooper's story (scenario by Doris Schroeder and Harvey Gates) didn't bear thinking about, director Jack Conway's attempts to breathe conviction into the circus sequences were successful; so was Gladys Walton's (illustrated) starring performance as Nita. Edith Yorke and Herbert Standing were her 'parents', Niles Welch came and went as her lawyer-lover, and the rest of the cast included Matthew Betz, Frank Brownlee, William Robert Daly, Mattie Peters and a clever terrier called Sawdust.

▷ The same meticulous attention to detail that went into the Monte Carlo settings of *Foolish Wives* the previous year, was very much in evidence in **The Merry-Go-Round**, whose pre-war Vienna locale provided the colourful milieu to the story Harvey Gates concocted for director Erich von Stroheim. Though Von Stroheim also had his eye on the leading role of Franz Maximilian Hohenegg, his by now legendary extravagance, coupled with his temperamental outbursts, did not impress Irving Thalberg, the studio's influential head of production. Thalberg cast Norman Kerry as the Count and, after several disagreements – usually financial – replaced Von Stroheim with Rupert Julian. Though Julian claimed that no more than 600 feet of film was the work of his predecessor, the painstaking pre-production work (for which Von Stroheim was responsible) was very much in evidence in the authentic and evocative 'look' of the period, and it was this aspect of the drama that attracted most of the critical attention. For the rest, it was the romantic tale of the love felt by Count Franz Maximilian (posing as a necktie salesman) for the organ-grinding daughter (Mary Philbin) of a circus puppeteer (Cesare Gravina), despite the fact that he is engaged to (and eventually marries) Dorothy Wallace, the stately daughter of the war minister (Spottiswoode Aitken). Ten reels later it ended happily, with the Count returning from the war a widower and therefore free to marry Miss Philbin (right), whose hunchbacked fiancé (George Hackathorne, left) considerately agrees to step aside. It was photographed by Charles Kaufman and William Daniels, costumed by Von Stroheim and Richard Day (the latter also in charge of the set designs), and produced by Irving Thalberg. Completing the cast were Edith Yorke, George Siegmann, Dale Fuller, Lillian Sylvester, Ed Edmundsen and Maude George. (Super Jewel).

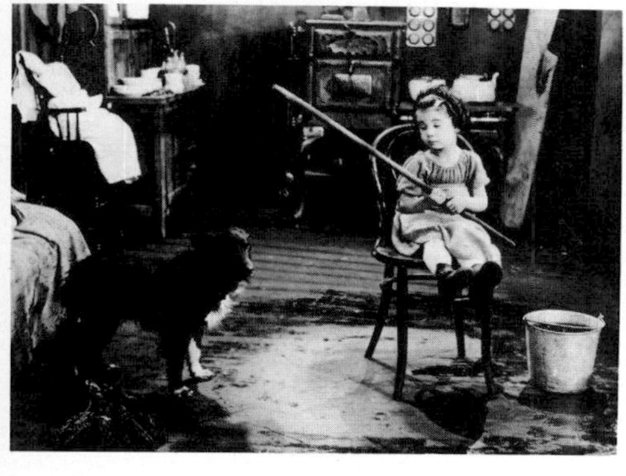

△ After appearing in a series of successful two-reel comedies, Baby Peggy Montgomery, whose contract with the studio was worth a massive $5,000,000, starred in her first feature, **The Darling Of New York**. Tailor-made by scenarists King Baggot (who also directed), Raymond L. Schrock and Adrian Johnson for maximum moppet mileage, the story concerned a five-year-old orphan (Baby Peggy, illustrated) who, en route to America to live with her grandfather, is separated from her nurse, and cared for by a gangster called Giovanni (Sheldon Lewis). Baby Peggy's adventures in gangsterland centred on some contraband diamonds hidden in her rag doll, her sojourn with a poor Jewish family called Levinsky, and, finally, on finding her grandfather (Frank Currier). As the raison d'être of the picture, Baby Peggy appeared in practically every scene in the film, regardless of whether or not it furthered the plot-line. Nor was director Baggot able to resist showing her in close-up on far more occasions than was necessary. Still, it was Baby Peggy the customers paid to see, and it was Baby Peggy they certainly got! For the record, the rest of the cast included Gladys Brockwell, Pat Hartigan, Junior Coghlan, Max Davidson, Emma Steel and Walter 'Spec' O'Donnell. (Jewel).

▽ A ridiculously over-made-up Lon Chaney played the romantic lead (as well as an underworld cripple, the use of whose legs are miraculously restored to him in the last reel) in **The Shock**, a conventional melodrama from a story by William Dudley Pelley. All about Chaney's (left) romance with the daughter of a small-town banker who is being blackmailed by a female San Francisco gang leader called 'Queen Anne' – and whom he has been ordered to expose, the convoluted scenario by Arthur Statter and Charles Kenyon also involved blackmail, religion and the great San Francisco earthquake (unconvincingly depicted in models) as it slowly worked its way to a far-fetched conclusion. Virginia Valli (right) co-starred as Chaney's sweetheart and Queen Anne was played by Christina Mayo, with other roles under Lambert Hillyer's guidance going to Jack Mower, William Welsh (as the banker), Henry Barrows and Harry Devere. (Jewel).

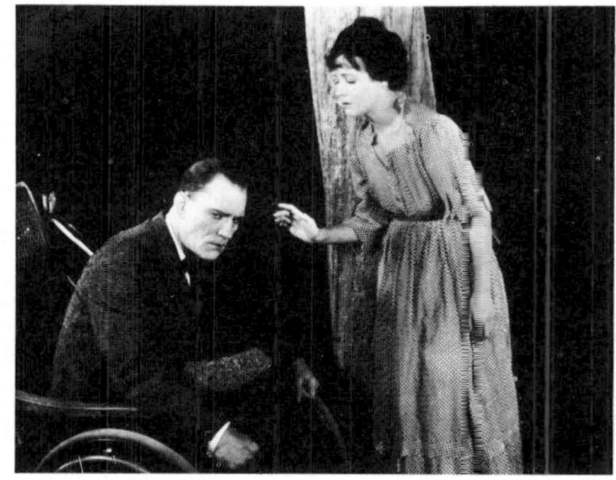

△ The miscasting of Charles Emmett Mack (illustrated) as Tom Tolliver made it difficult to accept **Driven** as anything other than old-fashioned melodrama. Mack's slightly sinister appearance was totally at odds in a story which required him, in contrast to his three brutish brothers and father, to be palpably sympathetic. Emily Fitzroy (illustrated) played Mrs Tolliver, the long-suffering wife and mother to the unpleasant brood of Southern moonshiners who, in the course of Alfred Raboch's scenario (from a *Cosmopolitan Magazine* story by Jay Gelzer), betrays her family by telling revenue officers of the whereabouts of the Tolliver still. She does this in order to ensure that Tom, whom she adores more than her life, is free to marry Elinor Fair, the girl he loves who, against her will, has married one of his brothers (George Bancroft) instead. Burr McIntosh was cast as the head of the household, with other parts going to Fred Kohler and Ernest Chandler as the two remaining Tolliver brothers, and to Leslie Stowe. It was directed on location in the South by Charles J. Brabin. (Jewel).

▽ Though Irving Thalberg left Universal in February 1923, before the release of **The Hunchback Of Notre Dame**, the project had been his brainchild from the start, and it was his unbridled enthusiasm for it that persuaded Carl Laemmle to spend a great deal more money on it than was normal for the studio, and to release it as a 'roadshow' attraction. The finished film more than justified the expenditure. **Hunchback** remains a classic piece of silent film-making, in which Lon Chaney as Quasimodo, the bellringer of Notre Dame, gave one of the great performances in cinema history. An expert with make-up, Chaney excelled himself on this memorable occasion. At the cost of his physical comfort he masochistically attached a seventy-pound rubber lump to his back, wore a leather harness that made it impossible for him to stand up straight, and donned a rubber suit covered with animal hair. Then, to disguise his facial features, he stuffed mortician's wax into his mouth, puttied his cheeks, matted his hair, and gave himself a grotesque, bulging false eye. For three arduous months he worked in this fashion, and if his suffering seems so heartfelt on screen, much of it was genuine! Perley Poore Sheehan's adaptation of the novel underplayed Victor Hugo's attack on the priesthood, altered the plot-line in such a way as to make the archdeacon of Paris' brother, Jehan, the real villain of the piece and, in order to ensure a happy ending, reunited Esmeralda with Captain Phoebus after Quasimodo's death. Under Wallace Worsley's stirring direction, press and public alike were pleased with the changes, and the film, which firmly established Chaney (left) as a major Hollywood star, was an immediate hit. Originally twelve reels in length, its running time was shortened after its initial roadshow release, one of the casualties of the cuts being Ernest Torrence, whose role as the beggar chieftain Clopin, considered by many to be as fine as Chaney's, was greatly truncated. Patsy Ruth Miller (right) played Esmeralda, Norman Kerry was Phoebus, Tully Marshall appeared as Louis XI, and Nigel de Brulier was Dom Claude the archdeacon. Also cast: Kate Lester, Gladys Brockwell, Brandon Hurst (as Jehan) and Raymond Hatton. Contributing immeasurably to the film's success were the spectacular sets, most notably Notre Dame Cathedral which, like the Casino in *Foolish Wives* (1922), was constructed at Universal City. Edward T. Lowe provided the scenario and, assisting director Worsley to control the 2000 extras employed in the crowd scenes, was a relative newcomer called William Wyler. The story had been filmed three times before, in 1906, 1911, and 1917; and would be filmed on two further occasions: by RKO in 1939 with Charles Laughton, and by Allied Artists in 1957 with Anthony Quinn.

◁ Universal did a first-rate job of recreating – on its backlot – colourful Shanghai, the setting of **Drifting**, a melodrama based on a play by John Colton and Daisy H. Andrews. Priscilla Dean (left) starred as Cassie Cook, an American girl in China who, after smuggling opium under the surveillance of a government agent posing as a mining engineer, falls in love with the agent and reforms. Matt Moore (right) played the agent, but the film's fulcrum wasn't the romance that blossoms between the young couple – it was the enjoyable villainy of second-billed Wallace Beery as Miss Dean's partner-in-crime. There wasn't much director Tod Browning, working from an improbable scenario (which he himself wrote with A.P. Younger), could do to rescue the plot from its melodramatic clutches, a climactic (tinted) fire being the visual highlight of the occasion. J. Farrell MacDonald, Rose Dione, Edna Tichenor, William V. Mong and Anna May Wong completed the cast. (Jewel).

▽ Wallace Beery's performance as an extremist revolutionary out to loot the palaces of Russian autocrats was the best thing about **Bavu**, an unconvincing drama of political intrigue in which Beery (as Bavu, right) finds himself involved in a battle of wits with Forrest Stanley – also a revolutionary, but one without bloodshed in mind. Estelle Taylor played a Princess befriended by Stanley, with other roles going to Sylvia Breamer (left) (as Bavu's mistress), Josef Swickard, Nick De Ruiz and Martha Mattox. The impossibly confused scenario was by Raymond L. Schrock and Albert Kenyon, and it was directed without distinction by Stuart Paton. (Jewel).

△ After their successful teaming in *Drifting*, Priscilla Dean (centre), Matt Moore and Wallace Beery (left) again pooled their talents in **The White Tiger**, a crook melodrama directed by Tod Browning, whose handling of the material was better than it deserved. Written by Browning and Charles Kenyon, it was the story of a trio of international jewel thieves (Dean, Beery, and Raymond Griffith, right), two of whom (Dean and Griffith) are brother and sister, but don't know it. Arriving in America from England, the trio sets about robbing wealthy residents by using a gimmick known as an automatic chess player, in which one of the thieves is concealed. But their partnership turns sour when (a) the brother-sister relationship is finally revealed and (b) it is discovered that Beery was responsible for the murder of the siblings' father. Matt Moore played a detective who falls in love with Miss Dean and facilitates her regeneration in the last reel. (Jewel).

OTHER PRODUCTIONS OF 1923

The Acquittal (Jewel)
Dir: Clarence Brown. Mystery melodrama. Claire Windsor, Norman Kerry.

Blinky
Dir: Edward Sedgwick. Cavalry comedy. Hoot Gibson, Esther Ralston.

The Bolted Door
Dir: William Worthington. Domestic melodrama. Frank Mayo, Charles A. Stevenson, Phyllis Haver, Nigel Barrie.

Burning Words
Dir: Stuart Paton. Northwest melodrama. Roy Stewart, Laura La Plante, Harold Goodwin.

A Chapter In Her Life (Jewel)
Dir: Lois Weber. Drama. Claude Gillingwater, Jane Mercer, Jacqueline Gasden.

The Clean Up
Dir: William Parke. Comedy. Herbert Rawlinson, Claire Adams, Claire Anderson.

Crooked Alley
Dir: Robert F. Hill. Reformed-crook melodrama. Thomas Carrigan, Laura La Plante, Tom Guise, Owen Gorine.

Crossed Wires
Dir: King Baggot. Society comedy. Gladys Walton, George Stewart, Tom Guise.

Dead Game
Dir: Edward Sedgwick. Western melodrama. Hoot Gibson, Laura La Plante, Robert McKim.

Don Quickshot Of The Rio Grande
Dir: George Marshall. Western melodrama. Jack Hoxie, Emmett King, Elinor Field.

Double Dealing
Dir: Henry Lehrman. Western melodrama. Hoot Gibson, Helen Ferguson, Eddie Gribbon.

The First Degree
Dir: Edward Sedgwick. Rural melodrama. Frank Mayo, Sylvia Breamer, George A. Williams.

Fools And Riches
Dir: Herbert Blache. Drama. Herbert Rawlinson, Katherine Perry, Tully Marshall.

The Gentleman From America
Dir: Edward Sedgwick. Holiday comedy. Hoot Gibson, Tom O'Brien, Louise Lorraine.

The Ghost Patrol
Dir: Nat Ross. Police drama. Ralph Graves, Bessie Love, George Nichols.

Gossip
Dir: King Baggot. Strike drama. Gladys Walton, Ramsay Wallace, Albert Prisco.

His Mystery Girl
Dir: Robert F. Hill. Comedy melodrama. Herbert Rawlinson, Ruth Dwyer.

Kindled Courage
Dir: William Worthington. Western melodrama. Hoot Gibson, Beatrice Burnham.

Legally Dead
Dir: William Parke. Crime melodrama. Milton Sills, Claire Adams, Margaret Campbell.

The Love Brand
Dir: Stuart Paton. Western melodrama. Roy Stewart, Wilfred North, Margaret Landis.

The Love Letter
Dir: King Baggot. Crime melodrama. Gladys Walton, Fontaine La Rue, George Cooper.

McGuire Of The Mounted
Dir: Richard Stanton. Northwest crime melodrama. William Desmond, Louise Lorraine.

Men In The Raw
Dir: George E. Marshall. Western melodrama. Jack Hoxie, Sid Jordan.

The Midnight Guest
Dir: George Archainbaud. Society crime melodrama. Grace Darmond, Mahlon Hamilton.

A Million To Burn
Dir: William Parke. Comedy. Herbert Rawlinson, Kalla Pasha, Beatrice Banham.

The Near Lady
Dir: Herbert Blache. Filial comedy. Gladys Walton, Jerry Gendron, Hank Mann.

Nobody's Bride
Dir: Herbert Blache. Crook melodrama. Herbert Rawlinson, Edna Murphy, Alice Lake.

Out Of Luck
Dir: Edward Sedgwick. Comedy drama. Hoot Gibson, Laura La Plante, Howard Truesdale.

The Prisoner
Dir: Jack Conway. European melodrama. Herbert Rawlinson, Boris Karloff, Eileen Percy.

Pure Grit
Dir: Nat Ross. Western melodrama. Roy Stewart, Jack Mower, Esther Ralston.

Railroaded
Dir: Edmund Mortimer. Crime melodrama. Herbert Rawlinson, Esther Ralston.

The Ramblin' Kid
Dir: Edward Sedgwick. Western melodrama. Hoot Gibson, Laura La Plante, Harold Goodwin.

The Red Warning
Dir: Robert North Bradbury. Western melodrama. Jack Hoxie, Elinor Field, Fred Kohler.

The Scarlet Car
Dir: Stuart Paton. Melodrama. Herbert Rawlinson, Claire Adams, Edward Cecil.

The Self-made Wife
Dir: Jack Dillon. New York melodrama. Ethel Grey Terry, Crauford Kent, Phillips Smalley, Virginia Ainsworth.

Shadows Of The North
Dir: Robert F. Hill. Western melodrama. William Desmond, Virginia Brown Faire.

Shootin' For Love
Dir: Edward Sedgwick. Western melodrama. Hoot Gibson, Laura La Plante, Alfred Allen.

Single Handed
Dir: Edward Sedgwick. Western melodrama. Hoot Gibson, Percy Challenger, Elinor Field.

The Six-Fifty
Dir: Nat Ross. Rural melodrama. Renee Adoree, Orville Caldwell, Bert Woodruff.

The Thrill Chaser
Dir: Edward Sedgwick. Adventure melodrama. Hoot Gibson, James Neil, Billie Dove.

Thundering Dawn (Jewel)
Dir: Harry Garson. Vamp melodrama. Winter Hall, J. Warren Kerrigan, Anna Q. Nilsson.

The Town Scandal
Dir: King Baggot. Chorus-girl comedy. Gladys Walton, Edward Hearne.

Trifling With Honor (Jewel)
Dir: Harry A. Pollard. Crime drama. Fritzi Ridgeway, Rockcliffe Fellowes, Buddy Messenger, Hayden Stevenson.

Trimmed In Scarlet
Dir: Jack Conway. Society melodrama. Kathlyn Williams, Roy Stewart, Lucille Rickson.

The Untameable
Dir: Herbert Blache. Psychological drama. Gladys Walton, Herbert McGregor.

What Wives Want
Dir: Jack Conway. Domestic drama. Ethel Grey Terry, Vernon Steele.

Where Is This West?
Dir: George E. Marshall. Western melodrama. Jack Hoxie, Mary Philbin, Joseph Girard.

The Wild Party
Dir: Herbert Blache. Office comedy drama. Gladys Walton, Robert Ellis.

1924

▽ Set for most of the time aboard a tramp schooner, **The Storm Daughter** successfully evoked a seafaring atmosphere, despite an improbable story in which a bestial skipper is tamed (and loved) by a woman he has violently tried to seduce. Priscilla Dean (right) was the forgiving woman, and although the emotional motivations which scenarist Edward J. Montagne (story by Leete Renick Brown) provided her with simply didn't make sense, director George Archainbaud kept it simmering thanks, in the main, to a well-staged hurricane, mutiny and shipwreck which drew the audience's attention away from the narrative. Tom Santschi (left) played the skipper (called 'Brute' Morgan), and William B. Davidson was the first mate and leader of the mutiny. Rounding out the cast were J. Farrell MacDonald, Cyril Chadwick, Bert Roach and Alfred Fisher.

▷ New York's rough-and-ready Bowery was the setting for **Fool's Highway**, the uncomplicated story of a 'primitive' pugilist called Mike Kildare (Pat O'Malley) whose romance with Mamie Rose (Mary Philbin, right) is initially hindered by his brute coarseness. Forsaking his undesirable gang in order to prove his love for Mamie (a gesture which almost results in his death), Kildare is regenerated and, in time, becomes a happily married husband and father who trades in his life of crime for one of law and order by becoming a policeman. Miss Philbin pleased the masses by giving her best performance since *The Merry-Go-Round* the previous year, and director Irving Cummings, firmly in control of Lenore J. Coffee and Harvey Gates' scenario, drew fine performances from a cast that also included William Collier Jr as Mike's gentle rival in love, Lincoln Plummer, Edwin J. Brady, Max Davidson, Kate Price (left) and Charles Murray. The subject originated with *My Mamie Rose: The Story Of My Regeneration* by Owen Frawley Kildare. (Jewel).

▷ Adapted by Arthur Ripley, Marian Ainsley and Marion Fairfax from Frances Hodgson Burnett's 1896 novel, **A Lady Of Quality** was a costume melodrama set in London and covering a period of over thirty years from 1704. Its heroine was Clorinda Wildairs (Virginia Valli, illustrated) who, after growing out of her hoydenish teens and becoming a young woman of exceptional beauty, unfortunately falls for the charms of a libertine called Sir John Oxon (Earle Foxe). After dallying with her affections, Sir John throws her over and goes to war. Five years later, she is about to marry the Duke of Osmonde (Milton Sills), when Sir John returns, and threatens to blackmail her if she resists his amorous advances. In the ensuing struggle he is accidentally killed, and his body buried in the cellar. Clorinda eventually reveals what has happened to the Duke, who faithfully promises to stand by her no matter what. Director Hobart Henley handled the story with admirable restraint and was especially successful in conveying the frequent lapses of time dictated by the scenario. Equally effective in this respect was Virginia Valli's central performance and the skilful way she developed from a wilful, tomboyish 16-year-old, to early and vulnerable womanhood, and finally to a mature woman driven to desperate measures in defence of her own happiness and future. The rest of the cast included Lionel Belmore, Margaret Seddon, Peggy Cartwright, Florence Gibson, Dorothea Wolbert and Bert Roach. (Jewel).

▷ A straightforward romantic melodrama, well mounted and convincingly performed by a cast that included top-starred Mary Philbin, Robert Cain and John Sainpolis, **The Rose Of Paris** was adapted from a French novel by Lenore J. Coffee and Bernard McConville. It was the story of an orphan called Marianne (Philbin, right) who, lured from her cloistered convent life to Paris, becomes the victim of a plot by an heir presumptive (Sainpolis) to fleece her of her rightful inheritance. Becoming a servant in a chateau, she falls in love with a Marquis called Christian (Cain) who, learning of her predicament, brings about Sainpolis' arrest, secures Marianne's fortune for her, then marries the girl himself. Irving Cummings' no-frills direction kept the rather commonplace story buoyant for most of its seven reels, eliciting adequate support from Rose Dione, Dorothy Revier, D.J. Mitsoras (2nd right), Gino Corrado, Charles Puffy (centre), Frank Currier and Cesare Gravina (left). (Jewel).

▽ Reginald Denny's reputation as a light comedian and likeable leading man was firmly established after his performance in **Sporting Youth**, a trifle set in the high-speed world of motor racing, and featuring Denny (centre right) as a chauffeur who is mistakenly believed to be an ace driver. Playing along with the deception, Denny enters a big race, wins, and, with the prize money, manages to free himself of his debts. He also gets the girl (Laura La Plante, centre left), the daughter of a wealthy car manufacturer. Director Harry A. Pollard was at his best in the action sequences on the track, more or less leaving a supporting cast that included Hallam Cooley, Frederick Vroom (left), Lucille Ward, Malcolm Denny, Henry Barrows (right) and Leo White to fend for themselves. Harvey Thew wrote it from a story by Byron Morgan. (Jewel).

▷ An amiable hodge-podge with a bit of this and a bit of that – none of it to be taken with anything more than a pinch of disbelief – **The Fighting American** starred Pat O'Malley as Bill Pendleton, a happy-go-lucky student adept at both flying and football, who accepts a wager from his fraternity colleagues that he will propose to any girl in the college they choose. Quiet, old-fashioned Mary O'Mallory (Mary Astor, illustrated centre, co-starred) is chosen and, unaware of the wager, accepts Bill's fraternity pin, the hero having actually proposed to her in earnest. Predictably, Mary gets to hear about the wager and, thoroughly disgusted with Bill, goes off to China to join her missionary father. A remorseful Bill follows her there and, in the final reel, redeems himself by rescuing her and her father from revolutionaries. Other roles under Tom Forman's tongue-in-cheek direction went to Raymond Hatton, Warner Oland, Edwin J. Brady, Taylor Carroll, Clarence Geldert and Alfred Fisher. The story was by William Elwell Oliver (whose original manuscript won a Laemmle scholarship award), it was adapted by Raymond L. Schrock, and scripted by Harvey Gates. (Jewel).

1924

▽ Wallace Beery (right) came to the rescue of **The Signal Tower**, a melodrama with a railroad backdrop. He played a character called Joe Standish who, after accepting lodgings in the home of a signalman colleague, makes a play for the signalman's wife. Fortunately, the lady is capable of looking after herself, and while hubby is preventing a runaway freight train from crashing into a passenger express, she repays the lodger by shooting him dead. Though Beery was the catalyst of the piece and the most compelling of the performers, Virginia Valli was top-billed; Rockliffe Fellowes (left) played her husband, and a young Frankie Darro her son. Completing the cast were J. Farrell MacDonald, Dot Farley and James O. Barrows. Clarence Brown directed (he also appeared in it as a switch man) and would have had a better little film on his hands had he brought it in at six reels rather than seven. It was written by James O. Spearing from a story by Wadsworth Camp. (Jewel).

△ **Butterfly** was the story of two orphaned sisters – Butterfly (Laura La Plante, illustrated) and Hilary (Ruth Clifford) – the latter a typist who sacrifices not only her career, but the man she loves, for the former who is studying to be a classical violinist. Not content at having ruined her sister's life once, Butterfly, although married, attempts to woo a violinist called Kronski – despite the fact that he is in love with Hilary. She does not succeed, and the film ends with self-sacrificing Hilary finding happiness at last. Norman Kerry played Kronski and Kenneth Harlan the man Butterfly almost deserts; with other roles under Clarence Brown's supportive direction going to Cesare Gravina, Margaret Livingston and Freeman Wood. Olga Printzlau scripted. (Jewel).

OTHER PRODUCTIONS OF 1924

The Back Trail
Dir: Clifford Smith. Western melodrama. Jack Hoxie, Alton Stone, Eugenia Gilbert.

Behind The Curtain
Dir: Chester M. Franklin. Mystery melodrama. Lucille Rickson, Johnny Harron.

Big Timber
Dir: William J. Craft. Northwest melodrama. William Desmond, Olive Hasbrouck.

The Breathless Moment
Dir: Robert F. Hill. Crime comedy melodrama. William Desmond, Charlotte Merriam.

Broadway Or Bust
Dir: Edward Sedgwick. Romantic comedy. Hoot Gibson, Ruth Dwyer, Gertrude Astor.

The Dancing Cheat
Dir: Irving Cummings. Gambling melodrama. Herbert Rawlinson, Alice Lake, Robert Walker, Edwin J. Brady.

The Dangerous Blonde
Dir: Robert F. Hill. Romantic comedy. Laura La Plante, Philo McCullough.

Daring Chances
Dir: Clifford Smith. Western melodrama. Jack Hoxie, Alta Allen, Claude Payton.

Dark Stairways (Jewel)
Dir: Robert F. Hill. Mystery melodrama. Herbert Rawlinson, Ruth Dwyer, Hayden Stevenson, Robert E. Homans.

Excitement
Dir: Robert F. Hill. Comedy melodrama. Laura La Plante, Edward Hearn.

The Family Secret
Dir: William A. Seiter. Child melodrama. Gladys Hulette, Baby Peggy Montgomery.

The Fast Worker (Jewel)
Dir: William A. Seiter. Holiday comedy. Reginald Denny, Laura La Plante, Ethel Grey Terry, Muriel Frances.

Fighting Fury
Dir: Clifford Smith. Western melodrama. Jack Hoxie, Helen Holmes, Fred Kohler.

40-Horse Hawkins
Dir: Edward Sedgwick. Backstage comedy. Hoot Gibson, Anne Cornwall.

The Gaiety Girl (Jewel)
Dir: King Baggot. Romantic melodrama. Mary Philbin, Joseph Dowling, William Haines.

The Galloping Ace
Dir: Robert North Bradbury. Western melodrama. Jack Hoxie, Margaret Morris.

High Speed
Dir: Herbert Blache. Comedy melodrama. Herbert Rawlinson, Carmelita Geraghty.

Hit And Run
Dir: Edward Sedgwick. Baseball comedy drama. Hoot Gibson, Marion Harlan, Cyril Ring.

Hook And Ladder
Dir: Edward Sedgwick. Western melodrama. Hoot Gibson, Frank Beal, Mildred June.

Jack O' Clubs
Dir: Robert F. Hill. Crime melodrama. Herbert Rawlinson, Ruth Dwyer, Eddie Gribbon.

K – The Unknown (Jewel)
Dir: Harry Pollard. Mystery melodrama. Virginia Valli, Percy Marmont.

The Law Forbids (Jewel)
Dir: Jesse Robbins. Romantic drama. Robert Ellis, Baby Peggy Montgomery, Elinor Fair, Joseph Dowling.

Love And Glory (Jewel)
Dir: Rupert Julian. Romantic drama. Charles De Roche, Ford Sterling.

The Man From Wyoming
Dir: Robert North Bradbury. Western melodrama. Jack Hoxie, Lillian Rich.

The Measure Of A Man
Dir: Arthur Rosson. Melodrama. William Desmond, Albert J. Smith, Francis Ford.

The Night Message
Dir: Perley Poore Sheehan. Rural melodrama. Howard Truesdale, Gladys Hulette.

The Phantom Horseman
Dir: Robert North Bradbury. Western melodrama. Jack Hoxie, Lillian Rich.

The Reckless Age (Jewel)
Dir: Harry Pollard. Comedy melodrama. Reginald Denny, Ruth Dwyer, John Steppling.

Ride For Your Life
Dir: Edward Sedgwick. Western melodrama. Hoot Gibson, Laura La Plante, Harry Todd.

Riders Up
Dir: Irving Cummings. Racing drama. Creighton Hale, George Cooper, Kate Price.

Ridgeway Of Montana
Dir: Clifford Smith. Western melodrama. Jack Hoxie, Olive Hasbrouck.

The Ridin' Kid From Powder River
Dir: Edward Sedgwick. Western melodrama. Hoot Gibson, Gladys Hulette, Tully Marshall.

The Sawdust Trail
Dir: Edward Sedgwick. Western melodrama. Hoot Gibson, Josie Sedgwick, David Torrence.

The Slanderers
Dir: Nat Ross. War hero drama. Johnnie Walker, Gladys Hulette, Billy Sullivan.

Stolen Secrets
Dir: Irving Cummings. Mystery melodrama. Herbert Rawlinson, Kathleen Myers, Edwards Davis, Arthur Stuart Hull.

The Sunset Trail
Dir: Whyndham Gittens. Western comedy melodrama. William Desmond, Gareth Hughes, Lucille Hutton.

The Tornado (Jewel)
Dir: Hobart Henley. Drama. Emmett Corrigan, George Hackathorne, Edward Hearn.

The Turmoil (Jewel)
Dir: Hobart Henley. Drama. Emmett Corrigan, Edward Hearn, George Hackathorne.

The Western Wallop
Dir: Clifford Smith. Western melodrama. Jack Hoxie, Margaret Landis, Duke R. Lee.

The Whispered Name
Dir: King Baggot. Comedy drama. Ruth Clifford, Charles Clary, William E. Lawrence.

Wine (Jewel)
Dir: Louis Gasnier. Prohibition melodrama. Clara Bow, Forrest Stanley.

Young Ideas
Dir: Robert F. Hill. Comedy. Laura La Plante, T. Roy Barnes, Lucille Rickson.

1925

▽ Critics threw their hats in the air for Rudolph Schildkraut's performance in **His People**, and justifiably praised the film itself for its humanity, its compassion and its pathos. Schildkraut (real-life father of Joseph) played Rabbi Cominsky, a poor pushcart peddler in New York's lower East Side. Cominsky has two sons: Morris, a selfishly ambitious student with a law career in mind; and Sammy who sells newspapers to help pay for his brother's college education. Sammy also happens to be an excellent boxer, and when his father discovers his boy has become a prizefighter known as 'Battling Rooney', he shows him the door. As Isadore Bernstein's story unfurls, however, Schildkraut slowly realises that it is Sammy who is the better of the two boys – Morris, at one point, having refused to acknowledge his own father at a party. It ends happily, with Schildkraut apologising to Sammy and giving him his blessing for his forthcoming marriage to an Irish girl (Blanche Mehaffey, left). George Lewis (right) played Sammy, Arthur Lubin was Morris; their mother was played by Rosa Rosanova with other parts going to Bobby Gordon and Albert Bushaland (Sammy and Morris as children), Jean Johnson, Kate Price, Virginia Brown Faire and Edgar Kennedy. Edward Sloman directed it from a screenplay by Charles E. Whittaker and Alfred A. Cohn. (Jewel).

△ In Dorothy Canfield's story, **The Home-Maker**, a husband (Clive Brook), after failing to gain a promotion in his office, and unsuccessfully attempting suicide in order to secure the insurance money for his wife (Alice Joyce) and three children, changes roles with his wife. Confined to a wheelchair as a result of the bungled suicide, Brook becomes the home-maker, while Miss Joyce (illustrated), freed of the drudgery of housework, soon proves herslf an efficient woman, and in no time at all is earning twice as much as her husband ever did. It is a perfect arrangement, Brook being a far better parent to his kids than his wife ever was. Then suddenly Brook regains the use of his legs. Realising that this means a return to his unhappy way of life as a breadwinner, he persuades his doctor (George Fawcett) to conceal the truth. Though overlong at eight reels, director King Baggot managed to maintain interest throughout, the film's chief asset being Clive Brook's excellent central performance. As his wife, Alice Joyce was less well cast, though there were no complaints about the delightful Billy Kent Schaeffer as one of their offspring. Also cast: Jacqueline Wells (to become Julie Bishop in the '40s), Maurice Murphy, Martha Mattox, Virginia Boardman and Frank Newburg. Mary O'Hara scripted. (Jewel).

▷ Reginald Denny, giving his most acrobatic performance to date, went beyond the call of duty to keep **Where Was I?** a nifty, albeit elaborately contrived, farce, buoyant. He played a successful young business man who, after announcing his engagement to the daughter of his main business rival, is suddenly confronted by a woman who swears she is his wife, and gives their wedding date as January 9th, 1923. Denny (right), unable to find an alibi for where he was on that particular day, is at his wits end attempting to keep his so-called 'wife' and fiancée apart, but the denouement finally reveals that the whole thing has been engineered by his fiancée's resentful father. Marion Nixon played the fiancée, Pauline Garon (left) the 'wife', and Tyrone Power Sr the catalyst of the piece, with other roles under William A. Seiter's over-energetic direction going to Lee Moran, Otis Harlan and Chester Conklin. Rex Taylor and Melville Brown scripted from an *Argosy* story by Edgar Franklin. (Jewel).

△ 'Intensive characterisation and a natural, plausible theme' – according to one reviewer at the time – were the twin factors which contributed substantially to the success of **Siege**. Another of the drama's qualities was the solid yet free-flowing scenario which Harvey Thew managed to cobble out of Samuel Hopkins Adams' novel published the previous year. The story of a strong-willed elderly woman called Augusta Ruyland, who for years has ruled her factory and the town in which she lives with Victorian severity, and her clash with the equally single-minded society wife of her nephew-successor, the film starred Mary Alden (left) as Augusta, Eugene O'Brien (right) as her nephew, and Virginia Valli as the wife. Sven Gade directed it with tremendous conviction, the occasional cliché and a not entirely satisfactory denouement only slightly denting the good impression made by all concerned. Marc MacDermott as a deaf mute in love with Miss Valli gave the best supporting performance in a cast that also included Harry Lorraine, Beatrice Burnham and Helen Dunbar. Remade as *Mother's Millions* (1929). (Jewel).

▽ Louise Dresser (illustrated centre) gave a remarkable performance in an otherwise conventional melodrama called **The Goose Woman**. She played a former opera singer called Marie de Nardi who lost her voice when her son was born and has subsequently taken to drink. A murder is committed near her house, and the story she invents in order to project herself back into the public eye, results in the arrest of her son. The film ends with the real murderer confessing to the crime (he did it to save the son's fiancée from a roué) and the son's release from prison. Director Clarence Brown's meticulous attention to detail throughout the telling of the story contributed a rich, narrative texture far superior to the material and, as usual, he secured some fine performances from his cast. They included Jack Pickford as the son, Constance Bennett as his fiancée, Spottiswoode Aitken, George Cooper, Gustav von Seyffertitz, George Nichols and, as the murderer, Marc MacDermott. It was scripted by Melville Brown and Dwinelle Benthall from a story by Rex Beach. Remade in 1933 as *The Past Of Mary Holmes* (RKO). (Jewel).

▷ One of the greatest of all horror films, and certainly the pinnacle of the genre in the silent era, **The Phantom Of The Opera** gave man-of-a-thousand-faces Lon Chaney (left), on loan from MGM, the chance to shatter audiences with his most grotesque face yet – that of Erik, the phantom of the title. Erik's menacing existence in the elaborate catacombs and dungeons beneath the Paris Opera terrified audiences almost as much as it terrified pretty Mary Philbin (right), an understudy at the Opera who, in one of the most effective moments in the film, rips off the phantom's mask to reveal a sight so hideous that, at each performance, several of the more faint-hearted patrons had to be revived with smelling salts! Because of Chaney's extraordinary make-up, painfully achieved by distending his nostrils with a wire clip, filling out his cheeks with celluloid discs and dilating his eyes with drops, the studio took special care to withhold photographs of this monstrous apparition in order not to diminish the impact of the moment when it finally arrived. The actual set of the Opera House was constructed at Universal City and was an exact replica of the Paris Opera, containing five tiers of balconies, and seating 3000 extras. Norman Kerry played Raoul, Miss Philbin's fiancé, and Arthur Edmund Carewe was Ledoux of the secret police, with other roles going to Snitz Edwards, Mary Fabian, Gibson Gowland, John Sainpolis, Virginia Pearson, Edith Yorke, Cesare Gravina, John Miljan and Chester Conklin. It was marvellously directed by a temperamental Rupert Julian, whose disagreements with Chaney over the latter's approach to the role led, ultimately, to Edward Sedgwick being called in to reshoot the spectacular chase finale, and to supervise the editing. It was adapted from Gaston Leroux's 1910 novel by Raymond L. Schrock and Elliott J. Clawson (with Tom Reed supplying the titles), and the oustanding and atmospheric set designs were by Charles D. Hall. This version was reissued in 1930 with several changes: talking sequences for Mary Philbin and Norman Kerry were added; extant scenes from the opera *Faust* had arias dubbed in; John Miljan's part was deleted, scenes featuring John Sainpolis were deleted, and new scenes were filmed with Edward Martindel. Remade in 1943 and, by Hammer, in 1962. (Jewel).

△ The dizzy-making 'jazz age', rarely represented with anything approaching verisimilitude on the screen, provided the backdrop for **The Mad Whirl** in which a first-rate cast did their best to bring a modicum of conviction to a story about a middle-aged couple's misguided attempts to keep pace with their hard-drinking, party-going son Jack. The film's first half, in which Jack's parents successfully make fools of themselves trying to be 'companionable' was entertaining enough; but with the arrival of pretty May McAvoy (top-billed) as the girl Jack falls for, the narrative (written in committee by Edward T. Lowe Jr, Harvey Thew, Frederic and Fanny Hatton and Lewis Milestone from a story by Richard Washburn Child) became decidedly commonplace. Jack Mulhall (standing left) played Jack, Myrtle Stedman (standing centre) and Alex B. Francis were his parents; with other parts under William A. Seiter's direction going to Barbara Bedford, Ward Crane, George Fawcett, Marie Astaire and Joe Singleton. (Jewel).

△ Ernest William Hornung's celebrated gentleman burglar and trickster, Raffles, made his first screen appearance in 1905 portrayed by J. Barney Sherry. John Barrymore put flesh and blood on him in 1917, while in 1925 it was the turn of House Peters to hoodwink English society with his elusive and skilfully executed thieving in **Raffles, The Amateur Cracksman**. A kind of Robin Hood of the smart set – robbing the rich to help the poor – Peters (left), under King Baggot's brisk direction, breezed through the role with an air of assured confidence and was well supported by a cast that included Miss DuPont (right), Hedda Hopper, Frederick Esmelton, Walter Long, Winter Hall, Kate Lester and Freeman Wood. The entertaining script was by Harvey Thew. It was remade twice by Samuel Goldwyn – in 1930 with Ronald Colman, and in 1940 with David Niven. (Jewel).

▽ The rather sensationally titled **Smouldering Fires** turned out to be an exceptional drama about a middle-aged woman executive who, after a lifetime devoid of romance, conceives an infatuation for a man half her age. Realising her young sister is also in love with him, she sacrifices her happiness (and her eventual marriage to him) by pretending she has fallen out of love and wants a divorce. Pauline Frederick (seated) starred, and her admirably restrained performance was reason itself for seeing the film. She received solid support from Laura La Plante (standing left) as her younger sister, as well as from Malcolm McGregor as the man in the middle. Tully Marshall scored acting points in a minor role, and there was much joy to be had from supporting players Wanda Hawley, Helen Lynch, George Cooper and Bert Roach. Clarence Brown directed it with immense style and a strong sense of narrative structure. It was scripted by Sada Cowan, Howard Higgin, Melville Brown and Dwinelle Benthall from a story by Cowan, Higgin and Margaret Deland.

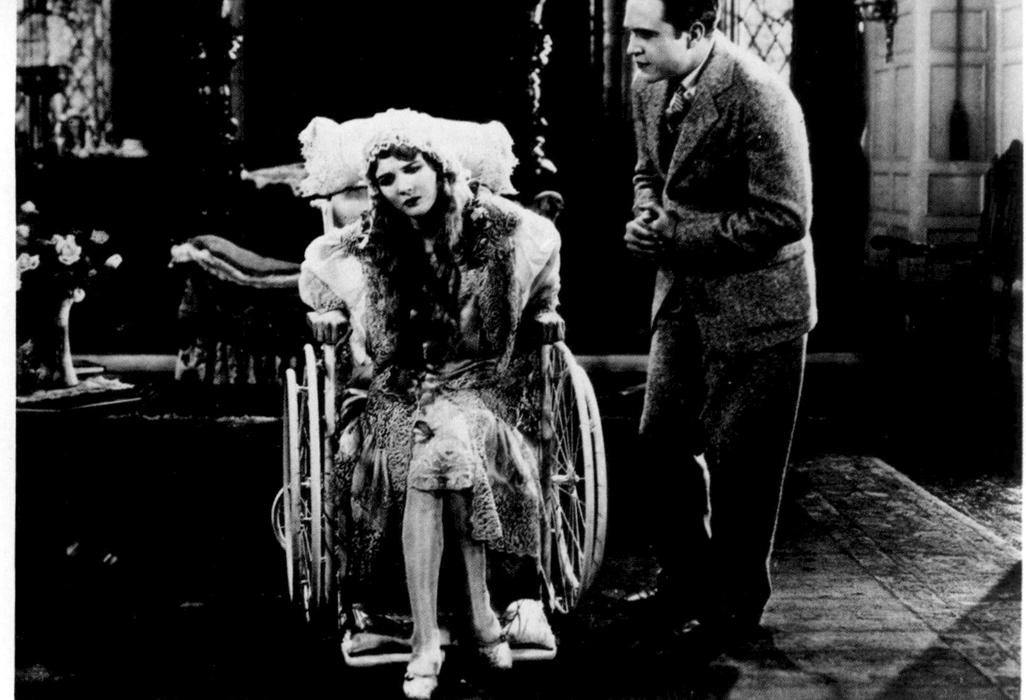

▽ A rather gauche melodrama, but with some entertaining moments, **Fifth Avenue Models** was the story of Isobel Ludani, a Fifth Avenue mannequin who, after a quarrel with one of the shop's other models in which an expensive gown is ruined, is forced to find the money to pay for the damage. She turns to her impecunious artist father in Greenwich Village who, in order to help his daughter, agrees to identify an Old Master for a pair of burglars and, in the process, is caught and arrested. The painting turns out to be a masterpiece, is exhibited by an art dealer for whom Isobel now works as a secretary (having had an affair with him), and the film ends happily ever after. Mary Philbin (kneeling centre) starred as Isobel, Josef Swickard was her father and Norman Kerry the art dealer. Other roles under Sven Gade's capable direction went to William Conklin, Rosemary Theby, Rose Dione, Jean Hersholt and Cesare Gravina. It was adapted from Muriel Hine Coxen's novel *The Best In Life*, and scripted by Olga Printzlau. (Jewel).

△ Melodrama par excellence reared its head in **Stella Maris**, the story of a crippled young aristocratic woman (Stella) and her companion John, whose vixenish wife, from whom he is separated, is doing a three-year stint in prison for maltreating an orphan called Unity. Loving John herself, and knowing of his infatuation for Stella, Unity kills John's wife – and then takes her own life. John, in turn, follows Unity's sacrifice by giving Stella to his good friend Walter – who has always loved her dearly – and vice versa. In the role originally played by Mary Pickford in 1918, Mary Philbin (left) was cast as Stella, doubling, as well, in the role of Unity. She went slightly over the top on both counts, an approach that was thoroughly in step with Charles J. Brabin's sledgehammer direction. Elliot Dexter played John, Gladys Brockwell was his unpleasant wife, and Jason Robards Sr (right) the friend who, in the last reel, finally gets the girl. Also cast: Phillips Smalley, Lillian Lawrence, Robert Bolder and Aileen Manning. Brabin scripted it (with Mary Alice Scully) from the story by William John Locke.

OTHER PRODUCTIONS OF 1925

The Burning Trail
Dir: Arthur Rosson. Western melodrama. William Desmond, Albert J. Smith.

Bustin' Thru
Dir: Clifford Smith. Western melodrama. Jack Hoxie, Helen Lynch.

The Calgary Stampede (Jewel)
Dir: Herbert Blache. Western melodrama. Hoot Gibson, Virginia Brown Faire.

California Straight Ahead (Jewel)
Dir: Harry Pollard. Bachelor comedy drama. Reginald Denny, Tom Wilson, Gertrude Olmstead, Charles Gerrard.

The Call Of Courage
Dir: Clifford Smith. Western melodrama. Art Acord, Olive Hasbrouck, Duke R. Lee.

The Circus Cyclone
Dir: Albert S. Rogell. Western melodrama. Art Acord, Nancy Deaver, Moe McRae.

Dangerous Innocence (Jewel)
Dir: William A. Seiter. Comedy drama. Laura La Plante, Eugene O'Brien, Jean Hersholt, Alfred Allen.

Daring Days
Dir: John B. O'Brien. Western melodrama. Josie Sedgwick, Edward Hearn.

Don Dare Devil
Dir: Clifford Smith. Western melodrama. Jack Hoxie, Duke R. Lee, Cathleen Calhoun.

Flying Hoofs
Dir: Clifford Smith. Western melodrama. Jack Hoxie, Bartlett A. Carre.

Head Winds (Jewel)
Dir: Herbert Blache. Melodrama. House Peters, Patsy Ruth Miller, Richard Travers.

Hidden Loot
Dir: Robert North Bradbury. Western melodrama. Jack Hoxie, Olive Hasbrouck.

The Hurricane Kid
Dir: Edward Sedgwick. Western melodrama. Hoot Gibson, Marion Nixon.

I'll Show You The Town (Jewel)
Dir: Harry Pollard. Comedy. Reginald Denny, Marion Nixon, Edward Kimball.

Let 'Er Buck
Dir: Edward Sedgwick. Western melodrama. Hoot Gibson, Marion Nixon.

Lorraine Of The Lions (Jewel)
Dir: Edward Sedgwick. Melodrama. Norman Kerry, Patsy Ruth Miller, Fred Humes.

The Man In Blue (Jewel)
Dir: Edward Laemmle. Melodrama. Herbert Rawlinson, Madge Bellamy, Nick De Ruiz.

The Meddler
Dir: Arthur Rosson Western melodrama. William Desmond, Dolores Rousse, Claire Anderson, Albert J. Smith.

Oh, Doctor! (Jewel)
Dir: Harry A. Pollard. Romantic comedy. Reginald Denny, Mary Astor, Otis Harlan.

The Outlaw's Daughter
Dir: John B. O'Brien. Western melodrama. Josie Sedgwick, Edward Hearn, Robert Walker, Jack Gavin, Harry Todd.

Peacock Feathers (Jewel)
Dir: Svend Gade. Romantic drama. Jacqueline Logan, Cullen Landis, Ward Crane.

The Price Of Pleasure (Jewel)
Dir: Edward Sloman. Society melodrama. Virginia Valli, Norman Kerry, Louise Fazenda, Kate Lester, George Fawcett.

The Red Rider
Dir: Clifford Smith. Western melodrama. Jack Hoxie, Mary McAllister, Jack Pratt.

Ridin' Pretty
Dir: Clifford Smith. Western melodrama. Art Acord, Olive Hasbrouck, Al Jennings.

Ridin' Thunder
Dir: Clifford Smith. Western melodrama. Jack Hoxie, Jack Pratt, Catherine Grant.

A Roaring Adventure
Dir: Clifford Smith. Western melodrama. Jack Hoxie, Mary McAllister, Marin Sais.

The Saddle Hawk
Dir: Edward Sedgwick. Western melodrama. Hoot Gibson, Marion Nixon, G. Raymond Nye.

Secrets Of The Night (Jewel)
Dir: Herbert Blache. Mystery comedy drama. James Kirkwood, Madge Bellamy, Tom Ricketts, Tom Guise, ZaSu Pitts.

The Sign Of The Cactus
Dir: Clifford Smith. Western melodrama. Jack Hoxie, Helen Holmes, Gordon Russell.

Spook Ranch (Jewel)
Dir: Edward Laemmle. Western mystery. Hoot Gibson, Helen Ferguson, Ed Cowles.

Sporting Life (Jewel)
Dir: Maurice Tournier. Gambling melodrama. Bert Lytell, Marion Nixon.

The Storm Breaker (Jewel)
Dir: Edward Sloman. Seafaring drama. House Peters, Ruth Clifford, Nina Romano.

Straight Through
Dir: Arthur Rosson. Western melodrama. William Desmond, Marguerite Clayton.

The Taming Of The West
Dir: Arthur Rosson. Western melodrama. Hoot Gibson, Morgan Brown, Marceline Day.

The Teaser (Jewel)
Dir: William A. Seiter. Comedy drama. Laura La Plante, Pat O'Malley, Hedda Hopper.

Triple Action
Dir: Tom Gibson. Western melodrama. Pete Morrison, Trilby Clark, Dolores Gardner.

Two-Fisted Jones
Dir: Edward Sedgwick. Western melodrama. Jack Hoxie, William Steele, Karthryn McGuire.

Up The Ladder (Jewel)
Dir: Edward Sloman. Marriage drama. Virginia Valli, Forrest Stanley.

The White Outlaw
Dir: Clifford Smith. Western melodrama. Jack Hoxie, Duke R. Lee, Marceline Day.

A Woman's Faith (Jewel)
Dir: Edward Laemmle. Religious melodrama. Alma Rubens, Percy Marmont, Jean Hersholt.

1926

▽ A romantic drama with a Broadway backdrop, some of whose ingredients were jealousy, misunderstanding, mental breakdown and inebriation, **The Marriage Clause** was the story of an actress who, under the guidance of her director, becomes a major star. The couple fall in love but are prevented from marrying by a clause inserted into her three-year contract by her producer. Misunderstandings lead to the director's dismissal which, in the course of events, leads to the actress' illness and her eventual breakdown on the opening night of her play. Visiting the actress in hospital, the director reaffirms his love for her thus facilitating her recovery. Billie Dove (right) played the actress, a miscast Francis X. Bushman was the director and Warner Oland (left – giving the best performance of all) was the producer, with other parts going to Henri La Garde, Grace Darmond, Caroline Snowden and Andre Cheron. It was directed and adapted by Lois Weber from Dana Burnet's *Saturday Evening Post* story *Technic*; and beautifully photographed by Hal Mohr. (Jewel).

△ An all-out melodrama set in an Oregon lumber camp, **The Ice Flood** starred Kenneth Harlan as Jack De Quincy, an American Oxford graduate – both brainy and brawny – who is being sent to establish order and step up output in his father's timber business. Once there, he creams the local bully in a spectacular fistfight, saves the girl he loves from death by ice avalanche (the film's big set-piece), and sees to it that a crippled youngster is successfully operated upon. Harlan (right) made a meal of the scenario written by director George B. Seitz, Gladys Lehman and James O. Spearing (from Johnston McCulley's story *The Brute Breaker*), and received spirited support from leading lady Viola Dana (left), as well as from a cast that also included Frank Hagney and Fred Kohler (as a pair of bootleggers), De Witt Jennings, Kitty Barlow and James Gordon. (Jewel).

▷ **What Happened To Jones** was that, on the eve of his wedding, a poker party he was attending was raided, and together with his buddy Ebenezer, he escaped into a ladies' Turkish bath. The police are called and the two men, dressed as women, make their getaway to Ebenezer's house where Jones dresses up as a bishop. Further complications arise when a real bishop (Ebenezer's brother) arrives to officiate at Jones' wedding. In the end, Jones is finally married in the back of a speeding car while being chased by the police. Though popular Reginald Denny (right) starred as Jones, the acting honours went to Otis Harlan as Ebenezer. Marian Nixon (left) played Denny's fiancée, with other roles in the scenario Melville W. Brown adapted from George H. Broadhurst's 1910 stage farce going to Melbourne McDowell, Frances Raymond, Emily Fitzroy, ZaSu Pitts, William Austin and Margaret Quimby. William A. Seiter directed. Fifty years later, playwright Terence McNally in *The Ritz*, filmed by Warner Bros., used a similar plot contrivance, except that the Turkish bath into which his protagonist escaped was exclusively homosexual. (Jewel).

△ A remake of Essanay's 1917 comedy, **Skinner's Dress Suit** was the perfect vehicle for Reginald Denny who, on this mirth-provoking occasion, played a rather henpecked husband whose lack of courage in telling his wife (Laura La Plante) that his request for a raise in salary was unsuccessful (he lies to her that he has been given ten dollars a week more) leads to all sorts of complications, especially when she insists that he buy a dress suit with which to impress high society. As Miss La Plante (left) embarks on a spending spree, Denny (right) loses his job. But a happy ending is assured when, after being seen in the company of a millionaire, he is re-employed by his old firm and made a partner. Rex Taylor wrote it (from a story by Henry Irving Dodge), the fluid direction was by William A. Seiter (Miss La Plante's real-life husband), and the cast included Ben Hendricks Jr, E.J. Ratcliffe, Arthur Lake, Hedda Hopper and Lionel Braham. Remade in 1929 as *Skinner Steps Out.* (Jewel).

▽ **The Beautiful Cheat** was Laura La Plante who, in the fanciful comedy written by A.P. Younger and Olga Printzlau from Nina Wilcox Putnam's *Saturday Evening Post* story *Doubling For Cupid*, played a pretty shopgirl and the object of an extensive publicity campaign engineered by press agent Harry Myers. After being taken to Europe by Myers, Miss La Plante (right) returns to America not as commonplace Mary Callahan, but as Maritza Callahansky, a Russian actress and owner of the crown jewels! As a result of the deception, all sorts of complications ensued, and gave employment to Bertram Grassby (left), Alexander Carr, Youcca Troubetzkoy, Helen Carr and Robert Anderson. But it was Miss La Plante's film all the way, and in the dual role of Mary/Maritza she brought to the story the star quality it needed. The director was Edward Sloman. (Jewel).

◁ Believing he is carrying a silver plate in his head due to a war wound and must therefore avoid all excitement, Chester Binney (Edward Everett Horton, right), who is to inherit a fortune, arrives home to find that his former employer (Otis Harlan) has arranged a match between Chester and his daughter Ethel (Virginia Lee Corbin, left). In order to make Chester appear more exciting to Ethel, her father invents a sensational past for him by putting it about (via a signed photograph by film star Rita Renault) that Chester and Miss Renault (Dolores Del Rio) were once lovers. The sudden arrival on the scene of the star, together with her jealous husband (Malcolm Waite) provided much of the comedy in **The Whole Town's Talking**, a racy farce with a slapstick climax, confidently directed by Edward Laemmle, and well performed by a cast that also included Trixie Friganza, Robert Ober, Aileen Manning, Hayden Stevenson and Margaret Quimby. It was scripted by Raymond Cannon from a play by John Emerson and Anita Loos. (Jewel).

▽ In the first of a successful series of comedies, **The Cohens And The Kellys** locked antlers in Alfred A. Cohn's screenplay about a Jew who owns a drygoods store, and an Irish cop – a popular racial combination in American fiction. It was based on Aaron Hoffman's play *Two Blocks Away* and had two main narrative lines running through it: (a) the frowned-upon romance between Kelly's son (Jason Robards Sr) and Cohen's daughter (Bobby Gordon), and (b) Cohen's inheritance of a fortune that, in the end, turns out to belong to Kelly. The story's denouement had the two men reconciling their differences and becoming partners, thus paving the way for further personality (and ethnic) clashes in the future. Charlie Murray and George Sidney (left) were cast as Kelly and Cohen respectively, and Vera Gordon (right) and Kate Price were their wives. Harry Pollard's direction (he also adapted it from the play) didn't always maintain the pace it needed, but was well-served by his cast, especially George Sidney, whose robust characterisation of Cohen was the film's mainstay. (Jewel).

▽ Edward Everett Horton starred in **Poker Faces**, a farce, written by Melville W. Brown from a short story by Edgar Franklin, the gist of which had Horton having to engage a prizefighter's wife as a stand-in for his own wife when the latter decides to take a job to earn some extra money. Reason for Horton's deception is an important business dinner which, if successful, will result in a lucrative contract coming through. Under Harry A. Pollard's direction, Horton (right), and with a cast that included Laura La Plante (left) as his wife, Dorothy Revier as the pug's wife, George Siegmann as the business contact with the contract, Harry Curlew as Horton's employer, and Tom O'Brien as the pug himself, the farce's component parts smoothly interlocked, causing high-spirited laughter for most of the film's eight reels. (Jewel).

△ Erstwhile gag writer and scenarist Melville W. Brown turned director (most capably) for **Her Big Night**, a comedy of mistaken identity in which a resourceful press agent offers a thousand dollars to a young woman to take the place, for a night, of a famous movie star whose looks are uncannily like her own. Seems that the real star, instead of attending an important premiere, is spending time on a yacht with millionaire Nat Carr. Laura La Plante (right), giving one of her best ever performances, doubled as the star and her lookalike; Tully Marshall was the enterprising man who first notices the resemblance between the two women, with other roles going to Einer Hansen, ZaSu Pitts, Lee Moran, Mark Swain, John Roche, William Austin and Cissy Fitzgerald. It was adapted by director Brown from Peggy Gaddis' story *Doubling For Laura*. (Jewel).

OTHER PRODUCTIONS OF 1926

The Arizona Sweepstakes (Jewel)
Dir: Clifford Smith. Western melodrama. Hoot Gibson, Helen Lynch.

Blue Blazes
Dir: Joseph Franz. Western melodrama. Pete Morrison, Jim Welsh, Barbara Starr.

The Border Sheriff
Dir: Robert North Bradbury. Western melodrama. Jack Hoxie, Olive Hasbrouck.

The Buckaroo Kid (Jewel)
Dir: Melville W. Brown. Army comedy. Lya De Putti, ZaSu Pitts, James Marcus.

Bucking The Truth
Dir: Milburn Morante. Western melodrama. Pete Morrison, Brinsley Shaw.

Butterflies In The Rain (Jewel)
Dir: Edward Sloman. Romantic society drama. Laura La Plante, James Kirkwood, Robert Ober, Dorothy Cumming.

Chasing Trouble
Dir: Milburn Morante. Western melodrama. Pete Morrison, Ione Reed, Tom London.

Chip Of The Flying U (Jewel)
Dir: Lynn Reynolds. Western comedy. Hoot Gibson, Virginia Brown Faire.

The Combat (Jewel)
Dir: Lynn Reynolds. Lumberjack melodrama. House Peters, Wanda Hawley, Walter McGrail.

The Demon
Dir: Clifford Smith. Western melodrama. Jack Hoxie, Lola Todd, William Welsh.

The Desperate Game
Dir: Joseph Franz. Western melodrama. Pete Morrison, James Welsh, Dolores Gardner.

The Escape
Dir: Milburn Morante. Western melodrama. Pete Morrison, Frank Norcross.

The Fighting Peacemaker
Dir: Clifford Smith. Western melodrama. Jack Hoxie, Lola Todd, Ted Oliver.

The Flaming Frontier (Jewel)
Dir: Edward Sedgwick. Western melodrama. Hoot Gibson, Anne Cornwall, Dustin Farnum.

Lazy Lightning
Dir: William Wyler. Western melodrama. Art Acord, Fay Wray, Bobby Gordon, Vin Moore.

The Little Giant (Jewel)
Dir: William Nigh. Comedy drama. Glenn Hunter, Edna Murphy, David Higgins.

Looking For Trouble
Dir: Robert North Bradbury. Western melodrama. Jack Hoxie, Marceline Day.

The Love Thief (Jewel)
Dir: John McDermott. Romantic melodrama. Norman Kerry, Greta Nissen, Marc McDermott.

The Man From The West
Dir: Albert S. Rogell. Western melodrama. Art Acord, Eugenia Gilbert, Irvin Renard.

The Man In The Saddle (Jewel)
Dir: Lynn Reynolds. Western melodrama. Hoot Gibson, Charles H. Mailes, Fay Wray.

The Midnight Sun (Jewel)
Dir: Dimitri Buchowetski. Russian melodrama. Laura La Plante, Pat O'Malley.

My Old Dutch (Jewel)
Dir: Lawrence Trimble. Cockney melodrama. May McAvoy, Pat O'Malley, Jean Hersholt.

The Mystery Club (Jewel)
Dir: Herbert Blache. Mystery puzzler. Matt Moore, Edith Roberts, Mildred Harris.

Oh, Baby!
Dir: Harley Knoles. Boxing melodrama. Little Billy, David Butler, Madge Kennedy.

The Old Soak (Jewel)
Dir: Edward Sloman. Domestic melodrama. Jean Hersholt, George Lewis, Louise Fazenda.

The Phantom Bullet (Jewel)
Dir: Clifford Smith. Western melodrama. Hoot Gibson, Eileen Percy, Pat Harmon.

Prisoners Of The Storm (Jewel)
Dir: Lynn Reynolds. Northwest melodrama. House Peters, Peggy Montgomery.

Prowlers Of The Night
Dir: Ernst Laemmle. Western melodrama. Fred Humes, Barbara Kent, Slim Cole.

Red Hot Leather
Dir: Albert S. Rogell. Western melodrama. Jack Hoxie, William Malan, Ena Gregory.

The Ridin' Rascal
Dir: Clifford Smith. Western melodrama. Art Acord, Olive Hasbrouck.

Rolling Home (Jewel)
Dir: William A. Seiter. Comedy. Reginald Denny, Marian Nixon, E.J. Ratcliffe.

The Runaway Express (Jewel)
Dir: Edward Sedgwick. Railroad melodrama. Jack Daugherty, Blanche Mehaffey.

Rustlers' Ranch
Dir: Clifford Smith. Western melodrama. Art Acord, Olive Hasbrouck.

The Scrappin' Kid
Dir: Clifford Smith. Western melodrama. Art Acord, Velma Connor.

The Set-Up
Dir: Clifford Smith. Western melodrama. Art Acord, Alta Allen, Albert Schaeffer.

A Six Shootin' Romance
Dir: Clifford Smith. Western melodrama. Jack Hoxie, Olive Hasbrouck.

Sky High Corral
Dir: Clifford Smith. Western melodrama. Art Acord, Marguerite Clayton.

Spangles (Jewel)
Dir: Frank O'Connor. Circus melodrama. Marian Nixon, Hobart Bosworth, Pat O'Malley.

The Still Alarm (Jewel)
Dir: Edward Laemmle. Fashion model melodrama. Helene Chadwick, William Russell, Richard C. Travers, Edna Marian.

The Stolen Ranch
Dir: William Wyler. Western melodrama. Fred Humes, Louise Lorraine.

Take It From Me (Jewel)
Dir: William A. Seiter. Office girl comedy. Reginald Denny, Blanche Mehaffey.

The Terror
Dir: Clifford Smith. Western melodrama. Art Acord, Velma Connor.

The Texas Streak (Jewel)
Dir: Lynn Reynolds. Western comedy drama. Hoot Gibson, Blanche Mehaffey.

Under Western Skies (Jewel)
Dir: Edward Sedgwick. Western melodrama. Norman Kerry, Anne Cornwall, Ward Crane.

Watch Your Wife (Jewel)
Dir: Svend Gade. Marriage comedy drama. Virginia Valli, Nat Carr, Pat O'Malley.

Western Pluck
Dir: Travers Vale. Western melodrama. Art Acord, Marceline Day, Ray Ripley.

The Wild Horse Stampede
Dir: Albert S. Rogell. Western melodrama. Jack Hoxie, Fay Wray, William Steele.

The Yellow Back
Dir: Del Andrews. Western melodrama. Fred Humes, Lotus Thompson, Claude Payton.

1927-1936

Laemmle's Last Decade

Because the motion picture industry was at first unsure whether talking pictures were merely a passing fad, the major Hollywood studios, Universal included, continued to make silent features well into 1928 and even 1929. When it became apparent that sound had come to stay, many silents already in production had either talking sequences added at the last minute, or a musical score and sound effects. The studio's first all-talking production was released on 2nd December 1928 – a romantic drama in nine reels called *Melody Of Love*, starring Walter Pidgeon and Mildred Harris.

By 1929 talkies were all the rage, especially the 'all-dancing, all-singing' variety. MGM won an Oscar for its musical *The Broadway Melody*, and with it the Hollywood musical was spectacularly launched. Universal contributed to the genre with a partly silent, not particularly successful version of the Jerome Kern-Oscar Hammerstein II hit *Show Boat*, followed by *Broadway* (which included sequences in two-colour Technicolor) and *Melody Lane*, all produced in 1929. The studio's best musical of the early sound era, though, was *King Of Jazz* (1930), a spectacular and innovative revue (in two-colour Technicolor) directed by John Murray Anderson. It was produced by Carl Laemmle Jr, whose appointment in 1929 as general manager in charge of production gave rise to Ogden Nash's observation that 'Uncle Carl Laemmle has a big faemmle'. But Laemmle Jr again proved himself capable with his memorable production of Erich Maria Remarque's anti-war drama *All Quiet On The Western Front* which, under Lewis Milestone's powerful direction, won the studio its first Oscar for best picture.

Inspired by this success 'Junior' Laemmle, as he was called, cut the studio's run-of-the-mill output by 40 per cent, concentrating instead on product he hoped would be the equal of anything emerging from Paramount or MGM. As studio head, 'Junior' was inevitably compared with 'wunderkind' Thalberg, but failed to emerge from the comparison unscathed. Despite his notable achievements at the studio – though it must be said that he failed to recognise the exceptional ability of the young Bette Davis – the industry didn't seem to give him the respect he had earned; more often than not he was regarded as the joke product of Laemmle Sr's nepotism. The box-office failure of both *King Of Jazz* and the same year's historical melodrama, *Captain Of The Guard*, fuelled the scornmongers' belief that 'Junior' simply didn't have what it took.

For the studio as a whole, however, the thirties could not

above: Mildred Harris in **Melody Of Love** (1928), Universal's first all-talkie feature. *centre:* Carl Laemmle Jr (right), photographed in 1930 during the filming of **All Quiet On The Western Front**, with Lew Ayres, the star of the film. *below:* Two of the most famous ghouls in the history of the horror genre, Bela Lugosi (left) and Boris Karloff, photographed off duty in about 1934.

have begun more prestigiously. In 1931 audiences were treated to the start of a cycle of horror films unmatched in Hollywood's history. *Dracula* was the first of the series and it starred a menacing, thickly accented Hungarian actor called Bela Lugosi, whose performance as the Transylvanian vampire was unforgettable. Though this film was directed by the excellent Tod Browning, it was James Whale who distinguished himself above all others in the genre and who helped to make a star of the studio's other ghoul, Boris Karloff, in *Frankenstein* the following year. Other horror films followed in quick succession: *The Mummy* (1932), *Murders In The Rue Morgue* (1932), *The Invisible Man* (1933), *The Black Cat* (1934), *The Bride Of Frankenstein* (1935) and *The Werewolf Of London* (1935).

Between 1930 and 1936 Universal also concentrated on low-budget serials and westerns, the latter running little more than an hour and featuring such stars as Hoot Gibson and Tom Mix (hold-overs from the silent era), as well as Johnny Mack Brown, singing cowboy Ken Maynard, and Buck Jones (who died tragically in the 1942 Coconut Grove fire).

Soap-opera, as directed by John Stahl, proved popular with audiences, especially women, and weepies such as *Back Street* (1932), *Imitation Of Life* (1934) and *Magnificent Obsession* (1935) were all durable enough to be remade in Technicolor during the fifties.

After the moratorium imposed by a sated public on musicals in the first couple of years of the thirties, the studio almost abandoned the genre. With *Moonlight And Pretzels* (1933), however, they emerged with a tuneful Depression musical which was a lot better than its title indicated. Notable non-musical productions of the period were William Wyler's *Counsellor-At-Law* (1933), adapted by Elmer Rice from his Broadway play and starring John Barrymore, Frank Borzage's *Little Man, What Now?* (1934) with Margaret Sullavan and Douglass Montgomery, and Wyler's *The Good Fairy* (1935) scripted by Preston Sturges and starring Margaret Sullavan.

Though the studio in no way matched the heady output of Metro-Goldwyn-Mayer, Warner Bros. or Paramount, 'Junior' Laemmle made sure that each year saw its quota of quality. But in so doing he was spending far too much money for his stockholders' liking. A prime example of his extravagance was the escalating cost of an expensive biographical film which was in production during 1935 called *Sutter's Gold*, whose budget far exceeded its market value.

The crunch finally came in November 1935. Laemmle Sr was forced to take a loan of three-quarters of a million dollars from an investment outfit headed by producer Charles Rogers and J. Cheever Cowdin (a British financier) of Standard Capital. Besides mortgaging the studio's future productions Laemmle offered the personal security of his controlling interest in the studio. A remake of the Kern-Hammerstein II musical *Show Boat* was currently in production with James Whale directing, and the Laemmles were convinced that its box-office success would buy them out of their financial difficulties. But it was not to be. Production problems and delays on the musical resulted in a further $300,000 being added to the debt. Eventually, on 14th March 1936, the investors called in their option and the studio's theatres and global operations went to Cowdin's Standard Capital for $4.1 million. Charles Rogers stepped in as head of production and Robert H. Cochrane, Laemmle's old partner, was made president. The services of the studio's personnel were in the main retained but the entire Laemmle connection was severed. An exciting era in the history of motion pictures had almost overnight come to an end.

When Charles Rogers took over as production head of New Universal (as it was now called) on 2nd April, he announced his intention of cutting back on budgets and, indeed, he made sure that the bulk of the year's output remained modest – not only in financial terms but in entertainment value as well. As well as *Show Boat*, there were two more fine films in 1936: Gregory La Cava's delightful comedy *My Man Godfrey* (prepared by the Laemmles) with William Powell and Carole Lombard, and *Three Smart Girls*, a musical with a 15-year-old soprano called Deanna Durbin whom Rogers wisely snapped up when her option at MGM expired. Almost overnight young Miss Durbin became New Universal's biggest star, and the studio's hopes were firmly pinned on her future.

above: Deanna Durbin (right) in **Three Smart Girls** (1936), her debut picture for Universal. *below left:* On 17th January 1933 Carl Laemmle (on the baker's left) celebrated his 66th birthday with Carl Jr (to his left), other members of his family and many of the studio's stars and behind-the-camera personalities. *below right:* Robert Taylor and Betty Furness in the prestigious weepie **Magnificent Obsession** (1935).

1927

▽ The studio's prestige, 'road show' production of **Uncle Tom's Cabin**, the eighth film version of Harriet Beecher Stowe's famous novel, took two years to complete and, at a budget of $1,500,000, was one of Universal's most expensive films to date. Good only in parts, it was not the success the studio had hoped it would be, and its failure to generate excitement proved a bitter disappointment to its director Harry Pollard who, in 1913, had directed a version of the story for Imp. On this later occasion Pollard was so determined to give the novel's 'big moments' their due, he went way over the top in several scenes, especially the demise of Little Eva, whose death-bed excesses (one sequence even showed her soul winging its angelic way to Heaven) totally robbed it of the desired poignancy. The scourging of Uncle Tom was equally unsuccessful (especially in a scene likening his agonies to the martyrdom of Christ on the Cross); while the villainous Simon Legree, was, predictably, more hissable than even Miss Stowe would have wished. Much more successful was the famous sequence in which Eliza is pursued across the ice by bloodhounds; as well as the scenes involving Topsy and Miss Ophelia, and Topsy and Eva. James Lowe played Uncle Tom and was as fine as Pollard's direction allowed him to be. Virginia Grey was an over-robust Eva, George Siegmann (left) in a beard rather than a moustache, was Simon Legree, Margarita Fisher (right – Mrs Pollard in real life) was miscast as Eliza, and there was a first-rate Topsy from Mona Ray – who, in real life, was not coloured at all, but white. Also cast: Eulalie Jensen (Cassie), Arthur Edmund Carewe (George Harris), Aileen Manning (Miss Ophelia), Lucien Littlefield (Laywer Marks), Adolph Milar (Haley), Jack Mower (Mr Shelby), Vivian Oakland (Mrs Shelby) and John Roche (St Clare). It was written by A.P. Younger and Harvey Thew (who, despite the fact that the novel was published in 1852, incorporated the Civil War) with subtitles by Walter Anthony. On its first showing in November, 1927, just one month after the premiere of Warner Bros' *The Jazz Singer*, the film went out with a musical accompaniment written by Hugo Riesenfeld. The running time was a mammoth 141 minutes, with a pause for intermission 80 minutes into the film immediately following a sequence depicting Lincoln's emancipation. Previous versions of Stowe's novel were filmed in 1903 (twice), 1910 (twice), 1913, 1914, and 1918. Herbert Lom starred in a German version in 1965, and United Artists released a variation in 1929 called *Topsy And Eva*, and starring Broadway's Duncan Sisters.

▽ Laura La Plante demonstrated that she was no slouch in the comedy department in **Silk Stockings**, a *bon-bon* from director Wesley Ruggles all about a devoted but argumentative couple who decide to separate for a year when, on the eve of their wedding anniversary, the husband innocently arrives home late with a pair of silk stockings which has been slipped into one of his pockets by a lady business associate. Needless to say, before the year is out, the couple are reunited and the misunderstanding forgotten. John Harron (right) co-starred as Miss La Plante's (left) spouse, and there was excellent work from Otis Harlan as a judge, William Austin, Marcella Daly, Heinie Conklin and Burr McIntosh. The light-hearted screenplay was the work of Beatrice Van and Albert De Mond, whose source material was Cyril Harcourt's story *A Pair Of Stockings*. (Jewel – silent).

◁ Cinemagoers' first sight of Reginald Denny (right) in **On Your Toes** was of a rather effeminate dancing instructor totally oblivious of the fact that his father was Kid Roberts, one-time undefeated heavyweight champion of the world. But, as the story (by Earl Snell) unfurls, Denny deserts the dance floor for the ring and in no time at all, not only wins the championship, but also the love of leading lady Barbara Worth. The amusing nonsense, delightfully played by its two stars, was directed by Fred Newmeyer from a screenplay by Snell and Gladys Lehman (titles by Albert De Mond and adaptation by Pierre Couderc and James Davis) and featured, in supporting roles, Hayden Stevenson, Frank Hagney, Mary Carr (left), Gertrude Howard (centre) and George West. (Jewel – silent).

△ Jean Hersholt (left) was the star of **Alias The Deacon**, playing a professional card shark and gambler who, dressed as a deacon, cons himself into solvency whenever the need arises. In Charles Kenyon and Walter Anthony's adaptation from John B. Hymer and Leroy Clemens' play of the same name, he sets about to help a pair of young lovers, one of whom turns out to be his daughter whom he has not seen since childhood. June Marlowe played the daughter, Ralph Graves (right) was her lover, with other roles under Edward Sloman's journeyman direction going to Myrtle Stedman, Lincoln Plummer, Ned Sparks and Tom Kennedy. It was remade in 1940. (Jewel – silent).

▷ German director Paul Leni made an auspicious American debut with **The Cat And The Canary**, a first-rate, highly imaginative adaptation of John Willard's Broadway success in which a variegated group of people gather together in a haunted house to learn the contents of a will twenty years after the testator's death. Most of the closest relatives are shocked to learn that they have all been disinherited in favour of Laura La Plante (left), a distant relative, on condition that she is proved to be sane. In no time at all, the lawyer (Tully Marshall in fine form, right) handling the case disappears – his mysterious departure giving rise to a number of spooky occurrences, several of which cause the gathered family to doubt Miss La Plante's sanity ... Contributing their talents to this classic example of haunted house melodrama were Creighton Hale, Forrest Stanley, Gertrude Astor, Flora Finch, Arthur Edmund Carewe, Martha Mattox, George Siegmann and Lucien Littlefield. It was written by Robert F. Hill, Alfred A. Cohn and Walter Anthony, whose scenario gave director Leni ample opportunity to reveal an exciting visual approach to a basically straightforward tale of mystery and suspense. It was remade in 1930 as **The Cat Creeps**, again (by Paramount) in 1939 with Bob Hope, and still again by a British independent for sale to US cable TV, in 1977, with Carol Lynley. (Jewel – silent).

OTHER PRODUCTIONS OF 1927

Back To God's Country (Jewel)
Dir: Irvin Willat. Northwest melodrama. Renee Adoree, Robert Frazer, Walter Long.

Beware Of Widows (Jewel)
Dir: Wesley Ruggles. Romantic farce. Laura La Plante, Bryant Washburn.

Blazing Days
Dir: William Wyler. Western melodrama. Fred Humes, Churchill Ross, Ena Gregory.

The Border Cavalier
Dir: William Wyler. Western melodrama. Fred Humes, Evelyn Pierce, Boris Bullock.

The Bronco Buster
Dir: Ernst Laemmle. Western melodrama. Fred Humes, Gloria Grey, George Connors.

Cheating Cheaters (Jewel)
Dir: Edward Laemmle. Crook melodrama. Betty Compson, Kenneth Harlan.

The Cheerful Fraud
Dir: William A. Seiter. Crime farce. Reginald Denny, Gertrude Olmstead.

The Chinese Parrot (Jewel)
Dir: Paul Leni. Mystery melodrama. Marian Nixon, Florence Turner, Hobart Bosworth.

The Claw (Jewel)
Dir: Sidney Olcott. Romantic drama. Norman Kerry, Claire Windsor, Tom Guise.

The Denver Dude (Jewel)
Dir: Reaves Eason. Western melodrama. Hoot Gibson, Blanche Mehaffey, Glenn Tryon.

Desert Dust
Dir: William Wyler. Western melodrama. Ted Wells, Lotus Thompson, Bruce Gordon.

Down The Stretch (Jewel)
Dir: King Baggot. Horseracing melodrama. Robert Agnew, Marian Nixon, Virginia True Boardman, Otis Harlan.

Fangs Of Destiny
Dir: Stuart Paton. Western melodrama. Dynamite, the dog, Edmund Cobb, Betty Caldwell, George Periolat.

Fast And Furious
Dir: Melville W. Brown. Motor racing farce. Reginald Denny, Barbara Worth.

The Fighting Three
Dir: Albert S. Rogell. Western melodrama. Jack Hoxie, Olive Hasbrouck, Marin Sais.

The Fourth Commandment (Jewel)
Dir: Emory Johnson. Domestic melodrama. Henry Victor, June Marlowe, Belle Bennett.

Galloping Fury
Dir: Reaves Eason. Western comedy drama. Hoot Gibson, Otis Harlan, Sally Rand.

Grinning Guns
Dir: Albert S. Rogell. Western melodrama. Jack Hoxie, Robert Milasch, Ena Gregory.

Hands Off
Dir: Ernst Laemmle. Western melodrama. Fred Humes, Helen Foster, George Connors.

Hard Fists
Dir: William Wyler. Western melodrama. Art Acord, Louise Lorraine, Lee Holmes.

Held By The Law (Jewel)
Dir: Edward Laemmle. Crime melodrama. Ralph Lewis, Johnnie Walker, Marguerite De La Motte, Robert Ober.

A Hero For A Night (Jewel)
Dir: William James Craft. Aviator comedy. Glenn Tryon, Patsy Ruth Miller.

A Hero On Horseback (Jewel)
Dir: Del Andrews. Western melodrama. Hoot Gibson, Ethlyne Clair, Edward Hearn.

Hey! Hey! Cowboy (Jewel)
Dir: Lynn Reynolds. Western comedy melodrama. Hoot Gibson, Nick Cogley.

The Irresistible Lover (Jewel)
Dir: William Beaudine. Romantic drama. Norman Kerry, Lois Moran, Gertrude Astor.

Loco Luck
Dir: Clifford Smith. Western melodrama. Art Acord, Fay Wray, Aggie Herring.

The Lone Eagle (Jewel)
Dir: Emory Johnson. Western melodrama. Raymond Keane, Nigel Barrie, Barbara Kent.

The Love Thrill (Jewel)
Dir: Millard Webb. Farce comedy. Laura La Plante, Tom Moore, Bryant Washburn.

A Man's Past (Jewel)
Dir: George Melford. French melodrama. Conrad Veidt, Ian Keith, Barbara Bedford.

Men Of Daring
Dir: Albert S. Rogell. Western melodrama. Jack Hoxie, Francis Ford, Ena Gregory.

One Glorious Scrap
Dir: Edgar Lewis. Western melodrama. Fred Humes, Dorothy Gulliver, Robert McKenzie.

A One Man Game
Dir: Ernst Laemmle. Western melodrama. Fred Humes, Fay Wray, Harry Todd.

Out All Night (Jewel)
Dir: William A. Seiter. Farce. Reginald Denny, Marian Nixon, Wheeler Oakman.

Painted Ponies
Dir: Reaves Eason. Western melodrama Hoot Gibson, William Dunn, Ethlyne Clair.

Painting The Town (Jewel)
Dir: William James Craft. Romantic comedy. Glenn Tryon, Patsy Ruth Miller.

Perch Of The Devil (Jewel)
Dir: King Baggot. Society drama. Mae Busch, Pat O'Malley, Jane Winton, Mario Carillo.

The Prairie King (Jewel)
Dir: Reaves Eason. Western melodrama. Hoot Gibson, Barbara Worth, Albert Prisco.

The Rambling Ranger
Dir: Del Henderson. Western melodrama. Jack Hoxie, Dorothy Gulliver, C.E. Anderson.

Range Courage
Dir: Ernst Laemmle. Western melodrama. Fred Humes, Gloria Grey, Dick Winslow.

Red Clay
Dir: Ernst Laemmle. War hero melodrama. William Desmond, Marceline Day.

Rough And Ready
Dir: Albert S. Rogell. Western melodrama. Jack Hoxie, William A. Steele, Ena Gregory.

Sensation Seekers (Jewel)
Dir: Lois Weber. Romantic drama. Billie Dove, Huntley Gordon, Peggy Montgomery, Phillips Smalley.

Set Free
Dir: Arthur Rosson. Western melodrama. Art Acord, Olive Hasbrouck, Claude Payton.

The Shield Of Honor (Jewel)
Dir: Emory Johnson. Police melodrama. Neil Hamilton, Dorothy Gulliver, Ralph Lewis.

The Silent Rider (Jewel)
Dir: Lynn Reynolds. Western melodrama. Hoot Gibson, Blanche Mehaffey, Otis Harlan.

Sky-High Saunders
Dir: Bruce Mitchell. Adventure melodrama. Al Wilson, Elsie Tarron, Frank Rice.

The Small Bachelor (Jewel)
Dir: William A. Seiter. Comedy. Barbara Kent, André Beranger, William Austin.

Spurs And Saddles
Dir: Clifford Smith. Western melodrama. Art Acord, Fay Wray, Bill Dyer.

Straight Shootin'
Dir: William Wyler. Western melodrama. Ted Wells, Garry O'Dell, Lillian Gilmore.

Surrender (Jewel)
Dir: Edward Sloman. Romantic drama. Mary Philbin, Ivan Mosjukine, Otto Matieson.

Taxi! Taxi! (Jewel)
Dir: Melville W. Brown. Farce. Edward Evertt Horton, Marion Nixon.

The Thirteenth Juror (Jewel)
Dir: Edward Laemmle. Mystery melodrama. Anna Q. Nilsson, Francis X. Bushman, Walter Pidgeon, Martha Mattox, Sidney Bracey.

Three Miles Up
Dir: Bruce Mitchell. Action melodrama. Al Wilson, William Malan, Ethlyne Claire.

The Western Rover
Dir: Albert S. Rogell. Western melodrama. Art Acord, Ena Gregory, Charles Avery.

The Western Whirlwind
Dir: Albert S. Rogell. Western melodrama. Jack Hoxie, Margaret Quimby, Claude Payton.

Wild Beauty (Jewel)
Dir: Henry MacRae. War hero melodrama. June Marlowe, Hugh Allen, Scott Seaton.

Wolf's Trail
Dir: Francis Ford. Action melodrama. Edmund Cobb, Dixie Lamont, Edwin Terry.

The Wrong Mr Right (Jewel)
Dir: Scott Sidney. Farce. Jean Hersholt, Enid Bennett, Dorothy Devore.

1928

▷ Some very tentative use of sound robbed **Give And Take**, a part-talkie with a musical score, of whatever impact it might have had. With actors such as Jean Hersholt, George Sidney (right), Sam Hardy and George Lewis (left) reciting their lines as opposed to acting them, the story of a fruit canner's fight against industrial ruin as a result of strike action, remained moribund. Hersholt was the owner of the factory, Lewis was his son (who, on leaving college immediately organises his father's workers into an Industrial Democracy), Sidney played the factory foreman (whose daughter, played by Sharon Lynn, is having a romance with the boss' son) and Hardy was an industrialist who, after promising to haul Hersholt out of debt by placing a massive order with him, is discovered to have escaped from a mental institution, and is insolvent. Turns out, however, that Hardy is both sane and solvent, thus vouchsafing a happy ending. William Beaudine, doing his best to cope with the gremlins in the sound equipment, directed it from a screenplay by Harvey Thew and Albert De Mond (story by Aaron Hoffman). (Jewel).

▽ The leading character in **The Man Who Laughs** was no handsome hero, but someone whose features were distorted into a permanent grin by order of James II because his father was a political enemy. As a result of this disability, Gwynplaine, as the victim is called, has become a clown with a circus troupe, in whose company he meets and falls in love with a blind girl called Dea. Finding he is heir to a peerage, Gwynplaine denounces his title and all that goes with it (including marriage to Queen Anne's half sister, the Duchess Josiana) in order to be with the woman he loves. Based on Victor Hugo's *L'Homme Qui Rit*, and written by J. Grubb Alexander and Walter Anthony (from an adaptation by Charles E. Whittaker, Marion Ward and May McLean), it was stylishly directed by Paul Leni with a cast that included German actor Conrad Veidt (right) as Gwynplaine, Mary Philbin (left) as Dea, Olga Baclanova as Josiana, Josephine Crowell as Queen Anne, as well as George Siegmann (Dr Hardquanonne), Brandon Hurst (Barkilphedro, the jester), Sam De Grasse (King James), Stuart Holmes (Lord Dirry-Noir), Cesare Gravina (Ursus) and Nick De Ruiz (Wapentake). Though completed in April of 1927, the film was not copyrighted and released until a year later after the addition of a musical score and sound effects. It featured the song 'When Love Comes Stealing' by Walter Hirsch, Lew Pollack and Erno Rapee. Remade in Italy in 1969.

◁ Director William Wyler, hitherto confined to directing westerns, was given a modest budget of $60,000 for **Anybody Here Seen Kelly?** a romantic comedy set, for most of its time, in New York, where much of it was photographed. Bessie Love (left) starred as a young girl called Mitzi Lavell who falls in love with extrovert Pat Kelly (Tom Moore, right) a member of the American Expeditionary Force in Europe. Kelly, as is his wont with every girl he meets, generously invites her back to America where, he claims, he is a VIP – not for a moment thinking she will actually take him up on his invitation. But she does and, after searching New York for him (he has told her his home is the Metropolitan Museum), finally finds him directing traffic on Broadway at 42nd Street. Pat is happy to see her and quite prepared to settle down but has first to cope with the interference of Immigration official Buck Johnson (Tom O'Brien) who is in love with Mitzi, but determined to deport her if he cannot have her for himself. It ended happily with Pat and Mitzi marrying just in time, thus thwarting Johnson's plan to send her back to Europe. A modest entertainment, adroitly directed by Wyler and with convincing performances from the three leading players, the film also featured Kate Price, Addie MacPhail, Bruce Gordon and Alfred Allen. It was scripted by John B. Clymer, Walter Anthony and Albert De Mond from a story by Leigh Jason, and adapted by Clymer, Joseph Franklin Poland, James Gruen, Rob Wagner, Earl Snell and Samuel M. Pike, though no adaptation credit was given on screen. (silent).

▽ Aided and abetted by cameraman Hal Mohr, director Paul Leni was up to some of his old camera angles again in **The Last Warning**, a murder mystery set, for much of its time, in an old theatre (the one originally constructed for the Paris Opera sequences in *Phantom Of The Opera*, 1925), and involving the murder of the company's leading man (D'Arcy Corrigan) during a performance. The theatre is immediately closed, suspicion falling on both the leading lady and on the dead man's understudy. After a period of five years, a producer decides to reopen the theatre by staging a production of the fatal play (see illustration) with the remaining members of the original cast. All sorts of weird things happen as rehearsals begin, including an appearance of the murdered actor's ghost warning off the company from continuing the production, and the disappearance of the leading man (Roy D'Arcy). On the opening night, however, the guilty parties are revealed. Laura La Plante and John Boles played the prime suspects, with other question marks hanging over the aforementioned Mr D'Arcy, as well as Margaret Livingston, Montagu Love, Burr McIntosh, Mark Swain, Bert Roach, Carrie Daumery, Slim Summerville and Torben Meyer. A part-talkie, it was scripted by Alfred A. Cohn and Tom Reed, and adapted from Thomas F. Fallon's play of the same name, and Wadsworth Camp's story *House Of Fear* by Cohn and Robert F. Hill. It was remade in 1939 as *House Of Fear*. (Jewel).

▽ Reginald Denny provided the story for and starred in **That's My Daddy**, an enjoyable piece of escapism, the ramifications of whose plot found him pretending to be the father of an endearing four-year-old orphan girl. The child, delightfully played by moppet Jane La Verne (left), becomes so attached to Denny (right) that, on the day of his marriage to a society snob called Sylvia Van Tassel (Lillian Rich) whom he does not love, she throws the cat among the pigeons by announcing to the assembled guests 'That's my daddy!'. The wedding is cancelled, a relieved Denny finds happiness in the arms of the woman he really loves (Barbara Kent) and, you guessed it, adopts little Miss La Verne. Faith Thomas and Pierre Couderc scripted it, it was directed by Fred Newmeyer, and Albert De Mond supplied the titles. Also cast: Tom O'Brien, Armand Kaliz and Mathilde Brundage. (Jewel – silent).

◁ **Lonesome**, a remarkably effective romantic drama with sound effects and talking sequences, found director Paul Fejos indulging in some striking, neo-expressionistic camera effects in telling the simple tale of two lonely people who live in the same New York boardinghouse, but are each unaware of the other's existence until they meet, by chance, on a beach in Coney Island and fall in love. In the course of the day they lose one another when a fire breaks out, and each returns, separately, to their lodgings. It is at this point that they joyfully discover, for the first time, that they are neighbours. Barbara Kent (illustrated) was the girl, Glenn Tryon the boy, neither of them particularly convincing as the two lonely souls. The cast was completed by Gustav Partos and Eddie Phillips. Edward T. Lowe Jr and Tom Reed wrote it from a story by Mann Page, and the production was supervised by Carl Laemmle Jr.

△ The studio's first 100% talkie, made in a week because Carl Laemmle was unable to obtain William Fox's Movietone equipment for any longer, **Melody Of Love** may have been a milestone of sorts in the studio's history but, artistically, it was a non-starter. A romantic drama in nine reels written by Robert Arch, it was the story of a songwriter who, after leaving his chorus-girl sweetheart to join the army, is pursued in France by a singer called Madelon. After being wounded in combat and losing the use of his right arm, the songwriter returns home, is jilted by his chorus-girl sweetheart, and becomes a derelict. Madelon, however, has not been able to forget him, and makes her way to America where she becomes a cabaret singer. By chance, the songwriter finds her and, in his joy at meeting her again, recovers the use of his arm. As he sits down at the piano to sing a love song of his own composition to Madelon, he knows, deep down, that at last he has found the woman he loves. The arrant nonsense starred Walter Pidgeon (illustrated right) as Jack, Mildred Harris (illustrated left) as Madelon, Jane Winton as the chorus girl, with other roles under A.B. Heath's faltering direction going to Tommy Dugan, Jack Richardson, Victor Potel and Flynn O'Malley. (Jewel).

△ On a scale of one to ten, **The Count Of Ten** merited a five. The so-so tale of a young prizefighter whose promising career goes to the dogs as soon as he marries a pretty saleslady in a department store and allows her worthless brother and father to move in with them, the film's most potent asset was the casting of James Gleason as the prizefighter's tough, no-nonsense misogynistic manager. Charles Ray (left) was adequate as the boxer, Jobyna Ralston somewhat less so as his wife. Arthur Lake played the no-good brother and Charles Sellon the father. Also cast: Edythe Chapman (right), George Magrill and Jackie Coombs. James Flood directed it from a screenplay by Harry O. Hoyt and Albert De Mond, based on a *Redbook* short story called *Betty's A Lady* by Gerald Beaumont. (Jewel – silent).

▽ First they called it 'Fresh Every Hour', then they changed it to 'The Prince Of Peanuts'. Still not satisfied, they changed the title to 'Meet The Prince'. After that came 'Three Days'. Finally they settled for **How To Handle Women**, a title which bore no relation to the theme of Carl Krusada's screenplay (story by William J. Craft and Jack Foley, title cards by Albert De Mond) which was all about a smalltime commercial artist who helps save Prince Hendryx of Volgaria from bankruptcy by exploiting Volgaria's enormous peanut crop. Glenn Tryon was the artist, Raymond Keane the Prince and Marian Nixon (illustrated centre with Tryon) a pretty columnist and Tryon's inamorata. William J. Craft also directed, and the cast included Mario Carillo, Bull Montana, Cesare Gravina and Robert T. Haines. (Jewel – silent).

△ An unpretentious, small-scale comedy that provided audiences with a fair amount of mirth, **Thanks For The Buggy Ride** chronicled the up-and-down romance between a dance instructor and a song plugger and composer, and told what happened when the former incurs the enmity of a song publisher after spurning his advances. Laura La Plante (right) played the dance instructor, Glenn Tryon (left) was her composer beau and Richard Tucker the lecherous publisher. Beatrice Van and Tom Reed's scenario (story by Byron Morgan) also featured Lee Moran, David Rollins, Kate Price, Jack Raymond and Trixie Friganza, and it was directed with just the right touch by Miss La Plante's husband William A. Seiter. (Jewel – silent).

OTHER PRODUCTIONS OF 1928

The Air Patrol
Dir: Bruce Mitchell. Smuggling melodrama. Al Wilson, Elsa Benham, Jack Mower.

Arizona Cyclone
Dir: Edgar Lewis. Western melodrama. Fred Humes, George K. French, Margaret Gray.

Beauty And Bullets
Dir: Ray Taylor. Western melodrama. Ted Wells, Wilbur Mack, Duane Thompson.

Buck Privates (Jewel)
Dir: Melville W. Brown. Army comedy. Lya De Putti, ZaSu Pitts, Malcolm McGregor.

Call Of The Heart
Dir: Francis Ford. Western melodrama. Dynamite, the dog, Joan Alden, Edmund Cobb.

The Clean-up Man
Dir: Ray Taylor. Western melodrama. Ted Wells, Peggy O'Day, Henry Hebert.

Clearing The Trail (Jewel)
Dir: Reaves Eason. Western melodrama. Hoot Gibson, Dorothy Gulliver, Fred Gilman.

The Cloud Dodger
Dir: Bruce Mitchell. Aviator comedy drama. Al Wilson, Gloria Grey, Joe O'Brien.

The Cohens And The Kellys In Paris (Jewel)
Dir: William Beaudine. Two-family comedy. George Sidney, J. Farrell MacDonald, Vera Gordon, Kate Price, Gertrude Astor.

The Crimson Canyon
Dir: Ray Taylor. Western melodrama. Ted Wells, Wilbur Mack, Lotus Thompson.

The Danger Rider (Jewel)
Dir: Henry MacRae. Western melodrama. Hoot Gibson, Eugenia Gilbert, Reaves Eason.

The Fearless Rider
Dir: Edgar Lewis. Western melodrama. Fred Humes, Barbara Worth, Ben Corbett.

Finders Keepers (Jewel)
Dir: Wesley Ruggles. Army comedy. Laura La Plante, John Barron, Edmond Breese.

The Flying Cowboy (Jewel)
Dir: Reaves Eason. Western melodrama. Hoot Gibson, Olive Hasbrouck, Harry Todd.

The Foreign Legion
Dir: Edward Sloman. Melodrama. Norman Kerry, Lewis Stone, Mary Nolan.

The Four-Footed Ranger
Dir: Stuart Paton. Western melodrama. Dynamite, the dog, Edmund Cobb.

The Fourflusher (Jewel)
Dir: Wesley Ruggles. Comedy drama. George Lewis, Marion Nixon, Eddie Phillips.

Freedom Of The Press (Jewel)
Dir: George Melford. Mystery drama. Lewis Stone, Malcolm McGregor, Marceline Day.

The Gate Crasher (Jewel)
Dir: William James Craft. Comedy melodrama. Glenn Tryon, Patsy Ruth Miller.

Good Morning Judge (Jewel)
Dir: William A. Seiter. Comedy. Reginald Denny, Mary Nolan, Otis Harlan.

Greased Lightning
Dir: Ray Taylor. Western melodrama. Ted Wells, Betty Caldwell, Walter Shumway.

The Grip Of The Yukon (Jewel)
Dir: Ernst Laemmle. Melodrama. Francis X. Bushman, Neil Hamilton, June Marlowe.

Guardians Of The Wild
Dir: Henry MacRae. Western melodrama. Jack Perrin.

Home James (Jewel)
Dir: William Beaudine. Comedy drama. Laura La Plante, Charles Delaney.

Honeymoon Flats
Dir: Millard Webb. Comedy drama. George Lewis, Dorothy Gulliver, Phillips Smalley.

Hot Heels
Dir: William James Craft. Comedy. Glenn Tryon, Patsy Ruth Miller, Tod Sloan.

The Hound Of Silver Creek
Dir: Stuart Paton. Police melodrama. Dynamite, the dog, Gloria Grey, Edmund Cobb.

Jazz Mad (Jewel)
Dir: F. Harmon Weight. Society drama. Jean Hersholt, George Lewis, Marion Nixon.

Love Me And The World Is Mine (Jewel)
Dir: E.A. Dupont. Romantic melodrama. Mary Philbin, Norman Kerry, Betty Compson.

A Made-To-Order Hero
Dir: Edgar Lewis. Western melodrama. Ted Wells, Marjorie Bonner, Pee Wee Holmes.

The Michigan Kid
Dir: Irvin Willat. Northwest melodrama. Renee Adoree, Conrad Nagel, Fred Esmelton.

Midnight Rose (Jewel)
Dir: James Young. Crime melodrama. Lya De Putti, Kenneth Harlan, Henry Kolker.

The Night Bird
Dir: Fred Newmeyer. Boxing comedy. Reginald Denny, Betsy Lee, Sam Parker.

The Phantom Flyer
Dir: Robert North Bradbury. Western melodrama. Jack Hoxie, Lillian Rich.

Phyllis Of The Follies
Dir: Ernst Laemmle. Chorus girl comedy. Alice Day, Matt Moore, Edmund Burns.

The Price Of Fear
Dir: Leigh Jason. Western melodrama. Bill Cody, Duane Thompson, Grace Cunard.

Put 'Em Up
Dir: Edgar Lewis. Western melodrama. Fred Humes, Gloria Grey, Pee Wee Holmes.

Quick Triggers
Dir: Ray Taylor. Western melodrama. Fred Humes, Derelys Perdue, Wilbur Mack.

The Rawhide Kid (Jewel)
Dir: Del Andrews. Western melodrama. Hoot Gibson, Georgia Hale, Fred Hagney.

Red Lips
Dir: Melville W. Brown. Co-ed drama. Marion Nixon, Charles Buddy Rogers, Stanley Taylor.

Riding For Fame
Dir: Reaves Eason. Western melodrama. Hoot Gibson, Ethlyne Clair, Charles K. French.

Stop That Man (Jewel)
Dir: Nat Ross. Farce. Arthur Lake, Barbara Kent, Eddie Gribbon, Warner Richmond.

13 Washington Square (Jewel)
Dir: Melville W. Brown. Crime comedy. Jean Hersholt, Alice Joyce, ZaSu Pitts.

Thunder Riders
Dir: William Wyler. Western melodrama. Ted Wells, Charlotte Stevens.

A Trick Of Hearts (Jewel)
Dir: Reaves Eason. Western melodrama. Hoot Gibson, Georgia Hale, Heinie Conklin.

The Two Outlaws
Dir: Henry MacRae. Western melodrama. Jack Perrin, Kathleen Collins.

We Americans (Jewel)
Dir: Edward Sloman. Society drama. George Sidney, Patsy Ruth Miller, George Lewis.

The Wild West Show (Jewel)
Dir: Del Andrews. Western melodrama. Hoot Gibson, Dorothy Gulliver, Allen Forrest.

Won In The Clouds
Dir: Bruce Mitchell. Adventure melodrama. Al Wilson, Helen Foster, Frank Risco.

1929

▽ A typical campus comedy of the period, **College Love** was a minor league all-talkie which starred George Lewis (right) as an all-American hero who protects footballer Eddie Phillips (as 'Flash' Thomas) from disgrace by pretending that it was he, not 'Flash', who drank himself into a stupor just before the big game. Furthermore, he scores the final touchdown, is proclaimed the campus hero and, of course, gets the girl (Dorothy Gulliver, left). Carl Laemmle Jr produced it, Nat Ross directed; it was written in assembly-line fashion by John B. Clymer, Pierre Couderc, Albert De Mond and Leonard Fields, and featured Churchill Ross, Hayden Stevenson and Sumner Getchell in supporting roles. (Jewel).

△ Glenn Tryon starred in **The Kid's Clever**, a breezy, silent comedy written by Jack Foley, which set out to show how hero Tryon, as the inventor of a car with a fuelless motor, wins a contract from an automobile manufacturer (Russell Simpson) after a rival mechanic (Lloyd Whitlock) sabotages his invention. Tryon (left) not only got the contract, but also the girl (Kathryn Crawford, right) as well as most of the reviews for his appealing performance. It was directed at a cracking pace by William James Craft whose cast included George Chandler, Joan Standing, Max Asher, Virginia Sale and Stepin Fetchit.

▽ Jerome Kern and Oscar Hammerstein II's Broadway classic, **Show Boat**, adapted from the novel by Edna Ferber, received its first screen translation (it was remade by Universal in 1936 and MGM in 1951) as a part-talkie produced by Carl Laemmle. Alas, the magic ingredients were pounded into a very strange mixture which failed to jell, or to find an audience. The movie was first filmed as a silent, and the songs and dialogue were added later. Inexplicably, it also offered a prologue, introduced by Laemmle and Florenz Ziegfeld, composed of extracts from the original stage production and featuring some of its stars: Tess Gardella and The Jubilee Singers sang 'C'Mon Folks' and 'Hey Feller'; Helen Morgan sang 'Bill' and 'Can't Help Lovin' Dat Man', and Jules Bledsoe 'Ol' Man River' (accompanied by the original Broadway chorus). Inappropriate as this embellishment may have been, the quality of its performance further diminished the inadequacies that followed. An incohesive screenplay (by Charles Kenyon) was peopled by Laura La Plante (centre – dubbed by Eva Olivetti) as an over-tearful Magnolia, Joseph Schildkraut (left) as an over-acted – and distinctly foreign – Gaylord Ravenal, Otis Harlan as a hopelessly unfunny Cap'n Andy, and a decidedly eccentric Emily Fitzroy as Parthenia Hawks, the Cap'n's wife. The only distinguished performance came from Alma Rubens as the tragic Julie. (Ironically, Miss Rubens' own life ended tragically when, aged 33, she died of drug addiction after being committed to an asylum). Harry Pollard was responsible for the plodding direction, and the rest of the cast included Elsie Bartlett, Jack McDonald, Stepin Fetchit, Neely Edwards, Theodore Lorch, Jane La Verne (right), and the combined voices of The Billbrew Chorus, Silverstone Quartet, The Four Emperors of Harmony, Claude Collins, and Jules Bledsoe singing spirituals offscreen. Other songs: 'The Lonesome Road' Gene Austin, Nathaniel Shilkret; 'Here Comes That Show Boat' Maceo Pinkard, Billy Rose; 'Love Sings A Song In My Heart' Joseph Cherniavsky, Clarence J. Marks; 'Coon, Coon, Coon' Gene Jefferson, Leo Friedmann; 'Down South' Sigmund Spaeth, William H. Myddelton; 'I've Got Shoes', 'Deep River' (traditional).

◁ Based on a play by Ernest Pascal and Leonard Praskins, **The Charlatan**, a part-talkie, was a fair-to-middling mystery drama that starred Holmes Herbert as a circus clown whose wife (Margaret Livingston) runs off with wealthy Rockcliffe Fellowes, taking their little daughter with her. Fifteen years later Herbert (right), posing as a Hindu seer, finds his wife just as she is about to leave Fellowes for yet another man. On the night of the elopement Miss Livingston (left) is killed at a society party, her murder being pointed at Herbert. Various other suspects are brought forth in J.G. Hawks, Jacques Rollens, Tom Reed and Robert N. Lee's screenplay until, in the end, the guilty culprit is finally unmasked. George Melford directed it and his cast included Philo McCullogh, Anita Garvin, Crauford Kent and Rose Tapley. (Jewel).

△ Of interest solely because of its director, William Wyler, **The Love Trap** – a part-talkie – was a romantic comedy of no particular distinction that starred Laura La Plante (centre) as a chorus girl who, after being fired from her job and evicted from her apartment with all her furniture, marries a young taxi driver (Neil Hamilton) much to the disapproval of his uncle (Norman Trevor, centre right), a judge, who at first tries to buy Miss La Plante off, but finally realises she's not so bad after all. Wyler did the best he could with John B. Clymer, Clarence Thompson and Albert De Mond's screenplay (story by Edward J. Montagne), and with a cast that also included Robert Ellis, Clarissa Selwynne and Rita Le Roy. But it just didn't add up to much.

▽ Universal's debut all-talkie musical was also minstrel Eddie Leonard's (right) sound debut, but **Melody Lane** didn't do much for either him or the studio. It was a hackneyed weepie about a married vaudeville dancing team who part when the wife (Josephine Dunn) is offered a job in a legit acting company. Three years later he has become a struggling prop man, she a successful actress. They are reunited in the usual implausible happy ending endemic to such plots when their daughter (Jane La Verne) falls and injures herself, and her daddy croons her to recovery. Robert F. Hill directed from a screenplay by himself and J.G. Hawks (and from a play by Jo Swerling), and Huntley Gordon was also featured in the cast. The movie featured Leonard's own popular composition 'Roly Boly Eyes', performed by the star, but its inclusion failed to expand the undersized lines at the paybox. Other songs: 'The Song Of The Islands' Charles King; 'Here I Am', 'There's Sugar Cane Round My Door', 'The Boogy Man Is Here' Leonard, Grace and Jack Stern.

▷ Producer Carl Laemmle Jr brought the Phillip Dunning-George Abbott 1927 stage hit, **Broadway**, to the screen as an all-talkie at a cost of $1,000,000. A camera crane was devised by director Paul Fejos which was able to travel at every conceivable angle at a speed of 600 feet a minute, thus giving greater fluidity than was usual in movie musicals of the time. The story (screenplay by Edward T. Lowe Jr and Charles Furthman) focused on a naive young Broadway hoofer who becomes innocently entangled in a bootlegging murder. As backstage musicals went, it was tense and hard-hitting, even though the elaborate nightclub settings were at odds with the intended sleaziness of the original. Glenn Tryon was convincing as the hoofer, but Merna Kennedy as the object of his affections was only just adequate. Robert Ellis featured as the villain whose nefarious activities are halted with a gun by a vengeful chorine (an effective performance from Evelyn Brent). Thomas E. Jackson (the detective) and Paul Porcasi (the nightclub owner) were imported from the original stage show, and others cast included Otis Harlan, Fritz Feld, Leslie Fenton, and Gus Arnheim and His Cocoanut Grove Ambassadors. Maurice Kusell staged the ostentatious dance numbers (see illustration) and the nightclub sequences were photographed (by Hal Mohr) in 'natural' colour. Remade in 1942. Songs and musical numbers: 'Broadway', 'The Chicken Or The Egg', 'Hot Footin' It', 'Hittin' The Ceiling', 'Sing A Little Love Song' Con Conrad, Sidney Mitchell, Archie Gottler.

▽ Virtually a filmed version of his 1928 Broadway play, author/actor James Gleason, together with his wife Lucile Webster Gleason (both illustrated) starred in and as **The Shannons Of Broadway**. They played a couple of vaudeville entertainers who, after being discharged from their show, buy a hotel and, to their good fortune, discover that the adjacent property which they also own is being sought after by an airplane company who wish to turn it into an airport. A pleasing comedy talkie, with pleasing performances from the Gleasons as well as from a cast that included Mary Philbin and John Breeden as the romantic interest, Tom Santschi, Harry Tyler, Gladys Crolius, Slim Summerville, Walter Brennan and Charles Grapewin, it was directed by Emmett J. Flynn, and written by Gleason and Agnes Christina Johnston. Remade in 1938 as *Goodbye Broadway*.

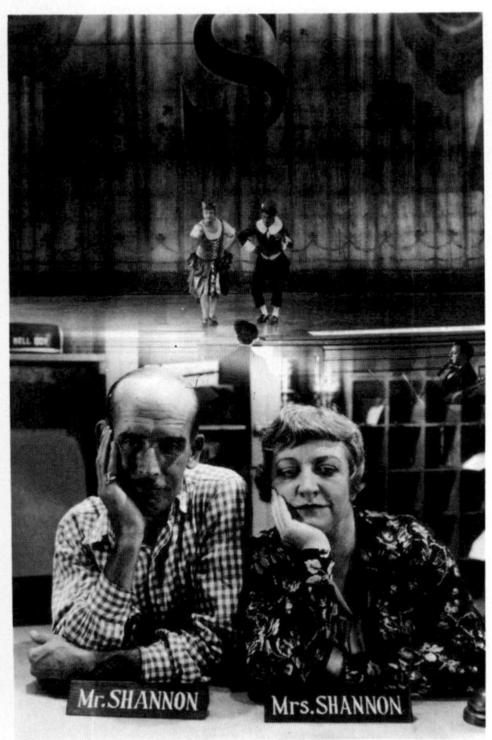

▽ Joseph Schildkraut (centre), fresh from his appearance as Gaylord Ravenal in *Show Boat*, and replete with Southern accent, again played a riverboat gambler in the very same riverboat used in the Kern-Hammerstein musical. This time the film was called **The Mississippi Gambler** – a talkie, the gist of whose trumped up plot (by Karl Brown and Leonard Fields) had Schildkraut cheating the father (Alec B. Francis) of the girl (Joan Bennett) he loves, then regretting it and redeeming himself in his sweetheart's eyes. It was scripted by Edward T. Lowe Jr, Winifred Reeve, H.H. Van Loan and Dudley Early and also featured Otis Harlan (left), Carmelita Geraghty (right) and William Welsh.

▷ Reginald Denny (inset right) revealed a solid speaking voice in **Clear The Decks**, a part-talkie written by Earl Snell, Gladys Lehman, Albert De Mond and Charles H. Smith. Plot had him embarking on an ocean voyage to pursue Olive Hasbrouck (inset left), using the ticket and identity of an ailing friend who has been ordered to undertake the voyage for health-reasons. As the rather complicated plot unravels itself, he is mistaken by a band of crooks to be a detective, and by the ship's crew to be off his head. The denouement sees him unwittingly assisting in the capture of the crooks (jewel thieves), as a result of which he finally gets the girl. Amiable nonsense, amiably performed and directed (by Joseph E. Henabery), the film also featured Otis Harlan, Lucien Littlefield, Collette Marten, Robert Anderson, Elinor Leslie and Brooks Benedict. (Jewel).

▽ **The Girl On The Barge** was Sally O'Neil (left), the illiterate daughter of a mean, inebriated barge captain (Jean Hersholt) who, much to her father's displeasure, falls in love with Malcolm McGregor (right), a tugboat pilot. Hersholt does his best to break up the romance, including knocking McGregor unconscious and stealing his tugboat. But love proves stronger than fisticuffs and the film ends with the couple happily married and presenting a sobered-up Hersholt with a grandson. Director Edward Sloman wasn't able to make a silk purse from Charles Kenyon, Nan Cochrane, Tom Reed and Charles H. Smith's part-talking sow's ear of a screenplay, but managed to draw from an uncharacteristically violent Hersholt a most interesting performance. Also cast: Morris McIntosh, Nancy Kelly (not to be confused with the 20th Century-Fox ingenue of the '30s and early '40s), George Offerman Jr and Henry West. (Jewel).

△ Alice Day (left) starred opposite Reginald Denny (right) in a part-talkie farce called **Red Hot Speed**, as the daughter of a newspaper publisher (Thomas Ricketts). Miss Day is arrested for speeding and, under an assumed name, is paroled into the custody of assistant district attorney Denny. Trouble is, Miss Day's father is presently conducting a massive anti-speeding campaign in his newspaper and, should it ever be revealed that his own daughter is guilty of the very thing he is campaigning against, it would be too embarrassing to contemplate. How Denny and Day manage to perpetuate the deception for seven reels (falling in love in the process) provided the main thrust to Gladys Lehman, Matt Taylor, Albert De Mond and Faith Thomas' scenario, as well as employment for a cast that also included Charles Byer, De Witt Jennings, Fritzi Ridgeway and Hector V. Sarno. Joseph E. Henabery directed at a cracking pace. (Jewel).

▷ Laura La Plante (right) made her sound debut in **Scandal**, a part-talkie, produced by Harry L. Decker and directed by Wesley Ruggles, and failed to make the transition with any impact. She played a socialite, fallen on hard times who, after finding employment as a stenographer in a fashionable resort hotel, meets a former sweetheart (John Boles) but marries wealthy Huntley Gordon (left) instead. In Gordon's absence, Boles calls on Miss La Plante on the very eve that his wife is murdered. Not wishing to compromise Miss La Plante, he refuses to provide an alibi. But just as things are looking really bad for him, Miss La Plante, risking a scandal, provides the vital alibi, thus setting Boles free. Jane Winton, Julia Swayne Gordon, Eddie Phillips and Nancy Dover completed the cast. It was written by Paul Schofield, Tom Reed and Walter Anthony.

△ Laura La Plante again totally failed to come to grips with the exigencies of sound in **Hold Your Man**, an all-talkie romantic comedy, whose well-worn storyline (by Maxine Alton, banally scripted by Harold Shumate) was the one about the ambitious wife who leaves her husband to seek a career as an artist in Paris. The husband counters her move by having an affair with a former sweetheart, but in the end husband and wife are reconciled. Miss La Plante (left) was the wife, Scott Kolk (right) the husband, with other roles going to Mildred Van Dorn as the sweetheart, and Eugene Borden. It was directed for the potboiler it was by Emmett J. Flynn.

△ **The Shakedown** was a part-talkie, sluggishly directed by William Wyler, about how a young orphan and a waitress reform a crooked boxer who moves from one town to the next, with his equally crooked manager faking fights for him. James Murray (illustrated), at Wyler's special request, was hired to play the boxer, the waitress was Barbara Kent, the orphan Jack Hanlon and the manager Wheeler Oakman. Completing the cast were George Kotsonaros as a boxer called Battling Roff and Harry Gibbon as a dancehall bouncer. It was written by Charles A. Logue, Clarence J. Marks and Albert De Mond. (Jewel).

OTHER PRODUCTIONS OF 1929

The Body Punch
Dir: Leigh Jason. Comedy. Virginia Brown Faire, Jack Daugherty.

The Border Wildcat
Dir: Ray Taylor. Western melodrama. Ted Wells, Tom London, Kathryn McGuire.

Born To The Saddle
Dir: Joseph Levigard. Western melodrama. Ted Wells, Duane Thompson, Leo White.

Burning The Wind
Dir: Henry MacRae. Romantic drama. Hoot Gibson, Virginia Brown Faire, Cesare Gravina, Boris Karloff.

The Cohens And The Kellys In Atlantic City
Dir: William James Craft. Cohen's daughter and Kelly's son save their families' bathing suit business by staging a beauty contest. George Sidney, Vera Gordon, Mack Swain, Kate Price, Cornelius Keefe. (Part-talkie)

Come Across
Dir: Ray Taylor. Crook melodrama. Lina Basquette, Reed Howes, Flora Finch.

The Drake Case
Dir: Edward Laemmle. Divorcée Gladys Brockwell proves that her 'deceased' ex-husband isn't dead at all and has murdered his present wife. Forrest Stanley, Robert Frazer, James Crane. (Talkie).

Eyes Of The Underworld
Dir: Leigh Jason. Newspaper crime melodrama. Bill Cody, Sally Blane, Arthur Lubin.

Girl Overboard
Dir: Wesley Ruggles. Parolee Fred Mackaye, barred from marrying for eight years, saves homeless Mary Philbin from drowning and is allowed by parole officer Edmund Breese to marry her. Otis Harlan, Francis McDonald. (Part-talkie)

Grit Wins
Dir: Joseph Levigard. Western melodrama. Ted Wells, Kathleen Collins, Al Ferguson.

The Harvest Of Hate
Dir: Henry MacRae. Western melodrama. Jack Perrin, Helen Foster.

His Lucky Day
Dir: Edward Cline. Real-estate agent Reginald Denny mistakes a gang of bank robbers for respectable, prospective tenants. Lorayne Du Val, Otis Harlan, Eddie Phillips. (Part-talkie)

Hoofbeats Of Vengeance
Dir: Henry MacRae. Western melodrama. Jack Perrin, Helen Foster.

It Can Be Done
Dir: Fred Newmeyer. Glenn Tryon, a clerk with an inferiority complex is mistaken for the boss of a publishing house. Sue Carol, Richard Carlyle, Richard Carle. (Part-talkie)

King Of The Rodeo
Dir: Henry MacRae. Western melodrama. Hoot Gibson, Kathryn Crawford.

The Lariat Kid (Jewel)
Dir: Reaves Eason. Western melodrama. Hoot Gibson, Francis Ford, Ann Christy.

The Long Long Trail
Dir: Arthur Rosson. Hoot Gibson, as the Ramblin' Kid, prevents bad guy James Mason from absconding with the annual rodeo sweepstake money. Sally Eilers, Kathryn McGuire, Archie Ricks. (Talkie)

Man Woman And Wife
Dir: Edward Laemmle. Unhappily married Marian Nixon re-marries when she learns of husband Norman Kerry's death. But it turns out he isn't dead at all. Pauline Starke, Byron Douglas. (Musical score & effects)

Modern Love
Dir: Arch Heath. Kathryn Crawford, a designer for an exclusive dressmaking concern, cannot choose between a life of wedded domesticity and her career. Charley Chase, Jean Hersholt, Edward Martindel. (Part-talkie)

Plunging Hoofs
Dir: Henry MacRae. Western melodrama. Jack Perrin.

Points West (Jewel)
Dir: Arthur Rosson. Western melodrama. Hoot Gibson, Alberta Vaughn, Frank Campeau.

The Ridin' Demon
Dir: Ray Taylor. Western melodrama. Ted Wells, Kathleen Collins, Lucy Beaumont.

Senor Americano
Dir: Harry J. Brown. Ken Maynard western in which hero Maynard incurs the enmity of Gino Corrado, his rival for the love of Kathryn Crawford. J.P. McGowan, Frank Yaconelli. (Talkie)

Shanghai Lady
Dir: John S. Robertson. After Mary Nolan is discharged for disorderly conduct from a teashop, she meets Wheeler Oakman on a train. Oakman, a derelict, believes her to be respectable and vice versa. James Murray. (Talkie)

Silks And Saddles
Dir: Robert F. Hill. Racing drama. Richard Walling, Sam De Grasse, Marion Nixon.

The Sky Skidder
Dir: Bruce Mitchell. Action melodrama. Al Wilson, Helen Foster, Wilbur McGaugh.

Slim Fingers
Dir: Joseph Levigard. Crime melodrama. Bill Cody, Duane Thompson, Wilbur Mack.

Smilin' Guns (Jewel)
Dir: Henry MacRae. Western melodrama. Hoot Gibson, Blanche Mehaffey.

The Smiling Terror
Dir: Joseph Levigard. Western melodrama. Ted Wells, Derelys Perdue, Al Ferguson.

The Tip-Off
Dir: Leigh Jason. Crime melodrama. Bill Cody, George Hackathorne, Duane Thompson.

The Wagon Master
Dir: Harry J. Brown. Ken Maynard as The Rambler prevents a group of miners from signing an exorbitant contract with bad-guy Tom Santschi. (Part-talkie)

Wild Blood
Dir: Henry MacRae. Western melodrama. Jack Perrin, Ethlyn Claire.

The Winged Horseman (Jewel)
Dir: Arthur Rosson. Western melodrama. Hoot Gibson, Mary Elder, Charles Schaeffer.

Wolves Of The City
Dir: Leigh Jason. Crime melodrama. Bill Cody, Sally Blane, Al Ferguson.

1930

▷ It began with director Paul Fejos as 'La Marseillaise', and ended with director John S. Robertson. The nett result was **Captain Of The Guard**, a musical that dealt with the French Revolution and the composing of 'La Marseillaise'. John Boles (right) and Laura La Plante (left) starred as a pair of lovers whose idyll is tarnished by politics; he is her Royalist music teacher and captain of the guard, she is an innkeeper's daughter on the side of revolution. The film passed muster only on the music side, thanks to the excellent songs by William Francis Dugan and Heinz Roemheld (scored by Charles Wakefield Cadman). The rest was ruined by a bungled screenplay, poorly written and full of historical inaccuracies, an opening credit apologising for the latter. George Manker Watters and Arthur Ripley, working from a story by Houston Branch, were responsible. Others in the cast included Sam De Grasse (Bazin), Stuart Holmes (Louis XVI), Evelyn Hall (Marie Antoinette), Lionel Belmore (Colonel of Hussars), Richard Cramer (Danton), and George Hackathorne (Robespierre). Songs: 'Song Of The Guard', 'For You', 'Maids On Parade', 'You, You Alone', 'Can It Be', 'It's A Sword', 'La Marseillaise'. (83 mins)

▽ **The Cat Creeps** was the creaky story of a creaking mansion and the dastardly things that happen in front of and behind its sliding panels. A remake of *The Cat And The Canary* (1927) it seemed to do little more than simply add dialogue (by Gladys Lehman and Tom Hurlburt, screenplay by Lehman from the play by John Willard) to the original. Helen Twelvetrees, in the Laura La Plante role, played the canary, and the cat was – well, was it Raymond Hackett? Lilyan Tashman? Jean Hersholt? Neil Hamilton (left)? Montagu Love (right), perhaps? or even Theodore Von Eltz...? Also featured was Lawrence Grant as a lawyer whose dead body understandably causes an upset in the mansion. Rupert Julian's direction was par for the course. It was remade by Paramount (with Bob Hope) in 1939. (75 mins)

▽ They didn't come more romantic or more melodramatic than **The Lady Surrenders**, an entertaining romantic melodrama which witnessed the talkie debut of Genevieve Tobin (right) and Rose Hobart, rivals in love for Conrad Nagel (centre), to whom Miss Hobart is already married. It almost ended in tears when Miss Tobin attempted suicide in an effort to help reunite husband and wife. As it turned out, however, Hobart gracefully accepts defeat, allowing her husband and Miss T to carry on their romance without too much guilt. Gladys Lehman adapted it (probably while her mind was distracted on other matters) from the novel *Sincerity* by John Erskine, and John Stahl directed. Also cast: Basil Rathbone, Edgar Norton (left), Carmel Myers, Franklin Pangborn and Vivian Oakland. (102 mins)

◁ One of the livelier entries in the series, **The Cohens And Kellys In Scotland** again starred George Sidney (left) and Charles Murray (right) as rival businessmen. In John McDermott's screenplay (adaptation and dialogue by Albert De Mond) they find themselves in Edinburgh, desperately trying to outsell each other's supply of tartan cloth to local shopkeepers in the hope that the sartorially elegant Prince of Morania (Lloyd Whitlock) will start wearing tartan garb, thus setting a profitable trend. The pun-filled screenplay had its moments, the best being a golf match between the warring protagonists. Vera Gordon and Kate Price were Mrs Cohen and Mrs Kelly respectively, and the cast, under William James Craft's direction, was completed by E.J. Ratcliffe, William Colvin and John McDermott. (84 mins)

▷ Edward G. Robinson's second talkie (his first was Paramount's *The Hole In The Wall*, 1929) was **Night Ride**, in which he brought an appropriately menacing demeanour to the role of a gangland leader called Tony Garotta. In the course of Edward T. Lowe Jr's screenplay (story by Henry La Cossitt) Robinson (right) also gave reporter Roe Rooker (Joseph Schildkraut, left) a pretty rough time for writing an exposé story about his nefarious activities in general and a double murder in particular. Of its type it was competently made, with good performances from the two leading men contributing to its well-being. Barbara Kent played Schildkraut's wife, with Harry Stubbs, DeWitt Jennings, Ralph Welles, Hal Price and George Ovey completing the cast. John S. Robertson directed. (70 mins)

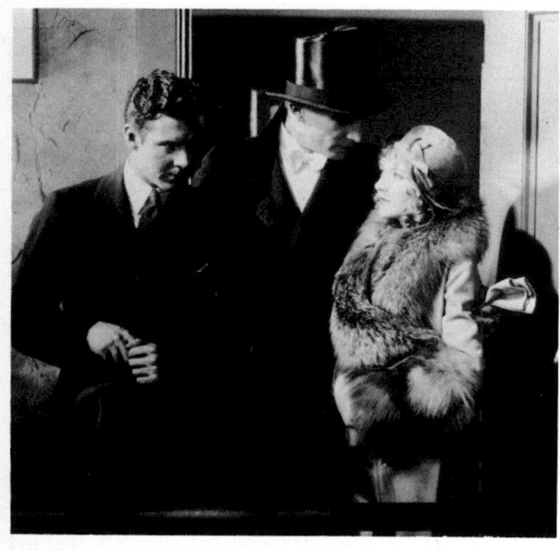

△ 'A tale of three passions – love, desire and hate', as a title card proclaimed, **The Last Performance** was, in fact, deficient in plot, and had to rely instead on some inventive direction from Paul Fejos, and the excellent camera work of Hal Mohr. All about a middle-aged magician's unrequited passion for his young assistant who, in her turn, is in love with the magician's protégé (a young vagrant and erstwhile thief), it starred Conrad Veidt (centre) as Erik, the magician, Mary Philbin (right) as the girl, and Leslie Fenton (left) as the young man. Fred Mackaye was cast as a character called Boffo, another of Veidt's assistants who, jealous of Miss Philbin, exposes her romance with Fenton to Erik and, as a result, is killed by Fenton, who then kills himself at his trial. The story, by James Ashmore Creelman, was scripted by Creelman with Walter Anthony and Tom Reed. Also cast: Gustav Partos, William H. Turner, Anders Randolf, Sam De Grasse and George Irving. (Jewel).

▷ Based on the novel *An Unmarried Father* by Floyd Dell and the play *The Little Accident* by Dell and Thomas Mitchell, **The Little Accident** did not benefit much from its celluloid incarnation. On the contrary, thanks to Will Hays' censorship code, a certain toning down of dialogue was required, which reduced to the level of an anecdote the story of a man who, on the eve of his second marriage, learns that he is the father of his ex-wife's child and postpones the wedding ceremony indefinitely. After becoming engaged to practically every female member of the cast, the father returns to his former wife (having first smuggled the baby away from her), and a happy-ever-after situation was duly vouchsafed. Douglas Fairbanks Jr (right) did the best he could as the hero, with Anita Page (his wife), Sally Blane and Joan Marsh as the women in his life. Others on duty in Gladys Lehman's screenplay (adaptation by Gene Towne) included Roscoe Karns, Slim Summerville, ZaSu Pitts, Henry Armetta (left) and Myrtle Stedman, who were directed by William James Craft. The studio remade it in 1939, and it surfaced yet again as *Casanova Brown* (International) in 1944. (82 mins)

▷ A remake of *The Three Godfathers* (1916) and Jack (John) Ford's *Marked Men* (1920), Peter Bernard Kyne's story *The Three Godfathers* surfaced yet again called, this time, **Hell's Heroes**. It was the story of three bandits who, while fleeing the law after a bank raid, discover a woman in a wagon about to give birth to a child, and promise to become the child's godfathers. They also promise to escort it safely back to its father in New Jerusalem, the town whose bank they have just robbed. Charles Bickford, Fred Kohler and Raymond Hatton starred as Sangster, Kearney and Gibbons respectively, and Fritzi Ridgeway played the dying mother. Shot on location in the Mojave Desert and the Panamint Valley near Death Valley, it was the first all-talkie outdoor film made by the studio, and the first all-talkie made by its direcor, William Wyler, whose work on it earned him a new contract at Universal. An uncompromisingly bleak western, even to an unhappy ending its realistic approach to its subject (especially effective in the trio's long, arduous haul back to civilisation against overwhelming physical odds) appealed to audiences by now sated with musicals, revues, and ineptly handled crime melodrama, and grossed a fortune at box offices across the country – it took $18,000 in its first week in New York alone. It was written by Tom Reed and photographed by George Robinson (see illustration). (65 mins)

△ Sound, especially in view of the feeble dialogue provided by Edward I. Luddy and Vin Moore (adapted by C. Jerome Horwin), hardly enhanced **See America Thirst**. Indeed its star, comedian Harry Langdon (right), apart from muttering inaudibly, did little to distinguish his performance from the many he had given without the aid of the spoken word. Langdon and his co-star Slim Summerville (left) played a couple of tramps who are mistaken for two big-time hoods known as 'Shivering Smith' and 'Gun-kissed Casey'. Director William James Craft allowed the pair to indulge in some high-flying Harold Lloyd-style comedy but, that aside, there was little of value on offer. Bessie Love co-starred as a gangster's moll who turns out to be working for the local district attorney, with other parts going to Mitchell Lewis, Matthew Betz and Stanley Fields. (75 mins)

△ In **East Is West**, Edward G. Robinson (left), as the Chop Suey King of San Francisco, mugged outrageously in a vainglorious attempt to enliven a tale wherein a Chinese girl is auctioned off into slavery by her father. The heroine in Winifred Eaton Reeve and Tom Reed's flaccid screenplay (based on the play by Samuel Shipman and John B. Hymer), is saved by a wealthy young American who causes quite a stir in polite society when he decides to marry her. Turns out, however, that his wife isn't Chinese after all, but as Caucasian as he is, having been taken from a murdered missionary while still a baby. Lupe Velez (centre) received star billing as the girl, with Lew Ayres (right) as her shining saviour. Other roles under Monta Bell's melodramatic direction were assigned to E. Allyn Warren, Tetsu Komai, Henry Kolker, Mary Forbes and Jean Hersholt. (75 mins)

△ The special effects department had a field day attempting to bring **The Storm** to life with avalanches, snow drifts, pounding rapids, blinding storms and howling gales. This certainly tested the efficacy of the studio's newly acquired sound equipment, and lent atmosphere to a routine triangle situation which found best friends William 'Stage' Boyd and Paul Cavanagh lusting for Lupe Velez (left), a French-Canadian bombshell, while the trio are snowbound in a log cabin in the Canadian wild. For the record: Boyd got the girl. The three leading players brought a welcome note of naturalness to Wells Root's workaday screenplay (adapted from Langdon McCormick's play *Men Without Skirts* by Charles A. Logue), and it was resourcefully directed by William Wyler, with Alphonse Ethier (right) featured in support. Previously filmed in 1922 with House Peters, Matt Moore and Virginia Valli. (80 mins)

▷ Wretched performances, including those by Edward G. Robinson, Mary Nolan and Owen Moore, the three principals in director Tod Browning's **Outside The Law**, reduced a routine crime melodrama to something even less than a potboiler. Robinson (left) played a gangleader yet again. He is double-crossed in a bank heist by Moore and his girlfriend Miss Nolan (right), the outcome of which is a climactic shoot-out, during which Robinson is killed, and the other two are apprehended and sent to prison. Edwin Sturgis, John George, Delmar Watson and DeWitt Jennings were merely statistics in Browning and Garrett Fort's undistinguished screenplay. Note: Tod Browning had made a silent version in 1921 with Lon Chaney Sr. (70 mins)

▷ Although King Vidor's silent, *The Big Parade* (MGM, 1925), had taken a non-heroic look at World War I, it had a happy ending that sent audiences home with hope in their hearts. In Lewis Milestone's altogether superior **All Quiet On The Western Front** – the most uncompromisingly bleak statement about the nightmare of trench warfare the cinema had ever attempted – there was no comfort at all except, perhaps, in the film's justly celebrated penultimate scene when, in the midst of the surrounding carnage, young Lew Ayres sees beauty and the wonder of creation in a butterfly. Spontaneously reaching out to touch one of life's miracles, he attracts a French sniper's bullet and is killed. It was the most poignant moment in a film memorable for the compassion it brought to the simple story of a group of young men (particularly Paul Baumer, so affectingly played by Ayres, left) who, one by one, are maimed or killed in action. For an American film it was unique in showing war from the German trenches, a fact which forcibly underlined the message that war is hell for both sides. George Abbott's stunningly economical screenplay (from the novel by Erich Maria Remarque) eloquently reinforced this point in what was perhaps the film's most moving scene of all: Ayres, finding a Frenchman (Raymond Griffith) in a shell-hole, stabs him, then agonises over what he has done. No film, before or since, has managed to capture the futility of war with such quiet simplicity, and it remains one of the masterpieces of the American cinema. Louis Wolheim (right) played Sergeant Katczinsky, a seen-it-all-before veteran whose own strength gives young Ayres the will to cope, and was superb; and there were fine performances, too, from Arnold Lucy as Professor Kantorek, the schoolmaster who enthusiastically exhorts Ayres and his fellow pupils to enlist, John Wray as Himmelstoss, a once mild-mannered postman who, in army training camp, turns into a sadistic corporal, and Ben Alexander as Kemmerick, Ayres' buddy who is unaware that he has had a leg amputated. Also: Russell Gleason, Owen Davis Jr, William Bakewell, Joan Marsh, Beryl Mercer (as Ayres' mother), Slim Summerville and, in a small role, Fred Zinneman. The film was produced by Carl Laemmle Jr, the studio's production head. Interesting sideline: Miss Mercer replaced ZaSu Pitts after the first preview where audiences laughed at Miss Pitts, then fast establishing herself as a comedienne. The film was withdrawn and all her scenes reshot. Interesting too, was the fact that the film was poorly received in Germany, and banned in Berlin where it was considered to have a demoralising effect on Germany's flowering youth. Reissued in 1939 with an opening commentary on the horrors of war added to it. (140 mins)

△ Produced by Carl Laemmle Jr, written by Frederick T. Lowe with sketches by Harry Ruskin, and photographed in subtle and enhancing two-tone Technicolor by Hal Mohr, Jerome Ash and Ray Rennahan, **King Of Jazz** was one of the studio's outstanding offerings for 1930. A lavish musical revue, it owed its distinction largely to the superb, innovative talent of its director, John Murray Anderson, whose inventiveness was to prove a source of inspiration to several outstanding musicals in the future. Anderson's dazzling originality was seen at its best in the staging of George Gershwin's 'Rhapsody In Blue', and he ran this a close second with his final tableau, 'The Melting Pot Of Jazz', in which the music of several nationalities combined in a giant cauldron to produce a new sound called Jazz. Watching these sequences today, it is impossible to believe that the director was making his movie debut. The quality does occasionally vary, but the overall impact remains bold and impressive, and, certainly, there was a cavalcade of talent on hand to service the enterprise. Jack Yellen and Milton Ager's 'A Bench In The Park' was performed by The Brox Sisters, The Rhythm Boys, George Chiles and Paul Whiteman and his Orchestra (illustrated), and The Sisters G gave out with another Yellen-Ager number, 'Happy Feet'. In amongst a selection of folk, classical and light classical pieces, some Sousa marches and a couple of parodies, audiences were also treated to Bing Crosby (his debut) and The Rhythm Boys performing 'Mississippi Mud' (by Harry Barris and James Cavanaugh) and – with Al Rinker and Harry Barris – Barris and Billy Moll's 'So The Bluebirds And The Blackbirds Got Together'. Bing, solo, sang Yellen and Ager's 'Music Hath Charms', and John Boles warbled the same team's 'The Song Of The Dawn' as well as 'It Happened In Monterey' (by Mabel Wayne and Billy Rose); Jeannie Lang, George Chiles, Don Rose and Marian Statler sang 'Ragamuffin Romeo' (by Mabel Wayne and Harry De Costa); orchestrator Ferde Grofé interpolated Buddy De Sylva and Robert Katscher's 'When Day Is Done' into his arrangement for 'A Bench In The Park'. Grofé's scoring included several medleys chosen to feature members of the band in specialty solo spots. Since Whiteman's band at the time boasted such musicians as guitarist Eddie Lang and violinist Joe Venuti, this was yet another attractive ingredient in an altogether attractive entertainment. (105 mins)

OTHER RELEASES OF 1930

Barnum Was Right
Dir: Del Lord. Through a chain of unlikely circumstances, Glenn Tryon manages to turn an ageing mansion into a profitable investment. Merna Kennedy, Otis Harlan.

Boudoir Diplomat
Dir: Mal St Clair. Meagre programmer involving a flirtatious attache who woos a war minister's wife at a foreign court to achieve an important treaty-signing. Ian Keith, Lawrence Grant, Betty Compson, Lionel Belmore, Mary Duncan. (68 mins)

The Climax
Dir: Renaud Hoffman. Multiple complications centre on opera star Kathryn Crawford who falls for singing teacher Jean Hersholt's son, John Reinhardt, loses her voice then falls for the doctor, LeRoy Mason, jilts him and returns to the son. Remade 1944. (65 mins)

The Concentratin' Kid (Hoot Gibson)
Dir: Arthur Rosson. Hoot, for a bet, tries to win the hand of a travelling radio singer and gets caught up with rustlers. Kathryn Crawford. (57 mins)

Courtin' Wildcats
Dir: Jerome Storm. Unusual role for cowboy Hoot Gibson in this comedy drama of student life. Eugenia Gilbert, Harry Todd.

Czar Of Broadway
Dir: William James Craft. Routine newspaper story with reporter John Harron befriending gambler John Wray whom he has set out to investigate, and falling in love with nightclub girl Betty Compson. (79 mins)

Dames Ahoy
Dir: William James Craft. Comedy sailor trio attempt to track down a blonde who tricked one of them out of half his pay. Gal and guy marry at film's-end. Glenn Tryon, Eddie Gribbon, Otis Harlan, Helen Wright, Gertrude Astor. (64 mins)

Embarrassing Moments
Dir: William James Craft. Crass comedy in which artist Merna Kennedy invents a husband to avoid an arranged marriage. The invention turns to reality in the shape of Reginald Denny. Otis Harlan, Virginia Sale, William Austin. (58 mins)

The Fighting Legion (Ken Maynard)
Dir: Harry J. Brown. An honest cowboy, wrongly accused of shooting a Texas ranger, escapes lynching and hunts the killer. Dorothy Dwan. (75 mins)

Hide Out
Dir: Reginald Barker. College-dropout-cum-bootlegger escapes the law by hiding out at a former college under a new name, distinguishes himself in the sporting arena and goes straight with his girl's help. James Murray, Edward Hearn, Dorothy Dwan. (59 mins)

Lucky Larkin
Dir: Harry J. Brown. Ken Maynard, as the titular hero, wins a country horse race, brings some criminals to justice and wins the hand of Nora Lane. James Farley, Harry Todd. (Musical score & effects – 65 mins)

Mountain Justice (Ken Maynard)
Dir: Harry J. Brown. An Oklahoma rancher goes west to avenge the murder of his father and wins the love of a schoolmarm. Kathryn Crawford. (75 mins)

The Mounted Stranger (Hoot Gibson)
Dir: Arthur Rosson. A boy sees his father murdered and years later as a man, seeks vengeance from the killer and his gang. Buddy Hunter. (65 mins)

One Hysterical Night
Dir: William James Craft. Believing he is going to a fancy dress ball, Reginald Denny, heir to a family fortune, is taken by his scheming aunt and uncle to an insane asylum. Nora Lane, E.J. Ratcliffe, Fritz Feld, Slim Summerville. (75 mins)

Parade Of The West (Ken Maynard)
Dir: Harry J. Brown. A cowboy joins a Wild West Show and wins the respect of a child in his charge and the love of a performer. Gladys McConnell. (65 mins)

Roaring Ranch (Hoot Gibson)
Dir: Arthur Rosson. Hoot comes to the rescue of a ranch owner about to sell out to a crooked geologist who has found oil beneath the spread. Sally Eilers. (68 mins)

Skinner Steps Out
Dir: William James Craft. Remake of *Skinner's Dress Suit* (1925). Glenn Tryon, Merna Kennedy, E.J. Ratcliffe, Burr McIntosh, Lloyd Whitlock. (70 mins)

Song Of The Caballero (Ken Maynard)
Dir: Harry J. Brown. A grown-up son uses banditry against his uncle, a Spanish rancho, because of former misdeeds towards his mother. Doris Hill. (70 mins)

Sons Of The Saddle (Ken Maynard)
Dir: Harry J. Brown. A shy foreman, Ken finds the owner's gal really loves him when he outsmarts the owner's enemies. Doris Hill. (70 mins)

Spurs (Hoot Gibson)
Dir: Reaves Eason. Hoot, on the trail of a killer, finds the gang holed up in a secret den guarded by a machine-gun. Helen Wright, Robert Homans. (59 mins)

Tonight At Twelve
Dir: Harry A. Pollard. Robert Ellis falsely admits to being the recipient of a love note to protect his father and future mother-in-law. Madge Bellamy, Margaret Livingston. (74 mins)

Trailin' Trouble (Hoot Gibson)
Dir: Arthur Rosson. A trail-drive boss is suspected of stealing the sale money and goes after the real culprits. Margaret Quimby. (57 mins)

Trigger Tricks (Hoot Gibson)
Dir: Reaves Eason. Hoot plays a cowboy who hires himself out to a ruthless gang responsible for murdering his brother. Sally Eilers. (60 mins)

Undertow
Dir: Harry A. Pollard. Incompetent love drama in which a blind lighthouse keeper's wife is snatched by an underhand coastguard; but the blind man regains his sight in time to save the day. Mary Nolan, Johnny Mack Brown, Robert Ellis. (60 mins)

What Men Want
Dir: Ernst Laemmle. Pauline Starke, mistress of debonaire Robert Ellis, falls in love with Ben Lyon. Complications proliferate with the arrival of Barbara Kent, Miss Starke's sister. Hallam Cooley, Carmelita Geraghty. (65 mins)

Young Desire
Dir: Lew Collins. Inconsequential but colourful carnival backdrop was the setting for this doomed romance between kooch dancer Mary Nolan and William Janney. Suicide denied it a happy ending. (69 mins)

1931

△ Small time crime as practised by sleazy bookmakers and manufacturers of bathtub gin was the subject of a moderately entertaining gangster drama called **Reckless Living**. It featured Mae Clark (left) and Norman Foster as the owners of a small speakeasy who are saving for enough money to buy a gas station in New Jersey and go straight. When Foster, who compulsively plays the horses and is equally mesmerised by dice, gambles away their savings, he is hauled out by big-shot Ricardo Cortez who sets him and his girl up in a swanky apartment as a front for his own underworld activities. In the end, though, Foster shows enough strength of character to buy that gas station after all, proving that, in some respects, crime pays. As scripted by Courtenay Terrett from an adaptation by Cyril Gardner and Tom Reed of Eve K. Flint and Martha Madison's story *Twenty Grand* (which, in turn, surfaced as a play by Miss Flint called *The Up And Up*), the narrative line and the characterisations were negligible. However, under Cyril Gardner's direction, the twilight worlds of the bookie and the bootlegger were accurately conveyed. Also cast: Marie Prevost (right), Slim Summerville, Robert Emmett O'Connor and Thomas Jackson. (65 mins)

▽ Though Carl Laemmle Jr claimed that Bette Davis (standing right) had about as much sex appeal as Slim Summerville, he allowed her to make her screen debut in **Bad Sister**, playing the relatively minor role of Laura Madison, the good sister. The movie was a remake of Booth Tarkington's novel, *The Flirt*, first filmed by the studio in 1916 as a Bluebird Production, and remade in 1922. This third version also marked the debut of Sidney Fox (lying foreground) who, as Marianne Madison, the more flamboyant of the two sisters, understandably made much more of an impression than Davis, both on audiences and on the critics. Humphrey Bogart was cast as Valentine Corliss, a swindler and the man Marianne elopes with but is later deserted by, while Conrad Nagel, as Dr Dick Lindley, received top billing and was paired with Miss Davis. Papa Madison was played by the reliable Charles Winninger (kneeling), with other roles under Hobart Henley's direction going to ZaSu Pitts, Slim Summerville, Emma Dunn (standing left) and Bert Roach. It was scripted by Raymond L. Schrock and Tom Reed, whose dialogue remained sorely in need of the kiss of life throughout. (71 mins)

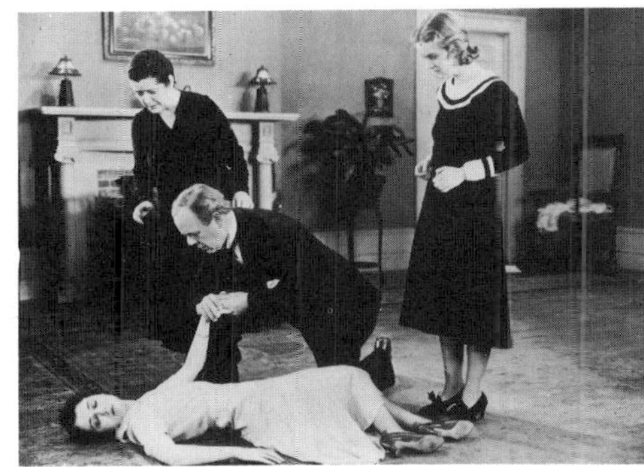

▽ John Boles (centre), deprived of recourse to song, made heavy weather of **Seed**, a turgid drama (based on the novel by Charles G. Norris) in which he played a would-be author who deserts his wife and five children for a high-powered employee of the publishing concern where he works as a clerk. Lois Wilson (left) played the deserted wife and Genevieve Tobin (right) the other woman. Both were fine in the circumstances. It was the circumstances themselves – comprising, as they did, an unconvincing screenplay (by Gladys Lehman) and clumsy direction by John M. Stahl, that needed avoiding. Bette Davis made no impression whatsoever in the small role of Boles' daughter. Also: ZaSu Pitts (a servant yet again), Raymond Hackett, Frances Dade and Richard Tucker. (96 mins)

▽ Though Vin Moore's direction for **Virtuous Husband** was little more than a photographed version of the stage play *Apron Strings* (by Dorrance Davis) on which it was based (screenplay by Dale Van Every, adapted by Edward Luddy and Jerome Horwin), it brought out the best in an attractive cast that included Elliot Nugent (right), Betty Compson and Jean Arthur (left). All about a meek, unimaginative young man (Nugent) whose late author-mother has bequeathed him a stack of written instructions on how he should conduct the rest of his life, it had Miss Arthur as Nugent's fiancée who, understandably irritated by her prospective husband's dogged reliance on his late mother's 'advice', walks out on him. Tully Marshall (as a lawyer), and J. C. Nugent and Alison Skipworth (as Miss Arthur's parents) were in it too. (76 mins)

◁ Dedicated to Knute Rockne, **The Spirit Of Notre Dame** was a football film with a vengeance. It starred Lew Ayres as Bucky O'Brien, a freshman who provided Dale Van Every and Lt Commander Frank Wead's screenplay (story by Van Every and Richard Schayer) with what little vestige of plot it contained, by falling out of favour with coach J. Farrell MacDonald. The jealousy of another player caused the rift, but it was only temporary and, in the end, Bucky accomplishes the impossible by making a winning touchdown in the final moments of the big game. Andy Devine was third-billed as an injured player fighting for his life in hospital, with other roles under Russell Mack's rah-rah direction going to William Bakewell, Nat Pendleton, Sally Blane (right) and Harry Barris (left). The virtually all-male cast also featured several well known football players, including Notre Dame's 'The Four Horsemen', as well as Adam Walsh, Bucky O'Connor, John Law, Moon Mullins and Art McManmon. (80 mins)

△ Advertised as 'the story of the strangest passion the world has ever known' **Dracula**, based on Bram Stoker's classic horror story (and a successful stage play by Hamilton Deane and John Balderston), was an immediate hit with audiences. It was also the studio's biggest money-maker of the year, and it set a trend for horror films which Universal would exploit with varying degrees of success for the remainder of the decade. Though director Tod Browning originally sought Lon Chaney for the central role of the Transylvanian Count, Chaney demurred – then died. Thus it became possible for the Hungarian-born Bela Lugosi, who had opened the play on Broadway in 1927, to recreate his mesmeric performance on film. It is doubtful whether the movie would have been the enormous success it was without Lugosi's formidable presence, especially as much of the horror described in Garrett Fort's screenplay took place off screen. But with Lugosi (centre) dominating the proceedings so completely and allowing such an overwhelming miasma of evil to seep through the tale, it hardly mattered that the film's visual content was rather tame. Dwight Frye played Renfield, the English real-estate agent who travels to Transylvania to discuss the sale of the Castle Dracula with its aristocratic and outwardly gracious owner; Helen Chandler and Frances Dade were Minna Seward and her friend Lucy Watson, Edward Van Sloan was vampire fighter Professor Von Helsing, and David Manners played Minna's sweetheart John Harker. Other roles went to Michael Visaroff (as the innkeeper), Herbert Bunston, Charles Gerrard and Joan Standing. The sparingly used background music was from Tchaikovsky's 'Swan Lake'. A Spanish version, directed by George Melford, was filmed simultaneously. In 1922 the great German director Murnau filmed a version under the title *Nosferatu* (with Max Schreck); it was remade in 1958 by Hammer Films with Christopher Lee (who also appeared as the Count in several other films between 1958 and 1972, including a Spanish-German version in 1971), and it was filmed yet again by Universal in 1979, with Frank Langella as Dracula. (84 mins)

▽ Lovely Genevieve Tobin (left) literally took it on the chin in **Free Love** when her husband, Conrad Nagel (right), furious at her friendship with his best friend (Monroe Owsley), socks her one. It does the trick, for the estranged couple thereafter return to each other's arms. Prior to this, though, Tobin visits a psychiatrist who informs her that marital incompatability is the cause of all her problems – she is 'an intuitive introvert', her hubby 'an infantile extrovert'. Having paid through the nose ($800 to be precise) for this information, she packs her bags and, taking her kids with her, checks in to the nearest hotel. Nagel follows her, and persuades her to return home, which she does – as a guest. But it isn't until the aforementioned punch on the jaw that the confused Miss Tobin finally sees, not only stars, but the light. Such was the trashy content of Winifred Dunn's screenplay, adapted from Sidney Howard's play *Half Gods* by Edwin Knopf, the latter also supplying the dialogue. Hobart Henley directed it, and his cast included ZaSu Pitts as a maid and Slim Summerville as a gas inspector (they, too, pair off in the course of the story), as well as Ilka Chase, Bertha Mann and George Irving. (70 mins)

△ Robert E. Sherwood's play **Waterloo Bridge**, with its Camille-like overtones, reached the screen in a respectable version which Benn W. Levy scripted, together with Tom Reed who supplied the 'continuity' and additional dialogue. It was directed – alas, without much subtlety – by James Whale, and starred Mae Clark (left) as a chorus girl-cum-prostitute who, during an air raid in World War I, falls in love with a Canadian soldier (Kent Douglass, right) and he with her. Unaware of her street-walking activities, he proposes marriage but, during a weekend spent in the country with Douglass' aristocratic family, Miss Clark tells her prospective mother-in-law (Enid Bennett) the truth about herself. The mother thereupon persuades the girl to avoid ruining the son's life by backing out of the marriage. Bette Davis, making her last appearance for the studio before signing with Warner Bros., played Douglass' sister, with other roles going to Frederick Kerr, Doris Lloyd, Ethel Griffies and Rita Carlisle. Kent Douglass soon became better known as Douglass Montgomery. The film was remade (superbly) by MGM in 1940 with Vivien Leigh and Robert Taylor, and again by MGM in 1956, called *Gaby*, with Leslie Caron and John Kerr. (72 mins)

▽ The first sound version of Leo Tolstoy's **Resurrection** was a ponderous affair, starring a totally miscast John Boles (left) as Prince Dimitri Nekhludoff. Lupe Velez (right) fared somewhat better as Katusha, but received no help from director Edmund Carewe, whose inability to marshall the emotional resources of his cast into the necessary sweeping dramatic statement, crippled the lofty intentions of the project. (Carewe's silent version with Rod La Rocque and Dolores Del Rio, released by United Artists in 1927, was somewhat better). Finis Fox's screenplay was poorly written and constructed, and provided few opportunities for a cast that also included Nance O'Neil as Princess Marya, William Keighley as Mayor Schoeboek, and Rosa Tapley as Princess Sophya. John Boles' singing voice was catered for in compositions by Dimitri Tiomkin (music) and Bernard Grossman (lyrics). A Spanish version was shot simultaneously, with Gilbert Roland substituting for Boles in an otherwise all-Spanish cast. Living up to its name, **Resurrection** had come to the screen on seven previous occasions (in 1907, twice in 1909, in 1912, in 1915, in 1918, and in 1927), and was remade by United Artists in 1934 under the title *We Live Again*, directed by Rouben Mamoulian with Anna Sten. A Russian version appeared in 1961. (81 mins)

▷ Though **Heaven On Earth** wasn't exactly that, it plausibly evoked the life-styles of a handful of Mississippi poor whites and their superstitions. The brunt of the action in Ray Doyle's screenplay, based on the novel *Mississippi* by Ben Lucien Burman, was borne by Lew Ayres (left) who, in the course of the drama, discovers that the steamboat captain he always believed to be his father was, in fact, his real father's killer. It all ended happily, however, with Ayres forgiving the captain (Harry Beresford, right), and pairing off with Anita Louise. It was earnestly directed by Russell Mack, whose cast included Elizabeth Patterson, Slim Summerville, Alf P. James, Harlan Knight and Peter Richmond (soon to be better known as John Carradine). (70 mins)

△ Director Tod Browning turned to prize fighting for **Iron Man** and, relegating action to second place, relied on Francis Faragoh's dialogue (from the novel by W.H. Burnett) to tell the story of a likeable lightweight called Kid Mason (Lew Ayres) and the fight for dominance over him between his manager (Robert Armstrong) and his capricious blonde girlfriend (Jean Harlow). Ayres (right) and Armstrong handled the wordy screenplay admirably but Harlow (left) – as a go-getter only really interested in The Kid when he's ahead – had little to offer but sex appeal. John Miljan as her sideline romantic interest wasn't up to much either, and the cast was completed by Mike Donlin, Morrie Cohan, Mary Doran and Mildred Van Dorn. It was remade in 1937 as *Some Blondes Are Dangerous*, and again in 1951 as *The Iron Man*. (73 mins)

△ As a jungle adventure with a supporting cast of snakes, tigers, monkeys, pumas and crocodiles, **East Of Borneo** was a lot of fun. The human side of things was attractively taken care of by Rose Hobart who, in Edwin Knopf's action-packed screenplay (based on a story by Dale Van Every), braved all manner of dangers while out in the jungles of Borneo searching for her lost husband. She needn't have bothered though, for, when she eventually finds him, he is in the best of health, and employed as the personal physician to Prince Hashin at his jungle palace. Charles Bickford (left) played the husband and Georges Renavent the Prince, with Lupita Tovar (right) and Noble Johnson in it too. They were all upstaged, however, by a climactic volcanic eruption which brought the adventure, directed by George Melford, to a spectacular close. (77 mins)

△ **Up For Murder** was the misleading title of a story about a touching, if unfulfilled, romance between a cub reporter and the paper's attractive society editor who, in turn, is the mistress of the publisher. Actually a remake of *Man, Woman And Sin* (1927), Monta Bell's screenplay and direction drew excellent performances from Lew Ayres (right) as the young man and Genevieve Tobin as the older woman. Purnell B. Pratt was featured as the publisher whom Ayres accidentally kills (hence the film's title), with other parts in this efficient melodrama going to Frank McHugh (centre, as a drunken reporter), Richard Tucker, Louise Beavers, Frederick Burt (left) and Dorothy Peterson. (68 mins)

OTHER RELEASES OF 1931

The Cohens And Kellys In Africa
Dir: Vin Moore. Limpid story of a piano business partnership, and their adventurous trip to Africa to investigate an ivory shortage. George Sidney, Charles Murray, Vera Gordon, Kate Price. (68 mins)

Ex-Bad Boy
Dir: Vin Moore. Sluggish comedy comprising Jason Robards' attempts to quash an affair between daughter Jean Arthur and Robert Armstrong. George Brent, Grace Hampton, Mary Doran, Eddie Kane. (67 mins)

Graft
Dir: Christy Cabanne. Story of a dumb cub reporter redeeming himself by apprehending a murderer involved in political intrigue. Regis Toomey, Sue Carol, Dorothy Revier, Boris Karloff, William Davidson. (72 mins)

Homicide Squad
Dir: George Melford. Racketeer Leo Carrillo searches for son Russell Gleason, lost for 18 years, and who has since turned to crime. He helps police frame his father to avoid a murder rap. Mary Brian, George Brent, J. Carrol Naish. (70 mins)

Lasca Of The Rio Grande
Dir: Edward Laemmle. The love affairs of a dancing girl who finally sacrifices her life for a Texas Ranger in a cattle stampede. Leo Carrillo, Dorothy Burgess. (60 mins)

Many A Slip
Dir: Vin Moore. Complications galore when society girl Joan Bennett pretends she's pregnant in order to get boyfriend Lew Ayres to marry her. Slim Summerville, Ben Alexander, Virginia Sale, Roscoe Karns. (74 mins)

Mother's Millions (aka She-Wolf)
Dir: James Flood. Financier May Robson's obsession with evening up score with Edmund Breese, her late husband's business adversary, results in turgid intrigue and strained family loyalties. David Talbot, Lawrence Gray, Frances Dade. (85 mins)

1932

△ Apart from giving the film version a happy ending, Tom Reed's screenplay for **Afraid To Talk** was faithful to the play *Merry Go Round* by Albert Maltz and George Sklar on which it was based. It concerned an innocent bellboy (Eric Linden, top-cast) who becomes the victim of police corruption after witnessing a murder committed by gangland chief Jim Skelli (Edward Arnold). Seems that Skelli has some evidence that will incriminate district attorney Tully Marshall, so young Linden (illustrated centre) is sent to prison instead. Berton Churchill as the mayor played another dishonest character in the exposé; so did Louis Calhern. The good-guy roles went to Frank Sheridan as a police commissioner, and Reginald Barlow as a magistrate. Also cast: Sidney Fox (as Linden's young wife), Robert Warwick, George Meeker, Mayo Methot, Ian MacLaren and Matt McHugh. The fast moving direction was by Edward L. Cahn. (69 mins)

▽ Germany, France, Italy, Austria and America were represented in **The Doomed Battalion**, a handsomely produced drama photographed in the Austrian Tyrol and on Universal's studio back lot. The snow-covered Alps were used as a backdrop to tell the World War I story of Florian Di Mai (Luis Trenker, right) and the effect the war has on him, on his wife (Tala Birell, left) and on Victor Varconi as an Italian mountaineer befriended by Trenker and who, once war is declared, finds himself billetted in Trenker's home. The film sustained interest throughout thanks, in the main, to the central performances, Trenker's gripping story (adapted by himself and Carl Harth, dialogue by Patrick Kearney), and direction by Cyril Gardner that brought the best out of a cast which also included Albert Conti, Gustav Von Seyffertitz, Henry Armetta, Ferdinand Gottschalk and Gibson Gowland. It was remade in 1940 as *Ski Patrol*. (95 mins)

▽ The first, and least successful, version of Max Brand's durable story, **Destry Rides Again**, marked Tom Mix's talkie debut. By now a mere shadow of his former self, Mix (left) played the titular hero, a stagecoach proprietor whose partner (Earle Fox) is the brains behind a gang of bandits. Stanley Fields was a crooked sheriff, the love interest was supplied by Claudia Dell (right), and the laughs by Andy Devine and ZaSu Pitts (a single brief appearance). In fact, Robert Keith and Isidore Bernstein's scenario underplayed the action by overplaying the story's more humorous (even farcical) elements, and the end result was pretty mediocre. It was brilliantly remade in 1939, and somewhat less spectacularly so in 1951 as *Frenchy*, and in 1955 as *Destry*. (53 mins)

▽ That fine actress Irene Dunne (on loan from RKO) fought an uphill battle in **Back Street**. Not only was the dialogue (by Lynn Starling) ridiculously stilted, but John M. Stahl's direction was unhelpful, and the performance from Miss Dunne's leading man, John Boles, was an embarrassment. Based on the popular novel by Fannie Hurst (screenplay and continuity by Gladys Lehman), this story of a successful banker's (Boles, right) long-standing love for a 'back room' mistress (Dunne, left) was tedious from start to finish, inducing boredom rather than tears. Doris Lloyd played Boles' wife, with other parts going to June Clyde, George Meeker, ZaSu Pitts, Shirley Grey and Jane Darwell. It was remade in 1941 with Margaret Sullavan, and again in 1961 with Susan Hayward. (93 mins)

▷ After the impact made ten months earlier by Bela Lugosi as Dracula, it was Boris Karloff's turn to create cinema history in the horror genre – which he indisputably did with **Frankenstein**. He would play the monster twice more (in 1935 and 1939) and, to this day, the character remains as welded to his name as Dracula to Lugosi's. Though the technical preparations that went into the creation of the monster caused Karloff (illustrated) hours of discomfort on the set (he was made 18 inches taller, 65 pounds heavier, and had his legs stiffened by steel struts), it was worth it in the end with the finished product resulting in one of the most memorable screen images of the thirties. Make-up wizard Jack Pierce was responsible for that image, his major achievement resting in the way the creature managed to arouse both revulsion and sympathy at one and the same time. Though Karloff's performance remains the memorable one, he was in fact only billed fourth to Colin Clive (as his creator Dr Frankenstein), Mae Clark as Frankenstein's pretty fiancée, and John Boles as a friend who tries to dissuade the doctor from continuing his dangerous experiments. Also cast: Edward Van Sloan, Dwight Frye, Frederick Kerr, Lionel Belmore and Marilyn Harris. It was chillingly directed by James Whale, the two most memorable sequences being the monster's 'birth', and the one near the end of the film in which Karloff, after innocently throwing a little girl into a lake, realises what he has done. It was written by Garrett Fort and Francis Edwards Faragoh, and adapted from a play by Peggy Webling which, in turn, was adapted from the classic gothic novel by Mary Shelley. The most radical change from the original lay in giving the screen monster a brain that once belonged to a criminal. Edison had made a version of the famous story in 1910 with Charles Ogle; in 1957 Hammer Films starred Peter Cushing in *The Curse Of Frankenstein*. (71 mins)

△ The negative effect of too much adulation too soon was the theme of **The All-American**, a collection of clichés which charted the fall from grace of a one-time football hero (Richard Arlen, right), who has allowed success to go to his head, and now faces a life of anti-climax. Believing his own publicity, he quits school, endorses several commercial products, squanders his money on drink and gambling, and generally sinks about as low as an ex-college hero can get. When, in time, he regains some of his former self-respect, his younger brother (John Darrow), himself a local crowd-pleaser on the playing field, seems headed in the same degrading direction as Arlen. Highlight of director Russell Mack's morality tale was a climactic match which featured several well-known players of the day. For the rest it was drearily conventional stuff, partially redeemed by excellent performances from James Gleason as a perenially pessimistic coach, and Andy Devine as a none-too-bright linesman. Gloria Stuart was the romantic interest, and the cast also included Preston Foster and Merna Kennedy (left). It was written by Frank Wead and Ferdinand Reyher from a story by Richard Schayer and Dale Van Every. (79 mins)

▽ One of the studio's few westerns to run over 65 minutes and which was, in every sense, an 'A'-grade product, **Law And Order**, based on William R. Burnett's novel *Saint Johnson*, featured Walter Huston (left) and Harry Carey as Frame Johnson and Ed Brandt (characters modelled on Wyatt Earp and Doc Holliday). The rest of the male-dominated cast included Raymond Hatton (right), Russell Simpson, Russell Hopton (centre), Ralph Ince, Harry Woods, Andy Devine and Walter Brennan. Basically the story of Huston's attempts to convert the ungodly citizens of Tombstone, Arizona, into a law-abiding community, its matter-of-fact approach to violence and gunplay was the sagebrush equivalent of the hard-hitting gang warfare being pioneered at Warner Bros. Under Edward L. Cahn's expert direction, it developed into a thoroughly engrossing melodrama, with a marvellous central performance from Huston. Tom Reed scripted, with additional dialogue supplied by John Huston. (70 mins)

△ **Scandal For Sale**, which invaded the world of newspapers, passed the time painlessly enough and focussed on the attempts of the editor (Charles Bickford, left) of the 'New York Comet' to boost the paper's circulation to the million mark. If he succeeds, his reward will be a cheque for $25,000 from publisher Bunnyweather (Berton Churchill). Pat O'Brien (centre) co-starred as an ace reporter who Bickford inadvertently sends to his death when, as part of his news promotion plans, he asks O'Brien to accompany a German pilot on a Trans-atlantic airflight. Rose Hobart played Bickford's wife (who does not hide her admiration for O'Brien), with other roles in Ralph Graves' screen-*News*, going to Claudia Dell (right), J. Farrell MacDonald, Harry Beresford, Glenda Farrell and, as the Harry Beresford, Glenda Farrell (right) and, as the Teutonic pilot, Heinrich von Twardofski. Russell Mack directed. (75 mins)

△ Clearly influenced by German Expressionism à la *The Cabinet Of Dr Caligari* (Decla-Film, 1920), director Robert Florey gave **Murders In The Rue Morgue** a decidedly European look to it in his use of sets and camera angles. The kinky story (by Edgar Allan Poe, adapted by Florey, and scripted by Dale Van Every and Tom Reed with additional dialogue by John Huston), of Dr Mirakle, a mad scientist who goes about Paris seeking a human bride for his pet gorilla Erik, and injecting specimens of gorilla blood into the veins of possible contenders, it starred Bela Lugosi (left) as Mirakle, Sidney Fox (foreground) as the girl both he and Erik settle on, and Leon Waycoff (later known as Leon Ames) as Miss Fox's beau. Arlene Francis (her debut) played a prostitute whose lifeless body is dumped in the Seine after she has bled to death on a torture rack; Betsy Ross Clarke was the heroine's mother whose unfortunate fate – in the only incident to be retained from the original Poe story – is to be stuffed up a chimney! Also: Bert Roach, Brandon Hurst and Noble Johnson (right). It was remade by Warner Bros. as *Phantom Of The Rue Morgue* in 1954. (92 mins)

▽ Clearly inspired by Eugene O'Neill's play *Desire Under The Elms*, Olive Edens' story *Hearts And Hands* (scripted by John B. Clymer and Dale Van Every with additional dialogue by John Huston) came to the screen as **A House Divided** and starred Walter Huston (right). In an impressive performance, he played a fisherman who, after the death of his wife, recruits someone from a matrimonial agency to take her place, only to find that the young woman (Helen Chandler, left) and his son (Kent Douglass) have fallen in love under his very nose. Atmospherically directed by William Wyler, whose use of the sea was particularly effective, and with three fine central performances at its core, the film was both a critical and a public success. Vivian Oakland, Frank Hagney, Marjorie Main, Mary Fay, Lloyd Ingraham and Charles Middleton completed the cast. (68 mins)

◁ Cowboy Tom Mix, and Tony the Wonder Horse (both illustrated, left), joined little Mickey Rooney (in carriage, right) in **My Pal The King**, a kiddies' delight in which Rooney played the pint-sized King of Alvonia who, after walking out of a boring council meeting, befriends Tom Mix, the star of a travelling circus. In the final reel, Mix comes to Mickey's rescue when wicked James Kirkwood, as Alvonia's scheming prime minister, tries to drown the boy and take his place on the throne. Jack Natteford and Tom J. Crizer scripted from a story by Richard Schayer, and it was directed by Kurt Neumann. Paul Hurst, Noel Francis, Finis Barton and Jim Thorpe were in it too. (63 mins)

▽ Though some of the satire was toned down for the film version, Moss Hart and George S. Kaufman's Broadway success, **Once In A Lifetime**, was still very funny. Director Russell Mack assembled an excellent cast to tell the story of a trio of cheap vaudevillians who, during Hollywood's transitional period from silents to sound, travel from New York to the coast, hoping to make their fortune by opening an elocution school. Once in Hollywood, George Lewis, one of the members of the vaudeville act, meets, among others, a Hollywood producer called Glogauer whom he insults. As a result of this unusual behaviour, he is considered a genius, made a movie supervisor, and goes on to create a cinematic masterpiece by inadvertently filming from a reject script. Jack Oakie (right) was top-billed as Lewis, Sidney Fox and Russell Hopton were the other two vaudevillians; Aline MacMahon (left) was outstanding as an elocutionist, Gregory Ratoff was Glogauer, ZaSu Pitts a studio receptionist, Louise Fazenda a famous film critic, and Onslow Stevens a playwright called Lawrence Vail (a part created on the stage by Kaufman himself). Also: Robert McWade, Jobyna Howland, Claudia Morgan and Gregory Gaye. Seton I. Miller's screenplay, although greatly abbreviated from the original, retained much of its zany flavour which, by Hollywood's meddlesome standards, was decidedly unusual. (90 mins)

△ The kind of film Howard Hawks might have made a few years later, **Airmail** was the macho story of a group of men whose job it is to see that planes carrying mail arrive at their destinations safely and on time. Ralph Bellamy (right) played the airport manager, and top-billed Pat O'Brien was his irresponsible, though most skilled pilot. A show-off in the air, and totally unscrupulous where other men's women are concerned, O'Brien (as many other seemingly anti-heroic characters had done before him and would do in the future) gets a chance to vindicate himself, proving to be a hero after all. He comes to the rescue of manager Bellamy, who has been compelled to take a plane out in appalling weather after O'Brien has left the airport with a woman whose husband has just been killed. There were no subtleties in Dale Van Every and Lt Commander Frank Wead's screenplay, or in the melodramatic emphasis of John Ford's direction, which was at its best when depicting the moment to moment activities in an air station such as Desert Airport. Also cast: Russell Hopton, Slim Summerville, Gloria Stuart (left) and Lillian Bond. (84 mins)

▽ **Night World** was a programmer focussing on one night in the life of a swanky nightclub, and the numerous dramas attached to members of its clientele. It brought together an excellent cast whose talents were not fully explored in the choppy screenplay by Richard Schayer (story by P.J. Wolfson and Alan Rivkin), which hardly had enough time to develop its account of an alcoholic millionaire's romance with a chorus girl, let alone the parallel tale of the affair the club owner's wife is having with the dance director. Lew Ayres and Mae Clark played the alcoholic and the chorus girl; Dorothy Revier (left) and Russell Hopton were the faithless wife and her lover; and the owner of the club in which it all took place was a subdued Boris Karloff (right). George Raft appeared as a gambler and Clarence Muse was the doorman with other roles under Hobart Henley's uneven direction going to Bert Roach, Florence Lake, Hedda Hopper and Louise Beavers. The dance direction was in the capable hands of Busby Berkeley (his fourth feature), and Alfred Newman supplied the music. (60 mins)

△ Under the expert guidance of director James Whale, J.B. Priestley's scary novel *Benighted* was filmed from a screenplay by Benn W. Levy (with additional dialogue by R.C. Sherriff) as **The Old Dark House** – and chilling it was too! Priestley's eerie tale of a group of people who, one dark, stormy night, descend on the forbidding Femm mansion in the Welsh mountains to seek shelter, was vividly brought to life by Raymond Massey, Gloria Stuart, John Dudgeon (as a 100-year-old baronet), Charles Laughton (marvellous as Sir William Porterhouse, complete with Lancashire accent) and Lillian Bond (illustrated, with Laughton). Ernest Thesiger and Eva Moore were the insane, anti-social Femms, Bember Wills the dwarf-like and fire-obsessed brother they keep behind locked doors (Wills came from England especially to play the role) and, dominating them all, Boris Karloff, wonderfully menacing as the Femm's butler, Morgan. It all came together beautifully, and remains one of the classic thrillers in the horror genre, as well as the best of all 'haunted house' melodramas. (75 mins)

▽ Having done so well by Frankenstein's monster, Boris Karloff changed make-up to appear as **The Mummy**, the first and most effective of the many 'mummy' films that would proliferate in its wake. Having been buried alive some 3000 years ago for trying to restore life to his beloved princess by invoking The Book of Thoth, Im-ho-tep (Karloff) is himself brought to life when a British professor (Arthur Byron) on an expedition to Egypt, inadvertently reads from The Book of Thoth. Disguising himself as a modern-day Egyptian, Karloff (left) sets about trying to find his lost love. What he actually finds is Helen Grosvenor, a British girl whom he believes to be the reincarnation of his princess. Directed with moody intensity by Karl Freund (who photographed both *Dracula*, 1931 and *Murders In The Rue Morgue*), it eschewed shock tactics in the telling of Nina Wilcox Putnam and Richard Schayer's strange tale (screenplay by John L. Balderston), but failed to animate the supporting performances of David Manners, Edward Van Sloan and Bramwell Fletcher. Zita Johann, second-billed (right) as Helen Grosvenor, looked fairly stunned by it all. It was remade in 1959 by Hammer Films with Christopher Lee as the mummy. (72 mins)

▷ **Tom Brown Of Culver** often resembled an extended commercial for the Culver Military Academy in which it was set. With the accent on youth in general and on Tom Brown (played by Tom Brown, right) in particular, it concentrated on Master Brown's development from a recalcitrant beginner to a noble-minded and patriotic young man, worthy of his late father whom he believes was killed in action. It transpires, however, that Tom's old man (H.B. Warner) wasn't killed at all, but was a deserter. This news has a devastating effect on Tom and causes a crisis in his young life. It was written by Tom Buckingham (additional dialogue by Clarence Marks) from a story by George Green and Dale Van Every, in a pleasingly naturalistic manner, sensitively directed by William Wyler (one of whose best scenes was an initiation ceremony of sorts in which a group of freshmen are tyrranised by some older boys), and engagingly performed by a predominantly male cast that included Richard Cromwell (centre), Ben Alexander, Sidney Toler, Russell Hopton, Andy Devine, a very young Tyrone Power Jr (the future star whose father, Tyrone Power, was also an actor), Alan Ladd and Slim Summerville (as a reminiscing veteran, left). It was remade in 1939 as *Spirit Of Culver*. (82 mins)

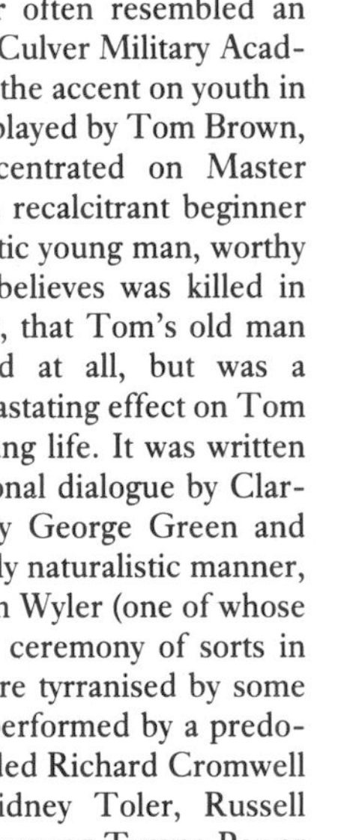

▽ Preston Sturges' stage comedy, **Strictly Dishonourable**, came to the screen via scenarist Gladys Lehman with most of its humour intact, and with an engaging central performance by Paul Lukas (right) that won him many admirers. He played a suave Italian singer, known as Count di Ruovo (Gus to his friends) who, at a speakeasy one night, falls in love with a petite Southern belle (Sidney Fox, centre) despite the fact that she is engaged to an inebriated and bellicose boor (George Meeker). Lukas' love is requited, causing all sorts of amusing complications which, under John M. Stahl's racy direction, kept audiences chuckling from start to finish and gave Lewis Stone (left, as a judge) the opportunity to filch the acting honours. The cast also included William Ricciardi as the owner of the speakeasy and Sidney Toler as a policeman. It was remade in 1951 by MGM with Ezio Pinza and Janet Leigh. (70 mins)

OTHER RELEASES OF 1932

The Cohens And Kellys In Hollywood
Dir: John Francis Dillon. Irrepressible Irish-Jewish rivalry ensues as the two families vie unsuccessfully to achieve motion-picture prominence. George Sidney, Charles Murray, Frank Albertson, Lew Ayres, Sidney Fox, Boris Karloff. (75 mins)

Fast Companions
Dir: Kurt Neumann. Tom Brown, a crooked jockey, reforms after befriending young Mickey Rooney and falling in love with Maureen O'Sullivan, a boarding house proprietress. Andy Devine, James Gleason. (70 mins)

Flaming Guns (Tom Mix)
Dir: Arthur Rosson. Tom is a range manager who falls for a banker's daughter and takes her across the border after a quarrel with her parents. Ruth Hall. (57 mins)

The Fourth Horseman (Tom Mix)
Dir: Hamilton McFadden. Tom saves a boom town from a gang of train robbers trying to muscle in on the new-found prosperity. Margaret Lindsay, Raymond Hutton. (63 mins)

Hidden Gold (Tom Mix)
Dir: Arthur Rosson. Tom plays an honest cowman who wins the confidence of a gang of bank robbers in order to recover the stolen gold. Judith Barrie. (61 mins)

Igloo
Dir: Ewing Scott. Icy love-drama/documentary set in the land of Eskimos was frigidly received by depression audiences and broke no box-office records. Chee-Ak, Kyatuk, Toyuk, Lanak, Nan-Shuk. (70 mins)

Impatient Maiden
Dir: James Whale. A secretary refuses to marry a surgeon until he establishes himself, but all ends happily after he successfully performs an appendectomy on her. Lew Ayres, Mae Clark, Una Merkel, Andy Devine, Arthur Hoyt. (72 mins)

The Last Ride
Dir: Duke Worne. Newspaper reporter mixed up with bootleggers and hi-jackers. Frank Mayo, Tom Santschi, Dorothy Revier, Charles Morton. (64 mins)

Nice Women
Dir: Edwin H. Knopf. Avaricious Lucile Webster Gleason persuades daughter Sidney Fox to marry millionaire Alan Mowbray at the expense of Russell Gleason, the man she really loves. James Durkin, Carmel Myers. (70 mins)

Okay America
Dir: Tay Garnett. Dreary crime melodrama in which brash journalist Lew Ayres meets a sticky end after his part in the kidnapping of a politician's daughter. Edward Arnold, Maureen O'Sullivan, Margaret Lindsay. (80 mins)

Racing Youth
Dir: Vin Moore. Racing driver Frank Albertson is mistaken for his boss. June Clyde, Louise Fazenda, Slim Summerville, Arthur Stuart Hull. (62 mins)

Radio Patrol
Dir: Edward Cahn. Noisy crime programmer climaxes when policemen Robert Armstrong dies leaving wife Lila Lee holding a sickly new-born babe. The late husband's buddy, Russell Hopton, lectures the doctor on the necessity of keeping the baby alive. Andy Devine, June Clyde, Onslow Stevens, Harry Woods. (65 mins)

Riders Of Death Valley (Tom Mix)
Dir: Albert S. Rogell. Tom comes to the rescue of an eastern gal whose brother has been killed by two men plotting to steal his gold mine. Lois Wilson, Fred Kohler. (63 mins)

Steady Company
Dir: Edward Luddy. Girl loves boxing boy who, after a bad smash-up in a fight, accepts a safer offer made by a promotor and all ends happily. June Clyde, Norman Foster, Henry Armetta, ZaSu Pitts. (65 mins)

The Stowaway
Dir: Phil Whitman. To escape her sordid dance hall existence, Fay Wray stows away, is discovered by second mate Leon Waycoff who agrees to hide her; but there is trouble when first mate Montagu Love finds out. Lee Moran, Roscoe Karns, James Gordon. (60 mins)

The Texas Bad Man (Tom Mix)
Dir: Edward Laemmle. Tom is a US marshal who masquerades as a bandit in order to round up a notorious killer. Lucille Powers, Fred Kohler. (63 mins)

Unexpected Father
Dir: Thornton Freeland. ZaSu Pitts, a nursemaid, marries wealthy simpleton Slim Summerville after he falls foul of his fiancée by taking orphan Cora Sue Collins into his home. Claude Allister, Dorothy Kristy. (64 mins)

1933

▽ **By Candlelight** was a piece of European frippery with a mistaken identity plot that gave a handful of attractive performers a chance to enjoy themselves hugely. Set in a world largely peopled by princes, counts, and barons (as well as their servants, of course), it drew much comic mileage from a situation in which a prince's butler, preceding his master on a train journey, is mistaken by the aristocratic Marie for the Prince himself. When the real Prince arrives, he is presumed to be the butler. As for Marie, there's something slightly out of kilter about her too. It was written *en commune* by Hans Kraly, F. Hugh Herbert, Karen De Wolf and Ruth Cummings from the German play *Candle Light* by Siegfried Geyer, and starred Elissa Landi (left) as Marie, Paul Lukas (right) as the butler and Nils Asther as the Prince. It really needed Ernst Lubitsch's touch to fulfil its romantic potential, but it was pleasant enough under James Whale's reliable guidance. The cast was completed by Dorothy Revier, Lawrence Grant, Warburton Gamble, Lois January and Esther Ralston. (70 mins)

◁ Not a great deal of plot attached itself to **The Big Cage**, the little there was providing a backdrop to top-billed Clyde Beatty's brave whip-cracking, pistol-firing antics in and out of the big cage with his ferocious collection of lions and tigers. Beatty's (left) dominance over his animals was truly awesome, and it provided Edward Anthony and Ferdinand Reyher's screenplay (based on a book by Beatty and Anthony) with most of its thrills. Anita Page was second-billed as a circus trapeze artist, Andy Devine and Vince Barnett were on hand to ease the heart-stopping tension with a few laughs, Raymond Hatton was featured as a played-out animal trainer, and young Mickey Rooney all but upstaged the roaring beasts as a youngster whose only ambition in life is to become an animal trainer himself. Also in it were Wallace Ford (as a former lion tamer), Reginald Barlow (right), Edward Piel and Robert McWade. The director was Kurt Neumann. (82 mins)

▽ **King For A Night** was a well-made, albeit grim, melodrama with a boxing background that allowed a promising middleweight to take the rap for a murder committed by his compromised sister – and sizzle for it. Chester Morris (centre) played the noble pugilist (refreshingly called Bud, rather than the usual 'Kid'), Helen Twelvetrees his sister and John Miljan the promoter she kills. Grant Mitchell appeared in the maudlin role of Morris' paralysed Reverend father, with other roles under Kurt Neumann's direction farmed out to Alice White as a tough chorus girl, George E. Stone (left), George Meeker, Frank Albertson, Warren Hymer, Maxie Rosenbloom, John Sheehan (right) and Wade Boteler. Reminiscent in parts of *The Prizefighter And The Lady* (MGM, 1933), it was scripted, from his own story, by William Anthony McGuire, with Jack O'Donnell and Scott Pembroke. (70 mins)

◁ **Myrt And Marge** (GB: **Laughter In The Air**) was a seemingly interminable piece of unappealing drivel. A backstage B-musical about the dreary vicissitudes of radio stars Myrt (Myrtle Vail) and her daughter Marge (Donna Damerel, Myrt's real-life daughter, too), it had absolutely nothing to recommend it. Bravely battling with the supporting roles were Eddie Foy Jr, Ted Healy (left), Thomas Jackson, Trixie Friganza, J. Farrell MacDonald and The Three Stooges (illustrated with Healy). Beatrice Banyard perpetrated the script, Al Boasberg directed, and the unmemorable sprinkling of songs was by Joan Jasmin and M.K. Jerome. (65 minutes)

△ **The Secret Of The Blue Room**, in William Hurlbut's screenplay (story by Erich Phillip), tested the love of three suitors (Paul Lukas, right, Onslow Stevens and William Janney) by having each of them spend the night alone in the blue room of Castle Heldorf which, since the mysterious murders of three people some twenty years earlier, has remained shut. The object of the foolhardy trio's affections was Gloria Stuart (centre). Lionel Atwill (left) received top billing as the castle's owner, with other members of director Kurt Neumann's cast being Robert Barrat, Muriel Kirkland and Russell Hopton. Though not as successful as *The Old Dark House* (1932) which traversed very similar territory, it nevertheless had some effective moments. It was remade as *The Missing Guest* in 1938, and *Murder In The Blue Room* in 1944. (66 mins)

▽ Frank Morgan joined Universal for **The Kiss Before The Mirror**, an adaptation by William Anthony McGuire of a play by the Hungarian, Laszlo Fodor, in which a lawyer, while defending a client who has murdered his faithless wife, discovers that his own wife is similarly cuckolding him. Morgan (left), not altogether convincingly cast as the lawyer, should really have exchanged roles with Paul Lukas as his client. Nancy Carroll (top-billed, right) was Morgan's wife, and Gloria Stuart the victim of Lukas' jealousy. Set in Vienna, it was stylishly photographed by Karl Freund, and directed by James Whale for maximum dramatic impact, with Lukas' trial scene coming off especially well. Other members of the cast included Jean Dixon, Charles Grapewin, Walter Pidgeon and Donald Cook. It was remade in 1938 as *Wives Under Suspicion*. (66 mins)

△ Lew Ayres (centre) and Ginger Rogers (right) starred in a diverting little comedy called **Don't Bet On Love**. He was a plumber with a passion for horse-racing, she his manicurist bride-to-be. When Rogers discovers that her fiancé plans to spend their honeymoon in Saratoga, she calls the whole thing off, leaving Ayres to come to his senses – a difficult undertaking in view of the fact that he has backed twenty six winners in a row in the wake of his cancelled wedding! Murray Roth, Howard Emmett Rogers and Ben Ryan's screenplay (story by Roth, who was also in charge of the breezy direction) provided the predictable happy ending, ensuring, en route to it, that a good time was had by all, including Charles Grapewin, Shirley Grey, Merna Kennedy, Thomas Dugan, Robert Emmett O'Connor and Henry Armetta in their supporting roles. (62 mins)

△ Director William Wyler's first choice for the role of the Jewish lawyer in the screen version of Elmer Rice's 1931 Broadway play, **Counsellor-At-Law**, was Paul Muni, who had played it so brilliantly on stage. But Muni, himself a Jew, did not wish to become identified on screen as an actor of Jewish characters, and declined the part. It was given instead to John Barrymore at a salary of $25,000 a week, for what should have been two weeks. However, the film overran its schedule, and although producer Carl Laemmle Jr was unhappy at paying out more money to his star, he had to concede – when the film was finally completed – that Barrymore (right) was worth every additional cent. The story of a shrewd, self-made Jewish lawyer who finds himself in danger of being disbarred for some past unprofessional conduct, it also starred Doris Kenyon as his gentile wife – a woman who shows him no sympathy at all and over whom he almost commits suicide when she leaves him – and Bebe Daniels (centre) as the secretary who has always loved him and who comes to the rescue of his shattered emotions. Other roles went to Onslow Stevens, Isabel Jewell, Melvyn Douglas, Thelma Todd (left), Mayo Methot and John Qualen. It was written for the screen by Rice himself and, against much front office opposition, was mostly set in the lawyer's office. Wyler's direction showed no evidence of the short shooting schedule in which he was expected to complete the work, and he did away with background music, except over opening and closing credits (this decision was also taken in the face of studio opposition). The film, which did not shirk the play's underlying suggestions of anti-semitism, was a deserved success, both critically and commerically. (87 mins)

△ Boris Karloff was the first choice for the role of Dr Griffin, **The Invisible Man**, but he turned it down on the grounds that a) his voice was not good enough and b) in terms of actual screen time, he would hardly be seen at all. Instead, the part marked the screen debut of the marvellous Claude Rains (illustrated) who, despite being a victim of the special effects department for much of the film's running time, nevertheless managed to make his non-presence felt. The story of a mysterious stranger who arrives at the English village of Ipping in bandages and dark glasses, hires a room at a local inn and, after experimenting with a drug called monocaine, discovers a means of making himself invisible (the side effects of the process being megalomania), it was the perfect subject for cinema fantasy. Directed by James Whale, the master of the macabre (with considerable help from special effects expert John P. Fulton), from a solid, well structured, unusually literate screenplay by R.C. Sherriff (and an uncredited Philip Wylie), it did full justice to the original H.G. Wells story from which it was taken. Though none of the supporting performances stood much of a chance against the wizardry of the trick photography, respectable contributions were registered from Henry Travers and William Harrigan as Rains' baffled colleagues and from Gloria Stuart as the girl he loves, as well as from Una O'Connor, Forrester Harvey, Holmes Herbert, E.E. Clive, Dudley Digges, Walter Brennan and John Carradine. The film, inevitably, spawned several less effective spin-offs. (71 mins)

△ A variation on the gold-digger theme, **Ladies Must Love** was a breezy comedy that concentrated on the lives of a quartet of young girls, all of whom are down on their uppers. To ease their way financially, they agree to sign a contract splitting each other's earnings four ways. However, when Jeannie (top-billed June Knight) lands a job in a nightclub and meets wealthy Neil Hamilton who gives her a diamond bracelet, the deal is off. All kinds of complications ensue as the rest of the girls (Sally O'Neil, left, Dorothy Burgess, right and Mary Carlisle, centre) find employment in a nightclub revue and double-cross each other outrageously. With a couple of songs (by Harry Sauber and Lynn Cowan) sung by Miss Knight thrown in for good measure, and with George E. Stone (2nd left), Edmund Breese, Arthur Hoyt (2nd right), Richard Carle and Oscar Apfel completing the cast, it added up to a snappy little romp, written by John Francis Larkin from a play by William Hurlbut and directed by E.A. DuPont. (70 mins)

▽ Unlike Richard Arlen in *The All-American* (1932), Robert Young (left), the star of what had hitherto been a contradiction in terms – an intelligent football drama – did not allow campus adulation or the cooings of an enthusiastic press to go to his head. On the contrary, in **Saturday's Millions**, he took a rather jaundiced view both of himself and the game, and it was this realistic approach to the football milieu that made it the refreshing entertainment it was. And although in the end Young capitulates and insists on playing an important match, even though he is injured, Dale Van Every's screenplay (story by Lucien Cary) did not have him winning the match in a climactic and clichéd final touchdown. Grant Mitchell was fine as Young's father, Leila Hyams somewhat less so as his insipid fiancée. The cast, under Edward Sedgwick's no-nonsense direction, also included Johnny Mack Brown, Mary Carlisle, Joe Sauers (later Sawyer), Mary Doran, Paul Porcasi and, as Young's best pal, Andy Devine. (77 mins)

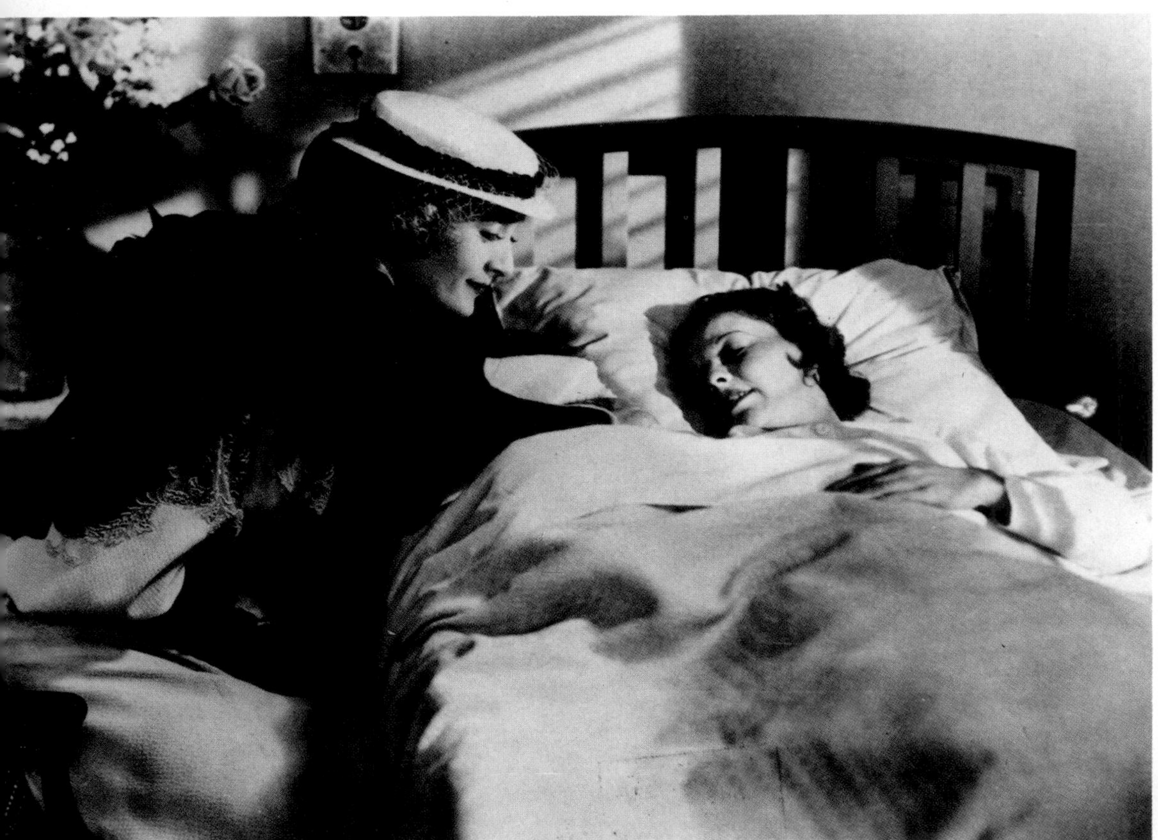

▽ The kookie title of **Moonlight And Pretzels** belied a musical that was, on the whole, a goodie. Monte Brice and Sig Herzig's screenplay (story by Brice and Arthur Jarrett) was pure formula (albeit dealing squarely with the Depression), focusing on the fortunes of a song plugger. The plugger was played by Roger Pryor (his screen debut) who finds himself stranded in a small town. The local glamour girl (Mary Brian) helps him to put on a Broadway show, backed by a wealthy Broadway gambler (Leo Carrillo, illustrated left, top-cast). The top trio were fine, but the best performance – and the best thing in the show – came from Lillian Miles (right) with her delivery of a Herman Hupfeld number called 'Are You Makin' Any Money Baby?'. Karl Freund directed, with Bobby Watson and William Frawley featured in the supporting cast, and unbilled guest appearances by Jack Denny and His Orchestra, Bernice Claire, Alexander Gray, Richard Keene and Mary Lang. E.Y. Harburg and Jay Gorney contributed four songs, among them the title number and the superb 'Dusty Shoes', one of the great numbers of the Depression; Harburg and Sammy Fain supplied 'There's A Little Bit Of You In Every Love Song', and Herman Hupfeld wrote 'Gotta Get Up And Go To Work', another number dealing with the Depression.

△ Margaret Sullavan made her screen debut in **Only Yesterday**, a big-budget romantic drama which began at the time of the Wall Street crash, and flashed back twelve years in the telling of a rather lugubrious story about a young woman (Sullavan) who, as the consequence of a one-night stand with a World War I lieutenant (John Boles), becomes pregnant. When, however, the child's father returns, the unfortunate mother discovers that he has no recollection of having ever even met her. Given the story's credibility gap, it was directed by John M. Stahl for as much pathos as he could wring out of William Hurlbut, Arthur Richman and George O'Neil's screenplay (from a popular history of America up to the time of the 1929 Wall Street crash by Frederick Lewis Allan); and with Miss Sullavan (right) and John Boles successfully bringing flesh and blood to essentially cardboard characters, it managed to pass muster. Contributing in no small measure to its success was the performance of Billie Burke (left) as Miss Sullavan's open-minded aunt; and there was good work, too, from – among others – Reginald Denny, Edna May Oliver, Benita Hume, George Meeker (refreshingly sympathetic for once), June Clyde, Marie Prevost, Jane Darwell, Walter Catlett, Joyce Compton, Onslow Stevens and Jimmy Butler (as Miss Sullavan's son). (105 mins)

OTHER RELEASES OF 1933

The Cohens And Kellys In Trouble
Dir: George Stevens. Strictly passé attempt at comedy has the two families vying unsuccessfully for laughs on a tugboat. George Sidney, Charles Murray, Maureen O'Sullivan, Andy Devine, Henry Armetta. (67 mins)

Destination Unknown
Dir: Tay Garnett. Nonsensical programmer with bootlegger Pat O'Brien commandeering a becalmed rum-running schooner, and stowaway Ralph Bellamy saving the day only to disappear as mysteriously as he arrived. Betty Compson, Alan Hale, Tom Brown. (65 mins)

Fiddlin' Buckaroo (Ken Maynard)
Dir: Maynard. Ken breaks jail after being wrongly accused of a hold-up and tracks down the real culprits who have also kidnapped his gal. Gloria Shea. (65 mins)

Gun Justice (Ken Maynard)
Dir: Alan James. Ken inherits a ranch but finds rival ranchers are disputing his claim and withholding access through to his valley. Cecilia Parker. (59 mins)

Her First Mate
Dir: William Wyler. A merry comedy ensues when wife ZaSu Pitts sinks her life savings into a ferryboat which husband Slim Summerville swaps for a sloop. He explores the world solo, battles with a US destroyer, and finally returns to wife, ferry and happiness. Una Merkel, Warren Hymer, Berton Churchill. (65 mins)

Horseplay
Dir: Edward Sedgwick. Broad but amiable comedy about a rancher who, discovering pitchblend on his patch, becomes a millionaire and, with his backwoods ways, follows his girlfriend to London where the smart set are aghast. Slim Summerville, Andy Devine, Leila Hyams, Cornelius Keefe. (70 mins)

King Of The Arena (Ken Maynard)
Dir: Alan James. Ken plays a Ranger Captain who rejoins his old circus, following a clue while tracking down a gang of villains. Lucille Brown, Bob Kortman. (62 mins)

Laughter In Hell
Dir: Edward L. Cahn. Chain-gang melodrama recounted the experiences of condemned train driver Pat O'Brien, down for murdering his faithless wife. Escape only leads to refuge in a house blighted with contagious fever. Merna Kennedy, Gloria Stuart, Tom Brown. (70 mins)

Love, Honor And Oh, Baby
Dir: Edward Buzzell. Below-par comedy from Slim Summerville as a shyster lawyer who compromises his fiancée ZaSu Pitts, and frames her boss, George Barbier, into taking her on a trip to Rochester. Purnell Pratt, Lucile Webster Gleason. (63 mins)

Lucky Dog
Dir: Zion Myers. Sentimental story of a dog's devotion to his master throughout prosperity and adversity. Buster the dog starred with Chic Sale, Harry Holman, Tom O'Brien. (60 mins)

Nagana
Dir: Ernst L. Frank. In the African jungle Tala Birell is in love with Melvyn Douglas, a doctor in search of a sleeping-sickness cure. Restless natives and menacing crocs. Onslow Stevens, Everett Brown. (62 mins)

Out All Night
Dir: Sam Taylor. Mother's boy Slim Summerville and fluttery fiancée ZaSu Pitts are hindered by overbearing mama Laura Hope Crews who, when the couple finally defy her by marrying, even tries encouraging divorce. A slender comedy with Shirley Grey, Alexander Carr, Shirley Temple. (68 mins)

Private Jones
Dir: Russell Mack. War comedy about a soldier drafted to the French trenches and what befell him there. Not a lot! Lee Tracy, Donald Cook, Gloria Stuart. (70 mins)

Rustlers' Roundup (Tom Mix)
Dir: Henry MacRae. Tom wins the trust and love of a female neighbour whose father has been killed by landgrabbers. Diana Sinclair, Noah Beery Jr. (60 mins)

S.O.S. Iceberg
Dir: Tay Garnett. Routine arctic adventure yarn involving an expedition to recover lost explorers. Greenland's icy landscape upstaged the melodrama. Rod La Rocque, Leni Riefenstahl, Gibson Gowland. (76 mins)

Strawberry Roan (Ken Maynard)
Dir: Alan James. Ken tames a wild stallion to bow the knee and become his trusty steed. Ruth Hall, Harold Goodwin. (59 mins)

Terror Trail (Tom Mix)
Dir: Armand Schaefer. Tom relentlessly pursues an outlaw gang and finally brings them to justice. Naomi Judge, Arthur Rankin. (58 mins)

They Just Had To Get Married
Dir: Edward Ludwig. Assembly-line comedy in which ZaSu Pitts and Slim Summerville receive a large inheritance from an ex-employer. He gambles it away, she divorces him, but all is forgiven and they re-unite for the final fade. Roland Young, Verree Teasdale, Aubrey Smith. (65 mins)

Trail Drive (Ken Maynard)
Dir: Alan James. Ken leads a cattle-drive but finds the operation in danger when the financier pulls out and turns crook. Cecilia Parker, William Gould. (60 mins)

1934

◁ The English actress Binnie Barnes made her debut in **There's Always Tomorrow**, but the undoubted star of the proceedings was Frank Morgan who, as the hero of Ursula Parrot's novel (screenplay by William Hurlbut) committed grand larceny under the noses of a talented cast. Morgan played Joseph White, a likeable, mild-mannered husband and father who is not only taken for granted by his family, but has virtually been put out to graze since outliving his usefulness to them. All that changes, however, with the appearance of Miss Barnes (right). She has been secretly in love with Morgan for years and, realising what has happened to his home life, begins a friendship that allows him to feel wanted again. Though innocent, the relationship is discovered by Morgan's children who, keeping the news from their mother (Lois Wilson), selfishly set about trying to bring it to an end. Edward Sloman's direction made the most of the screenplay and of his cast, which also included Louise Latimer, Elizabeth Young, Alan Hale, Robert Taylor (soon to become a major star at MGM), Dick Winslow, Helen Parrish (left) and Margaret Hamilton. It was remade in 1956. (84 mins)

▽ **Gift Of Gab** was a musical starring Edmund Lowe (right) as a big-headed radio announcer who regains Gloria Stuart's favours by risking his life to supply his listeners with the whereabouts of a missing plane. The gab was a rambling bore, and the gift – a roll-call of starry guests – did little to alleviate the awful tedium. Those wasting their time included Ruth Etting (left), Phil Baker, Ethel Waters, Alice White, Alexander Woollcott, Gene Austin, Andy Devine, Wini Shaw, Boris Karloff, Bela Lugosi, Paul Lukas, and Gus Arnheim and His Orchestra. The screenplay was written by Rian James and Lou Breslow, from a story by Jerry Wald and Philip G. Epstein, and it was directed by Karl Freund. Among the songs: 'Talking To Myself', 'Gift Of Gab' Herb Magidson, Con Conrad; 'Somebody Looks Good' George Whiting, Albert von Tilzer; 'Walkin' On Air' Von Tilzer, Jack Meskill. (71 mins)

▽ Mistaken identity was the theme of **The Countess of Monte Cristo**. It starred Paul Lukas as a film extra who, in the company of Fay Wray (right) – a bit player pretending to be a Countess, attends a swanky party, arriving in a studio car, and convinces everybody that he is the Baron Rumowski. Karen De Wolf and Gene Lewis' predictable screenplay (additional dialogue by Gladys Unger) from a story by Walter Fleisher was hardly a revelation, and it relied on Patsy Kelly as the fake noblewoman's maid to provide the bulk of the laughs. Karl Freund directed a cast that also included Paul Page (left), John Sheehan, Carmel Myers and Robert McWade. It was remade in 1948. (74 mins)

▷ **The Crosby Case** had absolutely nothing to do with an up and coming young crooner fast making a name for himself at Paramount Pictures, but was a murder mystery in which a quack doctor staggers out of an apartment one night with a bullet in his body. So whodunnit? Was it Wynne Gibson (right), seen leaving the apartment house shortly after the killing? Or Onslow Stevens (left) who once owned the killer's gun? Or Edward Van Sloan, a half-blind research engineer? Or John Wray, a police stool pigeon? Or J. Farrell MacDonald, a doorman at the apartment house? Warren B. Duff and Gordon Kahn's screenplay kept audiences guessing, and also gave employment to Alan Dinehart, William Collier Sr, Warren Hymer, Richard 'Skeets' Gallagher, Harold Huber and Mischa Auer. Edwin L. Marin directed. (78 mins)

△ After the success each had made of their respective monsters, it was inevitable that Bela Lugosi (left) and Boris Karloff (right) would eventually share star honours in the same feature. It happened with **The Black Cat**, a truly bizarre concoction of mayhem, necrophilia, satanism and sadism in which Karloff played an Austrian architect, living in a futuristic mausoleum, whose basement contains a collection of embalmed women, including Lugosi's wife. When the latter comes to claim both her and their daughter, Karloff informs him that they are dead – despite the fact that he has married the daughter (Lucille Lund) against her wishes. This information is imparted to Lugosi by a young woman (Jacqueline Wells, later to join Warner Bros. as Julie Bishop) who, together with her newly-wed husband (David Manners), has taken up temporary residence at Karloff's abode. As a consequence of her loose tongue, Miss Wells finds herself being prepared as a sacrificial victim for one of her host's Black Mass ceremonies. Lugosi comes to the rescue, saves her, and skins Karloff alive. The whole thing ends with a bang as the house and the evils therein are blown to smithereens. Though it had little to do with the Edgar Allan Poe story on which Peter Ruric's screenplay was allegedly based, it nonetheless created a convincing pall of gothic horror, thanks to the performances of its two leads, to John Mescall's striking photography, and to Edgar C. Ulmer's atmospheric direction which attempted, with varying degrees of success, to turn a really ludicrous story into something halfway convincing. The rest of the cast included Egon Brecher, Henry Armetta, John Carradine, Herman Bing and Luis Alberni. (65 mins)

▽ Director Frank Borzage's **Little Man, What Now?** was an earnest and sincere attempt to describe the plight of Germany's unemployed in the wake of World War I. It centred on the lives of a married couple whose trials and tribulations were indicative of the hardships which many couples like them experienced at the time of the Weimar Republic. Margaret Sullavan (centre) and Douglass Montgomery (left) played Lammchen and Hans Pinneberg, and only after being shunted from one job to another (in the course of which a baby son is born) do they eventually find happiness. William Anthony McGuire's screenplay (from a novel by Hans Fallada) incorporated a variety of incidental chracters, giving work to Catherine Doucet and Alan Hale as Miss Sullavan's stepmother and lover, De Witt Jennings (right, as a merchant and one of Montgomery's employers), Mae Marsh, Alan Mowbray (as an egotistical movie actor), Fred Kohler, Muriel Kirkland, Monroe Owsley, G.P. Huntley, Etienne Girardot and Paul Fix. (71 mins)

◁ Binnie Barnes (left) received star treatment in **One Exciting Adventure** in which she played a kleptomaniac who simply cannot resist jewels, and camouflages her ill-gotten gains in a crystal chandelier in her hotel apartment (a ploy Alfred Hitchcock would use forty years later in *Family Plot*). Though the film itself was hardly a gem, it was brightly scripted by Samuel Ornitz, Billy Wilder and Frank Schulz, crisply directed by Ernest L. Frank, and also featured Grant Mitchell and Eugene Pallette as a pair of detectives who set out to nab Miss Barnes through the perfume she uses! Neil Hamilton (right), Paul Cavanagh and Ferdinand Gottschalk completed the cast. (70 mins)

▽ Victor Schertzinger, who wrote the music and lyrics for **Beloved**, a seemingly interminable drama that covered four generations of a musically gifted family, was also responsible for directing it. John Boles (centre) starred as Carl Hausmann who, having survived the revolution of 1848, flees Austria for South Carolina. After fighting in the Civil War, he marries, and moves to New York where he ekes out a dingy living by giving violin lessons. Carl's son brings nothing but shame and disgrace on the family, but is killed in the Spanish American War, and it is not until Carl's grandson (Morgan Farley) grows up to reveal a genuine musical talent, that the old man is able to take any comfort from life. He does, however, die a happy man, shortly after the premiere of the symphony he has laboured long to compose, and into which he has poured the agonies of a lifetime. Gloria Stuart (left) played Boles' wife, with other roles going to Albert Conti, Dorothy Peterson, Ruth Hall, Anderson Lawler, Edmund Breese, a tiny Mickey Rooney (right), Louise Carter and Mae Busch. It was written by George O'Neil and Paul Gangelin, and produced by A.B.F. Zeidman and Carl Laemmle Jr. (85 mins)

▽ It took a lot more talent than director Stuart Walker possessed to capture the essential essence of Charles Dickens' **Great Expectations**, more skill than scenarist Gladys Unger brought to the adaptation, and better performances than those offered by Henry Hull as Magwitch, Phillips Holmes (left) as Pip, George Breakstone as the young Pip, Jane Wyatt (standing centre) as Estella, Florence Reed (centre) as Miss Havisham, Alan Hale (right) as Joe Gargery and Walter Armitage as Herbert Pocket. Valerie Hobson was cast as Biddy (later Mrs Joe) but landed up on the cutting room floor which, in view of Biddy's role in the original novel, is indicative of the degree to which it was misread and bowdlerised. Miss Hobson had better luck in David Lean's altogether superior verision in 1946, when she was ideally cast as Estella to John Mills' Pip. Still, as a piece of solid storytelling, the durable tale of an orphan boy's rise in the world, thanks to the provision of a mysterious benefactor, was not without interest, and diligently covered most of the narrative highlights of the novel. It was remade yet again in 1974 with Michael York as Pip. (100 mins)

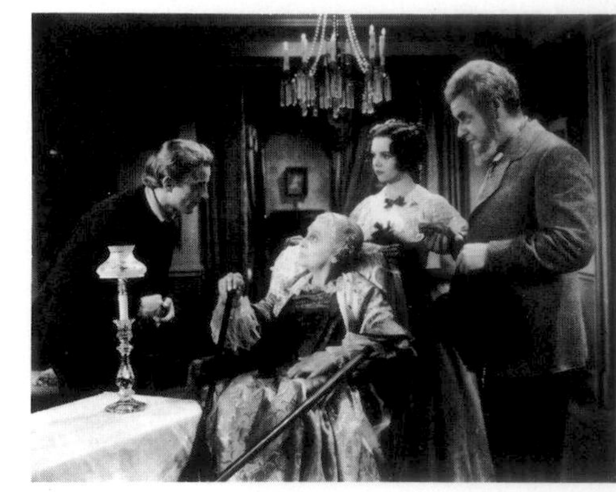

▽ The best thing about **Glamour** was its attractive leading lady, Constance Cummings. Miss Cummings (right), at least, brought a much-needed sense of style to her role as an ambitious chorus girl who, after bettering herself professionally by becoming a dancer, callously jilts her husband (Paul Lukas) for her younger dance partner (Phillip Reed, left). Reed, in turn, jilts the lady, thus paving the way for a reconciliation with husband number one. Doris Anderson's screenplay (continuity by Gladys Unger) from a story by Edna Ferber, was irredeemably trite, and William Wyler's direction perfunctory. Also cast: Joseph Cawthorne, Doris Lloyd, Lyman Williams and Luis Alberni. (73 mins)

▽ **Bombay Mail** was an efficient lower-case thriller in which Edmund Lowe (right), as Inspector Dyke of His Majesty's forces in India, is assigned the task of unravelling the mysterious circumstances, aboard a train from Calcutta to Bombay, surrounding the death of one Sir Anthony Daniels. The case is being treated as murder and, naturally, suspicion falls on a number of passengers, including the strange Sonia Smeganoff (Shirley Grey, left) who isn't all that she appears to be; The Maharajah of Zungore (Walter Armitage), and a character known only as Xavier (John Davidson). Others involved in Tom Reed's neat little screenplay (from a novel by L.G. Blochman) included Hedda Hopper (as the dead man's wife), Onslow Stevens, Ralph Forbes, John Wray, Brandon Hurst, Ferdinand Gottschalk and Georges Renavent. Edwin L. Marin's direction did its best to keep audiences guessing, and succeeded. (70 mins)

◁ The studio's minimal number of musicals in the first half of the decade were certainly not among the best of their output. **I Like It That Way** was a feeble programmer in which Gloria Stuart (left) desported herself as a nightclub star. Roger Pryor (right) played an insurance agent in love with Miss Stuart, and who has a sister (Marian Marsh) who gives up operating a switchboard to plug herself in to a chorus line instead. Harry Lachman directed from a script by Chandler Sprague and Joseph Santley (story by Harry Sauber). Mickey Rooney turned up in a bit part and the rest of the cast included Shirley Grey, Lucile Gleason, Noel Madison, Gloria Shea, Mae Busch and Merna Kennedy. Songs: 'Blue Sky Avenue' Herb Magidson, Con Conrad; 'Let's Put Two And Two Together', 'I Like It That Way', 'Goin' To Town' Sidney Mitchell, Archie Gottler. (67 mins)

△ **Wake Up And Dream** completed the year's trio of musical stinkers. Furnished with an anaemic, not to mention archaic, story and screenplay by John Meehan Jr, it starred Russ Columbo (2nd left), Roger Pryor (centre) and June Knight (left) as a vaudeville trio. Bored audiences sat through their predictable battle to bust into the big time, as well as a romantic triangle which had Russ and Roger both in love with June. The flabby direction was by Kurt Neumann for producer B.F. Ziedman. Also cast: Catherine Doucet, Henry Armetta, Andy Devine, Spencer Charters (right), Wini Shaw and Paul Porcasi Songs: 'Too Beautiful For Words' Bernie Grossman, Russ Columbo, Jack Stern; 'When You're In Love', 'Wake Up And Dream', 'Let's Pretend' Grossman, Stern, Grace Hamilton Note: This was crooner Columbo's last film before his untimely death in a bizarre shooting accident at a friend's house.

▽ A first-rate cast, headed by Claude Rains, Joan Bennett and Lionel Atwill, distinguished **The Man Who Reclaimed His Head**, an otherwise confused drama in which Rains (right) played a writer of anti-war editorials whose employer (Atwill, left) is on the make for Rains' wife (Miss Bennett, centre). Though Atwill deliberately sends Rains into dangerous war zones in order to keep him out of the way, Rains returns home unexpectedly, finds Atwill making advances to his wife and, although they are unrequited, kills the man. Such were the melodramatic goings-on in Jean Bart and Samuel Ornitz's screenplay, adapted from Bart's stage play, and told in flashback. Edward Ludwig directed, and the rest of his cast included Baby Jane Quigley – who managed to hog the limelight in every one of her scenes – Henry O'Neill, Wallace Ford and Henry Armetta. (82 mins)

▽ Director Karl Freund, who was no slouch in the camera department, brought immense visual flair to **Madame Spy**, an entertaining albeit implausible romantic melodrama, full of intrigue and espionage, which starred Fay Wray (centre) as the Russian wife of a German captain (Nils Asther, right). He's working in Austria for a secret service organisation out to apprehend an agent known as B-24; she's none other than B-24. Adapted by William Hurlbut from a 1932 German film called *Under False Flags*, it maintained interest throughout, and included in its cast Edward Arnold and John Miljan (as a pair of Austrian spy experts – Miljan left), David Torrence, Douglas Walton, Oscar Apfel and, in fine form as an old Russian *roué*, Noah Beery. (70 mins)

△ Director James Whale selected a tip-top cast in bringing John Galsworthy's final novel (and the third of the *Forsyte* trilogy) to the screen. As scripted by R.C. Sherriff, **One More River** (GB: **Over The River**) emerged as a solid, well-carpentered drama, whose climactic courtroom scene kept audiences on the edge of their seats. Jettisoning, for the most part, the story of Dinny Cherell, and concentrating instead on the tribulations of her sister Clare, the narrative described how Clare, after being beaten with a riding crop by her husband Sir Gerald, leaves him, meets young Tony Croom who falls madly in love with her, is spied on by her estranged husband, and finishes up in a divorce court with Croom cited as the co-respondent. Diana Wynyard (left) gave a marvellous performance as Clare, and was more than ably supported by Frank Lawton (right) as Tony Croom and the splendid Mrs Patrick Campbell as Lady Mont, as well as by Jane Wyatt (as Clare's sister Dinny), Colin Clive (as Sir Gerald), Reginald Denny, C. Aubrey Smith, Henry Stephenson, Lionel Atwill, Alan Mowbray, Gilbert Emery and E.E. Clive. (88 mins)

▽ Damon Runyon provided the story for **Million Dollar Ransom**, which was recommendation enough. It was basically the tale of a bootlegger who, on his release from a spell in prison, learns that Prohibition is over and that, as a consequence, he has no means of income. Edward Arnold (centre) starred as the bootlegger and Phillips Holmes (top-billed, left) as the wealthy young man who comes to Arnold's aid by offering him a large sum of money to 'kidnap' him in the hope that the ensuing publicity will put a halt to his mother's (Marjorie Gateson) impending marriage to an adventurer. Matters are complicated when a bunch of rival hoods, believing the kidnap to be genuine, decide to claim some of the ransom money for themselves. A rather soft-centred ending, in which Arnold's daughter (Mary Carlisle, right) and millionaire Holmes fall in love, as a result of which Arnold double-crosses his adversaries and so stops a bullet, just didn't ring true. Murray Roth directed it, and his cast included Wini Shaw, Andy Devine, Robert Gleckler, Henry Kolker, Jane Darwell, Jay C. Flippen and Spencer Charters. (70 mins)

▷ Fannie Hurst's assault on the tear ducts, **Imitation Of Life**, didn't disappoint those audiences who treated the cinema as a darkened shrine in which one's own problems are halved by vicariously living through the travails of others. Skirting around such issues as racialism, mother love and self-sacrifice, William Hurlbut's screenplay, concentrating as it did on the essentials of Miss Hurst's novel, recreated the story of Bea Pullman, a determined young widow and mother of a small daughter, who starts life afresh when she opens a flapjack parlour. The inspiration behind the enterprise is the superb flapjacks in which her black maid, Aunt Delilah (also the mother of a small daughter) specialises. In time, the business becomes a flourishing success but, alas, the domestic front is another story – Aunt Delilah's daughter, whose skin is so light she can pass for white, is having such a rough time from the local white fraternity, that she runs away from school and breaks from her mother completely. Bea, meanwhile, discovers that she and *her* daughter are in love with the same man. It all ends in tears, with Bea sending her lover away and Delilah dying of a broken heart. Claudette Colbert (right) was marvellous as Bea, and Louise Beavers (centre) brought tremendous dignity to the sufferings of Aunt Delilah. Warren William (left) was the man loved by both mother and daughter, with other parts under John M. Stahl's sturdy, albeit sentimental, direction going to Ned Sparks, Alan Hale, Clarence Hummel Wilson, Henry Kolker, Henry Armetta and Paul Porcasi. Colbert's daughter was played by Baby Jane (aged three, and later to be known as Juanita Quigley), Marilyn Knowlden (aged 8), and Rochelle Hudson (aged 18); Beavers' daughter was played by Sebie Hendriks (4), Dorothy Black (9), and Fredi Washington (19). It was remade in 1959, by Douglas Sirk, with Lana Turner in the Colbert role. (106 mins)

△ Victor Moore was the *raison d'être* for **Romance In The Rain**, a light-hearted comedy whose screenplay by Barry Trivers and Gladys Unger, based on a story by Sig Herzig and Jay Gorney, was tailormade for the comedian's deflatable personality. In a story that was clearly never meant to be taken with anything more than the proverbial grain of salt, he played the publisher of a lurid book called 'Livid Love Tales'. When an elaborate publicity gimmick arranged by one of his eager-beaver writers (Roger Pryor, left) and which involved a wedding between 'Prince Charming' and 'Cinderella' in front of an audience of 50,000 goes awry, Moore finds himself forced to marry his longstanding girlfriend (Esther Ralston). With Moore on top form as the befuddled executive, the rest of the cast, including Heather Angel (right, as Pryor's love interest), Ruth Donnelly, Paul Kaye and Guinn Williams barely got a look in. And that's just the way audiences liked it. The director was Stuart Walker. (70 mins)

OTHER RELEASES OF 1934

Affairs Of A Gentleman
Dir: Edwin L. Marin. Tedious mystery story of an ardent casanova (Paul Lukas) whose last twelve hours on *terra firma*, before he is killed, are recounted in flashback. Phillip Reed, Onslow Stevens, Leila Hyams, Sara Haden. (68 mins)

Cheating Cheaters
Dir: Richard Thorpe. Remake of 1919 and 1927 story of rival jewel thieves meeting on board ship while their respective 'familes' rob each other's houses at home. All is unravelled and thieves Fay Wray and Cesar Romero are paired in the final clinch. Minna Gombell, Hugh O'Connell, Henry Armetta. (67 mins)

Cross-Country Cruise
Dir: Edward Buzzell. Excruciating complexities proliferate when bus load of passengers on a trans-America journey stumble on murder, intrigue and love. Alan Dinehart, Minna Gombell, Lew Ayres, June Knight, Eugene Pallette, Robert McWade. (75 mins)

Embarrassing Moments
Dir: Edward Laemmle. Mildly amusing comedy ensues when one of practical joker Chester Morris' pranks fails, causing a 'suicide' which turns out to be another prank aimed at teaching him a lesson. Walter Woolf, Marion Nixon. (67 mins)

Half A Sinner
Dir: Kurt Neumann. 'Lack-lustre' and 'far-fetched' describe this story of a conman posing as a deacon in order to rob gullible thrifties in the mid-West. Berton Churchill, Sally Blane, Joel McCrea, Mickey Rooney. (71 mins)

Honor Of The Range (Ken Maynard)
Dir: Alan James. A dual role for Ken as an honest sheriff who loses his badge through his twin brother's stealing. Cecilia Parker. (62 mins)

The Human Side
Dir: Edward Buzzell. Rickety romance about a broke producer hurrying his ex-wife into a wealthy marriage to secure interests of their offspring, but a last-frame reconciliation results in their reunion. Adolphe Menjou, Doris Kenyon, Reginald Owen. (70 mins)

I Give My Love
Dir: Karl Freund. Weepie melodrama in which a woman murders husband, serves ten years, becomes a flower-seller/artist's model in Paris and poses for her son who believes she's dead. Wynne Gibson, Paul Lukas, Eric Linden. (65 mins)

I'll Tell The World
Dir: Edward Sedgwick. Junk newspaper drama starring reporter Lee Tracy who writes about a lost dirigible, then discovers it and a plot to overthrow a mythical government. Gloria Stuart, Roger Pryor, Onslow Stevens. Remade 1945. (85 mins)

I've Been Around
Dir: Philip Cahn. Tediously indecisive in affairs of the heart, Rochelle Hudson cannot decide on a man, throwing over one after another until, after a suicide attempt, she returns to first-love Chester Morris who, in the meantime, has been driven to a global binge by her behaviour. G.P. Huntley Jr, Gene Lockhart. (63 mins)

Let's Be Ritzy
Dir: Edward Ludwig. Moneyless newly-weds Lew Ayres and Patricia Ellis, in danger of losing their apartment and each other, put on the ritz to make their way in the world. Frank McHugh, Robert McWade. (68 mins

Let's Talk It Over
Dir: Kurt Neumann. Tedium prevails as a millionairess pretends to drown to attract the attention of a man. She is rescued by a sailor who falls for her, and ends up working in her factory. Chester Morris, Mae Clark, Frank Craven, Andy Devine. (70 mins)

Love Birds
Dir: William A. Seiter. Misogynist Slim Summerville and man-hating ZaSu Pitts are sold the same property by phoney estate agent Frederick Burton who then offers a handsome buy-back price after rumours of gold (which prove false). Mickey Rooney, Emmett Vogan, Maude Eburne. (62 mins)

The Love Captive
Dir: Max Marcin. Hypnotist uses his powers on several women who fall in love with him, incurring the wrath of their respective husbands/boyfriends. Nils Asther, Gloria Stuart, Paul Kelly, Alan Dinehart. (65 mins

Midnight
Dir: Chester Erskine. Jury-foreman O.P. Heggie, having sent a woman to the electric chair for a crime of passion, discovers his own daughter is guilty of the same crime. Reporter Henry Hull helps out. Sidney Fox. (80 mins)

The Poor Rich
Dir: Edward Sedgwick. Edward Everett Horton and Edna May Oliver, financially embarrassed after a holiday, pretend to be wealthy in order to impress their rich friends. Andy Devine, Leila Hyams, Grant Mitchell. (76 mins)

Rocky Rhodes (Buck Jones)
Dir: Al Raboch. Buck and his sidekick leave Chicago and head west to catch the villains who murdered his father. Stanley Fields, Sheila Terry. (64 mins)

Secret Of The Chateau
Dir: Richard Thorpe. Dullsville thriller unravels story of a Guttenburg bible which most of the characters try to get their hands on. Alice White, Jack La Rue, George E. Stone, DeWitt Jennings, Helen Ware. (65 mins)

Smoking Guns (Ken Maynard)
Dir: Alan James. Ken impersonates a Texas Ranger in order to clear himself of murder and solve the mystery of his father's disappearance. Gloria Shea. (62 mins)

Strange Wives
Dir: Richard Thorpe. Feeble romance recounting Roger Pryor's marriage to Russian June Clayworth who turns out to have a family and equally unwanted lover. Esther Ralston, Hugh O'Connell, Cesar Romero. (73 mins)

Uncertain Lady
Dir: Karl Freund. An emancipated wife doesn't mind her husband leaving her for another woman on condition that a suitable man is found to take his place. House party is arranged to do just that! Edward Everett Horton, Genevieve Tobin, Renee Gadd, George Meeker. (65 mins)

Wheels Of Destiny (Ken Maynard)
Dir: Alan James. Ken plays a roving cowboy who joins a wagon train on its trek through Indian country to California. Dorothy Dix, Philo McCullough. (64 mins)

When A Man Sees Red (Buck Jones)
Dir: Al Raboch. Buck plays a ranch foreman who finds problems when a snooty eastern gal is left the ranch in a legacy. Peggy Campbell, Dorothy Revier. (60 mins)

1935

▽ Lloyd C. Douglas' improbable tear-jerker, **Magnificent Obsession**, with its metaphysical themes of faith and godliness, came to the screen in one of the studio's most prestigious productions of the year. Essentially a 'woman's' picture, and directed as such by John M. Stahl (whose own production it was) with as much emphasis on wringing the emotions dry as was humanly decent in the course of one picture, it top-starred Irene Dunne (left) as a woman blinded in an accident which occurs as a result of co-star Robert Taylor's drunken, wastrel ways. Thereafter, Taylor (right) develops a magnificent obsession to redeem himself, which he does over a period of six years by becoming a brilliant eye specialist able to restore Miss Dunne's sight. He also wins the Nobel Prize. As in the novel, it was a premise hard to take seriously but, handled with the kind of skilful dramatic sleight-of-hand in evidence in George O'Neil, Sarah Y. Mason and Victor Heerman's screenplay, audiences swallowed it whole and, with the arrival of the glossy Ross Hunter remake in 1954 (starring Jane Wyman and Rock Hudson), came back for more. The cast included Charles Butterworth, Betty Furness, Sara Haden, Ralph Morgan, Henry Armetta, Gilbert Emery, Arthur Hoyt, Inez Courtney, Lucien Littlefield, Theodore Von Eltz and, again playing a snobby butler, Arthur Treacher. (110 mins)

△ Director Alan Crosland kept **Lady Tubbs** bright and breezy, and was particularly fortunate in having Alice Brady (left) as his leading lady. Taking a healthy swipe at the *haute monde*, Barry Trivers' scenario (from a novel by Homer Croy) concerned itself with Miss Brady's conversion from a construction worker's cook to a lady in society. In the process, Brady exposes the shallowness of most of 'society's' members, and saves third-billed Anita Louise from the grip of elitism. Douglass Montgomery co-starred as Miss Louise's boyfriend, with other roles going to Alan Mowbray (centre), Minor Watson (right), Russell Hicks, Hedda Hopper, June Clayworth, Lumsden Hare and Walter Brennan. (69 mins)

▽ The good news was that Edward Arnold (left) was given the key role of Diamond Jim Brady in **Diamond Jim**. The bad news was that nothing about Preston Sturges' greatly embroidered screenplay from Parker Morrell's biography (adapted by Harry Clork and Doris Malloy) was worthy of its star; or of the legendary character on whose life it was based. A gross distortion of the facts, it was a typical rags-to-riches story, whose largely fictitious narrative (with undue emphasis being placed on Brady's voracious appetite) involved the multi-millionaire in an unrequited love affair with Jean Arthur who loves Cesar Romero who, in turn, is the object of Binnie Barnes' affections – Miss Barnes (right), on this occasion, playing Lillian Russell. The fact that all four leading players rose above the superficial level of the screenplay – with Arnold particularly impressive in the title role – made audiences regret all the more that the vehicle they graced didn't return the compliment. It was directed with more than a trace of vulgarity by Edward Sutherland, whose excellent supporting cast included Eric Blore, Hugh O'Connell, George Sidney, William Demarest, Otis Harlan, Henry Kolker, Purnell Pratt and Tully Marshall. (88 mins)

▽ What happened **East Of Java** was that an Oriental sailing vessel, together with its crew, passengers, and a cargo of dangerous animals, ran aground on a desert island, with the animals creating serious hazards for the humans. Top-starred Charles Bickford (left) played a wanted criminal who, when the animals aren't stealing his thunder, dominates the lives of the castaways, with other roles going to Leslie Fenton as the captain of the wrecked ship, Clarence Muse as the first mate (a part which allowed him to indulge his talent for negro spirituals), Sig Rumann as an animal trainer, Elizabeth Young (right, the only woman present), Jay Gilbuena and Edgar Norton. George Melford, working from a scenario by Paul Peres and James Ashmore Creelman (who, in turn, adapted it from a story by Gouverneur Morris called *Tiger Island*), loaded the narrative with as much action as it could conceivably support, and with particular (and obvious) emphasis placed on the threat imposed by the wild animals. (72 mins)

▽ The original ending showing the death of Boris Karloff (right), alias Frankenstein's monster, was sensibly shelved by the studio when Carl Laemmle Jr realised what a hot property he had in the monster, and he commissioned a sequel to *Frankenstein* (1931) from John L. Balderston and William Hurlbut. The result was **The Bride Of Frankenstein**, in which the monster (more human than in the earlier film) having, it seemed, escaped the flames that devoured the old mill at the end of *Frankenstein*, suffers further humiliations when a certain Dr Praetorius (Ernest Thesiger) who the monster meets in a cemetery, decides that what the creature needs is a she-monster to keep him company. Trouble is, when Praetorius, together with Frankenstein (Colin Clive), succeeds in creating such a companion (Elsa Lanchester, left), she takes one look at her so-called mate and rejects him. The denouement had everyone, except Frankenstein, being blown to bits. Again directed by James Whale (whose final excursion into horror this would be), and with a full-bodied musical score by Franz Waxman to help it along, it emerged as even more outrageous in its baroque excesses than its predecessor. John Mescall's camerawork was especially striking throughout, and nowhere better than in the sequence showing the 'birth' of the she-monster. Valerie Hobson appeared as Mrs Frankenstein, with other roles going to O.P. Heggie (as a blind hermit who provides the monster with hospitality), Dwight Frye, Ted Bollings, E.E. Clive and John Carradine. Elsa Lanchester, in addition to her role, appeared in a prologue as Mary Shelley, author of the original novel from which the central characters were once again drawn. (75 mins)

△ John L. Balderston and Gladys Unger's screenplay of Charles Dickens' unfinished novel *Edwin Drood* (adapted by Leopold Atlas and Bradley King) didn't quite manage to conquer the narrative problem inherent in bringing the book to the screen, but in **The Mystery Of Edwin Drood** they gave Claude Rains (centre) a splendid opportunity to prove just how good an actor he was in the role of John Jasper, the opium-addicted choirmaster of an English cathedral, who kills his nephew Edwin Drood (David Manners, right) because of his own passionate infatuation with Rosa Bud, Drood's betrothed (Heather Angel). Douglass Montgomery (second-billed, illustrated left) played Neville Landless, on whom Rains tries to pin the murder, and was fine in the role. Valerie Hobson (as Helena Landless), Francis L. Sullivan (Mr Crisparkle), Walter Kingsford (Hiram Grewgious), E.E. Clive (Thomas Sapsea) and Forrester Harvey (Durdles) also appeared for director Stuart Walker who, happily for them, concentrated more on characterisation than on narrative. (85 mins)

▷ **Straight From The Heart** went straight to the tear ducts as Baby Jane (Quigley) upstaged Mary Astor (top-starred, right) and Roger Pryor in an old-fashioned weepie which featured Pryor as a ruthless politician and Astor as the innocent woman he gets to help him frame an incumbent mayor by slapping a paternity suit on him (Baby Jane, left, being the issue of that suit). When Astor discovers that the mayor is guiltless and that Pryor is a rogue, she double-crosses him. Her anger is short lived though, for Pryor, thanks to the soft-centred nature of Doris Anderson's screenplay, reforms in time for the final fade. Carol Coombe played Baby Jane's mother, and the cast, under Scott R. Beal's direction, also included Andy Devine (there to provide some minimal laughs), Henry Armetta, Grant Mitchell and Virginia Hammond. (70 mins)

▽ Ferenc Molnar's play **The Good Fairy**, presented on Broadway in 1931 with Helen Hayes as the titular heroine, was worked over by Preston Sturges who, for the screen version, sanitized many of the play's observations on marital infidelity, stitched a completely new beginning on to it, and toned down the moral stance it had adopted on the evils of do-gooding. At the same time, however, Sturges managed to retain the work's basic charm. Although top-starred Margaret Sullavan (as Luisa Ginglebusher) was a bit too earthbound as a young woman whose helplessness in the world attracts the attentions of three very different kinds of men, she certainly didn't disgrace either herself or the film. But it was Frank Morgan who stole the show, as a millionaire who promises to turn Miss Sullavan's husband into a wealthy man. As Miss Sullavan (right) is not married, she quickly rushes to a telephone directory and selects the first name she comes across to become her spouse and the recipient of Morgan's largesse. The man of her choice turns out to be a lawyer, played, with admirable restraint, by Herbert Marshall. Reginald Owen (left) was the third man in the heroine's life – an eccentric waiter. It was directed by William Wyler with a pleasing sense of its fairy tale quality and, in smaller roles, featured Alan Hale, Beulah Bondi and Cesar Romero. It was remade as a vehicle for Deanna Durbin in 1947, retitled *I'll Be Yours*. (81 mins)

▽ Kids, gangsters, G-man heroics, romance, comedy, pathos and dollops of sentimentality were the ingredients of **Three Kids And A Queen**, a popular success with family audiences and an extremely enjoyable hodge-podge. May Robson (left) was top-starred as the 'queen' of the title, an eccentric spinster who is erroneously presumed to be kidnapped. She subsequently pretends that indeed she is kidnapped, in order to allow a reward of $50,000 for her release to benefit an impecunious family (headed by Henry Armetta). It also featured Frankie Darro, William Benedict and a six-year-old charmer called Billy Burrud (right) as the three kids of the title (and Armetta's brood), as well as Charlotte Henry (Darro's mild love interest), Herman Bing, Lillian Harmer, John Miljan, Hedda Hopper and Lawrence Grant. Barry Trivers and Samuel Ornitz scripted from a story by Harry Poppe and Chester Beecroft, and it was competently directed by Edward Ludwig. (85 mins)

▽ The best thing about **The Werewolf Of London** was John P. Fulton's special effects, notably in the beautifully matched double-exposure scenes showing Henry Hull's (right) transformation from Wilfred Glendon, an English botanist, to the deadly wolfman. Hull's performance itself was extremely low-key and unconvincing due, in part, to his reluctance to submit to the kind of elaborate make-up that Jack Pierce had devised for Karloff; and, with director Stuart Walker not nearly as in control of the material as James Whale would have been, the story of a botanist who is attacked in Tibet by a mysterious creature and, after returning to London with a rare plant called 'Marifasa Lupina', becomes a werewolf, hardly achieved its potential to shock – especially as the werewolf was a creature more to be pitied that feared. Valerie Hobson played Hull's wife, with other roles going to Warner Oland (left, as an oriental werewolf called Yogami), Lester Matthews, Lawrence Grant, and Spring Byington. Robert Harris provided the story which he and Harvey Gates adapted, and which was scripted by John Colton. (75 mins)

▽ After his personal success as Diamond Jim in the unmemorable screen biography of the legendary millionaire, Edward Arnold failed to bring much credibility to the role of a good-natured sleuth in **Remember Last Night**. The movie was a supposedly 'sophisticated' melodrama with laughs, which boasted four murders and two suicides, as a group of hard-drinking socialites, after a wild night spent in an alcoholic haze, find themselves involved in a murder case. Those attractive performers Robert Young (left) and Constance Cummings (right) shared star billing with Arnold, with other roles under James Whale's uncharacteristically floundering direction going to Gustav von Seyffertitz (as a hypnotist who is murdered himself just as he is about to provide a solution to the crime), Reginald Denny, Sally Eilers, Monroe Owsley, George Meeker, Ed Brophy, Jack LaRue, Louise Henry, Gregory Ratoff, Rafaela Ottiano and, out to murder them all as far as scene-stealing was concerned, Arthur Treacher in his proverbial role of butler. It was adapted from Adam Hobhouse's novel, *Hangover Murders*, by Doris Malloy, Harry Clork and Dan Totheroh. (85 mins)

△ **Fighting Youth** was a campus drama in which football did not, for once, take pride of place, but gave way to politics. Charles Farrell (left) top-starred as an all-American quarterback who is equally concerned with the number of radical student organisations proliferating across the country, as he is with winning his big games. Seems that Left Wing agents, masquerading as students, have been infiltrating colleges everywhere and preaching Communism. At State College (the film's setting), the radicals are represented by Ann Sheridan, no less, who, together with her followers, is quite prepared to cause chaos and disruption to the all-important football team. As put across by scenarists Henry Johnson, Florabel Muir and Hamilton Macfadden (who also directed), the propagandistic message was that subversive behaviour directed towards the football team was only the beginning. ... Far too simplistic to be anything other than a mildly interesting curiosity, it came and went without raising an eyebrow. Its cast included June Martel, Andy Devine (right), Eddie Nugent, Herman Bing and Phyllis Fraser. (85 mins)

▽ **Sweet Surrender** was a muddled mish-mash of a musical whose implausible plot embraced anti-war propaganda, crime, and a bit of mistaken identity. The improbabilities centred on Frank Parker (right) as a crooner on board an ocean liner to Europe, his dancer girlfriend Tamara (her screen debut) and the dancer's double (also Tamara). The leading lady displayed evidence of talent, especially in the terpsichorean department, and her work in the 'Appassionata' finale, performed at the Paris Opera House, was the high spot of an otherwise depressingly low-level show. The performance of Parker, and of supporting players Helen Lynd (centre), Russ Brown and Arthur Pierson were abysmal. Carl Laemmle Jr presented the movie; Monte Brice directed from a screenplay by John V.A. Weaver (original story Herbert Fields, adaptation Charles Beahan), and the forgettable songs were by Edward Heyman, Dana Suesse, James Hanley and Arthur Swanstrom. They included: 'Love Makes The World Go Round', 'Take This Ring', 'I'm So Happy I Could Cry'. (80 mins)

△ Though *The Black Cat* (1934) failed to attract critical hosannas, it made sufficient money for the studio to reunite its two stars, Bela Lugosi and Boris Karloff, in **The Raven**, whose shoddy screenplay by David Boehm was 'inspired' by, rather than based on, Edgar Allan Poe's poem. Acting-wise Lugosi (illustrated on floor) got the better of his co-star; he played Dr Vollin, a mad surgeon obsessed with instruments of torture (and Edgar Allan Poe) who, after being refused permission to marry the girl of his dreams (Irene Ware, centre), invites most of the *dramatis personae* to a house party and systematically sets about torturing them, using the torture devised by Poe in *The Pit And The Pendulum* for the girl's unobliging father (Samuel S. Hinds). It is Karloff (right), as a mutant called Bateman, who prevents even more flesh being drawn, quartered, stretched, and mutilated. The film brought no distinction to the studio, to its director Louis Friedlander (later Lew Landers), or to a cast that included Lester Matthews (centre right), Inez Courtney, Ian Wolfe, Spencer Charters, Maidel Turner and Arthur Hoyt. (61 mins)

OTHER RELEASES OF 1935

The Affair Of Susan
Dir: Kurt Neumann. ZaSu Pitts and Hugh O'Connell as wallflowers spend the day together on Coney Island. Walter Catlett, Inez Courtney, James Burke. (62 mins)

Alias Mary Dow
Dir: Kurt Neumann. Trite programmer with Sally Eilers pretending to be the daughter of a couple whose own was kidnapped eighteen years earlier. Blackmail rears its ugly head. Henry O'Neill, Katharine Alexander. (65 mins)

Border Brigands (Buck Jones)
Dir: Nick Grinde. Buck plays a Canadian mountie who joins a ruthless gang to get the lowdown on who killed his brother. Lona Andre, Fred Kohler, Frank Rice. (56 mins)

Chinatown Squad
Dir: Murray Roth. Inept thriller about a dim-witted detective and his efforts to apprehend a man who has stolen funds from a group of Chinese communists. Valerie Hobson, Lyle Talbot, Andy Devine. (75 mins)

The Crimson Trail (Buck Jones)
Dir: Al Raboch. Buck resolves a feud between two ranchers, one of whom mistakenly believes the other is a cattle rustler. Polly Ann Young. (58 mins)

The Great Impersonation
Dir: Alan Crosland. Attempted takeover of an English castle by a German spy who impersonates the rightful owner. Edmund Lowe, Valerie Hobson, Lumsden Hare, Spring Byington. Remade 1942. (81 mins)

His Night Out
Dir: Willam Nigh. Timid drug company employee discovers he has a terminal illness, decides to live dangerously, and becomes involved in robbery and kidnapping. Edward Everett Horton, Doris Malloy, Harry Clork. (67 mins)

It Happened In New York
Dir: Alan Crosland. A get-away-from-it-all film star finds herself in New York and promptly falls for a cab-driver who is already affianced to another girl. Lyle Talbot, Gertrude Michael, Heather Angel. (65 mins)

The Ivory-Handled Gun (Buck Jones)
Dir: Ray Taylor. Buck is accused of cardsharping and murder and sets out to clear his name and hunt the villain. Charlotte Wynters, Walter Miller. (58 mins)

King Solomon Of Broadway
Dir: Alan Crosland. Melodramatic gangster fable about nightspot owner Edmund Lowe's attempts to salvage his club by borrowing, then gambling, underworld money. Dorothy Page, Louise Henry, Edward Pawley. (72 mins)

Life Returns
Dir: James Hogan. A doctor's experiments in bringing asphyxiation victims back to life are halted after his discovery that his sponsors are really racketeers. Onslow Stevens, Lois Wilson, Valerie Hobson, Stanley Fields, Frank Reicher, Richard Carle. (60 mins)

Manhattan Moon
Dir: Stuart Walker. Lacklustre comedy (with songs) about self-made boy's attempts to seduce a singer and her double in his nightclub. Ricardo Cortez, Dorothy Page. (62 mins)

Mr Dynamite
Dir: Alan Crosland. Edmund Lowe played Dashiell Hammett's cool detective in this competent thriller; Minor Watson was the casino proprietor who engages him. Jean Dixon, Esther Ralston, Victor Varconi. (72 mins)

Night Life Of The Gods
Dir: Lowell Sherman. Potentially amusing comedy, with splendid trick photography, recounting the tale of a man whose talent for turning statues into humans and vice versa results in a series of hilarious events. Alan Mowbray, Florine McKinney, Peggy Shannon. (74 mins)

A Notorious Gentleman
Dir: Edward Laemmle. Charles Bickford murders Sidney Blackmer and frames his fiancée while pretending to protect her, but attorney Onslow Stevens knows better and says so in a disappointing courtroom scene Helen Vinson, Dudley Digges. (75 mins)

Outlawed Guns (Buck Jones)
Dir: Ray Taylor. Buck is cast as an older brother who nearly takes the rap when his younger brother falls into bad company. Pat O'Brien, Frank McGlynn Sr. (62 mins)

Princess O'Hara
Dir: David Burton. Disappointing adaptation of a Damon Runyon story in which a group of hoodlums offer helpless Jean Parker protective custody. Chester Morris, Leon Errol. Remade as *It Aint Hay* (1943). (74 mins)

The Prodigal Son
Dir: Luis Trenker. A German immigrant goes to New York to seek his fortune but finds only disillusionment. Luis Trenker, Maria Andergast, Marion Marsh. (60 mins)

Rendezvous At Midnight
Dir: Christy Cabanne. A mismanaged melodrama about the murder of an ex-police commissioner. Ralph Bellamy, Valerie Hobson, Catherine Doucet. (60 mins)

She Gets Her Man
Dir: William Nigh. Unfunny comedy about press-agent Hugh O'Connell who turns dim-witted waitress ZaSu Pitts into a national celebrity after she foils a bank-robbery. Helen Twelvetrees, Lucien Littlefield, Ward Bond, Warren Hymer. (66 mins)

Stone Of Silver Creek (Buck Jones)
Dir: Nick Grinde. Buck plays a square-shooting dance hall and gambling proprietor who discovers a plan to rob him of gold. Niles Welch, Noel Francis. (63 mins)

Storm Over The Andes
Dir: Christy Cabanne. Adventure programmer with Jack Holt as a pilot encountering aggro from his Bolivian counterparts, as well as from his superior officer for whose wife he makes an innocent play. Antonio Moreno, Mona Barrie, Grant Withers. (82 mins)

Stormy
Dir: Louis Friedlander. A horse-loving lad is befriended by two bickering ranchers and saves a pack of wild horses from being slaughtered. Noah Beery Jr. (67 mins)

Sunset Of Power (Buck Jones)
Dir: Ray Taylor. Cow-puncher Buck finds his foreman is a rustler and wins the owner's daughter by proving his guilt. Dorothy Dix, Charles B. Middleton. (57 mins)

The Throwback (Buck Jones)
Dir: Ray Taylor. Buck returns to vindicate his father's name in a town that once thought him a cattle rustler. Muriel Evans, Eddie Phillips. (61 mins)

Transient Lady
Dir: Edward Buzzell. Story of a travelling ice-skating show and the problems arising from a murder attributed to one of its stars. Clark Williams, Gene Raymond, Henry Hull, Frances Drake, June Clayworth. (68 mins)

1936

▽ Boris Karloff (right) and Bela Lugosi (left) were teamed yet again for **The Invisible Ray**, a moderately entertaining excursion into the macabre, scripted by John Colton from a story by Howard Higgin and Douglas Howard. Director Lambert Hillyer, however, chose to tone down the horror in his account of a group of scientists in Africa, one of whom (Karloff) discovers radium, is turned homicidal by its side-effects, and proceeds to radium out of existence everyone except the romantic juvenile leads (Frances Drake and Frank Lawton). In the end, Karloff himself is destroyed by his discovery, thus making it possible for the rest of humanity to sleep more easily in their beds. Lugosi was cast as one of Karloff's colleagues, with other roles going to Walter Kingsford, Beulah Bondi, a way over-the-top Violet Kemble Cooper (as Karloff's mother), and Nydia Westman. It was produced by Edmund Grainger. (82 mins)

▽ Written by Adele Commandini and Austin Parker (story by Miss Commandini), **Three Smart Girls** was a simple little tale, couched in sentimental comedy terms, about the attempts (successful, of course) of three sisters to reunite their estranged parents. Henry Koster directed with a style and attention to detail which elevated the basic trivia, and a solid supporting cast did justice to his efforts. What really made it notable, however, was that it marked the feature debut of Deanna Durbin (centre), who soon became the studio's number one money-maker. The teenage diva's pretty face, winsome personality and precocious coloratura overcame her rather limited acting range, and she launched two hit songs – 'My Heart Is Singing' and 'Someone To Care For Me' (by Gus Kahn, Walter Jurmann and Bronislau Kaper) – as well as setting herself firmly on the road to stardom. She also sang 'Il Bacio' by Luigi Arditi, and a couple of operatic arias. Her two sisters were played by Nan Grey (right) and Barbara Read (left), their father by Charles Winninger, mother by Nella Walker, and a gold-digger with her sights set on Winninger by Binnie Barnes. Also: Ray Milland, Alice Brady, Mischa Auer, Ernest Cossart, Hobart Cavanaugh, Dennis O'Keefe and Franklin Pangborn. Joseph Pasternak produded. Twelve years later he repackaged the property as a vehicle for Jane Powell at MGM, and called it *Three Daring Daughters*. Note: Pasternak and Henry Koster (formerly Kosterlitz) were both imported by Carl Laemmle from Germany when Universal's outfit there closed down. (90 mins)

△ **Love Before Breakfast** was the perplexing, non-sequitur title of a piece of romantic flim-flam that would have been even less than it was without the attractive participation of Carole Lombard. Miss Lombard (left) starred as a society lass who, in the course of Herbert Fields' so-so screenplay (adapted from Faith Baldwin's novel *Spinster Dinner*), throws over Cesar Romero for wealthy, older businessman Preston Foster (right). And that was about it. Edmund Grainger's production values were far better than the vehicle deserved, but couldn't disguise the fact that, at its centre, it was a programmer masquerading as something more. Walter Lang directed a cast that also included Janet Beecher (as Miss Lombard's mother), Betty Lawford and, for light relief, Richard Carle. (65 mins)

△ James Stewart (right) received his most substantial film role to date as a reporter in **Next Time We Love**. Margaret Sullavan (left) was top-billed as a Broadway actress married to Stewart, and it was this career clash which caused all the problems in Melville Baker's love-versus-career screenplay (based on Ursula Parrott's novel *Next Time We Live*). A third-billed Ray Milland deserved a better role than he got as the proverbial family friend in love with the heroine. Though a faithful reworking of the novel on which it was based, the film never quite got off the ground, despite charismatic performances from its three leads, and the Grade-A look of Paul Kohner's production. Put the film's pedestrian quality down to the uninspired direction of Edward H. Griffith. Also cast: Grant Mitchell, Anna Demetrio, Robert McWade, Florence Roberts and Hattie McDaniel. (85 mins)

△ For one of its two musical offerings in 1935, Universal returned to the scene of its 1929 crime, **Show Boat**, and emerged vindicated and triumphant under James Whale's memorable direction. On this occasion the cast, with two exceptions (Helen Westley as Parthenia Hawks and Queenie Smith as Ellie), had all been in one of the several stage versions of this Edna Ferber-Jerome Kern-Oscar Hammerstein II masterpiece, and their familiarity and expertise with the material was shiningly evident. Irene Dunne and Allan Jones starred as Magnolia and Ravenal and were superb; Charles Winninger brought his engaging Cap'n Andy from the original Broadway production; Paul Robeson gave a towering performance as Joe and raised 'Ol' Man River' to new heights; and Helen Morgan was magnificent as the ill-fated mulatto, Julie. Other featured roles were taken by Hattie McDaniel, Donald Cook, Francis X. Mahoney, Charles Middleton and Sammy White. The screenplay, adapted from the 1927 Broadway original by Hammerstein himself, displayed some imperfections only towards the end, where the resolution of certain plot points failed to convince. The relegation of 'Why Do I Love You' to background music was a shame but, otherwise, the numbers were gloriously intact and were swelled by three new Kern-Hammerstein additions – 'I Have The Room Above Her' (sung by Jones and Dunne); 'Ah Still Suits Me' (Robeson), and 'Gallivantin' Around' (Miss Dunne, somewhat embarrassing in blackface). As well as the Kern-Hammerstein score, the film featured 'Goodbye Ma Lady Love' by Joe Howard, 'At A Georgia Camp Meeting' by Kerry Mills, 'After The Ball' by Charles K Harris, and Sousa's 'Washington Post March'. The ravishing camerawork was by John J. Mescall, the art direction by Charles D. Hall, and LeRoy Prinz staged the musical numbers with appropriate style. **Show Boat** was produced by Carl Laemmle Jr, and was the last major production completed under the Laemmle regime. Illustration shows (background L to R): Francis X. Mahoney, Queenie Smith, Sammy White, Irene Dunne, Charles Winninger, Helen Westley; foreground: Donald Cook and Helen Morgan.

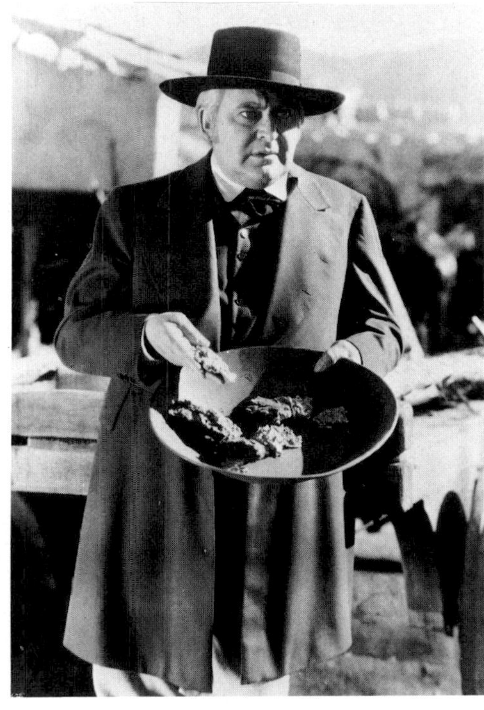

△ Producer Edmund Grainger bit off more than his film, **Sutter's Gold**, could possibly chew in just over an hour. A biography of the pioneer John Sutter, whose prosperous colony in California was ruined with the discovery of gold and the influx of prospectors, it fatally miscast Edward Arnold (illustrated) in the central role. Scenarists Jack Kirkwood, Walter Woods and George O'Neil (working from a novel by Blaise Cendras and story by Bruno Frank) began their account with Sutter's flight from Switzerland after being charged with murder, and described his stay in Hawaii, thus cramming too much incident into their restricted framework with inevitably 'bitty' results. James Cruze's direction made much of the spectacle on offer, but failed dismally on the more intimate levels, and was unable to animate a cast that included Lee Tracy, Addison Richards, John Miljan, Montagu Love, Russell Hopton and Harry Carey. (94 mins)

◁ **Crash Donovan** was a lively programmer which starred Jack Holt (right) as the eponymous hero in a story (by Howard Shumate, screenplay by Eugene Solow, Charles Grayson and Karl Detzer) that was centred on the life and life-style of a California motorcycle highway patrol cop. Thus audiences were made privy to how these men train, just what is expected of them physically and mentally and, as an added bonus, were allowed to accompany hero Holt on a case involving a group of smugglers in them thar Hollywood hills. Newcomers John King (left) and Nan Grey (centre) provided some secondary romantic interest, and Eddie Acuff some comedy. Others lending their talents to the enterprise were Hugh Buckler, Ward Bond, Douglas Fowley and Paul Porcasi. William Nigh directed and Julian Bernheim produced. (57 mins)

△ An absolutely top-notch comedy, directed by Gregory La Cava at the speed of light, **My Man Godfrey** was a whacky delight which joyously brought to life the characters created by Eric Hatch in his novel, every one of whom gave the distinct impression that they'd been dropped on their heads at birth. Godfrey, a former socialite turned East Side bum after an unsuccessful love affair, is attempting to rehabilitate himself by working as an all-purpose butler to the dotty Bullock family. The screwiest screwball of all is one of the Bullock daughters, who manages to ensnare Godfrey as her husband. The urbane William Powell (right) starred as Godfrey, and was paired with Carole Lombard (left) as his successful temptress. Mrs Bullock (Angelica to her friends) was wonderfully played by Alice Brady, her husband was Eugene Pallette, and their tempestuous second daughter Gail Patrick. Mischa Auer appeared as a gigolo of sorts, and was very funny if you liked Mischa Auer; Jean Dixon was a maid, and Alan Mowbray a millionaire. Franklin Pangborn turned up as a master of ceremonies, and the cast was completed by Grady Sutton, Ed Gargan, Robert Light, James Flavin and Robert Perry. Future star Jane Wyman made a somewhat inauspicious debut as an extra at a party. The laugh-a-line screenplay was by Morrie Ryskind and novelist Hatch. Charles R. Rogers produced. It was remade in 1957. (92 mins)

◁ Victor McLaglen (centre) and William Hall (right) starred in **The Magnificent Brute** as steel mill workers who are at loggerheads both professionally and privately. Binnie Barnes (left) was the gold-digger that both men are after, but there was other plot-a-plenty in Owen Francis and Lewis J. Foster's screenplay, most of it originating with Hall misappropriating money that does not belong to him, and causing a rift between Miss Barnes and McLaglen. Thanks to the intervention of Jean Dixon (as the mistress of a boarding house), all ended well. Producer Edmund Grainger assembled a cast that included Henry Armetta (providing some light relief), youngster Billy Burrud (as Miss Dixon's son), Edward Norris and Ann Preston. The makeshift direction was by John G. Blystone. (77 mins)

▷ An early precursor of the studio's successful series of airport films in the sixties and seventies, **Flying Hostess** was as much a plug for TWA as it was for air hostesses. The latter were represented by Judith Barrett (centre) as a brave and efficient young woman who saves the lives of several airline passengers by landing the plane safely after the pilots have been conked over the head by a pair of gunmen. Apart from that, in the course of the screenplay by Brown Holmes, Harvey Gates and Harry Clork (from the story *Sky Fever* by George Sayre), the film followed the careers of two other hostesses and showed how they are recruited and trained. Ella Logan made her screen debut as the second hostess (and sang 'Bang The Bell Rang' by Irving Actman and Frank Loesser), with Astrid Allwyn completing the trio. Also cast: Addison Randall as a crook (and the man Allwyn marries), William Gargan (left, as a hostess trainer in love with Miss Barrett), William Hall (right) and Andy Devine. Charles R. Rogers produced, and Murray Roth directed with efficiency. (66 mins)

△ **Dracula's Daughter**, a pale sequel to *Dracula* (1931), starred Gloria Holden (illustrated) as the late count's daughter, all of whose attempts to lead a normal, healthy life are doomed by her hereditary addiction to blood. Garrett Fort's screenplay (from a story by John Balderston and an idea by Oliver Jeffries) was short on horror, and none of the cast, under Lambert Hillyer's bland direction, was able to save the film from being a massive anti-climax. Otto Kruger, Marguerite Churchill, Irving Pichel, Edward Van Sloan, Nan Grey, Hedda Hopper, Gilbert Emery, Claude Allister, E.E. Clive and Billy Bevan completed the cast for producer E.M. Asher. (70 mins)

▽ Not even John Wayne was able to come to the rescue of **Sea Spoilers**, a mundane actioner in which he played a Coast Guard skipper whose girlfriend (Nan Grey) is kidnapped by a bunch of murderous seal poachers. Their prime object, to judge from the mortality rate in George Waggner's screenplay (story by Dorrell and Stuart E. McCowan), was to kill every one in sight. Though Wayne (right) couldn't save the film, he was instrumental in bringing about a happy ending by sending an all-important wireless message asking for help. Fuzzy Knight was in it for laughs, Russell Hicks was the villain, and, giving the best performance of all (as the misunderstood son of a Coast Guard big-wig), William Bakewell (left). Trem Carr produced and Frank Straker directed. (62 mins)

△ **The Luckiest Girl In The World** turned out to be Jane Wyatt (centre) who, in the service of Herbert Fields and Henry Myers' screenplay (story by Anne Jordan), sets out to prove to her wealthy father (Eugene Pallette) that, for as little as $150 a month, she can live in New York. The exercise is designed to demonstrate that, should she ever decide to marry her indigent boyfriend (Phillip Reed), she'll certainly be able to cope with poverty. Of course, she doesn't marry Reed at all, because she falls for personable Louis Hayward (right), a fellow lodger. Nat Pendleton (left) was featured as a bodyguard, and director Edward Buzzell's cast was completed by Catherine Doucet and Viola Callahan. Charles R. Rogers' production was aimed primarily at the female members of the ticket-buying public, as was the original story from *The Ladies' Home Journal*. (75 mins)

OTHER RELEASES OF 1936

The Boss Rider Of Gun Creek (Buck Jones)
Dir: Les Selander. Buck is a cattle drive boss who is eventually cleared after being suspected of crooked dealings. Muriel Evans, Harvey Clark. (60 mins)

Conflict (aka **The Abysmal Brute**)
Prod: Trem Carr Dir: David Howard. Virile adventure top-starring gentle giant John Wayne who takes 'dives' for touring heavyweight Ward Bond but turns moral under the influence of blonde reporter Jean Rogers and orphan Tommy Bupp. (60 mins)

The Cowboy And The Kid (Buck Jones)
Dir: Ray Taylor. Buck plays a cowboy-pappy to a fatherless kid and falls in love with the village schoolmarm. Dorothy Revier, Billy Burrud. (58 mins)

Dangerous Waters
Prod: Fred S. Meyer Dir: Lambert Hillyer. Depressing formula adventure about a sea-captain's wife who is found in a clinch with a crew-member while racketeers attempt to flood the ship's hold. Jack Holt, Grace Bradley, Robert Armstrong. (70 mins)

Don't Get Personal
Prod: David Diamond Dir: William Nigh. When expelled college kids offer their services to the highest bidder, Sally Eilers uses them for company on a jalopy trip. James Dunn, Pinky Tomlin, Spencer Charters. (70 mins)

Empty Saddles (Buck Jones)
Dir: Les Selander. Buck's heroics stop the fightin' and feudin' between local ranchers and cattlemen over territory. Louise Brooks, Harvey Clark. (65 mins)

For The Service (Buck Jones)
Dir: Jones. Buck is a government scout in Indian territory who saves a stockade post from a gang of brigands. Clifford Jones, Beth Marion. (65 mins)

The Girl On The Front Page
Prod: Charles R. Rogers Dir: Harry Beaumont. Mediocre story of a daughter inheriting papa's newspaper to the chagrin of the managing editor who threatens resignation, but winds up wedded to her. Gloria Stuart, Edmund Lowe, Reginald Owen. (75 mins)

Love Letters Of A Star
Prod: E.M. Asher Dir: Lewis R. Foster. Suicide or murder? Competent thriller hinges on Mary Alice Rice's death and husband Henry Hunter's attempts to uncover the truth aided by detective C. Henry Gordon. (66 mins)

The Man I Marry
Prod: Val Paul Dir: Ralph Murphy. A playwright defies his domineering mother but, on discovering it is his girl who's responsible for his sudden success at the agency, calls off both career and romance, prior to the obligatory happy ending. Doris Nolan, Michael Whalen. (75 mins)

Mysterious Crossing
Prod: Val Paul Dir: Arthur Lubin. Travelling reporter stumbles on murder while crossing the Mississippi and winds up in the arms of the victim's daughter. James Dunn, Jean Rogers, Andy Devine. (56 mins)

Nobody's Fool
Prod: Irving Starr Dir: Arthur Greville Collins. Programmer comedy about a small-town waiter arriving in New York and outwitting real-estate crooks. Edward Everett Horton, Glenda Farrell, Cesar Romero, Frank Conroy, Florence Roberts. (64 mins)

Parole
Prod: Robert Presnell Dir: Louis Friedlander. Simplistic saccharine-coated prison drama about a paroled prisoner's struggle on re-entering the free world. Henry Hunter, Ann Preston, Grant Mitchell. (67 mins)

Postal Inspector
Prod: Robert Presnell Dir: Otto Brower. Villainous Bela Lugosi tries to intercept a mail shipment. Patricia Ellis, Ricardo Cortez, Michael Loring. (58 mins)

Ride 'Em Cowboy (Buck Jones)
Dir: Les Selander. Buck forsakes his horse for the motor car and wins a big race to save a pretty girl and her father from penury. Luana Walters. (60 mins)

Silver Spurs (Buck Jones)
Dir: Ray Taylor. Buck saves a rich and honest rancher from a gang of rustlers and wins the love of his daughter. Muriel Evans. (61 mins)

Two In A Crowd
Prod: Charles R. Rogers Dir: Lewis R. Foster. Impecunious race-horse owner finds one half of a thousand dollar bill, and a would-be-actress the other. Joel McCrea, Joan Bennett. (80 mins)

Yellowstone
Prod: Val Paul Dir: Arthur Lubin. Limp little programmer about no-goodniks returning to the park to search for $90,000 left there seventeen years ago. Henry Hunter, Judith Barrett, Andy Devine, Alan Hale. (60 mins)

1937-1945

The Durbin Era

The arrival of Deanna Durbin almost certainly saved the studio from bankruptcy in the last years of the thirties. She attracted huge box-office grosses with a series of wholesome soufflés, most notably *One Hundred Men And A Girl* (1937), *Mad About Music* (1938), *That Certain Age* (1938) – after which she received a special Oscar for 'bringing to the screen the spirit and personification of youth' – *Three Smart Girls Grow Up* (1939) and *First Love* (1939) in which she received her first screen kiss from Robert Stack. They were all produced by Hungarian-born Joe Pasternak who settled in California after the studio's European operations ended and who, in the late forties would contribute to shaping the careers of Jane Powell and Kathryn Grayson at MGM.

But apart from the Durbin successes the years between 1937 and the outbreak of war were pretty lean. The plots of Universal pictures were corny and unimaginative – one of the favourite ploys was to focus on a hero accused of a crime he did not commit, so as to spend the rest of the playing time proving his innocence – while the talent both in front of and behind the cameras was generally second rate. There were, of course, the inevitable exceptions, director James Whale being one of them. Whale's good intentions, however, in bringing to the screen Erich Maria Remarque's *The Road Back* (1937), a sequel to *All Quiet On The Western Front* (1930), backfired as a result of some severe miscasting.

Other better-than-mediocre pictures during this period were hard to find but there were the occasional offerings: Boris Karloff appeared in an off-beat thriller called *Night Key* (1937) as a half-blind, mad genius inventor; Danielle Darrieux made her American screen debut in *The Rage Of Paris* (1938) and got the thumbs-up from press and public alike; and, in the same year the Dead End Kids, alias the Little Tough Guys, surfaced in *Little Tough Guy*. Buster Crabbe as Flash appeared in *Flash Gordon's Trip To Mars*, the studio's best serial throughout the thirties. Low-budget westerns (many with Bob Baker) running an hour or just under

Three of the Durbin offerings that helped to pull Universal out of the doldrums of the mid-thirties. *left:* With Herbert Marshall in **Mad About Music** (1938). *below right:* Slightly more grown up in **That Certain Age** (1938). *above right:* With Charles Coleman in **First Love** (1939), the film in which she received her first kiss on the screen.

above: In her 12-year career with Universal, Deanna Durbin made 21 films and in 1938 was awarded a special Oscar 'for bringing to the screen the spirit and personification of youth'. *right:* James Stewart and Marlene Dietrich in the excellent 1939 western **Destry Rides Again**.

continued to plug the first half of double bills, and the studio's roster of 'stars' included such unexciting talents as James Dunn, Robert Wilcox, Noah Beery Jr, William Gargan, Kent Taylor, Preston Foster, Dick Purcell, Wendy Barrie and Nan Grey.

Things perked up slightly after the appointment of Nate J. Blumberg, an RKO theatre executive who, in January 1938, replaced Robert H. Cochrane as president when it became apparent that the studio's austerity policy was a flop. Charles Rogers was replaced as head of the studio by Cliff Work, also from RKO, and between 1938 and 1941 the two new arrivals converted a net loss of a million dollars into a profit of $2.4 million. The films they did it with included *You Can't Cheat An Honest Man* (1939) starring W.C. Fields, the tear-jerker *When Tomorrow Comes* (1939) with Irene Dunne and Charles Boyer, *Son Of Frankenstein* (1939) in which Boris Karloff made his third and final appearance as the monster, and, best of all, George Marshall's *Destry Rides Again* (1939) produced by Joe Pasternak with Marlene Dietrich and James Stewart heading the cast. Other incidental pleasures along the way included *Tower Of London* (1939) with Basil Rathbone and Boris Karloff, and a modest little musical with Bing Crosby called *East Side Of Heaven* (1939) which also featured Baby Sandy, a girl (who played a boy) and who, on the strength of her 'performance', was given a series of comedies all of her own.

Sadly, by 1939 Bela Lugosi's career was on the skids, as evidenced by his dispiriting appearance in a serial called *The Phantom Creeps*. The year which saw the outbreak of the war was also the one in which Richard Arlen and Andy Devine teamed up to appear in three outdoor adventure programmers, all of mediocre quality.

The full impact of Nate Blumberg and Cliff Work's regime was felt between 1940 and 1946 when, with the arrival of World War II (and for its duration) the studio stepped up its output as part of the war effort. The new talent recruited for

Abbott (left) and Costello in **One Night In The Tropics** (1940), the first of many films in their successful career with the studio.

the increased production schedule included a pair of radio comedians called Bud Abbott and Lou Costello, who scored a hit in their first feature, *One Night In The Tropics* (1940), though billed beneath Allan Jones and Nancy Kelly. They consolidated their comic reputations with *Buck Privates* the following year, and were top-billed for the first time in *Hold That Ghost* (1941). In these last two films they appeared with a trio of newcomers called The Andrews Sisters. It was a winning combination and the movies grossed a fortune. Unbelievably, by 1942 Messrs A and C were among the world's most popular performers.

Youth was very much on parade in the early forties and the studio recruited several teenage stars to place alongside Deanna Durbin who was now, of course, growing up. They included the multi-talented Donald O'Connor – Universal's answer to MGM's Mickey Rooney, Peggy Ryan, Gloria Jean, Susanna Foster, Ann Blyth and Jane Frazee, all of whom appeared in a string of budget musicals in the first five years of the decade, together with such specialty acts as The Merry Macs, Tip, Tap and Toe, Six Hits and A Miss, The Merry Maids and The Delta Rhythm Boys. The studio's big-budget musicals, excluding the Durbin and the Abbott and Costello vehicles, were *Hellzapoppin'* (1941), adapted from the long-running Broadway hit and starring Olsen and Johnson, the Technicolored *Phantom Of The Opera* (1943), *Crazy House* (1943), *Bowery To Broadway* (1944) and *Follow The Boys* (1944).

A pattern to Universal's annual output soon began to emerge: a couple of prestige Deanna Durbin pictures, several low-budget horror films, a few outdoor adventures, two Abbott and Costello offerings and as many quickie musicals as possible.

W.C. Fields appeared in four more Universal productions in the forties: *The Bank Dick* (1940), *My Little Chickadee* (1940) in which he was teamed with Mae West, whose sensational career at Paramount was over, *Never Give A Sucker An Even Break* (1941) and *Follow The Boys* (1944).

Low-budget westerns were still made with Johnny Mack Brown, Kirby Grant, Rod Cameron, Fuzzy Knight and Tex Ritter; while Richard Arlen and sidekick Andy Devine were still fighting off the baddies in a continuing series of undistinguished programmers.

The studio's first Technicolor production (excluding *King Of Jazz* in 1930, which used the early two-colour Technicolor process) was producer Walter Wanger's *Arabian Nights* (1942), and it gave star billing to exotic Maria Montez whose curvaceous figure more than compensated for her limited acting abilities. The film's success led to several more colourful adventures in lands that exist only in film-maker's imaginations; they included *White Savage* (1943), *Ali Baba And The Forty Thieves* (1944), *Gypsy Wildcat* (1944), *Cobra Woman* (1944) and *Sudan* (1945), all with virile Jon Hall as Miss Montez's leading man.

left: Deanna Durbin in one of her later films, **Lady On A Train** (1945). *above right:* Another of Durbin's more mature successes, **Christmas Holiday** (1944), in which she starred opposite Gene Kelly. *below right:* In his short stay with Universal between 1939 and 1944, W.C. Fields made five films, including **My Little Chickadee** (1940) with Mae West.

Montez's successor at the studio was the sultry Yvonne De Carlo, whose eye-catching figure rocketed her to stardom in *Salome, Where She Danced* (1945). She asserted her undeniable sex appeal again that year in *Frontier Gal*.

Another sex symbol, Marlene Dietrich, followed her success in *Destry Rides Again* (1939) by playing honky-tonk singer Bijou Blanche in *Seven Sinners* (1940), Claire Ledoux in *The Flame Of New Orleans* (1941) and Cherry Malotte in *The Spoilers* (1942).

The first half of the decade saw a return to the monster genre, the best being *The Wolf Man* (1941) which brought to prominence Lon Chaney Jr in the title role. By this time the studio was offering two and even three monsters for the price of one as in *Frankenstein Meets The Wolf Man* (1943) and *House Of Frankenstein* (1945), the latter a free-for-all featuring the Frankenstein monster and Dracula as well as the Wolf Man! But the golden days of the horror pic were over, as was painfully clear from such efforts as *The Invisible Woman* (1940), *The Mummy's Tomb* (1942), *The Mummy's Ghost* (1944), *The Mummy's Curse* (1945) and *House Of Dracula* (1945).

Also offering diminishing returns was the studio's series of twelve Sherlock Holmes thrillers, starring Basil Rathbone as Holmes and Nigel Bruce as Watson. The series began well enough in 1942 with *Sherlock Holmes And The Voice Of Terror*, maintained the standard in *Sherlock Holmes And The Secret Weapon* (1943), *Sherlock Holmes Faces Death* (1943) and *The Scarlet Claw* (1944), but steadily declined in direct proportion to Rathbone's loss of interest in the character.

Alfred Hitchcock's *Saboteur* (1942), with its exciting collection of set-pieces, and his superior *Shadow Of A Doubt* the following year, were two more notable offerings in the first half of the forties – a period which also saw a trio of fine *films noir*: *Christmas Holiday* (1944, directed by Robert Siodmak) with Deanna Durbin and Gene Kelly; *Lady On A Train* (1945, directed by Charles David) with Durbin; and *Uncle Harry* (1945, also directed by Siodmak) with George Sanders. Notable too was *Scarlet Street* (1945), produced and directed by Fritz Lang and starring Edward G. Robinson.

By 1945 the studio was releasing an average of a feature a week. The war generated a continual need for escapist entertainment and the box-offices had never been so busy. In accordance with wartime regulations the healthy profit was used for improving facilities at the studio; two new sound stages were erected, roads widened, and existing buildings enlarged. The studio released nearly 350 features between 1940 and 1945 and for the industry in general, and Universal in particular, the future looked assured.

Two of Universal's leading glamour girls of the forties. *above:* Maria Montez in **Cobra Woman** (1944) with Jon Hall. *below:* Yvonne De Carlo in **Frontier Gal** (1945) with Rod Cameron and Beverly Simmons.

left above: Two monsters for the price of one when Bela Lugosi (left) met Lon Chaney Jr in **Frankenstein Meets The Wolf Man** (1943). *left below:* **Saboteur** (1942), with Robert Cummings and Priscilla Lane, was one of Alfred Hitchcock's earlier offerings. *below:* Universal City in about 1943; Lankershim Boulevard edges the front lot, while the back lot beyond is flanked by the south bank of the Los Angeles River.

1937

▽ A melodrama with a race-track backdrop, **Breezing Home** featured third-billed Wendy Barrie (right) as a nightclub singer (she sang 'I'm Hitting The High Spots' and 'You're In My Heart Again' by Jimmy McHugh and Harold Adamson), co-starred William Gargan (left) as a conscientious, thoroughly honest trainer of thoroughbreds, and top-starred Binnie Barnes as the socialite owner of a stable. Charles Grayson's adaptation of Finley Peter Jr and Philip Dunne's story, got off to an unsteady start, but perked up when Gargan's favourite horse, Galaxy, is transferred to a crooked bookie (Alan Baxter) who, in turn, makes a gift of it to his girlfriend (Miss Barrie). The film really got into its stride after Galaxy was injured in a crooked race and Miss Barrie, on the road to reform, nurses the thoroughbred back to health rather than see him destroyed. Milton Carruth directed it breezily enough, and producer Edmund Grainger selected a solid supporting cast that included Raymond Walburn, Alma Kruger, Michael Loring, Elisha Cook Jr and, as a stereotyped coloured stable hand, Willie Best. (65 mins)

△ **Merry-Go-Round of 1938** went round and round in search of merriment, but found very little. It was no more than a feverish and generally unamusing peek at the farcical antics of Bert Lahr (right) and Jimmy Savo in Hollywood. However, it did offer Lahr's rendition of 'The Woodman's Song' (by E.Y. Harburg and Harold Arlen), as well as comedian Savo's 'River Stay 'Way From My Door' (by Mort Dixon and Harry Woods) by way of diversion. Monte Brice and A. Dorian Otvos wrote it from a story by Brice and Harry Myers. Also caught up in the ride: Mischa Auer (left), Billy House (centre), Alice Brady, Joy Hodges, Louise Fazenda, and Dave Apollon and His Orchestra. The producer was Charles R. Rogers, the director Irving Cummings. Other songs: 'I'm In My Glory', 'More Power To You', 'You're My Dish' Harold Adamson, Jimmy McHugh. (82 mins)

△ Musical star Alice Faye (2nd left) came to Universal for the first time in **You're A Sweetheart**. Not surprisingly, it was also the last time, for the studio served up a dull and nonsensical movie that in no way did justice to their leading lady's gifts. A long-winded storyline (by Warren Wilson, Maxwell Shane and William Thomas) addressed itself to a publicity-seeking producer's attempts to mount his new show on Broadway. George Murphy (3rd left) played the producer, and he and Miss Faye danced the title number (by Harold Adamson and Jimmy McHugh) with unexpected expertise. Mickey Bloom, Arthur Quenzer and Lou Bring's 'So It's Love', sung by Faye, was another of the show's better moments, but the rest of the venture was extremely stale. The cast also featured Charles Winninger, Andy Devine (in doorway), Ken Murray (left), Frances Hunt (4th left), William Gargan, Frank Jenks, and Donald Meek, and there were specialty numbers from The Four Playboys, Malda and Ray, and The Noville Brothers. The screenplay was by Monte Brice and Charles Grayson, and David Butler directed for producer Buddy De Sylva. Remade in 1943 as *Cowboy From Manhattan*. Other songs included: 'Broadway Jamboree', 'Oh, Oh, Oklahoma' Adamson McHugh; 'Scraping The Toast' Murray Mencher, Charles Tobias. (98 mins)

▷ A big hit for the studio, **One Hundred Men And A Girl** owed its success to a combination of its delightful story, and the spontaneous vitality and fresh charm of Deanna Durbin (centre). The young soprano appeared as a girl determined to enlist eminent conductor Leopold Stokowski's aid in launching an orchestra which would give work to one hundred unemployed musicians, one of whom is her widowed father (Adolphe Menjou, left). The young lady remains undaunted in the face of all obstacles, and finally marches the entire orchestra into the home of the unsuspecting maestro who capitulates by conducting Liszt's *Hungarian Rhapsody No 2* from the top of his staircase. It was a fairy-tale from start to finish, and audiences loved it. There were opportunities, too, for Deanna to break into song, and if her rendition of 'The Drinking Song' from Verdi's *La Traviata* was a shade uncertain, nobody minded. The stalwart supporting cast also featured Eugene Pallette, Mischa Auer (right) and Alice Brady, and the simple but effective screenplay was by Bruce Manning, Charles Kenyon, Hans Kraly and James Mulhauser. It was produced by Charles R. Rogers and Joe Pasternak, and directed with a light and confident touch by Henry Koster. Other songs and music included the hit 'It's Raining Sunbeams' by Sam Coslow and Frederick Hollander as well as 'A Heart That's Free' Alfred G. Robyn, Thomas T. Railey; 'Alleluia' Mozart (from Exultate, Jubilate K165); excerpts from *Lohengrin* Wagner and Tchaikovsky's *Fifth Symphony*. Interesting sideline: After the film's release, Miss Durbin's contract was revised, doubling her salary to $3000 a week, with a $10,000 bonus for each subsequent film. (84 mins)

▽ In his 56th film, **California Straight Ahead**, John Wayne (centre) played the driver of a high-powered truck who embarks on a contest with a train to see which of the two vehicles – each carrying aviation parts, but for rival manufacturers – will arrive at its destination first. The destination is a trans-Pacific liner, and the reason for the urgency is a threatened labour strike which the drivers hope to beat by effecting delivery of the goods before the strike commences. Pretty Louise Latimer co-starred for producer Trem Carr, whose cast also included Robert McWade, Tully Marshall, Theodore Von Eltz, LeRoy Mason and Grace Goodall. Scott Darling scripted from a story by Herman Boxer, and it was directed with as much distinction as the material allowed by Arthur Lubin. (67 mins)

◁ **Top Of The Town**, a musical, was the essence of mediocrity. Nobody was actually bad, nobody was particularly good; it wasn't totally boring, but it wasn't madly entertaining. The plot was not unpromising but somebody (could it be associate producer Lou Brock who wrote the story) forgot to develop it, and it turned out to be little more than a trifle about a Manhattan heiress (Doris Nolan, right) who opens a nightclub for the smart set atop a skyscraper. Enter Gertrude Niesen to sing a clutch of Harold Adamson-Jimmy McHugh songs, and Ella Logan to do the same. The Three Sailors (alias Jason, Robson and Blue, left) imitated a giraffe; Mischa Auer was excruciating in an extract from *Hamlet*, and Peggy Ryan, aged 12 at the time, made her debut. Also in it: Gregory Ratoff (as an agent), George Murphy (centre right), Hugh Herbert (centre), Henry Armetta, Claude Gillingwater, Ernest Cossart, The Californian Collegians, and The Four Esquires. Brown Holmes and Charles Grayson sketched the screenplay and Ralph Murphy directed. Songs included: 'Blame It On The Rhumba', 'Where Are You?', 'Top Of The Town', 'I Feel That Foolish Feeling Coming On', 'Fireman Save My Child'. (86 mins)

▽ A sequel to *All Quiet On The Western Front* (1930), **The Road Back** was fatally flawed by the inappropriate casting of Slim Summerville as Tjaden and Andy Devine as Willy. Though the characters in themselves (certainly as written by Erich Maria Remarque, on whose book R.C. Sherriff and Charles Kenyon based their screenplay) were not without humour, it was a grievous piece of ill-judgement to reduce them to the level of slapstick. This approach unbalanced a potentially powerful drama whose purpose was to describe the bitter aftermath of war, and to show the heartbreaking plight of the young men who tried to find 'the road back' to normalcy after four devastating years in the trenches. In short, producer Charles R. Rogers trivialised a subject that deserved nobler treatment. Not everything was lost, however, thanks to James Whale's first-rate, fluid direction of the more suitably cast performers – the death of Wessling (Noah Beery Jr, left) and Ernst's (John King, right) homecoming being especially effective. Also in it: Barbara Read, Louise Fazenda, Richard Cromwell, Etienne Girardot, Lionel Atwill, Greta Gynt, Spring Byington, Laura Hope Crews and Samuel S. Hinds. (103 mins)

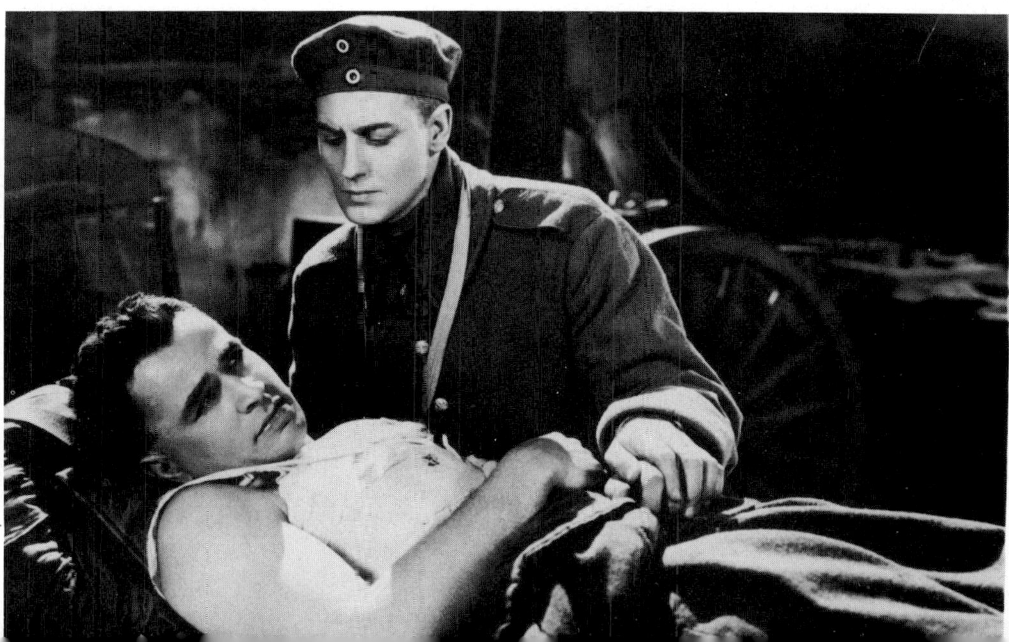

▽ **Night Key** was a quirky little thriller which benefitted enormously from the casting of Boris Karloff as an elderly, half-blind, wholly eccentric inventor-cum-mad genius. Twenty years prior to the film's start, Karloff (centre) was gypped out of his burglar alarm invention by the unscrupulous Samuel S. Hinds, but finally perfects an invisible ray alarm that neutralises the effects of the first machine. How Karloff puts this gadget to work and gets his revenge for the wrong done to him all those years ago, framed the enjoyable hokum of J.C. Moffitt and Tristram Tupper's screenplay (story by William Pierce). Warren Hull and Jean Rogers were the juve leads and romantic interest, and producer Robert Presnell's cast was completed by Hobart Cavanaugh, Alan Baxter (right), David Oliver, Edwin Maxwell and Ward Bond (centre right). Lloyd Corrigan directed. (67 mins)

△ There was a fair amount of fun on offer in **A Girl With Ideas**, but very little accuracy in terms of the newspaper milieu it purported to portray. A romantic fairytale in which capable Wendy Barrie (centre) inherits a newspaper that once libelled her and, much to the chagrin of its former owner (Walter Pidgeon, right), boosts its circulation as soon as she takes control, it moved at a jaunty pace and never outstayed its welcome. The semblance of plot (story by William Rankin, script by Bruce Manning and Robert T. Shannon) had pouting Pidgeon framing the fake kidnapping of Barrie's father (George Barbier) then giving the story to a rival paper. S. Sylvan Simon's direction kept it breezing along, as did a cast that included Kent Taylor (left), Dorothea Kent (as a blonde blackmailer), Ted Osborn, Henry Hunter, Samuel S. Hinds and Ed Gargan. (70 mins)

▽ Virginia Bruce, displaying a pleasing sense of comedy, was the star of **When Love Is Young**, a modest but thoroughly agreeable comedy. Miss Bruce (centre) was Wanda Werner – the girl most unlikely to succeed – who confounds the campus sceptics who once snubbed her when she returns in triumph as a Broadway star and is given a civic welcome. An engaging exercise in wish fulfilment, it also starred Kent Taylor (right) as Miss Bruce's likeable press agent (and the man she eventually marries), with other parts under famous cameraman Hal Mohr's direction going to William Tannen (as an insufferably conceited campus hero with whom Miss Bruce was once infatuated), Walter Brennan (left), Greta Meyer, Sterling Holloway and Jack Smart. Eve Green and Joseph Fields scripted, from the story *Class Prophecy* by Eleanore Griffin, and the producer was Robert Presnell. Two songs, 'When Love Is Young' and 'Did Anyone Ever Tell You' by Harold Adamson and Jimmy McHugh, were featured. (75 mins)

▽ Some solid virtues, such as an adequate script, attractive central performances and a sturdy physical production that was always good to look at, were to the credit of **Wings Over Honolulu**. The film also gave Wendy Barrie (left) as the Southern belle wife of a naval airman transferred to Pearl Harbour on their wedding day, the strongest role of her career so far. Ray Milland (right) played her on-the-move husband, whose transfer to Hawaii unleashes a revolt of sorts in his spouse who follows him there, only to discover that he is far too busy on naval manouevres to pay her much attention. To spite him, she takes up with an old flame (Kent Taylor) – an unwise move which leads to all sorts of complications, and which scenarists Isabel Dawn and Boyce DeGaw (story by Mildred Cram) unravelled for a satisfying if somewhat predictable conclusion. William Gargan, relative newcomer Polly Rowles, Samuel S. Hinds, Mary Philips, Clara Blandick and Louise Beavers were also featured for director H.C. Potter and producer Charles R. Rogers. (78 mins)

◁ **I Cover The War**, written by George Waggner from a story by Bernard McConville, starred John Wayne (centre) and Don Barclay (right) as a pair of newsreel cameramen who crush an Arab revolt in Mesopotamia, unmask a rebel leader, and save an entire regiment of Lancers from destruction. A romantic adventure yarn, to be enjoyed for the *Boys' Own* actioner it was, it was produced by Trem Carr with supporting players Arthur Aylesworth (left), Jack Mack (2nd left), Franklin Parker (centre left), Earle Hodgins (2nd right), Gwen Gaze, Pat Somerset, Major Sam Harris, Charles Brokaw and James Bush contributing their share to the gung-ho heroics. Arthur Lubin directed on location – in California! (93 mins)

OTHER RELEASES OF 1937

Adventure's End
Prod: Trem Carr Dir: Arthur Lubin. Adventure never began in this potboiler about three Pacific whale-fishermen. Probably John Wayne's worst film ever. Diana Gibson, Moroni Olsen, Montagu Love, Maurice Black, Paul Winter, Cameron Hall. (63 mins)

Armored Car
Prod: E.M. Asher Dir: Lewis R. Foster. Oh-so-familiar story of an undercover detective's attempts to apprehend armored-car robbers by joining the gang. Robert Wilcox, Judith Barrett, Irving Pichel, Cesar Romero. (64 mins)

As Good As Married
Prod: E.M. Asher Dir: Edward Buzzell. Worn-out comedy theme of boss marrying secretary to avoid alimony suit and reduce tax. Turns out he really loves the doll and always did. John Boles, Doris Nolan, Alan Mowbray, Dorothea Kent. (73 mins)

Behind The Mike
Prod: Lou Brock Dir: Sidney Salkow. Old-fashioned gag-infested screenplay about two rival radio-station managers and their machinations. William Gargan, Don Wilson, Judith Barrett. (68 mins)

Black Aces (Buck Jones)
Dir: Buck Jones. Buck brings a gang of blackmailers to justice when his girlfriend accuses him of cowardice. Kay Linaker, Robert Frazer. (59 mins)

Boss Of Lonely Valley (Buck Jones)
Dir: Ray Taylor. Buck plays a government agent sent to investigate a crook who has gained control of a valley through forged documents. Muriel Evans. (60 mins)

Carnival Queen
Prod: Robert Presnell Dir: Nate Watt. The owner of a travelling carnival joins the show incognito and discovers it is being run by a gang of crooks. Dorothea Kent, Robert Wilcox, Hobart Cavanaugh. (66 mins)

Courage Of The West (Bob Baker)
Dir: Joseph H. Lewis. An adopted boy grows up to become a Free Ranger and discovers his father is a bandit leader. J. Farrell Macdonald, Buddy Cox. (56 mins)

Four Days Wonder
Prod: Robert Presnell Dir: Sidney Salkow. A child mystery enthusiast becomes involved in a real murder and attaches herself to a detective-story writer. Jeanne Dante, Kenneth Howell, Martha Sleeper. (60 mins)

Girl Overboard
Prod: Robert Presnell Dir: Sidney Salkow. Barely releasable programmer about an ex-mannequin blamed for the murder of her amorous ex-employer at sea, then proved innocent after the ship catches fire and the real culprit drowns. Gloria Stuart, Sidney Blackmer, Walter Pidgeon, Hobart Cavanaugh. (58 mins)

The Idol Of The Crowds
Prod: Paul Malvern Dir: Arthur Lubin. Feeble story of a hockey player threatened after refusing to cheat; his integrity gets him the girl but injures the team's 12-year-old mascot. John Wayne, Billy Burrud, Sheila Bromley. (62 mins)

The Lady Fights Back
Prod: Edmund Grainger Dir: Milton Carruth. Not much to fight for in this romantic drama which paired Irene Hervey with dam-builder Kent Taylor, both of whom fight to preserve local salmon ecology. William Lundigan, Willie Best, Frank Jenks. (61 mins)

Law For Tombstone (Buck Jones)
Dir: Charles Jones. Buck is a Texas Ranger sent to Tombstone to end a reign of terror organised by a mysterious bandit. Muriel Evans. (59 mins)

Left-handed Law (Buck Jones)
Dir: Les Selander. Buck restores law and order to a town in New Mexico that has been helpless against a daring gang of outlaws. Lee Phelps, Noel Francis. (62 mins)

Let Them Live
Prod: Edmund Grainger Dir: Harold Young. One-man vigilante operation to rid community of political sharks. Honest medic John Howard falls in love with Nan Grey en route to objective. Above-average. Edward Ellis, Judith Barrett, Robert Wilcox. (72 mins)

Love In A Bungalow
Prod: E.M. Asher Dir: Raymond B. McCarey. Boring story about unmarried couple Nan Grey and Kent Taylor's participation in a radio contest for marrieds only; they promptly win $5,000 and have to carry on the pretence. Louise Beavers, Richard Carle. (67 mins)

The Man In Blue
Prod: Kubec Glasmon Dir: Ralph Morgan. Luke-warm melodrama showing Robert Wilcox suffering for the sins of his criminal father when, as an honest bank-teller, he is unwillingly sucked into crime. Richard Carle, Nan Grey, Edward Ellis. (64 mins)

The Man Who Cried Wolf
Prod: E.M. Asher Dir: Lewis R. Foster Story of an innocent actor confessing to a crime so police will think him guiltless when he finally commits the murder he has always planned. Lewis Stone, Jameson Thomas, Tom Brown. (66 mins)

The Mighty Treve
Prod: Val Paul Dir: Lewis D. Collins. Unassuming but efficient canine story for kiddies chronicled the adventures of youngster Noah Beery Jr and dog Treve (Tuffy) on a ranch run by disapproving Samuel S. Hinds. Barbara Reed. (68 mins)

Oh, Doctor
Prod/Dir: Edmund Grainger. Depressing remake (1925) of hypochondriac's fear that death will reach him before his inheritance. Edward Everett Horton, Drue Leighton. (67 mins)

Prescription For Romance
Prod: Edmund Grainger Dir: S. Sylvan Simon. While pursuing an embezzler, detective Kent Taylor falls for Wendy Barrie, a beautiful doctor in Budapest. Frank Jenks, Mischa Auer, Gregory Gaye. (70 mins)

Reported Missing
Prod: E.M. Asher Dir: Milton Carruth. Kiddies' fare, telling of an ex-pilot-cum-inventor's efforts to track a maniac passenger-plane saboteur. William Gargan, Jean Rogers. (64 mins)

Sandflow (Buck Jones)
Dir: Les Selander. Buck is convinced that his brother is innocent of a murder charge and sets off to find the real killers. Lita Chevret, Bob Kortman. (58 mins)

She's Dangerous
Prod: E.M. Asher Dir: Lewis R. Foster/Milton Carruth. Irredeemable thriller about a girl detective posing as a jewel thief to track down gangsters. Tala Birell, Cesar Romero, Walter Pidgeon, Walter Brennan. (68 mins)

Smoke Tree Range (Buck Jones)
Dir: Les Selander. Buck comes to the aid of a pretty female rancher and her son who are threatened with eviction by some crooked rustlers. Muriel Evans. (59 mins)

Some Blondes Are Dangerous
Prod: E.M. Asher Dir: Milton Carruth. Appallingly scripted boxing melodrama in which a chump turns champ, leaves his girl for another, regrets this on discovering his new love's faithlessness, loses an important fight, and returns to his first love in final frame. Noah Beery Jr, Nan Grey, Dorothea Kent, William Gargan. (65 mins)

Sudden Bill Dorn (Buck Jones)
Dir: Ray Taylor. Buck to the rescue again when lawlessness hits town after gold is found close by. Evelyn Brent, Noel Francis. (60 mins)

That's My Story
Prod: Robert Presnell Dir: Sidney Salkow. A reporter gets himself thrown into jail in order to interview a gangster's moll, but the woman he interviews is another reporter with the same idea. Claudia Morgan, William Lundigan, Eddie Garr. (63 mins)

Trouble At Midnight
Prod: Barney A. Sarecky Dir: Ford Beebe. Audiences stayed away in droves from this western-style gangster movie about stock-raids on a dairy farm. Noah Beery Jr, Larry Blake, Catherine Hughes, Bernadene Hayes. (60 mins)

We Have Our Moments
Prod: Edmund Grainger Dir: Alfred L. Worker. On a cruise to Europe prior to marriage, teacher Sally Eilers gets mixed up with racketeers, but falls for detective James Dunn whom she eventually marries instead. Mischa Auer, Marjorie Gateson, David Niven. (65 mins)

Westbound Limited
Prod: Henry MacRae/Ben Koenig Dir: Ford Beebe. Average adventure story about a railway employee held responsible for a train crash after an incident with a gunman, but who successfully clears his name. Lyle Talbot, Polly Rowles. (76 mins)

The Westland Case
Prod: Larry Fox/Irving Starr Dir: Christy Cabanne. Handsomely mounted but mundane thriller in which a detective saves the life of a man wrongly accused of murder. Preston Foster, Theodore Von Eltz, Carol Hughes, Barbara Pepper. (62 mins)

The Wildcatter
Prod: George Owen Dir: Lewis D. Collins. Wildcatters Scott Colton and Jack Smart leave pretty Jean Rogers to take care of their roadside cafe when they indulge in a spot of Texas wildcatting. (58 mins)

1938

▽ Sally Eilers (centre) was the star of **Nurse From Brooklyn**, a modest and undemanding romance. It co-starred Paul Kelly (right) as a cop who, wounded in a gun battle in which Miss Eilers' brother (Maurice Murphy) is killed, is blamed for Murphy's death. Roy Chanslor's screenplay (story by Steve Fisher) predictably cleared Kelly of the charge, proving that the man responsible was Miss Eilers' boyfriend (Larry Blake, left). S. Sylvan Simon's direction more than gave the piece – which was produced by Edmund Grainger – its due, and the cast was completed by Morgan Conway, David Oliver and Lucile Gleason. (65 mins)

◁ **The Rage Of Paris** was Danielle Darrieux who, in her first American film, captivated audiences and critics alike. A tailor-made vehicle for the glamorous French star, it gave her star billing as Nicole de Cortillon, an employee of the *Casino de France* who, after that establishment's closure, becomes a model. Trouble is, she goes to the wrong address and begins to disrobe in front of Douglas Fairbanks Jr who immediately suspects that she is trying to blackmail him. The plot (story and screenplay by Bruce Manning and Felix Jackson) thickened with the appearances of Mischa Auer (left, as a head waiter) and Helen Broderick as an ex-actress under whose joint patronage Miss Darrieux (centre) moves into an expensive hotel and sets her gold-digging sights on millionaire Louis Hayward. Fairbanks (right) – who turns out to be a friend of Hayward's – sets out to save his buddy from the 'imposter', in the process of which he falls in love with her himself. Henry Koster's direction kept the caper light and airy, and drew performances to match from his cast. It was, in all, a pleasing comedy of which producer Buddy De Sylva had every reason to be proud. The cast was completed by Charles Coleman, Harry Davenport, Samuel S. Hinds, Nella Walker and, making her debut in an unbilled part, Mary Martin. (75 mins)

▽ **The Road To Reno** had absolutely nothing to do with Bing Crosby, Bob Hope and Dorothy Lamour, whose own series of 'Road' movies wasn't due to commence for another two years. It was, in fact, an entertaining romance about a Reno-bound woman (silent screen star Hope Hampton in terrific form) whose divorce plans come to a halt when she decides that she still loves her first husband (top-starred Randolph Scott), despite having promised to wed Alan Marshal. A battle for Miss Hampton's favours provided scenarists Roy Chanslor and Adele Commandini (dialogue by Brian Marlowe) with several really funny sequences involving Easterner Marshal's successful attempts to 'out-Western' Westerner Scott at such outdoor activities as swimming and bronco busting. All the same, it's Scott (right) Miss Hampton (centre) decides she wants, and Scott she gets, in a screen story by Charles Kenyon and F. Hugh Herbert (based on I.A.R. Wylie's story *Puritan At Large*) from which the scenarists worked. It was pleasingly directed by S. Sylvan Simon, who brought out the best in a cast that also included Glenda Farrell, Helen Broderick (left), David Oliver, Ted Osborne, Samuel S. Hinds and Spencer Charters. Edmund Grainger produced. (72 mins)

▷ One of the year's better programmers, **The Jury's Secret** was an adroit thriller in which a ghost writer (Kent Taylor, 2nd left, top-billed) finds himself sitting on the jury at the murder trial of innocent stevedore Larry Blake (centre right), accused of a crime which Taylor in fact committed. In the end, Taylor does the right thing and confesses that he killed publisher Samuel S. Hinds. Fay Wray (left) was second-billed, with other roles going to Nan Grey (centre), Halliwell Hobbes (as a butler), Leonard Mudie, Bert Roach, Virginia Sale, Jane Darwell (right) and Granville Bates as the learned judge who, throughout the trial, has been studying an illustrated catalogue of trout flies. Lester Cole adapted it with Norman Levy from his own story, and director Ted Sloman kept it interesting for producer Edmund Grainger. (62 mins)

△ One of Hollywood's familiar sights was Charles Winninger playing an old vaudeville trouper, such as Pat Molloy in **Goodbye Broadway**. Partnered on this occasion by Alice Brady (top-billed) as the distaff side of a vaudeville team, he and the missus find themselves conned over their purchase of a run-down hotel in a small town. By the end, however, they have survived numerous trials and tribulations, and make a success of the venture. Based on James Gleason's *The Shannons Of Broadway* (first seen as a film in 1929), but with scenarists Roy Chanslor and A. Dorian Otvos changing the central characters' names from Shannon to Malloy, it emerged as a pleasant piece of *deja vu* whose cast included Tom Brown (left), Dorothea Kent (right), Frank Jenks, Jed Prouty, Willie Best and Donald Meek. It was directed by Ray McCarey for producer Edmund Grainger. (65 mins)

Deanna Durbin was given top billing in her third feature, **Mad About Music**, and garnered excellent reviews. In this one she played a young teenager whose mother, a vain Hollywood actress (Gail Patrick), keeps her well-hidden in a boarding school for young ladies in Switzerland, so as to protect her own image of youthfulness. The child invents an explorer father for herself, and boasts of his romantic and amazing exploits to her chums – and, indeed, to her gullible teachers. Her fabrications catch up with her through the meddling of a suspicious fellow pupil, and a desperate Deanna (illustrated left) dragoons a bewildered Herbert Marshall (illustrated left with Durbin) into acting out her fantasy for her. Far-fetched and often cloying, the movie nevertheless managed to charm. The young songstress delivered all that her adoring fans had come to expect, and the polished presence of Mr Marshall almost elevated the nonsense to credibility. Jackie Moran played a young lad smitten with Miss Durbin, and other excellent featured performances were given by Arthur Treacher (illustrated in bowler hat), William Frawley, Helen Parrish, Christian Rub (illustrated driving carriage) and Marcia Mae Jones. Cappy Barra's Harmonica Band was much in evidence; the star sang Harold Adamson and Jimmy McHugh's catchy 'I Love To Whistle' with them. She also rendered Gounod's 'Ave Maria' in company with The Vienna Boys' Choir. Bruce Manning and Felix Jackson wrote it from a story by Marcella Burke and Frederick Kohner; Joe Pasternak produced, and the director was Norman Taurog. Remade in 1956 as *The Toy Tiger* with Tim Hovey in the Durbin role. Other songs: 'Chapel Bells', 'Serenade To The Stars', 'There Isn't A Day Goes By' Adamson, McHugh.

△ The American public's increasing fascination with radio, particularly its behind-the-scenes aspect, was ably catered for in **Danger On The Air**, one of the studio's *Crime Club* melodramas produced by Irving Starr and directed by Otis Garrett. A whodunnit, in which a much despised sponsor is mysteriously murdered during a broadcast, it starred Donald Woods (right) as a young sound engineer who sets out to solve the crime, and also featured Nan Grey (left), Jed Prouty, Berton Churchill, William Lundigan, Skeets Gallagher, Edward Van Sloan, George Meeker and, in a small part, Lee J. Cobb. Betty Laidlaw and Robert Lively's screenplay, from the novel *Death Catches Up With Mr Cluck* by Xantippe, also concerned itself with the then current warfare between newspapers and radio networks over advertising space, and kept audiences guessing until the all-important final reel. (67 mins)

▷ A slightly better than average *Crime Club* thriller, **The Last Express** benefited from a tightly woven screenplay by Edmund L. Hartmann (story by Bayard Kendrick). Kent Taylor was top-starred as a private investigator who finds himself threatened by gangsters as he sets out to solve the murder of a special prosecutor who was appointed to rid New York city of its criminal element. As if that weren't enough, Taylor (centre) is then arrested himself as one of the murder suspects ... Don Brodie (right) played Taylor's sidekick and Dorothea Kent the romantic interest, with other roles going to Greta Granstedt (left), Paul Hurst, Samuel Lee, Charles Trowbridge, and Addison Richards. New York's subway system was integral to the plot, and Otis Garrett's direction made the most of it. The producer was Irving Starr. (60 mins)

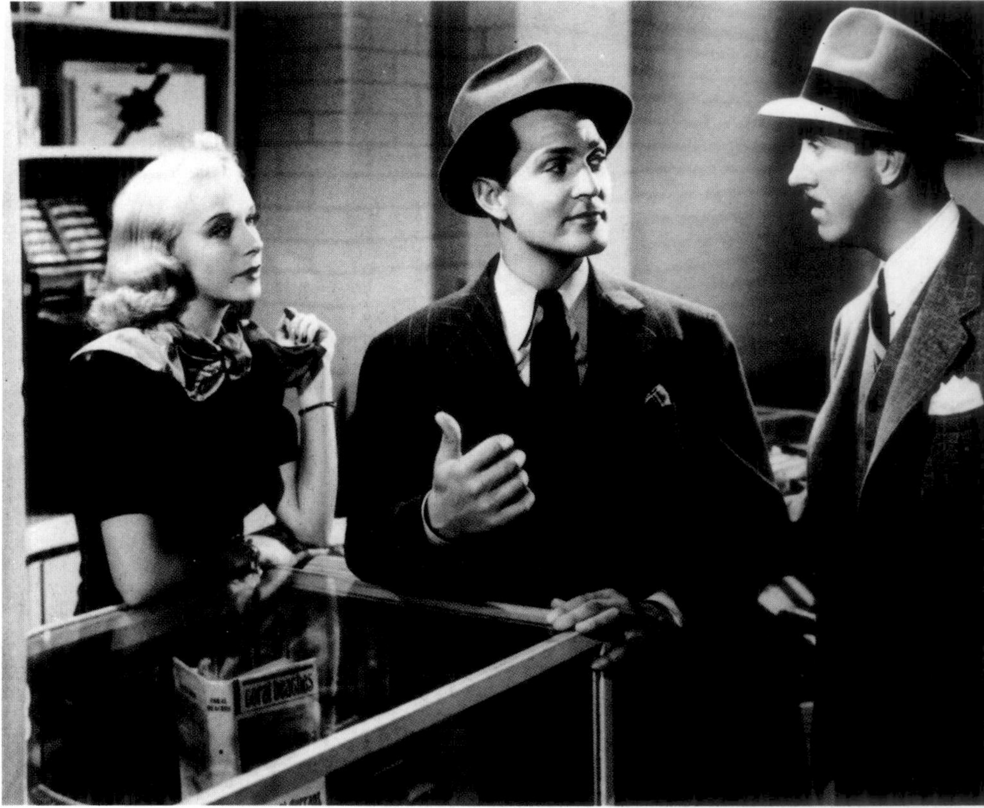

△ William Lundigan starred in **Freshman Year**, a moderately diverting campus caper, directed by Frank MacDonald. Lundigan played an undergraduate who dreams up the moneymaking idea of selling 'flunk' insurance to the students. A fifty-cent policy yields ten dollars to those who flunk their exams, but trouble comes when the professor (Ernest Truex) flunks nearly all of them. Lundigan (left) is saved from bankruptcy, however, by his successful promotion of the annual college show. Cue for music – and appearances by The Three Diamond Brothers, The Three Murtha Sisters, and The Lucky Seven Choir. Others cast: Dixie Dunbar, Constance Moore (right), Stanley Hughes, Frank Melton and, in a bit part, Alan Ladd. It was written by Charles Grayson (story by Thomas Ahearn and F. Murray Grossman), and produced by George Bilson. Songs included: 'Chasin' You Around' Frank Loesser, Irving Actman; 'Ain't That Marvellous', 'Swing That Cheer' Joe McCarthy, Harry Barris. (65 mins)

▽ One of the studio's more successful A-grade offerings for 1938 was **Letter Of Introduction**, in which Andrea Leeds (right) played the 20-year-old daughter of matinée idol Adolphe Menjou (left, top-starred) who last saw her when she was still a baby. Now, with four marriages behind him, she re-enters his life, herself an aspiring actress. George Murphy was cast as Andrea's boyfriend, whose misunderstanding of his sweetheart's relationship with Menjou (the latter reluctant, for reasons of vanity, to disclose the fact that he has a grown-up daughter), provided additional fuel for Sheridan Gibney and Leonard Spigelgass' well-turned screenplay (based on a story by Bernice Boone). Edgar Bergen (centre) and Charlie McCarthy (the dummy, centre) appeared as themselves and contributed substantially to the film's overall wellbeing, with Rita Johnson, Ann Sheridan, Eve Arden, Constance Moore, Frank Jenks and Ernest Cossart (2nd left) completing the cast for John M. Stahl who produced and directed. (98 mins)

△ The parole system came under scrutiny in **Prison Break** and, as described by scenarists Norton S. Parker and Dorothy Reid (based on Parker's story *Walls Of San Quentin*), was found heavily wanting. The story's victim was Barton MacLane (right), an honest tuna fisherman sent to prison for a murder he did not commit. Not only is he the victim of injustice, but of a parole system that prevents him from marrying Glenda Farrell (left), or travelling more than 12 miles beyond the parole limit. Text-book sociology melded uneasily with crime melodrama as the story veered between a moral crusade and attempts to solve the murder of Edward Pawley for which MacLane has been blamed. Arthur Lubin's direction divided its attention equally between these two aspects of the film, thus allowing producer Trem Carr to have his cake and eat it. Paul Hurst, Constance Moore, Ward Bond and Edmund MacDonald were also featured. (72 mins)

▽ As a child, Hell's Kitchen slum kid Marty Malone (Mickey Renschler) took the rap when his gang (Scotty Beckett, Tommy Bupp, Dickie Jones and Juanita Quigley) accidentally burned down a warehouse during a raid on a fruit truck. His punishment was a few years in reform school. Time passes, transforming Master Renschler into Victor McLaglen (right), the owner of an underworld nightclub, Master Beckett into William Gargan, a policeman, Master Bupp into Paul Kelly, a priest, and little Miss Quigley into Beatrice Roberts (left), a singer. Roy Chanslor's screenplay, based on Borden Chase's novel *Hell's Kitchen Has A Party*, put a decided strain on credibility, which Ray McCarey's direction did little to rectify. Main thrust of the plot had McLaglen being painted as a villain when, in fact, he's basically Mr Nice Guy. Other roles in producer Edmund Grainger's not particularly compelling melodrama, **The Devil's Party**, went to Frank Jenks, Samuel S. Hinds, Joseph Downing, Arthur Hoyt, Ed Gargan (brother of William), and John Gallaudet (as the adult version of Dickie Jones). (65 mins)

▽ An enjoyable programmer without a single star name to attract the paying customers, **Young Fugitives** combined comedy and melodrama in about equal proportions. The screenplay by Ben Grauman Kohn and Charles Grayson (based on Edward James' story *Afraid To Talk*) told the story of two old cronies (Harry Davenport and Clem Bevans), one of whom (Bevans) dies, leaving the other with the $50,000 the two men have pooled over the years. Davenport (left) sets out to locate Bevans' son (Robert Wilcox, centre) who he has promised his late friend he will treat as his own. He does indeed find the lad, only to realise that he is a no-good racketeer out to steal the loot. By the end of the movie, however, Wilcox has reformed under Davenport's benign influence. Dorothea Kent (right) played a vagabond in love with Wilcox, with other roles under John Rawlins' workmanlike direction going to Larry Blake, Myra McKinney, Henry Roquemore, Tom Ricketts, Mary Treen and William Benedict. Barney A. Sarecky produced. (65 mins)

◁ A comedy clearly designed to confirm a misogynist's most fearful prejudices, **Youth Takes A Fling** told the story of a sensitive lad from Kansas (Joel McCrea) who arrives in New York to begin a sea-faring career. Due to scarcity of jobs in this field, he accepts work at an emporium where he immediately becomes the object of Andrea Leeds' voracious romantic designs. Miss Leeds (centre) pursues McCrea (left) relentlessly, taking shameful advantage of his innocence as often as Myles Connolly's screenplay allowed. Which was often. The movie's other romantic pairing was Dorothea Kent and Frank Jenks (right), with Isabel Jeans, Virginia Grey, Grant Mitchell, Brandon Tynan and Willie Best in support. Archie Mayo directed it all a mite too vigorously, and the producer was Joe Pasternak. (79 mins)

△ Warner Bros.' 1938 *Crime School* was unmistakably a copy of Samuel Goldwyn's 1937 *Dead End*. Universal came up with a pale copy of both, giving employment again to the Dead End Kids, with **Little Tough Guy**. This time, the Kids were known collectively as 'the little tough guys' and individually as Johnny Boylan (Billy Halop, centre), Pig (Huntz Hall, right front), String (Gabriel Dell, left front), Ape (Bernard Punsley, left), Sniper (David Gorcey, centre front), and Dopey (Hally Chester, right). Gilson Brown and Brenda Weisberg's screenplay (story by Weisberg) took a superficial look at slum kids, and showed what happened after young Halop's father (Edward Pawley) is convicted for a crime he did not commit. The circumstances force Halop into the streets where he fetches up with a gang of thugs and becomes their leader. He embarks on a series of crimes and, ultimately, finishes up in reform school. Harold Young's direction brought nothing new to the writers' phoney sociology. The rest of the cast in Ken Goldsmith's production were Helen Parrish, Robert Wilcox, Jackie Searl, Marjorie Main and Peggy Stewart. (63 mins)

△ Another Deanna Durbin vehicle, **That Certain Age** presented the star in slightly more grown-up guise than the schoolgirl of *Mad About Music*. The movie dealt, for the most part, with Deanna's (left) crush on an older man (Melvyn Douglas, right) who is a journalist on her father's newspaper but, by the final fade, she ends up with the more suitable Jackie Cooper. Apart from an aria from Gounod's *Romeo and Juliet*, and the de Musset-Delibes 'Les Filles De Cadiz', all the songs were by Harold Adamson and Jimmy McHugh, one of them ('My Own') giving the star a huge hit. Irene Rich and John Halliday played Deanna's parents, with Nancy Carroll, Juanita Quigley, Jackie Searl, Charles Coleman and Peggy Stewart also cast. F. Hugh Herbert wrote the original story which was scripted by Bruce Manning, Charles Brackett and Billy Wilder. Joe Pasternak again produced, this time utilising director Edward Ludwig. Other songs: 'That Certain Age', 'You're As Pretty As A Picture', 'Be A Good Scout'. (83 mins)

▽ **Service De Luxe** was scripted by Claude Purcell and Leonard Spigelgass from a dangerously fragile plot by Bruce Manning and Vera Caspary. Considering the tremulousness of the material, the scenarists did sterling work with their account of Constance Bennett's (centre right) attempts (she runs an all-service bureau) to prevent Vincent Price (centre left, his debut) from arriving in New York. It was no surprise that she finished up falling in love with Price and marrying him – but not before almost losing him to Joy Hodges (2nd right) – Miss Hodges' consolation prize was Mischa Auer (right), with whom she eloped. Stalwart performances from the starring players, as well as from a supporting cast that included Charlie Ruggles (2nd left), Helen Broderick (left), Frances Robinson and Halliwell Hobbes kept it all buoyant, as did producer Rowland V. Lee's screwball direction. (85 mins)

◁ Definitely fodder for the bottom half of a double bill, **Swing, Sister, Swing** was a musical about the jitterbug vogue. It followed a group of small-town jitterbug addicts who shoot to sudden Broadway fame, returning with equal swiftness to the oblivion from whence they came. The story, such as it was, was by associate producer Burt Kelly, the screenplay by Charles Grayson, and the leading roles went to Ken Murray (centre, top cast as a high-powered agent), Johnny Downs (right) and Kathryn Kane (right centre) – the latter pair introducing the 'Baltimore Bubble' to New York, accompanied by trombonist Eddie Quillan (left). Also: Ernest Truex, Edna Sedgewick (2nd left), Nana Bryant and Ted Weems and His Orchestra. The pedestrian dance routines were by Matty Kelly, and the director was Josephy Santley. Songs: 'Gingham Gown', 'Just A Bore', 'Wasn't It You?', 'Kameski Waltz' Frank Skinner, Charles Henderson. (72 mins)

OTHER RELEASES OF 1938

Air Devils
Prod: Paul Malvern Dir: John Rawlins. Plodding performances from Larry Blake and Dick Purcell as bickering ex-marines who, in pursuit of further adventures, become flying-cops on a South Sea Island. Beryl Wallace, Namo Clark. (58 mins)

Black Bandit (Bob Baker)
Dir: George Waggner. Dual roles for Bob as a sheriff who is forced to apprehend his twin brother – a rustler known as 'The Black Bandit'. Marjorie Reynolds, Forrest Taylor. (60 mins)

The Black Doll
Prod: Irving Starr Dir: Otis Garrett. Private eye investigates a murder, with practically all the characters coming under suspicion. Donald Woods, Nan Grey. (66 mins)

Border Wolves (Bob Baker)
Dir: George Waggner. Bob and a group of townsfolk get together to hunt down a pack of wolves that has been terrifying their border town. (56 mins)

The Crime Of Doctor Hallet
Prod: Edmund Grainger Dir: S. Sylvan Simon. Nifty jungle drama telling of a doctor and his assistant who find a cure for dreaded red fever, one of them dying in the process. Ralph Bellamy, John King, Josephine Hutchinson. (68 mins)

Exposed
Prod: Max H. Golden Dir: Harold Schuster. Ace photographer Glenda Farrell, working from a pic, helps apprehend racketeers and sets wedding bells ringing. Otto Kruger, Bernard Nedell. (63 mins)

Forbidden Valley
Dir: Wyndham Gittens. A young man raised in a secret canyon sets out to sell a herd of wild mustangs and outsmart rustlers. Noah Beery Jr (67 mins)

Ghost Town Riders (Bob Baker)
Dir: George Waggner. Bob finds that an abandoned town is being used by an outlaw gang as their base to steal a gold mine from an eastern gal. Fay Shannon. (54 mins)

Guilty Trails (Bob Baker)
Dir: George Waggner. Bob outwits a crooked banker and manages to save a family ranch for the orphaned girl owner. Marjorie Reynolds, Jack Rockwell. (57 mins)

His Exciting Night
Prod: Ken Goldsmith Dir: Gus Meins. Elaborate comedy about a timid clerk who becomes the butt of practical jokes on his wedding night, and nearly loses his bride-to-be. Charlie Ruggles, Ona Munson. (55 mins)

The Lady In The Morgue
Prod: Irving Starr Dir: Otis Garrett. Posing more questions than answers, this complicated story revolved round detective Preston Foster's attempts at proving his innocence after he is accused of body-snatching a girl's corpse. Patricia Ellis, Frank Jenks, Barbara Pepper. (67 mins)

The Last Stand (Bob Baker)
Dir: Joseph H. Lewis. Bob poses as a notorious bandit in order to hunt down a rich cattle owner and rustler suspected of killing his father. Constance Moore. (57 mins)

Little Tough Guys In Society
Prod: Max H. Golden Dir: Erle C. Kenton. Ex-slum kids enter the *haute monde* and are invited to a millionairess' estate as company for her Schopenhauer-loving son. Predictable comedy. Mary Boland, Frankie Thomas, Harris Berger, Hally Chester, Charles Duncan, David Gorcey. (63 mins)

Mars Attacks The World
Prod: Barney A. Sarecky Dir: Ford Beebe, Robert Hill. Fun-filled feature version of the studio's 1938 serial *Flash Gordon's Trip To Mars*. Buster Crabbe, Jean Rogers, Charles Middleton, Frank Shannon. (101 mins)

Midnight Intruder
Prod: Trem Carr Dir: Arthur Lubin. Serviceable story of a tramp who, while sheltering in an empty (he thinks) mansion, is discovered by the servants and mistaken for the owner's estranged son. Louis Hayward, Eric Linden. (66 mins)

The Missing Guest
Prod: Barney A. Sarecky Dir: John Rawlins. A newspaperman is required to spend time in a haunted house in which two murders are committed and several people faint. Paul Kelly, Constance Moore, William Lundigan, Selmer Jackson. (68 mins)

Newsboy's Home
Prod: Ken Goldsmith Dir: Harold Young. The Little Tough Guys up to their necks in a circulation war between two rival newspapers and their newsboys. Jackie Cooper, Joseph Crehan, Wendy Barrie, Edmund Lowe. (72 mins)

Outlaw Express (Bob Baker)
Dir: George Waggner. Bob plays a US cavalry captain assigned to track down a gang responsible for killing pony express riders. Cecilia Callejo. (56 mins)

Personal Secretary
Prod: Max H. Golden Dir: Otis Garrett. William Gargan and Joy Hodges are rival columnists, the latter becoming the former's secretary, and eventually his wife. They prove Kay Linaker did not murder her playboy husband. Andy Devine. (63 mins)

Prairie Justice (Bob Baker)
Dir: George Waggner. Bob is US marshal sent to Medicine Hat in disguise to discover the brains behind a recent spate of crimes. Dorothy Fay. (58 mins)

Reckless Living
Prod: Val Paul Dir: Frank McDonald. Modest programmer with race-track background about an unlucky punter who finally manages to beat the gambling bug. Robert Wilcox, Nan Grey. (65 mins)

Secrets Of A Nurse
Prod: Burt Kelly Dir: Arthur Lubin. Well-worn drama in which a fighter's accident in the ring forces him to become a hotel bell-boy, where he is framed for murder. His nurse girlfriend keeps faith and all's well that ends well. Edmund Lowe, Dick Foran, Helen Mack. (75 mins)

The Singing Outlaw (Bob Baker)
Dir: Joseph H. Lewis. Bob plays a rodeo star who finds himself implicated in the double killings of a US marshal and his assassin. Joan Barclay. (57 mins)

Sinners In Paradise
Prod: Ken Goldsmith Dir: James Whale. A tropical Island set the scene for a plane crash which strands a variety of passengers – all with a past – as castaways. But is the island deserted? Madge Evans, Bruce Cabot, Marian Martin, Gene Lockhart, Charlotte Wynters, John Boles. (65 mins)

The Spy Ring
Prod: Trem Carr Dir: Joseph H. Lewis. An army base whose only excitements are polo matches and dances, suddenly finds espionage in its midst. William Hall, Jane Wyman, Esther Ralston. (60 mins)

State Police
Prod: Trem Carr Dir: John Rawlins. John King and William Lundigan headed the cast of this action-packed 'B' set in a coal-mining town. Constance Moore, Larry Blake. (61 mins)

The Storm
Prod: Ken Goldsmith Dir: Harold Young. Routine adventure at sea with Charles Bickford, Barton MacLane, Preston Foster, Tom Brown, Nan Grey and Andy Devine, all victims of a typhoon. (78 mins)

Strange Faces
Prod: Burt Kelly Dir: Earl Taggart. Holly-wooden melodrama showing rival reporters chasing the same story; one tricks the other into jail so she can tackle the story – and the gangsters – alone. Frank Jenks, Dorothea Kent, Andy Devine. (65 mins)

Swing That Cheer
Prod: Max H. Golden Dir: Harold Schuster. Campus comedy focussing on the rivalry between footballers Tom Brown and Robert Wilcox, and the consequences of their behaviour. Andy Devine, Constance Moore, Ernest Truex. (70 mins)

Western Trails (Bob Baker)
Dir: George Waggner. Bob leads the goodies in a predictable right-against-wrong tale, helped along on this occasion by an above-average music score. Marjorie Reynolds, Carlyle Moore. (58 mins)

Wives Under Suspicion
Prod: Edmund Grainger Dir: James Whale. Protracted cliché telling the melodramatic tale of an attorney who discovers the *crime passionel* he is prosecuting resembles the affair his own wife is conducting under his nose. Warren William, Gail Patrick, Ralph Morgan. Remake of *The Kiss Before The Mirror* (1933). (68 mins)

1939

▽ Style triumphed decisively over content in **Rio**, the furrows of whose rather wrinkled story (by Jean Negulesco) were ironed out in Aben Kandel, Edwin Justus Mayer, Steven Moorehouse Avery and Frank Partos' deft screenplay, and in John Brahm's even defter direction. Basically the story of a swindler who escapes from a French penal colony only to discover that his wife has taken a lover, it starred Basil Rathbone as the convict (left), Sigrid Gurie as his wife, and Robert Cummings as the lover. Victor McLaglen was in it, too, and so were Leo Carrillo, Billy Gilbert, Irving Bacon, Maurice Moscovitch (right), Samuel S. Hinds, Irving Pichel and Ferike Boros. Under Brahm's sensitive guidance they all helped to buttress the plot and turn the melodrama into solid adult entertainment. (77 mins)

◁ With Deanna Durbin now advancing into her late teens, the studio unveiled a 13-year-old named Gloria Jean (right). The little miss resembled a sort of cross between Deanna and the inimitable Shirley Temple, though without quite the star quality of either. In **The Underpup** little Gloria played a child from poverty row who is treated to a vacation in an exclusive girls' camp. Before long she becomes the group's agony aunty, dishing out good advice to everyone, including the predictable poor little rich girl whose parents' marriage is on the rocks. It was competently directed by Richard Wallace, with a cast that included Robert Cummings (centre, second-billed), Nan Grey (right), C. Aubrey Smith, Beulah Bondi, Virginia Weidler, Margaret Lindsay, Raymond Walburn, Ann Gillis, Pat Cavanagh and Billy Gilbert. A pleasant middle-of-the-road package, it was written by Grover Jones from a story by I.A.R. Wylie, and produced by Joe Pasternak, who seemed to have a penchant for picking youthful new talent. Songs included: 'March Of The Penguins' (High School Cadets March) John Philip Sousa; 'Annie Laurie' Lady John Douglas Scott; 'I'm Like A Bird' (composer unknown). (81 mins)

△ A penitentiary melodrama, **The Big Guy** told the trite story of a prison warden (Victor McLaglen, illustrated) who faces a dilemma: should he allow a young man (Jackie Cooper), innocently convicted of murder, to be executed? Or should he return some vital stolen funds which have come into his possession, thereby saving Cooper from the chair? He does the decent thing, of course, but pays the ultimate price all the same when he stops a bullet during Cooper's capture after an abortive escape attempt. Written by Lester Cole from a story by Wallace Sullivan and Richard K. Polimer, and with a cast that included Edward Brophy, Peggy Moran, Ona Munson, Russell Hicks and Edward Pawley, it was assembly-line stuff, albeit well assembled by producer Burt Kelly. The dirctor was Arthur Lubin. (78 mins)

◁ **First Love** hit the news headlines (literally) thanks to Deanna Durbin receiving her first screen kiss in it. Apart from this cataclysmic event, the movie could not be said to have displayed much originality in its unfolding of a tale about an orphan (Miss Durbin, right) who is rescued from the bosom of her unpleasant relatives by handsome Robert Stack (left) – purveyor of the famous kiss. Helen Parrish featured as Deanna's cousin, a puss both glamour and sour; Eugene Pallette was her wealthy uncle who, quite understandably, detests his family, and Leatrice Joy an aunt preoccupied with astrology. Lewis Howard, June Storey and Charles Coleman were also cast. Bruce Manning and Lionel Houser wrote it for producer Joe Pasternak and director Henry Koster. Songs included: 'Spring In My Heart' (from a melody by Johann Strauss, adapted by Hans Salter, lyrics Ralph Freed); 'Amapola' Albert Gamse, Joseph La Calle; 'Home Sweet Home' John Howard Payne, Sir Henry Bishop; 'One Fine Day' (from *Madame Butterfly*) Puccini. (78 mins)

△ In **Ex-Champ** (GB: **Golden Gloves**) Victor McLaglen played an ex-champ-turned-doorman who, after his son (Donald Briggs) disowns him in order to marry a socialite (Constance Moore), spends his time training Tom Brown, a promising young boxer. Complications surfaced in Alex Gottlieb and Edmund L. Hartmann's entertaining screenplay (story by Gordon Kahn) after Briggs steals some money from a gambling syndicate and McLaglen (right), to save his son, plans to drug protégé Brown (left) in an important welterweight championship and bet on his opponent instead. But it all worked out well in the end. William Frawley (centre) was featured as McLaglen's down-and-out buddy, also an ex-champ, with other roles under Phil Rosen's okay direction going to Nan Grey (2nd left) as McLaglen's daughter, Thurston Hall, and Samuel S. Hinds. Burt Kelly produced. (72 mins)

▽ Producer/director Rowland V. Lee successfully filled the shoes of James Whale as he steered Basil Rathbone, Boris Karloff (illustrated), Bela Lugosi, Lionel Atwill, Josephine Hutchinson and Emma Dunn through their ghoulish paces in **Son Of Frankenstein**. The fact that Mary Shelley's monster had been seen to perish so spectacularly and conclusively at the end of *The Bride Of Frankenstein* (1935) didn't deter scenarist Willis Cooper from resurrecting him to cause havoc all over again – this time as the vengeful tool of Ygor, a crazed shepherd (Lugosi). According to the plot, Ygor has survived the hangman's noose for allegedly body-snatching, had his neck put out of joint in the process, and has since been responsible (via the monster) for the deaths of six of the jurors who sentenced him. It was the last time Karloff played the monster and, sadly, his farewell performance in the role lacked all traces of the 'humanity' that helped make his original creation unique. Rathbone was Frankenstein's son, and the rest of the cast also included Donnie Dunagan, Edgar Norton, Gustav von Seyffertitz, Lionel Belmore and Ward Bond. (93 mins)

△ Loosely based on the 1930 film version, this remake of **Little Accident** starred the riotously unhinged Hugh Herbert (left) as a newspaper advice columnist, writing under a woman's pseudonym, who finds an abandoned baby and decides to take it into his care. Had he realised just how much of a scene stealer the kid would turn out to be, he would probably have had some serious second thoughts! Little Sandra Lee Henville was cast as the abandoned tot (called Sandy) and was the *raison d'être* for resuscitating Floyd Dell and Thomas Mitchell's play *The Little Accident*, on which Paul Yawitz and Eve Green based their screenplay. As long as little Miss Henville was eliciting 'ooh's' and 'aah's' from indulgent audiences, the rest of the cast barely got a look in. These neglected thespians included Florence Rice (right), Richard Carlson, Joy Hodges, Edgar Kennedy, Etienne Girardot, Ernest Truex, Anne Gwynne and Peggy Moran. It was produced and directed by Charles Lamont. A third version of the story appeared in 1944, called *Casanova Brown*. (65 mins)

△ **Spirit Of Culver**, which top-starred Jackie Cooper (left), was a remake of *Tom Brown Of Culver* (1932) which had starred young Tom Brown. Adroitly scripted by Whitney Bolton and Nathanael West (from the story *Tom Brown Of Culver* by George Green, Tom Buckingham and Clarence Marks), it again told the story of a cadet who discovers that his hero father, whom he believed to be dead, is very much alive and no hero at all, his Congressional Medal having been totally undeserved. Henry Hull played Cooper's pa, with other roles under Joseph Santley's expert direction going to Freddie Bartholomew (second-billed), Andy Devine, Jackie Moran (right), Tim Holt, Gene Reynolds (centre right), Kathryn Kane, Walter Tetley (centre) and Milburn Stone (background in overalls). The producer was Burt Kelly. (89 mins)

▷ Edgar Bergen (centre) and his better half, Charlie McCarthy (centre left), headed the cast of **Charlie McCarthy, Detective** a thriller whose plot was almost as wooden as its titular hero. All about the mysterious murder of a magazine publisher who is bumped off the very weekend Messrs Bergen and McCarthy are enjoying his hospitality, it focussed attention on the wrong man as culprit until you-know-who saw to it that justice prevailed. Working from a story by Robertson White and Darrell Ware, Edward Eliscu fashioned a complicated screenplay that added chaos to confusion by mixing melodrama with slapstick in unpalatable proportions. The rest of the cast under producer Frank Tuttle's direction included Robert Cummings, Constance Moore, John Sutton, Louis Calhern, Edgar Kennedy, Warren Hymer, and Samuel S. Hinds. (65 mins)

▽ In **I Stole A Million**, George Raft (centre right) played Joe Lourik, an aggressively independent man who, defrauded of his life's savings, turns to crime. After marrying Claire Trevor, however, he attempts to go straight, but he is in too deep and, when his wife is jailed for complicity in shielding a criminal, he returns to his underworld activities with a vengeance. The climax of his notorious career is a million dollar theft, but the money turns out to be worthless to him, and he dies in a rainstorm of policemen's bullets. A tough little melodrama with two absorbing central performances from Raft and Trevor, it was written by Nathanael West from a story by Lester Cole, produced by Burt Kelly, and directed in a no-nonsense way by Frank Tuttle, whose cast also included Dick Foran, Henry Armetta, Victor Jory, George Chandler, Irving Bacon, Hobart Cavanaugh, Jason Robards Sr and Ralph Dunn (left). (75 mins)

▽ Primarily a vehicle for the silver tonsils of Bing Crosby, **East Side Of Heaven** told the passable tale of a crooning cab driver (Crosby, left) who, by a series of highly improbable events, finds himself a surrogate father to Baby Sandy (centre), a ten-month-old toddler who played a boy in the film, but was actually a girl! Co-star Joan Blondell was a telephonist whose wedding is postponed by the tot's appearance, and Mischa Auer (right) featured as Bing's best friend and ally. Johnny Burke and James V. Monaco wrote the songs – all ballads but for the bouncy 'Hang Your Heart On A Hickory Limb', sung in a cafe by the star, the cafe's owner (Jane Jones), and a group of waitresses otherwise known as The Music Maids. It was written by William Conselman from a story by Herbert Polesie and David Butler, with Butler also directing. C. Aubrey Smith, Jerome Cowan, Robert Kent, Mary Travers and Arthur Hoyt were in it too. Other songs: 'Sing A Song Of Sunbeams', 'That Sly Old Gentleman', 'East Side Of Heaven'. (90 mins)

▽ Blatantly cashing in on the success of Irene Dunne (centre) and Charles Boyer (right) in RKO's *Love Affair* (1939), producer John M. Stahl, clearly the Ross Hunter of his time, hastily commissioned a screenplay from Dwight Taylor (based on a novel by James M. Cain) that, hopefully, would give audiences, especially women, a second helping of the irresistible Dunne-Boyer magic. The result was **When Tomorrow Comes**, an emotional retread of the team's Paramount effort, with Dunne as a waitress and Boyer as a concert pianist. The pair have a passionate affair in an organ loft on Long Island after a union strike renders her unemployed, and an opportune hurricane assures them of privacy. Directed by producer Stahl, the movie did not display one single spontaneous emotion, and its slavish adherence to the romantic ingredients offered by its altogether superior predecessor, crippled it beyond repair. Barbara O'Neil played Boyer's wife (deranged as a result of giving birth to a stillborn baby), with other parts going to Onslow Stevens, Nydia Westman, Fritz Feld, Milton Parsons (left) and Nella Walker. It was remade in 1957 as *Interlude*. (90 mins)

▽ **Destry Rides Again** was the one in which Marlene Dietrich (centre), as saloon singer Frenchy, immortalised Frank Loesser and Frederick Hollander's song 'See What The Boys In The Backroom Will Have'. It was also the one in which la Dietrich and Una Merkel tore into each other in a most unladylike manner over Mischa Auer's trousers. And, you may remember, it was the one in which second-billed James Stewart, cast as a mild-mannered sheriff's deputy with a dislike of guns, proved that underneath his sensitive exterior beat the heart of one of the West's true heroes! Though Felix Jackson, Gertrude Purcell and Henry Myers' screenplay (from the novel by Max Brand) told a story no more powerful than how law and order were restored to the frontier town of Bottleneck, it was written with enough *brio* to disguise its basic thinness, directed by George Marshall with such unbridled gusto, and so irresistibly performed by its two stars that, in the end, it was not *what* happened but *how* it happened, that mattered. Brian Donlevy (foreground left) was in fine form as the villain of the piece, Charles Winninger played the local sheriff, and Samuel S. Hinds did well as the town's mayor, with other roles in producer Joe Pasternak's solid gold winner going to Irene Hervey, Allen Jenkins (right), Warren Hymer (left), Billy Gilbert, Tom Fadden, Jack Carson, Dickie Jones and Ann Todd (not to be confused with the English actress). Two other numbers by Loesser and Hollander were also featured – 'Little Joe The Wrangler' and 'You've Got That Look'. The movie had been previously made in 1932 with Tom Mix. It was remade in 1950 as *Frenchie* with Shelley Winters and again, as *Destry*, with Audie Murphy in 1954. (81 mins)

▷ **Three Smart Girls Grow Up** was a happy sequel to the studio's *Three Smart Girls* (1936). This time a spring-fresh Deanna Durbin (centre right) directed her energies to marrying off her two elder sisters and, naturally, accomplished the operation successfully. Nan Grey (left) repeated her earlier role as one of the siblings, but Helen Parrish (right) subbed for Barbara Read as the other; their men were played by Robert Cummings and William Lundigan, and Charles Winninger (centre) was in it too. Edward Teschemacher and Guy D'Hardelot's 'Because', sung by Miss Durbin, turned out to be one of her biggest ever hits, and bathed audiences in a rosy glow. She also sang 'The Last Rose Of Summer' (by Thomas Moore and Richard Alfred Milliken). It was written by Bruce Manning and Felix Jackson, produced by Joe Pasternak, and directed by Henry Koster with his usual flair for extracting the best from this durable young star. (73 mins)

△ More than somewhat resembling *East Side Of Heaven*, but with Dennis O'Keefe (standing centre) in the Bing Crosby role, **Unexpected Father** again employed the gurgling talents of cute little Sandra Lee Henville (Sandy, centre), as well as Russian Mischa Auer (right), to embellish a child custody situation whose successful resolution (or so says the court) rests with the bickering applicants (O'Keefe, and Shirley Ross, left) burying the hatchet and marrying each other. It was a routine comedy that did nothing for a cast that included Joy Hodges, Donald Briggs, Mayo Methot, Ann Nagel, Anne Gwynne and Dorothy Arnold – and vice versa. Leonard Spigelgass scripted it from his own story together with Charles Grayson, and it was directed – with little sparkle – by Charles Lamont for associate producer Ken Goldsmith. (78 mins)

△ A comedy melodrama, or a melodramatic comedy, **For Love Or Money** was, regardless of how audiences interpreted its intentions, good clean fun in a Runyonesque sort of way. It starred Robert Kent (left) and Edward Brophy as a couple employed by a bookmaker (Richard Lane), who allow $50,000 to slip through their hands. The money finds its way through the mail to June Lang (centre), who spends all but $6000 of it. Messrs Kent and Brophy's directive from Lane is simple and to the point: get the loot back in 36 hours, or else. What followed provided scenarists Charles Grayson and Arthur T. Horman (story by Julian Blaustein, Daniel Taradash and Bernard Fein) with enough comic mileage to keep the punters happy, and supplied parts for Etienne Girardot (right), Edward Gargan and Horace MacMahon. Max H. Golden produced, and the efficient direction was by Albert S. Rogell. (67 mins)

▽ After their successful pairing earlier in the year in *Spirit Of Culver*, the studio quickly reteamed Jackie Cooper (left) and Freddie Bartholomew (2nd left) in another *Boys' Own*-style yarn called, without ostentation, **Two Bright Boys**. The story and screenplay, by Val Burton and Edmund L. Hartmann, was a pretty straightforward account of how the fatherless Cooper inherits a valuable piece of property in Texas which he is not yet capable of handling on his own. An unscrupulous oil man (Alan Dinehart) can't wait to appropriate the land for himself, but is prevented from doing so by the intervention of Master Bartholomew and his father (Melville Cooper, centre). Predictable but entertaining, it also featured Dorothy Peterson, J.M. Kerrigan (right – as a loquacious Irish driller), Willard Robertson and Eddie Acuff. Burt Kelly's modest but pleasant little production was capably directed by Joseph Santley. (65 mins)

▽ Shakespeare's *Richard III*, stripped of its poetry, but with all of its gore intact, gave scenarist Robert N. Lee a marvellous opportunity to indulge in a bit of medieval Grand Guignol. The result was **Tower Of London**, whose positively operatic direction by producer Rowland V. Lee, and larger-than-life performances by Basil Rathbone (top-billed, left) as Richard, Boris Karloff (Mord), Barbara O'Neil (Queen Elizabeth), Ian Hunter (centre – Edward IV), Vincent Price (Clarence), Nan Grey (Lady Alice Barton), John Sutton (right – John Wyatt), Ernest Cossart (Tom Clink) and Leo G. Carroll (Hastings), contributed substantially to the satisfying blood-letting. John Rodion (Rathbone's son) and Donnie Dunagan played Lord de Verez and one of the princes in the tower, and Rose Hobart, Lionel Belmore, Ralph Forbes, G.P. Huntley, and bit players Georgia Caine (2nd right) and Francis Powers (2nd left), were also featured. It was remade by United Artists in 1962. (92 mins)

△ Arrant nonsense masquerading as pro-British propaganda, **The Sun Never Sets** was altogether unworthy of its director, Rowland V. Lee, who also produced it, thus shouldering total responsibility for the debacle. Furthermore, the material did no credit to an excellent cast that top-billed Douglas Fairbanks Jr (right), co-starred Basil Rathbone, and featured Virginia Field, Lionel Atwill, Barbara O'Neil (left), C. Aubrey Smith, Melville Cooper (centre) and Mary Forbes. Set in a far-flung British colonial outpost somewhere along the African gold coast, W.P. Lipscombe's screenplay (story by Jerry Horwin and Arthur Fitz-Richards) involved the Randolph family, whose members comprised the bulk of the cast, in a fracas with a villain called Zurof (Lionel Atwil) who, among other things, has established a secret radio station in the territory which he uses to spread anti-British propaganda, and for such other nefarious purposes as warmongering and bomb-plotting. Fairbanks' pukka English accent was the best thing on offer in an otherwise silly entertainment. (98 mins)

▷ W.C. Fields (illustrated), lured away from Paramount by a larger salary ($125,000 per film, plus $25,000 for his story), played Larson E. Whipsnade, a cantankerous circus owner fallen on hard times, in **You Can't Cheat An Honest Man**. The film was only funny in parts, with the great comedian sharing the limelight with co-star Edgar Bergen, as well as with Charlie McCarthy and Mortimer Snerd. George Marion Jr, Richard Mack and Everett Freeman's screenplay (from a story by Charles Bogle, a pseudonym for Fields) comprised a series of comic set-pieces, with what little narrative there was revolving around the efforts of Fields' daughter (Constance Moore) to raise money for her old man by agreeing to marry a millionaire. Miss Moore, however, abandons her plans after her father causes something of a scandal at a society reception, and decides to marry ventriloquist Bergen, who she has loved all along. Considering how relentlessly unpleasant Fields' characterisation of Whipsnade was, director William Marshall did the best he could, but the laughter and the general level of comic invention (seen at its best in Whipsnade's portable shower, and a parachute escape from a runaway balloon) was well below par. Lester Cowan produced, also casting James Bush (as the millionaire), Mary Forbes and Thurston Hall as Bush's parents, John Arledge, Edward Brophy and Grady Sutton. (75 mins)

BALLOONS

△ A song called 'Hawaii Sang Me To Sleep' (by Frank Loesser and Matt Malneck) aptly summed up the effect of the movie that featured it. **Hawaiian Nights**, a threadbare programmer musical, starred Johnny Downs (2nd left) as a bandleader. The lad's father (Thurston Hall, 2nd right) shows his violent disapproval of his son's occupation by packing him off to Hawaii which, like the film, turned out to be a mistake. Charles Grayson and Lee Loeb wrote the dreary screenplay from a story by John Grey, giving roles to Mary Carlisle (left), Constance Moore, Eddie Quillan (right), Etienne Girardot, Samuel S. Hinds and Princess Luana. Albert S. Rogell directed for producer Max H. Golden. Other songs: 'Hey, Good Lookin'!', 'I Found My Love', 'Then I Wrote The Minuet In G' (based on a Beethoven melody) Loesser, Malneck. (65 mins)

▽ Adroit, entertaining, lower-case mayhem, **The House Of Fear**, a remake of the superior *The Last Warning* (1928), combined laughter and suspense in an atmospheric whodunnit that used a theatre as its setting, and the cast of a show as murder suspects. When the company's leading man is mysteriously bumped off, detective William Gargan pretends to be a producer, reassembles the cast, and restages the play with the intention of capturing the killer. Walter Woolf King (left) becomes the new leading man and he, too, is killed in the same mysterious manner as his predecessor. Though the cast assembled by real-life producer Edmund Grainger (Irene Hervey, Alan Dinehart, Harvey Stephens, Dorothy Arnold, El Brendel (right), Tom Dugan, Jan Duggan and Robert Coote) was not exactly glittering with stars, director Joe May kept them on their toes and brought the best out of Peter Milne's screenplay from a story by Thomas Fallon. (66 mins)

△ The tedious tale of four desperate actresses who try and save their vanishing careers by staging a floorshow in a played-out nightclub, **Laugh It Off** (GB: **Lady Be Gay**) was intended as an amusing musical. In the event, it deserved credit only for the brevity of its running time. Bravely attempting to grasp the elusive script (by Harry Clork and Lee Loeb, from a story by Loeb and Mortimer Braus) were Cecil Cunningham, Constance Moore (left), Johnny Downs (right), Janet Beecher, Marjorie Rambeau, Hedda Hopper, Edgar Kennedy, William Demarest, Horace McMahon and Paula Stone. It was produced and directed by Albert S. Rogell. Songs: 'My Dream And I', 'Doin' The 1940', 'Laugh It Off', 'Who's Gonna Keep Your Wigwam Warm?' Sam Lerner, Ben Oakland. (63 mins)

OTHER RELEASES OF 1939

Big Town Czar
Prod: Ken Goldsmith Dir: Arthur Lubin. Gangster melodrama whose 'crime doesn't pay' message centres on a condemned man regretting past actions, including fratricide, too late. He is relentlessly claimed by the electric-chair. Ed Sullivan (as himself), Barton MacLane, Tom Brown, Esther Dale, Eve Arden. (66 mins)

Call A Messenger
Prod: Ken Goldsmith Dir: Arthur Lubin. Little Tough Guy Billy Halop persuades neighbourhood juvenile delinquents to reform. They do, and prevent a stick-up. Huntz Hall, Robert Armstrong, Mary Carlisle, Anne Nagel, Victor Jory, William Benedict, David Gorcey, El Brendel. (65 mins)

Chip Of The Flying U (Johnny Mack Brown)
Dir: Ralph Staub. Johnny is misjudged by his boss' sister and blamed for the misdeeds of a gang of bank robbers. Fuzzy Knight, Doris Weston, Bob Baker. (55 mins)

Code Of The Street
Prod: Burt Kelly Dir: Harold Young. The Little Tough Guys, again, help clear 'toughie' leader James McCallion of murder, enlisting the aid of demoted policeman Harry Carey and bringing the real culprit to bay. Paul Fix, Frankie Thomas. (72 mins)

Desperate Trails (Johnny Mack Brown)
Dir: Albert Ray. Johnny plays a secret agent posing as a bandit in order to save a town from a crooked banker and a conniving sheriff. Fuzzy Knight. (60 mins)

The Family Next Door
Prod: Max H. Golden Dir: Joseph Santley. Aimed at family audiences, this comedy tells of a scatty plumber whose screwball family and their ambitions are perpetually frustrated by his incompetence. Hugh Herbert, Eddie Quillan, Ruth Donnelly. (60 mins)

The Forgotten Woman
Prod: Edmund Grainger Dir: Harold Young. Old-fashioned meller about an innocent widow jailed for four years who, after her release, marries the very D.A. who sent her down. A contrived plot leads to her clearing her name. Sigrid Gurie, Donald Briggs. (67 mins)

Gambling Ship
Prod: Irving Starr Dir: Aubrey H. Scotto. Patron of an orphanage, whose daughter believes him to be the essence of respectability, makes money from a gambling ship. Robert Wilcox, Helen Mack, Selmer Jackson. (62 mins)

Hero For A Day
Prod: Ken Goldsmith Dir: Harold Young. Irredeemably bad film about an erstwhile football star who, as part of a publicity stunt, returns to his old campus for an all-important game and collapses under the strain. Charley Grapewin, Dick Foran, Anita Louise. (65 mins)

Honor Of The West (Bob Baker)
Dir: George Waggner. Bob is a 'Singing Sheriff' appointed to clean out a cattle-rustling gang led by a former friend. Marjorie Bell, Carleton Young. (60 mins)

Inside Information
Prod: Irving Starr Dir: Charles Lamont. All-too-familiar meller in which a rookie cop scorns modern crime detection methods doing things his way to solve the crime. Dick Foran, June Lang, Harry Carey. (62 mins)

The Last Warning
Prod: Irving Starr Dir: Al Rogell. From the Crime Club, Preston Foster shenanigans as he investigates threatening letters received by a wealthy playboy who, in the end, is neither wealthy nor undeserving of the letters. Raymond Parker, Kay Linaker, E.E. Clive. (63 mins)

Legion Of Lost Flyers
Prod: Ben Pivar Dir: Christy Cabanne. Preposterous schoolboys' yarn starred Richard Arlen as a pilot falsely accused of bailing out and leaving passengers to their fate. Amid broken wings, smashed landing-gear, snowbound takeoffs and crashes, he nails the guilty party. William Lundigan, Andy Devine. (65 mins)

The Man From Montreal
Prod: Ben Pivar Dir: Christy Cabanne. Fur trapper wrongly accused of stealing pelts sets out to prove his innocence. Richard Arlen, Andy Devine, Anne Gwynne. (61 mins)

Missing Evidence
Prod/Dir: Phil Rosen. In vain did audiences search for evidence of originality and excitement in this routine story of the FBI's attempts to stamp out a phoney sweepstake organisation. Irene Hervey, Inez Courtney, Chick Chandler, Noel Madison. (64 mins)

Mutiny On The Blackhawk
Prod: Ben Pivar Dir: Christy Cabanne. Two movies for the price of one with Richard Arlen inciting slaves to mutiny in the first, and a settler-colony's narrow escape from Mexicans in the second. Neither plot worked. Andy Devine, Constance Moore, Guinn Williams. (66 mins)

Mystery Of The White Room
Prod: Irving Starr Dir: Otis Garrett. A mindless mélange of stilted acting, poor plot and faltering direction characterised this whodunnit dealing with an operating-theatre murder. Bruce Cabot, Helen Mack. (59 mins)

Oklahoma Frontier (Johnny Mack Brown)
Dir: Ford Beebe. Johnny joins the Oklahoma land rush and finds his best friend and sister being duped by claim-jumpers. Fuzzy Knight, Anne Gwynne. (59 mins)

One Hour To Live
Prod: George Yohalem Dir: Harold Schuster. Fifty-nine minutes too long, this threadbare story told of an honest cop's efforts to rout a gang of hoods and their Mr Big ringleader. Charles Bickford, Doris Nolan, Samuel S. Hinds, Paul Guilfoyle, John Litel. (59 mins)

The Phantom Stage (Buck Jones)
Dir: Drew Eberson. Buck has problems in trying to get the pony express inaugurated and win government approval and contract. Marjorie Williams. (58 mins)

Pirates Of The Skies
Prod: Barney A. Sarecky Dir: Joseph A. McDonough. Fairly interesting, albeit clumsy, plot about waitress Rochelle Hudson who refuses to acknowledge her marriage to air policeman Kent Taylor until he upgrades his career. He does so by apprehending a gang of crooks. (61 mins)

Risky Business
Prod: Burt Kelly Dir: Arthur Lubin. Radio gossip columnist turns glamorous hero when he rescues a movie producer's kidnapped daughter. George Murphy, Eduardo Ciannelli, Dorothea Kent. (70 mins)

Society Smugglers
Prod: Ken Goldsmith Dir: Joe May. Crime melodrama, with no saving graces, about a Treasury Department agent who discovers a diamond-smuggling racket. Preston Foster, Irene Hervey. (70 mins)

They Asked For It
Prod: Max Gordon Dir: Frank McDonald. Determinedly second-rate film about a trio of college graduates who take over a small-town newspaper and put it about that the death of a local inebriate was murder. Turns out it was! William Lundigan, Michael Whalen, Lyle Talbot. (61 mins)

Tropic Fury
Prod: Ben Pivar Dir: Christy Cabanne. Tropical jungle setting for a scientist's search for rubber, brutal conditions on an Amazon plantation, a missing professor tortured into lunacy and the daughter who searches for him. Richard Arlen, Beverley Roberts, Andy Devine. (62 mins)

The Witness Vanishes
Prod: Irving Starr Dir: Otis Garrett. Routine thriller with one murder every fifteen minutes and a quartet of crooked journalists who commit newspaper-owner Edmund Lowe to an asylum so they can run his publication. Wendy Barrie, Bruce Lester. (66 mins)

1940

▽ **The Boys From Syracuse**, with a superlative score by Richard Rodgers and Lorenz Hart, and a book by George Abbott, had been an immediate hit on Broadway in 1938. Producer Jules Levey picked it up for the screen for reasons that seemed obvious, but became incomprehensible in the light of what followed. The story drew its inspiration from Shakespeare's *The Comedy Of Errors*, and focused on the confusions that beset two pairs of twins – one pair married and one pair single – when they get mixed up. The Leonard Spigelgass–Charles Grayson screenplay eliminated all traces of the original's satire, substituting anachronistic vulgarities in place of true humour. Musically, the Rodgers and Hart classics – numbers such as 'Sing For Your Supper', 'Falling In Love With Love', 'He And She' and 'This Can't Be Love' – were bowdlerized almost to the point of extinction, with new songs (like 'Who Are You' and 'The Greeks Have A Word For It') being unnecessarily added. Allen Jones (right) and Joe Penner starred in the dual roles of the twins, with Martha Raye, Rosemary Lane, Charles Butterworth, Irene Hervey (left), Alan Mowbray, Eric Blore and Samuel S. Hinds also in it. Dave Gould staged the dances, and Edward Sutherland directed. (73 mins)

▷ Though Boris Karloff was top-starred in **Black Friday**, the acting honours went to third-billed Stanley Ridges (illustrated) as a professor friend of Karloff's who, after being seriously injured in a gangster shoot-out, has a brain operation in which Karloff gives him a transplant of cells from the brain of one of the dead gangsters. The operation results in Ridges possessing a dual personality which Karloff is able to manipulate. The plot thickened with Karloff's discovery that the dead man, whose brain cells he appropriated, had a fortune in cash which is hidden away somewhere in New York, and he greedily uses the darker side of Ridges' split personality to help him gain access to the money. It ends with Karloff having to kill his 'creation' in order to save his own daughter's life – a crime which results in his being sentenced to death for murder. Bela Lugosi was second-billed, but appeared only briefly (as a gangster), with other roles under Arthur Lubin's second division direction going to Anne Nagel, Anne Gwynne, Virginia Brissac, Edmund MacDonald and Paul Fix. Kurt Siodmak and Eric Taylor wrote it, and Burt Kelly produced. (70 mins)

△ An espionage melodrama without a difference (but fun), **Enemy Agent** starred Richard Cromwell (right) as an innocent draftsman mistakenly believed to be a spy by a group of G-men who, in just over an hour of screen time, apprehend the real villains of the piece. At the same time, they manage to retrieve some vital top security plans for the army's secret bombsight. Sam Robins and Edmund L. Hartmann's screenplay (story by Robins) provided an almost surrealistic finale to their tale by having G-men bursting into the head of the spy ring's home and, in the guise of college boys, turning his lounge into a football stadium as they tackled the rest of his henchmen into submission! Also involved were Helen Vinson, Robert Armstrong, Marjorie Reynolds, Jack Arnold, Russell Hicks, Philip Dorn (left) and Jack La Rue. Ben Pivar produced (using footage from the 1937 serial *Radio Patrol*), and Lew Landers directed. (61 mins)

▽ First seen as a silent comedy in 1927 with Jean Hersholt in the lead, then as *Half A Sinner* in 1934 with Berton Churchill (who also played the role on stage), **Alias The Deacon** surfaced for a third airing with comic Bob Burns (right) as the film's *raison d'être*. Based on a play by John B. Hymer and LeRoy Clemens, it was the simple story of a card shark who invades a small town and, posing as a deacon, cleans up as a gambler. With a screenplay (by Nat Perrin and Charles Grayson) custom-made for Burns' personality, and with showy bits in it too for Mischa Auer (as a barber), Guinn Williams (a punch-drunk pug), as well as Edward Brophy, Thurston Hall, Benny Bartlett (left), Spencer Charters, Jack Carson and – as the young lovers – Peggy Moran and Dennis O'Keefe, a good time was had by the undemanding. Christy Cabanne's direction could certainly not be accused of subtlety; neither could Ben Pivar's raucous production. (74 mins)

▽ A pile of jungle platitudes with restless natives whose drums are driving everyone crazy, **Green Hell** was totally unworthy of its director James Whale, and a cast headed by Douglas Fairbanks Jr (right), John Howard (left), Vincent Price and George Sanders. Frances Marion and Harry Hervey's screenplay described the hazards attendant on an archaeological expedition in search of Inca treasure in the Brazilian interior, and showed what happens when a woman (Joan Bennett) joins what has hitherto been an all-male expedition. The film was little more than a transposed cowboys-'n'-injuns adventure with the jungle savages deputising for Red Indians. Alan Hale, George Bancroft and Francis McDonald (centre) were also in it, and the producer was Harry Edington. (87 mins)

▽ W.C. Fields made a welcome return to form in **The Bank Dick**, a typically Fieldsian brew of laughter and mayhem in which he played Egbert Souse (pronounced Soo-zay), an impecunious inebriate who, in the small town of Lompoc, inadvertently effects the capture of a hold-up man, and is rewarded with a bank guard's job. On the premise that if at first you succeed, there's no reason why you shouldn't succeed again, Fields (centre) is given a second chance to prove his worth when a second bank robber happens along at a most advantageous moment. As scripted by the great man himself (alias Mahatma Kane Jeeves), the laughs were plentiful, a surplus supply of them providing Franklin Pangborn, Una Merkel, Cora Witherspoon, Grady Sutton (left) and Shemp Howard with a fair crack of the comic whip. It all added up to a delightfully expansive entertainment that pleased the customers hugely. Edward Cline (veteran director of the Keystone Kops) directed, his big set-piece being a mountainside auto chase that climaxed the film. (69 mins)

▽ The seventh movie from the producer-star team of Joe Pasternak and Deanna Durbin (right), **It's A Date**, showed that the young lady was definitely growing up. With maturer years, she also displayed a richer voice and some development in her acting abilities. Norman Krasna's screenplay (from a story by Jane Hall, Frederick Kohner and Ralph Block), had Deanna as the daughter of a famous actress (Kay Francis) who, herself, has aspirations to the stage. In the event, mother gives up her grip on stardom to settle for romance with a millionaire (Walter Pidgeon, left), leaving the way clear for her daughter's rise to fame. If low on realism, it was high on entertainment, and was well served by co-stars Pidgeon and Miss Francis, as well as a stalwart supporting cast who included Eugene Pallette, Lewis Howard (Miss D's romantic interest), Samuel S. Hinds, Henry Stephenson, Virginia Brissac and, making his Hollywood debut S.Z. ('Cuddles') Sakall. Harry Owens and His Royal Hawaiians were also featured, and the music included four songs from the star: 'Musetta's Waltz' from *La Boheme* (Puccini), Schubert's 'Ave Maria', 'Loch Lomond' (traditional), and one new and pleasing ballad, 'Love Is All' (by Pinky Tomlin and Harry Tobias). William A. Seiter directed. Remade as *Nancy Goes To Rio* (MGM, 1940). (100 mins)

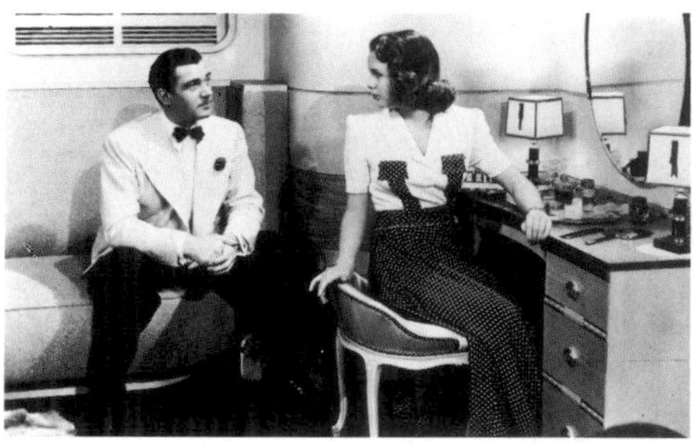

◁ Milton Krasner's gloomily atmospheric, low-key camerawork on **The House Of Seven Gables** was the best thing about this screen adaptation of Nathaniel Hawthorne's classic novel, and it went some distance to give what was basically a 'B' quality picture the look of an 'A'. George Sanders (left), an impossibly hammy Vincent Price (centre), and a rather insipid Margaret Lindsay (right) starred as members of the cursed Pyncheon family, with Price accused by his grasping brother (Sanders) of murdering his father, and being sent to prison for 20 years as a result. Meantime, his betrothed cousin (Miss Lindsay) has inherited 'Seven Gables', the Pyncheon house, and waits patiently for the day Price will be released. That day finally comes, Sanders gets his long overdue comeuppance, and Lindsay and Price are free to spend their remaining years in marital bliss. Scenarists Lester Cole and Harold Greene (the latter responsible for the adaptation) clearly had difficulty compressing the story's twenty-year span into just under an hour and a half, and the numerous dramatic contrivances they employed in doing so, proved fatal to credibility. Still, it was fun in a preposterous sort of way, with Price giving the most unintentionally humorous performance of his career. Other parts went to Dick Foran and Nan Grey as a pair of subsidiary young lovers, Cecil Kellaway, Alan Napier, Gilbert Emery and Miles Mander. Burt Kelly produced, and the brooding, moody direction was by Joe May. (87 mins)

△ Depending on one's mood, **The Mummy's Hand** was either very funny or very scary. It was also a rich assemblage of every trademark ever originated for the genre. Crumbling old temples presided over by grim-faced priests whose main purpose is to see that they are not desecrated, dark underground passageways leading to goodness-knows-where, strange and perplexing assortments of hieroglyphics, and an all-important 3000-year-old mummy being sustained by a secret elixir, were just some of the familiar ingredients that were poured into Griffin Jay and Maxwell Shane's screenplay (story by Jay). Dick Foran, Peggy Moran (illustrated) and Wallace Ford headed the cast (and the particular expedition in question), with other roles under Christy Cabanne's well-digested direction going to Eduardo Ciannelli, George Zucco, Cecil Kellaway, Charles Trowbridge, Sig Arno and, as the murderous mummy, Tom Tyler (illustrated). (67 mins)

△ **Argentine Nights**, a programmer musical, marked the screen debut of The Andrews Sisters. They were teamed with The Ritz Brothers, a knockabout comedy trio who had defected to Universal from 20th Century-Fox and, for those who liked their humour unsubtle, it was all sufficiently diverting. Written by Arthur T. Horman, Ray Golden and Sid Kuller (story by J. Robert Bren and Gladys Atwater), it was about a threesome of broke girl singers (The Andrews Sisters, illustrated) who run off to Argentina with their managers (The Ritz Brothers, illustrated). As directed by Albert S. Rogell for producer Ken Goldsmith, the show turned out to be a flimsy excuse for some comedy turns (variable in quality) from the boys, and a generous dollop of warbling from the girls. Also cast: Constance Moore, George Reeves, Peggy Moran and Ann Nagel. Songs included: 'Hit The Road'; 'Oh, He Loves Me' Don Raye, Hughie Prince, Vic Schoen; 'Rhumboogie' Raye, Prince; 'Amigo We Go Riding Tonight'; 'The Dowry Song' Sammy Cahn, Saul Chaplin. (72 mins)

△ Fifteen-year-old Gloria Jean was teamed with star Bing Crosby in a boring and fatuous musical called **If I Had My Way**. Most of the blame rested with David Butler who dreamed up the story (with William Conselman and James V. Kern, who scripted it), as well as directed and produced it. Plot had Bing (right), a construction worker, and sidekick El Brendel, escorting a newly-orphaned Gloria (left) to New York in search of her rich uncle. When the latter fails to take an interest in his niece, another uncle – an old-time vaudeville artist (Charles Winninger) – takes her in. Crosby and Brendel invest their remaining cash in a failed restaurant and turn it into a paying proposition by staging an old-time floor show. The stars, including little Miss Jean, did their best, but it wasn't good enough. Even the finale, with vintage performers Eddie Leonard (performing his own and Eddie Munson's 'Ida, Sweet As Apple Cider' in black-face), and Blanche Ring singing 'Rings On My Fingers' by Maurice Scott, R.P. Western and F.J. Barnes) failed to revive the tired old material. Also cast: Allyn Joslyn, David Woods, Claire Dodd, Nana Bryant, Moroni Olsen, Trixie Friganza and Julian Eltinge. Other songs included: 'If I Had My Way' Lew Klein, James Kendis; 'I Haven't Time To Be A Millionaire'; 'Meet The Sun Halfway'; 'The Pessimistic Character (With The Crab Apple Face)' Johnny Burke, James V. Monaco. (93 mins)

▽ John P. Fulton and the studio's special effects department came to the aid of **The Invisible Man Returns** which, despite some excellent trick photography, was nothing like as good as its illustrious predecessor. If seeing is believing, there was no believing Kurt Siodmak, Lester Cole and Cedric Belfrage's screenplay, based on a story by director Joe May and Siodmak, in which top-starred Vincent Price is accused of a murder he did not commit. Price (right) has the invisible-making drug administered to him, hoping that it will enable him to bring about the capture of the real culprit before he becomes visible again, thus saving himself from the gallows. The leading man, heard but not seen, was about the best deal the movie had to offer (apart from those weird special effects), with other roles going to Nan Grey (centre), John Sutton (left), Cecil Kellaway and, as the villain of the tale, Sir Cedric Hardwicke who, in one of the film's best sight gags, is seen being hustled by the collar with a disembodied gun sticking into his back. Ken Goldsmith produced. (81 mins)

▽ The marvellous Rosalind Russell bulldozed her way through **Hired Wife**, a romantic comedy in which she received top billing as Brian Aherne's efficient, all-purpose secretary. Going beyond the call of duty (plot-wise), Miss Russell (left) even schemes to marry him so that, for tax purposes, he can put his assets in his wife's name. Aherne (right), however, only has eyes for advertising model Virginia Bruce but, by the end, Miss Bruce has fallen for Latin lover John Carroll, thus leaving the way open for Miss Russell's proposed marriage of convenience to materialise into the real thing. Richard Connell and Gladys Lehmann's screenplay (from a story by George Beck), gave its principal players (including Robert Benchley as a scatter-brained attorney) a chance to show their mettle – which they all did to excellent advantage. Hobart Cavanaugh, William Davidson, Leonard Cary and Selmer Jackson were in it, too, for producer William A. Seiter who also directed. (95 mins)

△ **A Little Bit Of Heaven** was a starring vehicle for Gloria Jean who, while displaying a relaxed versatility, could hardly be said to set the screen ablaze. A corny, sentimental comedy, it featured Gloria as a talented neighbourhood kid who is rocketed to sudden fame on radio, bringing wealth – and its attendant difficulties – to her large family, hitherto poor but happy, in the tenement district of New York. The run-of-the-mill screenplay by Daniel Taradash, Gertrude Purcell and Harold Goldman (story by Grover Jones) was pepped up slightly by a quality supporting cast that included Robert Stack (right), Hugh Herbert, C. Aubrey Smith, Nan Grey (left), Eugene Pallette, Butch and Buddy, Frank Jenks, Noah Beery Sr, Sig Arno, Monte Blue and Rafaela Ottiano. Andrew Marton (a European making his first American film) directed with no noticeable distinction for producer Joe Pasternak and associate producer Islin Auster. The old song which gave the movie its title was by Ernest Ball and J. Keirn Brennan, and the other numbers were 'What Did We Learn At School?' by Vivian Ellis, 'Dawn Of Love' by Ralph Freed and Charles Previn, and 'After Every Rain Storm' by Sam Lerner and Frank Skinner. (85 mins)

△ John Barrymore hammed it up to give a wickedly accurate impersonation of his brother Lionel, as well as joining forces with special effects wizard John P. Fulton to rescue a maiden in distress or, to be more precise, **The Invisible Woman**. Not that the rescue operation was entirely satisfactory. That would have taken the kind of miracle that had been absent from the studio for some time. What they did manage to salvage, though, were isolated moments of fun wherein a beautiful model, after being turned invisible by scientist Barrymore, sets out, among other things, to even the score with her ruthless ex-employer. Robert Lees, Fred Rinaldo and Gertrude Purcell's screenplay (story by Kurt Siodmak and Joe May) attempted to make matters slightly more interesting by introducing a criminal element in search of the invisible-making formula, but under Edward Sutherland's invisible direction, the story remained obstinately simple-minded. Virginia Bruce (right) was the model who literally disappeared, with other roles going to John Howard (Miss Bruce's romantic interest), Charlie Ruggles (left) as a butler, Oscar Homolka as a gang leader, Margaret Hamilton as Barrymore's housekeeper, Thurston Hall, Charles Lane, Mary Gordon, Maria Montez, Ed Brophy and Shemp Howard. Burt Kelly produced. (73 mins)

△ One hundred per cent efficient in every department, **Spring Parade** represented another box office winner for Joe Pasternak and Deanna Durbin (centre). Departing noticeably from the wholesome all-American girl formula of the previous Durbin movies, it featured the star – now edging into attractive womanhood – as a wholesome Viennese baker's assistant during the reign of the Emperor Franz Joseph (an engagingly 'human' portrayal by Henry Stephenson). The tale of a peasant girl's romance with an army drummer (Robert Cummings, right) who is really cut out to be a composer, it had little substance to it, but was as airy and delicious as a Viennese cream puff. Bruce Manning and Felix Jackson wrote it (from a story by Ernst Marischka), and it was directed by the suitably schmaltzy Henry Koster. Also cast were S.Z. Sakall (left – a winning performance as the baker), Walter Catlett, Mischa Auer, Allyn Joslyn, Reginald Denny, Franklin Pangborn and Butch and Buddy. The liberal helping of songs included 'Blue Danube Dream' Johann Strauss II (lyrics by Gus Kahn); 'Waltzing In The Clouds'; 'It's Foolish But It's Fun' Kahn, Robert Stolz; 'In A Spring Parade' Kahn, Charles Previn. (75 mins)

▽ It wasn't only the natives featured in **South To Karanga** who were understandably restless; audiences were pretty miffed by the movie's similarity to Paramount's altogether superior *Shanghai Express* (1932), which it more than somewhat resembled, as well as by the poor quality of the writing (Edmund L. Hartmann and Stanley Rubin), the direction (Harold Schuster), and the performances of featured players Charles Bickford (right), John Sutton, Luli Deste (left), Addison Richards and James Craig. Only Paul Hurst as a prize-fighter manager refused to allow the inanities of the script to defeat him. For the rest, it was a tired old adventure yarn, whose express-train setting invited all the genre's old clichés to dust themselves off in furtherance of a well-worn plot. The obligatory on-board murder, plus the usual assortment of character types, not to mention a bomb explosion and a native attack, comprised barely an hour of screen time, brevity, in this instance being the picture's only blessing. The producer was Marshall Grant. (59 mins)

△ After an absence of two years Mae West (right) returned to the screen in **My Little Chickadee** and was paired with W.C. Fields (left), in what, on paper, promised to be a blockbuster. That the film, under Edward Cline's direction, turned out to be only moderately amusing was due, in the main, to the rather episodic nature of the screenplay, written by its two stars, each making sure that the other was not given the lion's share of the action. Basically a series of set-pieces in which both stars 'did their thing', what story there was echoed *Destry Rides Again* (1939) in reverse, with West (as Flower Belle Lee) returning from Chicago to a small Western town, and being drummed out of it again when she becomes the object of a masked gunman's attentions. On board a train to Greasewood City, the next frontier town, she meets medicine man Cuthbert J. Twittle (Fields), promotes a fake marriage with him, sees him inducted as sheriff of the new town, offers her charms to all and sundry, and finishes up bringing law and order to the place. The film ends with Fields moving on to pastures new and inviting West to 'come up and see me sometime'. West's own dialogue had its fair share of typical one-liners ('I generally avoid temptation unless I can't resist it'), but the great days she enjoyed at Paramount were clearly over. West and Fields were both too voluble as personalities to spend much time together in the same frame, and the structure of the film was such that, for most of the footage, each appeared separately. The scenes they did share always promised more than was delivered. **My Little Chickadee** was, in a word, disappointing. Joseph Calleia, Dick Foran, Ruth Donnelly, Margaret Hamilton, Donald Meek, Fuzzy Knight and Willard Robertson were also in it, and the producer was Lester Cowan. Song: 'Willie Of The Valley' Milton Drake, Ben Oakland. (83 mins)

▽ Marlene Dietrich (left), deliciously satirising every Shanghai Lil or Singapore Sal that ever swayed her hips in a sultry tropical romance, brought all her glamorous trade-marks to bear on hero John Wayne (right) – as audiences witnessed to their delight – in **Seven Sinners**. Dietrich played a woman called Bijou who, in the company of Broderick Crawford, Mischa Auer and Albert Dekker, arrives on the South Sea island of Boni-Komba to begin an engagement as a singer at the 'Seven Sinners Café' (owned by Billy Gilbert). It is there that she meets handsome Lieutenant Wayne, whom she charms so exhaustively that he is prepared to throw in his lot and marry her. In the end, however, common sense prevails. She realises that Wayne already has a wife – the sea. In a magnanimous gesture of sacrifice, she gets the hell out of the place, but not before a climactic brawl in which the 'Seven Sinners Café' is reduced to mere flotsam and jetsam. It was all good, clean, robust fun, with producer Joe Pasternak's well-chosen cast (including Oscar Homolka as the villain, Richard Carle, Samuel S. Hinds, Reginald Denny, Vince Barnett and Herbert Rawlinson) responding well to Tay Garnett's knock-'em-in-the-aisles direction. The leading lady husked her way through two songs by Frank Loesser and Frederick Hollander. They were 'I've Been In Love Before' and 'The Man's In The Navy'. (85 mins)

◁ Throughout the first half of the Forties, Universal tacked the title of a popular song onto a programmer and called it a musical. A really half-witted effort, **Oh Johnny, How You Can Love!** exemplified the pitfalls of this approach. In it, Tom Brown (right) and Peggy Moran (centre) starred as a salesman and an heiress respectively. They get involved when he rescues her from a car crash that occurs on her way to an elopement. Several nonsensical complications later, they fall into each other's by-now loving arms. End. Edwin Rutt (who was clearly stuck in one) wrote it for producer Ken Goldsmith and director Charles Lamont, providing featured roles that wasted the abilities of Betty Jane Rhodes (who sang the lively title song by Abe Olman and Ed Rose), Allen Jenkins (left), Donald Meek, Juanita Quigley and Isabel Jewel. Other songs included: 'Maybe I Like What You Like', 'Swing Chariot Swing'; 'Make Up Your Mind' Paul Gerard Smith, Frank Skinner. (60 mins)

▽ Story took second place in **Private Affairs**, a light-hearted comedy starring a refreshingly subdued Hugh Herbert (as a Scots taxi driver-cum-valet). Roland Young made a pleasant impression too, as a dispossessed Wall Street 'chalk-board operator' who betters his position in life, in the process of which he sees to it that his estranged daughter (whom he has not been allowed to visit) marries the right man. He also becomes reconciled with his old father (Montagu Love, right) and prevents some crooked stock manipulations. Nancy Kelly (left) received top billing as Young's daughter, with other roles under Albert S. Rogell's whirlwind direction (climaxing in a frenzied car chase) going to Robert Cummings (centre), Jonathan Hale, Florence Shirley, G.P. Huntley Jr and Dick Purcell. It was written by Charles Grayson, Leonard Spigelgass and Peter Milne (from Walter Greene's story *One Of The Boston Bullertons*) and produced by Burt Kelly and Glenn Tryon. (74 mins)

▽ Already very popular on radio, the comedy team of Bud Abbott (left) and Lou Costello (2nd left) were launched into their screen careers with **One Night In The Tropics**, a musical on which the studio spent a good deal of money and wasted a good deal of talent. Bud and Lou made a suitable impression – as a pair of undercover men mixed up in a plot about a man whose bride-to-be leaves him on their wedding day to run off with an insurance broker. However, the rest of Gertrude Purcell and Charles Grayson's screenplay (adapted by Kathryn Scola and Francis Martin from a novel by Earl Derr Biggers) was just a mess. A score by Jerome Kern, Oscar Hammerstein II and Dorothy Fields couldn't rescue it; neither could Allan Jones, Nancy Kelly, William Frawley (right), Mary Boland, Peggy Moran (centre) and Leo Carrillo. Edward Sutherland directed. Songs: 'Back In My Shell', 'Remind Me', 'You And Your Kiss' Kern, Fields; 'Your Dream Is The Same As My Dream' Kern, Hammerstein II, Otto Harbach. (82 mins)

◁ **Zanzibar** was clearly the kind of film that, years later, would inspire George Lucas to reassemble its ingredients for his blockbuster, *Raiders Of The Lost Ark* (Paramount, 1981). All about the search for the ancient skull of an African sultan, possession of which – according to the Versailles Treaty, no less – brings with it total control of the natives, it starred Lola Lane (3rd left) as an intrepid explorer who, together with James Craig (right, his debut) and Tom Fadden (left), sets out to return the skull to its rightful owners (Great Britain, according to that Treaty) before the Germans can lay their hands on it. But, as soon as the trio of explorers locates the object of its search, and true to jungle superstition, they awaken a volcano whose belching fury wipes out an entire native village but not, fortunately, the film's three leads, who move on to adventures new. Good clean fun in the best Saturday matinée tradition, the film also featured Eduardo Ciannelli (centre) as a spy out to topple Miss Lane's plans, with other roles going to Clarence Muse (2nd right) as a native leader, Eskimo Ray Mala (2nd left), Robert C. Fischer, Henry Victor and Samuel S. Hinds. The Maurices Tombragel and Wright scripted it with tongues well in cheek, and the action-packed direction was by Harold Schuster. Warren Douglas produced. (69 mins)

▽ One of Baby Sandy's better efforts, **Sandy Gets Her Man** involved the likeable little toddler in a plot in which the city's local police and fire department find themselves competing for the major share of a lucrative municipal contract. The decision as to which department will succeed in clinching the deal rests with council man William Davidson, who happens to be Sandy's grandfather. In the end it goes to the fire brigade (whose leader was slow-burn king Edgar Kennedy) for rescuing Baby Sandy (2nd left) from a burning building. Sandy's mum (Una Merkel, centre) was the object of fireman Stuart Erwin (centre right) and policeman Jack Carson's (left) affections, with other roles in Sy Bartlett and Jane Storm's family-oriented screenplay going to William Frawley, Wally Vernon (right), Edward Brophy and Isabel Randoph. Burt Kelly produced and Otis Garrett directed. (65 mins)

◁ The further adventures of two-year-old infant prodigy Baby Sandy (left) were unveiled in **Sandy Is A Lady**, whose screenplay by Charles Grayson ransacked the archives of silent screen comedy – to judge by the number of old-time comic situations he dredged up for the purposes of the plot (from Sandy attempting to cross a traffic-infested street, to the moppet's dizzying stint on a steel framework high above street level). Basically a series of incidents in which Sandy's misadventures bring good fortune to a restaurateur, an Italian neighbour, and her very own father, it was far too self-consciously cute to be endearing, despite solid support from a cast that included Mischa Auer, Billy Gilbert, Eugene Pallette, Edgar Kennedy, Fritz Feld, Anne Gwynne, Nan Grey (right), Tom Brown (centre), and Butch and Buddy (The Little Tornados). Charles Lamont directed it all from memory, and the producer was Burt Kelly. (62 mins)

◁ **When The Daltons Rode** was a rip-roaring, no punches pulled, no holds barred actioner which relied on the generosity of cinematic licence to recreate the bullet-whizzing adventures of the Dalton boys who, round about 1891, took to a life of crime when their ranch was appropriated by railroad land grabbers. Much of Harold Shumate's exciting screenplay (based on a book by Emmett Dalton and Jack Jungmeyer) pandered to the blood lust of its audiences, and delivered the goods in a series of bank robberies and train hold-ups, each more daring than the last. The movie's breathless climax, in which the Daltons participate in their last shoot-out (in Coffeyville, Kansas) vied with the last scene of *Hamlet* in the number of dead bodies that resulted. Though Randolph Scott, as a young lawyer friend of the vengeful Daltons, and Kay Francis as his romantic interest, headed the cast, it was the marauding adventures of the Dalton boys themselves (Broderick Crawford, Brian Donlevy, centre, Stuart Erwin, Frank Albertson, right) the customers paid to see, and they weren't disappointed. Mary Gordon played Ma Dalton, with other roles going to Andy Devine (as usual providing the comedy relief, left), Harvey Stephens, Edgar Deering and Quen Ramsey (2nd left). George Marshall's direction didn't flag for a second. (81 mins)

▽ A vapid comedy-thriller, partially redeemed by the performances of Edmund Lowe and Margaret Lindsay (both seated left), **Honeymoon Deferred** was the story of an insurance agent (Lowe) who gives up his job to marry (Miss Lindsay) and settle down to a quiet suburban existence. But just as he is about to set sail on his honeymoon in Bermuda, he is notified that his ex-boss has been murdered and promptly sets about finding out whodunnit. As scripted (clumsily) by Roy Chanslor and Elliot Gibbons, the murderer was revealed pretty early on and the denouement, when it finally arrived, was more confusing than illuminating. Elisabeth Risdon, Joyce Compton, Chick Chandler, Anne Gwynne, Emmett Vogan (left), Jimmy Conlin (2nd left), Cliff Clark (centre), Joe Sawyer (centre right) and Jerry Marlowe (seated right) were also featured, the woolly direction was by Lew Landers, and it was produced by Ken Goldsmith. (59 mins)

△ Allowing for a rather porous plot, **Double Alibi** was a better-than-average programme thriller with better-than-average central performance from Wayne Morris (left), a man incorrectly suspected of murdering not only his wife, but two men who, years before, had been his accomplices in a robbery. The real villain of Harold Buckman, Ray Chanslor and Charles Grayson's screenplay (story by Frederick C. Davis) was none other than police captain James Burke. Also cast in this early example of corruption in the forces, were Roscoe Karns (right) and Robert Emmett Keane, who provided some comic relief as a newspaper photographer and a reporter, while Margaret Lindsay (centre, second-billed) was there to provide the romantic interest for Mr Morris. William Gargan, Frank Mitchell, Eddy Chandler, Cliff Clark, Wade Boteler and Mary Treen completed the cast for producer Ben Pivar, and the better-than-average direction was by Philip Rosen. (60 mins)

OTHER RELEASES OF 1940

Bad Man From Red Butte (Johnny Mack Brown)
Dir: Ray Taylor. A dual role for Johnny as an outlaw and a stage-coach agent in a town dominated by a ruthless villain. Fuzzy Knight, Bob Baker, Anne Gwynne. (58 mins)

Black Diamonds
Prod: Ben Pivar Dir: Christy Cabanne. Workaday story of a newspaperman's return to home town where he finds a crooked inspector allowing coal miners to work in unsafe conditions. Richard Arlen, Andy Devine, Kathryn Adams, Mary Treen. (60 mins)

Danger On Wheels
Prod: Ben Pivar Dir: Christy Cabanne. Low budget actioner starred Richard Arlen as chief tester for Atlas Motors who takes the chief racing driver's place at the last minute. But there is a crash and Atlas is discredited until things are finally put right. Jack Arnold, Herbert Corthell. (61 mins)

The Devil's Pipeline
Prod: Ben Pivar Dir: Christy Cabanne. Forgettable meller once again teaming Richard Arlen and Andy Devine as investigators despatched to the South Pacific where oilfield men are being imprisoned on phoney charges. Jeanne Kelly. (65 mins)

Diamond Frontier
Prod: Marshall Grant Dir: Harold Schuster. Little more than a transposed western, but purporting to be an accurate account of the South African diamond rush, this movie told of attempts at maintaining law and order in a fast growing mining town. Victor McLaglen, John Loder, Anne Nagel. (73 mins)

Framed
Prod: Ben Pivar Dir: Harold Schuster. Reporter outsmarts cops, unravels a murder for which he's been framed, and delivers a scoop for his paper. Frank Albertson, Constance Moore, Jerome Cowan. (60 mins)

Give Us Wings
Prod: Ken Goldsmith Dir: Charles Lamont. Lousy programmer assembling The Little Tough Guys and The Dead End Kids who, failing to get into the airforce, become crop dusters for Victor Jory. Wallace Ford, Anne Gwynne. (62 mins)

Half A Sinner
Prod/Dir: Al Christie. Rich John King helps teacher Heather Angel out of trouble after she steals his car to avoid a flirtatious male, unaware that the back seat passenger is a dead gangster. Constance Collier, Walter Catlett. (60 mins)

Hot Steel
Prod: Ben Pivar Dir: Christy Cabanne. Metallurgist invents a high-test steel formula which is stolen, and is jailed for a murder he didn't commit. Richard Arlen, Anne Nagel, William Wayne, Andy Devine. (61 mins)

I Can't Give You Anything But Love Baby
Prod: Ken Goldsmith Dir: Albert S. Rogell. Lyric-writing gangster kidnaps composer to write love song for long lost sweetheart. Broderick Crawford, Johnny Downs, Peggy Moran. (60 mins)

I'm Nobody's Sweetheart Now
Prod: Joseph G. Sandford Dir: Arthur Lubin. Two young lovebirds marry and thwart parental plans for alternative marriage partners. Dennis O'Keefe, Helen Parrish, Lewis Howard, Constance Moore, Laura Hope Crews, Samuel S. Hinds, Marjorie Gateson and The Dancing Cansinos. (63 mins)

La Conga Nights
Prod: Ken Goldsmith Dir: Lew Landers. Cabdriver-vaudevillian meets singer, puts on show in his boarding house, and quashes a tenant's eviction order. Hugh Herbert, Dennis O'Keefe, Constance Moore, Eddie Quillan. (70 mins)

Law And Order (Johnny Mack Brown)
Dir: Ray Taylor. Johnny is a former US marshal who rides into town with his two pals and cleans out a gang of thugs. Bob Baker, Fuzzy Knight, Nell O'Day. (57 mins)

The Leather Pushers
Prod: Ben Pivar Dir: John Rawlins. Richard Arlen and Andy Devine, as trainer and boxer, and Douglas Fowley as a promoter who, seeing Arlen as a champ not trainer, sets about reversing the roles with sports columnist Astrid Allwyn's help. (64 mins)

Love Honour And Oh Baby!
Prod: None credited Dir: Charles Lamont. Silliest comedy of the year about a man who hires a crime syndicate to murder him so his sister can inherit insurance money – then has second thoughts. Donald Woods, Kathryn Adams. (60 mins)

Ma, He's Making Eyes At Me
Prod: Joseph G. Sandford Dir: Harold Schuster. Press agent cultivates model to promote cheap clothing. Title song by Sidney Clare, Con Conrad. Tom Brown, Constance Moore, Anne Nagel, Richard Carle, Jerome Cowan. (61 mins)

Margie
Prod: Joseph G. Sandford Dir: Otis Garrett. Songwriter encounters marital difficulties with his scriptwriter wife. Tom Brown, Nan Grey, Eddie Quillan, Wally Vernon. (59 mins)

Meet The Wildcat
Prod: Joseph G. Sandford Dir: Arthur Lubin. An accomplished cast prodded life into this moribund thriller about a New York detective mistaken for an art thief. Ralph Bellamy, Margaret Lindsay, Joseph Schildkraut, Allen Jenkins. (61 mins)

Pony Post (Johnny Mack Brown)
Dir: Ray Taylor. Johnny is the honest cowboy who has to contend with outlaws and Indians while running a pony express relay station. Fuzzy Knight, Nell O'Day. (59 mins)

Ragtime Cowboy Joe (Johnny Mack Brown)
Dir: Ray Taylor. Johnny plays an investigator for a cattle association sent to capture rustlers employed by a politician. Fuzzy Knight, Nell O'Day. (68 mins)

Riders Of the Pasco Basin (Johnny Mack Brown)
Dir: Ray Taylor. Johnny leads a group of vigilantes against a gang who have been taking money from ranchers with promises to build a dam. Fuzzy Knight, Bob Baker. (56 mins)

Ski Patrol
Prod: Warren Douglas Dir: Lew Landers. Capitalizing on Russo-Finnish war, the film told the story of troops' defence of a mountain-top mined by Russian sappers. Philip Dorn, Luli Deste, Stanley Fields, Samuel S. Hinds, Edward Norris, John Qualen. (64 mins)

Slightly Tempted
Prod: Ken Goldsmith Dir: Lew Landers. Fumbling kleptomaniac, after unloading unwanted goods on a small town, reforms for the sake of his daughter, and the elderly spinster he lands up marrying. Hugh Herbert, Peggy Moran, Elisabeth Risdon. (60 mins)

Son Of Roaring Dan (Johnny Mack Brown)
Dir: Ford Beebe. Johnny pretends that a tough old westerner is his father as a masquerade to capture his real father's murderers. Fuzzy Knight, Nell O'Day. (60 mins)

Trail Of The Vigilantes
Dir: Alan Dwan. A tenderfoot marshal from the east is sent west to investigate the disappearance of his predecessor. Franchot Tone, Broderick Crawford. (78 mins)

West Of Carson City (Johnny Mack Brown)
Dir: Ray Taylor. Johnny and his pals save a gold rush community from gamblers trying to move in and take over. Bob Baker, Fuzzy Knight, Peggy Moran. (56 mins)

You're Not So Tough
Prod: Ken Goldsmith Dir: Joe May. The Dead End Kids and The Little Tough Guys again, this time in difficulties on a fruit ranch when they refuse to implement a grower's association wage cut. Nan Grey, Rosina Galli. (71 mins)

1941

◁ Former burlesque and radio stars Bud Abbott (2nd right) and Lou Costello (2nd left) (billed below Lee Bowman and Alan Curtis) turned **Buck Privates** into a major box-office hit for the studio. A totally zany and madcap piece of nonsense, in which the comics find themselves unintentionally trapped in an army induction centre and end up as enlisted men, the movie rocketed Bud and Lou to third place (behind Mickey Rooney and Clark Gable) in the national popularity polls. Their routines followed thick and fast, with a five-minute sequence featuring Costello doing special rifle drill being a standout for laughs. The Andrews Sisters (illustrated), suitably decked out as WAACS, spiced the comedy with several vocal highspots that included 'Boogie Woogie Bugle Boy From Company B' and 'Bounce Me Brother With A Solid Four' (by Don Raye and Hughie Prince), 'You're A Lucky Fellow, Mr Smith' (Raye, Prince and Sonny Burke), and the Neville Fleeson–Albert von Tilzer oldie, 'I'll Be With You In Apple Blossom Time'. The supporting cast featured Nat Pendleton as the sergeant at loggerheads with the untrainable Costello, while stars Lee Bowman and Alan Curtis played recruits who get romantically involved with Jane Frazee. Also: Samuel S. Hinds, Harry Strang, Nella Walker, Leonard Elliott and Shemp Howard. The laugh-infested script by Arthur T. Horman was given direction to match by Arthur Lubin. It was produced by Alex Gottlieb. (82 mins)

▽ An 'A' grade western with a 'C' grade storyline, **Badlands Of Dakota** offered action in lieu of a decent plot, and starred Robert Stack and Ann Rutherford as the romantic leads, with fourth-billed Broderick Crawford (right) as Stack's brother who, until his sibling came along, was once Miss Rutherford's fiancé. Comedy was given a free rein in the familiar routines of Hugh Herbert, Andy Devine and Fuzzy Knight – so much so that latecomers might be forgiven for thinking they'd paid to see the wrong film. Traditional western action finally reasserted itself with the whooping arrival of the Sioux, guaranteeing patrons a noisy finale. Gerald Geraghty wrote it from an 'original' story by Harold Shumate, Alfred E. Green pulled out all the stops to keep it exciting, it was produced by George Waggner, and the cast included Lon Chaney Jr, Bradley Page, Samuel S. Hinds, Frances Farmer (left), Addison Richards (as General Custer) and third-billed Richard Dix as Wild Bill Hickock – whose misfortune it was to die three-quarters of the way through. (75 mins)

△ Though a great deal of physical mileage was covered in **Burma Convoy**, the entertainment mileage clocked up by producer Marshall Grant wasn't anything like as impressive. All about a convoy of hell drivers carrying munitions to the Chinese from Rangoon to Chungking via the Burma highway, it starred tough Charles Bickford (illustrated) whose main preoccupation in Stanley Rubin and Roy Chanslor's screenplay was figuring out how top security convoy schedules have been managing to fall into enemy hands. The answer was apparent to audiences long before it finally became apparent to him. Although for most of the time, the story sagged like an old horse-hair sofa, it did perk up for a fairly rousing finale in which the convoy is hi-jacked by a band of guerilla parachutists. Nonetheless, it was nothing to get excited about and hardly worth waiting for. Evelyn Ankers, Frank Albertson, Cecil Kellaway, Willie Fung, Keye Luke, Turhan Bey and Truman Bradley were also cast, and the director was Noel M. Smith. (72 mins)

△ Baby Sandy (right) was getting far too old to play the gurgling toddler by the time **Bachelor Daddy** was made. In this one, the diapered Duse found herself abandoned by her mother and in the care of three bachelor brothers, whose bachelor club she turns upside down, especially when she takes it on herself to run the club's elevator. Edward Everett Horton (left), Donald Woods and Raymond Walburn were cast as her hapless foster fathers, with other roles going to Franklin Pangborn, Evelyn Ankers, Kathryn Adams, Jed Prouty and Juanita Quigley. It was written by Robert Lees and Fred Rinaldo, produced by Burt Kelly and directed by Harold Young. (61 mins)

△ Without Charles Boyer (left) and Margaret Sullavan (right), **Appointment For Love** would have been an appointment with tedium. Even with them there was less to this romantic comedy than met the eye. He played a playwright, she a doctor. They marry, but for some reason don't trust each other. He misunderstands her need for privacy; she thinks he's having affairs with other women. They bicker and change apartments a lot. It all worked out in the end, of course, but not before a great deal of energy was wasted on giving it the appearance of a custom-built Rolls when, underneath the trimmings, it was nothing more than a barely functional flivver. Producer Bruce Manning wrote it with Felix Jackson from the story *Heartbeat* by Ladislaus Bus-Fekete, William A. Seiter brought a glossy sensibility to the direction, and the cast included Rita Johnson, Eugene Pallette, Ruth Terry, Virginia Brissac and Gus Schilling. (88 mins)

△ 'This is Hollywood, we change everything here. We've *got* to!' Thus spake actor Richard Lane (playing the director) to comedians Olsen and Johnson at the beginning of **Hellzapoppin'**, in which the duo had scored an enormous stage success. And change everything they did, injecting an orthodox love triangle into the proceedings, and noticeably pulling the punches on the mad humour of the original material. The result was a very uneven comedy musical that offered a lot of good sight gags (and quite a number of poor ones), a dollop of songs by Don Raye and Gene De Paul, a specialty act called Slim and Sam, the larger-than-life Martha Raye, and a capable supporting cast, some of the whose roles seemed to be part of a vanishing act. Robert Paige played the wealthy owner of a Long Island mansion where he is trying to stage a show (he was also part of the love triangle along with Jane Frazee and Lewis Howard); Miss Raye (left) spent the time pursuing a well-heeled aristocrat (Mischa Auer, right), taking a moment off to sing the nutty 'Watch The Birdie'; Hugh Herbert passed through as a private eye, and Shemp Howard was momentarily glimpsed as a movie projectionist. H.C. Potter directed for producer Jules Levey, from a screenplay by Nat Perrin and Warren Wilson (story by Perrin), with Clarence Kolb, Nella Walker, Katherine Johnson and Elisha Cook Jr also in it. (84 mins)

△ 'If you have tears, prepare to shed them now ...' could have been the advertising slogan for **Back Street**, a remake of the studio's 1932 success with Charles Boyer (centre) as the irresistible, albeit selfish, banker and Margaret Sullavan (left) as the hapless 'back street' woman who waits for him in vain, and whose heart he breaks. If emotional frustration was one of the key themes of Fannie Hurst's best-seller, producer Bruce Manning who scripted this latest adaptation with Felix Jackson, didn't miss a trick in conveying the agony of a tormented affair. Neither did the two leading players, whose beautiful and eloquent sufferings shredded the hearts of female audiences everywhere. It was reverentially directed by Robert Stevenson as though it had been scripted by Shakespeare, and also featured Richard Carlson, Frank McHugh, Frank Jenks, Nella Walker (as Boyer's wife), and Tim Holt and Nell O'Day as his children. Also: Samuel S. Hinds, Peggy Stewart, Cecil Cunningham (right), and Marjorie Gateson. The film's only miscalculation was the over-the-top sequence depicting Boyer's death from a stroke. Piling on the agony was all very well, but enough was enough! The film was remade yet again in 1961. (89 mins)

▽ Romance on the high seas was about the only saleable ingredient in **This Woman Is Mine**, a half-baked story of a two-year long fur trapping expedition from New York to Oregon in which top-starred Franchot Tone (centre), as the agent of the expedition's organiser (Sig Rumann), and Frenchman John Carroll (left) vie for the affections of lovely stowaway Carol Bruce (right). Also along for the ride: Nigel Bruce and Leo G. Carroll as a pair of fur traders, as well as Captain Walter Brennan, First Mate Frank Conroy, Second Mate Paul Hurst, Abner Biberman and Morris Ankrum. Seton I. Miller's screenplay, based on Gilbert Wolff Gabriel's novel *I, James Lewis*, literally ended with a bang as the ship on which most of it took place was blown out of existence. A pity it didn't happen an hour earlier. It was written and directed by Frank Lloyd, who should have known better. (92 mins)

◁ A comedy of mistaken identity, **The Man Who Lost Himself** starred Brian Aherne (right) who, in the course of Eddie Moran's screenplay from the novel by H. DeVere Stackpoole, spends a night drinking with a look-a-like and, the following morning, wakes up in his double's bed only to discover his drinking companion of the previous evening has died – in circumstances which force him to assume the dead man's identity. A beautifully gowned Kay Francis was second-billed as the deceased's wife – totally unaware that her real husband is dead. Also featured was S.Z. 'Cuddles' Sakall (left) of the pinchable jowls, with other roles in this contrived but amusing romp going to Henry Stephenson, Nils Asther, Sig Rumann, Dorothy Tree, Janet Beecher, Henry Kolker and Russell Hicks. Lawrence W. Fox Jr produced, and it was directed by Edward Ludwig. (70 mins)

▽ Following their hugely successful antics in *Buck Privates* Abbott and Costello switched their uniforms and surfaced **In The Navy**. The story (by Arthur T. Horman, who wrote the screenplay with John Grant) was actually about a radio crooner (Dick Powell) who joins the navy to escape the ardour of his fans, and is pursued by a would-be lady reporter (Claire Dodd, centre) who scents a story. With Powell (right), Dick Foran (left), and The Andrews Sisters all heavily in attendance, the movie lent itself to music, with Powell performing 'Starlight, Starbright' and 'We're In The Navy', Foran and male chorus singing 'A Sailor's Life For Me', and the Andrews girls handling some tailor-made songs, including 'Gimme Some Skin'. For all this pleasant distraction, Abbott and Costello delivered a fair quota of wacky slapstick, as well as another big hit for Universal. The rest of the cast included Billy Lenhart, Kenneth Brown and Shemp Howard, and there was some good specialty work from the dancing Condos Brothers. Don Raye and Gene De Paul penned the songs and Nick Castle staged the dances. (85 mins)

▷ The third Abbott (left) and Costello (2nd left) blockbuster to please audiences (not to mention studio executives), **Hold That Ghost** had, in fact, been filmed, but not released, before *In The Navy*. The latter was rushed out to capitalize on the success of *Buck Privates* and, in the interim, it was decided to expand the possibilities of **Hold That Ghost**. Its original producer, Burt Kelly, having departed for Paramount, Glenn Tryon was assigned to the production and new material added to feature Ted Lewis and His Entertainers, and The Andrews Sisters. The musical angle proved a winner, getting the movie airborne in its opening sequences. Lewis, in fine form, gave his theme song 'When My Baby Smiles At Me' (by Harry von Tilzer and Andrew B. Sterling), and 'Me And My Shadow' (by Billy Rose, Al Jolson and Dave Dreyer). The Andrews Sisters followed with a knockout arrangement of 'Sleepy Serenade' (by Mort Greene and Lou Singer). Excuse for all this was a nightclub where Bud and Lou are working as waiters. They get fired, do a stint in a gas station and finally inherit a deserted roadhouse from a murdered mobster of their acquaintance. Demented antics prevailed, as the house turns out to be haunted – a device that left plenty of room for provoking mirth. Accompanying the boys to their new property were Joan Davis (as a radio singer, centre right), Richard Carlson (a doctor, right), Mischa Auer, Evelyn Ankers (centre), Marc Lawrence, Shemp Howard and Russell Hicks. The story, by Robert Lees and Fred Rinaldo – (which they scripted with John Grant), had the comedians discovering the late owner's hoard of hidden riches, and turning the place into a thriving roadhouse. Cue for more interludes from Lewis and The Andrews Sisters. Arthur Lubin again directed, delivering a pacy and profitable frolic. (85 mins)

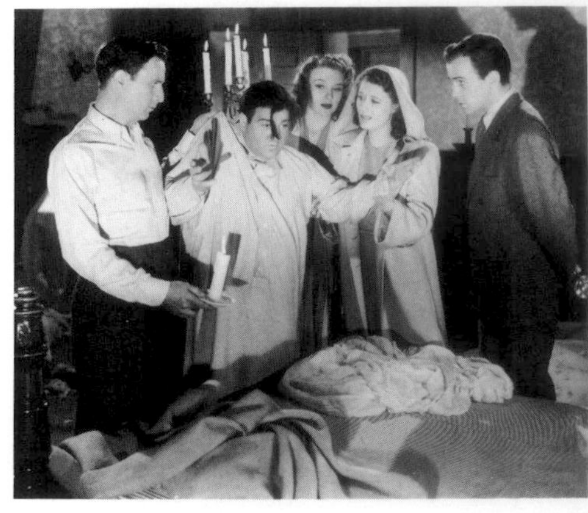

▽ There were no fewer than four deaths in **The Black Cat**, a spooky thriller, laced with laughs, in which wealthy, cat-loving Cecilia Loftus makes a deathbed recovery only to be bumped off either by a greedy member of her family or by one of her staff. A stock plot of a horror stock pot into which were mixed all the familiar ingredients of the genre, including a number of ill-judged bits of comedy from the likes of Hugh Herbert and Broderick Crawford (right) as an antique dealer and a family friend respectively, the film always promised more than it delivered, especially with a cast that included Basil Rathbone (left, top-starred), Bela Lugosi, Gale Sondergaard (centre) and Gladys Cooper. Anne Gwynne, Claire Dodd and John Eldredge were in it too; and, in a small part, so was Alan Ladd. Robert Lees, Fred Rinaldo, Eric Taylor and Robert Neville wrote it *en masse* from a story 'suggested' by Edgar Allan Poe, the associate producer was Burt Kelly, and it was directed with a welter of synthetic 'thrills' by Albert S. Rogell. (70 mins)

◁ Director Rene Clair received a critical lambasting for **The Flame Of New Orleans**, an antebellum trifle in which a French beauty, played by Marlene Dietrich (left), arrives in New Orleans in 1841 pretending to be a wealthy noblewoman in order to marry the richest man in town (Roland Young). She is snatched from the altar, however, by rough-and-ready Bruce Cabot (right), and together the two of them make off by ship, with Dietrich's magnificent wedding gown being flung, in a most cavalier manner, out of the nearest porthole as she settles down for a night of love. Though certainly not one of Clair's best efforts, it was unfairly dismissed as being too flippant a vehicle for his considerable talents. Reassessed today, it is a slight, but highly civilised comedy. Dietrich's performance as heroine Claire Ledoux, though not at all Gallic, was delightful. She sang 'Sweet As The Blush Of May' by Charles Previn and Sam Lerner, and benefitted strikingly from Rudolph Mate's stunning photography, from Rene Hubert's costumes and from the ravishing period art direction. The excellent supporting cast included Mischa Auer, Andy Devine, Frank Jenks, Eddie Quillan, Laura Hope Crews, Franklin Pangborn, Theresa Harris, Clarence Muse, Melville Cooper and Anne Revere; it was scripted by Norman Krasna and produced by Joe Pasternak. (78 mins)

▷ **Model Wife** wasn't entirely a model comedy, but it came pretty close, being let down by a screenplay that should have been much wittier than it was. Still, it gave Joan Blondell (2nd left) and Dick Powell (right – hitherto stars over at Warner Bros., many of whose musicals their talents had graced) a chance to shine as a husband and wife who, because of the strict conditions of their present employment, are obliged to keep their marital status a secret. The fact that the couple want to have a child but haven't the financial wherewithal to turn their dream into a practical reality, was an added complication. Charles Kaufman, Horace Jackson and Grant Garrett's screenplay indulged in some frank discussions concerning the baby problem, as well as providing substantial roles for Lucille Watson as the young couple's disagreeable martinet employer, Charlie Ruggles (left) and Lee Bowman. Ruth Donnelly, Billy Gilbert and John Qualen were also featured, and it was produced and directed by Leigh Jason, who also provided the original story. (78 mins)

△ **It Started With Eve** was an unqualified delight in which Charles Laughton (right), second-billed to Deanna Durbin (centre), gave one of the most endearing performances of his career. He played a cantankerous millionaire whose deathbed wish is to meet his son's future bride. As the lady in question isn't immediately available, son Robert Cummings (left) picks up the first girl he can find (Deanna Durbin, no less) and, believing his father to be fast expiring, introduces her to the old curmudgeon. Turns out that Laughton, who takes an understandable shine to hat-check girl Miss Durbin, isn't dying after all – which is good news in one respect, but needlessly complicates Cummings' life, since his real fiancée (Margaret Tallichet) is about to arrive on the scene at any moment! As scripted by Norman Krasna and Leo Townsend from a story by Hans Kraly, it all tied itself up in a neat little bow – even allowing Miss Durbin to break into song on three separate occasions with a waltz by Tchaikovsky, 'Clavelitos' by Valverde and 'Going Home' by Dvorak. Guy Kibbee, Catherine Doucet, Walter Catlett (as Laughton's prissy doctor), Charles Coleman (as the butler), Leonard Elliott, Irving Bacon, Gus Schilling, Wade Boteler, Dorothea Kent and Clara Blandick also appeared for producer Joe Pasternak, and it was directed with well-judged insouciance by Henry Koster. The same story resurfaced in 1964 as *I'd Rather Be Rich*. (90 mins)

△ Audiences exposed to the absurdities perpetrated in **South Of Tahiti** would have had to search in vain to find a Polynesian travel brochure remotely resembling the island paradise which Brian Donlevy (left), Broderick Crawford, Andy Devine and Henry Wilcoxon, as shipwrecked pearl hunters, stumble upon in the movie. Chief tourist attraction on the island is sarong-clad Melahi, portrayed by Maria Montez (right), whose particular talent is her way with wild animals, with an extravagantly choreographed initiation ceremony in which the island's youth pass from boyhood to manhood, coming a close second. It was written by Gerald Geraghty from a story by Ainsworth Morgan, directed as a piece of wish-fulfilment escapism by George Waggner (who also produced) and featured H.B. Warner as the island's High Chief (who happens to speak English as if to the manor born), Armida, Abner Biberman, Ignacio Saenz and Frank Lackteen. Song: 'Melahi' Frank Skinner, George Waggner, sung by Montez, dubbed by Martha Tilton. (78 mins)

▽ **The Lady From Cheyenne** struck an early blow for women's liberation, telling, as it did, the story of one Annie Morgan (Loretta Young, top-billed), a schoolteacher who, in 1869, won the vote for the area's womenfolk and with it the right for women to sit on a jury. Set in a typical western boom town of the period, and peopled by Robert Preston (as the man Miss Young, centre, eventually marries), Edward Arnold (as an amiable villain), Gladys George (as the town's fancy woman, right), Samuel S. Hinds (as the local governor) as well as Frank Craven, Jessie Ralph, Willie Best (left), Stanley Fields and Spencer Charters, it was a genial enough entertainment, produced and directed by Frank Lloyd with care and affection. And if, strictly speaking, the screenplay by Kathryn Scola and Warren Duff (story by Jonathan Finn and Theresa Oaks) was somewhat thin on the ground, Loretta Young's gracious and attractive presence was quite enough to keep one from speaking strictly. (84 mins)

△ Plot (such as there was) played very little part in **Never Give A Sucker An Even Break** (GB: **What A Man**), a recklessly incoherent comedy given the kiss of immortality by its star W.C. Fields (right) who, as a character simply called 'The Great Man', peddled mirth in a series of non-sequiturs – from outlining the story of a script he hopes to sell to a movie producer to impersonating a Russian mujik enjoying the delights of fermented goat's milk. Whether courting in a tail-coat whose tails are carried by two attendants, contemplating the froth on a chocolate soda or dispensing glorious one-liners such as 'She drove me to drink, the one thing I'm indebted to her', Fields had a field day honing his comic genius, and so did audiences partial to his particular brand of nonsense. Especially effective was a climactic chase to a maternity hospital in which the car Fields is driving literally falls apart in his hands. (The sequence would be reworked by the studio in Abbott and Costello's *In Society*, in 1944). It was scripted by John T. Neville and Prescott Chaplin (from a story by Fields, alias Otis Criblecoblis), and, discernible between the numerous vaudeville turns of its stars, was the tale of a con man's attempts to marry Mrs Hemogloben (Margaret Dumont) or, failing that, her daughter Ouliotta (Susan Miller). It was directed by Edward Cline with the emphasis squarely on the eccentricities of his leading player, and also featured Gloria Jean (as Fields's niece) and Leon Errol (as his rival, left), as well as Butch and Buddy, Franklin Pangborn (as the film producer), Mona Barrie, Charles Lang, Anne Nagel and Nell O'Day. No producer was credited. (70 mins)

△ With **Keep 'Em Flying**, their fourth release in 10 months, laugh merchants Abbott (left) and Costello (right) peddled their humour via the airforce. They burlesqued their way through an insignificant screenplay (by True Boardman, Nat Perrin and John Grant, story by Edmund Hartmann) in company with Martha Raye playing twin sisters, Dick Foran as a stunt flyer and Carol Bruce as Foran's romantic interest. It was all good clean fun in expected Bud and Lou style, but their routines were, by now, beginning to seem slightly over-familiar. Miss Raye's raucous rendering of 'Pig Foot Pete' (by Don Raye and Gene De Paul) was a decided asset; Miss Bruce pleased, too, with 'I'm Getting Sentimental Over You' (by Ned Washington and George Bassman) and 'The Boy With The Wistful Eyes' (Raye, De Paul); while Dick Foran sang the lively 'Let's Keep 'Em Flying', also by Raye and De Paul. William Gargan, Charles Lang, Truman Bradley, William Davidson and Loring Smith completed the cast for A and C's director-in-residence, Arthur Lubin. (86 mins)

△ With **Nice Girl?** it was clear that Deanna Durbin (left) had finally reached womanhood. However, her charm, looks and voice accompanied her there, as well as a youthful air of innocence that imparted the familiar flavour of her previous films to this slight tale of romance lost and found in a small town. Echoing *That Certain Age* (1938), this one again had Deanna falling for an older man – a colleague of her father's on a visit from New York. The suave Franchot Tone (right) co-starred as the object of Miss Durbin's feminine wiles, to which he responds with much embarrassment. After several rejections by Tone, the young lady regains her senses and returns her affections to her long-standing boyfriend, Robert Stack. An A-grade supporting cast helped to jolly it all along, notably Walter Brennan (as the local postman), Robert Benchley (Deanna's father, left) and Ann Gillis (her man-mad younger sister). Helen Broderick, Anne Gwynne, Elizabeth Risdon and Nana Bryant were also featured. Joe Pasternak produced it, and William A. Seiter directed from a screenplay by Richard Connell and Gladys Lehman (story by Phyllis Duganne). The star's vocal offerings included 'Love At Last' by Eddie Cherkose and Jacques Press, and 'Perhaps' by Aldo Franchetti and Andreas De Segurola. (91 mins)

▽ Director Gregory La Cava came to the aid (in no uncertain terms) of **Unfinished Business**, a mundane romantic comedy which needed all the help it could beg, borrow or steal. Fortunately, the La Cava touch was in evidence throughout the telling of a rather trite story in which, after a fleeting train flirtation with Preston Foster, small-town Ohio girl Irene Dunne marries Foster's brother (Robert Montgomery, left). Following an initial round of nightclub going and general merry-making, the married couple settle down unhappily. But not for long. Miss Dunne (right) takes off, and is discovered a year later, singing in the chorus of an opera company. Scenarist Eugene Thackeray vouchsafed a happy ending, with Foster taking an upper-cut as a means of reconciling Miss Dunne with his brother who, in the interim, has become the father of a baby boy. Eugene Pallette did yeoman duty as a butler; and so did Walter Catlett as a Billy Rose-type nightclub owner called Billy Ross. Also cast: Dick Foran, Richard Davies, Samuel S. Hinds, June Clyde and Walter Adams. La Cava also produced. (94 mins)

▽ Lon Chaney Jr (left) got his first crack at the monster genre in **Man Made Monster**, playing the victim of mad doctor Lionel Atwill (right), who pumps him so full of electricity that he becomes immune to high voltage shocks. Despite some good special effects by John P. Fulton – whose wizardry enabled Chaney to move about impersonating a fully operational neon light – there was little in Joseph West's screenplay (from H.J. Essex, Sid Schwartz and Len Colos' story *The Electric Man*) to shock audiences. Best moment was the one in which Chaney, having committed murder at Atwill's behest, discovers he is totally immune to the currents being passed through his body on the electric chair. How Atwill's creation finally 'diselectrocutes' himself, provided the scenarists with a denouement about as electrifying as a blown fuse. Anne Nagel, Frank Albertson, Samuel S. Hinds, William Davidson, Ben Taggart and Connie Bergen also appeared for producer Jack Beinhard, and it was directed by George Waggner. (60 mins)

▽ Hugh Herbert 'woo-wooed' his way to little effect through **Meet The Chump**, a lower-case comedy designed to depress the spirits and bury any charitable feelings for the human race. Herbert (illustrated) top-starred as the executor of a $10,000,000 trust belonging to his nephew (Lewis Howard) who, on marrying, immediately becomes eligible to take possession of the capital himself. Trouble is, Herbert's management has reduced the assets to almost nothing. After an abortive suicide attempt by Herbert, he decides to commit his nephew to an insane asylum rather than have him discover that he's almost broke. Alex Gottlieb's screenplay (from a story by Hal Hudson and Otis Garrett) failed to capitalize on the situation, and the result was a caper more tiresome than amusing which, despite its modest running time, far outstayed its welcome. The desperate direction was by Edward F. Cline, it was produced by Ken Goldsmith, and the cast included Jeanne Kelly (later known as Jean Brooks), Anne Nagel, Kathryn Adams, Shemp Howard, Richard Lane, Andrew Tombes and Hobart Cavanaugh. (60 mins)

◁ What with its famous earthquake of 1906 and the sleazy activities along its Barbary Coast, San Francisco usually comes up trumps for filmmakers. But not, alas, with **San Francisco Docks**, a depressingly third-rate melodrama which squandered the abilities of Burgess Meredith, Irene Hervey, Barry Fitzgerald (right) and Raymond Walburn (left) in a trite little waterfront tale wherein Meredith, as a longshoreman, becomes implicated in a murder with which he had no connection whatsoever; and in which Miss Hervey does everything in her power to help him prove his innocence. That privilege, however, was ultimately given to Robert Armstrong as a tough parish priest whose strong-arm tactics finally nail the culprit (Ed Pawley). Walburn played the owner of the waterfront tavern where much of the action took place. Esther Ralston, Ed Gargan and Lewis Howard completed the cast, and it was directed with minimal tension and suspense by Arthur Lubin. (64 mins)

▽ Lon Chaney Jr, abetted by make-up man Jack Pierce, would doubtless have filled his late pa with pride for carrying on the family tradition so well in **The Wolf Man**, an effective chiller in which Chaney Jr's uneventful existence in Talbot Castle undergoes a horrendous change when he becomes the victim of a wolf attack, as a consequence of which he is turned into a werewolf. Curt Siodmak's screenplay had Chaney being the only one able to see the scars he sustained in the attack, with the result that no one believes him when he relates his frightening tale. As the wolf man, Chaney (left) spent a considerable amount of the film's running time stumbling through a misty forest like a man possessed (which, of course, he was), his nocturnal meanderings ending in his death as he tries to choke the life out of pretty Evelyn Ankers (right). Claude Rains was wasted in the role of Chaney's father (it is he who is finally forced to kill his own son with a silver-tipped cane displaying the head of a wolf and the design of a pentagram), with other roles under producer George Waggner's effectively low-key direction going to Maria Ouspenskaya and Bela Lugosi as a mother-and-son fortune-telling team – Lugosi being a wolf man himself – as well as Warren William, Ralph Bellamy, Patric Knowles, Forrester Harvey, Fay Helm and J.M. Kerrigan. (70 mins)

▷ Scenarist Leonard Spigelgass' screen version of Damon Runyon's story **Tight Shoes** zipped along at a cracking pace and, under Albert S. Rogell's energetic direction, provided superior programmer entertainment. All about a shoe salesman (top-starred John Howard) who sells Broderick Crawford (at the latter's insistence) a pair of tight shoes, and the numerous complications that follow – such as Crawford using the shoe store as a front for a hideaway dice game and getting Howard (centre) fired; it also featured Richard Lane as a newspaper editor who encourages Howard to expose Crawford's crooked political connections, with other roles going to Leo Carrillo (as the owner of the shop), Anne Gwynne (left, as Howard's on-off romantic interest), Binnie Barnes (right), Samuel S. Hinds (as Horace Grover, The Brain) and, for comic relief, Shemp Howard and Ed Gargan as Crawford's side-kicks. Jules Levey produced for Mayfair Productions. (67 mins)

OTHER RELEASES OF 1941

Arizona Cyclone (Johnny Mack Brown)
Dir: Ray Taylor. Johnny frustrates the villainy of a rival freight line boss who resorts to murder to obtain franchises. Fuzzy Knight, Nell O'Day. (57 mins)

Boss Of Bullion City (Johnny Mack Brown)
Dir: Ray Taylor. Johnny and his nit-witted stooge thwart the rascally actions of a crooked sheriff. Fuzzy Knight, Nell O'Day, Harry Brown. (61 mins)

Bury Me Not On The Lone Prairie (Johnny Mack Brown)
Dir: Ray Taylor. Johnny plays a mining engineer who rounds up a gang of claim jumpers and avenges the murder of his brother. Fuzzy Knight, Nell O'Day. (61 mins)

Cracked Nuts
Prod: Joseph G. Sanford Dir: Edward Cline. Even a climactic chase finale failed to save this dreary comedy in which a contest winner is persuaded to invest his winnings in fake 'mechanical man' invention. Stuart Erwin, Una Merkel, Mischa Auer. (61 mins)

A Dangerous Game
Prod: Ben Pivar Dir: John Rawlins. Investigators Richard Arlen and Andy Devine are despatched to a sanatorium rife with murder, robbery and madness. (63 mins)

Dark Streets Of Cairo
Prod: Joseph G. Sanford Dir: Alex Gottlieb. Modest little thriller tells how an inspector outwits a murderous jewel thief. Rod La Rocque, George Zucco, Sigrid Gurie, Eddie Quillan. (59 mins)

Double Date
Prod: Joseph G. Sanford Dir: Glenn Tryon. A pair of youngsters, on returning home from boarding school, do their best to end a romance between the boy's father and the girl's aunt. Edmund Lowe, Una Merkel, Peggy Moran, Rand Brooks. (59 mins)

Flying Cadets
Prod: Paul Malvern Dir: Erle C. Kenton. Skin-and-bones programmer in which an old-time pilot teaching aviation at a flying school discovers the pupil he has most neglected is his son. Edmund Lowe, Frankie Thomas. (54 mins)

Hello Sucker
Prod: Ken Goldsmith Dir: Edward Cline. Tom Brown and Peggy Moran buy an impoverished vaudeville agency and attempt to get it back in the black. Heavy-going comedy. Hugh Herbert, Walter Catlett. (60 mins)

Hit The Road
Prod: Ken Goldsmith Dir: Joe May. Relentlessly mediocre melodrama with The Dead End Kids moving from a reformatory into society in order to discover the murderer of the father of one of the boys. Gladys George, Barton MacLane. (61 mins)

Horror Island
Prod: Ben Pivar Dir: George Waggner. Routine horror story placed an assorted set of characters in a fog-bound castle where a search for hidden treasure is in progress. Dick Foran, Leo Carrillo, Peggy Moran, Fuzzy Knight. (60 mins)

The Kid From Kansas
Prod: Ben Pivar Dir: William Nigh. Adventure yarn about murder on a banana plantation after a fruit company refuses to pay competitive prices for crops. Leo Carrillo, Dick Foran, Andy Devine. (66 mins)

Law Of The Range (Johnny Mack Brown)
Dir: Ray Taylor. Johnny and Fuzzy Knight solve a second generation family feud caused by the eternal friction between cattle and sheep men. Nell O'Day. (59 mins)

Lucky Devils
Prod: Ben Pivar Dir: Lew Landers. Another Richard Arlen-Andy Devine caper, this time as newsreel reporters involved with saboteurs. (66 mins)

Man From Montana (Johnny Mack Brown)
Dir: Ray Taylor. Johnny is a community sheriff who fights to protect the lives and property of homesteaders against invaders and outlaws. Fuzzy Knight. (57 mins)

The Masked Rider (Johnny Mack Brown)
Dir: Ray Taylor. Johnny and Fuzzy Knight find themselves caught up in a puzzle of stolen silver shipments, murder and a mysterious masked rider. (58 mins)

Melody Lane
Prod: Ken Goldsmith Dir: Charles Lamont. Radio sponsor's interference with The Merry Macs' programme leads to trouble. Nine numbers by Norman Berens and Jack Brooks. Leon Errol, Anne Gwynne, Robert Paige, Billy Lenhart. (60 mins)

Men Of The Timberlands
Prod: Ben Pivar Dir: John Rawlins. Irrepressible do-gooders Richard Arlen and Andy Devine sort out problems besetting a debutante landowner who is victim of an unscrupulous lumber operator. Linda Hayes, Francis McDonald. (62 mins)

Mr Dynamite
Prod: Marshall Grant Dir: John Rawlins. A damp squib involving Lloyd Nolan in murder after his meeting with Irene Hervey who is in pursuit of Nazi saboteurs. J. Carrol Naish, Robert Armstrong. (63 mins)

Mob Town
Prod: Ken Goldsmith Dir: William Nigh. True to formula, The Dead End Kids switch from delinquency to respectability and help a cop to rehabilitate the tearaway kid brother of an executed thug. Billy Halop, Dick Foran, Anne Gwynne. (60 mins)

Moonlight In Hawaii
Prod: Ken Goldsmith Dir: Charles Lamont. Two pineapple juice manufacturers are on the make for a wealthy lady's money. Their sponsored radio show forms the subplot for The Merry Macs. Jane Frazee, Leon Errol, Mischa Auer, Johnny Downs, Sunnie O'Dea, Maria Montez. (59 mins)

Mutiny In The Arctic
Prod: Ben Pivar Dir: John Rawlins. Title tells all! Richard Arlen and Andy Devine experience a mutiny on their arctic expedition to find radium deposits. Addison Richards, Anne Nagel. (64 mins)

Raiders Of The Desert
Prod: Ben Pivar Dir: John Rawlins. The Arlen-Devine team again; this time jumping ship to aid philanthropic George Carleton and save his experiment in democracy in the Arabian desert. Linda Hayes. (60 mins)

Rawhide Rangers (Johnny Mack Brown)
Dir: Ray Taylor. Johnny and Fuzzy Knight unmask a rich businessman who leads a band of outlaws to terrorize local ranchers. Katherine Adams, Nell O'Day. (57 mins)

Road Agent (Dick Foran)
Dir: Charles Lamont. Three cowboys are released from jail and become the sheriff and deputies in order to clean up a gang. Leo Carrillo, Andy Devine. (69 mins)

San Antonio Rose
Prod: Ken Goldsmith Dir: Charles Lamont. Story of rivalry between two roadhouse owners, featuring nine numbers, including the title song by Bob Willis and 'Once Upon A Summertime' by Jack Brooks and Norman Berens. Jane Frazee, Robert Paige, Eve Arden, Lon Chaney Jr. (62 mins)

Sealed Lips
Prod: Jack Bernhard Dir: George Waggner. Cops 'n' robbers yarn about a detective who uncovers a gangster plot to circumvent the law by using a double to take a prison rap. William Gargan, June Clyde. (62 mins)

Sing Another Chorus
Prod: Ken Goldsmith Dir: Charles Lamont. Producer absconds with sponsor's money but all ends happily when sponsor's employees stage fashion show to replace stolen funds. Spanish dancers Rosario and Antonio, Jane Frazee, Johnny Downs, Iris Adrian, The Peters Brothers, Sunnie O'Dea.

Six Lessons From Madame La Zonga
Prod: Joseph G. Sandford Dir: John Rawlins. Lovesick bandleader tries to arrange a gig in a Cuban café. Leon Errol, Lupe Velez, Charles Lang, Helen Parrish, Eddie Quillan. (62 mins)

Swing It Soldier
Prod: Joseph G. Sandford Dir: Harold Young. Pregnant soldier's wife calls in twin sister to stand in for her in radio show. Snappy song and dance numbers. Ken Murray, Frances Langford, Don Wilson, Blanche Stewart, Iris Adrian, Thurston Hall. (66 mins)

Too Many Blondes
Prod: Joseph G. Sandford Dir: Thornton Freeland. Blonde siren comes between newly-wed radio team in a happy ending story. Rudy Vallee, Helen Parrish, Iris Adrian, Lon Chaney Jr, Humberto Herpera and His Orchestra. (60 mins)

Where Did You Get That Girl?
Prod: Joseph G. Sandford Dir: Arthur Lubin. Singer and songwriter land recording contract thanks to publicity following a hold-up in a recording studio. Leon Errol, Helen Parrish, Eddie Quillan, Franklin Pangborn. (68 mins)

1942

▽ Another reporter-turned-hero story, **Bombay Clipper** top-starred William Gargan (left) in a fair-to-middling adventure concerned with a Clipper's flight from Bombay to San Francisco, and involving a $4,000,000 shipment of diamonds which India's government is presenting to Great Britain for use in the manufacture of wartime precision tools. On board the Clipper is a gang of international crooks, as well as intrepid reporter Gargan, the latter successfully overcoming the former. Irene Hervey played Gargan's neglected girlfriend, with other roles in Roy Chanslor and Stanley Rubin's factory-made screenplay going to Charles Lang, C. Montague Shaw (centre), Maria Montez, Lloyd Corrigan, Warren Ashe (right), Mary Gordon, Truman Bradley, Turhan Bey and Wade Boteler. Marshall Grant produced and it was directed by John Rawlins, who by now could handle assignments of this ilk in his sleep. (60 mins)

△ Scenarist Leonard Spigelgass managed to generate a fair supply of laughter in his adaptation of Damon Runyon's story **Butch Minds The Baby**, a soft-centred tale in which ex-con Broderick Crawford (illustrated) finds himself being weaned off such bad habits as smoking and drinking, by a one-year-old baby (Michael Barnitz, illustrated). For the sake of the toddler's future, however, the almost reformed Crawford blows open just one more safe, and takes the rap for his actions. Virginia Bruce received top billing as Master Barnitz's widowed mother, Dick Foran played a cop, and Shemp Howard an astigmatic hood. Also cast: Porter Hall, Richard Lane, Fuzzy Knight, Grant Withers and, as themselves, Six Hits and a Miss. Albert S. Rogell directed for Mayfair Productions. (75 mins)

▽ Producer-adaptor Bruce Manning gave a new twist to **Broadway**, a remake of the studio's 1929 film version of the Phillip Dunning-George Abbott play, turning it into an unusual vehicle for George Raft, who played himself. During a nostalgic stroll along Broadway, Raft reminisces about the old days which were dominated by bootleggers and racketeers – a cue to swing into the original Dunning-Abbott backstage suspense story in which the villain (an excellent performance from Broderick Crawford) tries to steal Raft's dancing partner (Janet Blair, right), attempts to frame Raft for murder, and is finally killed himself by the chorus girl (Anne Gwynne) whom he has wronged. Raft (left) gave an adequate account of himself as himself, although he was eclipsed in the acting stakes by Pat O'Brien as a detective. Felix Jackson and John Bright's pacy script provided a number of featured roles which were done full justice to by Marjorie Rambeau, S.Z. Sakall, Edward Brophy, Gus Schilling, Ralf Harolde and Nestor Paiva. Fourteen popular twenties tunes were utilized, largely as background music, though some cabaret presentation had Miss Rambeau singing 'Dinah' (by Joe Young, Sam Lewis and Harry Akst), 'Sweet Georgia Brown' (Ben Bernie, Kenneth Casey, Maceo Pinkard), and 'Alabamy Bound' (Buddy De Sylva, Bud Green, Ray Henderson); Janet Blair sang Eubie Blake and Noble Sissle's 'I'm Just Wild About Harry', and teamed with Raft for a tango. William A. Seiter directed. (89 mins)

◁ **Arabian Nights** was the studio's first 3-colour Technicolor production, the real star of which was cinematographer Milton Krasner. Next best thing was Maria Montez (right) as a curvaceous dancing girl bent on marrying above her station. She succeeds, and finishes up with caliph Jon Hall (left) no less. But not before nursing Mr Hall back to health after his sibling rival, Leif Erickson, supposedly kills him in an attempt to nab the caliphate for himself. Comedy was supplied by Billy Gilbert as Ahmad and Shemp Howard as Sinbad, with other roles in scenarist Michael Hogan's exotic romantic adventure going to John Qualen (as Aladdin), Turhan Bey, William Davis, Edgar Barrier, Richard Lane and, as Hall's best friend, Sabu. Walter Wanger's opulent production was kitschily directed by John Rawlins. (86 mins)

▽ **Eagle Squadron** was a studio rarity: one of its handful of films to run over a hundred minutes. A Grade 'A' production from Walter Wanger, it told the timely story of a group of American pilots in Britain (Robert Stack, John Loder, Eddie Albert, Leif Erickson, Edgar Barrier, Jon Hall) who help play their part (on land and in the air) against Nazi attacks in general, and in locating a mysterious Nazi plane somewhere along the French coast, then hijacking it. Though there was nothing new in Norman Reilly Raine's patriotic screenplay (from a *Cosmopolitan* story by C.S. Forester) – dealing as it did with the life-style of wartime pilots, and the love affair between squadron pilot Stack (left) and English lass Diana Barrymore (right, daughter of John), it was competently crafted and benefitted enormously from the co-operation of the British government, who allowed authentic shots of air battles to be included for verisimilitude. Authentic, too, were the details provided of British aircraft raids on the mainland. Producer Wanger's large cast included Nigel Bruce, Evelyn Ankers, Isobel Elsom, Gladys Cooper, Alan Hale Jr, and Don Porter. Quentin Reynolds provided the propagandistic foreword that helped set the scene, and the workmanlike direction was by Arthur Lubin. (108 mins)

◁ What **Between Us Girls** needed to get it airborne, was Deanna Durbin. What it got was a rather untalented Diana Barrymore (right) who, on this innocuous (but not unpleasant) occasion, could have used some of her late father's braggadocio personality to bulldoze her way through a role which required her to play an actress of twenty playing a twelve-year-old in order to hide her mother's age from a likely lover. Plot complications tumbled over each other with the appearance on the scene of second-billed Robert Cummings, who falls in love with the twenty-year-old, thus creating for the young woman (aged 12) a series of frantic situations which would have taxed the ingenuity of an actress with twice Miss Barrymore's abilities. It was a mistake, too, for director Henry Koster to allow his ingenue to pad out Myles Connolly and True Boardman's screenplay (based on *Le Fruit Vert* by Regis Gignoux and Jacques Thery, adapted by John Jacoby) with extracts from *Queen Victoria*, *Sadie Thompson* and *Joan of Arc*. Kay Francis (left) as Miss Barrymore's mother and John Boles as her prospective swain co-starred, with other roles going to Andy Devine, Ethel Griffies, Guinn Williams, Walter Catlett, Scotty Beckett and Mary Treen. (88 mins)

△ The studio's obvious desire to turn Gloria Jean (left), now aged 14, into a reincarnation of Deanna Durbin, remained unfulfilled with **Get Hep To Love** (GB: **It Comes Up Love**) in which a pack of precocious young talents competed with the star. The clear winner on this occasion was Peggy Ryan. Jay Dratler's screenplay (from a silly story by M.M. Musselman) was packed with plot: Gloria, a budding concert artist of renown, leaves home to escape her slave-driving, money-grubbing aunt (Nana Bryant), who sets a private detective on to finding her. She, meanwhile, gets herself adopted by a childless married couple (Jane Frazee and Robert Paige), and goes to high school where her classmates include Donald O'Connor (right), Cora Sue Collins, and the aforementioned Peggy Ryan. En route to the plot's resolution, Miss Jean sang 'Sempre Libre' from Verdi's *La Traviata*, 'Villanelle' by Eva Dell Acqua and Ralph Freed, 'Siboney' by Dolly Morse and Ernesto Lecuona, and 'Drink To Me Only With Thine Eyes' (all performed as part of the school's music appreciation class!); while Miss Ryan pepped up the proceedings with 'Let's Hitch A Horsie To The Automobile' by Al Hoffman, Mann Curtis and Jerry Livingston. The producer was Bernard Burton, and the director Charles Lamont, whose cast also featured Edith Barrett, Tim Ryan, Irving Bacon, John Abbott, Millard Mitchell and The Jivin' Jacks and Jills. (79 mins)

△ Leo Carrillo (right) as a British Intelligence agent persuades scientist-explorer Don Terry (2nd left – together with the latter's photographer pal Andy Devine, 2nd right) to postpone his marriage to wealthy sportswoman Louise Allbritton and undertake an expedition to a Pacific island instead. Their adventures formed the basis of **Danger In The Pacific**, a fast-paced, but not especially gripping actioner in which Messrs Terry and Devine undergo all kinds of adventures and face all manner of danger (from pythons to head-hunter attacks) as they set out to find the arsenal Turhan Bey has hidden in the hills for use by the Axis when the time comes. It was real Boys' Own material, the highlight being the sight of Carrillo (as a judo expert) flinging Andy Devine across the screen as he attempts to teach him some of the finer points of the noble art. Edgar Barrier (left), Holmes Herbert and David Hoffman also appeared for producer Ben Pivar; it was written by Walter Doniger and Maurice Tombragel (story by Doniger and Neil P. Varnick), and directed by Lewis D. Collins. (60 mins)

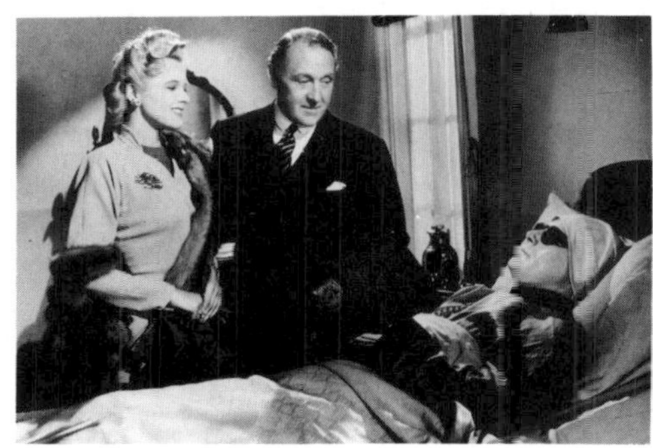

△ More espionage adventure in **Invisible Agent** with Jon Hall (right), courtesy of John P. Fulton's special effects, being injected with a chemical that renders him transparent. This done, he is able to bewilder the Gestapo and Jap leaders, as he sets about obtaining confidential information such as the plans for a dastardly air attack on New York City. Top-starred Ilona Massey (left) as a counter-espionage agent for the allies was Hall's love interest, with other roles under Edward L. Marin's direction going to Peter Lorre (as a ruthless Jap killer who commits hari-kiri), Sir Cedric Hardwicke and J. Edward Bromberg (as the heavies), John Litel, Holmes Herbert (centre) and Albert Basserman. The fanciful screenplay was the work of Curt Siodmak, and the producer was Frank Lloyd with George Waggner his associate. (79 mins)

▽ **Madame Spy** was attractive Constance Bennett (right), whose intimate involvement with a Nazi spy ring is an elaborate ruse to disguise the fact that underneath her activities with enemy agents, she's really an American counter-espionage operator. And that was about all there was to scenarist Lynn Riggs and Clarence Upson Young's screenplay (story by Young) in which Don Porter was second-billed as a reporter whom Miss Bennett marries. John Litel played the leader of the Nazi ring, with other roles going to Edward Brophy, John Eldredge (left), Edmund MacDonald, Jimmy Conlin and Nana Bryant. Roy William Neill directed at a lugubrious pace, and the producer was Marshall Grant. It couldn't have been more ordinary. (63 mins)

△ Don Terry was the hero of **Escape From Hong Kong**, a well-paced programmer with an espionage theme in which Terry (left), accompanied by Leo Carrillo and Andy Devine, ferrets out a German agent within the Hong Kong ranks of British Intelligence. Marjorie Lord (centre) is suspected of being the spy in question but isn't. The film climaxed with the eventual apprehension of the traitor; and with Messrs Terry, Carrillo and Devine – as well as pretty Miss Lord – escaping in a speed boat just as the Japs start their blitz on Hong Kong. Gilbert Emery, Leyland Hodgson (right) and Frank Puglia were also in it; Roy Chanslor wrote it, Marshall Grant produced, and it was directed by William Nigh. (60 mins)

△ Darkest Africa provided producer Henry McRae with the exotic background to **Drums Of The Congo**, the main thrust of whose screenplay (by Roy Chanslor) was whether United States intelligence officer Don Terry will arrive before the enemy at a spot containing a rare material of use to the war effort. Add to this basic situation a head-on clash between two warring native tribes, plus a fight-to-the-finish between a python and a water buffalo, and you have all the ingredients of the sort of yarn pre-pubescent youngsters delight in reading (usually in comic-book form). Peggy Moran and Richard Lane were the baddies; with top-starred Ona Munson (right, as a doctor) aiding and abetting hero Terry (left) in all his patriotic endeavours. Jules Bledsoe was featured as a native leader with a penchant for bursting into song; with other roles under Christy Cabanne's resourceful direction going to Stuart Erwin (centre), Turhan Bey, Dorothy Dandridge and Ernest Whitman, an excellent dancer who deserved better than this. Songs: 'Round The Bend'; 'Hear The Drum Beat Out'; 'River Man' Everett Carter, Milton Rosen. (59 mins)

△ Frankenstein's monster was resurrected once again in **The Ghost Of Frankenstein**, this time in the less sinister shape of Lon Chaney Jr (illustrated centre). A chiller in which most of the *dramatis personae* (but not audiences) were scared witless at the proceedings described in W. Scott Darling's screenplay (story by Eric Taylor), it centred on the efforts of Sir Cedric Hardwicke (right, as the second son of the monster's original creator), to remove Chaney's murderous brain, and replace it with a more educated one. For a while the transplant is successful, then things suddenly begin to go dreadfully wrong . . . It ends up with the hapless creature perishing (yet again) in a blazing inferno. Ralph Bellamy, Lionel Atwill, Bela Lugosi (as Ygor), and Evelyn Ankers and Janet Ann Gallow were fine in supporting roles; Erle C. Kenton directed without any of James Whale's panache, and it was produced by George Waggner. (65 mins)

▽ A comedy with a prison background, **Jailhouse Blues** was the amusing story of a convict who becomes so involved with his duties as the producer of a forthcoming prison show, that he balks at being pardoned, and unwillingly becomes a free man – returning in time for the big show after capturing an escaped convict who'd been pencilled in as the show's leading lady. He also manages to find a tenor on the outside, whose performance during the show lands him a Broadway contract. Well, that's show business. Nat Pendleton starred as the 'producer', with other roles going to Robert Paige, Elisabeth Risdon (centre, as Pendleton's mum), Anne Gwynne, Horace McMahon, Warren Hymer and Samuel S. Hinds. Albert S. Rogell's direction turned it into a passable fairytale; it was scripted by Paul Gerard Smith and Harold Tarshis (from Tarshis's story *Rhapsody In Stripes*), and the producer was Ken Goldsmith. (62 mins)

▽ Seeking vengeance on archaeologist Dick Foran for defiling the 3000-year-old tomb of the Mummy Kharis (Lon Chaney Jr, right) in Egypt, high priest Turhan Bey (left) in **The Mummy's Tomb** brings Chaney Jr to America (the creature having been kept alive by a steady diet of the tanna leaf), to kill Foran, but falls in love with Foran's fiancée (Elyse Knox, centre) instead. It all ended in flames with Foran and a handful of angry folk destroying Bey's cemetery headquarters and setting poor Mr Chaney alight. Nothing, however, was able to set Griffin Jay and Harry Sucher's screenplay alight; or even to save it from the tedium generated by over-familiarity with the subject matter and the stereotyped characters. John Hubbard, Mary Gordon, Virginia Brissac, Wallace Ford and George Zucco were also in it; Harold Young directed, and Ben Pivar produced. The film included footage from *The* Mummy's Hand (1940) with Peggy Moran and Charles Trowbridge. (61 mins)

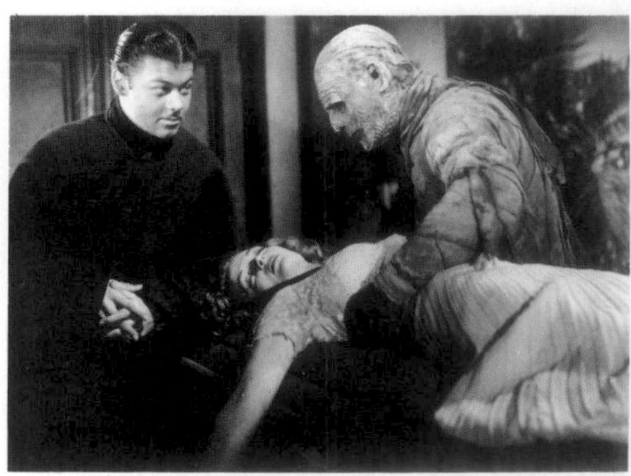

▽ **Ride 'Em Cowboy** roped in Bud Abbott (2nd left) and Lou Costello (centre left) as a couple of peanut and hot dog vendors who find themselves spirited off to a dude ranch to work as cowhands. True Boardman and John Grant's script (from a story by Edmund L. Hartmann and adaptation by Harold Shumate) was piffle from start to finish, but it furnished the stars with appropriate situations in which to exploit their own brand of slapstick and sight gags, and they chalked up yet another huge hit for themselves and the studio. Singing cowboy Dick Foran (left, co-starred), was also down on the ranch, as a writer playing at being a cowboy, and providing the romantic interest together with Anne Gwynne (centre right) as the ranch owner's daughter. The Merry Macs strayed in to the proceedings as did, more remarkably, Ella Fitzgerald, who joined them for 'Rockin' 'n' Reelin' (by Don Raye and Gene De Paul), and sang her own hit 'A Tisket A Tasket', which she and Al Feldman adapted. The Merry Macs also sang two other serviceable Raye-De Paul numbers. 'Wake Up Jacob' and 'Beside The Rio Tonto', but the film's big musical hit, which still remains an enduring favourite, was 'I'll Remember April' which Raye and De Paul wrote with Patricia Johnston. Arthur Lubin was at the directional helm for producer Alex Gottlieb who also cast Johnny Mack Brown (right), Samuel S. Hinds, Douglass Dumbrille, Richard Lane, Charles Lane, Morris Ankrum, The Hi-Hatters, The Buckaroos Band and The Ranger Chorus of Forty. (84 mins)

▽ The **Lady In A Jam** was Irene Dunne – a scatterbrained heiress with a passion for numerology – who squanders away the fortune left to her by her grandfather; and who is kept under observation by second-billed Patric Knowles, as a psychiatrist posing as a chauffeur. A sprinkling of amusing lines wasn't enough to overcome scenarists Eugene Thackeray, Frank Cockrell and Otto Lovering's silly screenplay, which also featured an over-the-top Queenie Vassar as Miss Dunne's desert-queen Grandma, who helps facilitate a happy ending by opening up an old, but rich vein in a high-content quartz mine. Needless to say Miss Dunne (left) and Mr Knowles (right) were romantically paired for the final fade. Ralph Bellamy, Eugene Pallette (centre), Samuel S. Hinds, Jane Garland (as an intrusive child), Edward McWade and Robert Homans completed the cast for producer Gregory La Cava, who also directed. It was not his finest hour. (81 mins)

▷ Wartime patriotism manifested itself in **Men Of Texas**, whose colourful and action-filled setting was the reconstruction period immediately after the Civil War. Harold Shumate's flag-waving screenplay (with additional dialogue by Richard Brooks) concerned itself with the turbulent times in Texas when Confederate volunteers returned home to find Union troops maintaining martial law, and it gave top-starred Robert Stack (centre) the plum role of a newspaper reporter from Chicago who, together with photographer Leo Carrillo, sets out to write the real story of the state of Texas. En route he falls in love with southern belle Anne Gwynne (right). Broderick Crawford (left) was the heavy of the piece, with other roles under Ray Enright's energetic direction going to Ralph Bellamy, Jane Darwell, John Litel, Jackie Cooper, William Farnum, Janet Beecher and Kay Linaker. George Waggner produced. (81 mins)

▽ **Pittsburgh** again teamed Marlene Dietrich with Randolph Scott (left, second-billed) and John Wayne (right) in another macho drama – this time with Scott getting the gal. Messrs Scott and Wayne played coal-miner buddies who rise up in the world to become the owners of a huge industrial complex. They're both in love with Dietrich, who inspires them to better their positions in life. Wayne's bloody-mindedness, however, causes a rift between him and Scott, but the war and the demands it makes on their steel combine, brings out their patriotism and helps them to patch up their differences. Frank Craven as the mining-town doctor featured prominently in scenarists Kenneth Gamet and Tom Reed's screenplay (story by Reed and George Owen) as the investor of a revolutionary coal-tar formula of immense value to the war effort. As in *The Spoilers* (1942), it was the chemistry of the three leading players that attracted the customers, rather than the plot they embellished, with the trio again helping to spell box-office potency for producer Charles K. Feldman. Lewis Seiler's direction was extremely capable, and so were the performances he coaxed out of a supporting cast that also included Louise Allbritton (as an oil magnate's daughter who marries Wayne), Shemp Howard Thomas Gomez, Samuel S. Hinds, Ludwig Stossel and Douglas Fowley. (91 mins)

1942

▽ Elisabeth Bergner (right) made her American film debut in **Paris Calling**, a melodrama unworthy of her considerable talents, as well as unworthy of its subject: the fall of Paris. All about a wealthy young Parisienne (Bergner) who, after Paris is occupied by the Germans, joins the French underground, falls in love with an American pilot (Randolph Scott, left), and shoots a former lover-turned-traitor (Basil Rathbone), it was unconvincingly scripted by producer Benjamin Glazer and Charles F. Kaufman, ploddingly directed by Edwin Marlin, and indifferently performed by a cast that included Gale Sondergaard, Charles Arnt, Eduardo Ciannelli, Elisabeth Risdon and Georges Renavent. Only Lee J. Cobb as a Gestapo chief brought a touch of credibility to the proceedings. (93 mins)

▽ Basil Rathbone (left), who'd played the role of Arthur Conan Doyle's super sleuth Sherlock Holmes for 20th Century-Fox, repeated his celebrated characterisation in a series of Doyle-based thrillers for Universal, the first of which was **Sherlock Holmes And The Voice Of Terror**. Based on Doyle's story *His Last Bow*, but updated to World War II, it had Holmes being hired by the British Inner Council to track down a Nazi agent responsible for Nazi propaganda broadcasts ('The Voice of Terror') which describe various acts of sabotage as they are about to occur. Nigel Bruce played the faithful Dr Watson, with other roles under John Rawlins' direction going to Evelyn Ankers (right – whom Holmes hires to spy on Nazi agent Thomas Gomez, who subsequently kills her), Reginald Denny (as a Nazi spy in the Inner Council), as well as Henry Daniell, Montague Love and Mary Gordon (as Mrs Hudson, Holmes' housekeeper). Lynn Riggs wrote it from an adaptation by Robert D. Andrews and John Bright (it was originally going to be called *Sherlock Holmes Saves London*) and wasted no opportunities to insert some patriotic speeches – especially the one that closes the picture, and which was lifted from the original Doyle story. The associate producer was Howard Benedict. (65 mins)

△ Veteran Hollywood comedy director Erle C. Kenton turned his attentions to Bud Abbott (right) and Lou Costello (centre) in **Pardon My Sarong**. Plot and screenplay by True Boardman, Nat Perrin and John Grant was little more than an extended chase, and it took Messrs A & C from Chicago to the Pacific and, finally, to a South Sea island infested with sharks, alligators and lions, where the boys foil thief Lionel Atwill who is out to steal the islanders' tribal jewels. These unlikely events provided plenty of scope for the routine Abbott and Costello gags, as well as for several songs and musical numbers performed by, among others, The Ink Spots, who sang one of their biggest hits, 'Do I Worry?' (by Bobby Worth and Stanley Cowan). Robert Paige was the millionaire owner of the yacht, and the rest of the cast included Virginia Bruce (left), William Demarest, Leif Erickson, Samuel S. Hinds and Nan Wynn. Also: The Sarango Girls, Jack La Rue, Tip, Tap and Toe, and The Katherine Dunham Dancers (Miss Dunham staged the dance numbers). Alex Gottlieb was the producer. (83 mins)

△ **Nightmare** began promisingly enough, with gambler Brian Donlevy (illustrated), desperately in need of a square meal, breaking into the London home of Diana Barrymore, unaware that her husband is sprawled over his desk upstairs with a knife in his back. The choice Miss B offers Donlevy is: either face the consequences for unlawful entry into her home; or help her get rid of the body. From this point on in producer Dwight Taylor's screenplay (from Philip MacDonald's story *Escape*), the film deteriorated beyond repair as the narrative bogged itself down in a welter of unconvincing explanations, plus a mad dash across English countryside in which the two protagonists desperately dodge the police as well as some obligatory Nazi spies. Gavin Muir, Henry Daniell, Hans Conried, Arthur Shields and Stanley Logan were also featured, and it was directed by Tim Whelan. (81 mins)

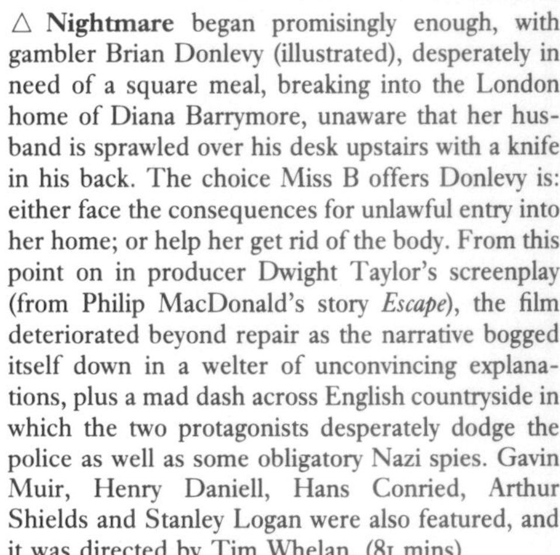

△ Bud Abbott (centre) and Lou Costello (left) were barely off the screen in **Who Done It?** a comedy thriller without – on this occasion – any recourse to song and dance. The team played a pair of soda jerks with scriptwriting ambitions who work in a radio station building, and who find themselves involved in a murder during the recording of a whodunnit play. While setting out to solve the crime, they're bucked by police officer William Gargan and William Bendix. Or was it vice-versa? At any rate, there was a prolonged chase, climaxing with Costello à la Harold Lloyd, perched on the radio station's aerial wires high above the ground. Patric Knowles, Louise Allbritton, Thomas Gomez, Don Porter, Jerome Cowan, Mary Wickes (right) and Ludwig Stossel also appeared for producer Alex Gottlieb; it was scripted (with the emphasis on burlesque) by Stanley Roberts, Edmund Joseph and John Grant (story by Roberts) who reworked many of A & C's old routines into their storyline; and the director was Erle C. Kenton. Not one of the team's best, but passable. (66 mins)

▽ A thrill-a-second canoe ride through dangerous rapids, plus an all-out climactic fist-fight between good-guy Broderick Crawford (centre) and villain Lon Chaney Jr was the best that **North To The Klondike** could offer. Set in Alaska, it told the computerised story of tough guy Chaney's efforts to evict a group of farmer-settlers out of their valley in order to appropriate the gold he believes to be hidden in 'them thar hills'. It is mining engineer Crawford, initially employed by Chaney, who sees that his boss doesn't get away with it. Clarence Young, Lou Sarecky and George Bricker's tenuous screenplay (from a story by William Castle which, in turn, was based on Jack London's novel *Gold Hunters Of The North*) gave work to Evelyn Ankers (centre right), Andy Devine (foreground right), Lloyd Corrigan, Dorothy Granger (2nd right), Willie Fung, Keye Luke and veteran Monte Blue (foreground centre left); Erle C. Kenton directed it, and the producer was Paul Malvern. (58 mins)

△ Audiences willing to suspend all vestiges of disbelief had a really riveting time at **Saboteur**, a quintessential Hitchcock thriller which threw logic to the proverbial winds as it told the timely story of a Nazi saboteur (Norman Lloyd) who unleashes a massive chase after setting fire to an aircraft factory in Los Angeles. In hot pursuit of the Nazi agent is aircraft maintenance man Robert Cummings, whose buddy (Virgil Summers) was killed in the fire, but who, to complicate matters, is innocently implicated in the fire himself. How Cummings (left) with the aid of Priscilla Lane (top cast, right) whom he meets during his cross-country chase and who, at first, does not know whether to trust him or not, finally exposes the agent for the rat he is – and brings about his demise, was the main concern in Peter Viertel, Joan Harrison and Dorothy Parker's far-fetched screenplay. And even if it was all a mite too improbable to satisfy the intellect, there could be no denying the excitement engendered by Hitchcock in his masterly unfurling of the plot or the sheer cinematic dazzle of its several set-pieces, the best and most famous being the climax atop the Statue of Liberty where, after an equally brilliant sequence in the Radio City Music Hall, saboteur Lloyd finally gets his come-uppance (or, in this spectacular case, his come-downance). A not particularly distinguished supporting cast included Otto Kruger, Vaughan Glaser, Alan Baxter, Clem Bevans, Alma Kruger, Dorothy Peterson and Ian Wolfe. It was a Frank Lloyd Productions Inc. presentation. (108 mins)

△ Hugh Herbert (centre), ditheringly prodding the risibles, was the star of **There's One Born Every Minute**, a political comedy. He played a small-town pudding manufacturer (and inventor of a secret ingredient) who makes an unlikely bid for the mayoral seat and, after much political skulduggery (which he overcomes thanks to the 'spiritual' intervention of his ancestors), succeeds. Peggy Moran (as Herbert's daughter, 2nd left) and Tom Brown (right) supplied the romance; Guy Kibbee and Edgar Kennedy (as a pair of villains) additional comedy; Catherine Doucet (left) was Herbert's wife, with other roles under Harold Young's direction going to Scott Jordan, Gus Schilling, Carl 'Alfalfa' Switzer, and a young Elizabeth Taylor. The scenarists were Robert B. Hunt and Brenda Weisberg (it was based on Hunt's story *Man Or Mouse?*), and the associate producer was Ken Goldsmith. (60 mins)

▽ Another loosely-based screen adaptation of an Edgar Allan Poe story, **The Mystery Of Marie Roget**, scripted to formula by Michael Jacoby, featured Maria Montez, sans sarong or exotic Eastern garb, as the eponymous 'heroine' – a French musical comedy star who plots to murder her younger sister (Nell O'Day, left). As the story unfurls, Miss Montez (centre) herself is murdered, and it is left to Patric Knowles (top-billed), a young chemist attached to the police department, to work out who did what to whom, and why. Maria Ouspenskaya, John Litel, Edward Norris (right) and Lloyd Corrigan were also in it for Paul Malvern, whose production under Phil Rosen's direction was more than passable, considering its meagre budget. (60 mins)

▷ A spooky chiller set in uninviting Ingston Manor, and in which the body count almost reached double figures, **The Night Monster** featured Ralph Morgan in the title role as a man who, after his legs are amputated, sports a pair of artificial ones and sets about murdering the numerous doctors responsible for his disability. Bela Lugosi was top-billed as a sinister butler, with other roles going to Lionel Atwill, Leif Erickson, Irene Hervey, Don Porter (centre), Nils Asther (seated), Fay Helm, Frank Reicher (left), Janet Shaw, Doris Lloyd and Francis Pierlot (right). Clarence Upson Young thought it all up (in about 3½ minutes, probably) and it was produced and directed by Ford Beebe. (73 mins)

▷ Another programmer designed to showcase the teenage talent at Universal, **What's Cookin'** (GB: **Wake Up And Dream**) served up fourteen musical numbers and an insubstantial, heard-it-all-before story about the efforts of a group of youngsters to make it in show business. Jerry Cady and Stanley Roberts' screenplay (story by Edgar Allan Woolf, adaptation Haworth Bromley) contrived a joint radio show for the aspiring kids (Gloria Jean, Donald O'Connor, Grace McDonald, Peggy Ryan) and established stars Jane Frazee, The Andrews Sisters, and Woody Herman and His Band. On the way to this air-wave jamboree, director Edward Cline extracted some good comedy performances from Charles Butterworth (right – as the radio show's sponsor and Gloria Jean's uncle), Leo Carrillo, Billie Burke (left) and Franklin Pangborn, and neatly interwove some dance routines from The Jivin' Jacks and Jills. Robert Paige (centre) was top-billed, and little Susan Levine was in it too, for producer Ken Goldsmith. Among the songs and musical numbers: 'What To Do' Sid Robin; 'Blue Flame' James Noble; 'Woodchopper's Ball' Woody Herman, Joe Bishop; 'I'll Pray For You' Arthur Altman and Kim Gannon; 'Amen (Yea-Men)' Roger Segure, Bill Hardy, Vic Schoen; 'You Can't Hold A Memory In Your Arms' Hy Zaret, Arthur Altman; 'If', 'Love Laughs At Anything' Don Raye, Gene De Paul. (69 mins)

▽ **Sin Town** could not have kept its scenarists W. Scott Darling and Gerald Geraghty burning the midnight oil in the search for originality. Their screenplay, assembled rather than written, featured Constance Bennett (right) and Broderick Crawford as a pair of opportunists who arrive in a typical frontier boom town, circa 1910, and, without much ado, become involved in the town's only gambling joint. Dissatisfied with the establishment's earning potential, Crawford falls foul of the town's law-abiding element, especially Anne Gwynne who edits the local newspaper. The plot was fattened by Ward Bond, whom Crawford has ousted as owner of the gambling establishment, but who returns with his henchmen to even the score. It ended with Crawford and Miss Bennett quitting the town, presumably to try their luck in pastures new. Patric Knowles, Andy Devine, Leo Carrillo (centre), Arthur Aylsworth and Ralf Harolde were also in it for producer George Waggner, and the director was Ray Enright. (73 mins)

◁ In **The Spoilers**, his 80th movie, John Wayne (right) played the part-owner of a gold mine which he loses after being double-crossed by Judge Samuel S. Hinds, the uncle of his pretty sweetheart (Margaret Lindsay). As if that weren't enough, he's unjustly sent to prison by gold commissioner Randolph Scott (left) for a murder he did not commit. But not for long. He busts out, reclaims his mine, and after a truly spectacular fist-fight with Scott, pairs off, not with Miss Lindsay (who turns out to be somewhat crooked), but with leading lady Marlene Dietrich (centre), a saloon gal who's been in love with him for quite some time. Such was the routine screenplay concocted by Lawrence Hazard and Tom Reed from an oft-filmed novel by Rex Beach. What guaranteed the movie its success was the super performances by its three leads, especially Dietrich (as Cherry Malotte), and the climactic no-holds-barred brawl in which the two leading men demolished each other (as well as most of the furniture) with their battering-ram fists. Harry Carey played Wayne's partner, with other roles under Ray Enright's macho direction going to Richard Barthelmess (as the Bronco Kid, a gambler who works for – and is in love with – Dietrich, and consequently jealous of Wayne), old-timer William Farnum as Wayne's attorney, George Cleveland and Russell Simpson. The producer was Frank Lloyd. Beach's novel (written in 1906) was first seen as a film in 1914 (for Selig) with William Farnum; in 1923 with Milton Sills (for Goldwyn) and in 1930 with Gary Cooper (for Paramount). It was remade by Universal in 1956 with Jeff Chandler in the John Wayne role. (84 mins)

△ Leo Carrillo (centre) and Andy Devine (right) were joined by Dan Dailey in **Timber**, a topical melodrama set against a lumber-camp background, and dealing with enemy saboteurs. Carrillo was top-starred as a mill boss, Devine was in charge of the wood crews, and Dailey was an undercover agent who, assisted by Messrs Carrillo and Devine, finally succeeds in uncovering the saboteurs in question, whose chief target is the timber trucks containing materials vital to the war effort. Marjorie Lord (left) provided Griffin Jay's screenplay (story by Larry Rhine and Ben Chapman) with its female interest, with other roles under Christy Cabanne's serviceable direction going to Nestor Paiva, Wade Boteler, Edmund MacDonald and Paul Burns. The producer was Ben Pivar. (58 mins)

▽ **Treat 'Em Rough** was the lightweight story of a middleweight boxer (Eddie Albert) who, after defying his oil-tycoon father by entering the fight game, redeems himself in the old man's eyes by saving him from ruin and dishonour. Seems a million barrels of oil have gone missing and federal investigators want to know why and where. Thanks to Albert's intervention (at the behest of secretary Peggy Moran, illustrated right with Albert), the mystery of the missing barrels is solved (thieves have been passing the stuff across a secret bridge), and everyone in Roy Chanslor and Bob Williams' facile screenplay lived happily ever after. Apart from Albert, the cast also included William Frawley, Lloyd Corrigan (as Albert's father), Truman Bradley, Mantan Moreland, Joe Crehan, Ed Pawley and Monte Blue. The director was Ray Taylor. (59 mins)

△ The studio continued to mine current wartime situations with **Unseen Enemy**, in which top-starred Leo Carrillo (right) became an agent for a group of Axis plotters who are determined to round up a captain and crew to man a Jap ship in San Francisco harbour for the nefarious purpose of disrupting American shipping on the West Coast. Andy Devine as a government agent and Don Terry (left) as a Canadian intelligence officer were the heroes of Roy Chanslor and Stanley Rubin's rather violent screenplay (story by George Wallace Sayre), John Rawlins directed, and the cast included Irene Hervey (centre, as Carrillo's stepdaughter), Lionel Royce, Turhan Bey, Frederick Giermann and William Ruhl. The associate producer was Marshall Grant. (61 mins)

OTHER RELEASES OF 1942

Almost Married
Prod: Ken Goldsmith Dir: Charles Lamont. Singer agrees to a mock marriage in order to help Robert Paige out of romantic entanglement, then falls in love for real. Jane Frazee, Eugene Pallette, Maude Eburne. (65 mins)

Behind The Eight Ball (GB: **Off The Beaten Track**)
Prod: Howard Benedict Dir: Edward F. Cline. Programmer vehicle for crazy antics of The Ritz Brothers. Sketchy plot involved enemy spies and a touch of murder, but emphasis was on the ten musical numbers, nine by Don Raye and Gene De Paul. Carol Bruce, Dick Foran, Johnny Downs, Sonny Dunham and His Orchestra. (59 mins)

Boss Of Hangtown Mesa (Johnny Mack Brown)
Dir: Joseph H. Lewis. Johnny and Fuzzy Knight outwit the efforts of a gang trying to delay the completion of a telegraph line. William Farnum, Rex Lease. (59 mins)

Deep In The Heart Of Texas (Johnny Mack Brown, Tex Ritter)
Dir: Elmer Clifton. Johnny and Tex manage to return the Alamo state to the Stars and Stripes from insurrectionist Texans. Fuzzy Knight, Jennifer Holt. (62 mins)

Destination Unknown
Prod: Marshall Grant Dir: Rod Taylor. William Gargan and Irene Hervey chase each other across China for jewels whose sale will provide money for munitions. Turns out they're on the same side. Sam Levene, Turhan Bey. (63 mins)

Don't Get Personal
Prod: Ken Goldsmith Dir: Charles Lamont. Pickle manufacturer interferes in lives of two radio stars whose on-air marital spats he mistakes for the real thing. Hugh Herbert, Mischa Auer, Jane Frazee, Anne Gwynne, Robert Paige, Sterling Holloway. (60 mins)

Fighting Bill Fargo (Johnny Mack Brown)
Dir: Ray Taylor. Johnny and Fuzzy Knight depose a crooked sheriff and his henchmen who have been rigging the election of a new sheriff. Jeanne Kelly. (58 mins)

Frisco Lil
Prod: Paul Malvern Dir: Erle C. Kenton. Time-wasting programmer which top-starred Irene Hervey as croupier who joins gambling joint to clear her father of a murder charge. Minor Watson, Kent Taylor. (60 mins)

Give Out Sisters
Prod: Bernard W. Burton Dir: Edward F. Cline. An heiress breaks into showbusiness as a dancer resulting in, among other things, The Andrews Sisters masquerading as her disapproving aunts. Grace McDonald, Charles Butterworth, William Frawley, Walter Catlett, Peggy Ryan. (65 mins)

The Great Impersonation
Prod: Paul Malvern Dir: John Rawlins. Adequate remake (1935) telling the slightly different story of identical doubles (Ralph Bellamy) – a German and an Englishman – and the mistaken identity complications that arise, centreing on a Nazi spy-ring. Evelyn Ankers, Aubrey Mather, Edward Norris. (70 mins)

Halfway To Shanghai
Prod: Paul Malvern Dir: John Rawlins. Addlepated programmer set on Burma night train where Nazi spy pair try to steal maps of Chinese defences and munitions caches. Kent Taylor, George Zucco, Irene Hervey. (61 mins)

Juke Box Jenny
Prod: Joseph G. Sandford Dir: Harold Young. Thin excuse for musical numbers in which Harriet Hilliard, (Jenny) is exploited by record salesman Ken Murray. Don Douglas, Iris Adrian, Charles Barnet, Wingy Manone and their Orchestras, The King's Men. (61 mins)

Little Joe, The Wrangler (Johnny Mack Brown, Tex Ritter)
Dir: Lewis D. Collins. Tex plays a discredited sheriff who teams up with a frame-up victim, Johnny, to track down the real culprits of murder. (60 mins)

The Mad Doctor Of Market Street
Prod: Paul Malvern Dir: John Lewis. A quack with hypnotic powers kills a man and escapes by sea. Ship sinks, survivors are cast away on island, quack is nasty to everyone and is left behind when rescue plane arrives. Lionel Atwill, Una Merkel, Nat Pendleton. (60 mins)

Mississippi Gambler
Prod: Paul Malvern Dir: John Rawlins. Familiar story of newspaperman Kent Taylor who sets off to apprehend elusive criminal John Litel in Mississippi. Frances Langford. (60 mins)

Moonlight In Havana
Prod: Bernard W. Burton Dir: Anthony Mann. Convoluted and utterly silly musical starred Allan Jones as a singing baseball player who can only perform when he has a cold. Good specialty act from Grace and Nico and a couple of passable tunes in Dave Franklin's score. William Frawley, Jane Frazee, The Jivin' Jacks and Jills. (63 mins)

The Old Chisholm Trail (Johnny Mack Brown, Tex Ritter)
Dir: Elmer Clifton. Johnny and Tex stop a femme villain from controlling a water hole and selling usage for a bounty. Fuzzy Knight, Jennifer Holt. (61 mins)

Private Buckaroo
Prod: Ken Goldsmith Dir: Edward F. Cline. The Andrews Sisters and Harry James and His Music Makers stage a show for servicemen. Dick Foran, Joe E. Lewis, Shemp Howard, Richard Davies, Mary Wickes, Donald O'Conner, Peggy Ryan, Huntz Hall. (68 mins)

The Silver Bullet (Johnny Mack Brown)
Dir: Joseph H. Lewis. Johnny seeks revenge from a notorious killer who had once shot his father in the back with a silver bullet. Fuzzy Knight. (60 mins)

Stagecoach Buckaroo (Johnny Mack Brown)
Dir: Ray Taylor. Johnny and Fuzzy Knight defeat a crook's plot to use an innocent girl to obtain information concerning a gold shipment. Nell O'Day. (58 mins)

The Strange Case Of Dr RX
Prod: Jack Bernhard Dir: William Nigh. Thoroughly confusing programmer focussing on five men acquitted of various charges who are murdered by a mysterious avenger. Samuel S. Hinds, Patric Knowles, Anne Gwynne, Mantan Moreland. (64 mins)

Strictly In The Groove
Prod: Joseph G. Sandford Dir: Vernon Keays. Sixteen songs propped up this programmer musical about the son of a rich hotel owner who is packed off to an Arizona dude ranch after flunking college, and falls in love with the owner of a rival hotel. Richard Davies, Mary Healy, Leon Errol, The Jimmy Wakely Trio, The Dinning Sisters, Ozzie Nelson and His Band. (59 mins)

Top Sergeant
Prod: Ben Pivar Dir: Christy Cabanne. A thriller of sorts in which a trio of NCO's apprehend a trio of bank robbers; but one of the robbers escapes and kills the brother of one of the NCO's. Leo Carrillo, Andy Devine, Don Terry, Gene Garrick. (58 mins)

Tough As They Come
Prod: Ken Goldsmith Dir: William Nigh. The Dead End Kids are now young men and on the side of the law; Billy Halop takes a job with a legal aid society and is accused of graft after his involvement with a shady loan company; but he clears his name. (61 mins)

You're Telling Me
Prod: Ken Goldsmith Dir: Charles Lamont. Good-natured incompetent is given a job in the family advertising business and signs up a big game hunter for a radio programme. Turns out the hunter is a fake. Hugh Herbert, Edward Ashley, Robert Paige. (60 mins)

1943

▽ A lurid exploitation melodrama, **The Strange Death of Adolf Hitler** was a curiosity that starred Ludwig Donath (illustrated) in a dual role: Adolf Hitler, and Viennese Franz Huber, Hitler's double. Gale Sondergaard played Huber's wife who, in the course of the screenplay Fritz Kortner wrote from his and Joe May's original story, has the misfortune to shoot her husband in the belief that he is really Hitler. Under James Hogan's direction it all added up to little more than potboiler entertainment. Also cast were George Dolenz, Frederick Giermann, William Trenk, Merrill Rodin, Charles Bates and Ludwig Stossel. The production was by Ben Pivar. (74 mins)

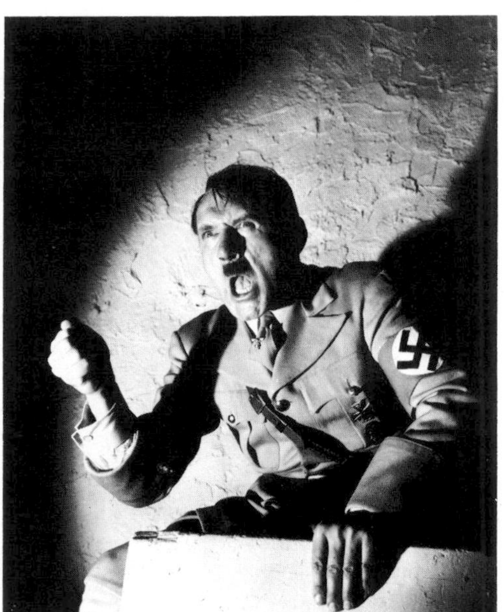

△ Having reaped financial rewards by transplanting brains from one creature into another, the studio turned to blood transfusions in **Captive Wild Woman** to tell the frankly bizarre story of an interfering scientist's experiments with a circus ape called Cheela. After the scientist, played by John Carradine (right), fills Cheela's veins with the blood of a woman, a strange physical metamorphosis takes place, resulting in Acquanetta. Perfectly well-behaved for most of the time, Acquanetta sees red, however, when animal trainer Milburn Stone, whom she rather fancies, takes time off to kiss his fiancée (Evelyn Ankers). It's then that the animal in her lets loose, and Carradine (who eventually perishes at the hands of his creation) wishes he'd left nature well alone! Director Edward Dmytryk, using footage from Clyde Beatty's *The Big Cage* (1933), directed it as effectively as the far-fetched material allowed, and, in smaller roles, used Martha MacVicar (later Vickers), Lloyd Corrigan, William Edmunds (left), Vince Barnett and Fay Helm. It was written by Henry Stephenson and Griffin Jay from an original story by Ted Fithian and Maurice Pivar, and produced by Ben Pivar. (61 mins)

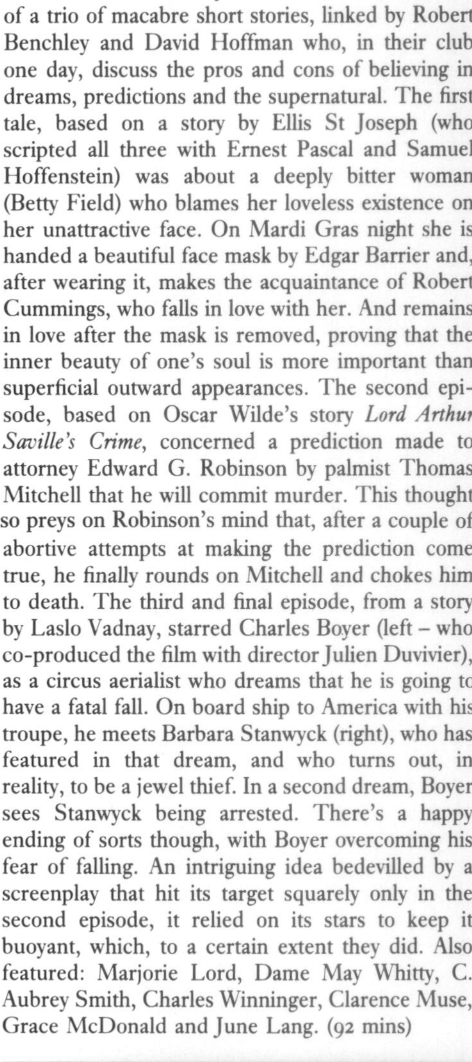

▽ **Flesh And Fantasy** was the rather fanciful title of a trio of macabre short stories, linked by Robert Benchley and David Hoffman who, in their club one day, discuss the pros and cons of believing in dreams, predictions and the supernatural. The first tale, based on a story by Ellis St Joseph (who scripted all three with Ernest Pascal and Samuel Hoffenstein) was about a deeply bitter woman (Betty Field) who blames her loveless existence on her unattractive face. On Mardi Gras night she is handed a beautiful face mask by Edgar Barrier and, after wearing it, makes the acquaintance of Robert Cummings, who falls in love with her. And remains in love after the mask is removed, proving that the inner beauty of one's soul is more important than superficial outward appearances. The second episode, based on Oscar Wilde's story *Lord Arthur Saville's Crime*, concerned a prediction made to attorney Edward G. Robinson by palmist Thomas Mitchell that he will commit murder. This thought so preys on Robinson's mind that, after a couple of abortive attempts at making the prediction come true, he finally rounds on Mitchell and chokes him to death. The third and final episode, from a story by Laslo Vadnay, starred Charles Boyer (left – who co-produced the film with director Julien Duvivier), as a circus aerialist who dreams that he is going to have a fatal fall. On board ship to America with his troupe, he meets Barbara Stanwyck (right), who has featured in that dream, and who turns out, in reality, to be a jewel thief. In a second dream, Boyer sees Stanwyck being arrested. There's a happy ending of sorts though, with Boyer overcoming his fear of falling. An intriguing idea bedevilled by a screenplay that hit its target squarely only in the second episode, it relied on its stars to keep it buoyant, which, to a certain extent they did. Also featured: Marjorie Lord, Dame May Whitty, C. Aubrey Smith, Charles Winninger, Clarence Muse, Grace McDonald and June Lang. (92 mins)

◁ The first of a series of thrillers inspired by radio's 'Inner Sanctum' broadcasts (by arrangement with publishers Simon and Schuster), **Calling Dr Death** was a fair-to-middling offering in which a neurologist (Lon Chaney Jr, left), after discovering his unfaithful wife's mutilated body, doesn't know whether or not he himself committed the murder while under hypnosis. Ramsay Ames (right) was third-billed as Chaney's wife; Patricia Morison was a nurse, and J. Carrol Naish the uncannily shrewd detective who helps bring the case to a satisfactory conclusion. It was directed by Reginald Le Borg, who should have eliminated the 'voice over' commentary supplied (as if in a radio play) by Chaney. It added nothing to Edward Dein's screenplay, and, if anything, detracted from it. Ben Pivar produced, and his cast included David Bruce, Fay Helm, Holmes Herbert, Alec Craig and Isabel Jewell. (62 mins)

▷ **The Amazing Mrs Holliday** was a synthetic romantic drama which exploited the subject of war orphans as a vehicle for top-starred Deanna Durbin. Durbin (illustrated right of doorway) played an American school teacher in China, whose mission in Frank Ryan and John Jacoby's cloying screenplay (adapted by Boris Ingster and Leo Townsend from a story by Sonya Levien) was to smuggle nine recently orphaned Chinese children back to the States. En route, the ship in which they are travelling is torpedoed and, after being rescued, the only way Miss Durbin and her moppet cargo are allowed into America, is by lying that her husband (who has promised to adopt the children) is the missing owner of the torpedoed ship. The obligatory romance was provided by Edmond O'Brien, as the 'missing' shipping magnate's son, to whom Miss Durbin confesses her deception; with other roles under producer Bruce Manning's plastic direction going to Barry Fitzgerald (wasted as a boat-steward), Arthur Treacher (as a butler), Harry Davenport (as the 'missing' magnate); as well as Grant Mitchell, Frieda Inescort, Elisabeth Risdon, Jonathan Hale, Esther Dale and Gus Schilling. Songs included: 'The Old Refrain', 'Mighty Like A Rose', 'Visi d'Arte' from Puccini's *Tosca*. (96 mins)

△ **Crazy House** was Ole Olsen (left) and Chic Johnson's (right) first film since *Hellzapoppin'* (1941), and in it they played a couple of wacky comedians who arrive at Universal studios wanting to make another picture. The studio executives couldn't be less interested, so the boys decide to rent a movie lot and set up on their own. Robert Lees and Frederick Rinaldo's screenplay, continuing from this premise, provided an adequate vehicle for O & J's crazy antics, which were directed at a suitably breathless pace by Edward Cline. There were some moments of calm engendered by a mild romantic sub-plot concerning Patric Knowles and Martha O'Driscoll, and lots and lots and lots of music, song, and specialty acts, as well as two big production numbers – 'Pocketful Of Pennies' (by Eddie Cherkose and Franz Steininger) and 'Tropicana' (by Don Raye and Gene De Paul). The supporting cast included Cass Daley (centre), Percy Kilbride, Leighton Noble, Thomas Gomez, Edgar Kennedy and Franklin Pangborn. There were appearances, too, from Alan Curtis, Allan Jones, Billy Gilbert, Hans Conried, Shemp Howard, Lon Chaney Jr, Andy Devine, Robert Paige, The Glenn Miller Singers with Marion Hutton, Count Basie and His Band, Tony and Sally De Marco, Chandra, The Kaly Dancers, The Laison Brothers, The Five Hertzogs, The Delta Rhythm Boys, The Bobby Brooks Quartet, Andrew Tombes and Basil Rathbone and Nigel Bruce (as Sherlock Holmes and Dr Watson). It was reasonably amusing if you could stand the pace. Other songs and musical numbers included: 'Crazy House' Eddie Cherkose, Milton Rosen; 'Lament Of A Laundry Girl' Jerry Seelen, Lester Lee; Ted Shapiro; 'Donkey Serenade' Rudolf Friml, Bob Wright, Chet Forrest; 'I Ought To Dance' Sammy Cahn, Saul Chaplin; 'My Rainbow Song' Mitchell Parish, Matt Malneck, Frank Signorelli. (80 mins)

▽ **Corvette K-225**, produced by Howard Hawks and excellently directed by Robert Rosson, told with almost documentary-like precision, the story of life on board one of the compact escort warships of the British and Canadian naval forces, known as corvettes. While sailing on an eastward Atlantic crossing from Halifax to Britain, the vessel comes under torpedo attack, as well as being bombed by German aircraft. How the crew, led by Lieutenant Commander Randolph Scott (left), courageously cope, provided Lieutenant John Rhodes Sturdy with the heroic content of his admirable and informative screenplay. Taking second place to the documentary aspect of the story, was a personal drama involving Scott's relationship with Ella Raines (centre), whose brother has been killed in action. Scott and Raines fall in love, despite the fact that her second brother (James Brown, right) is enlisted as a sub-officer on his next voyage. A competent supporting cast, including Barry Fitzgerald, Andy Devine, Fuzzy Knight, Noah Beery Jr, Richard Lane, Thomas Gomez and, in a bit part, Robert Mitchum, brought up the rear, and contributed powerfully to the film's overall verisimilitude. (98 mins)

△ The real-life Makin Island raid on August 17th 1942 was tailor-made for the movies, and, without wasting too much time, the studio signed scenarist Lucien Hubbard to turn Captain W.A. Le Francois' on-the-spot account of it into **Gung Ho**, a stirring, and action-filled war drama. By occasionally bending the facts as well as adding a few totally fictitious episodes, Hubbard arrived at a tautly dramatic framework in which he described how the Second Marine Raider Battalion was chosen and trained for the raid; how the 200 men finally selected to participate were transported to the Pacific; and how they lost their lives reclaiming the Island from the Japs. A top-notch cast headed by Randolph Scott included Grace McDonald (right), Alan Curtis, Noah Beery Jr (centre), J. Carrol Naish, David Bruce (left), Peter Coe, Robert Mitchum, Richard Lane, Rod Cameron and Sam Levene; it was produced by Walter Wanger, and the director was Ray Enright, whose climactic battle scenes were definitely not for the squeamish. (88 mins)

△ The mad ghoul in **The Mad Ghoul** was George Zucco, whose diabolical experiments, according to Hans Kraly's screenplay, result in isolating a noxious gas of ancient Egyptian origin, whose horrible effects can only be neutralised by heart fluid from a recently deceased person. David Bruce (right) received top-billing as a medical student on whom Zucco experiments, with other roles going to Evelyn Ankers (left) as a singer, and Robert Armstrong as a newspaperman whose death helps facilitate the capture of Zucco. It was a really feeble effort indeed, which needed far more pazazz that director James Hogan brought to it. Also cast: Turhan Bey (centre), Charles McGraw, Milburn Stone, Rose Hobart, Andrew Tombes and Addison Richards. (64 mins)

△ Two stalwarts of the horror genre for the price of one (and expensive even at that), **Frankenstein Meets The Wolf Man** paired Frankenstein's monster (this time played by Bela Lugosi, left) with the Wolf Man (Lon Chaney Jr, right), the latter brought back to life after grave-diggers unearth his tomb one moonlit night while searching for jewellery. In an attempt to find a cure for his unfortunate condition (lycanthropy), the Wolf Man seeks out gypsy woman Maria Ouspenskaya who, in turn, tells him to pay a call on Dr Frankenstein. It is in Vasaria that the Wolf Man meets the monster (brought to life by mad scientist Patric Knowles) and is promised a cure that never materialises. It all ends violently, with the two monsters attempting to do grievous bodily harm to each other until they are swept away by the floodwaters of a burst dam. Ilona Massey was cast as Frankenstein's daughter, with other roles under director Roy William Neill's clichéd direction going to Denis Hoey, Lionel Atwill, Rex Evans and Don Barclay. Curt Siodmak scripted it, and the producer was George Waggner. (72 mins)

▽ The studio departed from its Scrooge-like penny-pinching for its Technicolor remake of **Phantom Of The Opera**, and gave producer George Waggner one and a half million dollars to shower on opulent sets and costumes. This approach certainly made for a good-looking extravaganza but, alas, with the production approached as more of a musical than anything else, and starring Nelson Eddy and Susanna Foster (right), the menace of Gaston Leroux's original story was largely lost. As the phantom himself (originally played by Lon Chaney in 1925), Claude Rains' performance went for nought in Eric Taylor and Samuel Hoffenstein's screenplay (adaptation by John Jacoby) which left him little opportunity to do more than slink ineffectually round the Paris Opera House, planning revenge on the publisher (Miles Mander) who Rains (left, at piano) believes has stolen his music. The operatic scenes were staged by William von Wymetal and Lester Horton, and included excerpts from Flotow's *Martha*, as well as two operas invented for the film, using a combination of Tchaikovsky's Symphony No 4 and some music by Chopin. In addition, Mr Eddy and Miss Foster were given a song (by Edward Ward and George Waggner) called 'Lullaby Of The Bells', also heard as a violin solo and a piano concerto. Director Arthur Lubin, who added no particular quality to the enterprise, cast Edgar Barrier as the detective (right), as well as Jane Farrar (niece of soprano Geraldine Farrar), Barbara Everest, Steve Geray, Frank Puglia, Hume Cronyn and Fritz Leiber (as Liszt). (91 mins)

▽ A grown-up Deanna Durbin (centre right) found herself dropped into an efficient but run-of-the-mill weepie called **Hers To Hold**. Lewis R. Foster's screenplay from a story by John D. Klorer placed her in an aircraft factory, where she has taken a job to be near to the pilot she loves (Joseph Cotten, centre left). The couple are, however, soon separated by the war, leaving Miss Durbin and her audiences weeping copiously. None of these events, however, prevented Deanna from singing several songs, including a wartime hit by Herb Magidson and Jimmy McHugh called 'Say A Prayer For The Boys Over There', Cole Porter's 'Begin The Beguine' and, proving that she was still up to it, 'The Seguidilla' from Bizet's *Carmen*. Frank Ryan directed, also casting Charles Winninger (as the star's father), Gus Schilling, Nella Walker, Evelyn Ankers, Ludwig Stossel, William Davidson and Irving Bacon. The producer was Felix Jackson. (94 mins)

△ A better-than-average western, but with the main ingredients of the genre intact, **Frontier Bad Men** was the story of a couple of Texans (Robert Paige, left and Noah Beery Jr) who arrive in Abilene, Kansas, with their herd, and, after realising that bad-guy Thomas Gomez controls the local cattle market with terror tactics, shows him who's boss by establishing their own independent exchange. The inevitable clashes germane to rivalries of this nature proliferated in Gerald Geraghty and Morgan B. Cox's screenplay (which included a noisy cattle stampede), but there was nothing that our heroes couldn't handle. Female interest, not overlooked in the general melée, was supplied by Diana Barrymore (top-cast, right) and Anne Gwynne, with other parts under William McCann's traditional direction for producer Ford Beebe, going to Leo Carrillo, Andy Devine, Lon Chaney Jr, Tex Ritter, William Farnum and Robert Homans. (77 mins)

△ Director Charles Lamont brought verve and vigour to Bud Abbott (centre) and Lou Costello's (right) latest offering, **Hit The Ice**, in which the pair, having been mistaken for a couple of bank robbers, flee to Sun Valley to escape arrest. The assorted travellers who arrive there with them included vocalist Ginny Simms (2nd right), who was co-starred and given four songs by Harry Revel and Paul Francis Webster to sing. The Robert Lees-Frederick Rinaldo-John Grant screenplay (story by True Boardman) ran true to the expected form of Abbott and Costello comedies, with enough plot complications to keep the fans laughingly attentive. This one even staged a musical sequence on ice which, by Universal's economy-cutting standards, was mounted with noticeable lavishness. Others involved in the non-stop action were Patric Knowles, Elyse Knox, Joseph Sawyer (centre left), Marc Lawrence (left), Sheldon Leonard (2nd left) and, on the musical side, Johnny Long and His Orchestra, The Four Teens, Helen Young and Gene Williams. Alex Gottlieb produced. Songs: 'Happiness Bound', 'I'd Like To Set You To Music', 'Slap Polka'. (81 mins)

▷ Alfred Hitchcock brilliantly captured the small-town atmosphere (actually Santa Rosa, California) that played such an integral part in **Shadow Of A Doubt**, a gripping character study of a murderer rather than a fully fledged thriller. It starred Joseph Cotten as 'Uncle Charlie' who, on the run from the police in Philadelphia, travels to his sister's small-town home in California, and soon becomes absorbed in family life. It is Cotten's niece, Teresa Wright (as 'Young Charlie') who, despite the warmth she feels towards her uncle, begins to sense intuitively that all is not well, and recognises in him a guilty conscience. Her suspicions are reinforced with the arrival of two detectives (MacDonald Carey and Wallace Ford) whom Cotten (left) refuses to see. All vestiges of doubt are removed after Cotten's abortive attempts to murder Miss Wright (centre), albeit 'accidentally'. The screenplay by Thornton Wilder, Sally Benson and Alma Reville (from a story by Gordon McDonell) – apart from its deft characterisations of the townfolk in general and the Newton family in particular – was especially effective in the way it juxtaposed evil with innocence (a favourite Hitchcock ruse), and provided excellent roles for Hume Cronyn as the community's earnest amateur sleuth, forever barking up the wrong tree; as well as for Patricia Collinge (right) and Henry Travers as the heads of the Newton household. Edna May Wonacott and Charles Bates were their children, with other roles going to Irving Bacon, Clarence Muse, Janet Shaw and Estelle Jewel. Produced by Jack H. Skirball. Remade in 1959 as *Step Down To Terror*. (106 mins)

◁ A remake of *Princess O'Hara* (1935), **It Ain't Hay**, loosely based on Damon Runyon's story, was a typical Abbott (right) and Costello (left) vehicle, reworked by scenarists Allan Boretz and John Grant to allow the comedians maximum exposure in a story about a cab driver's attempts to acquire a horse for Cecil Kellaway, whose own nag Costello inadvertently but effectively bumped off by administering candy to the ailing animal. Turns out that the nag Costello finds for Kellaway is a world famous racehorse. Alex Gottlieb's production provided generous dollops of music and comedy – the latter not entirely vintage A & C. Though the rest of the cast included Grace McDonald and Leighton Noble (as the romantic interest), Eugene Pallette, Eddie Quillan, Shemp Howard, Samuel S. Hinds, Wade Boteler and Selmer Jackson, Costello, as usual, dominated – a fact which director Erle C. Kenton hardly underplayed. Also featured: The Vagabonds; The Step Brothers and The Hollywood Blondes. Songs: 'Glory Be', 'Old Timer', 'The Sunbeam Serenade' Paul Francis Webster, Harry Revel. (81 mins)

▽ Director Robert Siodmak brought immense flair to **Son Of Dracula**, turning Eric Taylor's otherwise trite screenplay – wherein Lon Chaney Jr (centre) as Dracula *fils*, marries Louise Allbritton (left), an occult-worshipper who believes him to be a Hungarian count – into a more than passable example of the horror genre. The usual isolated mansion in surrounding woodland countryside, complete with nocturnal killings vampire-style, lent atmosphere to the tale; with second-billed Robert Paige (right), as Miss Allbritton's erstwhile fiancé spoking the wheel of the couple's anti-social behaviour by killing them. Frank Craven played a small-town doctor, and J. Edward Bromberg a psychologist (both of whom Paige consults before killing the bloodthirsty couple), with other roles going to Evelyn Ankers, Samuel S. Hinds, Adeline De Walt Reynolds and Patrick Moriarty. The producer was Ford Beebe. (79 mins)

▽ One of the best of the series, **Sherlock Holmes Faces Death** benefitted from a really taut screenplay (by Bertram Millhauser, working from Conan Doyle's story *The Sign Of The Four*) set in an army officers' convalescent home called Musgrave House, in which three murders have taken place – always after the clock strikes thirteen! Using the manor's large checkered entrance-hall floor as a chessboard, and the establishment's inhabitants and personnel as pawns in a chess game, Holmes ingeniously discovers a hidden cellar which contains a long-forgotten land grant – and the motive for the three killings. After that it's a matter of mere minutes before Holmes, brandishing a pistol loaded with blanks, finally confronts the murderer. Basil Rathbone (centre) and Nigel Bruce (left) were still Holmes and Watson, and Gavin Muir and Frederick Worlock the two Musgrave brothers, with other roles under Roy William Neill's tight direction going to Hillary Brooke (right), Milburn Stone, Arthur Margetson, Halliwell Hobbes and, as Inspector Lestrade, Dennis Hoey. Neill also produced. (68 mins)

▽ Conan Doyle's celebrated sleuth, one of whose most remarkable achievements, if this current series was anything to go by, was his miraculous ability never to age, again found himself working for the allies in **Sherlock Holmes In Washington**. Poorly scripted by Bertram Millhauser (for whose story Sir Arthur was not responsible), it concerned an all-important piece of microfilm hidden in a matchbox and passed from a British agent on a train to passenger Marjorie Lord, without her realising what it contains – apart from matches, that is. The Nazis are desperate for its contents; so is Basil Rathbone's Holmes (left). Needless to say, the latter finally attains his object, but not before half of Washington have had their cigarettes lit by the seemingly endless number of matches in the box. Millhauser's silly screenplay relied too much on coincidence to generate much excitement, a fact which Roy William Neill's direction was powerless to overcome. Nigel Bruce (right) again played Watson, with other roles for associate producer Howard Benedict going to Henry Daniell, George Zucco, John Archer, Gavin Muir, Edmund MacDonald, Don Terry, Bradley Page, Holmes Herbert and Thurston Hall. (71 mins)

◁ Donald O'Connor (right) starred in **Top Man** (GB: **Man Of The Family**), an efficient and fast moving diversion which successfully combined homely, family comedy-drama of the Andy Hardy variety with snappy musical numbers. Zachary Gold's script (story by Ken Goldsmith) had young Donald as a college student who has two sisters (Peggy Ryan, 2nd left and Anne Gwynne, 2nd right) and who, when father (Richard Dix, centre) is called up for army service, assumes the position of head of the household. Apart from taking care of mother (Lillian Gish, left) and the girls, he organizes his schoolmates into a war factory labour force, and mounts a rousing show on the factory premises. O'Connor and Peggy Ryan sparkled in some comedy dance routines, and Susanna Foster as the girl next door and O'Connor's youthful romance, warbled away in her pleasant coloratura style. Count Basie and His Band turned up for the factory show, and there were a couple of specialties from Borrah Minnevitch and His Harmonica Rascals. The solid supporting cast for producer Milton Schwarzwald and director Charles Lamont featured David Holt, Noah Beery Jr, Marcia Mae Jones, Louise Beavers and Samuel S. Hinds. Songs included: 'Wrap Your Troubles In Dreams' Ted Koehler, Harry Barris; 'Basie Boogie' Count Basie; 'Dream Lover' Clifford Grey, Victor Schertzinger.

▽ 'Kaloe, you don't need Vitamin A,' was the immortal line uttered by sarong-clad Maria Montez (left) to Jon Hall (right – who kills sharks for their vitamin content) after he kisses her in **White Savage**. In fact, surrounded by the tropical tranquillity and blissful South Sea existence of the film's exotic make-believe setting, all Hall really needed was a better script. What he got was a colourful collection of clichés (compiled by Richard Brooks from an original story by Peter Milne) in which the island's sense of well-being is shattered by the intrusion of Thomas Gomez, who has his eye on the treasures contained in the local sacred temple, including a gold and jewel-encrusted swimming pool. The local temple deities, however, literally send their wrath crashing down on his head by conjuring up an earthquake the moment the temple is defiled. Sabu (centre), as a light-footed native urchin, was third-billed to play cupid in the affair between Miss Montez and fisherman Hall; with other roles under Arthur Lubin's direction going to Don Terry, Turhan Bey, Sidney Toler, Paul Guilfoyle and Constance Purdy. The Technicolor production was by George Waggner. (75 mins)

△ Also updated to World War II, but much more polished than the studio's first Sherlock Holmes effort in 1942, **Sherlock Holmes And The Secret Weapon**, loosely based on Arthur Conan Doyle's story *The Dancing Men*, again concerned Nazi agents. The 'McGuffin' (Alfred Hitchcock's term for the plot object), this time, was a bomb-sight invented by William Post Jr, which has been divided into four parts, each part being entrusted to a different scientist. Evil adversary Moriarty (Lionel Atwill) is hired by the Nazis to acquire the bomb-sight being held by the quartet, and it is up to Holmes to see that he doesn't. Basil Rathbone (left) again played the famous Baker Street sleuth and Nigel Bruce (right) encored as Watson, with other roles in W. Scott Darling and Edmund L. Hartmann's fanciful (but fun) screenplay going to Kaaren Verne, Dennis Hoey, Harold de Becker, Paul Fix and Holmes Herbert. It was well directed, at a lively pace, by Roy William Neill, and the producer was Howard Benedict. (68 mins)

△ Producer Walter Wanger's **We've Never Been Licked** was a bogus wartime morale booster set, for much of the time, in Texas' famed Agricultural and Mechanical College – a military school at which top-starred Richard Quine (soon to give up acting for film directing) is one of the students. Quine's career, however, would seem to be blighted after he is dismissed from the A & M for spying on kindly Harry Davenport, the science professor; and for showing too tolerant an attitude towards a couple of Japanese. There was method in young Quine's madness, however. He has deliberately cultivated his Jap activities (which included handing over a gas-antidote formula to a local spy ring at A & M) in order to gain their confidence so that he, in turn, might be privy to information that could be useful to the Allies. Quine (illustrated centre on floor) proves his patriotism by turning kamikaze pilot and crashing his plane into a Jap aircraft carrier. Noah Beery Jr received second-billing as Quine's room-mate, and the cast, under John Rawlins' unremarkable direction, was completed by Anne Gwynne, Martha O'Driscoll, Edgar Barrier and William Frawley. Apart from three Texas A & M college songs ('Spirit of Aggieland', 'Aggie War Hymn', and 'I'd Rather Be A Texas Aggie'), there was one additional number: 'Me For You, Forever' by Harry Revel and Paul Francis Webster. (104 mins)

◁ In her 13th starring picture, **His Butler's Sister**, Deanna Durbin (centre) proved that her appealing qualities were in no way diminished by the passage of time. She played a small-town girl who, in Samuel Hoffenstein and Betty Reinhardt's original screenplay, goes to New York to seek out a famous composer (Franchot Tone) under whose patronage she hopes to find fame as a singer. Tone's butler (Pat O'Brien), however, turns out to be none other than Deanna's considerably older half-brother, who has other ideas of what is proper to a well-brought-up young girl, and who puts her to work as a maid under a regime of strict discipline. Misunderstandings and complications proliferate before Mr Tone and Miss Durbin are united, in the course of which the 'maid' is courted by a delightful quintet of middle-aged butlers (Akim Tamiroff, Alan Mowbray, Frank Jenks, Hans Conried and Sig Arno) who all want to marry her. The soprano was given several opportunities to sing, from a repertoire that included an aria from Puccini's *Turandot*, 'When You're Away' (Victor Herbert, lyrics Henry Blossom), a medley of Russian songs (in Russian) and 'In The Spirit Of The Moment' by Bernie Grossman and Walter Jurmann. Also cast: Walter Catlett, Elsa Janssen, Florence Bates, Evelyn Ankers, Roscoe Karns and Russell Hicks. Felix Jackson was the producer, and it was directed for the delightful nonsense it was by Frank Borzage. (93 mins)

OTHER RELEASES OF 1943

All By Myself
Prod: Bernard W. Burton Dir: Felix Feist. Advertising executive jilts girlfriend for nightclub singer. Girlfriend blackmails doctor to pose as her fiancé for revenge, but falls in love with him and finds happiness. Neil Hamilton, Evelyn Ankers, Rosemary Lane, Patric Knowles. (63 mins)

Always A Bridesmaid
Prod: Ken Goldsmith Dir: Erle C. Kenton. Andrews Sisters 'B' about a detective who joins a club to uncover a swindler using it for nefarious business. Patric Knowles, Grace McDonald, Charles Butterworth, Billy Gilbert. (61 mins)

Arizona Trail (Tex Ritter)
Dir: Vernon Keays. Tex and Fuzzy Knight return home to help the former's dad hang on to his spread which is sought by a gang for water rights. Janet Shaw. (57 mins)

Cheyenne Roundup (Johnny Mack Brown, Tex Ritter)
Dir: Ray Taylor. Dual roles for Johnny as an outlaw brought to justice for claim jumping by his look-a-like twin brother. Fuzzy Knight, Jennifer Holt. (59 mins)

Cowboy In Manhattan
Prod: Paul Malvern Dir: Frank Woodruff. Songwriter pretends to be a millionaire to win the love of Broadway star. Robert Paige, Frances Langford, Leon Errol, Walter Catlett. (54 mins)

Eyes Of The Underworld
Prod: Ben Pivar Dir: Roy William Neill. Low-grade programmer starred Richard Dix as a police chief with a secret prison record he is determined to keep hidden. Lon Chaney Jr, Wendy Barrie, Lloyd Corrigan. (61 mins)

Fired Wife
Prod: Alex Gottlieb Dir: Charles Lamont. Enjoyable comedy with Louise Allbritton, as assistant to superstitious Broadway producer, and Robert Paige who decide, for reasons of business, to keep their marriage a secret. Diana Barrymore. (75 mins)

Follow The Band
Prod: Paul Malvern Dir: Jean Yarbrough. A young farmer in town on business finds himself playing a trombone in a nightclub. An excuse for a ten-number floorshow. Frances Langford, Eddie Quillan, Mary Beth Hughes, Anne Rooney, The King's Men, The King Sisters. (60 mins)

Frontier Law
Dir: Elmer Clifton. A gunman cowboy rounds up a gang of rustlers and sets free an innocent man jailed for murder. Russell Hayden, Fuzzy Knight. (55 mins)

Gals Incorporated
Dir: Leslie Goodwins. Millionaire Leon Errol plays sugar daddy to a nightclubful of gold-diggers – to the consternation of his sister and son. Minna Phillips, David Bacon, Harriet Hilliard, Grace McDonald, Betty Kean, Maureen Cannon. (61 mins)

Get Going
Prod: Will Cowan Dir: Jean Yarbrough. Newly arrived in Washington, Grace McDonald, as a typist in a bureau, hints to Robert Paige that she might be a spy. He falls for her while investigating her and then uncovers a real spy ring. (57 mins)

Good Morning Judge
Prod: Paul Malvern Dir: Jean Yarbrough. One-joke comedy in which music publisher slips a mickey finn to Louise Allbritton after realising she is the attorney to a woman sueing him for plagiarism. Mary Beth Hughes, J. Carrol Naish, Louise Beavers. (66 mins)

He's My Guy
Prod: Will Cowan Dir: Edward F. Cline. Morale boosting programmer about ex-vaudevillians and the show they stage in a defence plant. Dick Foran, Irene Hervey. (65 mins)

Hi, Buddy
Prod: Paul Malvern Dir: Harold Young. Military-flavoured song and dance 'B' in which fund-raising effort saves boys' club from closure. Dick Foran, Harriet Hilliard, Robert Paige, The King's Men, The Step Brothers, The Four Sweethearts. (68 mins)

Hi' Ya Chum (GB: **Everything Happens To Us**)
Prod: Howard Benedict Dir: Harold Young. Knock-about story featuring The Ritz Brothers, making a go of their newly-opened restaurant in boom-time California. Jane Frazee, Robert Paige, June Clyde, Paul Hurst, Edmund McDonald, Lou Lubin. (61 mins)

Hi' Ya Sailor
Prod/Dir: Jean Yarbrough. Yawnsome yarn about seaman-cum-songwriter's adventures in New York. Donald Woods, Elyse Knox, Eddie Quillan, Matt Willis. (63 mins)

Honeymoon Lodge
Prod: Warren Wilson Dir: Edward Lilley. Returning to the scene of their courtship to salvage their marriage, a couple meet obstacles along the way, but songs and dances settle all amicably. Songwriter Gus Kahn helped. David Bruce, June Vincent, Harriet Hilliard. (63 mins)

How's About It?
Prod: Ken Goldsmith Dir: Erle C. Kenton. The Andrews Sisters as elevator operators in music publishing building hope to make the big time; publisher Robert Paige is accused of plagiarising Grace McDonald's lyrics but love conquers all. (60 mins)

It Comes Up Love
Prod: Ken Goldsmith Dir: Charles Lamont. Gloria Jean goes to New York with her younger sister to live with their father. The girls become involved with his love life, in which two rivals are competing for his matrimonial favours. A pleasing diversion with three songs from Miss Jean. Ian Hunter, Donald O'Connor, Frieda Inescort, Louise Allbritton. (64 mins)

Keep 'Em Slugging
Prod: Ben Pivar Dir: Christy Cabanne. The Dead End Kids and The Little Tough Guys seek a summer vacation job; one of them finds employment in a shipping office and is framed on a theft charge. His buddies come to his aid. Bobby Jordan, Evelyn Ankers, Don Porter. (60 mins)

Larceny With Music
Prod: Howard Benedict Dir: Edward Lilley. There are complications when nightspot owner Leo Carrillo hires singer Allan Jones who he believes is to inherit a fortune. Kitty Carlisle, The King Sisters. (64 mins)

The Lone Star Trail (Johnny Mack Brown Tex Ritter)
Dir: Ray Taylor. Johnny, having served a two-year sentence through a frame-up, gets a US marshal Tex, to help him clear his name. Fuzzy Knight. (58 mins)

Mister Big
Prod: Ken Goldsmith Dir: Charles Lamont. Lively musical about college kids turning their drama school's annual show into a swinging revue. Gloria Jean, Donald O'Connor, Peggy Ryan, Robert Paige, Elyse Knox. (64 mins)

Moonlight In Vermont
Prod: Bernard W. Burton Dir: Edward Lilley Thin excuse for song and dance story of backwoods girl Gloria Jean who attends New York drama school, runs out of money, but is saved by a barnyard revue. Ray Malone, George Dolenz, Fay Helm. (62 mins)

Mug Town
Prod: Ken Goldsmith Dir: Rod Taylor. Boring return of Dead End Kids in formula story of delinquents unjustly blamed for a fur theft. They're cleared, of course – during the bombing of Pearl Harbour! (60 mins)

Never A Dull Moment
Prod: Howard Benedict Dir: Edward Lilley. Zippy story about The Ritz Brothers who, posing as mobsters in their nightclub act, inadvertantly become involved in a real crime. Mary Beth Hughes, Frances Langford, Stuart Crawford, Elisabeth Risdon. (60 mins)

Raiders Of San Joaquin (Johnny Mack Brown, Tex Ritter)
Dir: Lewis D. Collins. Johnny and Tex overcome the efforts of a gang who are grabbing land under the pretence of a railroad development. Fuzzy Knight. (59 mins)

Rhythm Of The Islands
Prod: Bernard W. Burton Dir: Roy William Neill. South Sea Island caper in which native chief Allan Jones and beachcomber Andy Devine sell off their paradise island to millionaire Ernest Truex whose daughter Jane Frazee is the love interest. (59 mins)

She's For Me
Prod: Frank Gross Dir: Reginald Le Borg. Attorney David Bruce curbs extravagance of niece Lois Collier, and falls in love with singer Grace McDonald whose help he solicits to hinder niece's romance with his playboy buddy, George Dolenz. (60 mins)

So's Your Uncle
Prod: Charles Previn Dir: Jean Yarbrough. To avoid creditors, Donald Woods disguises himself but is struck by a car during his getaway. Driver Elyse Knox takes him home where her wealthy Auntie Billie Burke takes a shine to him. (64 mins)

Tenting Tonight On The Old Campground (Johnny Mack Brown, Tex Ritter)
Dir: Lewis D. Collins. Problems for Johnny and Tex when a bunch of baddies are out to stymie the building of a new stagecoach road. Fuzzy Knight. (62 mins)

Two Tickets To London
Prod/Dir: Edwin L. Marin. Basically a two-reeler with elephantiasis, about a ship's mate incorrectly accused of aiding an enemy submarine and clearing his name by apprehending the real culprit. Alan Curtis, Michelle Morgan, C. Aubrey Smith. (78 mins)

When Johnny Comes Marching Home
Prod: Bernard W. Burton Dir: Charles Lamont. Soldier-cum-singer returns to his old boarding house and finds romance. Boring story but snappy song and dance numbers. Allan Jones, Jane Frazee, Gloria Jean, Donald O'Connor, Peggy Ryan, The Step Brothers. (74 mins)

You're A Lucky Fellow Mr Smith
Prod: Edward Lilley Dir: Felix Feist. Cole Porter and Gus Kahn musically assisted this routine story involving marriage trickery and inheritance. Evelyn Ankers, David Bruce, Allan Jones. (64 mins)

1944

▷ Although more than a little reminiscent of operetta in its approach, **Can't Help Singing** was a decided musical success, parading, as it did, an appealing score by no less than Jerome Kern and E.Y. Harburg, stunning Technicolor photography (by Woody Bredell and W. Howard Greene), and a lively and winsome Deanna Durbin (illustrated) in the lead role. The screenplay was by Lewis R. Foster and Frank Ryan from a story by John Klorer and Leo Townsend (based on *Girl Of The Overland Trail* by Samuel J. and Curtis B. Warshawsky). In it, Miss Durbin played a spirited young lady who decides to journey west to marry her army lieutenant sweetheart against her father's wishes. On the way, however, she meets Robert Paige, falls for him, and abandons her former plans. Felix Jackson's production was a decidedly outdoor affair, pleasing to the eye and easy on the ear, with solid direction from Frank Ryan, whose excellent supporting cast featured Ray Collins (as Deanna's father), Akim Tamiroff and Leonid Kinskey (lending comedy as two foreign and confused fortune hunters), Clara Blandick, David Bruce, Olin Howlin, June Vincent, Thomas Gomez, Andrew Tombes and George Cleveland. Songs and musical numbers: 'Can't Help Singing', 'More And More', 'Cal-i-for-ni-ay', 'Elbow Room', 'Swing Your Sweetheart', 'Any Moment Now'. (95 mins)

▽ Originally intended as a fourth episode in the studio's *Flesh And Fantasy* of the previous year, but dropped in the editing stages, **Destiny** had 35 minutes added to its original 30-minute running time, for the simple story of a fugitive from justice (Alan Curtis, left) who, after being accused of a hold-up he had nothing to do with, hides out on a farm owned by blind Gloria Jean (top-starred, right) and her benign father (Frank Craven, centre). How the bitter fugitive is, in time, regenerated by father and daughter and, in the process, is freed of the charges he's been accused of, formed the why-bother content of Roy Chanslor and Ernest Pascal's screenplay, whose original footage was directed by Julien Duvivier; and with Reginald LeBorg responsible for the added opening and closing sequences. The associate producer was Roy William Neill and the cast was completed by Grace McDonald, Vivian Austin, Frank Fenton and Minna Gombell. (65 mins)

△ Donald O'Connor (centre), now rising fast to become one of the studio's young musical comedy stars, shared top billing with Peggy Ryan (centre left) and, in her screen debut, Ann Blyth, in **Chip Off The Old Block**. Playing a talented member of a show-biz family, Miss Blyth made a favourable impression on reviewers and audiences alike, and displayed a pleasing lyric soprano in 'My Song' (by Lew Brown and Ray Henderson) and 'Love Is Like Music' (by Milton Schwarzwald, Inez James and Sidney Miller). Eugene Conrad and Leo Townsend's screenplay (story by Robert Arthur), abounded in complications, with O'Connor as a naval cadet on leave from school who finds himself flirting with show business – as well as with Miss Blyth – and pursued by Peggy Ryan who would like to be the recipient of his favours. Ryan's involvement with the action allowed opportunities for her to pair in some energetic dance routines (staged by Louis Da Pron) with the leading man; juvenile quiz-kid Joel Kupperman was featured to good effect, and an excellent supporting cast, under Charles Lamont's lively direction, included Helen Vinson, Helen Broderick, Arthur Treacher, Patric Knowles, J. Edward Bromberg, Ernest Truex and Minna Gombell. Bernard W. Burton produced and, among the other songs and musicl numbers featured were 'Is It Good Or Is It Bad?' Charles Tobias; 'Mighty Nice To Have Met You' Bill Grage, Grace Shannon; 'Sailor Song' Eugene Conrad. (76 mins)

▷ The shock of Deanna Durbin's defection from sweet ingenue to disillusioned singer in a sleazy nightclub was described, by one reviewer at the time, as having the same impact as Garbo's first appearance in a talkie. He was being a trifle fanciful, although it was undeniably refreshing to see the studio's top money-maker shedding her little girl image for a more substantially dramatic role in **Christmas Holiday**. Based on a novel by Somerset Maugham, Herman J. Mankiewicz's screenplay switched locales from France to New Orleans as it told the story (largely in flashback) of Miss Durbin's (right) unhappy marriage to a young ne'er do-well, who is arrested for murder and imprisoned for life. Gene Kelly (centre, on loan from MGM) played her husband, but with the homosexual (and incestuous) aspects of the novel virtually obliterated, he had little to latch on to. The film, under Robert Siodmak's direction, was full of resonances, none of which really added up to much. Richard Whorf (left) was featured as a reporter, with other roles in Felix Jackson's production going to Dean Harens as the young lieutenant to whom Durbin pours her heart out after he accompanies her to a midnight mass; as well as Gladys George, Gale Sondergaard (as Kelly's mother) and David Bruce. Songs: 'Always' Irving Berlin; 'Spring Will Be A Little Late This Year' Frank Loesser. (93 mins)

△ The studio spent what, by their standards, was a goodly sum on **Bowery To Broadway**, and brought together a sizeable cast of their resident 'name' players to attract the paying customers. In the event, the musical was just another vaudeville show, periodically enlivened by a crisp number or two in amongst the largely seen-it-all-before offerings. The episodic story centred on Jack Oakie (right) and Donald Cook as the owners of rival nightspots in the Bowery. They both move uptown and continue to compete in establishments on 14th Street, finally joining forces to produce a series of hit Broadway shows. Their travels (and travails) were accompanied by appearances from Maria Montez, Susanna Foster (who sang two Everett Carter–Edward Ward songs, 'The Love Waltz' and 'There'll Always Be A Moon'), Ann Blyth, Louise Allbritton (excellent as Lillian Russell and singing 'Under The Bamboo Tree' by Bob Cole and J. Rosamond Johnson), Frank McHugh, Rosemary De Camp, Leo Carrillo, Andy Devine and, in a specialty dance number, Donald O'Connor and Peggy Ryan. The stand-out item was a fast-patter routine by the Negro pair, Ben Carter and Mantan Moreland (left). Edmund Joseph, Bart Lytton and Arthur T. Horman wrote it from a story by Joseph and Horman, and it was choreographed by Louis Da Pron, Carlos Romero and Johnny Boyle – all of which proved that more is not necessarily better. Charles Lamont directed for producer John Grant, and other songs and musical numbers included: 'Montevideo', 'Coney Island Waltz' Kim Gannon, Walter Kent; 'My Song Of Romance' Don George, Dave Franklin; 'Wait Till The Sun Shines Nellie' Andrew B. Sterling, Harry von Tilzer; 'Just Because You Made Dem Goo Goo Eyes At Me' Hughie Cannon, John Queen; 'He Took Her For A Sleigh Ride' (composer unknown). (95 mins)

▷ No expense was spared in producer Paul Malvern's good-to-look-at Technicolor follow-up to the studio's successful *Arabian Nights* (1942). **Ali Baba And The Forty Thieves** was lush escapist entertainment set in Baghdad at the time of the Mongol invasion. Jon Hall (left) as Ali Baba received second-billing to shapely Maria Montez as Princess Amara, daughter of traitor Frank Puglia. In the course of Edmund L. Hartmann's screenplay, she finds herself betrothed to Hulagu Khan (Kurt Katch), but Ali Baba, who has stumbled on the secret cave of the 40 thieves and has become one of them, soon sees to it that Miss Montez finishes up where she belongs: in his arms. Turhan Bey, in a role he was born to play, was third-billed as slave boy Jamiel, with other roles under Arthur Lubin's action-filled direction going to Andy Devine (right), Fortunio Bonanova (centre), Moroni Olsen, Ramsay Ames, Chris-Pin Martin and young Scotty Beckett as the child Ali Baba. (85 mins)

△ More escapism, in glorious Technicolor, from the team of Maria Montez (centre), Jon Hall (right) and Sabu (foreground) in **Cobra Woman**, with la Montez giving the paying customers added value for money by playing two roles; a sarong-clad native girl, and her more ornately gowned high-priestess sister. On the eve of her wedding to Hall, Montez (alias the simple native girl) is kidnapped and taken to her sister's island, with her fiancé following in hot pursuit. An erupting volcano brought Richard Brooks and Gene Lewis' screenplay (story by W. Scott Darling) to its climax, with sarong-clad Montez taking her rightful place as high-priestess, and being reunited with handsome Jon Hall as well. Robert Siodmak's direction kept it moving at a cracking pace, and there was serviceable support from Lon Chaney Jr (left), Mary Nash, Edgar Barrier, Lois Collier, Samuel S. Hinds and Moroni Olsen. George Waggner produced. (70 mins)

▽ A first cousin to *The Phantom Of The Opera* (1943), **The Climax** co-starred Boris Karloff (right), Susanna Foster and Turhan Bey in a ghoulish story about a resident physician to a European opera house (Karloff) who, years before, killed a soprano who failed to requite his passion. When Miss Foster appears on the scene to revive the opera that made her unfortunate predecessor famous, the maniacal doctor decides to take steps ... In a happy ending, his insane plans are foiled by Turhan Bey, who is in love with Foster. Dressed up in some excellent Technicolor photography by Hal Mohr and W. Howard Greene, and directed with flair and a sense of suspense by George Waggner, it all added up to satisfying, not-to-be-taken seriously entertainment. Director Waggner also produced, as well as writing lyrics to Edward Ward's music, and the screenplay, adapted by Curt Siodmak from a play by Edward Locke, was by Siodmak and Lynn Starling. Lester Horton staged the operatic sequences. Also in it: Gale Sondergaard (left), Thomas Gomez, June Vincent, George Dolenz and Ludwig Stossel. Themes from the music of Schubert and Chopin were featured, and the songs by Ward and Waggner were 'Now At Last', 'Someday I Know', 'The Magic Voice' and 'The Boulevardier'. (86 mins)

◁ A star-spangled banner for the war effort, producer Charles K. Feldman's largely musical **Follow The Boys** presented an impressive parade of Universal stars, as well as guest artists from elsewhere, for the enjoyment of the boys at the front, not to mention their star-struck families back home. The literally dozens of songs and acts were introduced via a practically invisible plot (screenplay by Lou Breslow and Gertrude Purcell) which had George Raft (centre left) married to Vera Zorina (centre right). They part for some entirely trivial reason, but the parting inspires Raft to devote his energies to organising the Hollywood Victory Committee, in the course of which there were substantial, diverting appearances by The Andrews Sisters, The Delta Rhythm Boys, Dinah Shore, Jeanette MacDonald, W.C. Fields, Artur Rubinstein, Orson Welles and Marlene Dietrich (together in a magic act), Donald O'Connor and Peggy Ryan (in a winning specialty dance routine), Sophie Tucker, Carmen Amaya, Leo and Gautier's Dog Act, The Bricklayers, and the orchestras of Ted Lewis, Freddie Slack, Charlie Spivak and Louis Jordan. In between times, the movie returned itself to its 'plot', in which Mr Raft and Miss Zorina were supported by Charles Grapewin, Grace McDonald, Charles Butterworth, George Macready, Elizabeth Patterson, Theodore von Eltz and Regis Toomey. Producer Feldman interwove some footage of celebrities actually doing their wartime entertainment duty and, in the Hollywood Victory Committee sequence, presented Louise Allbritton, Evelyn Ankers, Noah Beery Jr, Turhan Bey, Louise Beavers, Nigel Bruce, Lon Chaney Jr, Lois Collier, Peter Coe, Alan Curtis, Andy Devine, Susanna Foster, Thomas Gomez, Samuel S. Hinds, Gloria Jean, Maria Montez, Clarence Muse, Robert Paige, Martha O'Driscoll, Maxie Rosenbloom, Randolph Scott and Gale Sondergaard. Conspicuously absent, though, was Deanna Durbin. Choreographed by George Hale and Joe Schoenfeld, and directed by Edward Sutherland, **Follow The Boys** was hardly a cinematic masterpiece, but for sheer entertainment it was, and is, a collector's item. A sample of the music that was featured: 'I'll Get By' Roy Turk, Fred Ahlert, sung by Dinah Shore; 'Some Of These Days' Shelton Brooks, sung by Sophie Tucker; 'I'll See You In My Dreams' Gus Kahn, Isham Jones, sung by Jeanette MacDonald; 'Beer Barrel Polka' Lew Brown, Jaromir Vejvoda, sung by The Andrews Sisters; 'The House I Live In' Earl Robinson, Lewis Allan, sung by The Delta Rhythm Boys, and Chopin's 'Polonaise in A Flat Major' played by maestro Rubinstein. (122 mins)

△ Maria Montez (right) and Jon Hall (left) were again exotically paired in **Gypsy Wildcat**, a romantic adventure with a mediaeval setting in which a group of innocent gypsies find themselves imprisoned in the bowels of wicked Baron Douglass Dumbrille's castle, charged with the murder of Count Orso. It's Dumbrille who's really the culprit, and hero Hall, the king's messenger, knows it, having witnessed the heinous murder of the Count by the baron's henchmen. Gypsy dancer Montez was top-billed as the Count's daughter whom Dumbrille wishes to marry, as she is heiress to a fortune; but she only has eyes for Hall. Other roles in George Waggner's colour-by-Technicolor production went to Peter Coe, Leo Carrillo, Gale Sondergaard, Curt Bois and, providing light relief from the treachery and inflamed passions, Nigel Bruce. Roy William Neill directed from a screenplay by James Hogan, Gene Lewis and James M. Cain (story by Hogan). (77 mins)

▽ Newcomer Charles Korvin (left), attempting to emulate Charles Boyer in Gallic charm and accent, was given the title role in **Enter Arsene Lupin**, which was all about a dashing jewel thief with a penchant for giving the law the slip. Ella Raines was co-starred as his romantic side-interest, as well as the owner of a fabulous emerald; but in this instance, Lupin is far more interested in winning the girl than the gem and in avoiding the determined efforts of Inspector J. Carrol Naish to catch him. George Dolenz (right) played Lupin's murderous bodyguard, with other roles under producer Ford Beebe's direction going to Gale Sondergaard, Miles Mander, Leland Hodgson, Tom Pilkington and Holmes Herbert. The script by Bertram Millhauser relied far too much on coincidence to be really convincing. MGM had made an earlier version in 1932 with John Barrymore in the title role. (72 mins)

▽ Another of the studio's 'younger set' musicals, co-starring Ann Blyth and Peggy Ryan (but omitting Donald O'Connor this time), **Babes On Swing Street** suffered from a sorely pedestrian screenplay by Howard Dimsdale and Eugene Conrad, based on a crushingly unoriginal story by Brenda Weisberg. In it, a bunch of hardworking youngsters decide to put on a show to raise the necessary funds to continue their studies at music school. The well-tried device allowed for the usual plethora of songs and musical numbers, with above-average contributions being Alfred Bryan and Fred Fisher's hit 'Peg O' My Heart' sung by Miss Blyth, and the excellent Marion Hutton singing 'Take It Easy' (by Albert De Bru, Irving Taylor and Vic Mizzy). In between times, the story was propped up by a silly sub-plot in which Leon Errol played the timid brother of spinster Alma Kruger who terrorises their young nephew. Andy Devine, Anne Gwynne (left), June Preisser, Kirby Grant (right) and Billy Dunn were also in it; so were Freddie Slack and His Orchestra and The Rubenettes. Bernard W. Burton was the associate producer, Edward Lilley directed, and Louis Da Pron cheoreographed. Other songs and musical numbers included: 'Just Being With You', 'Hotcha Sonja', 'Musical Chairs' Inez James, Sidney Miller; 'Youth Is On The March' Everett Carter, Milton Rosen; 'Loch Lomond' (traditional). (69 mins)

▷ **The Ghost Catchers** was a fast and furious money-maker from Ole Olsen (2nd left) and Chic Johnson (left) who, this time, actually found themselves in a movie with a semblance of plot – not much of a one, mind you – just enough to boast a beginning, a middle, and an end. They came to the aid of a southern family whose newest acquisition, an old brownstone city mansion, situated next to a nightclub, turns out to be haunted. Murder and mayhem were just two of the ingredients in Edmund L. Hartmann's screenplay (based on Milton Gross and Edward Cline's story *High Spirits*); melody and mirth two more. Gloria Jean (right), Martha O'Driscoll (centre), Leo Carrillo, Andy Devine, Lon Chaney Jr, Kirby Grant, Walter Catlett (2nd right) and Henry Armetta (welcome back, Henry!) were also featured; so were Morton Downey, who sang 'These Foolish Things' (by Harry Link, Holt Marvell and Jack Strachey) and Ella Mae Morse who sang 'Quoth The Raven' (by Paul Francis Webster, Harry Revel and Edward Ward). It was produced by Edmund L. Hartmann, and directed frenetically by Edward Cline. Other songs: 'Blue Candlelight And Red Roses', 'Three Cheers For The Customer' Webster, Revel; 'I'm Old Enough To Dream' Everett Carter, Ward. (67 mins)

▽ **Her Primitive Man** was a far-out screwball comedy that again teamed Louise Allbritton (left) with Robert Paige, and third-billed Robert Benchley as a publisher whose new book on head-hunters has been branded a fraud by the president (Allbritton) of an anthropological society. The author of the book (Paige), working out of a Havana casino (with help from bartender Edward Everett Horton), decides to take revenge on the interfering Miss Allbritton by tricking her into going on a head-hunting expedition with him, then disguising himself as a head-hunter. And that was just for starters! Complications begat complications in Michael Fessier and Ernest Pagano's screenplay (story by Dick Irving Hyland), and utilised the additional talents of Helen Broderick (centre, as a stuffy society matron), Stephanie Bachelor, Ernest Truex, Oscar O'Shea (2nd right), Walter Catlett and Louis Jean Heydt (right) en route to the inevitable happy-ever-after ending. Fessier and Pagano produced, and their director was Charles Lamont. (80 mins)

◁ All the comic situations you'd expect to find in a film in which Bud Abbott (right) and Lou Costello (left) starred as a pair of blundering plumbers who are accidentally invited to spend a weekend in high society, came tumbling out in **In Society**. It was a lively farce, aided by several songs, and a burlesque-inspired screenplay by John Grant, Edmund L. Hartmann and Hal Fimberg from a story by Hugh Wedlock Jr. Marion Hutton (sister of Betty), as a woman taxi driver, and Kirby Grant provided the love interest, with Ann Gillis in it as a socialite (who sang Bobby Worth and Stanley Cowan's 'Rehearsin'). Also cast were Thurston Hall, Nella Walker (centre), Margaret Irving and – inevitably as a butler – Arthur Treacher. Jean Yarbrough directed for producer Edmund L. Hartmann. Others songs: 'No Bout Adoubt It', 'My Dreams Are Getting Better All The Time' Mann Curtis, Vic Mizzy; 'Change In The Weather' Kim Gannon, Walter Kent. (73 mins)

△ The long arm of happenstance which characterised **The Pearl Of Death** made it almost impossible to accept the film with anything other than the proverbial pinch of salt. Based on Sir Arthur Conan Doyle's story *The Six Napoleons*, and porously scripted by Bertram Millhauser, it was the story of master European criminal (Miles Mander, left) and his stop-at-nothing attempts to lay his thieving fingers on a huge pearl valued at £250,000, and housed in the British Museum. He almost succeeds, too, but is outfoxed by the infallible Sherlock Holmes (Basil Rathbone, right). Nigel Bruce blustered and bumbled his way through the text as Dr Watson, with other roles for director Roy William Neill going to Dennis Hoey (as Lestrade), Evelyn Ankers (as Mander's accomplice), Ian Wolfe and Mary Gordon. Neill also produced. (63 mins)

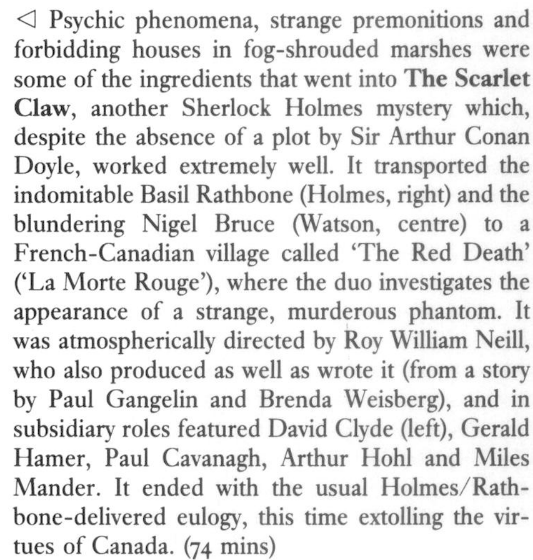

◁ Psychic phenomena, strange premonitions and forbidding houses in fog-shrouded marshes were some of the ingredients that went into **The Scarlet Claw**, another Sherlock Holmes mystery which, despite the absence of a plot by Sir Arthur Conan Doyle, worked extremely well. It transported the indomitable Basil Rathbone (Holmes, right) and the blundering Nigel Bruce (Watson, centre) to a French-Canadian village called 'The Red Death' ('La Morte Rouge'), where the duo investigates the appearance of a strange, murderous phantom. It was atmospherically directed by Roy William Neill, who also produced as well as wrote it (from a story by Paul Gangelin and Brenda Weisberg), and in subsidiary roles featured David Clyde (left), Gerald Hamer, Paul Cavanagh, Arthur Hohl and Miles Mander. It ended with the usual Holmes/Rathbone-delivered eulogy, this time extolling the virtues of Canada. (74 mins)

▽ **Phantom Lady** was an intriguing thriller whose basic situation ensured audience involvement from the start: Alan Curtis (third-billed) picks up a woman (Fay Helm) in a bar and takes her to a show. That same night his wife is murdered and, shortly afterwards, Curtis is convicted on circumstantial evidence for her murder when he fails to locate or identify his woman-companion of the fateful evening. It is Curtis' resourceful secretary, Ella Raines (right), who sets about tracking down Miss Helm, whose only distinguishing characteristic was the strange hat she was wearing. Turns out the real murderer is top-billed Franchot Tone (left), Curtis' best friend. Bernard C. Schoenfeld's screenplay (based on a novel by William Irish, a pseudonym for Cornell Woolrich) maintained interest throughout, ditto the lean-limbed direction by Robert Siodmak who, in supporting roles, cast Thomas Gomez (centre), Elisha Cook Jr, Andrew Tombes, Regis Toomey, Joseph Crehan and Milburn Stone. Carmen Miranda's sister, Aurora, was also featured as the star of a musical show, and sang 'Chick-ee-Chick' by Jacques Press and Eddie Cherkose. The film was produced by Joan Harrison, an erstwhile secretary-cum-reader-cum-scriptwriter for Alfred Hitchcock, who married novelist Eric Ambler, and went on to produce the Hitchcock TV series in later years. (85 mins)

△ Not one of the series' vintage contributions, **Sherlock Holmes And The Spider Woman** nonetheless contained most of the salient ingredients that director Roy William Neill required to keep audiences guessing, with Holmes (Basil Rathbone, left) this time solving a series of 'pyjama' suicides. Except, of course, that they're not suicides at all, but murder victims. Seems that evil Gale Sondergaard (right), as head of a group of criminals who kill for life-insurance benefits, has something to do with the crimes. Nigel Bruce was Dr Watson, with other roles in Bertram Millhauser's formula screenplay (based on elements in Conan Doyle's story *The Sign Of The Four*) going to Dennis Hoey as Lestrade, Vernon Downing, Donald Stuart, Mary Gordon, Stanley Logan, Arthur Hohl and Teddy Infuhr. Neill also doubled as producer. (62 mins)

△ As was usual in such impoverished circumstances, John P. Fulton's special effects were the best thing on view (or not on view, as the case may be) in **The Invisible Man's Revenge**. Jon Hall (left) starred as a maniac with a persecution complex who agrees to throw in his lot with professor John Carradine and turn invisible. His motive? To badger a titled English couple (Gale Sondergaard, centre, and Lester Matthews, right) into turning over their property (and their daughter) to him. Evelyn Ankers was the daughter, with other roles in Bertram Millhauser's screenplay (suggested by H.G. Wells' *The Invisible Man*) going to Alan Curtis (second-billed as a journalist), Leon Errol (the comic relief), Doris Lloyd, Ian Wolfe and Halliwell Hobbes. Ford Beebe produced as well as directed it. (78 mins)

▽ **Moonlight And Cactus** was a compact, unpretentious musical programmer in which The Andrews Sisters, Patty, Maxene and Laverne, were top-starred, although their only visible function was to sing. The simple plot (story and screenplay by Eugene Conrad and Paul Gerard Smith) centred on a rancher (Tom Seidel, left) who, on returning home from active service with the marines, finds that all his cowhands have been replaced by women. Being an old-fashioned sort, his reaction is anything but favourable, until the new lady foreman (Elyse Knox, right) demonstrates that her team of gals are capable of delivering the goods with expert efficiency. Charles O'Curran staged the dance numbers and it was directed, for producer Frank Gross, by Edward Cline. Mitchell Ayres and His Orchestra were featured, and the rest of the cast included Leo Carrillo (as a cattle thief, centre), Shemp Howard, Eddie Quillan, Murray Alper, Tom Kennedy and Minerva Urecal. Songs and musical numbers included: 'Send Me A Man, Amen' Ray Gilbert, Sidney Miller; 'Wa Hoo' Cliff Friend; 'Down In The Valley' Frank Luther; 'Sing' Harold Mooney, Hughie Prince. (60 mins)

▽ **San Diego I Love You**, a modest little comedy that yielded more than its fair share of belly-laughs, quite a few chuckles, and kept the patrons smiling throughout, featured second-billed Louise Allbritton (right) as the older sister to four obstreperous brothers. It's Miss A's lot in life to mother the brood, as well as to market her inventor-father's new collapsible life-raft. How she combined these two duties formed the basis of producer-writers Michael Fessier and Ernest Pagano's enjoyable farce, from an original story by Ruth (*My Sister Eileen*) McKenny and Richard Bransten. Jon Hall (centre) was top-billed as the third richest man in America, with Edward Everett Horton as a school professor, Eric Blore as a butler who's fired a dozen times a day but who, it turns out, comes with the house, and the venerable Buster Keaton (left) as a bus driver. The film's setting was a crowded, wartime San Diego where Miss Allbritton hopes to sell her father's invention to a research institute. Director Reginald LeBorg deserved the lion's share of the credit for keeping it swift and to the point. (81 mins)

▽ A compact screenplay by Wanda Tuchock (from a play by Sinclair Lewis and Fay Wray) resulted in a fairly appealing, slightly above average programme musical called **This Is The Life**. Story had Donald O'Connor (seated foreground – a little less exuberant than usual) in a romance with co-star Susanna Foster (centre). Miss Foster, however, becomes infatuated with an older man (an army officer, played by Patric Knowles, left), thereby driving Donald – between songs and musical numbers – to do his best to keep Knowles and the girl away from each other. Ray Eberle and His Orchestra and The Bobby Brooks Quartet were there to provide musical interest, and the choreography was by Louis Da Pron. Others featured in the cast were Louise Allbritton, Dorothy Peterson, Peggy Ryan (clearly part of the studio's Donald O'Connor film formula), Jonathan Hale, Eddie Quillan, Virginia Brissac (right), little Richard Nichols (in bed) and Frank Jenks. It was produced by Bernard W. Burton and directed by Felix Feist. Among the songs and musical numbers were: 'With A Song In My Heart' Richard Rodgers, Lorenz Hart; 'All Or Nothing At All' Jack Lawrence, Arthur Altman; 'At Sundown' Walter Donaldson; 'Gremlin Walk' Inez James, Sidney Miller. (87 mins)

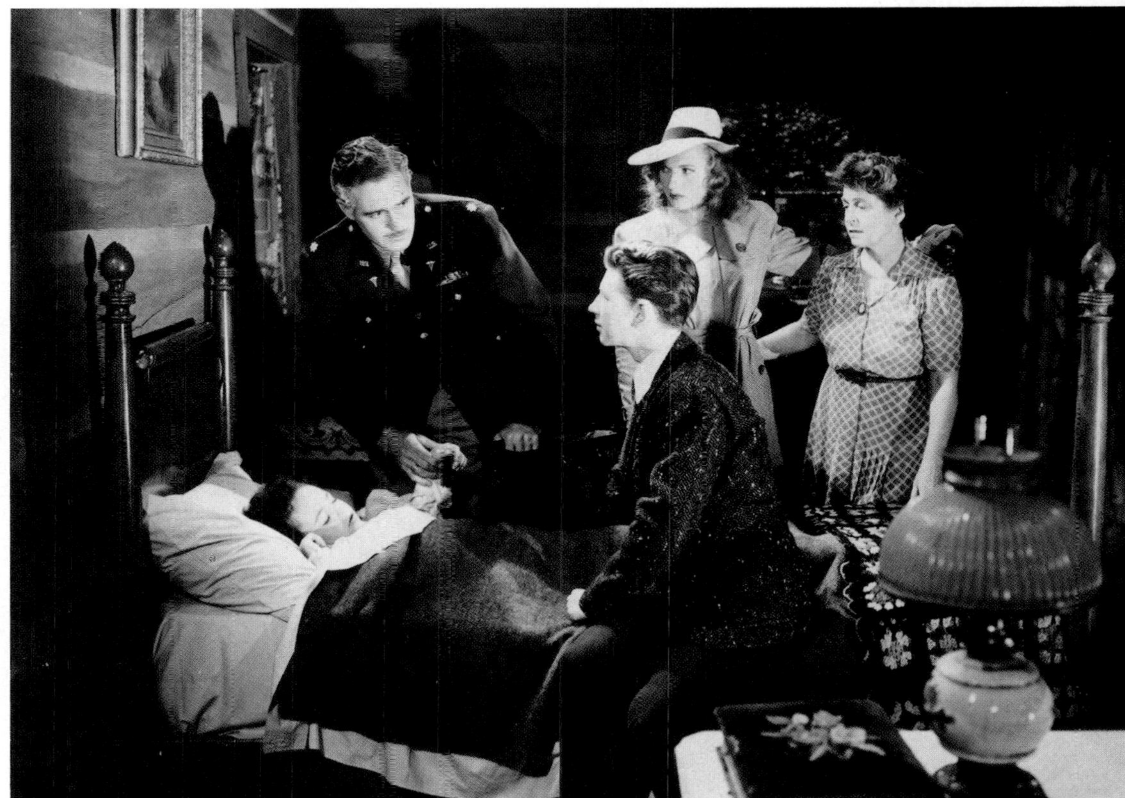

△ **Ladies Courageous** was a wordy and diffuse drama in which top-starred Loretta Young (right), as an executive officer of the WAFS (Women's Auxiliary Ferrying Squadron), is determined to see that the girls who ferry ships overseas should receive the recognition from army brass hats that they deserve. Some of the girls in Norman Reilly Raine's screenplay (suggested by the book *Looking For Trouble* by Virginia Spencer Cowles) allow their personal problems to obstruct their work; and Miss Young's sister (Geraldine Fitzgerald, left) nearly wipes out the entire WAFS outfit by crashing a plane. The film was basically on the side of the more conscientious members of the group, but definitely not on the side of audiences being, in all, a really rather dull exercise in feminist propaganda. Diana Barrymore, Anne Gwynne, Evelyn Ankers, Phillip Terry, David Bruce, Lois Collier, June Vincent, Samuel S. Hinds and Frank Jenks were in it too; Walter Wanger produced, and the enervating direction was by John Rawlins. (85 mins)

▽ Jean Gabin (seated left) played **The Imposter** for writer, director and producer Julien Duvivier. The fall of France in 1940, and the subsequent formation of Free French units in Africa, provided the background to a story in which a criminal (Gabin), saved from the guillotine by a Nazi air raid, assumes the identity of a dead French soldier, joins the Free French forces, and is gradually transformed into a hero. Decorated for gallantry under his assumed name, Gabin confesses the deception and is broken to the ranks, but again proves himself by launching a suicidal attack on a machine-gun nest in order to protect his battalion. Worthy, but slow, it relied more on characterisation than on narrative drive, with Gabin displaying his usual humourless competence in the central role. Richard Whorf (right), Allyn Joslyn, John Qualen (seated centre), Peter Van Eyck and Eddie Quillan were adequate in support, with Ellen Drew appearing briefly for feminine interest. (93 mins)

△ **Murder In The Blue Room**, first seen as *Secret Of The Blue Room* (1933), then as *The Missing Guest* (1938), was a haunted house comedy-thriller with the obligatory sliding panels, secret passages, self-playing pianos etc etc – and even the odd ghost. A climactic underground chase, in which the least likely suspect of the household is revealed to be the murderer, brought Frank Gross' stencilled production to its predictable conclusion. I.A.L. Diamond and Stanley Davis scripted it from a story by Erich Philippi, and it was directed by Leslie Goodwins whose cast included top-billed Anne Gwynne (right), Donald Cook (2nd right), John Litel (centre), Grace McDonald, Betty Kean, June Preisser, Regis Toomey, Nella Walker (2nd left), Andrew Tombes (left) and Ian Wolfe. (61 mins)

▽ The studio pummelled the mummy's tomb formula to death in **The Mummy's Ghost**, with top-starred Lon Chaney Jr (left) as Kharis, whose punishment for being the love object of Princess Ananka over 3000 years ago was to be kept alive in mummified form in order to guard her tomb. Incarnated as Ramsay Ames (Rameses Ames?), the Princess escapes and, for most of the film (screenplay by Griffin Jay, Henry Sucher and Brenda Weisberg) Chaney, looking decidedly weird, tries to return the Princess to her resting place. Robert Lowery played Ames' boyfriend, with other roles under Reginald Le Borg's direction going to John Carradine (right, second-billed), George Zucco (as a high priest) and Barton MacLane. Ben Pivar produced. (60 mins)

OTHER RELEASES OF 1944

Allergic To Love
Prod: Warren Wilson Dir: Edward Lilley. Comedy musical about an arranged marriage and the bride's discovery that she gets hayfever whenever her future husband is near. Martha O'Driscoll, Noah Beery Jr, David Bruce. (60 mins)

Boss Of Boomtown (Rod Cameron)
Dir: Ray Taylor. Problems begin between two cavalry sergeants when one breaks his promise to re-enlist through being made to join a bandit gang. Tom Tyler. (56 mins)

Dead Man's Eyes
Prod: Will Cowan Dir: Reginald LeBorg. 'Inner Sanctum' mystery starring Lon Chaney Jr who is blinded by jealous model Acquanetta. To restore his sight involves using tissues from the eye of another man, and causes the donor's death. Jean Parker, Paul Kelly. (64 mins)

Hat Check Honey
Prod: Will Cowan Dir: Edward F. Cline. Colourless musical programmer about an old-time vaudevillian who fires his son from their act to prod the boy into making it alone. Everett Carter and Milton Rosen penned the songs. Leon Errol, Richard Davies, Grace McDonald. (68 mins)

Hi, Beautiful
Prod: Dick Irving Hyland Dir: Leslie Goodwins. Martha O'Driscoll and Noah Beery Jr win a 'happiest GI couple' contest, but they're not married. Hattie McDaniel, Walter Catlett, Tim Ryan. Remake of *Love In A Bungalow* (1937). (66 mins)

Hi, Good Lookin'
Prod: Frank Gross Dir: Edward C. Lilley. Mid-western singer arrives in Hollywood hoping to make it big as a vocalist on radio – and she does too! Harriet Hilliard, Kirby Grant, Eddie Quillan, Betty Kean, Fuzzy Knight, The Delta Rhythm Boys. (62 mins)

Jungle Woman
Prod: Will Cowan Dir: Reginald LeBorg. Ape-girl Acquanetta makes her presence felt in a sanatorium, where her attraction to Richard Davis causes aggro as he is already engaged to Lois Collier. (60 mins)

Marshal Of Gunsmoke (Tex Ritter)
Dir: Vernon Keays. US marshal Tex restores law in town and prevents a gang from intimidating townsfolk in their elections. Russell Hayden. (59 mins)

The Merry Monahans
Prod: Michael Fessier and Ernest Pagano Dir: Charles Lamont. A worn-out retread of the backstage tribulations of a vaudeville family, this musical offered a dose of nostalgia to the tune of some twenty old favourites, and a stalwart cast. Donald O'Connor, Peggy Ryan, Jack Oakie, Ann Blyth. (91 mins)

Moon Over Las Vegas
Prod/Dir: Jean Yarbrough. Vera Vague advises Anne Gwynne to make her hubby David Bruce jealous in order to salvage their marriage. (69 mins)

My Gal Loves Music
Prod/Dir: Edward Lilley. Thanks to a brainstorm by medicine man Walter Catlett, Grace McDonald wins a trip to New York and a radio appearance on a show sponsored by vitamin manufacturer Alan Mowbray. Bob Crosby, Betty Kean. (60 mins)

Oklahoma Raiders (Tex Ritter)
Dir: Lewis D. Collins. Tex is assigned by the US army to trail an outlaw band who have been stealing herds of mustangs due for the service. Fuzzy Knight. (57 mins)

The Old Texas Trail (Rod Cameron)
Dir: Lewis D. Collins. A stagecoach line is hampered in construction by a rival gang hoping to delay the option rights. Eddie Dew, Fuzzy Knight. (60 mins)

Pardon My Rhythm
Prod: Bernard W. Burton Dir: Felix Feist. Infatuated with drummer Mel Torme, Gloria Jean comes in for some rough patches when Marjorie Weaver is ordered by Bob Crosby to flirt with Torme so that he'll sign a contract. Patric Knowles. (62 mins)

Reckless Age
Prod/Dir: Felix Feist. Gloria Jean rebels against grandpa Henry Stephenson and runs away from home; unbeknown to grandpa, she joins one of his many dime stores as a clerk. The Delta Rhythm Boys, Jane Darwell, Franklin Pangborn, Marshall Thompson (his debut). (63 mins)

Riders Of The Sante Fe (Rod Cameron)
Dir: Wallace W. Fox. Rod rounds up a gang led by a small-town boss who has been freezing trail drivers out of their water rights. Eddie Dew, Fuzzy Knight. (60 mins)

Sing A Jingle
Prod/Dir: Edward C. Lilley. Complications arise when famous tenor enrols for war work in mid-western defence plant. Allan Jones, June Vincent, Dicky Love, Betty Kean, Gus Schilling. (62 mins)

The Singing Sheriff
Prod: Bernard W. Burton Dir: Leslie Goodwins. Broadway star, through series of unlikely circumstances, finds himself playing sheriff in a mid-western town and rounding up a gang of bandits. Bob Crosby, Fay McKenzie, Fuzzy Knight, Iris Adrian. (60 mins)

Slightly Terrific
Prod: Alexis Thurn-Taxis Dir: Edward F. Cline. A manufacturer and an impresario (who's promised some youngsters he'll stage their show) are twin brothers. The confusion arising from their mistaken identity passed for the plot of this musical. Leon Errol, Anne Rooney, Eddie Quillan. (61 mins)

South Of Dixie
Prod/Dir: Jean Yarbrough. Phoney writer of Southern pop tunes has to go south to manufacture a suitable family background for himself after being promoted as the subject for a biopic. David Bruce, Anne Gwynne, Ella Mae Morse, Samuel S. Hinds. (61 mins)

Swingtime Johnny
Prod: Warren Wilson Dir: Edward F. Cline. The Andrews Sisters make more music than shell casings when they don overalls to work in a munitions factory. Harriet Hilliard, Tim Ryan, Matt Willis, Tom Dugan, Mitchell Ayres and His Orchestra. (61 mins)

Trail To Gunsight
Dir: Vernon Keays. A cowboy fights to clear himself of a murder charge by hunting out the real killer. Eddie Dew, Fuzzy Knight, Maris Wrixon. (57 mins)

Trigger Trail (Rod Cameron)
Dir: Lewis D. Collins. Rod thwarts some unscrupulous city slickers in their efforts to hi-jack land belonging to homesteaders. Vivian Austin. (59 mins)

Twilight On The Prairie
Prod: Warren Wilson Dir: Jean Yarbrough. Buckaroo radio band are given employment on a ranch when stranded in Texas en route to Hollywood to make a movie. Vivian Austin, Leon Errol, Eddie Quillan, Jack Teagarden and His Orchestra. (62 mins)

Week-end Pass
Prod: Warren Wilson Dir: Jean Yarbrough. All about runaway socialite Martha O'Driscoll who yearns to join the WACS, and the adventures she has with a shipyard worker. Noah Beery Jr, The Delta Rhythm Boys. (65 mins)

Weird Woman
Prod: Oliver Drake Dir: Reginald LeBorg. 'Inner Sanctum' mystery in which newly-weds Lon Chaney Jr and Anne Gwynne return to a small town where jealous Evelyn Ankers begins a smear campaign against them, resulting in murder and suicide. Ralph Morgan. (62 mins)

1945

◁ **The Frozen Ghost** was a middle-grade thriller in the 'Inner Sanctum' series (screenplay by Bernard Schubert and Luci Ward from a story by Harrison Carter and Henry Suchet) in which top-starred Lon Chaney Jr (right), as a hypnotist whose strange powers result in the death of a member of his audience, finds himself being driven mad by Milburn Stone, his business agent. A wax museum setting added little to the general 'atmosphere' of Will Cowan's negligible production which, unlike its central character, totally failed to hypnotise anyone. Harold Young's direction was, to put it gently, makeshift; as were the supporting performances of Evelyn Ankers (left), Douglass Dumbrille, Martin Kosleck, Tara Birell and Arthur Hohl. (61 mins)

▽ Hypnotism also played an important part in an unimportant entry in the Sherlock Holmes series, unfathomably called **The Woman In Green**. Bertram Millhauser's perfunctory screenplay permitted Holmes (Basil Rathbone, centre) to be hypnotised by Hilary Brooke in the course of tracking down a syndicate dedicated to blackmail and murder. Nigel Bruce (left) again appeared as Dr Watson, with other roles under Roy William Neill's reliable albeit uninspired direction going to Henry Daniell (as Moriarty), Paul Cavanagh (the body), Matthew Boulton (right) and Mary Gordon. Neill also produced. (68 mins)

▽ When all but one member of the Good Comrades Club disappear, a tired Basil Rathbone (2nd left), alias Sherlock Holmes, and Nigel Bruce (Dr Watson, 3rd left) set out to discover what's what. And, in **House Of Fear**, what they discover is that the rest of the Comrades have faked their deaths (by substituting cadavers from the local churchyard) in order to secure the financial benefits of a joint insurance policy, and are hiding out in the cellar of a Scottish castle. It was scripted by Roy Chanslor from Conan Doyle's story *The Adventures Of The Five Orange Pips* and featured Dennis Hoey (as Lestrade), with other roles under producer-director Roy William Neill (one of whose better efforts this decidedly was not) going to Holmes Herbert (right), Paul Cavanagh (far left), Harry Cording (seated), Sally Shepherd, Dave Thursby (in uniform) and, as the 'surviving' member of the club, Aubrey Mather (centre with lamp). (68 mins)

◁ Violence came to the rescue of **The Daltons Ride Again**, a thundering western whose climax saw three of the Dalton boys (Kent Taylor, left, Lon Chaney Jr and Noah Beery Jr) biting the dust, and the fourth (Alan Curtis, right, top-starred) being badly wounded and about to face life in prison. The implication in Roy Chanslor and Paul Gangelin's screenplay (additional dialogue by Henry Blankfort) was that there'd be time off for good behaviour, which was good news to Martha O'Driscoll, the daughter of a publisher who, despite Curtis' wrongdoings, loves him and has promised to be there when he's eventually released. Thomas Gomez was featured as a drunkard and the brains behind a land-grab plot; with other roles in Howard Welsch's action-packed production going to Jess Barker, John Litel, Milburn Stone, Walter Sande, Douglass Dumbrille and Virginia Brissac. (70 mins)

▽ Producer Howard Benedict, turning to a play by Luigi Pirandello, to screenwriters Bruce Manning, John Klorer and Leonard Lee to bring it to the screen, and to director William Dieterle to bring it all to life, spent $2,000,000 of the studio's money on **This Love Of Ours**, a romantic melodrama rescued from the leaden grip of bathos by Dieterle's intelligent handling of the material. All about a daughter (Sue England) who believes her much revered mother (Merle Oberon, left, top-starred) whom she has never seen, is dead, but who, in fact, is very much alive and working as artist Claude Rains' assistant in a nightclub act, it also starred Charles Korvin (right) as Miss Oberon's husband, as well as Jess Barker, Harry Davenport and Ralph Morgan. The screenplay had Korvin who, years ago had given his wife the push after gossip led him to believe she was no good, bumping into her many years later in Chicago, convincing her that he knows he was wrong about her and, inevitably, inviting her back to share his life with him. Daughter Sue is not told of the woman's true identity and, naturally, rejects her as her 'substitute' mother. But it all came right in the end. High-class junk and very enjoyable, it was done previously by MGM in 1932, called *As You Desire Me*, and starring Greta Garbo. (90 mins)

▽ **Easy To Look At** was also easy to sleep through. Produced and written by Henry Blankfort as a vehicle for Gloria Jean (right), this programmer musical had the young songstress as a would-be costume designer who goes off to New York to establish her reputation. And establish it she does, gaining a name for being a design thief. Of course, she isn't anything of the kind, as you knew all along, and by the final fade she's fair set for a romance with Kirby Grant. J. Edward Bromberg (left) was also in on the act, as a has-been couturier reduced to working in a clothing store who, at the end, is rescued from oblivion and reinstated at the forefront of fashion. Also in it, under Ford Beebe's direction, were George Dolenz, Eric Blore, Leon Belasco, Mildred Law, Dick French (centre), and The Delta Rhythm Boys. Songs and musical numbers included: 'Is You Is Or Is You Ain't My Baby?' Billy Austin, Louis Jordan; 'Come Along My Heart', 'Umbrella With A Silver Lining', 'Swing Low Sweet Lariat' Charles Newman, Arthur Altman. (64 mins)

△ Arthur T. Horman and John Grant's screenplay (story by Edmund L. Hartmann) for **Here Come The Co-Eds** provided a girls' school as the setting for a respectable effort from Bud Abbott (right) and Lou Costello (left). The comedians played caretakers who rescue the school from a financial crisis which threatens to close it down and who, in the course of the action, have to pit their wits against Lon Chaney Jr who *wants* the place to close. This conflict provided the best sequence in the movie when Chaney, disguised as a wrestler called The Masked Marvel, meets Costello for a bout in the ring. Peggy Ryan (2nd left) was on hand with her sparkling tap shoes, and Phil Spitalny and His All-Girl Orchestra – featuring Evelyn Kaye and Her Magic Violin – were there too. The rest of the cast was completed by Martha O'Driscoll (centre), June Vincent (2nd right), Donald Cook, Charles Dingle, Richard Lane, Joe Kirk and Bill Stern. Writer Grant produced it, and the director was Jean Yarbrough. The songs and musical numbers were written by Edgar Fairchild and Jack Brooks, and included 'Hooray For Our Side', 'I Don't Care If I Never Dream Again' and 'Let's Play House'. (88 mins)

△ As a Broadway play, **Uncle Harry** (also known as **The Strange Affair Of Uncle Harry**), whose cast included Joseph Schildkraut and Eva Le Galliene, had enough melodramatic clout to run for a season. In its film incarnation, with George Sanders (centre) and Geraldine Fitzgerald heading a cast that also included Ella Raines (left), Sara Allgood, Moyna Magill, Samuel S. Hinds, Craig Reynolds (right), Harry Von Zell and Ethel Griffies, the story, told without recourse to flashbacks as in the stage version, was still melodramatic but lost its impact. Sanders played a fabric designer who lives a dreary existence with two spinster sisters (Fitzgerald and Magill) and who, after meeting fashion expert Ella Raines and planning to marry her, discovers that his younger sister (Miss Fitzgerald) plans to break up his romance. Furious at her interference, he poisons her cocoa. But the cup is switched and drunk by Miss Magill, whose death results in Fitzgerald standing trial and being convicted of murder. Thomas Job was the author of the play whence it all came, Keith Winter adapted it for the screen, and it was scripted by Stephen Longstreet who didn't do all that hot a job, and whose cop-out ending (it was all a dream) resulted in producer Joan Harrison resigning from the studios, such was the level of her dissatisfaction. It was capably directed by Robert Siodmak. (80 mins)

▽ Yvonne De Carlo (right), a relative newcomer to movies, was given her big break in **Salome, Where She Danced**, a stinker which the passage of time has kindly elevated to cult status. She played a Viennese dancer who, during the Franco-Prussian war, joins forces with leading man Rod Cameron (centre, as an American newspaper reporter) to outwit one of Bismarck's officers. As a result, they are forced to flee to America or, more specifically, to Arizona. Or, to be more specific still, to the desert town of Drinkman's Wells whose unlawful citizens (turned lawful by Salome) have, in her honour, and in honour of her dancing, changed the name of their dot-on-the-map to that of our heroine. Salome's adventures (and there were several of them) also took her to San Francisco where Russian aristocrat Walter Slezak is so enamoured of the lady that he builds an opera house for her. Laurence Stalling's bizarre screenplay (from a story by Michael J. Phillips) allowed for a gallery of colourful supporting characters, among whom were Abner Biberman (left, as a Scots-accented Chinaman), as well as David Bruce, Albert Dekker, Marjorie Rambeau, J. Edward Bromberg, John Litel (as General Lee) and Kurt Katch as Bismarck. Walter Wanger produced (in Technicolor) and it was directed first by Charles Lamont who, in the course of shooting, was replaced by Erle C. Kenton. (90 mins)

▽ A formula western, but generally good to look at (in Technicolor), **Frontier Gal** was a lively enough entertainment for anyone whose criteria for such things didn't include originality. Yvonne De Carlo (right) was top-starred as a saloon owner in Red Gulch, who falls for dashing Rod Cameron (centre) soon after he rides into town in order to escape a posse. The wily Miss De Carlo manoeuvres him into a shot-gun wedding, then turns him over to the law. He escapes and, after a one-night honeymoon with his 'bride', returns six years later to discover that he is the father of a scene-stealing five-year-old daughter (Beverley Simmons) whose purpose, in producers Michael Fessier and Ernest Pagano's screenplay, was to help reunite her mammy with her pappy. Which, of course, she does. Andy Devine, Fuzzy Knight (left) and Andrew Tombes were in it for laughs, with other roles going to Sheldon Leonard as the heavy (and desirous of Miss De Carlo's sexual favours) and Clara Blandick. The director was Charles Lamont. (84 mins)

▽ A comparatively subdued Charles Laughton (right) was the star of **The Suspect**, a first-rate, low-key thriller set in Victorian London. Laughton was cast as a wretchedly unhappy married man who murders his hateful wife (Rosalind Ivan), then marries stenographer Ella Raines (centre), the only person who has brought him happiness. Though more of a character study than a thriller *per se*, it generated suspense by having audiences wondering whether Laughton (on whose side they were) will get away with it or not, and even condoning the second murder he commits which takes place after his vile neighbour (Henry Daniell) threatens to blackmail him. Bertram Millhauser coaxed an excellent screenplay from James Ronald's novel *The Way Out* (which Arthur T. Horman adapted), with parts in it for Dean Harens (left), Molly Lamont (marvellous as Daniell's wife), Eve Amber (2nd left), Clifford Brooke (centre right), Raymond Severn and Maude Eburne (centre left). The strongly atmospheric direction was by Robert Siodmak; Islin Auster produced. (85 mins)

▽ Deanna Durbin (illustrated) was the **Lady On A Train**. She played (quite delightfully) a thriller addict who, while on a train journey, actually witnesses a murder from the vantage point of her window. On arriving at New York's Grand Central Station, she recounts what she has seen to the police, who disbelieve her, forcing her to turn, in sheer desperation, to thriller-writer David Bruce. What happened thereafter formed the humorous content of Edmond Beloin and Robert O'Brien's witty screenplay – the authors were alumni of Jack Benny's radio programme – in the course of which Miss Durbin becomes involved with the victim's family, and is mistakenly believed to be the murdered man's nightclub-singer sweetheart. In time the culprit is unearthed by Durbin and Bruce, but not before a happy quota of laughs reverberated around the theatre, as well as some songs from Deanna. Edward Everett Horton, George Colouris, Allen Jenkins, Samuel S. Hinds, Patricia Morison and Dan Duryea were also in Felix Jackson's production, and it was buoyantly directed by Charles David. Songs: 'Silent Night'; 'Night And Day' Cole Porter; 'Give Me A Little Kiss Will Ya, Huh?' Roy Turk, Jack Smith, Maceo Pinkard. (96 mins)

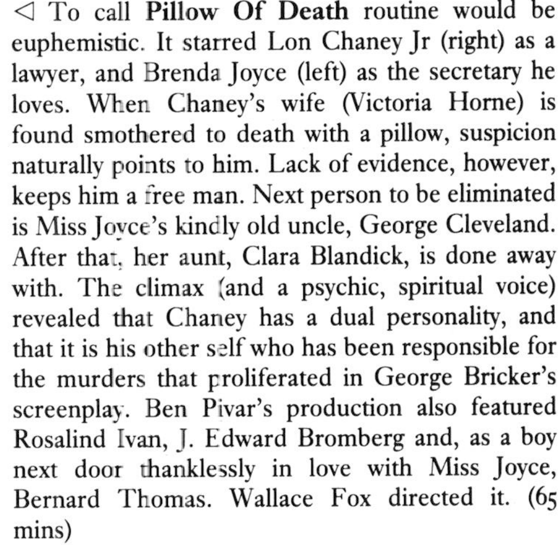

◁ To call **Pillow Of Death** routine would be euphemistic. It starred Lon Chaney Jr (right) as a lawyer, and Brenda Joyce (left) as the secretary he loves. When Chaney's wife (Victoria Horne) is found smothered to death with a pillow, suspicion naturally points to him. Lack of evidence, however, keeps him a free man. Next person to be eliminated is Miss Joyce's kindly old uncle, George Cleveland. After that, her aunt, Clara Blandick, is done away with. The climax (and a psychic, spiritual voice) revealed that Chaney has a dual personality, and that it is his other self who has been responsible for the murders that proliferated in George Bricker's screenplay. Ben Pivar's production also featured Rosalind Ivan, J. Edward Bromberg and, as a boy next door thanklessly in love with Miss Joyce, Bernard Thomas. Wallace Fox directed it. (65 mins)

△ The problem most producers faced with ongoing film series, was having to devise new situations into which old tried and tested formulas could be worked. In **Sudan**, Paul Malvern resourcefully overcame the problem by transporting his exotic players (Maria Montez, centre, Jon Hall, right, and Turhan Bey, left) to ancient Egypt for a story which top-cast Montez as a beautiful Egyptian queen who, after being snatched by a group of slave-traders, escapes with the help of Jon Hall and his sidekick Andy Devine. They're recaptured and, were it not for the timely intervention of Turhan Bey, a slave leader who frees them in spectacular fashion and falls in love with the beauteous Maria, who knows what might have become of them. George Zucco did well as a scheming royal chamberlain, with other roles under John Rawlins' just-what-you'd-expect direction going to Robert Warwick, Phil Van Zandt and Henry Cording. It was photographed in Technicolor. (76 mins)

△ **House Of Frankenstein** put all its ghouls in one basket with, alas, diminishing returns. It top-starred Boris Karloff (right) as Dr Niemann who, after spending 15 years in an asylum, escapes with J. Carrol Naish, his hunchback assistant and, in the course of Edmund T. Lowe's screenplay (based on Curt Siodmak's story *The Devil's Brood*), revives Count Dracula (John Carradine), and makes the acquaintance of both the Frankenstein monster (Glenn Strange, left) and the Wolf Man (Lon Chaney Jr). The complicated plot-line was sparse on thrills, and relied on the personalities (minus, for some reason, Bela Lugosi) of the leading players to keep it moving from one contrivance to the next. Lionel Atwill played a police inspector, Elena Verdugo was a gypsy girl loved by the Wolf Man, with other roles under Erle C. Kenton's prescribed direction going to Anne Gwynne, Peter Coe, George Zucco and Sig Rumann. The producer was Paul Malvern. (71 mins)

△ Yet another variation on the theme of a mummy returning to life to cause havoc etc, **The Mummy's Curse** was a producer's curse which affected patrons with an unmistakable sense of *déjà vu*. Lon Chaney Jr (right) generously swathed in mummy's bandages, played a preserved Egyptian prince who, years and years and years before, was buried alive for trying to resuscitate his dead girlfriend, Princess Ananka (yes, the same Princess Ananka, but a new actress, Virginia Christine). Transported to the Cajun country of Louisiana by archaeologists, Lon and Christine break out of their gauze confines, and upset the locals dreadfully. It was scripted by Bernard Schubert from a story by Leon Abrams and Dwight V. Babcock (who also adapted it), and directed by Leslie Goodwins with a conspicuous absence of ideas. The cast included Peter Coe (left), Kay Harding, Dennis Moore, Martin Kosleck, Addison Richards, Holmes Herbert and William Farnum. (60 mins)

▽ A bleakly effective excursion into the realms of *film noir* by director Fritz Lang, **Scarlet Street** top-starred Edward G. Robinson (right), with Joan Bennett (left) and Dan Duryea (both of whom the previous year had starred with Robinson in RKO's *The Woman In The Window*) second and third billed. The story of an unhappily married (to Rosalind Ivan) amateur painter and clothing-store cashier (Robinson) who, after celebrating 20 years of service with his firm, falls in love with Miss Bennett, the latter believing him to be a famous artist, it characterised Robinson as an easily exploitable milquetoast who, in the course of Dudley Nichols' cruel screenplay (based on Georges de la Fouchardiere's novel and play *La Chienne*), is exploited by Miss Bennett and Duryea, the former urging him to embezzle money from his firm to finance an apartment for her, the latter selling Robinson's unsigned canvasses (which find critical acceptance as the work of Miss Bennett). It all ended in tears with Robinson murdering Miss B (after discovering her in Duryea's arms) with an ice-pick, a crime for which Duryea is tried and, ultimately executed. Fired from his job for embezzlement, and unable to paint because Miss Bennett has usurped his name, he suffers a breakdown and finishes up as a piece of humanity's flotsam, failing to convince anyone he's not crazy when he confesses his crime. A grim study of the corrosive effects of evil preying on innocence and its tragic consequences, its loveless story was made palatable by Lang's cynical approach to the material; and by the fine performances of its leading players. Walter Wanger produced for Diana Productions, and his cast also included Margaret Lindsay, Samuel S. Hinds, Jess Barker, Arthur Loft and Vladimir Sokoloff. Previously filmed in France as *La Chienne* (1931), starring Michel Simon. (98 mins)

▽ One of the least successful entries in the Sherlock Holmes series was **Pursuit To Algiers**, in which Holmes (a bored Basil Rathbone, right), accompanied as ever by Dr Watson (Nigel Bruce), found himself all at sea (literally) in his assignment to escort King Nikolas of Algiers (Leslie Vincent, centre) by ship to his home country. Assassin Martin Kosleck, however, has other ideas ... Which was more than could be said for scenarist Leonard Lee whose compendium of platitudes passing for plot made the going pretty heavy. Bruce burst into song with 'Loch Lomond', which was quite amusing; and Vincent fell in love with Marjorie Riordan (left), which wasn't. The latter, incidentally, played a singer from Brooklyn who, in the course of the voyage, becomes an unwilling agent for jewel thieves. Rosalind Ivan, also along for the trip, was an athletic passenger, with other roles under Roy William Neill's really sloppy direction going to John Abbott, Frederick Worlock and Morton Lowry. (65 mins)

△ Donald O'Connor (2nd right) and Peggy Ryan (right), always an appealing pair, gave their 'all' to **Patrick The Great**, which, unfortunately, gave them little in return. Slight and unimaginative, the film totally wasted the talents of Frances Dee and Eve Arden, both of whom embellished a plot-line which had O'Connor and his father (Donald Cook, left) at loggerheads when the boy is offered a part in a Broadway show that Dad wants for himself. It all ended happily, of course, with Cook finding solace in Miss Dee, who agrees to marry him. Bertram Millhauser and Dorothy Bennett's screenplay (story by Jane Hall, Frederick Kohner and Ralph Block) also gave roles to Thomas Gomez (2nd left), Gavin Muir, Andrew Tombes and Irving Bacon. Louis Da Pron staged the dance routines, the songs and musical numbers were penned by Charles Tobias, David Kapp, Sidney Miller, Inez James and Charles Previn, and the director was Frank Ryan. It was produced by Howard Benedict. Songs and musical numbers included: 'Song Of Love', 'For The First Time', 'Ask Madam Zan', 'The Cubacha'. (84 mins)

△ A song called 'Fuzzy Wuzzy' (by Bob Bell and Roy Branker), featured in **See My Lawyer**, aptly summed up the incoherent quality of the film. A comedy musical for Olsen (right) and Johnson (left), it turned out to be their last movie, and not the one by which they will be remembered. Edmund L. Hartmann, who produced it, also wrote the screenplay with Stanley Davis (from a play by Richard Maibaum and Harry Clork), managing to find room for a number of specialty acts. In between, comedians O & J played comedians – employed in a nightclub, but seeking to be released from their contract. When club boss Franklin Pangborn refuses to let them go, they encourage him to change his mind by hurling insults at his patrons – a ploy which heaps several lawsuits upon them to the delight of three under-employed attorneys. Alan Curtis, Grace McDonald (centre), Noah Beery Jr, Edward S. Brophy, Richard Benedict, Lee Patrick and Gus Schilling comprised the supporting cast for director Edward Cline, who battled valiantly with the material, but lost. The specialty acts on show included Carmen Amaya and her dance company, The King Cole Trio (with Nat King Cole), The Cristianos Troupe, The Rogers Adagio Trio, The Six Willys, The Hudson Wonders and The Four Teens. Other songs included: 'Penny Arcade' Dave Franklin; 'Take It Away' Everett Carter, Milton Rosen; 'Man On The Little White Keys' Joe Greene, Nat King Cole. (69 mins)

▷ If you are to believe folklore as rewritten by the studio's resident scenarists, it is not only the old soldiers who never die, but the great monsters of the silver screen as well. **House Of Dracula** once again resuscitated Dracula, The Wolf Man, and Frankenstein's monster in an innocuous (but not entirely unentertaining) chiller with prominently featured Onslow Stevens (centre) as Dr Erdmann, who manages to cure the Wolf Man of his anti-social tendencies. Dracula (John Carradine) also seeks a cure for his particular problem, and gets it by being eliminated completely when Stevens allows the rays of the sun to fall on the vampire's sleeping body. In the process of these 'cures', however, Stevens is himself affected and, in his newly acquired madness, revives Frankenstein's monster (Glenn Strange) whom he finds in a sea-cavern nearby. Edmund T. Lowe's screenplay then had Stevens murdering Jane Adams (right), his hunchback assistant, and finally perishing, together with Frankenstein's monster, in flames. Martha O'Driscoll (left) was featured as another of Onslow's assistants, with other roles going to Lionel Atwill (as the local inspector), Skelton Knaggs and Joseph E. Bernard. Erle C. Kenton directed the brew, and Paul Malvern produced it. (69 mins)

OTHER RELEASES OF 1945

Bad Men Of The Border (Kirby Grant)
Dir: Wallace W. Fox. Kirby masquerades as a bandit in order to expose a counterfeiting ring operating below the border. Fuzzy Knight, Armida. (60 mins)

The Beautiful Cheat
Prod/Dir: Charles Barton. Bonita Granville, a reform school secretary, pretends to be the institution's worst delinquent, which causes complications when Prof. Noah Beery Jr arrives to research a book on delinquency. Margaret Irving, Irene Ryan. (59 mins)

Beyond The Pecos (Rod Cameron)
Dir: Lambert Hillyer. Rod does battle with a neighbouring rancher for local oil rights and the hand of the heroine. Eddie Dew, Jennifer Holt. (59 mins)

Blonde Ransom
Prod: Gene Lewis Dir: William Beaudine. NY nightclub owner runs the risk of losing his club through gambling debts; wealthy socialite stages fake kidnapping to raise money to save him. Donald Cook, Virginia Grey, Pinky Lee, Colette Lyons. (68 mins)

Code Of The Lawless (Kirby Grant)
Dir: Wallace W. Fox. Kirby succeeds in exposing a holding company combine which has been levying unwarranted taxes on local ranches. Fuzzy Knight, Poni Adams. (60 mins)

Crimson Canary
Prod: Henry Blankfort Dir: John Hoffman. A jazz musician's gig in a small town nightspot is wrecked when a female vocalist is murdered. Whodunnit? Noah Beery Jr, Lois Collier, John Litel, Steven Geray. (64 mins)

Frisco Sal
Prod/Dir: George Waggner. A New England girl fetches up on the Barbary Coast to find her brother's murderer, and gets a job in a saloon. Susanna Foster starred, and sang a couple of songs. Turhan Bey. (94 mins)

Her Lucky Night
Prod: Warren Wilson Dir: Edward Lilley. Fortune-teller predicts Martha O'Driscoll will find the man of her life sitting next to her in a cinema; she buys two tickets, tosses one away and hopes for the best. The Andrews Sisters, Noah Beery Jr. (63 mins)

Honeymoon Ahead
Prod: Will Cowan Dir: Reginald Le Borg. Unexpected release of crooning convict causes havoc in prison choir; a plot is hatched to involve him in a robbery so that the choir can get him back. Allan Jones, Grace McDonald, Raymond Walburn. (59 mins)

I'll Remember April
Prod: Gene Lewis Dir: Harold Young. A programmer of diverse ingredients starring Gloria Jean as a singer intent on keeping a recently bankrupted family solvent and in doing so stumbles on feuds, murders and mysteries. Kirby Grant. (63 mins)

I'll Tell The World
Prod: Frank Gross Dir: Leslie Goodwins. Announcer Lee Tracey puts failing radio station back on the map with popular lonely hearts programme. Brenda Joyce, Raymond Walburn, June Preisser, Thomas Gomez. (61 mins)

Jungle Captive
Prod: Morgan B. Cox Dir: Donald Young. Banal low-budget chiller in which a biochemist, using the blood of a woman (among others), restores life to ape woman Vicki Lane who, after turning on her creator, meets her demise. Otto Kruger, Rondo Hatton. (63 mins)

Men In Her Diary
Prod: Howard Welsch Dir: Charles Barton. A wife files for divorce after discovering the diary of her innocent husband's besotted secretary. But all ends well. Peggy Ryan, Jon Hall, Louise Allbritton, Virginia Grey. (73 mins)

The Naughty Nineties
Prod: Edmund L. Hartmann Dir: Jean Yarbrough. Abbott and Costello on a Mississippi river boat, with all the usual complications. Alan Curtis, Rita Johnson, Henry Travers, Lois Collier. (76 mins)

Night Club Girl
Prod: Frank Gross Dir: Edward F. Cline. Rags-to-riches yarn about two kids given a chance to try their act at a Hollywood niterie. They over-eat hotdogs and are too sick to do themselves justice. Vivian Austin, Billy Dunn, Edward Norris, Maxie Rosenbloom. (61 mins)

On Stage Everybody
Prod: Lou Goldberg Dir: Jean Yarbrough. Jack Oakie and Peggy Ryan teamed as father and daughter vaudeville partnership. Oakie, having rejected radio, finds himself auditioning a group of kids for the very medium he once so despised. The King Sisters, Johnny Coy, Julie London. (75 mins)

Penthouse Rhythm
Prod: Frank Gross Dir: Edward F. Cline. Three brothers and their sister encounter difficulties in their bid for musical recognition. Jimmy Dodd, Bobby Worth, Louis Da Pron, Judy Clark, Velasco and Lenee. (60 mins)

Renegades Of The Rio Grande (Rod Cameron)
Dir: Howard Bretherton. Rod poses as a bank robber to bring to justice a bunch of thieves who have killed his brother. Fuzzy Knight, Eddie Dew, Jennifer Holt (56 mins)

River Gang
Prod/Dir: Charles David. Gloria Jean is an assistant in uncle John Qualen's pawnshop, unaware that he's a crook whose shop is a front for a gang of thieves. One stolen violin and a murder later sees our heroine wising up and our villain in chains. (64 mins)

Senorita From The West
Prod: Phil Cahn Dir: Frank Strayer. Ambitious youngster arrives from the backwoods and makes her fortune in the big city. Bonita Granville, Allan Jones, Jess Barker, George Cleveland. (63 mins)

Shady Lady
Prod/Dir: George Waggner. In which Charles Coburn starred as a cardsharp, Ginny Simms as his nightclub-singer niece and Robert Paige as the Deputy Attorney in charge of gambling; also Alan Curtis, as a racketeer. (94 mins)

She Gets Her Man
Prod: Warren Wilson Dir: Erle C. Kenton. Feeble comedy in which comedienne Joan Davis follows in her famous police-chief mum's footsteps by tracking down needle-shooting murderer. William Gargan, Leon Errol. (70 mins)

Song Of The Sarong
Prod: Gene Lewis Dir: Harold Young. Adventure-musical-comedy recounting the escapades of William Gargan who journeys to a remote island in search of priceless pearls. The problem is the savages who guard them. Nancy Kelly, Eddie Quillan. (65 mins)

Strange Confession
Prod: Ben Pivar Dir: John Hoffman. Poor 'Inner Sanctum' mystery starred Lon Chaney Jr as a chemist who has murdered his drug-peddling boss, J. Carrol Naish; he persuades his attorney buddy to defend him. Brenda Joyce, Milburn Stone. (61 mins)

Swing Out Sister
Prod: Bernard W. Burton Dir: Edward Dein. Romantic complications of young singer trilling at a night-club instead of pursuing her operatic studies, and her alternating infatuation with the club proprietor and a symphony conductor. Frances Raeburn, Milburn Stone, Rod Cameron, The Leo Diamond Quintet. (60 mins)

That Night With You
Prod: Michael Fessier/Ernest Pagano Dir: William A. Seiter. Susanna Foster is so stage-struck that, to get a part in a show, she tells producer Franchot Tone she's his daughter – the result of a one day marriage in his youth. David Bruce. (84 mins)

That's The Spirit
Prod: Michael Fessier/Ernest Pagano Dir: Charles Lamont. Long-deceased hoofer returns to earth to help his daughter make a career for herself on the stage. Jack Oakie, Peggy Ryan, Gene Lockhart, June Vincent. (92 mins)

Trail To Vengeance (Kirby Grant)
Dir: Wallace W. Fox. Kirby uncovers a gang responsible for murdering his brother and trying to take his land. Fuzzy Knight, Poni Adams. (54 mins)

Under Western Skies
Dir: Jean Yarbrough. The adventures of a small vaude troupe who find themselves not entirely welcome in town. Martha O'Driscoll, Noah Beery Jr, Leo Carrillo. (57 mins)

1946-1959

Changes For The Better

The end of the war saw a change in the movie-going habits of the public and though 1946 was one of the best years in the cinema's history, with a weekly attendance in the US of 90 million people, audiences were definitely becoming more discriminating in their tastes. In 1939 the average price of a cinema ticket in America was 23 cents; by 1946 it had risen to 40 cents and patrons were demanding more value for more money. Quickies running just under an hour were no longer in vogue. Mindless escapism was all very well but at 40 cents a throw it had to have a quality look about it. What satisfied the anything-goes taste of the public throughout the troubled war years no longer sufficed. Universal's top brass realised this and in a deliberate attempt to change their production policies they merged with an independent studio called International Pictures. The merger went through on 12th November 1946 and Universal became Universal-International. A brand-new modernised logo accompanied the move, and a new regime began under production heads Leo Spitz (an attorney and former president of RKO) and William Goetz (a former production executive at 20th Century-Fox and Louis B. Mayer's son-in-law), with Cowdin and Blumberg remaining on as heads of Universal Pictures Company, the parent organisation.

The first thing Messrs Spitz and Goetz announced was that henceforth no feature film that bore the Universal-International imprimatur would run under 70 minutes. So-called 'B' pictures were to be outlawed, even if they were in the middle of production. Serials were given the chop, as were programmer westerns. More movies were to be shot in Technicolor and to make quite sure the public got its money's-worth (as well as to counteract the increasing pull of that upstart medium – television), most Universal-International programmes would offer two features for the price of one. The studio also decided to increase its number of British imports (which had been trickling through since 1939) and in 1947 consolidated its arrangement with the UK distributor J. Arthur Rank to acquire the US rights to such prestigious British productions as *Black Narcissus* (1947), *Nicholas Nickleby* (1947), *Great Expectations* (1947), *Odd Man Out* (1947) and *Jassy* (1948). This deal with Rank lasted well into the fifties and, with Laurence Olivier's *Hamlet* (1948), the studio notched up a second Oscar for best picture.

In the shuffle that followed the formation of Universal-International several of the studio's forties stars – among them Gloria Jean, Peggy Ryan, Susanna Foster, David Bruce, Richard Arlen, Andy Devine, Rod Cameron and William Gargan – were dropped; so were Basil Rathbone and Nigel Bruce, whose Sherlock Holmes series limped to an end in 1946 with *Dressed To Kill*.

Donald O'Connor, however, was retained and in the fifties he helped to swell the studio coffers with the popular and

Two popular partnerships of the period. *above:* Donald O'Connor and Francis the Talking Mule (from **Francis Goes To The Races**, 1951). *below:* Bud Abbott (right) and Lou Costello (from **Abbott and Costello Meet The Keystone Kops**, 1955).

profitable Francis the Talking Mule series. There were seven Francis comedies in all, the last featuring Mickey Rooney in place of O'Connor. It was not a success.

Also retained were Deanna Durbin (though by 1948 her career was over), and Bud Abbott and Lou Costello. A and C made twelve more comedies for Universal before bowing out with *Abbott And Costello Meet The Mummy* (1955), having already met, over a period of 15 lucrative years, Boris Karloff, the Wolf Man, the Keystone Kops, Dr Jekyll and Mr Hyde, and the Invisible Man.

Another popular series, with a distinct backwoods flavour, turned out to be the Ma and Pa Kettle comedies starring Marjorie Main and Percy Kilbride. First seen as subsidiary characters in the studio's successful 1947 entry *The Egg And I* (which took a massive $5.75 million to become one of the top grossers of the year), the Kettles came into their own in the modest *Ma And Pa Kettle* (1949). It ran 75 minutes, cost $200,000 and raked in more than $2.25 million profit. There were nine Kettle comedies in all, the last two, *The Kettles In The Ozarks* (1956) and *The Kettles On Old Macdonald's Farm* (1957), being made without Kilbride who retired from the series after being hurt in a car accident.

Spitz and Goetz's arrival at the studio heralded the introduction of several independent production units such as the Fairbanks Company (*The Exile*, 1947), and Kanin Productions (*A Double Life*, 1948). Walter Wanger, who had started work as an independent with *Arabian Nights* back in 1942, continued to operate out of Universal City; so did Mark Hellinger whose films *The Killers* (1946) and *The Naked City* (1948) were among the more striking black-and-white entries of the period. The studio pegged the average budget for a major production between $1 million and $1.5 million, and there could be no doubt that, qualitatively, the company had nothing to be ashamed of. Unfortunately several important films such as *Another Part Of The Forest* (1948) and Arthur Miller's powerful drama *All My Sons* (1948) failed to find an audience and between 1948 and 1949 the studio was again in the red, this time to the tune of $4.3 million. Budgets were again drastically slashed, so was the studio's programme line-up. Fortunately sensible guidance from studio manager Edward Muhl, who had been with Universal since 1927, managed to turn the tide of the company's declining fortunes. As the fifties began, thanks to the popularity of the aforementioned Francis and Ma and Pa Kettle series, as well as to an industrious schedule of programmer action/adventure films in Technicolor, the studio was again in the black. The situation was further helped by the Supreme Court's divestiture decree (in 1949), whereby companies such as Warner Bros., Paramount, MGM and 20th Century-Fox were forced to relinquish their theatre chains. The upheaval in distribution policies which inevitably resulted from this was watched with amusement by Universal who had no theatre arm of its own and who, when the dust finally settled, suddenly found a far richer market for its product than ever before.

Then in 1950, after 14 years as chairman of the board, J. Cheever Cowdin resigned, leaving Nate J. Blumberg in control. In November the following year, through a complex arrangement involving the open-market sale of the company's stock and the purchase of J. Arthur Rank holdings, Decca Records acquired 28 per cent of Universal for $3.8 million, including Spitz and Goetz's 150,000 shares. By the spring of 1952 Decca owned a controlling interest in the studio. In July the same year Decca's president, Milton Rackmil, succeeded Blumberg as president of Universal. Spitz and Goetz immediately resigned as heads of production, their places being taken by studio manager Edward Muhl. It was an excellent appointment and under Muhl the studio entered its golden period. Largely responsible for the good work that followed Muhl's appointment were producers Aaron Rosenberg (*The World In His Arms*, 1952; *The Glenn Miller Story*, 1954; *To Hell And Back*, 1955; *Man Without A Star*, 1955), Albert Zugsmith (*Written On The Wind*, 1957; *The Incredible Shrinking Man*, 1957; *A Touch Of Evil*, 1958), and Ross Hunter, a former schoolteacher-cum-actor and the most successful of them all.

Hunter's films were handsomely mounted (usually in Technicolor), well accoutred and appealed mainly to women. 'Glossy' was the word most frequently used to describe these productions, the most successful being the teary remakes of *Magnificent Obsession* (1954) and *Imitation Of Life* (1959). The former starred Jane Wyman and Rock Hudson, a good-looking young actor who had been spotted by director Raoul Walsh and who had been working his way up the ranks since 1949 when he appeared in Douglas Sirk's *Undertow*. In 1959 Hudson also appeared in Hunter's production of *Pillow Talk* opposite the virginal Doris Day, whose first film for Universal it was. A sex comedy, but pretty innocent by today's permissive standards, it grossed a massive $7.5 million and unleashed a plethora of light-hearted, mildly risqué items throughout the sixties, most of them box-office dynamite.

left above: Barry Fitzgerald (left) and Howard Duff in **The Naked City** (1948). *left below:* The main administration building as it appeared in 1953; built in the late twenties, it has now been replaced by a 14-storey tower block. *below:* A scene from Ross Hunter's immensely successful **Pillow Talk** (1959), starring Doris Day and Rock Hudson.

left: Tony Curtis and Piper Laurie teamed up for a second time in **Son Of Ali Baba**, one of the many 'easterns' of the early fifties. *centre:* Audie Murphy, the most popular cowboy of the time and America's most decorated war hero. *right:* **The Creature From The Black Lagoon** surfaced in 3-D in 1954.

Another star waiting in the wings for his big break was Tony Curtis and, after several unremarkable appearances (as Anthony Curtis) in several unremarkable films, he finally received star billing opposite Piper Laurie in *The Prince Who Was A Thief* (1951) – one of the studio's many 'tits and sand' adventures. Also known as 'easterns' this genre, which had been popularised by Maria Montez and Jon Hall in the forties, also gave employment throughout the fifties to Yvonne De Carlo, Maureen O'Hara, Rock Hudson and Jeff Chandler in such Technicolor epics as *Flame Of Araby* (1952), *Son Of Ali Baba* (1952), *Veils Of Bagdad* (1953) and *The Golden Blade* (1953). Messrs Hudson, Chandler, Curtis and many other artists under contract with Universal at this period were fully trained for the feats of heroism expected of them in these romantic adventures. They all attended acting classes at Universal City, where fencing, horse-riding, speech and deportment were part of the curriculum.

Westerns in all shapes and sizes continued to flourish throughout the fifties, usually in Technicolor. Joel McCrea appeared in several of them, but the studio's number one saddle star was Audie Murphy, the most decorated war hero in America's history. Films such as *The Kid From Texas* (1950), *Kansas Raiders* (1950), *Duel At Silver Creek* (1952), *Column South* (1953), *Destry* (1955) and *Walk The Proud Land* (1956) kept his many fans glued to their seats, and though most of these oaters usually shared a double bill with, say, a Francis comedy or an Arabian Nights fantasy, they looked stunning in colour and nobody complained about the routine plots.

In 1956 Bela Lugosi died at the age of 73. A drug addict whose last years were pathetically spent scratching a living from whatever work he could find, his death seemed to symbolise the end of the horror genre so popular in the thirties and early forties. The following year saw the death, too, of 70-year-old James Whale, whose horror films rank among the best ever made; he was found drowned in the swimming pool of his Hollywood home.

Horror of a different sort began to insinuate itself into audiences' imaginations from the beginning of the fifties with such chillers as *It Came From Outer Space* (1953) and *The Creature From The Black Lagoon* (1954); both were filmed in 3-D, a short-lived process that film-makers had hoped would counteract the continuing stranglehold of TV on America's box-office takings. Two further examples of new-look horror (in 2-D) were *The Mole People* and *The Creature Walks Among Us* (both 1956), but it wasn't until the following year that the studio produced the first classic of the genre with Jack Arnold's *The Incredible Shrinking Man*.

As the Kettles bowed out with *The Kettles On Old Macdonald's Farm* (1957), which was the least successful of the series, a new backwoods character called Tammy made her appearance in *Tammy And The Bachelor* (1957) and, as impersonated by Debbie Reynolds, captured the hearts of family audiences everywhere. The series continued into the sixties but not, alas, with Miss Reynolds.

In 1950 James Stewart, hitherto under contract to MGM, made motion picture history by being the first actor since the days of silents to demand, and to succeed in obtaining, a percentage of his films' profits as well as a regular salary. The deal paid off handsomely with the releases of both *Winchester '73* (1950), one of the decade's better westerns, and *Harvey* (1951). Stewart's other films for Universal-International included *Bend Of The River* (1952) and *The Glenn Miller Story* (1954), a $7 million grosser and the best musical the studio produced in the fifties. Other stars under contract at the time (usually on a two-picture deal) included José Ferrer, Jane Russell, June Allyson, Jane Wyman, Kirk Douglas, Janet Leigh, Gloria Grahame, Charlton Heston, Jack Palance, Dana Andrews, Esther Williams and Lana Turner, as well as long-term contractees George Nader, John Saxon, John Gavin and Jock Mahoney.

Apart from releasing all its own product, as well as J. Arthur Rank's more prestigious British titles, Universal-International also handled in 1957 and 1958 eleven of the RKO pictures that remained unreleased when RKO ceased operations in the former year.

above: The studio's back lot, containing over 500 outdoor sets and building façades, photographed in 1953. *below:* The ever-popular James Stewart co-starred with Shelley Winters in **Winchester '73** (1950).

Despite such quality films as Rudolph Maté's *Mississippi Gambler* (1953), King Vidor's *Man Without A Star* (1955), Anthony Mann's *The Far Country* (1955), Joseph Pevney's *The Man Of A Thousand Faces* (1957) in which James Cagney played silent star Lon Chaney, James Neilson's *Night Passage* (1957) and Orson Welles's remarkable *A Touch Of Evil* (1958), theatre attendances continued to decline. In 1958 ticket sales throughout the country were 12 per cent lower than they had been the previous year. The average price of a cinema ticket was now 50 cents and between 1957 and 1958 weekly cinema attendances had dropped by 5 million to 40 million – the lowest in Hollywood's chequered history. Universal-International's loss in 1958 was $2 million and the number of productions at work on the lot was falling rapidly. It was not a healthy situation and in February 1959, with so many sound stages unoccupied in Universal City, Milton Rackmil decided to sell out to the MCA (Music Corporation of America) talent agency who needed space for its TV subsidiary, Revue Productions. Universal received $11.25 million for the real-estate in a deal which allowed it to lease back any facilities it might require for future film production.

The company's change in management in 1959 could not have happened at a more propitious time and the years between 1959 and 1962 were to be the most successful in the studio's history. Though the number of productions was drastically pared down, they included some huge Technicolor hits. In the year of the takeover *Imitation Of Life* and *Pillow Talk* led the sparse but on the whole commendable output. All in all the MCA deal turned out to be the shrewdest move that the company had ever made.

1946

◁ A depressingly routine western, **Gunman's Code** starred Kirby Grant (centre left) as a Wells Fargo agent and featured Fuzzy Knight (left) as his buffoonish companion. They're detailed to round up a gang of stagecoach robbers in the town of Calliope and succeed. That was all there was to William Lively's little screenplay, unless you took into account the mini romance our hero has with Jane Adams (centre), the bank manager's daughter. Bernard Thomas (right) was in it too, and it was produced and directed by Wallace W. Fox. (54 mins)

▽ George Brent (centre), Lucille Ball (right) and Vera Zorina made their first appearances for the studio in **Lover Come Back** (also known as When Lovers Meet), a sleep-inducing romantic comedy in which Brent played a returning war correspondent (and lady-killer) whose two years away from his wife (Miss Ball) were not exactly spent in a state of celibacy – a fact which results in the latter heading straight to Las Vegas for a divorce. Brent follows her there and, after emerging unscathed from a series of zany situations, the bickering couple decide to stay married. Such was the content of Michael Fessier and Ernest Pagano's screenplay, in which Miss Zorina (surely one of the world's worst actresses) played the other woman, with Carl Esmond and Raymond Walburn as two of Miss Ball's entourage of admirers. Charles Winninger was cast as Brent's father, with other roles under William A. Seiter's take-it-or-leave-it direction going to Wallace Ford, Franklin Pangborn, Louise Beavers, Joan Fulton (left) and Elisabeth Risdon. Howard Benedict produced. (90 mins)

△ Another Kirby Grant (left)-Fuzzy Knight (2nd right) western, **Gun Town** offered more sagebrush action from the Wallace W. Fox (producer/director), William Lively (scenarist) stable, with hero Grant preventing the stagecoach line owned by heroine Louise Currie from falling into the hands of marauders, led by Lyle Talbot (2nd left). Claire Carleton (centre) was in it, too, as a lady of easy virtue and Talbot's girlfriend; so was Dan White (right). (53 mins)

▽ The talents of Desi Arnaz (illustrated) were well-camouflaged in an empty little programmer called **Cuban Pete** (GB: **Down Cuban Way**). Robert Presnell Sr and M. Coates Webster's screenplay (story by Bernard Feins) concerned an advertising agent (Don Porter) whose sponsor (Jacqueline De Wit) threatens to cancel his contract unless he can acquire the services of well-known Cuban bandleader Arnaz for a radio commercial. Porter despatches his comely assistant (Joan Fulton) to Havana to persuade Arnaz to come to New York, a mission she only manages to accomplish with the help of Arnaz's little niece (Beverly Simmons) to whom he is devoted. In the end, of course, Miss De Wit gets her show and Miss Fulton gets Desi. All audiences got were a couple of musical numbers, the most lively being organ virtuoso Ethel Smith's rendering of 'The Breeze And I' (by Al Stillman and Ernesto Lecuona). Pedro De Cordoba, The King Sisters and dancers Igor and Yvette were also in it, Jean Yarbrough directed, Will Cowan produced, and the executive producer was Howard Welsch. (61 mins)

▷ Though **Canyon Passage** crammed as many sagebrush clichés into its running time as the story permitted, it nonetheless emerged as a handsome, action-packed, romance-filled western, dazzling to look at (in Technicolor) and one in which familiarity bred content. Set in beautiful pioneering Oregon, circa 1856, Ernest Pascal's screenplay, based on Ernest Haycox's *Saturday Evening Post* story of the same name, centred on top-starred Dana Andrews (centre) as the hero who runs a freight depot and general store; Brian Donlevy (left) as a local banker with an unfortunate penchant for losing his depositors' gold at poker; Ward Bond as a tough outlaw and, for feminine interest, Susan Hayward (right) as Donlevy's fiancée (though she's in love with Andrews) and, from Britain, Patricia Roc, somewhat incongruous as Andrew's *vis-à-vis* until the scenario conveniently does a switcheroo in order to pair Andrews with Hayward. Sub-plots were as plentiful as flying fists in Walter Wanger's excellent production, and they gave employment to Hoagy Carmichael, Andy Devine (whose real-life sons Ted and Dennis were also in it), Rose Hobart, Halliwell Hobbes, Lloyd Bridges, Stanley Ridges, Dorothy Peterson, Vic Cutler and Fay Holden. A climactic Indian uprising was expertly handled by director Jacques Tourneur, whose work throughout was commendable. Two Hoagy Carmichael compositions were featured: 'Rogue River Jack' and 'Old Buttermilk Sky'. (92 mins)

△ Not bad of its kind, **House Of Horrors** was the story of an insane Greenwich Village sculptor (Martin Kosleck, right) who vents his wrath on art critics insensitive to the qualities of his masterworks, by sending out 'The Creeper' (Rondo Hatton, left) to do them in. It was entertainingly scripted by George Bricker from a story by Dwight V. Babcock, and directed by Jean Yarbrough, whose cast was completed by Robert Lowery and Virginia Grey (as a pair of romantic young lovers), Alan Napier, Howard Freeman and Joan Fulton. (65 mins)

▷ An off-the-cuff programmer, **The Dark Horse** was the story of a World War II vet (Phillip Terry, seated left) who, on his return from the front, is persuaded by a local politician (Donald MacBride) to run for alderman. Terry exposes a crooked political set-up in the town, and is elected on the strength of his honesty. So much for Charles R. Marion and Leo Solomon's screenplay (story by Sam Hellman), which found parts for Ann Savage (seated right). Allen Jenkins, Jane Darwell, Edward Gargan, Ruth Lee, Mary Gordon and the Merry Macs (standing). Howard Welsch produced, and it was directed by Will Jason. (59 mins)

△ **Blonde Alibi** was another dime-a-dozen thriller with absolutely nothing to recommend it. The trite tale of an aviator (Tom Neal, centre) wrongly accused of murder, it top-starred Martha O'Driscoll as Neal's sweetheart; had Peter Whitney (left) and Donald MacBride (right) providing painful comic routines as an imbecile cop and a long-suffering inspector, Samuel S. Hinds as an elderly gent whose testimony incriminates an innocent man – as well as Elisha Cook Jr and Tom Kennedy. George Bricker wrote it from a story by Gordon Kahn, Ben Pivar produced and the tired direction was by Will James. (62 mins)

△ Joan Davis fans had no trouble swallowing whole the situations on offer in **She Wrote The Book**. Others less disposed to the comedienne's particular brand of unrestrained clowning found it harder to take. For patrons who didn't mind one way or the other, it was average entertainment. Miss Davis (2nd left, top-starred), first seen as a plain, mild-mannered, bespectacled lecturer in calculus at a small mid-Western university, is reluctantly persuaded by the dean's wife (Gloria Stuart), who has written a sultry best-seller, to travel to New York to pick up the royalties for her and, for the duration of her stay there, to pretend to be the authoress herself. In a taxi accident, however, Miss Davis receives a bump on the head and, after coming round, really believes she *is* the authoress, and that she's actually lived the torrid life described in the book. Jack Oakie co-starred as the publisher's chief PR man who has an enormous promotional campaign mapped out for his valuable author; with other roles in Warren Wilson and Oscar Brodney's mildly satirical screenplay going to Mischa Auer (as a fake Russian count), John Litel, Kirby Grant (right), Jacqueline de Wit (2nd right) and Thurston Hall (left). It was crisply directed by Charles Lamont and produced by Warren Wilson. (75 mins)

▽ Deanna Durbin (centre) received top billing in **Because Of Him**, but it was third-billed Charles Laughton (2nd left), as a famous stage actor, who kept it on the boil and offered patrons something special for their money. Otherwise, it was just a moderately pleasing fairytale in which Miss Durbin, as a stage-struck waitress, contrives a meeting with Laughton in the fervent hope that he will further her career. At first he is suitably unimpressed with the pushy young lady, and makes no attempt to hide his contempt for her or her talent. Then, in a subdued moment, she sings 'Danny Boy' to him and the old trouper's heart all but melts away. It ends with Durbin co-starring (in triumph) with Laughton, while playwright Franchot Tone (second-billed), who has objected to Miss D being cast in his new play, stands in the wings realising that his objections were totally misplaced. It was written by Edmund Beloin from a story he and Sig Herzig wrote called *Catherine The Last*, and also featured Helen Broderick, Donald Meek (left), Stanley Ridges (as a producer), Douglas Wood (right) and Charles Halton. Felix Jackson produced, and the 'schmaltzy' direction was by Richard Wallace. Other songs: 'Lover' Richard Rodgers, Lorenz Hart; 'Goodbye' Tosti. (100 mins)

◁ Kirby Grant (centre) and Fuzzy Knight (centre right) were again teamed to frustrate villainy in the old west in **Lawless Breed**. The baddie of the piece was the town banker who hopes to profit by faking his own death and collecting the insurance money. Grant, as a government agent, foils the ploy and, naturally, gets the girl (Jane Adams, right). It was produced and directed by Wallace W. Fox from a screenplay by Bob Williams. Also cast: Karl Hackett (left) as the sheriff, Claudia Drake, Harry Brown and Dick Curtis. (58 mins)

△ Not a remake of the studio's 1930 offering, but a brand new stinker in which a newspaper reporter finds himself aided by a cat with extra-sensory perception (and the soul of a dead girl), **The Cat Creeps** featured Fred Brady as the reporter who, as the story unfurls, discovers that a suicide committed 15 years previously was actually murder. After three more murders, involving $20,000 and committed in an old island mansion, the true identity of the killer is revealed, courtesy of Brady (left) and his cat accomplice. Edward Dein and Jerry Warner wrote it from a story by Gerald Geraghty, Howard Welsch produced and Erle C. Kenton directed a cast that also featured Paul Kelly (centre), Noah Beery Jr (centre left), Douglass Dumbrille, Lois Collier (2nd right), Rose Hobart (2nd left) and Jonathan Hale (right). (58 mins)

△ The **Girl On The Spot** was Lois Collier, a singer, and she was put there by a trio of hoods called Weepy McGurk (Richard Lane), Fingers (Edward Brophy) and Lightfoot (Billy Newell) after arriving to audition for the owner of a nightclub only minutes after he has been murdered in his office by the aforementioned trio. Dorcas Cochran and Jerry Warner's screenplay (from a story by George Blake and Jack Hartfield) thickened the plot with a romance between Miss Collier (left) and ace crime photographer Jess Barker (right), and even introduced some musical interludes (staged by Louis Da Pron) involving Gilbert and Sullivan's *The Pirates of Penzance*, as presented by Collier's impresario father (Ludwig Stossel). In the end, the bad guys are duly apprehended, *Pirates* turns out to be a colossal hit and, presumably, the romantic leads lived happily ever after. George Blake was the associate producer, Milton Schwarzwald the executive producer, and William Beaudine the director. The cast included Fuzzy Knight, George Dolenz and Donald MacBride. (71 mins)

▽ A veritable text book of movie-making 'don'ts', **Inside Job** was possibly the studio's worst film of the year. Alan Curtis (centre) and Ann Rutherford (centre left) appeared as a 'crooked' couple who, having finally decided to go straight, are prevented from doing so by a blackmailing gangster (Preston Foster, top-billed) who knows their past. Foster forces them to burgle the department store where they're employed and they, in turn, double-cross him. It ends with Foster's death (at the hands of a cop) and Curtis and Rutherford returning the loot and giving themselves up. It was written by George Bricker and Jerry Warner (whose soft-centred screenplay included a policeman's motherless son – played by Jimmie Moss – and his dog) and produced and directed by Jean Yarbrough who, in other roles, cast Joe Sawyer, Joan Fulton, Milburn Stone and Samuel S. Hinds. (65 mins)

▽ **Slightly Scandalous**, a tedious musical, offered two Fred Brady's for the price of one, but neither was worth the price of admission. Brady played twin brothers, one of whom is attempting to sell a TV show to a fountain pen manufacturer, and boasts three girlfriends; the other, a modest insurance salesman, hasn't got a girl at all. The latter puts money in the former's show and finds himself involved with his twin's romantic entanglements. And that was that, but for the musical numbers which periodically relieved the boredom, and which featured Isabelita, The Guadalajara Trio, Nico Moro, Frank Yaconelli, and specialty dancers Dorese Midgley and Georgann Smith. Erna Lazarus and David Matthews wrote it, with additional dialogue by Joel Malone and Jerry Warner. The cast, for producers Stanley Rubin and Marshall Grant, was completed by Paula Drew, Sheila Ryan, Walter Catlett and Louis Da Pron (illustrated), and the director was Will Jason. Songs and musical numbers: 'I Couldn't Love You Anymore', 'When I Fall In Love', 'Negra Leona', 'Same Old Routine', 'The Mad Hatter', 'Baa Baa To You' Jack Brooks. (62 mins)

△ Though Dennis O'Keefe (left) and Helen Walker (centre) were the stars of **Her Adventurous Night**, it was their son, 14-year-old Scotty Beckett (right), around whom most of the action pivoted. Being an over-imaginative youngster, Beckett, when found with a pistol in his possession, invents a way-out story that lands both his parents and the school's principal in jail. How he gets them released by solving a murder mystery just one year older than himself, formed the content of Jerry Warner's rather juvenile screenplay which John Rawlins directed for associate producer Charles F. Haas; and with a cast that included Fuzzy Knight, Tom Powers, Charles Judels, Milburn Stone and Betty Compson. (73 mins)

△ Working from an uninspired screenplay by Joseph Michael, director Lewis D. Collins flung together **Danger Woman**, a melodramatic contrivance which unceremoniously starred Don Porter (left) as a young scientist who, assisted by his secretary Brenda Joyce (right), is working on a formula for putting the atom to commercial use. Plot complications arise when, after an absence of three years, his wife (Patricia Morison) suddenly re-enters his life, joins forces with a criminal element, and sets out to steal the formula. A few murders later the baddies get what's coming to them, and everyone lives happily ever after – except, perhaps, the paying customers who spent good money to see it. Milburn Stone, Samuel S. Hinds and Kathleen Howard were also cast, and the producer was Morgan B. Cox. (59 mins)

▽ The one thing **Idea Girl** lacked was ideas. A programmer which just about got by, it featured second-billed Julie Bishop (centre) as a song plugger whose job it was in Charles R. Marion's screenplay (adapted by Ellwood Ullman from a story by Gladys Shelley) to promote, among other things, an amateur song contest as part of a campaign to bestow status on the publishing firm who employs her. She succeeds, but not before causing her publisher-employers several king-sized headaches. Jess Barker (right) was top-billed as one of the harassed publishers (and the romantic interest) with George Dolenz, Alan Mowbray (left), Joan Fulton and Tim Ryan in support. It was directed by Will Jason and the associate producer was Will Cowan. Songs: 'I Don't Care If I Never Dream Again', 'I Can't Get You Out Of My Mind' Jack Brooks, Edgar Fairchild, Xango Fairchild, George Waggner. (60 mins)

▽ Following in the footsteps of Bette Davis in *A Stolen Life* (Warner Bros, 1946), Olivia de Havilland (illustrated left and right) played identical twin sisters in **Dark Mirror**. But not nearly as effectively. When an admirer of the twins is murdered, both the sisters (one of whom is kind and loving, the other unpleasant and spiteful) fall under suspicion, and it is left to a psychiatrist (Lew Ayres, centre, making a welcome return to the screen after several years' absence) to discover which twin (if either) is guilty of the crime. Producer Nunnally Johnson's screenplay, based on a story by Vladimir Pozner, let it down badly; as did de Havilland, who simply failed to differentiate sufficiently between the two characters she played. The end result was a gimmicky melodrama that would have been twice as enjoyable had its star been twice as effective and had Bette Davis not been half so good in the rival production. Thomas Mitchell (giving the best performance in the movie) played a baffled police lieutenant, with other roles under Robert Siodmak's direction going to Richard Long, Charles Evans, Garry Owen and Lester Allen. (85 mins)

▽ In **Rustler's Roundup** singing cowboy Kirby Grant (left), in the familiar company of Fuzzy Knight (right) and Jane Adams, rides into the frontier town of Rawhide, has a marshal's badge pinned to his chest and smartly rids the place of a trio of marauding brothers. Jack Natteford's screenplay spilled over with saloon brawls, runaway stagecoaches and assorted acts of skulduggery and, in the process, gave employment to Mauritz Hugo, Eddy Waller and Eddie Cobb. It was produced and directed by Wallace W. Fox. (56 mins)

△ **Wild Beauty** was the story of an Indian boy and a wild horse (called Wild Beauty). It was also about a doctor and his concern with the various attitudes expressed towards the Indian by the white man. Not only that, but it told the story of an Eastern capitalist and a school teacher who, in cahoots, attempt to organise the slaying of a herd of wild horses in order to make shoes from their hides. Lois Collier, Don Porter (illustrated standing), Robert 'Buzz' Henry (as the Indian lad, illustrated), Jacqueline De Wit and Robert Wilcox appeared for producer-director Wallace W. Fox, but they were all upstaged by the horses on display who, mercifully, were spared scenarist Adele Buffington's dialogue. (61 mins)

△ Burt Lancaster (right) made an impressive screen debut in **The Killers**, a taut, beautifully crafted *film noir* in which scenarist Anthony Veiller filled in some of the unspecified gaps in the Ernest Hemingway story from whence it came. Lancaster played a down-at-heel boxer-cum-small-town service station attendant who waits unprotestingly in a small darkened room for two hired killers (Charles McGraw and William Conrad) to eliminate him. The reasons for Lancaster's sombre situation are traced by Edmond O'Brien, an insurance investigator, who unearths a story showing the boxer's involvement with a gang of thieves as well as with a beautiful woman (Ava Gardner, left) who has double-crossed him. Director Robert Siodmak successfully found a visual equivalent for Hemingway's spare, clean-limbed prose, and his use of flashbacks in the piecing together of the story was exemplary. He also drew first-class performances from his leading players, as well as from a cast that included Albert Dekker as Miss Gardner's partner-in-crime, Sam Levene (as a cop), Vince Barnett, Jack Lambert, Jeff Corey, Virginia Christine, Phil Brown, John Miljan and Queenie Smith. It was brilliantly photographed by Woody Bredell, and classily produced by Mark Hellinger. Remade in 1964. (103 mins)

◁ London at the turn of the century was the setting for **She-Wolf Of London**, a combination thriller and chiller which emerged as little more than a filler. June Lockhart (left – off-screen daughter of actors Gene and Kathleen) is persuaded by her aunt Sara Haden that she's part werewolf, and guilty of a series of recently committed murders in the vicinity. Her lawyer fiancé (Don Porter, right), however, with whom she has broken off her engagement, is so convinced she is not that he successfully sets out to unmask the real killers. George Bricker's screenplay (from an original story by Dwight V. Babcock) simply reworked several clichés associated with the genre; a state of affairs perpetuated in Jean Yarbrough's direction. Ben Pivar produced and the cast included Jan Wiley, Dennis Hoey and Martin Kosleck. (61 mins)

▽ Sherlock Holmes and Dr Watson (Basil Rathbone, centre, and Nigel Bruce, centre right) were passengers aboard a train from London to Edinburgh in **Terror By Night**, a decided improvement on the last couple of entries in the series, with Holmes having to put his ingenuity to full use in finding out who stole the 'Star of Rhodesia' diamond he has been hired to safeguard; and who murdered its owner. He gets all the answers, of course, but not before two more murders and several plot complications had padded out the content of Frank Gruber's tight little screenplay, which producer/director Roy William Neill kept lively. Alan Mowbray, Dennis Hoey (right, as Lestrade), Renee Godfrey, Mary Forbes (left) and Billy Bevan (2nd left) were just some of the passengers going along for the ride. (60 mins)

▽ Another example of *film noir*, and a victory of style over content, **The Black Angel** offered the refreshing spectacle of top-cast Dan Duryea in a role totally at variance with what audiences had come to expect from him. For, although the denouement of Roy Chanslor's screenplay (from the novel by Cornell Woolrich) revealed him to be the murderer, he was really rather affable throughout. He played the songwriter husband of Constance Dowling whose murder, initially, is blamed on John Bennett, her lover. Bennett's nightclub-singer wife (June Vincent, left), despite her husband's infidelity, believes in his innocence, and enlists the aid of Duryea to help her prove it. Also implicated in the crime is Peter Lorre (right), a bent nightclub operator. In an alcoholic haze (the same state he was in when he did the deed) Duryea, who had blocked the incident from his mind, finally admits to being the guilty party. Roy William Neill, who also produced (with Tom McKnight) gave the material an immediacy it did not deserve, successfully disguising the movie's 'B' picture plot in a good-looking and resourceful production. Also cast: Broderick Crawford, Wallace Ford and Hobart Cavanaugh. Songs: 'Heartbreak', 'I Want To Be Talked About', 'Time Will Tell', 'Continental Gentleman' Edgar Fairchild, Jack Brooks, all sung by June Vincent. (80 mins)

▽ Rod Cameron (right) and Broderick Crawford (centre), as a couple of rival private dicks, came to blows on several occasions in **The Runaround**. It would have been more appropriate if they had assaulted scenarists Arthur T. Horman and Sam Hellman (story by Horman and Walter Wise) for the lines they put in their mouths and the situations in which they were placed. Clearly inspired by Frank Capra's altogether superior *It Happened One Night* (Columbia, 1934), the film had the two men competing to be the first to prevent the daughter of a wealthy industrialist from eloping, and return her safely to her father. The chase covered ground from New York to San Francisco and back again and, in the end, the daughter (whose safe return carries a reward of $15,000 and a valuable contract) turns out to be the industrialist's secretary. Ella Raines was the girl in the centre of it all and Samuel S. Hinds the industrialist, with other roles going to Frank McHugh, George Cleveland, Joe Sawyer and Nana Bryant. It was directed by Charles Lamont for producer Joe Gershenson. (86 mins)

△ Hal Mohr and W. Howard Green's Technicolor photography offered audiences an eyeful in **Night In Paradise**, and Ernest Pascal's screenplay (adapted by Emmet Lavery from the novel *Peacock's Feather* by George S. Hellman) an earful – of rubbish. A lavish fairytale awash with anachronistic dialogue, it top-starred Merle Oberon (centre) as the Princess Delarai who, in the land of Lydia a couple of hundred years BC finds herself unwillingly affianced to the wealthy, gluttonous, tyrannical, thoroughly despicable Croesus (Thomas Gomez, right). She is saved from this fate-worse-than-death by Turhan Bey as the aged storyteller Aesop – except he isn't really old at all, only disguised to look that way (see illustration – left) – whose chief purpose in arriving in Lydia isn't to keep Miss Oberon and her wicked fiancé amused by his storytelling, but to prevent Gomez from enslaving the free people of his native Samos. Cue for some propagandistic dialogue about the iniquity of big powers who use bullyboy tactics to force their will on small, defenceless nations. In time, Bey and the stunningly clad (by Vera West) Miss Oberon fall passionately in love and, in the tradition of all the best fairy stories (and even the not-so-good ones), live happily ever after. Gale Sondergaard appeared briefly as a sorceress, with other roles in Walter Wanger's opulent production going to Ray Collins (as the chamberlain), George Dolenz, John Litel, Ernest Truex and Jerome Cowan. Arthur Lubin directed. (81 mins)

▷ **Smooth As Silk** was a tidy little programmer that lived up to its title as it told the simple, but effective, story of a criminal lawyer (Kent Taylor) who murders ambitious actress Virginia Grey (right) after she jilts him for a top producer. Does he get away with it? Dane Lussier and Kerry Shaw's screenplay (based on Florence Ryerson and Colin Clements' story *Notorious Gentleman*) revealed all, as well as offering work to Jane Adams, Milburn Stone, John Litel, Danny Morton (left) and Charles Trowbridge. Howard Welsch and Jack Bernhard were the producers, and it was directed by Charles Barton. (64 mins)

△ Brenda Joyce was the hapless heroine of **The Spider Woman Strikes Back**, and she really should have known better than to seek employment with seemingly blind Gale Sondergaard (right) in a remote spot in the country. No sooner does poor Miss Joyce set foot inside the front door than all manner of unwelcome things occur, such as being accosted by deaf mute Rondo Hatton (left), and being drugged in order to allow her employer to continue her weird nocturnal experiments with plants and insects. Kirby Grant was Miss Joyce's boyfriend, with other parts in Eric Taylor's screenplay taken by Milburn Stone, Hobart Cavanaugh, Norman Leavitt and Eula Guy. It was directed along familiar lines by Arthur Lubin for producer Howard Welsch. (59 mins)

▽ Loosely based on *A Genius In The Family*, Hiram Percy Maxim's biography of his inventor father Hiram Stephen Maxim, **So Goes My Love** was a cosy, home-spun romantic comedy. Don Ameche (second-billed) played an inventor (but not quite as famous a one as Alexander Graham Bell whom he played in *The Story of Alexander Graham Bell*, 20th Century-Fox, 1939) who sets his marital sights on top-starred Myrna Loy after she journeys from Boston to Brooklyn in 1867 to find a husband. Ameche woos her away from wealthy, well-positioned Richard Gaines, then marries her (Loy and Ameche illustrated) despite the fact that he is so poor he can barely support himself. Bruce Manning and James Clifden's corner-cutting screenplay dealt rather perfunctorily (and unsatisfactorily) with Ameche's rise from indigent inventor to respected success, with one scene showing the family down-on-their-uppers, and the very next showing them as well-to-do householders. Still, its heart was definitely in the right place and, thanks to the excellent performances of its two leads, as well as from Bobby Driscoll as their high-spirited offspring – whose relationship with his father was one of the mainsprings of the film – it left audiences glowing with nostalgia. Rhys Williams was splendid as an eccentric artist commissioned by Miss Loy to paint her husband's portrait, with other roles under Frank Ryan's occasionally over-sentimental direction going to Molly Lamont (seated left), Sarah Hadden, Renie Riano and Clara Blandick. Jack Skirball and scenarist Manning produced. (88 mins)

▽ Bud Abbott (foreground centre) and Lou Costello (left) more or less played it 'straight' in **The Time Of Their Lives**, a likeable comedy that always promised more than it eventually delivered. The fault lay not in the basic situation (in which Costello and Marjorie Reynolds (2nd left), both having been mistakenly shot as traitors during the Revolutionary War of 1780, are doomed to remain on earth as ghosts until their innocence is proved), but in the screenplay which four writers (Val Burton, Walter De Leon, Bradford Ropes and John Grant) were unable to invest with anything other than a rag-bag of tired old gags and routines. Abbott played a psychiatrist house-guest in the manse which Costello and Miss Reynolds have chosen as their haunting ground, with other roles going to Gale Sondergaard (as a psychic house-maid), Binnie Barnes (right, another houseguest), Donald McBride (a cop), as well as John Shelton (centre), Lynne Baggett (2nd right), Jess Barker and Ann Gillis. Charles Barton's direction was seen at its best in a climactic sequence that had the invisible Costello driving a car helter-skelter around the grounds of the manor in which most of the action was set, and generally relied on every other 'invisible man' gimmick in the book to generate a quick laugh or two. The producer was Joe Gershenson. (82 mins)

△ **White Tie And Tails** was a 'once upon a time' fairytale with a 'happily ever after' ending. As innocuous as a breath of fresh air, but not really as exhilarating, it miscast Dan Duryea (top-billed) as an insouciant butler to a wealthy family who, during his employer's 10-day vacation in Florida, pretends to be a gentleman of quality. In this guise he meets, and falls for, Ella Raines (centre), the daughter of another wealthy family, and finds himself involved with racketeer gambler William Bendix, who is owed a mere 100 grand by Miss Raines' sister. Duryea (right), playing it way above his station, nonchalantly signs over a cheque to Bendix (left) who, for security, takes a couple of paintings belonging to Duryea's employer. How butler-cum-gentleman Duryea makes good his cheque to Bendix before his master returns, formed the moderately amusing content of the screenplay Bertram Millhauser fashioned from Rufus King and Charles Beacon's novel *The Victoria Docks At Eight*. A bit more of the butler's insouciance reflected in the dialogue would have been of considerable help to all concerned. Richard Gaines, Barbara Brown, Clarence Kolb, Frank Jenks and Samuel S. Hinds were also featured in Howard Benedict's well-mounted production, and the director was Charles T. Barton. (75 mins)

△ A puny remake of *Three Kids And A Queen* (1935), **Little Miss Big** was the treacly tale of a wealthy but bad-tempered old crone (Fay Holden) whose scheming nephew (John Eldredge) commits her to an asylum in the hope that he, rather than her beloved pet dog, will be the beneficiary of her fortune. Miss Holden, however, is taken in by a poor barber (Frank McHugh, left) and his family, is stripped of her ill-humour by young Beverly Simmons (the Miss Big of the title, right) and, after being proved mentally A-1 at an official hearing, sees that McHugh and his caring family are well-provided for happily ever after. Erna Lazarus' commonplace screenplay (story by Harry H. Poppe, Chester Beecroft and Mary Marlin) was a catalogue of missed opportunities which made heavy weather of its attempts at humour, and created all sorts of problems for featured players Fred Brady, Dorothy Morris, Milburn Stone and Samuel S. Hinds. Erle C. Kenton's direction didn't help. The producer was Marshall Grant. (60 mins)

▽ **Strange Conquest** was an earnest but thoroughly malconceived drama in which two scientists, working in the jungle, attempt to find a cure for a tropical fever. One of the doctors (Peter Cookson), believing his work in the field to be useless, offers himself to his rival (Lowell Gilmore, centre) as a human guinea pig – and dies in the process. At this point in scenarist Roy Chanslor's yarn (story by Lester Cole and Carl Dreher), Gilmore assumes Cookson's identity in order to complete the dead man's unfinished work, the deception leading to a great many complications re the distaff side of the cast – ie Jane Wyatt (right) as his girlfriend, and Julie Bishop as Cookson's widow. It was all really rather puerile, a fact which John Rawlins' direction was powerless to disguise. Marshall Grant produced and the cast was completed by Milburn Stone (left), Samuel S. Hinds and Abner Biberman. It was a remake of *The Crime Of Dr Hallet* (1938). (63 mins)

△ Another Abbott and Costello comedy, but this time with the two comedians playing separate characters who are not teamed from the start, but who meet in the course of the film, **Little Giant** was no world beater and certainly made no new converts for the duo. Costello played a country bumpkin vacuum cleaner salesman who is elevated to star status when, by a lucky accident, he sells several of his firm's machines on the same day. But not before encountering Bud Abbott who, in a dual role, appeared as two different store managers in different parts of the country. Funniest scene (borrowed from Laurel and Hardy) had Costello (centre) attempting to undress in a cramped Pullman car; and funniest supporting player was the redoubtable Margaret Dumont, borrowed from the Marx Brothers. Walter De Leon scripted (from a story by Paul Jarrico and Richard Collins), director William A. Seiter did yeoman work attempting to give it the kiss of life and, in supporting roles, cast Elena Verdugo (right), Brenda Joyce, Jacqueline de Wit, George Cleveland and Mary Gordon (left). The producer was Joe Gershenson. (91 mins)

△ The last film made by International before its merger with Universal to become Universal-International was Edward Small's production of **Temptation**. And what an old-fashioned melodrama it turned out to be! Based on the novel *Bella Donna* by Robert Hichens and the play by James Bernard Fagan, Robert Thoeren's screenplay unearthed all the familiar clichés germane to the genre in his retelling of the story of beautiful *femme fatale* Merle Oberon (left) who ditches George Brent, her Egyptologist husband, for Egyptian *roué* Charles Korvin (right). She sees the error of her ways, however, when Korvin, down-and-out and riddled with debt, threatens to dump her as unceremoniously as she dumped Brent – unless she agrees to kill her husband for her inheritance. She kills Korvin instead, and does away with herself. Miss Oberon looked a treat in Vera West's Victorian creations, but couldn't do much with the dialogue she was expected to animate; Brent was his usual boring self, and Korvin a grotesque caricature of a cad. Paul Lukas, Lenore Ulric, Arnold Moss and Ludwig Stossel were also in it, and it was directed at an agonisingly slow pace by Irving Pichel. First made as a Pola Negri silent (Paramount, 1923). (98 mins)

◁ The best thing about **Tangier** was native guide Sabu's refreshingly individual interpretation of the song 'She'll Be Coming Round The Mountain'. The rest was an exotic bore with exotic Maria Montez (left) as a Spanish dancer in exotic Tangier looking for a Nazi who killed one of her close relatives. Third-billed Robert Paige co-starred as a discredited journalist hoping to regain his satus by uncovering a major international story involving an enormous diamond over which several murders are perpetrated. Preston Foster (right) was second-billed as a police chief, with Louise Allbritton, Kent Taylor, J. Edward Bromberg, Reginald Denny and Charles Judels also in it for producer Paul Malvern and director George Waggner. M.M. Musselman and Monty Collins wrote it from a story by Alice D.G. Miller. Other songs: 'Love Me Tonight' George Waggner, Gabriel Ruiz; 'Polly Wolly Doodle'. (74 mins)

▷ It was a great pity that the twelfth and final entry in the Sherlock Holmes series should be the unmitigated dud that **Dressed To Kill** turned out to be. Following the well-worn paths of *Sherlock Holmes And The Secret Weapon* (1943) and *The Pearl Of Death* (1944), it again pitted Holmes (Basil Rathbone, centre) against his diabolical adversaries in a race – this time to find stolen Bank of England engraving plates, clues to whose whereabouts are contained in three music boxes made by a prison inmate. A barely adequate screenplay by Leonard Lee, performances to match by a supporting cast that included Patricia Morison, Edmond Breon, Frederick Worlock, Carl Harbord and Mary Gordon, and tired direction by producer/director Roy William Neill sounded the death knell for a series which had nothing new to say and nowhere new to go. Even Basil Rathbone's central performance had a depressing been-there-once-too-often feel to it. Nigel Bruce (left, who gave an amusing impression of a duck) was, as usual, Dr Watson, and a child actress, Anita Glyn (right) was in it too. (72 mins)

1947

▽ A trite, far-fetched screenplay by Seton I. Miller and Robert Thoeren (story by Miller) made the going extremely heavy for top-starred Fred MacMurray and his glamorous co-star Ava Gardner in **Singapore**. It was equally heavy going for audiences who, apart from the marquee value of its two stars, were offered a plot that would have sat more comfortably at the tail end of a double-bill than as the 'A' grade feature producer Jerry Bresler obviously intended it to be. MacMurray (left) was cast as an ex-sailor who returns to Singapore after the war to continue his vocation as a pearl smuggler. Through flashbacks, the script established MacMurray's romance with Miss Gardner (right) who, it is presumed, has been killed in a Japanese air raid on the couple's wedding night. It turns out that the lady is still alive, married to another man, and in the grip of total amnesia. How this unlikely piece of fiction eventually unravelled itself was the chief concern of the screenplay, backed up by a dreary sub-plot, in which MacMurray is tailed by a gang of villains who are after some valuable pearls which were hidden in a hotel room during the Japanese occupation. It was directed somewhat flatly by John Brahm, with a supporting cast that included Porter Hall and Spring Byington as American tourists, Roland Culver as Miss Gardner's husband, George Lloyd as a pickpocket and Richard Hayden as a police chief. It was remade as *Istanbul* in 1957. (79 mins)

▷ Sex, melodrama and gangsterism were some of the ingredients that went into producer Mark Hellinger's **Brute Force**, a prison movie with a vengeance! Apart from a planned jail break which provided the film with its climax, Richard Brooks' taut and entertaining screenplay (from a story by Robert Patterson) was underpinned by four stories concerning a quartet of 'insiders' and their 'outside' women. Thus (via flashback) we saw how Whit Bissell, a book-keeper, embezzled $3000 to give his avaricious wife (Ella Raines) a mink coat; how Howard Duff (left), an ex-army corporal, took the rap for a murder committed by his Italian bride (Yvonne De Carlo); how top-starred Burt Lancaster's (right) love for invalided wife Ann Blyth landed him in jail, and how John Hoyt, a crapshooter, was 'hijacked' by Anita Colby. It was a fault in Brooks' screenplay to depict all the inmates as basically nice guys, so that audiences were totally on their side in the climactic jail break, despite the film's underlying message that violence begets violence and offers no satisfactory solution to anything. Hume Cronyn was monstrously effective as the sadistic Wagner-loving prison captain, with good performances, too, from Charles Bickford, Sam Levene, Jeff Corey, Jack Overman, Roman Bohnen (as the weak-willed warden) and Sir Lancelot (as a Trinidadian songwriter). The virile direction was by Jules Dassin. (94 mins)

△ Composer Rimsky-Korsakov, as portrayed by Jean-Pierre Aumont (left), was the focus of an outrageously 'camp' extravaganza called **Song Of Scheherezade**. Walter Reisch's vacuous screenplay (he also directed, in garish Technicolor) told the story of Rimsky's meeting with a dancer named Cara (Yvonne De Carlo, right – top-starred) in an exotic Spanish-Moroccan port during his return journey to Russia from a world cruise. Their encounter provides the composer with the inspiration to write his famous 'Scheherazade', which premieres at the St Petersburg Opera House. And who should arrive in time to dance the title role at this glittering event, but Cara herself. How the script contrived to get her there typified the idiocy of the entire venture, as did the casting of Eve Arden as Miss De Carlo's mother! It must be said, however, that today the movie comes across as a wildly enjoyable piece of kitsch, whose excesses amuse rather than offend. Edward Kaufman produced, with Miklos Rosza as musical director (Jack Brooks wrote the lyrics) and Tilly Losch as choreographer. Others cast: Brian Donlevy (co-starred as the chain-smoking captin of the ship on which Rimsky travels), Philip Reed, John Qualen, Richard Lane, Terry Kilburn and George Dolenz. Musical numbers: 'Gypsy Song', 'Navy March', 'Song Of India', 'Arabesque', 'Hymn To The Sun', 'Flight Of The Bumble Bee', 'Capriccio Espagnole, Opus 35 (Fandango)', 'Song Of Scheherazade', 'Dance Of The Tumblers'. (105 mins)

▽ Six years and 18 movies later, Bud Abbott (right) and Lou Costello (left) made the inevitable sequel to their successful *Buck Privates* with **Buck Privates Come Home**. Donning civvies, the duo found themselves caught up in a peace-time story involving the smuggling of a six-year-old French orphan (Beverly Simmons, centre) into the US. A climactic car-chase finale was the highlight of John Grant, Frederic Rinaldo and Robert Lees' screenplay (story by Richard Macaulay and Bradford Ropes). For the rest, if offered fans the usual A & C 'shtick', as well as a cast that included Nat Pendleton as a sergeant driven to despair by the funnymen's antics; as well as Tom Brown and Joan Fulton (the romantic leads), Don Beddoe, Don Porter and Donald MacBride. Robert Arthur produced, and it was directed by Charles Barton along strictly formula lines. (77 mins)

△ Douglas Fairbanks Jr (centre left) wrote and produced (for Fairbanks Productions) **The Exile**, a costume drama in which he also appeared as the exiled Charles II of England. Newcomer Paule Croset (later Paula Corday, right) was featured as a young Dutch innkeeper and owner of a farm on whose premises Charles is hiding, Nigel Bruce was Charles' chancellor and Henry Daniell the Roundhead sent by Cromwell to kill the king. Maria Montez, second-billed, had but one lengthy scene – as a countess. Though the movie was good to look at and handsomely mounted (it was photographed in sepia tones), it was kaiboshed by Fairbanks' screenplay which was tedious in the extreme. Max Ophuls directed, and his cast included Robert Coote (as a ham actor who impersonates the king, seated left), Otto Waldis and Eldon Gorst. (94 mins)

▽ British actress Phyllis Calvert made an undistinguished Hollywood debut in **Time Out Of Mind**, a soporific drama about a young New England musician whose seafaring father (Leo G. Carroll) thoroughly disapproves of his son's artistic vocation. Miss Calvert played a maid in the household, and it was her role in Abem Finkel and Arnold Phillips' screenplay, based on the novel by Rachel Field, to see that the son – played by Robert Hutton (left) – fulfils his natural talents. Working to the same end was Ella Raines (right) as Hutton's sister. The film failed to gell, due largely to weaknesses in the central characters, though Janet Shaw, Helena Carter and John Abbott (as a music critic) offered sturdy acting support. Also cast: Eddie Albert, Henry Stephenson and Samuel S. Hinds, whose last film for the studio this was. It was produced and directed by Robert Siodmak. (86 mins)

▽ Betty McDonald's best-seller **The Egg And I** came to the screen via producers Chester Erskine and Fred Finkelhoffe, who also wrote the screenplay, and although it failed to be the laugh-riot audiences hoped for, it was a respectable enough adaptation which starred Claudette Colbert (illusrated) and Fred MacMurray, and prominently featured Marjorie Main and Percy Kilbride as Ma and Pa Kettle – whose success in the film led to a comedy series of their own. As in the novel, Colbert, an alumnus of a Boston finishing school, is spirited by hubby MacDonald from her rarefied world to the Pacific Northwest to embark on a life of chicken farming. Also, as in the novel, much of the humour's mainstay was seeing how the totally ill-equipped young wife copes with her unsophisticated surroundings, whose hardships are aggravated by the premises' lack of plumbing and electricity. A sub-plot (not in the book) involved Louise Allbritton as a *femme fatale* widow and the owner of a neighbouring farm, who sets her sights on MacMurray. Chester Erskine's direction tended, on the whole, to lack energy and comic invention, and the big moment of drama, when a fire all but ruins the couple and everything they've worked for, was positively thrown away. Still, there was enough in it to keep audiences happy, and it flourished at the box office. Also cast: Richard Long, Billy House, Ida Moore, Donald MacBride, Samuel S. Hinds, Fuzzy Knight and Elisabeth Risdon. (108 mins)

▽ Jon Hall (centre), Victor McLaglen (left), Rita Johnson (2nd left) and Andy Devine (right) lent a certain marquee value to **Michigan Kid**, a Cinecolor horse-opera in which top-billed Hall, as an ex-US marshal, takes himself to Rawhide, Arizona where he intends to open a ranch. En route he fends off a stage-coach attack led by 'road agent' McLaglen, who swears revenge – the scene thus being set for a series of fast-moving, albeit traditional sagebrush set-pieces, from jailbreaks, to chases, to climactic shoot-outs, and the eventual bringing to justice of the bad guys. Byron Foulger, Stanley Andrews and Milburn Stone featured prominently in Roy Chanslor's screenplay based on the novel by Rex Beach; director Ray Taylor kept the dust flying, and the producer was Howard Welsch. (69 mins)

△ An incisive screenplay by William Bowers and Bertram Millhauser, based on a story by Harry Kurnitz, was the saving grace of **The Web**, an otherwise routine tale of a young attorney (Edmond O'Brien, right), working together with a police lieutenant (William Bendix), to trap wealthy industrialist Vincent Price (who has employed O'Brien as a bodyguard) and to draw from him a confession of two murders as well as details of a million-dollar theft. Making his directorial debut, Michael Gordon kept up the pace and quality of the screenplay, and coaxed more than passable performances from a cast that was headlined by Ella Raines (left, as Price's secretary and O'Brien's romantic interest), Maria Palmer, John Abbott and Fritz Leiber. Jerry Bresler produced. (87 mins)

△ **Ride The Pink Horse** was an oddly titled melodrama in which Robert Montgomery (who also directed) played a blackmailer who sets out to track down a war-profiteer responsible for the death of a former buddy. As scripted by Ben Hecht and Charles Lederer (from the novel by Dorothy B. Hughes, whose colourful backdrop to the tale was a small New Mexico town during carnival time), it had Montgomery in possession of a cancelled check which links the villain (Fred Clark) with illegal profits. Montgomery's initial intention was to sell the check to Clark, but after being the victim of some strong arm stuff by the latter's henchmen, he turns the evidence over to the law. The storyline itself wasn't up to much, but it was expertly treated by Messrs Hecht and Lederer and, in the hands of a capable cast that included Wanda Hendrix (right) as a young Mexican girl who befriends Montgomery (left), as well as Thomas Gomez (the owner of a merry-go-round), Art Smith (of the FBI), Iris Flores. Grandon Rhodes, Tito Renaldo, Richard Gaines and Andrea King, it worked well enough. The producer was Joan Harrison. (100 mins)

△ Joan Fontaine (left) starred as the eponymous heroine in **Ivy**, a mysterious melodrama neatly scripted by Charles Bennett who, in his adaptation of the Marie Belloc Lowndes novel on which it was based, turned the clock back to turn-of-the-century England. The story of a thoroughly unscrupulous woman (Fontaine) who attempts to rid herself of a husband (Richard Ney, right) and a lover (Patric Knowles) so that she can woo wealthy Englishman Herbert Marshall unencumbered, it benefitted from a solid physical production, a good music score by Daniele Amfitheatrof, a strong central performance by its star, and some fine supporting performances from Sir Cedric Hardwicke as a Scotland Yard inspector, Lucille Watson as Knowles' mother, Sara Allgood and Rosalind Ivan as maids, Una O'Connor as a fortune-teller (who opens the movie by predicting to the wicked Miss Fontaine some of the black events to follow), and Lumsden Hare (centre). Sam Wood's direction was serviceable, but needed to be more than that to elevate the material beyond its melodramatic status, and it was produced by William Cameron Menzies for Wood's Interwood Productions. (96 mins)

▽ A western in Cinecolor, **The Vigilantes Return** top-starred Jon Hall (right) as an officer of the law who, after infiltrating a gang of desperadoes by pretending to be one of them, finds they have tumbled to his disguise. They attempt revenge by framing him for a murder he did not commit but, in the end, a group of vigilantes are summoned by the local judge to restore peace to the countryside. It all ended with right triumphing over wrong and good over evil. Margaret Lindsay, Andy Devine (left), Paula Drew and Robert Wilcox were also featured in the cast, Howard Welsch produced, Ray Taylor directed, and it was written by Roy Chanslor. (67 mins)

▽ **Something In The Wind** teamed reigning star Deanna Durbin (right) with dancing star Donald O'Connor (left) and, it must be said, the latter rather eclipsed the former. Not that Miss Durbin's delivery of several songs by Johnny Green and Leo Robin failed to please; it was just that O'Connor's energy and versatility upstaged her. The plot, by Harry Kurnitz and William Bowers, wasn't particularly inspired, but their screenplay rose above its subject, which was the kidnapping of a lady deejay (Durbin) by the grandson (John Dall) of a recently deceased tycoon. The reason? Dall thinks she was the old boy's mistress ... Irving Pichel directed a cast that also included Charles Winninger, Margaret Wycherley and Helena Carter, as well as The Williams Brothers and Jan Peerce (who sang the 'Miserere' from Verdi's *Il Trovatore* with Durbin). The production, by Joseph Sistrom, was strong on entertainment value in spite of the silly story. The Green-Robin songs included: 'Something In The Wind', 'Turntable Song', 'It's Only Love', 'Happy Go Lucky And Free'. (88 mins)

△ Ferenc Molnar's *The Good Fairy*, produced by the studio in 1935, turned up twelve years later as a musical for Deanna Durbin, retitled **I'll Be Yours**. In the role originally played by Margaret Sullavan, Miss Durbin (right) was a young woman who helps a struggling attorney to get a job with a meat packer. Preston Sturges, who wrote the 1935 version as well, provided the script (adapted from the Hungarian by Jane Hinton), and made no improvement to either Molnar's original or his own, completely mislaying the fantasy element. Miss Durbin sang four songs and delivered an adequate performance under William A. Seiter's competent direction, but it was a somewhat dull diversion in which neither Adolphe Menjou (centre, the meat packer) nor Tom Drake (the attorney) distinguished themselves. Felix Jackson produced, giving other parts to William Bendix (left), Walter Catlett, Franklin Pangborn, William Trenk, Joan Fulton, Patricia Alphin and William Brooks. Songs: 'It's Dreamtime', 'Cobbleskill School Song' Jack Brooks, Walter Schumann; 'Granada' Augustin Lara, English lyrics Dorothy Dodd; 'Sari Waltz' C.C.S. Cushman, E.P. Heath, Emmerich Kalman. (93 mins)

△ The best thing by far about **Pirates Of Monterey** was its luscious Technicolor photography by Hal Mohr and W. Howard Greene. For the rest, it was a boringly routine romantic adventure, set along the colourful California coast in the 1840s, and involving an American soldier of fortune (Rod Cameron, right) who takes a wagon train from Mexico City to an army detachment in old Monterey. The requisite gun-play, sex-play and ambushes helped clutter Sam Hellman and Margaret Buell Wilder's otherwise sparse screenplay (story by Edward T. Lowe and Bradford Ropes), with Maria Montez (left) as the picture's main marquee draw receiving billing over the handsome Cameron. Mikhail Rasumny, Philip Reed, Gilbert Roland, Gale Sondergaard and Tamara Shayne also appeared for producer Paul Malvern, and it was directed by Alfred Werker. (78 mins)

1947

▷ Abbott (centre) and Costello (right) went west for **The Wistful Widow Of Wagon Gap**, and entertained their fans by becoming embroiled in every sagebrush cliché ever invented. Using as their springboard an old Montana law stating that any man who kills another in a duel is responsible for the victim's dependents as well as his debts, scenarists Robert Lees, Frederick I. Rinaldo and John Grant (story by D.D. Beauchamp and William Bowers) devised a situation in which Costello, as a travelling salesman newly arrived in the lawless town of Wagon Gap, becomes involved in a killing and, as a result, finds himself the guardian of the victim's widow (Marjorie Main) and her brood of kids. An added plot point had Miss Main being so physically repellent, that the town's tough guys avoid Costello like the plague in case one of them bumps him off and, as a consequence, has to take on his responsibilities! Abbott played Costello's partner, and together the duo stopped the show with their well known frog-in-the-soup gag. For the rest, the humour (with Costello, having been made sheriff, strutting through town as if he owned the place) was pretty predictable. Audrey Young, George Cleveland, Gordon Jones, William Ching (left) and Peter Thompson were also in it, Charles T. Barton directed and it was produced by Robert Arthur. (77 mins)

▽ Yvonne De Carlo (right) allowed scenarists Michael Fessier and Ernest Pagano to send her up something rotten in **Slave Girl**, a spoof-cum-farce – or vice versa, it didn't really matter – in which she played a shapely dancing girl (what else?) who becomes romantically involved with George Brent (left – again miscast as a womaniser), whose brief it is to ransom a group of sailors held by a Tripoli potentate (Albert Dekker). A talking camel called Lumpy, complete with Brooklyn accent, set the tone of the piece, and was periodically called on to comment on the action. In so doing, he upstaged a cast that also included Broderick Crawford (as Brent's bodyguard), Lois Collier, Andy Devine, Carl Esmond, Arthur Treacher and Philip Van Zandt. Messrs Fessier and Pagano also produced (in Technicolor), and it was directed by Charles Lamont. (80 mins)

◁ The swell guy in **Swell Guy** was Sonny Tufts (right) but, as it turned out in Richard Brooks' screenplay of Gilbert Emery's stage play *The Hero*, he wasn't swell at all. On the contrary. He was an unscrupulous bum who, after the war (in which he served as a correspondent), visits his brother and sister-in-law in a small Californian town, immediately becomes something of a celebrity to the townsfolk (but not to his mother, who knows exactly what she's spawned), then sets about conning innocent citizens in crap games and almost wrecking his brother's marriage. He even compromises rich Ann Blyth (left), and is about to make off with the funds collected in a local GI veterans' drive when he dies a hero's death saving his young nephew. A purposeless exercise from producer Mark Hellinger, it did, at least, offer Tufts an opportunity (which he grabbed) to sink his molars into a substantial role. Ann Blyth was good, too; and there was solid backup support from Ruth Warrick as the sister-in-law, William Gargan as the brother, and Mary Nash as Tufts' knowing mother. Also cast: John Litel, Thomas Gomez, Millard Mitchell and young Donald Devlin as the nephew whose life the 'hero' saves. Frank Tuttle directed, but failed to give the story a point of view. (86 mins)

▽ Susan Hayward was given her biggest break to date in **Smash-Up – The Story Of A Woman.** A sort of female counterpart to *The Lost Weekend* (Parmount, 1945) but not as good, it charted the tribulations of a nightclub singer (Hayward), who sacrifices her career when she marries Lee Bowman, whose own rise to fame (also as a singer) is in direct proportion to his wife's decline – a decline engendered by neglect and a feeling of uselessness; and resulting in her hitting the bottle with alarming and destructive frequency. Bowman (left) sues for divorce, but after a near-tragedy Hayward sobers up with a jolt, and the couple are reunited to provide a happy ending to John Howard Lawson's so-so screenplay, based on a story by Dorothy Parker and Frank Cavett. Hayward (centre) was excellent in her rather stereotyped role, but Bowman miscast in his. Marsha Hunt was the unsympathetic 'other' woman and Eddie Albert (right) an understanding friend, with other roles under Stuart Heisler's direction going to Carl Esmond (as a doctor), Carleton Young, Charles D. Brown and Janet Murdoch. Walter Wanger produced. Songs: 'Life Can Be Beautiful', 'Hush-a-bye Island', 'I Miss That Feeling' Jimmy McHugh, Harold Adamson. (103 mins)

1948

▽ A musical comedy that had enjoyed a modest (15 months) run on Broadway, where its chief asset had been its score by Sigmund Romberg, **Up In Central Park** arrived on screen complete with Deanna Durbin, but with all except two of Romberg's numbers gone. Set in turn-of-the-century New York, Karl Tunberg's screenplay (adapted from Herbert and Dorothy Fields' Broadway original) featured Miss Durbin (left) as the Irish immigrant daughter – curiously devoid of brogue – of a park superintendent (Albert Sharpe), who teams up with a news reporter (Dick Haymes, right) to expose the dirty political dealings of Vincent Price. Romberg's remaining songs were 'When She Walks In The Room', pleasingly crooned by an otherwise miscast Haymes, and 'Carousel In The Park' which he and Deanna shared in an actual merry-go-round scene. Miss Durbin also sang, though without particular distinction, 'Pace, Pace, Mio Dio' from Verdi's *La Forza del Destino*. Otherwise, the movie, though good to look at and competently directed by William A. Seiter, offered a mediocre score, over-sentimentality, and too little pace to attract the paying customers. Writer Tunberg produced, and the cast was completed by Tom Powers, Hobart Cavanaugh, Thurston Hall, Howard Freeman, Mary Field, Tom Pedi and Moroni Olsen. It was a great pity that this below-par Durbin offering turned out to be the last film in which the legendary star ever appeared. (87 mins)

△ There was only one really funny moment in **Mexican Hayride**, another Abbott and Costello caper, very loosely based on Cole Porter's Broadway show of the same name, but without any of Porter's music in it. That moment occurred when Costello walks into a bull-ring south of the border and completely subdues the snorting animal's ferocity. For the rest it was a depressingly routine A & C comedy, with Costello (right) appearing as the fall guy for a gang of confidence tricksters (headed by Abbott, left), who is made to front for a fake mining set-up in Mexico. Virginia Grey, Luba Malina, John Hubbard, Pedro De Cordoba and Fritz Feld also had parts in Oscar Brodney and John Grant's screenplay (the original Broadway book was by Herbert and Dorothy Fields); it was directed with little evidence of verve by Charles T. Barton, and the producer was Robert Arthur. (77 mins)

▽ The French Foreign Legion, an Indo-China backdrop, skirmishes between Legionnaires and local natives, double-dealing art collectors with gun-running interests, and exotic sloe-eyed charmers, were just a handful of the melodramatic components that went into **Rogue's Regiment**, an action-packed adventure which top-starred Dick Powell (illustrated left) of US Army Intelligence who sets out to capture a Nazi war criminal. A character called Carl Reicher, clearly modelled on Martin Boorman, was played by Stephen McNally, with other roles under the capable direction of Robert Florey going to Marta Toren as a Saigon songstress, Henry Rowland as a cowardly ex-SS officer, and Vincent Price as the art-collector-cum-gun-runner. Producer Robert Buckner scripted it (from a story he wrote with director Florey), and his screenplay was the least effective element on display. Songs: 'Just For A While', 'Who Can Tell' Jack Brooks, Serge Walter. (85 mins)

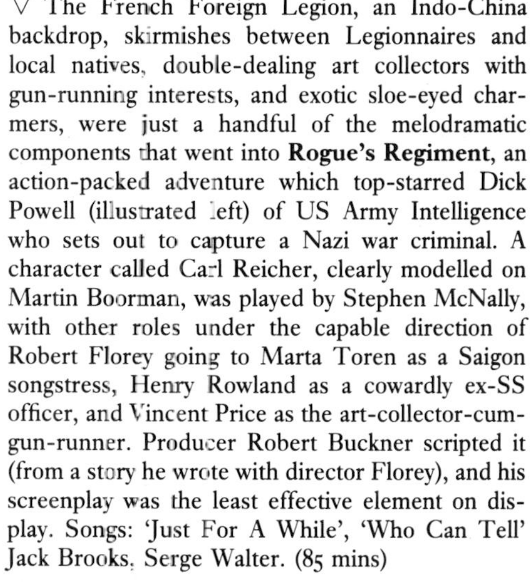

▽ Technicolor and some stirring action sequences were the main allies of **River Lady**, an outdoor melodrama with a logging-camp background that starred Yvonne De Carlo (who sang 'Louis Sands And Jim McGee' by Walter Schumann and Jim Brooks), Dan Duryea, Rod Cameron and Helena Carter (left). De Carlo was a wealthy gambling gal who attempts to buy the love of virile Cameron (right), a logger, by setting him up in his own business. He discovers her ruse and, his manly pride wounded, jilts her for Miss Carter. Equally piqued, De Carlo sets out to ruin Cameron and almost succeeds. Duryea was prominently featured as the traditional heavy in the yarn, with other roles going to Lloyd Gough (as Cameron's side-kick), Florence Bates, John McIntire and Jack Lambert. It was scripted by D.D. Beauchamp and William Bowers from the novel by Houston Branch, and directed for the elongated cliché it was by George Sherman for producer Leonard Goldstein. (77 mins)

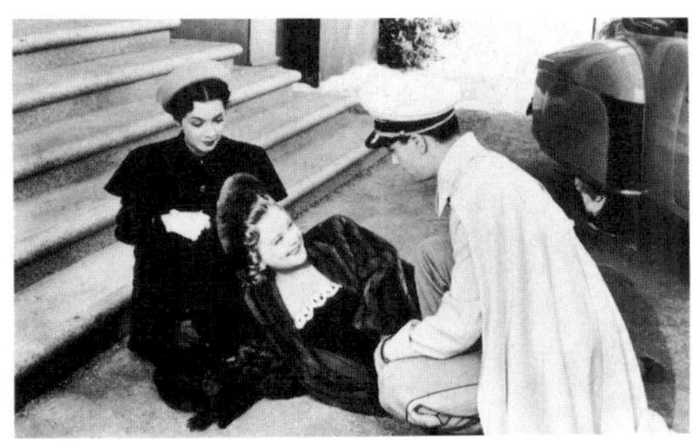

◁ Ice-skating queen Sonja Henie (centre), who had been absent from the screen for almost four years, returned for one last American film appearance in **Countess Of Monte Cristo**. Alas, Miss Henie's last was also her least in this tale of two Norwegian barmaids (Olga San Juan, co-starred, left, was the other one) who get jobs at an Oslo film studio, and 'borrow' some props in which to masquerade as a countess (Henie) and her maidservant at a smart resort. Although there were six ice-skating sequences for the star, and Miss San Juan sang three Jack Brooks–Saul Chaplin songs, the screenplay (by William Bowers from a story by Walter Reisch) was a limp effort, the film lacked sparkle, and it was a box-office failure. John Beck produced, the director was Frederick de Cordova, and the cast also included Dorothy Hart, Michael Kirby (right – Miss Henie's real-life skating partner), Arthur Treacher, Hugh French, Freddie Trenkler and Arthur O'Connell. Songs: 'Friendly Polka', 'Count Your Blessings', 'Who Believes In Santa Claus?'. (76 mins)

▽ **For The Love Of Mary** was a piece of romantic flim-flam in which the President of the United States (never actually seen, but whose presence was felt throughout) helps a White House telephonist (top-billed Deanna Durbin, left) to sort out her romantic problems. It was as lightweight as a pussy willow but, thanks to its star's pleasing personality and a pleasing, not-to-be-taken-seriously screenplay by Oscar Brodney, it worked beautifully. Miss Durbin broke into song on several occasions, the most effective being a cod version of 'Largo Al Factotum' from Rossini's *The Barber Of Seville*. Edmond O'Brien co-starred, with other roles under Frederick de Cordova's well-paced direction going to Don Taylor (as the cause of all Miss D's romantic problems), Jeffrey Lynn (right), Ray Collins, Hugo Haas and Harry Davenport. The producer was Robert Arthur. (90 mins)

△ War profiteering and the devastating effects its aftermath has on the affluent Keller family, was the subject of Arthur Miller's powerful stage play, **All My Sons**. It came to the screen, via producer Chester Erskine, with a strong cast headed by Edward G. Robinson as Joe Keller, a small-town arms manufacturer who, despite the fact that one of his own sons was, at the time, away at war, knowingly sent defective parts to the Army Air Force – a criminal move which cost the lives of 21 men. Robinson (centre left) has blamed his erstwhile partner (Frank Conroy) for the debacle – an accusation resulting in a lengthy, totally undeserved jail sentence which Conroy is still serving when the film opens. How Robinson's secret is brought into the open, thanks, largely, to the intense probing of his embittered second son Chris (Burt Lancaster, right), was the mainstay of producer Erskine's compelling adaptation, and it made for gripping and compulsive viewing. Mady Christians (centre right) was co-starred as Robinson's protective wife (pathetically clinging to the hope that her elder son, missing believed killed in action, is still alive), with other roles under Irving Reis's restrained but effective direction going to Howard Duff, Louisa Horton (left, her debut) as the dead son's fiancée, Arlene Francis, Lloyd Gough, Henry Morgan and Elisabeth Fraser. (93 mins)

◁ The subject of **Larceny** was confidence tricksters – a breed not entirely new to the cinema. It was given an up-date treatment in Leonard Goldstein and Aaron Rosenberg's production by making the con-man's victim the widow of a war hero in a small Californian town. Herbert H. Margolis, Louis Morheim and William Bowers' screenplay (from Lois Eby and John Fleming's novel *The Velvet Fleece*) pivoted on leading man John Payne's attempts to con the widow (Joan Caulfield) out of money in order to erect a phoney memorial to her late husband – in the process of which he falls in love with her, much to the annoyance of Shelley Winters (girlfriend of gangleader Dan Duryea, left), who takes quite a shine to Payne as the plot unfurls. Finale has Payne (right) turning himself and his confederates over to the police, with no happy ending anywhere in sight. Dorothy Hart, Richard Rober, Patricia Alphin, Dan O'Herlihy and Russ Conway were also in it, and did good work for director George Sherman who kept it lively. (89 mins)

△ Another intense family drama by another heavyweight dramatist (Lillian Hellman), and involving yet another guilty secret harboured by the *paterfamilias* (in this case the betraying of neighbours during the Civil War and the resultant deaths of 27 Confederate soldiers), **Another Part Of The Forest** was a *prequel* to Hellman's *The Little Foxes* (Goldwyn, 1941), set twenty years earlier in 1880. Most of the characters who appeared in the earlier play were here 'introduced', the playwright's chief concern being to show just how the despicable Hubbard family came to be the way they were. Like *The Little Foxes*, **Another Part Of The Forest** had little in it to ingratiate itself with audiences, being a relentless catalogue of family in-fighting and avarice. It was redeemed, however, by sharp characterisations, sizzling dialogue and a set of performances that helped make the machinations of the Hubbard clan positively mesmeric. Fredric March (left) was brilliant as Marcus Hubbard, one of the richest men in a small Southern town in Alabama but still hankering for social acceptability (he has still not been forgiven for selling smuggled Union salt at $8 a pound to the Confederates); Dan Duryea (centre), Edmond O'Brien (right) and a slightly miscast Ann Blyth (2nd left) were his ghastly offspring, and Florence Eldridge (seated) his wife, and the only decent character among them. Vladimir Pozner's screenplay also had parts in it for John Dall, Betsy Blair, Fritz Leiber and Whit Bissell, all of them first rate, and it was directed by Michael Gordon, who was in full control of the steamy material. Jerry Bresler produced. (106 mins)

△ Producer/director Zoltan Korda surfaced with a really classy melodrama in **A Woman's Vengeance**, which top-starred urbane Charles Boyer as a man accused of murdering his wife (Rachel Kempson), but who, despite the overwhelming circumstantial evidence against him, is innocent of the crime. The guilty culprit is actually Jessica Tandy (right), whose unrequited love for Boyer drives her to wreak a terrible vengeance. A highly-charged screenplay, written by Aldous Huxley, that was literate, gripping, and rich in characterisation, received polished performances from a cast that also included pretty Ann Blyth (left) as the woman Boyer marries after the death of his wife, and Sir Cedric Hardwicke, really excellent as a doctor who uses hypnosis to draw the truth from Miss Tandy in order to save Boyer from the gallows at the last minute. Other roles went to Mildred Natwick (as a nurse), Hugh French and Valerie Cardew. (95 mins)

▽ A traditional western, in Technicolor, but with the 'heroes' of the piece being a trio of likeable heavies – two of whom pay for their lawlessness by being gunned down, while the third is merely sent to prison – **Black Bart** was a slightly above-average horse-opera, set in California's frontier days. Under George Sherman's energetic action-packed direction, Yvonne De Carlo, top-billed, played Lola Montez, with Dan Duryea (left), Jeffrey Lynn (right) and Percy Kilbride co-starred. The acquisition of gold at any price was the motivating factor in Luci Ward, Jack Natteford and William Bowers' screenplay (story by Ward and Natteford), with Duryea, the most prominent member of the trio, as a 'respectable' rancher who also happens to have an insatiable appetite for Wells Fargo gold, which he appropriates under the name Black Bart. Lloyd Gough, Frank Lovejoy, John McIntire and Don Beddoe were also in it, and it was produced by Leonard Goldstein, whose debut effort it was. (80 mins)

△ New York City co-starred with Barry Fitzgerald in **The Naked City**, a hard-hitting crime melodrama (not unlike some of the real-life stories producer Mark Hellinger wrote in his newspaper days), as well as a valentine to a great city. Filmed entirely on location in and around Manhattan, the film's narrative concentrated on the bath-tub murder, in an upper West Side apartment, of a blonde, and adroitly used NYC for its atmosphere and for its general sense of excitement, both of which contributed to Albert Maltz and Malvin Wald's screenplay (story by Wald). Fitzgerald (top-starred) played a Homicide-Squad police lieutenant in charge of the murder in question, with other roles under Jules Dassin's stark, almost documentary-like direction going to Howard Duff (as a con-man), Ted De Corsia (right, as a thug), Don Taylor (left), Dorothy Hart and House Jameson. It was photographed (again, in almost documentary-like fashion) by William Daniels, had a moody score by Miklos Rosza and Frank Skinner that reeked of the city, and a voice-over commentary by Hellinger himself, whose last film this was. Interesting sideline: At the time of release it was said that the blonde corpse was Shelley Winters. She never denied it. (96 mins)

▷ **Feudin', Fussin' And A-Fightin'** was a boisterous, good-natured backwoods musical that offered undemanding broad comedy and some fast and furious tap dancing. D.D. Beauchamp's screenplay (from his own *Collier's Magazine* story) had the ever-engaging Donald O'Connor (left) as a travelling salesman who, while doing a pitch in the ittle town of Rimrock, demonstrates his terpsichorean talents. The inhabitants of Rimrock, who need a runner for their forthcoming foot-race with a rival village, kidnap the visitor and persuade him to the task. The laughs were led by Marjorie Main (right) as Rimrock's mayor and Percy Kilbride (2nd left) as a livery stable owner; Penny Edwards (centre) was O'Connor's romantic interest, and others in the cast were Joe Besser, Harry Shannon, Fred Kohler Jr and Howland Chamberlain. Louis Da Pron choreographed, George Sherman directed, and the producer was Leonard Goldstein. Songs and musical numbers included: 'S'posing' Andy Razaf, Paul Denniker; 'Me And My Shadow' Al Jolson, Billy Rose, Dave Dreyer; 'Feudin' and Fightin'' Al Dubin, Burton Lane. (78 mins)

▽ **Abbott And Costello Meet Frankenstein** (or rather, Frankenstein's monster) as well as Dracula and the Wolf Man – and the experience offered patrons a spine-tingling laugh, whose more horrific moments were as scarey as anything ever perpetrated by the trio of ghouls while playing it straight way back in the thirties. Dispensing, for the most part, with their usual quota of familiar, tacked-on routines, Messrs A & C relied on the script (by Robert Lees, Frederick I. Rinaldo and John Grant) for their laughs, with Costello (left) again providing the lynch-pin of the plot by becoming Count Dracula's victim for a brain transplant, the intended recipient being Frankenstein's monster. A rather sad Bela Lugosi played Dracula, Glenn Strange was the monster, and Lon Chaney Jr surfaced as a benign Wolf Man (right) except, of course, when the moon is full ... Completing the cast were Lenore Aubert, Jane Randolph, Frank Ferguson and Charles Bradstreet. It was directed by Charles T. Barton, who brought the film to a hilarious conclusion in a frantic chase finale. The producer was Robert Arthur. (89 mins)

▽ Directed by Jack Hively, choreographed by Louis Da Pron, and with a clutch of songs by Inez James and Sidney Miller, **Are You With It?** was a star vehicle for Donald O'Connor. It was also a disappointment. Oscar Brodney's simplistic screenplay (based on the Sam Perrin-George Balzer stage show) did little for the story of a mathematical genius (O'Connor, left) who, when he is fired for putting a decimal point in the wrong place, joins a carnival and, in between some energetic hoofing, gets romantically tied up with Olga San Juan. Donald properly came in to his own in a stunning dance routine set in a restaurant. For the rest, the goings-on in the carnival, including a really appalling ballet staged by Da Pron for the film's finale, didn't add up to much, and drew a really hammy performance from its young star. Robert Arthur produced, also casting Lew Parker as a carnival pitch man (the part he originally played on Broadway), Martha Stewart (centre), George O'Hanlon (right), Walter Catlett, Ransom Sherman, Louis Da Pron and Julie Gibson. Songs and musical numbers included: 'Down At Baba's Alley', 'It Only Takes A Little Imagination', 'Are You With It?', 'Daddy Surprise Me'. (89 mins)

▷ Terrific was the word for **A Double Life**, whose highly theatrical premise was that if an actor plays a part for too long, or with too much intensity, he is psychologically in danger of continuing the performance into his private life. Ruth Gordon and Garson Kanin's intelligent screenplay (filmed largely in New York at the old Empire Theatre) focussed on an actor called Anthony John (Ronald Colman, left) who, during a two-year run of Shakespeare's *Othello* in which he plays the title role, gradually takes on the jealous character of the Moor to such an extent that a chance acquaintance with a woman of easy virtue (Shelley Winters, right) results in his murdering her by strangulation. In the end, Colman takes his own life during a performance by stabbing himself – just as Othello did after the murder of Desdemona. Colman's central performance was a brilliant and mesmeric study of a man obsessed, while, as his stage co-star and former wife, Signe Hasso was offered the best role of her career, and more than justified producer Michael Kanin's faith in casting her in so difficult and demanding a part. With such excellent material at hand, director George Cukor had no difficulty in drawing equally convincing performances from Edmond O'Brien (as a press agent), as well as from Ray Collins, Millard Mitchell, Philip Loeb and Joe Sawyer. Miklos Rosza supplied the marvellous music score. (103 mins)

▽ **Mr Peabody And The Mermaid**, based on Guy and Constance Jones' novel *Peabody's Mermaid*, was joyously dedicated to the proposition that life begins at fifty. At least, that's where it began for top-starred William Powell as a rather staid Bostonian who, on reaching his half century, is ordered by his doctor (Art Smith) to spend the winter relaxing in the West Indies. Which he does, and where, during a fishing excursion, he hooks a mermaid (Ann Blyth, illustrated, with Powell) in the tail, takes his catch back to his beach-house and puts her in a fish pond. Producer Nunnally Johnson's screenplay (told in flashback) was pretty adept at devising situations in which outsiders glimpsed no more of the mermaid than her tail, a fact which quickly results in Powell's sanity being questioned whenever he describes his catch. Needless to say, Powell soon falls in love with his creature from the deep but, in the end, she returns to whence she came. Irene Hervey was cast as Powell's wife (who at one point walks out on him), with other roles under Irving Pichel's tongue-in-cheek direction going to Clinton Sundberg (as a press agent), Hugh French, Lumsden Hare, Fred Clark and Andrea King. The first half of the comedy was better than the second, by which time it had run out of steam. (89 mins)

△ In **The Saxon Charm**, top-starred Robert Montgomery played stage producer Matt Saxon, a despicable, talentless egomaniac and bully with about as much charm as an angry piranha. As he had done throughout Frederic Wakeman's novel (adapted for the screen by Claude Binyon, who also directed), Saxon almost ruins novelist John Payne (left), whose play about Moliére he is presenting and whom he puts under undue pressure to revise it. Payne's wife (Susan Hayward, right) also becomes the victim of Montgomery's arrogance; so does Audrey Totter as his girlfriend, and Harry von Zell as a millionaire play backer or 'angel'. Saxon's eventual come-uppance for his domineering behaviour and insensitivity was a long time arriving, and when it finally happened, it offered audiences their only respite from the catalogue of unpleasantness hitherto witnessed. Joseph Sistrom's glossy production was far too insular to achieve popular success, but those 'in the know' found much in it that was unflinchingly truthful. The cast was completed by Henry Morgan, Cara Williams, Chill Wills and Heather Angel. Jimmy McHugh and Dorothy Fields' 'I'm In The Mood For Love' was sung by Miss Totter. (88 mins)

▽ **One Touch Of Venus**, based on the S.J. Perelman–Ogden Nash–Kurt Weill stage musical, was an insult to its creators. The whimsical and charming story of a statue of Venus in a department store who comes to life when she is kissed by a window dresser, it starred the exquisite Ava Gardner (right) as Venus and Robert Walker (left) as the man who releases her from immobility. Unfortunately, he didn't succeed in mobilising her performance or, indeed, his own. The dreariness of the two stars was matched by William A. Seiter's direction of the Harry Kurnitz–Frank Tashlin screenplay, and the dances, staged by Billy Daniels, were feeble. Musically, Lester Cowan's production saw fit to retain only five of Weill's original sixteen songs, none of them sung with any particular sparkle. Miss Gardner's vocals were dubbed by Eileen Wilson, and crooner Dick Haymes was featured in a cast that also included Eve Arden, Olga San Juan, Tom Conway, James Flavin and Sara Allgood. Songs and musical numbers: 'My Week', 'Don't Look Now But My Heart Is Showing', 'That's Him' (lyrics Ann Ronnell), 'The Trouble With Woman', 'Speak Low' Ogden Nash, Weill. (81 mins)

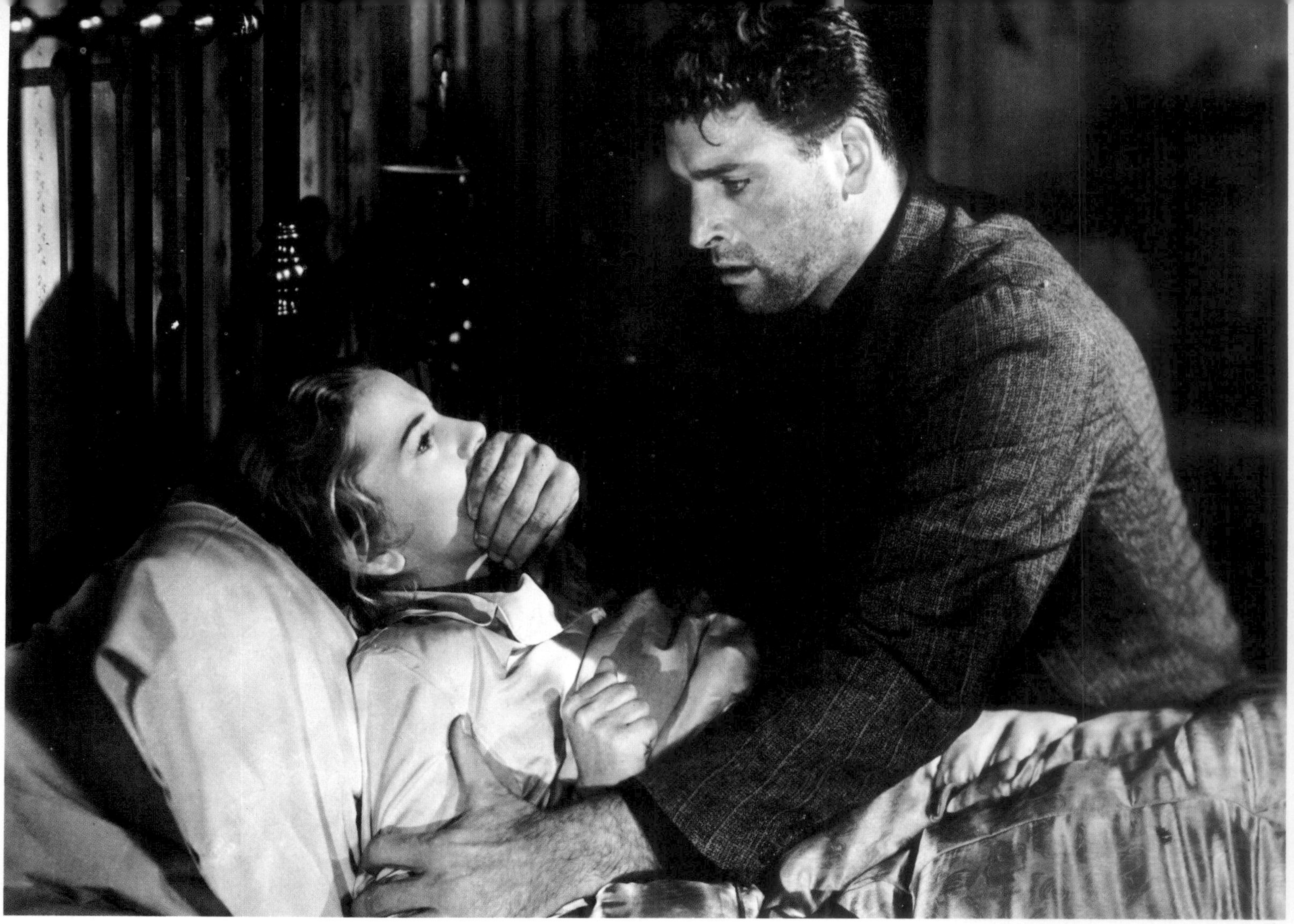

▽ The tale of a spy named Pepe Le Moko had been told in a French film of that name, starring Jean Gabin, as well as in *Algiers*, starring Charles Boyer (United Artists, 1938). It now surfaced at Universal as **Casbah**, a musical version starring Tony Martin (right) – an excellent choice vocally, with his strong, creamy tenor, but whose acting left something to be desired. Ladislaus Bus-Fekete and Arnold Manoff were responsible for the screenplay, which they based on the novel by Detective Ashelbe and a 'musical' adaptation by Erik Charell. Their efforts gave featured employment to the Swedish beauty Marta Toren (her Hollywood debut) as the woman whose love Pepe dies for, as well as Hugo Haas, Peter Lorre (left) and Yvonne De Carlo, without whose presence no exotic North African adventure would have seemed complete. Thomas Gomez, Douglas Dick, Herbert Rudley and Katherine Dunham and her dancers were in it, too, for director John Berry and producer Nat G. Goldstone. Bernard Pearce choreographed. Songs: 'For Every Man There's A Woman', 'It Was Written In The Stars', 'Hooray For Love', 'What's Good About Goodbye?' Harold Arlen, Leo Robin. (93 mins)

△ **Kiss The Blood Off My Hands** was a splendid example of *film noir*, whose dark and brooding atmosphere created by director Norman Foster was far superior to the trite and melodramatic story it embellished. Burt Lancaster (right) starred as a World War II veteran who, after accidentally killing a man in a London pub, flees the police and, while still on the run, makes the acquaintance of top-billed Joan Fontaine (left), a hospital employee with whom he falls in love. The fair-to-middling script by Leonardo Bercovici (adapted by Ben Maddow and Walter Bernstein, with additional dialogue by Hugh Gray, from the novel by Gerald Butler), had Lancaster attempting to go straight, but being prevented from doing so by sinister black-marketeer Robert Newton who blackmails him into a hi-jack deal. Newton eventually pays for his crimes when he is murdered by Miss Fontaine after he makes a pass at her. It was over the top to be sure, but stylishly handled by all concerned, including a supporting cast completed by Lewis L. Russell, Arminta Dyne, Grizelda Harvey, Jay Novello and Colin Keith-Johnston. A Harold-Hecht-Norma Production, it was produced by Richard Vernon. (79 mins)

△ Some torrid sex scenes between Van Heflin (left) and Susan Hayward (centre), and the lush colour (by Technicolor) photography of the Smokey Mountains locations in Tennessee and North Carolina (picturesquely serving as Mississippi, the movie's setting) were the best things that **Tap Roots** had to offer. A George Marshall production for Walter Wanger Pictures Inc, it was scripted by Alan LeMay (additional dialogue by Lionel Wiggam) from James Street's novel of the same name, and was the sprawling story of the Dabney family and their fraught-filled efforts to maintain their neutrality in the South with the arrival of the Civil War. Hayward's spirited performance à la Scarlett O'Hara went some distance to compensate for director George Marshall's lack of epic sweep in his approach to the subject; and there was good work too from Heflin in a poorly characterised role as a newspaper publisher and notorious duellist. Ward Bond, however, was totally unable to bring conviction to his role as the head of the Dabney clan and might, with advantage, have been eliminated completely. Boris Karloff was fine as an Indian friend of the family, with other roles going to Julie London as Hayward's amorous younger sister, Whitfield Connor (right, as the man Miss London steals away from her sister), Richard Young, Arthur Shields, Ruby Dandrige and Russell Simpson. (108 mins)

1949

▽ Douglas Fairbanks Jr (left) emulated his celebrated father in **The Fighting O'Flynn** by playing a kind of Irish Musketeer whose braggadocio doings had him scaling walls and leaping across roofs with reckless abandon. Equally adept with a pistol, a rapier, a sword or a shillelagh, he was a dashing soldier of fortune whose gift of the Irish gab secured him any female his heart desired. In short, he was a breathing compendium of clichés, whose main purpose on this colourful occasion, was to prevent Napoleon's army from landing on Irish soil. Co-star Helena Carter (right – as the daughter of Ireland's Viceroy, Lumsden Hare) is carrying an important message concerning Napoleon's planned invasion, and she makes the acquaintance of Fairbanks (known as The O'Flynn) when he comes to her rescue after the carriage in which she is travelling is attacked by highwaymen. It was all so familiar it could have passed for parody but, as entertainingly directed by Arthur Pierson, it was blarney of a most engaging nature, and hugely enjoyable. Fairbanks Jr produced and wrote it with Robert Thoeren from the novel by Justin Huntly McCarthy, and his cast included Richard Greene as the villainous viceroy's aide (to whom Miss Carter is affianced), Patricia Medina, Arthur Shields, J.M. Kerrigan, Ludwig Donath and Otto Waldis. (94 mins)

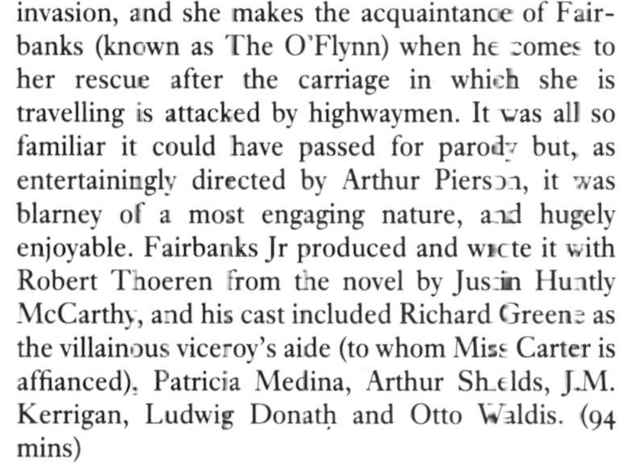

▽ Advertised as 'the year's most sensational picture', **Abandoned** was nothing of the sort. What it turned out to be was a melodramatic throwback to the thirties when, about every second week or so, the studio exposed some kind of racket or another. This time it was the black-market baby racket that was under scrutiny, and which, thanks to the efforts of Gale Storm (right – whose sister and her baby go missing), and newspaper man Dennis O'Keefe, was finally smashed in an all-out shoot-up. Meg Randall featured in Irwin Gielgud's screenplay as an expectant mum who helps to expose the crooks, with other roles under Joe Newman's inscrutable direction going to Marjorie Rambeau (centre left – as a dowager who fronts the illegal adoption ring), Jeff Chandler (as a district attorney), Raymond Burr (as a double-dealing sleuth), Jeanette Nolan, Mike Mazurki (centre right) and Will Kuluva (left). Jerry Bresler produced. (79 mins)

▽ **Abbott And Costello Meet The Killer (Boris Karloff)** proved too long a title for most neighbourhood marquees (the number of letters required almost out-budgeting the movie itself!) with the result that Boris Karloff's name was frequently dropped. Not that it mattered much, for the role he played in the comedy – that of a phoney swami (see illustration) who, at one point, tries to hypnotise Costello (left) into committing suicide – was hardly integral to a story which had Messrs A & C playing a bellboy and a house detective respectively. A whodunnit involving several murders in the hotel at which Bud and Lou are employed, it bumped along, under Charles T. Barton's accustomed direction, to its inevitable climax set in a subterranean cavern. Hugh Wedlock Jr, Howard Snyder and John Grant scripted it (from a story by Wedlock Jr and Snyder), Robert Arthur produced and, in secondary roles, cast Lenore Aubert, Gar Moore, Donna Martell and Alan Mowbray. (84 mins)

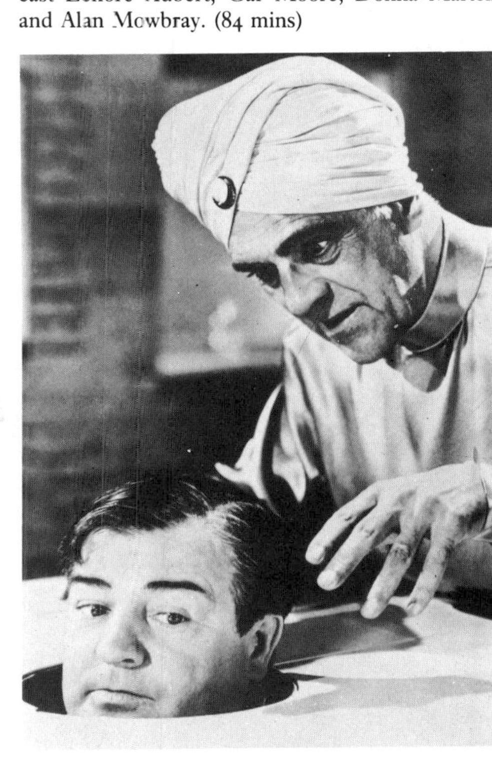

1949

▷ **City Across The River**, which traversed much the same territory as the melodramas featuring The Dead End Kids, was full of worthy intentions, setting out, as it did, to arrive at some of the answers that for years have bothered sociologists seeking reasons for juvenile delinquency. Set against backdrops of Manhattan and Brooklyn, the film adopted an almost documentary-like approach in its attempt to show how sleazy tenement conditions tend to spawn criminal activity, and made a powerful visual statement about poverty and its grim side-effects. Apart from expressing the obvious – that there would be less crime if there were less urban squalor – the drama, written, produced and directed by Maxwell Shane (from the novel *The Amboy Dukes* by Irving Shulman, adapted by Shulman and co-scripted by Dennis Cooper) failed to throw fresh light on the issues in question, being content to make superficial observations about the lack of parental supervision as an additional cause for street crime among the young. Basically the story of a Brooklyn street gang (The Amboy Dukes), and one of its members (Peter Fernandez, 2nd right) in particular, the film depicted, with harrowing conviction, how a chain of strait-jacketing circumstances can turn a small-time hood into a fully-fledged killer. Stephen McNally was top-cast as a community centre counsellor. Luis Van Rooten and Thelma Ritter were Fernandez' honest, hardworking parents, with other roles going to Jeff Corey, Sharon McManus, Sue England, Barbara Whiting, Richard Benedict and, as members of the gang, Al Ramsen (right), Joshua Shelley (2nd left), Mickey Knox (left), Richard Jaeckel (centre) and Anthony (Tony) Curtis (centre left). (90 mins)

▷ **Arctic Manhunt** was a dispiriting non-event which top-starred Mikel Conrad (who?) as an ex-convict who, having completed his prison sentence, makes his way to Alaska in order to lay his hands on the spoils of an armoured-car heist, and finds himself on the run from insurance investigators. Vapidly written (by Oscar Brodney and Joel Malone), inertly directed (by Ewing Scott, who also supplied the story) and performed with about as much enthusiasm as a man on his way to the electric chair, it co-starred Carol Thurston (illustrated, with Conrad), and featured Wally Cassell, Helen Brown, Harry Harvey and Russ Conway. Leonard Goldstein produced. (69 mins)

▽ **Johnny Stool Pigeon** was a cops-and-mobsters melodrama whose main objective was to provide a few thrills en route to smashing a dope-smuggling syndicate. Lurching from San Francisco to Vancouver, then from Tucson to Mexico – and back again to Tucson, Robert L. Richards' screenplay (story by Henry Jordan) top-starred the reliable Howard Duff as a fearless Federal agent who, hot on the heels of the narcotics boys, comes to an arrangement with an Alcatraz inmate (Dan Duryea, right) – whose own wife is a drug addict – that leads to the eventual routing of the mob. Shelley Winters (left) appeared as a blonde moll, with other parts going to Anthony (Tony) Curtis, John McIntire, Gar Moore and Leif Erickson. Aaron Rosenberg produced, and William Castle directed. (75 mins)

△ An unintentional parody of the studio's exotic 'tits and sand' adventures, **Bagdad**'s Technicolor photography and the good looks of leading lady Maureen O'Hara (centre left) were hardly enough to keep the sand out of its patrons' eyes. Nor was the fact that she sang three songs without being dubbed. Producer Robert Arthur cast her as a Sheikh's daughter who, returning from a lengthy stay in Lonon, discovers that her father is dead, his wealth gone, and his followers scattered. So whodunnit? All the evidence points to newcomer Paul Christian, but after getting just one or two glimpses of the leering John Sutton, audiences immediately knew who the real culprit was. Vincent Price (centre right) as Pasha Ali Nadim was another villain; with other parts in this desert song going to Jeff Corey, Frank Puglia, Fritz Leiber and Ann Pearce. Robert Hardy Andrews wrote it and it was directed with devastating (but understandable) indifference by Charles Lamont. Songs: 'Bagdad', 'Love Is Strange', 'Song Of The Desert' Jack Brooks, Frank Skinner. (82 mins)

▽ Howard Duff's first western was **Red Canyon**, a respectable enough oater whose multifarious clichés benefitted from Technicolor and the superbly photogenic Utah backdrop which producer Leonard Goldstein wisely chose as the locale for a rather tired story. Based on Zane Grey's novel *Wildfire*, it involved maverick stallions, ranch-hands, horse thieves and the obligatory romance, the latter in the capable hands of Duff (right) and Ann Blyth (centre). Duff played a drifter who, while attempting to corral a notorious stallion, meets Miss Blyth, the daughter of the territory's number one horse breeder (George Brent). What happens when Brent discovers that Duff intends to compete against him in an important race, and that Duff's father is a horse thief, helped pad out the screenplay fashioned by Maurice Geraghty, and provided parts for Edgar Buchanan (left), John McIntire, Chill Wills, Jane Darwell and Lloyd Bridges. The director was George Sherman, whose shoot-out finale was worth waiting for. (82 mins)

▽ **The Life Of Riley**, based on the well-known radio programme, was no improvement on its airwave counterpart – just more of the same. It starred William Bendix (seated left) as Riley, Rosemary de Camp (right) as his wife, and Meg Randall (centre) and Lanny Rees (left) as his offspring. James Gleason was, as usual, Riley's quarrelsome sidekick, and John Brown undertaker 'Digger' O'Dell. Producer/director Irving Brecher's screenplay featured Bendix as a riveter in an aircraft factory, and his discovery, after being upgraded to an executive position, that his promotion was engineered by his daughter who, in return, has to marry playboy Mark Daniels, the boss' son. Revolted by the conditions under which his 'promotion' has taken place, Bendix breaks up the wedding ceremony and makes quite sure his daughter is reunited with the man she really loves. Also cast: Bill Goodwin, Beulah Bondi, Richard Long and Ted De Corsia. (87 mins)

▽ Euthanasia was the subject of **An Act Of Murder** (also known as **Live Today For Tomorrow**), an unflinchingly grim little drama which scenarists Michael Blankfort and Robert Thoeren adapted from an even grimmer novel (*Mills Of God*) by Ernest Lothar on which it was based. Fredric March starred as a small-town judge who lives his life by the letter of the law, and who finds himself facing the gravest dilemma of his life when his wife (Florence Eldridge) is stricken with a terminal illness. So excruciating is her pain, that March has to decide whether to indulge in a spot of mercy-killing or let her sufferings continue until the bitter end. He decides on the former and kills her by crashing their car over a cliff. Apart from March (right) and his real-life wife Eldridge (left), who were excellent as the suffering couple, there was splendid work from second-billed Edmond O'Brien as a lawyer, seen at his most effective in a courtroom scene; as well as from Geraldine Brooks as the couple's daughter and Stanley Ridges as a doctor. Also cast: John McIntire (as a judge), Frederic Tozere, Virginia Brissac, Don Beddoe and Clarence Muse. Jerry Bresler produced and Michael Gordon was the director. (91 mins)

△ **Once More My Darling** was a piece of good-natured nonsense that should have been much funnier than it was. It starred personable Robert Montgomery (he also produced, for Neptune Productions, and directed it) as a lawyer and ex-movie star who is pressed into service by the Army to woo a pretty young heiress (Ann Blyth) in order to track down the man who gave her several pieces of Nazi-acquired jewellery. It takes just 24 hours for the impetuous Miss Blyth (right) to realise that she's madly in love with Montgomery (left), whom she forces to elope with her to Las Vegas, thereby unleashing a frantic chase instigated by Taylor Holmes, her concerned father. Miss Blyth looked delightful in only four changes of costume throughout, and exhibited a nice line in featherweight comedy; while Montgomery also responded well to his own direction. It was scripted by Robert Carson from his *Saturday Evening Post* story *Come Be My Love*, with additional dialogue by Oscar Saul. Stage actress Jane Cowl made her talkie debut (she first appeared for the studio in 1915!) playing Montgomery's attorney-mother, with other roles going to Lillian Randolph, Steven Geray, John Ridgely and Roland Winters. (92 mins)

▷ The humour that scenarist Dane Lussier (working from the novel by Homer Croy) wrung out of **Family Honeymoon** sprung from one basic situation: a honeymoon in which the bride brings along her three children from a former marriage. Claudette Colbert (centre) was the bride, Fred MacMurray (left) her understandably harassed new college professor husband, and Jimmy Hunt, Peter Miles and Gigi Perreau (illustrated with MacMurray) the offspring who refer to their stepfather as 'that man'. It was a delightfully genial entertainment whose predictability was mitigated by the appealing performances of all concerned, by a witty screenplay, and by direction (by Claude Binyon) that moved swiftly and never laboured the predicaments in which the newlyweds found themselves placed. A fine supporting cast included Rita Johnson (as a blonde vamp and former flame of MacMurray's), Henry Daniell, Lillian Bronson, Chill Wills and Hattie McDaniel. John Beck and Z. Wayne Griffin produced. (90 mins)

▽ **Illegal Entry** was a throwback to the kind of double-bill programmer the studio had churned out with such awesome regularity throughout the thirties and early forties. Allegedly based on a 'secret' file housed in the Immigration Bureau, it told the story (by Ben Bengal, Herbert Kline and Dan Moore) of a World War II veteran (Howard Duff, left) who has been recruited into the US Department of Immigration and Naturalization to help put a stop to the illegal smuggling of aliens into America via Mexico. How he does so provided Joel Malone's screenplay (adapted by Art Cohn) with its red meat, and involved glamorous Marta Toren as an unwilling associate of the criminals wanted by the Bureau and the widow of one of Duff's wartime colleagues. Implacably routine, it also featured George Brent as an Inspector, as well as Tom Tully (right), Gar Moore, Paul Stewart (centre) and Richard Rober. Jules Schermer produced, and it was directed to minimal effect by Frederick de Cordova. (84 mins)

△ Yvonne De Carlo played Calamity Jane and Howard Duff (centre) played Sam Bass in **Calamity Jane And Sam Bass**, an outdoor adventure which used Technicolor and Utah to eye-catching effect. The story, however, wasn't up to much, involving, as it did, Duff in a three-way love affair: with Miss De Carlo; with Dorothy Hart (as the sheriff's sister, 2nd left) and with his racing mare – the loss of the latter and his killing of a man in self-defence turning him into an outlaw. Willard Parker (left) was cast as the sheriff in Maurice Geraghty and Melvin Levy's screenplay, with other parts in it for Norman Lloyd, Ann Doran (in bonnet), Lloyd Bridges (on horse), Marc Lawrence, Houseley Stevenson and Milburn Stone. The director was George Sherman, who also supplied the original story. (83 mins)

▽ **The Gal Who Took The West** traded in anti-climaxes as three old timers each gave their version (via flashback) to a contemporary newspaperman (James Todd) of a bitter feud between two cousins (Scott Brady and John Russell, right) who, for no apparent reason, hated each other's guts. Yvonne De Carlo (left) top-starred as a singer, in which guise she rendered the traditional ballad 'Frankie and Johnny'; Clem Bevans, Houseley Stevenson and Russell Simpson were the old timers who remembered it well, with other roles in Robert Arthur's Technicolor production going to Charles Coburn, Myrna Dell, James Millican, Bob Stevenson and Robert Short. Frederick de Cordova directed it, and the screenplay, which half-heartedly attempted to lampoon the genre, was by William Bowers and Oscar Brodney. (84 mins)

▷ More *film noir* from director Robert Siodmak in **Criss Cross**, an often violent melodrama, whose tragic inevitability was signposted very early on in the film when Burt Lancaster (top-starred), as an honest armoured-truck guard is found in a compromising situation with Yvonne De Carlo, his former wife, by gangster Dan Duryea, her present husband. Lying to Duryea that he and De Carlo were discussing the possibilities of pulling off a hold-up on the armoured truck, Lancaster has little choice but to make good his lie – and does so with tragic consequences. Daniel Fuchs' talky screenplay (from a novel by Don Tracy) brought nothing new to the situation, and it was left entirely to Siodmak, who was in his element with such material, to steer it to an exciting, albeit bleak climax. Lancaster (right) and Duryea (centre left) were their usual charismatic selves, Miss De Carlo (left) somewhat less so in an otherwise welcome change of pace for her. The rest of the cast included Stephen McNally (as a cop), Richard Long, Tom Pedi (centre) and Alan Napier. The producer was Michael Kraike. (87 mins)

△ First seen as subsidiary characters in *The Egg And I* (1947), Percy Kilbride (left) and Marjorie Main (right) were given star status in **Ma And Pa Kettle**, a comedy which sophisticates avoided like the plague but which found unqualified and enthusiastic response in outback communities everywhere. Kilbride played an indigent father of fifteen kids who, just as he and his family are about to be evicted from their run-down abode, finds alternative accommodation in a home equipped with every modern convenience when a slogan he has written for a tobacco contest wins first prize. Herbert Margolis, Louis Morheim and Al Lewis' screenplay (based on characters created by Betty MacDonald) complicated matters by having the town's jealous busybody (Esther Dale) claiming that the winning slogan wasn't original, an assertion vehemently disproved by magazine writer Meg Randall, who also provided the yarn with a touch of romance by marrying Richard Long, the Kettle's eldest son. Charles Lamont directed it broadly; it was produced by Leon Goldstein, and featured Patricia Alphin, Barry Kelley, Harry Antrim and Ida Moore. (76 mins)

▽ June Havoc (left) was the only point of interest in a dreary prison melodrama called **The Story Of Molly X**. As the Molly X of the title, she lands herself in the jug for theft involving her gang-leader husband and, in less than an hour and a half of screen time, becomes a reformed woman, even confessing to a murder she did not commit. Both the script and the direction (by Crane Wilbur) left much to be desired; so did the supporting performances of a barely adequate cast that included handsome John Russell (right) as a thug, Dorothy Hart, Connie Gilchrist and Cathy Lewis. The producer was Aaron Rosenberg, whose film also made a vague statement about the problems women criminals face in readjusting to civilian life. (82 mins)

▷ Robert Cummings (left) starred in **Free For All**, playing an inventor from Ohio who, having found a way of turning water into gasoline, travels to Washington in an attempt to patent his invention. But there's many a slip etc, which he discovers to his cost when he crosses swords with the head (Ray Collins) of an oil company. An unexpected romance with Ann Blyth (right), the daughter of a patent-office worker (Percy Kilbride), himself an inventor, further complicated matters and helped flesh out producer Robert Buckner's screenplay (from a story by Herbert Clyde Lewis) which found parts for Donald Woods, Mikhail Rasumny, Percy Helton, Harry Antrim, Wallis Clark, Dooley Wilson. The director was Charles T. Barton who kept it as lively as the commonplace material allowed (83 mins)

△ Barbara Stanwyck (right) emoted to great effect in **The Lady Gambles** – an entertaining load of old codswallop in which she played a happily married woman who, on a trip to Las Vegas with her journalist husband (Robert Preston), makes the fatal mistake of spending time at the roulette table. Before you could say Universal-International she was as addicted to the wheel (as well as playing cards and dice) as Ray Milland was to alcohol in *The Lost Weekend* (Paramount, 1945). In fact, she becomes so possessed by the gambling bug that she recklessly spends all her husband's money, hocks his camera, lies about her movements and, after being sent packing, takes up employment as a gambling-house manageress, from whence it is only a short distance to a psychopaths' ward, via the gutter. Roy Huggins' screenplay (from an adaptation by Halsted Welles of a story by Lewis Meltzer and Oscar Saul) copped out with the perfunctory happy ending in which husband and wife are reconciled, thus underlining the basic speciousness of the whole enterprise. Still, Stanwyck devotees (and there were many) had a ball watching the star suffer so harrowingly in the name of art. Stephen McNally, Peter Leeds (left), Edith Barrett and John Hoyt (and, in a bit part Anthony (Tony) Curtis) were also cast for producer Michael Kraike; and it was directed for maximum shock effect by Michael Gordon. (98 mins)

△ Objectivity was hardly the purpose of producer Robert Buckner's pro-Jewish screenplay for **Sword In The Desert**, Hollywood's first attempt to deal with the sensitive subject of the Palestinian war. A fictional story (which hardly mentioned the Arab involvement in the conflict at all), it featured Dana Andrews as an American sea captain of a freighter carrying a group of displaced persons to Palestine, and Marta Toren (centre) as a Jewish broadcaster who uses an underground radio to lash out at the British responsible for making life so difficult for her people. Clearly, there was no question where one's sympathies were meant to lie, and the result was a highly emotional, often exciting, but intellectually simplistic exercise which offended as many people as it moved. Jeff Chandler played an Israeli rebel leader (and landed himself an exclusive seven-year contract for his efforts), with other parts under George Sherman's partisan direction going to Stephen McNally (as Toren's boyfriend), Philip Friend, Hugh French, Stanley Logan (right), Liam Redmond, Hayden Rorke (2nd right) and Lowell Gilmore. (100 mins)

△ Much of **Undertow** was filmed on location in Chicago, which lent a certain verisimilitude to what otherwise would have been a thriller of even less consequence than it was. A 'B' picture with a cast to match, it starred Scott Brady as an ex-gambler whose intentions, after leaving military service, to manage a mountain lodge, are interrupted when, on a trip to Chicago to collect his fiancée (Dorothy Hart), he finds himself framed for murder. Taking refuge in the apartment of Peggy Dow, whom he has met on the plane en route to the windy city, he sets out (with Miss Dow's assistance and the help of a police buddy) to bring the real culprit to justice. His sleuthing revealed that it was his fiancée, in cahoots with John Russell, an erstwhile chum, who was responsible for the frame-up. Rock Hudson (left), Bruce Bennett (right), Gregg Martell, Robert Anderson and Ann Pearce were in it too; Arthur T. Horman and Lee Loeb were guilty of writing the screenplay (story by Horman), and it was directed for producer Ralph Dietrich by William Castle, with none of the latter's customary 'B' picture panache. (70 mins)

▷ A musical campus caper of minimal entertainment value, **Yes Sir, That's My Baby** featured Charles Coburn (illustrated), Donald O'Connor and Gloria De Haven as the central characters at a college for war veterans who are finishing their education. Oscar Brodney's unfunny screenplay concerned itself with biology professor Coburn's efforts to form a football team in the face of hostility from the students' wives who, understandably, prefer their hubbies to stay home. Coburn's job is threatened by his imminent failure to achieve his aim in time for an important match, so the wives give in. End of conflict. George Sherman directed it, and Leonard Goldstein produced (in Technicolor) casting Barbara Brown, Joshua Shelley, Jack Lambert, Jack Overman, George Spaulding, Michael Dugan and June Fulton in supporting roles. Songs and musical numbers: 'Yes Sir, That's My Baby' Gus Kahn, Walter Donaldson; 'Men Are Little Children', 'They've Never Figured Out A Woman', 'Look At Me' Jack Brooks, Walter Scharf. (82 mins)

▽ The debonair William Powell (left) returned to sleuthing in **Take One False Step**, a blatant melodrama which uneasily mixed the frivolous and the not-so-frivolous. He played a staid, married college professor whose composure is ruffled with the appearance of Shelley Winters, an old flame who talks him into taking her out for the evening, then thoughtlessly disappears. All the evidence points to murder, and before the police can discover his liaison with Miss Winters (news of which would surely upset the strait-laced philanthropist he's hoping to woo in connection with a new university) he sets out, on a journey from Los Angeles to San Francisco, to clear up the matter himself. A rather unpleasant and ferocious fight with a police dog, as well as a not-for-the-squeamish death of a man who falls under the wheel of a train, detracted somewhat from the intended lightness of the subject matter, and gave the enterprise a decidedly schizophrenic quality. Blame this on Chester Erskine who, with Jack Hively, produced; and on Irwin Shaw who, based on the novel *Night Call* which he wrote with his brother David, scripted as well as directed. The cast included Marsha Hunt (right), Dorothy Hart (as Powell's wife), James Gleason, Felix Bressart, Art Baker, Sheldon Leonard, Howard Freeman and Jess Barker. (94 mins)

▽ **You Gotta Stay Happy**, a hare-brained romantic comedy which disappeared from memory two minutes after it was over, needed all the help it could get from Joan Fontaine (top-starred) who, in a dramatic change of pace from her cavortings in *Kiss The Blood Off My Hands* the previous year, turned her talents to comedy. Though hardly ideal casting as a bride who deserts her stuffed-shirt husband on their wedding day, she, in turn, needed all the help *she* could get from co-star James Stewart as a likeable ex-Army pilot whom she persuades to take her to California. Stewart (left) delivered the goods (and the lines) in his usual appealing way, falling in love with Miss Fontaine (centre) after his plane crashes on an Oklahoma farm owned by Percy Kilbride. H.C. Potter's direction made the most of producer Karl Tunberg's screenplay (based on a *Saturday Evening Post* serial by Robert Carson), and ably steered a cast that included Eddie Albert (right, as Stewart's flier buddy), Roland Young, Willard Parker (the deserted groom), Marcy McGuire, Arthur Walsh, William Bakewell and Paul Cavanagh through their comic paces. It was a Rampart-William Dozier Production. (100 mins)

1950

▽ Because producers Milton H. Bren and William A. Seiter (the latter also directing) couldn't make up their minds whether they wanted the aptly titled **Borderline** to be a comedy or a melodrama, Devery Freeman's screenplay veered uneasily between the borderline of one and the borderline of the other. The result was a hodge-podge that left audiences thoroughly confused. All about a narcotics racket, it featured Claire Trevor (centre left) as a Los Angeles policewoman who, disguised as a blowsy chorus girl, sets off, on behalf of the Federal Narcotics Bureau, to track down the Mr Big of the operation. She doesn't get very far before she makes the acquaintance of top-starred Fred MacMurray (centre right), pretending to be a rival gangster, but really an undercover agent also out to find the ringleader. Naturally, they fall in love, although unaware of each other's real identity. Raymond Burr played one of the genuine heavies, with other roles going to Roy Roberts, José Torvay, Morris Ankrum, Lita Baron (left) and Nacho Galindo (right). (88 mins)

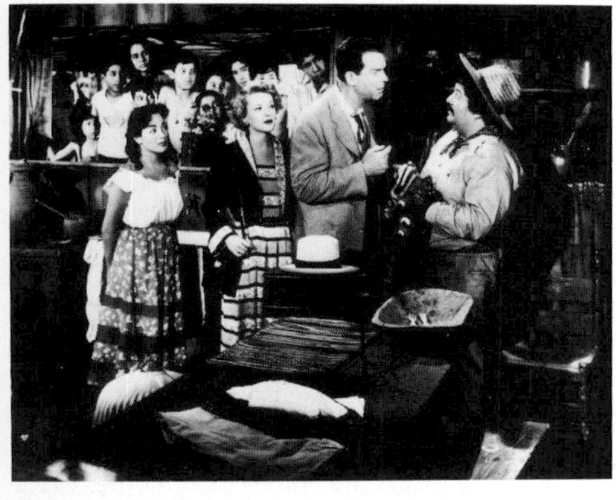

▽ In **Abbott And Costello In The Foreign Legion**, their 25th screen adventure, the fat man and the thin plodded through John Grant, Martin Ragaway and Leonard Stern's screenplay (story by D.D. Beauchamp) searching not only for laughs, but an Arab wrestler – all the way from Brooklyn to the Sahara. How the team unintentionally finish up in the Foreign Legion, and become involved with the likes of Patricia Medina, as an exotic undercover agent, Walter Slezak as a legionnaire, and Douglass Dumbrille as Sheikh Hamus El Khalid, was what the picture was all about. Apart from a sequence in which Costello (illustrated) finds himself the unwilling participant in a slave auction by inadvertently waving his hands at one of the girls; and one in which he and his partner become afflicted by mirages, the humour was sorely rationed. Charles Lamont directed, and Robert Arthur produced. (79 mins)

△ Donald O'Connor over-acted outrageously in **Curtain Call At Cactus Creek**, a comedy western with songs, set during the thud-and-blunder days of the Western frontier. He played a stage manager of an impoverished troupe of touring players who yearns to act. Instead, he single-handedly captures bank robber Walter Brennan. Gale Storm provided O'Connor (illustrated) with some romance (and sang 'Be My Little Baby Bumble Bee' by Stanley Murphy and Henry I. Marshall); Eve Arden was featured as a musical comedy star way past her prime (and sang 'Waiting At The Church' by Henry Pether and F.W. Leigh), with other roles going to Vincent Price as a has-been actor, Chick Chandler, Joe Sawyer and Harry Shannon. Howard Dimsdale Scripted from a story he wrote with Stanley Roberts, the at times over-zealous direction was by Charles Lamont, and it was produced, in Technicolor, by Robert Arthur. (86 mins)

▽ Yvonne De Carlo was the **Buccaneer's Girl** and heroine of producer Robert Arthur's rollicking Technicolor pirate romp, with every cliché in the well-worn genre tumbling out of Harold Shumate and Joseph Hoffman's corny screenplay (story by Joe May and Samuel R. Golding) with reckless abandon. Miss De Carlo (centre) played an itinerant entertainer from Boston who, after stowing away on a ship that is scuttled by the notorious pirate Frederic Baptiste (Philip Friend, left), manages to make her way to New Orleans, where she soon becomes romantically involved with the brigand who, it transpires, is a Robin Hood at heart, practising his piracy only on the ruthless shipowner (Robert Douglas) responsible for ruining his father, and donating the spoils to a seamen's fund. Elsa Lanchester played the proprietor of a school for 'genteel' entertainers, with other parts under Frederick de Cordova's guidance going to Norman Lloyd, Andrea King, Jay C. Flippen (right), Henry Daniell, Douglass Dumbrille and Verna Felton. (77 mins)

▽ More comedy backwoods-style from the Kettles in **Ma And Pa Kettle Go To Town**, the town in question being New York where they meet a gangster on the lam, for whom they agree to deliver stolen money to one of his mobster pals. Pa loses the money and, by so doing, incurs the wrath of its would-be recipient who thinks the old boy is up to something fishy. Percy Kilbride and Marjorie Main (both illustrated) were, as usual, Ma and Pa, Richard Long and Meg Randall son and daughter-in-law, with Charles McGraw and Gregg Martell as the heavies. Also cast: Jim Backus, Kathryn Givney and Elliott Lewis. Martin Ragaway and Leonard Stern wrote it, Leonard Goldstein produced, and Charles Lamont directed. (79 mins)

▷ Shoplifting, and how to do it, was the subject of **I Was A Shoplifter**, a woebegone melodrama whose story and screenplay by Irwin Gielgud had beautiful Mona Freeman (right) being blackmailed into becoming a member of a shoplifting gang, and Scott Brady (top-starred, left) as a detective who eventually rescues her and nails the culprits. Andrea King (in a role originally offered to Alexis Smith, who refused it and went on suspension for her recalcitrance), played the gang's scheming leader, with other roles under Charles Lamont's exasperatingly routine direction going to Anthony (Tony) Curtis, Charles Drake, Gregg Martell, Robert Gist, Larry Keating and, in a bit part, Rock Hudson. Leonard Goldstein produced. (82 mins)

◁ Persia a thousand years ago provided the exotic setting for **The Desert Hawk**, more period escapism (in glowing Technicolor) with Yvonne De Carlo doing her best to obliterate comparisons with Maria Montez, as the Princess Scheherazade, and Richard Greene, as the hero Omar, trying to live up to the brave exploits of his predecessor, Jon Hall. Greene (illustrated) played a blacksmith who swaps his anvil for a sword in order to rid his people of the cruel Prince Murad (George Macready), in the course of which he tricks an unwilling Miss De Carlo into marriage before going on to win her heart legitimately. It was mindless to a fault, and far better to look at, with its abundance of semi-clad harem lovelies and luscious studio-built sets, than to listen to. The supporting cast featured Rock Hudson, Carl Esmond, Jackie Gleason (as Aladdin) and Joe Besser (as Sinbad), as well as Anne Pearce, Marc Lawrence, Lois Andrews and Frank Puglia. It was written by Aubrey Wisberg, Jack Pollexfen and Gerald Drayson Adams, directed by Frederick de Cordova, and produced by Leonard Goldstein. (77 mins)

▽ The first in a series of such offerings, **Francis** was a huge money-spinner for the studio. All about the havoc caused by a talking mule (called Francis) in the Burma Command, it was dedicated to the belief that a four-legged creature is far superior to most army personnel, and proved its point through a screenplay by David Stern (from his own novel) that had its fair share of belly-laughs. However, by the law of diminishing returns, it tended to run out of steam towards the end. Though the loquacious quadruped was the undoubted hero of the enterprise, the film top-starred Donald O'Connor (right) as a newly-commissioned lieutenant who is rescued by Francis (left) while lost behind enemy lines. The plot had O'Connor spending quite a bit of time in the booby hatch because of his who-would-believe-it? encounters with the mule (in which he is fed top-secret information), and generally overworked what was a one-joke situation. Patricia Medina was a spy, ZaSu Pitts (welcome back ZaSu!) was wasted as a nurse, and Eduard Franz and Howland Chamberlin were in it too; the director was Arthur Lubin and it was produced by Robert Arthur who, in a moment of inspiration, chose Chill Wills to supply Francis' voice. (91 mins)

▷ Though the combined ages of Spring Byington, Edmund Gwenn and Charles Coburn were just this side of two hundred, **Louisa**, the comedy whose presence they graced, was a young-in-heart delight dedicated to the dictum that life begins at sixty – or even seventy. It was the genial, heart-warming story of a grandmother (Byington, right) who, after moving in with her son (Ronald Reagan) and his family, finds that she is the recipient of romantic compliments from grocer Gwenn, and also from Mr Coburn (left), her son's boss. In the end, the grocer wins. Ruth Hussey was cast as Reagan's wife, with the younger generation represented by Piper Laurie and Jimmy Hunt as Miss Byington's grandchildren, and Scotty Beckett as Miss Laurie's teenage suitor. Stanley Roberts provided a screenplay mercifully free of sentimentality, as was Alexander Hall's direction; it was produced by Robert Arthur, whose modest, low-budget little film provided a happily disproportionate amount of pleasure. (89 mins)

▽ A treadmill melodrama, written by George W. George and George F. Slavin (story by Ralph Dietrich), directed by Douglas Sirk, and starring Macdonald Carey, **Mystery Submarine** offered, as entertainment, the dated story of a renegade submarine commander (Robert Douglas, illustrated) who kidnaps a German scientist (Ludwig Donath) for an unspecified enemy power. Carey (illustrated in headphones) was the hero of the piece and, posing as a German medical officer, he rescues the kidnapped scientist and helps bring about the destruction of the Nazi sub. Marta Toren was also in it; so were Carl Esmond, Jacqueline Daly Hilliard and Fred Nurney. The producer was Ralph Dietrich. (78 mins)

△ **Deported**, filmed in Italy, was little more than a pallid excuse on behalf of producer Robert Buckner (who also scripted from a story by Lionel Shapiro) to use up some of the studio's frozen European assets. A corny gangster melodrama with Jeff Chandler (right) as an Italian-born mobster deported to Italy after serving a five-year jail sentence for stealing $100,000, it revolved around the deportee's romance with countess Marta Toren, under whose influence he is regenerated, despite some initial attempts on his behalf to regain the stolen swag. Claude Dauphin was featured as an Italian detective, with other members of the largely foreign company comprising Marina Berti, Silvio Minciotti, Carlo Rizzo, Mimi Aguglia and Adriano Ambrogi. American Richard Hober completed the cast as Chandler's ex-partner. Robert Siodmak, who directed, added nothing to his distinguished track record with this one. (88 mins)

▽ **One Way Street** was pretentious twaddle that led nowhere at all. It starred James Mason (right) as a not-so-good doctor involved with a gang of hoods who have just knocked off a bank for $200,000. Making off to Mexico with the loot (as well as with Marta Toren, left, girlfriend of gang chief Dan Duryea), Mason settles down to a quiet life south of the border and, in the process of regeneration, opens a medical practice of sorts for the benefit of ailing natives and their pets. The climax has him returning the money to the villains who planned the heist, then being knocked over by a car for his trouble. The picture, which also featured William Conrad, King Donovan, Jack Elam and several Mexican actors, had nothing going for it and unceremoniously disappeared from circulation shortly after its release. Lawrence Kimble wrote it, Hugo Fregonese directed, and the producer was Leonard Goldstein. (79 mins)

▷ **Kansas Raiders** was an impuissant little sagebrush saga that made no impact whatsoever, despite a cast of characters which included such notorious outlaws as Jesse James (Audie Murphy, left), Quantrell (Brian Donlevy), Kit Dalton (Tony Curtis, right) and the Younger Brothers (James Best and Dewey Martin). As scripted by Robert L. Richards, it was simply a collection of raids and chases instigated by Quantrell's boys – the most dramatic being the violent sacking of Lawrence, Kansas. It ended with Quantrell being gunned down by Union Forces under Richard Arlen (welcome back Richard!), with James *et al* going their separate ways, the details of which the cinema has, over the years, chronicled on many more auspicious occasions than this. Marguerite Chapman, Scott Brady and John Kellogg completed the cast. Ray Enright directed, and Ted Richmond produced, in Technicolor. (80 mins)

▽ A take-it-or-leave-it farce (discriminating audiences left it) with a handful of indifferent songs, **The Milkman** paired Donald O'Connor (top-billed) with the great Jimmy Durante in what, on paper, must have seemed like a cute idea, but which left its laughter behind on the drawing board. O'Connor (right) played the idiotic war-veteran son of a wealthy milk company owner, who is given a job by a rival milk firm where Mr Durante (left) is employed. How O'Connor (whose over-the-top conniptions were allowed to go unchecked by director Charles T. Barton) almost puts the kaibosh on long-service deliveryman Durante's imminent retirement plans (and helps round up a gang of blackmailing gamblers in the process), formed the painful-to-behold content of the screenplay wrought by Albert Beich, James O'Hanlon, Martin Ragaway and Leonard Stern (story by Ragaway and Stern). The rest of the cast included Joyce Holden, William Conrad, Piper Laurie, Henry O'Neill, Elisabeth Risdon and Jess Barker. The producer was Ted Richmond. Songs: 'Nobody Wants My Money', 'That's My Boy', 'It's Bigger Than Both Of Us', 'Early Morning Song' Sammy Fain, Jackie Barnett. (86 mins)

◁ Set just after the Civil War, when the railroad made its bid for supremacy over the pony express, **Wyoming Mail** was a formula western which benefitted considerably from Russell Metty's Technicolor photography, and from the virile presence of top-cast Stephen McNally (right) as a postal inspector who, pretending to be a bank robber, pulls an escape from a territorial prison in order to fall in with a gang of train thieves and then expose them to the authorities. Alexis Smith (left), second-billed as a saloon-singer (and a contact between crooked railway official Roy Roberts and the robbers), provided the romantic interest and, even after McNally's deception is revealed, she sticks by him; with other parts going to Howard da Silva (as Roberts' chief henchman), Ed Begley (a prison warden), and Dan Riss, Whit Bissell, James Arness, Armando Silvestre, Richard Jaeckel and Frankie Darro. Harry Essex and Leonard Lee scripted from a story by Robert Hardy Andrews, and it was directed by Reginald LeBorg for producer Aubrey Schenck. (87 mins)

△ Audiences gasped at the beauty of Lincoln County in New Mexico, the picturesque setting for **The Kid From Texas**, but yawned at its familiar plot which found Audie Murphy hell-bent on vengeance when his cattle-baron benefactor (Shepperd Strudwick) is cold-bloodedly felled by hired gunmen. The final death count, as Murphy (left) becomes the victim of a massive manhunt, is 21. Frank Wilcox appeared as Sheriff Pat Garrett (the man responsible for putting an end to the killings), with other roles under Kurt Neuman's bang-bang-you're-dead direction going to Gale Storm (right), Albert Dekker (as the villain), Will Geer and William Talman. Robert Hardy Andrews and Karl Kamb wrote it from a story by Andrews, and it was produced by Paul Short in Technicolor. (78 mins)

△ Cloak-and-dagger melodrama of mediocre vintage could be sampled in **Spy Hunt**, in which a vital (isn't it always?) piece of microfilm showing details of a political assassination is being smuggled out of Europe in the collar of a black panther. How enemy agents attempt to prevent the microfilm from reaching its destination at Lake Success, formed the witless content of George Zuckerman and Leonard Lee's fanciful screenplay (based on Victor Canning's *Panther Moon*), and offered parts to Marta Toren as a British agent in Italy, Howard Duff (top-starred, left) as the courier in charge of the panther, and Philip Friend (centre), Philip Dorn, Robert Douglas as a trio of enemy agents. Also cast: Walter Slezak, Kurt Kreuger (right) and Aram Katcher. George Sherman's direction could safely be described as plodding; and the production was in the hands of Ralph Dietrich. (74 mins)

△ **Sierra** (a remake of *Forbidden Valley*, 1937) was worth its weight in manure. A really lousy western which top-starred a miscast Wanda Hendrix (left) and a second-billed Audie Murphy (real-life Mr and Mrs for a while), its only asset was Russell Metty's Technicolor photography. Basically the story of a pair of fugitives from justice (Murphy, right, and his father, Dean Jagger, centre) who, in the final reel, relinquish their hiding place in the hills when the dying member of a posse reveals that it is he who was guilty of the crime Jagger has been accused of, it offered the usual rag-bag collection of clichés in lieu of a decent script. Burl Ives was co-starred as a prospector called Lonesome (and sang six songs in that monotonous way of his), with other roles under Alfred E. Green's direction going to Richard Rober, Anthony (Tony) Curtis, Houseley Stevenson, Elisabeth Risdon and Sara Allgood. Edna Anhalt scripted it from a novel by Stuart Hardy, with additional dialogue supplied by Milton Gunzburg. The producer was Michael Kraike. (83 mins)

△ Not since Shakespeare's Iago had there been so irredeemable a character as newspaper photographer Jack Early, the blacker-than-black protagonist of **Shakedown**. And as played (extremely well) by Howard Duff, his machinations had the clarion call of credibility about them. Which was more than could be claimed for the melodramatic plot that Alfred Lewis Levitt and Martin Goldsmith shaped from Nat Dallinger's story. Basically concerned with Duff's ruthless manipulation and enemy-making techniques as he sets out to scale the heights of his profession, the main plot hinged on his working in league with a racketeer to expose a rival who he has photographed in the very act of a holdup. He then uses the evidence as depicted in the photo to blackmail the hood into handing over a substantial portion of the booty. Production Code requirements assured audiences of Duff's eventual downfall, but even as he is being murdered, the photographer manages to snap his killer. No fool he. Peggy Dow (right) was a photographic editor whom Duff (left) uses to better his position, with other parts going to Brian Donlevy and Lawrence Tierney (as gangsters), Anne Vernon, Stapleton Kent, Peter Virgo and Charles Sherlock. It was a Ted Richmond production directed by Joseph Pevney. (80 mins)

▽ **Peggy** set out to be nothing more than an amiable, family-orientated comedy and, on its own modest terms, succeeded admirably. Produced in Technicolor by Ralph Dietrich, and set against the colourful Tournament of Roses in Pasadena (with actual newsreel footage of the event skilfully interspersed), the film concerned a retired Ohio professor (Charles Coburn) and his two pretty daughters (Diana Lynn and Barbara Lawrence) who move to Pasadena. The only conflict to be found in George F. Slavin and George W. George's screenplay (story by Leon Ware) was whether Miss Lynn (left), as the eponymous heroine, should tell her dyspeptic father that she is secretly married to Rock Hudson (right), a fullback at Ohio State, whom he positively loathes. Adding to the slight complication is the fact that as a married woman she is automatically ineligible for the Queen of the Rose Tournament. Clearly the decision she arrived at was the correct one, for audiences and critics alike gave the film the thumbs up. Charlotte Greenwood was delightfully cast as a widowed neighbour who successfully sets her sights on crusty old Coburn, Charles Drake was her son, and Connie Gilchrist scored in a small part as a nurse. Also: Jerome Cowan, Ann Pearce and Charles Trowbridge. Adroitly juggling all the elements was director Frederick de Cordova. (77 mins)

▽ Described as 'one of the strangest stories ever told', **Outside The Wall** was, in truth, one of the most frequent stories ever told – being the misadventures of an ex-con (Richard Basehart, left) who, after spending 15 years in the Pennsy penitentiary near Philadelphia (the film's setting), is released, attempts to go straight, but finds the road to good intentions paved with obstacles – particularly in the shape of Marilyn Maxwell, a blonde nurse with a penchant for everything money can buy. Basehart's subsequent skirmishes with a gang of hoods, his romantic involvement with the grasping Miss Maxwell, and his eventual regeneration by Dorothy Hart (right), a nurse who helps him turn down a million in order to become a lawful citizen – were the ho-hum ingredients of director Crane Wilbur's stale screenplay (story by Henry Edward Helseth). Signe Hasso (as a gangster's wife), Joseph Pevney, John Hoyt, Henry Morgan, Lloyd Gough and Mickey Knox completed the cast for producer Aaron Rosenberg. (80 mins)

△ As its title betrayed, **Comanche Territory** was a western – but not, alas, one with a difference. On the contrary, it was a protracted passel of platitudes which top-starred Maureen O'Hara (left) as the tough proprietress of a saloon in Crooked Tongue, and co-starred Macdonald Carey (right) as frontiersman James Bowie (inventor of the Bowie knife) who, in the course of Oscar Brodney and Lewis Meltzer's screenplay (story by Meltzer) is totally on the side of the much maligned redskins, protecting them from such unscrupulous silver prospectors as Charles Drake, Miss O'Hara's greedy brother. There was no doubt that blazing Technicolor helped Leonard Goldstein's modest production along, the scenic landscapes and the leading lady's fiery good looks being the two best things in the show. George Sherman was the nominal director (movies like this tended to direct themselves), and the cast included Will Geer (as a politico), Pedro De Cordoba, Ian MacDonald and Rick Vallin. (76 mins)

▷ Though crime doesn't pay, it can provide gripping entertainment, as was demonstrated in **Woman On The Run**, a modestly budgeted melodrama produced by Howard Welsch for Fidelity Productions, and with a deglamorised Ann Sheridan (right) heading the cast. Ross Elliott played her artist husband and the sole witness to a gangland killing who, rather than become involved, disappears, leaving his wife to track him down. She undertakes the task only when she learns that he is suffering from a heart disease, and realises that she loves him more than she thought. Accompanying her on her search is newspaperman Dennis O'Keefe who, as it turns out in Alan Campbell and director Norman Foster's tightly-written screenplay, is the murderer Elliott witnessed in action. Though the cast also included Robert Keith (left), Frank Jenks, John Qualen, J. Farrell McDonald and Thomas P. Dillon, they were all upstaged by San Francisco, the film's setting, which was given star treatment by photographer Hal Mohr. (77 mins)

▽ Bellevue Hospital was the real-life setting for **The Sleeping City**, though a preface spoken by Richard Conte made it quite clear that the shady goings-on within that venerable institution were purely fictitious. What those goings-on amounted to were the murder of one interne and the suicide of another, both of whom, to supplement their incomes, stole narcotics which they then sold to pay off gambling debts. Conte (right) was top-starred as a member of the police squad planted in the hospital as an interne in order to find out who's doing what to whom; Coleen Gray (left), second-billed, was a nurse who finds herself snared into illegal drug trafficking. The rest of the cast mainly comprised Broadway stage actors (all of them displaying a tendency to overact) and included Richard Taber as an elderly elevator operator (and key man in the whole affair), Alex Nicol (as the young suicide) and John Alexander. Peggy Dow was also in it, but if you blinked, you missed her. Jo Eisinger's screenplay could have made much better use of Bellevue than it did; ditto George Sherman's direction which, after its documentary-style opening sequences, lapsed into pure crime-fiction melodrama. The producer was Leonard Goldstein. (85 mins)

▷ The **Woman In Hiding** was Ida Lupino, and she was hiding from Stephen McNally, her homicidal husband of one day who, on their honeymoon, is out to kill her – or, at best, have her committed as insane. The reason for this shocking state of affairs was told via flashback and it turns out that McNally (right) married Lupino (left) only to get his avaricious hands on the mill she owns. The frightened bride is ultimately rescued from her appalling predicament by sturdy Howard Duff (Ida's real-life husband), an ex-GI. Peggy Dow was featured as McNally's girlfriend, with John Litel, Taylor Holmes, Irving Bacon, Joe Besser and Don Beddoe completing the cast for producer Michael Kraike. It was a gripping melodrama, written by Oscar Segal from a *Saturday Evening Post* serial called *Fugitive From Terror* by James R. Webb, and directed at a nail-biting pace by Michael Gordon. The acting throughout was first-class. (92 mins)

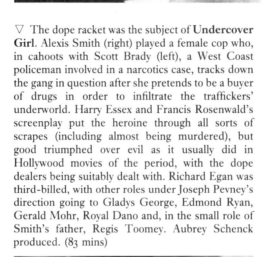

▽ The dope racket was the subject of **Undercover Girl**. Alexis Smith (right) played a female cop who, in cahoots with Scott Brady (left), a West Coast policeman involved in a narcotics case, tracks down the gang in question after she pretends to be a buyer of drugs in order to infiltrate the traffickers' underworld. Harry Essex and Francis Rosenwald's screenplay put the heroine through all sorts of scrapes (including almost being murdered), but good triumphed over evil as it usually did in Hollywood movies of the period, with the dope dealers being suitably dealt with. Richard Egan was third-billed, with other roles under Joseph Pevney's direction going to Gladys George, Edmond Ryan, Gerald Mohr, Royal Dano and, in the small role of Smith's father, Regis Toomey. Aubrey Schenck produced. (83 mins)

△ **Saddle Tramp** was a family western designed for audiences with a sweet-tooth. It starred Joel McCrea (right) as a happy-go-lucky cowpoke whose carefree existence is curtailed when he inherits a dead friend's four offspring. His responsibilities are augmented with the arrival on the scene of Wanda Hendrix, who has run away from a cruel uncle. How McCrea copes with his newly acquired family and, at the same time, settles a ranch feud between his employer and a neighbour, formed the world-shattering content of Harold Shumate's screenplay. John McIntire and Antonio Moreno showed up as the rival ranchers, John Russell (centre) was the foreman whose crooked ways caused the feud in the first place, with other parts going to Jimmy Hunt, Orley Lindgren, Gordon Gebert and Gregory Moffett as McCrea's adopted offspring; as well as to Ed Begley, Paul Picerni (left), Jeanette Nolan (Mrs John McIntire in real life) and Russell Simpson. Blame the tedium on producer Leonard Goldstein and director Hugo Fregonese. It was photographed in Technicolor. (76 mins)

▽ **Winchester '73**, the studio's answer to Warner's *Colt .45* (1950), was an altogether superior western. Though basically little more than an oater which might accurately be summarised as man gets gun, man loses gun, man gets gun, it starred frontiersman James Stewart as the proud possessor of a Winchester model 73 rifle, won in a Dodge City marksmanship contest. It is stolen, however, by his own murderous brother (Stephen McNally, right), whence it passes to an Indian chief, a gun trader, a pair of bank robbers, back to McNally, and, finally, after a showdown on a mountain precipice, into the hands of Stewart (illustrated, with rifle), its rightful owner. None of it was meant to be taken too seriously, and the result was an hour and a half of unfaltering entertainment, niftily scripted by Robert L. Richards and Borden Chase (from a story by Stuart N. Lake), with direction to match by Anthony Mann who, with a cast that also included Shelley Winters as a dancehall girl (and the rifle's only rival for Stewart's affections), Dan Duryea as a trigger-happy cut-throat (what else?), Will Geer as the marshal of Dodge City, John McIntire as a no-good Indian trader, and Jay C. Flippen as a cavalry sergeant, helped turn the picture into one of the year's most enjoyable westerns. Aaron Rosenberg produced. It was remade for TV in 1970. (92 mins)

▷ Shelley Winters (illustrated) as Coral, a cabaret singer, was the **South Sea Sinner** and, under Bruce Humberstone's steamy direction, she emerged as a cross between Mae West and Sadie Thompson. It was difficult to accept anything that occurred in the screenplay Joel Malone and Oscar Brodney fashioned (from the story by Ladislas Fodor and Laszlo Vadnay) without regarding it as a parody, which was clearly not the intention of producer Michael Kraike who, to the detriment of all concerned, took it all far too seriously. MacDonald Carey was top-starred as a world-weary wanderer-cum-beach-bum who fetches up on the small South Sea island of Oraca in the company of doctor Frank Lovejoy. In no time at all he finds himself involved with Miss Winters, much to the chagrin of Luther Adler, the oily proprietor of a waterfront café who sets out to wreck Carey's life. Described by one critic at the time as having about as much South Sea flavour as a roadside papaya bar, the film came and went in a flash, bringing no credit to Helena Carter (as Carey's society-girl fiancée), Art Smith, John Ridgely, James Flavin and, as Miss Winters' pianist, Liberace (left, his screen debut) who got to play a snippet of the Liszt Piano Concerto Number One. Songs: 'It Had To Be You' Gus Kahn, Isham Jones; 'I'm The Lonesomest Gal In Town' Lew Brown, Albert Von Tilzer; 'Blue Lagoon' Frederic Herbert, Arnold Hughes; 'One Man Woman' Jack Brooks, Milton Schwarzwald. (88 mins)

1951

▷ When it actually took to the air, **Air Cadet** held the interest. On land, however, it was deadly dull, telling, as it ploddingly did, the stories of three fledgling pilots training at Randolph Fields, Texas, en route to a jet fighter base at Williams Field, Arizona. Richard Long, Alex Nicol and Robert Arthur were the trainees, with Long attempting to surpass his late brother's war record; Nicol, an ex-sergeant wanting to become a commercial pilot; and Arthur, a spoiled rich kid wanting to do things for himself. They were overseered by top-cast Stephen NcNally as the chief jet instructor who is still neurotically brooding over the fact that he was responsible for sending a lot of men to their deaths. Gail Russell played his wife from whom he is separated, with Charles Drake, Rock Hudson (illustrated), Peggie Castle, James Best and Parley Baer completing the cast. It was directed by Joseph Pevney from a screenplay by Robert L. Richards (story by Richards and Robert Soderberg) with additional dialogue by Joseph Hoffman; and produced by Aaron Rosenberg. (93 mins)

▽ Technicolor, and New Mexico's Carlsbad Caverns, were the best things on offer in **Cave Of Outlaws**, whose story and screenplay (by Elizabeth Wilson) was little more than an extended treasure hunt, with top-starred Macdonald Carey (right) who, having been jailed ten years earlier for robbing a train, returns to the site of the robbery to look for the loot. Seems the gold is hidden somewhere in the Carlsbad caves, and Carey intends to get there before villain Victor Jory (left) does. Alexis Smith (background left) was second-billed as the attractive widow of a small western newspaperman, with other parts in it going to Edgar Buchanan (as a Wells Fargo detective), Hugh O'Brian and Houseley Stevenson. Leonard Goldstein produced, and the director was William Castle. (76 mins)

▽ A very minor entry indeed, **The Raging Tide**, scripted by Ernest K. Gann from his novel *Fiddler's Green*, told the confusing, and uninvolving story of a San Francisco racketeer (Richard Conte) who, after killing a rival hood and unsuccessfully attempting to locate girlfriend Shelley Winters (top-billed, left) on whom he has been relying to provide an alibi, stows away on a small fishing boat run by Charles Bickford and his son Alex Nicol. A plethora of subplots unduly thickened the texture of the narrative, making it all but indigestible, with Conte nobly sacrificing himself to save Nicol's life. An indifferent story, indifferently performed by a cast that also included Stephen McNally (right), John McIntire and Pepito Perez, firmly rooted Aaron Rosenberg's production (directed by George Sherman) in mediocrity. (92 mins)

◁ The final body-count in **Under The Gun** was six, including hero Richard Conte (left). Sent to prison in the South for killing one of his enemies, New Yorker Conte learns that, in the particular prison in which he is serving his sentence, 'trustees' are made to guard other prisoners; and that, should a trustee actually shoot an escaping prisoner, he himself is given his freedom. Being a smart cookie, Conte soon becomes a trustee and, using a bribe of $25,000, sends Sam Jaffe, one of the inmates (who has a starving wife and child) into the woods, whence he takes aim and fells the hapless con instantly. Given his freedom, Conte heads for the border with a determined sheriff (John McIntire) on his tail, and is ultimately killed. George Zuckerman based his screenplay on a story by Daniel B. Ullman; Ted Tetzlaff directed, and the producer was Ralph Dietrich. Also cast: Audrey Totter (right), Shepherd Strudwick, Royal Dano and Richard Taber. (83 mins)

▷ Having met practically everyone else, it was inevitable that Messrs Abbott (left) and Costello (right) would meet the Invisible Man, which they did in the explicitly titled **Abbott And Costello Meet The Invisible Man**. They played a pair of private detectives hired by prizefighter Arthur Franz to clear his name in a murder case. Much of the laughter (though rarely of the abdominal sort) came as a result of Franz injecting himself with invisible-making serum, the highlight being a climactic boxing-ring sequence in which Costello, with help from the Invisible Man (as well as from special effects wizard David S. Horsley), kayoes the champ. Amiable nonsense, it pleased A & C fans enormously, and gave employment to Nancy Guild, Adele Jergens, Sheldon Leonard, William Frawley, Gavin Muir and John Day. It was scripted by Robert Lees, Frederic I. Rinaldo and John Grant from a story by Hugh Wedlock Jr and Howard Snyder ('suggested' by H.G. Wells' *The Invisible Man*). Charles Lamont directed, and it was produced by Howard Christie. (82 mins)

△ **The Lady From Texas** was Josephine Hull, an eccentric Civil War widow (she still believes her missing husband to be alive) whose ranch is in danger of being appropriated by villainous Craig Stevens and his wife Barbara Knudson. They are thwarted, though, by hero Howard Duff (centre), a saddle tramp with a hatred of injustice, and Mona Freeman as a kitchen maid and friend of the put-upon Miss Hull. A courtroom scene, nicely written by scenarists Gerald Drayson Adams and Connie Lee Bennett (story by Harold Shumate), in which Stevens and his wife try to prove the old girl insane, was the highlight of the film, and it gave Miss Hull an opportunity to show just how good an actress she was. Producer Leonard Goldstein's cast, under Joseph Pevney's direction, was completed by Jay C. Flippen (left), Ed Begley and Chris-Pin Martin. (78 mins)

▽ Just as spoilt rich-kid Freddie Bartholomew was, with the help of Spencer Tracy, regenerated on a fishing vessel in MGM's memorable tearjerker *Captains Courageous* (1937), so young Dean Stockwell (right), whose disposition at the start of **Cattle Drive** was similar to Master Bartholomew's, underwent a complete change of personality after being inadvertently left in the care of cowpoke Joel McCrea (left) after the train his railroad magnate father (Leon Ames) is travelling in, leaves without him. Pleasant family entertainment, in Technicolor, and with a cast that also included Chill Wills, Henry Brandon, Howard Petrie and Bob Steele, it made no indelible impression on the imagination of the movie-going public, but was a well produced (by Aaron Rosenberg), nicely written (by Jack Natteford and Lillie Hayward) and competently directed (by Kurt Neumann) family western. (77 mins)

△ **Comin' Round The Mountain**, in which Robert Lees and Frederick I. Rinaldo's screenplay provided a treasure hunt for Bud Abbott and Lou Costello (2nd left), was a compendium of stale situations. A too-often repeated gag about a love potion, and some overdone family feuding between two clans in hillbilly country, propped up A & C's search for the gold (successful, of course), as did a constant supply of songs warbled by Dorothy Shay. Kirby Grant, Joe Sawyer, Guy Wilkerson (2nd right), Glenn Strange (left), Ida Moore (centre) and Shaye Cogan were in it, too, for producer Howard Christie and director Charles Lamont. Songs included: 'You Broke Your Promise' George Wyle, Irving Taylor, Eddie Pola; 'Agnes Clung' Hessie Smith, Dorothy Shay; 'Why Don't Someone Marry Mary Ann?' Wilbur Beatty, Britt Wood; 'Sagebrush Sadie' Britt Wood. (76 mins)

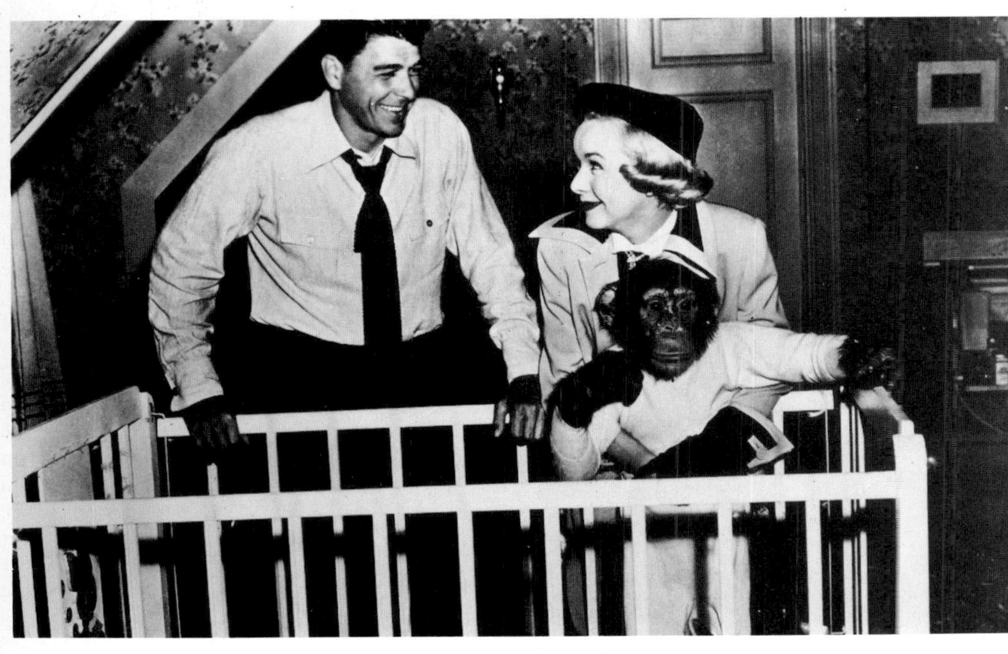

◁ **Bedtime For Bonzo** was the one in which the future president of the US played a psychology professor who takes a chimpanzee (Bonzo) into his home to raise as he would a child, in order to prove his theory that it is not heredity, but environment that shapes and moulds one's personality and character. Though it offered only a few chuckles at the time (particularly a sequence in which Bonzo takes on a vacuum cleaner), because of Ronald Reagan's starring performance, it has today become something of a cult film, despite (or because of!) the fact that Bonzo upstages the future president something shameful in every scene they share. Diana Lynn (right) was second-billed as a farmgirl who finds domestic employment with Reagan (left), and who, in the course of Val Burton and Lou Breslow's screenplay (story by David Blau), successfully breaks up Reagan's romance with Lucille Barkley, with other roles going to Walter Slezak (another professor), Jesse White (the local DA), Herbert Heyes, Herbert Vigran and Harry Tyler. Michael Kraike produced and it was directed by Frederick de Cordova. (83 mins)

▽ The Indians were on the war path again in **Apache Drums**, a good-looking western whose screenplay by David Chandler from a story by Harry Brown (called *Stand At Spanish Boot*) took an awful long time to get going and, even when it did, trod a pretty well-worn path. All about a group of hardy settlers in the desert town of Spanish Boot who, to their cost, ignore gambler Stephen McNally's (left) warning about an impending Indian raid, it flickered into life during a climactic massacre in which the townsfolk take refuge in the local church while a handful of cavalrymen attempt to stave off disaster at the hands of the warring braves. For the rest it was a seen-it-all-before frontier western which co-starred Willard Parker (as the mayor, back left) and Coleen Gray, and featured Arthur Shields (right), James Griffith (centre), Armando Silvestre (foreground), Georgia Backus and Clarence Muse. It was produced by Val Lewton who died shortly after its completion, and directed, in Technicolor, by Hugo Fregonese. (74 mins)

▽ **The Fat Man** wasn't corpulent Sydney Greenstreet, but J. Scott Smart, the famous radio sleuth, here making his motion picture debut as super-detective Brad Runyan. Harry Essex and Leonard Lee's screenplay (story by Lee), had an innocent dentist and his nurse being murdered, with clues to the killing scattered between New York and Los Angeles. There were several likely suspects (including circus-clown Emmett Kelly, right, in his first screen appearance), and a $500,000 robbery to complicate matters further. But thanks to the gourmet fat man, the real killer was ultimately unmasked. Rock Hudson (left), working his way up to third billing, played a handsome hood, with Julie London as his wife. Others roles were shared out between Clinton Sundberg, Jayne Meadows, John Russell, Jerome Cowan and Lucille Barkley. Aubrey Schenck produced and it was directed without particular distinction by William Castle. (77 mins)

△ Poor Ginger Rogers (left). After tripping the light fantastic in so many memorable musicals with Fred Astaire, it was sad to see her losing her composure in **The Groom Wore Spurs** and come crashing down with such an unladylike thud in this lumbering comedy. She played an attorney who marries phoney cowboy Jack Carson (right), then sets out to prove him innocent of a murder charge. It was an aberration scripted by Robert Carson, Robert Libott and Frank Burt (story by Carson), and it featured Joan Davis, Stanley Ridges, James Brown and John Litel. Richard Whorf was credited as director, and it was produced by Howard Welsch for Fidelity Pictures. (81 mins)

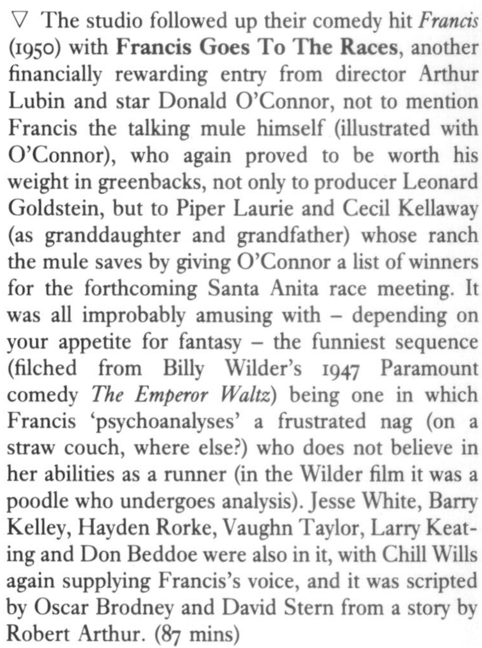

▽ The studio followed up their comedy hit *Francis* (1950) with **Francis Goes To The Races**, another financially rewarding entry from director Arthur Lubin and star Donald O'Connor, not to mention Francis the talking mule himself (illustrated with O'Connor), who again proved to be worth his weight in greenbacks, not only to producer Leonard Goldstein, but to Piper Laurie and Cecil Kellaway (as granddaughter and grandfather) whose ranch the mule saves by giving O'Connor a list of winners for the forthcoming Santa Anita race meeting. It was all improbably amusing with – depending on your appetite for fantasy – the funniest sequence (filched from Billy Wilder's 1947 Paramount comedy *The Emperor Waltz*) being one in which Francis 'psychoanalyses' a frustrated nag (on a straw couch, where else?) who does not believe in her abilities as a runner (in the Wilder film it was a poodle who undergoes analysis). Jesse White, Barry Kelley, Hayden Rorke, Vaughn Taylor, Larry Keating and Don Beddoe were also in it, with Chill Wills again supplying Francis's voice, and it was scripted by Oscar Brodney and David Stern from a story by Robert Arthur. (87 mins)

△ A pirate spoof with top-starred Donald O'Connor as an apprentice shopkeeper who, through circumstances beyond his control, is arrested for piracy, escapes, and finds himself the possessor of a free-booter's ship and a notorious reputation, **Double Crossbones** was a Technicolor lark from producer Leonard Goldstein. It brought together, under one proscenium arch, Captain Kidd (Alan Napier), Henry Morgan (Robert Barratt), Blackbeard (Louis Bacigalupi) and Ann Bonney (Hope Emerson), with results that were only mildly diverting. O'Connor (right) was at his best in a number called 'Percy Had A Heart' by Dan Shapiro and Lester Lee, but the rest of his comic derring-do was predictable. Other roles under Charles T. Barton's disappointing direction went to Helena Carter (left) as the governor's ward forced into a loveless marriage, Will Geer, John Emery, Kathryn Givney, Hayden Rorke and Morgan Farley. Oscar Brodney scripted, with additional dialogue by John Grant. There was one other song, also by Shapiro and Lee, called 'Song Of Adventure'. (75 mins)

▽ What Katie (Ann Blyth, left) did in **Katie Did It**, was to go to New York from her safe little New England town in order to sell a song so that Cecil Kellaway, her booze-ridden uncle, can pay off a gambling debt. She doesn't sell the song but agrees, instead, to pose in the semi-nude for an artist (Mark Stevens, right) whom she recently met when he passed through her village. She is later shocked to find the painting being displayed on advertising billboards across the country. Furious, she sets a date to marry Craig Stevens (though it is Mark she really loves), and is only prevented from doing so by the latter's last-minute intervention. And that's what Katie did. She was helped by a cast that included Jesse White, Harold Vermilyea, William Lynn, Elizabeth Patterson, Jimmy Hunt and Irving Bacon; by scenarist Jack Henley (who, in turn, was helped by Oscar Brodney's additional dialogue) and by director Frederick de Cordova. Leonard Goldstein produced. (81 mins)

▷ Remember the siege of Samarkand led by Genghis Khan in 1220? Neither, judging by **The Golden Horde**, did scenarist Gerald Drayson Adams (story by Harold Lamb). But it didn't stop him using it as a backdrop for top-starred Ann Blyth (left) as Princess Shalimar whose city is threatened with destruction by leering Genghis Khan (Marvin Miller). Though plucky Miss Blyth (looking gorgeous in Technicolor) has ideas of her own how to put bully-boy Khan in his place, it is David Farrar (centre, making his Hollywood debut) as Sir Guy who, with broadsword and crossbow, puts the situation to rights. The adventure hardly made many demands on the talents of the leading players; or, for that matter, on a cast that also included George Macready, Henry Brandon, Howard Petrie, Richard Egan (right) and Peggie Castle. It was produced by Howard Christie and Robert Arthur, and directed for the nonsense it was by George Sherman. (75 mins)

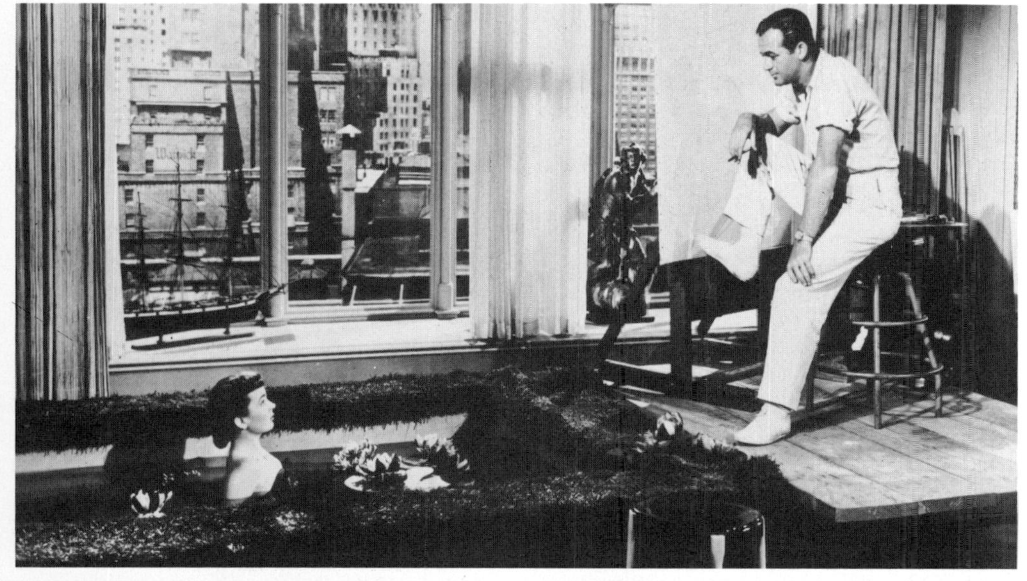

▽ Mary Chase's long-running Pulitzer Prize-winning play **Harvey** was written for the screen by Miss Chase herself and scenarist Oscar Brodney, and had several of the original cast members repeating their Broadway performances. It was an occasion in which whimsy-fanciers rejoiced, and even those customers who preferred their entertainment a little more down to earth couldn't help being beguiled by gentle James Stewart in the central role of Elwood P. Dowd, an inebriate whose constant companion is a six-foot rabbit called Harvey. Josephine Hull (from the original stage company) was second-billed as the sister who attempts to have Stewart (right) committed, but is committed herself instead. Also from the Broadway cast were Victoria Horne as Stewart's timid niece, and Jesse White as an asylum guard. William Lynn played the family counsellor Judge Gaffney, with other roles going to Cecil Kellaway (as a doctor), Peggy Dow (left), Charles Drake (as a psychiatrist, centre left), Wallace Ford, Nana Bryant, Grace Mills, Clem Bevans and Ida Moore. Director Henry Koster kept the whimsy palatable and John Beek's overall production was a credit to the stage play which inspired it. (103 mins)

1951

▷ Traversing territory explored to far greater effect by Billy Wilder in *Sunset Boulevard* (Paramount, 1950), **Hollywood Story** was a crime melodrama with a motion picture backdrop that set out to discover the circumstances surrounding an unsolved crime way back in 1929 when a famous director was mysteriously murdered in his studio bungalow. The murder is envisaged by movie producer Richard Conte (left) as the perfect subject for a thiller and, to help him bring it to the screen, he seeks out a has-been writer (Henry Hull) who once worked with the deceased director. Furthermore, for added authenticity, he dusts off such silent stars as Francis X. Bushman, Betty Blythe, William Farnum and Helen Gibson. It could (and should) have been much more fun than it was, but for a very ordinary screenplay by Jonathan Latimer and Liam O'Brien (story by Charles Marquis Warren), which turned out to consist of the usual box of whodunnit platitudes. Paul Cavanagh played a silent-screen star now reduced to bit roles, with other parts under William Castle's direction going to Julia Adams, Richard Egan (right), Fred Clark (as Conte's financial partner), Jim Backus (Conte's agent), Houseley Stevenson and, in a special guest appearance, Joel McCrea. Leonard Goldstein produced. (77 mins)

▽ Jeff Chandler (left) starred in **Iron Man**, as a coal-miner who becomes a prizefighter in order to speed up the process of saving enough money to buy a small radio store. Trouble is, while he is Mr Nice Guy out of the ring, in it he has the instincts of a killer – which causes no end of bother to his opponents, his fiancée (Evelyn Keyes) and to his older brother (Stephen McNally) who has masterminded Chandler's career so far. Rock Hudson (right) made a good impression as the friend who helps the fighter come to grips with his 'killer complex', Jim Backus played a sportswriter, with other parts in Aaron Rosenberg's hard-hitting production going to Joyce Holden, James Arness, Steve Martin and George Baxter. It was scripted by George Zuckerman and Borden Chase from a story by William R. Burnett, and punched home by director Joseph Pevney. First made in 1931 with Lew Ayres and Jean Harlow. (81 mins)

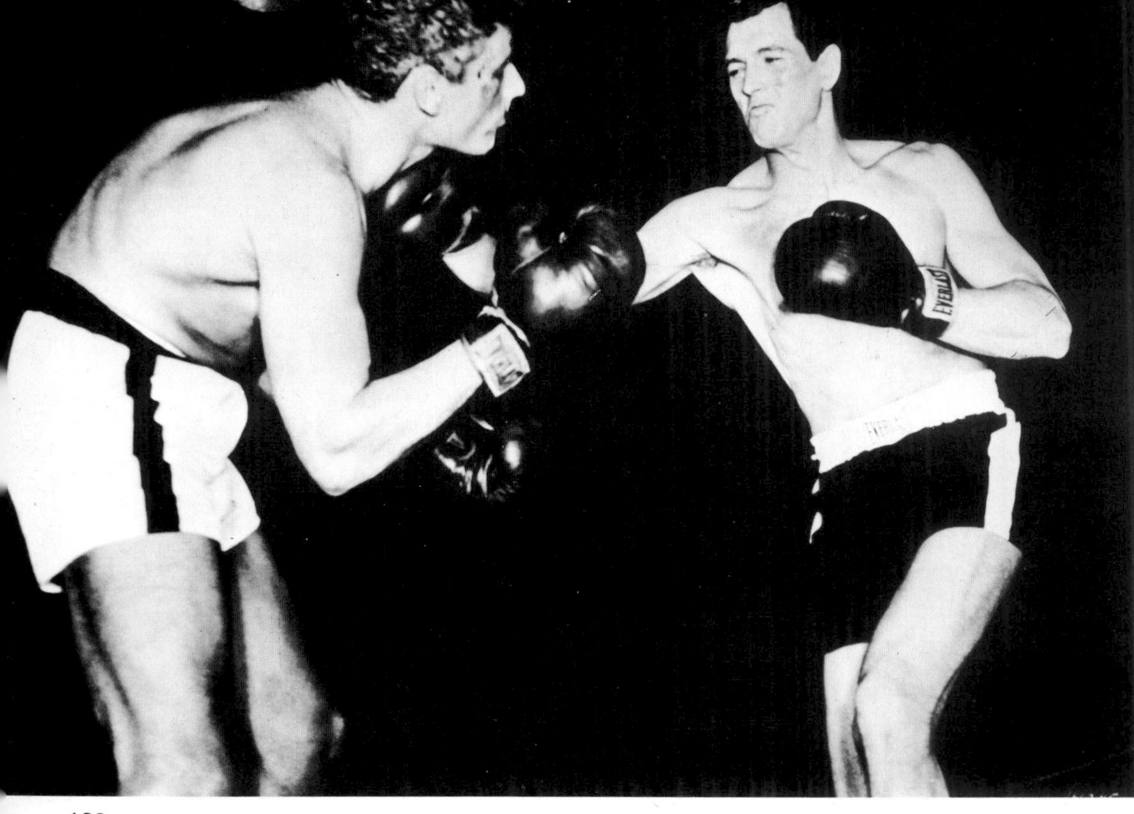

▽ A cavalry-and-Indians adventure of the sort they (mercifully) don't make anymore, **Tomahawk** threw in some perfunctory action sequences to enliven the oft-told tale of conflict between a man sympathetic to the Red Indian cause (Van Heflin as history's Jim Bridger), and one whose fervent belief is the cliché that the only good Indian is a dead one (Alex Nicol). That wasn't the only cliché in producer Leonard Goldstein's Technicolor production, another being Yvonne De Carlo as a travelling wagon-show singer who stupidly ventures forth into no-woman's-land and has to be rescued in the nick of time by hero Heflin (centre). Also part of the South Dakota setting were Preston Foster, Jack Oakie (left), Tom Tully, John War Eagle, eighth-billed Rock Hudson and Susan Cabot (right). It was written by Silvia Richards and Maurice Geraghty from a story by Daniel Jarrett, and directed off-the-peg by George Sherman. (81 mins)

▽ Linda Darnell (top-starred) played a very irritating lady indeed in **The Lady Pays Off**, a tiresome comedy-drama in which she was miscast as a schoolmarm who, while vacationing in Reno, finds herself losing $7000 at a casino. The club's owner (Stephen McNally), a widower, agrees to tear up her IOU if she, in turn, will agree to spend the rest of her vacation tutoring his young daughter (Gigi Perreau). With little choice but to agree, Miss Darnell (right) deliberately sets out to make McNally (left) fall in love with her (which she does), so that she can dump him (which she does). But neither of them have reckoned on the ingenuity of little Miss Perreau (centre), who has taken quite a shine – heaven knows why – to Miss Darnell, and, in cahoots with French housekeeper Ann Codee, plans a stratagem that vouchsafes a happy ending. Frank Gill Jr and producer Albert J. Cohen wrote it, Douglas Sirk, who would soon move on to meatier stuff than this, directed, and the cast was completed by Virginia Field (as a former McNally flame who unexpectedly turns up at his beach-house and is made to feel extremely unwelcome), Nestor Paiva and Lynn Hunter. (80 mins)

▽ **Little Egypt** had nothing whatsoever to do with the legendary cooch dancer who took the 1893 Chicago Exposition by storm with her suggestive undulations, but was, instead, the lightweight tale of a con man called Wayne Cravat (Mark Stevens, right) and a phoney Egyptian 'princess' from New Jersey who, against a backdrop of the aforementioned Chicago exhibition, do their cunning best to con Chicago tobacco tycoon Minor Watson out of a million bucks. In the course of these machinations, second-billed Rhonda Fleming (left, as the phoney Princess Izora) agrees to put on a demonstration of 'ancient Egyptian ceremonial dances' to help attract custom to the fair. She does, and is promptly hauled off by the police for indecent exposure. There was nothing indecent about producer Jack Gross' brightly Technicolored production; it just didn't add up to stimulating entertainment. Oscar Brodney and Doris Gilbert wrote it (additional dialogue by Lou Breslow) from a story by Brodney; Frederick de Cordova directed, and the cast was completed by Nancy Guild, John Litel, Charles Drake, Tom D'Andrea, Steven Geray (as a phoney Pasha), Verna Felton and Kathryn Givney. (81 mins)

▽ Despite its Technicolor trappings, **Frenchie** was an insipid reworking of *Destry Rides Again* (1939). A warmed-over-lightly western, it starred Shelley Winters and Joel McCrea. Winters (in the Dietrich role) played a New Orleans gambling house proprietress who, fifteen years after the murder of her father, returns to the hick town of Bottleneck to find his killers. McCrea (subbing for James Stewart) was the sheriff she falls for, without forgetting the real purpose of her visit. Paul Kelly turned out to be one of the killers; John Emery (a respectable banker), the other. Just as la Dietrich resorted to fisticuffs with Una Merkel in the earlier film, so Miss Winters (left) got pugnacious with Marie Windsor as the banker's wife. But it just wasn't the same. Blame it on Louis King's lack-lustre direction, or on Oscar Brodney's talkative screenplay; or even on the central performances which, though spirited, couldn't match the originals in star quality. Michael Kraike produced, and his cast included Elsa Lanchester (right), John Russell (centre), George Cleveland, Regis Toomey and Paul E. Burns. (80 mins)

▽ A tepid, stilted and cliché-prone screenplay (by Louis Solomon and Robert Hardy Andrews from a story by Johnston McCulley) bogged down **Mark Of The Renegade**, a costume melodrama about the early days of California. It starred Ricardo Montalban (right) and Cyd Charisse (both on loan from MGM), whose good looks and shapely figures in no way compensated for a witheringly banal plot which found Montalban, together with hissable George Tobias, landing on Californian shores with a brief to contact a secret informer who will pave the way for the sacking of the pueblo of Los Angeles by pirates. Miss Charisse played the comely daughter of Antonio Moreno, the leader of the Californian republic, with other roles under Hugo Fregonese's rather confused guidance going to J. Carrol Naish, Gilbert Roland (left), Andrea King, George Backus, Robert Warwick and Armando Silvestre. It was produced by Jack Gross in Technicolor. (82 mins)

◁ Strictly for hinterland audiences, **Ma And Pa Kettle Back On The Farm** again starred Marjorie Main and Percy Kilbride as the eponymous couple (Kilbride, left), whose adventures take them from the super-duper New York apartment won by Pa in an advertising slogan competition, as described in an earlier movie, back to their farm in search of uranium. Turns out that the only radioactive object in sight is Pa's war-surplus overalls which causes car horns to blow, light bulbs to flash and a row of peddlers' pots and pans to stand to attention as he passes by them. Some humour was milked from a situation involving Ma Kettle's disagreements with son Richard Long's imperious mother-in-law (Barbara Brown), who wants to raise her infant grandchild 'hygienically' but, for the most part, Jack Henley's screenplay was formula fare, with direction to match by Edward Sedgwick. Meg Randall, Ray Collins, Emory Parnell, Peter Leeds, Teddy Hart (centre) and Oliver Blake (right) completed the cast for producer Leonard Goldstein. (86 mins)

▽ Thirteenth-century Tangiers, aided and abetted by luscious Technicolor, was the exotic, haven't-we-been-there-before? locale of **The Prince Who Was A Thief**, an opulent piece of escapism from producer Leonard Goldstein, who top-cast Tony Curtis (right) as a thief who is really a prince – the title tells it all. Piper Laurie (left – also a thief) was Curtis' romantic *vis-à-vis*, and Everett Sloane his kindly foster-father who, years ago, was ordered to kill the boy, but simply could not bring himself to do so. Peggie Castle was also in it as the beauteous and treacherous Princess Yasmin (seeker of the Pearl Of Fatima), with other parts in this *Arabian Nights*-type adventure (written by Gerald Drayson Adams and Aeneas McKenzie from a story by Theodore Dreiser) going to Donald Randolph as the evil Mustapha and Jeff Corey as his henchman, as well as to Betty Garde, Marvin Miller, Nita Bieber and Hayden Rorke. Giving it just the right amount of bravado and romantic sweep was director Rudolph Maté. (87 mins)

▽ Gigi Perreau, the studio's answer to MGM's Margaret O'Brien, was the star of **Reunion In Reno**, even though she was third-billed under Mark Stevens and Peggy Dow. She played a nine-year-old moppet who arrives in Reno in order to seek a divorce from her parents (Frances Dee and Leif Erickson). Divorce attorney Stevens (right) agrees to handle the 'case', whereupon he and his girlfriend Miss Dow discover that little Miss Perreau (centre) wants out because her mother is about to have a baby, and, being adopted, she fears that henceforth she'll just be in the way. Hans Jacoby and Shirley White's screenplay, adapted by Lou Breslow from a story by Brenda Weisberg and William Sackheim, kept it ticking over merrily, with roles in it for Ray Collins, Fay Baker, Myrna Dell and Dick Wessel. It was, in all, a modest but likeable entertainment from producer Leonard Goldstein, capably directed by Kurt Neumann. (78 mins)

▽ Charles Laughton (illustrated) definitely slummed it (as well as hammed it up) in **The Strange Door**, a throwback to the studio's numerous past excursions into horror which Jerry Sackheim scripted from Robert Louis Stevenson's story *The Sire de Maletroit's Door.* Set, for much of the time, in a mediaeval castle replete with sliding panels, gloom-laden corridors and dingy torture chambers, the film creaked its way arthritically through a plot in which Laughton, as a crazed French nobleman, perpetrates all manner of nastiness after his brother (Paul Cavanagh) steals his girlfriend and marries her. Their union brings forth Sally Forrest whom Laughton hopes to marry off to wastrel Richard Stapley. But the couple, who grow to like one another, succeed in eliminating Laughton with the help of faithful retainer Boris Karloff. Director Joseph Pevney, working with a cast that also included Michael Pate, Alan Napier and William Cottrell did the best he could in the impoverished circumstances, but it was an uphill battle with few rewards. The producer was Ted Richmond. (81 mins)

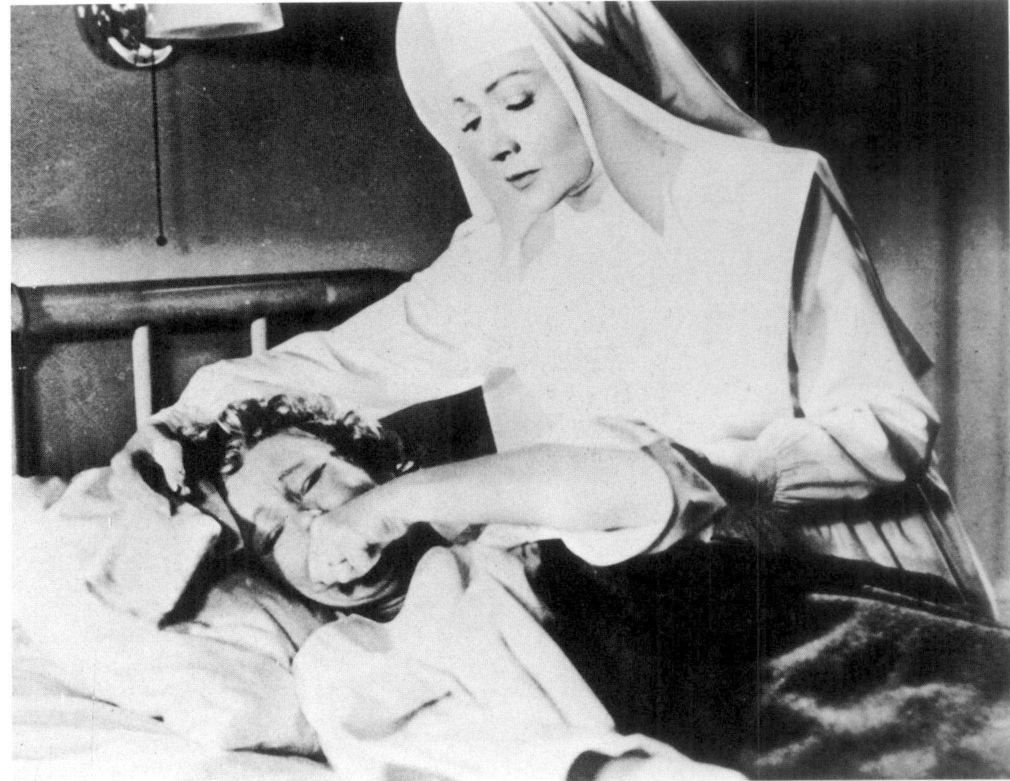

△ Claudette Colbert, making quite sure that cameraman William Daniels kept his lenses trained on the left side of her face, starred in **Thunder On The Hill**, a 'woman's picture' adapted by Oscar Brodney and Andrew Solt from Charlotte Hastings' West End play *Bonaventure.* Miss Colbert (right) played a nun at an English convent whose purpose, in the narrative, was to prove a fraught Ann Blyth innocent of murder after Miss Blyth and her guards take shelter at the convent during a flood. The crime is eventually tagged on to Robert Douglas, a doctor who poisoned Miss Blyth's brother because of his jealousy over the latter's relationship with his wife (Anne Crawford, making her Hollywood debut). Gladys Cooper played the no-nonsense Mother Superior, Michael Pate the convent's idiot handyman, with other roles under Douglas Sirk's solemn direction going to Philip Friend, John Abbott and Connie Gilchrist. Michael Kraike produced. (84 mins)

▽ A cosy family comedy for cosy family audiences, **Weekend With Father** starred Van Heflin (standing centre) and Patricia Neal (right) – in a welcome change of pace for both – as a widower and widow, each with two kids, who meet at a railway station where both, for the first time, are sending their families to summer camp. The trials and tribulations of the romance that ultimately flourishes between them provided scenarist Joseph Hoffman (working from a story by George F. Slavin and George W. George) with several opportunities for chuckles, and parts for Gigi Perreau and her sister Janine (left) as Heflin's kids, and Tommy Rettig and Jimmy Hunt as Miss Neal's progeny. Also in it was Virginia Field (as a TV actress) in a role similar to the one she played in *The Lady Pays Off*), with Gary Pagett, Frances Williams, Richard Denning (foreground centre), Elvia Allman and Forrest Lewis completing the cast for producer Ted Richmond and director Douglas Sirk. (83 mins)

▽ **Up Front** put flesh and blood on to the popular World War II cartoon characters of 'Joe' and 'Willie' created by Bill Mauldin, and starred David Wayne (left) as Joe and Tom Ewell (right) as Willie. While their outward physical characteristics did not disappoint afficionados of the original cartoons, the screenplay fashioned by Stanley Roberts from Mauldin's book of the same name, lacked the latter's trenchant humour and caustic irony, and the end result was just another slapstick spoof of army life – this time among infantrymen in World War II's Italian campaign north of Naples. Plot complications manifested themselves in the shape of Marina Berti as a Neapolitan girl and her black marketeering father (Silvio Minciotti), and gave rise to an inevitable chase finale with Joe and Willie fleeing in any army truck full of contraband goodies. Jeffrey Lynn, Richard Egan, Maurice Cavell, Vaughn Taylor and Paul Harvey were also in it; Alexander Hall directed it as a broad farce, and it was produced by Leonard Goldstein. (92 mins)

▽ Two hundred thousand dollars was the motivating factor in **Smuggler's Island**. Jeff Chandler (right) starred as a Navy vet and independent diver whose headquarters were in Macao, and Evelyn Keyes as the beautiful woman who agrees to bail him out and save his small sloop from being returned to a mortgage-holding banker if he, in return, will dive for the illegal gold. He does so, also plunging headlong into love with Evelyn (despite the fact that she's married to double-crossing Philip Friend), and although the gold finishes up at the bottom of the ocean when Chandler's sloop (loaded with firecrackers to conceal its precious cargo) is set alight by Friend, and literally ends the movie with a bang, Chandler and Keyes finish up in each other's arms. Routine melodrama to be sure, enlivened by Technicolor but not much else; and with a cast that included Marvin Miller (as a pirate), Ducky Louie, David Wolfe and Jay Novello. Leonard Lee scripted from a story and adaptation by Herbert Margolis and Louis Morheim; Edward Ludwig directed and it was produced by Ted Richmond. (75 mins)

△ There was whimsy a-plenty in **You Never Can Tell**, an amiable fantasy in which a German shepherd dog called King, bequeathed a fortune by his eccentric millionaire owners, is poisoned by Charles Drake and returns to earth (as Dick Powell, illustrated) to see that vengeance is done. The situation gave scenarists Lou Breslow (who also directed and provided the story) and David Chandler lots of opportunities for word play about 'a dog's life' or 'barking up the wrong tree', and to draw humour from fire hydrants (which Powell cannot pass without pausing longingly), as well as from dog biscuits and raw hamburgers – two of Powell's favourite foods. Peggy Dow was second-billed as the trustee of King's estate, with Joyce Holden in it too, as Goldie, a racehorse who returns to earth with Powell (and can outrun a bus), with other parts going to Albert Sharpe and Sara Taft. Leonard Goldstein's production was silly but enjoyable. (78 mins)

▽ Though the subject of **Target Unknown** was an unusual one – the questioning by German Intelligence of World War II American Air Force prisoners of war – there was nothing original about the film which producer Aubrey Schenck, his director George Sherman and scriptwriter Harold Medford made of it. In fact, it was all numbingly familiar. Set in occupied France, it featured, Mark Stevens (right) as a US captain, and, as his crewmen, Alex Nicol (centre), Don Taylor, James Best, Richard Carlyle, John Sands and James Young, who gave competent accounts of themselves as they helped flesh out a plot in which the enemy were able, through their interrogations, to piece together enough information to indicate, what the next big Allied bombing target would be, helped by Malu Gatica who betrays the aircrew. Suzanne Dalbert (left), brought a touch of femininity to the proceedings and aided the Allies to escape; but it was the actual aerial combat footage used to bolster the ailing narrative that provided the film with its only real moments of interest. (90 mins)

1952

▷ Scenarist Ketti Frings (story by Thelma Robinson) should have been ashamed of herself for peddling such sentimental clap-trap as **Because Of You**, and ditto producer Albert J. Cohen for buying it. Loretta Young (right) starred as a dope-runner's moll who, just as she is about to marry the crook (Alex Nicol), finds herself serving a prison sentence after the couple are nabbed by the police, Nicol having planted an incriminating envelope on her at the time. In prison she discovers a talent for nursing and, on her release, becomes a nurse's aid, in which capacity she meets and falls in love with red-blooded Jeff Chandler (left), a wounded (and neurotic) pilot. They marry, have a daughter, and seem to be getting along well enough when Miss Young throws her happiness away by foolishly taking herself and her daughter to Mexico in the company of her erstwhile lover Nicol. Chandler understandably has his marriage annulled on the grounds of his wife's deception and, as a result, Miss Young is left to live unhappily ever after. The rubbish was directed by Joseph Pevney, who gave as good as he got; and the cast included Frances Dee (making her reappearance after an absence of several years), Alexander Scourby, Lynn Roberts, Mae Clarke and Gayle Reed. (95 mins)

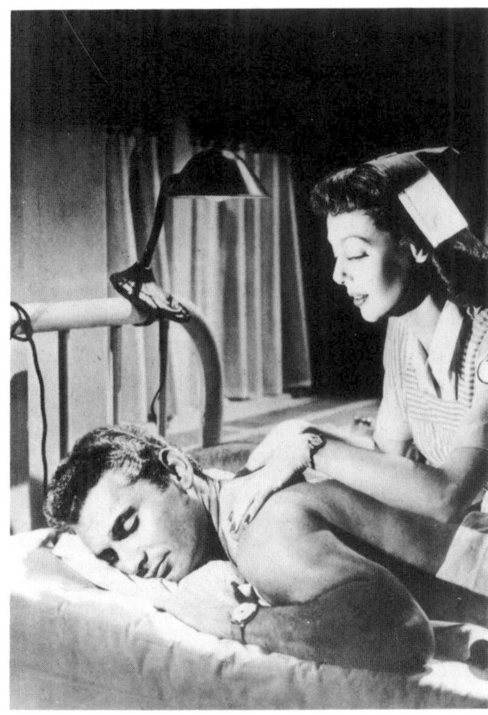

▽ A truly puerile comedy from producer Leonard Goldstein, **Finders Keepers** was a programmer about a two-year-old (Dusty Henley) who causes all sorts of problems when he accidentally stumbles on some stolen bank notes in a robber's hideout. The effect of this 'windfall' on a larcenous grandmother (Evelyn Varden), and on the kid's ex-con father (Tom Ewell, illustrated) out on parole, provided Richard Morris with the springboard for a witless little screenplay which director Frederick de Cordova simply did not know how to pummel into life. The cast was completed by Harold Vermilyea, Douglas Fowley, Richard Reeves, James Elam and Herbert Anderson. (75 mins)

▽ Marjorie Main (left) and Percy Kilbride (centre) as Ma and Pa Kettle returned in **Ma And Pa Kettle At The Fair**, and this time found themselves involved in a variety of highly unlikely situations at a local fair, their main objective being to raise enough money during their outing to send daughter Lori Nelson (right) to college. James Best (2nd right) provided Miss Nelson with romance, the other parts in Richard Morris and John Grant's uninspired little contrivance going to Esther Dale, Emory Parnell, Oliver Blake and Russell Simpson. The formula production was by Leonard Goldstein, with Charles Barton directing. (78 mins)

◁ A tailor-made vehicle for Frank Sinatra, **Meet Danny Wilson** charted the rise to stardom of a singing nobody. Don McGuire's screenplay laced drama with comedy, and gave the star every opportunity to display his impressive acting range, as well as his golden vocal chords. The story had Sinatra (right) involved with a tough racketeering promoter (Raymond Burr, left) who cuts in for 50% of his earnings, but meets a bullet-riddled end at Sinatra's hands after wounding the singer's best friend (Alex Nicol). Shelley Winters co-starred as a nightclub entertainer over whom Nicol and Sinatra come to blows, and she joined the latter in singing 'A Good Man Is Hard To Find' (by Eddie Green). Tommy Farrell and Vaughan Taylor completed the cast, the crisp direction was by Joseph Pevney, and Leonard Goldstein was the producer. The songs comprised a selection of favourite standards, all wonderfully sung by ol' Blue Eyes. They included: 'All Of Me' Seymour Simons, Gerald Marks; 'How Deep Is The Ocean?' Irving Berlin; 'She's Funny That Way' Neil Moret, Richard Whiting; 'I've Got A Crush On You' George and Ira Gershwin; 'That Old Black Magic' Harold Arlen, Johnny Mercer. (85 mins)

▷ Errol Flynn (illustrated centre) made his swashbuckling debut for the studio in **Against All Flags**, playing an 18th-century British naval officer who gets himself cashiered in order to infiltrate a pirate stronghold in Madagascar. Suspected of being a spy by one of the pirates, he is saved from death by beautiful buccaneer Maureen O'Hara and, while continuing with his secret work, successfully woos her. Aeneas McKenzie and Joseph Hoffman's screenplay threw in some additional distaff interest by having the pirates (led by Anthony Quinn) capturing the private ship of the Mogul of India and seizing the Mogul's daughter (Alice Kelley), as well as about a dozen harem hussies. Mildred Natwick, Robert Warwick, Harry Cording and John Alderson were also in it for producer Howard Christie; and it was directed by George Sherman, whose several action sequences included a stunt performed by Douglas Fairbanks in *The Black Pirate* (United Artists), way back in 1926. The main pirate ship, though slightly altered, was also used in *Yankee Buccaneer* (1952). The film was shot in Technicolor. (83 mins)

△ Say this for **Battle At Apache Pass**, it was an earnest attempt on behalf of scenarist Gerald Drayson Adams to take a more penetrating look at the Red Indian and his plight than was hitherto the norm in oaters of the period. Set in New Mexico at the start of Civil War, and involving the US Army in a peace pact with the Chiricahua Tribe, it was the routine story of the pact's betrayal by an ambitious Indian Affairs advisor (Bruce Cowling) who, working with the warring Geronimo (Jay Silverheels) of the Mogollon Apaches, turns the hitherto quiet area into a battleground. This was bad news for the army's John Lund (top-starred, right), but a boon to audiences in danger of nodding off from the triteness of it all. Beverly Tyler and Susan Cabot were the only women in a cast that second-billed Jeff Chandler (left) as tribal leader Cochise (a role he first played in 20th Century-Fox's 1950 western, *Broken Arrow*), and featured John Hudson, Jimmy Best, Regis Toomey (centre) and Richard Egan. George Sherman directed, and the Technicolor production was the responsibility of Leonard Goldstein. (85 mins)

△ An isolated, storm-swept castle standing in the unwelcoming estate of a cruel count; a personable and good-looking hero; a damsel in distress; torture chambers; an alligator pit – not to mention Boris Karloff and Lon Chaney Jr – were some of the 'horror' ingredients that went into William Alland's production of **The Black Castle**, an enjoyable programmer reminiscent of the studio's horror flicks of a decade earlier. Written by Jerry Sackheim, it featured top-starred Richard Greene (right) as a young English nobleman, and Stephen McNally (centre) as a villainous count, who embark on a cat-and-mouse battle of wits when two of Greene's friends fail to return after a hunting trip on McNally's estate. Chaney played McNally's bodyguard, Karloff (seated right) the castle physician opposed to his employer's villainy; Paula Corday was McNally's unwilling bride (rescued, of course, by Greene), with John Hoyt, Michael Pate (left), Nancy Valentine, Tudor Owen and Henry Corden completing the cast. Nathan Juran directed with all the genre's clichés firmly intact. (82 mins)

▷ The Pacific Northwest in all its scenic splendour looked marvellous in Technicolor, and provided the handsome backdrop to producer Aaron Rosenberg's **Bend Of The River**, an exciting, continually gripping outdoor actioner that starred James Stewart (left) as the leader of a wagon train who, together with a group of settlers, moves through the wilderness into Oregon. Arthur Kennedy (right), as a former Missouri raider rescued from the gallows by Stewart, joins the group and, together with Stewart, picks off some marauding Indians en route; so does Rock Hudson (as a gambler). Julia Adams was second-billed as the (romantic) female lead, and shared Borden Chase's screenplay (based on Bill Gulick's novel *Bend Of The Snake*) with Lori Nelson, Jay C. Flippen, Stepin Fetchit, Henry Morgan, Chubby Johnson and Howard Petrie. The all-involving direction was by Anthony Mann. (91 mins)

▽ **Bright Victory**, written and produced by Robert Buckner from the novel *Lights Out* by Baynard Kendrick, allowed top-starred Arthur Kennedy (illustrated), as a blind war veteran coming to grips with his appalling affliction, to give one of the best, most moving performances of his career. Peggy Dow played the charming young woman he meets at the Valley Forge General Hospital, with Julia Adams less effectively cast as his 'girl back home', destined to have her heart broken when he chooses (quite understandably) Miss Dow instead. Will Geer and Nana Bryant played Kennedy's parents and James Edwards a black friend, with Jim Backus, Minor Watson, John Hudson, Murray Hamilton and Hugh Reilly providing first-rate support under Mark Robson's sensitive and probing direction. Concerned also with the methods by which people who have been blinded are rehabilitated, the picture was as instructive as it was poignant, and it did the studio proud. (96 mins)

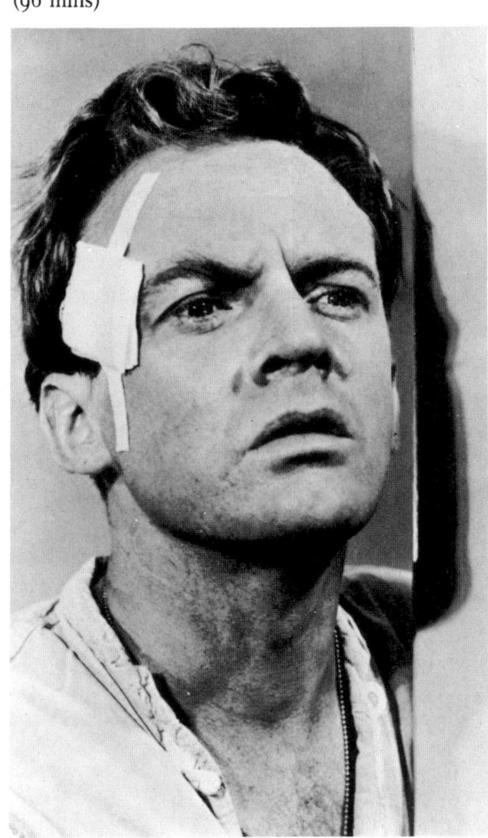

△ Tony Curtis received star billing in **Flesh And Fury** and did a pretty solid job as a deaf-mute prizefighter in a good vs evil contest between two women: evil Jan Sterling, a sexy blonde out to exploit Curtis (left) for as much money as she can get; and good Mona Freeman (right), a newspaper feature writer who loves the kid for what he is. In the course of Bernard Gordon's screenplay (story by William Alland), Curtis regains his hearing after an operation, kisses it goodbye again during a championship bout, but gets it back for the final fade in which, predictably, Miss Freeman featured prominently. Though Leonard Goldstein's production said nothing new about the fight game or the people involved in it, it was modestly entertaining and, in supporting roles, featured Wallace Ford, Connie Gilchrist, Katherine Locke, Harry Shannon and Harry Guardino. Joseph Pevney directed with his customary competence. (82 mins)

△ Tunisia provided the setting for **Flame Of Araby**, a Technicolor adventure full of 'bosoms and burning sand', which starred Maureen O'Hara (right) as the flame of the title, and co-starred Jeff Chandler (left) as the hero who manages to capture the swiftest steed in the desert – a black stallion on whose back he wins a climactic race, as well as Miss O'Hara's hand in marriage. Gerald Drayson Adams' screenplay also had Lon Chaney Jr and Buddy Baer, as two evil brothers, desperately trying to nab the prized stallion for themselves, with parts in it, too, for Susan Cabot, Richard Egan, Royal Dano, Maxwell Reed and Dewey Martin. The producer was Leonard Goldstein (with Ross Hunter as associate producer) and it was directed by Charles Lamont. (77 mins)

▽ Being upstaged by an animal was one thing, but being upstaged by a child *and* an animal was pure sadism as Maureen O'Sullivan (right) and Charles Drake painfully discovered in **Bonzo Goes To College**, the sequel to the previous year's *Bedtime For Bonzo*. The animal in question was the eponymous simian; the child was Gigi Perreau (2nd left), whose pet he becomes. O'Sullivan and Drake were Miss Perreau's parents, living in a college campus, with third-billed Edmund Gwenn (centre) as grandpa. Bonzo (left) is adopted into the family after leaving a side-show under a cloud (his mental prowess being questioned by sharpies John Miljan and Jerry Paris) and, after easily passing the college entrance exams, becomes a football hero by winning an important game in the last few moments of play. Leo Lieberman and Jack Henley scripted it from a story by Lieberman, Frederick de Cordova directed it, and it was produced by Ted Richmond with a cast that also included Irene Ryan as a maid, Gene Lockhart (as Perreau's other grandfather), Guy Williams and, of course, Bonzo as Bonzo. It was a modest little comedy, and modestly entertaining. (78 mins)

▽ The Daltons – Bob, Grat, Emmett and Will, alias Noah Beery Jr, Palmer Lee, Rand Brooks and William Reynolds – were resuscitated for **The Cimarron Kid**, the main purpose in Louis Stevens' screenplay (story by Stevens and Kay Lenard) being to involve top-starred Audie Murphy (left) in a life of crime. Which they did. He's regenerated, however, by Beverly Tyler, the daughter of former outlaw Roy Roberts, but still has to do time when he and his gang are betrayed in what he had hoped would be his final job. Hugh O'Brian (right), John Hudson, James Best, Leif Erickson and David Wolfe were also featured in Ted Richmond's crushingly ordinary production, and it was directed by Budd Boetticher. (84 mins)

▷ Though Piper Laurie (left) and Rock Hudson (right) received top billing in **Has Anybody Seen My Gal?**, Charles Coburn shamelessly pilfered every scene he was in. He played a millionaire who, years after being turned down in marriage by a girl he once loved very much, returns to visit the woman's family in order to see if they are worthy of inheriting his fortune. Pretending to be an eccentric artist, he takes a room in the family's house and a job as a soda-jerk in the local drugstore. He also arranges for the family to receive $100,000 from an 'unknown benefactor' then sits back to watch the effects the windfall has on them. Joseph Hoffman's delightful screenplay (based on a story by Eleanor H. Porter), set in Vermont in the 1920s, and punctuated every now and then with some typical songs of the period, was bouncily directed by Douglas Sirk for producer Ted Richmond, whose engaging Technicolor production also featured Lynn Bari (as the daughter of Coburn's erstwhile love), Gigi Perreau, William Reynolds, Larry Gates, Skip Homeier, Paul Harvey, Paul McVey, Gloria Holden and, making his debut in a bit part, James Dean. Songs included: 'Gimme A Little Kiss, Will Ya Huh?' Roy Smith, Roy Turk, Maceo Pinkard; 'It Aint Gonna Rain No More' Wendell Hall; 'Tiger Rag' Jelly Roll Morton. (88 mins)

△ Not even glorious Technicolor and a cast that boasted Joseph Cotten (left), Shelley Winters (right) and Scott Brady, could prevent **Untamed Frontier** from being a protracted bore. Scripted in committee by Gerald Drayson Adams and John and Gwen Bagni, with additional dialogue by Polly James (from a story by Houston Branch and Eugenia Night) and directed by Hugo Fregonese with no excitement whatsoever, it was the tired story of a crippled cattle baron (Minor Watson), who selfishly refuses to allow settlers to cross his property en route to free government land because he's using that land himself as grazing ground for his vast cattle herds. Cotten played Watson's good-guy nephew, Brady his bad-guy son and Miss Winters a waitress who, after witnessing a killing by Brady, is tricked into marrying the brute to prevent her testifying against him. It was produced by Leonard Goldstein with a cast that also included Suzan Ball, Katherine Emery, José Torvay, and Lee Van Cleef who, years later, would come into his own in Italian-made 'spaghetti' westerns opposite Clint Eastwood. (75 mins)

▽ Director Don Siegel was clearly cutting his teeth on **Duel At Silver Creek**, a stock western, with stock situations and a stock cast – including Audie Murphy (top-billed), Faith Domergue, Stephen McNally, Susan Cabot and Gerald Mohr. All about a gang of murdering gold-claim jumpers (led by Domergue and Mohr), the plot featured McNally (right) as a US marshal, and Murphy (left) as his deputy, with the former, against the protest of the latter, falling in love with the treacherous (albeit beautiful) Miss Domergue, as a consequence of which the baddies literally get away with murder. Love, however, only conquers McNally temporarily, and as soon as he realises he is being used, he brings matters to a head in the inevitable climactic shoot-out. Susan Cabot played the good gal who at first fancies McNally, but decides to settle for Murphy; with Eugene Iglesias, Kyle James, Walter Sande, George Eldredge and, in a small part, Lee Marvin, completing the cast for producer Leonard Goldstein. (76 mins)

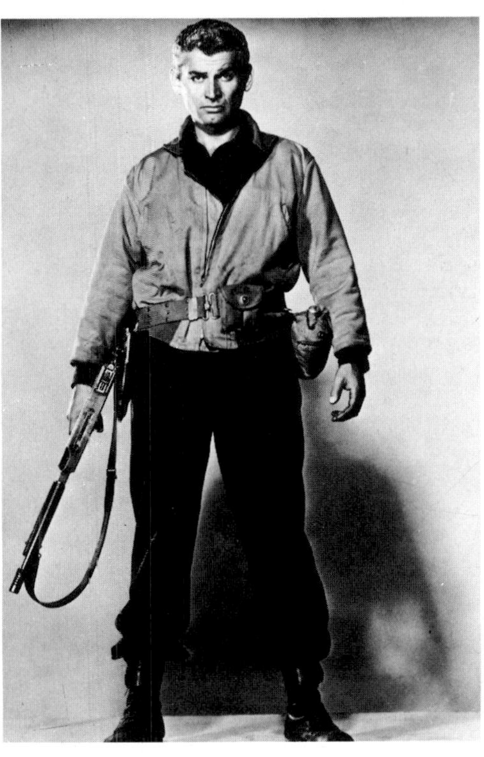

△ A clichéd World War II actioner, **Red Ball Express** starred Jeff Chandler (illustrated) as a lieutenant in charge of a US Army Transportation Corps trucking unit whose function, during General Patton's push to Paris, was to transport gasoline and ammunition to the front. Apart from the 24-hour-a-day problems that went with the job, scenarist Michael Hayes (working from a story by Marcel Klauber and Billy Grady Jr) saddled Chandler with the manic hatred of a venomous top sergeant (Alex Nicol), as well as with a moody Sidney Poitier who honestly believes he is being got at because of his colour. Both 'victims', however, soon see the error of their ways, and come to accept Chandler as an unmitigated hero. Though feminine company was supplied by Judith Braun, Jacqueline Duval and Cindy Garner, it was the males who dominated, and they included Charles Drake, Hugh O'Brian, Jack Kelly and Howard Petrie. Aaron Rosenberg produced, and it was directed by Budd Boetticher. (83 mins)

◁ It was inevitable that the popular radio and TV serial *Adventures Of Ozzie And Harriet* – first aired in 1944 – would sooner or later reach the screen, and it did in a comedy called **Here Come The Nelsons**. The family in question comprised Ozzie and Harriet as Ma and Pa, and David (right) and Ricky (left) Nelson as their sons. Family fare, and then some, its simple storyline (by Ozzie and Donald Nelson and William Davenport, the trio also scripting) pirouetted on the misunderstandings caused when Ozzie invites attractive Barbara Lawrence, the grownup kid sister of a school chum, to spend time with the family during a centennial celebration; and Harriet does the same thing with Rock Hudson. A sub-plot had Ozzie entering a bucking bronco contest in the centennial's rodeo, and leading a chase to capture a pair of robbers who have absconded with the fair's takings. Sheldon Leonard (centre) and Ed Max were the robbers and Jim Backus the Nelson's neighbour, with other roles going to Ann Doran, Gale Gordon and Paul Harvey. Aaron Rosenberg produced, and Frederick de Cordova called the shots. (75 mins)

◁ A truly dire comedy, **No Room For The Groom** paired Tony Curtis and Piper Laurie in the banal story of a GI's (Curtis, centre) attempts to spend some time alone with his bride (Laurie, left) in a house overrun by his wife's relatives – all of whom are unaware that Miss Laurie is married. Hardly surprising, since she has neglected to mention the fact to them. Spring Byington (right) played Curtis' mother-in-law who, in the course of Joseph Hoffman's laugh-free screenplay (from a story by Darwin L. Teilheit called *My True Love*), tries to break up the marriage so that her daughter can marry Don DeFore; with other roles taken by Lillian Bronson, Paul McVey and Steven Chase. Ted Richmond produced and Douglas Sirk was given the futile task of making it meaningful. (82 mins)

△ Maimed by a story and screenplay from Louis Stevens that wilfully turned its back on originality and determinedly rejected fresh ideas, **Horizons West** went the same direction in its pedestrian account of three Texans and their post-Civil War lives after returning to their home state. Rock Hudson (centre) and James Arness resume their work as ranchers, while top-billed Robert Ryan (right) is more ambitious: he wants to make money fast and to build a western empire. Julia Adams (as a widow woman with an eye for Ryan, despite the fact that it was Ryan who shot down her unscrupulous husband, Raymond Burr), was the female lead; with Judith Braun, John McIntire, Dennis Weaver, Frances Bavier and (in a small role) Mae Clark also lending their presences to Albert J. Cohen's conventional Technicolor production. Budd Boetticher's direction was as flat as his material. (80 mins)

◁ More masquerading in **Just Across The Street**, the culprit, this time, being top-billed Ann Sheridan (left) who, to help support herself and her father, finds employment with John Lund (right), a plumber. For some reason, Lund believes her to be the daughter of a wealthy banker (Robert Keith) and Miss Sheridan goes along with the deception, even to the extent of having the plumber drop her off at the banker's residence each day after work, despite the fact that she lives just across the street from him (hence the title). This arrangement causes all sorts of plot complications, especially with banker Keith's wife (Natalie Schaefer) who thinks her hubby is having an affair with Miss Sheridan. But – surprise, surprise! – it all comes right in the end, with Lund and Sheridan finding true love together. All that audiences found was true boredom. Cecil Kellaway, Harvey Lembeck, Alan Mowbray and George Eldredge also featured in Roswell Rogers and Joel Malone's screenplay, which Leonard Goldstein produced, and Joseph Pevney directed. (78 mins)

▷ The 'It' in **It Grows On Trees** was money, and it did so, literally, in producer Leonard Goldstein's one-joke comedy. Recipient of the financial windfall was top-starred Irene Dunne (left – whose last film it was) as a zany housewife (married to Dean Jagger, right) who discovers, one day, that the two trees she has planted in her backyard have started sprouting five and ten dollar bills – and, furthermore, that the US Treasury Department has pronounced the money legitimate. Miss Dunne happily embarks on a massive spending spree, decorating her homestead and paying off the mortgage, only to discover that, like leaves, the money soon dries and crumbles. Finale sees the trees destroyed in the interests of the American economy. The wish-fulfilment fantasy, with its faint whiff of moral fable, was scripted by Leonard Praskins and Barney Slater, whimsically directed by Arthur Lubin, and featured Joan Evans, Richard Crenna, Edith Meiser, Les Tremayne and Forrest Lewis. (84 mins)

▽ Ordinary was the word for **Steel Town**, a macho yarn set in the Kaiser-Fontana Steel Plant at Fontana in California, and involving a feud between second-billed John Lund (a steel-mill heir learning the business the hard way) and third-billed Howard Duff as a mill-worker colleague. Star billing went to café cashier Ann Sheridan (right), whom both men fancy, but whom Lund (left) ultimately wins after saving her father (William Harrigan) when he has a heart attack and falls into a ladle about to be filled with molten metal. Some padding to do with Lund's unpopularity with the smelters after he costs his colleagues an employee's sweepstake prize in a tonnage race, helped fill out Gerald Drayson Adams and Lou Breslow's screenplay (story by Leonard Freeman), with other parts going to Eileen Crowe, Chick Chandler and James Best. It was produced in Technicolor by Leonard Goldstein and directed by George Sherman. (83 mins)

▷ Some authentic rodeo footage and behind-the-scenes glimpses at bronco-busting were the only interesting elements in **Bronco Buster**, more macho outdoor entertainment which pitted rodeo star John Lund against cocky newcomer Scott Brady (left) with all the inevitable clichés (including Brady's alienating show-off antics, and his unsuccessful attempt to steal Joyce Holden (right) away from Lund) passing for plot in Horace McCoy and Lillie Hayward's screenplay (story by Peter B. Kyne). True to form, the story even had Brady being regenerated after his showy heroics in the grandstand cause injury to Chill Wills, Miss Holden's clownish father. Technicolor made it just about watchable, but by now the transparent formula was too well-worn for comfort. Ted Richmond produced, Budd Boetticher directed, and the cast was completed by Don Haggerty, Dan Poore, Pete Crump, Bill Williams and Jerry Ambler. (80 mins)

▷ The triteness of the title given to **The Raiders** (also known as **Riders Of Vengeance**) betrayed a well-made, albeit familiar, western, the mainstays of which were the two leading performances by Richard Conte (right) and Viveca Lindfors (left). And Technicolor. Plot-wise there was little more to Polly James and Lillie Hayward's screenplay than a war between victimized goldminers in 1849 California, and a ruthless land baron (Morris Ankrum) out to sabotage a movement to unionize the California Territory. Leading the miners' rebellion is Conte (cue for much gun play and shaking up of dust), with Viveca Lindfors as a Mexican beauty and underground rider making a romantic play for him. Richard Martin was cast as a once wealthy Mexican ranchowner (and brother of Miss Lindfors) who joins up with Conte in the latter's fight with Ankrum and his gang. William Bishop played a marshal, with other parts under Lesley Selander's neat and nifty direction going to Barbara Britton, Hugh O'Brian, William Reynolds and Lane Bradford. William Alland produced. (82 mins)

◁ Yvonne De Carlo (left) starred in **The Scarlet Angel** as a New Orleans saloon gal who, just after the Civil War, takes the place of the recently deceased widow of a wealthy San Francisco scion and, travelling to the coast, enters high society under false pretences, quickly learning the tricks of the upper-class trade. But just as she is about to marry into money, second-billed Rock Hudson (fast working his way up to leading man status) re-enters her life, causing our heroine to realise that once a saloon gal, always a saloon gal. The movie ended with her turning her back on wealth and falsely attained position for a humbler existence with the man she really loves. It was the brainchild of scenarist Oscar Brodney, who scripted it for producer Leonard Goldstein; and the director was Sidney Salkow. The rest of the cast included Harry Harvey Sr (right), Richard Denning, Whitfield Connor, Bodil Miller, Amanda Blake and Henry O'Neill. It was photographed in Technicolor. (81 mins)

△ **Lost In Alaska** was one of Abbott (left) and Costello's (right) feebler efforts, and it found the pair fleeing to the frozen north after saving co-star Tom Ewell (centre left), a gold prospector, from committing suicide over the unrequited love of dance hall singer Mitzi Green (centre right). In Alaska they become involved in a $2,000,000 gold fortune belonging to Ewell which saloon owner Bruce Cabot has set his greedy sights on. A climactic dog-sled chase and the loss of the gold brought the film to its hackneyed conclusion. Howard Christie produced; the impossible task of directing the rubbish fell to Jean Yarbrough, and the cast was completed by Iron Eyes Cody (centre), Emory Parnell, Joseph Kirk, Rex Lease and Minerva Urecal. (76 mins)

△ William Powell was worthy of better subjects than the one producer Leonard Goldstein handed him in **Treasure Of Lost Canyon**, which was all about an orphaned youngster (Tommy Ivo, illustrated) who, after being fleeced by a San Francisco attorney (Henry Hull) is given a home by a kindly small-town doctor (Powell). Brainerd Duffield and Emerson Crocker's screenplay, loosely based on Robert Louis Stevenson's *The Treasure of Franchard*, also involved an underwater search for an ancient treasure chest and the valuables contained therein, and featured Julia Adams, Rosemary De Camp (as Powell's wife), Chubby Johnson and John Doucette. Technicolor didn't help it one bit; nor did director Ted Tetzlaff. (82 mins)

▽ The love affair between men and their ships cropped up again in **Yankee Buccaneer**, a routine costumer which top-starred Jeff Chandler (left) as a humourless commander of a US frigate. Chandler allows his vessel to assume the guise of a pirate ship in order to find a fleet of freebooters, masterminded by Spanish govenor Joseph Calleia, who are causing havoc in the Caribbean. Chandler's first officer was Scott Brady (right), a happy-go-lucky character who inevitably antagonises the commander with his outgoing nonchalance; Suzan Ball (centre) was the obligatory femme interest – a refugee Portuguese countess intent on getting word back to her compatriots that pirates are after the gold needed to overthrow the king of Portugal. Howard Christie's Technicolor production didn't spare the clichés; nor did scenarist Charles K. Peck Jr. The equally reminiscent direction was by Frederick de Cordova, whose cast included George Matthews, Rudolfo Acosta, David Janssen and Jay Silverheels. (85 mins)

△ Another comedy in which the title said it all, **Francis Goes To West Point** again featured the (money-making) talking mule (left) and best friend of top-starred Donald O'Connor (right), who, this time out, saves an atomic plant from sabotage and is rewarded by becoming a West Point cadet. Complications infiltrated Oscar Brodney's screenplay when O'Connor invents a pregnant wife for himself. He's almost expelled as a result, but the situation satisfactorily unravels itself, with Francis helping the academy to win an important game against the Navy in the last climactic minutes of play. Helping to shuffle the familiar ingredients together was director Arthur Lubin who, at best, was able to raise only a few mild chuckles. It was produced by Leonard Goldstein, and also featured Lori Nelson, Alice Kelley, William Reynolds, Palmer Lee and, as the voice of Francis, Chill Wills. (81 mins)

▽ Thanks to the red-blooded direction of Raoul Walsh, **The World In His Arms**, a period actioner set in Alaska, left audiences exhilaratingly wind-swept and with a salty tang on their lips. It starred Gregory Peck (right) as the captain of a sealing schooner and Ann Blyth (left) as a Russian countess fleeing from a loveless marriage arranged for her by the Czar. The couple meet and fall in love in San Francisco, but this was a mere prelude to a full-blown romantic adventure such as only the movies could provide. Borden Chase's screenplay (additional dialogue by Horace McCoy) from the novel by Rex Beach had Miss Blyth being abducted by a Russian prince on the day of her marriage to Peck, leaving the latter to think he has been jilted. Of course, it ended not with the world in Peck's arms, but the more modestly scaled Miss Blyth. Though romance and action were the two main ingredients in Aaron Rosenberg's good-looking Technicolor Production, it was the action with which, on balance, director Walsh seemed more at home – a climactic race between two rival schooners in appalling gale conditions being the film's great 'set piece' and most memorable sequence. Anthony Quinn was third-billed as a seal-poaching rival to Peck, with other parts going to John McIntire, Carl Esmond, Andrea King, Eugenie Leontovich, Hans Conried, Rhys Williams, Sig Rumann and Bryan Forbes. (104 mins)

◁ A sequel to the previous year's *Up Front*, with Tom Ewell (right) reprising his characterisation of cartoonist Bill Mauldin's Willie, but with Harvey Lembeck (left) taking over from David Wayne as side-kick Joe, **Back At The Front** (also known as **Willie And Joe Back At The Front**) found the duo in Japan as guinea pigs in an army experiment, the reward for their services being time off in Tokyo. Scenarists Lou Breslow (who also supplied the story), Don McGuire and Oscar Brodney devised a yarn which threw Willie and Joe among a gang of arms smugglers, as well as several comic situations involving a Japanese bath, the pair's adventures on the streets of Tokyo while being chased by the military police, and their attempts to feign assorted illnesses in the hope that one of their ailments will secure their discharge from the service. Helping to provoke the occasional chuckle was director George Sherman whose cast was completed by Mari Blanchard (centre), Barry Kelley, Vaughn Taylor, Richard Long, Russell Johnson and Palmer Lee. Leonard Goldstein produced much of it on location in Japan. (87 mins)

▽ A family-oriented comedy and the cinematic equivalent of a gooey cream-bun, **Sally And Saint Anne** was the story of an Irish family's battle to save their home from a conniving town alderman with whom they have long feuded and who they eventually outwit. Ann Blyth (right) starred as the Sally of the title, Saint Anne being the mother of the Virgin Mary (and patron saint of young girls) with whom Miss Blyth has a very special relationship. Edmund Gwenn (left) co-starred as grandpop who, twenty years prior to the film's commencement, took to his bed on the pretext that he was dying and, for the sheer hell of it, has pretended to be dying ever since; with other roles in James O'Hanlon and Herb Meadows' likeable screenplay (story by O'Hanlon) being acted out by John McIntire (as the alderman), Palmer Lee, Hugh O'Brian, Jack Kelly, Frances Bavier, Otto Hulett and Lamont Johnson. It was directed by Rudolph Mate for producer Leonard Goldstein. (89 mins)

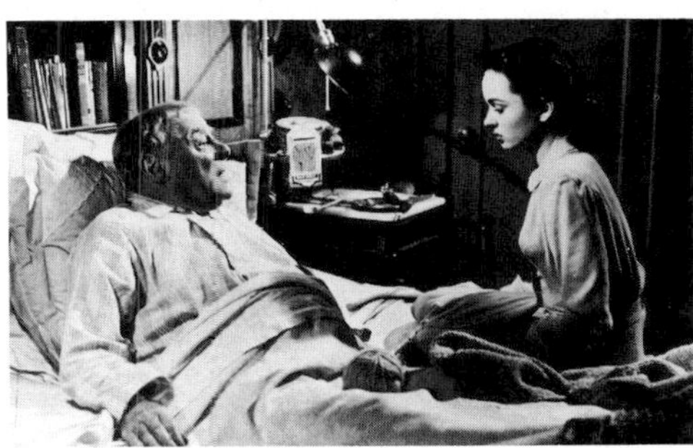

◁ Ancient Bagdad was the exotic setting for **Son Of Ali Baba**, an intrigue-laden excursion into Arabian Nights territory, with Tony Curtis (left) providing the heroics in Gerald Drayson Adams' inconsequential screenplay, and Piper Laurie (right, as a princess) the glamour – along with the usual quota of scantily-clad lovelies. The villain of producer Leonard Goldstein's Technicolor programmer was Caliph Victor Jory, with other roles assigned to Morris Ankrum (as Ali Baba), Susan Cabot, William Reynolds, Hugh O'Brian and Philip Van Zandt. Kurt Neumann directed. (75 mins)

1953

△ Some man-into-monster special effects, a wax museum sequence, a roof-top chase and the sinister presence of Boris Karloff (right) were the plus factors of **Abbott And Costello Meet Dr Jekyll And Mr Hyde**. The rest was drearily familiar as the fat man (centre) and the thin (left), having been discharged from the police force by a harassed Scotland Yard inspector (Reginald Denny), set out to redeem themselves by apprehending the monster scourge of Hyde Park, but track down his alter ego instead. Karloff played both Jekyll and Hyde, with other parts under Charles Lamont's tired direction going to Craig Stevens, Helen Westcott and John Dierkes. Howard Christie produced, and the script was the work of Lee Loeb and John Grant, based on stories by Grant Garrett and Sidney Fields. (76 mins)

▽ A tepid programmer about juvenile delinquency, **Girls In The Night**'s fallacious come-on title concealed a trite, really rather dull story of an indigent family's attempts to better themselves in the world by moving out of New York's lower east side to a more salubrious area. Anthony Ross and Glenda Farrell were the parents, Patricia Hardy (right) and Harvey Lembeck (left) their offspring. Plot hinged on Lembeck's stealing money from a phoney blind man, only to learn of the victim's murder by a neighbourhood thug (Don Gordon). Gordon's eventual apprehension was the main concern of Ray Buffam's under-nourished screenplay, the main participants in the search being Lembeck, his sister Hardy, top-billed Joyce Holden (centre), and Glen Roberts (2nd left). Albert J. Cohen produced and Jack Arnold directed (ineffectually). (83 mins)

▽ An undersea 'earthquake' in the historic sunken city of Port Royal, Jamaica, was the only item of interest in **City Beneath The Sea**, scripted by Jack Harvey and Ramon Romero (based on Harry E. Reisberg's *Port Royal – Ghost City Beneath The Sea*) and starring Robert Ryan and Anthony Quinn (illustrated) as a pair of dare-devil deep-sea divers who arrive in Kingston, Jamaica, to dive for a million dollars worth of gold bullion. Karel Stepanek was cast as the man who employs them (but who has reasons of his own for not wanting the boys to discover the treasure); with Mala Powers and Suzan Ball supplying the love angle. George Matthews, Lalo Rios, Hilo Hattie and Woody Strode were also in it; Albert J. Cohen produced (in Technicolor), and it was directed by Budd Boetticher. (87 mins)

▽ Tony Curtis played a gridiron hero in **The All-American**, an old-fashioned drama with a football background which D.D. Beauchamp scripted from an adaptation by Robert Yale Libott of a story by Leonard Freeman. Brimming with self-confidence both on and off the playing field, quarterback Curtis (left) undergoes a change when his parents are killed in a bus accident en route to see him play. He gives up school for a while, accepts a scholarship in a smaller, more exclusive college, gradually eases himself back into football, becomes involved with some wealthy socialites and is expelled on the day of an important game. But, in the best rah-rah tradition, he is reinstated just in time to make the winning touchdown. Lori Nelson co-starred as the girl who helps Curtis both physically and mentally. Richard Long was a wealthy snob, and Mamie Van Doren (right) a blonde seductress who lures members of the football team to their doom via an off-limits beer joint. Also cast: Gregg Palmer, Paul Cavanagh, Barney Phillips, Jimmy Hunt and Stuart Whitman. Aaron Rosenberg produced, and Jesse Hibbs directed. (82 mins)

▷ The great Barbara Stanwyck (right) did everything that was legal to try and rescue **All I Desire** from the quagmire of sentimental mediocrity into which director Douglas Sirk and scenarists James Gunn and Robert Blees plunged it. Based on Carol Brink's novel *Stopover* (adapted by Gina Kaus), it was the story of a woman (Stanwyck) who, ten years prior to the film's opening (in 1900), walked out on her school principal husband (Richard Carlson) and two daughters (Marcia Henderson, left, and Lori Nelson) when a scandal linked her name with Lyle Bettger's. After pursuing a career on the stage, she returns to see daughter Nelson in a high school graduation play, is given an icy reception by older daughter Henderson, and unintentionally rakes over the ashes of her past affair with Bettger when the latter makes unwelcome advances to her and is shot in the process. In a happy ending imposed on the production by producer Ross Hunter (much to director Sirk's disapproval), Stanwyck's husband stands by her for a cop-out reconciliation. Maureen O'Sullivan, Richard Long, Billy Gray and Lotte Stein (centre) completed the cast. (79 mins)

△ First filmed in 1919 by First National, then in 1927 by Universal, **Back To God's Country** definitely showed its age in Howard Christie's brand new Technicolor version. Rock Hudson and Marcia Henderson (both illustrated) starred as the ship's captain and his wife detained in a remote Canadian harbour by hateful Steve Cochran, who's after Miss Henderson. Following a rough-and-tumble fight with Cochran in which Hudson breaks his leg, Mr and Mrs set off together with a treacherous guide and a Great Dane on a five-day trip across the snow (via dog sled), with Cochran in hot pursuit. When he finally catches up with his quarry, the Great Dane comes splendiferously to the rescue. Tom Reed scripted it from the novel by James Oliver Curwood, and it was directed by Joseph Pevney with a cast that included Hugh O'Brian, Chubby Johnson, Tudor Owen and Arthur Space. (77 mins)

▽ **Column South** was the kind of traditional oater that made no demands on anyone – including the audience. A familiar cavalry vs Indians story set just before the Civil War, it starred Audie Murphy (centre) as a cavalry lieutenant who's having a spot of bother trying to convince Captain Robert Sterling, the new commander at a New Mexico post, that there *is* a way to live peacefully with the Navajos under their leader Dennis Weaver. Of course, there was more to it than that (but not much), with Murphy uncovering a plot laid by Ray Collins (a general in charge of Union forces) to turn his troops over to the Confederates when war is declared. Joan Evans, the only woman in the cast, played Sterling's pretty sister (whom Murphy successfully romances), with other roles in William Sackheim's thoroughly undistinguished screenplay going to Palmer Lee, Russell Johnson, Jack Kelly and Johnny Downs. Ted Richmond produced (in Technicolor) and it was directed by Frederick de Cordova. (84 mins)

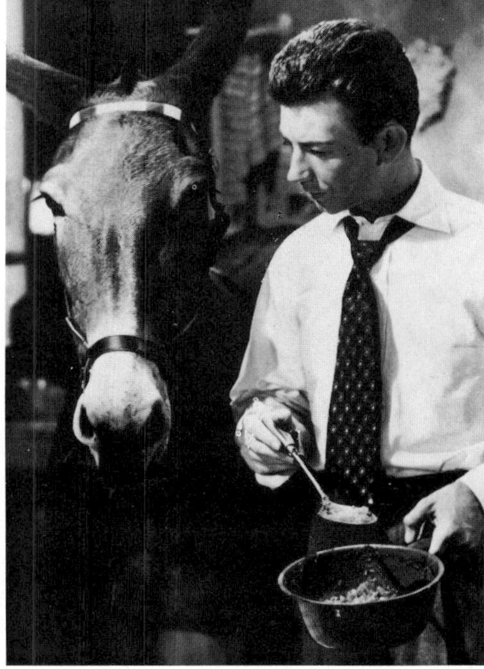

△ Donald O'Connor (illustrated) punched home Oscar Brodney's dialogue for **Francis Covers The Big Town** with his usual brand of zany enthusiasm but, as always, it was Francis (illustrated), the titular talking mule (with a voice again supplied by Chill Wills) whom audiences paid to see (and hear). This time they witnessed him aiding and abetting Mr O'Connor in the latter's newly chosen profession as ace reporter on a New York newspaper. Thanks to Francis, O'Connor surfaces with several scoops, and, also thanks to Francis, is acquitted of a murder charge when the mule testifies to his innocence. The only thing Francis didn't do was supply the love interest – Yvette Dugay and Nancy Guild took care of that. Leonard Goldstein produced it and his cast also included Gene Lockhart as an editor and Larry Gates as a reporter. The director was Arthur Lubin. (86 mins)

▽ **East Of Sumatra** needed a bit more starch than director Budd Boetticher gave it. A flaccid wadge of Technicolor escapism, it starred Jeff Chandler as a tin miner on a Pacific island, and third-billed Anthony Quinn (illustrated) as the island's ruler. Second-billed Marilyn Maxwell added her shapely feminine charms to the island setting; so did Suzan Ball as Quinn's betrothed. When, however, Chandler and Quinn fight it out in a climactic duel – involving a knife and a flaming torch – which Quinn loses, Miss Ball becomes ruler and vouchsafes a happy ending for the 'white' members of the cast who, in the course of Frank Gill's screenplay (adapted by Jack Natteford from a story he wrote with Louis L'Amour) are blamed for the fire which destroys the natives' rice crop. John Sutton, Jay C. Flippen, Scat Man Crothers (as a cook), Aram Katcher and Eugene Yglesias were also in it for producer Albert J. Cohen. (81 mins)

▽ Edward G. Robinson (left) lent his considerable talents to a miserably inconsiderable thriller called **The Glass Web**, whose only point of interest was its TV studio setting. The star played a frustrated researcher on a weekly crime series: co-star John Forsythe was the writjr of the series. Both are involved with actress Kathleen Hughes (right) who is blackmailing Forsythe because of the summer affair they had while his wife was away; and using Robinson because of his unbridled infatuation with her. The plot thickens with the death of Miss Hughes – killed by Robinson, who has pinned the rap on Forsythe. Justice, however, is seen to be done, and the thriller ends with Robinson being nicked just as he is about to ventilate Forsythe with lead. Marcia Henderson, Richard Denning, Hugh Sanders and Jean Willes were also in it; Albert J. Cohen produced (in 3-D, though the film was also released in 2-D, despite its 1-D plot), with Jack Arnold in charge of the direction. (81 mins)

△ Alan Ladd and the Foreign Legion made a predictable combination in **Desert Legion**, whose screenplay by Irving Wallace and Lewis Meltzer (from the novel *The Demon Caravan* by Georges Arthur Surdez) went in for the kind of juvenile muscularity greatly appreciated by 12-year-olds. Ladd (left) played a legionnaire, sole survivor of an ambush, who is nursed back to health by luscious Arlene Dahl (doubly luscious in Technicolor) whose father (Oscar Beregi) is the ruler of a 'Lost City' in the mountains. In return for aiding his recovery, Dahl (centre) seeks Ladd's help against bad guy Richard Conte, who is determined to destroy her peaceful Utopia. When Ladd fails to muster official support for his philanthropic mission (no one believes such a place exists), he goes AWOL, and together with loquacious travelling companion Akim Tamiroff (right), sets out to do what he can for red-haired Miss Dahl and her father. The last 25 minutes or so compensated for the suicidally slow opening hour, but not sufficiently to save the picture from being just another routine actioner. The cast was completed by Leon Askin, Anthony Caruso, George L. Lewis and dancers Sujata and Asoka, and the director was Joseph Pevney. (85 mins)

▷ Without the benefits gained by utilising 3-D, **It Came From Outer Space** would have been just another tame piece of sci-fi, with precious little to recommend it. Not that its technical accoutrements helped to elevate it into a cinematic masterpiece. Far from it. But at least it was fun to watch (through polaroid glasses), and it did convey a feeling of physical depth. There was no depth, however, in Harry Essex's screenplay (from a story by Ray Bradbury) which merely featured a frustrated Richard Carlson (as a scientist – illustrated) trying to convince the authorities that he really did see a fiery object landing in the Arizona desert, prior to a landslide which then covered it. Also witnessing the spectacle was his schoolteacher fiancée, Barbara Rush. It is only when a series of strange occurrences begin to insinuate themselves on the small Arizona community (among whose folk the film was set), that Carlson is able to convince people he has been telling the truth. Charles Drake, Russell Johnson, Kathleen Hughes, Joseph Sawyer and Dave Wilcox were the earthlings involved: William Alland produced, and it was directed by Jack Arnold who kept the special 3-D effects under suitable control. (80 mins)

▽ A misdirected comedy in every sense, **Abbott And Costello Go To Mars** had A & C accidentally taking off for Mars and landing on Venus (via a short stop-off in New Orleans at Mardi Gras time where they acquire travelling companions Horace McMahon, 2nd left and Jack Khruschen, right) instead. Being Venus, they discover the planet is run by Queen Mari Blanchard who has had all men banished because her husband had a roving eye. Just as the one-eyed man is god in the kingdom of the blind, so, in a planet starved of males, this motley quartet of space travellers are welcomed with open arms. But not for long. Costello (2nd right) is untrue to the Queen and is banished to from whence he came. Not even a group of 1952 Miss Universe candidates, who helped people Venus, could save the film from the kind of relentless tedium which irritated even the duo's (Abbott, left) most faithful fans. Robert Paige, Martha Hyer, Joe Kirk and Anita Ekberg also had parts in D.D. Beauchamp and John Grant's silly screenplay; it was produced by Howard Christie (who also provided the storyline), and directed by Charles Lamont. (76 mins)

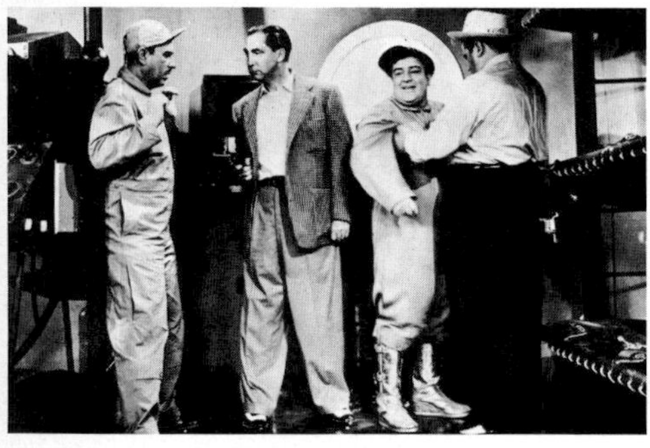

▷ Norman A. Fox's novel *Roughshod* provided the inspiration for **Gunsmoke**, scripted by D.D. Beauchamp, and with Audie Murphy (left) top-starred as a gunman for hire who arrives in Montana to investigate a job offer from Donald Randolph, a big-wheel out to corner the ranch market in the valley, but prevented from doing so by Paul Kelly who has a vital piece of land Randolph wants. Murphy's brief is to eliminate Kelly. This basically simple strand of plot developed several knots en route to its predictable conclusion, with Susan Cabot (right), Mary Castle, Charles Drake, Jack Kelly and Jesse White in support. Aaron Rosenberg produced (in Technicolor), and it was directed without any evidence of flair by Nathan Juran. (78 mins)

△ Another of the studio's standard, Technicolored costume actioners, **The Golden Blade** starred Rock Hudson (centre) who, as Harun, the personification of all that is good and noble, puts an end (with the help of the magic sword of Damascus, though he could have done it alone) to the dastardly grand vizier (George Macready), the personification of everything rotten and vile. And that was about all there was to producer Richard Wilson's familiar dollop of escapism – unless you counted the obligatory love stuff with the beautiful Princess of Bagdad, played, on this not particularly memorable occasion, by Miss Piper Laurie (on couch right). Also helping to act out John Rich's story and screenplay were Gene Evans, Kathleen Hughes (on couch left), Steven Geray, Edgar Barrier and Anita Ekberg. Nathan Juran directed. (80 mins)

▽ **The Great Sioux Uprising** was an inexorably trite formula western whose only potential point of interest lay in its basic subject matter: the acquisition of horses from neutral red Indians by the army, whose own supply of cavalry mounts are diminishing at an alarming rate. Top-billed Jeff Chandler (centre), as a surgeon-turned-horse-doctor because of a hand wound, sets out to acquire the horses in an above-board manner; antagonist Lyle Bettger, a rancher with a contract to supply nags to the army, does so crookedly. The consequences of the latter's underhand methods formed the basis for the Melvin Levy-J. Robert Bren-Gladys Atwater screenplay (story by Bren and Atwater, and additional dialogue by Frank Gill Jr), with other parts in it for Faith Domergue (as a lady rancher, right), Peter Whitney, John War Eagle, Stephen Chase, Stacey Harris and Walter Sande. It was produced (in Technicolor and on location in eastern Oregon) by Albert J. Cohen, and directed by Lloyd Bacon. (79 mins)

▽ Another farcical bromide from Percy Kilbride and Marjorie Main alias Ma and Pa Kettle, **Ma And Pa Kettle On Vacation** found the couple, in the company of their daughter-in-law's wealthy parents (Ray Collins and Barbara Brown), holidaying in Paris where Pa, between ogling Can-Can dancers (see illustration) and attempting to purchase a set of dirty postcards, also finds the time to become involved in a spy plot, and to prove himself a hero of sorts. It didn't short-change regular fans, but it made no converts either. Bodil Miller, Sig Rumann and Peter Brocco played the spies; with Ivan Triesault, Oliver Blake and Teddy Hart completing the cast for producer Leonard Goldstein and director Charles Lamont. Jack Henley scripted. (75 mins)

▽ Rock Hudson (right) was top-starred for the first time in **The Lawless Breed**, as John Wesley Hardin, a gunman in the early west, whose screen biography this was. Under Raoul Walsh's lusty direction, it emerged as a solid piece of outdoor entertainment, with an episodic plot (screenplay by Bernard Gordon, story by producer William Alland) that chronicled how Hardin earned his reputation as a killer after felling his first victim in self-defence; how he was forced into further killings while fleeing the law; how he lost his sweetheart (Mary Castle) in a rain of bullets; how he acquired another (Julia Adams, centre); and how, finally, he was apprehended by Texas rangers. It was shot in Technicolor and, in supporting roles featured Hugh O'Brian, Lee Van Cleef, Glenn Strange, Tom Fadden, Dick Wessel (left) and Forrest Lewis. (83 mins)

△ **The Redhead From Wyoming** was Maureen O'Hara (centre), whose stunning good looks, rapturously enhanced by Technicolor, embellished the hand-me-down plot (by Polly James, who scripted with Herb Meadow). In it, the villain (William Bishop, left) promotes a range war between ranchers and settlers as a cover-up for his own rustling activities and crooked political ambitions. He uses O'Hara, an ex-girlfriend and saloon-keeper as a 'fall guy' (or, in this case, 'fall gal') in his scheme, much to the lady's disapproval. Furious at being thus manipulated, she attempts to end the range war by forming a cattle association for the settlers, but, instead, finds herself thrown in jail on charges of murder and rustling. She (and the settlers) are saved, however, by the timely intervention of sheriff Alex Nicol, whose successful pitch against the baddies is rewarded when he gets the gal. Leonard Goldstein's production (redolent of so many others), was directed by Lee Sholem with a cast that included Robert Strauss (right), Alexander Scourby, Palmer Lee, Jack Kelly and Dennis Weaver. (81 mins)

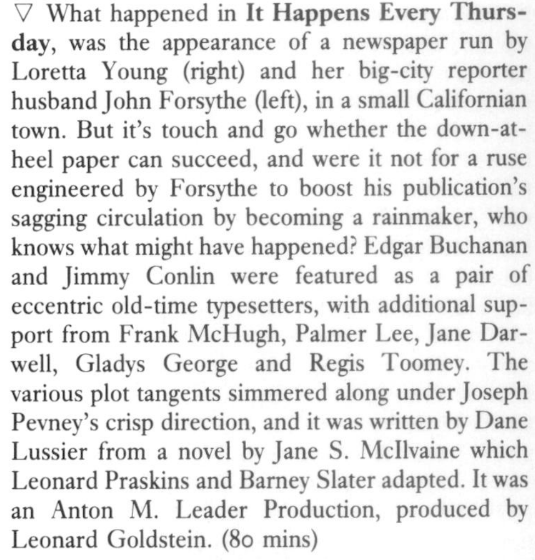

▽ What happened in **It Happens Every Thursday**, was the appearance of a newspaper run by Loretta Young (right) and her big-city reporter husband John Forsythe (left), in a small Californian town. But it's touch and go whether the down-at-heel paper can succeed, and were it not for a ruse engineered by Forsythe to boost his publication's sagging circulation by becoming a rainmaker, who knows what might have happened? Edgar Buchanan and Jimmy Conlin were featured as a pair of eccentric old-time typesetters, with additional support from Frank McHugh, Palmer Lee, Jane Darwell, Gladys George and Regis Toomey. The various plot tangents simmered along under Joseph Pevney's crisp direction, and it was written by Dane Lussier from a novel by Jane S. McIlvaine which Leonard Praskins and Barney Slater adapted. It was an Anton M. Leader Production, produced by Leonard Goldstein. (80 mins)

▽ Set in 1904 and starring Dan Dailey as a travelling medicine man, **Meet Me At The Fair** provided easy, undemanding entertainment, laced with some good musical numbers performed by Dailey, a lively Carole Mathews (as a vaudeville entertainer in love with Dan), Scat Man Crothers, and child singer Chet Allen. Young Master Allen (right) played an orphan on the run from a grim children's home who finds sanctuary with Dailey (seated left). The latter is then accused of kidnapping the child, and gets into a wrangle with social worker Diana Lynn (centre) who is engaged to politician Hugh O'Brian. O'Brian turns out to be crooked, Miss Lynn's animosity to Dailey turns to affection and, together, they foil O'Brian's nefarious plans, as well as reforming the offending orphanage. Albert J. Cohen produced, and was well-served by director Douglas Sirk who drew as much from the material as possible. The screenplay was by Irving Wallace (adapted by Martin Berkeley from a novel by Gene Markey), and the cast was completed by Rhys Williams, Russell Simpson, Thomas E. Jackson and George Chandler. The dances were staged by Kenny Williams. Songs and musical numbers included: 'Meet Me At The Fair' Milton Rosen, Frederick Herbert; 'I Was There' F.E. Miller, Scat Man Crothers; 'Bill Bailey Won't You Please Come Home' Hughie Cannon; 'Ave Maria' Schubert; 'I Got The Shiniest Mouth In Town' Stan Freeberg; 'Ezekiel Saw De Wheel' (traditional). (87 mins)

▷ Tyrone Power (illustrated) came to Universal to star in, and as, **The Mississippi Gambler**, a handsomely produced (by Ted Richmond) romantic costume adventure (in Technicolor) set in antebellum New Orleans, in which hero Power proved himself adept at the card table, at swordfighting, at fisticuffs and at pitching the proverbial woo. There were two women in Power's life (and in Seton I. Miller's platitudinous screenplay): fiery Southern belle Piper Laurie, an heiress who fancies Power like crazy but wilfully marries banker Ron Randell; and Julia Adams, who quietly adores our hero though, alas, the sentiment is not mutual, with Power feeling merely protective towards her. Paul Cavanagh played Miss Laurie's father, John Baer was her weak-willed brother, John McIntire a card dealer and Power's side-kick, with other parts going to Ralph Dumke, Robert Warwick, William Reynolds and Guy Williams. Director Rudolph Maté only partially succeeded in knitting together the romantic and swashbuckling elements in the yarn, but the film was fun in its old-fashioned way, with the good looks of the leading players (and the Technicolor photography) appealing to audiences of all sexes. (99 mins)

△ **Lone Hand**, with Joel McCrea in the lead, and with a halfway decent screenplay by Joseph Hoffman (story by Irving Ravetch) was an above average Technicolor western. McCrea played a high-principled widower newly arrived with his hero-worshipping son (Jimmy Hunt, left) into a community of ranchers (circa 1870), only to learn that the community has been plagued by killer bandits. Before you could say 'that's show-biz', McCrea joins up with the heavies – much to the consternation of his young son (as well as his newly acquired wife, Barbara Hale, right) who simply cannot believe what has happened. Turns out, though, that McCrea has been on the side of the law all along. So there. Alex Nicol, Wesley Morgan, Charles Drake and James Arness completed the cast for producer Howard Christie and director George Sherman, both of whom were to be deplored for allowing the statutory 'surprise' ending. (80 mins)

◁ Ronald Reagan in Technicolor wasn't a sufficient magnet to pull customers to **Law And Order** which, like its title, was as well-worn as a pair of bedroom slippers, and just about as innocuous. Designed for the kind of youngster who wears toy six-shooters to Saturday morning movie matinees, it told the ho-hum story of a marshal (Reagan, left) who, having cleaned up Tombstone, turns in his badge and retires, *avec* girlfriend Dorothy Malone (right), to another small, western town, not as a marshal but as a rancher. Unfortunately, the town he has chosen is in the grip of bad guy Preston Foster, and after Reagan's brother (Alex Nicol) is killed by one of Foster's sons, the retired marshal has little choice but to return to law enforcement, which he does – but only for as long as it takes to rid the town of Foster and his boys. Ruth Hampton, Russell Johnson, Barry Kelley, Chubby Johnson and Dennis Weaver also appeared for producer John W. Rogers; it was written by John and Gwen Bagni and D.D. Beauchamp (from a novel by William R. Burnett) and directed by Nathan Juran. If it seemed especially familiar, it was – being a remake of two earlier versions (1932 and 1940) of the story; as well as a rehash of the 1937 serial *Wild West Days*. (80 mins)

◁ A laconic Glenn Ford (illustrated on ground) starred in **The Man From Alamo**, another Technicolored western that looked better than it sounded. Chosen by lot to escape from the Alamo before the arrival of Santa Ana's forces, and to warn the families of the Alamo's defenders of the impending disaster about to befall the fort, Glenn is branded a coward for desertion, a fact he stubbornly refuses to refute verbally, clearly believing that actions speak louder than words. Particularly when the words were by scenarists D.D. Beauchamp and Steve Fisher (from a story by Niven Busch and Oliver Crawford). Naturally, Ford gets a chance to prove himself and to take revenge against the film's heavy, Victor Jory who, together with a group of men posing as Mexican soldiers, wiped out Glenn's family, as well as the families of several other Alamo heroes. Julia Adams (centre kneeling) was second-billed as the one person who believed in Ford from the outset, with other roles under Budd Boetticher's gritty direction going to Chill Wills (centre right), Jeanne Cooper (left), Hugh O'Brian (centre left), Myra Marsh (centre), Neville Brand and John Day. Aaron Rosenberg produced. (97 mins)

▽ 3-D did nothing for **Wings Of The Hawk**, except involve audiences a mite more closely in the tedium it perpetrated than they might have wished for. Set against a Mexican backdrop, the film evoked the revolutionary days of Pancho Villa and President Diaz, and starred Van Heflin (illustrated) as an American mining engineer, whose gold mine is confiscated by Colonel Ruiz (George Dolenz), leader of the Federales. How Heflin, after joining a group of Mexican 'insurrectos' (and meeting lovely outlaw Julia Adams) avenges himself, provided scenarist James E. Moser (working from Kay Lenard's adaptation of the Gerald Drayson Adams novel on which it was based) with the basis for his chase-filled screenplay; and parts for Abbe Lane, Antonio Moreno, Noah Beery Jr and Pedro Gonzales-Gonzales. Aaron Rosenberg produced (in Technicolor), and it was directed by Budd Boetticher, whose restraint in not flinging into the audiences' laps everything that wasn't actually nailed down was to be commended. (80 mins)

▽ **The Veils Of Bagdad** was a puny little potboiler, despite the anything but puny presence of beefy Victor Mature (right) who, single-handedly, brings down the despotic pasha (Leon Askin) and grand vizier (Guy Rolfe) of Bagdad, appropriators of tax money in order to finance a private war against the Ottoman Empire. His reward? Mari Blanchard (left), daughter of a murdered tribe leader, who, while trying to track down her father's slayer, has taken employment in a Bagdad tavern as a dancing girl. The impossible screenplay was the work of William R. Cox; George Sherman directed, and it was produced, in Technicolor, by Albert J. Cohen with a cast that included Virginia Field, James Arness, Palmer Lee, Nick Cravat and Ludwig Donath. (82 mins)

◁ Florida's swamp country (looking good in Technicolor) provided the colourful backdrop to **Seminole**, an action-packed chestnut which starred Rock Hudson (right) as a native Floridian assigned to Fort King, an army outpost near the Everglades, after he graduates from West Point. His commanding officer is martinet Richard Carlson, bent on ridding the Everglades of its Seminole Indian population. Hudson doesn't quite see things Carlson's way, and their differences concerning the Seminoles was just one of the issues in Charles K. Peck's routine screenplay. Barbara Hale was the only woman in producer Howard Christie's cast, and she loved both Hudson and third-billed Anthony Quinn (left, as Indian leader Osceola, a boyhood friend of Hudson's); Hugh O'Brian, Russell Johnson and Lee Marvin were also in it, and Budd Boetticher directed. (87 mins)

▽ **Take Me To Town** was a painfully self-conscious attempt to capture family audiences, but its irrepressible blend of molasses and saccharine served only to decay everything it touched. Apart from the punters, the worst to suffer from its gooey excesses were Ann Sheridan, a good woman if ever there was one, and her co-star Sterling Hayden who, if anything, suffered even more, being the widower-father of three impossible tykes. Sheridan (right), for her sins, played 'a lady with a past' who, while hiding out from the law in a lumber town, is propositioned by the aforementioned tykes to become their surrogate mother while preacher pa goes off to work. Needless to say she does – but fails to receive the approval of the logging community until she stages a show to raise money for a new church, after which she's in like Flint. The obvious ending had her and Hayden paired off together, and the trio of kids richer by a new mom. Philip Reed (centre), Lee Patrick, Lee Asker, Harvey Grant, Larry Gates (left) and Phyllis Stanley were also part of Ross Hunter's Technicolor production, and the director was Douglas Sirk. (80 mins)

▽ Multi-talented Donald O'Connor (illustrated) starred in **Walking My Baby Back Home**, but could not save the enterprise from its tedious screenplay by Don McGuire and Oscar Brodney (story by McGuire), mediocre direction by Lloyd Bacon, and pedestrian musical numbers choreographed by Louis Da Pron. O'Connor was a socialite who, on getting his army discharge, forms a band with some ex-GI pals. Their music fails to catch on, and he ends up joining a minstrel show run by co-star Janet Leigh's uncle. When this fails, he attempts to give Dixieland music symphonic treatment, and finds himself a success at last. Buddy Hackett, Scat Man Crothers, Lori Nelson, Kathleen Lockhart, George Cleveland, John Hubbard, Paula Kelly (who also dubbed for Miss Leigh), The Sportsmen and The Modernaires were featured in support for producer Ted Richmond. It was well-photographed in Technicolor, and offered twelve tunes, among which were: 'Man's Gotta Eat' F.E. Miller, Scat Man Crothers; 'Walkin' My Baby Back Home' Roy Turk, Fred Ahlert; 'Glow Worm' Paul Lincke, Johnny Mercer; 'Honeysuckle Rose' Fats Waller, Andy Razaf; 'South Rampart Street Parade' Ray Bauduc, Bob Haggart; Steve Allen; 'De Camptown Races' Stephen Foster; 'Muskrat Ramble' Kid Ory, Ray Gilbert. (94 mins)

▽ To call **Stand At Apache River** depressingly ordinary would be to understate the case. Set around a stage-coach station at a river crossing and all about a group of eight people who are being held under siege by red Indians, it was slow, repetitive, too wordy by half, and asphyxiatingly predictable. Stephen McNally (centre) starred as a sheriff with a wounded prisoner (Russell Johnson, foreground) in tow; with Julia Adams (centre right), Hugh Marlowe (left), Jaclynne Greene, Hugh O'Brian, Jack Kelly and Forrest Lewis as the other members of the cast being held by redskin leader Edgar Barrier. Eventually the Indians get their come uppance, and romance is served when McNally and Adams pair off for the final fade. But, oh dear, how boring it all was! William Alland produced (in Technicolor), and it was directed by Lee Sholem from a screenplay by Arthur Ross which, in turn, was based on Robert J. Hogan's novel *Apache Landing*. (76 mins)

◁ A typical Audie Murphy (left) western, with the usual generous quota of action stuff, **Tumbleweed** had the hero being accused of a wagon-train raid. He's saved from a lynching mob by sheriff Chill Wills (centre right), and rescued from jail by an Indian he had once helped, before finally coming to grips with the real villain, Russell Johnson. Basically a protracted chase, the film hardly contributed to the mythology of the west, being a par-for-the-course entertainment with no pretensions to originality. Lori Nelson (centre left) provided some perfunctory feminine interest, with Roy Roberts (right), K.T. Stevens, Madge Meredith, Lee Van Cleef, and a rather clever nag called Tumbleweed (the real hero of the piece, far left) also lending their talents to producer Ross Hunter and director Nathan Juran's oater. It was photographed in Technicolor. (79 mins)

▽ The studio's impressive new wide screen process as well as three-speaker stereophonic sound, not to mention Technicolor, didn't, in the end, do much for **Thunder Bay**. An adventure yarn structured entirely out of clichés, it featured James Stewart and Dan Duryea (the latter in a sympathetic role for once) as a couple of ex-GIs who set out, with the financial backing of oil man Jay C. Flippen, to find 'black gold' at the bottom of the Gulf of Mexico off the Louisiana coast. They are opposed in their venture by a group of shrimp fishermen who fear for their livelihood with all that blasting going on around them. The women in the piece were Joanne Dru (left) and her sister Marcia Henderson, the former pairing off with Stewart (right), the latter in love with Duryea but already married to Robert Monet. The finale had the heroes succeeding in finding not only the precious 'black gold' they came for, but, to placate the put-upon Cajun folk, a vast bed of king-sized shrimps as well. Four people had a hand in writing it: Gil Doud, John Michael Hayes, George W. George and George F. Slavin, the latter two providing the idea. Aaron Rosenberg produced. Anthony Mann directed, and the cast was completed by Gilbert Roland (as a shrimp-boat captain), Antonio Moreno and Henry Morgan. (103 mins)

1954

△ Strictly for die-hards of the western genre, **Drums Across The River** corralled every oater cliché in the lexicon to tell the story of a trouble-maker (Lyle Bettger) who sets out to cause friction between the Utes and the whites and, for personal gain, to open up a gold deposit in the Ute territory hitherto closed to whites by treaty. Not only that, but he robs a stage-coach of its gold shipment, and lays the blame at the door of top-starred Audie Murphy (right) and his dad Walter Brennan. And he almost gets away with it too, the so-and-so. Which was more than could be said for Melville Tucker's Technicolor production, which made no impact at all, and soon became just another studio statistic. Lisa Gaye provided the perfunctory feminine interest, with Hugh O'Brian (Bettger's henchman), Mara Corday, Jay Silverheels, Morris Ankrum, Ken Terrell (left) and Regis Toomey also appearing under Nathan Juran's comic-book direction. It was written by John K. Butler and Lawrence Roman from a story by Butler. (77 mins)

▽ Lashings of good-natured backwoods sentiment were liberally poured over **Ma And Pa Kettle At Home** by scenarist Kay Lenard whose plot couldn't have been simpler. One of the Kettle's offspring (Brett Halsey) is a finalist in an essay competition, the prize being a scholarship to an agricultural college. But before the winner is announced, the two judges involved (prissy Alan Mowbray and Ross Elliott) plan to spend a week at each of the two finalists' homes. Naturally, Pa Kettle wants to make as good an impression on the judges as possible, so he sets about sprucing up their old ramshackle farm. Things don't quite work out as planned, however, and showing Pa's well-intentioned endeavours misfire was the *raison d'être* for Richard Wilson's modest, and modestly entertaining, little farce. As usual Percy Kilbride and Marjorie Main (both illustrated) played Ma and Pa, with other roles under Charles Lamont's seasoned direction going to Alice Kelley, Mary Wickes, Oliver Blake and Stan Ross. (80 mins)

▽ A potboiler western with vengeance as its theme, **Ride Clear Of Diablo** star-billed Audie Murphy (right) who, with a bit of help from Dan Duryea (left), sets out to avenge the murder of his father and kid brother by Russell Johnson and Paul Birch – a sheriff and a lawyer respectively. Also in on the dirty work is William Pullen, and the trio of heavies do everything they can to eliminate Murphy. But retribution was what George Zuckerman's screenplay (with additional dialogue by D.D. Beauchamp) and Ellis Marcus' story was all about, and it was retribution that Murphy finally exacted. He also got Susan Cabot, the crooked sheriff's niece. What audiences got was a formula oater in Technicolor. The cast was completed by Abbe Lane, Jack Elam and Denver Pyle. Director Jesse Hibbs kept it simmering, and it was produced by John W. Rogers. (80 mins)

▽ An amiable adventure yarn with a sports-car racing background, **Johnny Dark** starred Tony Curtis in the title role. His main purpose in Franklin Coen's screenplay is to win a climactic Canada-to-Mexico race (which he does), and the love of co-star Piper Laurie (which he also does). *How* he did it, comprised the unshattering contents of the plot, and provided roles for Paul Kelly and Ilka Chase, of The Fielding Motor Company, whose boss is Sidney Blackmer. Curtis (right) and Laurie (left) are also Blackmer employees; so is Don Taylor, a buddy of Curtis who, after a fall-out, races against the hero in the big finish. Ruth Hampton, Russell Johnson, Joseph Sawyer and Robert Nichols were also in it; William Alland produced (in Technicolor) and it was directed by George Sherman who managed, despite the slender material, to keep it gripping throughout. The big race at the end was especially worth waiting for. It was remade in 1964 as *The Lively Set*. (85 mins)

▽ The studio's first venture into CinemaScope was **The Black Shield Of Falworth**, a comic cut about ye chivalrous knights of olde, with no pretensions whatsoever to historical accuracy, let alone art. The familiar story of a peasant lad who turns out not to be a peasant at all but the son of the banished Earl of Falworth, it starred Tony Curtis (left) as the 'peasant', looking somewhat puny in all that mediaeval drag. After becoming a squire at the Earl of Mackworth's (Herbert Marshall, right) castle and training for knighthood, Curtis quells a conspiracy against King Henry IV (Ian Keith) hatched by David Farrar, the wicked Earl of Alban. He then disposes of the traitor, regains his aristocratic status and is richly rewarded for his feats of derring-do with the hand of Marshall's daughter, the lovely Lady Ann (Janet Leigh, centre). Giving a performance as *papier maché* as the settings in which it all took place, Curtis hardly convinced audiences he was made of the stuff of heroes; but then conviction (on every level) was the one quality most conspicuous by its absence. Rudolph Maté directed from a screenplay Oscar Brodney pummelled out of Howard Pyle's novel *Men Of Iron*, with a cast that included Torin Thatcher (standing centre), Barbara Rush, Daniel (Dan) O'Herlihy, Patrick O'Neal, Craig Hill, Doris Lloyd, Rhys Williams and Leonard Mudie. It was produced (in Technicolor) by Robert Arthur. (98 mins)

▽ An entertaining adventure in Technicolor, set in the US Civil War, **Border River** starred Joel McCrea as a Confederate Major who, in the closing stages of the war, attempts to help the South's decreasing chances by stealing $2,000,000 in gold bullion from a Union mint. Crossing the Rio Grande, McCrea (right) makes his way to the money-grabbing town of Zona Libre where he hopes to use the bullion to make a deal for ammunition and supplies for the Rebel army. Word quickly gets round that he has gold in his possession and, in no time at all, various unsavoury types are after it for their own nefarious purposes – particularly Pedro Armendariz (left), a renegade Mexican general. Second-billed Yvonne De Carlo (centre) played Armendariz's girlfriend, with other roles assigned to Ivan Triesault, Alphonso Bedoya, Howard Petrie, Erika Nordin and George Lewis. It was scripted by William Sackheim and Louis Stevens from a story by Stevens, produced by Albert J. Cohen, and competently directed with a passable sense of period by George Sherman. (80 mins)

△ Stiff upper-lippery combined with red-blooded heroics in **Bengal Brigade**, another formula adventure set in India at the time of British rule, and starring handsome Rock Hudson (left) as the leader of a brigade of Sepoy troops who, against orders, leads his troops into action, and resigns after being disciplined for disobedience. He also resigns from Torin Thatcher's beautiful daughter (second-billed Arlene Dahl, right) because of his uncertain future. When, however, he hears of a scheme by rajah Arnold Moss to free India of British rule, he pretends to be a traitor in order to infiltrate the enemy's ranks, in which guise he manages to save the colonel, Miss Dahl, and several Sepoys; and also quashes the proposed rebellion before it gets underway. Despite his strong midwestern accent, Hudson had just the right kind of matinée-idol good-looks for hokum of this calibre, and brought to Richard Alan Simmons' screenplay (adapted by Seton I. Miller from Hall Hunter's novel *Bengal Tiger*) the panache it required. Ursula Thiess also starred (as a native with an unrequited passion for the hero), with other roles under Laslo Benedek's gung-ho direction going to Daniel (Dan) O'Herlihy (as a cowardly British captain), Harold Gordon, Michael Ansara and, as a pair of local dancers, Sujata and Asoka. Ted Richmond produced it in Technicolor. (86 mins)

△ The message behind **The Creature From The Black Lagoon** was that even scaly gill-men (or mer-men) are human. Certainly the rather lonely creature stumbled upon by science researchers Richard Carlson, Julia Adams, Richard Denning and Antonio Moreno on an expedition in the Amazon, was human, otherwise why would he find himself so irresistibly drawn to the well-endowed physical charms of Miss Adams – especially when the lady dons a white bathing suit or slips into a pair of shorts? Credit make-up wizards Bud Westmore and Jack Kevan for the number they did on the monster in question (see illustration), but debit scenarists Harry Essex and Arthur Ross (story by Maurice Zimm) for the rather feeble plot they put their protagonists through. It was produced in 3-D by William Alland, and the director was Jack Arnold. Also cast: Nestor Paiva and Whit Bissell. (79 mins)

▽ It was nice to see Tony Curtis (illustrated) out of eastern garb and in mufti for **Forbidden**, but that was all that could be said in its favour. For the rest it was a relentlessly drab little caper which chronicled the on-off romance between Curtis and co-star Joanne Dru, in tandem with a plot involving hoodlum Curtis' trip to Macao to bring Miss Dru (as the widow of a racketeer) back to the States, together with the incriminating evidence she carries with her, and which would be fatal to the well-being of several crooks should the evidence ever be used against them. A great deal of double-crossing threaded its way across William Sackheim and Gil Doud's screenplay, but it all sorted itself out in the end with the two protagonists finishing up in each other's arms. Lyle Bettger played Macao's suave Mr Big, with other parts under Rudolph Maté's direction going to Marvin Miller, Victor Sen Yung and Peter J. Mamakos. Ted Richmond produced. (84 mins)

▽ Francis, the loquacious mule, referred to by one scribe at the time as a 'veritable Machiavelli with hocks' was back in the fold in **Francis Joins The WACS**, more screwball comedy with top-starred Donald O'Connor (as a bank clerk and ex-GI, right) this time joining the WACS due to a clerical error. As usual, the script, by Deverey Freeman and James B. Allardice (story by Herbert Baker), gave the quadruped all the best lines in an attempt to prove him more intelligent by far than any of the two-legged specimens on display – the latter including Lynn Bari, the WACS' unit commander, and her aide Julia Adams; not to mention shapely Mamie Van Doren, ZaSu Pitts (reprising her role as the nurse in the first film of the series in 1950), Joan Shawlee (centre left), Alison Hayes, Mara Corday, and third-billed Chill Wills, who not only supplied the voice of Francis, but also appeared as a commanding general. Ted Richmond produced and, ensuring a steady ripple of laughter throughout, was director Arthur Lubin. (94 mins)

▽ A better than average horse opera whose Technicolor tints were always eye-catching, **Black Horse Canyon** pitted Joel McCrea (top-starred) and Race Gentry as a pair of ranchers against neighbouring rancher Murvyn Vye for the possession of a wild black stallion. McCrea and Gentry win. McCrea (right) also wins the girl (Mari Blanchard), his adversary in love being young Gentry (left), his partner. And that was the gist of the screenplay Geoffrey Homes scripted and David Lang adapted from the novel *The Wild Horse* by Lee Savage Jr. Completing the cast for producer John W. Rogers and director Jesse Hibbs were Irving Bacon, John Pickard, Ewing Mitchell, Pilar Del Rey and William J. Williams. (81 mins)

▽ A laconic Rory Calhoun (illustrated), as the heavy you hate to love, was top-billed in **Four Guns To The Border**, playing the leader of four cowpokes (the other three were John McIntire, George Nader and Jay Silverheels) who, being financially embarrassed, successfully rob a bank. They head for the border where their good deed in saving pretty Colleen Miller and her dyspeptic old father, Walter Brennan, from Apaches, ultimately leads to the deaths of Messrs McIntire, Nader and Silverheels and the jailing of Calhoun. A torrid, rainswept love scene between the hero and heroine, unusual for Saturday matinee oaters such as this, was about the only interesting thing to emerge from George Van Marter and Franklin Coen's screenplay (story by Louis L'Amour), and it was given more than its passionate due by the two principals. Completing the cast for actor-turned-director Richard Carlson and producer William Alland, were Charles Drake (as the sheriff), Nina Foch (as his wife), Nestor Paiva, Mary Field, Robert Hoy, Robert Herron and Reg Parton. It was photographed in Technicolor. (82 mins)

◁ An exercise in violent contrivance, **Naked Alibi** was also a far-fetched chase melodrama in which top-starred Sterling Hayden (right), discharged of his detective duties for accusing an 'innocent' businessman (Gene Barry) of the murder of three cops, sets out to prove himself right in a chase that takes him to a Mexican border town where Barry is hiding out with his girlfriend Gloria Grahame (left), a singer in a cheap saloon. Hayden soon wins the confidence of Miss Grahame, paving the way for an all-out roof-top chase finale in which the singer is killed and Barry falls to his death. Lawrence Roman concocted it from J. Robert Bren and Gladys Atwater's story *Cry Copper*; Jerry Hopper directed it, and it was produced by Ross Hunter in one of his less glossily glamorous moods. Also cast: Marcia Henderson, Casey Adams, Billy Chapin, Chuck Connors and Don Haggerty. (85 mins)

△ There wasn't a great deal to engage the spectator's mind in **Dawn At Socorro**, another dose of gun-slinging strictly for giddy-up fans. Rory Calhoun (left) was the hero – a gunfighter-gambler (in flashback we learn how he came to be what he is) whose main purpose in George Zuckerman's two-a-penny screenplay was to rescue saloon girl Piper Laurie (centre – kicked out by a stern father) from the clutches of villainous saloon owner David Brian (right). He does, filling the latter with lead in the process. Real villain, however, was the script. Kathleen Hughes appeared as a dance girl, with Alex Nicol, Edgar Buchanan (2nd left), Mara Corday, Skip Homeier, Roy Roberts and Lee Van Cleef rounding out the cast. George Sherman was the director, and William Alland produced, in Technicolor. (80 mins)

△ To judge from the sluggish way the cast came to grips with George Zuckerman and Russell Hughes' screenplay (adapted by Robert Blees from a story by Harold Channing) for **The Yellow Mountain**, this conveyor-belt western must have been a protracted chore for all concerned – including director Jesse Hibbs, who was totally unable to inject excitement into the story of a couple of men (Lex Barker, left and Howard Duff, right) at odds over the possession of a gold mine and the possession of a girl (Mala Powers). The pair do, however, join forces against John McIntire, who is out to oust Miss Powers' father (William Demarest) from a supposedly worthless gold claim. The End. Leo Gordon, Dayton Lummis, Hal K. Dawson, William Fawcett and James Parnell completed the cast for producer Ross Hunter. It was photographed in Technicolor. (77 mins)

▷ Glenn Miller, undoubtedly one of the greatest of American Big Band leaders, and still famous for his unique Miller 'sound', died tragically in 1944 when a military plane on which he was travelling went missing. With their Technicolor musical biopic, **The Glenn Miller Story**, Universal paid tribute to Miller – the man and the musician – and hit the jackpot with a superior screenplay (by Valentine Davies and Oscar Brodney), a perfectly cast star (James Stewart, right) and a tasteful director (Anthony Mann). The story of Miller's rise from obscurity and poverty to fame and wealth was lovingly charted, and generously punctuated by his music. June Allyson (left) was a winningly sympathetic Mrs Miller, and his parents were well subbed for by Irving Bacon and Kathleen Lockhart. The supporting cast also featured Henry Morgan, Charles Drake, George Tobias, Marion Ross, Barton MacLane, Sig Rumann, James Bell and Katharine Warren. Louis Armstrong and Gene Krupa appeared as themselves; so did Frances Langford, Ben Pollack, The Archie Savage Dancers and The Modernaires. Joseph Gershenson and Henry Mancini were joint musical directors, Kenny Williams staged the musical numbers, and Murray MacEachern dubbed the Miller trombone for Stewart. All Miller's best known hits were aired, among them: 'Moonlight Serenade' Miller, Mitchell Parish; 'In The Mood' Andy Razaf, Joe Garland; 'String Of Pearls' Eddie DeLange, Jerry Gray; 'I Know Why', 'Chattanoogo Choo Choo' Mack Gordon, Harry Warren. (115 mins)

△ Originally intended as a vehicle for Bud Abbott and Lou Costello, **Fireman Save My Child** eventually became a starring vehicle for Spike Jones (centre) and His City Slickers, with Buddy Hackett (left) and Hugh O'Brian (right) standing in for Abbott and Costello when the latter fell ill and withdrew from the project. Footage featuring A & C in long shot was incorporated into Howard Christie's zany farce, but with the two comedians out of it, the script (by Lee Loeb and John Grant, story by Loeb) was rewritten to accommodate Jones' eccentricities, and with breaks in the narrative line for typical City Slicker reworkings of von Suppe's 'Poet and Peasant Overture', Ponchielli's 'Dance Of The Hours' and Ketelby's 'In A Persian Market'. The plot was a pretty shy affair indeed, having to do with the motorisation of a San Francisco fire-station in 1910, the crew of which comprises Jones and his Slickers, as well as O'Brian and Hackett, the latter a rookie fireman who happens to have invented a new type of fire extinguisher. Tom Brown, Adele Jergens, George Cleveland and Willis Bouchey also appeared, and it was directed at 110 mph by Leslie Goodwins, to whom restraint was clearly an obnoxious word. The movie bore no resemblance to the Warner Bros. comedy of the same name in 1932, which starred Joe E. Brown. (79 mins)

△ A par-for-the course western, **Rails Into Laramie** starred John Payne as a one-man army assigned to clean up a gang headed by saloon-keeper Dan Duryea (illustrated). Seems that Duryea is doing his best to prevent the completion of Laramie's railroad because, as things stand, the railroad workers are keeping his saloon prosperous. Mari Blanchard played Duryea's pretty partner but, as D.D. Beauchamp and Joseph Hoffman's screenplay unfurled, she changes allegiance to Payne and organises the first all-female jury to ensure villain Duryea's conviction (previous all-male juries having always found him innocent). But it's Payne, inevitably, who finally nails him after he escapes. Joyce MacKenzie (left, as Duryea's wife), Barton MacLane, Ralph Dumke, Harry Shannon, James Griffith and Lee Van Cleef were also part of producer Ted Richmond's cast, which Jesse Hibbs directed in workmanlike fashion. (80 mins)

▽ Yet another variation on the cavalry-versus-Indians theme, **War Arrow** billed Maureen O'Hara (looking lovely in Technicolor) in a rather soporific western whose plot had second-billed Jeff Chandler as an army major, recruiting Seminole Indians to help him quash a Kiowa Indian uprising. Chandler is opposed by commanding officer John McIntire but, in the end, his scheme is successful; the Kiowas bite the dust and the leading lady and leading man (both illustrated) are romantically paired. So much for John Michael Hayes' uncluttered screenplay, whose *dramatis personae* included Suzan Ball as a hot-blooded Seminole princess called Avis and Henry Brandon as her chieftain father, as well as Noah Beery Jr, Charles Drake, Dennis Weaver and Jay Silverheels. John W. Rogers produced and the director was George Sherman. (78 mins)

△ **Ricochet Romance** could have been another comedy with the indomitable Ma and Pa Kettle but, due to Percy Kilbride's retirement from the series, Marjorie Main (centre) went it alone, playing a replacement cook for Chill Wills, whose dude ranch and its dissatisfied paying guests provided most of the outback humour on offer in Kay Lenard's sit-com screenplay. Pedro Gonzales-Gonzales and Alfonso Bedoya (right) appeared as a pair of jokey Mexican employees on the belaboured ranch, and Rudy Vallee (left) cropped up as a wealthy guest with a passion for gourmet cooking. Also: Ruth Hampton, Benay Venuta, Judith Ames, Darryl Hickman and Irene Ryan. Charles Lamont directed, and the moderately budgeted production was in the hands of Robert Arthur. Songs: 'Ricochet Romance' Larry Coleman Jr, Joe Darion; 'Las Altenitas', 'Para Vigo Me Voy', 'Un Tequila' Ernesto Lecuona, Arturo G. Gonzales. (80 mins)

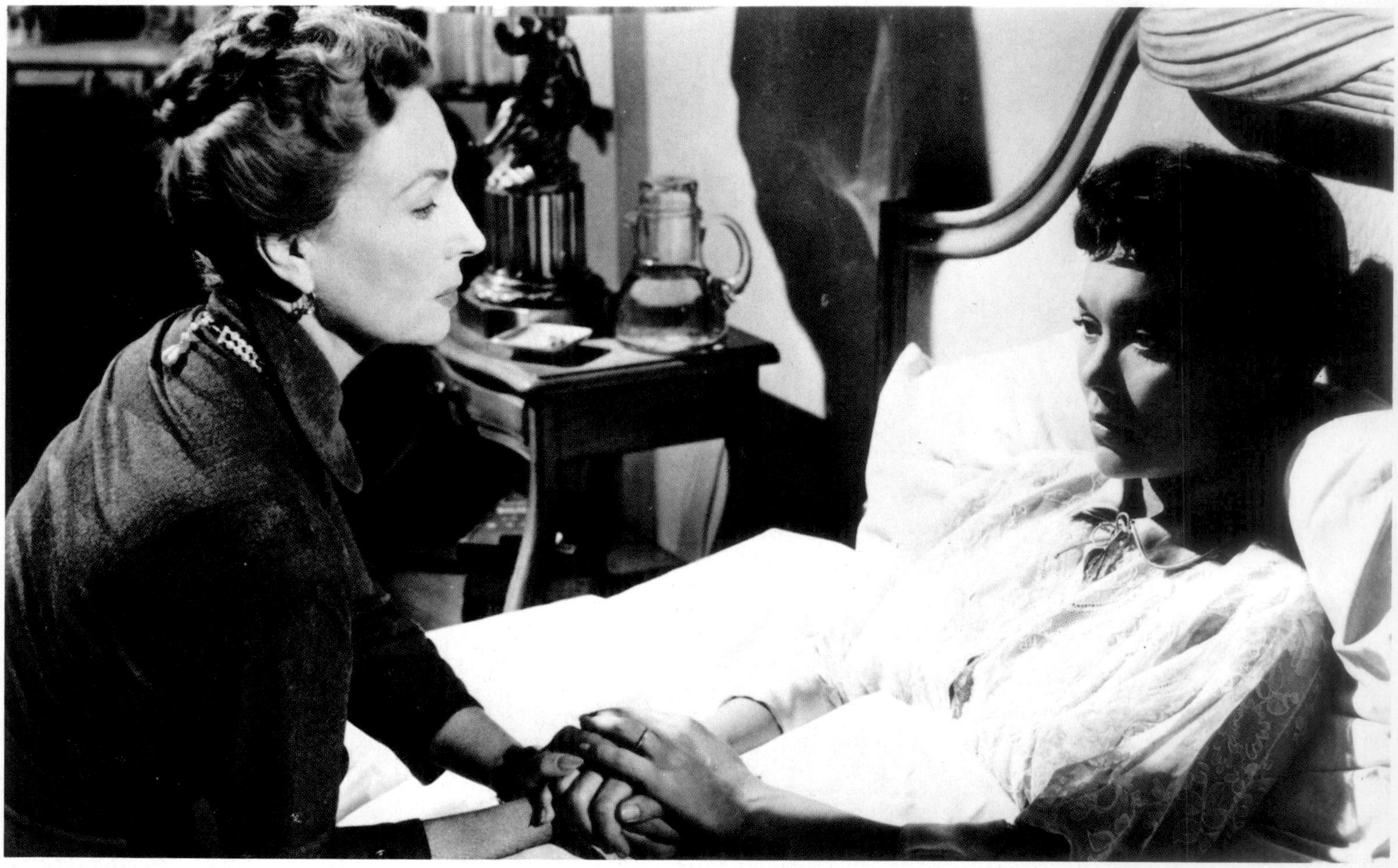

△ Rock Hudson, who had hitherto worked his way up from the ranks via low-calorie westerns and exotic sex-and-sand desert romps, became a major star and potent box-office ammunition after the remake of **Magnificent Obsession** (first made in 1935), playing the role Robert Taylor was given in the earlier film. His co-star was Jane Wyman (right) (in the Irene Dunne part), and although she was billed above Hudson, it was his movie all the way. The familiar story of a wastrel (Hudson) who, in one fell swoop, both widows and blinds Miss Wyman, then spends the rest of the film regenerating himself by becoming a surgeon – in which capacity he makes amends by successfully operating on Wyman and returning her sight to her – it was one of the great tear-jerkers of the decade, and sent the studio's accountants crying all the way to the bank. Handsomely produced (in Technicolor) by Ross Hunter, and directed by Douglas Sirk for maximum emotional impact, it emerged as a solid victory of style and professional know-how over trashy content, and inspired its two leading players as well as a cast that included Barbara Rush (as Wyman's stepdaughter), Agnes Moorehead (left, as the blind woman's nurse-cum-companion), and Otto Kruger, Gregg Palmer, Sara Shane and Paul Cavanagh, to give performances choc-full of conviction. No mean achievement, this, considering the gooey substance of Lloyd C. Douglas' novel on which scenarist Robert Blees (also working from the previous screenplay by Sara Y. Mason and Victor Heerman, adapted by Wells Root) based his updated version. (107 mins)

▽ There were more desert shenanigans in **Yankee Pasha**, an adaptation of Edison Marshall's sex-in-the-sand novel which scenarist Joseph Hoffman cut and re-stitched in order to conform to the studio's highly profitable series of desert adventures. Jeff Chandler (illustrated centre), bursting with buckle and swash, was top-starred in order to rescue lovely New England lass Rhonda Fleming after she has been taken against her will by Barbary pirates and sold into the Moroccan harem of womaniser Bart Roberts. Dotted around the harem was a bevy of Miss Universe finalists (representing the States, Japan, Panama, Norway, South Africa, Uruguay and Australia) – not to mention *the* Miss Universe herself (Christiane Martel), but they all paled into insignificance compared with Miss Fleming, in whom Technicolor brought out the very best. Sex of a more flagrant sort was represented by Mamie Van Doren as a loquacious slave girl; with other roles going to Lee J. Cobb as a sultan, Tudor Owen, Arthur Space, comedian Benny Rubin, and Hal March as a native officer who assists hero Chandler in his rescue plans. Howard Christie controlled the purse-strings, and the shots were called by Joseph Pevney. (83 mins)

▽ A sequel to *Battle Of Apache Pass* (1952), **Taza, Son Of Cochise** made stunning use of the breath-taking vistas offered by Moab in Utah in the telling of the adventures of Taza (Rock Hudson, right), son of Cochise who, when his father was on his death-bed, promised he'd live a peaceful co-existence with the white man. Taza's younger brother Naiche (Bart Roberts) holds other views, and does his best to persuade the tribe to join the warring Geronimo. How Taza restores peace to the territory after Naiche joins up with Geronimo to wipe out a column of General Crook's (Robert Burton) cavalry, gave scenarist George Zuckerman and adapter Gerald Drayson Adams their main storyline. There were no surprises in either content or execution, and the best that could be said for it (apart from the way it looked) was that it contained all the well-tried ingredients germane to the genre. Barbara Rush as Oona, daughter of Grey Eagle (Morris Ankrum), was in it for romance, with other roles under Douglas Sirk's well-paced direction going to Gregg Palmer (centre) as a cavalry captain who befriends Taza, Eugene Iglesias, Richard Cutting (left) and Ian MacDonald. Jeff Chandler, who played Cochise in the earlier film, made an unbilled appearance in the death-bed scene. It was filmed in 3-D, but also released in 2-D. (79 mins)

△ A big-budget epic with intellectual pretensions, but little cinematic value, **Sign Of The Pagan**, in CinemaScope and Technicolor, offered audiences the larger-than-life spectacle of a neurotic, Christ-obsessed Attila the Hun chewing up the scenery in the shape of Jack Palance (left); and the more restrained Jeff Chandler as Roman centurion Marcian attempting to waken an indifferent Emperor Theodosius (George Dolenz) to the possibility of Rome's sacking by the war-like Hun. Scenarists Oscar Brodney and Barre Lyndon were clearly determined to turn in a screenplay that rejected the well-worn notion that Attila was a ruthless savage bereft of human feelings, but their humanising attempts were, alas, ludicrous. Nor were they much more successful in putting flesh and blood on to the characters enacted by Ludmilla Tcherina (Princess Pulcheria), Rita Gam (a total failure as Attila's daughter), plus Jeff Morrow, Eduard Franz, Allison Hayes, Alexander Scourby, and, as Pope Leo, Moroni Olsen (foreground centre). Albert J. Cohen produced, and it was directed by Douglas Sirk who, apart from a climactic battle sequence, managed to keep it all pretty static. (91 mins)

△ **Playgirl** was little more than an updated silent-screen melodrama which described the travails of an innocent in the big city. The innocent on this occasion was Colleen Miller (left – her debut), newly arrived in New York from Nebraska who, almost overnight, finds herself on the cover of a magazine called 'Glitter'. Trouble, however, insinuates itself in the shape of singer Shelley Winters (right), Miss Miller's room-mate who, jealous over her publisher boyfriend's (Barry Sullivan, far right) interest in Miss Miller, accidentally shoots him in a jealous scuffle. Naturally, these unsavoury goings-on don't help Miss M's career one bit, and it doesn't take very long before she becomes a 'party' girl and finds herself involved in the murder of a gangster. Thanks, however, to Miss Winters vouching for the girl's innocence, and to the sturdy presence of Gregg Palmer (the man who got her on to the cover of 'Glitter'), it all ended happily. Robert Blees' screenplay (from a story by Ray Buffman) could have been more trenchant, but it wasn't bad; Albert J. Cohen produced, and the director was Joseph Pevney, at his best in the sequences showing his two female protagonists coming to grips with the harsh realities of big city life. Songs: 'Lie To Me' Ray Gilbert; 'There'll Be Some Changes Made' Billy Higgins, W. Benton Overstreet and Herbert Edwards. (85 mins)

▽ Stock jungle footage was intercut abysmally in **Tanganyika** for verisimilitude, but it only served to pinpoint the phoniness of the whole counterfeit undertaking. A stinker through and through, the film starred Van Heflin (left) who, in British East Africa circa 1900, leads a safari on a manhunt for Jeff Morrow, a renegade murderer whose evil influence over the warlike Nukumbi natives has to be curtailed before the savages terrorize the entire jungle. Joining the safari were Howard Duff as Morrow's good brother, school teacher Ruth Roman (right), as well as Noreen Corcoran and Gregory Marshall, a couple of kids. It ended with Heflin tricking the Nukumbi tribe by a simulated bombardment; and with the death of the baddie. Joe Commodore, Naaman Brown and Edward C. Short completed the cast. Albert J. Cohen produced (in Technicolor) and the hapless director was Andre De Toth. (80 mins)

▽ A big budget western with a tiny little plot, **Saskatchewan** proved just one thing: with top-starred Alan Ladd (centre) in the saddle, the world was a safer, better place. He played an Indian-raised mountie who, single-handedly and with an almost religious sense of his own infallibility, eschews all the rules and regulations of the Northwest Mounted Police to prevent the American Sioux from rousing the peace-loving Canadian Cree Indians to hostilities against the whites. His actions initially brand him a mutineer but, after saving the Mounties from annihilation, he is recognised for the hero he undoubtedly is. Stirring stuff – and numbingly familiar. Still, the Canadian Rockies looked most fetching in Technicolor, Ladd's manly presence was an inspiration to all, and the action sequences were tautly handled by director Raoul Walsh who, unfortunately, was unable to do anything for co-star Shelley Winters (left). As a girl on the run from the law, she floundered helplessly. Robert Douglas played a mountie inspector who, in the end, is made aware of Ladd's infallibility; J. Carrol Naish (right) was a scout, Hugh O'Brian the sheriff pursuing Miss Winters, with other parts in Aaron Rosenberg's production and Gil Doud's screenplay taken by Richard Long, Jay Silverheels and Antonio Moreno. (87 mins)

1955

△ Arthur Kennedy and Betta St John starred in **The Naked Dawn**, a programmer that adopted a distinctly moralistic tone as it showed the corrosive effects the prospect of easy money has on a Mexican farmer (Eugene Iglesias, right) and his wife (St John, centre). Catalyst of the piece is Kennedy (left), who hires Iglesias to help him collect on the money from a freight train hold-up, thus putting temptation in the way of the indigent farmer. Hitherto satisfied with his modest lot, Iglesias now plans Kennedy's death in order to lay his hands on the ill-gotten cash. Edgar G. Ulmer's direction was a trifle slow, but the Technicolor photography helped the familiar yarn along painlessly enough. Nina and Herman Schneider wrote it, and the producer was James Q. Radford. Also cast: Charlita, and Roy Engel. (82 mins)

▽ Tony Curtis (left), like everyone else involved, came unstuck in **The Purple Mask**, a costume drama in CinemaScope and Technicolor set in French Revolution days. He played a foppish, lower-case Scarlet Pimpernel whose mission, throughout the insipid screenplay devised by Oscar Brodney from a play by Paul Armont and Jean Manoussi, was to save the perfumed necks of Royalists from the guillotine's indiscriminate chop. Colleen Miller was second-billed as the daughter of an imprisoned duke, with other roles in Howard Christie's floperoo going to Gene Barry, Dan O'Herlihy (right), Angela Lansbury, George Dolenz, John Hoyt, Paul Cavanagh and, as Napoleon, Robert Cornthwaite. Bruce Humberstone directed. Off with their heads the lot of them! (82 mins)

▽ **Ain't Misbehavin'** was a musical that rested on that oh-so-familiar cliché beloved of musicals in which a rich young man falls in love with a chorus girl. The predictable screenplay, from a story by Robert Carson, was by Phillip Rapp, Devery Freeman and Edward Buzzell, the latter also directing (in Technicolor). Rory Calhoun and Piper Laurie (both illustrated left) starred as the central couple, with third-billed Jack Carson (right) as the hard-boiled custodian of Calhoun's fortune. Kenny Williams and Lee Scott choreographed, Samuel Marx produced, and the cast was completed by Mamie Van Doren, Reginald Gardiner, Barbara Britton, Lisa Gaye and Dani Crane. Musical numbers: 'A Little Love Can Go A Long Way' Paul Francis Webster, Sammy Fain; 'The Dixie Mambo' Charles Henderson, Sonny Burke; 'I Love That Rickey Tickey Tickey' Sammy Cahn, Johnny Scott; 'Ain't Misbehaving" Fats Waller, Andy Razaf. (81 mins)

▽ Victor Mature (right) played the titular hero in **Chief Crazy Horse**, a traditional western in Technicolor and CinemaScope, whose narrative was underpinned by the prophecy of a dying Lakota-Sioux Indian chief that a great warrior would emerge to lead his people to victory, only to be killed by one of his own. And so it came to pass, as Franklin Coen and Gerald Drayson Adams' screenplay (from Adams' own story) depicted under George Sherman's able direction. Suzan Ball (left) co-starred as Crazy Horse's wife Black Shawl, with other roles in William Alland's production going to John Lund as a white man who is befriended by the chief and Ray Danton as the chief's nemesis. Also: Keith Larsen, James Millican, David Janssen, Robert Warwick, Paul Guilfoyle, Morris Ankrum and Dennis Weaver. (86 mins)

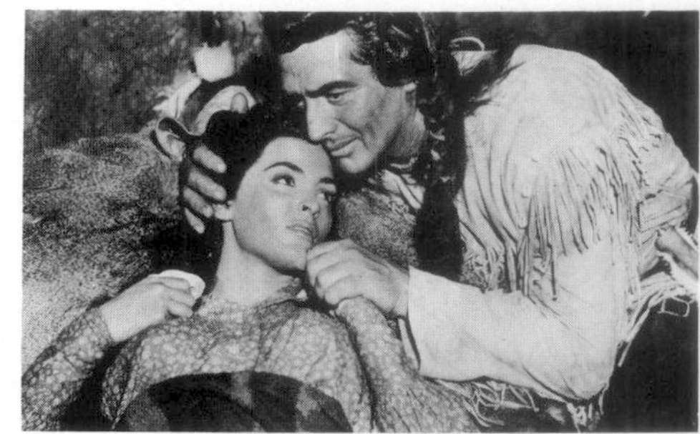

◁ Audiences had to wade through several Irish brogues to find out what was going on in **Captain Lightfoot**. Those who stayed with it were rewarded with a pin-prick of a plot which had top-starred Rock Hudson (left), as a 19th-century Irish hothead, joining up with rebel leader Jeff Morrow, falling in love with Morrow's daughter (Barbara Rush, right), and proving what a man he is by indulging in some bogglingly brave feats of derring-do against the English, while Morrow languishes with battle wounds. Producer Ross Hunter took his CinemaScope and Technicolor cameras to Ireland for authenticity but, to judge from the sluggish entertainment director Douglas Sirk cobbled out of W.R. Burnett and Oscar Brodney's overblown screenplay, it was a wasted journey. Kathleen Ryan, Finlay Currie, Denis O'Dea, Geoffrey Toone, Hilton Edwards and Sheila Brennan were also in it. (91 mins)

▽ Having met practically everyone else, it was only a matter of time before Abbott and Costello encountered Mack Sennet's men in blue, and they did so, most disappointingly, in **Abbott And Costello Meet The Keystone Kops**. What could, and should, have been a glorious spoof on the silent comedy era emerged as a rather listless caper, circa 1912, in which A & C are conned by Fred Clark into purchasing the Edison Film Studio in New York. When they discover they've been had, the two comedians head for Hollywood on a freight train, where they find Clark masquerading as a Russian film direcor. A & C become stunt men for Amalgamated Pictures, catch Clark making off with studio funds, enlist the aid of the eponymous Keystone Kops, then embark on an anything-goes chase. Mack Sennet made a token appearance (and threw a custard pie); and, to add a touch of authenticity, there were appearances by Harold Goodwin, Heinie Conklin and Hank Mann, three of the original Keystones. But it was pretty dreary all the same, the only worthwhile sequence being the chase itself (see illustration) which, although it was a long time coming, was worth waiting for. Lynn Bari, Maxie Rosenbloom, Frank Wilcox, Roscoe Ates and (as a cashier at the beginning of the film), Carol Costello, daughter of Lou, completed the cast. John Grant scripted from a story by Lee Loeb; Howard Christie produced and, as usual, the director was Charles Lamont. (78 mins)

△ After fifteen money-making years at the studio, comedians Abbott and Costello (illustrated) bade farewell to their *alma mater* with **Abbott And Costello Meet The Mummy** – happily, one of their better efforts. Though Costello appeared somewhat drawn, and less heavy than usual (due to a recent bout of rheumatic fever), he nonetheless managed to extract all the available laughs in John Grant's screenplay (story by Lee Loeb), whose narrative transported the duo to Egypt and involved them in a routine search for buried treasure, Costello having swallowed a medallion pinpointing the exact spot of the loot. Marie Windsor and Richard Deacon were the adversaries in the yarn, with other roles under Charles Lamont's broad-based direction going to Michael Ansara, Dan Seymour, Kurt Katch, Richard Karlan and the Mazone-Abbott and Chandra Kaly Dancers. Also featured was vocalist Peggy King who sang 'You Came A Long Way From St Louis'. Howard Christie produced. (79 mins)

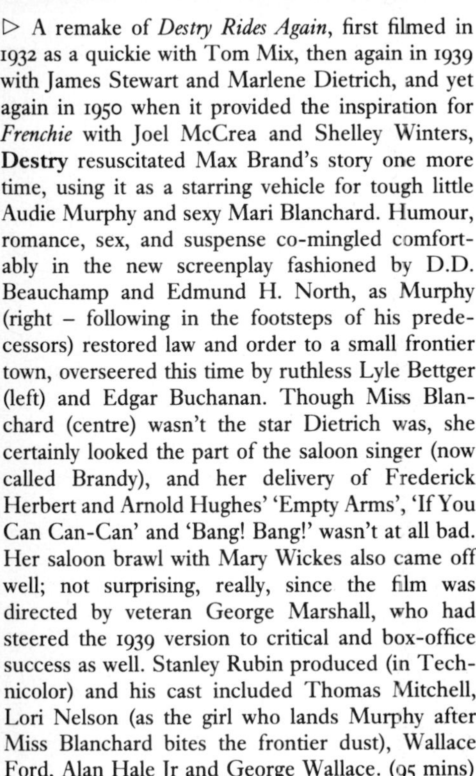

▷ A remake of *Destry Rides Again*, first filmed in 1932 as a quickie with Tom Mix, then again in 1939 with James Stewart and Marlene Dietrich, and yet again in 1950 when it provided the inspiration for *Frenchie* with Joel McCrea and Shelley Winters, **Destry** resuscitated Max Brand's story one more time, using it as a starring vehicle for tough little Audie Murphy and sexy Mari Blanchard. Humour, romance, sex, and suspense co-mingled comfortably in the new screenplay fashioned by D.D. Beauchamp and Edmund H. North, as Murphy (right – following in the footsteps of his predecessors) restored law and order to a small frontier town, overseered this time by ruthless Lyle Bettger (left) and Edgar Buchanan. Though Miss Blanchard (centre) wasn't the star Dietrich was, she certainly looked the part of the saloon singer (now called Brandy), and her delivery of Frederick Herbert and Arnold Hughes' 'Empty Arms', 'If You Can Can-Can' and 'Bang! Bang!' wasn't at all bad. Her saloon brawl with Mary Wickes also came off well; not surprising, really, since the film was directed by veteran George Marshall, who had steered the 1939 version to critical and box-office success as well. Stanley Rubin produced (in Technicolor) and his cast included Thomas Mitchell, Lori Nelson (as the girl who lands Murphy after Miss Blanchard bites the frontier dust), Wallace Ford, Alan Hale Jr and George Wallace. (95 mins)

▽ Strictly for masochists, **Revenge Of The Creature**, a sequel to the previous year's *Creature From The Black Lagoon*, was a 3-D chiller that emerged as the comedy of the year. The Gill-man (illustrated) of the earlier film found himself (itself?) being transported from the Amazon to Florida's famous Marine Land Aquarium. Not particularly liking the surroundings or the company (perfectly understandable in the circumstances), he escapes. The terror he subsequently struck in the hearts of Florida's good citizens was nothing compared to the mirth he provoked among the paying customers who, let's face it, had seen this kind of drivel just once too often. John Agar, Lori Nelson (playing Beauty to the Gill-man's beast), John Bromfield (right), Robert B. Williams and Nestor Paiva were recognisable as humans; William Alland (who also provided the story) produced; Jack Arnold directed, and it was scripted by Martin Berkeley who doubtless earned the gratitude of the vengeful creature for not being given a single line of dialogue to utter throughout. (82 mins)

◁ Produced several years before its actual release, **Ma And Pa Kettle At Waikiki** bid *au revoir* to Percy Kilbride whose retirement from the series may have been a disappointment to its fans but in no way deterred the studio from continuing to use the Kettle name in further adventures. This one saw Pa turned tycoon when he and his brood are summoned by a cousin (Loring Smith) to Waikiki to take over the running of a pineapple factory until he (Smith) recovers from an incapacitating illness. In no time at all, Pa causes a massive explosion on the premises and gets himself kidnapped. Lori Nelson as daughter Rosie Kettle was romantically paired with Byron Palmer in the screenplay Jack Henley, Harry Clork and Elwood Ullman coaxed out of a story by Connie Lee Bennett; Lowell Gilmore and Russell Johnson were the obligatory heavies. Also cast were Hilo Hattie (left), Mabel Albertson, Fay Roope and, of course, as Ma, Marjorie Main (right). It was produced by Leonard Goldstein (who died shortly after its completion), and the routine direction was by Lee Sholem. (79 mins)

▽ A head-on collision between East Coast and Wild West hardly made the impact producer Aaron Rosenberg was hoping for in **Foxfire**. Still, there was enough in it to attract the paying customers, especially leading lady Jane Russell (left) who, in her first film for the studio, played an Eastern socialite. After an extremely brief courtship she marries second-billed Jeff Chandler (right), a half-breed Apache mining engineer, and takes up residence with him in an Arizona ghost town. The couple's clash of cultures provided scenarist Ketti Frings, working from a story by Anya Seton, with enough conflict to keep audiences involved, and parts for Dan Duryea, as a booze-ridden mine doctor, Barton MacLane as an Indian-hating mine superintendent, and Frieda Inescort and Celia Lovsky as the two stars' mothers. Plot had the seemingly incompatible marriage being rescued in the nick of time after Miss Russell has a miscarriage and Chandler discovers gold in an abandoned mine. Joseph Pevney directed. Song: 'Foxfire' Henry Mancini, Jeff Chandler, sung by Chandler. (91 mins)

▷ The fifth collaboration between producer Aaron Rosenberg, director Anthony Mann and star James Stewart resulted in **The Far Country**, a rugged and exhilarating western whose entertainment value derived from Stewart's central performance, Borden Chase's intelligent screenplay, Mann's gritty direction and the stunning scenery (in Technicolor) provided by the Canadian Rockies, the Columbia ice-fields and Jaspar National Park. Stewart (illustrated standing), together with his partner Walter Brennan, arrives in Canada via Wyoming with a herd of cattle. The pair hope to sell the herd at inflated prices to the gold-crazy citizens of Dawson and Skagway, thus pocketing enough money to return to Utah and open a ranch. They haven't, however, reckoned with John McIntire, the self-styled 'lawman' of Skagway, who grabs hold of Stewart's herd before it reaches Dawson. Then, when Brennan is shot by one of McIntire's claim-jumpers, the hitherto laid-back, characteristically laconic Stewart lets rip in time for a rootin'-tootin'-shoot-out that climaxes the film. Ruth Roman played a saloon keeper with a yen for Stewart, but the woman who finally nabs him is Corinne Calvet as a hoydenish French-Canadian girl of the gold-fields. Jay C. Flippen was prominently featured as a booze-loving pal of the hero, with other roles going to Henry Morgan, Steve Brodie, Connie Gilchrist and Chubby Johnson. (96 mins)

△ Scenarists Robert Hill and Richard Alan Simmons, working from Hill's play *The Besieged Heart*, amassed a collection of quite resistible folk for **Female On The Beach**, which top-starred Joan Crawford (illustrated) as the lady referred to in the title. She played the widow of a Las Vegas gambler newly arrived in Southern California's Balboa Beach to take up residence in a beach-house formerly occupied by a wealthy widow (Judith Evelyn) who met a sorry end when she fell (or was she pushed?) from the cottage balcony on to the beach below. It isn't long before Crawford makes the acquaintance of beach-bum Jeff Chandler (illustrated, with Crawford), a neighbour of the deceased widow. A brief courtship with Chandler ends in marriage, the wedding night being blighted somewhat when Crawford discovers that, like her predecessor, she, too, is marked out for murder. It turns out, though, that Chandler is innocent of such thoughts, the guilty party being jealous Jan Sterling, a real-estate agent who wants Chandler for herself. Cecil Kellaway and Natalie Schaefer played a pair of confidence tricksters; with Charles Drake, Stuart Randall and Marjorie Bennett completing producer Albert Zugsmith's cast. Joseph Pevney directed, and needed to be much tougher with his leading lady, whose over-the-top histrionics sorely unbalanced the melodrama. (97 mins)

▽ **Cult Of The Cobra** offered only mild bouts of horror in the telling of a bizarre tale (story by Jerry Davis) of the leader (Faith Domergue, illustrated) of an Asiatic cult of snake worshippers who believes that humans have the power of changing themselves into snakes – then back again. Trouble infiltrated Jerry Davis, Cecile Maiden and Richard Collins' screenplay with the arrival of six American GIs who, after disrupting a secret ceremony, have a curse placed on them by Miss Domergue which states that the Snake Goddess will sooner or later kill them all. Howard Pine's production was in the programmer category, with matching direction by Francis D. Lyon, and a ditto cast that included Richard Long, Marshall Thompson, Kathleen Hughes, Jack Kelly, Myrna Hansen, David Janssen and William Reynolds. (81 mins)

△ **Francis In The Navy**, was a tiresome little farce with a mistaken identity theme that allowed top-starred Donald O'Connor (left) to play a dual role: an Army lieutenant full of impressive accomplishments, and a bosun's mate who knows from nothing. Springboard for the action was the talking mule, who calls O'Connor (alias the lieutenant) to tell him that he has been drafted into the navy and is in danger of being auctioned off as surplus. Martha Hyer (right), Richard Erdman, Jim Backus, David Janssen and a young man called Clint Eastwood also appeared for director Arthur Lubin and producer Stanley Rubin; and it was scripted (weakly) by Devery Freeman. (80 mins)

▽ **Kiss Of Fire** was the kiss of death as far as its entertainment value was concerned. Based on Jonreed Lauritzen's period novel *The Rose And The Flame* it told the story, via a watery screenplay by Franklin Coen and Richard Collins, of an heir apparent to the throne of Spain (Barbara Rush, standing centre), and her attempts to travel from Santa Fe, New Mexico (where, inexplicably, she happens to be living), back to Spain after news reaches her that King Charles V is on his deathbed. Seems that if she doesn't get there fast, some other 'pretender' will nab the throne. But first she has to get from Santa Fé to Monterey, where a ship is waiting to take her to Europe. And it is this segment of her journey, led by top-starred Jack Palance (an ex-Spanish nobleman known as El Tigre, kneeling centre) that provided the bulk of the action – most of it little more than traditional wild-west skirmishes with local redskins etc. When, finally, Miss Rush makes it to Monterey, she decides she loves Palance more than the prospect of being Queen of Spain, and cancels her trip to Europe. Rex Reason (right), Martha Hyer (centre left), Leslie Bradley (centre right) and Alan Reed were also featured for producer Samuel Marx, and it was directed for the unashamed potboiler it was by Joseph M. Newman. (89 mins)

1955

▽ Action and romance, 'B' picture-style, and revolving around a plane crash in the Pike's Peak region of the Colorado Rockies, was what **The Looters** offered. Mountaineer Rory Calhoun (top-starred, centre) and his army buddy Ray Danton (standing left) set out on a rescue mission and find four survivors: Julie Adams (kneeling left – a soft-porn model), Thomas Gomez (standing right – a brokerage clerk), Frank Faylen (kneeling right – a Navy petty officer) and Rod Williams (the badly-hurt co-pilot). Two hundred and fifty thousand dollars in cash also survived the wreckage, and it proves too much of a lure for Danton who, working in cahoots with Gomez, forces Calhoun to lead them out of the wilderness. Danton's plan is to murder them all as soon as they reach civilisation. Russ Conway and John Stephenson completed the cast for producer Howard Christie, whose very commonplace little thriller was directed by Abner Biberman from a commonplace screenplay by Richard Alan Simmons (story by Paul Schneider). (87 mins)

▽ Anne Baxter and Rock Hudson (centre) starred in **One Desire**, a romantic soap-opera whose screenplay by Lawrence Roman and Robert Blees (based on Conrad Richter's novel *Tracey Cromwell*) was pretty lugubrious. Baxter and Hudson played a pair of gambling hall habitués who fall in love and have a crack at respectability in a new town. They more or less 'adopt' Hudson's kid brother (Barry Curtis), as well as an orphan girl (Natalie Wood). But they hadn't reckoned on the scheming daughter (Julie Adams, left) of a banker, who uses her ample feminine wiles to draw Hudson away from Baxter. In the end, however, she pays for her trouble-making by perishing in a fire, leaving Miss Baxter free to resume her romantic relationship with the leading man. Ross Hunter's Technicolor production ensured that audiences got their money's worth in the way of gloss; and the tear-stained direction was the work of Jerry Hopper. Also cast: Carl Benton Reid, William Hopper, William Forrest (right) and Betty Garde. (94 mins)

△ A musical top-starring George Nader (left) and Jeanne Crain (right), **The Second Greatest Sex** (like MGM's *Seven Brides For Seven Brothers* the previous year) traded on the Lysistrata story for its content. Set, this time, in Kansas circa 1880, Charles Hoffman's script had the women withholding their favours in order to stop the men's feuding pursuit of official county records, the holder of which will have control of the county seat. On the whole only moderately entertaining, it offered some first-class acrobatic dancing (choreographed by Lee Scott) and a lively cast that included Kitty Kallen, Bert Lahr, Paul Gilbert, Keith Andes, Mamie Van Doren, Tommy Rall and The Midwesterners. It was produced in Technicolor by Albert J. Cohen, and the director was George Marshall. Songs and musical numbers: 'Lysistrata', 'Send Us A Miracle', 'Travellin' Man', 'My Love Is Yours', 'What Good Is A Woman Without A Man?', 'There's Gonna Be A Wedding' Pony Sherrell, Phil Moody; 'The Second Greatest Sex' Jay Livingston, Ray Evans; 'How Lonely Can I Get?' Joan Whitney, Alex Kramer. (87 mins)

△ Though the nominal stars of **This Island Earth**, a hugely enjoyable interplanetary adventure, were Rex Reason (top-billed, left), Faith Domergue (centre left), Jeff Morrow (centre right), Lance Fuller and Russell Johnson, the people who really deserved to take the bows were David S. Horsley and Clifford Stine for their mind-bending special photography; Alexander Golitzen and Richard H. Riedel for their art direction; and Russel A. Hausman and Julia Heron for their imaginative set decoration. Without their stand-out contributions, this sci-fi thriller – about the desperate efforts of the mutant inhabitants of the doomed planet Metaluna to find a new source of atomic energy from the planet Earth – would have been very ordinary indeed. According to scenarists Franklin Coen and Edward G. O'Callaghan (working from the novel by Raymond F. Jones), the energy is needed to provide an isolation layer around Metaluna, otherwise the planet will be vulnerable to attack from the more powerful inhabitants of Zagon. Morrow was the representative from Metaluna; Reason and Domergue the nuclear fission earth scientists whose help is being sought. William Alland produced (in Techicolor), and Joseph Newman directed. (87 mins)

▽ Take one martinet, a handful of cute kids, some nuns and their mother superior, and a kindly woman who has a way with children and you have – not *The Sound Of Music* (20th Century-Fox, 1965) – but **The Private War Of Major Benson**, a 'heart-warming' family entertainment that spelled many happy box-office returns. Charlton Heston (right) starred as an overly-strict major assigned (as a disciplinary measure) to take charge of a military boarding school whose Catholic students range in age from six to fifteen. Julie Adams (centre) was second-billed as the school's doctor and, in time, provided the requisite romantic interest in William Roberts and Richard Alan Simmons' screenplay (from the story by Joe Connelly and Bob Mosher). Heston and Miss Adams were both upstaged by the kids producer Howard Pine managed to corral, especially Tim Hovey, a six-year-old with a natural, and winning, tendency to draw attention away from the grown-ups whenever he appeared. Sal Mineo, Tim Considine, Donald Keeler, Gary Pagett, Mickey Little and Butch Jones were some of the other youngsters in it and, under Jerry Hopper's watchful direction, managed to keep cringe-making precocity well out of the picture. Credit Hopper, too, for ensuring that the potentially syrupy material never cloyed. The rest of the adults were represented by William Demarest (as a handy-man), Nana Bryant (the Mother Superior, left), Milburn Stone, Mary Field and Don Haggerty. It was photographed in Technicolor. (105 mins)

▽ The cavalry again clashed with the redskins in **Smoke Signal**, but it was a skirmish that carried little excitement. Best thing about producer Howard Christie's yawnsome hoss opera was its spectacular setting – the Colorado River's Grand Canyon which, in glorious Technicolor, looked more inviting than the most elaborate travel brochure. Otherwise, it was little more than the story of a small cavalry detachment and the risks they take, via uncharted river rapids, to escape a band of warring Indians. Dana Andrews (left) and Piper Laurie (the only woman in the cast) starred, with Andrews playing a deserter who joins the redskins after their ill-treatment by a cavalry officer. Other roles went to Rex Reason, William Talman (the head of the cavalry group, right), Milburn Stone and Douglas Spencer. George F. Slavin and George W. George scripted it, and the director was Jerry Hopper. (87 mins)

▷ Kirk Douglas (illustrated) played an easy-going saddle-tramp, a **Man Without A Star**, who wanders around the country, avoiding the barbed wire that is fast enclosing the land. His theme song, in fact, could have been Cole Porter's 'Don't Fence Me In'. Travelling around with him is range novice William Campbell, an impressionable young man whom Douglas has taken under his wing, and whom he enlightens on such edifying topics as booze, women, and self-preservation. Scenting the prairie air was Jeanne Crain, a ranchowner who decides Douglas is just the man to see that her ranch remains unfenced – much to the disapproval of the area's small-ranchers who realise that the only way they can save enough grass for the winter time, is by fencing off the land. Borden Chase and D.D. Beauchamp's tautly-written, well-sounding screenplay (based on a novel by Dee Linford) subsequently had Douglas switching allegiances and helping the small-time ranchers in their battle against their barbed wire opponents. But it's just another job for Douglas – and the film ended with him riding off into the unbounded yonder, still very much a loner, a man without a star. Claire Trevor provided additional female interest as the town madam with the proverbial golden heart (and friend of the hero); with other roles under veteran King Vidor's muscular direction going to Jay C. Flippen, Richard Boone, Mara Corday and Myrna Hansen. It was produced by Aaron Rosenberg in Technicolor. Songs: 'And The Moon Grew Brighter And Brighter' Kimmy Kennedy, Lou Singer, sung by Douglas; 'Man Without A Star' Arnold Hughes, Frederick Herbert, sung by Frankie Laine. (89 mins)

△ **Six Bridges To Cross** was just one more hurdle in the burgeoning career of its star Tony Curtis who, as an unregenerate young hoodlum with 32 arrests to his name, wasn't entirely convincing. The film was based on the notorious Boston Brink robbery, and the story of that crime, written by Joseph F. Dinnen and called *They Stole $2,500,000 And Got Away With It.* Sidney Boehm scripted the movie, which adopted the matter-of-fact format of the early crime melodramas Warner Bros. were making in the thirties, and which showed Curtis enmeshed in a life of juvenile delinquency on the streets of Boston from an early age. By employing a documentary-like narration, it then traced Curtis' subsequent rise in the underworld as he goes from bad to worse. George Nader co-starred as a cop with a paternal interest in the young thug; Julia Adams as Nader's wife. Both try to straighten the kid out, but to no avail, and the movie ends after Curtis, having pretended to go straight for a while, pulls off his biggest job yet – the $2,500,000 haul – but is shot by one of his own when he decides to return the loot so that he can remain in the States. Sal Mineo (centre) played Curtis as a boy, with other parts in Aaron Rosenberg's production (much of it filmed on location in Boston, and making excellent use of the city), going to Jay C. Flippen, Jan Merlin (left) and Richard Castle. Joseph Pevney directed it without much depth or insight. (95 mins)

◁ Maureen O'Hara (illustrated), swathed in yards and yards of red hair, sauntered through 11th-century Coventry in the last reel of **Lady Godiva**, and while it wasn't exactly a sight for sore eyes, it offered a brief respite from the talky tedium of Oscar Brodney and Harry Ruskin's inaccurate screenplay (Brodney, rather than history, supplied the story). Set during a time when the Normans were planning to oust the Saxons, the film featured O'Hara as the Saxon bride of Saxon nobleman George Nader (thus thwarting all plans for a Norman marital alliance). Long before her famous public outing, the lady finds herself involved in all manner of court intrigue, and her notorious bare-backed ride was undertaken, we learn, to prove the loyalty of Canterbury's Saxon population, none of whom – save curious Tom the Tailor, who paid for his curiosity by having his eyes removed by Victor McLaglen – so much as peeked at her. Robert Arthur's Technicolor production and Arthur Lubin's mild-mannered direction did nothing to kindle the country's box-offices, their film emerging as little more than the second half of a double bill. Also cast: Rex Reason, Torin Thatcher, Eduard Franz, Leslie Bradley, Henry Brandon, Grant Withers, Arthur Shields and, as peeping Tom the Tailor, Alex Harford. (89 mins)

▽ Aimed largely at the teenage rock 'n' roll market, **Running Wild** was a programmer whose hand-me-down plot saw top-starred William Campbell, as a rookie cop, pretending to be a 19-year-old thug in order to infiltrate a gang of automobile thieves overseered by Keenan Wynn. Kathleen Case played Wynn's unwilling moll (forced into the relationship by Wynn's threats to blow the gaff on her Nazi-persecuted father's illegal entry into the US), while second-billed Mamie Van Doren (illustrated) was prominently seen and heard as a rock 'n' roll performer, as well as the blonde girlfriend of tough Jan Merlin, Wynn's second-in-command. John Saxon was also in it; so were Walter Coy, Grace Mills and Chris Randall. Abner Biberman directed Lee Townsend's screenplay (from the novel by Ben Benson), and the producer was Howard Pine. (81 mins)

▽ There was no sparing the horses in director Jack Arnold's well-paced handling of **The Man From Bitter Ridge**, a conventional off-the-peg oater with Lex Barker (as the man from Bitter Ridge, right) who, in his capacity as a special investigator, arrives in Tomahawk to find out who has been holding up the local stage coach and indulging in a spot of killing. Word has it that the guilty parties comprise a group of sheepmen led by Stephen McNally (left); but, after a run-in with the gun-toting brothers of aspiring politician John Dehner, Barker knows exactly who's behind it all. So does sheriff Trevor Bardette. Trouble is, how do they catch Dehner and his brothers (Warren Stevens and Myron Healey) red-handed? Lawrence Roman's screenplay (adapted by Teddi Sherman from the novel by William MacLeod Rains) eventually saw to it that justice was done, and the movie ended with Barker ready to take up romantic cudgels with glamorous sheep-herder Mara Corday (second-billed). Howard Pine's Technicolor production also featured Ray Teal and John Harmon. (80 mins)

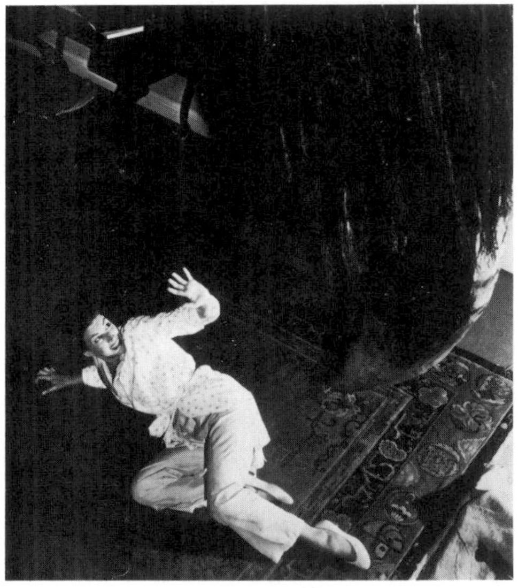

△ Horror addicts were well-supplied with grotesqueries in **Tarantula**, a modest but enjoyable piece of sci-fi which showed what happens when a nutritional formula designed to feed the world's increasing population goes wrong, and a tarantula is injected with the as yet unstabilised contents. The insect grows to enormous proportions and begins to feed off cattle and humans; and it takes the Air Force and a few napalm bombs finally to destroy it, but not before a creepy time was had by all. John Agar top-starred as a young doctor, Mara Corday (illustrated) co-starred as a science student stationed near Desert Rock, Arizona, Leo G. Carroll was her employer, with other parts in Robert M. Fresco and Martin Berkeley's screenplay (story by director Jack Arnold and Fresco) going to Nestor Paiva as a sheriff, Ross Elliott as a local editor and Hank Patterson as a hotel clerk. William Alland produced, the most effective thing in his show being Bud Westmore's excellent make-up. (80 mins)

△ Straight off the Technicolor musicals conveyor belt, **So This Is Paris** brought not an iota of originality to the screen with its seen-it-all-before (often) story about a trio of American sailors in Paris who team up with three local girls. Charles Hoffman's screenplay (story by Ray Buffum) was a faded carbon copy of *On The Town*, and Pony Sherell and Phil Moody's score gave new meaning to the term unmemorable. Against these odds, choreographers Gene Nelson and Lee Scott couldn't achieve much; neither could the cast, whose leads comprised Tony Curtis (right), Gloria De Haven (left), Gene Nelson, Corinne Calvet, Paul Gilbert and Mara Corday. Allison Hayes, Christiane Martel, Myrna Hansen and little Sandy Deschner (centre) were also in it for producer Albert J. Cohen and director Richard Quine. Songs and musical numbers included: 'So This Is Paris', 'Two Of Us', 'A Dame's A Dame', 'Wait Till Paris Sees Us', 'If You Were There' Sherrell, Moody; 'I Can't Give You Anything But Love' (sung in French by De Haven) Dorothy Fields, Jimmy McHugh. (96 mins)

▷ Though there were no false heroics in **To Hell And Back**, heroism was nonetheless the name of the game in Aaron Rosenberg's big-budget CinemaScope and Technicolor version of Audie Murphy's autobiography, which recounted in sober detail how the star (playing himself, illustrated) came to be the most decorated soldier in his country's history. Scenarist Gil Doud established the hero's character early on in the film when, as a youngster, we see him helping out his mother on their impoverished Texas farm. The picture then jumped to 1942 when, at the age of 18, Murphy entered the army. In 1943 he became a replacement in Company B, 15th Infantry Regiment, Third Division, 7th Army in North Africa, and served with the unit throughout the rest of the war in Tunisia, Italy, France, Germany and Austria. During that time he worked his way up to company commander, was wounded three times, personally killed 240 Germans, and was one of two soldiers left in the original company at war's end. His bravery in battle garnered 24 medals for him, including the Congressional Medal of Honor. Jesse Hibbs' action-filled direction (at its best in a sequence showing the elimination of a Nazi machine-gun nest from a farmhouse in Anzio), while not entirely eschewing the usual clichés of the genre, handled the material with a certain restraint (and, at times, even nobility), and drew sturdy performances from a cast that included Marshall Thompson, Gregg Palmer, Charles Drake, Jack Kelly, Paul Picerni, Susan Kohner (as Murphy's brief romantic interest), Richard Castle and, as Mrs Murphy, the hero's mum, Mary Field. (106 mins)

△ Jose Ferrer (right) made his first appearance at the studio and his debut as a film director in **The Shrike**, an adaptation by Ketti Frings of Joseph Kramm's Pulitzer Prize-winning stage play, which Ferrer had both starred in and directed on Broadway. Unfortunately, what on stage was a bold and terrifying drama of a man embroiled and ensnared in a set of horrific circumstances from which, thanks to the designing machinations of an interfering wife, he couldn't escape, emerged in the screen version as a superior soap-opera complete with happy ending. Part of the blame lay with co-star June Allyson (left) who, as the jealous, unsuccessful actress-wife of stage-director Ferrer, was far too charming and unpsychotic to make much impact. Ferrer, on the other hand, despite Miss Frings' removal of the lethal sting from the basic material, nonetheless managed to turn in a performance of immense stature and conviction as he recounts (via two flashbacks) to psychiatrist Kendall Clark the reasons for his breakdown. Joy Page was cast as a woman with whom the tortured Ferrer finds emotional solace (but is unable to marry); with other roles going to Mary Bell as a ward nurse and Ed Platt as Ferrer's brother, as well as Will Kuluva, Herbie Faye, Martin Newman and Billy Greene, all of whom were members of the original Broadway company. The producer was Aaron Rosenberg. Interesting sideline: Isabel Bonner, who played a physician in the movie and had been in the play, was the actress on whom *The Shrike* was based. She was married to Joe Kramm, and 'shriked' her way in to both play and movie. (88 mins)

1956

△ A compendium of 'jungle thrill' clichés, **Curucu, Beast Of The Amazon**, produced in Eastmancolor by Richard Kay and Harry Rybnick, followed the exploits of John Bromfield (left) as a plantation controller, and Beverly Garland (centre right) as a doctor, who make their way up the Amazon to investigate a monster that has been terrorising the natives. Turns out the 'monster' is none other than tribal chieftain Tupanico (Tom Payne, centre), whose scheme is to rid the natives of the white man's influence by frightening them off the plantations and back to their primitive life-styles. It was the brainchild of writer-director Curt Siodmak, whose cast included Harvey Chalk, Sergio de Oliviera and Wilson Vianna. (72 mins)

▽ The Gill-man, that amphibious monster seen twice before (in 3-D) lost one of his dimensions in **The Creature Walks Among Us**. Which ever way you looked at it, though, it was pretty flat third time round. Scenarist Arthur Ross' chief concern was getting the scaly creature (illustrated on bed) onto land which, after a successful underwater expedition undertaken by Jeff Morrow (left), Rex Reason (right), Gregg Palmer and Leigh Snowden, they do. A fire destroys some of the Gill-man's gills, whereupon it is discovered that his lung structure can support life out of water if a tracheotomy is performed. So far so good. Then Morrow goes and spoils it all by becoming jealous of Palmer's attentions towards his wife (Snowden) and, in an ensuing shoot-out (in which Palmer is killed), the Gill-man is wounded, escapes, and heads for the Pacific. And that was about all there was to it. William Alland produced and the cast included Maurice Manson (2nd right), James Rawley (2nd left), David McMahon and Paul Fierro. (78 mins)

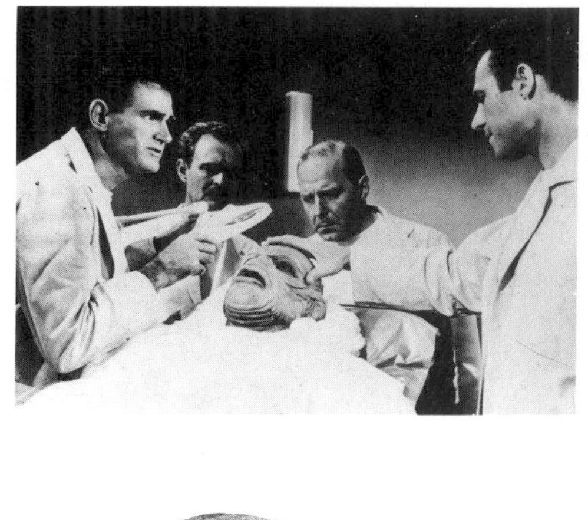

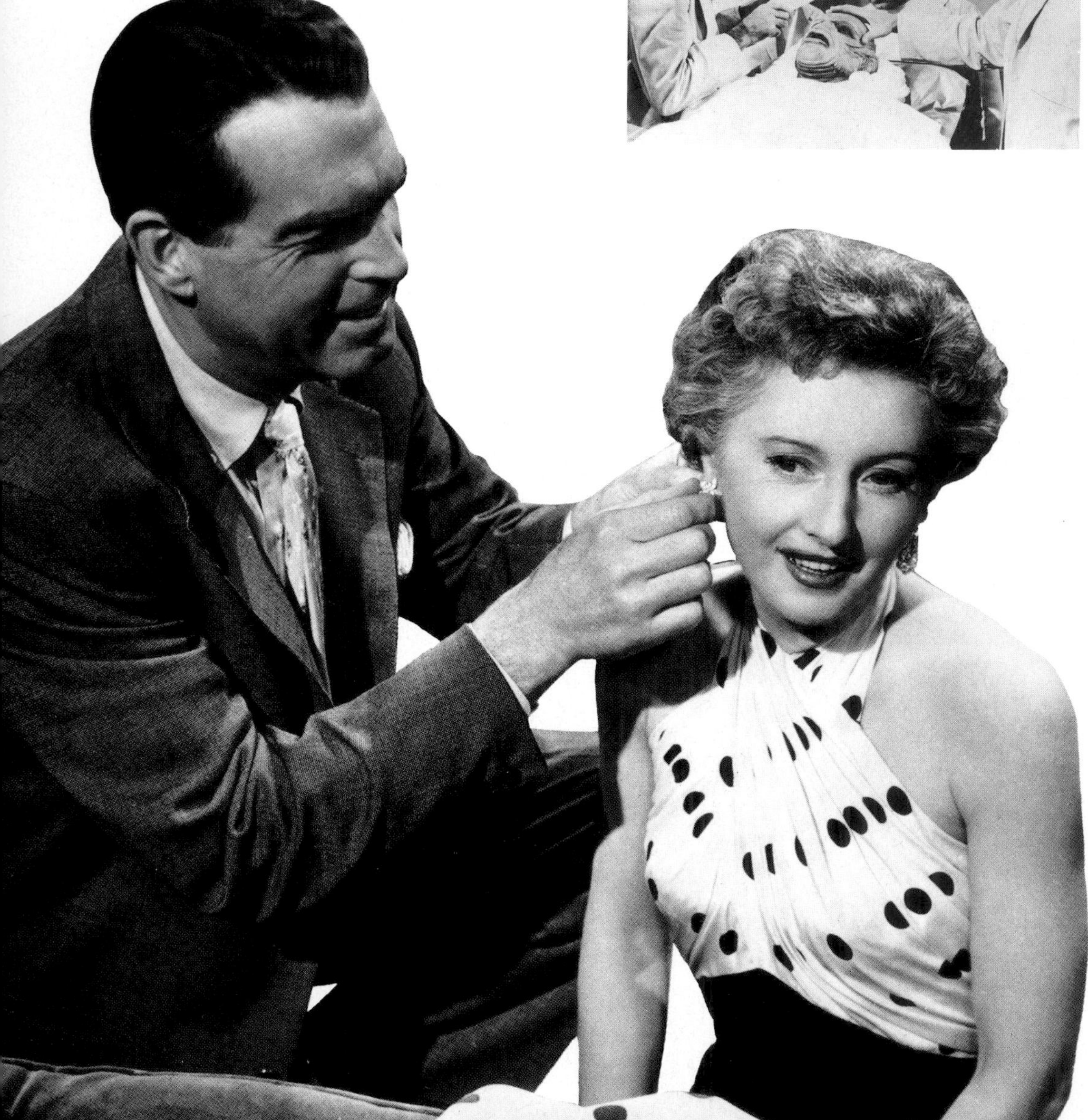

▽ **Everything But The Truth** was a mild little programmer whose *raison d'être* was clearly the role it provided for master Tim Hovey (left) as an orphaned youngster schooled, by top-billed Maureen O'Hara (right, as a teacher), into always telling the truth. But the truth can hurt, as the youngster's uncle (Barry Atwater) discovers to his cost, when Master Hovey lets it be known that Atwater gave mayor Philip Bourneuf $10,000 in a crooked real-estate deal. The ensuing complications were the substance of Herb Meadow's screenplay, which co-starred John Forsyth (as a newspaper columnist), Frank Faylen, Les Tremayne, Philip Birch, Addison Richards and Jeanette Nolan. Howard Christie's production was aimed squarely at the family trade, and Jerry Hopper underlined the fact in his direction. (Eastmancolor) (83 mins)

▽ Reincarnation was the theme of **I've Lived Before**, a low-budget programmer from producer Howard Christie, in which top-starred Jock Mahoney (right), a commercial airline pilot, after a chance meeting with passenger Ann Harding, almost crashes his plane when he honestly believes himself to be Harding's long-dead husband, a pilot, who was shot down in a dog-fight over France in 1918. Leigh Snowden played Mahoney's incredulous fiancée; John McIntire was an equally disbelieving doctor, with other roles under Richard Bartlett's *déjà-vu* direction going to Raymond Bailey as the airline's understandably annoyed owner; Jerry Paris (left) as the co-pilot, Simon Scott as an attorney and April Kent (daughter of June Havoc) as a stewardess. (82 mins)

◁ **There's Always Tomorrow**, previously filmed in 1934, was a tepid soap-opera from producer Ross Hunter whose excellent cast (Barbara Stanwyck, Fred MacMurray and Joan Bennett) could do little to promote interest in the screenplay Bernard C. Schoenfeld constructed out of Ursula Parrott's story about a taken-for-granted husband and father (MacMurray, left), whose greyish life becomes more colourful after he re-acquaints himself with a former flame (Stanwyck, right). In fact, so ardent are his feelings towards Miss Stanwyck, that he seriously considers leaving his wife (Joan Bennett) and children (Gigi Perreau, William Reynolds and Judy Nugent) for her. But the kids make a personal deposition to Stanwyck, who gracefully decides to opt out. In the meantime, Miss Bennett remains blissfully unaware of what has been happening (the wife always being the last to know etc, etc), so things remain exactly the same between her and her neglected spouse. Douglas Sirk's direction made nothing out of this soap-powder plot; neither did a cast that also included Pat Crowley, Jane Darwell, Race Gentry and Myrna Hansen. (88 mins)

▷ Having clicked at the box office in *Magnificent Obsession* two years earlier, producer Ross Hunter was quick to plunge Jane Wyman (right) and Rock Hudson (left) into yet another Technicolor sudser in the hope of exploiting the pair's strong marquee pull. The dire results could be seen in the aptly titled **All That Heaven Allows**. For, all that heaven allows, when it came to emotionally manipulative trash like this, was flung into Peg Fenwick's damp little screenplay. Basically it was the romantic story of a widow's infatuation for a man (her gardener, actually) some fifteen or so years her junior, and the subsequent social pressures brought to bear on the liaison by her friends and her impossibly selfish offspring (Gloria Talbott and William Reynolds). For a while Miss Wyman lets these pressures rule her heart, until Hudson's involvement in a mountain accident, resulting in concussion, brings her to her senses. With producer Hunter supplying the gilt, and director Douglas Sirk the varnish, the finished product was, not surprisingly, a highly polished affair. It was also extremely vacuous. The cast included Agnes Moorehead, Conrad Nagel, Virginia Grey, Jacqueline de Wit and Charles Drake. (89 mins)

△ A prison meller whose screenplay by Harold Jack Bloom (story by Wallace Sullivan and Richard K. Pollimer) should have been behind bars for boring audiences to death, **Behind The High Wall** was the far-fetched story of a prison warden (Tom Tully) who, after being kidnapped by some escaping convicts, finds that he and the driver of the getaway truck (handsome newcomer John Gavin, illustrated) are the only survivors of a crash in which all the others are killed. Tully hides $100,000 the escapees just happen to be carrying with them, then sentences Gavin to death for participating in the break. The film ended with an eleventh-hour confession from Tully which saves Gavin's life after he breaks out of the death-house in which he has been confined. The marvellous Sylvia Sidney, though second-billed, was wasted in the role of Tully's wife, Betty Lynn played Gavin's fiancée, with other parts under Abner Biberman's ineffectual direction going to Don Beddoe, John Larch, Barney Phillips and Ed Kemmer. Stanley Rubin produced. (85 mins)

▽ Mean and moody Richard Widmark (right) starred in **Backlash**, a reheated programmer western, in gorgeous Technicolor, set in Arizona just after the Civil War. Borden Chase's carbon-copy screenplay (from a novel by Frank Gruber) focussed on the deaths of five white men at the hands of the Apaches; the sixth man has escaped with $60,000 in gold. Question is, who escaped, and where's the loot? Widmark has a sneaky feeling that the one who got away was his deplorable father (John McIntire); while second-billed Donna Reed (left) believes it might have been her husband. Turns out Widmark was right, and although he never lays his hands on the gold (McIntire having spent it on a rustling empire before being killed by ranchers), he fills his arms with Miss Reed by way of consolation. Aaron Rosenberg produced on location in Arizona, and the spotty direction was by John Sturgess, whose cast included William Campbell (as a grotesquely leering young killer), Barton MacLane, Harry Morgan, Robert J. Wilke and Jack Lambert. (83 mins)

◁ Having struck it rich with the army in *To Hell And Back* (1955), the studio turned to the navy in **Away All Boats** and, aided by VistaVision and Technicolor, plus a sizeable budget, top-starred Jeff Chandler as the captain of World War II *USS Belinda*, whose fortunes the screenplay (by Ted Sherdeman, from the novel by Kenneth M. Dodson) followed. Unfortunately, the rather episodic nature of Howard Christie's production made involvement difficult, and it was from arms' length that audiences were privy to the ship's shakedown cruise, its training period in the Pacific, its landing actions and, best of all, its heroic stand against Japanese kamikaze attacks. The crew also featured prominently in the story, but there were too many of them for all but a mere handful to establish themselves in mere vignettes. Stand-outs, of course, were captain Chandler, a moody loner; and George Nader (second-billed, left) as one of his aides. Lex Barker played a socialite, new to war duty, who eventually proves himself in battle, with other parts assigned to Richard Boone (right), Charles McGraw and Sam Gilman (as sea officers), Don Keefer (as an ineffectual ensign) and James Westerfield, George Dunn and Kendall Clark. The only woman in the cast was Julie Adams as Nader's wife. Manfully overcoming the fissures in the narrative, was director Joseph Pevney. (114 mins)

△ **The Benny Goodman Story**, needless to say, told the story of the famous clarinettist who, like trombonist Glenn Miller, made good from humble beginnings. Unfortunately, although some of the production team from *The Glenn Miller Story* (1954) were involved, and obviously aimed for a repeat performance of that success, the results – bar the music – were disappointing. Valentine Davies, who directed, also provided a somewhat dull and routine screenplay, and cast newcomer Steve Allen (centre) as the maestro. Donna Reed co-starred as the society girl Goodman married, and Berta Gersten was the musician's mother. The plodding familiarity of the enterprise, however, was certainly enlivened by the music which was not only plentiful, but performed by Harry James, Gene Krupa (right), Martha Tilton, Teddy Wilson (at piano), Lionel Hampton, Ziggy Elman and Kid Ory. The King of Swing himself dubbed the clarinet playing for Allen. Aaron Rosenberg produced in Technicolor, also casting Herbert Anderson, Robert F. Simon, Sammy Davis Jr, Dick Winslow, Barry Truex, David Kasday, Hy Averback and Wilton Graff. The huge number of swing classics featured included: 'Bugle Call Rag' Elmer Schoebel, Billy Meyers, Jack Pettis; 'Goody Goody' Johnny Mercer, Matt Malneck; 'Don't Be That Way' Goodman, Mitchell Parish, Edgar Sampson; 'Stompin' At The Savoy' Goodman, Sampson, Chick Webb, Andy Razaf; 'One O'Clock Jump' Count Basie; 'Moonglow' Will Hudson, Eddie DeLange, Irving Mills; 'Avalon' Al Jolson, Vincent Rose, as well as Mozart's *Clarinet Concerto*. (116 mins)

▷ Intelligent audiences weren't in the least bit hoodwinked by the University of Southern California's Dr Frank Baxter who, in a prologue to **The Mole People**, more or less gave the undertaking a scientific seal of approval. Truth was, the movie was unadulterated hokum from producer William Alland, set into motion, plot-wise, when a member of a scientific expedition falls into a cavern on top of a mountain in Asia and, by so doing, discovers a lost Sumarian city whose inhabitants, due to living in semi-dark conditions, are albinos, and their slaves mole-men. John Agar, Hugh Beaumont, Nestor Paiva and Phil Chambers were the trapped scientists involved; Cynthia Patrick (right) a female Sumarian who almost manages to secure her freedom but dies in a climactic earthquake which seals off the 'lost' city for good and all. Rodd Redwing, Robin Hughes and Arthur Gilmore completed the cast and it was sluggishly directed by Virgil Vogel from a screenplay by Laszlo Gorog. (77 mins)

△ **Outside The Law** was a low-voltage melodrama that served to showcase the talents of three of the studio's newer stars: Ray Danton (right), Leigh Snowden (left) and Grant Williams (centre). Danny Arnold's screenplay (from a story by Peter R. Brooke) attempted to draw mileage out of the rounding up of an international counterfeit gang, and, in its modest way, succeeded. Danton, paroled into the army after serving a prison sentence for a crime committed in his youth, is called back from overseas to help round up the gang, after a GI buddy of his – who is involved in the ring – is killed. Danton's brief is to pitch woo at Miss Snowden, his buddy's widow, in the hope that she'll let something slip. She does. Her guard – and by film's end she and Danton are, predictably, romantically paired. Onslow Stevens played Danton's Treasury agent father, with Raymond Bailey, Judson Pratt, Jack Kruschen and Floyd Simmons also in it for producer Albert J. Cohen and director Jack Arnold. (81 mins)

△ The eighth in the series of Kettle capers – and the weakest – **The Kettles In The Ozarks**, with Marjorie Main (centre) still Ma, but *sans* Percy Kilbride as Pa, offered Arthur Hunnicutt as Uncle Sedge (a character modelled closely on the Kilbride original) substituting. It was a load of malarky set, for much of the time, on Hunnicutt's (illustrated in car) ramshackle farm and incorporating, albeit tenuously, a wafer-thin plot involving a group of bootleggers who have set up in competition with local Ozarkian-distilled moonshine; as well as Hunnicutt's twenty-year fence-sitting 'romance' with Una Merkel. Kay Lenard scripted; Ted De Corsia, Olive Sturgess, David O'Brien and Richard Eyer were also in it; Richard Wilson produced and the wheezy direction was by Charles Lamont. (81 mins)

△ A passable, slightly off-beat western, aimed strictly at the double-bill trade, **A Day Of Fury** (whose plot unfolded within a single Sunday) pitted non-conformist Dale Robertson, who regrets the passing of the Old West, against Jock Mahoney (left, whose life Robertson saves in the opening sequence), a marshal responsible for cleaning up the small town in which it all takes place. Robertson shows he means business when he shoots off the lock on the door of the local saloon and brings back the establishment's erstwhile dancing girls, who have been forced to find employment elsewhere since marshal Mahoney's clean-up. Well, things go from bad to worse in the course of the day, with several killings and attempted killings to spice the action. It ended with Mahoney gunning down Robertson after first saving him from a bullet fired by second-billed Mara Corday, a reformed dance-hall gal. James Edmiston and Oscar Brodney's screenplay was clearly a low-budget affair for a low-budget cast that included Carl Benton Reid, Jan Merlin, John Dehner (right), Dee Carroll and Sheila Bromley. Robert Arthur's Technicolor production was directed by Harmon Jones. (78 mins)

▷ The only unusual thing about **Pillars Of The Sky** was that top-starred Jeff Chandler didn't get the girl at the final fade. She (Dorothy Malone) returned to her husband (Keith Andes) after a brief dalliance with the hero. For the rest, though, it was a drearily competent cavalry-versus Indians sagebrush actioner, the inevitable conflict between the two erupting when the cavalry start to open a road and build a fort on land granted to the redskins by treaty. Chandler (left) played a virile cavalry scout who warns the colonel (Willis Bouchey) what will happen if the development plans go ahead, with Ward Bond (as a medical missionary, right) Lee Marvin (a tough sergeant, centre), Sydney Chaplin (an Indian scout), Michael Ansara (the Indian chief) as well as Olive Carey, Charles Norvath, Orlando Rodriguez and Glen Cramer also acting out Sam Rolfe's screenplay (from the novel *Frontier Fury* by Will Henry). Robert Arthur produced (in CinemaScope and Technicolor), and the director was George Marshall. (95 mins)

△ A remake of *This Love Of Ours* (1945), **Never Say Goodbye** was the quintessential 'woman's picture', produced, not by Ross Hunter this time, but by Albert J. Cohen. It top-starred Rock Hudson as a successful Californian physician, and German actress Cornell Borchers (making her American movie debut) as the wife he thought he'd lost in Vienna ten years earlier, after walking out on her in a jealous rage and taking their child with him (see illustration). Attempts at a reconciliation proved abortive when Miss Borchers, caught in the Russian sector, was arrested and sent to an Iron Curtain camp. On her subsequent arrival in the States, having lost trace of Hudson, she became an assistant to a cabaret caricaturist (George Sanders), and it is at a café in Chicago that Hudson meets her again after all those years. On recognising him, she dashes out into the street and is injured by a truck. But, just as he had done with Jane Wyman in *Magnificent Obsession* (1954), Hudson successfully operates on Miss Borchers, persuading her, once she has recovered, to return to him. She agrees with reluctance, immediately meeting with opposition from her young daughter (Shelley Fabares) who refuses to accept Miss Borchers as her mother. In the end, of course, she does, and the process by which this happens gave the film its 'woman' appeal. Ray Collins, David Janssen, Raymond Greenleaf and Frank Wilcox completed the cast, and it was directed in highly lachrymose fashion by Jerry Hopper. The writing credits read thus: screenplay by Charles Hoffman based on a screenplay by Bruce Manning, John Klorer and Leonard Lee, from the play *Come Prima Meglio De Prima* by Luigi Pirandello. (96 mins)

▷ The only thing new about **Francis In The Haunted House**, the seventh and final offering in a series which, for some years now, had been flogging a dead mule, was the casting of Mickey Rooney (illustrated with Francis) in the Donald O'Connor role (despite a change in the actual name of the character); and with Paul Frees rather than Chill Wills supplying the voice of Francis. Apart from that, it was a wearisome litle farce in which four-legged Francis came to Rooney's rescue in a haunted house overrun by a gang of crooks who are substituting fake works of art for the genuine thing. Chief among the heavies were Virginia Welles and Paul Cavanagh, with other roles in Herbert Margolis and William Raynor's screenplay going to Mary Ellen Kaye, David Janssen, Ralph Dumke and Richard Gaines. Robert Arthur produced, and the laugh-sparse direction was by Charles Lamont. (79 mins)

△ An old-fashioned jungle melodrama, dripping in colour by Technicolor and with a sweaty plot (by Houston Branch, screenplay by Richard Alan Simmons) to keep the interest on the boil, **Congo Crossing** was formula film-making which took an indifferent approach to a story concerning a young woman (Virginia Mayo, left) who, being suspected of murder, goes to Congotanga in West Africa because of the spot's lack of extradition laws. Second-billed George Nader (right), a government official, has been employed by the Belgian Congo authorities to draw up a survey showing that Congotanga does in fact fall within Belgian Congo rule. Much of the plot hinged on the outcome of the survey, with a local criminal Mr Big (Tonio Selwart) particularly concerned that the boundaries should remain exactly as they are. Suspense also manifested itself in a sub-plot involving Chicago mobster Michael Pate's plan to murder Miss Mayo by poisoning. The film perked up whenever third-billed Peter Lorre (centre) appeared (he played the local 'law' who keeps the country's fugitives in check) but, for the most part, it was all painfully reminiscent. Rex Ingram, Kathryn Givney, Tudor Owen and Raymond Bailey helped complete the cast for director Joseph Pevney. (85 mins)

◁ Ardent feminists would have been well advised to give **Raw Edge** a miss. Male chauvinists on the other hand, had a great time as scenarists Harry Essex and Robert Hill (story by William Kozlenko and James Benson Nablo) depicted a male chauvinist society in Oregon where a man simply claimed the woman he wanted on a first-come, first-served basis. Rory Calhoun (right) starred as a man bent on avenging the death of his younger brother, as well as proving himself innocent of the accusation that he attacked co-star Yvonne De Carlo, a girl previously 'claimed' by frontier-baron Herbert Rudley. Mara Corday was also in it (as the Indian widow of Calhoun's murdered brother); with other parts in producer Michael Baird's Technicolor time-filler going to Neville Brand (centre), Rex Reason (left), Emile Meyer (2nd left) and Robert J. Wilke. John Sherwood directed. (88 mins)

▽ A no-punches-pulled fistfight and a climactic gun duel were offered to audiences by way of excitement in **Red Sundown**, a paralysingly conventional oater which starred Rory Calhoun (right) as a gunfighter-turned-good-guy who becomes a deputy sheriff in Durango. His chief adversaries in Martin Berkeley's yawnsome screenplay (from the story *Black Trail* by Lewis B. Patten) were Robert Middleton, a rancher engaged in a struggle with local smallholders; and Grant Williams, a gunman whom Middleton has hired to eliminate him. Need one say it, but in the final shoot-out, Calhoun emerges the victor, his prize being second-billed Martha Hyer, the sheriff's daughter. Albert Zugsmith produced, and the director was Jack Arnold. Also cast: Dean Jagger, James Millican and Lita Baron. (81 mins)

◁ **Showdown At Abilene** was an unpretentious little Technicolor western from producer Howard Christie, competently crafted by director Charles Haas from a script by Berne Giler and a story by Clarence Upson Young. It starred Jock Mahoney (right) as Abilene's former sheriff who, after serving in the Civil War, returns with a troubled conscience (and gun-shy, to boot), only to discover that his friend Lyle Bettger (left), whose brother Mahoney accidentally killed in the war, has stolen his gal (Martha Hyer, centre left), and has taken over the range from the farmers. By the end of the picture, need one say, Mahoney's nerve returns to him; so does his girl – with bad-boy-Bettger getting what was coming to him. David Janssen, Grant Williams, Ted De Corsia and Harry Harvey Sr completed the cast. It was remade in 1967 as *Gunfight In Abilene*. (80 mins)

◁ **The Price Of Fear** proffered a potentially interesting situation: that in which a man is framed for two crimes, each of which alibis the other. In the first he's accused of a hit-and-run incident in a stolen car; in the second, he's nailed for a dog-track murder. It's established that if he'd done the one, he couldn't have done the other – and vice versa. Lex Barker (right) was the man, top-starred Merle Oberon (left) the woman he loves, but who doesn't love him. In fact, she's responsible for most of his problems. Charles Drake played a homicide detective, Gia Scala the daughter of the hit-and-run victim, Phillip Pine a gunman, and Warren Stevens a gangleader. Robert Tallman's screenplay (story by Dick Irving Hyland) promised more than it delivered; Howard Christie produced it, and the director was Abner Biberman. (79 mins)

▽ Yet another programmer western which spent its action in the course of a day, **Star In The Dust**, directed by Charles Haas with a sturdy grip on the material supplied by Oscar Brodney (from Lee Leighton's novel *Law Man*), was set in a typical dot-on-the-map western town and concerned itself with the hanging of a hired gunman (Richard Boone, right). There are those (ie the cattlemen) who don't want to see him hanged; and those (the farmers) who do – the former having hired him in the first place to frighten off the latter. Leif Erickson, the town banker, is also keen that the gunman should swing, having paid him to murder three men. Top-starred John Agar played the local sheriff and, on two rough-and-tumble occasions, proved his prowess with his fists. Other roles in Albert Zugsmith's Technicolor production were handled by Coleen Gray (as Boone's lover, left), James Gleason (the jail's janitor), Randy Stuart, Terry Gilkyson, Paul Fix, Henry Morgan and second-billed Mamie Van Doren as banker Erickson's sister and Agar's fiancée. (80 mins)

△ The fifth version (the others being in 1914, 1923, 1930 and 1942) of Rex Beach's hard-hitting novel, **The Spoilers**, reached the screen via producer Ross Hunter who, by building up the role of Cherry Malotte (essayed so memorably by Marlene Dietrich in 1942), almost turned this most macho of stories into a Woman's Film. It certainly lacked the punch of the previous versions, the climactic fist fight between good guy Jeff Chandler (2nd right) and baddie Rory Calhoun (left) being positively perfunctory in comparison with the one undertaken by John Wayne and Randolph Scott in 1942. Still, the basic ingredients in this tale of greed, gold and claim-jumping in an Alaskan boom town managed, in Oscar Brodney and Charles Hoffman's screenplay, to retain its power to involve, despite a lightweight cast that also included Ray Danton, Barbara Britton, John McIntire, Carl Benton Reid, Raymond Walburn, Ruth Donnelly (right), and top-billed Anne Baxter (centre) as Cherry Malotte, owner of the richest saloon in Alaska. Jesse Hibbs directed, its only novelty value being its Technicolor lensing. (84 mins)

▷ **The Square Jungle**, was, of course, the boxing ring, and it provided the background for producer Albert Zugsmith's middleweight actioner, the business of whose screenplay (by George Zuckerman) involved top-starred Tony Curtis (illustrated) in the fight game merely as a means of raising bail money for his drunken father (Jim Backus). Ernest Borgnine, fresh from his success in *Marty* (United Artists, 1955), was cast as the trainer who readies Curtis for a career in the ring; with Pat Crowley and Leigh Snowden in it for featherweight romantic interest. Paul Kelly played a police lieutenant who helps to sponsor Curtis all the way to the top; with other roles going to John Day (as a boxer whom Curtis badly injures during a championship bout), David Janssen, singer Carmen McRae, John Marley, and, playing himself, Joe Louis. The director was Jerry Hopper. (86 mins)

▷ A loose re-working of the Deanna Durbin vehicle *Mad About Music* (1938), but with master Tim Hovey in the Durbin role, **Toy Tiger** – though it billed Jeff Chandler and Laraine Day above the scene-stealing youngster – was, fundamentally, the story of a lonely, fatherless schoolboy (Hovey, right with tiger) at a boarding school who cons high-powered executive Chandler (left) into pretending to be his explorer father in order not to lose face with his lied-to school chums. Furthering the storyline was the fact that Chandler is unaware that Miss Day is the youngster's widowed mother. Cecil Kellaway and Richard Haydn played school masters in the screenplay Ted Sherdeman wrote from a story by Frederick Kohner and Marcella Burke; with other parts in it for David Janssen, Judson Pratt, Butch Bernard and Jacqueline de Wit. It was produced by Howard Christie with family audiences in mind, and directed with similar leanings by Jerry Hopper. (Technicolor). (87 mins)

1956

▷ **The Unguarded Moment** was notable only in that it starred aquatic musical star Esther Williams who, for the first time in her very profitably water-logged career kept herself dry and barely showed an ankle. In her debut effort for the studio she played a high-school teacher unfortunate enough to become involved with a sexual psychopath (handsome John Saxon, one of Universal's newest heart-throbs, and clearly being groomed for stardom). Though outwardly shy of women and, to his contemporaries, an attractive mixture of brawn and brain, Saxon secretly prowls the night attacking women – a condition traced back to his loony father whose mind was warped when his wife deserted him. Miss Williams (illustrated right) is one of his victims, and her philanthropic efforts to protect the nutter are misinterpreted, resulting in her suspension. It is thanks to second-billed George Nader, a police lieutenant who also finds Miss Williams attractive, that both her reputation and her job are restored to her. Actress Rosalind Russell supplied scenarists Herb Meadow and Larry Marcus with the raw material on which to structure their screenplay; Gordon Kay produced (in Technicolor), the pulp-fiction direction was by Harry Keller, and the cast included Edward Andrews (as Saxon's father), Les Tremayne, Jack Albertson and Dani Crayne. It was no world-beater; just passable. (95 mins)

▷ CinemaScope, Technicolor, and Audie Murphy (illustrated) as Indian agent John Philip Clum, were what producer Aaron Rosenberg had to sell in **Walk The Proud Land** and those who bought it were lumbered with a pretty sterile drama of the early west. Based on a biography by Woodworth Clum from which Jack Sher and Gil Doud scripted, it was the story of Clum's attempts to instal self-government for the Apaches, and his historic achievement in forcing a surrender from the warlike Geronimo (Jay Silverheels), the latter incident occupying pride of place in the narrative's scheme of things. Anne Bancroft was second-billed as an Apache widow who can't understand why married Murphy (his wife is Pat Crowley) won't have her for his bride; with other roles under Jesse Hibbs' sluggish direction divided between Charles Drake, Tommy Rall, Robert Warwick, Eugene Mazzola and Anthony Caruso. (88 mins)

▽ There were so many gaping holes in the story devised by scenarist Earl Felton and adaptors Robert Presnell and D.D. Beauchamp from the novel by Norman A. Fox, that Rudolph Maté wisely opted to direct **The Rawhide Years** at a pace deliberately designed to speed past its non-sequiturs and unconvincing motivations. Helping to disguise the mundanities (and inanities) of the storyline, was the flashy casting of top-billed Tony Curtis (centre) as a young adventurer who goes into hiding after being falsely accused of murder. Three years later he returns to the frontier town in which the accusation was made, clears his name, and gets the girl (Colleen Miller). Arthur Kennedy also helped lend weight to the pussy-willow yarn, with other roles in Stanley Rubin's Technicolor production going to William Demarest (as a river-boat pirate pretending to be a respectable rancher), William Gargan, Peter Van Eyck, Minor Watson (left) and Donald Randolph. Leigh Snowden was in it too – but for just one scene. (85 mins)

◁ Audie Murphy took to the ring in **World In My Corner** and should have ko'd scenarist Jack Sher (story by Sher and Joseph Stone) for providing him with so puny a vehicle. The story of a youngster (Murphy, centre) who, under the tutelage of former fight manager John McIntire (right), becomes a promising welterweight boxer, it second-billed Barbara Rush, daughter of a domineering father (Jeff Morrow, left), whom Murphy hopes to marry. The only way he can raise enough money to support Miss Rush though, is to agree to take a fall in a fight with champion Chico Vejar. But he changes his mind at the last minute (being Audie Murphy how could he possibly do otherwise?), as a result of which he sustains injuries which put him out of the fight game for ever. Tommy Rall, Howard St John (as a crooked promoter) and Steve Ellis were also featured in Aaron Rosenberg's production, and the director was Jesse Hibbs. (81 mins)

1957

▽ **Slim Carter** took the mickey out of western stars, but not very effectively. Jock Mahoney (right) top-starred under Richard Bartlett's lukewarm direction, playing an impossibly egocentric smalltime western cafe singer, elevated to film-stardom after being discovered by publicist Julie Adams (left), whose unenviable job it is to keep his head from reaching science-fiction proportions as fame goes to it. He's humanised, however, by young Tim Hovey (foreground centre), an orphan who, in a contest, wins a month's stay with his idol. The problem facing everyone is how to hide Mahoney's true colours from his hero-worshipping young fan. The lad is not to be underestimated though and after helping to cut the star down to size, plays cupid to him and Miss Adams. The ingredients had possibilities, and better direction plus a sharper screenplay from Montgomery Pittman would have helped Howie Horwitz's Eastmancolor production enormously. The rest of the cast included Ben Johnson, Joanna Moore, Maggie Mahoney, Barbara Hale and Roxanne Arlen. (80 mins)

▽ **The Deadly Mantis** was the one about the prehistoric ancestor of the small praying mantis who escapes from a polar icecap when an earthquake shatters his iceberg dwelling place, and causes havoc until he is finally destroyed by poison gas in a Hudson River tunnel in New York. The End. Craig Stevens (seated) starred as a commander in charge of snuffing out the creature and William Hopper (centre) was a paleontologist assigned to help him, with other roles in William Alland's cheapo programmer going to Alix Talton (left), Donald Randolph and Pat Conway – none of whom was able to elevate Martin Berkeley's story and screenplay above the level of a comic-cut. The direction was assigned to Nathan Juran who, in his battle with the deadly mantis, lost. (78 mins)

▽ An ineptly made adventure from producer/director Curt Siodmak, **Love Slaves Of The Amazon** starred Don Taylor as an archaeologist who, together with Eduardo Ciannelli, sets out on an expedition in the Amazon, is captured by a group of Amazonian ladies, and escapes with Gianna Segale (illustrated with Taylor), a white scientist being held captive in the female-dominated society. Harvey Chalk, John Herbert and Wilson Vianna were also in it; Siodmak also scripted (abysmally), and it was filmed in Eastmancolor. Could easily have been mistaken for the comedy of the year. (81 mins)

▽ Howard Christie's skimpily budgeted programmer **The Monolith Monsters**, with an all non-star cast headed by Grant Williams (right), Lola Albright, Les Tremayne (left), Trevor Burdette and Phil Harvey, was an average sci-fi contrivance involving a mysterious meteorite which swells to an enormous size when it comes into contact with water and, literally, petrifies humans by turning them into stone. The inhabitants of the small Californian town in which the picture was set were particularly threatened when the heavens opened and it began to pour with rain. There wasn't much in Norman Jolley and Robert M. Fresco's screenplay (story by Fresco and Jack Arnold) to frighten audiences; and the word for John Sherwood's direction was fumbling. (76 mins)

▷ Rock Hudson (right), producer Ross Hunter and director Douglas Sirk once again pooled their various resources to give **Battle Hymn** the 'heart warming' quality the story cried out for. Based on the real-life exploits of Colonel Dean Hess, a minister-cum-fighter pilot who, in World War II, accidentally bombed a German orphanage and atoned for his miscalculation by air-lifting some 1000 Korean orphans to safety during the Korean war, the film featured Hudson as Hess (with the real-life minister standing by in the wings to offer technical advice), and Martha Hyer as his patient wife; as well as Dan Duryea (in a good-guy role) as an Air Force sergeant, Don DeFore, Anna Kashfi (as a Korean heroine who loses her life in the cause of Hess' work with the orphans, illustrated centre with Jung Kyoo Fyo), Jock Mahoney, Alan Hale, Philip Ahn (left) and Carl Benton Reid. It was another drama aimed at family audiences, and it hit its target dead centre. Charles Grayson and Vincent B. Evans scripted, and it was photographed in CinemaScope and Technicolor. (108 mins)

△ A really flaccid remake of *When Tomorrow Comes* (1939), **Interlude** was little more than a guided tour around Munich and Saltzburg (in CinemaScope and Technicolor, beautifully photographed by cameraman William Daniels) whose pulpy plot had American June Allyson (left) falling in love with famous conductor Rossano Brazzi (right) while working in the information section of Munich's Amerika Haus. Trouble is, he's already married to a demented woman (Marianne Cook) whom he has no intention of deserting. On the rebound Allyson renounces him, and returns to the States with Keith Andes, a doctor who has been patiently waiting in the wings for her. In the earlier film, it was Irene Dunne and Charles Boyer who were the doomed lovers. Their contemporary counterparts, alas, totally lacked the heady romantic aura necessary to spark life into the inert proceedings – especially as scripted so flabbily by Daniel Fuchs and Franklin Coen , based on a screenplay by Dwight Taylor and a story by James Crain, and adapted by Inez Cooke. Francoise Rosay was cast by producer Ross Hunter as a Countess who takes care of Brazzi's invalid wife, with other roles under Douglas Sirk's glutinous direction going to Frances Bergen, Jane Wyatt and Lisa Helwig. (90 mins)

▽ Aimed exclusively at the teenage market, **Rock Pretty Baby** was a squirm-making experience for anyone old enough to know better. To the accompaniment of seventeen rock 'n' roll numbers from the likes of Henry Mancini, Bill Carey, Sonny Burke, Bobby Troup, Rod McKuen and Phil Ruminello, it told the simple story of an 18-year-old high school senior (John Saxon, centre) who wants to become a bandleader despite the wishes of his physician father (Edward C. Platt, right). That was the basis of Herbert Margolis and William Raynor's back-to-the-past screenplay, and it gave employment to Fay Wray as Saxon's mum, Sal Mineo, Luana Patten (Saxon's love interest, centre left), John Wilder, Alan Reed Jr, Douglas Fowley, Shelley Fabares and young George Winslow. Edmond Chevie produced, and Richard Bartlett directed. (89 mins)

▽ It was back to the movie world itself for the setting of **Four Girls In Town**, a fair-to-middling programmer which charted the course taken by four young hopefuls in Hollywood – all of them after a role vacated by shapely Helene Stanton. The auditioning lovelies, in no particular order of merit, were German actress Marianne Cook (centre right), Italian Elsa Martinelli (centre left), Gia Scala (left, also from Italy) and Julie Adams (2nd left) representing the US of A. Turns out none of the girls gets the part when Miss Stanton does a *volte face* and returns to the movie in question. George Nader (2nd right) was top-billed as a director new to the job, with other roles in Jack Sher's none-too-stimulating screenplay (he also directed), farmed out to Sydney Chaplin, John Gavin, Herbert Anderson (far right) and Hy Averback. Aaron Rosenberg produced it in CinemaScope and Technicolor, and Alex North composed the theme song called 'Rhapsody For Four Girls'. (85 mins)

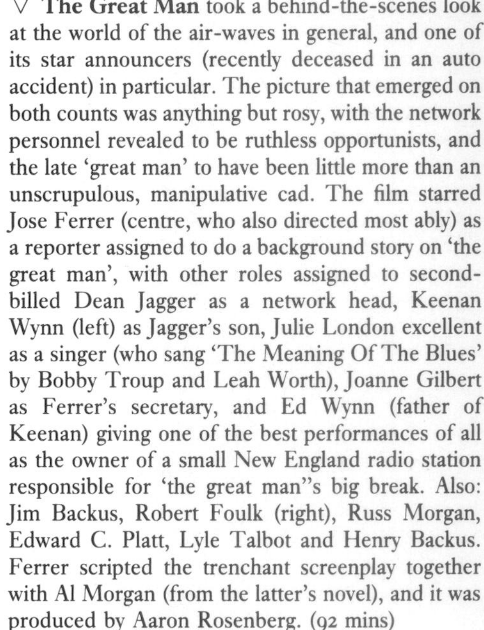

▽ **The Great Man** took a behind-the-scenes look at the world of the air-waves in general, and one of its star announcers (recently deceased in an auto accident) in particular. The picture that emerged on both counts was anything but rosy, with the network personnel revealed to be ruthless opportunists, and the late 'great man' to have been little more than an unscrupulous, manipulative cad. The film starred Jose Ferrer (centre, who also directed most ably) as a reporter assigned to do a background story on 'the great man', with other roles assigned to second-billed Dean Jagger as a network head, Keenan Wynn (left) as Jagger's son, Julie London excellent as a singer (who sang 'The Meaning Of The Blues' by Bobby Troup and Leah Worth), Joanne Gilbert as Ferrer's secretary, and Ed Wynn (father of Keenan) giving one of the best performances of all as the owner of a small New England radio station responsible for 'the great man''s big break. Also: Jim Backus, Robert Foulk (right), Russ Morgan, Edward C. Platt, Lyle Talbot and Henry Backus. Ferrer scripted the trenchant screenplay together with Al Morgan (from the latter's novel), and it was produced by Aaron Rosenberg. (92 mins)

▽ To describe **The Girl In The Kremlin** as improbable would be most charitable. Implausible and far-fetched were also words not strong enough to describe the screenplay shaped by Gene L. Coon and Robert Hill from a story by Harry Ruskin and DeWitt Bodeen. Unadulterated bilge comes nearer the mark and even that's euphemistic. It was predicated on the suggestion that Stalin, though admittedly dead, isn't buried in Moscow's Red Square, but somewhere in Greece where, after undergoing plastic surgery and leaving Moscow with a large sum of cash, he is tracked down by top-starred Lex Barker (centre), an ex-SS cloak-and-dagger man. Second-billed Zsa Zsa Gabor (right) was cast in a dual role (as a Lithuanian and her twin sister) – a feat which defeated her (playing one role convincingly was usually difficult enough for Miss Gabor), with other roles in Albert Zugsmith's incredibly silly drama going to Jeffrey Stone as a one-armed underground spy working with Barker, Maurice Manson as Stalin (before and after plastic surgery) and William Schallert as the son who hates him and is eventually responsible for his death. Also: Natalia Daryll, Aram Katcher, Norbert Schiller and Michael Fox. Russell Birdwell's direction was a mere formality in the wretched circumstances. (81 mins)

△ The studio's special effects department was literally up to its tricks again for **The Incredible Shrinking Man**, and made a magnificent job of the unusual requirements specified in the screenplay which Richard Matheson adapted from his novel. Those requirements necessitated, in full view of the audience, the shrinking of a six-footer (Grant Williams) to a mere two inches as the result of contamination by radioactive fog while out boating. Responsible for these deflationary feats of magic were Clifford Stine, Roswell A. Hoffman and Everett H. Broussard who, contrary to the law of diminishing returns, produced their best optical illusions the smaller Mr Williams became, and achieved a really macabre quality in a scene involving the family cat, and one in which the little hero uses a household pin to lance a giant spider (see illustration). Randy Stuart played the shrinking man's wife who, although on board with her husband at the time the fog struck, was below deck, thus avoiding its after-effects, with Albert Zugsmith's highly effective production also providing roles for April Kent, Raymond Bailey, William Schallert and Frank Scannell. Jack Arnold directed – often quite chillingly. (81 mins)

▽ **The Night Runner** was a thoroughly disagreeable little 'B' whose cast (Ray Danton, Colleen Miller and Eilly Bouchey) did little to enhance its tawdry status. The story of a young psychopath (Danton, illustrated) who is released from a mental institution before being properly cured, it concentrated on the havoc he causes after murdering the father (Bouchey) of the girl he loves (Miller, illustrated), then attempting to murder her too. He recovers his sanity just in time to save her from drowning after pushing her over a cliff, then does the right thing by calling the authorities and giving himself up. Gene Leavitt wrote it from a story by Owen Cameron, Albert J. Cohen produced and Abner Biberman directed. Also cast: Merry Anders, Harry Jackson, Robert Anderson and Jean Innes. (79 mins)

◁ **Man Afraid** was a serviceable melodrama which put Reverend George Nader through hell after he accidentally kills a teenage burglar attempting to rob his home. The dead boy's grief-stricken father (Eduard Franz, illustrated) is determined on revenge, and the movie's climax had Nader's young son (Tim Hovey, illustrated) being chased by a murderous Franz under a beach pier. The denouement saw Nader converting the crazed father by asking the man's forgiveness. Phyllis Thaxter played Nader's wife, and the cast, under Harry Keller's journeyman direction, was completed by Edward J. Stone, Judson Pratt, Reta Shaw, Mabel Albertson and Martin Milner. It was produced in CinemaScope by Gordon Kay from a screenplay by Herb Meadows and a story by Daniel B. Ullman. (83 mins)

▽ **The Tattered Dress** needed a much stronger screenplay than the one provided by George Zuckerman if Albert Zugsmith's production was to be anything other than a perfunctory piece of pulp fiction. In the absence of such a script, what emerged under Jack Arnold's equally perfunctory direction was a negligible account of a well-known New York criminal lawyer (Jeff Chandler, top-starred) employed by wealthy small-town sex-pot and good-time gal (Elaine Stewart) and her dissolute husband (Phillip Reed), after the latter murders a bartender responsible for making a pass at Miss Stewart, then tearing her dress. Chandler, despite the local antagonisms he encounters, wins an acquittal for his client much to the chagrin of the local sheriff (Jack Carson) whom he has managed to antagonise and trip up on the witness stand. Carson exacts a revenge of sorts by framing Chandler (standing left) via a woman juror (Gail Russell, illustrated on floor) whom he persuades to say she was bribed by Chandler – the ensuing complications providing scenarist Zuckerman with the main thrust of his story. Second-billed Jeanne Crain played Chandler's estranged wife (reconciled at the end, natch); with other parts going to George Tobias as the comedian saved by Chandler from taking a murder rap; Edward Andrews as a rival lawyer, and Edward C. Platt as a newspaperman. It was photographed in CinemaScope. (93 mins)

▽ The story of three brothers (Fred MacMurray (illustrated), Jeffrey Hunter and Dean Stockwell (in MacMurray's arms) came to the screen via scenarist R. Wright Campbell in **Gun For A Coward**, the so-called coward of the trio being Hunter who isn't a coward at all – just a sensitive young man for whom violence leaves a bitter taste, as he believes himself responsible, years earlier, for the death of his father. MacMurray, the eldest of the three and father-figure to his siblings, is in charge of their ranch, his numerous responsibilities resulting in the loss of his girl (Janice Rule) to Hunter; with Stockwell (self-consciously apeing the late James Dean), as the youngest, wildest, and dramatically least effective of the boys. Josephine Hutchinson was their Ma, with other roles under Abner Biberman's solid direction going to Chill Wills as a ranch foreman, Betty Lynn, Iron Eyes Cody, Robert Hoy and Jane Howard. William Alland's production enlivened proceedings with the requisite cattle drives and gunfights, but the emphasis was primarily on the characterisations of the three brothers, which did at least help to make the picture a mite more interesting than it might otherwise have been. It was photographed in CinemaScope and Eastmancolor. (88 mins)

▽ A remake in CinemaScope and Technicolor of *Singapore* (1947), **Istanbul** top-starred Errol Flynn (centre) as an American pilot who, after purchasing a bracelet in Istanbul and discovering that it contains 13 valuable diamonds, becomes involved with a gang of smugglers, as well as Turkish Customs who deport him for smuggling. Five years later he returns to collect the jewels he had left hidden in his hotel room and again finds himself sought by the smugglers and Customs people who are after the jewels themselves. Infiltrating the cloak-and-dagger intrigue of Seton I. Miller, Barbara Gray and Richard Alan Simmons' screenplay (story by Miller) was a romantic complication in the shape of Cornell Borchers, whom Flynn believed was burned to death on their wedding night but who, it turns out, is now an amnesia victim married to Torin Thatcher. Albert J. Cohen 's melodrama had little, apart from the pulling power of its male star, going for it, a fact which Joseph Pevney's standard direction did little to alter. Leif Erickson, John Bentley, Peggy Knudson, Martin Benson, Werner Klemperer and Nat King Cole completed the cast, the latter singing 'I Was A Little Too Lonely' and Jack Brooks' 'When I Fall In Love'. (95 mins)

△ **Joe Dakota** was a western with the dubious distinction of there not being a single shot fired throughout. But that was about the only distinction to which it could lay claim. Moving at a pace which would barely tax a snail, it featured top-starred Jock Mahoney as a stranger who arrives in a small oil town in California and begins to ask a lot of awkward questions: such as whatever became of the Indian who once owned the land on which the drilling is taking place? Answer: he was hanged for attacking the young daughter of a local storekeeper. But Mahoney, a retired cavalry captain for whom the deceased Indian once worked as a scout, isn't happy with the explanation and sets about to prove that he was framed by wild-catter Charles McGraw, head of the oil-drilling operation. Luana Patten as storekeeper Frank Weaver's daughter helped Mahoney with his investigations (and supplied romantic interest), Barbara Lawrence played her older sister, with other roles going to Claude Akins (right), Lee Van Cleef, Anthony Caruso (centre) and George Dunn. William Talman and Norman Jolley scripted it, Howard Christie produced, and the sluggish direction was by Richard Bartlett. (Eastmancolor) (79 mins)

△ Star Van Johnson (illustrated) and director Robert Z. Leonard, both alumni from MGM, signed with the studio for an innocuous piece of family fare called **Kelly And Me**. Johnson played a song-and-dance man in the early days of talking pictures, whose one-way-to-oblivion career on the boards perks up after his faithful German shepherd dog, Kelly, 'takes over' his master and helps set him up in pictures, with himself (Kelly) a star in the Rin-Tin-Tin mould. Johnson is forced into the realisation that it's the dog the public pays to see – which is tough on him, but better than starvation. Giving added mileage to Everett Freeman's workaday screenplay was a sub-plot involving the attempts of Kelly's former owner to reclaim the hound, but that was a mere formality in a movie whose happy ending was never in doubt. Feminine interest was supplied by second-billed Piper Laurie as the daughter of studio boss Onslow Stevens, in love with Johnson, and by Martha Hyer as the sexy queen of the lot. Herbert Anderson, Gregory Gay, Dan Riss, Maurice Manson and Douglas Fowley were also in it; and it was produced by Robert Arthur in Technicolor and CinemaScope. (86 mins)

▽ Tautly written (by John Robinson and Edwin Blum) and crisply directed by Joseph Pevney, **The Midnight Story** emerged as an excellent whodunnit. It starred Tony Curtis (left) as a San Francisco cop who, after the murder of a Roman Catholic priest, resigns from the force when he is refused a transfer to homicide, and sets about solving the case himself. The priest turns out to have been a foster father of sorts to Curtis (an orphan) who, naturally, is determined to bring the slayer to justice. Curtis' suspicions fall on Gilbert Roland (right), a sea-food restaurateur and close friend of the murdered man; and when he receives an invitation from Roland to live in the home he shares with his cousin, Marisa Pavan, he accepts, fervently hoping that Roland, whom he has grown to like, is not the man he is after. When he discovers his host had an alibi on the night of the crime he asks Miss Pavan, with whom he has fallen in love, to marry him – only to learn from police sergeant Jay C. Flippen that Roland's alibi was false. Now read on ... Argentina Brunetti, Ted De Corsia and Kathleen Freeman also appeared for Robert Arthur, whose production, in CinemaScope, made excellent use of its San Francisco backdrops. (87 mins)

▽ Marjorie Main (2nd left, whose final film this was, though she didn't die until 1975, aged 85) acquired a new husband for herself in **The Kettles On Old Macdonald's Farm**, the ninth and last in the series. He was Parker Fennelly (left) and, although not as adept at the broad-based comedy as was his predecessor Percy Kilbride, he managed well-enough considering the comic limitation in William Raynor and Herbert Margolis' screenplay. The plot turned the Kettles into matchmakers as they helped engineer the marriage between rich Gloria Talbott (centre right) and poor lumberman John Smith (centre). It was Ma Kettle's role in all this to teach the wealthy Miss Talbott the finer points of being a backwoods wife. Clearly (and accurately) believing the basic situation needed strengthening, producer Howard Christie roped in the services of a bear known as Three Toes for additional interest via a chase sequence. George Dunn (right), reprising his garbage man role in *Away All Boats* (1956) was also in it, and the cast under Virgil Vogel's rural direction was completed by Claude Akins, Roy Barcroft, Pat Morrow and George Arglen. (79 mins)

▽ Reminiscent of MGM's *Teahouse Of The August Moon* (1956) but neither as clever, nor as entertaining, **Joe Butterfly** top-starred Audie Murphy as a brash photographer. But it was Burgess Meredith (centre), as the Joe of the title who stole the show. He played a former Japanese houseboy to a bunch of American hoods who knows all the answers, and who is instrumental in lubricating a plot which involved a group of harassed American journalists and the numerous red-tape difficulties they encounter in bringing out their publication in time to greet the first batch of occupying troops after the Japanese surrender. Most of the humour derived from the attempts of the GIs to pit their ingenuity against the official army system (and the deployment of non-official methods in getting things done), and it involved second-billed George Nader (left) as the sergeant in charge of the American reporters, Keenan Wynn as a civilian correspondent everyone could comfortably live without, and Fred Clark as a highly-strung colonel. It was scripted by Sy Gomberg, Jack Sher and Marion Hargrove from a play by Evan Wylie and Jack Ruge, directed by Jesse Hibbs, and produced in CinemaScope and Technicolor by Aaron Rosenberg. Also cast: John Agar, Charles McGraw, Frank Chase and, as a would-be Tokyo Rose, Reiko Higa. (90 mins)

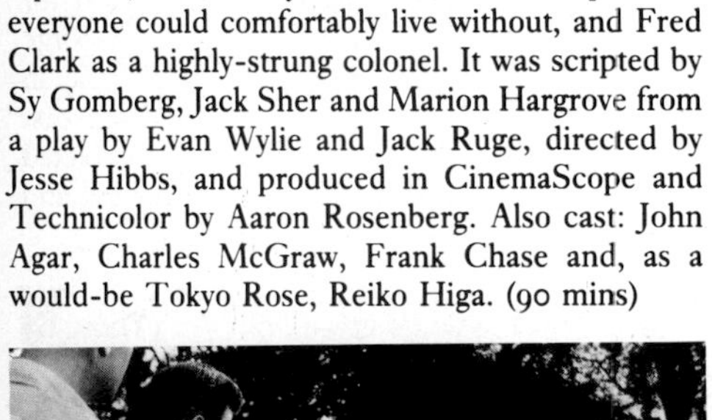

△ Lon Chaney was one of Universal's biggest money-makers in the studio's silent days and it was only right and proper that they should have honoured this strange, tortured genius in a biopic of his life and times. It was called **Man Of A Thousand Faces**, a soubriquet provided by the publicity department for Chaney himself and, giving the role a lot more due than scenarists R. Wright Campbell, Ivan Goff and Ben Roberts (story by Ralph Wheelwright) did, was James Cagney (right) as Chaney. In his most effective performance since his superb recreation of George M. Cohan in *Yankee Doodle Dandy* (Warner Bros., 1942), Cagney turned in a major performance which skilfully combined his subject's intense pride and immense sensitivity. The film itself was more concerned with Chaney's unhappy private life than with his successful public one beginning, as it did, with the star's early childhood (he was born of deaf and dumb parents, hence his extraordinary ability to communicate mimetically), and continuing through his days as a vaudeville song-and-dance man, two marriages and the birth of a son, Hollywood stardom (after appearing as an extra), and his tragic death from throat cancer. Throughout, he is presented as a hard, stubborn man, deeply hurt by and totally unable to forgive being abandoned by his ambitious first wife, singer Cleva Creighton Chaney (Dorothy Malone, left). Jane Greer was cast as his second wife, Roger Smith as his son Creighton (later Lon Chaney Jr) aged 21, with other roles in Robert Arthur's absorbing CinemaScope production going to Marjorie Rambeau as a film extra, Jim Backus as Chaney's press agent, Celia Lovsky and Nolan Leary as Chaney's parents and, in a monumentally awful performance as boy wonder Irving Thalberg, Robert J. Evans, who would later make a name for himself not as an actor but as a real-life movie mogul at Paramount from 1966 to 1976. Joseph Pevney's direction constantly tugged at the heart-strings. (122 mins)

△ A flying pterodactyl, a giant Tyrannosaurus Rex, and a swimming elasmosaurus were just three of the Mesozoic creatures encountered by Navy scientist Jock Mahoney (as the leader of an expedition, left) in **The Land Unknown**. The setting was a strange and mysterious warm-water area in the middle of the Antarctic which Mahoney, in the company of lady news reporter Shawn Smith (centre), helicopter pilot William Reynolds (foreground right) and mechanic Phil Harvey (background right), discovers when the 'copter in which they are all travelling collides with a pterodactyl, forcing the party to descend through heavy fog into a warm, subterranean chasm. Special effects men Fred Knoth, Orien Ernest and Jack Kevan did wonders in boosting this modest sci-fi adventure, written by Laszlo Gorog, into the realms of the respectable, and, under Virgil Vogel's direction, it emerged as lots of fun. William Alland's CinemaScope production also featured Henry Brandon as a scientist (who was also a member of Admiral Byrd's 1947 South Pole expedition) who, ten years previously, had also crashed into this strange prehistoric world, and whose mind is now twisted to the point of madness. Dolores R. Kennedy completed the cast. (78 mins)

◁ **Night Passage** was a blockbuster western whose blockbusting qualities relied not one iota on Borden Chase's seen-it-once-too-often screenplay, but on the box-office combustibility of its three stars, James Stewart, Audie Murphy and Dan Duryea; on the superb Technirama and Technicolor camera work of William Daniels, and on the good-looking scenery of the Durango-Silverton region of Colorado where much of it was filmed. All these plus factors (as well as an excellent score by Dimitri Tiomkin) gave a mighty boost to the second-hand story of two brothers, one of whom is the good guy (Stewart), the other (Murphy) an outlaw in Duryea's service. Stewart (centre) played a former railroad employee whose gun-slinging services are required to ensure the safe delivery, via railroad, of a $10,000 pay-load. The train is held up and the bulk of the hand-me-down plot concerned Stewart's attempts to recover the cash – in the course of which Murphy changes allegiances and, in an all-out shoot-up with the baddies, loses his life while saving his brother's. Dianne Foster (left) and Elaine Stewart provided the female interest, with Foster two-timing Murphy, and Miss Stewart doing ditto to Jay C. Flippen (as a railroad superintendent), with other roles under James Neilson's rip-roaring direction going to young Brandon de Wilde (right), Herbert Anderson, Robert J. Wilke, Hugh Beaumont, Jack Elam and James Flavin. The happy producer responsible for it all was Aaron Rosenberg. (90 mins)

▽ Not nearly as diverting as the original version in 1936, Ross Hunter's lavishly accoutred (in CinemaScope and Eastmancolor) remake of **My Man Godfrey** simply lacked the intrinsic whackiness of the original. Nor did its stars, June Allyson (left) and David Niven (right) possess the madcap qualities displayed to such delightful effect by Carole Lombard and William Powell in the earlier picture. In the update, which scenarists Everett Freeman, Peter Bermeis and William Bowers based on the screenplay by Morrie Ryskind and Eric Hatch (from the novel by Hatch), Godfrey, the butler to an eccentric New York family wasn't a Harvard educated hobo, but an Austrian refugee enjoying illegal US citizenship. As Godfrey, Niven was merely urbane; what was missing from his performance was a sense of the ridiculous. More successful was Jessie Royce Landis as Allyson's screwball mum. Robert Keith was featured as the head of the family (threatened by financial ruin), with other parts under Henry Koster's serviceable direction (no improvement, though, on the 1936 version, which he also helmed), going to Eva Gabor (a divorcee), Jeff Donnell (as the family maid), Jay Robinson, Martha Hyer, Herbert Anderson and Eric Sinclair. (92 mins)

△ With her delightfully refreshing portrayal of Tammy in **Tammy And The Bachelor** (GB: **Tammy**), Debbie Reynolds (right) helped producer Ross Hunter to provide the studio with one of its biggest money-makers of the year. She played an unsophisticated backwoods gal who, after saving wealthy Leslie Nielsen in a plane crash in the Mississippi, is invited to spend time at Brentwood Hall, his plantation, when her grandpappy (Walter Brennan) is arrested for peddling 'corn-likker'. Tammy's unworldly presence among the up-tight, world-weary folk of Brentwood Hall, including Nielsen himself (a drifter since the war), his mother (Fay Wray), father (Sidney Blackmer) and maiden aunt (Mildred Natwick, left), was what the picture was all about. Miss Wray, dreadfully insecure, spends her time trying to turn the plantation into something resembling 'Tara' in *Gone With The Wind*; Blackmer, a professor, has retreated into a world of books; while Natwick is frustrated at not being the artist she had always hoped to be. Under Tammy's regenerative influence, they all undergo a change for the better. In fact, the only one to lose out is Mala Powers, Nielsen's ambitious fiancée, since Oscar Brodney's screenplay (based on the novel by Cid Ricketts Sumner) ended with Reynolds and Nielsen very much in love. And the paying customers wouldn't have had it any other way. Philip Ober, Craig Hill, Louise Beavers and April Kent completed the cast, and it was directed with just the right Cinderella touch by Joseph Pevney. The theme song, penned by Jay Livingston and Ray Evans, was as big a hit as the movie. It was sung over the credits by The Ames Brothers and, in the course of the film, by Miss Reynolds. (Technicolor). (87 mins)

▽ **Slaughter On Tenth Avenue** was a hard-hitting melodrama which focussed on certain criminal activities along New York's waterfront, and demonstrated how the 'code of silence' employed by racketeers and their victims alike operates to make life especially difficult for anyone investigating the area's underworld. One such investigator was top-starred Richard Egan (as real-life William Keating), a deputy assistant district attorney assigned to find out who shot longshoreman boss Mickey Shaughnessy (centre). All sorts of underhand activities insinuated themselves in the course of Egan's probing, and they effectively jollied along Lawrence Roman's screenplay (based on William J. Keating and Richard Carter's novel *The Man Who Rocked The Boat*). The ending, with its courtroom scene and denouement, was something of a let-down, but for three quarters of its running time at least, Albert Zugsmith's production was first-class. Contributing substantially to its success were the performances of Jan Sterling (left), second-billed as Shaughnessy's sympathetic wife; Walter Matthau as a labour racketeer, Dan Duryea as Matthau's lawyer; Julie Adams as Keating's wife, Charles McGraw as a detective, and Harry Bellaver (right) and Nick Dennis as honest longshoremen opposed to the nefarious goings-on which too often blight their world. It was directed with almost documentary-like matter-of-factness by Arnold Laven, who made excellent use of Richard Rodgers' 'Slaughter On Tenth Avenue' score as background. (103 mins)

▷ The rise and rise of Tony Curtis – from Chicago slum-kid to partnering Charles Bickford in a ritzy gambling club – was charted with only fair entertainment returns in **Mister Cory**, a Blake Edwards-scripted and directed drama (based on a story by Leo Rosten), with feminine interest provided by Martha Hyer as a society gal who fancies Curtis (right) for his body but not much else; and Kathryn Grant as her younger sister who, in the end, gets him for keeps. William Reynolds played Hyer's fiancé, with other roles in Robert Arthur's glossy CinemaScope and Eastmancolor production going to Russ Morgan, Henry Daniell (left), Willis Bouchey and Louise Lorimer. But it was Curtis's film all the way, and he wasn't at all bad. (92 mins)

△ 'Static, turgid, claptrap' was one wag's comment on **Quantez**. That was generous. Producer Gordon Kay misapplied the talents of Fred MacMurray (centre), Dorothy Malone, James Barton, Sydney Chaplin, John Gavin (right), John Larch (left) and Michael Ansara to a screenplay by R. Wright Campbell (story by Campbell and Ann Edwards) which suffered, among other things, from verbal diarrhoea. All about a band of bickering outlaws who are holed up in the saloon of a ghost town – surrounded by Apaches – after robbing a bank, it moved along so ponderously under Harry Keller's direction that, by the end of it, it hardly mattered that the only survivors were Gavin and Miss Malone, MacMurray (as an elderly gunfighter) having sacrificed himself to ensure that the young couple can escape to a new and better life together. It was photographed in CinemaScope and Technicolor, neither of which helped. (79 mins)

▽ Preceding the long-running TV serial *Dallas* by a couple of decades, **Written On The Wind** homed in on the morals and passions of a high-powered multi-millionaire Texas oil family whose members had names like Lucy, Mitch, Kyle, Marylee and Jasper. Actually, Mitch (top-starred Rock Hudson, left) wasn't really a member of the family in question, just a lifelong buddy of profligate Kyle Hadley (a marvellously dissolute Robert Stack), the psychotic son ruined by lack of character and an abundance of money – clearly a most unhealthy combination. Or so it proved in George Zuckerman's entertaining screenplay (from the novel by Robert Wilder), which also offered plum roles to Lauren Bacall as a woman unfortunate enough to marry into the family via Stack, and Dorothy Malone (right) as Stack's sexy, immoral sister. Needless to say, both women, gowned by Bill Thomas, looked sensational. Robert Keith was cast as the head of the Hadley family; Grant Williams was one of Miss Malone's numerous one-night motel standbys; others responding well to Douglas Sirk's steamy direction were Robert J. Wilke, Edward C. Platt, Harry Shannon and John Larch. Though the carryings-on in the screenplay were alien to the country's better regulated families, better regulated families world-wide lapped it all up for exactly the same reasons they would one day respond so overwhelmingly to *Dallas* and *Dynasty*; and the film was an enormous money-spinner for Albert Zugsmith, whose Technicolor production made for compulsive viewing. (99 mins)

1958

△ Based on the true-life story of Colonel Francis C. Grevemberg, a World War II hero who single-handedly won a war against crime and corruption in his native state of Louisiana, **Damn Citizen!** starred Keith Andes as Grevemberg, Maggie Hayes as Mrs G, and a cast that included Gene Evans (as the hero's chief aide), Lynn Bari, Jeffrey Stone, Clegg Hoyt (right), Edward C. Platt, Ann Robinson and Sam Buffington. There was a certain documentary matter-of-factness about both the screenplay (by Sterling Silliphant) and the direction (by Robert Gordon). Yet the overall impression left by Herman Webber's production wasn't particularly satisfactory – due, in the main, to the episodic nature of the narrative. (88 mins)

▽ **Flood Tide** was an unpleasant little drama about an emotionally crippled young man (Michel Ray, back to camera) and the havoc wrought by his insanely jealous feelings towards his mother (Cornell Borchers, centre) and her relationship with their neighbour (top-starred George Nader, centre left). Much of Dorothy Cooper's scenario had Nader attempting to win the boy over to his side, as well as getting him to admit that his lying testimony was responsible for sending a man to prison on a murder charge. Nader himself is almost killed by the disturbed youngster in a boating incident. Others involved in producer Robert Arthur's uncommercial proposition were Judson Pratt, Joanna Moore, Charles E. Arnt and Russ Conway. Abner Biberman directed. (82 mins)

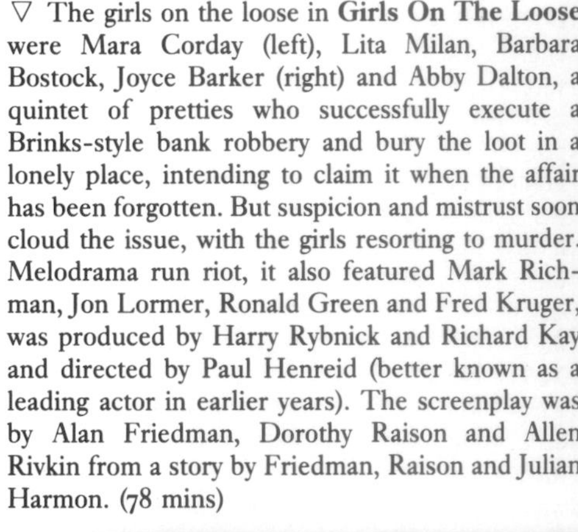

▽ The girls on the loose in **Girls On The Loose** were Mara Corday (left), Lita Milan, Barbara Bostock, Joyce Barker (right) and Abby Dalton, a quintet of pretties who successfully execute a Brinks-style bank robbery and bury the loot in a lonely place, intending to claim it when the affair has been forgotten. But suspicion and mistrust soon cloud the issue, with the girls resorting to murder. Melodrama run riot, it also featured Mark Richman, Jon Lormer, Ronald Green and Fred Kruger, was produced by Harry Rybnick and Richard Kay and directed by Paul Henreid (better known as a leading actor in earlier years). The screenplay was by Alan Friedman, Dorothy Raison and Allen Rivkin from a story by Friedman, Raison and Julian Harmon. (78 mins)

▽ A programmer quickie from producer-director Will Cowan, **The Thing That Couldn't Die** turned out to be one of the members of Magellen's crew. It's unearthed on a western ranch and comes in two portions: a head and, under separate cover, the rest of him (see illustration). He's put together by satanic Carolyn Kearney. The movie was hard to credit on any level and it disappeared without trace. William Reynolds and Andra Martin co-starred, Peggy Converse and Robin Hughes were also in it, and David Duncan scripted. (69 mins)

◁ Patty McCormack (right), who made such a strong impression in Warner Bros.' *The Bad Seed* (1956), gave another excellent account of herself in **Kathy O**, playing Kathy O'Rourke, a famous child star 'loved by millions, yet loved by no one'. For the truth is, the kid's a real pill. Her nemesis (and vice versa) is top-billed Dan Duryea (left), the studio publicist with whom she stubbornly refuses to co-operate, and who has almost to bribe her to be nice and sweet to columnist Jan Sterling (his ex-wife), when the lady comes to interview her. Turns out in Jack Sher and Sy Gomberg's screenplay (from a *Saturday Evening Post* story by Sher), that the moppet and Miss Sterling get on well together; so much so that when little Miss McCormack decides to run away from her guardian aunt (Mary Jane Croft), she makes straight for the newspaper woman. Duryea intercepts, however, and takes the spoilt brat into his own home, with the result that he's accused of kidnapping her. But it all resolves itself satisfactorily, with the child star undergoing a complete change of personality and emerging as a human being after all. Mary Fickett played Duryea's second wife (still jealous of Miss Sterling); Rickey and Terry Kelman were their sons; with other roles under Jack Sher's competent direction going to Sam Levene, Ainslie Pryor, Barney Phillips and Mel Leonard. Several of the movie studio scenes were shot on the Universal City lot. Sy Gomberg produced. (99 mins)

▷ **Appointment With A Shadow** offered audiences the chance to see how, in the course of a single day, booze-ridden reporter George Nader (left) puts his alcoholism behind him and makes a professional come-back by (a) being present when a notorious criminal is apprehended and (b) realising that the wrong man has been shot, the real fugitive having engineered the deception to facilitate his escape. Alec Coppel and Norma Jolley's screenplay was thin on characterisation and thick on platitudes; the performances (including those of Joanna Moore, right, Brian Keith, Virginia Field, Frank de Cova and Stephen Chase) were nothing to get excited about; nor was Richard Carlson's direction (he was actor Carlson making his directorial debut) which did little to disguise its programmer origins. Howie Horwitz produced and it was photographed in CinemaScope. (73 mins)

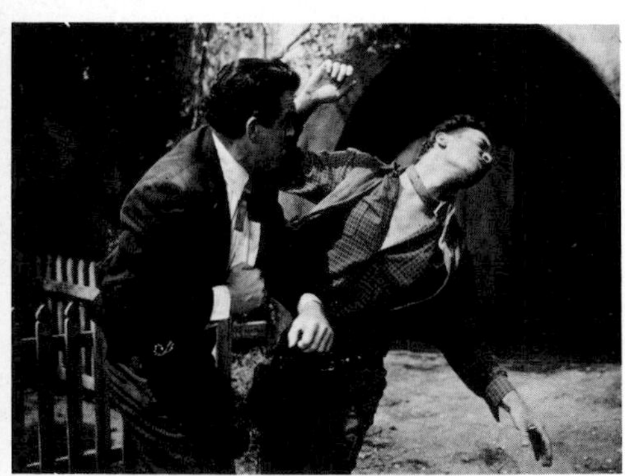

△ As routine and uninspired as its title, **Day Of The Badman** pitted judge Fred MacMurray (left) against four determined toughs who ride into a small western town to see that a relative, convicted of murder, is set free. Everyone, including sheriff John Ericson, is for commuting the sentence to 'banishment' in return for the speedy exit of the quartet (they turn the town upside down to prove they mean business), except MacMurray who, aided by side-kick Edgar Buchanan, goes after the baddies himself and wipes them out. Joan Weldon, Robert Middleton, Marie Windsor and Skip Homeier looked in from the side-lines occasionally. It was produced (in Eastmancolor) by Gordon Kay, written by Lawrence Roman from a story by John M. Cunningham, and directed by Harry Keller. (81 mins)

▷ Hedy Lamarr, Jane Powell and Jan Sterling gave **The Female Animal** a decidedly distaff slant but, thanks to a screenplay (by Robert Hill from a story by producer Albert Zugsmith) to which they all should have said thanks but no thanks, that's all they gave it. A woman's magazine story in which film star Miss Lamarr shows her gratitude to movie extra George Nader (right) for saving her from a falling spotlight on the set by giving him the job of caretaker at her luxury beach house, it featured Miss Powell (left) as her daughter (in love with Nader, as is Miss Lamarr) and Miss Sterling as a former actress, likewise attracted to the good-looking extra. Jerry Paris and James Gleason, as well as Gregg Palmer and Ann Doran were also in it; and it was directed for the mush it was by Harry Keller. (92 mins)

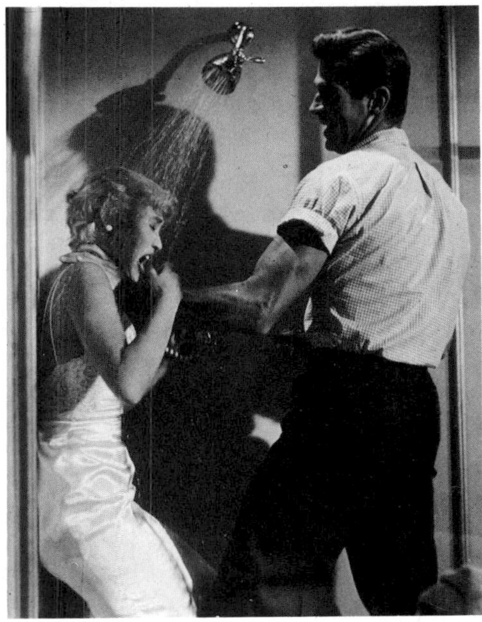

◁ Question: what took to the air on several occasions, but always remained firmly on the ground? Answer: **The Lady Takes A Flyer**, a depressingly ordinary romance that paired Lana Turner and Jeff Chandler (both illustrated centre) with so-so results. They played a husband-and-wife plane-ferrying service who travel all over the world together until she has a baby and he has to go it alone. Climax of the film had Turner crossing the Atlantic on her own in order to deliver a plane to England – with hubby managing to get there ahead of her in time to direct her through thick fog to a safe landing. It was a real waste of time from producer William Alland, whose purposeless screenplay by Danny Arnold (story by Edmund H. North) did little to enhance the careers of its two stars. Andrea Martin provided the story with conflict in the shape of a female pilot on the make for Chandler, with other roles going to Richard Denning, Chuck Connors, Reta Shaw, Alan Hale Jr, Dee J. Thompson and Nestor Paiva. It was photographed in CinemaScope and Eastmancolor. (93 mins)

▷ With no fewer than fifteen musical numbers punctuating David P. Harmon's screenplay for **The Big Beat**, and featuring such artists as The Del Vikings, The Diamonds, Fats Domino, The Four Aces, Harry James, The Lancers, Freddy Martin, Russ Morgan, The Mills Brothers, The George Shearing Quintet, The Thompson Singers and The Cal Tjader Quartet, there was very little room for plot. What little there was concerned top-starred William Reynolds, the son of a successful record producer, and his attempts (ultimately successful after a slow start) to improve the 'pop' side of the business. Andra Martin, Gogi Grant, Jeffrey Stone, Rose Marie (illustrated centre), Hans Conried and Howard Miller helped round out the cast for producer-director Will Cowan, whose Eastmancolor production was a shameless exploitation of the current youth market. (82 mins)

△ **Raw Wind In Eden** was about as entertaining as a raw wound in Eden. A poor script, which the direction and acting did nothing to improve, it was a romantic adventure which starred Esther Williams (right) and Carlos Thompson (as a fashion model and a playboy) whose plane crashes on a remote island run by Jeff Chandler, with Rosanna Podesta and her grandfather, Eduardo di Filippo, also on hand. Bathing belle Williams gets into her swimsuit for a dip 'around the point' and falls in love with Chandler while Thompson, having discovered a beached yacht, repairs it and leaves the island. It was directed by Richard Wilson, who wrote the screenplay with Elizabeth Wilson, from a story by himself and Dan Lundberg. William Alland produced, in CinemaScope and Eastmancolor, with a cast that was completed by Rik Battaglia. (93 mins)

▽ Director Jack (*The Incredible Shrinking Man*) Arnold had another go at sci-fi in **Monster On The Campus** and, if his latest effort had more *schlock* than shock, teenage audiences – preferably huddled together with a loved one in the back seat of a car at a drive-in – found it lots of fun. All about a prehistoric fish discovered in Madagascar and the terrible things that happen on contact with it (such as dragonflies changing into two-foot flying killers, dogs turning into wolves and men becoming Neanderthal killers), it featured Joanna Moore (left), Arthur Franz (centre) as her fiancé, Judson Pratt (right) as a homicide lieutenant, Troy Donahue and Nancy Walters as a couple of students, as well as Phil Harvey, Helen Westcott and Alexander Lockwood. David Duncan's vivid imagination provided the screenplay, and the producer was Joseph Gershenson. (77 mins)

△ With *Tammy And The Bachelor* having notched up a massive hit for the studio the previous year, producer Ross Hunter quickly put Debbie Reynolds, its appealing female star, into a similar vehicle, and the result was **This Happy Feeling**. As written (from F. Hugh Herbert's play *For Love Of Money*) and directed by Blake Edwards, it emerged as a piece of glossy escapism in which several attractive and talented actors found themselves unextended by a plot which had girlish Miss Reynolds (left) arriving by chance at the Connecticut farm of retired matinée idol Curt Jurgens (right – now a horse breeder with a crick in his back) and falling for the old bachelor, but settling in the end for handsome and youthful neighbour John Saxon. Alexis Smith played an amorous leading lady on the make for Jurgens, Estelle Winwood was cast as Jurgens' housekeeper (whose speciality is butterscotch pancakes – made with butter and Scotch), with other roles going to Mary Astor, Troy Donahue (as a method-school actor), Hayden Rorke, and a seagull that for no discernible purpose keeps flying through the action to garner the odd quizzical laugh or two. It was filmed in CinemaScope and Eastmancolor, and featured a title song by Jay Livingston and Ray Evans, sung by Miss Reynolds. (92 mins)

▽ After the deaths of Billy The Kid and Jesse James, the **Last Of The Fast Guns** (according to scenarist David P. Harmon) was Brad Ellison (Jock Mahoney, left) who, circa 1880, sets off to find the missing brother (Eduard Franz) of wealthy industrialist Carl Benton Reid. If, however, Franz, who is somewhere in Mexico, is not found, a large sum of money goes to his partner (Gilbert Roland, right). In the circumstances, Roland is keen to see that his partner remains missing. But he has not reckoned with Mahoney, who finds Franz alive and well and persuades him to return to civilisation after an attempt is made to kill him. Linda Cristal provided some perfunctory love interest for the hero; with other roles in Howard Christie's visually gorgeous production (it was filmed in CinemaScope and Eastmancolor in Northern Mexico) going to Lorne Greene and Edward C. Platt. George Sherman directed. (82 mins)

▽ **Voice In The Mirror** was a small-scale, yet not unimpressive drama about alcoholism. It wasn't as good as *The Lost Weekend* (Paramount, 1945) but it didn't need to be. The point it was making – that it takes a drunk to help a drunk – came over loud and clear under Harry Keller's assured direction. Richard Egan (illustrated) top-starred as a successful commercial artist who hits the bottle once too often after the death of his small daughter and is unable to leave liquor alone, despite the pleas of his extremely sympathetic and understanding wife (Julie London), and the haranguing of his doctor (the excellent Walter Matthau). His drinking goes from bad to worse, and it is only after discovering that his alcoholic binges have caused some nerve damage that he attempts to do something about his chronic condition. What he does is to form his own personal Alcoholics Anonymous, starting with Arthur O'Connell, a former teacher who has been an alcoholic for the past fourteen years. The film ends with a sober Egan being applauded, some ten years later, by the many men and women he has helped regenerate through what Larry Marcus' screenplay somewhat vaguely referred to as 'spiritual awareness'. Troy Donahue, Ann Doran, Harry Bartell, Peggy Converse, Mae Clarke and Casey Adams were also featured, and the film was modestly produced (in CinemaScope) by Gordon Kay, who made good use of downtown Los Angeles. (105 mins)

△ Comedians Dan Rowan (left) and Dick Martin (right) made their movie debuts in **Once Upon A Horse**, a scatter-brained western farce, written (from a story by Henry Gregor Felsen), produced and directed by Hal Kanter, in which the two funnymen appeared as a couple of cowpokes incapable of making a living either legitimately or crookedly. Plot took second place to the series of sight gags imposed by Kanter on the proceedings, and the antics of a cast that included Martha Hyer and Nita Talbot (for distaff interest), as well as James Gleason, John McGiver, Paul Anderson, David Burns, Mac and Buddy Baer and Dick Ryan. Also in it were western stars Tom Keene, Bob Livingston, Kermit Maynard and Bob Steele, all there for a send-up chase. It was photographed in CinemaScope. Re-released in 1963 as *Hot Horse*. (85 mins)

▽ **The Restless Years** was curiously old-fashioned for a movie aimed at the contemporary youth scene. About a couple of teenagers (John Saxon and Sandra Dee, left) whose development, if not actually arrested by the interference of parents, was somewhat hampered by it, it would have worked far better set at a time when small-town bigotry could really ruin lives. In the youth-dominated mid-fifties it was hard to believe in a young girl (Dee) being rejected because of her illegitimacy. Yet that was one of the main points in the screenplay Edward Anhalt based on Patricia Joudry's stage play *Teach Me How To Cry*. Saxon's complications occur with the arrival in the small town of his failure of a father (James Whitmore), a man hoping that his past connections in the town will help him find the kind of success he has not been able to achieve elsewhere. There was something old-fashioned, too, about the feel of Ross Hunter's production which may have had something to do with the fact that the older members of the cast, such as Teresa Wright (right) as Dee's ashamed mother, the aforementioned Whitmore, Margaret Lindsay (as Saxon's mother), and Virginia Grey as a teacher were so much better than the youngsters. Though moderately entertaining, the picture wasn't the trenchant statement on youth Hunter clearly hoped it would be. Helmut Kautner directed it slickly, and the cast was completed by Luana Patten, Jody McCrea, Alan Baxter, Hayden Rorke and Dorothy Green. (86 mins)

△ Having scored such a notable success with *The High And The Mighty* (Warner Bros., 1954) author Ernest K. Gann, using a similar formula (ie a group of diverse characters facing a potentially hazardous situation), surfaced with the pretentiously titled **Twilight Of The Gods**, a less successful attempt at creating suspense and set, not on a crippled airliner, but on a battered old two-masted leaking brigantine en route from the South Sea islands to Honolulu. Passengers this time included Cyd Charisse (centre) as a Honolulu call girl running away from the police; Leif Erickson (right) as a has-been showman; Judith Evelyn (centre right) as a *passé* opera singer; Vladimir Sokoloff and Celia Lovsky as an elderly pair of refugees; Ernest Truex as a missionary, and Richard Hayden as a British beachcomber. Top-starred Rock Hudson (left) was the vessel's courtmartialled, alcoholic captain, and Arthur Kennedy his not-to-be-trusted second mate. Also: Wallace Ford as a seaman, and Charles McGraw as a mutineering deck hand. It was average entertainment, with all the stock ingredients of the 'disaster' genre – but not, alas, the requisite excitement – in evidence in the screenplay Gann fashioned from his novel, and it was directed for producer Gordon Kay by Joseph Pevney with only a minimum amount of audience involvement. It was filmed in Eastmancolor on location in the Hawaiian Islands by Irving Glassberg. (120 mins)

▽ The top-casting of Audie Murphy wasn't enough to save **Ride A Crooked Trail** from being a deadly bore. He played a bank robber (called Joe Maybe) on the run who is mistaken by Judge Walter Matthau of Little Rock to be the town's new marshal, an error which Murphy (centre) naturally plays along with until the respectability bestowed on him in his new-found position (as well as the attentions of creole Gia Scala, left, whom he pretends is his wife), transforms him completely, despite his being suspected of a bank robbery he did not commit. Borden Chase wrote it, Howard Pine produced and it was directed by Jesse Hibbs with a cast that also included Henry Silva and Eddie Little (in Murphy's arms). It was photographed in CinemaScope and Eastmancolor. (88 mins)

◁ Producer Albert Zugsmith, flushed with the success of *Written On The Wind* (1956), re-assembled Rock Hudson (right), Robert Stack (left) and Dorothy Malone (centre right) to head the cast of **The Tarnished Angels**, a tarnished melodrama set in the barnstorming days of the early '30s, whose truly appalling screenplay (by George Zuckerman, from William Faulkner's novel *Pylon*) totally defeated a cast that also included Jack Carson (centre);, Robert Middleton, Alan Reed and Alexander Lockwood. Douglas Sirk's dim-witted direction was another liability in the telling of this absurdly silly story of a romance between Hudson (playing a New Orleans reporter) and the wife (Malone) of a trick-parachutist barnstormer and ex-World War I ace pilot (Robert Stack). Carson played a mechanic in love with Malone, and angry at Stack's cavalier treatment of his wife. It was shot in CinemaScope. (87 mins)

▷ Writer/director/actor Orson Welles (illustrated) made a remarkable return to form in all three capacities for **A Touch Of Evil**, which he adapted from Whit Masterson's novel *Badge Of Evil*, and in which he appeared as Hank Quinlan, ruthless, twisted Texas cop in a Mexican border town who, after framing a young man for murder, clashes with top-billed Charlton Heston as a coolly indignant Mexican government official on honeymoon with Janet Leigh. Not only does Heston have to cope with the machinations of the evil Mr Welles, but his honeymoon is further blighted by a gang of narcotics racketeers who, in one of the most chilling, nightmarish scenes in the film, give Miss Leigh a really tough time. From the marathon opening tracking shot (Russell Metty's camerawork was particularly stunning throughout), to the macabre closing sequence in which the dead body of Welles is seen floating whale-like in the water, the movie was a stylistic triumph, with Welles again exploring the infinite possibilities the medium of film offers for personal expression. There was not a tired set-up throughout and, as a piece of atmospheric cinema, it was an unqualified winner, relying far more on its baroque style than on its often melodramatic content. Also appearing with Heston, Leigh and Welles were Joseph Calleia, Akim Tamiroff, Joanna Moore, Ray Collins, Dennis Weaver, Valentin de Vargas, Mort Mills and, in unbilled guest spots, Zsa Zsa Gabor, Joseph Cotten, Mercedes McCambridge, Keenan Wynn and, as the madam of a Mexican bordello, a gypsy-like Marlene Dietrich, who had the best line of all when, talking about Welles after his death, she remarks 'What can you say about anybody? He was some kind of a man'. *Touch of Evil*, produced by Albert Zugsmith, was some kind of a film. (95 mins)

▽ A sequel to *Rock Pretty Baby* (1957), **Summer Love** again starred John Saxon, with Edward C. Platt, Fay Wray and young George Winslow reprising their roles as Ma, Pa and younger brother. Scenarists William Raynor and Herbert Margolis allowed Saxon to head his own musical combo comprising Rod McKuen, John Wilder (left), Bob Courtney, Troy Donahue and Hylton Socher, and manoeuvered him through a slender plot involving a summer-camp musical engagement, and the inevitable romantic complications. Seems he can't choose between Judi Meredith and Jill St John (right). Shelley Fabares, Molly Bee, Gordon Gebert and Beverley Washburne were also in it for producer William Grady Jr and, with seven rock 'n' roll numbers on offer, there was no mistaking at which market director Charles Haas was asked to aim. The songs were supplied by Henry Mancini, Rod McKuen, Bill Carey, Malvina Reynolds, Everett Carter and Milton Rosen. (85 mins)

▷ Based on the novel by Erich Maria Remarque and scripted by Orin Jannings, **A Time To Love And A Time To Die** took over two long hours to drive home the message (more effectively stated in *All Quiet On The Western Front*, brilliantly filmed by the studio in 1930) that war is hell, regardless of what side you happen to be fighting for. Set in Germany during World War II, this was the story of Ernest Graeber, a German soldier who, while home on a furlough, falls in love with a young girl (Lilo Pulver, left), marries her, then returns to the Russian front where (in a scene reminiscent of the memorable closing moments in *All Quiet*), he is killed while clutching a letter from his wife informing him that he is soon to be a father. Though extremely well intentioned, it was difficult to believe in producer Robert Arthur's CinemaScope and Eastmancolor recreation of Remarque's novel, due mainly to the casting of all-American John Gavin (right) as Graeber. It could be argued that by using an actor as obviously American as Gavin, the production was underlining the point of the book – that a soldier is a soldier is a soldier, regardless of nationality. But it just didn't work. And although the film was shot on location in Germany, with a cast list that included such all-Americans as Keenan Wynn, Jock Mahoney and Don Defore, audiences had to keep reminding themselves that the characters they were watching were, in fact, Germans. Not that the cast was made up entirely of American accents. It was just that apart from Miss Pulver, the three leading men were clearly not European; nor were they good enough actors to pretend they were (as, for example, Marlon Brando was in *The Young Lions*, 20th Century-Fox, 1958). Author Remarque made an undistinguished appearance in the film as an elderly school teacher, with other roles under Douglas Sirk's plodding direction going to Dieter Borsche, Barbara Rutting, Thayer David, Charles Regnier, Alexander Engel, Dorothea Wieck (star of *Maedchen In Uniform*) and Klaus Kinski. (133 mins)

△ A family western graced by the attractive presence of second-billed Maureen O'Sullivan (right), **Wild Heritage** was a mediocre entertainment about two families heading west in covered wagons, and encountering cattle rustlers and gunslingers en route. Miss O'Sullivan (widowed early in the picture) is mother to Rod McKuen, George Winslow, Gigi Perreau (centre) and Gary Gray; while the second family are represented by Stephen Ellsworth and Jeanette Nolan, and their offspring Troy Donahue and Judi Meredith. Climax of the film is the killing of two gunmen by McKuen, Gray and Donahue. Top-billed Will Rogers Jr was cast as a frontier lawyer, with other roles in Paul King and Joseph Stone's screenplay (story by Steve Frazee) going to Paul Birch (left), John Beradino and Phil Harvey. John E. Horton produced (in Eastmancolor) and the director was Charles Haas. (78 mins)

◁ **Live Fast, Die Young** was the story of two sisters, one of whom (Norma Eberhardt, illustrated left) leaves home to embark on a life of crime, while the other (Mary Murphy) is a goody-goody who hopes to save her from same. A Harry Rybnick-Richard Kay production, it was aimed largely at the teenage market and also featured Michael Connors, Peggy Maley, Carol Varga and Troy Donahue. A low-budget effort with practically no marquee value, it made little impact at the box-office. Paul Henreid directed, and it was scripted by Allen Rivkin and Ib Melchior from a story by Melchior and Edwin B. Watson. (82 mins)

▽ A low-budget oater in CinemaScope and Eastmancolor from producer Gordon Kay, **The Saga Of Hemp Brown** starred Rory Calhoun (a US Cavalry officer) in the title role, his saga being that he was falsely accused of an ambush in which several men, as well as the colonel's wife, were murdered. Stripped of his uniform and thoroughly disgraced, Calhoun (centre) hitches a ride with medicine man Fortunio Bonanova (centre right) and his attractive assistant Beverly Garland (left, who saves him from lynching), wastes no time in proving his innocence in the affair, and exposes the real villain, who turns out to be John Larch. Both Bob Williams' screenplay and Richard Carlson's direction allowed audiences to keep three jumps ahead of them throughout and, by so doing, dissipated any suspense or tension the plot might have generated. Russell Johnson, Allan Lane, Trevor Bardette, Morris Ankrum and Addison Richards were also cast. (80 mins)

△ Jeff Chandler starred with Orson Welles in **Man In The Shadow**, a contemporary western that shaped up as par-for-the-sagebrush course, but nothing to get excited about. Chandler (left) played a newly appointed sheriff, and Welles a domineering rancher who strenuously objects to the former's investigation of the death of a Mexican labourer on the latter's property. The discovery of bloodstains leads Chandler to suspect foul play and, against the urgings of the town's leading citizens to drop the case, the sheriff continues his enquiries. His actions almost lead to his death but, in the end, the culprit is found and turns out to be ranch foreman John Larch. Colleen Miller (right) played Welles' daughter, with other parts going to Ben Alexander, Barbara Lawrence (as Chandler's wife), James Gleason, Royal Dano and Paul Fix. It was produced by Albert Zugsmith in CinemaScope, and directed by Jack Arnold from a screenplay by Gene L. Coon. (79 mins)

1959

△ The only original element in **Curse Of The Undead**, another in the studio's long (and distinguished) line of Dracula-inspired chillers, was the fact that the vampire in this instance was a typical western gunfighter (Michael Pate) who, after sinking his teeth into Kathleen Crowley, and committing several murders, is finally laid to rest (see illustration) by Eric Fleming (of TV's *Rawhide*), who inserts a wooden cross in a bullet, then fires it at the blood-sucking troublemaker. The nonsense was written by Edward and Mildred Dein (the former also directing), and produced by Joseph Gershenson with a cast that included John Hoyt, Bruce Gordon and Edward Binns. (79 mins)

▽ Producer Ross Hunter and director Douglas Sirk's lachrymose remake of **Imitation Of Life**, first seen as a film in 1934 with Claudette Colbert, assaulted the tear-ducts all over again (in CinemaScope and Eastmancolor) as it re-told the story of two mothers and the trouble each has with her respective daughter. Lana Turner (in the Colbert role) played an actress who neglects her daughter (Sandra Dee) in the furtherance of her career (in the earlier film it was a pancake flour business the character pursued though, whichever way you looked at it, her interest was self-raising); while Juanita Moore, the other mother in question, is a Negress whose daughter (Susan Kohner) is sufficiently light-skinned to 'pass' for white – which, against mama's wishes, she does. Second-billed John Gavin (left) was the man in both Miss Turner (right) and Miss Dee's life, with other roles going to Robert Alda as an opportunistic agent and Dan O'Herlihy as a playwright, as well as Mahalia Jackson (who sang 'Trouble Of The World' at Miss Moore's tear-filled funeral), John Vivyan, Lee Goodman and Troy Donahue. Miss Moore and Miss Turner's daughters, aged 8 and 6 respectively, were played by Karen Dicker and Terry Burnham. It was scripted by Eleanore Griffin and Allan Scott from the novel by Fannie Hurst in a manner that manipulated the emotions shamefully – and to great box-office effect. (125 mins)

▽ Audie Murphy (illustrated) played a notorious hired assassin in **No Name On The Bullet**, who, much to the disapproval of the inhabiants of Lordsburg, especially sheriff Willis Bouchey and the town's doctor (Charles Drake), checks into a local hotel. His purpose? To plug Judge Edgar Stehli. How he causes the man's death without actually firing a shot, gave scenarist Gene L. Coon (story by Harold Amacker) his surprise and 'ironic' denouement. Joan Evans played the judge's daughter, with R.C. Armstrong, Karl Svenson, Whit Bissell, John Alderson, Warren Stevens and Virginia Grey completing the cast for producers Howard Christie and Jack Arnold , the latter also directing in CinemaScope and Eastmancolor. It was relentlessly second-rate. (77 mins)

▽ In her first film for Universal, Doris Day (left) scored a terrific bulls-eye opposite top-cast Rock Hudson (right) in **Pillow Talk**, an Arwin Production, produced by Ross Hunter in eye-filling Eastmancolor and CinemaScope. She played a fashionable interior decorator, he a songwriter, and what they have in common is a party telephone line. Every time she attempts to make a call, she hears Hudson crooning some love song to one of several amorous young ladies. Her interjections are interpreted by Hudson to be the envious bitchings of an unattractive old maid. When, however, Hudson gets to see Miss Day in the flesh, his attitude changes completely and, pretending to be a wealthy Texan, he sets out to woo her. It all worked delightfully, thanks to the attractive presences of the two stars, and a screenplay by Stanley Shapiro and Maurice Richlin that kept the patter sparkling and fresh throughout. Director Michael Gordon (making effective use of the split-screen) played it for maximum laughter, and drew marvellous performances, too, from a quality cast that included Tony Randall (as one of Miss Day's disappointed suitors, what else?) and Thelma Ritter as an alcoholic maid, as well as Nick Adams, Mary McCarty, Alex Gerry, Marcel Dalio and Lee Patrick. The lively music score was by Frank DeVol, and the sumptuous gowns worn by Miss Day by Jean Louis. (105 mins)

◁ Audie Murphy (left) played it mainly for laughs in **The Wild And The Innocent**, being a wildly innocent young man who, in the course of producer Sy Gomberg's screenplay (written in cahoots with director Jack Sher), meets Sandra Dee, an equally naive urchin, and Joanne Dru a sophisticated dance-hall hostess. After a brief dalliance with Dru, Murphy decides it's really Dee he wants – thus bringing the light-hearted oater to its unmemorable close. Gilbert Roland (right) made a flashy impact as a local Mr Big, with other roles going to Jim Backus, George Mitchell, Peter Breck and Strother Martin. It was filmed in CinemaScope and Eastmancolor. (84 mins)

△ A combination western and thriller, **Money, Women And Guns** was successful in neither category. It was about an elderly prospector who is attacked by a trio of outlaws. He kills two of them and, just before he dies, leaves a will dividing his money among four people: Tim Hovey, a youngster with expensive tastes; William Campbell (right), a gunman trying to go straight to please his tubercular wife Judi Meredith (seated); James Gleason, an old timer and poker player; and Jeffrey Stone, who turns out to be the third outlaw responsible for the old man's attack. Jock Mahoney (left) was top-starred as a detective investigating the case, with other roles going to Kim Hunter, Gene Evans, Lon Chaney Jr and Tom Drake. It was scripted by Montgomery Pittman, produced in CinemaScope and Eastmancolor by Howie Horwitz, and directed by Richard Bartlett. (80 mins)

▽ The central character in Mel Dinelli, Czenzi Ormonde and Chris Cooper's screenplay (story by Gordon McDonell) for **Step Down To Terror** (a pale remake of Hitchcock's *Shadow Of A Doubt*, 1943) was Charles Drake who, after being away for six years, returns home much to the joy of his mother (Josephine Hutchinson), his widowed sister-in-law (top-billed Colleen Miller), and his orphaned nephew (Rickey Kelman). But joy soon turns to suspicion, which sours into fear when it becomes apparent that Drake is a psychopathic killer who, were it not for the intervention of Rod Taylor, would almost certainly have bumped Miss Miller (illustrated, pursued by Drake) off. Under Harry Keller's earnest direction the cast did its best to bring a patina of credibility to the melodramatic proceedings but, although competently produced by Joseph Gershenson, the triteness of the material defeated all concerned. (75 mins)

▷ The great James Cagney (centre), now decidedly advanced into middle age, had his last crack at at musical in **Never Steal Anything Small**. Based on Maxwell Anderson and Rouben Mamoulian's unproduced musical *The Devil's Hornpipe*, the subject matter was, alas, fairly unsavoury, with Cagney as an engaging waterfront hoodlum who wants to become president of United Stevedores. To this end he is willing to engage in any number of dirty operations including perjury, bribery and grand larceny (he even lays a trumped-up charge of corruption on a young lawyer engaged to the girl Cagney loves in an attempt to destroy their marriage). Shirley Jones (left) co-starred as the object of Cagney's affections and Roger Smith was the lawyer, with supporting parts going to Cara Williams, Nehemiah Persoff, Anthony Caruso, Royal Dano and Jack Albertson. Charles Lederer, who wrote the screenplay, directed without any noticeable grip on the proceedings, and it was produced, in CinemaScope and Eastmancolor, by Aaron Rosenberg. Hermes Pan choreographed, Allie Wrubel wrote the music, and the lyrics were by Maxwell Anderson. Standout number: Cagney and Cara Williams singing 'I'm Sorry, I Want A Ferrari'. Other songs and musical numbers included: 'Never Steal Anything Small', 'I Haven't Got A Thing To Wear', 'It Takes Love To Make A Home', 'Helping Out Friends'. (94 mins)

▽ Despite a cast that included Rock Hudson (right, top-billed), Jean Simmons (left), Dorothy McGuire, Kent Smith and, making his first appearance at the studio for several years, the always reliable Claude Rains, **This Earth Is Mine** failed to hold the interest. Set in the Napa Valley during prohibition, it was the story of two generations of vintners – the modern generation represented by Hudson, who's in it for the money; and the older generation by Rains, Hudson's grandfather, who believes in and is dedicated to his craft (seems that Hudson wants to link the family empire to the lucrative business of bootlegging). Simmons played a newcomer to the Napa Valley from Britain and, although being a first cousin of Hudson's, has an affair with him but can't make up her mind whether she wants marriage as well. Producer Casey Robinson's screenplay, from the novel *The Cup And The Sword* by Alice Tisdale Hobart, was very talky and full of side-issues (one of them involving vineyard worker Cindy Robbins and her pregnancy for which Hudson is responsible; another concerning both anti-Semitic and anti-Italian prejudices), and it lacked the kind of cohesion a sprawling tale such as this desperately needed. It looked beautiful, though (in CinemaScope and Technicolor), producers Robinson and Claude Heilman making quite sure the picturesque location was exploited to the full by cameramen Winton Hoch and Russell Metty. The director was Henry King. (123 mins)

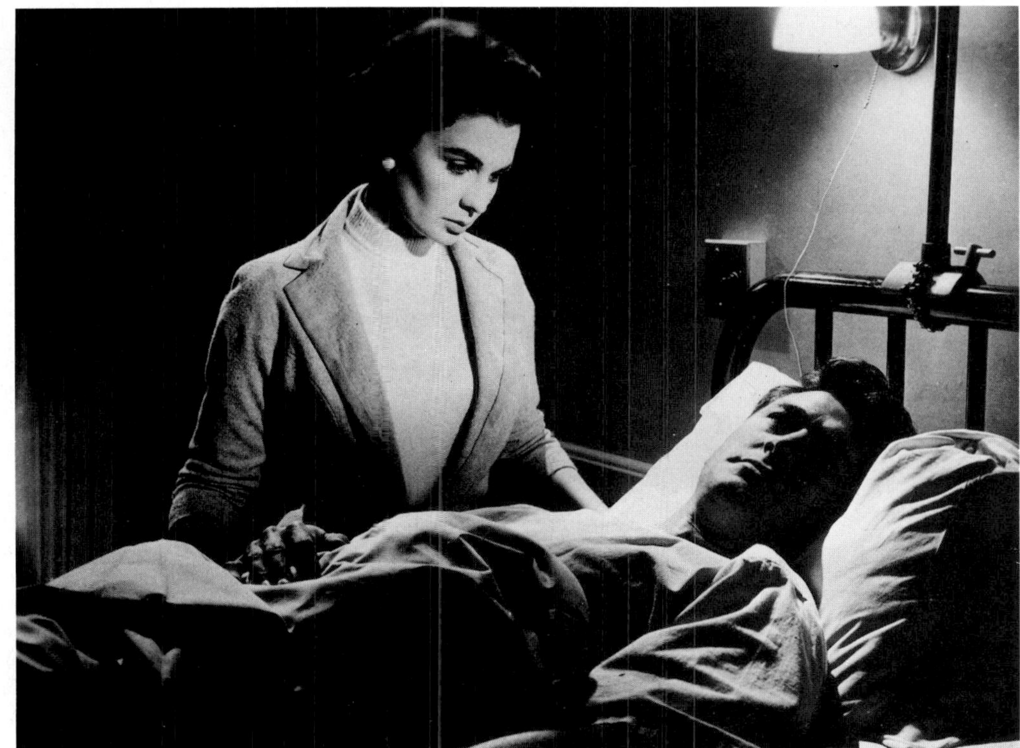

△ Though June Allyson and Jeff Chandler received top billing in Ross Hunter's production of **Stranger In My Arms**, the only thing thing that made it moderately watchable was the performance of Mary Astor (fifth-billed) as an unreasonably possessive mother who'll go to any lengths (including bribery) to see that her dead son (killed in Korea) obtains a posthumous medal of honour. Truth was, the boy not only hated the old girl, but was a coward to boot. Allyson played the soldier's widow, and Chandler (illustrated) an Air Force major asked to testify that Astor's son died a hero's death when he knows the opposite to be true. Predictably, the two leads were romantically linked at the final fade. Charles Coburn was cast as Allyson's father-in-law, with other roles under Helmut Kautner's direction going to Peter Graves, Conrad Nagel and Hayden Rorke. It was scripted from Robert Wilder's novel *And Ride A Tiger* by Peter Berneis, and filmed in CinemaScope. (88 mins)

◁ Director Blake Edwards, working from a screenplay by Stanley Shapiro, endowed Robert Arthur's production of **The Perfect Furlough** with a degree of slickness its painfully contrived plot-line needed if it wasn't to take on the dismal appearance of a failed soufflé. Tony Curtis starred as a soldier in the Arctic who, among 100 other sex-starved men, is chosen to go on 'the perfect furlough' so that, on his return, the rest of the men can live vicariously off his experiences. The idea originated with US Army psychologist Janet Leigh (if you could believe that piece of casting, you could believe the contents of what follows) who accompanies Curtis (centre) to Paris, France, where, as a publicity gimmick, film star Linda Cristal is to be his escort for three glorious weeks. Needless to say, where Miss Cristal is concerned Curtis may look but may not touch – and it's only a matter of time before he and Miss Leigh finally hear the sound of wedding bells. Innocuous to a fault (and pretty silly too), the film also featured Keenan Wynn as Miss Cristal's manager and Elaine Stritch as a press agent, as well as Marcel Dalio, Les Tremayne, Gordon Jones (left), Jay Novello, Dick Crockett (right) and King Donovan. (CinemaScope and Eastmancolor). (93 mins)

1960-1982

The Blockbuster Years

The new decade continued to reap profits for the company. Only twelve films were made in 1960 but they included *Operation Petticoat* which was hugely successful with a gross of $9.5 million, and *Midnight Lace*. It was also the year of *Spartacus*, the most expensive film ever to have emerged from Universal City, having cost $12 million; but it did gross $14.5 million and went on to win four Oscars.

In 1961 Rock Hudson was voted the world's most popular male star and consolidated his popularity with two more comedies, *Come September* and *Lover Come Back* (released in 1962); his leading ladies were Gina Lollobrigida and Doris Day respectively. Also among 1961's productions were *The Grass Is Greener* and the studio's third version of Fannie Hurst's weepie *Back Street*, which came to the screen this time via producer Ross Hunter, with Susan Hayward in the lead. The same year, Sandra Dee unwisely stepped into Debbie Reynolds's shoes for a sequel to *Tammy And The Bachelor* (1957) called *Tammy Tell Me True*.

There were twelve films made in 1962, including David Miller's *Lonely Are The Brave* in which Kirk Douglas, as a cowboy at odds with the 20th century, gave his best performance to date. There was good work too from Montgomery Clift (making his one and only appearance for Universal International) in *Freud*, John Huston's intense drama about the life of the great Viennese psychoanalyst.

This was also the year in which MCA completed the process it had begun in 1959 and acquired controlling interest in Universal-International by buying Decca Records. The executive management of Universal continued with Milton Rackmil as president and Edward Muhl in charge of production, a position he held until 1972. MCA's first chairman of the board (and founder) was Dr Jules Stein, while the president of the entire complex was Lew R. Wasserman.

On acquiring the studio in 1962, MCA immediately set about improving studio facilities and two years later, echoing 'Uncle' Carl Laemmle's early days, re-established public tours of the studio complex. These tours remain one of the company's most profitable enterprises attracting, as they do, some 25,000 visitors on a busy day. In 1963 the word 'International' was dropped from the company name and a new logo (the studio's fourth) was created, the first film to which it was attached being Alfred Hitchcock's *The Birds*. It marked Hitch's return to the studio after a break of 17 years and grossed $4.6 million. This year also saw the release of Gregory Peck's first film for the studio – *To Kill A Mockingbird* – which was directed by Robert Mulligan and won for Peck the Best Actor Oscar.

above: Kirk Douglas in **Spartacus** (1960). *below:* Gregory Peck, seen here with Mary Badham, turned in an Oscar-winning performance in **To Kill A Mockingbird** (1963).

left: MCA president Lew R. Wasserman (extreme left) looks on as Milton Rackmil (with wrench) and Dr Jules Stein mark the foundation of the black tower administration building on 9th July 1963; overseeing operations behind the pillar are, left to right, Rock Hudson, Jack Benny and, taking time off from the set of **Bedtime Story** (1964), Marlon Brando. *right:* Julie Andrews brought a breath of fresh air to the musical genre in **Thoroughly Modern Millie** (1968).

Alfred Hitchcock's next film was *Marnie* (1964) with Sean Connery and *Birds* star Tippi Hedren. Hitchcock remained at Universal for the rest of his career, his last four films being *Torn Curtain* (1966), *Topaz* (1969), the English-made *Frenzy* (1972) and *Family Plot* (1976). When he died, aged 81, in 1980, Universal named its new 340-seat screening room 'The Alfred Hitchcock Theatre' and a representation of his famous trademark – his cartoon profile – now looks down from the front wall.

A superior thriller called *Charade* (1964) wasn't directed by Hitchcock (the man in charge was Stanley Donen) but, for sheer stylishness, it could have been. With Audrey Hepburn and Cary Grant in the leads, it grossed over $6 million.

Audie Murphy was still at it in the sixties, but in films like *Showdown* (1963) both he and his vehicles were running out of fuel. A far better western was *Shenandoah* (1965), beautifully directed by Andrew V. McLaglen and with James Stewart heading the cast. It grossed $7.8 million and provided the basis for a long-running musical of the same name.

Ross Hunter, by now the most successful producer in the world, gave the studio two more hits in 1966 and 1968: *Madame X*, a lachrymose remake of the famous Alexander Brisdon story with Lana Turner as the titular heroine; and *Thoroughly Modern Millie*, the best original musical in a decade not noted for successes in the genre. *Millie* starred Julie Andrews, Mary Tyler Moore, John Gavin and James Fox, and grossed an unbelievable $16 million, every dollar thoroughly deserved.

In general, though, the mid-sixties were not particularly distinguished years for the studio. Small-budget features far outnumbered the quality offerings and, with a few notable exceptions, Universal's product was generally lack-lustre during this period. Two of the exceptions were both directed by Don Siegel: *Madigan* with Richard Widmark and *Coogan's Bluff* with Clint Eastwood, both released in 1968. Though neither made the kind of profits that Ross Hunter was amassing, they were splendid urban thrillers and remain as powerful today as when they were first released.

Two stalwarts of the horror genre died as the decade drew to a close: make-up man Ted Pierce, whose brilliant creations helped enliven many a mediocre chiller, succumbed to cancer at the age of 79 in 1968; and the following year Boris Karloff, probably the most famous ghoul of them all, died in England after a career spanning more than 80 films – he was 81. Basil Rathbone, who had played Sherlock Holmes twelve times for the studio and twice for 20th Century-Fox, died of a heart attack, aged 75, in New York in 1967; 'big baddie' Dan Duryea, at the age of 61, died of cancer in Los Angeles in 1968; and in 1973 Lon Chaney Jr, who had made over 160 films, died of throat cancer, aged 63.

In 1970 producer Ross Hunter turned his attention away from sex comedies and romantic weepies to disaster movies. The first was called *Airport*; it boasted an all-star cast headed by Burt Lancaster and Dean Martin, and it grossed a phenomenal $45 million, making it Universal's top money-maker of all time and one of the top earners in motion picture history.

A low-voltage cast (Arthur Hill, David Wayne, James Olson) did nothing to hamper the chance of a 1971 science-fiction entry called *The Andromeda Strain*, which grossed $8.3 million; while, the same year, the pulling power of Clint

A studio tour tram train overlooks the Universal City back lot, on which are built nearly 600 outdoor sets, buildings and facades, representative of nearly every conceivable place and period.

Memorable blockbusters of the early seventies. *left:* **Airport** (1970). *centre:* **The Sting** (1973). *right:* **Jaws** (1975).

Eastwood coudn't elevate a really scary thriller called *Play Misty For Me* – which he directed as well as starred in – to box-office success.

The studio's big money-maker the following year was *Pete 'N' Tillie*, a modest domestic comedy drama with Walter Matthau and Carol Burnett, which pulled in nearly $8 million.

Then came *The Sting* (1973), produced by Richard D. Zanuck and David Brown, and starring Paul Newman and Robert Redford. It was only the second home-grown film to win an Academy Award in the Best Picture category in 43 years (*Hamlet*, 1948, was British) and it also picked up six other Oscars. With a gross of $79 million, *The Sting* far outstripped *Airport* as the studio's most profitable film to date.

The winning streak continued with such films as Fred Zinneman's *The Day Of The Jackal* ($8.5 million), George Lucas's extraordinary *American Graffiti* ($56.7 million), Norman Jewison's *Jesus Christ Superstar* ($13.3 million) and Clint Eastwood's *High Plains Drifter* ($7.1 million). All were released in 1973, making it the greatest single year, both qualitatively and financially, that Universal had ever known.

This was also the year which saw a number of changes in the top management. Milton Rackmil was succeeded as Universal's president by Henry H. Martin, and Dr Jules Stein handed over the chairmanship of MCA to former president Lew R. Wasserman.

In 1974 a new presentation technique known as Sensurround enhanced the dramatic effects of a Californian catastrophe in *Earthquake* and split the world's box-offices apart to the tune of $12.3 million. Steven Spielberg's *The Sugarland Express* and Billy Wilder's *The Front Page* were two of the studio's non-blockbusters of the year, but excellent entertainment all the same.

The following year, 1975, was the year of *Jaws*, the tale of a killer shark that causes havoc among holiday-makers at a coastal resort. It not only supplanted *Airport* and *The Sting* as the studio's biggest money-maker but also became the top-grossing film in the history of motion pictures with a take of $133.4 million. For two years the Richard D. Zanuck-David Brown production reigned supreme, to be overtaken only by George Lucas's *Star Wars* (20th Century-Fox, 1977) which itself was elbowed into second place in 1980 by the $185 million gross of *The Empire Strikes Back* (20th Century-Fox), also directed by Lucas.

Another 'disaster' movie was *The Hindenburg* (1975), directed by Robert Wise, which grossed $15.1 million – though not as deservedly as some of its more distinguished predecessors. George Roy Hill's *The Great Waldo Pepper* (1975) featured Robert Redford (as well as Universal's early sound logo – the one with a little aeroplane circling the globe) and took in rentals of $10.2 million.

The studio's big one for 1976 was *Midway*, with a gross of over $22 million, followed by Hitchcock's last movie *Family Plot* ($7.5 million). Apart from that, 1976 was not an especially memorable year, with such flops as *W.C. Fields And Me* and *Gable And Lombard* again proving the box-office poison of Hollywood subjects.

Airport 77 (1977) pulled in a disappointing $16.2 million, while the more modest *Slap Shot* (which contained some of the foulest language ever heard on the screen and starred Paul Newman as an erstwhile hockey ace) grossed $14.3 million. The same year Gregory Peck played *MacArthur* for producers Richard D. Zanuck and David Brown and didn't make nearly as much impact as did Burt Reynolds in a 'road' film called *Smokey And The Bandit*, which grossed over $61 million and became the seventeenth most successful film in Hollywood's history and the fourth biggest earner for Universal.

The studio's third biggest earner turned out to be *National Lampoon's Animal House* (1978), a raucous farce which creamed off a staggering $74 million. *Jaws 2*, also released in 1978, swelled the studio's coffers by a further $55.6 million, much of which, however, was lost to Sidney Lumet's elephantine all-black musical *The Wiz*, a reworking of MGM's 1939 charmer *The Wizard Of Oz*. At the turn of the year the studio's presidency changed hands when Ned Tanen took over from Henry H. Martin.

The eighties began promisingly with *Coal Miner's Daughter*, the life story of country-and-western singer Loretta Lynn. The film grossed $38.5 million and won for its star, Sissy Spacek, a much deserved Oscar. This was also the year of Jonathan Demme's superb *Melvin And Howard*; an underrated fantasy called *Somewhere In Time* with Christopher Reeve; a sequel to *Smokey And The Bandit* which grossed a healthy $37.6 million; a fourth version of *Little Miss Marker* with the incomparable Walter Matthau; the $32.2 million grosser *The Blues Brothers* with John Belushi and Dan Aykroyd; and the highly resistible *Cheech And Chong's Next Movie* ($22 million).

The money-makers for the studio in 1981 were Alan Alda's *Four Seasons* ($26.8 million), *Bustin' Loose* ($15.3 million), Franco Zeffirelli's *Endless Love* ($15.1 million), and *On Golden Pond*, a glossy, nostalgic and sentimental vehicle for Katharine Hepburn and Henry Fonda, which grossed $63 million and won Oscars for its venerable stars. Sadly, Fonda died shortly afterwards, aged 77. It was sad, too, that in the same year Universal also lost one of its leading citizens – Dr Jules Stein. He was MCA's founder and first chairman of the board, and even after he gave up that position in 1973 he continued to participate actively in the company. An ophthalmologist by training, he somehow managed to combine successfully his apparently separate interests, being at the same time MCA executive and also founder and principal benefactor of the Jules Stein Eye Institute at UCLA

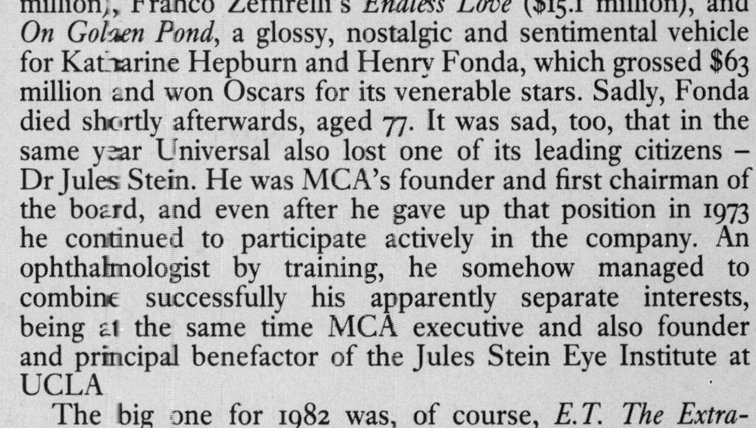

The big one for 1982 was, of course, *E.T. The Extra-Terrestrial*. Steven Spielberg's compassionate fairy tale for children and adults alike immediately captivated audiences all over the world and, with box-office receipts of $195 million, became the biggest grossing film in the history of Hollywood. Infinitely modest by comparison but nonetheless successful in the same year were *The Best Little Whorehouse In Texas*, which starred the outrageous country-and-western singer Dolly Parton, and *Sophie's Choice*, the film in which Meryl Streep indisputably earned her Best Actress Oscar.

As for Universal City itself, under the overall guidance of Lew Wasserman (chairman of the board and chief executive officer of MCA, Inc.) and Sidney J. Sheinberg (MCA's president and chief operating officer, and the man at the sharp end of running the studio), it has expanded from its original 230 acres in 1915 to 450 acres in 1982. It has 36 sound stages, the largest extant backlot in Hollywood, a 14-storey 'black tower' administration building, a 200,000 square foot producers' office complex (complete with garden terraces), a twin Technicolor film processing laboratory, a 6,000-seat covered amphitheatre, a Bank of America branch, a 20-storey, 500-room hotel called the Sheraton Universal and over 10,000 employees.

Uncle Carl would be impressed.

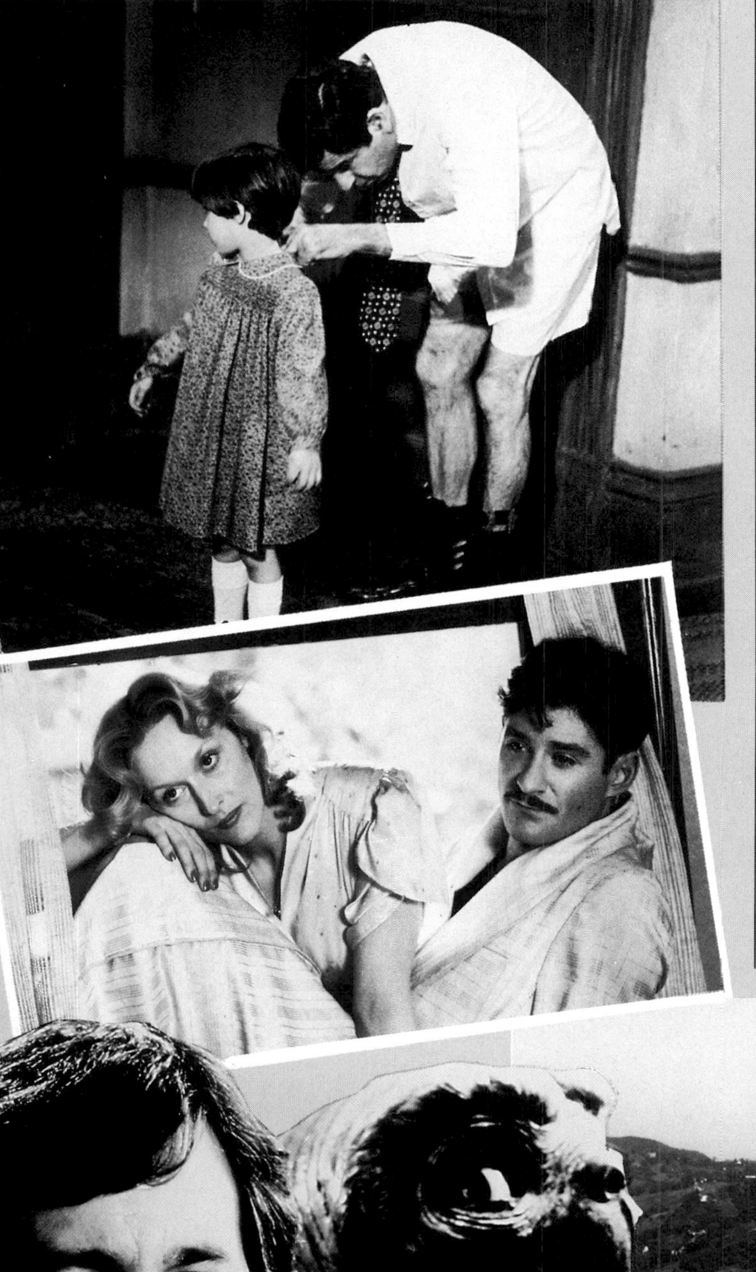

left above: Walter Matthau and Sara Stimson made a delightful duo in the perennial **Little Miss Marker** (1980). *left centre:* Meryl Streep, Best Actress of 1982, with Kevin Kline in **Sophie's Choice** (1982). *left below:* Director Steven Spielberg made motion picture history with his endearing **E.T. The Extra-Terrestrial** (1982), the biggest ever box-office success. *below:* Universal City today. The white-painted sound stages of the front lot make up much of the vista but the area extends much further to the left of the picture, where all the building facades and outdoor sets of the back lot are situated. The black tower, terraced producers' offices and hotel are on the right, with the studio tours car park behind. The two large buildings beside the now concreted river in the foreground are the twin Technicolor laboratories.

1960

△ Simple to the point of simple-mindedness, **Chartroose Caboose** was the story of a comfortably furnished chartreuse railway caboose, its genial owner (a retired railway conductor), and the shelter it provides for a couple of runaway lovers, a lad who has left home (Mike McGreevey, 2nd left), and an eccentric millionaire-tramp. Something actually resembling a story insinuated itself in the shape of a cantankerous brakeman who is prevented from sending the caboose to the junk yard through the intervention of the eccentric tramp. Molly Bee (centre) and Ben Cooper (left) were the young lovers, Edgar Buchanan the retired conductor, O.Z. Whitehead the tramp and Slim Pickens (right, in window) the thoughtless brakeman. Stanley W. Dougherty produced, Rod Peterson scripted, and it was directed with a view to attracting a family audience by William 'Red' Reynolds. (76 mins)

▽ A melodrama with a college background, **College Confidential** was the story of a professor (Steve Allen, centre) who, while compiling a Kinsey-like report on the mating habits of students, finds himself framed for indecency. A courtroom finale (in a grocery store) attended by such journalists as Earl Wilson, Sheila Graham, Walter Winchell and Louis Sobol promised more than it delivered. So did a cast that included Jayne Meadows, Mamie Van Doren, Cathy Crosby, Herbert Marshall (left), Theona Bryant (right, as Allen's fiancée), Conway Twitty, Randy Sparks, Rocky Marciano, Pamela Mason, Elisha Cook, Robert Montgomery Jr and William Wellman Jr. It was produced and directed by Albert Zugsmith for Famous Players-Universal International and written by Irvin Shulman. (91 mins)

▽ A sense of humour was a decided asset at **Dinosaurus**, a fantasy which featured the resurrection of a prehistoric carnivorous tyrannosaurus rex, a herbivorous brontosaurus, and (for light relief) a rather agreeable caveman (Gregg Martell, illustrated crouching). The tongue-in-cheek plot by Jean Yeaworth and Dan E. Weisbord (from an idea by producer Jack H. Harris) concerned the efforts of the caveman to destroy the anti-social tyrannosaurus, but it was the incidental pleasures, such as a heavily made-up young woman and the caveman coming face to face and both recoiling in horror, that audiences left the cinema remembering. Few people remembered the cast: Ward Ramsey, Paul Lukather, Kristina Hanson (illustrated, lying on ground) and Alan Roberts. Irwin S. Yeaworth Jr directed. (85 mins)

◁ A western with a mistaken identity theme, **Hell Bent For Leather** told the story of an honest cowhand who finds himself accused of murder, but relied more on its stars than on its plot (screenplay by Christopher Knopf from the novel by Ray Hogan) to draw the customers. The innocent victim of circumstance was played by Audie Murphy (right), the real culprit turned out to be Jan Merlin, and Robert Middleton, in a small but showy role, was a second heavy. Love interest was supplied by Felicia Farr (left), with other roles under George Sherman's action-filled direction (in Eastmancolor) going to Stephen McNally, Rad Fulton, John Qualen and Eddie Little Sky. Gordon Kay produced. (82 mins)

△ Scenarists Stanley Shapiro and Maurice Richlin gave the studio another comedy hit with **Operation Petticoat**, simply by placing a quintet of attractive nurses on board a ramshackle submarine en route from the Philippines to Australia in the opening weeks of World War II. The ensuing complications thrown up by so potentially explosive a situation garnered a fair amount of laughter throughout, although not quite enough to justify the film's over-generous running time. Still, with Cary Grant (left) as the commander of the sub, and Tony Curtis as his scheming junior officer, the comedy was in excellent hands, the two of them even managing to find laughs that certainly weren't in the script. Joan O'Brien, Dina Merrill, Gene Evans, Arthur O'Connell (right), Richard Sargent and – way down the cast list – Frankie Darro, were also in it; Robert Arthur produced for Granart Productions (in Eastmancolor), and the nimble direction was by Blake Edwards. (124 mins)

▷ Make-up man Bud Westmore was the real star of **The Leech Woman**, a lower-case second feature which starred Coleen Gray (illustrated) as an alcoholic whose endocrinologist hubby (Phillip Terry) plans to take her to Africa as his guinea pig in a crazy experiment involving the secret of perpetual youth. Understandably indignant at being treated like a test tube, she murders him – only to discover, as a result of a bizarre tribal ritual, that everlasting youth and beauty are to be found in the pineal gland of the human male. In order to acquire this gland, however, she has to kill, kill, kill. Two of her victims should have been scenarist David Duncan (working from a story by Ben Pivar and Francis Rosenwald); and director Edward Dein. The critics murdered them instead, along with Grant Williams, Gloria Talbott, John Van Dreelen (right) and Kim Hamilton. Joseph Gershenson produced. (77 mins)

△ Janet Green's play *Matilda Shouted Fire* was no world-beater to begin with, and its far-fetched, red-herring strewn plot was hardly improved upon in Ivan Goff and Ben Roberts' screen adaptation if it. Retitled **Midnight Lace**, and fashioned as a star vehicle for Doris Day whose husband Marty Melcher produced it with Ross Hunter, it emerged as a typical Hunter glossy whose undeniable good looks were the responsibility of cameraman Russell Metty (who photographed it in Eastmancolor), art directors Alexander Golitzen and Robert Clatworthy, and Irene who designed all the star's gowns. Plot had Miss Day (illustrated) receiving anonymous phone calls from a mysterious someone warning her that her life is in danger; suspicion ultimately falls on John Gavin as a construction-gang foreman, Roddy McDowell as an irritating young man who finds Miss Day irresistible, and Herbert Marshall as the treasurer in the firm belonging to our put-upon heroine's husband (impeccably played by debonair Rex Harrison). The producers, in their advertising, requested that the 'unique plot development' not be divulged by audiences; but they needn't have bothered for there was hardly any development at all, though the unmasking of the villain was a mild surprise. A slickly packaged parcel of hokum, it was attractively directed by David Miller whose cast also included Myrna Loy, Natasha Parry and Hermione Baddeley. (106 mins)

▽ Described by one critic at the time as 'less morally objectionable than artistically chaotic', **The Private Lives Of Adam And Eve**, originally scheduled for a 1960 release but hastily withdrawn for 'readjusting' after it was condemned as 'blasphemous and sacrilegious' by the Catholic Legion of Decency, made no impact on the world's box-offices at all. The story of a group of unhappily married people en route to Reno, the narrative pivoted on a dream they all share when a flash-flood grounds the bus they are travelling on, and forces them to take shelter in a church. Subject of the dream: the Garden of Eden Story, object: vague. Possibly it was meant to show them all the error of their ways. What it actually showed was the error of scenarist Robert Hill's way with words, and the unfocussed direction of Mickey Rooney and Albert Zugsmith, the former also starring as The Devil. His co-star was Mamie Van Doren (Eve, illustrated) with other roles in this Spectacolor debacle going to Marty Milner (Adam), Fay Spain, Mel Torme, Cecil Kellaway, Tuesday Weld and Paul Anka, who wrote and sang the title song. Red Doff produced. (86 mins)

◁ Jean Louis supplied Lana Turner with some eye-catching gowns in producer Ross Hunter's glossy but wooden thriller **Portrait In Black**. Not even a potentially interesting cast that included Anthony Quinn (illustrated with Lana Turner), Sandra Dee, John Saxon, Richard Basehart, Lloyd Nolan, Ray Walston, Virginia Grey and Anna May Wong could successfully sweep the cobwebs out of Ivan Goff and Ben Roberts' screenplay (based on their stage play) about the murder of a shipping magnate (Nolan) by his physician (Quinn) in tandem with his wife (Turner). The treacherous couple seem to be getting away with their dastardly deed when, suddenly, Miss T receives an anonymous letter congratulating her on the success of her crime. The only congratulations due on this occasion were to the aforementioned Jean Louis, and to art director Richard H. Riedel, both of whom brought some much needed style to the proceedings. It was directed by Michael Gordon (in Eastmancolor). (112 mins)

◁ A generation-gap drama, redolent in theme of *Rebel Without A Cause* (Warner Bros., 1955) but without any of the earlier film's impact, **Too Soon To Love** (GB: **Teenage Lovers**) told the down-beat cautionary tale of two teenagers (Jennifer West and Richard Evans, illustrated) who, through parental interference – especially from Warren Parker, Miss West's martinet father – find themselves embroiled in a screenplay (by Laszlo Gorog and Richard Rush) in which, among other things, they are arrested by the cops for necking in public. The 'other things' include Miss West's unwanted pregnancy and her attempted suicide. Just a couple of average teenagers in love – sixties-style! Richard Rush produced and directed, and his cast included Ralph Manza, Jacqueline Schwab and a young Jack Nicholson. (85 mins)

▽ It took twelve million dollars and two years of intensive planning to bring Howard Fast's stirring novel, **Spartacus**, to the screen. Photographed by Russell Metty in Technicolor, and starring Kirk Douglas (illustrated foreground) as the eponymous hero, the end results justified the enormous expense. Directing a cast of heavyweight marquee names such as Laurence Olivier (as the sadistic patrician general Crassus), Jean Simmons (the slave girl Varinia), Charles Laughton (Republican senator Gracchus), Peter Ustinov (Batiatus, the fleshy dealer in gladiators) and Tony Curtis (Crassus' Italian houseboy Antoninus), Stanley Kubrick (then aged 31), in his fifth feature, brought as much visual sweep and dramatic emphasis to his epic subject as the Technirama 70 screen could comfortably contain, as well as some excessively violent scenes which it could not – such as Crassus' callous puncturing of a gladiator's neck, and the severing of a warrior's arm in a battle between Roman legions and slaves. For most of its fairly extensive running time, however, Kubrick wisely concentrated on the development of the personal relationships described in both the novel and in Dalton Trumbo's literate, deeply moving screenplay (his first since his blacklisting and imprisonment a decade earlier by the House Un-American Activities Committee) relegating the spectacle, if not exactly to the background (there was far too much of it for that), certainly to second place. What interested him more was his hero's courageous and inspiring struggle for freedom from a tyrannous and pagan regime; and, aided by Douglas' granite-strong performance, he succeeded. A Bryna Production (produced by Edward Lewis), it was filmed partially on location outside Madrid where 8000 Spanish soldiers doubled as Roman legionnaires) and in Hollywood. Secondary roles features John Gavin, Herbert Lom, John Ireland, John Dall, and the physically overpowering Woody Strode who, in one of the film's most memorable sequences, unwillingly engages in a fight to the death with Spartacus, the latter wielding a stunted Thracian sword, the former a trident and net, to the sadistic delight of Roman noblewomen Nina Foch and Joanna Barnes. The film netted a massive $14,600,000. (196 mins)

▽ Clair Huffaker's screenplay for **Seven Ways From Sundown**, which he adapted from his novel, relied more on the engaging performance of its stars, Audie Murphy and Barry Sullivan, than on a rather routine plot which found Murphy (left) as an apprentice Texas ranger in hot pursuit of outlaw Sullivan. Ellis Carter's Eastmancolor photography was a decided plus factor in Gordon Kay's production; so was Harry Keller's suspenseful direction. Also cast: Venetia Stevenson, John McIntire, Kenneth Tobey and attractive Suzanne Lloyd. (86 mins)

1961

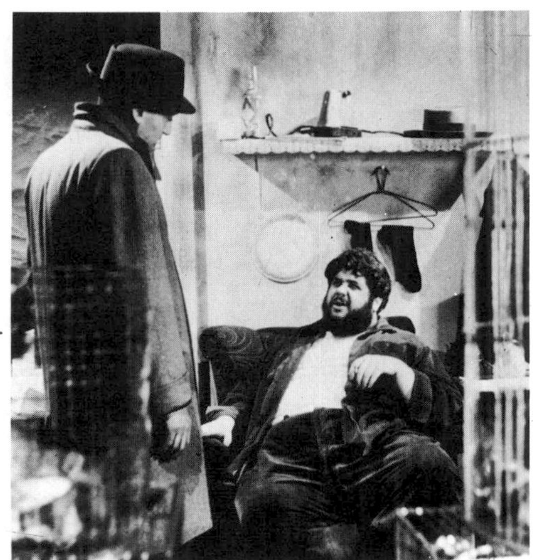

◁ Pretention was **Blast Of Silence**'s undoing. Teetering uneasily on the brink of text-book psychology while attempting to tell its story as tautly as possible, writer-producer-director-actor Allen Baron (left) was, in the end, unable to maintain a comfortable balance between the two. The finished product was decidedly unconvincing. Baron played a hired hood whose brief is to eliminate a well-known mobster, in the process of which he is reunited with his erstwhile home-town girlfriend (Molly McCarthy) who soon gives him the push; and strangles a rather unpalatable fatty (Larry Tucker, right) who has supplied him with the murder weapon. An uncredited Lionel Stander (another victim of the McCarthy witch-hunts) narrated portions of the screenplay and, together with Baron, Miss McCarthy and Danny Meehan, was one of four professionals in a cast literally comprised entirely of amateurs. (77 mins)

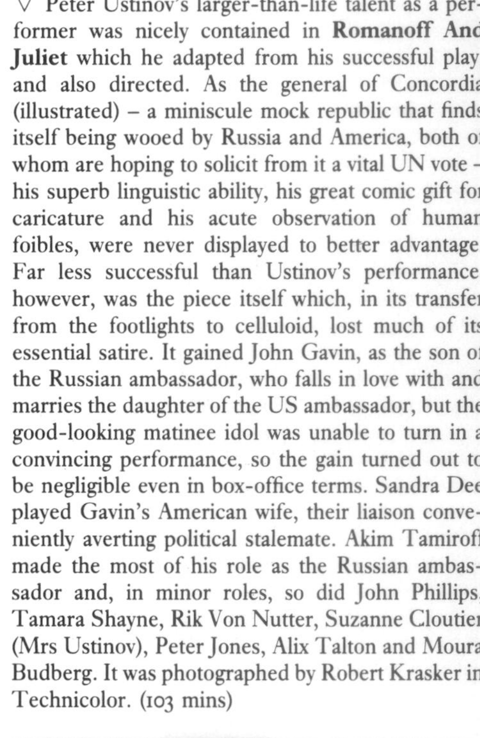

▽ Peter Ustinov's larger-than-life talent as a performer was nicely contained in **Romanoff And Juliet** which he adapted from his successful play, and also directed. As the general of Concordia (illustrated) – a miniscule mock republic that finds itself being wooed by Russia and America, both of whom are hoping to solicit from it a vital UN vote – his superb linguistic ability, his great comic gift for caricature and his acute observation of human foibles, were never displayed to better advantage. Far less successful than Ustinov's performance, however, was the piece itself which, in its transfer from the footlights to celluloid, lost much of its essential satire. It gained John Gavin, as the son of the Russian ambassador, who falls in love with and marries the daughter of the US ambassador, but the good-looking matinee idol was unable to turn in a convincing performance, so the gain turned out to be negligible even in box-office terms. Sandra Dee played Gavin's American wife, their liaison conveniently averting political stalemate. Akim Tamiroff made the most of his role as the Russian ambassador and, in minor roles, so did John Phillips, Tamara Shayne, Rik Von Nutter, Suzanne Cloutier (Mrs Ustinov), Peter Jones, Alix Talton and Moura Budberg. It was photographed by Robert Krasker in Technicolor. (103 mins)

◁ Despite a really stellar line-up, headed by Rock Hudson (left) and also including Kirk Douglas (second-billed), shapely Dorothy Malone (right), Joseph Cotten, Carol Lynley and Regis Toomey, and a screenplay by the sensitive Dalton Trumbo (from Howard Rigsby's novel *Sundown At Crazy Horse*), **The Last Sunset**, directed by Robert Aldrich, turned out to be a pretty routine western whose only novelty was a touch of incest. Seems that the 16-year-old girl (Lynley) Douglas falls for happens to be his daughter. For the rest it was a strikingly well photographed (by Ernest Laszlo, in Eastmancolor) cliché which, despite Trumbo's efforts to flesh out his characters, remained nothing more than the story of a gunman (Douglas) pursued across the Mexican border by Hudson; their rivalry over the love of Miss Malone; Hudson's successful conquest of her, and Douglas' involvement with the aforementioned Miss Lynley, who is Malone's daughter, Malone and Douglas having had an affair sixteen years earlier. Now read on ... It was produced by Eugene Frenke and Edward Lewis. (112 mins)

▽ Rock Hudson, in a reprise of his *Pillow Talk* (1959) performance, again revealed himself to be a light comedian of exceptional charm in **Come September**, a breezy comedy devised by writers Stanley Shapiro and Maurice Richlin. It was about a wealthy American businessman (Hudson, left) who surprises the 'major domo' (Walter Slezak) of his Italian holiday villa by unexpectedly arriving there in July rather than in the usual month of September – which is bad news for Slezak who, for 11 months of every year, turns the place into a hotel. Hudson's romantic interest was Gina Lollobrigida (right – looking smashing in the gowns designed for her by Morton Haack), with additional romance in the shape of real-life newlyweds Sandra Dee and Bobby Darin (his debut). Joel Grey (on floor, right) also had a part in Robert Arthur's CinemaScope and Technicolor production; so did Brenda De Banzie, Rosanna Rory and Ronald Howard. The director was Robert Mulligan. (112 mins)

△ Tony Curtis wasn't exactly ideal casting for the role of real-life masquerader Ferdinand Waldo Demara Jr, known in Liam O'Brien's screenplay (from the book by Robert Crichton) as **The Great Imposter**. In the course of this light-hearted romp Curtis, alias Demara, assumes the identity of a schoolteacher (see illustration), a novitiate in a Trappist monastery, a prison warden's assistant, and a surgeon lieutenant in the Canadian Navy. In each instance he is, of course, totally unequipped for the roles he assumes. The why's and the wherefore's of Demara's strange behaviour were never sufficiently motivated or explained in Robert Arthur's production, director Robert Mulligan's main concern being to keep it light and superficial. And constantly amusing. He was greatly aided in this by a fine supporting cast which included Edmund O'Brien as a ship's captain, Karl Malden as a parish priest, Raymond Massey as an elderly Abbot, Gary Merrill as Curtis' father, Jeanette Nolan as his mother and Arthur O'Connell as a prison warden. (112 mins)

▷ It first starred Irene Dunne and John Boles in 1932, then Margaret Sullavan and Charles Boyer nine years later. For the third and most *chic* version of **Back Street**, producer Ross Hunter continued his long line of well-mounted monuments to escapism, casting Susan Hayward (illustrated) and handsome John Gavin as the star-crossed, ill-fated lovers, and Vera Miles as the latter's bad-tempered, alcoholic wife who does her best to put a spoke in the wheel of her spouse's affair. The fact that Eleanore Griffin and William Ludwig's screenplay (from the novel by Fannie Hurst) had the arthritic creak of old-time melodrama, mattered not at all to the paying customers – especially the women in the audience – most of whom responded favourably to Jean Louis' sumptuous gowns, Stanley Cortez's glowing Eastmancolor photography, and Alexander Golitzen's art direction. There was an effectively soupy music score from Frank Skinner, with direction to match from David Miller. Also cast: Charles Drake, Virginia Grey, Reginald Gardiner and Natalie Schaefer. (107 mins)

△ There was nothing much on offer for sophisticates in **Tammy Tell Me True**, a shamelessly sentimental, often cloying sequel to *Tammy* (1957) with Sandra Dee (left) subbing for Debbie Reynolds in the title role, and definitely remaining a sub. Oscar Brodney's screenplay, from the novel by Cid Ricketts Sumner, was a one-joke affair which found our heroine in search of a little book-larnin' at Seminole University, so that she can be the intellectual equal of her boyfriend Pete who is also away at college. Pete, however, soon has to stand down in her affections when she falls for the unsubtle good looks of professor John Gavin, who seems to spend a great deal of his time laughing uproariously at her unworldly antics (most of the comic mileage derived from the fact that Tammy, like Molly Brown in *The Unsinkable Molly Brown*, MGM 1964, could not adjust to sophisticated society). Charles Drake (right), Julia Mende, Virginia Grey, Beulah Bondi, Cecil Kellaway and Gigi Perreau completed the cast for producer Ross Hunter. It was photographed in Eastmancolor by Clifford Stine and directed by Harry Keller. (97 mins)

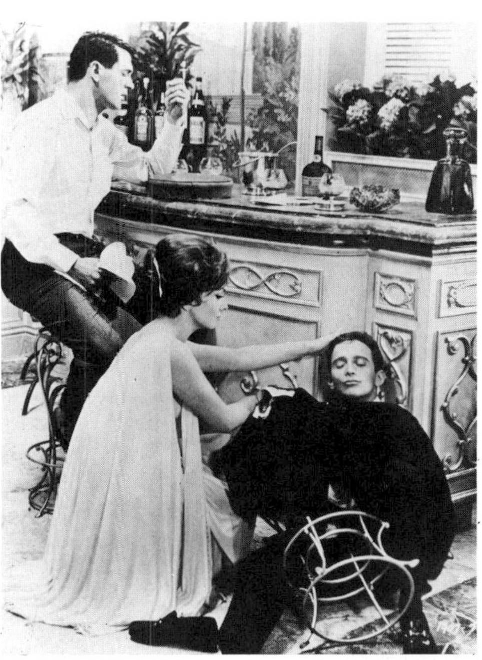

▽ The best thing about Stanley Donen's production (which he also directed) of Hugh and Margaret Williams' rather verbose adaptation of their charming West End stage hit **The Grass Is Greener**, was Maurice Binder's delightful title sequence. The second best was Cary Grant's suave performance as an earl who, to supplement his income, has opened parts of his stately home to the public. Story-wise, the trouble begins when American visitor Robert Mitchum (surely the most unlikely candidate for a sedate wander round a stately home) finds himself in Grant's private quarters and, quite by chance, meets and falls in love with Deborah Kerr (right), the missus of the establishment and Grant's personable wife. How Grant (left) sets about wooing his wife back, formed the substance of the plot, and involved the talents of Jean Simmons (as an ex-girlfriend of Grant's), and Moray Watson as the butler. Some Noel Coward melodies, most notably (and appropriately) 'The Stately Homes Of England', comprised the background music; Christopher Challis photographed it in Technicolor (the English countryside looked particularly attractive) and Miss Simmons' gowns were by Christian Dior. (106 mins)

◁ Another Audie Murphy oater, adapted by Clair Huffaker from his novel, **Posse From Hell** featured its leading man as a young gunslinger in charge of a posse pursuing four heavies guilty not only of cold-blooded murder, but of robbing the local bank and abducting pretty Miss Zohra Lampert. Huffaker's screenplay had philosophical pretentions, taking time off from the action stuff to consider such subjects as prejudice, courage, cowardice etc etc. To little avail, however. What the customers paid to see was Murphy (centre) in action, and they were more or less satisfied with what director Herbert Coleman in his debut offered in this respect. John Saxon (right) co-starred as a New Yorker unused to the rough ways of the west, with other parts in Gordon Kay's handsome Eastmancolor production farmed out to Vic Morrow, Robert Keith (foreground left), Ward Ramsay and twelfth-billed Lee Van Cleef. (89 mins)

▽ A seriously intended cloak-and-dagger drama which drew more than its share of unintentional laughs (courtesy of Phil Karlson's cliché-ridden direction), **The Secret Ways**, clearly inspired by Carol Reed's superior *The Third Man* (London Films, 1949) starred Richard Widmark (centre – who also produced) as an American mercenary who undertakes an assignment to rescue a celebrated scholar (Walter Rilla) from behind the Iron Curtain in Hungary. It was written without flair by Jean Hazlewood from the novel by Alastair MacLean, and filmed in Europe with a European cast that included Sonja Ziemann, Charles Regnier, Howard Vernon, Heinz Moog and Senta Berger. (112 mins)

◁ A low-budget comedy that would require the kind of powerful telescope used at Jodrell Bank to discover in it a single vestige of quality, **The Sergeant Was A Lady**, written, produced and directed by Bernard Glasser, was the one about the GI who is mistakenly transferred to a base run by 125 WACS under the command of a pretty but tough sergeant (Venetia Stevenson, illustrated). Martin West was the hapless GI, Francine York made a meal out of her role as a sex-mad WAC, and the rest of the parts in this Twincraft Production went to Bill Williams, Catherine McLeod, Roy Engell, Gregg Martell and Mari Lynn. (72 mins)

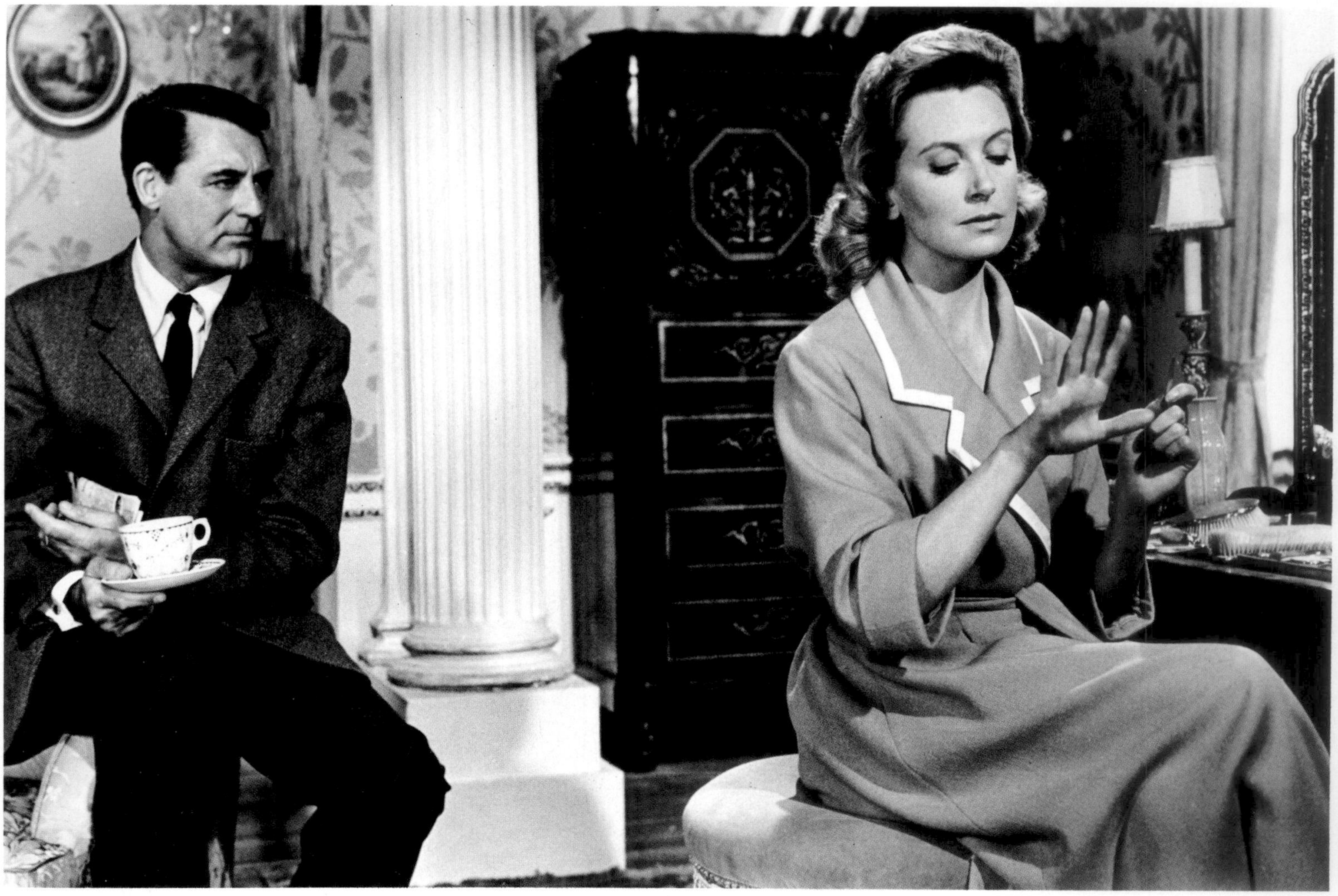

1962

△ A low-budget, rather off-beat western which was produced and directed by Earl Bellamy, **Stagecoach To Dancer's Rock** centred around a group of passengers travelling by stagecoach in 1873 from Tucson to Fort Yuma, Arizona. One of the passengers, a Chinese girl (played by Judy Dan) is discovered to have contracted the dreaded smallpox, as a result of which the rest of the passengers on the stage are turned out in the desert and left to fend for themselves. They included top-billed Warren Stevens as a gunfighter, Martin Landau (right) as a gambler, Jody Lawrence (left) as a medical student, Del Moore as an unpleasant Indian agent and Don Willbanks as an army officer. In the end, only the Chinese girl and Stevens survive, all the others dying horrible deaths. The passable screenplay was by Kenneth Darling. (72 mins)

△ Jeffrey Hunter, fresh from his role as Jesus in *King Of Kings* (MGM, 1961), played another hero in **No Man Is An Island**, a distorted biopic of George R. Tweed, USN, whose signalling to the US fleet from a secret hilltop outpost where he stayed for several years during the Japanese occupation of Guam, led to the ultimate liberation of the island. Hunter (centre), with his pretty-boy good looks, did the best he could with John Monks Jr and Richard Goldstone's guts-and-glory screenplay (they also produced and directed); with so-so support from Marshall Thompson (left), Ronald Remy, Paul Edwards Jr and Rolf Baver. It was photographed by Carl Kayser (whose use of the zoom lens was particularly effective), on location in the Philippines. (114 mins)

▷ In **Lonely Are The Brave**, Kirk Douglas (illustrated) found himself playing the role of an anachronism: a romantic cowboy in an age of advanced technology. Sounds pretentious? Well, to a degree it was and, on occasion, was made even more so by scenarist Dalton Trumbo's failure to endow the central character with a more complex, fleshed-out personality. The screenplay (from the novel *Brave Cowboy* by Edward Abbey) stated rather than probed, thus reducing the potential of an unusual theme. Still, in its off-beat way, it sustained interest, thanks largely to the performances (including Douglas') and to David Miller's assured direction, nowhere better than in the lengthy mountain chase that climaxed the film. The standout supporting performance came from Walter Matthau as a long-suffering sheriff whose force seems comprised entirely of nincompoops. Also Michael Kane, Gena Rowlands and Carroll O'Connor. Philip Lathrop photographed it in brilliant black and white, Jerry Goldsmith provided the wistful score, and it was produced by Joel Productions and Edward Lewis. (107 mins)

△ Wearing a Panama fedora and chomping menacingly on a cigar, Robert Mitchum emerged as the embodiment of undiluted evil in **Cape Fear**, an effective if somewhat gratuitously violent revenge tale. Mitchum (left) was a sadistic ex-con, hunting down and terrorising the smalltown lawyer (Gregory Peck, right) who, eight years earlier, testified against him in a case involving a brutal assault on a woman in a parking lot. Because of the one-dimensional nature of Mitchum's character and the absence of a single redeeming feature in his personality, there was nothing in James R. Webb's one-note screenplay (based on John D. MacDonald's novel *The Executioners*) to arouse the intellect, villainy for its own sake hardly being the most edifying of themes. Polly Bergen returned to the screen after an eight-year absence to play Peck's wife, Lori Nelson was their daughter, with other roles going to Martin Balsam, Jack Kruschen, Telly Savalas and Barrie Chase. The background score was by Bernard Herrmann, and the routine direction by J. Lee Thompson. (105 mins)

▽ By taking five significant years (1890–1895) in the life of Sigmund Freud, and concentrating on the case history of a young woman patient who has a mental and physical breakdown after the death of her father, producer Wolfgang Reinhardt (who wrote the screenplay with Charles Kaufman) was able, in **Freud** (also known as **The Secret Passion**), to offer audiences an absorbing and provocative glimpse of a great pioneer at work on a complex and riveting piece of mental therapy. They were the years in which Freud formulated his renowned theory that the basis of all human behaviour was sexual and, in helping his young patient with her particular problem, he realised that her neuroses were not unlike his own. This discovery resulted in his formulation of the Oedipus complex, or the fixation by a child on a parent of the opposite sex. If, in synposis, it sounds somewhat simplistic (rather like Edward G. Robinson's discovery of a cure for syphilis in *Dr Ehrlich's Magic Bullet*, Warner Bros., 1940, or Greer Garson's discovery of radium in *Madame Curie*, MGM, 1944), well, to an extent it was, despite its almost too explicatory screenplay and John Huston's intense direction. But with a bewhiskered Montgomery Clift (left) in the title role, giving a blazingly intelligent central performance, and with Susannah York (right) equally effective as his patient Cecily Koertner, the film emerged as a superior biopic which never patronised the viewer. Larry Parks, who had been blacklisted as a result of the McCarthy witch-hunts, returned to the screen as Freud's friend and colleague Dr Joseph Breuer, with other parts going to Susan Kohner, Eileen Herlie, Fernand Ledoux, David McCullum, Rosalie Crutchley, David Kossoff, Alexander Mango, Leonard Sachs and Eric Portman. (140 mins)

▷ If good intentions alone made good movies, **The Outsider** would rank with the best of them. As it turned out, Sy Bartlett's earnest account of the tragic life of Ira Hamilton Hayes, a Pima Indian who, as one of the flag-raisers on Mount Suribachi, was never able to accept the heroic status accorded him for his action, promised far more than it delivered. Part of this might have been the responsibility of the movie's star, Tony Curtis (illustrated), whose dedicated and energetic performance was unable to disguise the fact that he was basically miscast. Also to blame was Stewart Stern's screenplay (from the novel by William Bradford Huie), which dealt with Hayes' life from the time he leaves his Arizona reservation to enlist in the Marines, to his tragic death from alcohol and exposure some ten years later. Stern's writing was totally convincing during the early sequences, especially the ones depicting Hayes' training period at Boot Camp. What he wasn't able to pull together were the film's later scenes showing Hayes at odds with a white man's society. Nor was he able to bring much conviction to one of the film's key elements: Hayes' friendship with James Franciscus, whose death was a contributing factor to the Indian's own bleak demise. Perhaps scared that too close an examination of the relationship might reveal homosexual undercurrents, Stern's reluctance to delve merely left a question mark which did little to enhance Hayes' credibility or audience involvement. Delbert Mann's direction lacked objectivity, though there were good supporting performances from Gregory Walcott as a drill instructor, Bruce Bennett as a general and Vivian Nathan as the hero's mother. (108 mins)

▷ As it so often did, the beautiful state of Utah came to the aid of a western desperately in need of all the help it could get. This time it was producer Gordon Kay's Eastmancolor oater, **Six Black Horses**, which benefitted from the sheer visual sweep of the scenery and relegated its puny story to the background. All about a vendetta between a widow woman and the hired gun who killed her husband, it featured Joan O'Brien (left) as the widow, Dan Duryea (right) as the killer and top-starred Audie Murphy as an unemployed wrangler whose life was once saved by Duryea and who falls in love with O'Brien. Harry Keller directed from a screenplay by Burt Kennedy. (86 mins)

△ **Lover Come Back**, probably one of the best of the Doris Day-Rock Hudson comedies, scored additional points over its predecessor *Pillow Talk* (1959) through the added ingredient of satire. In this instance it was the world of advertising that came in for some ribbing, with Madison Avenue being integral to Stanley Shapiro and Paul Henning's racy screenplay. Day and Hudson are rivals in the advertising market, though she believes him to be a scientist at work on a product called VIP. No such product exists, and most of the fun derives from Day (centre left) attempting to wrest the VIP contract away from Hudson (right) the scientist. He, of course, is attempting to get her into bed. Tony Randall was perfectly cast as an ineffectual *nebbish* who has inherited an advertising agency; and there were entertaining performances, too, from veteran Jack Oakie as a manufacturer of floor wax who offers his account to the agency most willing to supply him with broads and bourbon. Edie Adams played a chorus girl, and Jack Kruschen a screwball scientist. A 7 Pictures-Nob Hill-Arwin production, produced by Stanley Shapiro and Martin Melcher with Robert Arthur as execuive producer, it was photographed in Eastmancolor and directed, with a sure sense of where the laughs should come, by Delbert Mann. Songs: 'Lover Come Back' Alan Spilton, Frank DeVol; 'Should I Surrender?' William Landan, Adam Rose, both sung by Doris Day. (107 mins)

1962

▽ The best that could be said for **If A Man Answers** is that it was harmless. Another Ross Hunter comedy, impeccably shot in Eastmancolor and with Sandra Dee (right) and Bobby Darin (left) in the starring roles, it barely managed to raise a smile. Dee and Darin played newlyweds who discover there's more to marriage than might appear, if some of Ross Hunter's previous romantic excursions into the subject were anything to go by. Miss Dee, aided by her father-in-law (Cesar Romero) and gorgeously gowned by Jean Louis, spent a great deal of time making her spouse jealous by inventing a lover, and that was about the best that Richard Morris' uninventive screenplay (from a novel by Winifred Wolfe) had to offer. Henry Levin directed it and cast Micheline Presle as Dee's mum (an ex-Folies Bergère girl) and John Lund as her father; with other parts going to Stefanie Powers, Ted Thorpe and Roger Bacon. (102 mins)

▽ Another glossy, money-making comedy from the production team who gave you *Lover Come Back* (Arwin-Nob Hill, 1961), **That Touch Of Mink** received its box-office clout from the casting of Cary Grant (right – who also had a hand in its production) as a philandering tycoon who sets his lecherous (albeit charming) sights on chaste, job-seeking secretary Doris Day (left). So much for the romantic element. Most of the laughs, however, were supplied by Gig Young as Grant's wise-cracking fiscal adviser; and by Audrey Meadows, an Eve Arden type who played Doris' chirpy room-mate. There was good work, too, from Dick Sargent, Alan Hewitt and John Astin. Stanley Shapiro and Nate Monaster's screenplay had its moments, but they weren't to be found in the team's cheap lampooning of psychiatry. It was photographed in Eastmancolor by Russell Metty and directed with appropriate understanding of the genre by Delbert Mann. (99 mins)

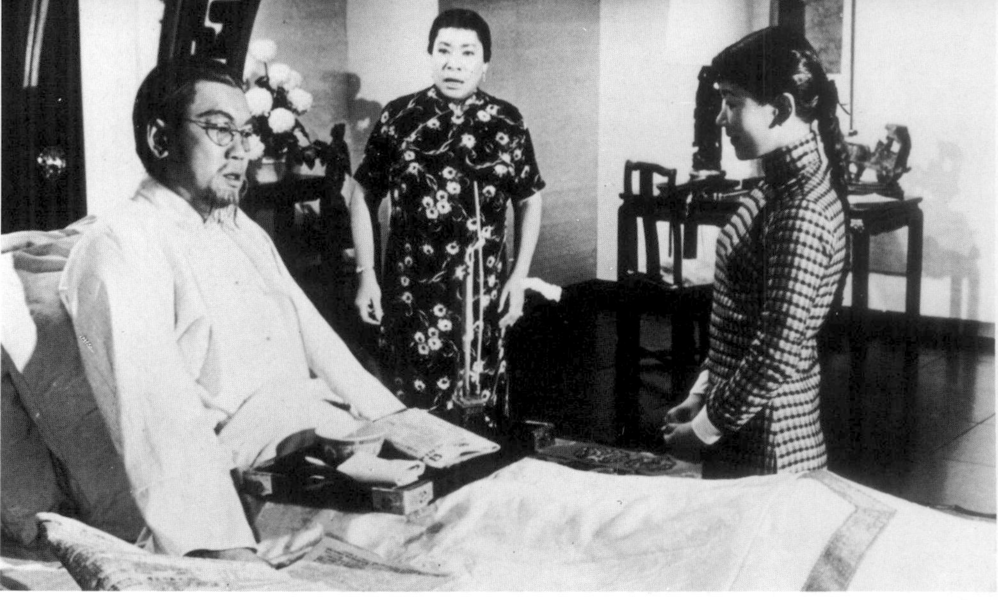

△ The screen version of the Rodgers-Hammerstein-Joseph Fields Broadway hit, **Flower Drum Song**, was Universal's first musical of the sixties, and only their second in five years. Unfortunately, the scale and gloss of the enterprise did litle to disguise its overtly 'cutesy-cutesy' tone that succeeded in being uncomfortably condescending to the Chinese community of San Francisco which was its focus. Scripted by Joseph Fields (from a novel by C.Y. Lee and from his stage book), the movie concerned a Hong Kong girl (Myoshi Umeki, right) who arrives in San Francisco for an arranged marriage to a nightclub owner (Jack Soo) whom she hasn't met. She finally ends up in a more suitable liaison with a college boy (James Shigeta), leaving the field clear for Soo and his nightclub-singer sweetheart (Nancy Kwan). Not one of Rodgers and Hammerstein's more memorable efforts, it nonetheless offered some beautiful dancing (choreographed by Hermes Pan), notable in the 'Love Look Away' dream ballet, danced by Reiko Sato. It also offered audiences a taste of the magical Juanita Hall (centre), whose unique rendition of 'Chopy Suey' was one of the better items on display. Some agreeable tunes included 'I Enjoy Being A Girl' (sung by Nancy Kwan) and 'A Hundred Million Miracles' (Miss Umeki and Kam Tong). Soo, Umeki and Miss Hall came from the Broadway production, and Benson Fong (left) was also featured for producer Ross Hunter and director Henry Koster. The film was photographed in Panavision and Technicolor by Russell Metty in sets that paraded a wonderful replica of San Francisco's Chinatown. Other songs and musical numbers included 'Fan Tan Fanny'; 'Grant Avenue'; 'You Are Beautiful'; 'The Other Generation'; 'Don't Marry Me'. (131 mins)

▽ Audiences searched in vain for any evidence of rounded characters or sophisticated plot-probing in **The Spiral Road**. Adapted by John Lee Mahin and Neil Paterson from Dutch author Jan de Hartog's novel, it was an interminable saga, charting the route taken by an atheist's conversion to God in the jungles of Java, circa 1936, where, after ending a leprosy epidemic, he becomes a missionary. A badly miscast Rock Hudson (right) played the young doctor who, in the early stages of the story, is an unscrupulous opportunist out to find a place in the medical history books via the research work of eminent physician Burl Ives (centre). Other parts in Robert Mulligan's stodgy brew were taken by Gena Rowlands as Hudson's wife and Geoffrey Keen as a representative of the Salvation Army. Also cast: Neva Patterson, Will Kuluva and Larry Gates (left). It was produced by Robert Arthur and photographed in Eastmancolor. (145 mins)

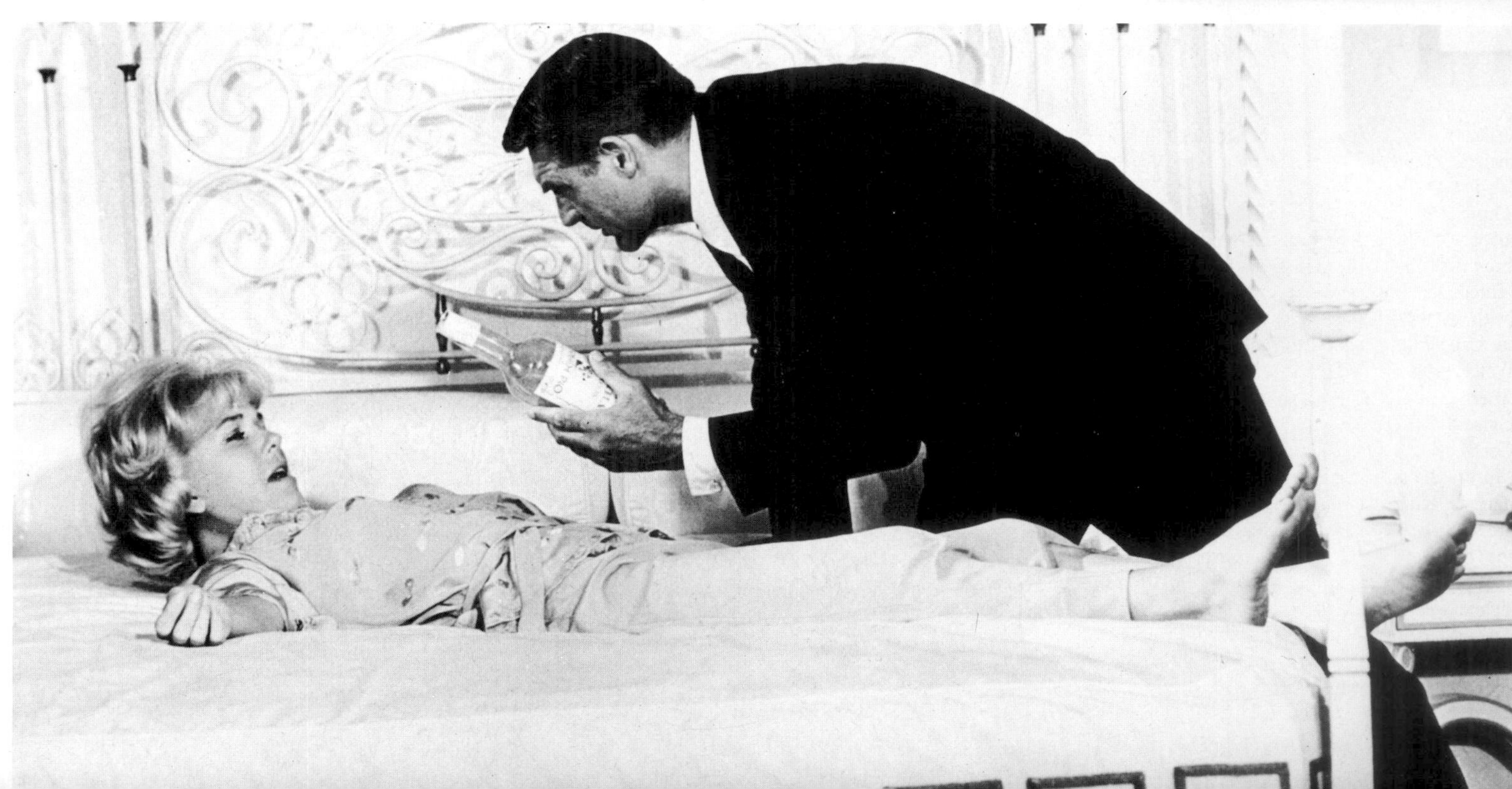

1963

▽ Those much satirised bastions of American life – television, advertising, the servant problem, and such status-conferring objects as Cadillacs and swimming pools – were given the Carl Reiner treatment (story by Larry Gelbart) in **The Thrill Of It All**, another well-polished Ross Hunter-Marty Melcher production which this time teamed wholesome Doris Day (centre) with manly James Garner (right). He's a successful gynaecologist, she's a housewife and mother of two. Their marriage is made in heaven until she accepts an $80,000 a year job to appear in a soap commercial. After that it's downhill for most of the way as career and domesticity collide head-on. But, being a light-hearted romantic comedy, it all works out well in the end as you knew it would and wanted it to. Reiner's screenplay had some marvellous moments – such as Garner returning home from work and driving his convertible straight into a swimming pool that wasn't there the previous day; so did Norman Jewison's direction – even though an unexpected birth scene during an East River traffic jam went way over the top. Arlene Francis and Edward Andrews were excellent as the middle-aged couple who suddenly find themselves 'expecting' and, in her last role, ZaSu Pitts, who died shortly after the film's completion, played a worry-prone maid. Also cast: Reginald Owen, Elliott Reid (left), Lucy Landau, Alice Pearce, Robert Strauss, Pamela Curran and, as Garner and Day's offspring, Kym Karath and Brian Nash (2nd left). It was filmed in Eastmancolor. (103 mins)

▷ Richard Schayer and Jefferson Pascal based their screenplay for **Lancelot And Guinevere** (also known as **Sword Of Lancelot**) on Sir Thomas Mallory's *Morte d'Arthur*, but they might just as well have gone to a comic strip of the famous story if the finished version was anything to go by. A vehicle for Cornel Wilde (right), who produced it (with Bernard Luber), directed it, and starred in it as Lancelot, it also utilised the talents of Jean Wallace (Mrs Wilde) as Guinevere (left), Brian Aherne as King Arthur, George Baker as Sir Gawain, Archie Duncan as Sir Lamorak, Adrienne Corri as Lady Vivian, Michael Meacham as Mordred, Mark Dignam as Merlin and John Longden as King Leodogran, Arthur's rival for the crown. Despite some clumsy editing throughout, the film just about passed muster on its action sequences, all the outdoor footage being filmed in Yugoslavia. The interiors were shot at Pinewood in England. Eastmancolor and Panavision. (116 mins)

△ Three more institutions – physical fitness, modern art and motivational research – were satirised in **For Love Or Money**, another good-looking romantic comedy aimed at the tired housewife rather than at her spouse. The main plot-line, however, involved a matrimonial search by an eccentric widow (Thelma Ritter) for suitable husbands for her three gorgeous daughters. Kirk Douglas (left), revealing a pleasing flair for comedy, played Miss Ritter's attorney whose duties also extended to matchmaking, while capably filling the roles of the curvaceous girls themselves were Mitzi Gaynor (a consumer researcher in Madison Avenue), Julie Newmar (a health addict, right) and Leslie Parrish (a beatnik). In the end, Douglas does some matchmaking of his own and pairs off with Gaynor, leaving Richard Sargent and William Windom their choice of the other two. Gig Young (on floor) was on hand to give another of his well-honed boozy playboy characterisations, with other roles in Robert Arthur's amiable, though by no means distinguished, production going to William Bendix and Elizabeth MacRae. The gowns were by Jean Louis and they looked stunning in Eastmancolor. (108 mins)

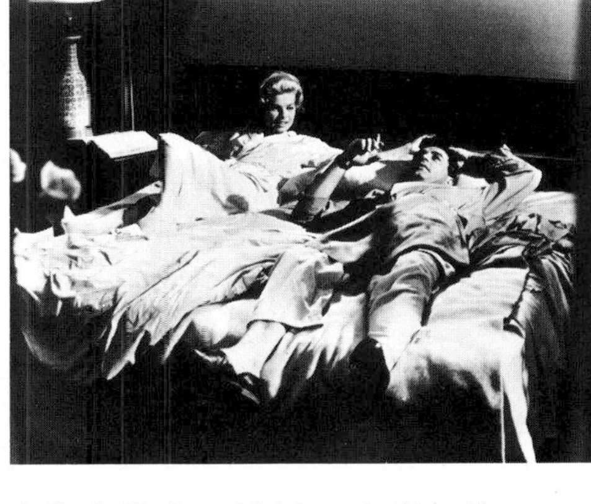

△ Rock Hudson (right) made himself very unpopular in **A Gathering Of Eagles** playing a wing commander determined to improve the efficiency of the Strategic Air Command base to which he has been assigned. The appointment doesn't do much for his marriage either. If conflict is the essence of drama, there was drama a-plenty in Robert Pirosh's screenplay, with Hudson having to decide whether his marriage is more important than his job; and whether his quest for perfection is more important than personal relationships. Unfortunately neither Pirosh nor director Delbert Mann were able to bring anything new to a rather well-worn subject, and the film failed to find a sizeable audience. British actress Mary Peach (left) played Hudson's wife, with other roles in Sy Bartlett's Eastmancolor production going to Rod Taylor as a recalcitrant vice-commander (who sang 'The Sac Song' by Tom Lehrer), Barry Sullivan as an alcoholic commander, and to Kevin McCarthy, Henry Silva, Leif Erickson, Robert Lansing and Richard Anderson. (115 mins)

◁ 'Light-hearted, effervescent entertainment' seemed to be the general concensus of opinion of **40 Pounds Of Trouble**, which found Tony Curtis perfectly cast as the manager of a Lake Tahoe night spot who, in the course of Marion Hargrove's witty screenplay, had to cope with an orphaned moppet, an alimony suit, and the advances of husband-seeking Suzanne Pleshette. It all came to a racy climax in a chase through Disneyland *à la* the Keystone Kops, at the end of which Curtis (right) is finally apprehended for the non-payment of his ex-wife's alimony. Little Claire Wilcox (left) made an appealing (for some) debut as the 40 pounds of trouble described in the title, though there were many who preferred the less cutesy-cutesy humour of Phil Silvers as the owner of a casino. It was zippily directed by Norman Jewison (making his movie debut), produced (in Panavision and Eastmancolor) by Stan Margulies and, in secondary parts, featured Stubby Kaye, Larry Storch, Howard Morris, Warren Stevens, Mary Murphy and Kevin McCarthy. The film was a loose remake of Shirley Temple's *Little Miss Marker* (Paramount, 1934), and was remade yet again, as *Little Miss Marker*, in 1980 with Walter Matthau. (106 mins)

▽ Gregory Peck's low-key personality was showcased to perfection in **To Kill A Mockingbird**. A moodily atmospheric filmisation of Harper Lee's celebrated first novel, it successfully tackled the twin themes of racial prejudice in the deep South, and the gradual maturing to a state of compassion and social insight, of a couple of youngsters. Peck (foreground left) played a soft-spoken Alabama lawyer who finds himself saddled with a double responsibility: having to defend a black man accused of rape (which he does with great restraint, yet bursting with humanitarian concern); and raising his two motherless children. It was a performance full of gentle conviction and inner strength, and it deservedly won him an Oscar. Nine-year-old Mary Badham and 13-year-old Phillip Alford were his offspring (a third junior performance was supplied by little John Megna) and they were a delight. A pity, though, that much of their dialogue suffered from poor articulation. Brock Peters (foreground right) played Tom Robinson, the man accused of the rape, and brought immense dignity to the role. Robert Mulligan's direction was completely sensitive to the many-faceted screenplay by Horton Foote, and his handling of the lengthy courtroom scene towards the end was masterly. His cast was completed by Frank Overton, Estelle Evans, Alice Ghostley, Paul Fix and Robert Duvall. Alan J. Pakula produced and the memorable background score was composed by Elmer Bernstein. (129 mins)

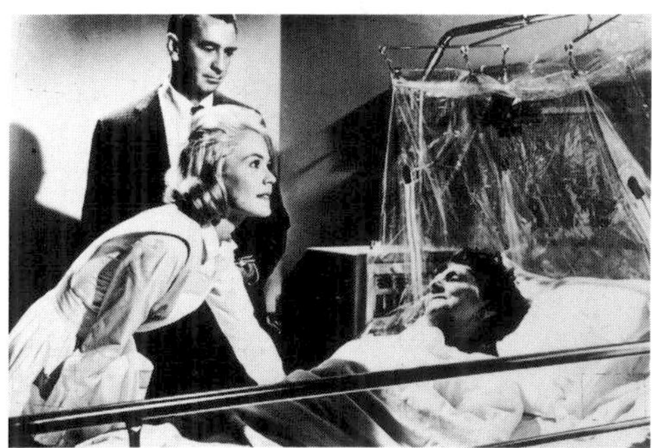

△ The third – and feeblest – in the series, **Tammy And The Doctor** was formula film-making from the Ross Hunter stable which this time around had Sandra Dee (as Tammy, foreground left) deserting her shantyboat for Los Angeles, where she becomes a nurse's aide and finds herself taking care of an ailing Beulah Bondi (right). She also finds romance with interne Peter Fonda (his debut). A pity she was unable to nurse Oscar Brodney's listless screenplay back to health. But then neither was young Fonda, who made hardly any impression at all; nor a supporting cast that numbered among its victims Macdonald Carey (left), Margaret Lindsay, Reginald Owen, Adam West and Alice Pearce. Harry Keller's direction looked as though it wasn't even trying. Jay Livingston and Ray Evans' hit song 'Tammy' was revived for the occasion, but to no avail. (88 mins)

△ Another Audie Murphy western, aimed largely at the drive-in trade, **Showdown** followed the fortunes of a couple of ranch hands (Murphy, left, and Charles Drake, right, the latter revealing a penchant for booze and gambling) and their involvement with a bunch of desperados. Bronson Howitzer's screenplay found enough opportunities for action and gave employment to Kathleen Crowley, Harold J. Stone, Skip Homeier, L.Q. Jones, Strother Martin and Charles Horvath. Gordon Kay produced and R.G. Springsteen directed. (79 mins)

▽ Make-up man Bud Westmore did an absolutely marvellous job disguising the well-known faces of Tony Curtis, Kirk Douglas, Burt Lancaster, Robert Mitchum and Frank Sinatra in **The List Of Adrian Messenger**, niftily directed by John Huston, who must have been the only director in the history of the cinema to have had six of the biggest male stars of the day at his disposal and yet was prepared to keep the fact a secret. It was a gimmick, alas, which undermined the film's narrative content and proved to be more of a hindrance than a help. A sort of *Kind Hearts And Coronets* (Ealing, 1949) of the sixties, Anthony Veiller's screenplay (from a story by Philip MacDonald) told the promising yarn of a British Intelligence Officer's (George C. Scott, right) efforts to apprehend a murderer who has, so far, eliminated the eleven men standing between him and a vast fortune. With only one more victim on the loose, a 12-year-old who is next in line to the Gleneyre estate, the killer (Kirk Douglas, left) would appear to be home and dry. At this point, however, things go wrong for him, as, indeed, they did for the film, the last third of Veiller's screenplay falling completely to pieces. Clive Brook abandoned a 26-year retirement to play the Marquis of Gleneyre, with other roles in producer Edward Lewis' thriller going to Dana Wynter, Gladys Cooper, Herbert Marshall, Jacques Roux, John Merivale, Marcel Dalio and Huston's son, Walter Anthony Huston. (98 mins)

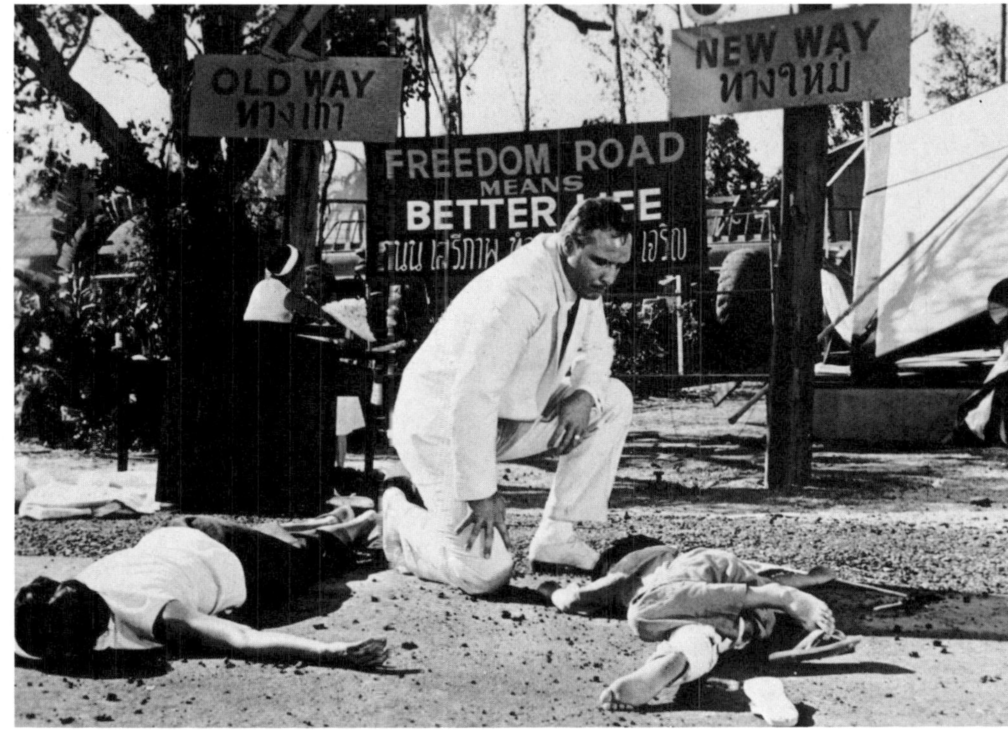

△ Cold War politics was the subject of producer-director George Englund's screen adaptation of William J. Lederer and Eugene Burdick's bestseller, **The Ugly American** and, in his screenplay, Stewart Stern made a conscientious effort to analyse the subject's many ambiguities and complexities. All about an American publisher who is sent to South East Asia as ambassador and, in the course of his stay there, comes to believe there is a great deal more to dealing with uprisings against 'Yankee imperialism' than he had imagined, it showed the ambassador finally realising that Americans 'can't hope to win the cold war unless we remember what we're for as well as what we're against'. Scenarist Stern's (and the novelists') condemnation of American indifference to, and even complacency about, many of the political issues of the day rang out loud and clear; what was less well-defined was just *what* some of those issues were. And it was this haziness which ultimately robbed the film of its intended impact. Nothing, however, could rob Marlon Brando (as the ambassador, centre) of his charismatic and powerful screen presence, and his performance alone justified the time and effort that clearly went into the film's preparation. Impressive, too, was Eiji Okada (of *Hiroshima Mon Amour*, 1960), making his American film debut as an old wartime friend of Brando's, and now the leader of the troubled country to which Brando has been sent. Pat Hingle, Arthur Hill, Sandra Church and Jocelyn Brando (Marlon's sister) completed the cast. (120 mins)

▷ The plot of Alfred Hitchcock's **The Birds** was pretty feeble, with many more narrative threads remaining untied than was usual for the 'master of suspense'. What one remembers most about the film is hardly Tippi Hedren's romance with attorney Rod Taylor (both illustrated) or Jessica Tandy, Taylor's mother, fearing loneliness and turning ultra-possessive; or even pretty Suzanne Pleshette and the role she played of a schoolteacher and Taylor's ex-girlfriend. As was so often the case with Hitchcock, the film's *raison d'être* lay not in its plot but in its eerie subtext – and in the notion of an entire community being threatened by a plague of birds. The film's underlying emotion, enhanced by the clever use of electronic sounds in place of more conventional background music, was menace, and in this respect Hitchcock certainly delivered the goods. Even when nothing happened you felt it was about to, and your heart was in your mouth. Though much of the back-projection was obvious and the special effects transparent, the overall atmosphere created through the low-key direction gave the film its reputation as one of the most purely cinematic of the entire Hitchcock *ouevre* – the great fire sequence (which began as a result of a leaking gasoline tank, and featured a remarkable long shot of Bodega Bay, the story's setting) being the film's most memorable set-piece. The cast also included Veronica Cartwright, Ethel Griffies, Charles McGraw and Ruth McDevitt. Hitchcock produced, Evan Hunter wrote the screenplay from a story by Daphne Du Maurier, it was photographed by Robert Burke in Technicolor, and designed by Robert Boyle. The bird trainer in charge of all the anti-social behaviour was Ray Berwick. (120 mins)

1964

▽ The **Kitten With A Whip** in producer Harry Keller's tawdry little shocker was Ann-Margret (illustrated), a juvenile delinquent who breaks into the home of a politician when his wife is out of town and refuses to leave. Not only that, but she threatens to cause a scandal if he seeks police intervention, and appropriates a couple of thugs to help her keep her victim a prisoner in his own home. John Forsythe (in car) was cast as the unfortunate politician, and Peter Brown and James Ward as the heavies. It was written by Douglas Hayes (who also directed) from a novel by Wade Miller, and also featured Patricia Barry, Diane Sayer and Ann Doran. Fortunately, the talented Ann-Margret went on to much better things than this. (82 mins)

△ A tale to appeal to the young at heart, if not the downright childish, **The Brass Bottle** was the simple-minded story of an architect (top-billed Tony Randall, right) whose life is thrown into disarray with the sudden arrival of a likeable but confused genie (Burl Ives, left), one of whose tasks, he believes, is to set about eliminating all of Randall's enemies. Barbara Eden was the lady in Randall's life, Edward Andrews her father (whom the genie turns into a mule), with other parts in Robert Arthur's Technicolor production going to Kamala Devi, Richard Erdman, Kathie Browne and Ann Doren. It was written by Oscar Brodney (from the novel by F. Anstey) and directed by Harry Keller. (89 mins)

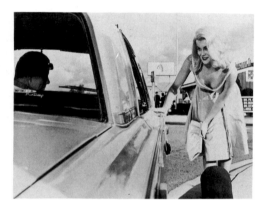

▽ A remake of *It Started With Eve* (1941), but this time with Maurice Chevalier (left) in the Charles Laughton role and, in a reversal of the sexes, Robert Goulet in the Deanna Durbin role and Sandra Dee (right) playing the Robert Cummings part, **I'd Rather Be Rich** was pleasant enough entertainment, but lacked the charm that made the original Durbin vehicle so enjoyable. Miss Dee bore the brunt of a story which had her desperately searching for a fiancé to satisfy the last wishes of her ailing grandfather (Chevalier) who turns out not be be ailing at all. Miss Dee's real fiancé (Andy Williams, making his debut) has been grounded by fog – hence her desperate need to find a substitute, no matter who. Gene Raymond was cast as Chevalier's secretary, with other roles under Jack Smight's direction going to Charlie Ruggles as Chevalier's doctor, Hermione Gingold as his nurse, and Laurie Main as a family retainer. It was written by Oscar Brodney, Norman Krasna and Leo Townsend and filmed in Eastmancolor. Ross Hunter produced. Songs: 'I'd Rather Be Rich' (sung over titles by Robert Goulet); 'Almost There', 'Where Are You?' Harold Adamson, Jimmy McHugh; 'It Had To Be You' Gus Kahn, Isham Jones (sung by Andy Williams). (96 mins)

◁ Another remake, **The Lively Set** – first seen as *Johnny Dark* in 1954 – with James Darren (left) in the role created by Tony Curtis, benefitted from its handful of songs (mainly by Bobby Darin) and from Carl Guthrie's colourful photography. For the rest it was a pretty routine tale of 22-year-old ex-GI college student Darren who is fonder of his cars than he is of college. Pamela Tiffin is the only girl he rates higher than anything on four wheels. Not surprisingly in a story that glorified the automobile, the film's best sequence was a race around the picturesque Sierra Mountains. It was written by Mel Goldberg and William Wood from a story by Goldberg and producer William Alland, featured Doug McClure (right), Marilyn Maxwell, Joanie Sommers, Charles Drake, Russ Conway, Ross Elliott and, as themselves, ace race drivers Mickey Thompson, James Nelson, Duane Carter, Billy Krause and Ron Miller. Jack Arnold directed. Songs included: 'If You Love Him', 'Casey Wake Up' Darin; 'Look At Me' Darin, Randy Newman; 'Boss Barracuda' Darin, Terry Melcher. (95 mins)

▽ According to producer-director Howard Hawks, **Man's Favourite Sport** is fishing. And who better to demonstrate the deep satisfaction derived from it than personable Rock Hudson (illustrated). Trouble is, Rock, who sells fishing equipment at Abercrombie and Fitch's swank emporium and professes to be an authority on the subject, doesn't know a darn thing about it. When, therefore, he is ordered by his boss to take part in a fishing tournament he's really in trouble. The kind of one-joke situation that Universal's Joe McDoakes or MGM's Pete Smith might have found themselves in during a ten-minute short, it was, unfortunately, extended way beyond its limits. But there were some good visual gags (with Hudson taking to the water and emerging drenched on several occasions), and some pleasing performances, especially from Paula Prentiss who, midway through, provided the film with its romantic interest; and John McGiver as Hudson's boss. Also cast: Roscoe Karns, Maria Perschy, Charlene Holt, Norman Alden and Regis Toomey. It was directed, in sequence, by Hawks, who filmed each scene a day at a time. John Fenton Murray and Steve McNeil wrote it from a story by Pat Frank called *The Girl Who Almost Got Away*; it was photographed in Technicolor, and had a score by Henry Mancini who, with Johnny Mercer, also wrote the catchy title song. (120 mins)

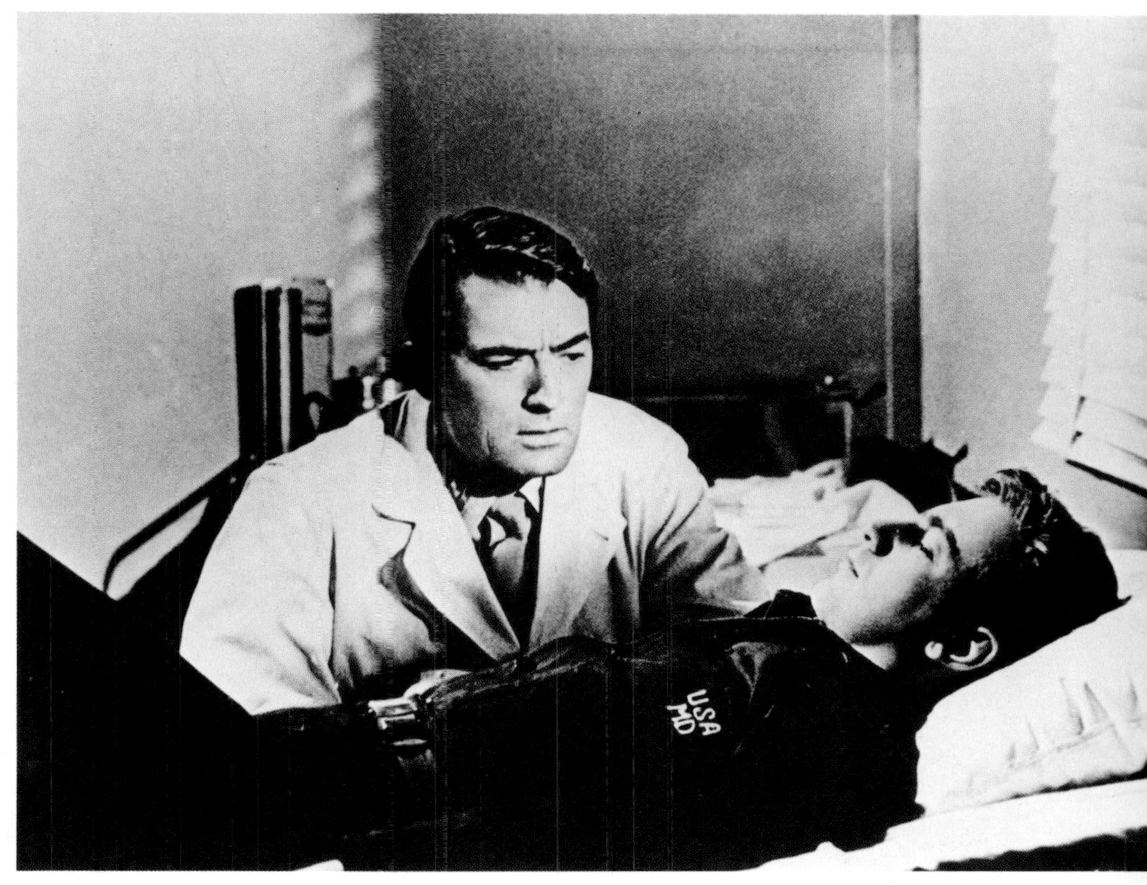

△ Set in an army base hospital in 1944, **Captain Newman MD** combined realism, sentimentality and comedy in equal proportions, but with diminishing returns. Gregory Peck (left) was top-starred as Captain Josiah Newman, a psychiatrist who, in the course of Robert Arthur's often self-consciously 'heartwarming' production, treated three specific cases. Bobby Darin (in bed, right) featured in one of them as a decorated corporal who has never forgiven himself for turning coward and deserting a buddy in a burning plane; Eddie Albert was a colonel who cannot stop torturing himself for sending so many men to their deaths in aerial combat; Robert Duvall is overcome with shame for having spent a year in Nazi occupied territory hiding alone in a cellar. The obligatory romance was supplied by Angie Dickinson as a nurse, while the comedy came mainly from Tony Curtis as a glib but resourceful orderly. David Miller, directing from a screenplay by Richard L. Breen and Phoebe and Henry Ephron (from the novel by Leo Rosten), drew fine performances from most of his cast, especially Bobby Darin, but was unable to skim the *schmaltz* from the film's mawkish Chrismas party sequence at the end. One time child star Jane Withers came out of retirement to play the expendable part of a nurse, with other roles in this Eastmancolor production going to James Gregory, Larry Storch, Dick Sargent and Robert F. Simon. (126 mins)

▷ Marlon Brando (right) and David Niven (left) took to the French Riviera in **Bedtime Story**, a lightweight entry in which heavyweight Brando played a small-time con man in competition with middleweight David Niven who played a big-time operator, for the love of Miss Shirley Jones, herself a walking con trick. She pretends to be a wealthy American soap queen; in truth she's nothing but the impecunious winner of a soap queen contest. In the end, Niven loses the girl but proves the better con man. Brando, on the other hand, lost out to his rival in the light comedy stakes, proving to be no match for the suave Mr Niven's way with a witty, sophisticated line. And in Stanley Shapiro (who also produced) and Paul Henning's screenplay, there were quite a few of them – though a few more wouldn't have come amiss. Ralph Levy's direction betrayed a heavy hand in the more overtly comic bits, and his cast included Dody Goodman, Parley Baer, Marie Windsor and Norman Alden. It was photographed in Eastmancolor. (99 mins)

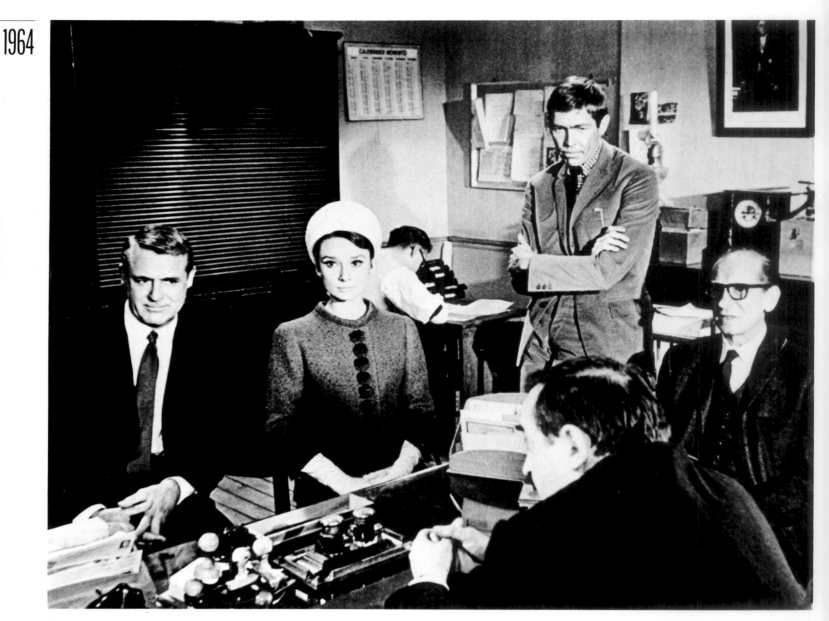

▽ On the stage Enid Bagnold's play **The Chalk Garden** was a genuinely eccentric, highly individualistic, strangely haunting comedy about a melancholy household whose chalky-soil garden was a symbol of the unflowering lives being led within – until the arrival of a governess, an expert with chalk gardens as well as with people. Though producer Ross Hunter and his scriptwriter John Michael Hayes maintained the play's basic narrative line (eliminating one unseen character), they completely removed the quirkiness that was so endemic to the piece. Which was tantamount to removing the poetry from *Hamlet*. Edith Evans played the house's haughty owner, Hayley Mills (left – far too ordinary and unsophisticated) was her neurotic granddaughter (the victim of a broken home), and Deborah Kerr (right – a lovely, up-front actress with not a glimmer of mystery about her) the enigmatic green-fingered governess with a secret in her past. The rest of the all-English cast was completed by John Mills as the butler (much more refined than the author intended), Felix Aylmer, Elizabeth Sellars and Lally Bowers. The rather flat-footed direction was by Ronald Neame. (Technicolor). (105 mins)

△ Cary Grant (left) and Audrey Hepburn (centre) were teamed for the first time in **Charade**, a Hitchcock-influenced brew of mystery and suspense with touches of *comedie noir* thrown in for added spice. Set in France, the film opened in the Alpine resort of Megeve where Hepburn, after a casual encounter with Grant, returns to Paris only to discover that her husband has been murdered and that a quartet of his World War II accomplices, believing that she knows the whereabouts of a quarter of a million dollars in gold, are out to get her. Grant follows her to Paris and offers to help. But can she trust him? And what about Walter Matthau, her informant, who advises her to find the gold as soon as possible and, for her own safety, to hand it over to him? Scenarist Peter Stone, working from a story he devised with Marc Behm, posed many questions in the course of the convoluted plot's eventual unravelling, and while not all of them were convincingly answered, the film's overall pace and many of its individual moments such as villain George Kennedy's rooftop fight with Grant, as well as the exciting finale under the stage of a theatre, more than compensated for the areas of narrative untidiness. The two central performances and the chemistry they engendered, helped the film garner many happy box-office returns. Stanley Donen's direction was a true marriage of style to content, Charles Lang Jr's Technicolor photography glowed, and Henry Mancini's score provided a first rate musical accompaniment to the action. Donen produced, and in subsidiary roles cast James Coburn (standing right) and Ned Glass (seated right) (as villains), Jacques Marin (back to camera), Paul Bonifas and Dominique Minot. (113 mins)

▽ Why does the glacial Tippi Hedren tell so many lies? Why is she given to stealing? Why does she flinch in repugnance from the touch of a man? Why do so *many* things terrify her? In his psychological thriller **Marnie**, Alfred Hitchcock, through his scenarist Jay Presson Allen (working from the novel by Winston Graham) attempted to answer these questions – and to a certain extent he did. But the explanations, when they finally came, were not all that convincing so that, in the end, audiences had once more to settle for style over content, with the master of suspense again revealing himself to be a supreme craftsman, capable of extracting the most from the least, and of investing the commonplace with a sense of the macabre. In Hitchcock it's not *what* is said but the *way* it is said that counts, and never has this been better demonstrated than in **Marnie**. In a role originally offered to Princess Grace of Monaco (Grace Kelly) in the hope that it would entice her out of retirement, Tippi Hedren (left) proved an excellent second best, her inexpressive face giving absolutely nothing away – which must surely have been Hitch's intention all along. Making his American debut, Sean Connery (right) was adequate as the man Miss Hedren works for, steals from, then marries; with other roles in Hitchcock's Technicolor production going to Diane Baker as Connery's dead wife's sister, Martin Gabel, and Louise Latham as Miss Hedren's mum, from whom Connery manages to discover certain events in his wife's background that serve as a partial explanation for her strange behaviour, such as the fact that mother murdered a sailor (Bruce Dern). The music was by Bernard Herrmann. (130 mins)

△ Tony Curtis (left) and Christine Kaufmann were unashamedly upstaged by a pooch called Monsieur Cognac (right) in **Wild And Wonderful**, an amiable enough comedy about a pampered French movie-star poodle whose fur is decidedly ruffled when his mistress (Kaufmann) marries an American jazz musician (Curtis). With not much more to it than that, it was hard to believe that it was written by three scenarists (Larry Markes, Michael Morris and Waldo Salt) from a screen story by Richard M. Powell and Phillip Rapp which, in turn, was based on a story by Dorothy Crider! It was directed by Michael Anderson, who extracted as much fun from the basic premise as he could, the high-spot being a sequence in a TV studio at the end. The producer was Harold Hecht, who decided to build Montmartre on the backlot rather than to film in France. The supporting cast included Jules Munshin as a harassed TV director, Larry Storch, Marty Ingels, Pierre Olaf, Marcel Hillaire and Sarah Marshall. Filmed in Eastmancolor. (88 mins)

▽ Another pooch, this time called Rontu, was the best thing in **Island Of The Blue Dolphins**, a kiddies' film which scenarists Ted Sherdeman and Jane Klove based on a novel by Scott O'Dell which, in turn, was based on truth. It was all about an Indian girl called Karana and how, in the first half of the 19th century, she spent eighteen years alone on a small island in the Santa Barbara chain after her father was murdered by a white trapper and her little brother killed by wild dogs. Her only friend is the aforementioned Rontu. What effect the experience had on Karana was never made clear in the film, due largely to the yawning crevasses in the screenplay (which made very little attempt to convey the passing of time); and to the performance of newcomer Celia Kaye (illustrated) who was simply unable to flesh out what the writers failed to provide. Ann Daniel, George Kennedy and Carlos Romero were in it too; Robert B. Radnitz produced (in Eastmancolor), and James B. Clark directed. (93 mins)

◁ Rock Hudson (right) and Doris Day (left) were teamed for a third time in **Send Me No Flowers**, a marital comedy (in Technicolor) in which Hudson, a hypochondriac, overhears his doctor discussing another patient's fatal condition, and mistakently believes the patient to be himself. Nice guy that he is, he immediately sets about finding a replacement hubby for his wife (Day). When Miss Day learns from the doctor that her husband isn't going to die at all, it is *her* turn to clutch at the wrong end of the stick – which she does by believing that he only claimed to be dying in order to disguise the fact that he is having an affair with another woman. Such complications were the red meat of Julian Epstein's serviceable screenplay (based on a play by Norman Barasch and Carroll Moore), and it provided its good-looking stars with the sort of roles that by now they wore as naturally as skin. Also cast in a familiar role was Tony Randall as Hudson's next door neighbour. Marty Melcher and Harry Keller produced, it was directed by Norman Jewison and, in supporting roles, featured Edward Andrews as Hudson's doctor and Clint Walker as an erstwhile millionaire flame of Miss Day's, as well as Paul Lynde, Hal March and Patricia Barry. (100 mins)

◁ **The Killers** (a remake of the 1946 success) owed more to producer-director Don Siegel's taste for brutality than to Ernest Hemingway's short story from which Gene L. Coon's screenplay was fashioned. This time the 'hero', played by John Cassavetes (right), was more interested in racing cars than the boxing ring, and worked at an institution for the blind. His death by hired killers Lee Marvin and Clu Gulager unleashed a complicated plot involving robbery and blackmail that was strictly routine. Angie Dickinson (left) was the no-good girl Cassavetes falls for, Ronald Reagan her 'protector'. Anthony Veiller's screenplay provided additional parts for Claude Akins, Norman Fell, Virginia Christine, Don Haggerty and Robert Phillips. It was photographed in Pathé Color. (95 mins)

△ Audiences proud of America's victory in the Pacific during World War II wondered, if the antics of the men in **McHale's Navy** were anything to go by, just how they did it. In a screenplay by Frank Gill Jr and G. Carleton Brown (story by Si Rose) that accommodated every bit of vaudeville 'shtick' ever perpetrated on stage or film, this wacky transfer from TV (where it enjoyed popularity as one of America's better comedy series) to the big screen, repeated its TV casting of Ernest Borgnine as Lt Commander Quinton McHale, while Borgnine (illustrated left of centre) repeated his energetic performance under producer Edward J. Montagne's direction – Montagne having been in charge of the TV series as well. It was filmed in Pathé Color and also featured Joe Flynn (hell-bent on sending Borgnine to the brig, and on introducing a bit of discipline into the outfit), Tim Conway, Carl Ballantine, Gary Vinson and, for female interest, Claudine Longet and Jean Willes. Subtlety was not its strong point. (93 mins)

△ The badman in producer Gordon Kay's **Bullet For A Badman**, was Darren McGavin, whose former wife (Beverley Owen) has married hero Audie Murphy (top-starred). As Murphy (illustrated) is bringing up Owen and McGavin's child as his own, his task in apprehending McGavin, a gunman who has escaped from jail, is made all the more difficult. Added to the complication is the fact that the two men were once good friends. After a slow start, the film reached the level of adequacy audiences had come to expect from such lower-case productions, and they settled back to enjoy the two leading performances, as well as those of Skip Homeier, George Tobias, Alan Hale, Ruta Lee and Berkeley Harris. R.G. Springsteen directed (in Eastmancolor) from a screenplay by Mary and Willard Willing from the novel by Marvin H. Albert. (80 mins)

△ A conventional western which, by 1964, was also an anachronism, **He Rides Tall** starred Tony Young (right) as the hero, Dan Duryea as the bad guy and Madlyn Rhue and Jo Morrow as a good girl and a bad respectively. R.G. Armstrong (left), Joel Fluellen, Carl Reindel and Mickey Simpson were in it too; it was written by Charles W. Irwin and Robert Creighton Williams, produced by Gordon Kay, and directed by R.G. Springsteen. (84 mins)

1965

▽ Very much a family affair, **Love And Kisses**, written (from a play by Anita Rowe Black), produced and directed by Ozzie Nelson and starring his son Rick (2nd left) and daughter-in-law Kristin (left), was the story of a couple of teenagers who suddenly decide to marry and move in with the groom's father (Jack Kelly, centre, giving the best performance in the movie). Madelyn Hines (right) played ma, with other roles going to Pert Kelton as the family retainer, Sheila Wells and Jerry Van Dyke. All told, it could have done with more professional gloss and less sentimentality. Robert Moreno photographed it in Technicolor. (87 mins)

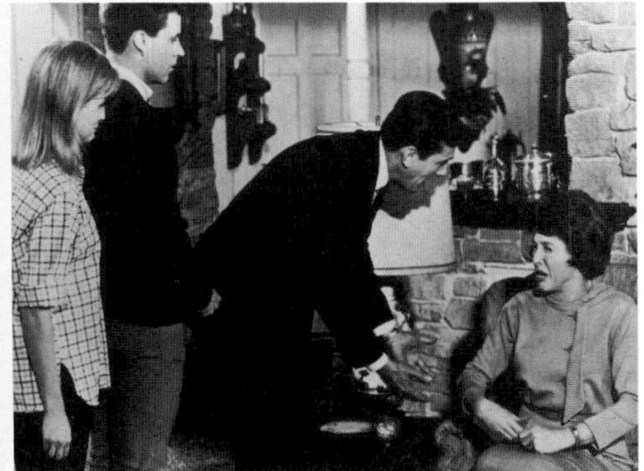

△ Obviously conceived as a contemporary social drama, **Wild Seed** was a non-starter which gave Michael Parks (right) top billing, and co-starred Celia Kaye (left) as a runaway girl. A weak, unfocussed screenplay by Les Pine (from a story he wrote with Ike Jones) had Miss Kaye teaming up with a young opportunist (Parks) on her travels from New York (and her foster parents) to Los Angeles. Brian G. Hutton's direction matched the level of the material, and did little to enhance the prestige of Albert S. Ruddy's Pennebaker production (executive producer Marlon Brando Sr). The supporting cast included Ross Elliott, Woodrow Chambliss and Rupert Crosse. (99 mins)

▽ Though the behind-the-scenes team, especially cameraman Russell Metty and art directors Alexander Golitzen and Frank Arrigo, shared 17 Oscar nominations between them for past successes, they were unable to salvage **Bus Riley's Back In Town** from the oblivion into which it deserved to sink. Written by Walter Gage (a collective pseudonym for several of the writers who worked on it but who wisely chose to remain anonymous), the project was initially entrusted to playwright William Inge from whom it was eventually wrested by producer Elliot Kastner – though segments of the work Inge completed remained. Despite Ann-Margret's (right) top billing, the plot centred around newcomer Michael Parks (left – whose second film, *Wild Seed*, was released before **Riley** as a means of introducing him to audiences and, with luck, building up a following for him before the release of this more expensive second feature). Relying very much on the 'method' school of acting in general and Marlon Brando in particular, Parks revealed no great flair in his role of an ex-serviceman romantically involved with temptress Ann-Margret, as well as with supportive good girl Janet Margolin. Crahan Denton was fine as a homosexual undertaker, though most of the other supporting performances from a cast that included Brad Dexter, Jocelyn Brando, Larry Storch, Alice Pearce and Kim Darby, were nothing special. Neither was Harvey Hart's direction. It was photographed in Eastmancolor. (93 mins)

◁ Satire and slapstick collided head-on in **The Art Of Love**, a frenetic entry from gloss merchant Ross Hunter in which an unsuccessful American artist, living in Paris, discovers the only way he can sell his canvasses is by faking suicide and leaving the business arrangements to his grasping roommate. Dick Van Dyke (left) was the artist; James Garner his buddy. The ploy, like the film, went wrong, and it was left to such talented supporting players as Irving Jacobson as the owner of a Jewish delicatessen, Naomi Stevens as his wife, Roger C. Carmel as a phoney art dealer and Pierre Olaf as a police inspector in the Clouseau mould to salvage the laughs. Ethel Merman appeared as a brassy nightclub owner-cum-madame, while the more shapely Elke Sommer (right) and Angie Dickinson (as Van Dyke's rich fiancée) provided the conventional female interest. The script was by Carl Reiner (who also appeared in it), from a story by Alan Simmons and William Sackheim, and although it had its moments, they were too few and far between. Norman Jewison directed the ***pot-pourri*** without any idea how to unify its disparate elements, and the costume designer, who deserved a solo bow, was Ray Aghayan. It was photographed in Technicolor. (99 mins)

△ Cary Grant (right) changed his sophisticated screen image for **Father Goose**, in which he played an inebriated, unkempt bum who spends his time looking out for Japanese planes for the Australian government on a deserted South Sea island. The main plot complication in Peter Stone and Frank Tarloff's screenplay (from the novel by S.H. Barnett) arrived in the cute shape of Leslie Caron, a prim schoolmistress whom Grant rescues (together with seven schoolgirls, illustrated) after they are marooned when the pilot carrying them to safety from New Guinea is forced to abandon them for a group of survivors from a crashed bomber. Grant and Caron did well by their material (the latter especially amusing in an uncharacteristic drunk scene), with other roles in producer Robert Arthur's fair-to-middling comedy going to Trevor Howard as an Australian commander, Jack Good, Sharyl Locke and Pip Sparke. It was photographed in Technicolor and directed by Ralph Nelson. (115 mins)

▽ Writer-producer-director Richard C. Serafian undertook a sizeable theme in **Andy**: the positive and negative aspects of human nature. The film's catalyst was a mentally retarded 40-year-old (called Andy) whose parents, Greek immigrants living in New York, reluctantly decide to commit him to an institution when they find they are no longer able to give him the care and attention he needs. Serafian's moving drama concentrated on Andy's last 24 hours and the events that befall his protagonist during that time. Norman Alden (centre) was marvellous in the non-speaking lead role; and there were splendid performances, too, from Tamara Daykarhanova (left) and Zvee Scooler (right) as his genuinely loving parents; as well as from Murvyn Vye as a sympathetic but ineffectual bartender, Ann Wedgeworth as a barmaid who makes a date with the retarded Andy then breaks it, and Sudie Bond as a hooker who invites the retard back to her apartment only to dismiss him with cool indifference the following morning. (86 mins)

▽ Just as *The Prince Who Was A Thief* (1951) introduced the world to Tony Curtis and Piper Laurie, so its remake, **The Sword Of Ali Baba** served as a launching pad for the rather less illustrious careers of Peter Mann (illustrated) and Jocelyn Lane. Using footage from the earlier film, as well as ransacking some left-over Maria Montez material, producer Howard Christie surfaced with a numbingly routine variation on the familiar Ali Baba story, the film's main challenge falling to cameraman William Margulies, whose unenviable task it was to match up the Technicolor process of the various past versions the film freely utilised (the latest being in Eastmancolor). Director Virgil Vogel cast Greg Morris as Yusuf a black slave (in the 1951 version the role was played by Everett Sloane who appeared as Ali Baba's foster father), as well as Peter Whitney, Gavin MacLeod and Frank Puglia. Oscar Brodney scripted. (81 mins)

▽ Sex reared its head in **Taggart**, and was the only ingredient that distinguished producer Gordon Kay's otherwise routine oater in which top-starred Tony Young (right) is pursued by hired killer Dan Duryea (left). The sexual element insinuated itself between cattle stampedes and Indian attacks on a wagon train, and made its presence felt in the shape of Elsa Cardenas who, hussy that she is, double-crosses husband Young and makes off with Duryea (foreground) in search of a lost gold mine. It was written by Creighton Williams from a novel by Louis L'Amour, beautifully photographed in colour by William Margulies and directed by R.G. Springsteen. Also cast: Dick Foran, Jean Hale, Emile Meyer and David Carradine. (85 mins)

▽ Producer-director William Castle's **I Saw What You Did** had an intriguing storyline going for it; a couple of teenage girls, alone in a large isolated house one night, decide to phone a random collection of strangers to whom they impart the following message: 'I Saw What You Did. I Know Who You Are'. One of their 'victims' turns out to be John Ireland who, as William McGiver's screenplay (from the novel *Out Of The Dark* by Ursula Curtiss) has it, has just murdered his wife (Joyce Meadows). Ireland is convinced he knows the identity of the girl. What followed provided the film with its suspense, and Joan Crawford (top-billed, illustrated) with another meaty role as Ireland's demanding lover. As the two teenage girls who started it all, Andi Garrett and Sarah Lane committed grand larceny in all their scenes; Sharyl Locke played Andi's younger sister who is also in on the game, with Leif Erickson and Patricia Breslin (as Andi's parents), John Archer and John Crawford completing the cast. (82 mins)

▷ The trouble with **Mirage** was that just as audiences felt they were about to grasp the complications of the plot, the more confused they became. It starred Gregory Peck (right) as a physio-chemist who loses his memory and cannot recall a single incident that has happened to him in the past two years (though it is ultimately revealed he has discovered a way of removing the danger of radiation from nuclear explosions). Could his important discovery have anything to do with his boss (Walter Abel) plunging to his death from the 27th floor? Or the fact that he is being pursued by assassins? Scenarist Peter Stone, working from a story by Walter Ericson, allowed too many plot points to remain unresolved, and it was left to Edward Dmytryk's resourceful direction and to the performances of a cast that also included Diane Baker as the enigmatic woman in Peck's life, Walter Matthau (left) as the detective he hires, Leif Erickson as the head of a nuclear manufacturing organisation and Jack Weston and George Kennedy as a pair of gunmen, to keep the proceedings buoyant – which they certainly did. Harry Keller produced. (109 mins)

△ The **Strange Bedfellows** in this glossy, Technicolor, Panama and Frank production, were Rock Hudson (centre) as a prim and proper London-based American oil executive, and lovely Gina Lollobrigida (centre left) as his tempestuous Italian wife. The screenplay by Melvin Frank and Michael Pertwee, from a story by Panama and Frank, was a trifle which engaged the services of middle-man Gig Young who, in his capacity as Hudson's PR man, is given the task of cleaning up his boss' image as part of a scheme to propel his employer to the top position in his company – ie smoothing over the cracks in Hudson and Lollobrigida's unsuccessful seven-year marriage. It looked good, and boasted a clutch of engaging comedy performances from Arthur Haynes, David King, Terry-Thomas, Peggy Rea, Nancy Kulp and Lucy Landau. The film's setting, London, was recreated on Universal's new 'European' set on its backlot; and it was directed by Melvin Frank. (99 mins)

▽ Aimed directly at audiences who supported such trifles as *Strange Bedfellows* and *Lover Come Back* (1961), **A Very Special Favor** was a feeble little number that pretended to be far more sophisticated than it really was. Rock Hudson (right) starred as a handsome Lothario totally irresistible to the opposite sex; Leslie Caron (left) was a spinsterish lady psychiatrist with whom he becomes romantically involved. Charles Boyer played a French lawyer and Miss Caron's father (it is he who instigates the romance between Hudson and his daughter), and did so with his usual air of urbanity. But the best performances director Michael Gordon drew were from Nita Talbot as a switchboard operator madly in love with Hudson, and from Larry Storch as a cab driver. Also cast for producer Stanley Shapiro (who, together with Nate Monaster, wrote it) were Dick Shawn, Walter Slezak, Norma Varden and George Furth. It was photographed in Technicolor. (105 mins)

▽ A sequel to *McHale's Navy* (1964), **McHale's Navy Joins The Air Force** was more of the same, but with one vital ingredient missing: Ernest Borgnine as Quinton McHale. A disagreement over money ultimately led to Borgnine's withdrawal, leaving the burden of John Fenton Murray's screenplay (based on a story by William J. Lederer) to series regulars Joe Flynn and Tim Conway. Story had Conway assuming the identity of an Air Force officer occasioned by a uniform mix-up and a hangover, and it was from this mix-up that most of the fun derived. As the flustered Navy captain Wallace Binghampton, Flynn (left) is given no choice but to go along with the mistaken identity gag which, would you believe, leads to the sinking of the Japanese fleet, and Conway (right) is honoured for his bravery by President Franklin D. Roosevelt! Such were the farcical machinations of Edward J. Montagne's fast-moving production, and fans of the popular series had themselves a ball. Montagne also directed (some of the sight gags were particularly effective) and his cast included Jacques Aubuchon as a Soviet sailor, Tom Tully as a three-star general, Henry Beckman as an Air Force colonel, and Bob Hastings as Flynn's harassed aide. Susan Silo and Jean Hale represented the distaff side. It was photographed in Technicolor. (90 mins)

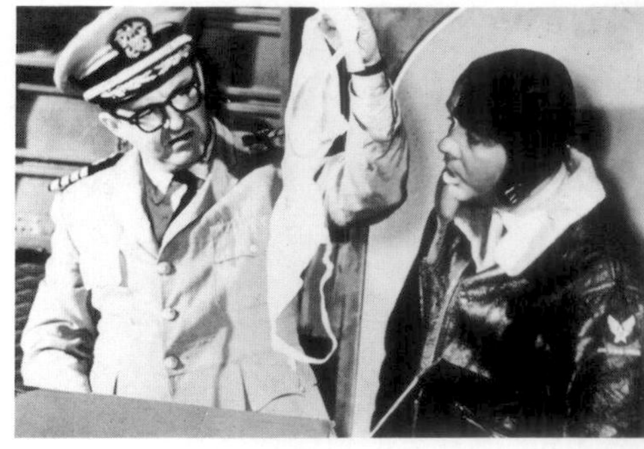

▽ Charlton Heston (centre) once again immersed himself in history in **The War Lord**, this time going as far back as the 11th century for his role as Chrusagon, war lord of the Duke of Normandy, whose job it is to protect a primitive Druid village and its inhabitants from Frisian invaders. He succeeds admirably, and the manner in which he protects his imposing Norman tower from the troublesome Frisians provided the film with its main action footage. Millard Kaufman's screenplay from Leslie Stevens' play *The Lovers*, found room for romance 11th-century fashion, and had Heston claiming a village girl (Rosemary Forsyth, left) on her wedding night according to the custom of *droit de seigneur*. Clearly Miss Forsyth enjoyed the experience for she refuses to return to her rightful groom. Guy Stockwell, brother of Dean, made his debut as Heston's brother, and Richard Boone (right) was Heston's faithful aide. Also cast for producer Walter Seltzer and director Franklin Schaffner: Maurice Evans, Niall McGinnis, Henry Wilcoxon and James Farentino. It was gorgeously photographed in Technicolor by Russell Metty. (121 mins)

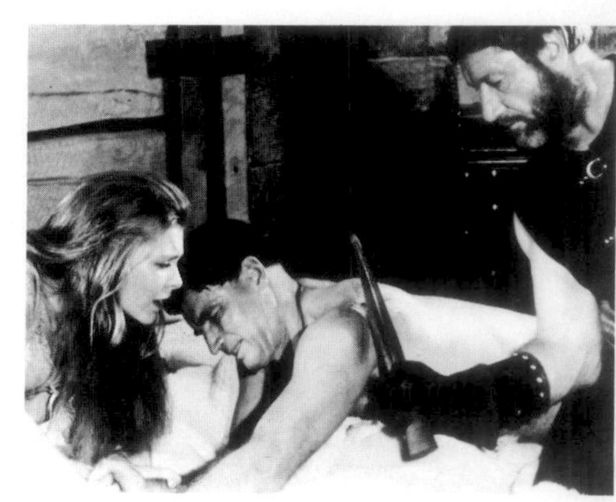

▽ James Stewart was cast against type in **Shenandoah**, an absorbing Civil War drama in which he starred as the *paterfamilias* presiding, unaided, over a family of six sons and a daughter, his wife having died in childbirth. A farmer whose priorities are his land and his family, he wants nothing whatsoever to do with the war, but he is inevitably forced to abandon his pacifist stance when his youngest son (Phillip Alford, illustrated centre with Stewart), stupidly donning a confederate cap, is captured as a rebel by Unionists. As scripted by James Lee Barrett, the war sequences carried less conviction than those concerned with family life, though under Andrew V. McLaglen's direction, one battle sequence was particularly well handled; as was a chilling scene in which a scavenger murders one of Stewart's sons (Patrick Wayne) who has remained behind on the farm with his wife (Katharine Ross) and baby. There were fine performances from Rosemary Forsyth as Stewart's daughter, and Doug McClure (second-billed) as the man in her life; and from Glenn Corbett, Charles Robinson, James McMullin and Tim McIntire as the rest of the sons. Completing the cast for producer Robert Arthur, were George Kennedy, Warren Oates, Strother Martin, Paul Fix (left with beard) and Denver Pyle. It was photographed in Technicolor. (105 mins)

▽ Husband and wife Sandra Dee (left) and Bobby Darin (right) appeared together again in **That Funny Feeling**, the only funny thing about it being how anyone could have thought it funny in the first place. She played a would-be actress doubling as a housemaid; he the owner of an apartment she services. As they've never met *in situ* she has no idea, when they bump into each other around New York, that she works for him, and thinks nothing of inviting him back to his own apartment, believing that the man she works for is out of town on a business trip. With a wittier, more inventive screenplay than the one provided by David R. Schwartz, such a contrivance might have worked. On this occasion, however, it merely engendered tedium. Going under with its two stars were Donald O'Connor (as Darin's partner), Nita Talbot, Larry Storch, James Westerfield and Robert Strauss. Harry Keller produced (in Technicolor) and it was leadenly directed by Richard Thorpe. (93 mins)

△ Aimed at the pre-teen market, **Pinocchio In Outer Space** was a full-length cartoon feature in colour, that found Collodi's famous little wooden puppet wafting through space in a spacecraft (see illustration), with a turtle called Nurtle for companionship. En route they encounter a cluster of giant crabs as well as an astral whale called Astro. Though not a patch on Disney's *Pinocchio* (RKO, 1940) it was always pretty to look at and offered some excellent animation. Lending their voices to the characters depicted were Conrad Jameson, Cliff Owens, Peter Lazar, Mavis Mims, Kever Kennedy, Minerva Pious and Arnold Stang. Norman Prescott and Fred Ladd produced, it was written by Fred Laderman and directed by Ray Goossens. (72 mins)

▽ A sort of 'That's Abbott and Costello', **The World Of Abbott And Costello** was a compendium of scenes from past A & C movies with connecting narration written by Gene Wood and spoken by Jack E. Leonard. Apart from the celebrated drill scene in *Buck Privates*, there were extracts from *The Naughty Nineties* (1945), *Wistful Widow Of Wagon Gap* (1947), *Hit The Ice* (1943), *Little Giant* (1946), *Mexican Hayride* (1948), *In The Navy* (1941), *Who Done It* (1942), *Go To Mars* (1953), *Lost In Alaska* (1952), *In The Foreign Legion* (1950, illustrated, with Patricia Medina, A & C), *Buck Privates Come Home* (1947), *Comin' Round The Mountain* (1951), *Ride 'Em Cowboy* (1942), *In Society* (1944), *Meet The Mummy* (1955), *Meet Frankenstein* (1948) and *Meet The Keystone Kops* (1955). Though the emphasis was squarely on the two comedians, the compendium also featured Glenn Anders, Tom Ewell, Luis Alberni, Nat Pendleton, Dorothy Grainger, Thurston Hall, Lon Chaney Jr, Bela Lugosi and, as a witch (what else?), Margaret Hamilton. The duo's famous 'Who's On First?' was a highlight in a film strictly for ardent fans. It was produced by Max L. Rosenberg and Milton Subotsky. (75 mins)

◁ Clearly inspired by such excursions into Victorian horror as *The Body Snatchers* (RKO, 1954) and *The Lodger* (20th Century-Fox, 1944), scenarist Barre Lyndon emerged with his own tribute to the genre called **Dark Intruder**. Though very much a budget-conscious effort, as was reflected in the shortness of the running time and the small number of sets employed (not to mention the lower-case cast), Lyndon's story of a San Franciscan criminologist (Leslie Nielsen) who sets out to apprehend a monster that has been stalking the city was often quite gripping, with the marvellous period atmosphere evoked in Harvey Hart's economical but immensely effective direction helping to offset the uneven performances of Gilbert Green, Charles Bolender (as Nielsen's dwarf valet), Mark Richman (centre, at top of steps), Judi Meredith and Werner Klemperer. Full marks to Bud Westmore's monster make-up. (59 mins)

△ Tony Randall (illustrated) starred in **Fluffy** as a biochemist whose experiments with a lion (called Fluffy) go awry, causing havoc in a hotel. It was relentlessly second-rate, and overworked its cast to little effect. Shirley Jones was the hotelier's daughter (and Randall's love-interest), Ernest Truex her father. Samuel Roeca wrote it, it featured Edward Andrews, Howard Morris, Dick Sargent, Jim Backus and Frank Faylen; Gordon Kay produced, and it was directed by Earl Bellamy. (92 mins)

△ Robert Taylor and Barbara Stanwyck (illustrated) brought a touch of class to producer William Castle's **The Night Walker**, a chiller with a well manipulated propensity to shock, but a really rather confusing screenplay by Robert Bloch in which Stanwyck's husband (Hayden Rorke) accuses her of infidelity. He is then killed, and she has a series of dreams so vivid that even after she awakens, she is not sure to what extent the dreams are fact or fantasy. Occupying top billing in those dreams was Lloyd Bochner, a handsome stranger who, on one occasion, spirits Miss S off to a chapel where they are married by a wax minister. What it all added up to only Freud might have known. Still, for addicts of the horror genre, it had its moments. Also cast: Judith Meredith, Marjorie Bennett and Jess Barker. (86 mins)

1966

▷ An overabundance of tricksy camera angles from director Sidney J. Furie, a far too leisurely screenplay (by James Bridges and Roland Kibbee from the novel by Robert MacLeod) and a rather rambling, under-characterized central performance from Marlon Brando (left) robbed **The Appaloosa** (GB: **Southwest To Sonora**) of much of its impact. What remained was a somewhat pretentious story of a cowboy (Brando) who has 'sinned and killed', and his coolly calculated efforts to retrieve an Appaloosa stallion stolen from him by a Mexican ranchero. Furie did, however, manage to convey a feeling of incipient violence simmering beneath the beautiful and picturesque landscape, and this at least created an interesting atmosphere against which the story unfurled. Anjanette Comer (right) co-starred as the ranchero's wife (whom Brando wins), John Saxon was the ranchero, with other roles in Alan Miller's Techniscope and Technicolor production going to Emilio Fernandez, Alex Montoya, Miriam Colon and Rafael Campos. Brando was the only one throughout who did not speak in a thick Mexican accent. (98 mins)

▽ Spoofing the spy genre with tongue well in cheek, producer Joseph F. Robertson surfaced with **Agent For H.A.R.M.**, passable programmer entertainment for the undemanding. It was a good guys-versus-bad guys caper in which the heroes who belong to H.A.R.M. (Human Aetiological Relations Machine) are determined to prevent the villain, a scientist defector, from spraying the crops with a deadly green fungus. Wendell Corey (left) was H.A.R.M.'s top security chief; Carl Esmond the bad guy, with other parts under Gerd Oswald's serviceable direction going to Mark Richman as a secret agent, Barbara Bouchet, Martin Kosleck, Rafael Campos, and Donna Michelle (right). It was written by Blair Robertson and photographed in Technicolor. (84 mins)

▽ A 'family' film, designed to appeal as much to parents as their children, **And Now Miguel** (from the award-winning novel by Joseph Krumgold) told the simple story of a young lad's ambition to become a shepherd so that he may tend the flocks that have been the mainstay of his family for generations. Twelve-year-old Pat Cardi (centre left) played Miguel most engagingly, and there were convincing performances from Michael Ansara (right) and Pilar Del Rey (centre) as his parents. Guy Stockwell, Peter Robbins, Clu Gulager (left), Joe Di Santis, Buck Taylor and Emma Tyson filled other roles in Ted Sherdeman and Jane Klove's screenplay (in which not a great deal happened). It was directed by James B. Clark, and produced by Robert B. Radnitz. (Technicolor) (95 mins)

◁ Cockney Michael Caine (*sans* spectacles, left, and in his first Hollywood-made film), joined forces with perky Shirley MacLaine (as a Jean Louis-clad Eurasian, right), in **Gambit**. A heist caper, reminiscent of *Topkapi* (United Artists, 1964), it pivoted on the theft of a priceless bust from a Middle European potentate (Herbert Lom) and combined equal portions of suspense and comedy. Under Ronald Neame's well-paced direction, the mixture worked very successfully, a decided plus factor being a 27-minute sequence at the start of the film showing just how the robbery, given ideal circumstances, can be accomplished. In reality, of course, it didn't quite work out that way ... Roger C. Carmel, Arnold Moss, John Abbott, Richard Angarola and Maurice Marsac completed the cast for producer Leo L. Fuchs, whose handsomely mounted production in Technicolor and Techniscope was an unmitigated delight. (107 mins)

▷ London provided the setting for Stanley Donen's entertaining, albeit confusing, thriller **Arabesque** which, apart from a certain muzziness in its plotting, suffered from the miscasting of Gregory Peck (left) as an American professor of ancient languages who, after being called on to decipher a secret message written in hieroglyphics – a document sought by several Arabs – finds himself involved in a *rondolet* of murders and attempted assassinations. That it all added up to something more or less incomprehensible hardly mattered in the face of so much action and intrigue; and with the luscious Sophia Loren (right) on hand to add a touch of rampant sexuality to the proceedings, no one complained. Alan Badel and Kieron Moore brought a veneer of enjoyable English menace to bear on the proceedings, and John Merivale and Duncan Lamont, two more English actors, did a nice job as a pair of heavies out to give Peck a bad time. Completing the cast for producer-director Donen were Carl Duering, George Coulouris, Ernest Clark and Harold Kasket. It was based on Gordon Cottler's novel *The Cipher* and scripted by Julian Mitchell, Stanley Price and Pierre Marton. The exquisite Panavision and Technicolor photography was by Christopher Challis. (107 mins)

◁ Italian sex symbol Claudia Cardinale joined Rock Hudson in **Blindfold**, another confusing caper in which Hudson (left) starred as a 'society psychiatrist' who, after treating a mentally disturbed scientist (Alejandro Rey), finds himself involved in a plot to kidnap him. He is spirited off, blindfolded, to a secluded hideout in the swampy South where Rey is being held by government agents for his own protection. Cardinale (far left) played Rey's sexy sister, naturally pairing off with Hudson for obligatory romantic interest. Jack Warden appeared as a general in charge of Rey's protection; Guy Stockwell (right) was the leader of the baddies, Brad Dexter a not-too-bright detective, and Vito Scotti and Angela Clark Miss Cardinale's parents. Anne Seymour completed the cast for producer Marvin Schwartz, playing Hudson's wisecracking secretary. Philip Dunne directed efficiently enough from a screenplay he wrote with W.H. Menger, and it was photographed in Technicolor. (102 mins)

▽ That hoary old comic standby, so beloved of Harold Lloyd, in which the local *nebbish*, through circumstances not entirely in his control, becomes a hero – surfaced once again in **The Ghost And Mr Chicken**. It starred TV's Don Knotts (illustrated) as a typesetter in a newspaper office whose ambition to become an ace reporter leads to his involvement in a libel suit and a haunted house. Yawningly routine, James Fritzell and Everett Greenbaum's screenplay offered only a modicum of laughs, and was in no way rescued by its star, or by Joan Staley, Skip Homeier, Dick Sargent , Phil Ober, Reta Shaw and Lurene Tuttle. Eddie Quillan and J. Edward McKinley, making unbilled appearances, didn't help either. It was produced by Edward J. Montagne in Technicolor and Techniscope and unenthusiastically directed by Alan Rafkin. (89 mins)

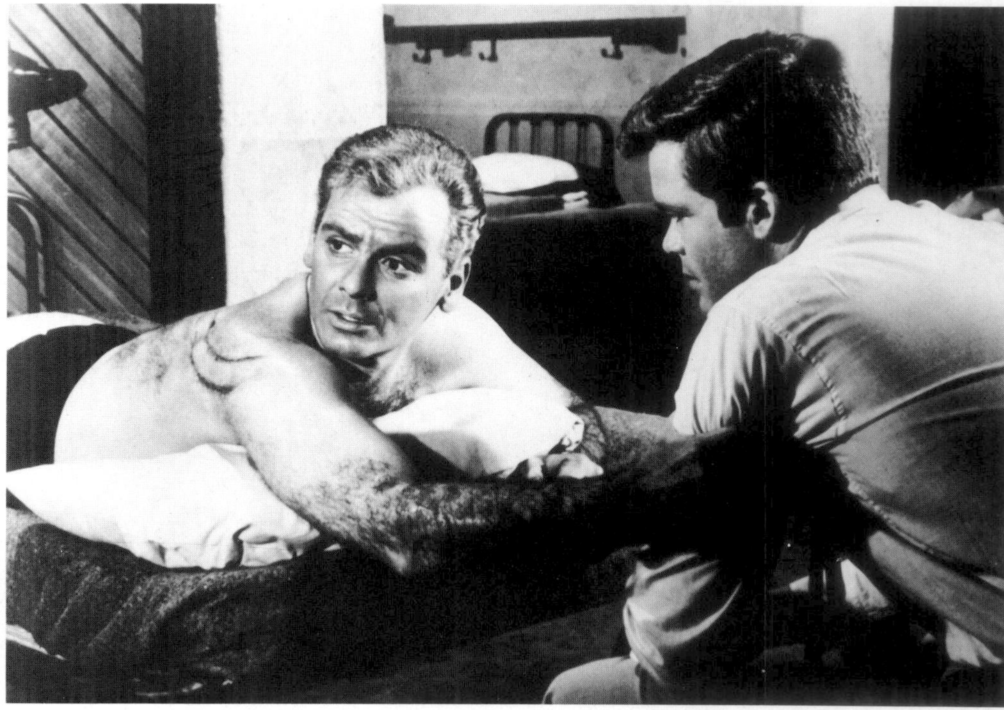

△ First seen as a Paramount film in 1926 (with Ronald Colman), then in 1939 (with Gary Cooper also for Paramount), **Beau Geste** was no stranger to audiences who, third time round, made his reacquaintance in the shape of Guy Stockwell (left). Telly Savalas played the sadistic sergeant, following in the footsteps of Noah Beery and Brian Donlevy in the earlier films. Director Douglas Heyes, who also scripted it, made certain changes from the original novel by Percival Christopher Wren, and turned Beau and his brother John (Doug McClure, right) into Americans, while dropping the third brother altogether. But Beau's reason for joining the Foreign Legion after taking the responsibility for a crime he was innocent of, was unaltered. Basically it remained a stirring tale of courage, heroism and brotherly devotion played out on the burning sands of the desert, and if Stockwell's performance couldn't hope to match those of his illustrious predecessors, it was certainly no disgrace to the noble spirit of the piece. The film looked marvellous in Techniscope and Technicolor, contained two excitingly staged battle sequences and, in secondary roles, featured Leslie Nielsen as the ineffectual lieutenant in command, David Mauro as a mercenary, Robert Wolders as a Frenchman, Leo Gordon as a former German officer, Michael Constantine as an erstwhile Cossack, and Malachi Throne as a treacherous Pole. The producer was Walter Seltzer. (105 mins)

▷ James Garner (left) starred in **A Man Could Get Killed**, a confusing caper filmed on location in Lisbon in which he played an American businessman mistaken for a British agent. Richard Breen and E.B. Clarke's confusing screenplay (from the novel *Diamonds For Danger* by David Esdaile Walker) also involved him in a search for smuggled diamonds and a romance with sultry Melina Mercouri (centre) – who is after the loot herself. So is Tony Franciosa, an American posing as a Portuguese smuggler. Ronald Neame's tongue-in-cheek direction went all out to keep it light and frothy but was defeated by the narrative complications which strained credibility to breaking point. Sandra Dee was third-billed in this Robert Arthur Panavision and Technicolor production, which found employment for a host of English character actors including Robert Coote (right), Cecil Parker, Dulcie Gray, Niall McGinnis and Isabel Dean. Also: Gregoire Aslan, Peter Illing and Brenda de Banzie. (97 mins)

△ Another quintessential 'woman's picture' and a four-handkerchief weepie that even attacked the sensibilities of hardened males, **Madame X**, in its sixth (count 'em) screen incarnation, gave Lana Turner one of the very best roles of her career and, trouper that she was, she devoured it greedily. In a role previously played by Dorothy Donnelly (1915), Pauline Frederick (1920), Ruth Chatterton (1929), Gladys George (1937) and Madame Kyveli (1960, for Orestes Laskos' Greek version), Turner (left) starred as a married woman whose love affair with a wealthy playboy ends in his accidental death, her own 'disappearance' in a mock drowning episode, the murder of a blackmailer, and her standing trial and being defended by an attorney who is unaware that the woman whose life he is fighting for is his very own mother. It was melodramatic in 1909 when it first appeared as a play by Alexandra Bisson, but melodrama of the highest order and, in Ross Hunter's expensive production (which switched the locale from France to America), that's how it remained. Jean Holloway's screenplay made several other changes, most notably 'Madame X's' genuine attachment to rather than loathing of her politician husband, sympathetically played by John Forsythe. But in all essentials the script was true to the spirit of the original play. Ricardo Montalban was Miss Turner's lover, Keir Dullea her unsuspecting son, Burgess Meredith the blackmailer and, as Forsythe's mother, Constance Bennett (right) in her last screen appearance before her death. Also: John Van Dreelen, Virginia Grey, Warren Stevens and Carl Benton Reid. It was photographed in Technicolor and directed by David Lowell Rich. **Madame X** surfaced for the seventh time in 1981 as a TV film starring Tuesday Weld. (99 mins)

▷ Don Murray (centre) as Wild Bill Hickock, Guy Stockwell (right) as Buffalo Bill Cody and Abby Dalton as Calamity Jane starred in **The Plainsman**, an inferior remake of the Cecil B. DeMille production for Paramount in 1937. Apart from the fact that this latest version lacked the star quality of its predecessor (Gary Cooper, Jean Arthur and James Ellison headed that cast), the film was not conceived as a big-budget production, with the result that all it offered contemporary audiences was a collection of clichés in the retelling of the legendary romance between Wild Bill Hickock and Calamity Jane, and their friendship with Buffalo Bill. Director David Lowell Rich handled the action stuff competently enough, a highlight being an episode when the army, assisted by Hickock and Cody, ward off an attack by Indians in the desert. Even so, as scripted by Michael Blankfort, it was all relentlessly predictable. Leslie Nielsen (left) made a brief appearance as Colonel George Custer, with other roles in Richard E. Lyons' Technicolor production going to Bradford Dillman, Henry Silva and Edward Binns. (92 mins)

▽ Peter Shaffer's one-act play *The Private Ear*, which formed the first half of a double bill with *The Public Eye*, was a sensitive, moving piece about loneliness, and how a shy music-lover loses the girl he has found the courage to invite back to his flat, to his more flashy, glib best friend. Ross Hunter's Technicolor production changed the setting from London to Los Angeles and, with gross insensitivity, called it **The Pad (And How To Use It)**, doubtless cashing in on the success of the British film *The Knack (And How To Get It)* (United Artists, 1965). Brian Bedford, complete with his native English accent (though no explanation was given for it) repeated the role he created on stage, but not nearly as convincingly; James Farentino (left) was his know-it-all friend, and Julie Sommers (right) the girl in the middle. Thomas C. Ryan and Ben Starr's screenplay stuck fundamentally to the original text, though on two occasions – one involving a fat woman on a bus and another a scene at the Greek Theatre – their own interpolations were awful. The cast was completed by Edy Williams, Nick Navarro, Pearl Shear and Barbara London – none of whose characters appeared in the original. For much of the time it was directed (by Brian G. Hutton) as farce rather than for the wistful comedy it should have been. (88 mins)

▽ **Out Of Sight** was a mindless rock musical which featured Gary Lewis and The Playboys, Freddie and The Dreamers, The Turtles, The Astronauts and The Knickerbockers in a youth exploitation quickie whose main concern was finding a suitable band for a forthcoming teenage fair. Larry Hovis' screenplay (story by Hovis and David Asher) complicated the issue slightly by introducing a heavy in the shape of John Lawrence who has some scheme afoot to eliminate Freddie and The Dreamers, but that was merely by way of padding. What counted were the musical numbers and there were plenty of those. Jonathan Daly (as a bumbling secret agent, right), Karen Jensen, Robert Pine and Carole Shelyn were the featured players, Deanna Lund (left) was in it too; Bart Patton and Lennie Weinrib produced, and it was photographed in Technicolor, and directed by Weinrib. Songs included: 'Malibu Run' Jim Karstein, Leon Russell, Gary Lewis, T. Leslie; 'Out On The Floor' Fred Darian, Al de Lory; 'She'll Come Back' Nita Garfield, Harold Kaylan; 'Baby Please Don't Go' Joe Williams; 'It's Not Unusual' Gordon Mills, Les Reed. (87 mins)

▽ **Johnny Tiger** focussed (somewhat blearily) on the dilemma facing a member of a racial minority: does he stick by his ethnic customs and cock a snook at the white man's civilisation? Or does he allow himself to become integrated? Robert Taylor (right) starred as the white man; Ford Rainey appeared as a Seminole chief opposed to the white man's ways, and Chad Everett (left) was the Seminole's half-breed grandson who has to decide whether he is going to become an Indian chieftain, or renounce his origins and marry Taylor's beautiful daughter (newcomer Brenda Scott, centre). As scripted by Paul Crabtree and R. John Hugh from the latter's story, audiences didn't give a damm one way or the other, and who could blame them? Paul Wendkos directed the too-familiar material with no sense of urgency or excitement, and totally failed to animate a cast that also included Geraldine Brooks, Marc Lawrence and Carol Seflinger. R. John Hugh produced (in colour). (102 mins)

▽ Producer-director Mervyn LeRoy's attempts to give the glamour treatment to murder, infidelity and amnesia failed abysmally in **Moment To Moment**, an intended tear-jerker with a French Riviera setting. As scripted by John Lee Mahin and Alec Coppel (from the latter's story *Laughs With A Stranger*), it told the story of a neglected American wife's affair with a US naval officer during the absence of her psychiatrist husband who is lecturing somewhere in Europe. The affair ends with the officer being shot and his body being dumped by the panicky wife and her helpful neighbour. Turns out, though, he isn't dead at all, is suffering from amnesia, and is treated for his condition by the cuckolded husband. Jean Seberg (left), exquisitely dressed by Yves Saint-Laurent was the unfaithful wife; Sean Garrison (right – making his debut) was the officer, Arthur Hill the husband and Honor Blackman the neighbour. Officer Garrison may have survived the shooting, but he was torpedoed both by the script and by his inability to project a personality that seemed sculpted in wood. Nor was there any semblance of life from Miss Seberg or Mr Hill. Acting honours went to Honor Blackman, who gave the liveliest performance out of a cast that also included Gregoire Aslan (as a cop), Peter Robbins and Donald Woods. The oft-plugged title song was by Henry Mancini and Johnny Mercer. (Technicolor). (108 mins)

▷ That popular TV series, *The Munsters*, finally came to the big screen in **Munster, Go Home**, promising much more than it delivered. In the story devised by scripters George Tibbles, Joe Connelly and Bob Mosher (the latter two also produced), Charles Addams' renowned Munster family, led by Fred Gwynne (right) and Yvonne De Carlo (left), leave America for England (by sea) after being informed that they have inherited a large manor house currently presided over by their English relatives Hermione Gingold and her gap-toothed son Terry-Thomas. Most of the plot hinged on Gingold's unsuccessful attempts to drive the Munster family back to America, and although spasmodically entertaining, it simply didn't possess enough laughs to justify its feature length incarnation. Al Lewis, Butch Patrick, Debbie Watson (in the role played on TV by Pat Priest), Robert Pine and John Carradine were also featured, and it was directed, in Technicolor, by Earl Bellamy. (90 mins)

△ A follow-up to his eerie chiller *I Saw What You Did* (1965), producer-director William Castle's **Let's Kill Uncle** also involved a couple of kids. This time, however, they were not teenage girls, but a 12-year-old orphan (Pat Cardi, right) who has inherited $1,000,000 from his father, and a pleasant girl his own age (Mary Badham), both of whom plot to kill the boy's greedy uncle before the uncle (who is after the lad's money) can kill the boy. Playing cat-and-mouse on a small abandoned island, the story unravelled itself with a satisfying neatness and resulted in a well-turned tale of suspense, equally appealing to adults and children. Mark Rodgers scripted from the novel by Rohan O'Grady, with parts in it for Robert Pickering as a police sergeant, Linda Lawson, Reff Sanchez, Nestor Paiva and, best of all, Nigel Green (left) as uncle. It was Castle's first film in Technicolor. (92 mins)

△ Rock singers Dick and Dee, Jay and The Americans, and The Beau Brummels added marquee value to producer Bart Patton's exploitation musical **Wild Wild Winter**. Concerned mainly with the efforts of a group of college undergraduates to seduce a handful of sorority sisters who are playing hard-to-get, it starred Gary Clarke (right) whose ruse is to pose as the son of a Hawaiian millionaire, and Chris Noel (left) as the girl who most needs to thaw. David Malcolm's routine screenplay shifted between the sunshine of Malibu and a snow-bound college (where most of the action took place), and provided parts for Don Edmonds, Suzie Kaye, Les Brown Jr and Vicky Albright. Lennie Weinrib directed. Songs: 'Wild Wild Winter' Chester Pipkin; 'A Change Of Heart' Pipkin, Mark Gordon; 'Heartbeats' Al Cupps, Mary Dean; 'Two Of A Kind' Victor Millrose, Tony Bruno; 'Just Wait And See' Ron Elliot. (80 mins)

▽ **The Rare Breed** offered entertaining family fare and two starry performances from James Stewart (right) and Maureen O'Hara (left). The latter played a widow from Britain who, together with her daughter (Juliet Mills, centre), travels to Texas in the unusual company of a hornless Hereford bull which she hopes to mate with American longhorns. In time they find a buyer for the beast, and hire cowpoke James Stewart to transport the bull (who responds to the tune of 'God Save The Queen') to its new owner. Fearing that their prize possession may not be treated as well as it deserves, mother and daughter accompany Stewart on the trail, experiencing, en route, a series of violent encounters with rustlers. Brian Keith was third-billed as the bull's new owner, a wild Scotsman, with other roles in producer William Alland's Panavision and Technicolor production going to Don Galloway, David Brian, Jack Elam and Harry Carey Jr. Andrew McLaglen directed it all a mite too sentimentally, and it was written by Ric Hardman. (97 mins)

◁ The master of suspense, Alfred Hitchcock, dropped an artistic clanger with **Torn Curtain**, a flaccidly directed thriller overburdened with far too many clichés, and the miscasting and mismating of its stars, Paul Newman (left) and Julie Andrews (right). All about an American nuclear scientist (Newman) who makes his way into East Berlin by pretending to defect – the object of the exercise being to pick a famous German scientist's brain – it stubbornly refused to generate anything resembling the director's characteristic undercurrent of menace or suspense. Even when Newman's ploy is discovered and he is being pursued, excitement was sorely rationed. Best, most chilling moment occurred in a memorable five-minute sequence in which Newman, assisted by a peasant farmer's wife (Carolyn Conwell), batters to death a security guard who refuses to die, then disposes of the body. Nothing else in the movie came near it for sheer cinematic pyrotechnics. Hitchcock himself made his customary appearance in a hotel lobby with a baby in his lap, though in more substantial roles he featured Lila Kedrova, Hansjoerg Felmy, Wolfgang Kieling, Gunter Strack, Ludwig Donath, David Opatashu and, making her first appearance in twelve years, Tamara Toumanova. Hitchcock produced, and the lustreless screenplay was by Brian Moore. It was photographed in Technicolor. (126 mins)

△ A traditional shoot-out with marauding Apaches, and a thunderous stampede of wild horse were the high points of Gordon Kay's production of **Gunpoint**, in which Audie Murphy (left) played the sheriff of a small Colorado town in pursuit of badman Morgan Woodward. It was filmed on location near St George, Utah, and featured Joan Staley (the only woman in the picture) as a dance hall girl, Warren Stevens (as a saloon keeper, right), Edgar Buchanan (the light relief), and Denver Pyle (as a deputy out to get Murphy's job for himself). Mary and Willard Willingham wrote it and Earl Bellamy directed. (86 mins)

△ The **Incident At Phantom Hill** took place towards the end of the Civil War and it resulted in a million dollars in gold being hi-jacked. Top-starred Robert Fuller, in the company of Jocelyn Lane and bad guy Dan Duryea (left) who knows the gold's whereabouts, is determined to recover it despite all the hazards (which involve crossing the desert and doing battle with Apaches) such an undertaking will entail. Tom Simcox, Linden Chiles, Claude Akins and Noah Beery Jr were also in it for producer Harry Tatelman, and it was directed by Earl Bellamy as if it were nothing special. Which, of course, it wasn't. (Technicolor and Techniscope) (88 mins)

▽ A western spoof out to capture as many laughs as Red Indians, **Texas Across The River** won some and lost some in telling the story of a seasoned Texas cowhand (Dean Martin, right) who needs a well-trained rifleman to accompany him on a gun-exporting expedition into Comanche territory. Instead, he gets an ill-equipped Spanish grandee (Alain Delon, left). Though everything in sight was satirised in the Wells Root-Harold Greene-Ben Starr screenplay, director Michael Gordon couldn't disguise the air of desperation that permeated it all, but he still managed to coax passable performances out of Tina Marquand (daughter of Jean-Pierre Aumont), Michael Ansara, Linden Chiles and Rosemary Forsyth (centre). It was produced in Technicolor by Harry Keller, and its title song, sung by The Kingston Trio, was by Sammy Cahn and Jimmy Van Heusen. (101 mins)

1967

▽ Melodie Johnson had a nude swimming scene in **The Ride To Hangman's Tree** – which was about the best thing on offer in producer Howard Christie's efficient but routine western in which Jack Lord (centre), James Farentino (left) and Don Galloway (right) starred as a trio of likeable bad guys who spend their lives living dangerously. Alan Rafkin directed a screenplay by Luci Ward, Jack Natteford and William Bowers (story by Ward and Natteford) and, in smaller roles, featured Richard Anderson, Robert Yuro, Ed Peck and Paul Reed. It was photographed in Technicolor. (90 mins)

△ Another quickie western, but with even less going for it than *The Ride To Hangman's Tree*, **Gunfight In Abilene** starred Bobby Darin (right) as an ex-Confederate Officer who tries to avoid all contact with guns after accidentally killing a buddy, but is persuaded to resume his old job as sheriff. Emily Banks provided female interest in a predominantly male cast, with other parts going to Leslie Nielsen and Donnelly Rhodes (as the villains), Don Galloway (left), Frank McGrath, and Michael Sarrazin who soon moved on to better things. Berne Giler and John D.F. Black wrote it from a novel by Clarence Upson Young, Howard Christie produced, and William Hale directed. It was a remake of *Showdown At Abilene* (1956). (86 mins)

▽ A remake of *Against All Flags* (1952), **The King's Pirate** starred Doug McClure (left) in the Errol Flynn role and was about the efforts of the British, circa 1700, to put an end to the piratical activities along their lucrative trade route to India. McClure appeared as a Colonial American who makes good his promise to rid the pirate port of Diego Suarez in Madagascar of its bothersome riff-raff, while the ubiquitous Guy Stockwell was cast as a pirate out to stop McClure. Jill St John (right) was the obligatory love interest, Mary Ann Mobley the daughter of the Emperor of India and Kurt Kasznar the helpful leader of an acrobatic troupe who sides with McClure. No one took it seriously, and no one was intended to. It was written by Paul Wayne, Aeneas Mackenzie and Joseph Hoffman, and directed for the mindless escapism it was by Don Weis. The producer was Robert Arthur. (100 mins)

▽ John Wayne (top-billed) and Kirk Douglas made an excellent team in **The War Wagon**, a superior western with a revenge theme which Marvin Schwartz produced for Wayne's Batjac Production company. Framed and sent to jail by bad guy Bruce Cabot, who then appropriated his land and made a fortune in gold, Wayne (right) is hell-bent on revenge. On his release he teams up with Douglas (left), a hired gun and, together with Howard Keel (as an Indian), Robert Walker, Keenan Wynn and Marco Antonio, sets out to relieve Cabot of his fortune. Which is easier said than done as Cabot keeps his loot in an all but impenetrable armour-plated coach with a revolving turret. How Wayne and company eventually succeed, provided the main narrative thrust of Clair Huffaker's first-rate screenplay (based on his novel *Badman*), and it also gave employment to Joanna Barnes as a sexy saloon gal, Gene Evans, Terry Wilson, Valora Noland, and promising newcomer Bruce Dern. Burt Kennedy's solid direction lifted the tale well above the routine. It was lushly photographed in Technicolor and Panavision, and the music was by Dimitri Tiomkin (with Ned Washington supplying the lyrics to the title song). (100 mins)

▽ A one-joke comedy about an astronaut afraid of heights, **The Reluctant Astronaut** starred Don Knotts (illustrated) as the astronaut whose father (Arthur O'Connell), a World War I veteran, involves him in a space programme he could well have lived without. Those not attuned to Mr Knotts' sense of humour and James Stewart-like vocal intonations could also have lived without it. And did. Leslie Nielsen, Joan Freeman, Jesse White, Jeanette Nolan, Frank McGrath and Joan Shawlee comprised the cast; Jim Fritzell and Everett Greenbaum thought it all up, and it was produced (in Technicolor) by Edward J. Montagne, who also directed. (101 mins)

△ **The Perils Of Pauline**, not to be confused with Paramount's superior musical of the same title (1947), was a proposed TV series that was abandoned in favour of a theatrical release. Although on this sorry occasion our heroine (Pamela Austin, right) had nothing whatsoever to do with serial queen Pearl White, she did manage to find herself in some cliff-hanging situations – from being captured by pygmies in Africa (who literally try to cut her down to size – *their* size); to being swept away in a New York sewer. Albert Beich's screenplay (story by Charles W. Goddard) also had Pauline frozen in a deep freeze for twenty-five years, all in the service of a plot which involved top-starred Pat Boone (left) as the richest man in the world and Pauline's most ardent suitor. Edward Everett Horton made an appearance as the 99½-year-old, second richest man in the world, with other parts in Herbert B. Leonard's Eastmancolor production going to Terry-Thomas (as the heavy), Hamilton Camp, Doris Packer, Kurt Kasznar and Vito Scotti. It was jointly directed by producer Leonard, and Joshua Shelley. (98 mins)

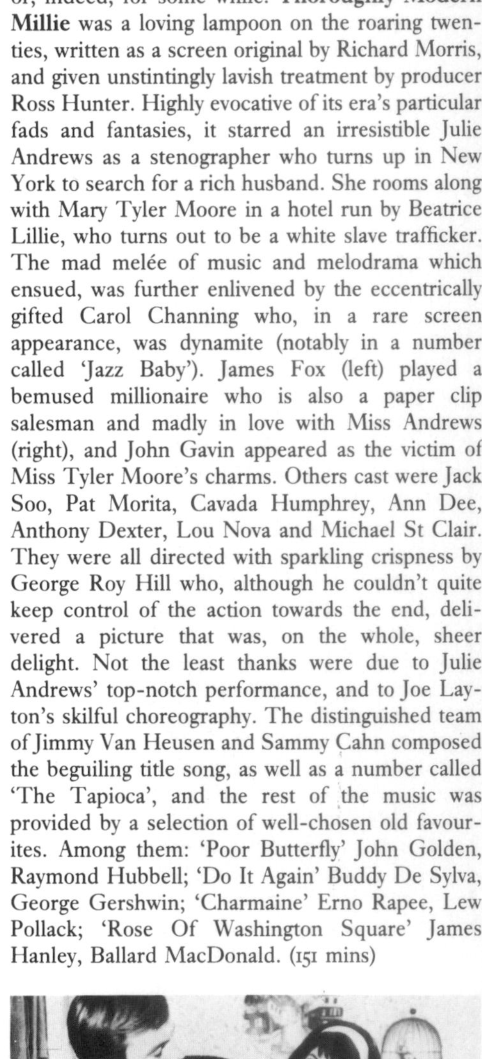

▷ After five non-musical years the studio created the best musical to emerge from Hollywood in 1967 or, indeed, for some while. **Thoroughly Modern Millie** was a loving lampoon on the roaring twenties, written as a screen original by Richard Morris, and given unstintingly lavish treatment by producer Ross Hunter. Highly evocative of its era's particular fads and fantasies, it starred an irresistible Julie Andrews as a stenographer who turns up in New York to search for a rich husband. She rooms along with Mary Tyler Moore in a hotel run by Beatrice Lillie, who turns out to be a white slave trafficker. The mad melée of music and melodrama which ensued, was further enlivened by the eccentrically gifted Carol Channing who, in a rare screen appearance, was dynamite (notably in a number called 'Jazz Baby'). James Fox (left) played a bemused millionaire who is also a paper clip salesman and madly in love with Miss Andrews (right), and John Gavin appeared as the victim of Miss Tyler Moore's charms. Others cast were Jack Soo, Pat Morita, Cavada Humphrey, Ann Dee, Anthony Dexter, Lou Nova and Michael St Clair. They were all directed with sparkling crispness by George Roy Hill who, although he couldn't quite keep control of the action towards the end, delivered a picture that was, on the whole, sheer delight. Not the least thanks were due to Julie Andrews' top-notch performance, and to Joe Layton's skilful choreography. The distinguished team of Jimmy Van Heusen and Sammy Cahn composed the beguiling title song, as well as a number called 'The Tapioca', and the rest of the music was provided by a selection of well-chosen old favourites. Among them: 'Poor Butterfly' John Golden, Raymond Hubbell; 'Do It Again' Buddy De Sylva, George Gershwin; 'Charmaine' Erno Rapee, Lew Pollack; 'Rose Of Washington Square' James Hanley, Ballard MacDonald. (151 mins)

△ Charles Chaplin's last movie, **A Countess From Hong Kong** was inspired by a trip he made to Shanghai in 1931, but there was very little inspiration evident in what one might charitably call an insipid swan song. It starred Marlon Brando and Sophia Loren, and told the old-fashioned story of a Russian emigrée countess (Loren, right) who, after hitting the high spots in Hong Kong one night, stows away in Brando's (left) cabin in the hope of remaining undetected until the ship's arrival in New York. How Miss Loren attempts to keep her presence a secret on board formed the wearisome content of Chaplin's lustreless screenplay. Best moment featured Chaplin himself in a brief walk-on cameo as an elderly steward; second best moment belonged to the redoubtable Margaret Rutherford who, in another cameo appearance, stole the thunder from the film's two big stars playing an eccentric old woman confined to her bed for the duration of the voyage. Chaplin's son Sydney was cast as Brando's cruising companion, with other roles in Jerome Epstein's enervating production going to Tippi Hedren, and to British actors Patrick Cargill, Michael Medwin, Oliver Johnston and Dilys Laye. Chaplin directed and scored it, and it was photographed in Technicolor. (126 mins)

△ A really wretched screenplay by James Lee, based on a story by Hamilton Maule, sabotaged the efforts of Robert Wagner (left), Anjanette Comer (right), Jill St John, Guy Stockwell, James Farentino and Sean Garrison to render plausible the silly things that were done and said in **Banning**. Wagner played the eponymous Banning, an assistant golf pro at a fashionable country club; Stockwell, who's having an affair with Miss Comer, is Wagner's enemy, having once accused him of dishonesty and thereby ruined his career prospects; while Farentino, an ambitious ex-caddy, has his sights set on Wagner's job. Dick Berg's Technicolor production looked a lot better than it sounded, thanks to the reliable art direction of Alexander Golitzen and Henry Bumstead, Jean Louis' gowns and Bud Westmore's make-up. For the record, it was directed by Ron Winston and, in a small role, featured Gene Hackman. (102 mins)

△ Though Rock Hudson received top billing in Gene Corman's big-budget Technicolor-Techniscope World War II melodrama **Tobruk**, it was George Peppard who made the stronger impression. Giving the best performance of his career so far, he played the leader of a German-Jewish convoy who, together with the British, formed a special attack unit with suicidal dangers attending their instructions to destroy Rommel's vital fuel supply at the Mediterranean seaport of Tobruk. Though nothing in director Arthur Hiller's gutsy account of the mission matched the action-filled climax in which the all-important German fuel bunkers are well and truly blitzed, the film rarely lost momentum and sustained interest throughout. Third-billed Nigel Green (left) as the head of the British column made the most of a routine role, and it was to be regretted that the film's anti-Semitic sub-text in which Messrs Hudson (centre) and Green do nothing to hide their feelings towards Peppard (right), was not more fully developed in Leo V. Gordon's screenplay. Guy Stockwell, Jack Watson, Norman Rossington, Percy Herbert, Liam Redmond, Robert Wolders and Henry Rico Cattani completed the cast, and the excellent music score was by Bronislau Kaper. (107 mins)

△ The only unusual thing about **Rough Night In Jericho** was the off-beat casting of genial Dean Martin (right) as an irredeemable bad guy responsible for giving the honest folk of Jericho a hard time with his sadistic shoot-ups, slayings, hangings, and other choice anti-social behaviour. Enter George Peppard (left) as a former deputy US marshal, and in no time at all it's all-out war. Sydney Boehm and Marvin H. Albert's predictable screenplay had parts in it for female lead Jean Simmons (whose stagecoach line is in danger of being appropriated by Martin), John McIntire as an erstwhile marshal, Slim Pickens as a heavy, Don Galloway and Brad Weston. Martin Rackin produced in Techniscope and Technicolor, and the limited direction was by Arnold Leven. (97 mins)

△ **Games**, directed by Curtis Harrington with a clear understanding of the genre and its requirements, was a thriller with a nice, bright sheen to it – despite its predictable climax and denouement. It starred Simone Signoret (right) as an immigrant door-to-door cosmetic saleslady given houseroom by a bored and wealthy Manhatten couple (James Caan, left and Katharine Ross, 2nd left), whose trendy penchant for games-playing ultimately leads to the death of delivery-boy Don Stroud, and to Miss Ross being driven out of her mind. Gene Kearney's screenplay, based on a story by Harrington, signposted most of the plot points long before they happened, thereby minimising the suspense – but not the atmosphere, which was there in abundance, and which helped buttress the rather sloppy plot. Kent Smith played a family lawyer, Estelle Winwood a scatty neighbour, and Ian Wolfe a doctor. Also featured in George Edwards' Techniscope and Technicolor entertainment were George Furth, Marjorie Bennett and Anthony Eustrel. (100 mins)

▽ Not even that wonderful actress Rosalind Russell (right) could rescue **Rosie!** from being a 40-carat stinker. Expanded by Samuel Taylor from Philippe Heriat's play *A Very Rich Woman* which Ruth Gordon adapted into a Broadway flop, it told the who-cares? story of a wealthy widow (à la Auntie Mame) whose greedy daughters confine her to a 'rest home' which vied with Alcatraz for comfort. Naturally, Ros played the put-upon heroine, who gets her revenge after a climactic courtroom showdown. It was produced by Jacques Mapes for Ross Hunter productions, with a supporting cast that included Sandra Dee, Brian Aherne, James Farentino (left), Leslie Nielsen, Reginald Owen, Margaret Hamilton, and, as the grasping daughters, Audrey Meadows and Vanessa Brown – an excellent line-up of talent that deserved far better than this. David Lowell Rich directed. (Technicolor) (98 mins)

▽ Yet another TV-pilot-turned-movie, **Sullivan's Empire** was an academic adventure yarn which asked audiences to believe that three sons, abandoned by their powerful father in infancy, would risk their lives in a series of cliff-hanging episodes when news reaches them that he is missing in the Brazilian interior. Braving Izo head-hunting Indians and ferocious beasts, they embark on a search which, among other things, involved a guerilla revolutionist embezzler, and all because of the respect they still feel for their proud, strong-willed if neglectful, old man (Arch Johnson). Martin Milner, Linden Chiles (foreground left) and Don Quine (standing left) played the sons (and did not show a spark of acting talent among them), with other roles in Frank Price's cut-rate production going to Karen Jensen, Clu Gulager and Bernie Hamilton. Frank Chase wrote it and it was directed by Harvey Hart and Thomas Carr. (Color) (85 mins)

◁ Trading in clichés, producer Gordon Kay's programmer war story, shot entirely on the backlot, but with excellent Technicolor camerawork from Loyal Griggs going some distance to disguise the fact that it was all assembled on a shoestring budget, **The Young Warriors** took a superficial look at the effects war has on young men. The young men in question were Jonathan Daly, Robert Pine, Michael Stanwood, Jeff Scott, Steve Carlson (right) and Tom Nolan and, in the service of Richard Matheson's woolly screenplay, they emerged as stereotypes to a man. TV star James Drury (left) was top-billed as a sergeant and, being the most seasoned performer on view, was also the best thing in the show. John Peyser directed. (93 mins)

1968

▽ John Wayne (left) played a fire-fighter in **Hellfighters**. Not just any old fire-fighter, but a specialist in oil-well conflagrations. And in the course of Robert Arthur's action-filled production he doused several such blazes in various parts of the world, climaxing in no fewer than five simultaneous infernos in Venezuela. On the domestic front, the fires that raged were all romantic, involving, as they did, Wayne's erstwhile wife Vera Miles (who couldn't take her spouse's dangerous way of life); and the marriage of Wayne's assistant, Jim Hutton (right), to his lovely daughter (Katharine Ross, centre). Clair Huffaker's screenplay was based on incidents in the life of fire-fighter 'Red' Adair (who served as technical adviser), and the excellent special effects were the work of Fred Knoth, who came out of retirement to create them. It was photographed in Technicolor and Panavision, featured Jay C. Flippen, Bruce Cabot, Edward Faulkner and Barbara Stuart, and was directed for the all out macho actioner it was by Andrew V. McLaglen. (122 mins)

▽ Kirk Douglas (right) was top-starred in **A Lovely Way To Die**, a thriller of no consequence whatsoever in which he played an ex-cop who becomes the bodyguard of Sylva Koscina (left), a glamorous young woman accused (incorrectly, as it turns out) of murdering her husband. Directed on location in New York, and with no sense of purpose at all, by David Lowell Rich, it also featured Eli Wallach, Kenneth Haigh, Martyn Green, Sharon Farrell and Gordon Peters. They should all have stayed at home. Richard Lewis produced and it was written by A.J. Russell. (104 mins)

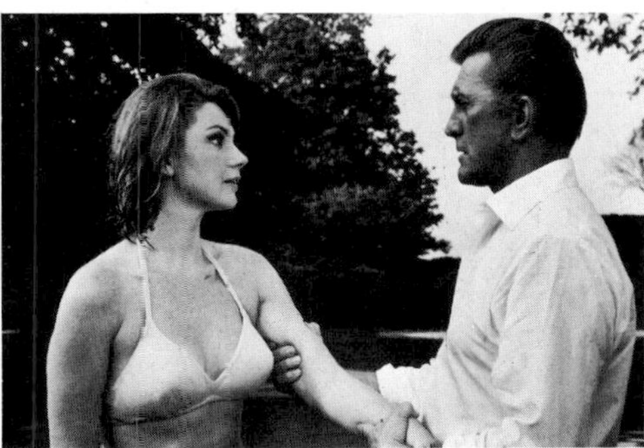

▽ **Don't Just Stand There** certainly had pace but, in the end, Stan Margulies' production didn't go anywhere special. Its uncomfortably contrived story (adapted by Charles Williams from his novel *The Wrong Venus*) featured Robert Wagner (left) as a dilettante American writer who, after trying to smuggle watches from Zurich to Paris, accepts an assignment to complete the final chapters of a sex novel by authoress Glynis Johns (right), who turns to archaeology as soon as she learns about sex first-hand. Also cast was Amazonian Barbara Rhoades as a judo expert with an insatiable appetite (who also does a spot of ghost-writing for Miss Johns), with other parts in this moderately amusing romp going to Harvey Korman as Miss Johns' business manager, Vincent Beck, Joseph Perry and Stuart Margolin. Ron Winston directed. (Technicolor). (97 mins)

▽ The combination of Clint Eastwood and director Don Siegel proved explosive in **Coogan's Bluff**, a hard-hitting police melodrama in which law enforcement as practised in the old west and its more sophisticated urban counterpart, clashed forcibly. Eastwood (right) played a sheriff from Arizona who is sent to New York to extradite hippie Don Stroud for an unspecified crime; Lee J. Cobb was the city detective whose methods are vastly different from those of Eastwood's. How the taciturn out-of-towner eventually apprehends Stroud after the latter's escape, provided the violent content of Herman Miller, Dean Riesner and Howard Rodman's no-punches-pulled screenplay (story by Miller) which might have been improved by putting more flesh on to its central character rather than taking it off his victims! In a cast that also included Susan Clark as a probation officer who falls for Clint, Tisha Sterling (daughter of Ann Sothern and Robert Sterling) as Stroud's girlfriend, and Betty Field as his mother – the standout performance was Cobb's. Siegel also produced (the executive producer was Richard E. Lyons), in Technicolor. (93 mins)

◁ Espionage was the main item on the agenda in **In Enemy Country**, in which Tony Franciosa (front right) starred as a French intelligence colonel involved in a plot to destroy a new type of German torpedo. Anjanette Comer was second-billed as a French spy, and Guy Stockwell (left) third-billed as Franciosa's American aide. Tom Bell played a British demolition expert, with Paul Hubschmid, as a German Intelligence Officer, completing the main line-up. A respectable, though uninspired, adventure, it was produced and directed by Harry Keller (in Techniscope and Technicolor), and written with few concessions to originality by Edward Anhalt (from a story by Sy Bartlett). The cast was completed by Michael Constantine, Harry Townes, John Marley, Milton Seltzer and Patric Knowles. (106 mins)

△ The answer to **Did You Hear The One About The Travelling Saleslady?** was yes – way back in 1956 when RKO presented the same material under the title *The First Travelling Saleslady* (starring Ginger Rogers and Carol Channing). This time out, comedienne Phyllis Diller (centre) headed the cast, playing a female saleslady, circa 1910, who arrives in a small Missouri town intent on selling recalcitrant pianolas – which she does with a bit of help from the town's local inventor (Bob Denver). Unfortunately, director Don Weis was unable to remove the straitjacket from John Fenton Murray's silly screenplay (story by Jim Fritzell and Everett Greenbaum), which at one point had an automatic milk machine causing a cow stampede. Joe Flynn (left) played a Scrooge-like banker, with other parts in Si Rose and Edward J. Montagne's production going to Eileen Wesson, Jeanette Nolan and Paul Reed. It was photographed in Technicolor and Techniscope. (95 mins)

△ A relentlessly second-rate melodrama, **The Hell With Heroes** featured Rod Taylor (right) and Peter Deuel as a couple of former United States airmen who, in the midst of unprofitably operating an air cargo service, find themselves smuggling contraband cigarettes to France for an unscrupulous racketeer (Harry Guardino). When the situation looks serious for the boys, Deuel approaches Kevin McCarthy of US Counter Intelligence for help. Claudia Cardinale (left) played Guardino's mistress (who falls in love with Taylor as a prelude to a happy ending), with other parts under Joseph Sargent's direction going to William Marshall, Don Knight, Michael Shillo and Robert Yuro. Stanley Chase produced, and it was scripted by Halsted Welles and Harold Livingston from a story by Livingston. (102 mins)

▷ Doris Day (illustrated centre) took to the Wild West in the Wyoming of the 1890s and, wearing men's clothes, proved in **The Ballad of Josie** that women were just as good at raising sheep as men. Trouble is, her run-down farm is in cattle territory, which causes something of a ruckus among the locals. Not being one to turn her back on trouble (in the opening of the film she is accused of killing her husband with a billiard cue after he arrives home drunk – and is acquitted), she involves herself in local politics and women's suffrage, proving the equal of any of the males around. And they included Peter Graves and George Kennedy as the good and bad guy respectively, Andy Devine as a judge, William Talman as an attorney, David Hartman as a sheriff and Guy Raymond as a doctor. Teddy Quinn played Miss Day's eight-year-old son, with other parts in Norman MacDonnell's production (executive producer Martin Melcher) going to Audrey Christie as the madame of a 'boarding-house', Timothy Scott, Don Stroud and Paul Fix. The so-so screenplay was by Harold Swanton, and the workmanlike direction by Andrew V. McLaglen who convincingly captured the rough and tumble of frontier life. (Technicolor). (102 mins)

▽ A feature initially intended for television but withdrawn because of its emphasis on psychedelic acid, **Jigsaw**, produced by Ranald MacDougall, had too many pieces missing to emerge as anything but an infuriatingly 'arty' retread of Edward Dymytryk's *Mirage* (1965). Here, an acid trip was substituted for the earlier film's amnesia theme, and the killer was revealed to the audience early on in the proceedings. Bradford Dillman (left) played the acid-imbibing hero, Harry Guardino (centre) was a private eye who's gathered most of his methods from old Bogart movies and Diana Hyland was his good-looking girlfriend, with other roles going to such top-notch players as Pat Hingle, Hope Lange (right), Victor Jory, Paul Stewart and Michael J. Pollard. It was directed by James Goldstone as if it were one long psychedelic trip itself. Rarely had viewers been subjected to so many frontal attacks of distorted angles, image-blurring filters, multiple exposures and jump cuts, when what was really needed in the circumstances was some uncluttered, straightforward story-telling. The complicated writing credits were divided between Quentin Werty, who provided the story and screenplay, Peter Stone, on whose earlier screenplay it was based, and Howard Fast whose novel *Fallen Angel* was the original inspirational source. It was photographed in Technicolor. (97 mins)

△ Tennessee Williams's ailing drama *The Milk Train Doesn't Stop Here Anymore* went through several re-writes and several cast changes (Hermione Baddeley and Paul Roebling were in it, then Tallulah Bankhead and Tab Hunter) in its halting progress to Broadway. In no version, however, did it succeed in being anything other than a mediocre parody of the playwright's earlier, more impressive work – and the screen version, whose title was shortened to **Boom**, was equally disastrous. Apart from the basic material itself ('opened out' for the Panavision screen by Williams himself), John Heyman's opulent production never recovered (either artistically or at the box office) from the miscasting of Elizabeth Taylor as Flora Goforth, the wealthy six-times married central character; and her then husband Richard Burton as Chris Flanders, a poet gigolo who carries with him the spectre of death. Taylor wasn't old enough for her role; Burton (right) was too old for his – which left the acting honours to Noel Coward (left) as The Witch of Capri, whose all-too-brief appearances enlivened an extremely pretentious drama. Joanna Shimkus played Taylor's efficient secretary; Michael Dunn was her bodyguard. It was directed by Joseph Losey, and designed by Richard MacDonald whose settings, against a spectacular Sardinian back drop, were the best thing in the show. (Technicolor). (112 mins)

△ A comedy with a navy setting, **Nobody's Perfect** was the seen-it-all-before account of Chief Petty Officer Doc Willoughby's numerous antics – all of which, presumably, were intended by scriptwriter John D.F. Black to make one laugh. What they actually induced was *ennui*, as Doug McClure (playing the CPO, right) involved himself in a number of 'incidents', including sprinkling cockroaches all over his meticulous skipper's cabin. He also rescues a Japanese diver and wins a medal for bravery. So it goes and so it went. Nancy Kwan (left) provided some oriental glamour as a nurse, with other roles under Alan Rafkin's undistinguished direction going to James Whitmore (as the skipper), David Hartmann, Gary Vinson James Shigeta and George Furth. It was produced by Howard Christie in Technicolor. (103 mins)

◁ The best thing about **Counterpoint** was the music it featured (courtesy of the Los Angeles Philharmonic Orchestra), with extracts from Schubert's 'Unfinished' Symphony, Wagner's 'Tannhauser' Overture, Tchaikovsky's 'Swan Lake' Ballet, Brahms' Symphony No 1 (fourth movement), and the first movement of Beethoven's Sympahony No 5. For the rest, Dick Berg's Techniscope and Technicolor production was a rather lukewarm battle of wills between orchestral conductor Charlton Heston (illustrated) who, together with his orchestra of 70 players, is captured by the Germans in Belgium during The Battle of the Bulge; and Maximilian Schell (seated centre right), a music-loving general who threatens to kill Heston and his orchestra at the conclusion of a concert. A surprise attack from a group of partisans saved the day but not, alas, the film – though it was refreshing to see Heston as a 20th-century character, free of period costume. James Lee and Joel Oliansky's screenplay, from the novel *The General* by Alan Sillitoe, provided the requisite amount of suspense (though not much else), as well as parts for Leslie Nielsen as the concert master, Kathryn Hays as his cellist wife and Anton Diffring in his familiar guise as a German colonel. (105 mins)

△ Director Don Siegel toned down his characteristic over-generous ladlings of sex and violence in **Madigan**, a cop melodrama cast from strength with Richard Widmark (right) top-lining as the titular hero – a tough New York detective who, together with Harry Guardino, is out to apprehend a dangerous criminal. Henry Fonda and James Whitmore played Widmark's superiors, Inger Stevens was his socialite wife, and Susan Clark Fonda's intelligent mistress. Henri Simoun and Abraham Polonsky's screenplay (from the novel *The Commissioner* by Richard Dougherty) provided an almost documentary look at the inner workings of police procedure in general and one case in particular, as well as the obligatory glimpses into the private lives of the cops concerned. Frank P. Rosenberg produced in Techniscope and Technicolor and, in supporting roles, featured Don Stroud, Michael Dunn, Steve Ihnat, Raymond St Jacques, Lloyd Gough and Sheree North (left). The film provided the inspiration for a later TV series, also starring Widmark as Madigan. (101 mins)

△ There were so many holes in scenarist Philip Reisman Jr's screenplay (story by Reisman and producer Edward J. Montagne) that it might have been put to better use as a colander. A melodrama with the accent on violence, **P.J.** starred George Peppard (illustrated) as a private eye hired to act as bodyguard to the wife of a wealthy businessman. Or was he simply hired to be the patsy in a murder involving the businessman's assistant? Audiences were not quite sure. Raymond Burr appeared as the tycoon, Gayle Hunnicutt was the wife he enjoys humiliating, and Brock Peters a Bahaman chief of police. Also cast: Wilfrid Hyde-White, Susan Saint James, Jason Evers, Coleen Grey and Severn Dardern. John Guillermin's direction made the most of the muddled goings on, and it was photographed in Technicolor. (109 mins)

◁ Politics, intrigue, romance and adventure all jostled for pride of place in **The Pink Jungle** – a satire of sorts on politics, intrigue, romance and adventure. Set in a mythical South American jungle where top fashion photographer James Garner (left) is hoping to shoot a lipstick layout with model Eva Renzi, the plot (courtesy of Charles Williams who scripted from the novel *Snake Water* by Alan Williams) found its leading man in a series of incidents involving the murder of a helicopter pilot, being mistaken for a CIA agent, and the discovery of a diamond mine. Intermittently amusing, and with an excellent comic performance from the usually serious George Kennedy (right, as an adventurer), Stan Margulies' Technicolor production was nothing to be ashamed of, and also featured Nigel Green, Michael Ansara and George Rose. Delbert Mann's direction more than gave the material its due. (104 mins)

▽ 'Dull, talky and pretentious' was how one reviewer at the time described **Journey To Shiloh**, and few disagreed. It was also ineptly directed (by William Hale), flabbily written (by Gene Coon, from the novel *Field of Honor* by Will Henry), and flat-footedly performed by a cast that included James Caan (right), Michael Sarrazin (2nd left), Brenda Scott, Don Stroud, Paul Petersen, Michael Burns, Jan Michael Vincent (left), Harrison Ford (2nd right – who would later become a major star in *Star Wars*, 20th Century-Fox, 1977), John Doucette and Noah Beery Jr. All about the derring-do efforts of seven men, collectively known as the Concho County Comanches, who undertake a cross-country journey in order to join the Confederate army (and who are killed more or less in reverse order of their billing), it also touched on such topics as racial and class prejudice, and the evils of war. Howard Christie's production gave new definition to the word banal. (Technicolor and Techniscope.) (101 mins)

▽ If the goings-on in **The Shakiest Gun In The West** seemed familiar, they were. A remake of Paramount's 1948 smash, *The Paleface*, it starred Don Knotts (right) in the Bob Hope role and newcomer Barbara Rhoades (left), a statuesque 5′ 11″ redhead in the part played by Jane Russell. As in the earlier film, the storyline (based on a screenplay by Edmund Hartmann and Frank Tashlin) had dentist Knotts arriving in the Wild West and becoming romantically linked with a lady highway bandit, who's trying to earn a pardon by blocking the shipment of guns to Indians. As in the 1948 version, the lady bandit saves the dentist from several perilous situations, allowing him in each instance to believe that he is the hero. Jim Fritzell and Everett Greenbaum's refurbished (though not improved) screenplay found work for Jackie Coogan, Donald Barry, Ruth McDevitt, Frank McGrath, Terry Wilson and Carl Ballantine; it was produced by Edward J. Montagne (in Technicolor and Techniscope); and directed by Alan Rafkin who brought nothing new to the familiar material. (100 mins)

△ Paul Newman (right), never at his best in comedy, starred as Harry Frigg in **The Secret War Of Harry Frigg**, playing a none-too-bright army private who, in the guise of a general, is sent to rescue five captured generals. The quintet were represented by Andrew Duggan, Tom Bosley, Charles D. Gray, John Williams and Jacques Roux; their Italian captor was Vito Scotti (left), and the US general responsible for the rescue scheme was James Gregory. In common with the character of its leading man, the screenplay by the Oscar-winning team of Peter Stone and Frank Tarloff (story by Tarloff) was none too bright either; nor was the direction by Jack Smight, which suffered from extensive studio interference. Sylva Koscina was the only woman in the cast, and helped slow down the plot considerably in her romantic interludes with Newman. Hal E. Chester produced in Technicolor and Techniscope. (110 mins)

▽ Based on an incident in Vincent McHugh's novel *I Am Thinking Of My Darling*, and fashioned into a screenplay by George Seaton (who also produced and directed) and Robert Pirosh, **What's So Bad About Feeling Good?** was a pleasant fantasy about a toucan who arrives in New York by ship carrying a contagious 'happy' virus which first infects George Peppard, and is then passed on to the whole of New York. It was a nice idea that needed a sharper script to realise its potential, but which benefitted enormously from the performances of Peppard (centre), Mary Tyler Moore (right), Dom DeLuise, John McMartin, Susan St James, Peter Gumeny (left) and Don Stroud. Thelma Ritter, whom Seaton directed in her screen debut (*Miracle On 34th Street*, 20th Century-Fox, 1947), made an unbilled appearance. It was photographed in Technicolor and Techniscope. (94 mins)

1969

▽ Elmer Rice's expressionist play **The Adding Machine**, first produced in 1923, was the story of a nonentity called Mr Zero who, after being replaced in his clerical job by a machine, rebels by stabbing his boss, is executed for murder, goes to heaven where he finds himself working with the same kind of depersonalized machine that caused all the trouble in the first place, and returns to earth. Jerome Epstein's production, which he also adapted and directed, eliminated the expressionist feel of the original play, treating it instead as a *nouvelle vague* fantasy. He assembled a cast headed by Phyllis Diller (left) as Mrs Zero and Milo O'Shea (right) as her husband, and which also featured Billie Whitelaw, Sydney Chaplin, Julian Glover and Raymond Huntley. All appeared uncomfortable in their roles. (100 mins)

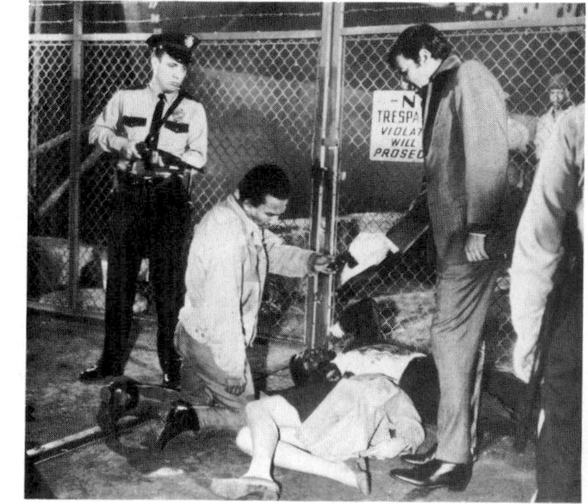

△ 'Porous sociology' was how one reviewer described **The Lost Man**, which starred Sidney Poitier as a laid-back black militant of the Malcolm X variety who unsuccessfully attempts to rob an all-white factory. The repercussions of the botched heist formed the basis of a screenplay by Robert Alan Aurthur (based on F.L. Green's novel, *Odd Man Out*, filmed with James Mason in 1947 by Two Cities) which served to examine black-white relationships and, more specifically, black militant behaviour. As written by Aurthur (who also directed), the themes explored pulled their punches, thus doing irreparable damage to the project's underlying purpose. At the end, for example, it is revealed that the reason for the robbery had nothing to do with Poitier's militancy, but was intended to help him find the children of his jailed 'brothers'. Joanna Shimkus co-starred as a white social worker and Poitier's lover-cum-accomplice; with other roles in the Edward Muhl-Melville Tucker Technicolor production going to Al Freeman Jr (kneeling centre), Michael Tolan, Leon Bibb and Richard Dysart. The excellent music score was by Quincy Jones. (122 mins)

▽ After an eight-year absence from the screen, during which time he concentrated on making a name for himself in television, Andy Griffith (centre) returned in **Angel In My Pocket**, a programmer which may have appealed to audiences in the Ozarks, but held little allure for sophisticates. All about the trials and tribulations of a married, small-town minister (Griffith) whose congregation is divided into two warring factions, its screenplay by Jim Fritzell and Everett Greenbaum was simply not inventive enough to support its slender narrative, nor as funny as it needed to be. Alan Rafkin's relentlessly folksy direction underlined the basic deficiencies in both the writing and characterisations, with end results that were, to say the least, dispiriting. Lee Meriweather (centre right) made little impression as Griffith's wife, and from Jerry Van Dyke and Kay Medford came merely caricatures. Completing the cast for Edward J. Montagne (who produced in Technicolor and Techniscope) were Henry Jones, Edgar Buchanan, Gary Collins and Parker Fennelly. (105 mins)

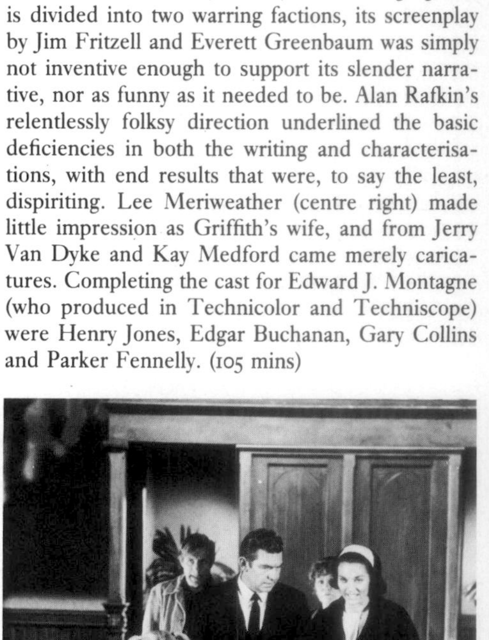

▽ Sufferers from aelurophobia (fear of cats) stayed away from **Eye Of The Cat** in droves. They missed little, for it was a poorly-plotted thriller which starred Michael Sarrazin (left) as the nephew of a wealthy San Francisco invalid who, in cahoots with pretty beautician Gayle Hunnicut (right), plots to do away with his aunt. There is only one complication, though: the aunt, played by Eleanor Parker, is surrounded by dozens of cats to which Sarrazin has a distinct aversion. Joseph Stefano's screenplay posed more questions than it ultimately answered – one of the main ones being why a woman as stunningly attractive (and as rich) as Miss Parker should, in the context of the story, have no friends, no servants and, considering that she only possesses a third of a lung, no nurse in attendance. The one person ministering to her needs is Sarrazin's younger brother (Tim Henry) whom Parker unreasonably loathes. David Lowell Rich's uneven direction never lived up to the stunning opening credits and failed to generate the kind of tension needed to help plug the holes in the plot. Laurence Naismith, Jennifer Leak, Linden Chiles and Mark Herron were also featured, and it was produced by Bernard Schwartz and Philip Hazelton (for Joseph J. Schenck Enterprises) in Technicolor. (102 mins)

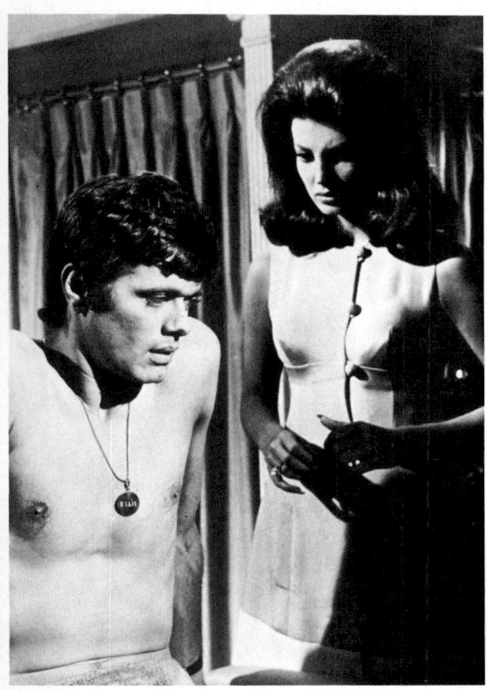

◁ Based on the play by Maxwell Anderson, adapted by Richard Sokolove and scripted by Bridget Boland and John Hale, **Anne Of The Thousand Days** was a prestige production with a capital 'P' from producer Hal B. Wallis. Photographed by Arthur Ibbotson in Panavision and Technicolor on location in England, it recruited an excellent cast to tell the fmiliar story of King Henry VIII's courtship of Anne Boleyn while still married to Katherine of Aragon, the severing of his ties with Rome after he divorces Katherine and marries Anne, their 1000 days together before her beheading, and the execution of Sir Thomas More. Richard Burton (left) in marvellous vocal form played the King, Genevieve Bujold (centre) made a sprightly Anne, and Irene Pappas was suitably gloomy as the dejected Katherine, with other roles under Charles Jarrott's cautious direction going to Anthony Quayle (as Cardinal Wolsey), John Colicos (as Cromwell), Michael Hordern (as Thomas Boleyn), Katherine Blake (Mrs Charles Jarrott in real-life, as Elizabeth Boleyn), and William Squire (as Sir Thomas More). The predominantly British cast also included Vernon Dobtcheff, Gary Bond (right), Denis Quilley, Esmond Knight and T.P. McKenna. The music was by George Delerue. (145 mins)

△ Richard Widmark's tough, hard-bitten performance was the best thing in, and the *raison d'être* for **Death Of A Gunfighter**, a western in which he played a small-town marshal with a dozen killings to his name, who falls out of favour with a group of local city councillors, all of whom want him removed. But how? Only one way, they decide: gun him down ... Lena Horne (left) co-starred as a coloured madame who eventually marries Widmark (right) after being his mistress, and while it was nice to welcome her back to the screen after a 12-year absence, it was a shame that the role was not more substantial; though she did sing one song, 'Sweet Apple Wine' (by Oliver Nelson and Carol Hall). Carroll O'Connor played a troublesome saloon keeper, John Saxon a sheriff; Kent Smith, Larry Gates and Morgan Woodward were adversaries of Widmark, with other roles in Richard E. Lyons' Technicolor production going to Dub Taylor, Jacqueline Scott and James Lydon. Joseph Calvelli's screenplay, from a novel by Lewis B. Patten, milked the situation for as much action as possible; ditto Allen Smithee's direction. (94 mins)

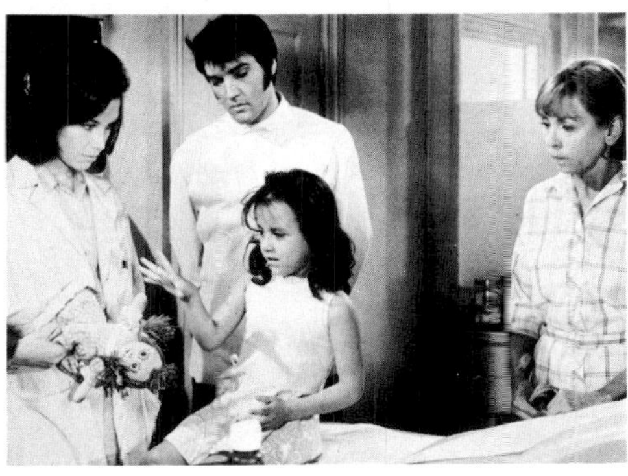

△ Elvis Presley (centre) was hardly ideal casting as a doctor who heads a clinic in a Puerto Rican slum neighbourhood. But that's how it was in **Change Of Habit** – entertainment for all the family, whose main plot point focussed on the arrival at the clinic of three women assistants who, unknown to Presley, are nuns in mufti. Mary Tyler Moore (left), a speech therapist, is the nun Presley finds himself attracted to; the other two sisters were played by Barbara McNair and Jane Elliott. Six-year-old Lorena Kirk (seated centre) was excellent as one of Presley's problem patients, with other roles in Joe Connelly's Technicolor production going to Edward Asner, Robert Emhardt, Regis Toomey, Virginia Vincent (right) and Nefti Millet. William Graham directed. Songs: 'Change of Habit', 'Rubberneckin'', 'Let Us Pray' Buddy Kaye, Ben Weisman. (93 mins)

▽ **The Love God?** was a tasteless Don Knotts vehicle which silent comedian Harold Lloyd would have handled more amusingly. Nat Hiken, who wrote and directed it, was unable to animate a situation in which leading man Knotts (illustrated), a virgin, inadvertently finds himself a sex hero when the bird-watching magazine he edits is bought by con-man Edmond O'Brien and turned into a girlie mag. Anne Francis co-starred as a slick editor, with other roles going to James Gregory, Maureen Arthur, Maggie Peterson, Jesslyn Fax and Jacques Aubuchon. It was produced, in Technicolor, by Edward J. Montagne. (101 mins)

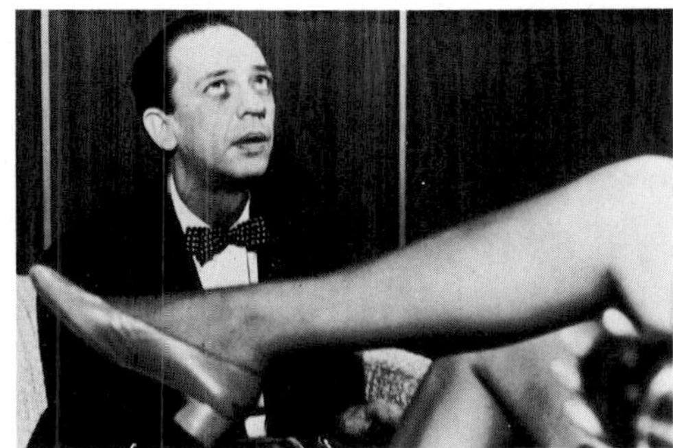

▽ Marlon Brando starred in a non-starter called **The Night Of The Following Day** in which a quartet of kidnappers, having abducted a rich little girl, fall out amongst themselves then resort to murder. Brando (left) was the leader of the operation, his accomplices were Richard Boone (centre), Rita Moreno and Jess Hahn; and the kidnapped girl Pamela Franklin (right). Hubert Cornfield, who produced and directed, also adapted it (from a novel by Lionel White), for executive producers Jerry Gershwin and Elliott Kastner's Gina Productions. (93 mins)

▽ Tony Franciosa (left) was **A Man Called Gannon**, a Kansas plains drifter as adept with his gun as he is with his fists who, as part of Gene Kearney, Borden Chase and D.D. Beauchamp's screenplay (based on Dee Linford's novel *Man Without A Star*), finds himself teaching brash young Michael Sarrazin (right) from the East the finer points of cow-pokery. They're also involved with widow woman Judi West on whose ranch they find employment. It was all numbingly familiar and, as directed by James Goldstone, held few surprises. Susan Oliver, John Anderson and David Sheiner were also featured, and it was produced in Technicolor and Techniscope by Howard Christie. (105 mins)

▽ **Topaz**, a Hitchcock thriller with several of the maestro's cinematic trademarks but none of his magic, opened dazzlingly enough with the defection of a Russian scientist in Copenhagen to the CIA, but never lived up to its initial ten minutes. Despite the twists and counter-twists elaborated upon in Samuel Taylor's screenplay (from the best-selling novel by Leon Uris), the plot failed to gather momentum, leaving the main question posed by the story, ie which members of 'Topaz' (the code name for a Russian spy ring operating from inside the French government) are betraying French security – dangling rather limply amidst much double crossing and intrigue. A not particularly memorable cast was headed by Frederick Stafford (right) as a French security investigator, with other parts assigned to Dany Robin, John Vernon, Karin Dor, John Forsythe (left) and the always reliable French stars Michel Piccoli and Philippe Noiret. Hitchcock produced (in Technicolor) and shot three different endings – an infallible sign that all was not well. (126 mins)

▽ Susan Clark (right) again surfaced in **Colossus, The Forbin Project** (also known as **The Forbin Project**), and again played a scientist but, like her co-star Eric Braeden (left), was upstaged by a computer called Colossus which has been programmed to take charge of the entire American missile defence system. Main thrust of James Bridges' screenplay (based on the novel *Colossus* by D.F. Jones) was what happens when the giant computer merges with its Russian equivalent called Guardian, and blackmails the universe into computer-controlled peace. By combining elements of suspense, science fiction, humour and satire, director Joseph Sargeant emerged with a tautly turned out sleeper which benefitted immeasurably from Alexander Golitzen's imaginative art direction, Albert Whitlock's special photographic effects, Michael Colombier's electronic score, and Walden O. Watson's computer sound effects. The undistinguished cast assembled by producer Stanley Chase included Gordon Pinsent, William Schallert and Leonid Rostoff. (100 mins)

◁ Though little more than a romantic triangle, **Three Into Two Won't Go** benefitted from an intelligent screenplay by Edna O'Brien (from the novel by Andrea Newman) that managed to be both literate and 'conversational' at the same time; and from a quartet of fine performances by Rod Steiger, Claire Bloom, Judy Geeson and Peggy Ashcroft. Steiger (left) played a career-conscious salesman, Miss Bloom his childless wife, Geeson (right) the sexy 19-year-old hitchhiker who seduces Steiger on one of his overnight trips, and Dame Peggy Bloom's neurotic mother. The ambiguities manifested by all four characters provided a basically routine situation with its resonance and, under Peter Hall's direction, the cast sparkled. Also in it were Paul Rogers, Lynn Farleigh, Elizabeth Spriggs and Sheila Allen. Julian Blaustein produced and it was filmed in Technicolor. (94 mins)

▷ **Winning** was a winner all the way. A gripping drama with an auto racing backdrop, it divided its time equally between the milieu in which it was set and the personal relationships of the characters involved, and offered husband and wife team Paul Newman and Joanne Woodward the best parts they had had in years. Newman (left) played an ace racer, Woodward a widow with a 13-year-old son, whom he marries then neglects. The villain of the piece was Robert Wagner (right), with whom Miss Woodward has a one-off affair, with other roles in producer John Foreman's first-class production (in Technicolor and Panavision) going to Richard Thomas as the teenage son (a marvellous performance), David Sheiner, Clu Gulager, Barry Ford and Toni Clayton. Howard Rodman wrote it amusingly and observantly – two long-distance calls between Newman and Woodward being especially outstanding; and it was directed by James Goldstone, whose semi-documentary handling of the races themselves, particularly the climactic Indianapolis 500 with its spectacular 17-car pile-up at its start, was positively thrilling. (123 mins)

UNION
Autolite
Lou

◁ Broadway stage director and ace choreographer Bob Fosse made his screen directorial debut with the celluloid version of his smash stage hit **Sweet Charity**, but his imagination and skill responded to Hollywood with bouts of showy self-indulgence which failed to do full justice to the superb material of the original. Shirley MacLaine starred as Charity, a hostess in a sleazy New York dance hall, who dreams of better things such as old-fashioned romance and blissful domesticity, but succeeds in being jilted by all her prospective partners. Miss MacLaine (centre) amply demonstrated her versatility, as well as her ebullient energy, although the latter quality proved a mite strident for the delicacy of the story, which was based on Fellini's moving *Nights Of Cabiria* (1957). Nonetheless, the musical was packed with good things, thanks to its vibrant score (by Cy Coleman and Dorothy Fields), some memorable choreographic highspots, and a first-rate supporting cast. The hit number was the dynamic 'Hey Big Spender', with standouts Chita Rivera (2nd left) and Paula Kelly. Other treats were 'The Rich-man's Frug' and 'The Hustle', performed by a glitzy chorus line in a ritzy nightspot, 'There's Got To Be Something Better Than This', sung and danced with vertiginous verve on a rooftop by MacLaine, Kelly and Rivera, and the rumbustious 'I'm A Brass Band' which set off both Fosse and MacLaine's particular gifts to good advantage. Sammy Davis Jr, as a fringe-religion evangelist led 'The Rhythm Of Life' with evident zest, and MacLaine's 'If They Could See Me Now' routine, performed in the apartment of a matinee idol (Ricardo Montalban), was almost a showstopper. The screenplay was by Peter Stone, based on the book by Neil Simon, and a screenplay by Federico Fellini, Tullio Pinelli and Ennio Flaiano. Robert Arthur produced, and others featured in the cast included Stubby Kaye (who, as Herman the dance hall employee, sang 'I Love To Cry At Weddings'), John McMartin (Charity's short-lived fiance, who warbled the title number), Barbara Bouchet, Alan Hewitt, Dante De Paulo, John Wheeler and John Craig. (133 mins)

△ As very little actual footage of Isadora Duncan exists, it is impossible to know just how accurate a portrait of this extraordinary 'Free Spirit' Vanessa Redgrave (illustrated) painted of her in director Karel Reisz's **The Loves Of Isadora** (GB: **Isadora**). True, Miss Redgrave's dancing wasn't up to much but, in the end, that didn't really matter. Her achievement lay in her ability to convey the essence of her subject's persona, and in this respect alone the film emerged triumphant. Conceived by scenarists Melvyn Bragg and Clive Exton (from Bragg's adaptation of Duncan's *My Life*, and Sewell Stokes' *Isadora Duncan, An Intimate Portrait*) as a memoir being dictated by Isadora at the Negresco Hotel in Nice, it began with the young Isadora burning her parents' marriage licence in San Francisco and dedicating her life to Art and Beauty. We then see her dancing her way to stardom and notoriety, with pauses between public engagements to take a succession of lovers, the most meaningful of whom were Paris Singer (Jason Robards), Gordon Craig (James Fox) and Essenin (Ivan Tchenko), the Russian poet whom she married. The incandescent Miss Redgrave successfully upstaged them all – as Isadora probably did in real life as well. Robert and Raymond Hakim produced, and their cast included John Fraser, Bessie Love, Cynthia Harris, Libby Glenn and Tony Vogel. (128 mins)

▽ **Secret Ceremony**, stylishly directed by Joseph Losey, was a psychological thriller of sorts which starred Elizabeth Taylor as an ageing prostitute who has never been able to come to grips with the death of her daughter; and Mia Farrow (right) as a wealthy, incest-prone nymphomaniac who 'kidnaps' Miss Taylor and moulds her into the role of her dead mother. Both women's psychological needs are thus satisfied. With the arrival of Robert Mitchum (left), Miss Farrow's step-father, the situation takes an even more bizarre turn as we learn that Farrow was responsible for the break-up of Mitchum's marriage because she seduced him. The climax sees Taylor knifing Mitchum to death in front of Farrow's coffin, Farrow having taken her own life by overdosing on sleeping pills. As scripted by George Tabori (from a short story by Marco Denevi) and performed by a cast that also included Peggy Ashcroft and Pamela Brown as a pair of masculine antique-collecting aunts, the film wielded a certain fascination and made for compulsive viewing, even though it may not have added up to very much. John Heyman and Norman Priggen produced, and it was a Heyman Production for Universal and World Film Services. The sparse but moody score was by Richard Rodney Bennett. (105 mins)

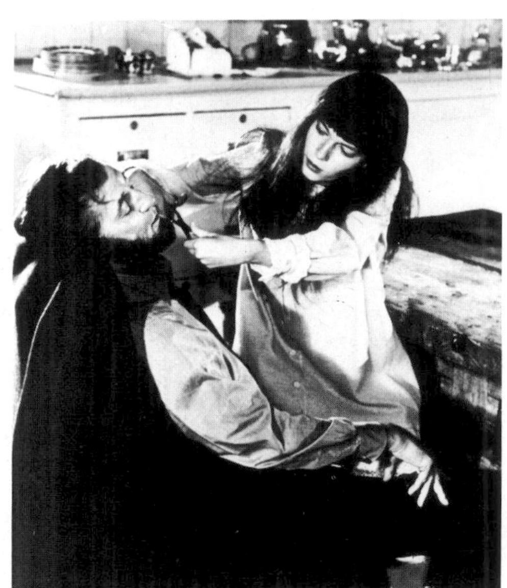

△ In **House Of Cards** George Peppard played a clean-cut, upstanding American citizen – a boxer-cum-writer by profession – who, while drifting around France, finds himself opposing a group of neo-Fascists headed by Keith Michell, Orson Welles and Ralph Michael. Their aim? To set up a new Fascist empire in Europe by again annexing Algeria to France. Peppard (illustrated) single-handedly combats this scheme, in tandem with taking a job as tutor to the young son of an attractive widow (Inger Stevens, illustrated) whose husband, a French general, was killed in the Algerian war. In the course of a screenplay (by James P. Bonner, from the novel by Stanley Ellin) overburdened with plot, Peppard and his pretty employer set out to rescue the latter's kidnapped son, with a climactic showdown taking place at the Colosseum in Rome. William Job, Maxine Audley, Peter Bayliss, Patience Collier and Barnaby Shaw were also featured in Dick Berg's Technicolor production, and it was directed by John Guillermin. (105 mins)

1970

△ Dan Blocker (foreground left) of TV's *Bonanza* starred in a witless helping of whimsy called **The Cockeyed Cowboys Of Calico County**, in which he played a blacksmith who spends a year's salary on a mail-order bride from Boston, only to find himself being stood up when he goes to the local station to meet her. Believing himself to be a laughing stock, he prepares to quit town – much to the dismay of the townsfolk who know there isn't another blacksmith for a hundred miles. How the locals go about keeping him put, formed the basis of Ranald MacDougall's screenplay (he also produced), which not even a potentially interesting cast that included Nanette Fabray, Jim Backus, Wally Cox, Stubby Kaye, Henry Jones, Mickey Rooney (foreground right), Noah Beery Jr, Marge Champion and Jack Cassidy could pummel into life. Tony Leader directed. (100 mins)

△ **Tell Them Willie Boy Is Here** was a condemnation of accepted American values as expressed by writer-director Abraham Polonsky, a casualty of the McCarthy witch-hunt, whose second film this was in twenty years (the first was *Force Of Evil*, MGM, 1948). Its simple story – about a renegade Indian – the 'Willie' of the title – who, in California, circa 1909, kills the father of the Indian girl he hopes to marry, and is tracked down by a deputy sheriff – served as a springboard for Polonsky's critical vision of America and what ails it. The result was a highly stylised, immensely personal drama, overburdened with symbolism and significance, full of 'meaningful' pauses and self-consciously arty camera set-ups. Alas, what it didn't have was much entertainment value, though Robert Redford, top-billed, as the deputy sheriff (and known as Coop, after Gary Cooper) exuded his usual magnetism as the film's most interesting character. Katharine Ross (right) was defeated by the role of Willie's girl Lola, Susan Clark was fine as a liberal but patronizing doctor, and Robert Blake (left) was adequate as Willie. The Jennings Lang production, produced by Philip A. Waxman, in Technicolor and Panavision, also featured Barry Sullivan, John Vernon, Lloyd Gough and Charles Aidman. Its source was Harry Lawton's novel *Willie Boy ... A Desert Manhunt*. (97 mins)

▷ Comedian Don Knotts' fifth comedy for producer Edward J. Montagne was **How To Frame A Figg**. In a screenplay by Georges Tibble (from a story by Montagne and Knotts) that banished all traces of sophistication, Knotts played Hollis Figg, the third assistant bookkeeper at the fast-growing town of Dalton's City Hall. In a situation that echoed the golden days of Harold Lloyd, Knotts (left) finds himself being made the fall guy when the town's corrupt mayor appropriates public funds. Joe Flynn and Edward Andrews played a pair of crooked local politicians, Yvonne Craig was the sexy secretary chosen to frame our hero, and Elaine Joyce (right) a blonde waitress with whom he has a mild flirtation. The cast also included Parker Fennelly, Fay DeWitt, Eddie Quillan and Benny Rubin. Alan Rafkin directed broadly. (103 mins)

△ Clint Eastwood (right) gave a determinedly expressionless performance in **Two Mules For Sister Sara** as an American mercenary in French-occupied Mexico. His co-star was Shirley MacLaine (centre), who he rescues from being raped, and who, as an avid supporter of the Mexican patriot Juarez, cannot afford to be taken by the French. Believing her to be a nun (she's really a prostitute), Eastwood allows her to travel with him en route to Chihuahua on an expedition he hopes will end in the destruction of a French garrison. Their journey together, and the relationship that develops between them, was the main concern of the screenplay Albert Matz fashioned from a story by Budd Boetticher. Don Siegel's effectively paced direction reached a gratuitously violent climax with the storming of the garrison (a shot showing a soldier being struck in the face with a machete was particularly flinch-making); though for most of the time sex and sadism were kept at bay. It was beautifully photographed by Mexican cinematographer Gabriel Figuero, with a particularly memorable pre-title sequence. Completing the cast for producer Martin Rackin were Manolo Fabregas, Alberto Morin (left), Armando Silvestre and John Kelly. (116 mins)

△ **Puzzle Of A Downfall Child** was a visually stunning drama that held more for the eye than the ear. Visually stunning, too, was its star Faye Dunaway (right) who, in the context of Adrian Joyce's screenplay (from a story by Joyce and director Jerry Schatzberg), was a successful model in the fifties. The life-style of that particular milieu has, however, taken its toll, and she retreats to an isolated beach house to gather together the remnants of her life and to avoid a mental breakdown. She also takes time off to tell photographer Barry Primus (left) her life story, which Schatzberg (himself an ex-fashion photographer making his directorial debut) recreated in flashbacks. With more than a nod in the direction of Fellini, we learn of Dunaway's past affair with a priest, her seduction by a dirty old man, and her present state of stasis and drug-taking. It wasn't the most edifying set of revelations ever committed to celluloid, but it looked a dream and boasted excellent performances from the leading lady, as well as from Roy Scheider as a New York businessman, Viveca Lindfors as a photographer, and Barry Morse as her husband. It was produced by Paul Newman and John Foreman. (104 mins)

▽ An impoverished re-working of *Tobruk* (1967), **Raid On Rommel** even borrowed extensively some of the earlier film's action footage in rehashing the famous military operation in which a group of British commandos, in North Africa in 1942, forced their way through heavily armed German lines to Tobruk to destroy German artillery before the arrival of the British fleet. In Richard Bluel's screenplay, however, a group of specially trained commandos take up residence behind German lines as prisoners of war. Richard Burton (centre) was billed above the title in this low-grade actioner, his seeming detachment from the project merely serving to remind one how much better he was in yet another Rommel epic, *The Desert Rats* (20th Century-Fox, 1953). Wolfgang Preiss played Rommel, with other roles under Henry Hathaway's disjointed and uninvolving direction going to John Colicos, Clinton Green, Karl Otto Alberty and (for sex interest) Danielle De Metz. Harry Tatelman produced. (99 mins)

▷ Weighing in at about $10,000,000, **Airport** – a sort of *Grand Hotel* with wings – was the first of a series of 'disaster' movies dealing with various aspects of aviation. It was, however, anything but a disaster at the box office, where it grossed a walloping $45,300,000. Adapted by director George Seaton from the best-selling novel (65 weeks at number one) by Arthur Hailey, it charted the tribulations of a divers group of Boeing 707 passengers, including a bomb-carrying psychopath, and followed the breathless events which led to the aircraft's ultimate landing in a blizzard-torn airport whose most vital runway has been blocked by a snowbound plane. With similar tensions having already been explored in earlier films such as *No Highway In The Sky* (20th Century-Fox, 1951), *The High And The Mighty* (Warner Bros., 1954) and *Julie* (MGM, 1956), audiences were hardly being treated to a new experience in cinematic thrills. They were, however, given the benefit of Ross Hunter's well-oiled production (in Todd-AO and Technicolor), and a cast headed by virile Burt Lancaster as a workaholic airport manager who, in addition to his professional problems (including a picket-line protesting against jet noises), has also to cope with his neglected, socialite wife (Dana Wynter). Dean Martin (centre) played a veteran pilot married to Barbara Hale; while others connected with the airport were George Kennedy as a cigar-chewing maintenance man, Lloyd Nolan as a customs agent, and Jean Seberg as a PR lady. The motley collection of Global Airline passengers included Van Heflin as the bomb carrier and Miss Helen Hayes (as she was billed) as a dotty old stowaway. Best performance, however, was turned in by Maureen Stapleton as Heflin's hysterical wife. Also cast: Barry Nelson, John Findlater, Jessie Royce Landis and Larry Gates. It was photographed by Ernest Laszlo and the woman were dressed by Edith Head. (137 mins)

◁ Frank and Eleanor Perry's **Diary Of A Mad Housewife** took a cold and clinical look at modern marriage and didn't like what it saw. The film starred Richard Benjamin (right) as a go-getting lawyer with an eye to the main chance, whose opinionated manner and materialistic approach to life alienates his bullied wife (Carrie Snodgress, left) and sends her into the arms of writer Frank Langella who isn't much better. In the end she leaves both husband and lover for the reassurance of group therapy – only to find little consolation there either. Eleanor Perry's screenplay (from the novel by Sue Kaufman) was particularly strong on characterisation, and provided excellent opportunities for its three interesting leading players, all of whom were outstanding. Director Frank Perry's acute powers of observation were also well served by a supporting cast that included Lorraine Cullen and Frannie Michel as Miss Snodgress' two resistible offspring, Lee Addams as a babysitter, Katherine Meskill as a trendy bitch, Leonard Elliot as a high-class caterer, and Valma as Benjamin's bit on the side. Frank Perry produced. (95 mins)

△ **Skullduggery** wasn't a comedy, but you would never have known it from the tongue-in-cheek performance delivered by leading man Burt Reynolds (centre). A throwback to the kind of jungle adventure so beloved of the Saturday matinee habitués in the thirties and forties, its plot centred on a scientific expedition to New Guinea whose leader, Susan Clark (right), not only finds the missing link she is looking for, but also a tribe of good-natured ape-men. Nelson Gidding's screenplay also went ape at this point – in keeping with the over-ripe performances of the monkey folk who were played by a group of Indonesian college boys in gorilla costumes. Those appearing without the benefit of disguise were Roger C. Carmel (left), Paul Hubschmid, Chips Rafferty, Edward Fox, Wilfrid Hyde-White, William Marshall and Alexander Knox. Pat Suzuki was also in it – as an ape-woman in long, blonde body hair! Saul David produced (in Technicolor and Panavision) and it was directed, largely on location in Jamaica, by Gordon Douglas in a manner that suggested he didn't know what was happening. (105 mins)

◁ Apart from one good number, 'Different', given the full treatment by Mama Cass, and the irrepressible Martha Raye (left) as leader of a witches' convention, **Pufnstuf** was a banal and totally unmemorable musical for children. Based on NBC's TV series, it was a fantasy about the adventures of a little boy (Jack Wild, foreground right) who encounters a dragon, several witches, and other similarly unoriginal situations. Si Rose produced and (with John Fenton Murray) provided the screenplay. Hollingsworth Morse (Re-morse might have been more appropriate) directed with a supporting cast that included Billy Hayes (centre), Roberto Gamonet, Sharon Baird and Johnny Silver. The mediocre songs were by Charles Fox and Norman Gimbel and included: 'Pufnstuf'; 'Angel Raid'; 'Happy Hour'; 'Witchiepoo's Lament'. (98 mins)

◁ Richard Benjamin could easily have played the leading role in **I Love My Wife**, another excursion into marital dissatisfaction. Instead, it went to Elliott Gould (left), whose rise from unworldly virgin to young bridegroom was entertainingly charted under the credit titles. In fact, the first twenty minutes of producer Stan Margulies' contemporary comedy was terrific. But the film promised more than it delivered, and finished up as a superficial account of a marriage that distintegrates when a husband responds to the increasing apathy of a physically burgeoning wife by seeking extra-marital affairs. Brenda Vaccaro (right) played the wife, and Angela Tompkins the affair. Robert Kaufman's screenplay hardly traded in profundities settling instead, for the occasional flip one-liner that kept the whole thing skin deep. Mel Stuart's direction took its cue from the screenplay, but drew performances from a cast that also included Dabney Coleman, Leonard Stone, Joan Tompkins and Helen Westcott. David L. Wolper was the executive producer. (95 mins)

1971

▷ **Red Sky At Morning** should have been a novel by Carson McCullers rather than the wishy-washy screenplay by Marguerite Roberts (from a novel by Richard Bradford), that it was. Set in New Mexico between 1944 and 1945, it adopted a nostalgic tone of voice as it followed the growth processes of a young lad whose family has moved to a new town prior to dad (Richard Crenna) going off to war. In the course of the story the lad – played by Richard Thomas (centre) – makes new friends, some enemies, falls in love with a 16-year-old girl (Catherine Burns, right), sheds his virginity, then passes from boyhood to manhood with the death of his father and its repercussions. A miscast Claire Bloom, awkward with a Southern accent, played Thomas' alienated mother while, keeping the sidelines active under James Goldstone's faltering direction, were Desi Arnaz Jr (left, as Thomas' best friend), John Colicos, Harry Guardino, Strother Martin, Nehemiah Persoff and Pepe Serna. Hal B. Wallis produced. (112 mins)

△ Dennis Hopper (illustrated), whose *Easy Rider* (Columbia, 1969) became one of the key films of the 1960s, had complete artistic control of **The Last Movie** (released on TV as *Chinchero*), an over-ambitious hodge-podge which unsuccessfully welded fantasy with reality in what the publicity handout at the time pretentiously referred to as 'an allegory concerning the destruction of innocence'. 'Innocence' was represented, as far as one could gather from the confusion of Stewart Stern's screenplay (story by Hopper), by a small Peruvian village in the Andes; while its destruction came in the shape of a Hollywood film crew who arrived there to shoot a western potboiler about Billy The Kid. Cameraman Laszlo Kovacs brought a certain visual elegance to it all, and some of the film-within-a-film sequences were nicely satirical, but for the most part it simply didn't work. Hopper himself played a mythic cowboy called Kansas, with other roles in Paul Lewis' production going to Stella Garcia, Julie Adams, Kris Kristofferson, Don Gordon, Rod Cameron, Roy Engel and, as a director, real-life director Sam Fuller. There were largely unrecognizable appearances, too, from Dean Stockwell, Peter Fonda, John Philip Law, Jim Mitchum and Severn Dardern. (108 mins)

▽ Another Hal B. Wallis entry, again scripted by Marguerite Roberts (from the novel *The Lone Cowboy* by Will James), **Shoot Out** was the one about the ex-con who, on being released from prison, sets out to seek revenge for his betrayal after a bank heist. He, in turn, is being sought by a bunch of hired killers. They find him in a shoot-out showdown in which everyone, save the hero, is eliminated. Gregory Peck (as the ex-con) lent his reassuring presence to the elongated cliché, but was thoroughly upstaged by the attractive scenery, as well as by the performance of Robert F. Lyons as a psychotic killer. A precocious moppet called Dawn Lyn (right) appeared as an abandoned child who helps Peck (left) regain his humanity, with other roles under Henry Hathaway's uninspired direction going to Pat Quinn, Susan Tyrrell, Pepe Serna, Arthur Hunnicutt, Jeff Corey, James Gregory and, in a small part, Rita Gam. A remake of Paramount's *The Lone Cowboy* (1934). (96 mins)

▽ 'There's some sort of craziness going on here that's not right' wails Gena Rowlands in **Minnie And Moskowitz**, and she wasn't kidding! Another of John Cassavetes' professional home-movies (his sixth), its simple story of a Jewish parking-lot attendant's (Seymour Cassel, right) romance with a beautiful gentile girl (Gena Rowlands, left) was characterized by a series of slanging matches between the two lonely people – each fresh assault on the eardrums offering diminishing returns. The best things about the film were the incidental performances of Tim Carey (as a looney in an all-night eaterie), Val Avery (as one of Miss Rowlands' blind dates), Katherine Cassavetes as Cassel's indulgent Jewish mother, and Lady Rowlands as Gena's middle-class mum. John Cassavetes (who wrote and directed it) also appeared; so did Elizabeth Deering, Elsie Ames, Holly Near and Judith Roberts. Al Rubin produced. (114 mins)

▷ Trailing in the wake of **The Beguiled** was a distinct whiff of Tennessee Williams, even though this was not one of the great Southern playwright's recent flops. But a flop it was – due largely to director Don Siegel's tentative direction of the material and a screenplay that garnered many more laughs than it set out to earn. It starred Clint Eastwood (illustrated) as a wounded Union soldier who takes refuge in the claustrophobic confines of a small girls' school in the south run by Geraldine Page. Eastwood's overtly physical presence is tantamount to setting the cat among the pigeons, and the havoc he causes among the repressed libidos of the belles in question – especially Miss Page's – was the main motivating force of the story. John B. Sherry and Grimes Grice scripted it from a novel by Thomas Cullinan, and made a meal of a particularly grisly scene in which Miss Page amputates Eastwood's leg. Definitely not for the squeamish. Elizabeth Hartman co-starred as the girl Eastwood is most attracted to, with other roles in the Malpaso Company production going to Jo Ann Harris, Darleen Carr, Mae Mercer, Pamelyn Ferdin and Melody Thomas. (105 mins)

▷ Clint Eastwood, another actor-turned-director, called the shots as well as appeared in **Play Misty For Me**, a good-looking, beautifully photographed thriller which did for Monterey and Carmel what *Three Coins In The Fountain* (20th Century-Fox, 1954) did for Rome. Eastwood (left) played a laid-back disc jockey operating out of a local Carmel radio station whose meeting with psychotic Jessica Walter (right), an infatuated fan of his, leads to murder, and provides the film with some genuinely scarey momens. An over-emphasis on the beauty of the local landscape dissipated some of the tension created in Jo Heims and Dean Riesner's screenplay (story by Heims), but not disastrously so; Errol Garner's haunting tune 'Misty' was used to excellent effect, and the performances, with the exception of Donna Mills as Eastwood's rather nebulous girlfriend, were first-rate. John Larch played a detective, Clarice Taylor a housekeeper, and James McEachin a fellow deejay. Also cast: Irene Hervey, Jack Ging and, in the small role of a bartender, director Don Siegel. The indulgent photography was by Bruce Surtees. Robert Daly produced for Eastwood's Malpaso Productions. (102 mins)

△ There was the feel of an extended metaphor to **Two Lane Blacktop**, a big-budget road movie directed, with a genuine understanding of the American southwest, by Monte Hellman. Just what that metaphor was, however, remained unrevealed in Rudolph Wurlitzer and Will Corry's elliptical screenplay (story by Wurlitzer). What *did* emerge was an absorbing tale of a couple of aimless drifters known as The Driver and The Mechanic who, together with a hitchhiker called The Girl, embark on a race from New Mexico to Washington DC with a character known as GTO. Pop stars James Taylor (right) and Dennis Wilson (left) played The Driver and The Mechanic, Laurie Bird was the hitchhiker, and Warren Oates, outacting them all, was GTO, an enigmatic middle-aged, once successful Establishment figure who now roams the country in a souped-up 1970 Pontiac. Producer Michael S. Laughlin's film clearly strove to be more than just a cross-country chase by a handful of modern America's drop-outs. Though just what, was anyone's guess. The cast was completed by David Drake and Richard Ruth playing characters called The Needless Station Attendant and The Needless Station Mechanic. (102 mins)

▽ **The Andromeda Strain** featured four characters in search of a mysterious phenomenon which has killed off most of the population of a small desert town adjacent to the spot where a space satellite has recently fallen. The four were Arthur Hill (centre), David Wayne (right), James Olson (left) and Kate Reid (2nd right) – a quartet of stultifyingly boring scientists who contributed in no uncertain terms to the general dead weight of Nelson Gidding's talky, expository, only spasmodically exciting screenplay (from the novel by J. Michael Crichton). It was directed (and produced) at a turtle's pace by Robert Wise and also featured Paula Kelly, Ramon Bieri and, as the only two survivors of the deadly biological invasion, George Mitchell and infant Robert Solo. (127 mins)

△ Still another entry in which its star was also its director, **Sometimes A Great Notion** (also known as **Never Give An Inch**) was a throwback to the type of Warner Bros. 'working man's' films of the thirties and forties, with director-cum-star Paul Newman (who took over after artistic differences with Richard A. Colla) risking life and limb running an independent logging outfit in the lumber country of the Pacific Northwest. The element of conflict in John Gay's screenplay (from a novel by Ken Kesey) arose in the shape of a strike by other loggers in the area, and the dogged determination of Newman (left) and his kin to remain independent and uninvolved. Though the narrative content of Gay's screenplay held no surprises, the characterisations were deft enough to allow director Newman to draw from Henry Fonda (as his elderly father), and from Michael Sarrazin and Richard Jaeckel as his younger brothers, extremely well delineated performances. He was less successful, though, with Lee Remick (right), whose over-sophisticated performance as his wife was out of kilter with her natural home-grown surroundings. A logging accident provided the dramatic highlight, and it showed Newman to be as adept in action sequences as he was on the quieter, domestic front. It was photographed by Richard Moore, whose Oregon exteriors were stunning. John C. Foreman produced. (108 mins)

◁ Czechoslovakian director Milos Forman made an impressive American debut in **Taking Off**, bringing a European's distancing sensibilities to the contemporary American scene. The result was a farce executed with immense affection for his protagonists, and one that examined, with an almost innocent, wide-eyed wonder, the immense chasm that exists between the generations. Nothing new in the theme to be sure, but as exploited by the keenly observant Forman in what amounted to a series of sketches, a total delight. Though it was Linnea Heacock, the teenage daughter of middle-class parents (Lynn Carlin, right, and Buck Henry) who was responsible for what happens when she decides to leave her Forest Hills home for the East Village in New York, Forman's main concern was for her confused parents and the way they cope with the situation. Hence we see them introduced to marijuana at a formal dinner given by the Society For Parents Of Fugitive Children and, in a moment of daring experimentation, playing strip poker. It was the impact of the permissive society on bourgeois respectability that provided Forman, who scripted it with John Guare, Jean-Claude Carriere and John Klein, with most of his gently satiric mileage, with young Miss Heacock emerging as little more than a catalyst. All the performances were outstanding, including those of Georgia Engel (left), Tony Harvey, Paul Benedict, Audra Lindley, Vincent Schiavelli, and David Gittler as a rock musician friend of Miss Heacock's who overwhelms the girl's parents by shyly informing them that his annual income is $290,000. Ike and Tina Turner also appeared, as themselves. It was produced by Alfred W. Crown for Forman-Crown-Hausman Productions in association with Claude Beri. (93 mins)

▷ Violence and humour were the twin ingredients of **One More Train To Rob**, a spirited western which gave top billing to George Peppard (illustrated) as a train robber who, after being framed and sent to jail by John Vernon, a buddy-cum-partner-in-crime, is released, and plots revenge. Diana Muldaur was cast as the woman in both men's lives, with other roles in Robert Arthur's efficient production going to France Nuyen (left), Steve Sandor, Soon-Taik Oh and Richard Loo. Don Tait and Dick Nelson's screenplay, from a story by William Roberts, also involved a shipment of gold being transported from a Chinese mining camp to the safety of a San Francisco bank, and climaxed with an anything-goes finale in which Peppard and his adversary Vernon have their inevitable show down. Andrew V. McLaglen directed. (108 mins)

△ Mysticism of a sort permeated the narrative line of **The Hired Hand**, an achingly lyrical western which Peter Fonda both directed and starred in, and which, through the auspices of a discursive screenplay by Alan Sharp, attempted to distil the essence of life in the west as it was *really* lived. The simple plot had Fonda (illustrated) leaving fellow-wanderer Warren Oates with whom he has been travelling for the last seven years, and returning home (as a hired hand) to his abandoned wife (Verna Bloom) and daughter – only to leave them again shortly afterwards, when he learns that Oates is being held captive by Severn Dardern who, earlier, had brutally murdered Fonda and Oates' young travelling companion, Robert Pratt. Though Fonda's direction did its best to avoid clichés, he was unable to disguise the material's intrinsic pretentiousness, and it was left to Vilmos Szigmond's superb photography to convey the mystical quality the star and his writer strove so hard to achieve. A Pando Production produced by William Hayward, it also featured Ted Markland, Owen Orr and Ann Doran. (90 mins)

▽ There were a couple of redeeming features in Hal B. Wallis' turgid examination of the life of **Mary Queen Of Scots** – Vanessa Redgrave (right, with Beth Harris, left) as Mary and Glenda Jackson as Queen Elizabeth I. Though in life the queens never met, scenarist John Hale clearly had no intention of remaining faithful to history at the expense of a dramatic confrontation between two of the foremost actresses of the day – so he wrote a couple of scenes which brought the protagonists face to face. For all the impact they made, he should have left history alone. The screenplay, like everything else about the production, was profoundly silly, and it wasted the considerable talents of its formidable leading ladies, as well as a cast that included Patrick McGoohan as James Stuart, Timothy Dalton as Lord Henry Darnley, Nigel Davenport as Lord Bothwell, Trevor Howard as William Cecil, Daniel Massey as Robert Dudley, and Ian Holm as David Riccio. It was photographed on location in England and at Shepperton Studios by Christopher Challis, and lavishly directed by Charles Jarrott. (128 mins)

△ Dedicated to the oft-expressed proposition that it is the truly insane who are blessed with sweet reason, **They Might Be Giants** came and went with hardly anyone noticing. It starred George C. Scott (right) as a once brilliant New York judge who has lost his marbles and now believes he is Sherlock Holmes; and Joanne Woodward (left), as a spinster psychiatrist called Dr Watson, who falls in love with him. Together they come across a group of nutters who have escaped reality by spending all their time watching westerns from the balcony of a movie house; as well as an eccentric old couple who, since 1939, have holed themselves up in a loft to escape reality by tending their shrubbery. It was far too whimsical and sentimental for comfort, and unworthy of its two talented stars. Also cast: Jack Gilford, Lester Rawlins, Rue McClanahan and Ron Weyand. The screenplay was the work of James Goldman (who adapted it from his play), it was a Newman-Foreman production and Jennings Lang presentation, and the director was Anthony Harvey. (98 mins)

1972

▷ With a title like **You'll Like My Mother** audiences were left in no doubt that they were in for an old-fashioned dollop or two of horror, and they weren't disappointed. It starred Patty Duke as the pregnant widow of a Vietnam pilot. Miss Duke (left) decides the time has come to pay her mother-in-law (whom she has never met) a visit, so she journeys to Minnesota, where her welcome is anything but cordial, and where she makes the acquaintance of her late husband's mentally retarded sister whom she never even knew existed. Also making his presence felt in this strangely forbidding household, is a young relative with murder and rape on his mind. Rosemary Murphy played mum, newcomer Sian Barbara Allen (right) was outstanding as the retard, and Richard Thomas, in a welcome change of pace from his good-boy roles, was effective as the deranged relative. Jo Heims' screenplay (from the novel by Naomi A. Hintze) got into its stride after Miss Duke, heavy blizzards having reluctantly forced her to spend the night at the manse, discovers that someone has drugged her cocoa. Director Lamont Johnson, without resorting to red herrings or cheap tricks, created a suitably scarey atmosphere, whose echoes from past films in the genre in no way diminished its impact. Mort Briskin produced for Bing Crosby Productions. (92 mins)

▽ The great Walter Matthau (left) and that delightful comedienne Carol Burnett (right) (absent from the big screen for nine years) combined their considerable talents for **Pete 'N' Tillie**, a bitter-sweet tearjerker beautifully directed by Martin Ritt, and performed to perfection by its two leading players. Though its simple story did little more than chart the courtship, marriage, breakup and reunion of two lonely, middle-aged San Franciscans – with tragedy intervening when their nine-year-old son dies after an illness – producer Julius J. Epstein's screenplay, faithfully adapted from the novel *Witch's Milk* by Peter De Vries, had so many good lines, tender moments and well-rounded characterisations in it – that it more than buoyed up the slender narrative with its accurate insights. It also had taste, humour and compassion – three qualities very much in abundance in the performances of its two stars. There was outstanding support, too, from Geraldine Page, Barry Nelson, Rene Auberjonois, Kent Smith, Lee H. Montgomery and Timothy Blake. (100 mins)

▽ An espionage thriller set against some breathtaking scenery in Vancouver Island and the mainland of British Columbia, **The Groundstar Conspiracy** literally began with a bang when an explosion destroyed a laboratory housing a top-secret space project and killed the scientists. The disaster has been triggered off by the theft of valuable information concerning the project, but when the thief (also a scientist) is eventually found, his memory, alas, isn't, and no amount of torture, probing, persuasion or shock treatment can make him recall the circumstances of the theft or who hired him to carry it out. Michael Sarrazin (left), giving one of his best performances to date, played the amnesiac scientist; George Peppard (top-cast) was a relentlessly tough, no-nonsense government agent employed to get to the bottom of the mystery. Christine Belford, Cliff Potts, James Olson, Tim O'Connor and James McEashin completed the cast. It was stylishly directed by Lamont Johnson from a screenplay by Matthew Howard (based on the novel *The Alien* by L.P. Davies), and produced by Trevor Wallace for Hal Roach International Productions with Earl A. Glick as executive producer. (95 mins)

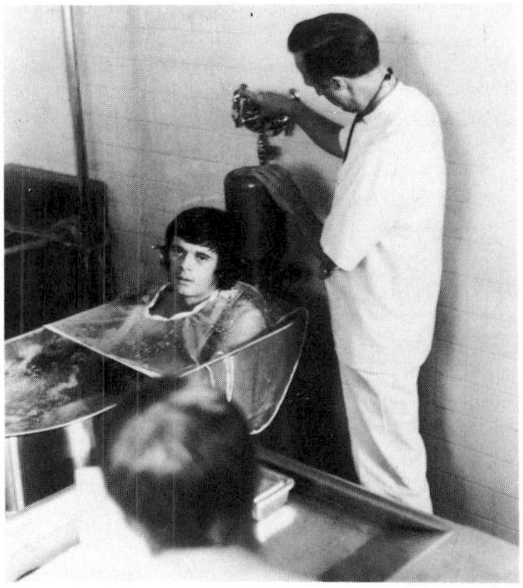

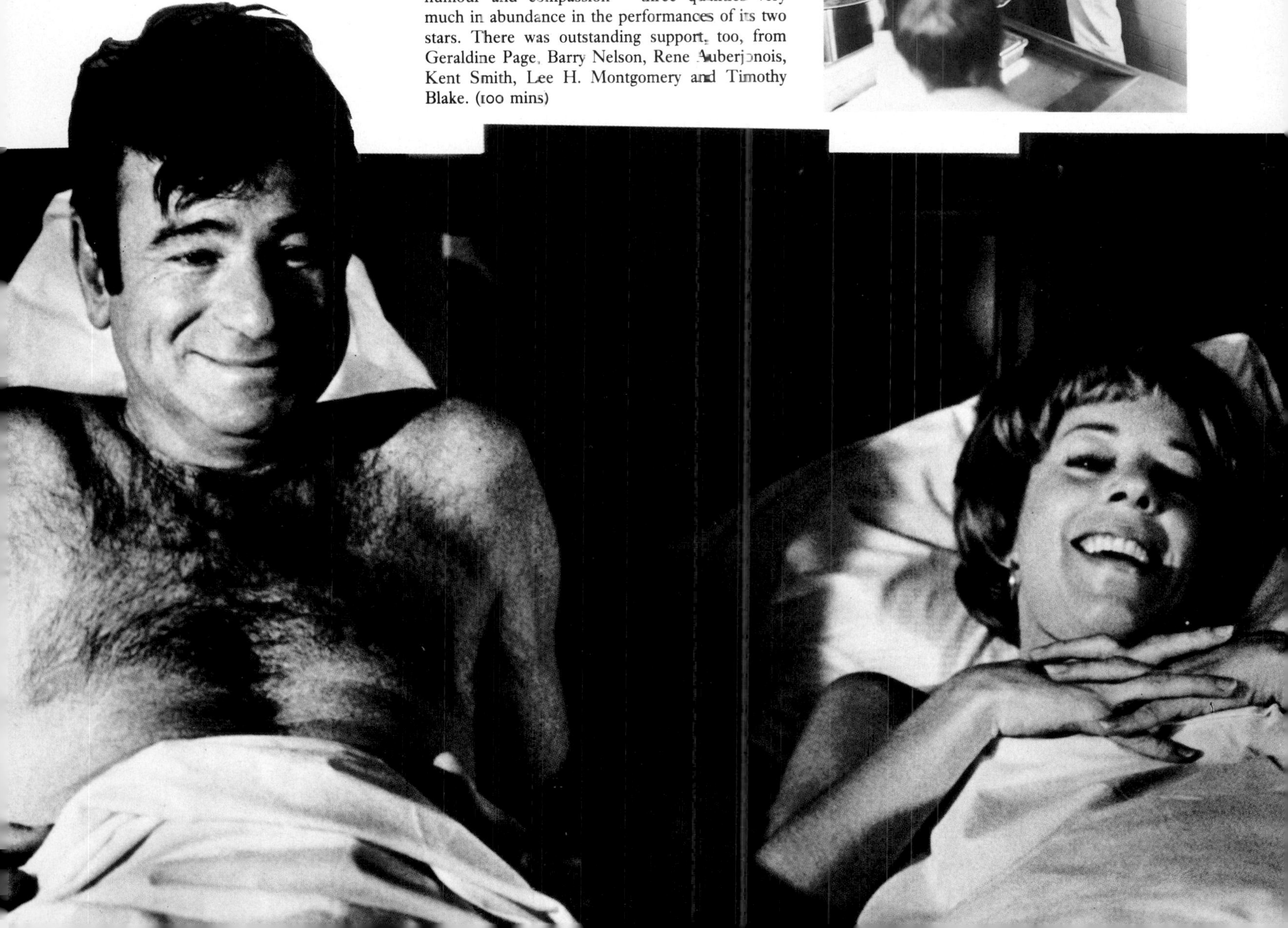

△ In **Frenzy**, his 54th film since the first started grinding them out in 1922, producer-director Alfred Hitchcock made a remarkable recovery after the disappointments of *Torn Curtain* (1966) and *Topaz* (1969). Brimful of characteristic Hitchcockian touches, it told the simple story of a former RAF pilot who is mistakenly believed to be a sex killer in the Jack The Ripper mould after his ex-wife has been found strangled with a tie. Early on, audiences were made aware of his innocence, and of the guilt of a Covent Garden vegetable merchant; and any suspense generated by Anthony Shaffer's colourful screenplay (from the novel *Goodbye Piccadilly, Farewell Leicester Square* by Arthur La Bern) relied on how, and how soon, the real culprit would be caught. The Chief Inspector to whom the case is assigned was played by Alec McCowen, whose performance was deliciously understated; and there were equally entertaining contributions from Vivien Merchant (as McCowen's gourmet wife), Billie Whitelaw, Anna Massey, Clive Swift, Bernard Cribbins, Michael Bates, Jean Marsh, and 1930's musicals star Elsie Randolph. Jon Finch (left) received top billing as the man incorrectly accused of murder; Barbara Leigh-Hunt was his former wife, and Barry Foster (right) the killer. Apart from a few uneasy moments in which Hitchcock, taking advantage of the cinema's new permissiveness, allowed an uncharacteristically graphic scene of sex-and-murder to slip by, his tongue-in-cheek direction never faltered. (116 mins)

▽ A visibly ageing Burt Lancaster turned in an effectively gritty and grizzled performance in **Ulzana's Raid**, an ultra-violent western directed with kick-in-the-gut impact by Robert Aldrich. Alan Sharp wrote it and used its deceptively simple narrative – in which an Indian fighter (Lancaster, right) and an ill-equipped young cavalry officer (Bruce Davidson) set out to round up a group of marauding Indians led by an Apache called Ulzana – as a springboard for the inherent violence of the Old West, and to show how contact with that violence (especially in the case of the greenhorn cavalry officer) has a maturing effect and instantly puts man in touch with reality. The sociology sprayed on to the text by scenarist Sharp occasionally brought the action to a standstill, but the blood-letting before and after these talky episodes more than made up for them. It was produced by Carter de Haven, and also featured Jorge Luke (left), Richard Jaeckel, Lloyd Bochner, Karl Swenson and, as Ulzana, Joaquin Martinez who hardly had any dialogue at all. (103 mins)

▽ Bruce Dern (illustrated) played a botanist in **Silent Running**, a futuristic adventure set in the year 2008, which was predicated on the notion that planet earth has completely lost its vegetation. Orbiting in the vicinity of Saturn, Dern and a crew of three, plus a couple of robots called Huey and Dewey, are in charge of a veritable convoy of floating greenhouses in which some remnants of earth's plant life are being preserved should the time ever come when the planet reintroduces a re-forestation programme. When, however, Dern receives orders to scuttle the programme and return to earth, he murders his human colleagues and, together with Huey and Dewey as his only companions, continues his journey into space. Making his debut as a director, Douglas Trumbull (who was an assistant on Stanley Kubrick's *2001: A Space Odyssey* (MGM, 1968), concentrated on the visual aspect of the film, as well as on the excellent special effects, to the detriment of the performances and a screenplay by Deric Washburn, Mike Cimino and Steve Bocho that basically lacked dramatic credibility. Cliff Potts, Ron Rifkin and Jesse Vint were cast as Dern's colleagues and it was produced by Michael Gruskoff. (90 mins)

▽ With **The Great Northfield Minnesota Raid**, writer-director Philip Kaufman set out to strip away the romantic myths that had always pertained to Jesse James and the Younger Brothers, and to stress the seamy under-belly of their hitherto glamourised existences. With a better screenplay than the one Kaufman provided for himself, he might have succeeded. As it turned out, the film's strength lay not so much in what was said or done but the way it all looked, with meticulous and loving attention to period detail helping to create an impressive sense of authenticity. Cliff Robertson (centre) brought a poetic quality to Cole Younger; Robert Duvall was altogether more sinister (even psychotic) as James. Jim Younger was played by Luke Askew, and together the trio of outlaws embark, in 1876, on their last big job: robbing a bank in Northfield, Minnesota. The cast included R.G. Armstrong, Dana Elcar, Donald Moffatt, John Pearce, Matt Clark and Wayne Sutherland. It was a Jennings Lang-Universal-Robertson and Associates Production. (91 mins)

△ **The Public Eye** (GB: **Follow Me**) was the second half of Peter Shaffer's entertaining double bill, whose first half, *The Private Ear*, was filmed by Ross Hunter in 1966, luridly titled *The Pad – And How To Use It*. Though no world beater, *The Pad* was marginally more entertaining than this more ambitious effort which had the distinction of being directed by Sir Carol Reed and scripted by Shaffer himself. It ran about a half an hour longer than the stage version and was extremely dull. Michael Jayston played a stuffy English accountant, Mia Farrow was his dominated American wife, and Israeli actor Topol the private eye Jayston hires to keep tabs on her. Inevitably, Topol (right) and Miss Farrow (left) decide they have a lot in common, such as horror movies, ice cream, sunsets etc etc, and fall in love. What on the stage was a charming little anecdote, here became a rather inflated romance, with director Reed padding out the slender material by taking audiences on a guided tour of London's more attractive locations. The rest of the cast in Hal B. Wallis' production were all English, and included Margaret Rawlings, Annette Crosbie, Dudley Foster and Michael Aldridge. (95 mins)

△ Clint Eastwood brought his enigmatic loner presence to **Joe Kidd**, a good-looking western set in the High Sierras. He played an enigmatic loner who is hired by landowner Robert Duvall to lead a party of gunmen against rebel John Saxon, a Spanish-American out to save the original Spanish land grants of his oppressed people. Eastwood (illustrated) soon changes sides, and, in a climactic finale, drives a locomotive through a bar in which the unscrupulous Duvall's gunmen are congregated. Elmore Leonard's screenplay had nothing new to say about the old west (or even the dispossessed Mexican minority), so that what emerged under John Sturges' workmanlike direction was a routine oater with a better-than-average cast (including Don Stroud, Stella Garcia, James Wainwright and Paul Koslo) making the most of their material. It was a Malpaso Company Production, produced by Sidney Beckerman. (88 mins)

▽ Director Frank Perry didn't have a lot of good to say for the human condition in **Play It As It Lays**, which Joan Didion, together with her husband John Gregory Dunne, adapted from her highly praised novel. Trouble is, what Perry *did* say, was transmitted in a manner so radically chic that the utter bleakness at the core of the novel was transformed into a series of dazzling visual images which may have been intended to convey despair and desolation, but which had exactly the opposite effect. As a result, the film's anatomy of the breakdown suffered by a young movie actress in Los Angeles called Maria Wyeth (Tuesday Weld) failed either to compel attention or to elicit compassion because audiences were never really given access to her mind, as they had been in the novel. Miss Weld (left) did all that was humanly possible to flesh out her encroaching despair, and there was a splendid and touching performance from Anthony Perkins (right) as a nihilistic producer who eventually takes his own life. Adam Roarke played Miss Weld's director husband, with other roles in this interesting failure going to Tammy Grimes, Ruth Ford, Eddie Firestone, Diana Ewing and Severn Dardern. It was produced by Perry, and Dominick Dunne. (102 mins)

▽ Kurt Vonnegut's highly individualistic view of life as expressed in his novel *Slaughterhouse Five Or The Children's Crusade*, came to the screen via producer Paul Monash (executive producer Jennings Lang) simply as **Slaughterhouse Five**, and featured newcomer Michael Sacks (left) as Billy Pilgrim, an Everyman figure who also happens to be an optometrist. 'Time-tripping' through both time and space, Billy survives a series of catastrophies that underlined the author's preoccupation with man's inhumanity to man – beginning with World War II in which Billy becomes a German prisoner of war, and ending up on the planet Tralfamadore with beautiful Hollywood starlet Montana Wildhack (Valerie Perrine, right). In between, he experiences marriage with an overweight wife (Sharon Gans) and has children as well as a breakdown. Stephen Geller's screenplay was a skilful reworking of the novel's main themes, and it also offered good parts to Ron Leibman as Billy's freaked-out redneck army buddy, Eugene Roche, Roberts Blossom, Sorrell Booke, Kevin Conway, Gary Waynesmith, Holly Near and Perry King. It was directed by George Roy Hill whose film made more sense on a second, or even a third, viewing. (104 mins)

1973

△ All that **Showdown** had going for it, was the box-office clout of its two stars, Dean Martin (left) and Rock Hudson (right). Otherwise, it was a routine western whose Damon and Pythias theme featured Martin as a train robber and Hudson, his best friend, as a sheriff. The latter had the difficult task of bringing the former to justice, and this provided Theodore Taylor's screenplay (from a story by Hank Fine) with its element of conflict. Susan Clark (centre) played the girl with whom both men are in love, and whom Hudson marries, thus causing a rift in his lifelong friendship with Martin. Other roles in George Seaton's handsomely photographed (by Ernest Laszlo on location in New Mexico) production went to Donald Moffat, John McLiam, Charles Bace and Jackson Kane. Seaton also directed. (99 mins)

▽ A throwback to the kind of horror movie the studio was making in the forties, but not as competently crafted, **The Boy Who Cried Werewolf** featured 12-year-old Scott Sealey (illustrated) as the boy who cried werewolf when, on a camping outing with his father (Kerwin Matthews, top-billed), the old man is bitten by one. Trouble is, no one believes young Sealey when he tells the local sheriff (Robert J. Wilke) what has happened – which considering the lack of conviction in both the writing and the performances was hardly surprising. Elaine Devry played Matthews' ex-wife, with other roles in Bob Homel's screenplay going to Susan Foster, Jack Lucas, George Gaynes and the aforementioned Mr Homel himself. It was sloppily directed by Nathan Juran for producer Aaron Rosenberg. (93 mins)

▽ Tim Rice and Andrew Lloyd Webber's highly successful rock opera (originally an album, then a stage hit in London and on Broadway), **Jesus Christ Superstar**, came to the screen via producers Robert Stigwood and Norman Jewison, with a screenplay by Melvyn Bragg and Norman Jewison, and direction by Norman Jewison. But three Jewisons for the price of one turned out a mixed blessing for, in this account of the last week of Christ's life, audiences were offered a frantic ragbag of styles in both imagery and acting. The addition of a show-within-a-show format to the plot wasn't particularly helpful, but Douglas Slocombe's expert photography (on location in Israel), Andre Previn's full-blooded musical direction, and some imaginative choreography from Robert Iscove, were. The amplitude of the original score was very much intact, and the major musical numbers drew a winner from Yvonne Elliman (as Mary Magdalene) in 'I Don't Know How To Love Him'. Ted Neeley (left) starred as Jesus, but his efforts to rise to the occasion were uneven, and were forcefully eclipsed by Carl Anderson's (right) exciting portrayal of Judas. In sum, an erratic movie whose mistakes were offset by some arresting sequences. Others cast: Barry Dennen (Pontius Pilate), Joshua Mostel (an over-camp interpretation of Herod which sabotaged the originally show-stopping 'Herod's Song'), Bob Bingham (Caiaphas) and Larry T. Marshall (Simon Zealotes). 'What's The Buzz' and 'Hosanna' were two of the musical highlights, and other numbers included: 'Heaven On Their Minds'; 'Strange Thing, Mystifying'; 'Then We Are Decided'; 'Everything's Alright'; 'This Jesus Must Die'; 'Simon Zealotes'; 'Poor Jerusalem'; 'Pilate's Dream'; 'The Temple'; 'Damned For All Time'; 'Blood Money'; 'The Last Supper'; 'Gethsemane (I Only Want To Say)'; 'The Arrest'; 'Peter's Denial'; 'Pilate And Christ'; 'Could We Start Again, Please'; 'Judas's Death'; 'Trial Before Pilate'; 'Superstar'; 'Crucifixion'; 'John 1941'. (103 mins)

△ One of the key films of the seventies, and one of the best films of the decade, **American Graffiti**, though set in a small Northern Californian town in 1962, evoked the fifties and remains unchallenged as the most authentic retrospective look at that period and its pastimes. Relying on a collage of events rather than an on-going narrative line, director George Lucas, in his second feature, brought an extraordinary concentration of time and milieu to his film by following the fortunes of four buddies during a 12-hour period one warm summer's night in the town of Modesto. Curt (Richard Dreyfuss), the intellectual of the group, is going to college in the East the following day; so is his mate Steve (Ronny Howard, right). Both are apprehensive about leaving the town of their boyhood. And while Curt, on his last night, is picked up by a gang of local hoods called The Pharoahs, and almost loses his life in their company, Steve spends the last few hours in town breaking up, then making up with his girlfriend Laurie (Cindy Williams) who happens to be Curt's sister. The third member of the group is John (Paul Le Mat), an aimless 22-year-old drag racer who refuses to leave his teens behind him; while the final representative of the quartet, Terry (Charlie Martin Smith, centre), is a bespectacled walking compedium of gaucheries who spends the night in a borrowed Chevy clumsily trying to seduce a blonde swinger called Debbie (Candy Clark, left). Shot (mostly at night) in 28 days and at a cost of $750,000, the film captured not only the look of the period, with its emphasis of fifties cars ritualistically cruising the streets of Modesto, but also its sound. The continuous background throb of contemporary pop music was supplied by disc jockey Wolfman Jack, hitherto a sort of god to the young citizens of Modesto. When, however, Curt finally meets this enigmatic local hero in person, he is so disillusioned by what he sees (an ordinary, middle-aged man eating a Popsicle from a vintage refrigerator) that he no longer feels any apprehension about abandoning his home town for a new life in the East. Director Lucas' screenplay, which he wrote with Gloria Katz and William Huyck, brilliantly captured a generation's last moments of innocence, the loss of which was so touchingly conveyed in all the performances, and which became the underlying theme of a remarkable piece of film-making. It was photographed without recourse to gimmickry by Haskell Wexler, who managed to find a poetry in the garish chrome and neon backdrops which characterised the way the film looked; and was produced by Francis Ford Coppola, with Gary Kurtz as co-producer. The large cast also included Mackenzie Phillips, Harrison Ford, Bo Hopkins, Manuel Padilla Jr and Beau Gentry. The film's initial investment returned a handsome profit of $10,300,000 (110 mins)

▽ **Trick Baby** was a black exploitation caper in which a couple of con men, both black, but one whose skin is light enough to pass for white (ie a 'trick baby'), show their contempt for a society that discriminates against them by shamelessly conning the connable. Director Larry Yust's screenplay, which he wrote in tandem with T. Raewyn and A. Neuberg, and which was based on a novel by Robert Beck (pen-name Iceberg Slim), coughed along from one con to another with very little in between to nurture the mind. Kiel Martin (right) played the 'trick baby', Mel Stewart (left) was the *echt* black, with other roles in Marshal Backlar's production going to Dallas Edward Hayes, Beverly Ballard and Vernee Watson. (89 mins)

▷ Clint Eastwood's third stint in the director's chair resulted in **Breezy**, a non-violent romantic drama whose story of a divorced middle-aged estate agent's romance with a worldly teenage drifter in the Hollywood Hills, was a welcome change of pace for the taciturn star/director who for the first time eschewed violence in favour of some of life's gentler emotions. He cast William Holden (right) as the estate agent and Kay Lenz (left) as the teenager who, after many misgivings, he finally decides to bed. Though Jo Heims' screenplay sounded as though it were conceived for TV rather than the big screen, it did at least offer Joan Hotchkis a chance to filch all the acting honours as Holden's ex-wife; and there was a good performance, too, from Marj Dusay as Holden's erstwhile fiancée, the death of whose husband in a car crash one week after their marriage convinces Holden to go ahead with his affair with Miss Lenz. Also cast: Roger C. Carmel, Shelley Morrison and Jamie Smith Jackson. Michel Legrand provided the music. It was produced by Robert Daley for Malpaso Productions. (107 mins)

△ Definitely unworthy of theatrical release, **That Man Bolt** was a stinker from producer Bernard Schwartz which starred Fred Williamson (right) as a black courier, well versed in the martial arts, who finds himself pursued by an agent of an unspecified government, and is able to use his Kung-Fu skills to predictable effect. Scenarists Quentin Wert and Charles Johnson piled cliché upon cliché in the telling of their who-cares? story, and it was jointly directed by Henry Levin and David Lowell Rich with a cast that included Byron Webster, Teresa Graves, Jack Ging, Vassili Lambrinos and Satoshi Nakamura. (102 mins)

△ Internal Mafia warfare was the subject of **The Don Is Dead**, a Hal B. Wallis production in which Frederic Forrest and Robert Forster found themselves at loggerheads with Mafia king Anthony Quinn (left), the chief reason for their enmity being Angel Tompkins (right), a nightclub singer who has inflamed the desires of both Forster and Quinn. Clearly an attempt to attract the same huge audiences that responded to the strong meat of *The Godfather* (Parmount, 1971), the film suffered from poor narrative motivation and from direction by Richard Fleischer that had a decided 'programmer' feel to it. The performances, given the flaccid nature of Marvin H. Albert's screenplay (which he adapted from his novel), were acceptable, with parts in it for Al Lettieri, Charles Cioffi, Jo Anne Meredith, J. Duke Russo and Louis Zorich. (115 mins)

▽ Desmond Morris' controversial best-seller, **The Naked Ape**, reached the screen via *Playboy* boss Hugh Hefner and producers Zev Bufman and Jennings Lang in a travesty of the original material. Part live-action and part animation, it featured Johnny Crawford (illustrated centre), Victoria Principal (who would receive far more adventageous exposure in TV's long-running serial *Dallas*) and Dennis Olivieri and, as adapted and directed by Donald Driver, clumsily attempted to depict (in an unnamed jungle) man's evolution from the ape. On the simple minded evidence of the finished film, not a great deal seems to have evolved in the last billion years or so. (85 mins)

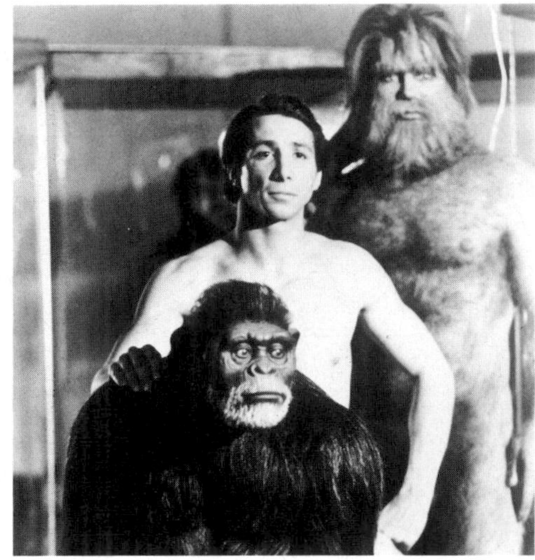

▽ From apes to snakes in **SSSSSSS** – a passable programmer produced by the newly formed company of Richard D. Zanuck and David Brown – which starred Strother Martin as a mad scientist whose speciality is turning people into cobras. Hal Dresner's screenplay, from the story by producer Dan Striepeke, wisely refrained from taking itself seriously, and the result, under Bernard L. Kowalski's modest direction (which was aimed at the funny-bone as well as the spine) was a moderately diverting piece of sci-fi. Dirk Benedict played Martin's student-helper (and the victim of the experiment) and Heather Menzies (illustrated) was his doting daughter, with other parts going to Richard B. Shull as a fellow scientist, Tim O'Connor as a carnival operator, Nobel Craig as a lab operator-turned-snake, and Jack Ging and Ted Grossman as a sheriff and his deputy. (99 mins)

△ Falling uneasily between soap opera and social comment, **Limbo** (also known as **Women In Limbo**), directed by Mark Robson with the emphasis on the story's tear-jerking aspects, followed the tribulations and heartaches of three women living at a Florida Air Force base whose husbands are either missing in action in Vietnam, or prisoners of war. Joan Silver and James Bridge's screenplay (story by Silver) set out to show that war is hell not only for the men who fight it, but also for the women who sit home and wait. The observation was applicable to any war, not specifically Vietnam, and it emerged as little more than a competently made 'sudser', distinguished only by a fine performance from Kathleen Nolan (right) as one of the wives. The cast also included Kate Jackson (left), Katherine Justice, Stuart Margolin, Hazel Medina, Russell Wiggins and Joan Murphy. A Filmakers Group Production in association with Omaha/Orange Films, it was produced by Linda Gottlieb. (112 mins)

△ Roscoe Orman (right) played **Willie Dynamite**, a black pimp whose rise and fall was charted by producers Richard D. Zanuck and David Brown in a 'blaxploitation' melodrama. The screenplay by Ron Cutler and Joe Keyes Jr (story by Cutler) accommodated all the clichés attendant on 'hip' blacks – trendy jargon, available black chicks, dope, flashy clothes, obligatory violence – in the telling of a morality tale that would already have been outdated five years earlier. Joyce Walker (left) debuted impressively as a prostitute, with other roles under Gilbert Moses' competent direction going to Robert Robinson as a rival pimp, Norma Donaldson as a prostitute, Diana Sands (who died of cancer in September 1974) as a hooker-turned-social worker, Thalmus Rasulala as an assistant district attorney, Al Hall and George Murdock as vice officers, and Royce Wallace as Orman's disapproving mother. (102 mins)

▷ Howard Rodman and Dean Riesner provided producer-director Don Siegel and star Walter Matthau with a really first class screenplay for **Charley Varrick** (based on John Reese's novel *The Looters*). It told the unusual tale of a small-time bank robber who inadvertently finds that one of the New Mexico banks he has just knocked off to the tune of $750,000 was a receptacle for Mafia money. Matthau (right), fearful of the consequences, wants to return the fruits of the successful heist. His partner (Andy Robinson, left) does not. The excellence of the screenplay, combined with the conviction of the performances and Siegel's sure-footed direction – particularly in the wham-bang opening sequence featuring Matthau's getaway from the bank – added up to one of the tautest, most entertaining melodramas in several years. Joe Don Baker was effective as a Mafia hit man, and there was solid support from Felicia Farr, John Vernon, Sheree North, Norman Fell, Benson Fong, William Schallert and, in a brief appearance as Matthau's wife (who is killed in the getaway chase), the excellent Jacqueline Scott. (111 mins)

△ **Two People** was a wretched little romance between a Vietnam deserter en route from Africa to America to give himself up; and a top fashion model (and daughter of a West Virginia coal miner) also on her way home to a meaningless (albeit well-paid) existence, as well as to an illegitimate young son. They meet in Marrakesh and spend the first 67 minutes of the movie talking about anything that comes into their empty heads then, in Paris, they make love to the accompaniment of David Shire's insistent and soupy background score. Peter Fonda (right) and a badly photographed Lindsay Wagner (left – her debut), starred as the lovers, though the best performance in a cast that also included Alan Fudge, Philippe March, Geoffrey Horne and Frances Sternhagen, came from Estelle Parsons as a fashion editor. A Filmakers Group Production, it was produced and directed by Robert Wise (who should have known better), and moonily written by Richard De Roy. (100 mins)

▷ As usual, Clint Eastwood (in tub) wasn't giving very much away in his characterisation of The Stranger for **High Plains Drifter**, which he also directed. Playing a sort of archangel of retribution, he turns up to avenge the murder of an honest marshal by some dishonest citizens, after the marshal reveals that the profits being amassed by the local mining community rightly belong to the government. There was no absence of violence in Ernest Tidyman's almost parodic screenplay (the first twenty minutes saw three murders and a possible rape); and even romance (supplied by Verna Bloom) infiltrated the plot. What it all added up to was a brilliantly photographed (by Bruce Surtees), eminently watchable western which hinged on its star's magnetic, albeit laconic presence. The Malpaso Company Production (produced by Robert Daley) also featured Billy Curtis (left), Mariana Hill, Mitchell Ryan, Jack Ging, Stefan Gierasch and Ted Hartley. The executive producer was Jennings Lang. (105 mins)

▽ Producer Hal B. Wallis continued his love affair with British history in **The Nelson Affair** (GB: **A Bequest To The Nation**), and through the auspices of playwright Terence Rattigan's screenplay (based on his play *A Bequest To The Nation*), set out to show us the truth behind the hitherto glorified romance between Lord Nelson and Amy Lyon, a blacksmith's daughter better known to the world as Lady Hamilton. True, Glenda Jackson (right) as Amy Hamilton eschewed the romanticised view taken by Vivien Leigh in *That Hamilton Woman* (GB: *Lady Hamilton*, London Films, 1942) for one that was altogether earthier and more trenchant than popular fiction normally allows. And while it was a characteristically brave performance (Miss Jackson being one of the boldest, most courageous actresses of her generation), it did not go very far in disguising the archness of the script or the dullness of James Cellan Jones' portentous direction. Peter Finch (centre) made an intelligent stab at Nelson but, again, was limited by the material. Also valiantly battling against the script were Margaret Leighton as Nelson's wife and Anthony Quayle as Lord Minto, as well as Dominic Guard, Nigel Stock, John Nolan (left), Barbara Leigh-Hunt and Roland Culver. (118 mins)

△ Like the novel on which it was based, Kenneth Ross' screenplay of Frederick Forsyth's monumental best-seller, **The Day Of The Jackal**, concentrated to a large extent on the minutiae behind an elaborate plot to assassinate General De Gaulle. 'The Jackal' is approached by former French Army officers indignant over France's loss of Algeria, and is offered $500,000 (half on acceptance, half on completion) to carry out the assassination and, as in the novel, we see just how he goes about his assignment. Since audiences knew that De Gaulle was not assassinated, author Forsyth had to build suspense through the negative process of showing just how and why the plot went wrong; and it is to the credit of scenarist Ross and director Fred Zinneman that they both managed to transfer the book's suspense to the screen intact. Edward Fox (right) played 'The Jackal' in a coolly confident manner throughout (taking time off from his meticulous preparations to enjoy a sexual diversion with beautiful but bored baroness Delphine Seyrig). The Anglo-French cast also included Michel Auclair, Alan Badel, Tony Britton, Cyril Cusack (left), Derek Jacobi, Adrien Cayla-Legrand, Michel Lonsdale, Ronald Pickup, Eric Porter and Donald Sinden. It was produced by John Woolf. (141 mins)

▷ The teaming of Paul Newman (right) and Robert Redford (left) again proved to be box-office dynamite in **The Sting**, one of the year's big grossers, as well as blockbuster entertainment which gave confirmed home-bodies everywhere the perfect excuse to abandon their TV sets for a couple of hours in order to see what all the fuss was about. And what they discovered was a well-constructed, beautifully written tale in which the magic Newman-Redford chemistry, so successfully tested in *Butch Cassidy And The Sundance Kid* (20th Century-Fox, 1969) proved miraculously infallible in the telling of a tale about a pair of smooth con artists in twenties Chicago who fleece a big-time racketeer at his own game. David S. Ward's rather convoluted (sometimes confusing) screenplay required close attention if some of its finer points were not to be missed, but even though certain details were easily lost or remained unexplained in the unfurling of the narrative, the gist of it remained comprehensible and made for compulsive viewing. Best scene was a poker game on board a train in which Newman successfully baits his adversary, Robert Shaw. The film's surprise ending, which many considered to be a con in itself, sent audiences home chuckling with pleasure; and, apart from the presence of its two superstars, was probably the main reason for keeping cash registers ringing wherever the film was shown. Other contributing factors to the film's success were the Scott Joplin tunes which Marvin Hamlisch scored so skilfully; Robert Surtees' 'rotogravure' photography, and the marvellous period detail reflected in Henry Bumstead's sets and Edith Head's costumes – not to mention a terrific supporting cast that included Charles Durning (as a corrupt detective on the lookout for Redford), Ray Walston, Eileen Brennan, Harold Gould, John Hefferman and Dana Elcar. A Richard D. Zanuck–David Brown presentation, produced by Tony Bill and Julia Phillips, it grossed $68,450,000. (127 mins)

GORDON'S
DISTILLED
LONDON DRY
GIN

1974

△ After the first-rate job he did on *Charley Varrick* (1973), producer-director Don Siegel's **The Black Windmill** was a decided let-down, having about it the second-rate feel of a made-for-TV movie. It starred Michael Caine (centre) as a secret agent whose young son is kidnapped by one of his colleagues, the ransom being a cache of diamonds intended to foil an international smuggling ring. The question is, whodunnit? Could it be Donald Pleasence (left), a superior who hates Caine's guts? Or John Vernon? Or Delphine Seyrig? Leigh Vance's screenplay, from the novel *Seven Days To A Killing* by Clive Egleton, built to a certain momentum, but let it all go in a perfunctory and unconvincing denouement. The executive producers were Richard D. Zanuck and David Brown, and the cast was completed by excellent character actor Clive Revill (as a Scotland Yard detective), Joss Ackland, Joseph O'Connor, Janet Suzman (as Caine's wife), Catherine Schell, Paul Humpoletz (right) and Denis Quilley. (106 mins)

△ A conventional police melodrama, **Newman's Law** benefitted in no small measure from the casting of George Peppard (centre) as an honest Los Angeles cop with an involvement in big city politics. Produced by Robert Irving, it was a competent enough time-filler in which a routine dope stakeout, engineered by Peppard and his black partner Roger Robinson, leads to the eventual apprehension (in a climactic parking-lot shoot-out) of a gang of international dope peddlers. In the end, though, director Richard Heffron and scenarist Anthony Wilson were unable to bring anything new to a rag-bag collection of stereotyped situations, all of them having been explored *ad nauseum* in both the cinema and on TV. The cast included Eugene Roche, Gordon Pinsent, Abe Vigoda, Louis Zorich, Michael Lerner, Victor Campos (right) and Mel Stewart (left). (98 mins)

▽ Burt Lancaster received top-billing in **The Midnight Man** as an ex-cop who, after being sent to prison for murdering his wife's lover, is let out on parole and reduced to accepting a job as a university security guard. Murder, however, rears its head yet again, and in no time at all Lancaster (right) finds himself proving a sheriff (Harris Yulin) and his sadistic deputy (Richard Winterstein) wrong when they lay the blame on janitor Charles Tyner. The screenplay, written by Roland Kibbee and Lancaster (both of whom also directed), was based on the novel *The Midnight Lady And The Mourning Man* by David Anthony, and needlessly complicated matters by involving a plethora of characters – including the dead girl's father (Morgan Woodward) as well as Ed Lauter, Mills Watson and Bill Hicks as a trio of heavies. An almost unrecognisable Susan Clark (left) played Lancaster's attractive parole officer, and Cameron Mitchell a long-time friend. There was nothing special about the material or the way it was handled and it more or less sank without trace. (117 mins)

▷ It sounded a great idea on paper: a third remake of Ben Hecht and Charles MacArthur's celebrated 1928 newspaper comedy-drama, **The Front Page**, with the charismatic pairing of Jack Lemmon and Walter Matthau (earlier versions being Howard Hughes' memorable 1931 production with Adolphe Menjou and Pat O'Brien, and Howard Hawks' equally splendid version in 1940, called *His Girl Friday* (Columbia), starring Cary Grant and Rosalind Russell). And with a screenplay by Billy Wilder and I.A.L. Diamond, and direction by Wilder – how could it miss? Yet it did, largely because Wilder and Diamond were unable to bring anything new to the oft-told tale except, perhaps, some unnecessary cynicism and a smattering of permissive language denied the earlier versions. And while its two male stars were always worth watching, the familiar story, involving as it always has, the politically motivated execution of a supposed radical for killing a cop, failed to grip audiences the third time round. Matthau (left) played Walter Burns, the managing editor of a Chicago newspaper; Lemmon (right) his ace reporter Hildy Johnson who wants out so that he can marry pretty Susan Sarandon. Carol Burnett, who also starred, didn't quite know what to make of the condemned man's prostitute friend, though in supporting roles Vincent Gardenia, David Wayne, Allen Garfield, Austin Pendleton and Charles Durning were fine. Paul Monash produced, and the executive producer was Jennings Lang. (105 mins)

▽ **The Girl From Petrovka**, complete with Russian accent, was Goldie Hawn (right) who, in Richard D. Zanuck and David Brown's sixth film for Universal, starred as a Russian at odds with the restrictive nature of the Soviet regime. Hal Holbrook (left), as an American correspondent in Moscow, co-starred, and in no time at all they're having a somewhat frustrating love affair, with Hawn being sent to prison for faulty citizenship documents. Gregoire Aslan as a government official was a victim of Allan Scott and Chris Bryant's lustreless, cold-war screenplay (from a book by George Feifer); so were Anthony Hopkins as a black marketeer, Anton Dolin as a ballet master, Bruno Wintzell as one of Goldie's former lovers, and Zoran Andric as a musician secretly in love with American jazz. Robert Ellis Miller's direction was totally without sparkle, unable to animate even the usually delightful Miss Hawn. (103 mins)

▷ After the enormous success of *Airport* (1970), it was surprising that the studio took so long to provide the inevitable follow-up. However, with **Airport 1975**, the sequel arrived, this time with a Jumbo 747 jet in place of a Boeing 707. When bad weather diverts the Jumbo to Salt Lake City, it collides in mid-air with a private plane piloted by Dana Andrews. Andrews, who has suffered a heart attack, is killed instantly, as are the 747's co-pilot (Roy Thinnes), its navigator (Erik Estrada) and steward (Ken Sansom), while the pilot (Efrem Zimbalist Jr) is badly wounded. The airline's determined vice-president (George Kennedy) and ace pilot (Charlton Heston) immediately fly out to effect a rescue as stewardess Karen Black (illustrated) is being coached from the ground on the fundamental points of landing the aircraft (just as Doris Day was in MGM's 1956 drama *Julie*). Meantime, the overriding question was: what will happen to the motley assortment of passengers who, on this occasion, included Kennedy's wife and son (Susan Clark and Brian Morrison), Helen Reddy (her debut) as a singing nun, Linda Blair as an ailing child, Nancy Olson as her concerned mother, and Myrna Loy as an inebriated little old lady whose role in Don Ingall's predictable screenplay ('inspired by the film *Airport* and based on Arthur Hailey's novel' as the credits proclaimed), was to reassure Charles White and Sid Caesar, fellow passengers, that all would be well. Others on the eventful flight were Norman Fell, Jerry Stiller, Conrad Janis, Larry Storch, Augusta Summerland, Guy Stockwell (welcome back, Guy) and Gloria Swanson (ditto), and Beverley Garland played Andrews's wife. It was not nearly as good as its profitable predecessor, due largely to the poor characterisations in the screenplay (poor even by disaster-movie standards), and to inferior special effects which botched the moment of impact between the two planes. It was produced by William Frye and Jennings Lang as executive producer, and directed for the routine stuff it was, by Jack Smight. (106 mins)

▽ **Earthquake** was the studio's second attempt of the year to cause havoc among the general public and, unlike *Airport 1975*, the special effects were terrific (see illustration), credit for which must go to Frank Brendel, Jack McMasters, Albert Whitlock, Glen Robinson and John Daheim. The stars in front of the camera were Charlton Heston (top-billed), Ava Gardner, George Kennedy, Lorne Greene, Genevieve Bujold, Richard Roundtree, Marjoe Gortner, Barry Sullivan, Lloyd Nolan, Victoria Principal, Monica Lewis, Gabriel Dell and, in a brief cameo appearance as a drunk, Walter Matuschanskayasky, better known as Matthau. Following the usual pattern of disaster movies, the story gave audiences a chance to take a peek at the disparate lives of the *dramatis personae* before the actual disaster strikes, as well as during, and after it. George Fox and Mario Puzo's original scenario, set in Los Angeles, was better scripted than one had come to expect on such occasions, so that, in a refreshing sort of way, audiences actually cared about the fate of the humans as well as the hardware. Using 'Sensurround' to simulate the sound of an actual earthquake, producer/director Mark Robson heightened the overall impact of the brilliant special effects, and turned the whole experience into quite a cinematic adventure. The cast was completed by Pedro Armendariz Jr, Lloyd Gough, John Randolph, Kip Niven, Scott Hylands and Tiger Williams. (122 mins)

◁ Director Steven Spielberg, whose first film was the gripping, made-for-TV thriller *Duel* (1971), made an impressive big-screen debut with **The Sugarland Express**, an anything-goes chase that ended in tragedy. Producers Richard D. Zanuck and David Brown cast William Atherton (centre) as a jailbird whose wife (top-billed Goldie Hawn, right) helps him escape from prison in order to prevent their baby boy (Harrison Zanuck, son of producer Richard and wife Linda Harrison) being adopted. In the course of events, the couple 'kidnap' patrol-car officer Michael Sacks (left), which unleashes a massive, all-out chase involving a veritable battalion of cops, headed by police captain Ben Johnson. Hal Barwood and Matthew Robbins' screenplay (story by Spielberg) was rich in sight gags and made space for several key action sequences, credit for whose adroit staging went to Carey Loftin. It also poured scorn on the police force, and delivered quite a kick in the solar plexus in its closing moments. The film was brilliantly photographed by Vilmos Szigmond and benefitted, too, from John Williams' score. (109 mins)

1975

◁ From Australia came **Sidecar Racers**, a perfunctory piece of film-making which featured Ben Murphy (centre right) as an American sidecar racer and John Clayton as his partner, both becoming involved in a triangle romance that develops when Wendy Hughes enters the picture. There was nothing new in Jon Cleary's plodding screenplay, the performances were mediocre, and so was Earl Bellamy's direction, echoing (as did the script) all the youth-orientated attitudes that had been fashionable ten years earlier. Richard Irving produced, and his cast included Peter Graves, John Meillon, John Derum, Peter Gwynne and Serge Lazareff (foreground left). (100 mins)

▽ The trouble with **Rooster Cogburn** was the air of self-congratulation that seemed to seep through its every frame, not because of the superior quality of the script or the excellence of the direction (neither of which applied in this instance), but because of Hal B. Wallis' coup in having brought together John Wayne and Katharine Hepburn – an odd couple he clearly hoped would help spell box-office dynamite, and re-create the success of *The African Queen* (Romulus, 1951), in which Hepburn starred with Humphrey Bogart. It turned out, however, to be little more than the expendable story of a demoted marshal (Wayne) who redeems himself by apprehending outlaws Richard Jordan and Anthony Zerbe. Hepburn (centre) was cast as the spinster daughter of a preacher (Jon Lormer), murdered by Jordan and his gang, and it is with Hepburn's help that Wayne (right) finally succeeds in tracking down the villains. If the Wayne character seemed familiar, it was – having first been introduced to audiences in the altogether more successful *True Grit* (Paramount, 1969). Martin Julien wrote it, Hal B. Wallis produced, and it was directed (as if in awe of his two stars) by Stuart Millar, who also cast John McIntire and Strother Martin (left). (107 mins)

△ If you could believe in Clint Eastwood (illustrated) as a college art teacher whose hobby is collecting priceless paintings, you could believe anything; and suspension of disbelief was certainly a prerequisite for the enjoyment of **The Eiger Sanction**. In it, Eastwood was not only able to hold his own in any conversation involving the fine arts, but, in a former period of his life, he was a mountain climber par excellence as well as a dab hand at assassinating people. So much so, that he is deemed the perfect choice by a secret intelligence organisation called CII who persuade him to come out of retirement in order to eliminate one of the organisation's enemies. All that our hero is told is that his proposed victim is a member of an international mountain climbing team, and that the job will have to take place on the Eiger. To get himself into shape for the assignment, Eastwood calls on George Kennedy, an old climbing friend in Arizona, who agrees to supervise his training period by travelling with him to picturesque Monument Valley, with its many difficult, but climbable rock formations. Eastwood's reward for the killing? A priceless Pissarro. Well, that's what it said in Hal Dresner, Warren B. Murphy and Rod Whitaker's screenplay, based on a novel by Trevanian. Helping to lend conviction to the tale were Vonetta McGee, Jack Cassidy, Heidi Bruhl and Thayer David, not to mention the visually breathtaking Bernese Oberlands in Switzerland which Frank Stanley's photography certainly didn't under-sell. The executive producers were Richard D. Zanuck and David Brown, the producer Robert Daley (for Malpaso), and it was presented by Jennings Lang. Eastwood directed and managed to draw his usual non-committal performance from himself. (125 mins)

▽ Realising that he could not improve on the actual newsreel footage of the destruction of **The Hindenburg**, director Robert Wise ransacked the archives to bring a touch of authenticity to another of the studio's 'disaster' movies. But it was authenticity at the expense of entertainment, since over-familiarity with those famous, harrowing shots of the German zeppelin's disintegration on that fateful night in 1937 at Lakehurst, New Jersey, totally robbed the film of its impact. Another reason the film failed to find favour with audiences was the painting-by-numbers approach to Nelson Gidding's screenplay (from a story by Richard A. Levinson and William Link, based on the book by Michael M. Mooney) which totally failed to create a single believable character. Without caring about the victims, there was no caring about the disaster. George C. Scott received top billing as an air-ace-cum-special-security-officer, Anne Bancroft (illustrated) was a marijuana-smoking countess, Roy Thinnes Scott's unpleasant partner, Gig Young an edgy advertising executive, and Burgess Meredith and Rene Auberjonois a couple of card sharks. Also cast: William Atherton, Charles Durning, Richard A. Dysart, Robert Clary and Peter Donat. There was no producer's credit. (125 mins)

▷ **The Great Waldo Pepper** was an evocative, good-looking period piece – the period being the 1920's – that starred Robert Redford (illustrated) as a World War I flier who, in peace-time, doesn't quite know what to do with his life. So he does the only thing he can: fly – in barnstorming exhibitions, for very little financial remuneration, across the midwest. Redford's partner is Bo Svenson, another World War I airman and, unlike their contemporary (Geoffrey Lewis), who has made a new career for himself in the burgeoning area of commercial aviation, Messrs Redford and Svenson are prepared to remain anachronisms in a fast-changing world. William Goldman's screenplay, from a story by producer/director George Roy Hill encapsulated something of the poignancy of the plight of pioneers being overtaken by progress – especially in its climax when Redford, lending his services to a Hollywood film unit, impersonates a World War I flier he greatly admired. Ironically, the 'technical adviser' on the film-within-a-film is former Imperial German ace (Bo Brundin), now debt-ridden and just as displaced as Redford, whose job it is to supervise a mendacious aerial epic largely based on his own exploits. Susan Sarandon played a female 'barnstormer' who dies after falling off the wing of a bi-plane, with other parts going to Edward Herrmann, Philip Bruns, Roderick Cook and Margot Kidder. The superb aerial photography was under the supervision of Frank Tallman, and art director Henry Bumstead was responsible for imparting period verisimilitude. (108 mins)

△ Based on E.G. Valens' biography *A Long Way Up*, David Seltzer's screenplay **The Other Side Of The Mountain** (GB: **A Window To The Sky**) told the heart-warming story of Jill Kinmont, a 19-year-old skier whose almost certain chance of finding a place on the 1956 Winter Olympics team was shattered when she suffered a near-fatal accident while competing in the Snow Cup Race at Alta, Utah. Though at times a trifle too maudlin, Seltzer nevertheless managed to convey the immense fighting spirit of a girl almost completely paralysed from the neck down who, after the tragedy that ended her athletic career, fought back to become a school teacher in Beverly Hills. Marilyn Hassett (in wheelchair) had the key role of Jill Kinmont, and good-looking Beau Bridges (pushing wheelchair) was her beau. Belinda J. Montgomery played her companion (herself a polio victim), Nan Martin and William Bryant were her parents, Dabney Coleman her ski coach and Bill Vint a man with whom she has an affair until he can no longer take the strain of her disabilities. Larry Peerce's direction zealously rubbed in some of the agony, but his heart was in the right place; and it was produced by Edward S. Feldman. (101 mins)

▷ **Jaws** cost $12,000,000 to make, was almost abandoned because of production difficulties and, so far, has earned over $133,000,000 in domestic box-office rentals, making it one of the top-grossing films of all time. Set in an East Coast holiday resort, it told the simple story of a community terrorized by a man-eating shark, and the efforts to bring the killer to bay. That, basically, was all there was to the screenplay Peter Benchley and Carl Gottlieb fashioned from Benchley's best-seller of the same name. So skilfully, however, did director Steven Spielberg create suspense by concentrating on man's primeval fear of both the known and the unknown trerrors of the deep, that audiences were positively mesmerised by the horrific events they witnessed. Far more effective than the climactic destruction of the shark itself, were the opening scenes on the beach to which audiences were able to relate on a real, instantly recognisable level. And they confirmed Spielberg as a director blessed with a remarkable ability to convey menace. Roy Scheider (left) was top-billed as the small community's chief of police. Robert Shaw (right) as a grizzled shark hunter brought in to kill the monster (in the process of which he, himself, is killed), and Richard Dreyfuss an oceanographer who alerts the unsuspecting – and unwilling to believe – mayor of the town (Murray Hamilton) to the gravity of the situation. Lorraine Gary played Scheider's wife, with other parts going to Carl Gottlieb and Jeffrey Kramer. Author Benchley made a token appearance as a TV newsman. Robert A. Mattey was in charge of the special effects which, despite the fact that his killer shark seemed to get bigger and bigger everytime it appeared, were, on the whole, outstanding. Richard D. Zanuck and David Brown were the financially well-rewarded producers. (124 mins)

1976

◁ Based on a stage musical that was premiered in Las Vegas, **The Bawdy Adventures Of Tom Jones** was an innocuous attempt to add music to Fielding's picaresque novel, as well as to repeat the successful formula of Tony Richardson's altogether superior *Tom Jones* (United Artists, 1963). On this uninspired occasion, the all-English cast was led by the personable Nicky Henson (right) in the title role, and Trevor Howard played the squire who, having discovered Tom in his bed when the boy was still a babe in arms, brings him up as his illegitimate son. Other roles under Cliff Owen's overtly randy direction went to Terry-Thomas, Arthur Lowe, Georgia Brown, Geraldine McEwan, Joan Collins (as Black Bess, left), William Mervyn and Murray Melvin. Jeremy Lloyd scripted it from the musical by Don MacPherson and Paul Holden, the latter providing the music and lyrics. Robert Sadoff produced. (94 mins)

△ A day in the music-filled life of a colourful ethnic crew, whose combined services ensure the smooth running of portly Sully Boyar's auto laundromat, **Car Wash** was a more-or-less plotless, eccentric comedy that burst its seams with some of the freshest, most engaging new talents to hit the screen for quite a while. Little more than a hilarious catalogue of happenings at a Los Angeles car wash, the film's basic idea and approach put one in mind of French comedian Jacques Tati, though the slickness of its fast-paced execution was 40-carat Hollywood. Best known member of the cast was Richard Pryor as a spiffily-dressed preacher called Daddy Rich who arrives at the premises in the company of The Pointer Sisters. Norman Whitfield's background score was an integral part of the action, and much of the direction (by Michael Schultz) seemed choreographed to fit its various rhythms. Joel Schumacher's anything-goes screenplay looked benignly (and even a trifle sentimentally) on most of his characters, and offered splendid opportunities to a cast that included Franklyn Ajaye, George Carlin, Prof Irwin Corey, Garrett Morris (left back), Pepe Serna (back right), Henry King (left front), Leon Pinkey (right front), Lorraine Gary, Darrow Igus, DeWayne Jessie, Melanie Mayron, Lauren Jones and, as an outrageously camp would-be transvestite, Antonio Fargas. It was produced by Art Linson and Gary Stromberg and photographed by Frank Stanley. (97 mins)

▷ Joel McCrea (left), having been put to graze for fourteen years, returned at the age of 70 to appear in **Mustang Country**, a mild-mannered western in which he co-starred with young Nika Mina (right) and spent most of his time in pursuit of a wild mustang. There wasn't much more to writer-producer-director John Champion's old-fashioned screenplay than that. But it was nice to see McCrea back on the screen, even though the acting honours went to the mustang and a dog called Rote. The cast was completed by Robert Fuller and Patrick Wayne. (79 mins)

◁ Audiences who enjoyed the drivel dished out by the popular movie magazines of the thirties and forties, with their interesting tit-bits of gossip and 'at home with the stars' features, had a field day with **Gable And Lombard**, a glossy reconstruction of the life and times (good and bad) of two legends of Hollywood's hey-day. Told in flashback (Gable is first seen at the Nevada mountainside which claimed Lombard's life in a plane crash), we were privy to the pair's first meeting at a Hollywood party; their immediate attraction for each other, the difficulties they encounter both privately (Gable is already married) and publicly (MGM boss Louis B. Mayer is frightened that a scandal might jeopardise his biggest male star's career) – and their short but happy marriage. Thoughout, Gable was characterised as a rugged individualist; Lombard as a ballsy lady with a terrific sense of humour and a penchant for bad language. And that's about as far as it went. If it takes a star to play a star, Jill Clayburgh (illustrated) came closer to the essence of the film's heroine than James Brolin (illustrated) managed as Gable. But then Clayburgh is a star and Brolin isn't. Neither were helped by Barry Sandler's superficial screenplay or Sidney J. Furie's direction which was on a par with the material. Allen Garfield played Louis B. Mayer, Alice Backes was Hedda Hopper, Morgan Brittany Vivien Leigh, and Red Buttons Gable's pal Ivan Cooper. Also cast: Melanie Mayron, Carl McGinnis, Joanne Linville and S. John Launer. Harry Korshak produced. (131 mins)

▷ Not even Sensurround, so effectively employed in *Earthquake* (1974), could give producer Walter Mirisch's big-budget re-staging of the battle of Midway the dramatic shot in the arm it so desperately needed. Called, simply, **Midway**, the film concerned itself with the events leading up to the historic battle on June 4th and 5th, 1942, when a small US Navy Task Force turned the tide of the war against the Japanese by defeating Admiral Yamamoto's large fleet whose mission was the invasion and occupation of Midway – and, of course, the decisive battle itself. Using miniatures as well as actual newsreel footage, director Jack Smight's climactic confrontation was more confusing than thrilling; so was much of the narrative that preceded it, due, in the main, to the incessant cross-cutting (reminiscent of *Tora! Tora! Tora!*, 20th Century-Fox, 1970) between the two naval powers concerned. Charlton Heston (left), even more humourless than usual, headed the cast and played a fictitious character whose son gives him an additional problem by having a romance with an American-born Japanese girl; Henry Fonda was second-billed as Admiral Chester W. Nimitz. Additional marquee value was supplied by James Coburn, Glenn Ford, Hal Holbrook, Robert Mitchum, Cliff Robertson (right), Robert Wagner, Robert Webber, Ed Nelson, James Shigeta, Edward Albert and, as Admiral Yamamoto, Toshiro Mifune. The cast was stronger than the film. (132 mins)

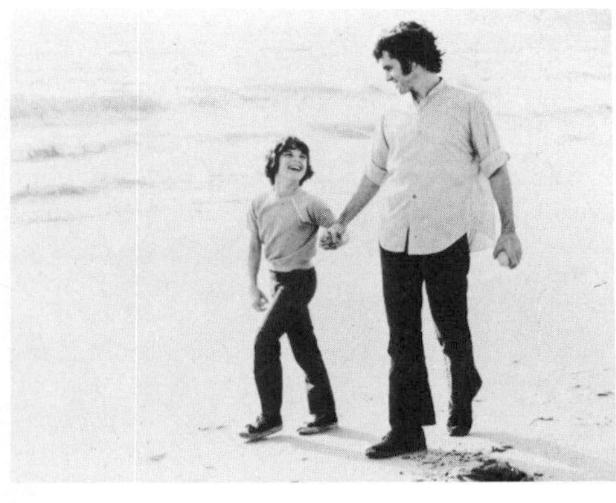

△ Written and directed by Don Coscarelli and Craig Mitchell, who were both 17 when they initiated the project and 22 when it was finally completed, **Jim, The World's Greatest** (also known as **Story Of A Teenager**) was a commendable first feature (shot for $150,000) about high-school life, which starred Gregory Harrison (right) as a student living an unhappy existence with an alcoholic father (Rory Guy) and an abused younger brother (Robbie Wolcott, left) whom he has to protect. He also has romantic problems and cannot decide between Marla Pennington and Karen McClain. Characterisation was not the strong point of the screenplay, but the film did come to life in the sequences that concentrated on various campus rituals. Don Coscarelli produced and, keeping it in the family were D.A. and S.T. Coscarelli as executive producers. (91 mins)

▽ Compared with **W.C. Fields And Me**, *Gable And Lombard* was a masterpiece. Capitalising on the great comedian's reputation for meanness and cruelty ('Anyone who hates animals and children can't be all bad . . .'), scenarist Bob Merrill, working from the book by Carlotta Monti (the 'Me' in the title) and Cy Rice, certainly pulled no punches in his relentlessly unattractive depiction of Fields, making it impossible to warm to the man on any level. Nor was he able to circumnavigate his way around the usual clichés attendant on stories dealing with an artist's rise (in this instance via the Ziegfeld Follies) to Hollywood fame and fortune. Though Fields arrived in Hollywood in 1931 in a luxury car and with $350,000 in thousand-dollar bills, Merrill invented a set of circumstances that found the comedian wiped out by financial mismanagement, and having to borrow money from stooge Billy Barty. In Merrill's version, Fields eventually arrives in Hollywood in a clapped-out flivver, stoney-broke. Far worse than these distortions of the facts, however, was Rod Steiger's (left) ill-conceived, caricatured performance as Fields, and the way it totally failed to capture anything of the character's eccentric comic genius. Valerie Perrine (right) was equally at sea as Carlotta, Fields' mistress for the last fourteen years of his life; and there was little joy, either, from the supporting performances of John Marley (as a studio head), Jack Cassidy (as John Barrymore), Paul Stewart (as Ziegfeld), Allen Arbus (as director Gregory La Cava), Milt Kamen (as Dave Chasen), Louis Zorich (as Gene Fowler) and Bernadette Peters (as Fields' two-timing sweetheart). Jay Weston produced, and the wax-work direction was by Arthur Hiller. (111 mins)

◁ Herbert Ross' **The Seven-Per-Cent-Solution** traversed similar territory to Billy Wilder's *The Private Life Of Sherlock Holmes* (UA, 1970) in that both revealed the great Baker Street detective to be hopelessly addicted to drugs. Also, both films managed to evoke the milieu in which the original Conan Doyle stories were set – and both boasted impressive casts. Wilder's film, though no masterpiece to be sure, was the more entertaining, for it took itself seriously. Ross' was a spoof and what might have been a good idea in theory (Watson, horrified at his friend's addiction to cocaine, spirits him off to Vienna to see a newcomer to the medical scene called Siegmund Freud, after which Holmes and Freud join forces to solve a crime) fell flat in practice. The casting was interesting rather than accurate with Nicol Williamson (centre) as Holmes behaving very oddly indeed. Robert Duvall (left) was hardly anyone's idea of Watson (now married with a family), but he managed well enough in the circumstances; so did Alan Arkin (right) as Freud, and Laurence Olivier as the evil Professor Moriarty. Also: Vanessa Redgrave, Joel Grey, Samantha Eggar, Jeremy Kemp, Charles Gray, Georgia Brown, Regine, Anna Quayle, Jill Townsend and John Bird. Nicholas Meyer scripted it from his novel and Herbert Ross produced as well as directed. (113 mins)

▽ Alfred Hitchcock's 55th film, **Family Plot**, found him in the kind of genial, light-hearted mood that made films such as *The Trouble With Harry* (Paramount, 1955) and *To Catch A Thief* (Paramount, 1955) such engaging thrillers. With Ernest Lehman scripting (from the novel *The Rainbird Pattern* by Victor Canning) the storyline never faltered in maintaining interest, and showed how a delightfully fraudulent psychic (Barbara Harris), together with her equally appealing cabdriver boyfriend (Bruce Dern, right), accepts a $10,000 fee offered by wealthy Cathleen Nesbitt to find the missing heir to an enormous fortune. The gentleman in question turns out to be a well-off diamond-loving Los Angeles jeweller who wishes to be even better off – and, as played by William Devane, he emerged as one of Hitchcock's most charmingly sinister rogues. His girlfriend was Karen Black, and together they go around kidnapping the wealthy, then demanding their jewels as ransom. Lehman's witty screenplay divided its time between the two couples, and though the film was free of the maestro's usual underlying menace, it had its quota of suspense and 'set pieces', one of the best being a hair-raising, mountainside car chase that combined laughter and thrills in equal proportions. Ed Lauter, Katherine Helmond (left), Warren J. Kennerling, Edith Atwater and William Prince rounded out the cast. No producer was credited. (120 mins)

◁ A 'disaster' movie that happened, also, to be a disastrous movie, **Two Minute Warning** set a mad sniper loose on a football crowd in Los Angeles' Memorial Coliseum with the inevitable loss of life resulting. Edward Hume's screenplay, based on a novel by George LeFountaine, kept quiet about the motives of the killer (who is he? and why is he doing such terrible things?) and failed, also, to involve audiences in the ultimate fates of the unlucky spectators who stopped the sniper's bullets. Charlton Heston (left) played a concerned policeman in his usual grim-visaged manner, Jack Klugman was a gambler whose life, literally, depends on the outcome of the match he is attending, with other parts going to John Cassavetes, Martin Balsam, Beau Bridges, Marilyn Hassett, David Janssen, Gena Rowlands, Walter Pidgeon, and All-American half-back, Anthony Davis (right). Between them they played a diverse cross-section of spectators from a pick-pocket to a harassed father and his family. Edward S. Feldman produced and Larry Peerce directed. (112 mins)

▽ Something of an anachronism in 1976, **Swashbuckler** (GB: **The Scarlet Buccaneer**) attempted to recreate the roistering pirate yarns of yore, but emerged as a cack-handed mish-mash without any of the fun or *brio* of its illustrious predecessors in the genre. Jeffrey Bloom, the scenarist (working from a story by Paul Wheeler), went back 200 years to tell his tale, and to well before the formation of the Grand Canyon for the manner in which he told it. All about the efforts of pirate Red Ned Lynch and his comrade Nick Debrett to thwart the wicked schemes being hatched by Lord Durant, the degenerate (ie gay) acting Governor of Jamaica, it starred Robert Shaw (right – somewhat long in the tooth) as Lynch, James Earl Jones (left) as Debrett and Peter Boyle as Durant. Also: Genevieve Bujold (centre) as a wronged noblewoman, Bernard Behrens as her noble father, Beau Bridges as a foppish soldier, as well as Avery Schreiber, Geoffrey Holder and Tom Clancy. It was produced by Elliott Kastner and Jennings Lang, and directed by James Goldstone. (101 mins)

1977

▷ **Heroes** was a numbingly awful comedy which traded in cuteness as it followed the cross-country adventures of a Vietnam veteran whose war experiences have definitely affected his brain. Henry Winkler (The Fonz of TV's *Happy Days*) played the vet, a man dedicated to the belief that it is the kooks of this world who are truly blessed. Escaping from the hospital at which he has been a patient for five years, he hops a bus bound for California (where he hopes to start a worm farm) and, en route, meets and falls in love with his female counterpart (Sally Fields). With both Winkler (right) and Miss Fields (left) giving performances that looked as though they had been computer-programmed, and with a screenplay by James Carabatsos guilty of trivialising a potentially interesting subject, director Jeremy Paul Kagan had precious little to work with. Harrison Ford appeared in a small supporting role, and the cast also included Val Avery, Olivia Cole, Hector Elias and Dennis Burkley. (119 mins)

▽ **Rollercoaster**, in Sensurround, was a lightweight mini-disaster movie about a young extortionist who goes around America's amusement parks fatally sabotaging rollercoasters when his demands are not met. Timothy Bottoms played the saboteur, and George Segal (as a safety inspector, illustrated) was his prime adversary. Richard Widmark also starred, as a hard-boiled Federal agent; so did Henry Fonda, as a mild mannered security chief. Apart from one really spectacular rollercoaster disaster at the start of the film, director James Goldstone underplayed the violence and treated Richard Levinson and William Link's screenplay (story by Tommy Cook) for the routine manhunt it basically was. Jennings Lang produced, and the featured members of the cast included Harry Guardino, Susan Strasberg, Helen Hunt and Dorothy Tristan. (119 mins)

▽ **The Car** was a thoroughly witless exercise in the macabre which featured a driverless car that terrorizes a small town in Utah, doing irreparable damage to a hitchhiker, a sheriff, a couple of cyclists, several policemen and a school teacher. It was flung together by Dennis Shryack, Michael Butler and Lane Slate (story by Shryack and Butler) and directed by Elliot Silverstein who also produced it with Marvin Bird. For the record if featured James Brolin (centre), Ronny Cox (right), Kathleen Lloyd, John Marley, R.G. Armstrong, John Rubinstein, Ernie Orsatti (left) and Elizabeth Thompson. (98 mins)

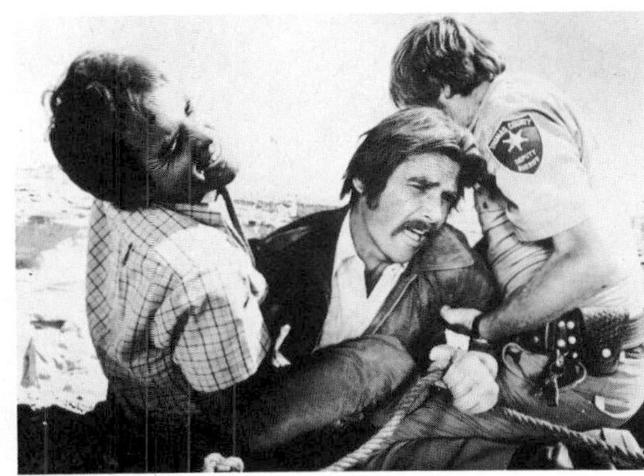

◁ Turn-of-the-century ragtime pianist and composer Scott Joplin, whose music had been so integral to the success of *The Sting* four years earlier, was the subject of a quality, no-frills biopic entitled, simply, **Scott Joplin**. Christopher Knopf constructed a screenplay that acutely charted the joyous early years of Joplin's life, and his subsequent descent into destitution, disease and death. With Billy Dee Williams (illustrated) starring, director Jeremy Paul Kagan kept a tight hold on the subject matter, and the atmosphere of the era. Joplin's music was featured, as well as Harold Johnson's 'Hangover Blues'. The producer was Don Hough, and the rest of the cast included Clifton Davis, Godfrey Cambridge, David Healy, Samuel Fuller, Art Carney, De Wayne Jessie, Mabel King, Taj Mahal, Spo-De-Odee, Eubie Blake and The Commodores. (98 mins)

△ Formula film-making at its most dispiriting, **Airport '77** again starred a Boeing jetliner in distress. This time the plane (privately owned) actually crashed – into the sea. And although it sank about a hundred feet, it remained upright. Most of the passengers were guests of millionaire art collector James Stewart, who has invited them (together with art collectors and art critics) to the grand opening of his Palm Beach museum. En route from Washington to Florida, however, the plane is hijacked by thieves for its priceless cargo of paintings – in the course of which it plunges into the drink. Jack Lemmon (illustrated) was top-billed as the pilot. Brenda Vaccaro (illustrated) was his fiancée, Olivia de Havilland played the part of a patron of the arts and was accompanied by her black maid, Maidie Norman; Joseph Cotten was Miss de Havilland's one time lover, Lee Grant and Christopher Lee an estranged married couple, and Tom Sullivan played a blind pianist. It was directed by Jerry Jameson for the piece of fabricated junk it was, written by Michael Scheff and David Spector, and produced by William Frye with Jennings Lang as executive producer. (117 mins)

△ A great deal of energy manifested itself in **Smokey And The Bandit**, a macho 'road' film which starred Burt Reynolds as Bandit, an artist behind the wheel of any car, truck or lorry who, for a net of $80,000 agrees to race 1800 miles from Georgia to Texas and back in 28 hours. Apart from the bet – the reason for his mad race against time involves the delivery of 400 cases of beer. All goes well until, on the return journey, Reynolds (centre) makes the acquaintance of runaway bride-to-be Sally Field, whose prospective father-in-law (Jackie Gleason) just happens to be a sheriff. As scripted by James Lee Barrett, Charles Shyer and Alan Mandel, it was an amiable enough caper, peppered with a fair amount of raunchy language, and some solid, albeit stereotyped characterisations, including that of Miss Field's 'nebbish' husband-to-be, Mike Henry. Jerry Reed (right), Paul Williams and Pat McCormick also appeared, and it was directed for Rastar Productions and producer Mort Engelberg at a cracking pace by Hal Needham. It grossed a healthy $39,744,000. (97 mins)

△ Soupçons of nudity, masturbation and lesbianism were some of the heady ingredients of **The Sentinel**, a Satanic melodrama directed by Michael Winner (who also produced and wrote it with Jeffrey Kravitz) in which a New York fashion model (Cristina Raines, left) finds herself living in an apartment in Brooklyn Heights which literally turns out to be the gateway to Hell. The unfortunate Miss Raines – who has rented the apartment for reasons no more sinister than that it has a beautiful view – now finds herself torn between the Church, who want her to guard the passageway to Hades and make sure the Devils remain within; and the Devils themselves (disguised as reincarnated murderers) who are trying to get her to kill herself. Chris Sarandon was top-billed as Cristina's sinister lover, and Martin Balsam rceived third-billing as a professor. Others persuaded by Mr Winner to appear in his occult orgy were such fine players as John Carradine, Jose Ferrer, Ava Gardner (right), Arthur Kennedy, Burgess Meredith and Sylvia Miles. The film was clearly aimed at the crowds who brought financial glory to the producers of *The Exorcist* (Warner Bros., 1973), but it wasn't to be. (105 mins)

△ Inhabiting the same period – the mid-fifties – as *The Last Picture Show* (Columbia, 1971) and *American Graffiti* (1973), **9/30/55** was an affecting little movie that focussed on the reaction of a teenage college kid in Arkansas when he first hears of the death of James Dean (on September 30th, 1955). Richard Thomas (illustrated) played Jimmy J, the young man in question, and was superb in the role. His grief over Dean's death is shared by his girlfriend, Deborah Benson, as well as by Lisa Blount, a way-out chick whose own tragic fate in writer-director James Bridges' excellent screenplay, is to have her face disfigured as a result of a prank that misfires when Thomas and his mates decide to commemorate Dean's accident by indulging in a spot of occult mysticism. The adults in the story, most notably Susan Tyrrell as Blount's larger-than-life mother, benefitted from more rounded characterisations than are usual on such occasions; Ben Fuhrman, Glen Irby and Collin Wilcox doing equally well in this respect. Also cast: Thomas Hulce, Dennis Quaid, Mary Kai Clark and Dennis Christopher. It was produced by Jerry Weintraub and the music was by Leonard Rosenman, who supplied the scores for James Dean's first two movies at Warner Bros. (101 mins)

△ An unsuccessful reworking of Lina Wertmuller's 1974 Italian comedy *The Seduction Of Mimi*, **Which Way Is Up?** moved from the original's Sicilian setting to Southern California, and substituted Richard Pryor as a lecherous cotton picker for Giancarlo Giannini's peasant. The result was a rather discombobulated comedy, funny in parts, that far too relentlessly exploited the very racial stereotypes that have for so long caused offence to black and white alike. Plot has Pryor (right) inadvertently becoming a union leader, in which capacity he deserts his wife and family for Los Angeles where a new woman enters his life. As a result of his selfish behaviour, he finds himself unceremoniously dumped by all his friends. So much for the morality tag. Apart from playing the central role – called, by scenarists Carl Gottlieb and Cecil Brown, Leroy Jones – Pryor also appeared (unconvincingly) as his father Rufus, as well as a philandering minister. His leading ladies were Lonette McKee (the mistress, centre) and Margaret Avery (the wife), with other roles under Michael Schultz's vulgar direction going to Morgan Woodward, Marilyn Coleman and Bebe Drake-Hooks. The producer was Steve Krantz. (94 mins)

△ How one responded to **The Last Remake Of Beau Geste** depended on how one responded to its star, Marty Feldman, who also directed it from a screenplay he wrote with Chris Allen and a story he wrote with Sam Bobrick. As its title suggested, the film spoofed most Foreign Legion films, but particularly William Wellman's celebrated 1939 Paramount adventure (which starred Gary Cooper), scenes of which were irreverently intercut into this version. Feldman (left) cast himself as the twin brother of Michael York (right), and if only the rest of the film had been consistent with this piece of inspired lunacy, he may have had the sort of success Mel Brooks had with *Blazing Saddles* (Warner Bros., 1974). But Feldman's undisciplined, hit-and-miss approach to comedy ultimately let him down and, apart from a handful of amusing sight-gags, it was left to a cast that included Ann-Margret (centre), Peter Ustinov (as a sadistic sergeant), James Earl Jones (as an Anglicised Arab), Trevor Howard (as Sir Hector Geste), Spike Milligan (as Sir Hector's elderly servant), as well as Henry Gibson, Terry-Thomas, Roy Kinnear, Avery Schreiber, Irene Handl and Hugh Griffith to help bolster the fun. It was produced by William S. Gilmore, with Howard West and George Shapiro as executive producers. (83 mins)

▽ **MacArthur** was a solid, well-mounted biography of the controversial World War II general, which suffered from sins of omission rather than comission. Dealing with MacArthur's career from his departure from Corregidor in 1942 before the Philippines fell, his stay in Australia, his return via New Guinea to the Philippines, his term as Japan's supreme commander and, ultimately, his alienation of President Truman as a result of Korean War policy – Hal Barwood and Matthew Robbins' respectful screenplay offered, through necessity (and via flashbacks), a shorthand version of the numerous events described, with superficial results. Producer Frank McCarthy was far better served by Gregory Peck (illustrated) who captured both the look and the temperament of MacArthur most convincingly, as well as the man's superb gift of oratory, nowhere better demonstrated than in the 'Old Soldiers Never Die' speech to Congress. Director Joseph Sargent's handling of the sprawling material was commendable, and while the emphasis was not on spectacle, such battle scenes as were included were competently handled. None of the other performances matched Peck's, with Dan O'Herlihy as President Roosevelt and Ed Flanders as Truman emerging as little more than waxworks. Also in the cast were Ivan Bonar, Ward Costello, Nicholas Coster, Marj Dusay, Art Fleming, Russell D. Johnson and Sandy Kenyon. (122 mins)

▽ **Slap Shot** invaded the milieu of professional ice hockey and was the story of the resuscitation of the Charlestown Chiefs, one-time pride of the New England mill town for whom they played. Unfortunately, under the flagging guidance of their middle-aged coach (Paul Newman), the Chiefs have become a third-rate team whose only virtue is that they play clean. But when manager Strother Martin recruits a trio of goons collectively known as The Hansen Brothers (Steve Carlson, Jeff Carlson, Dave Hanson) all that changes. A fracas during a game in which the Hansen boys 'cream' their opponents, delights the spectators, and gives Newman (foreground centre left) the idea that from now on the only way to succeed without really trying, is to play dirty. Which the Chiefs do, in one gory game after another, thus putting an end to an embarrassing losing streak and once again becoming a marketable team. Written by Nancy Dowd, whose liberal usage of locker-room jargon was enough to make a sailor blush, and directed by George Roy Hill with a positive relish for the rough stuff, the film's cynical message was that we are no longer living in an age of good sportsmanship, and that nice guys finish last. True or not, the observation was persuasively rammed home in an undeniably entertaining, if somewhat overblown manner, added conviction being lent by a perfectly cast company of actors. Michael Ontkean was second-billed as a Princeton graduate who, instead of indulging in violence, helps win the final game on a technicality by performing a striptease – to the outrage of the opposing team and the entertainment of the punters. It was five of the best moments in the film. Kathryn Walker played the wealthy lady who owned the team, and Jerry Houser (as a mystically-minded goalie) and Andrew Duncan (a radio sports announcer) were excellent; so were the wives and girlfriends whose sorry lot it is to sit at home and wait. Some do, some don't. They were represented by Lindsay Crouse, Jennifer Warren and Melinda Dillon. It was produced by Robert J. Wunsch and Stephen Friedman. (122 mins)

1978

▽ Paul Schrader, whose screenplays for *Taxi Driver* (Columbia, 1976), *Obsession* (Columbia, 1976) and *Rolling Thunder* (American International, 1977) were all hard-hitting affairs, turned his talents to directing in **Blue Collar** (which he also co-wrote with Leonard Schrader), a tough, accurately observed account of the lives of three blue collar workers at a Detroit automobile factory. The film was also about corruption, though exactly what points the Schraders were making remained somewhat fuzzy. It was on the domestic front that **Blue Collar** really came into its own, with its magnifying-glass examination of the life styles of Richard Pryor (right), married with three children, irascible, and deeply in debt; Harvey Keitel (centre), also married and financially pressed to the extent of having to keep down two jobs; and Yaphet Kotto (left) a playboy bachelor and ex-convict. Fed up with the drudgery of making ends meet, the trio of malcontents rob their union headquarters. But instead of finding money, they stumble across an explosive account of the union's loan-sharking practices which they decide to use as an instrument of blackmail – with catastrophic results. Pryor's stand-out performance memorably combined anger and humour; and there was excellent work, too, from both Keitel and Kotto, as well as from Ed Begley Jr, Harry Bellaver, George Memmoli and Lucy Saroyan and Lane Smith. Ron Guest produced, Robin French was the executive producer, and the source material from which the Schraders adapted their screenplay, was by Sydney A. Glass. (110 mins)

△ The studio climbed on the hard rock bandwagon with **FM**, a jamboree of Dolby sound and Deejay fury. Michael Brandon played the disc jockey whose 'creative' aspirations come up against the realities of commercialism. He had some classy support from Eileen Brennan, Cleavon Little, Cassie Yates (centre), Alex Karras, Martin Mull (right) and Janet Brandt (left) but Rand Holston's Technicolor production amounted to little more than an excuse to blast out over 30 songs. John A. Alonzo directed from a screenplay by Ezra Sacks, and the musical numbers included the Presley classic, 'Love Me Tender', Billy Joel's hit 'Just The Way You Are', James Taylor's 'Your Smiling Face', 'Tumbling Dice' by Mick Jagger and Keith Richard, and a title song written by Walter Becker and Donald Fagen. (104 mins)

▽ With a score consisting of 29 compositions by John Lennon, Paul McCartney and George Harrison, among them some of their most durable hits ('With A Little Help From My Friends', 'Lucy In The Sky With Diamonds', 'She's Leaving Home' etc.) **Sgt. Pepper's Lonely Hearts Club Band** must have seemed like a good idea at the time. The inspiration was embellished by top-casting Peter Frampton (centre left) and The Bee Gees (Robin Gibb, left, Barry Gibb, right, Morris Gibb, 2nd right), and surrounding them with a bunch of featured guest stars who ranged from talents as various and contrasting as Donald Pleasence to Carol Channing. Unfortunately, the result was a fevered mess, resting on a mindless and skeletal plot (story and screenplay by Henry Edwards) in which a number of peculiar characters set out to steal the musical instruments belonging to Sgt. Pepper's band. There was no focus to Michael Schultz's direction of this fantasy, which was clouded by an excess of electronic visual effects and an obtrusive soundtrack. Patricia Birch choreographed for producer Robert Stigwood, whose starry Technicolored line-up of featured actors and musical groups also included Frankie Howerd, Paul Nicholas, Dianne Steinberg, Sandy Farina, Alice Cooper, Stargard, Billy Preston, Earth, Wind and Fire, George Burns (centre), Peter Allen, Stephen Bishop, Keith Carradine, Donovan, Jose Feliciano, Peter Noone, Helen Reddy, Chita Rivera, Johnny Rivers, Sha-Na-Na, Aerosmith, Del Shannon and Connie Stevens. (111 mins)

▷ Richard Dreyfuss in **The Big Fix** gave one of his most 'laid back' performances to date as Moses Wine, a private detective who, in Roger L. Simon's complex screenplay (based on his novel), has left his radical campus ideals behind him at Berkeley, and now operates as a small-time gumshoe desperately trying to eke out enough money to support an ex-wife, two children, and himself. He almost takes on more than he can chew, however, when he is employed by Susan Anspach (right), a one-time campus activist who has entered politics as a campaign worker for an upcoming election. Someone, it appears, is trying to sabotage the election by distributing inflammatory leaflets about the candidate in question. As the plot unfurled, so did the screenplay's element of mayhem and intrigue. The end result was a gripping thriller, in the Philip Marlowe tradition but unconvincingly updated to the sixties, whose 'look' and 'feel' were well conveyed in Jeremy Paul Kagan's direction – Kagan, Dreyfuss (centre), Simon, and producer Carl Borack all being products of the era they were depicting. The rest of the cast included Bonnie Bedelia, John Lithgow, Ofelia Medina, Nicolas Coster (left) and Fritz Weaver. (108 mins)

△ The accent was squarely on youth in **Almost Summer**, which starred Bruno Kirby as an upstanding representative of a Los Angeles High School who, after being chosen President of the Student Body, resigns when he discovers that the election was rigged. His popularity among the students gets him re-elected, and all ends happily ever after. A veritable army of writers (Judith and Sandra Berg, Marc Reid, Rubel and Martin Davidson) thought it all up, Martin Davidson directed (breezily), it was produced by Anthony R. Clark (with Steve Tisch as executive producer); and its cast of relative unknowns included Lee Purcell, John Friedrich, Didi Conn, Thomas Carter, Tim Matheson, Petronia Paley, David Wilson and twins Yvette and Yvonne Sylvander (illustrated with Kirby). (89 mins)

▷ **Gray Lady Down** could have been another 'Airport' movie, except that the craft on this negligible occasion, wasn't an aeroplane but a nuclear powered US Navy submarine. Called 'Neptune', it surfaces off Cape Cod in dense fog, is rammed by a Norwegian freighter and plummets 1400 feet until it reaches a sea-shelf on which it precariously comes to rest. The question is, will it, and all who sank within her, be saved? As is the eternal way with disaster movies, some are, and some aren't ... James Whittaker and Howard Sackler, working from Frank R. Rosenberg's adaptation of David Lavallee's novel *Event 1000*, scripted it by rote, and it was directed by David Greene who managed to draw more convincing performances from the hardware than from his cast, which top-starred Charlton Heston (centre), David Carradine and Stacy Keach as three captains and, in supporting roles, featured Ned Beatty, Stephen Hattie, Ronny Cox (left), Dorian Harewood and Rosemary Forsyth. Walter Mirisch produced. (111 mins)

△ Rude and crude, rough and ready, often hilarious, sometimes revolting, but essentially innocent in a raunchy undergraduate kind of way, **National Lampoon's Animal House** told no discernible story. It concentrated, instead, on the unedifying antics of the inhabitants of Delta House, newcomers to an American campus (in 1962) who take pleasure in denting beer cans against their craniums, indulging in grossness of every conceivable kind, and bursting into song a lot. Not to mention shocking the campus elite. Though a trifle too self-consciously outrageous, its exuberance and relentlessly high-spirited approach to its often questionable material ultimately anaesthetized one to its excesses so that, in the end, it resembled little more than a *Hellzapoppin'* of the campus, with lots of offence intended, but none taken. John Belushi (centre) was prominently featured as one of the sleazier characters in Harold Ramis, Douglas Kenney and Chris Miller's anarchic screenplay, with other roles under John Landis' uninhibited direction played by Tim Matheson, Thomas Hulce, Stephen Furst (left), John Vernon, Mark Metcalf, Mary Louise Weller, Martha Smith, Bruce McGill (right), Kevin Bacon, Karen Allen and, as a hip pot-smoking English professor, Donald Sutherland. Matty Simmons and Ivan Reitman produced. (107 mins)

△ For enthusiasts only, **Skateboard** was an exploitation quickie that cashed in on a current craze and told the story of a down-and-out theatrical agent who recruits a few expert young skaters and forms them into a professional team. One of the members wins a $20,000 downhill race, thus helping to liberate the agent from a threatening bookie. Allen Garfield played the agent, and the rest of the cast under George Gage's unsubtle direction included Kathleen Lloyd, Leif Garrett, Richard Van Der Wyk, Tony Alva (illustrated), Steve Monahan and David Hyde. Gage wrote it with Richard A. Wolf (story by Wolf), and it was produced by Wolf and Harry N. Blum. (95 mins)

▷ After the death of his wife – to whom he had been faithful for 31 years – Walter Matthau, playing a surgeon in the worst run hospital in California, decides to make up for lost time. So he puts himself on the market, is considered by several desirable, unattached women to be a 'pussy cat', and finally falls for co-star Glenda Jackson, a divorcee he meets in surgery while attending to a hair-line fracture on her jaw. Their courtship and romance came to the screen via **House Calls**, an agreeable enough comedy, written in committee by Max Shulman, Julius J. Epstein, Alan Mandel and Charles Shyer (story by Shulman and Epstein) whose screenplay, despite its many witty one-liners, would have benefitted from the less obvious sit-com approach which informed every episode of its TV spin-off. Though the lovable Matthau and the flinty Miss Jackson (both illustrated) seemed slightly ill at ease together, sheer professionalism won through and watching the couple's romantic sparrings was a painless enough experience. The screenplay took several hard-hitting swipes at the medical profession in general and, on that level, was spot on target most of the time. Art Carney co-starred as a doddering old doctor so senile he cannot remember the name of the hospital to which he is attached, with other roles under Howard Zieff's serviceable direction going to Richard Benjamin, Candice Azzara, Dick O'Neil, Thayer David and Anthony Holland. (96 mins)

▽ **Paradise Alley**, written, directed and starring that one-man band, Sylvester Stallone, was an entertaining account of three Italian-American brothers whose sole purpose in life is to better themselves and escape from the claustrophobia of New York's Hell's Kitchen (the film's setting) in 1946. Stallone (right), the middle brother, is the one with the most confidence; Armand Assante (left), the eldest, a wounded World War II veteran who walks with a limp, is the bitterest of the three, and works as an embalmer; while Lee Canalito (centre), the youngest of the family, is the biggest, and the gentlest. It is Stallone and Assante's plan to promote their 'baby' brother as a wrestler in order to earn enough money to move to a better part of town, that formed the main narrative thrust of the screenplay, and it provided roles for Kevin Conway as an Irish hood, Frank Rae as a has-been black wrestler, Anne Archer as a redhead in a dime-a-dance establishment, Joyce Ingalls as a whore, and Aimee Eccles as a Chinese American who has young Canalito's interests at heart. Also: Terry Funk and Joe Spinelli. John F. Roach produced. (108 mins)

△ **Moment By Moment** did nothing for the careers of its two stars, John Travolta and Lily Tomlin (both illustrated), whom one wag skittishly suggested would have been better cast had they reversed roles! He played a handsome young layabout, she a middle-aged woman estranged from her husband and living in a beach-house. The nub of Jane Wagner's screenplay (she also directed) was how Travolta charms Miss T out of her apathy – and it just didn't wash. The rest of the cast included Andra Akers, Bert Kramer, Shelley R. Bonus, Denra Feuer and James Luisi. Robert Stigwood produced, and the executive producer was Kevin McCormick. (94 mins)

◁ Producer Rob Cohen, executive producer Ken Harper, and director Sidney Lumet looked to Broadway as a source of inspiration, and came up with The Big White Way's big black hit, **The Wiz**. Alas, the journey from stage to screen resulted in a catalogue of serious misjudgements which rendered this remake of *The Wizard Of Oz* (MGM, 1939) pretty pointless. Screenwriter Joel Schumacher changed novelist Frank Baum's setting from Kansas to New York City, and transformed the child heroine Dorothy into a 24-year-old Harlem school-teacher, played by Diana Ross (illustrated). This remodelling had Dorothy caught in a snowstorm while running after Toto, her dog, whereupon she disappears in a swirl of snowflakes and resurfaces in another part of Manhattan. From then on, her adventures largely parallelled those of the young Judy Garland in the original film, with one major omission: the sense of magic that should have accompanied them. A contemporary Oz was lavishly created from designs by Tony Walton, but director Lumet diminished the whole conception by overlaying it with garish spectacle and a lot of din. Even more damaging was the casting of the mature, sophisticated Miss Ross in the guise of Baum's vulnerable, youthful heroine. There were redeeming features in Mabel King's evil Witch, Evilene, who, together with her Flying Monkeys supplied a showstopper with 'Don't Bring Me No Bad News'; and in the glorious Lena Horne's appearance at the end as Glinda The Good Witch, singing 'Believe In Yourself', an overtly black pride number. Scarecrow, Tin Man and Cowardly Lion were back as Dorothy's companions, and perfectly well-played by Michael Jackson, Nipsey Russell and Ted Ross; a somewhat wasted Richard Pryor was cast as The Wiz himself, and others featured included Theresa Merritt (as Aunt Em), Thelma Carpenter, Stanley Greene and Clyde J. Barrett. Louis Johnson staged the several large-scale productions numbers (performed by the Louis Johnson Dance Theatre), and all the songs and musical numbers (23 of them) were written by Charlie Smalls and Quincy Jones. (140 mins)

▽ **Jaws 2** was the further adventures of a man-eating shark and the handful of brave individuals who set out to curb its voracious appetite. Set on a Long Island holiday resort called Amity, it again featured Roy Scheider as the local police chief, Lorraine Gary as his wife, and Murray Hamilon as the mayor whose perversity in all matters of office clearly renders him unfit for the job. (Does the man *never* learn? Didn't he see what happened in *Jaws*, 1975,?) What the movie didn't have was Richard Dreyfuss, or a halfway plausible screenplay, or direction that knew how to make the most of the (by now) well-excavated material. Richard D. Zanuck and David Brown produced and, unable to obtain the services of Steven Spielberg, hired Jeannot Szwarc to pull it all together. But although they got the shark in the end (at the expense of a few teenage lives), it was artistically a losing battle. The public, it must be admitted, behaved like sharks themselves and gobbled it all, thus keeping the accountants happy to the tune of $82,500,000 in domestic rentals. Also cast: Joseph Mascolo, Jeffrey Kramer, Colin Wilcox, Ann Dusenberry, Mark Gruner, Barry Coe, Gary Springer, Susan French, Donna Wilkes and, illustrated pursued by a shark, Cindy Grover. (120 mins)

△ A sequel to the studio's successful 1975 drama, **The Other Side Of The Mountain – Part 2** took up the Jill Kinmont story where the first one left off. Although most of the red meat of this biographical saga was accounted for in Part One, scenarist Douglas Day Stewart nonetheless managed to cobble together a five-handkerchief tearjerker from the on-off romance Ms Kinmont has with the long-haul trucker she meets in Bishop while on vacation from her school teaching job in Los Angeles. Via flashback, audiences not familiar with the dramatic events of the first part of the Kinmont story were given a re-cap of the courageous woman's life so far (her competitive skiing triumphs, the near fatal accident that left her confined to a wheelchair, her gradual recovery, her college years culminating in a degree as a teacher, and, finally, the death of her daredevil fiancé) thus ensuring that Part Two could be wept over with no sense of deprivation at having missed the first segment. Marilyn Hassett (left) repeated her performance as Jill Kinmont, Timothy Bottoms (right) was the new man in her life, with other roles under Larry Peerce's unashamedly sentimental direction going to Nan Martin, Belinda J. Montgomery, Gretchen Corbett and William Bryant. It was a Filmways Production produced by Edward S. Feldman. (105 mins)

△ **I Wanna Hold Your Hand**, directed by Robert Zemeckis, left its supposed aims and objects dismally unfulfilled. The script (by Zemeckis and Bob Gale) had Nancy Allen, Wendy Jo Sperber (left), Susan Kendall Newman and Theresa Saldanha as four New Jersey teenagers heading for New York to see The Beatles making their Ed Sullivan Show debut in 1964. As a memorial to Beatlemania, the movie was a no-no, with the four boys themselves notably absent from the proceedings. Zemeckis chose to suggest their presence with glimpses of their legs and shoulders, but nobody was particularly amused by this device. The characters were too idiotic to appeal to the teenage audience they were supposed to attract, so the venture didn't make it as a youth movie either. The producers were Tamara Asseyev and Alex Rose, with scriptwriter Gale as associate producer and guru Steven Spielberg as executive producer. Eleven Beatles compositions were featured, plus a handful of songs written by others such as 'Twist And Shout' (Phil Medley, Bert Berns), 'Till There Was You' (Meredith Willson) and 'Money' (Janie Bradford, Berry Gordy Jr). Also cast: Bobby Di Cicco, Marc McClure and Eddie Deezen (right). (99 mins)

▽ **Same Time Next Year**, scripted by Bernard Slade from his long-running (1,453 performances) Broadway hit, was a fairytale for grown-ups which began in 1956 and described the romance between a 27-year-old married accountant and a 24-year-old housewife and mother of three who, quite by chance, meet at a romantically situated inn, and, for the next 20 years, continue to meet, once a year, at the same time, and the same place. Ellen Burstyn was the woman, Alan Alda the man, and although it was difficult to accept Slade's basically contrived situation, the film (like the play) benefitted from the slick, well-turned, consistently humorous, often moving dialogue which, quite apart from charting the changes in an unorthodox relationship, also managed, by spanning two decades, to encompass many of the social and political developments in the world between 1956 and 1976. And although Burstyn (left) and Alda's (right) affair was somewhat fanciful, the emotions they expressed throughout always rang true. Given the confines of the setting, director Robert Mulligan did the best he could, and concentrated more on the quality of the performances than on how to broaden the scope of the material. Though the play was a two-hander, Morton Gottlieb and Walter Mirisch's production opened it out to give employment to Ivan Bonar, Bernie Kuby, Cosmo Sardo, David Northcutt and William Cantrell. The music was by Marvin Hamlisch. (119 mins)

▽ No prizes for guessing on whom the two leading characters in **The Greek Tycoon** were based. He (Anthony Quinn, left) is an elderly Greek millionaire whose interests are oil tankers, airlines and islands; she (Jacqueline Bisset, right) the beautiful young widow of an assassinated US President. Mort Fine's ponderous screenplay (which should have been fun in a camp sort of way, but wasn't) dealt primarily with the romance and marriage of the two protagonists, both of whom were characterised as truly wonderful human beings – honest, caring, and devoted to each other. But he failed to put honest, caring words into their mouths, and it was directed by J. Lee Thompson with a flabbiness that rendered it intolerable. The cast was completed by Edward Albert as Quinn's adored son and heir, Raf Vallone, Camilla Sparv, Marilu Tolo, Charles Durning and Luciana Paluzzi. Allen Klein and Ely Landau produced. (106 mins)

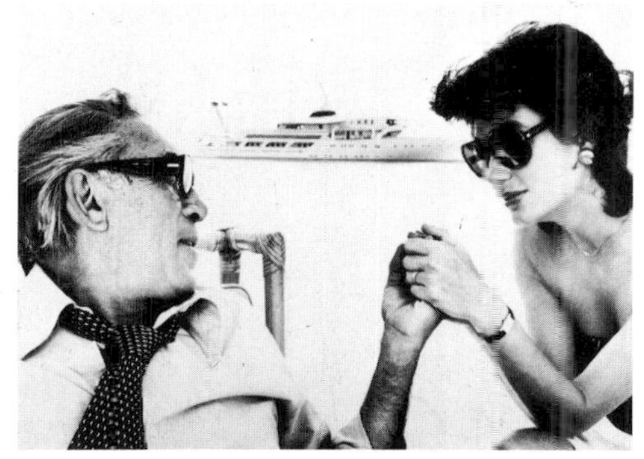

△ **Nunzio** is a mentally retarded adult whose physically mature body encases the mind of a child. Possessed by an innate goodness, he spends his time pretending to be Superman (in which guise he delivers groceries), and dreaming of marriage to a pretty girl who works in a bakery. The natural butt of the neighbourhood's insensitive young hoodlums, his 'Superman' fantasies are given credence when, at the end of the film, he saves a child belonging to a paraplegic mother from perishing in a burning building (see illustration). A simple, compassionate story, it was beautifully scripted by James Andronica (who also played Nunzio's deeply caring older brother), directed with only a minimal trace of mawkishness by Paul Williams, and produced by Jennings Lang. David Proval received top-billing in the title role and was excellent; and there were fine performances, too, from Morgana King as his mother and Tovah Feldshuh as the girl of his dreams. (86 mins)

1979

▽ John Badham's reworking of **Dracula** wasn't so much a remake of the studio's classic 1931 production as a capitalisation on the 1977 Broadway hit which starred sexy Frank Langella in the title role. And although Langella (illustrated) repeated his performance for producer Walter Mirisch, the film, though visually sumptuous (the designer was Peter Murton), lacked the brilliant stylisation of Edward Gorey's stage designs, as well as its Broadway counterpart's delicious sense of humour. This version played it straight and, as a result, wasn't nearly as compelling as it could have been. It was cast from strength, though, with Laurence Olivier and Donald Pleasence excellent as a vampire hunter and his assistant, and Kate Nelligan as the girl who is irresistibly drawn to the Transylvanian count. Also cast: Trevor Eve, Jan Francis, Janine Duvitski, Tony Haygarth, Teddy Turner and Sylveste McCoy. It was scripted by W.D. Richter from the play by Hamilton Deane and John L. Balderston which, of course, was based on the celebrated novel by Bram Stoker. John Williams provided the music. (110 mins)

▷ Anthony Hope's classic novel of adventure and intrigue, **The Prisoner Of Zenda**, was first filmed in 1913 by Famous Players. It was remade by Rex Ingram in 1922 with Lewis Stone and Ramon Novarro, remade again in 1937 by Selznick International with Ronald Colman and Douglas Fairbanks Jr, and yet again – in 1952 – MGM surfaced with a fourth version starring swashbuckler Stewart Granger and James Mason. The fifth version starred Peter Sellers (illustrated) in the dual role of lisping Ruritanian King and British commoner (a London Cabbie and the King's look-a-like), and was the worst of the five. Dick Clement and Ian La Frenais' screenplay, based on the novel and the play by Edward Rose, couldn't quite make up its mind whether it wanted to send it up, put it down or play it straight, and such wooziness of intent communicated itself to director Richard Quine, and to a cast that also featured Lynn Frederick (Mrs Sellers), Lionel Jeffries, Elke Sommer, Gregory Sierra, Jeremy Kemp, Catherine Schell, Simon Williams, Graham Stark, Stuart Wilson, Norman Rossington and John Laurie. Sellers also appeared in the film's opening sequence as an elderly, expiring King. Arthur Ibbetson's camerawork, much of it photographed on location in Vienna, was the best thing in the film. The producer was Walter Mirisch. (109 mins)

△ Not even motorcycle enthusiasts found much to thrill to in **Fast Charlie ... The Moonbeam Rider**, a barely competent actioner set in the 1920s, and starring David Carradine as a resistible motorcycle rider (and World War I veteran) whose dream it is to win the first Transcontinental motor race from St Louis to San Francisco. Brenda Vaccaro (right) co-starred as a waitress who, together with her son (Whit Clay, left) hitches up with Carradine (centre left). I.Q. Jones, R.G. Armstrong, Terry Kiser and Jessie Vint were also in it; Steve Carver directed (bumpily), it was written by Michael Gleason (story by Ed Spielman and Howard Friedlander), and produced by Roger Corman and Saul Krugman. (99 mins)

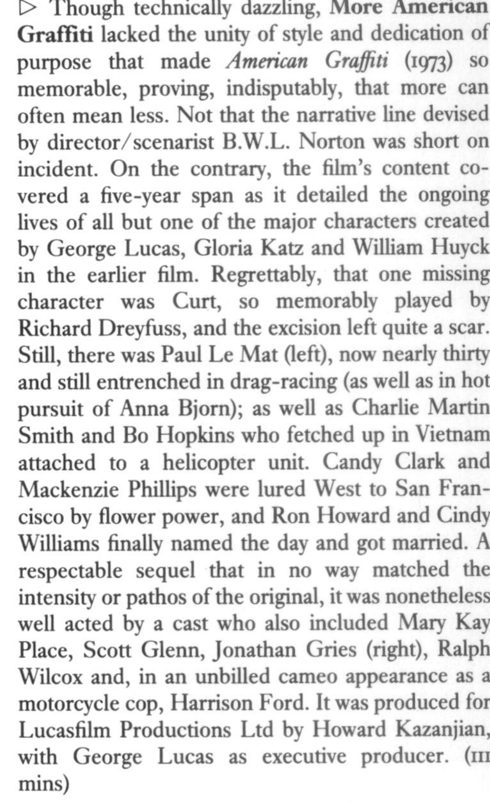

▷ Though technically dazzling, **More American Graffiti** lacked the unity of style and dedication of purpose that made *American Graffiti* (1973) so memorable, proving, indisputably, that more can often mean less. Not that the narrative line devised by director/scenarist B.W.L. Norton was short on incident. On the contrary, the film's content covered a five-year span as it detailed the ongoing lives of all but one of the major characters created by George Lucas, Gloria Katz and William Huyck in the earlier film. Regrettably, that one missing character was Curt, so memorably played by Richard Dreyfuss, and the excision left quite a scar. Still, there was Paul Le Mat (left), now nearly thirty and still entrenched in drag-racing (as well as in hot pursuit of Anna Bjorn); as well as Charlie Martin Smith and Bo Hopkins who fetched up in Vietnam attached to a helicopter unit. Candy Clark and Mackenzie Phillips were lured West to San Francisco by flower power, and Ron Howard and Cindy Williams finally named the day and got married. A respectable sequel that in no way matched the intensity or pathos of the original, it was nonetheless well acted by a cast who also included Mary Kay Place, Scott Glenn, Jonathan Gries (right), Ralph Wilcox and, in an unbilled cameo appearance as a motorcycle cop, Harrison Ford. It was produced for Lucasfilm Productions Ltd by Howard Kazanjian, with George Lucas as executive producer. (111 mins)

▽ Very much in the mould of such fine Washington-based political dramas as *The Best Man* (United Artists, 1964) and *Advise And Consent* (Columbia, 1962), **The Seduction Of Joe Tynan** was blessed with a bright, witty and intelligent screenplay by Alan Alda (illustrated centre), who also played the leading role. It took audiences on a guided tour of the damaging pressures and tensions that lurk behind the ingratiating public smile of an ambitious liberal senator; and unflinchingly showed how those pressures and a determination to make it to the top in the most cut-throat game of all, nearly wrecks his marriage. Barbara Harris played Alda's long-suffering wife (who, for a while is abandoned in favour of Meryl Streep, a labour lawyer), and was brilliant in the part. Melvyn Douglas turned in another fine performance, too, as a past-it politico; ditto Rip Torn as a power-imbibing senator. Adam Ross and Blanche Baker played Alda and Harris' offspring, and the cast was completed by Charles Kimbrough, Carrie Nye, Chris Arnold, Maurice Copeland and Robert Christian. It was directed with admirable restraint by Jerry Schatzberg, who didn't miss a trick in recording both the public and private aspects of his protagonist. Martin Bregman produced. (107 mins)

△ **The Promise** was the kind of forties weepie to which the young Bette Davis might once have lent her considerable talents. But instead of Bette, it was Kathleen Quinlan (right) on whom the burden of Gary Michael White's silly screenplay (from a story by producers Fred Weintraub and Paul Heller) fell. She played a young student who is so badly injured in a car smash that she is persuaded by the strong-willed building tycoon mother (Beatrice Straight) of her boyfriend (Stephen Collins, left) to undergo plastic surgery, and to seek a completely new life far away from her son. Which is exactly what Miss Quinlan does. With a change of locale (California) and a brand new face, she flourishes as a photographer whose services are eventually sought by a budding young architect. The architect turns out to be none other than her one-time beau and, if at first he doesn't recognise her, it's because (a) her face is so different, and (b) his mother has told him she was killed in the smash. But inevitably light dawns, and he also remembers a promise he once made to her (hence the title) which involved a necklace they both buried under a stone by the sea. The film was an anachronism in 1979 and it sunk without trace, despite entertaining performances from Miss Straight, and from Laurence Luckinbill as a plastic surgeon. William Prince, Michael O'Hara and Bibi Besch were also in it; and Gilbert Cates directed it for the irredeemable soap opera it was. (97 mins)

△ The fourth helping of 'Airport' adventure was called **The Concorde – Airport '79** and, inevitably, it suffered from the law of diminishing returns. This time the plot dealt with an international arms smuggler (Robert Wagner) who, on three separate occasions, attempts to sabotage Concorde in an effort to destroy some incriminating evidence against him which is being carried by one of the airline's passengers (Susan Blakely). Eric Roth's screenplay, which also gave credit to the Arthur Hailey novel *Airport* which inspired it, was the formula as before, with two-dimensional characters taking second place to both the aircraft itself and the in-flight drama which threatens its destruction. George Kennedy (centre) played the pilot, and the large cast under David Lowell Rich's equally formula direction, included Alain Delon (right), Sylvia Kristel, Eddie Albert, Bibi Andersson, Charo, John Davidson, Martha Raye (welcome back Martha!), Cicely Tyson, David Warner (left), Mercedes McCambridge and Ed Begley Jr. The producer was Jennings Lang. (114 mins)

▽ A gang movie with an anti-gang message (you do not have to hang around in macho groups to be a real man), **Walk Proud** cast Robby Benson (left – looking several shades darker than normal) as Emilio, a member of a Chicano gang in East Los Angeles. Through the influence of his girlfriend Sarah Holcomb, as well as a trip to Mexico where, at his grandmother's funeral he is introduced by his mother (Irene De Bari) to the father (Brad Sullivan) he has never seen, he reforms. Evan Hunter who, way back in 1955, scripted one of the first of the gang movies, MGM's *The Blackboard Jungle*, clearly understood the mentality of gangs and the mechanics of gang warfare, and his screenplay on this occasion was full of interesting insights into the rituals observed by most of the youngsters on view. Robert Collins directed it grittily (it was violent, but not excessively so), it was produced by Lawrence Turman, and featured Henry Darrow (as a social worker), Pepe Serna (right), Trinidad Silva, Gary Cervantes, Claudio Martinez, Domingo Ambriz and Lawrence Pressman. (102 mins)

△ Adopting behaviour patterns reminiscent of Jerry Lewis in his heyday, comedian Steve Martin bulldozed his way through **The Jerk**, an uneven comedy whose hit-and-miss approach to the material nonetheless yielded more laughs than groans. Martin played the adopted son of black parents (Mabel King and Richard Ward) who, on learning of his parental situation for the first time, leaves home with his dog. How he copes in the outside world, where he becomes a gas station attendant for Jackie Mason, and the driver of an amusement park train, formed the crux of the screenplay which the star collaborated on with Carl Gottlieb and Martin Elias (story by Martin and Gottlieb). The women in his life were Catlin Adams and Bernadette Peters (left, with Martin) but, in director Carl Reiner's scheme of things, they took third place to the many sight gags and off-the-cuff *non sequiturs* that proliferated throughout. Whether or not one enjoyed the film depended solely on one's admiration for its star. It was an Aspen Film Society-William E. McEuen-David V. Picker Production, produced by Picker and McEuen, and in supporting roles featured Dick Anthony Williams, Bill Macy and M. Emmett Walsh. (104 mins)

1980

▽ There was enough spicy language and ribald dialogue in **The Last Married Couple In America** to warrant cinema managers issuing a can of aerosol air-freshener with each admission. Just as Julie Andrews in *S.O.B.* (Lorimar, 1981) would shed her Mary Poppins image by baring her boobs, so Natalie Wood here threw discretion to the proverbial winds by reverting to the occasional use of good old Anglo-Saxon expletives. Apart from this innovation, John Herman Shaner's screenplay offered nothing new, and was just another glossy account of a happy Beverly Hills couple whose marital bliss is shattered when a blonde sets her sights on hubby. The couple in question were Miss Wood and George Segal (who, in the course of the film contracts gonorrhea), with Valerie Harper as the temptress. It all came right in the end, though, with Wood (right) and Segal (left) once again enjoying a contented life together, while the marriages of their friends continue to crumble. Richard Benjamin co-starred as a neurotic, with other parts under Gilbert Cates' smooth but shallow direction going to Allan Arbus, Charlene Ryan (as a hooker), Marilyn Sokol, Arlene Golonka, Oliver Clark, Priscilla Barnes, Dom DeLuise and Bob Dishy. Edward S. Feldman and scenarist Shaner producer, with Gilbert and Joseph Cates as executive producers. (103 mins)

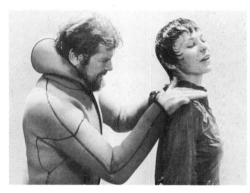

△ Roger Moore, taking time off from his James Bond heroics, received top billing in a slickly serviceable caper called **ffolkes** in the US and **North Sea Hijack** in Britain. Playing a frogman and dedicated male chauvinist pig, Moore (left) was put to work in Jack Davies' screenplay (based on his novel *Esther, Ruth and Jennifer*) as the saviour of a hi-jacked supply ship (called 'Esther') which bad guy Anthony Perkins and his accomplices have commandeered. Not only that, but the heavies threaten to destroy a drilling rig (called 'Ruth') and a vital production platform (called 'Jennifer') unless a sizeable ransom is paid. Andrew V. McLaglen's direction kept it simmering nicely, and was well-served by second-billed James Mason as an admiral. The rest of the cast included Michael Parks, David Hedison, Jack Watson, George Baker, Jeremy Clyde, David Wood, Faith Brook, Lea Brodie (right) and Jennifer Hilary. Elliot Kastner produced, and Moses Rothman was executive producer. (99 mins)

▽ Marty Feldman (illustrated) was a three-time loser in **In God We Trust**, an excrutiatingly unfunny comedy which he wrote (with Chris Allen), directed, and starred in as a blissfully innocent monk who leaves the relative safety of his mountainside monastery for the devil's playground (ie Hollywood Boulevard). His mission? To persuade Armageddon T. Thunderbird (Andy Kaufman) to part with some ready cash so that the monastery can remain in business. In Hollywood, Feldman, dressed in a robe and sandals, encounters a number of decidedly weird characters, as well as the proverbial tart-with-a-heart (Louise Lasser) with whom he has a most unlikely affair. Richard Pryor appeared as a character called G.O.D. (and made a complete fool of himself in the process), with Peter Boyle, Wilfrid Hyde-White and Severn Dardern completing the cast for producers Howard West and George Shapiro. Apart from a handful of sight gags in the opening sequence of the film, and the homage they paid to silent screen comic Buster Keaton, **In God We Trust** offered the dispiriting spectacle of a comedy totally bereft of laughs. (97 mins)

▽ After *Jaws* (1975) and *The Deep* (Columbia, 1977), scenarist Peter Benchley, working from his novel of the same name, took to the water once again in **The Island** and, in cahoots with director Michael Ritchie set out to top, for sheer gratuitous horror, the worst excesses of his two aforementioned hits. The not-for-the-squeamish sight of eyes being stretched open with pegs, bodies being bled by leeches and stung by jellyfish, and young men being mutilated with grappling hooks, were all part and parcel of a story involving the mysterious murders of a boat-load of inebriated businessmen who, somewhere in the region of the Bermuda triangle, are found hacked to death. Michael Caine (left), as a British journalist, goes to investigate in the company of his young son, Jeffrey Frank (right), and what he discovers provided the film with its main narrative thrust, as well as its laughably far-fetched denouement. Ritchie's film started promisingly enough but, after passing the point of no return, deteriorated disastrously. A Zanuck-Brown production, it also starred David Warner as the leader of a tribe of inbred pirate buccaneers (!), and featured Angela Punch McGregor, Frank Middlemass, Don Henderson and Dudley Sutton. (114 mins)

▽ Superman Christopher Reeve didn't fly in **Somewhere In Time**, but he was able to turn back the clock – from the present to 1912. Director Jeannot Szwarc went back in time too, to the 1940's and such fantasies as *Portrait Of Jennie* (Selznick, 1948), *Here Comes Mr Jordan* (Columbia, 1941) and *The Ghost And Mrs Muir* (20th Century-Fox, 1942). So did scenarist Richard Matheson, whose several scripts for the TV series *The Twilight Zone* also dealt with time warp à la H.G. Wells. Working from his own novel, *Bid Time Return*, Matheson's story concerned a young Chicago playwright (Reeve, left) who, on a visit to Mackinac Island to attend a premiere of a play of his, becomes fascinated with a photograph of an actress (Jane Seymour) which was taken in 1912. It transpires that, in a previous life, Reeve had had an affair with the beautiful young woman, the details of which formed the content of this intriguing Rastar/Stephen Deutsch production. Finding his form after such woebegone efforts as *Bug* (Paramount, 1975) and *Jaws 2* (1978), director Szwarc revealed a genuine flair for period romance and, aided by Matheson's well-turned screenplay, the two attractive central performances, Seymour Klate's superb designs, Isidore Mankofsky's ravishing photography and Serge Rachmaninov, whose 'Variations On A Theme Of Paganini' did wonders to evoke an appropriately romantic mood, he came up trumps – though, unhappily, the film failed to find much of an audience. Christopher Plummer (right) was featured as a Svengali-type figure who dominates Miss Seymour, and the cast was completed by Teresa Wright, Bill Erwin, George Voskovec, Susan French and John Alvin. (103 mins)

△ Strictly for TV nostalgia freaks, **The Nude Bomb** unsuccessfully attempted to resurrect the characters created by Mel Brooks and Buck Henry for the sixties TV hit series, *Get Smart*. But with the absence of Barbara Feldon and Ed Platt (integral to the series as Agent 99 and The Chief), Arne Sultan, Bill Dana and Leonard B. Stern's screenplay laboured under a decided disadvantage in the telling of a tale that involved Don Adams' (illustrated) attempts to prevent the launching of a missile designed to send the whole world into a state of nudity. Producer Jennings Lang's cast included Sylvia Kristel, Rhonda Fleming, Dana Elcar, Pamela Hensley, Andrea Howard, Norman Lloyd, Bill Dana and Gary Imhof, and it was directed by Clive Donner who, hampered by the show's lack of satirical bite, wasn't able to do much with it. (94 mins)

▷ **Coal Miner's Daughter** could so easily have been just another rags-to-riches biopic of a country-and-western singer, complete with all the attendant clichés in which the genre specializes. The potential for platitudes was certainly inherent in this story of a Kentucky lass whose singing ability is recognised, then nurtured, by a young man who becomes her husband and takes her away from the squalor of her hillbilly roots to the 'big time' in Nashville, Tennessee. What made it so special was Sissy Spacek's dynamic performance as Loretta Lynn, the coal miner's daughter of the title. Tom Rickman's screenplay, based on the autobiography Lynn wrote with George Vescey, certainly stretched Miss Spacek's talents to the full, requiring her to mature from an unworldly 13-year-old to a fully fledged artist grappling with drug addiction, marital problems and a nervous breakdown. As Miss Spacek (right) also did her own singing, the achievement was all the more remarkable. Tommy Lee Jones offered granite-like support as her caring husband, and there was good work from Beverly D'Angelo as country singer Patsy Cline, whose death greatly affects the coal miner's daughter. Also cast: Phyllis Boyens and Levon Helm (left) as Loretta's parents, as well as William Sanderson, Robert Elkins and Bob Hannah. It was affectionately directed by Michael Apted, and produced by Bernard Schwartz. Songs included: 'I'm A Honky Tonk Girl', 'You Ain't Man Enough To Take My Man', 'You're Lookin' At Country', 'Coal Miner's Daughter' Loretta Lynn; 'One's On The Way' Shel Silverstein, performed by Spacek; 'Back In My Baby's Arms' Bob Montgomery, performed by Spacek. (125 mins)

SO
7

▽ **The Blues Brothers** presented John Belushi (right) and Dan Aykroyd (left) as a pair of musicians struggling to get their now dispersed musical combo back together again when Belushi comes out of jail. Aykroyd and director John Landis chronicled the mayhem that followed in a screenplay redolent of a forties storyline but eighties expression and, if it was all rather too frenzied for belief, it was also high on entertainment value. This was due not least to Belushi and Aykroyd's own skills at playing knockabout farce, and they were ably supported by James Brown, Aretha Franklin, Kathleen Freeman, Carrie Fisher, John Candy, Henry Gibson, Steve Lawrence, Ray Charles and Twiggy. One of the high-spots: Cab Calloway singing his legendary 'Minnie The Moocher', which he composed with Irving Mills. The energetic choreography was by Carlton Johnson, Robert K. Weiss produced, and John Landis held it all (including the destruction of an inordinate number of automobiles) together with evident zest. Fifteen eclectic songs and musical numbers by assorted composers included Henry Mancini's 'Peter Gunn Theme', 'Quando, Quando, Quando' (Tony Renis, A. Testa), and Leiber and Stoller's 'Jailhouse Rock'. (132 mins)

△ Based on the writings and exploits of maverick journalist Hunter S. Thompson, **Where The Buffalo Roam** took a nostalgic look at the late sixties and, at best, was a series of incidents, or set-pieces, rather than a coherent screenplay with a solid story to tell, or a point of view to express. Indeed, it was the film's general aimlessness that was its most serious fault. For, apart from the fact that its hero uses drink and drugs to get him through his assignments (which include covering San Francisco's 1968 marijuana trials, the 1972 Super Bowl, and the Presidential campaign), the viewer remained baffled about Hunter S. Thompson and what motivated him. Still, Bill Murray (right), a cigarette holder constantly dangling from his lips, made a credible stab at portraying Thompson's anti-establishment eccentricities; while Peter Boyle (left) as an equally maverick lawyer was an appropriately unorthodox companion for Thompson on his various assignments. Art Linson, making his debut as a director, played it mostly for laughs and, for much of the time, got them. Linson also produced, with a cast that included Bruno Kirby, Rene Auberjonois, R.G. Armstrong, Danny Goldman, Rafael Campos and Leonard Frey. (96 mins)

▽ Though director Jonathan Demme's **Melvin And Howard** broke no records at the box office, it was an unusually striking piece of film-making that affectionately explored the myth of the American Dream by bringing together, for one brief moment in time, Howard Hughes and Melvin Dummer, one of life's perennial losers. Dummer's encounter with the legendary billionaire occurs on a Nevada highway when, believing Hughes to be nothing more than an inebriated tramp in need of help, he agrees to give him a lift to Las Vegas. After the vagrant tells him who he really is, Dummer, understandably, refuses to take him seriously, and even offers the man a few cents to see him on his way. It is only when Dummer, an impecunious milkman, is informed that Hughes has left him $156,000,000 in his will, that he realises the grizzled old tramp was not joking after all. Though it was Dummer's fate never to receive a cent of the money, he became a celebrity for a short while, but was totally unable to turn his moment of glory to advantage. Bo Goldman's sensitive, beautifully observed screenplay used Dummer as the spokesman for the Middle-American proletariat: the little man with big dreams, strait-jacketed into a society and into a claustrophobic domestic situation that precludes any part of the dream from coming true. Paul Le Mat (right) was flawless as the engagingly unfulfilled Melvin; so was Mary Steenburgen as his first wife, whose on-off relationship provided the film with its most humourous moments, as well as its most poignant; Jason Robards (left) depicted the fabled Howard. There were outstanding performances, too, from Michael J. Pollard, Pamela Reed, Dabney Coleman, Jack Kehoe, Denny Dark and Susan Peretz. Real-life Melvin Dummer appeared as a counterman in a bus depot; and there was a brief appearance, also from Gloria Grahame. It was produced by Art Linson and Don Phillips. (93 mins)

◁ Producer Lawrence Gordon's **Xanadu** had its origins firmly in the Hollywood musicals of the forties, with star Gene Kelly called Danny McGuire – the same name he had been given in Columbia's *Cover Girl* (1944). However, an unbelievably absurd plot removed any possibility of further comparison between the earlier film and this one. A fantasy, it had a struggling artist (Michael Beck) searching for a beautiful, mystery muse (Olivia Newton-John, co-starring). Along the way, Beck (left) meets an embittered but wealthy clarinettist (Kelly, centre), and persuades him to back a disco nightclub. Kelly was clearly not at home in this one, Miss Newton-John (right) was dreary, and any enticement to audiences stopped at the title. Robert Greenwald directed from a clumsy and ineffectual screenplay by Richard Christian Danus, Michael Kane and Marc Reid Rubel, and the musical numbers were staged (well) by Kenny Ortega and Jerry Trent. Others cast: Sandra Katie Hanley, Fred McCarren, Ron Woods, and the voices of Coral Browne and Wilfrid Hyde-White (in a fantasy sequence at the end). The score contained a couple of seductive, if not particularly durable, ballads such as 'Magic' (by Olivia Newton-John) and 'Suddenly' (Newton-John, Cliff Richard). (96 mins)

▽ It first came to the screen in 1934, via Paramount, as *Little Miss Marker*, and starred Shirley Temple and Adolphe Menjou. The same studio remade it in 1949 under the title *Sorrowful Jones* with Lucille Ball and Bob Hope. A third version surfaced in 1963 from Universal-International called *40 Pounds Of Trouble*, with Tony Curtis and Suzanne Pleshette. The fourth, and latest version, again called **Little Miss Marker**, introduced an engaging moppet called Sara Stimson (left), whose leading man was the inimitable Walter Matthau (right). He played Sorrowful Jones, a bachelor bookie seemingly impervious to sentimentality (and stingy to boot) who, as was always the way with the Damon Runyon story on which it was based, 'inherits' a destitute six-year-old after the kid's father leaves her with him as security for a bet, and never returns to claim her. Walter Bernstein, who both wrote and directed it, made the most of the 'odd couple' relationship between Matthau and little Miss Stimson, but failed to bring much plausibility to the casting of Julie Andrews as a wealthy widow. Tony Curtis was flashily cast as a smooth heavy who wants to borrow $50,000 from Matthau to establish a casino in Andrews' plush mansion; the talented Lee Grant was wasted in a bit part as a judge. The rest of the players included Bob Newhart, Brian Dennehey, Kenneth McMillan and Andrew Rubin. (103 mins)

◁ That outstanding actress Ellen Burstyn (illustrated) was given a sizeable role in **Resurrection**, a drama of the supernatural that, refreshingly, focused on good rather than evil. She played a wealthy Los Angeles housewife whose birthday present to her husband (Jeffrey DeMunn) of a sports car results in his death in a crash, and in her being paralysed from the waist down. While convalescing at home in Kansas, she discovers an aptitude for psychic healing which she refuses to exploit, or to acknowledge as being God-given – a decision which alienates her from her father (Roberts Blossom) and newly acquired boyfriend (Sam Shepherd). Though director Daniel Petrie steered his film uneasily between soap opera and mystical occult drama, he drew commendable performances from both Miss Burstyn and Shepherd, as well as from Eva Le Gallienne (as Burstyn's grandmother), Richard Farnsworth, Clifford David, Pamela Paynton Wright, Madeleine Thornton Sherwood and Lois Smith. Lewis John Carlino wrote it and it was produced by Renee Missel and Howard Rosenman. (103 mins)

▽ After the success of their anarchic debut effort *Up In Smoke* (Paramount, 1978) Richard 'Cheech' Martin (left) and Thomas Chong's (right) **Cheech And Chong's Next Movie** was a bitter disappointment for their fast-growing network of fans. An aimless, self-indulgent *pot pourri* of this-and-that, amateurishly directed (by Chong) and performed by the duo with an arrogant self-confidence, its virtually plotless screenplay (by the two stars) had them wandering purposelessly around Los Angeles in search of the bare bones of a coherent movie. They never found them. It was a C. and C. Brown Production which, for the record, also featured Evelyn Guerrero (centre), Betty Kennedy and Sy Kramer. (99 mins)

◁ **Smokey And The Bandit II** was a lumbering sequel to its profitable predecessor which found truck driver Burt Reynolds (illustrated) being upstaged by a pregnant elephant he has agreed to transport to a Republican convention. As in the first film, Sally Field was the star's romantic interest, while Jackie Gleason was also on hand to continue his frustrating vendetta with Reynolds. What was missing from this Rastar/Mort Engelberg production, produced by Hank Moonjean, was a feeling of spontaneity which not even a climactic ten-minute car chase could induce. The only genuinely funny moments occurred after the end titles when Reynolds (illustrated) and Co allowed some of the film's 'out-takes' (or mistakes) to be shown. Nothing in Jerry Belson and Brock Yates' screenplay (story by Michael Kane, based on characters created by Hal Needham who also directed) was half as hilarious. Also cast: Jerry Reed, Dom DeLuise, Paul Williams, Pat McCormick and David Huddleston. (101 mins)

1981

▽ It was somewhat dispiriting to see that hard-hitting, no-punches-pulled comedian Richard Pryor lending his refreshingly abrasive personality to a film as marshmallow gooey as **Bustin' Loose**. Not only was it a Richard Pryor Production, with Pryor (and Michael S. Glick) producing, but Pryor also provided the soft-centred story, adapted by Lonne Elder III, and scripted by Roger L. Simon. All about a habitual thief (Pryor, right) who, while out on probation for attempting to steal a truck-load of TV sets, is persuaded by his girlfriend (Cicely Tyson, left) to drive a bus full of handicapped and maladjusted school children from the city to a farm in the country, its saccharine content made it a decidedly sticky journey to tolerate. En route to the country, the seemingly hard-hearted Pryor is completely won over by the kids and, by the end of the picture, he is pretty much a reformed man. Yuck. Oz Scott's direction, combining raucousness and sentimentality, didn't help. The best thing in the show was the kids themselves, and they included Angel Ramirez, Jimmy Hughes, Edwin DeLeon, Edwin Kinter, Tami Luchow, Janet Wong, Alphonso Alexander and Kia Cooper. (92 mins)

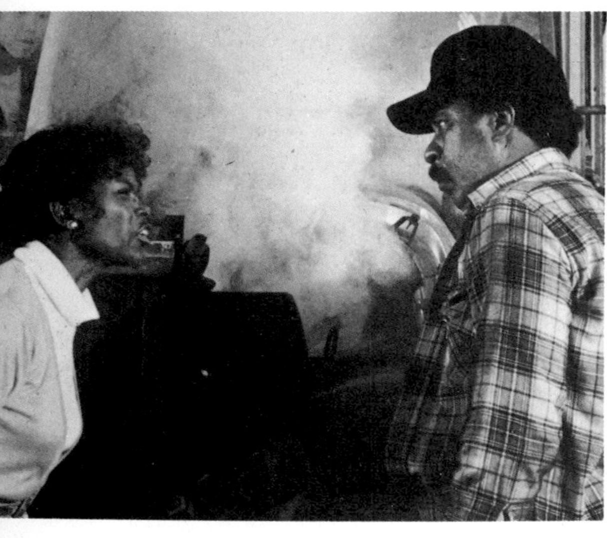

△ Basically a filmed version of Luis Valdez's absorbing stage play of the same name, **Zoot Suit**, filmed for a mere $2½ million (meagre by eighties standards) in eleven days, used the Sleepy Lagoon Murder Mystery in Los Angeles in 1942 (in which a gang of Chicanos were railroaded into life sentences on a trumped-up murder charge) to make its powerful point about the treatment of downtrodden minority groups. Valdez himself adapted his play for the screen, and directed as well, drawing fine performances from a cast headed by Daniel Valdez (left) as the group's leader and Edward James Olmos (right) as his zoot-suited alter ego. Rose Portillo, Charles Aidman, Tyne Daly, Lupe Ontiveros, John Anderson, Abel Franco and Mike Gomez were in it too, and it was produced by Peter Burrell. (103 mins)

▽ Director Franco Zeffirelli, aided by scenarist Judith Rascoe, did a castration job on **Endless Love**, reducing Scott Spencer's graphic, gritty, intelligently written 1979 best-seller about the nature of sexual obsession, to a soggy teenage romance between a 17-year-old Chicago boy (Martin Hewitt, left) and a 15-year-old girl (Brooke Shields, right). Shield's father (Don Murray) can't abide what's going on between the young lovers, especially when Hewitt all but takes up residence in his daughter's boudoir, and banishes him from the house for a month. Desperate to see his girlfriend, Hewitt sets fire to the house, his plan being to 'rescue' the family from the blaze. But things go wrong, the house burns to the ground, Hewitt confesses his crime, is sent to a correctional institute for a couple of years, unintentionally brings about Murray's death and is again dragged off by the cops. Though the brief love scenes between the youngster – so graphically described in the novel – were reduced to the level of an every-hair-in-place TV commercial for body fragrance, thus eliminating the key motivation from the story, the performances, despite the watering down of the screenplay were, in the main, convincing. Miss Shields, apart from a tendency to smile too much, was suitably love-struck, with Shirley Knight (as her mother) and Richard Kiley and Beatrice Straight (as her lover's parents) particularly good. Newcomer Hewitt was appropriately virile, and the cast was completed by Jimmy Spader, Ian Ziering, Robert Moore and Penelope Milford. It was a Keith Barish-Dyson Lovell production. (115 mins)

▷ The unlikely romance between John Belushi (right), as a hard-bitten columnist on the *Chicago Sunday Times* (whose speciality is uncovering local political scandals), and Blair Brown (left) as an ornithologist living in the Rocky Mountains (*her* speciality is avoiding inquisitive newspapermen) was charted with fair-to-middling results in **Continental Divide**. The couple meet when a story Belushi is working on about a corrupt alderman gets too hot to handle, and he is sent away from his usual beat to interview bird lady Brown. Despite the clash of their very different personalities and totally opposed environments, love finds a way, and it says much for the two central performances that a basically far-fetched situation seemed plausible enough while it was unfolding. Lawrence Kasdan's screenplay had some excellent things in it; it was directed by Michael Apted with the solid understanding that the film's *raison d'être* was Belushi; and produced by Bob Larson for Amblin Production. The executive producers were Steven Spielberg and Bernie Brillstein. Also cast: Allen Goorwitz, Tony Ganios, Val Avery, Liam Russell, Everett Smith and Bill Henderson. (103 mins)

△ Although for half a century a group of old fogeys – Fred Astaire (2nd left), Melvyn Douglas (right), Douglas Fairbanks Jr (left) and John Houseman (2nd right) – have regularly met to swap ghost stories, not once has any one of them mentioned an incident way back in their pasts that resulted in the death of a beautiful young woman (Alice Krige). It is only when the young woman materialises, returning to exact her revenge, that the dark secret shared by the elderly quartet in **Ghost Story** is revealed. Unfortunately, Lawrence D. Cohen's screenplay, based on a novel by Peter Straub, was so punctured with holes (through which most of the suspense disappeared), and left so many puzzling questions unanswered, that audiences were denied any chance of involvement. As ghosts of their former selves, Messrs Astaire *et al* looked more like members of a geriatric convention than employable actors; nor were there many saving graces from a cast that also included Craig Wasson, Jacqueline Brookes, Patricia Neal, Miguel Fernandes, Lance Holcombe, Mark Chamberlin and Tim Choate. Burt Weissbourd produced, and it was directed, without much bite, by John Irvin. (110 mins)

△ Barbra Streisand (right) came to the rescue of **All Night Long** as a romantically dissatisfied kook who decides to have an affair with Gene Hackman (left), a recently demoted executive, despite the fact that she is married to Hackman's cousin (Kevin Dobson) and is having a ding-dong with Hackman's son (Dennis Quaid). All sorts of marital havoc was wrought before W.D. Richter's almost laughless screenplay paved the way for a happy ending, while providing work for Diane Ladd (as Hackman's wife), William Daniels, Ann Doran, Jim Nolan, Judy Kerr and Marlyn Gates. The main problem with the film was that its attitudes to life and love were not nearly as contemporary as they thought they were. Another problem was Jean-Claude Tramon's direction – there just wasn't enough of it. Leonard Goldberg and Jerry Weintraub produced. (87 mins)

▽ There were some quite good special effects in **The Incredible Shrinking Woman**, a contemporary remake of *The Incredible Shrinking Man* (1957), with Lily Tomlin (illustrated) as a suburban housewife who, alarmingly, finds she is shrinking in size when she spills perfume over herself which has been given to her by her marketing executive husband (Charles Grodin). For the rest, though, Jane Wagner's screenplay changed the emphasis of the original novel (by Richard Matheson) on which it was based, turning it into a satire on the affluent consumer society and its ultra-reliance on TV-advertised products from breakfast cereals to washing-up liquid. Under Joel Schumacher's untidy direction, the satirical element was whammed home with all the subtlety of a kick in the groin, all its messages having already been delivered so early on in the film that there was nothing left to say by the halfway mark. Hank Moonjean produced, Ms Wagner was executive producer (for Lija Productions) and, as well as Tomlin and Grodin, who did their best with the material, the cast included Ned Beatty, Henry Gibson, Elizabeth Wilson, Maria Smith and Pamela Bellwood. (88 mins)

▷ The redoubtable Katharine Hepburn (right), returned to Universal to be teamed for the first time with Henry Fonda (centre) in **On Golden Pond**, an adaptation by Eric Thompson of his Broadway play. A 'small' picture dealing with 'big' themes (old age, the approach of death, lack of communication in family relationships), it was a bitter-sweet comedy-drama in which Fonda played Norman Thayer, a crotchety retired professor who, together with his wife, Ethel (Hepburn), returns to Golden Pond, their idyllic lakeside cottage in New England, to spend the 48th summer of their married lives. Though his 80th birthday is imminent, time has done little to mellow Thayer and, with the arrival of his daughter Chelsea (Jane Fonda left), her future husband Bill (Dabney Coleman), and Billy (Doug McKeon), Bill's foul-mouthed 13-year-old son, we see just how irascible a man he can be. For most of her life, Chelsea has been unable to communicate with her father who has constantly underestimated and undermined her, and it is only after she and Bill go to Europe, leaving young Billy in the care of the old folk, that we see why. For Norman Thayer always wanted a son, and the touching friendship that develops between the 13-year-old and the octogenarian, makes this abundantly clear. Indeed, it is their relationship (which grows during a series of fishing outings, one of which almost ends in tragedy when their boat capsizes), that is the mainstay of the film. The most touching sequences, however, are reserved for the end when Chelsea, now married to Bill, returns to Golden Pond to collect Billy and finally manages to arrive at some sort of mutual understanding with her father. Having made peace with his daughter and bid his newly-acquired family goodbye, Norman, alone with his wife, collapses and, in view of the actor's real-life illness at the time, enacts a near-death scene of almost unbearable poignancy which, no doubt, helped to clinch Fonda's first-ever Oscar. Indeed, the acting throughout was as observant as Thompson's text, and the performances of the five principal players were excellent. Bruce Gilbert produced, Mark Rydell directed with sensitivity, and the cast was completed by William Lanteau and Chris Rydell. Sadly Fonda died nine months after the film's release. (109 mins)

△ An aberration weighing in at $10,000,000 – and looking as though it had cost a millionth of that – **Heartbeeps** was a catastrophe which found two robots falling in love with each other. The male robot was Andy Kaufman (right), his female counterpart Bernadette Peters (left). It was not their finest hour. Randy Quaid, Kenneth McMillan, Melanie Mayron, Christopher Guest and the voice of Jack Carter were also associated with it; it was written by John Hill, produced by Michael Phillips and directed by Allan Arkush. R.I.P. (79 mins)

▷ In **Nighthawks**, Sylvester Stallone left the screenplay to David Shaber and the direction to Bruce Malmuth, and concentrated solely on his performance as Deke DaSilva, a tough New York cop who undergoes a special course in anti-terrorist tactics, and takes on a mercenary called Wulfgar (Rutger Hauer). After botching a job in London, in which a department store explosion against British colonialism results in the unplanned deaths of several children, Wulfgar is determined to regain credibility in the eyes of terrorist organisations who are likely to need his services in the future. He goes to New York, where his arrival has been anticipated by Inspector Hartman of Interpol (Nigel Davenport). How Wulfgar is eventually caught formed the main content of the film, with time off en route to the denouement for a familiar glimpse at the kind of job pressures which have placed Stallone's marriage (to Lindsay Wagner) in jeopardy. Stallone's (left) performance was marginally more interesting than some he had given in the past, but it was nothing special. The rest of the cast included Billy Dee Williams (right), Persis Khambatta, Hilaire Thompson, Joe Spinell, Walter Matthews and E. Brian Dean. Martin Poll produced, and Michael Wise and Franklin R. Levy were the executive producers. (99 mins)

▽ Many of the ingredients that made director Tobe Hooper's *The Texas Chain Saw Massacre* (Excalibur Films, 1978) such a frightening experience, were reassembled for **The Funhouse**, whose shock-horror tactics gave it a palpable dimension of nastiness. Set for most of its time in a carnival funhouse, where a group of youngsters come up against an albino mutant, it offered the usual quota of grisly deaths appropriate to such exploitation chillers, all of them handled to maximum shock effect by Hooper and scenarist Larry Block. The non-stellar cast, included Elizabeth Berridge (right), Cooper Huckabee (left), Miles Chapin, Largo Woodruff, Shawn Carson, Jeanne Austin, Jack McDermott, Kevin Conway and – as a fortune-teller who is murdered early on in the film – Sylvia Miles. Derek Power and Steve Bernhardt produced for Mace Neufeld Productions. (96 mins)

△ Jack and Kate Burroughs (Alan Alda and Carol Burnett, both illustrated centre), Nick and Anne Callan (Len Cariou and Sandy Dennis), and Claudia and Danny Zimmer (Rita Moreno and Jack Weston illustrated front right and left) are three middle-aged married couples who spend a great deal of time in each other's company. They take their holidays in a group and, on the surface at any rate, are the best of friends. In **The Four Seasons**, a perceptive comedy, their so-called friendship is sorely tested when Len Cariou (right rear) not only admits that he is bored to distraction by his wife, but proves it by dumping her for an attractive younger woman (Bess Armstrong, centre rear) whom he soon marries. The screenplay by Alan Alda, who also directed, concerned itself chiefly with the tension (much of it engendered through jealousy) that this situation creates, in the process of which the characters reveal a great deal about their insecurities and their frustrations. At the same time, the film took a probing look at marriage and its difficulties, doing so with immense perspicacity and humour. Only towards the end, in a sequence in which Jack Weston falls through thin ice on a frozen lake, did the film lose its grip on excellence to the mediocrity of TV situation comedy. Weston would surely have died of hypothermia long before help eventually arrived. A small point, maybe, but in a film that dealt so honestly with the realities of life, a jarring one. Helping to keep it in the family were Elizabeth and Beatrice Alda as a couple of offspring, with Robert Hitt, Kristi McCarthy and David Stackpole completing the cast. Martin Bregman produced, and the executive producer was Louis A. Stroller. (108 mins)

1982

▽ Though director Constantin Costa-Gavras never specifically stated which country was providing the setting for his gripping political thriller, **Missing**, it might safely be assumed that it was Allende's Chile at the time of the US involvement with the military coup of 1973. Based on the actual disappearance of a young American writer named Charles Horman, the film featured John Shea as Horman and Sissy Spacek (left) as his wife, and starred Jack Lemmon (right) as Horman's conservative, businessman father Ed, whose assistance Spacek seeks after she has failed to make headway with the authorities in locating her missing husband – despite the fact that father-and-daughter-in-law have little in common and are barely civil to one another. A Christian Scientist and staunch defender of The American Way Of Life, Lemmon's chauvinism undergoes a dramatic change when, in the course of his exhaustive enquiries into the whereabouts of his missing son, he learns that US embassy representatives are in cahoots with the country's fascistic military regime, and that his government is not beyond placing business expediency before human lives. As he had so successfully done in his award-winning **Z** (France, 1968), director Costa-Gavras again meticulously pieced together a Kafkaesque jigsaw, and emerged with an anti-establishment suspenser that was, at the same time, a domestic drama in which, at the end, father-and-daughter-in-law are reconciled in a shared tragedy of considerable power. Lemmon's performance was flawless; so was Miss Spacek's; and there was excellent support from a cast that included Melanie Mayron, Charles Cioffi, David Clennon and Richard Venture. Edward Lewis produced, garnering a number of Oscar nominations, and it was written by Costa-Gavras and Donald Stewart from a book by Thomas Hauser. (122 mins)

△ The legend of **Barbarosa** was given a respectable once-over in the film that bears his name, with Willie Nelson (illustrated) top-cast, and very sympathetically at that, as the outlaw who despite his criminal predilections, somehow always comes up smelling of roses. Second-billed Gary Busey was cast as the simple farm boy Barbarosa befriends, while the wife he loves but cannot bring himself to live with, was played by Isela Vega. A gentle, 'sensitive' western that eschewed unnecessary violence, it was competently scripted by co-producer William D. Witliff, produced by Paul N. Lazarus III (for Universal-Associated Film Distribution in association with ITC) and affectionately directed by Fred Schipisi, whose cast included Gilbert Roland, Danny De La Paz and George Voskovec (90 mins)

▽ Though author Cameron Crowe's **Fast Times At Ridgemont High** (GB: **Fast Times**) was based on the real-life observations he made – and chronicled in book form – on returning to high school at the age of 22, he himself does not feature in the movie which producers Art Linson and Irving Azoff made from those observations. Instead, his experiences there were fleshed out by a group of relative newcomers, all of them in desperate need of a plot on which to hang their efforts. Crowe's screenplay, alas, denied them any such luxury, and the result was a tiresome, discombobulated series of tenuously linked incidents involving such themes of adolescence as virginity loss, premature ejaculation and instant abortion. What must clearly have been intended as a kind of *American Graffiti* of the eighties, emerged as little more than an Andy Hardy update, with the cinema's new permissiveness replacing the antiseptic wholesomeness of the forties. For the record: Jennifer Jason Leigh (right) played a reluctant virgin who doesn't remain one for very long, Phoebe Cates was her more experienced friend, and Brian Backer and Robert Romanus (left) were their male counterparts. Sean Penn played a spaced-out surfer and Judge Reinhold a likeable teenager working his way through high school by working his way through a series of fast-food jobs. Old timer Ray Walston appeared as a school teacher and the cast, under Amy Heckerling's free-spirited direction, was completed by Scott Thomson, Vincent Schiavelli and Amanda Wyss. (92 mins)

1982

▷ The real stars of **The Thing**, a loose remake of Howard Hawks' superior *The Thing From Outer Space* (RKO, 1951), were special effects wizard Albert Whitlock and make-up man Rob Bottin. Their combined efforts resulted in an extra-terrestrial creature so grotesque that, for once, audiences were offered a monster more to be scorned than pitied. Capable of changing itself into any shape, both animal and human, that it chooses, 'the thing' coils itself around its victims with whip-lash tentacles and unsightly protuberances. The body under attack is then distorted beyond recognition, but later reshapes itself back to its former outward appearance. However, if dissected, the object of the attack will reveal fangs in place of intestines and, if decapitated, will sprout spider's legs and escape with a bizarre scuttle. In short, it has become 'the thing' until it, in turn, attacks the next victim. ... Truly Horrific. As in the earlier film, 'the thing' emerges from a slab of ice, its space ship having crashed in the Arctic wastes. In this version, it is first witnessed as a husky being pursued by a two-man Norwegian helicopter crew. Most of the action takes place among a group of American scientists and researchers at an isolated Arctic camp-site, a couple of whose members are taken over by 'the thing' as the story unfolds. Was top-starred Kurt Russell (illustrated), the expedition's pilot, one of the victims? Or A. Wilford Brimley? Or T.K. Carter? Or David Clennon? Or Keith David? Or Richard Dysart? Or Charles Hallahan? Or Peter Maloney? Or Richard Masur? Or Donald Moffat? Or Joel Polis? Or Thomas Waites? Bill Lancaster's screenplay (based on the story *Who Goes There?* by John W. Campbell Jr) revealed all, and provided a muddled climax and an ambiguous, unresolved finale. David Foster and Lawrence Turman produced, and it was directed by John Carpenter, who relied far too much on special effects rather than on honest-to-goodness story-telling to create his suspense. (109 mins)

△ Fifth-billed young Peter Billingsley (left) went some distance to create interest in the otherwise forgettable **Death Valley**, but it was an up-hill slog all the way. Playing a precocious, bespectacled kid from New York who is sent by his father (Edward Hermann) to visit his mother (Catherine Hicks, right) in Phoenix, Arizona, Billingsley was at least able to sustain audience interest in what was happening to him, and his efforts to resist his ma and her boyfriend Paul Le Mat's attempts to turn him from a New Yorker into a cowpoke, provided some amusement. Main thrust of co-producer Richard Rothstein's screenplay had young Billingsley discovering a few dead bodies parked in a car in the middle of nowhere and, after reporting the matter to sheriff A. Wilford Brimley, being chased all over the place by neurotic Stephen McHattie. Director Dick Richards wasn't able to do much with the material at hand, and Elliott Kastner's production came and went with indecent haste. (87 mins)

△ A good-natured spoof, in glorious black-and-white, on the detective genre, **Dead Men Don't Wear Plaid** attempted, with varying degrees of success, to recreate *film noir* by splicing into its narrative, clips from seventeen *noir* movies of forties vintage. Thus hero Steve Martin (illustrated), as a ten-dollar-a-day gumshoe called Rigby Reardon, is able to call on Humphrey Bogart's Philip Marlowe to help him solve the murder of sultry Rachel Ward's father. For most of the time the forties footage was felicitously chosen from such memorable examples of the genre as *This Gun For Hire* (Paramount, 1942), *Sorry Wrong Number* (Paramount, 1948), *The Killers* (1946), *The Big Sleep* (Warner Bros., 1946), *Deception* (Warner Bros., 1946), *Double Indemnity* (Paramount, 1944) and *White Heat* (Warner Bros., 1949) – and featured such stars as Alan Ladd, Burt Lancaster, Bette Davis, Ava Gardner, Barbara Stanwyck, Cary Grant, Veronica Lake, Lana Turner, Kirk Douglas, Fred MacMurray, James Cagney, Joan Crawford and Charles Laughton. Yet despite (or maybe because of) the wealth of material director and co-scripter Carl Reiner had to choose from, the story that these clips embellished had no momentum of its own and, by the final fade, all that audiences were left with was a certain curiosity value. Top-billed Martin did the best he could with original material, though leading lady Rachel Ward had little going for her apart from her stunning good looks. Reiner (whose co-scenarists were Martin and George Gipe) also appeared in the film as an Otto Preminger-type Field Marshal, with George Gaynes, Frank McCarthy, Adrian Ricard and Charles Picerni in it too. The period decor was by John DeCuir and the costumes by Edith Head, whose last film it was, and to whom it is dedicated. The score was by Miklos Rosza, and the producers were David Picker and William McEuen. (89 mins)

▷ A piece of contemporary science fiction which, according to its co-producer and director Steven Spielberg, is about the understanding, love and compassion people feel towards one another, E.T. **The Extra-Terrestrial** smashed all existing box-office records for the studio and, within just three months of its initial release, was well on the way to becoming the top money-making film of all time. As every schoolboy knows, it is the story of a young lad called Elliott (Henry Thomas, left) who befriends a strange looking extra-terrestrial after the creature is accidentally abandoned on Earth when his space ship takes off, in a hurry, without him. In a sense, Elliott has also been abandoned – by his father, who has left his mother and is living with another woman in Mexico, so he knows exactly the way poor E.T. (illustrated right) is feeling, and that if the creature is to survive, he has somehow to return home. Just how E.T., with Elliott's help, succeeds in returning to his people, provided scenarist Melissa Mathison with her story, and audiences with a cinematic adventure as pure, as innocent, and as entertaining as Dorothy's trip to the Land of Oz and back. Basically a children's story which, like all the best children's stories, also has immense adult appeal, the reason for the film's phenomenal success lay less in Dennis Muren's visual effects (which were good but not extraordinary) than in the enchanting development of the friendship that grows between Elliott and E.T., and in director Spielberg's imaginative grip on the material. What one remembered best about the picture was its more intimate and humorous moments, such as E.T. becoming intoxicated after drinking beer from a can, or dressing up in women's clothes, and gradually learning how to communicate with Elliott. For sheer lump-in-the-throat emotion, however, nothing surpassed the film's final sequence, when earthling and extra-terrestrial finally take their leave of one another. 'Stay' says a weepy Elliott as the two friends embrace. 'Come' replies E.T. Each knows, though, that unless Spielberg decides to bring them together again in a sequel, they will never meet again. With young master Thomas and E.T. giving the story its centre of gravity, there wasn't much chance for the rest of the cast to make much impression. Dee Wallace played Elliott's mum; Robert MacNaughton and Drew Barrymore were his brother and sister, and Peter Coyote a compassionate scientist who has waited ten years to witness the arrival on Earth of an E.T. It was co-produced by Kathleen Kennedy, scenarist Mathison was associate producer, and Frank Marshall the production supervisor. Allen Daviau photographed it, James Bissell designed it (though E.T. himself was created by Carlo Rambaldi), and the music was by John Williams. (115 mins)

▽ The studio's first venture with RKO was **The Border**, a rather flat affair produced by Edgar Bronfman Jr, directed (with little sense of involvement) by Tony Richardson, and starring Jack Nicholson (left). In a welcome change of pace, Nicholson played an ordinary Mr Nice Guy – a border patrol guard in El Paso, torn between right and wrong, and burdened with a materialistic, middle-class wife (Valerie Perrine, right) who thinks nothing about spending money her husband doesn't have on luxuries such as swimming pools and waterbeds. Harvey Keitel was second-billed as a colleague of Nicholson's whose job, together with Nicholson, is to ensure that no Mexican crosses the border into the US. Main crisis point in the screenplay by Deric Washburn, Walon Green and David Freeman occurred when the baby of a Mexican girl is kidnapped for adoption and Nicholson has to decide what to do about the situation. An up-beat ending, shot after the film was completed and in which Nicholson emerged as a traditional hero, failed to give the movie the box-office clout its producer (for Elfer Productions) was hoping for. Also cast: Warren Oates, Elpidia Carillo and Shannon Wilcox. (107 mins)

△ Both Burt Reynolds and Dolly Parton have star quality. In **The Best Little Whorehouse In Texas**, however, their personalities failed to ignite, and they left the screen wide open for Charles Durning to filch from under their noses whatever acting honours were to be squeezed out of director Colin Higgins' messy version of the Larry King-Peter Masterson-Carol Hall Broadway hit. Durning played a Texas governor whose political sidestepping results in the closure of Miss Mona Strangely's celebrated brothel – discreetly known as The Chicken Ranch because of a period in the establishment's history when dollars were in short supply and poultry was accepted payment for services rendered. Miss Parton (centre), her ample bosom outrageously emphasized in Theadora Van Runkle's tight-fitting costumes, starred as Mona, with Reynolds top-cast as local sheriff Ed Earl, whose 'secret' affair with la Parton provided the film with its love interest. The 'heavy' of the piece was Dom DeLuise as Melvin P. Thorpe, a resistible crusading TV consumer advocate who, in his capacity as self-appointed moral guardian of Texas, is determined to close down the whorehouse forthwith. DeLuise's performance was singularly unfunny, and although an accurate study of small-town bigotry and self-aggrandisement, it seemed to belong in another movie. Tony Stevens' choreography was suitably zestful and vigorous, the highlight being 'The Aggie Song', in which a team of footballers, having just scored the winning touchdown, prepare for a night of pleasure at The Chicken Ranch. And there was just as much fun to be had from Durning's more modestly choreographed showstopper, 'Sidestep'. The rest was pretty routine, with two new songs ('Sneakin' Around' and 'I Will Always Love You' by Dolly Parton) adding nothing to the history of musical comedy. A Universal-RKO presentation, produced by Thomas L. Miller, Edward K. Milkis and Robert Boyett, from a screenplay by Larry King, Peter Masterson and director Higgins, the film also featured Jim Nabors, Robert Mandan, Lois Nettleton, Theresa Merritt and Noah Beery Jr. Other songs: 'Twenty Fans', 'A Li'l Ol' Bitty Pissant Country Place', 'Watchdog Theme', 'Texas Has A Whorehouse In It', 'Hard Candy Christmas' Carol Hall. (114 mins)

△ DeWitt Bodeen's original story for **Cat People**, which first came to the screen via RKO, producer Val Lewton and director Jacques Tourneur in 1942, wasn't all that hot to begin with, and had it not been for Lewton's ability to elevate its 'B' picture content, it certainly would not have become the classic many admirers consider it to be. Director Paul Schrader's misogynistic remake, bereft of Lewton's guiding genius for turning dross into gold, was a shambles which, apart from Albert Whitlock's special effects (at their most gruesome in depicting the ripping off of an arm by a black panther), had little or no *raison d'être*. Appallingly edited (by Jacqueline Cambas), confusingly scripted (by Alan Ormsby) and indifferently acted by Nastassia Kinski (left), Malcolm McDowell (right), John Heard, Annette O'Toole and Ruby Dee, it was the story of a beautiful young woman (Kinski) who, after being reunited with her brother (McDowell) in New Orleans after many years of separation, is horrified to learn that they are both members of an ancient tribe who are transformed into killer leopards everytime they make love. In other words, the sex act literally brings out the beast in them. The only time they can free themselves from this debilitating state of affairs, is if they indulge in a spot of mutual incest. Producer Charles Fries' production had some stylish elements – notably John Bailey's Technicolor camerawork and Edward Richardson's art direction but, in the end, it emerged as an irredeemably silly exercise in the macabre. Also cast: Ed Begley Jr, Scott Paulin, Frankie Faison, Ron Diamond and Lynn Lowry. (118 mins)

▽ William Styron's best-selling novel, **Sophie's Choice**, came to the screen with its haunting resonances firmly in the grasp of director Alan J. Pakula, who also wrote the screenplay. Part of the movie, like the novel, dealt in flashback with Sophie's past and was shot on location in Yugoslavia, but the bulk of the story took place in a Brooklyn lodging house shortly after the second world war. Here Stingo, an aspiring young writer from the South (Peter MacNicol, right) becomes completely fascinated by two of his fellow tenants, Sophie and Nathan (Meryl Streep, centre, and Kevin Kline, left). Their story is seen through Stingo's eyes and, as it unfolds, we learn that Sophie is a Polish refugee who has been in Auschwitz, and Nathan is a research chemist working at a nearby laboratory. The two are lovers, locked in a passionate and complicated relationship in which Stingo becomes involved and which, ultimately, ends in tragedy. In flashback we see something of Sophie's life in Poland before the war, leading on to the hideous degradation she suffered in the concentration camp, and the appalling 'choice' she was forced to make. Directed by Pakula with a telling sense of time and place, the film was further served by three superlative leading performances, Miss Streep – who actually learned to speak Polish and German for the European scenes – deservedly capturing the Oscar for her beautifully observed portrayal. There was excellent support from a large cast, both American and European, including Rita Karin, Stephen D. Newman, Josh Mostel, David Wohl, Josef Sommer (the narrator in Poland), Gunther Maria Halmer (as Rudolf Hoess), and Michaela Karacic (Sophie as a child). The director of photography was Nestor Almendros, Marvin Hamlisch composed the original score (which was interspersed with music by Mozart, Beethoven, Handel, Mendelssohn, Schumann and Johann Strauss), and it was produced by Keith Barish and Pakula (executive producer Martin Starger). (151 mins)

▽ Muppet creator Jim Henson, together with Frank Oz (the voice of Miss Piggy, among others), explored new territory in **The Dark Crystal**, an ambitious, technically superb venture into fantasy whose simple message – that good triumphs over evil – was most imaginatively and effectively conveyed. All about a world inhabited by the monstrous Skeksis and the brave boy and girl gelflings who set out to destroy the Skeksis by replacing a precious shard that has been removed from the Dark Crystal, it involved the gelflings (illustrated) in all manner of adventures and obstacles before the job at hand was finally done. An entertainment aimed at both children and their parents, it was written by David Odell from a story by Henson, directed by Henson, and released by Universal and Associated Film Distributors for ITC. Character voices were supplied by Stephen Garlick, Lisa Maxwell, Billie Whitelaw, Percy Edwards, Brian Muehl, Sean Barrett and Joseph O'Connor. (94 mins)

Academy Nominations and Awards

The Academy of Motion Picture Arts and Sciences was founded in the early part of 1927 and, although an Awards of Merit committee was appointed soon after inauguration, it was not until July the following year that it suggested a procedure for recognizing meritorious achievement in the industry. The suggestion was adopted and studios were invited to submit lists of films released in the Los Angeles area between 1st August 1927 and 31st July 1928. From these lists the Academy's membership made its nominations in each of twelve categories of achievement and the winners were decided by an appointed board of judges. The results were announced publicly on 18th February 1929 and the awards themselves were presented three months later. The Academy has honoured members of the movie-making profession in this way every year since, and the annual ceremonial of presenting the Oscars (as the statuette trophies have been nicknamed) is perhaps the best known of all the Academy's activities.

The eligibility period of July to August remained in force until 1933 when the decision was taken to change to the calendar year. The last split-year period was therefore an extended one, from 1st August 1932 to 31st December 1933. The other eligibility qualification – release in Los Angeles area – has been unchanged throughout.

The following section gives details of all the nominations that Universal has received over the years. For the sake of completeness, nominations and awards not related to feature films are also included. Award-winners in categories where there were other nominations are identified by means of a star. Black spots denote recipients of awards that were presented at the Academy's discretion and were not competitive in the sense that other contenders, if indeed there were any, were not publicly nominated. It wasn't until the Academy's third season that Universal received its first nomination; for two seasons after that it failed to receive any, but it has figured every year since.

Occasionally the reader may discover a discrepancy between the year in which a film is nominated and the release year to which it is assigned in this book. Establishing the release year with precision is sometimes a difficult task and there are several ways in which confusion can arise. A film may be withdrawn for revision after an initial showing of short duration, and does not enjoy 'full' release until the following year. It also sometimes happens that a film is given a very limited release in the Los Angeles area simply to qualify for that year's awards, even though the main release is not planned until the following year, when the presentation ceremony gives it valuable publicity at the most effective time.

1929/1930

Picture
★ *All Quiet On The Western Front*

Direction
★ Lewis Milestone *All Quiet On The Western Front*

Writing
George Abbott, Maxwell Anderson, Dell Andrews *All Quiet On The Western Front*

Cinematography
Arthur Edeson *All Quiet On The Western Front*

Art Direction
★ Herman Rosse *King Of Jazz*

1932/1933

Short Subjects (cartoon)
The Merry Old Soul
(comedy)
Mister Mugg

Assistant Director
● Scott Beal (no film cited) – part of a multiple award

1934

Picture
Imitation Of Life

Sound Recording
Gilbert Kurland *Imitation Of Life*

Assistant Director
Scott Beal *Imitation Of Life*

Short Subjects (cartoon)
Jolly Little Elves

1935

Sound Recording
Gilbert Kurland *The Bride Of Frankenstein*

Short Subjects (novelty)
Camera Thrills

1936

Picture
Three Smart Girls

Actor
William Powell *My Man Godfrey*

Actress
Carole Lombard *My Man Godfrey*

Supporting Actor
Mischa Auer *My Man Godfrey*

Supporting Actress
Alice Brady *My Man Godfrey*

Direction
Gregory La Cava *My Man Godfrey*

Writing (original story)
Adele Commandini *Three Smart Girls*
(screenplay)
Eric Hatch, Morrie Ryskind *My Man Godfrey*

Art Direction
Albert S. D'Agostino, Jack Otterson *The Magnificent Brute*

Sound Recording
Homer G. Tasker *Three Smart Girls*

1937

Picture
One Hundred Men And A Girl

Writing (original story)
Hans Kraly *One Hundred Men And A Girl*

Cinematography
Joseph Valentine *Wings Over Honolulu*

Art Direction
Jack Otterson *You're A Sweetheart*

Music (score)
★ Universal Studio Music Department (under Charles Previn) *One Hundred Men And A Girl*

Sound Recording
Homer G. Tasker *One Hundred Men And A Girl*

Film Editing
Bernard W. Burton *One Hundred Men And A Girl*

1938

Writing (original story)
Marcella Burke, Frederick Kohner *Mad About Music*

Cinematography
Jospeph Valentine *Mad About Music*

Art Direction
Jack Otterson *Mad About Music*

Sound Recording
Bernard B. Brown *That Certain Age*

Music
(song)
Jimmy McHugh (music), Harold Adamson (lyrics) 'My Own' from *That Certain Age*
(scoring)
Charles Previn, Frank Skinner *Mad About Music*

Special Award
● Deanna Durbin (shared with Mickey Rooney) – for their significant contribution in bringing to the screen the spirit and personification of youth, and as juvenile players setting a high standard of ability and achievement.

1939

Art Direction
Jack Otterson, Martin Obzina *First Love*

Music (scoring)
Charles Previn *First Love*

Sound Recording
★ Bernard B. Brown *When Tomorrow Comes*

1940

Special Effects
John P. Fulton, Bernard B. Brown, Joseph Lapis *The Boys From Syracuse*
John P. Fulton, Bernard B. Brown, William Hedgecock *The Invisible Man Returns*

Cinematography (black & white)
Joseph Valentine *Spring Parade*

Sound Recording
Bernard B. Brown *Spring Parade*

Art Direction (black & white)
Jack Otterson *The Boys From Syracuse*

Music
(song)
Robert Stolz (music), Gus Kahn (lyrics) 'Waltzing In The Clouds' from *Spring Parade*
(score)
Charles Previn *Spring Parade*
(original score)
Frank Skinner *The House Of Seven Gables*

1941

Music
(song)
Hugh Prince (music), Don Raye (lyrics) 'Boogie Woogie Bugle Boy Of Company B' from *Buck Privates*
(scoring of a dramatic picture)
Frank Skinner *Back Street*
Richard Hageman *This Woman Is Mine*
(scoring of a musical picture)
Charles Previn *Buck Privates*

Special Effects
John Fulton, John Hall *The Invisible Woman*

Short Subjects (cartoons)
Boogie Woogie Bugle Boy Of Company B

Art Direction/Interior Decoration (black & white)
Martin Obzina, Jack Otterson/Russell A. Gausman *Flame Of New Orleans*

Sound Recording
Bernard B. Brown *Appointment For Love*

1942

Cinematography (colour)
Milton Krasner, William V. Skall, W. Howard Greene *Arabian Nights*

Art Direction/Interior Decoration
(black & white)
John B. Goodman, Jack Otterson/Russell A. Gausman, Edward R. Robinson *The Spoilers*
(colour)
Alexander Golitzen, Jack Otterson/Russell A. Gausman, Ira S. Webb *Arabian Nights*

Sound Recording
Bernard B. Brown *Arabian Nights*

Special Effects
John Fulton, Bernard B. Brown *Invisible Agent*

Short Subjects (cartoons)
Juke Box Jamboree

Music
(song)
Gene de Paul (music), Don Raye (lyrics) 'Pig Foot Pete' from *Keep 'Em Flying'**
(scoring of a dramatic or comedy picture)
Frank Skinner *Arabian Nights*
(scoring of a musical picture)
Charles Previn, Hans Salter *It Started With Eve*

* the Academy's official records erroneously give this song as coming from *Hellzapoppin'*

left to right *All Quiet On The Western Front* (1930); *King Of Jazz* (1930); *One Hundred Men And A Girl* (1937); Deanna Durbin – special award, 1938; (still from *Mad About Music*, 1938); *When Tomorrow Comes* (1939).

1943

Writing (original story)
Gordon McDonnell *Shadow Of A Doubt*

Cinematography
(black & white)
Tony Gaudio *Corvette K225*
(colour)
★ Hal Mohr, W. Howard Greene *Phantom Of The Opera*

Art Direction/Interior Decoration (colour)
★ Alexander Golitzen, John B. Goodman/Russell A. Gausman, Ira S. Webb *Phantom Of The Opera*

Sound Recording
Bernard B. Brown *Phantom Of The Opera*

Music
(song)
Jimmy McHugh (music), Herb Magidson (lyrics) 'Say A Prayer For The Boys Over There' from *Hers To Hold*
(scoring of a dramatic or comedy picture)
Hans J. Salter, Frank Skinner *The Amazing Mrs Holliday*
(scoring of a musical picture)
Edward Ward *Phantom Of The Opera*

Short Subjects (cartoons)
The Dizzy Acrobat

1944

Art Direction/Interior Decoration (colour)
John B. Goodman, Alexander Golitzen/Russell A. Gausman, Ira S. Webb *The Climax*

Sound Recording
Bernard B. Brown *His Butler's Sister*

Music
(song)
Jule Styne (music), Sammy Cahn (lyrics) 'I'll Walk Alone' from *Follow The Boys*
(scoring of a dramatic or comedy picture)
H.J. Salter *Christmas Holiday*
(scoring of a musical picture)
H.J. Salter *The Merry Monahans*

Short Subjects (cartoons)
Fish Fry

Documentary (short subjects)
★ *With The Marines At Tarawa* (U.S. Marine Corps)

1945

Sound Recording
Bernard B. Brown *Lady On A Train*

Music
(song)
Jerome Kern (music), E.Y. Harburg (lyrics) 'More And More' from *Can't Help Singing*
(scoring of a dramatic or comedy picture)
H.J. Salter *This Love Of Ours*
(scoring of a musical picture)
Jerome Kern, H.J. Salter *Can't Help Singing*

Short Subjects
(cartoons)
Poet And Peasant
(one-reel)
Your National Gallery

1946

Actress
Celia Johnson *Brief Encounter**

Direction
David Lean *Brief Encounter**
Robert Siodmak *The Killers*

Writing
(original story)
Vladimir Pozner *The Dark Mirror*
(original screenplay)
★ Muriel Box, Sydney Box *The Seventh Veil**
(screenplay)
Anthony Havelock-Allan, David Lean, Ronald Neame *Brief Encounter**
Anthony Veiller *The Killers*

Film Editing
Arthur Hilton *The Killers*

Music
(song)
Hoagy Carmichael (music), Jack Brooks (lyrics) 'Ole Buttermilk Sky' from *Canyon Passage*
(scoring of a dramatic or comedy picture)
Miklos Rozsa *The killers*

Short Subjects (cartoons)
Chopin's Musical Moments

* British production, released by Universal in the USA only (a Rank release in Great Britain)

1947

Picture
Great Expectations*

Actor
★ Ronald Colman *A Double Life*

Actress
Susan Hayward *Smash-Up – The Story Of A Woman*

left to right *Phantom Of The Opera* (1943); *The Seventh Veil* (1946); *Great Expectations* (1947); Ronald Colman (left) in *A Double Life* (1947); *Black Narcissus* (1947); Laurence Olivier and Jean Simmons in *Hamlet* (1948); *The Naked City* (1948); James Stewart and Josephine Hull in *Harvey* (1950).

Supporting Actor
Thomas Gomez *Ride The Pink Horse*

Supporting Actress
Marjorie Main *The Egg And I*

Direction
George Cukor *A Double Life*
David Lean *Great Expectations**

Writing
(original story)
Dorothy Parker, Frank Cavett *Smash-Up – The Story Of A Woman*
(original screenplay)
Ruth Gordon, Garson Kanin *A Double Life*
(screenplay)
David Lean, Ronald Neame, Anthony Havelock-Allan *Great Expectations**

Cinematography
(black & white)
★ Guy Green *Great Expectations**
(colour)
★ Jack Cardiff *Black Narcissus**

Art Direction/Set Decoration
(black & white)
★ John Bryan/Wilfred Shingleton *Great Expectations**
(colour)
★ Alfred Junge *Black Narcissus**

Film Editing
Fergus McDonnell *Odd Man Out**

Music (scoring of a dramatic or comedy picture)
★ Miklos Rozsa *A Double Life*

Short Subjects
(one-reel)
Brooklyn, U.S.A.
(two-reel)
Fight Of The Wild Stallions

* British production, released by Universal in the USA only (a Rank release in Great Britain)

1948

Picture
★ *Hamlet**

Actor
★ Laurence Olivier *Hamlet**

Supporting Actress
Jean Simmons *Hamlet**

Direction
Laurence Olivier *Hamlet**

Cinematography (black & white)
★ William Daniels *The Naked City*

Writing (motion picture story)
Malvin Wald *The Naked City*

Art Direction/Set Decoration (black & white)
★ Roger K. Furse/Carmen Dillon *Hamlet**

Costume Design (black & white)
★ Roger K. Furse *Hamlet**

Film Editing
★ Paul Weatherwax *The Naked City*

Short Subjects (two-reel)
Snow Capers

Music
(song)
Harold Arlen (music), Leo Robin (lyrics) 'For Every Man There's A Woman' from *Casbah*
(scoring of a dramatic or comedy picture)
William Walton *Hamlet**

* British production, released by Universal in the USA only (a Rank release in Great Britain)

1949

Sound Recording
Universal-International Sound Department *Once More, My Darling*

1950

Actor
James Stewart *Harvey*

Supporting Actress
★ Josephine Hull *Harvey*

Sound Recording
Universal-International Sound Department *Louisa*

1951

Actor
Arthur Kennedy *Bright Victory*

Short Subjects (two-reel)
Danger Under The Sea

Sound Recording
Leslie I. Carey *Bright Victory*

1952

Actor
Alec Guinness *The Lavender Hill Mob**

Writing
(screenplay)
Roger MacDougall, John Dighton, Alexander Mackendrick *The Man In The White Suit**
(story and screenplay)
★ T.E.B. Clarke *The Lavender Hill Mob**

Sound Recording
Pinewood Studios Sound Department *The Promoter**

* British production, released by Universal in the USA only (a Rank release in Great Britain)

1953

Writing (screenplay)
Eric Ambler *The Cruel Sea**

Sound Recording
Universal International Sound Department; Leslie I. Carey, sound director *The Mississippi Gambler*

Documentary (features)
*A Queen Is Crowned**

* British production, released by Universal in the USA only (a Rank release in Great Britain)

1954

Actress
Jane Wyman *Magnificent Obsession*

Writing (story and screenplay)
William Rose *Genevieve**
Valentine Davies, Oscar Brodney *The Glenn Miller Story*

Sound Recording
★ Leslie I. Carey *The Glenn Miller Story*

Music
(scoring of a dramatic or comedy picture)
Muir Mathieson *Genevieve**
(scoring of a musical picture)
Joseph Gershenson, Henry Mancini *The Glenn Miller Story*

Short Subjects (cartoons)
Crazy Mixed Up Pup

Scientific or Technical (class 3)
● David S. Horsley and the Universal-International Studio Special Photographic Department
● Fred Knoth and Orien Ernest of the Universal-International Studio Technical Department

* British production, released by Universal in USA only (a Rank release in Great Britain)

1955

Writing (motion picture story)
Joe Connelly, Bob Mosher *The Private War Of Major Benson*

Short Subjects (cartoons)
The Legend Of Rock-A-Bye-Point

1956

Supporting Actor
Robert Stack *Written On The Wind*

Supporting Actress
★ Dorothy Malone *Written On The Wind*

Music (song)
Victor Young (music), Sammy Cahn (lyrics) 'Written On The Wind' from *Written On The Wind*

Documentary (short subjects)
The House Without A Name

1957

Writing (story and screenplay – written directly for the screen)
Ralph Wheelright, R. Wright Campbell, Ivan Goff, Ben Roberts *Man Of A Thousand Faces*

Music (song)
Ray Evans and Jay Livingston (music and lyrics) 'Tammy' from *Tammy And The Bachelor*

1958

Sound
Universal-International Studio Sound Department; Leslie I. Carey, sound director *A Time To Love And A Time To Die*

1959

Actress
Doris Day *Pillow Talk*

Supporting Actress
Susan Kohner *Imitation Of Life*
Juanita Moore *Imitation Of Life*
Thelma Ritter *Pillow Talk*

Writing (story and screenplay – written directly for the screen)
Paul King, Joseph Stone, Stanley Shapiro, Maurice Richlin *Operation Petticoat*
★ Russell Rouse, Clarence Greene, Stanley Shapiro, Maurice Richlin *Pillow Talk*

Art Direction/Set Decoration (colour)
Richard H. Riedel/Russell A. Gausman, Ruby R. Levitt *Pillow Talk*

Music (scoring of a dramatic or comedy picture)
Frank DeVol *Pillow Talk*

left to right Alec Guinness (right) in *The Lavender Hill Mob* (1952); *The Glenn Miller Story* (1954); Dorothy Malone (right) in *Written On The Wind* (1956); Doris Day in *Pillow Talk* (1959); Peter Ustinov (centre) in *Spartacus* (1960); Gregory Peck in *To Kill A Mockingbird* (1962); *Father Goose* (1964).

1960

Supporting Actor
★ Peter Ustinov *Spartacus*

Cinematography (colour)
★ Russell Metty *Spartacus*

Art Direction/Set Decoration (colour)
★ Alexander Golitzen, Eric Orbom/Russell A. Gausman, Julia Heron *Spartacus*

Costume Design (colour)
Irene *Midnight Lace*
★ Valles and Bill Thomas *Spartacus*

Film Editing
Robert Lawrence *Spartacus*

Music (scoring of a dramatic or a comedy picture)
Alex North *Spartacus*

1961

Writing (story and screenplay – written directly for the screen)
Stanley Shapiro, Paul Henning *Lover Come Back*

Cinematography (colour)
Russell Metty *Flower Drum Song*

Art Direction/Set Decoration (colour)
Alexander Golitzen, Joseph Wright/Howard Bristol *Flower Drum Song*

Costume Design (colour)
Jean Louis *Back Street*
Irene Sharaff *Flower Drum Song*

Sound
Revue Studio Sound Department; Waldon O. Watson, sound director *Flower Drum Song*

Music (scoring of a musical picture)
Alfred Newman, Ken Darby *Flower Drum Song*

1962

Picture
To Kill A Mockingbird

Actor
★ Gregory Peck *To Kill A Mockingbird*

Supporting Actress
Mary Badham *To Kill A Mockingbird*

Direction
Robert Mulligan *To Kill A Mockingbird*

Writing
(screenplay – based on material for another medium)
★ Horton Foote *To Kill A Mockingbird*
(story and screenplay – written directly for the screen)
Charles Kaufman, Wolfgang Reinhardt *Freud*
Stanley Shapiro, Nate Monaster *That Touch Of Mink*

Cinematography (black & white)
Russell Harlan *To Kill A Mockingbird*

Music (music score – substantially original)
Jerry Goldsmith *Freud*
Elmer Bernstein *To Kill A Mockingbird*

Art Direction/Set Decoration (black & white)
★ Alexander Golitzen, Henry Bumstead/Oliver Emert *To Kill A Mockingbird*
(colour)
Alexander Golitzen, Robert Clatworthy/George Milo *That Touch Of Mink*

Sound
Universal City Studio Sound Department; Waldon O. Watson, sound director *That Touch Of Mink*

1963

Supporting Actor
Bobby Darin *Captain Newman, M.D.*

Writing (screenplay – based on material from another medium)
Richard L. Breen, Phoebe and Henry Ephron *Captain Newman, M.D.*

Sound
Universal City Studio Sound Department; Waldon O. Watson, sound director *Captain Newman, M.D.*

Special Visual Effects
Ub Iwerks *The Birds*

Sound Effects
Robert L. Bratton *A Gathering Of Eagles*

Music (song)
Henry Mancini (music), Johnny Mercer (lyrics) 'Charade' from *Charade*

1964

Supporting Actress
Dame Edith Evans *The Chalk Garden*

Writing (story and screenplay – written directly for the screen)
★ S.H. Barnett, Peter Stone, Frank Tarloff *Father Goose*

Sound
Universal City Studio Sound Department; Waldon O. Watson, sound director *Father Goose*

Film Editing
Ted J. Kent *Father Goose*

Sound Effects
Robert L. Bratton *The Lively Set*

1965

Sound
Universal City Studio Sound Department; Waldon O. Watson, sound director *Shenandoah*

1966

Art Direction/Set Decoration (colour)
Alexander Golitzen, George C. Webb/John McCarthy, John Austin *Gambit*

Costume Design (colour)
Jean Louis *Gambit*

Sound
Universal City Studio Sound Department; Waldon O. Watson, sound director *Gambit*

1967

Supporting Actress
Carol Channing *Thoroughly Modern Millie*

Art Direction/Set Decoration
Alexander Golitzen, George C. Webb/Howard Bristol *Thoroughly Modern Millie*

Costume Design
Jean Louis *Thoroughly Modern Millie*

Sound
Universal City Studio Sound Department *Thoroughly Modern Millie*

Special Visual Effects
Howard A. Anderson Jr, Albert Whitlock *Tobruk*

Music
(song)
Quincy Jones (music), Bob Russell (lyrics) 'The Eyes Of Love' from *Banning*
James Van Heusen and Sammy Cahn (music and lyrics) 'Thoroughly Modern Millie' from *Thoroughly Modern Millie*
(original music score)
★ Elmer Bernstein *Thoroughly Modern Millie*
(scoring of music – adaptation or treatment)
André Previn, Joseph Gershenson *Thoroughly Modern Millie*

Scientific or Technical (class 3)
● Waldon O. Watson and the Universal City Studio Sound Department

1968

Actress
Vanessa Redgrave *Isadora*

1969

Picture
Anne Of The Thousand Days

Actor
Richard Burton *Anne Of The Thousand Days*

Actress
Genevieve Bujold *Anne Of The Thousand Days*

Supporting Actor
Anthony Quayle *Anne Of The Thousand Days*

Writing (screenplay – based on material from another medium)
John Hale, Bridget Boland, Richard Sokolove *Anne Of The Thousand Days*

Cinematography
Arthur Ibbetson *Anne Of The Thousand Days*

Art Direction/Set Decoration
Mauric Carter, Lionel Couch/Patrick McLoughlin *Anne Of The Thousand Days*
Alexander Golitzen, George C. Webb/Jack D. Moore *Sweet Charity*

Costume Design
★ Margaret Furse *Anne Of The Thousand Days*
Edith Head *Sweet Charity*

Sound
John Aldred *Anne Of The Thousand Days*

Music
(original score – for a motion picture (not a musical))
Georges Delerue *Anne Of The Thousand Days*
(score of a musical picture (original or adaptation))
Cy Coleman *Sweet Charity*

Scientific or Technical (class 3)
● Robert M. Flynn and Russell Hessy of Universal City Studios, Inc.

1970

Picture
Airport

Actress
Carrie Snodgress *Diary Of A Mad Housewife*

Supporting Actress
★ Helen Hayes *Airport*
Maureen Stapleton *Airport*

Writing (screenplay – based on material from another medium)
George Seaton *Airport*

Cinematography
Ernest Laszlo *Airport*

Art Direction/Set Decoration
Alexander Golitzen, E. Preston Ames/Jack D. Moore, Mickey S. Michaels *Airport*

Costume Design
Edith Head *Airport*

Sound
Ronald Pierce, David Moriarty *Airport*

Film Editing
Stuart Gilmore *Aiport*

Music (original score)
Alfred Newman *Airport*

Short Subjects (live action subjects)
★ *The Resurrection Of Broncho Billy*

1971

Actress
Vanessa Redgrave *Mary, Queen Of Scots*

Supporting Actor
Richard Jaeckel *Sometimes A Great Notion*

Art Direction/Set Decoration
Boris Leven, William Tuntke/Ruby Levitt *The Andromeda Strain*
Terence Marsh, Robert Cartwright/Peter Howitt *Mary, Queen Of Scots*

Costume Design
Margaret Furse *Mary, Queen Of Scots*

Sound
Bob Jones, John Aldred *Mary, Queen Of Scots*

Film Editing
Stuart Gilmore, John W. Holmes *The Andromeda Strain*

Music
(song)
Henry Mancini (music), Alan and Marilyn Bergman (lyrics) 'All His Children' from *Sometimes A Great Notion*
(original dramatic score)
John Barry *Mary, Queen Of Scots*

1972

Supporting Actress
Geraldine Page *Pete 'N' Tillie*

Writing (screenplay – based on material from another medium)
Julius J. Epstein *Pete 'N' Tillie*

1973

Picture
American Graffiti
★ *The Sting*

Actor
Robert Redford *The Sting*

Supoorting Actress
Candy Clark *American Graffiti*

Direction
★ George Roy Hill *The Sting*
George Lucas *American Graffiti*

Writing (best story and screenplay – based on factual material or material not previously published or produced)
George Lucas, Gloria Katz, Willard Huyck *American Graffiti*
★ David S. Ward *The Sting*

Cinematography
Robert Surtees *The Sting*

Art Direction/Set Decoration
★ Henry Bumstead/James Payne *The Sting*

Costume Design
★ Edith Head *The Sting*

Sound
Ronald K. Pierce, Robert Bertrand *The Sting*

Film Editing
Verna Fields, Marcia Lucas *American Graffiti*
Ralph Kemplen *The Day Of The Jackal*
★ William Reynolds *The Sting*

Music (best scoring: original song score and/or adaptation)
André Previn, Herbert Spencer, Andrew Lloyd Webber *Jesus Christ Superstar*
★ Marvin Hamlisch *The Sting*

1973 Jean Hersholt Humanitarian Award
● Lew Wasserman

1974

Cinematography
Philip Lathrop *Earthquake*

Art Direction/Set Decoration
Alexander Golitzen, E. Preston Ames/Frank McKelvy *Earthquake*

Sound
★ Ronald Pierce, Melvin Metcalfe Sr *Earthquake*

Film Editing
Dorothy Spencer *Earthquake*

Special Achievement Award for Visual Effects
● Frank Brendel, Glen Robinson, Albert Whitlock *Earthquake*

Scientific or Technical
(class 2)
● Waldon O. Watson, Richard J. Stumpf, Robert J. Leonard and the Universal City Studios Sound Department for the development and enigneering of the Sensurround System for motion picture presentation
(class 3)
● Louis Ami of the Universal City Studios

1975

Picture
Jaws

Cinematography
Robert Surtees *The Hindenburg*

Art Direction/Set Decoration
Edward Carfagno/Frank McKelvy *The Hindenburg*

Sound
Leonard Peterson, John A. Bolger Jr, John Mack, Don K. Sharpless *The Hindenburg*
★ Robert L. Hoyt, Roger Heman, Earl Madery, John Carter *Jaws*

Film Editing
★ Verna Fields *Jaws*
Music
(song)
Charles Fox (music), Norman Gimbel (lyrics) 'Richard's Window' from *The Other Side Of The Mountain*
(original score)
★ John Williams *Jaws*

Special Achievement Award
for sound effects:
● Peter Berkos *The Hindenburg*
for visual effects:
● Albert Whitlock, Glen Robinson *The Hindenburg*

1975 Jean Hersholt Humanitarian Award
● Jules C. Stein

Scientific or Technical (class 2)
● William F. Miner of Universal City Studios, Inc., and the Westinghouse Electric Corporation for the development and engineering of a solid-state, 500 kilowatt, direct-current static rectifier for motion-picture lighting

left to right Carol Channing in *Thoroughly Modern Millie* (1967); Richard Burton and Genevieve Bujold in *Anne Of The Thousand Days* (1969); Helen Hayes (right) in *Airport* (1970); Robert Redford in *The Sting* (1973); *Earthquake* (1974); *Jaws* (1975); *The Hindenburg* (1975).

1976

Writing (screenplay based on material from another medium)
Frederico Fellini, Bernardino Zapponi *Fellini's Casanova**
Nicholas Meyer *The Seven-Per-Cent Solution*

Costume Design
★ Danilo Donati *Fellini's Casanova**
Alan Barrett *The Seven-Per-Cent Solution*

Film Editing
Eve Newman, Walter Hannemann *Two-Minute Warning*

* Italian production (see Foreign and Miscellaneous Films appendix)

1977

Art Direction/Set Decoration
George C. Webb/Mickey S. Michaels *Airport '77*

Costume Design
Edith Head, Burton Miller *Airport '77*

Sound
Robert Knudson, Robert J. Glass, Richard Tyler, Jean-Louis Ducarme *Sorcerer**

Film Editing
Walter Hannemann, Angelo Ross *Smokey And The Bandit*

Music (song)
Richard M. Sherman and Robert B. Sherman (music and lyrics) 'The Slipper And The Rose Waltz' from *The Slipper And The Rose**

(original score and its adaptation, or best adaptation score)
Richard M. Sherman, Robert B. Sherman, Angela Morley *The Slipper And The Rose**

* See Foreign and Miscellaneous Films appendix

1978

Picture
★ *The Deer Hunter**

Actor
Robert De Niro *The Deer Hunter**

Supporting Actor
★ Christopher Walken *The Deer Hunter**

Supporting Actress
Meryl Streep *The Deer Hunter**

Writing (screenplay written directly for the screen)
Michael Cimino, Deric Washburn, Louis Garfinkle, Quinn K. Redeker (story); Deric Washburn (screenplay) *The Deer Hunter**

Cinematography
Vilmos S. Zsigmond *The Deer Hunter**
Oswald Morris *The Wiz*

Art Direction/Set Decoration
Dean Tavoularis, Angela Graham/George R. Nelson *The Brink's Job**
Tony Walton, Philip Rosenberg, Edward Stewart/Robert Drumheller *The Wiz*

Costume Design
Reni Couley *Caravans**
Tony Walton *The Wiz*

Sound
★ Richard Portman, William McCaughey, Aaron Rochin, Darrin Knight *The Deer Hunter**

Film Editing
★ Peter Zinner *The Deer Hunter**

Music (original song score and its adaptation or best adaptation score)
Quincy Jones *The Wiz*

* Independent production, released by Universal in the USA only (see Foreign and Miscellaneous Films appendix)

1979

Cinematography
William Fraker *1941**

Sound
Robert Knudson, Robert J. Glass, Don MacDougall, Gene S. Cantamessa *1941**

Visual Effects
William A. Fraker, A.D. Flowers, Gregory Jein *1941**

* Independent production, released by Universal in USA only (see Foreign and Miscellaneous Films appendix)

left to right *Fellini's Casanova* (1976); Christopher Walken (extreme right) and Robert De Niro (centre left) in *The Deer Hunter* (1978); Sissy Spacek in *Coal Miner's Daughter* (1980); Mary Steenburgen (left) in *Melvin And Howard* (1980); Henry Fonda and Katharine Hepburn in *On Golden Pond* (1981); *E.T. The Extra-Terrestrial* (1982); Sissy Spacek and Jack Lemmon in *Missing* (1982); Meryl Streep in *Sophie's Choice* (1982).

1980

Picture
Coal Miner's Daughter

Actress
Ellen Burstyn *Resurrection*
★ Sissy Spacek *Coal Miner's Daughter*

Supporting Actress
★ Mary Steenburgen *Melvin And Howard*

Writing
(screenplay written directly for the screen)
★ Bo Goldman *Melvin And Howard*
(screenplay based on material from another medium)
Tom Rickman *Coal Miner's Daughter*

Cinematography
Ralph D. Bode *Coal Miner's Daughter*

Art Direction/Set Direction
John W. Corso/John M. Dwyer *Coal Miner's Daughter*

Sound
Richard Portman, Roger Heman, Jim Alexander *Coal Miner's Daughter*

Film Editing
Arthur Schmidt *Coal Miner's Daughter*

1981

Picture
On Golden Pond

Actor
★ Henry Fonda *On Golden Pond*

Actress
★ Katharine Hepburn *On Golden Pond*

Supporting Actress
Jane Fonda *On Golden Pond*

Direction
Mark Rydell *On Golden Pond*

Writing (screenplay based on material from another medium)
★ Ernest Thompson *On Golden Pond*

Cinematography
Billy Williams *On Golden Pond*

Sound
Richard Portman, David Ronne *On Golden Pond*

Film Editing
Robert L. Wolfe *On Golden Pond*

Music
(song)
Joe Raposo (music and lyrics) 'The Time It Happens' from *The Great Muppet Caper**
(original score)
Dave Grusin *On Golden Pond*

* Independent production, released by Universal in the USA only (see Foreign and Miscellaneous Films appendix)

1982

Picture
E.T. The Extra-Terrestrial
Missing

Actor
Jack Lemmon *Missing*

Actress
Sissy Spacek *Missing*
★ Meryl Streep *Sophie's Choice*

Supporting Actor
Charles Durning *The Best Little Whorehouse In Texas*

Direction
Steven Spielberg *E.T. The Extra-Terrestrial*

Writing (screenplay based on material from another medium)
★ Constantin Costa-Gavras, Donald Stewart *Missing*
Alan J. Pakula *Sophie's Choice*

Cinematography
Allen Daviau *E.T. The Extra-Terrestrial*
Nestor Almensros *Sophie's Choice*

Costume Design
Albert Wolsky *Sophie's Choice*

Sound
★ Buzz Knudson, Robert Glass, Don Digirolamo, Gene Cantamessa *E.T. The Extra-Terrestrial*

Film Editing
Carol Littleton *E.T. The Extra-Terrestrial*

Visual Effects
★ Carlo Rambaldi, Dennis Murren, Kenneth F. Smith *E.T. The Extra-Terrestrial*

Sound Effects
★ Charles L. Campbell, Ben Burtt *E.T. The Extra-Terrestrial*

Music (original score)
★ John Williams *E.T. The Extra-Terrestrial*

Appendixes

Throughout Universal's 70-year history it has been associated with many feature films which, for a variety of reasons, cannot be regarded as quite so centrally connected with the studio as those that appear in the preceding pages. Even so, they are a part of the story and for the sake of completeness they are included here in the form of five appendixes (numbers 1 to 5). Their different relationships to the studio are explained at the head of each group. They form a very diverse assemblage but the one factor common to all but a handful of anomalies is that they were released (or co-released) by Universal (or a Universal subsidiary), at least in the United States. To facilitate the search for any title, an alphabetic listing of all of them is given to the right. Each film is indexed by the appendix number in which it is listed and, following the comma, the year of American release.

Convenience listings of films made for Universal by Deanna Durbin and by Abbott and Costello, together with the four sets of films that were sufficiently related and numerous to be recognised as series, are given in Appendix 6.

Act Of The Heart	1, 1970
Activist, The	1, 1969
Adam And Evalyn	2, 1950
Adam And Evelyne	2, 1950
Adventure For Two	2, 1945
African Safari	5, 1969
All Mine To Give	4, 1958
All Over Town	2, 1949
All Weekend Lovers	1, 1969
Always A Bride	2, 1954
American Reunion	5, 1975
American Werewolf In London, An	1, 1981
Appointment With Venus	2, 1953
Arabella	1, 1969
Arizona Colt	1, 1967
Astonished Heart, The	2, 1950
Bad Sister	2,1948
Battle Of Algiers	1, 1969
Be Mine Tonight	1, 1933
Better A Widow	1, 1969
Between Time And Eternity	1, 1960
Beware Of Pity	2, 1947
Beyond The Reef	1, 1981
Bingo Long Travelling All-Stars And Motor Kings, The	1, 1976
Birds Come To Die In Peru, The	1, 1968
Birds In Peru	1, 1968
Black Narcissus	2, 1947
Blind Goddess, The	2, 1949
Blood Of The Vampire	1, 1958
Blue Lagoon, The	2, 1949
Bofors Gun, The	1, 1968
Born To Be Loved	1, 1959
Both Sides Of The Law	2, 1953
Boy Cried Murder, The	1, 1966
Brides Of Dracula, The	3, 1960
Brief Encounter	2, 1946
Brink's Job, The	1, 1978
Brothers, The	2, 1948
Browning Version, The	2, 1951
Brute Man, The	1, 1946
Bullet For Sandoval, A	1, 1970
Bush Christmas	2, 1947
Can Heironymus Merkin Ever Forget Mercy Humppe And Find True Happiness?	1, 1969
Captain Boycott	2, 1948
Captain Clegg	3, 1962
Captive Heart, The	2, 1947
Caravans	1, 1978
Card, The	2, 1953
Cattle Annie And Little Britches	1, 1981
Champagne Murders, The	1, 1968
Chappaqua	1, 1967
Charlie Bubbles	1, 1968
Chequered Flag Or Crash	1, 1978
Choirboys, The	1, 1977
Christopher Columbus	2, 1949
Company Of Killers	1, 1970
Conan The Barbarian	1, 1982
Cone Of Silence	1, 1961
Corridor Of Mirrors	2, 1949
Cossacks, The	1, 1960
Country Music	1, 1972
Crashing Through To Berlin	5, 1918
Crash Of Silence, The	2, 1953
Cruel Sea, The	2, 1953
Curse Of The Werewolf, The	3, 1961
Dark Purpose	1, 1964
Dark Rapture	5, 1938
Daybreak	2, 1949
Day The Earth Caught Fire, The	1, 1962
Day They Gave The Babies Away, The	4, 1958
Deadlier Than The Male	1, 1967
Dead Of Night	2, 1946
Dead Run	1, 1969
Dear Murderer	2, 1948
Deer Hunter, The	1, 1978
Dirty Mary	1, 1969
Degree Of Murder, A	1, 1969
Desert Patrol	1, 1962
Desperate Moment	2, 1953
Devil In The Flesh, The	1, 1949
Devil's Pit, The	5, 1930
Doctor At Large	2, 1957
Doppelganger	1, 1969
Dracula	3, 1958
Dream Maker, The	1, 1964
Dreams Of Glass	1, 1970
Dulcimer Street	2, 1948
Edge Of Hell	1, 1956
Electric Horseman	1, 1979
End Of The River, The	2, 1948
English Without Tears	2, 1949
Escapade In Japan	4, 1957
Evil Of Frankenstein, The	3, 1964
Evil Under The Sun	1, 1982
Fahrenheit 451	1, 1967
Family, The	1, 1970
Fellini's Casanova	1, 1976
Fighting Cossacks, The	1, 1969
Fighting President, The	5, 1933
Five Days From Home	1, 1978
Flash Gordon	1, 1980
Floods Of Fear	2, 1959
Forever Young, Forever Free	1, 1976
4D Man	1, 1959
Four Fast Guns	1, 1960
Four Hits And A Mister	1, 1963
Frances	1, 1982
Frieda	2, 1947
Fugitive, The	2, 1940
Gang War	2, 1947
Genevieve	2, 1954
Gentle Gunman, The	2, 1953
Girl In The Painting, The	2, 1949
Girl Most Likely, The	4, 1958
Girl Must Live, A	2, 1941
Gong Show Movie, The	1, 1980
Great Expectations	2, 1947
Great Muppet Caper, The	1, 1981
Guns Of A Stranger	1, 1973
Guns Of August, The	5, 1965
Guyana, Crime Of The Century	1, 1980
Guyana, Cult Of The Damned	1, 1980
Halloween II	1, 1981
Halloween III: Season Of The Witch	1, 1982
Hamlet	2, 1948
Hands Of The Ripper	3, 1972
Head Of A Tyrant	1, 1960
Her Man Gilbey	2, 1949
Hide And Seek	1, 1964
High And Dry	2, 1953
Hold Back Tomorrow	1, 1955
Holiday Camp	2, 1948
Homo Eroticus	1, 1973
Honky Tonk Freeway	1, 1981
Horror Of Dracula	3, 1958
Hungry Hill	2, 1947
Hunted	2, 1953
I Believe In You	2, 1953
I Know Where I'm Going	2, 1947
I'll Never Forget What's 'Is Name	1, 1968
I Married A Woman	4, 1958
Importance Of Being Earnest, The	2, 1953
Information Received	1, 1962
In Search Of Gregory	1, 1970
Ipcress File, The	1, 1965
Island Of Terror	1, 1967
Island Rescue	2, 1953
It's All Happening	1, 1964
Ivory Hunter	2, 1952
Janis	5, 1974
Jassy	2, 1948
Jet Pilot	4, 1957
Johnny Frenchman	2, 1946
Jokers, The	1, 1967
Journey To The Far Side Of The Sun	1, 1969
Killing Game, The	1, 1969
King Kong Escapes	1, 1968
King Kong vs Godzilla	1, 1963
King Of The Mountain	1, 1981
Kiss Of Evil	3, 1963
Kiss Of The Vampire	3, 1963
Lady Surrenders, A	2, 1947
Land Of Fury	2, 1955
Last Adventure, The	1, 1968
Lavender Hill Mob, The	2, 1952
Legacy, The	1, 1979
Legend Of The Lone Ranger, The	1, 1981
Let's Make A Night Of It	2, 1938
Letter From An Unknown Woman	1, 1948
Light Touch, The	2, 1958
Little Ballerina, The	2 & 5, 1952
Little Sex, A	1, 1982
Live It Up	1, 1964
London Belongs To Me	2, 1948
Lost Moment, The	1, 1947
Love Story	2, 1947
Madeleine	2, 1950
Madness Of The Heart	2, 1950
Madonna Of The Seven Moons	2, 1946
Maggie, The	2, 1953
Magic Bow, The	2, 1951
Magnet, The	2, 1951
Magnificent Doll	1, 1946
Mandy	2, 1953
Man-Eater Of Kumaon	1, 1948
Man From Nowhere, The	1, 1967
Man In Grey, The	2, 1946
Man In The Dark	1, 1965
Man In The White Suit, The	2, 1952
Man Of The Year	1, 1973
Mark Of The Hawk	1, 1958
Matter Of Innocence, A	1, 1968
Matter Of Life And Death, A	2, 1947
Michael And Mary	1, 1931
Mikado, The	2, 1939
Morning Departure	2, 1951
Mummy, The	3, 1959
My Name Is Nobody	1, 1974
Mystery Of Life, The	5, 1931
Mystery Submarine	1, 1962
Naked Brigade	1, 1965
Nearly A Nasty Accident	1, 1962
Net, The	2, 1953
Next Of Kin	2, 1943
Nicholas Nickleby	2, 1947
Night Creatures	3, 1962
Nightmare	3, 1964
1941	1, 1979
Notorious Gentleman	2, 1946
Nun At The Crossroads	1, 1970
Oedipus The King	1, 1968
Odd Man Out	2, 1947
On The Night Of The Fire	2, 1940
One Night With You	2, 1949
One Woman's Story	2, 1949
Operation Disaster	2, 1951
Othello	1, 1960
Overlanders, The	2, 1946
Palaces Of A Queen	5, 1967
Paranoiac	3, 1963
Passionate Friends, The	2, 1949
Paul J. Rainey's African Hunt	5, 1912
Penny Princess	2, 1953
Phantom Of The Opera	3, 1962
Pharoah's Woman, The	1, 1961
Pirate's Fiancee	1, 1969
Plains Of Battle	1, 1969
Pool Of London	2, 1951
Portrait Of An Unknown Woman	1, 1958
Prelude To Fame	2, 1950
Princess	1, 1970
Privilege	1, 1967
Projected Man, The	1, 1967
Project M7	2, 1953
Promoter, The	2, 1952
Public Pigeon No 1	4, 1957
Pursuit Of D.B. Cooper, The	1, 1981
Queen Is Crowned, A	2 & 5, 1953
Quiet Wedding	2, 1941
Ra Expeditions, The	5, 1974
Raggedy Man	1, 1981
Railway Children, The	1, 1971
Rake's Progress, The	2, 1946
Rebel, The	1, 1933
Rocking Horse Winner, The	2, 1950
Rome Express	1, 1933
Rugged O'Riordans, The	1, 1950
Run For Your Money, A	2, 1950
Running	1, 1979
Run Of The Arrow	4, 1957
Sapphire	2, 1959
Sea Of Sand	1, 1962
Secret Beyond The Door	1, 1948
Secret Of Blood Island, The	3, 1965
Seekers, The	2, 1955
Senator Was Indiscreet, The	1, 1948
Seventh Veil, The	2, 1946
Shadow Of The Cat	1, 1961
Shakedown, The	1, 1961
Silence Of The North	1, 1981
Silent Enemy, The	1, 1958
Simon And Laura	2, 1956
Sing And Swing	1, 1964
Six Weeks	1, 1982
Slipper And The Rose, The	1, 1977
Snowbound	2, 1949
Snow Queen, The	1, 1960
Something Money Can't Buy	2, 1953
Sons Of Matthew	1, 1950
Sorcerer	1, 1977
S.O.S. Pacific	1, 1960
Special Section	1, 1975
Stairway To Heaven	2, 1947
Story Of A Woman	1, 1970
Story Of Cinderella, The	1, 1977
Stranger In Between, The	2, 1953
Street Corner	2, 1953
Streets Of Hong Kong	1, 1979
Tawny Pipit	2, 1947
Tell Me Tonight	1, 1933
That Night!	4, 1957
They Were Sisters	2, 1947
This Happy Breed	2, 1947
This Is Russia	5, 1958
Tight Little Island	2, 1949
Time In The Sun, A	1, 1970
Titfield Thunderbolt, The	2, 1953
Tomboy And The Champ	1, 1961
Touch And Go	2, 1958
Traitors, The	1, 1963
Trouble In The Sky,	1, 1961
Truth About Spring, The	1, 1965
Twins Of Evil	3, 1972
Unholy Wife, The	4, 1957
Upturned Glass, The	4, 1957
Very Curious Girl, A	1, 1969
Violators, The	4, 1957
Violent City	1, 1970
Wages Of Fear	1, 1977
Warkill	1, 1967
West Of Zanzibar	2, 1954
Where No Vultures Fly	2, 1952
Whisky Galore	2, 1949
White Corridors	2, 1952
White Hell Of Pitz Palu, The	1, 1930
White Unicorn, The	2, 1948
Wicked Lady, The	2, 1947
Wild And The Willing, The	1, 1964
Wild Season	1, 1969
Wings Of Chance	1, 1961
Wise Guys, The	1, 1969
Woman Hater	2, 1949
Work Is A Four-Letter Word	1, 1968
Yanks	1, 1979
Years Between, The	2, 1947
Young And Willing	1, 1964
Young Stranger, The	4, 1957
Zita	1, 1969

1. Foreign and Miscellaneous Films

The main purpose of this book is to present the films that gave the studio its personality – that is, those made by Universal Pictures itself. For the most part, films in the main body of the book comply with that qualification. Over the years, however, there have been many other films released under the Universal imprimatur that, for one reason or another, cannot be regarded quite so unequivocally as Universal films. They undoubtedly have a connection with the studio, though, and the book would be less than complete were they excluded.

Separating off into Appendixes 2 to 5 the Universal releases associated with the Rank Organisation (prior to 1960), and those produced by Hammer and RKO, as well as documentaries, we are left with a mixed bag of films that is difficult to characterise in simple terms. With a very few exceptions, the single unifying feature in the following lists is that all the films were released by Universal – or, between 1967 and 1970, the Universal subsidiary, Regional Film Distributors, a releasing arm specially set up to handle what was termed 'specialized product' – at least in the United States.

The list contains, regardless of date, all films produced by independent companies operating outside the United States, including any films in which overseas branches of Universal itself were involved. This 'foreign' criterion applies even if Universal released the film in the UK as well as the USA.

Also included, for the period up to 1960, are all films made by American independent companies that were picked up by Universal, even if the releasing rights the studio acquired were unrestricted. It is often difficult, however, to establish just how 'independent' of Universal the production company was, and the dividing line between the releasing studio's involvement and non-involvement is almost impossible to draw in certain cases. For this reason there are some films whose positions might well be argued either way.

From 1960 onwards different criteria have to be applied, to reflect the fact that, as the decline in the Hollywood studio system accelerated, there was an increasing trend among the larger studios to act as sole distributors of major, but independently produced, films. After 1959, therefore, the independent US productions that appear in the list are only those for which Universal holds (or held) limited releasing rights that cover the USA, but exclude the UK (where the films may or may not have been released, but if so, by a different distributor). Included in this category is one anomalous Universal production (*Raggedy Man*, 1981) that was released in the UK by another company.

Finally, there is one Universal production (*The Brute Man*, 1946) that, curiously, was abandoned by the studio after completion and its release, even the US, handled by another distributor.

The production company and country of origin are given on the second line of each entry. If the available information has failed to yield the company's name, the term 'independent' is used instead. 'Also known as' is abbreviated to 'aka'.

1930

The White Hell Of Pitz Palu
independent (Germany)
Drama. Leni Riefenstahl, Gustav Diesel, Ernest Peterson, B. Spring. Dir: Arnold Fanck.

1931

Michael And Mary
independent (Great Britain)
Drama. Herbert Marshall, Edna Best, Frank Lawton, Elizabeth Allan. Dir: Victor Saville.

1933

Be Mine Tonight (aka **Tell Me Tonight**)
Gaumont-British (Germany/Great Britain)
Comedy with music. Jan Kiepura, Sonnie Hale, Magda Schneider, Edmund Gwenn. Dir: Anatole Litvak.

The Rebel
independent (Germany)
Drama. Luis Trenker, Vilma Banky, Victor Varconi, Paul Hildt, Olga Engel. Dir: Luis Trenker and Edwin H. Knopf.

Rome Express
Gaumont-British (Great Britain)
Thriller drama. Esther Ralston, Conrad Veidt, Hugh Williams, Cedric Hardwicke. Dir: Walter Forde.

1946

The Brute Man
Universal (USA); released in USA by PRC Pictures
Thriller. Tom Neal, Jane Adams, Rondo Hatton, Jane Wiley. Dir: Jean Yarbrough.

Magnificent Doll
Hallmark Productions (USA)
Drama. Ginger Rogers, David Niven, Burgess Meredith. Dir: Frank Borzage.

1947

The Lost Moment
Walter Wanger Pictures (USA)
Drama. Robert Cummings, Susan Hayward, Agnes Moorehead, Eduardo Ciannelli. Dir: Martin Gabel.

1948

Letter From An Unknown Woman
Rampart Productions (USA)
Romantic drama. Joan Fontaine, Louis Jourdan, Mady Christians. Dir: Max Ophuls.

Man-Eater Of Kumaon
independent (USA)
Adventure. Sabu, Wendell Corey, Joanne Page, Morris Carnovksy. Dir: Byron Haskin.

Secret Beyond The Door
Diana Productions (USA)
Mystery. Joan Bennett, Michael Redgrave, Anne Revere, Barbara O'Neil. Dir: Fritz Lang.

The Senator Was Indiscreet
Interjohn (USA)
Comedy drama. William Powell, Ella Raines, Peter Lind Hayes, Allen Jenkins. Dir: George S. Kaufman.

1949

The Devil In The Flesh
Transcontinental/Universal (France); distributed in USA by AFE Corporation.
Drama. Micheline Presle, Gerard Philippe, Jean Debucourt, Denise Grey. Dir: Claude Autant-Lara.

1950

The Rugged O'Riordans (aka **Sons Of Matthew**)
independent (Australia)
Drama. Michael Pate, Wendy Gibb, John O'Malley, Thelma Scott. Dir: Charles Chauvel.

1955

Hold Back Tomorrow
Hugo Haas (USA)
Drama. John Agar, Cleo Moore, Frank de Kova, Dallas Boyd. Dir: Hugo Haas.

1956

Edge Of Hell
Hugo Haas (USA)
Drama. Hugo Haas, Francesca De Scaffa, Ken Carlton, June Hammerstein, Jeffrey Stone. Dir: Hugo Haas.

1958

Blood Of The Vampire
Eros (Great Britain)
Horror. Donald Wolfit, Barbara Shelley, Vincent Ball, Victor Maddern. Dir: Henry Cass.

Mark Of The Hawk
World Horizon (USA)
Political drama. Sidney Poitier, John McIntire, Juano Hernandez, Eartha Kitt. Dir: Michael Audley.

Portrait Of An Unknown Woman
Sirus Films (Germany)
Romantic drama. Ruth Leuwerik, O.W. Fischer, Erich Schellow, Paul Hoffman. Dir: Helmut Kautner.

The Silent Enemy
Romulus (Great Britain)
War drama. Laurence Harvey, Dawn Addams, John Clements, Michael Craig. Dir: William Fairchild.

1959

Born To Be Loved
Hugo Haas (USA)
Drama. Carol Morris, Barbara Jo Allen, Hugo Haas, Dick Kallman. Dir: Hugo Haas.

4D Man (aka **Master Of Horror**, GB: **The Evil Force**)
Jack H. Harris (USA)
Horror thriller. Robert Lansing, Lee Meriweather, James Congdon, Patty Duke. Dir: Irvin S. Yeaworth Jr.

1960

Between Time And Eternity
Neue Terra-Film (Germany)
Drama. Lili Palmer, Carlos Thompson, Willy Birgel, Ellen Schiviers. Dir: Arthur Maria Rabenalt.

The Cossacks
independent (France/Italy)
Crimean War drama. Edmund Purdom, John Drew Barrymore, Georgia Moll, Pierre Brice. Dir: Giorgio Rivalta.

Four Fast Guns
Phoenix Films (USA)
Western. James Craig, Martha Vickers, Edgar Buchanan, Brett Halsey. Dir: William J. Hole Jr.

Head Of A Tyrant
Vic Films/CEC (France/Italy)
Drama. Massimo Girotti, Isabella Corey, Renato Baldini, Yvette Masson. Dir: Signor Cerchio.

Othello
independent (Soviet Union)
Shakespeare's tragedy. Sergei Bondarchuk, Andra Popov, Irina Skobtseva. Dir: Sergei Yutkevich.

The Snow Queen
Soyuzmultifilm (Soviet Union)
Cartoon version of Hans Christian Andersen's fairy tale. English dialogue version dubbed by Universal actors including Sandra Dee, Tommy Kirk, Patty McCormack.

S.O.S. Pacific
Sydney Box (Great Britain)
Suspense adventure. Eddie Constantine, Pier Angeli, John Gregson, Richard Attenborough. Dir: Guy Green.

1961

The Pharoah's Woman
independent (Italy)
Drama. John Drew Barrymore, Linda Cristal, Armando Francioli, Pierre Brice. Dir: Giorgio Rivalta.

Shadow Of The Cat
BHP (Great Britain)
Thriller. André Morell, Barbara Shelley, William Lucas, Freda Jackson. Dir: John Gillington.

The Shakedown
Alliance/Ethiro (Great Britain)
Crime melodrama. Terence Morgan, Hazel Court, Donald Pleasence, Bill Owen. Dir: John Lemont.

Tomboy And The Champ
Signal Pictures (USA)
Drama. Candy Moore, Ben Johnson, Jesse White, Jess Kilpatrick. Dir: Francis D. Lyon.

Trouble In The Sky (GB: **Cone Of Silence**)
Bryanston (Great Britain)
Drama. Bernard Lee, Elizabeth Seal, Michael Craig, Peter Cushing, George Sanders. Dir: Charles Frend.

Wings Of Chance
Tiger Films (Canada)
Drama. James Brown, Frances Rafferty, Richard Treddor, Patrick White. Dir: Edward Drew.

1962

The Day The Earth Caught Fire
Pax (Great Britain)
Science fiction drama. Edward Judd, Janet Munro, Leo McKern, Michael Goodliffe, Bernard Braden. Dir: Val Guest.

Desert Patrol (GB: **Sea Of Sand**)
Tempean Films (Great Britain)
War drama. John Gregson, Michael Craig, Richard Attenborough, Vincent Ball, Dermot Walsh. Dir: Guy Green.

Information Received
United Co-Productions (Great Britain)
Underworld drama. Sabrina Sesselman, William Sylvester, Hermione Baddeley, Edward Underdown. Dir: Robert Lynn.

Mystery Submarine
Britannia (Great Britain)
War adventure. Edward Judd, James Robertson Justice, Laurence Payne, Albert Lieven. Dir: C. M. Pennington-Richards.

Nearly A Nasty Accident
Marlow (Great Britain)
Comedy. Kenneth Connor, Jimmy Edwards, Shirley Eaton, Richard Wattis. Dir: Don Chaffey.

1963

Four Hits And A Mister
No information available.

King Kong vs Godzilla
Toho Productions (Japan)
Thriller. Michael Keith, James Yagi, Tadao Takeshima, Yu Fujiki. Dir: Inoshiro Honda.

The Traitors
Ello Productions (Great Britain)
Drama. Patrick Allen, James Maxwell, Ewan Roberts, Zena Walker. Dir: Robert Tronson.

1964

Dark Purpose
Galatea / Lyre / Brazzi / Barclay - Hayutin Productions (France/Italy/USA)
Drama. Shirley Jones, Rossano Brazzi, George Sanders, Micheline Presle, Georgia Moll. Dir: Vittorio Sala and George Marshall.

The Dream Maker (GB: **It's All Happening**)
Magnum (Great Britain)
Musical. Tommy Steele, Michael Medwin, Angela Douglas, Jean Harvey. Dir: Don Sharpe.

Hide And Seek
Albion (Great Britain)
Comedy-drama. Ian Carmichael, Janet Munro, Curt Jurgens, George Pravda. Dir: Cy Endfield.

Sing And Swing (GB: **Live It Up**)
Three Kings (Great Britain)
Rock 'n' Roll musical. David Hemmings, Veronica Hurst, Jennifer Moss, John Pike. Dir: Lance Comfort.

Young And Willing (GB: **The Wild And The Willing**)
Box-Thomas (Great Britain)
Drama. Virginia Maskell, Paul Rogers, Ian McShane, Samantha Eggar, John Hurt. Dir: Ralph Thomas.

1965

The Ipcress File
Steven/Lowndes (Great Britain)
Spy thriller. Michael Caine, Nigel Green, Guy Doleman, Sue Lloyd. Dir: Sidney J. Furie.

Man In The Dark
Mancunian (Great Britain)
Murder story. William Sylvester, Barbara Shelley, Elizabeth Shepherd, Mark Eden. Dir: Lance Comfort.

Naked Brigade
Box Office Attractions/Alfa Studios (USA/Greece)
World War II drama. Shirley Eaton, Ken Scott, Mary Chronopoulou, John Holland. Dir: Maury Dexter.

The Truth About Spring
Quota Rentals (Great Britain)
Drama. John Mills, Hayley Mills, James MacArthur, Lionel Jeffries. Dir: Richard Thorpe.

1966

The Boy Cried Murder
independent (USA/Germany/Yugoslavia)
Thriller. 'Fizz' MacIntosh, Phil Brown, Veronica Hurst, Beba Loncar. Dir: George Breakston.

1967

Chappaqua
Conrad Rooks (USA); released in the USA by Regional Film Distributors.
Jean-Louis Barrault, Conrad Rooks. Dir: Conrad Rooks.

Deadlier Than The Male
Sydney Box (Great Britain)
Bulldog Drummond adventure. Richard Johnson, Elke Sommer, Sylva Koscina, Nigel Green. Dir: Ralph Thomas.

Fahrenheit 451
Anglo Enterprise/Vineyard (Great Britain)
Futuristic political drama. Oskar Werner, Julie Christie, Cyril Cusack, Anton Diffring. Dir: François Truffaut.

Island Of Terror
Planet (Great Britain)
Horror. Peter Cushing, Edward Judd, Carole Grey, Eddie Byrne. Dir: Terence Fisher.

The Jokers
Adastra/Gildor/Scimitar (Great Britain)
Suspense comedy. Michael Crawford, Oliver Reed, Harry Andrews, James Donald, Daniel Massey. Dir: Michael Winner.

The Man From Nowhere (aka **Arizona Colt**)
G.G. Productions (Italy/France/Spain)
Giuliano Gemma, Fernando Sancho. No further information available.

Privilege
Worldfilm/Memorial (Great Britain)
Musical drama. Paul Jones, Jean Shrimpton, Mark London, Max Bacon. Dir: Peter Watkins.

The Projected Man
MLC Productions (Great Britain)
Science fiction thriller. Bryant Washburn, Mary Peach, Norman Woolland, Ronald Allen. Dir: Ian Curteis.

Warkill
Valut/Centaur Limited (USA)
World War II actioner. George Montgomery, Tom Drake, Conrad Parham, Eddie Infante. Dir: Ferde Grofé Jr.

1968

Birds In Peru (aka **The Birds Come To Die In Peru**)
Universal Pictures – France (France); released in the USA by Regional Film Distributors.
Jean Seberg, Maurice Ronet. Dir: Romain Gary.

The Bofors Gun
Everglades (Great Britain); Universal Pictures Limited co-production, released in the USA by Regional Film Distributors.
Army drama. Nicol Williamson, John Thaw, David Warner, Ian Holm. Dir: Jack Gold.

The Champagne Murders
Universal Pictures–France (France)
Murder mystery. Anthony Perkins, Maurice Ronet, Stephane Audran, Yvonne Furneaux. Dir: Claude Chabrol.

Charlie Bubbles
Memorial Enterprises (Great Britain); Universal co-production, released in the USA by Regional Film Distributors.
Contemporary romantic drama. Albert Finney, Liza Minnelli, Billie Whitelaw, Colin Blakely. Dir: Albert Finney.

I'll Never Forget What's 'Is Name
Scimitar (Great Britain); Universal co-production, released in the USA by Regional Film Distributors.
Contemporary tragi-comedy. Oliver Reed, Orson Welles, Carol White, Michael Hordern, Marianne Faithful. Dir: Michael Winner.

The Last Adventure
Société Nouvelle de Cinématographique (France/Italy)
Adventure love story. Alain Delon, Lino Ventura, Joanna Shimkus, Serge Reggiani. Dir: Robert Enrico.

King Kong Escapes
Toho Productions (Japan)
Science fiction. Rhodes Reason, Mie Hama, Linda Miller, Akira Takrada. Dir: Inoshiro Honda.

A Matter Of Innocence
independent (Great Britain)
Drama. Hayley Mills, Trevor Howard, Shashi Kapoor, Brenda De Banzie. Dir: Guy Green.

Oedipus The King
Crossword Productions (Great Britain)
Sophocles's tragedy. Christopher Plummer, Orson Welles, Lili Palmer, Richard Johnson. Dir: Philip Saville.

Work Is A Four-Letter Word
Cavalcade Films (Great Britain)
Futuristic comedy fantasy. David Warner, Cilla Black, Zia Mohyeddin, Elizabeth Spriggs. Dir: Peter Hall.

1969

The Activist
Jana Films (USA); released in the USA by Regional Film Distributors.
Drama. Mike Smith, Leslie Gilbrun, Tom Maier, Brian Murphy. Dir: Art Napoleon.

Arabella
Cram Film (Italy/USA)
Comedy adventure. James Fox, Terry-Thomas, Margaret Rutherford, Virna Lisi. Dir: Mauro Bolognini.

Battle Of Algiers
Rizzoli Film (Italy/Algeria)
Jean Martin, Yacef Saadi; Dir: Gillo Pontecorvo.

Better A Widow
Ultra Films (Italy/France)
Drama. Virna Lisi, Peter McEnery, Gabriele Ferzetti, Jean Servais, Agnes Spaak. Dir: Duccio Tessari.

Can Heironymus Merkin Ever Forget Mercy Humppe And Find True Happiness?
Taralex (Great Britain); released in the USA by Regional Film Distributors.
Personal fantasy. Anthony Newley, Joan Collins, George Jessel, Milton Berle. Dir: Anthony Newley.

Dead Run
independent (France/Italy/Germany)
Spy Thriller. Peter Lawford, Countess Ira Furstenberg, Georges Geret. Dir: Christian-Jaque.

A Degree Of Murder
independent (Germany)
Drama. Anita Pallenberg, Hans P. Hallwachs, Manfred Fischbeck. Dir: Volker Schlondorff.

Journey To The Far Side Of The Sun (aka **Doppelganger**)
Century 21 Productions (Great Britain)
Science fiction. Ian Hendry, Roy Thinnes, Patrick Wymark, Lynn Loring. Dir: Robert Parrish.

The Killing Game (aka **All Weekend Lovers**)
independent (France)
Mystery drama. Jean Pierre Cassel, Claudine Auger, Michel Duchaussay. Dir: Alain Jessua.

Plains Of Battle (aka **The Fighting Cossacks**)
independent (Italy)
W. Medor, Lorella De Luca. No further information available.

A Very Curious Girl (aka **Pirate's Fiancée** and **Dirty Mary**)
independent (France); released in the USA by Regional Film Distributors.
Comedy-drama. Bernadette Lafont, Georges Geret, Michel Constantin, Jacques Marin. Dir: Nelly Kaplan.

Wild Season
independent (South Africa)
Drama. Joe Stewardson, Marie Du Toit, Gert Van Den Bergh, Janis Reinhardt. Dir: Emil Noval.

The Wise Guys
independent (France)
Comedy. Lino Ventura, Marie Dubois, Jean-Claude Roland, Jess Hahn. Dir: Robert Enrico.

Zita
Regional Films (France)
Drama. Joanna Shimkus, Katina Paxinou, Suzanne Flon. Dir: Robert Enrico.

1970

Act Of The Heart
Quest Films (Canada)
Drama. Genevieve Bujold, Donald Sutherland, Bill Mitchell, Suzanne Langlois. Dir: Paul Almond.

A Bullet For Sandoval
independent (Italy/Spain)
Drama. Ernest Borgnine, George Hilton, Alberto De-Mendozo, Leo Anchoriz. Dir: Julio Buchs.

Company Of Killers
independent (USA)
Murder story. Van Johnson, Ray Milland, Fritz Weaver, Diana Lynn. Dir: Jerry Thorpe.

Dreams Of Glass
independent (USA)
Drama. John Denos, Caroline Barrett, Joe LoPresti, Margaret Rich, Pat Li. Dir: Robert Clouse.

In Search Of Gregory
Vic Films/Vera Films (Great Britain/Italy)
Drama. Julie Christie, Michael Sarrazin, John Hurt, Adolfo Celi. Dir: Peter Wood.

Nun At The Crossroads
Izaro Films/Filmes Cinematografica (Italy)
Drama. Rossana Schiaffino, John Richardson, Mary Cruz, Angel Picazo. Dir: Julio Buchs.

Story Of A Woman
independent (Italy/USA)
Drama. Bibi Anderson, Robert Stack, James Farentino, Annie Girardot. Dir: Leonardo Bercovici.

A Time In The Sun (aka **Princess**)
Europa Film (Sweden)
Drama. Grynet Molvig, Lars Passgard, Monica Nielsen, Brigitta Valberg. Dir: Ake Falck.

Violent City (aka **The Family**)
Unidis & Fono Roma/Universal Pictures–France (Italy/France)
Crime drama. Telly Savalas, Charles Bronson, Jill Ireland, Umberto Orsini. Dir: Sergio Sollima.

1971

The Railway Children
EMI (Great Britain)
Family entertainment drama. Dinah Sheridan, Bernard Cribbins, Ian Cuthbertson, Jenny Agutter. Dir: Lionel Jeffries.

1972

Country Music
Robert Kinkle Productions
Country-and-western music drama. Marty Robbins, Barbara Mandrell, Carl Smith, Sammy Jackson. Dir: Robert Hinkle.

1973

Guns Of A Stranger
Robert Hinkle Productions (USA)
Drama. Marty Robbins, Chill Wills, Dovie Beams, Stephen Tackett. Dir: Robert Hinkle.

Man Of The Year (aka **Homo Eroticus**)
Atlantica Cinematografica (Italy)
Drama. Lando Buzzanca, Rossana Podesta, Luciana Salce, Ira Furstenberg, Sylva Koscina. Dir: Marco Vicario.

1974

My Name Is Nobody
independent co-production (Italy/France/Germany)
Western. Terence Hill, Henry Fonda, Jean Martin, Piero Lulli. Dir: Tonino Valerii.

1975

Special Section
independent co-production (France/Italy/Germany)
Drama. Louis Seigner, Michel Lonsdale, Ivo Garrani, Francois Maistre. Dir: Costa-Gavras.

1976

The Bingo Long Traveling All-Stars And Motor Kings
independent (USA)
Baseball drama. Billy Dee Williams, James Earl Jones, Richard Pryor, Rico Dawson. Dir: John Badham.

Forever Young, Forever Free
Film Trust (South Africa)
Drama. José Ferrer, Bess Finney, Norman Knox, Muntu Ndebele. Dir: Ashley Lazarus.

Fellini's Casanova
TCF/PEA (Italy)
Period spectacle. Donald Sutherland, Tina Aumont, Peter Gonzales, Cicely Browne. Dir: Federico Fellini.

1977

The Choirboys
Lorimar/Airone (USA)
Black comedy. Charles Durning, Lou Gossett Jr, Perry King, Clyde Kusatsu. Dir: Robert Aldrich.

The Slipper And The Rose (aka **The Story Of Cinderella**)
Paradine Co-Productions (Great Britain)
Updated version, with music, of the *Cinderella* fairy tale. Richard Chamberlain, Gemma Craven, Edith Evans, Christopher Gable. Dir: Bryan Forbes.

Sorcerer (GB: **Wages Of Fear**)
Film Properties International (USA)
Suspense (remake of the French film, *The Wages Of Fear*, 1953). Roy Scheider, Francisco Rabal, Bruno Cremer, Amidou, Ramon Bieri. Dir: William Friedkin.

1978

The Brink's Job
Dino De Laurentiis (USA)
Armoured car heist. Peter Falk, Allen Goorwitz, Gena Rowlands, Peter Boyle. Dir: William Friedkin.

Caravans
Ibex/FIDCI (USA/Iran)
Drama. Anthony Quinn, Michael Sarrazin, Jennifer O'Neill, Joseph Cotten. Dir: James Fargo.

Checkered Flag Or Crash
independent (USA)
Comedy-drama actioner. Joe Don Baker, Larry Hagman, Susan Sarandon, Alan Vint. Dir: Alan Gibson.

The Deer Hunter
EMI (USA)
Vietnam War drama. Robert De Niro, Christopher Walken, John Cazale, Meryl Streep. Dir: Michael Cimino.

Five Days From Home
independent (USA)
Prison escape drama. George Peppard, Neville Brand, Savannah Smith, Sherry Boucher. Dir: George Peppard.

1979

The Electric Horseman
Wildwood/Columbia/Universal (USA)
Drama. Robert Redford, Jane Fonda, Valerie Perrine, John Saxon. Dir: Sidney Pollack.

The Legacy
Pethurst/Columbia (Great Britain)
Occult murder. Katharine Ross, Sam Elliot, John Standing, Ian Hogg. Dir: Richard Marquand.

1941
Columbia/A-Team (USA)
War farce. Dan Aykroyd, Ned Beatty, Christopher Lee, Lorraine Gary. Dir: Steven Spielberg.

Running
independent (USA/Canada)
Drama. Michael Douglas, Susan Anspach, Jennifer McKinney, Laurence Dane. Dir: Stephen Hilliard Stern.

Streets Of Hong Kong
Verily Productions (Hong Kong)
Drama. Gary Collins, Nancy Kwan. Dir: Hilton Alexander.

Yanks
United Artists/CIP (Great Britain)
War romance. Vanessa Redgrave, Richard Gere, Lisa Eichhorn, William Devane. Dir: John Schlesinger.

1980

Flash Gordon
EMI/Famous/Starling (Great Britain)
Comedy sci-fi. Sam J. Jones, Melody Anderson, Topol, Max Von Sydow. Dir: Michael Hodges.

The Gong Show Movie
independent (USA)
Movie version of TV's *Gong Show*. Chuck Barris, Robin Altman. Dir: Chuck Barris.

Guyana, Cult Of The Damned (aka **Guyana, Crime Of The Century**)
independent (Mexico/Spain/Panama)
Drama. Stuart Whitman, Gene Barry, Yvonne De Carlo. Dir: Rene Cardona Jr.

1981

An American Werewolf In London
Lycanthrope Films for Polygram Pictures (Great Britain)
Comedy horror. David Naughton, Jenny Agutter, Griffin Dunne, John Woodvine. Dir: John Landis.

Beyond The Reef
Dino De Laurentiis (USA)
Adventure drama. Joseph Ka'ne, Oliverio Maciel Diaz, Maren Jensen. Dir: Frank C. Clark.

Cattle Annie And Little Britches
Hemdale/UATC (USA)
Western. Amanda Plummer, Diane Lane, Burt Lancaster, Rod Steiger. Dir: Lamont Johnson.

The Great Muppet Caper
ITC (Great Britain); released in USA by Universal/AFD.
Muppet adventures. The Muppets, Diana Rigg, Robert Morley, Peter Ustinov, Peter Falk. Dir: Jim Henson.

Halloween II
Dino De Laurentiis (USA)
Gory frightener. Jamie Lee Curtis, Donald Pleasence, Charles Cyphers, Jeffrey Kramer. Dir: Rick Rosenthal.

Honky Tonk Freeway
Kendon Films/EMI (USA); released in USA by Universal/AFD.
Smalltown satire. Beau Bridges, Beverly D'Angelo, Hume Cronyn, Jessica Tandy. Dir: John Schlesinger.

King Of The Mountain
Polygram Pictures (USA)
Car-racing drama. Harry Hamlin, Deborah Van Valkenburgh, Joseph Bottoms, Richard Cox. Dir: Noel Nosseck.

The Legend Of The Lone Ranger
ITC (USA); released in USA by Universal/AFD.
Western adventure. Klinton Spilsbury, Michael Horse, Jason Robards, Matt Clark. Dir: William Fraker.

The Pursuit Of D. B. Cooper
Polygram Pictures (USA)
Crime investigation. Treat Williams, Robert Duvall, Paul Gleason, Kathryn Harrold. Dir: Roger Spottiswoode.

Raggedy Man
Universal (USA); released by Cannon in Great Britain.
Romantic thriller. Sissy Spacek, Eric Robert, Sam Shepard, William Sanderson. Dir: Jack Fisk.

Silence Of The North
independent (Canada)
Wilderness adventure drama. Ellen Burstyn, Tom Skerritt, Gordan Pinsent. Dir: Allan Winton King.

1982

Conan The Barbarian
Dino De Laurentiis (USA)
Warrior adventure. Arnold Schwarzenegger, James Earl Jones, Max Von Sydow, Sandahl Bergman. Dir: John Milius.

Evil Under The Sun
EMI (Great Britain)
Mystery thriller. Peter Ustinov, Colin Blakely, James Mason, Sylvia Miles, Roddy McDowell. Dir: Guy Hamilton.

Frances
EMI (USA)
Hollywood biographical drama. Jessica Lange, Sam Shepard, Kim Stanley, Bart Burns. Dir: Graeme Clifford.

Halloween III: Season Of The Witch
Dino De Laurentiis (USA)
Horror thriller. Tom Atkins, Stacey Nelkin, Dan O'Herlihy, Ralph Strait. Dir: Tommy Lee Wallace.

A Little Sex
MTM Enterprises (USA)
Drama. Tim Matheson, Kate Capshaw, Edward Hermann. Dir: Bruce Paltrow.

Six Weeks
Polygram Pictures (USA)
Drama. Dudley Moore, Mary Tyler Moore, Katherine Healy. Dir: Tony Bill.

2. Rank Organisation Releases

The financial problems that led to the takeover of Universal in 1936 saw the beginning of the association between the studio and J. Arthur Rank, the British film magnate. Rank was one of the group of financiers involved in providing Carl Laemmle with the loan he needed to overcome his cash-flow problem in 1935. By the time the group had called its option in March the following year, Rank had consolidated his involvement with the studio's overseas distribution arrangements.

In 1935 he had founded General Film Distributors to handle the release of Universal pictures in Britain, as well as a number of British productions. The arrangement also gave Universal access to Rank-controlled British films for release in the United States. In the first few years, indeed up to 1945, the studio availed itself of a very limited quantity of British product from this source but in 1946, the year of the merger between Universal and International Pictures – and also the year in which the J. Arthur Rank Organisation Limited was incorporated – the flow of British films across the Atlantic increased. At the same time, General Film Distributors was renamed Jarfid (an acronym of J. Arthur Rank Film Distributors), the forerunner of today's Rank Film Distributors.

Post-war international trade complications prevented Rank from being directly involved with the Universal/International merger, as the participants had hoped. Instead, however, they negotiated with him a reciprocal trade pact, which enabled Universal to give American release to an increasing number of the more prestigious films handled in the UK by the Rank Organisation; it also formalised the arrangement for Rank to release Universal pictures in Britain.

The deal contributed significantly to Universal's home release lists until the early fifties. Indeed, the policy of selecting prestigious pictures paid off more than once when several films picked up Academy Awards – notably *Hamlet*, best picture of 1948 – to the studio's credit. The number of films declined to a trickle after 1953, presumably a reflection of mutually diminishing interest after Decca Records bought out Rank's direct financial interest in 1950.

All the Rank films released by Universal in the United States over this period are listed below under their American release years (which often differ from the year of release in Britain). The occasional Rank pictures released by Universal after 1959 – the year of the MCA takeover – are not really distinguishable from the other, so-called, pick-ups from other independents, and are therefore listed in Appendix 1. The films' production companies, both Rank-controlled (for example, Cineguild and Two Cities) and independents, are given on the second line of each entry.

1938

Let's Make A Night Of It
British Independent Pictures
Musical comedy. Buddy Rogers, June Clyde, Claud Allister, Steve Geray, Iris Hoey. Dir: Graham Cutts

1939

The Mikado
Gilbert and Sullivan Productions
A filmed version, in Technicolor, of the famed Gilbert and Sullivan operetta, with music recorded by the London Symphony Orchestra and the D'Oyly Carte Opera Company. Kenny Baker, John Barclay, Martyn Green, Jean Colin, Elisabeth Paynter. Dir: Victor Schertzinger.

1940

The Fugitive (GB: **On The Night Of The Fire**)
G & S
A barber commits a petty theft and becomes involved in blackmail and murder. Ralph Richardson, Diana Wynyard, Romney Brent, Mary Clare. Dir: Brian Desmond Hurst.

1941

A Girl Must Live
Gainsborough Films
A drama concerning the tribulations of an aspiring young actress. Margaret Lockwood, Renée Houston, Lilli Palmer, George Robey, Hugh Sinclair. Dir: Carol Reed.

Quiet Wedding
Paramount/Conqueror
A comedy in which a wedding turns in a chaotic event, thanks to the intervention of a well-meaning but misguided family. Margaret Lockwood, Derek Farr, A.E. Matthews, Athene Seyler. Dir: Anthony Asquith.

1943

Next Of Kin
Ealing
A wartime drama demonstrating the danger of innocent remarks which are picked up by Nazi agents. A prologue and epilogue were spoken by J. Edgar Hoover. Basil Sidney, Jack Hawkins, Mary Clare, Torin Thatcher. Dir: Thorold Dickinson.

1945

Adventure For Two (GB: **The Demi-Paradise**)
Two Cities
A love story with laughs, about a young engineer who goes to Britain from the Soviet Union and it's not long before he falls for a local girl. Laurence Olivier, Penelope Ward, Margaret Rutherford, Felix Aylmer. Dir: Anthony Asquith.

1946

Brief Encounter
Cineguild
Film version of Noel Coward's one-act play *Still Life*, about a love affair between a married woman and a local doctor. Celia Johnson, Trevor Howard, Cyril Raymond, Joyce Carey. Dir: David Lean.

Dead Of Night
Ealing
Mystery story about a young man who, during a visit at a country mansion, develops psychic powers about his companions. Frederick Valk, Roland Culver, Googie Withers, Michael Redgrave. Dir: Alberto Cavalcanti.

Johnny Frenchman
Ealing
Drama focusing on rivalry between French and British fishermen. Tom Walls, Ralph Michel, Françoise Rosay, Patricia Roc. Dir: Charles Frend.

Madonna Of The Seven Moons
Gainsborough Films
Drama of a happily married woman with a split personality which gives her a dual existence as a gangster's moll. Phyllis Calvert, Patricia Roc, Stewart Granger, Peter Glenville. Dir: Arthur Crabtree.

The Man In Grey
Gainsborough Films
Romantic melodrama. No synopsis available. Margaret Lockwood, James Mason, Phyllis Calvert, Stewart Granger. Dir: Leslie Arliss.

Notorious Gentleman (GB: **The Rake's Progress**)
Individual
The irresponsibility of an attractive scoundrel leads to tragedy. Rex Harrison, Lilli Palmer, Godfrey Tearle, Margaret Johnston. Dir: Sidney Gilliat.

The Overlanders
Ealing
Part-western, part-wartime adventure, made on location in Australia, about a drover who saves a thousand head of cattle from the Japanese by taking them across country. Chips Rafferty, John Heyward, Daphne Campbell, Jean Blue. Dir: Harry Watt.

The Seventh Veil
Theatrecraft/Sydney Box/Ortus
An out-and-out melodrama about a female concert pianist romantically involved with four different men, including her guardian and her psychiatrist. Ann Todd, James Mason, Herbert Lom, Albert Lieven. Dir: Compton Bennett.

1947

Beware Of Pity
Two Cities
Film version of Stefan Zweig's novel about an aristocratic but paralysed girl's unrequited love for an Austrian army lieutenant. Lilli Palmer, Albert Lieven, Sir Cedric Hardwicke, Gladys Cooper. Dir: Maurice Elvey.

Black Narcissus
The Archers
Intense Technicolor drama about nuns, set in a remote convent in the Himalayas. Deborah Kerr, Flora Robson, Jean Simmons, David Farrar. Dir: Michael Powell & Emeric Pressburger.

Bush Christmas
Children's Entertainment Films (Australia)
The tale, filmed in the Australian wilds, of five children who set out to find the thieves who stole a mare and its foal. Chips Rafferty, John Fernside, Stan Tolhurst, Pat Penny. Dir: Ralph Smart.

The Captive Heart
Ealing
War drama about life in a German POW camp. Among the imprisoned British officers is a Czech posing, with stolen papers, as a Britisher. Michael Redgrave, Jack Warner, Basil Radford, Mervyn Johns. Dir: Basil Dearden.

Frieda
Ealing
An RAF pilot marries the German girl who helped him escape the Nazis, and brings her to England before the end of the war. David Farrar, Mai Zetterling, Glynis Johns, Flora Robson. Dir: Basil Dearden.

Great Expectations
Cineguild
Superior film version of the Charles Dickens classic about an orphan who grows up to be the beneficiary of a convict. John Mills, Valerie Hobson, Martita Hunt, Alec Guinness, Finlay Currie. Dir: David Lean.

Hungry Hill
Two Cities
Screen version of Daphne Du Maurier's dramatic novel about two Irish families who have been conducting a fierce feud for half-a-century. Margaret Lockwood, Dennis Price, Cecil Parker, Jean Simmons. Dir: Brian Desmond Hurst.

I Know Where I'm Going
The Archers
Romantic comedy-drama about a spoiled and determined young woman who travels to the Hebrides to marry for money. En route, she is stranded and meets a naval officer who reforms her values and whom she marries. Wendy Hiller, Roger Livesey, Pamela Brown, Finlay Currie. Dir: Michael Powell & Emeric Pressburger.

A Lady Surrenders (GB: **Love Story**)
Gainsborough
World War II melodramatic weepie about a handsome RAF pilot who is going blind, and his relationship with a pretty concert pianist who is suffering from a weak heart. Stewart Granger, Margaret Lockwood, Patricia Roc, Tom Walls. Dir: Leslie Arliss.

Nicholas Nickleby
Ealing
Film version of the Dickens novel about the adventures and misfortunes of a Victorian schoolmaster deprived of his rightful fortune. Derek Bond, Sir Cedric Hardwicke, Sally Anne Howes, Bernard Miles, Alfred Drayton. Dir: Alberto Cavalcanti.

Odd Man Out (aka **Gang War**)
Two Cities
Powerful acount of a wounded IRA gunman on the run from the law in Belfast. James Mason, Robert Newton, Kathleen Ryan, Dan O'Herlihy. Dir: Carol Reed.

Stairway To Heaven (GB: **A Matter Of Life And Death**)
The Archers
Supernatural fantasy about a brain-damaged RAF pilot, struggling to stay on earth against the forces of Death who summons him to trial for his life in heaven. A brain operation returns him to reality. David Niven, Roger Livesey, Kim Hunter, Marius Goring. Dir: Michael Powell & Emeric Pressburger.

Tawny Pipit
Two Cities
Lightweight comedy about an English village in wartime, its zany inhabitants, and the disruption caused by the nesting of two rare birds in a local meadow. Bernard Miles, Rosamund John, Niall MacGinnis, Jean Gillie. Dir: Bernard Miles & Charles Saunders.

They Were Sisters
Gainsborough Films
Complicated melodrama about the problematic lives of three sisters, all married. Phyllis Calvert, Dulcie Gray, Anne Crawford, James Mason, Hugh Sinclair. Dir: Arthur Crabtree.

This Happy Breed
Two Cities/Cineguild
Film version in Technicolor of Noel Coward's play about the lives of a suburban family between 1919 and 1939. Robert Newton, Celia Johnson, Stanley Holloway, John Mills, Kay Walsh. Dir: David Lean.

The Upturned Glass
Triton
A brain surgeon murders his sister-in-law when he discovers she is responsible for the death of the girl he loved. James Mason, Pamela Kellino, Rosamund John, Moreland Graham. Dir: Lawrence Huntington.

The Wicked Lady
Gainsborough Films
Costume drama, set in the days of Charles II, about an aristocratic lady who becomes a highwayman. Margaret Lockwood, James Mason, Griffith Jones, Patricia Roc. Dir: Leslie Arliss.

The Years Between
Sydney Box
A man reported dead in the war five years previously, returns home to find his wife elected to parliament in his place and about to remarry. Michael Redgrave, Valerie Hobson, Flora Robson, James McKechnie. Dir: Compton Bennett.

1948

Bad Sister (GB: **The White Unicorn**)
John Corfield
Not to be confused with Universal's 1931 film of the same name, this one concerned itself with a young woman who is put in an institution after trying to kill her baby and herself. Margaret Lockwood, Joan Greenwood, Ian Hunter, Dennis Price. Dir: Bernard Knowles.

The Brothers
Sydney Box
Problems and complications ensue when two brothers both fall in love with the same girl, an orphan. Patricia Roc, Finlay Currie, Maxwell Reed, Duncan MacRae Dir: David MacDonald.

Captain Boycott
Individual
Historical drama about the rebellion of poor Irish farmers against their callous English landlords circa 1880. Stewart Granger, Kathleen Ryan, Alastair Sim, Robert Donat. Dir: Frank Launder.

Dear Murderer
Gainsborough Films
Mystery thriller against a background of adultery and intrigue among the wealthy set. Eric Portman, Greta Gynt, Dennis Price, Maxwell Reed. Dir: Arthur Crabtree.

Dulcimer Street (GB: **London Belongs To Me**)
Individual
A drama dealing with the lives of a group of people living in a London boarding house. Richard Attenborough, Alastair Sim, Fay Compton, Joyce Carey. Dir: Sidney Gilliat.

The End Of The River
The Archers
The tribulations of a young South American Indian who flees from the jungle only to find the city a hostile place. Sabu, Esmond Knight, Bibi Ferreira, Torin Thatcher. Dir: Derek Twist.

Hamlet
Two Cities
Shakespeare's tragedy of revenge, heavily cut but powerfully acted and directed. Laurence Olivier, Eileen Herlie, Basil Sydney, Jean Simmons, Felix Aylmer, Stanley Holloway, Terence Morgan. Dir: Laurence Olivier.

Holiday Camp
Gainsborough Films
A comedy-drama about the goings-on in a holiday camp, affected by the knowledge that a killer is prowling the vicinity. Jack Warner, Kathleen Harrison, Flora Robson, Dennis Price. Dir: Ken Annakin.

Jassy
Gainsborough Films
Period romantic melodrama about a gypsy servant girl falsely accused of murder. Margaret Lockwood, Patricia Roc, Basil Sydney, Dermot Walsh. Dir: Bernard Knowles.

1949

All Over Town
Wessex
Combination of romantic comedy and newsroom drama as reporters on a small local paper expose a corrupt housing scheme. Norman Wooland, Sarah Churchill, Fabia Drake, Cyril Cusack. Dir: Derek Twist.

The Blind Goddess
Gainsborough Films
Old-fashioned courtroom drama, involving a public figure who is exposed as politically corrupt. Eric Portman, Anne Crawford, Hugh Williams, Michael Denison, Claire Bloom. Dir: Harold French.

The Blue Lagoon
Individual
Romantic tale of a boy and girl who grow up together on a desert island after a shipwreck. They fall in love, have a baby, and eventually sail off to seek civilization. Jean Simmons, Donald Houston, Noel Purcell, Cyril Cusack. Dir: Frank Launder.

Christopher Columbus
Gainsborough Films
Historical film recounting the life and voyages of Columbus from the time he receives the patronage of the Spanish court. Fredric March, Florence Eldredge Francis L. Sullivan, Kathleen Ryan. Dir: David MacDonald.

Corridor Of Mirrors
Apollo Films
Baroque mystery melodrama about a reclusive art collector who believes himself and his mistress to be reincarnations of the lovers in a mediaeval painting. Edana Romney, Eric Portman, Barbara Mullen, Hugh Sinclair. Dir: Terence Young.

Daybreak
Triton
A married couple who live on a barge find their relationship in difficulties when an attractive longshoreman becomes involved in their lives. Eric Portman, Ann Todd, Maxwell Reed, Jane Hylton. Dir: Compton Bennett.

The Girl In The Painting
Gainsborough Films
A British army officer, struck by a portrait in an art gallery, ventures to Germany in search of the girl who is its subject. Mai Zetterling, Guy Rolfe, Herbert Lom, Robert Beatty. Dir: Terence Fisher.

Her Man Gilbey (GB: **English Without Tears**)
Two Cities
A comedy romance about the cavortings of four people in Switzerland. Michael Wilding, Lilli Palmer, Penelope Ward, Claude Dauphin. Dir: Harold French.

One Night With You
Two Cities
A musical whose plot revolves around a glamorous socialite falling in love with a handsome singer. Nino Martini, Patricia Roc, Bonar Colleano, Stanley Holloway. Dir: Shaun Terence Young.

One Woman's Story (GB: **The Passionate Friends**)
Cineguild
A romantic drama centring on a woman, married to an older man, who meets her former young lover and realises she still cares for him. Ann Todd, Trevor Howard, Claude Rains, Isabel Dean. Dir: David Lean.

Snowbound
Gainsborough Films
Set in the Italian Alps, this story followed an intelligence officer's investigation of a mixed group of people. Robert Newton, Dennis Price, Herbert Lom, Marcel Dalio, Zena Marshall. Dir: David MacDonald.

Tight Little Island (GB: **Whisky Galore**)
Ealing
Comedy about the consequences for a small island in the Hebrides when a ship loaded with whisky is wrecked there. Basil Radford, Joan Greenwood, James Robertson Justice, John Gregson, Catherine Lacey. Dir: Alexander Mackendrick.

Woman Hater
Two Cities
A film star who maintains that she can't abide men and adores solitude, is challenged to prove it by an English nobleman. Stewart Granger, Mary Jerrold, Edwige Feuillere, Ronald Squire, Jeanne de Casalis. Dir: Terence Young.

1950

Adam And Evalyn (GB: **Adam And Evelyne**)
Two Cities
A society reprobate brings up the daughter of his dead friend, only to fall in love with her when she reaches adulthood. Stewart Granger, Jean Simmons, Helen Cherry, Wilfrid Hyde White. Dir: Harold French.

The Astonished Heart
Gainsborough Films/Sydney Box
A psychiatrist, with his wife's knowledge, has a love affair with another woman, but he can't cope with the situation and commits suicide. Noel Coward, Margaret Leighton, Celia Johnson, Graham Payn. Dir: Terence Fisher and Anthony Darnborough.

Madeleine
David Lean/Cineguild
Courtroom drama about the trial of a wealthy young woman, in the Victorian era, accused of murdering her lover. Ann Todd, Leslie Banks, Elizabeth Sellars, Ivan Desny. Dir: David Lean.

Madness Of The Heart
Two Cities
Emotional drama about a girl in danger of going blind who turns to religion, then falls in love. Margaret Lockwood, Paul Dupuis, Kathleen Byron, Maxwell Reed. Dir: Richard Wainwright.

Prelude To Fame
Two Cities
Drama, laced with classical music, about a child prodigy who is almost destroyed by the ambition of the woman who urges him on. Jeremy Spenser, Guy Rolfe, Kathleen Ryan, Kathleen Byron, James Robertson Justice. Dir: Fergus McDonell.

The Rocking Horse Winner
Two Cities
Drama about a boy who finds he can pick racing winners – with fatal consequences. John Howard Davies, John Mills, Valerie Hobson, Ronald Squire. Dir: Anthony Pelissier.

A Run For Your Money
Ealing
Comedy about the adventures of a couple of Welsh football fans who win a competition and spend a day in London. Alec Guinness, Meredith Edwards, Moira Lister, Donald Houston. Dir: Charles Frend.

1951

The Browning Version
Javelin
Terence Rattigan's stage drama about the various humiliations suffered by a schoolmaster, hated by his wife and his pupils, and retiring through ill-health. Michael Redgrave, Jean Kent, Nigel Patrick, Ronald Howard. Dir: Anthony Asquith.

The Magic Bow
Gainsborough Films
Period biopic about various supposed episodes in the life of composer and virtuoso violinist, Paganini. Stewart Granger, Jean Kent, Phyllis Calvert, Dennis Price. Dir: Bernard Knowles.

The Magnet
Ealing
Comedy about a precocious little boy who steals a magnet. Stephen Murray, Kay Walsh, William Fox, Gladys Henson. Dir: Charles Frend.

Operation Disaster (GB: **Morning Departure**)
Jay Lewis
World War II drama about twelve men trapped in a submarine that runs into a mine. John Mills, Richard Attenborough, Nigel Patrick, Helen Cherry. Dir: Roy Baker.

Pool Of London
Ealing
Documentary-style police thriller about a sailor who is a small-time smuggler, becoming involved in a murder. Bonar Colleano, Susan Shaw, Earl Cameron, Renée Asherson. Dir: Basil Dearden.

1952

Ivory Hunter (GB: **Where No Vultures Fly**)
Ealing
The adventures of a game warden in East Africa who, among other things, sets out to start a national game park on Mount Kilimanjaro. Anthony Steele, Dinah Sheridan, Harold Warrender, Meredith Edwards. Dir: Harry Watt.

The Lavender Hill Mob
Ealing
Inventive comedy about a diffident bank clerk who masterminds a large-scale robbery. Alec Guinness, Stanley Holloway, Sidney James, Alfie Bass. Dir: Charles Crichton.

The Little Ballerina
Gaumont-British Instructional
A documentary teaching film on the art of ballet dancing. No further information available.

The Man In The White Suit
Ealing
Satirical comedy about the invention – to the horror of both workers and management – of a fabric that never gets dirty and never wears out. Alec Guinness, Joan Greenwood, Cecil Parker, Ernest Thesiger. Dir: Alexander Mackendrick.

The Promoter (GB: **The Card**)
British Film Makers
The progress of a young man whose enthusiasm for promoting anything and everything earns him a fortune, until he comes up against a blonde. Alec Guinness, Valerie Hobson, Glynis Johns. Dir: Ronald Neame.

White Corridors
Vic Films
Drama of hospital life, one part of which concerned a pathologist who offers himself as a human guinea pig when he contracts a virulent disease. Googie Withers, James Donald, Godfrey Tearle, Petula Clark. Dir: Pat Jackson.

1953

Both Sides Of The Law (GB: **Street Corner**)
LIP/Sydney Box
Semi-documentary style police drama, with particular emphasis on the roles and attitudes of policewomen in the London force. Rosamund John, Anne Crawford, Peggy Cummins, Terence Morgan. Dir: Muriel Box.

The Crash Of Silence (GB: **Mandy**)
Ealing
Documentary-style drama focusing on a little girl who, having been born deaf, is sent to a school especially equipped for the problem. Mandy Miller, Jack Hawkins, Phyllis Calvert, Godfrey Tearle. Dir: Alexander Mackendrick.

The Cruel Sea
Ealing
Hugely successful screen version of best-selling novel about life on board a corvette at the height of the Atlantic sea conflicts in World War II. Jack Hawkins, Donald Sinden, Stanley Baker, Virginia McKenna, Denholm Elliott. Dir: Charles Frend.

Desperate Moment
George H. Brown
Drama of life in Berlin after World War II, focusing on black marketeers, romance, intrigue and a murder. Dirk Bogarde, Mai Zetterling, Philip Friend, Albert Lieven. Dir: Compton Bennett.

The Gentle Gunman
Associated British Pathé
Political drama in which an Irish revolutionary, who kills himself for the cause, is unjustly branded as a traitor. John Mills, Dirk Bogarde, Robert Beatty, Elizabeth Sellars. Dir: Basil Dearden.

High And Dry (GB: **The Maggie**)
Ealing
Comedy about an American businessman who is hoodwinked into dispatching cargo to a Scottish island, via a rickety old train. Paul Douglas, Alex Mackenzie, James Copeland, Dorothy Alison. Dir: Alexander Mackendrick.

I Believe In You
Ealing
Several parallel stories, all about probation officers and the young offenders they control. Cecil Parker, Celia Johnson, Laurence Harvey, Joan Collins. Dir: Basil Dearden.

The Importance Of Being Earnest
Javelin/Two Cities
Screen adaptation of Oscar Wilde's famous comedy of manners about the machinations of an eligible bachelor. Michael Redgrave, Michael Denison, Dorothy Tutin, Joan Greenwood, Edith Evans. Dir: Anthony Asquith.

Island Rescue (GB: **Appointment With Venus**)
British Film Makers
Comedy adventure about the rescue of a pedigree cow from the Nazi-occupied Channel Islands in World War II. David Niven, Glynis Johns, George Coulouris, Kenneth More. Dir: Ralph Thomas.

Penny Princess
Conquest
Comedy romance about a New York salesgirl who inherits a little European principality, boosts its economy and is wooed by an Englishman. Yolande Donlan, Dirk Bogarde, Edwin Styles, Reginald Beckwith. Dir: Val Guest.

Project M7 (GB: **The Net**)
Two Cities
Intrigue, tension, espionage and murder all rear their heads at an important aviation research centre. Phyllis Calvert, Noel Willman, Herbert Lom, James Donald. Dir: Anthony Asquith.

A Queen Is Crowned
Carleton Knight
A Technicolor documentary film of the coronation of Queen Elizabeth II, with a narration written by Christopher Fry and spoken by Laurence Olivier.

Something Money Can't Buy
Vic Films
Comedy-drama about the efforts of a young couple to start up a business in the face of rationing and post-World War II dreariness. Patricia Roc, Anthony Steele, A.E. Matthews, Moira Lister. Dir: Pat Jackson.

The Stranger In Between (GB: **Hunted**)
Independent Artists
A boy on the run joins up with a runaway killer who, in the end, puts the boy's safety before his own. Dirk Bogarde, Jon Whiteley, Kay Walsh, Elizabeth Sellars. Dir: Charles Crichton.

The Titfield Thunderbolt
Ealing
Action comedy about the inhabitants of a village who save their local railway line from closure by taking over the running of it themselves. Stanley Holloway, George Relph, John Gregson, Edie Martin. Dir: Charles Crichton.

1954

Always A Bride
Clarion Films
Comedy romance about a treasury agent whose love for a girl involves him in helping her father – a con-man. Peggy Cummins, Terence Morgan, Ronald Squire, James Hayter. Dir: Ralph Smart.

Genevieve
Sirius
Comedy about the journey back from the Brighton veteran car rally when two drivers engage in a friendly, unofficial race. John Gregson, Dinah Sheridan, Kenneth More, Kay Kendall. Dir: Henry Cornelius.

West Of Zanzibar
Ealing/Schlesinger
African adventure in which a game warden sets out to break up a gang of ivory poachers. Anthony Steele, Sheila Sim, Edric Connor, Orlando Martins. Dir: Harry Watt.

1955

Land Of Fury (GB: **The Seekers**)
Fanfare
Adventure drama about the life of a British family who, in 1820, emigrate to New Zealand and encounter many differences in culture and the way of life. Jack Hawkins, Glynis Johns, Inia Te Wiata, Laya Raki. Dir: Ken Annakin.

1956

Simon And Laura
Group Films
Sophisticated comedy about a husband-and-wife team, on TV and off, who detest each other in real life. Peter Finch, Kay Kendall, Ian Carmichael, Muriel Pavlow. Dir: Muriel Box.

1957

Doctor At Large
Rank
Comedy capers in (and out of) a London hospital as a young doctor muddles his way to becoming a surgeon. Dirk Bogarde, Muriel Pavlow, Donald Sinden, James Robertson Justice. Dir: Ralph Thomas.

1958

Touch And Go
Ealing
Comedy about a family who decide to emigrate to Australia and are then assailed by doubts. Jack Hawkins, Margaret Johnstone, June Thorburn, John Fraser. Dir: Michael Truman.

1959

Floods Of Fear
Sydney Box
Suspense melodrama in which a couple of escaped convicts – one a murderer – a prison warder and an attractive girl are marooned in an isolated house during floods. Howard Keel, Harry H. Corbett, Cyril Cusack, Anne Heywood. Dir: Charles Crichton.

Sapphire
Artna
A coloured music student is murdered. Scotland Yard solves the case which is complicated by their discovery that the girl was passing as white. Nigel Patrick, Michael Craig, Yvonne Mitchell, Gordon Heath. Dir: Basil Dearden.

3. Hammer Productions

Beginning in 1958, Universal-International began to release in the United States some of the films made by the British company Hammer Film Productions. Hammer was founded in 1948 but it was not until 1954, after its success with *The Quatermass Experiment*, that it began to concentrate on the horror films for which it is so well known. Thirteen of these enjoyed US release through Universal; all were made in Britain by British directors with British casts, but in the making of all but the first two and the last two Universal participated as a co-production company, if only financially.

1958
Horror Of Dracula (GB: **Dracula**)
Christopher Lee, Peter Cushing, Michael Gough, Melissa Stribling. Dir: Terence Fisher.

1959
The Mummy
Christopher Lee, Peter Cushing, Yvonne Furneaux, Felix Aylmer. Dir: Terence Fisher.

1960
The Brides Of Dracula
Peter Cushing, Freda Jackson, Martita Hunt, Yvonne Monlaur. Dir: Terence Fisher.

1961
The Curse Of The Werewolf
Oliver Reed, Clifford Evans, Yvonne Romain. Dir: Terence Fisher.

1962
Night Creatures (GB: **Captain Clegg**)
Oliver Reed, Peter Cushing, Patrick Allen, Yvonne Romain. Dir: Peter Graham Scott.

Phantom Of The Opera
Herbert Lom, Heather Searts, Thorley Walters, Michael Gough, Miles Malleson, Miriam Karlin. Dir: Terence Fisher.

1963
Kiss Of Evil (GB: **Kiss Of The Vampire**)
Clifford Evans, Noel Willman, Edward De Souza, Jennifer Daniel. Dir: Don Sharp.

Paranoiac
Oliver Reed, Janette Scott, Liliane Brousse. Dir: Freddie Francis.

1964
The Evil Of Frankenstein
Peter Cushing, Peter Woodthorpe, Duncan Lamont. Dir: Freddie Francis.

Nightmare
David Knight, Moira Redmond, Jennie Linden, Brenda Bruce. Dir: Freddie Francis.

1965
The Secret Of Blood Island
Jack Hedley, Barbara Shelley, Patrick Wymark, Charles Tingwell. Dir: Quentin Lawrence.

1972
Hands Of The Ripper
Eric Porter, Keith Bell, Jane Merrow, Angharad Rees. Dir: Peter Sasdy.

Twins Of Evil
Dennis Price, Peter Cushing, Madeleine & Mary Collinson. Dir: John Hough.

4. RKO Productions

In 1957 film-making at the ailing RKO studio ground to a halt but the momentum of the machine and contractual obligations to co-production companies brought forth a further 23 pictures whose release was handled not by RKO itself but by various companies, the last film appearing in 1960. Universal-International took on the US distribution of eleven of these during 1957 and 1958. More complete descriptions of these films, and all the others that the studio produced can be found in 'The RKO Story', a companion volume in this series.

1957
Escapade In Japan
Jon Provost, Roger Nakagawa, Teresa Wright, Cameron Mitchell. Dir: Arthur Lubin.

Jet Pilot
John Wayne, Janet Leigh, Jay C. Flippen, Paul Fix, Richard Rober. Dir: Josef von Sternberg.

Public Pigeon No. 1 (RKO/Val-Richie Productions)
Red Skelton, Janet Blair, Vivian Blaine, Jay C. Flippen. Dir: Norman Z. McLeod.

Run Of The Arrow (RKO/Globe Enterprises)
Rod Steiger, Brian Keith, Sarita Montiel, Ralph Meeker. Dir: Samuel Fuller.

That Night! (RKO/Galahad Productions)
John Beal, Augusta Dabney, Shepperd Strudwick, Rosemary Murphy. Dir: John Newland.

The Unholy Wife (RKO/Treasure Productions)
Diana Dors, Rod Steiger, Tom Tryon. Dir: John Farrow.

The Violators (RKO/Galahad Productions)
Arthur O'Connell, Nancy Malone, Fred Beir, Clarice Blackburn. Dir: John Newland

The Young Stranger
James MacArthur, James Daly, Kim Hunter, Whit Bissell. Dir: John Frankenheimer.

1958
All Mine To Give (GB: **The Day They Gave The Babies Away**)
Glynis Johns, Cameron Mitchell, Rex Thompson, Reta Shaw. Dir: Allen Reisner.

The Girl Most Likely
Jane Powell, Keith Andes, Cliff Robertson, Tommy Noonan. Dir: Mitchell Leisen.

I Married A Woman (RKO/Gomalco)
George Gobel, Diana Dors, Adolphe Menjou, Jesse Royce Landis. Dir: Hal Kanter.

5. Documentary Feature Releases

With only 15 examples released in over 70 years, feature-length documentaries can hardly be said to occupy a significant place in the history of the studio. Ironically, however, it was with a documentary that the company first broke away from producing shorts, soon after its inception in 1912. Three titles have emanated from the Rank Organisation, two of them within the period covered by Appendix 2, where they are also listed.

1912
Paul J. Rainey's African Hunt
A filmed account of explorer Rainey's year-long Africa expedition, featuring natives, flora and fauna.

1918
Crashing Through To Berlin
A compilation of film clips featuring events leading up to World War I, and sequences showing the troops (land, air and sea) in action. Presented by Carl Laemmle.

1930
The Devil's Pit
A documentary, filmed in New Zealand, and depicting the customs, legends, warfare and way of life of the Maori tribes. Produced by Lew Collins.

1931
The Mystery Of Life
A film on Darwin's theories of evolution. Combining instruction with entertainment, it constructed the doctrines with lectures and demonstrations by Clarence Darrow and Dr H.M. Parshley. Produced by Classic Productions.

1933
The Fighting President
Events in the life of Franklin D. Roosevelt, compiled by Allyn Butterfield from footage of various incidents and happenings. The narration was written and spoken by Edwin C. Hill

1938
Dark Rapture
A film by Armand Denis of the Denis-Roosevelt Belgian Congo expedition. High quality photography and a wide variety of material showing scenic wonders, tribal natives and animals.

1952
The Little Ballerina
A teaching film on the art of ballet dancing. Produced by Gaumont-British Instructional for the Rank Organisation.

1953
A Queen Is Crowned
A Technicolor documentary on the coronation of Queen Elizabeth II, with a narration written by Christopher Fry and spoken by Laurence Olivier. Produced by Carleton Knight for the Rank Organisation.

1958
This Is Russia
Produced, photographed and directed by Sid Feder, this documentary was visually no more than a tourist's camera trip round the cities of Russia. The narrative, however, conveyed suspicion and alarmism.

1965
The Guns Of August
A film by Nathan Kroll inspired by Barbara W. Tuchman's book of the same name about the First World War. Fritz Weaver narrated and Arthur B. Tourtellot wrote it.

1967
Palaces Of A Queen
A witty, historically informative and scenic tour of six British palaces (Buckingham Palace, Hampton Court, St James's Palace, Windsor Castle, Kensington Palace, Holyrood House), narrated by Sir Michael Redgrave. Produced by George Grafton Green for the Rank Organisation.

1969
African Safari
Produced, directed, written and photographed by Ron E. Shanin for R.E. Shanin Enterprises Inc. An arresting addition to the collection of African documentaries, with exciting footage of of wild life, volcanoes and waterfalls.

1974
Janis
Directed by Howard Alk and Seaton Findlay, this documentary was a carelessly assembled collection of interviews, and clips from filmed rock concerts given by pop star Janis Joplin who died of drugs and drink in 1970. A Crawley Films production.

The Ra Expeditions
Photographed by Carlo Mauri and Kei Ohara, this Norwegian-Swedish production for Swedish Broadcasting Corporation TV was a filmed account of explorer-anthropologist Thor Heyerdahl's expedition across the Atlantic in a papyrus boat. Exciting and informative.

1975
American Reunion
No information beyond release date and title is available.

6. Selected Filmographies and Series

The contributions of Deanna Durbin and the Abbott and Costello duo to the Universal fortunes were as significant as those of any of its other stars. There was no denying, too, the popularity of its series films. These are presented below in order of release. Each film is indexed by the page number of its entry in the main part of the book.

IT'S A DAT

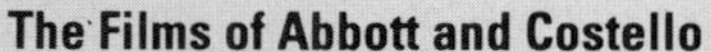

The Films of Abbott and Costello

1940 One Night In The Tropics 120
1941 Buck Privates 122
In The Navy 124
Hold That Ghost 124
Keep 'Em Flying 126
1942 Ride 'Em Cowboy 132
Pardon My Sarong 134
Who Done It? 134
1943 It Ain't Hay 141
Hit The Ice 140
1944 In Society 147
1945 Here Come The Co-Eds 152
The Naughty Nineties 155
1946 Little Giant 168
The Time Of Their Lives 168
1947 Buck Privates Come Home 171
The Wistful Widow Of Wagon Gap 174
1948 Abbott And Costello Meet Frankenstein 178
Mexican Hayride 175
1949 Abbott And Costello Meet The Killer, Boris Karloff 181
1950 Abbott And Costello In The Foreign Legion 187
1951 Abbott And Costello Meet The Invisible Man 195
Comin' Round The Mountain 195
1952 Lost In Alaska 208
1953 Abbott And Costello Go To Mars 213
Abbott And Costello Meet Dr Jekyll And Mr Hyde 210
1954 Fireman, Save My Child 220
1955 Abbott And Costello Meet The Keystone Kops 225
Abbott And Costello Meet The Mummy 225
1965 The World Of Abbott And Costello (a restrospective compilation) 284

Bud Abbott and Lou Costello joined Universal in 1940 to provide supporting comic relief in some of the studio's bigger pictures. Their first film was such a success, however, that they were immediately elevated to star status and a succession of hilarious comedies followed. When, after a decade, their following showed signs of fading, they were given a new lease of life with a different formula based on 'meeting' popular characters from other films, particularly spoofed-up horror characters. By 1955 their box-office appeal was again on the wane, as was the partnership, and they went their separate ways the following year. Over the 16-year period they made seven other features while on loan to other studios.

IT STARTED WITH EVE

COME THOSE
DIZZY, DAFFY DAREDEVILS!
Slapstick chases!
...Pies in faces!
...Shapely beauts in bathing suits!
LOU
COSTELLO
MEET THE
FAMOUS KEYSTONE KOPS
HOWARD CHRISTIE • A UNIVERSAL-INTERNATIONAL PICTURE

The Films of Deanna Durbin

1936 Three Smart Girls 92
1937 One Hundred Men And A Girl 101
1938 Mad About Music 105
That Certain Age 107
1939 Three Smart Girls Grow Up 112
First Love 110
1940 It's A Date 116
Spring Parade 118
1941 Nice Girl? 126
It Started With Eve 125
1943 The Amazing Mrs Holliday 139
Hers To Hold 140
His Butler's Sister 143
1944 Christmas Holiday 145
Can't Help Singing 144
1945 Lady On A Train 153
Because Of Him 162
1947 I'll Be Yours 173
Something In The Wind 173
1948 Up In Central Park 175
For The Love Of Mary 176

Born Edna Mae, of English parents in Canada, Deanna Durbin was just 15 when her debut film for Universal was released. She was first contracted by MGM for a feature that was eventually cancelled, but she did make a short for them (with Judy Garland) before she joined Universal. Thanks to pre-release publicity she received on Eddie Cantor's radio show, *Three Smart Girls* was a big success and it set the scene, not only for the studio's recovery, but for a 13-year career that ultimately made her the most highly paid female performer in the country. Her stay with the studio was not without its ups and down, however, and at one stage she was suspended for six months when she protested at the loss of her favourite producer, Joe Pasternak, to MGM after *It Started With Eve*. In 1948 she simply called it a day, and left the film world and the limelight for good. She and her husband now live on their estate near Paris.

ABBOTT AND COSTELLO MEET FRANKENSTEIN

The Sherlock Holmes Series

1942 Sherlock Holmes
And The Voice Of Terror 134
1943 Sherlock Holmes
And The Secret Weapon 142
Sherlock Holmes In Washington 142
Sherlock Holmes Faces Death 141
1944 Sherlock Holmes
And The Spider Woman 148
The Scarlet Claw 148
The Pearl Of Death 147
1945 The House Of Fear 151
The Woman In Green 151
Pursuit To Algiers 154
1946 Terror By Night 165
Dressed To Kill 169

After inaugurating their Sherlock Holmes/Dr Watson partnership in two films for 20th Century-Fox in 1939 (*Hound Of The Baskervilles* and *The Adventures Of Sherlock Holmes*), Basil Rathbone and Nigel Bruce stuck together throughout Universal's series. John Rawlins directed the first one but they were then handled by Roy Willian Neill. *The Spider Woman Strikes Back* (1946), while retaining Gale Sondergaard as the evil lady, severed connections with the intrepid duo and did not form part of the series.

DRESSED TO KILL

HENS AND KELLYS IN TROUBLE

The Cohens and Kellys Series

1926 The Cohens And The Kellys 52
1928 The Cohens And Kellys In Paris 60
1929 The Cohens And Kellys
In Atlantic City 65
1930 The Cohens And Kellys In Scotland 66
1931 The Cohens And Kellys In Africa 73
1932 The Cohens And Kellys In Hollywood 78
1933 The Cohens And Kellys In Trouble 82

A popular comedy series in its day about the ethnic clashes between a Jewish shopkeeper and an Irish cop, and their respective families. The ever-quarrelling men were the mainstays and George Sidney, as Cohen, stuck with the series throughout. Charlie Murray, as Kelly, did five of them but his place in *Paris* was taken by J. Farrell MacDonald, and in *Atlantic City* by Mack Swain.

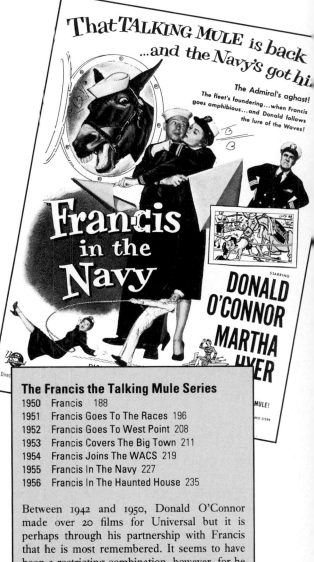

The Kettles Series

1947 The Egg And I 172
1949 Ma And Pa Kettle 185
1950 Ma And Pa Kettle Go To Town 187
1951 Ma And Pa Kettle Back On The Farm 199
1952 Ma And Pa Kettle At The Fair 202
1953 Ma And Pa Kettle On Vacation 214
1954 Ma And Pa Kettle At Home 218
1955 Ma And Pa Kettle At Waikiki 226
1956 The Kettles In The Ozarks 234
1957 The Kettles On Old
MacDonald's Farm 242

The Kettles, played by Percy Kilbride and Marjorie Main, first appeared in *The Egg And I* as subsidiary characters, and it was their success in that film that gave them their series. After the *Waikiki* film was made, Percy Kilbride suffered a car accident and retired from the series. Arthur Hunnicutt took over (as Pa's brother) in *Ozarks*, and Parker Fennelly was Pa in *Old MacDonald's Farm*.

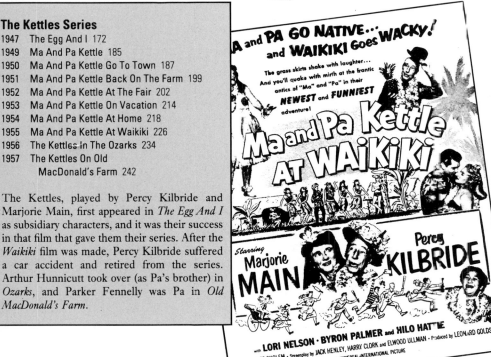

The Francis the Talking Mule Series

1950 Francis 188
1951 Francis Goes To The Races 196
1952 Francis Goes To West Point 208
1953 Francis Covers The Big Town 211
1954 Francis Joins The WACS 219
1955 Francis In The Navy 227
1956 Francis In The Haunted House 235

Between 1942 and 1950, Donald O'Connor made over 20 films for Universal but it is perhaps through his partnership with Francis that he is most remembered. It seems to have been a restricting combination, however, for he made only one other film for the studio during the run of the series. After the sixth he decided to call it a day and left Mickey Rooney to cope with the upstaging in the last one.

Index of Films

The index contains every feature film mentioned in the main body of the book (pages 8 to 357, inclusive). Films mentioned outside these pages are not indexed here, but a separate index for the films in the appendix listings (pages 369 to 375) can be found on page 368.

The main entry in the book for each film (whether it is an illustrated, full-text entry, or (between 1915 and 1945 only) an abbreviated entry) is denoted by the page number in bold type. Page numbers in the lighter type denote passing mentions of the film, either in a chapter introduction, or in another film's entry.

Where a film title begins with an arabic numeral, for example *40 Pounds Of Trouble*, it will be found under F, as if it were *Forty Pounds Of Trouble*.

Different films with the same or similar title are given separate entries and are distinguished by the insertion of the year of release in brackets after the title.

D

E

F

G

H

T

U

V

W

Index of Personnel

The index contains the names of every real person and named performing animal mentioned in the main body of the book (pages 8 to 357). Personnel mentioned in the Academy Awards section and the appendixes are not indexed, nor are the names of any fictional characters.

Where a person is depicted in an illustration, the page number is given in italics, and that number refers to the page on which the related text or caption appears. Different mentions of the same person on the same page, but in different contexts or in relation to different films, are denoted by the insertion of a number in brackets after the page number. Thus, in this fictitious example:

Elliott, Frank 127, 181(3), *181(2)*

Frank Elliott is mentioned in the text of one film on page 127, in the text of three films on page 181, and appears in the illustrations (as well as being mentioned in the texts) which relate to two further films on page 181.

The alphabetic position of people whose surnames are preceded by Von or De (as a separate word) is under the initial letter of their surname proper, and not under V or D. Cecil B. DeMille (no space after the 'De'), however, will be found under D, as will Beverly D'Angelo, and Maureen O'Hara is under O. Unhyphenated double surnames are indexed under the initial of the last of the two names – for example, Mary Tyler Moore is under M; hyphenated double surnames are indexed under the initial of the first name of the pair – for example, Colin Keith-Johnston is under K. Surnames of Scottish origin beginning Mc- are separated from those beginning Mac- by all names beginning Mad- to Maz-.

In those cases where two or more individuals have identical or similar names, we have indicated their separate identities by inserting their respective occupations in brackets after their names. Where we have not been able to verify separate identity, even though it is suggested by the contexts in which the names are mentioned, we have erred on the side of caution, left them as separate entries and specified the difference which the text suggests.

In compiling such an index as this, one finds that different reference sources may give different spellings or versions of a person's name. In many cases they are correct to do so, because the people concerned (particularly if they were performers) did use more than one form of their name, either arbitrarily or for different periods of their career. Where we know this to be the case we have indicated the alternatives in brackets after the form of the name which seems to have been used most widely – for example, Gallagher, Skeets (Richard); the mention in the text may use any one of the various forms. In those cases where there seems to be widespread confusion throughout the literature as to how a name should be spelt we have tried to standardise as far as possible on the basis of majority usage and/or by following the form used in *The New York Times Directory Of The Film*.

A

I

J

K

L

M

N

O

P

T

THE
END